Palgrave Macmillan Studies in Banking and Financial Institutions

Series Editor
Philip Molyneux, Bangor University, Bangor, UK

The Palgrave Macmillan Studies in Banking and Financial Institutions series is international in orientation and includes studies of banking systems in particular countries or regions as well as contemporary themes such as Islamic Banking, Financial Exclusion, Mergers and Acquisitions, Risk Management, and IT in Banking. The books focus on research and practice and include up to date and innovative studies that cover issues which impact banking systems globally.

Joshua Yindenaba Abor ·
Charles Komla Delali Adjasi
Editors

The Economics of Banking and Finance in Africa

Developments in Africa's Financial Systems

Volume 1

palgrave
macmillan

Editors
Joshua Yindenaba Abor
University of Ghana Business School
Accra, Ghana

Charles Komla Delali Adjasi
University of Stellenbosch Business School
Cape Town, South Africa

ISSN 2523-336X ISSN 2523-3378 (electronic)
Palgrave Macmillan Studies in Banking and Financial Institutions
ISBN 978-3-031-04161-7 ISBN 978-3-031-04162-4 (eBook)
https://doi.org/10.1007/978-3-031-04162-4

Cover illustration: Timothy Marks

This Palgrave Macmillan imprint is published by the registered company Springer Nature Switzerland AG
The registered company address is: Gewerbestrasse 11, 6330 Cham, Switzerland

Acknowledgements

Joshua Yindenaba Abor

To my wonderful wife, Dr. Patience Aseweh Abor and our lovely children, Ivana, Bastien and Venka for their love, support and encouragement. Also, to my parents, Abor Ndobire and Amina Tobga for their inspiration and commitment throughout my education. I also wish to appreciate my co-editor, Charles, and co-authors of the various chapters.

Charles Komla Delali Adjasi

To my wife Chewe Sakha Adjasi and our boys Delali and Dalitso for their love, support, encouragement and for tolerating Daddy's endless late nights. To my father W.O. K. Adjasi and my late mother D.A.M. Buachie (Auntie Mansah) for your blessings. I would like to thank my co-editor Joshua for the sterling initiatives and collaborative effort in getting this book project completed.

General

We the editors would like to thank all contributing authors for the high quality of their chapters. We wish to thank Prof. Helen Yitah, Dean of School of Languages and the Carnegie Writing Centre, University of Ghana, for the excellent work in proofreading and language editing. We also thank all the reviewers of various chapter as well as Ms. Angela Alu for providing editorial assistance.

The editors wish to specially appreciate the financial support provided by the following banks in completing this book project:

- Ecobank Ghana
- GCB Bank
- Stanbic Bank Ghana
- Agricultural Development Bank, Ghana
- CalBank
- Universal Merchant Bank
- Guaranty Trust Bank

Praise for *The Economics of Banking and Finance in Africa*

"The breadth of themes covered in this book is refreshing and quite extensive, from macroeconomic themes and analyses, through market structures and central bank performance, to such new themes as financial inclusion and FinTech, and the impact of COVID-19 on African financial systems. The scope of the volume is certainly remarkable as it helps us to appreciate recent developments in African financial systems. I am very happy to endorse it and recommend it to all those interested in understanding how finance in Africa works."

—Ernest Aryeetey, *Professor of Economics, Board Chair, African Economic Research Consortium & Former Vice-Chancellor, University of Ghana*

"This volume comes at a critical time to consolidate emerging evidence on the success of financial inclusion in all sectors of African economies. This emerging evidence, supported by the evolution of digital financial services, becomes an important input to development discourse. It now means that we can start formulating strong pillars for financial development in Africa. This book makes interesting contributions to the field of banking and finance."

—Prof. Njuguna S. Ndung'u, *Executive Director, African Economic Research Consortium and Former Governor, Central Bank of Kenya*

"This is a welcoming book on banking and finance in Africa. I commend the authors and the editors for covering the landscape and the depth of Africa's financial systems. The book provides an invaluable guide to scholars, policymakers, and graduate students on the theoretical, empirical and policy related issues in banking and finance in Africa. It is a must read for policymakers and researchers seeking to gain a deeper understanding of Africa's financial systems."

—Charles Amo-Yartey, Ph.D., *Senior Economist, International Monetary Fund, Washington DC, USA*

Contents

Notes on Contributors

Abor Joseph is a management and financial professional with over fifteen years of experience. He is currently the managing proprietor of Zuson Services; a business involved in haulage and product distribution. His professional life has largely been in the oil and gas industry as well as the integrated marketing communications industry. He worked as the General Manager of bulk oil distribution companies, such as Rama Energy Limited and Misyl Energy Company Ltd. He also worked as the General Manager of Nick Petroleum Ghana Limited, an oil marketing company. In addition, he worked as a Management and Financial Consultant at Resolve Medical Services. He holds M.Phil. in Finance degree and a Bachelor of Arts Degree in Accounting and Economics from the University of Ghana.

Abor Joshua Yindenaba is a financial economist with many years of expertise, mainly in development finance and economics research, as well as in senior-level practitioner, policy and consulting roles. He is a Professor of Finance and former Dean at the University of Ghana Business School. He is Adjunct Professor of Development Finance at the University of Stellenbosch Business School. He is an External Fellow at the Centre for Global Finance, SOAS University of London and a researcher with the African Economic Research Consortium as well as a Fellow of the Ghana Academy of Arts and Sciences. He has held Visiting Scholar positions at the International Monetary Fund (IMF), in Washington DC, and is a member of the Monetary Policy Committee of the Bank of Ghana.

Abor Patience Aseweh is a Senior Lecturer at the Department of Public Administration and Health Services Management, University of Ghana Business School. She holds a Ph.D. in Management from the Southampton Business School, University of Southampton, UK. Her research interests include issues in corporate governance, leadership and management. She has published in reputable international peer-refereed journals and serves as reviewer for a number of journals. He has also provided capacity building and consulting services for some organisations.

Abugre James Atambilla is a Senior Economic Development Officer in Ghana with vast experience in development finance, development planning and management, public policy administration and local governance and public financial management. He holds an M.Phil. in Economics from the University of Ghana and a Bachelor of Arts Degree in Integrated Development Studies (Economics and Entrepreneurship Development) from the University for Development Studies. He is a Ph.D. student in Finance at the University of Ghana Business School. He is a member of the Ghana Institute of Planners and Commonwealth Association of Planners.

Abugre Jessie A. is a lawyer with extensive experience in legal research, corporate and commercial matters and litigation. Jessie is intrigued by technology, loves everything science and tech and currently works with tech firms and startups. Her practice areas zero in on intellectual property, regulatory compliance and capital markets. She has experience representing high-profile clients in corporate and commercial matters and litigation. She holds a Bachelor of Laws degree from Kwame Nkrumah University of Science and Technology. She has an M.Phil. in Human Resource Management from the University of Ghana. Jessie is a member of the Ghana Bar Association and the International Academy of African Business Development.

Addae-Manu Richard is a nearly qualified Actuary and researcher in Development Finance, with close to twenty years of experience in the insurance industry. Richard's acquired skills include insurance pricing and valuation techniques, software application programming and project management. Richard has a keen interest in developing and growing the insurance sector in Africa and other emerging markets. Hence his research interests include insurance and financial market development. In addition, Richard enjoys family time and following the exploits of his favourite soccer teams.

Adjasi Charles Komla Delali is Professor of Development Finance and Economics at the University of Stellenbosch Business (USB) School in Cape Town South Africa, where he served as Head of Development Finance Programmes from January 2013–June 2017. He is also a Visiting Professor at ENSEA Cote d'Ivoire and an AFREXIM Bank Research Fellow. He has previously been a Visiting Professor at the Department of Economics, Econometrics and Finance, University of Groningen in the Netherlands. His research focuses on financial markets, firm productivity and household welfare development in Africa. He has published widely in reputable journals, a co-edited one book and co-authored another.

Afedzie Ekow is currently the Managing Director of the Ghana Stock Exchange and a member of the Council (Board) of the Exchange. He was educated at the University of Ghana, Legon, Ghana, where he obtained a master's degree in Business Administration (M.B.A.) in 1989 and a Master of Arts degree (M.A.) in Economic Policy Management. He also holds a bachelor's degree in Law (LL.B.) from Mountcrest University College and a Qualifying Certificate from the Ghana School of Law. He is a former Vice President of the African Securities Exchanges Association (ASEA) and currently a member of the Executive Committee of ASEA. He serves on the Boards of the Central Securities Depository (CSD) Ghana Ltd. and Ghana Investment and Securities Institute Ltd. Mr. Afedzie is also a member of the governing committees of Ghana Alternative Market (GAX) and Ghana Fixed Income Market (GFIM).

Agbloyor Elikplimi Komla is an Associate Professor in Finance at the University of Ghana Business School. He is also a research fellow in the Faculty of Economic and Management Sciences, University of Stellenbosch Business School, South Africa. He is a financial economist, chartered accountant and risk management expert. He has several years of teaching, research and consulting experience. Elikplimi has consulted for organisations including the International Finance Corporation (IFC), Ghana, Oil and Gas for Inclusive Growth (GOGIG) and the National Banking College. He is a researcher with the African Economic and Research Consortium (AERC).

Agoba Abel M. is a Lecturer in Finance at Coventry University, UK. He holds a Ph.D. in Finance degree and has over eight (8) years of teaching and research experience. He has developed and acquired extensive experience in outstanding communication, course development, research and publications, online course delivery and conference presentations. He is a member of the Institute of Chartered Accountants Ghana. Abel has experience in facilitating Corporate Finance, Statistical Analysis for Finance, among others. He has a proven excellence in organising short courses and training programs and serves as an external research fellow for Tesah Capital Ghana.

Agyei Samuel Kwaku is a Senior Lecturer of the Department of Finance of the University of Cape Coast. Dr. Agyei holds a Ph.D. and M.Phil. in Finance and Bachelor of Commerce degrees. He is a member, of the Institute of Chartered Accountants (Ghana). Dr. Agyei is currently the Vice-Dean of the School of Business, UCC. He teaches Accounting and Finance courses at both the graduate and undergraduate levels at the University of Cape Coast School of Business. His current research areas include financial literacy, behavioural finance, governance and welfare.

Agyeman Benjamin is a Ph.D. Finance student at the University of Ghana Business School. He holds an M.Phil. in Finance from the University of Ghana, a B.Sc. in Financial Mathematics from the University for Development Studies, and a Post-Secondary Education Certificate (Teachers' Cert 'A') from the University of Cape Coast. His research interests are in the areas of banking and finance, oil and gas finance, and corporate governance and finance. He is currently working on a number of book chapters with some renowned professors in the areas of project finance, sustainable and responsible investment, sustainable energy investment, and international corporate governance.

Ahmad Hassan Ahmad is at the School of Business and Economics, Loughborough University. Ahmad's research is in the areas of mobile money and financial inclusion and development in Africa, exchange rates and economic performance and fiscal policy in developing countries. He has published on these topics in journals including *Economics Letters*, *Journal of International Financial Markets, Institutions and Money*, *Review of Quantitative Finance and Accounting*, *Journal of Development Studies*, *The Manchester School*, *Review of Development Economics*, *Open Economies Review* and *Journal of Economic Surveys*.

Ajuwon Oluseye Samuel is a Lecturer in Economics at the University of Lagos, Nigeria. His areas of research are in macroeconomics and development finance, with a special focus on financing small businesses. He holds B.Sc. Economics from Obafemi Awolowo University, Nigeria, M.Sc. and M.Phil. in Economics from the University of Ibadan, Nigeria, and Ph.D. in Development Finance from the University of Stellenbosch Business School, South Africa.

Akinsola Foluso is a researcher and academic with over fifteen years of experience. He is currently a Lecturer in the Department of Economics at the University of Lagos. He obtained Ph.D. in Development Finance at the University of Stellenbosch Business School. He also has a Master's degree and a Bachelor's degree in Economics with honours from the University of Botswana. His areas of specialisation are International Economics, Monetary Economics and Development Finance. Dr. Akinsola has several publications in books and peer-reviewed academic journals.

Akotey Joseph Oscar has a Ph.D. in Development Finance from the University of Stellenbosch. His research interests include Development Finance, Risk Finance and Performance Evaluation. He has published in internationally accredited *3-Star* and *2-Star* journals. He has also made presentations at various international conferences such as the Centre for the Study of Africa Economies, Oxford University, WEI Conference at Harvard University, the Economic Society of South Africa and the Global Development Finance Conferences. He currently teaches *International Finance, Project Finance, Financial Derivatives* and *Corporate Governance* at KNUST School of Business, Kwame Nkrumah University of Science and Technology, Ghana.

Alagidede Imhotep Paul is a metaeconomist, a transdisciplinary scholar and professor at the University of the Witwatersrand, South Africa, and the Simon Diedong Dombo University of Business and Integrated Development Studies, Wa, Ghana. His research and teaching interests transcends traditional academic boundaries, delving into the possibilities and limits of human consciousness. He is an accomplished entrepreneur, a philanthropist and policy maker. Imhotep is the President and Chancellor of the multidimensional network of social enterprises called the Nile Valley Multiversity, the Grand Editor of the Journal of Indigenous and Shamanic Studies, Editor-in-Chief of the Journal of Construction and Built Environment and Executive Director of AREF Consult.

Alu Angela A. is currently awaiting the determination of her Ph.D. with the Department of Finance at the University of Ghana Business School. She holds an M.Phil. in Finance and B.Sc. in Administration (Banking and Finance) from the University of Ghana Business School. Her primary research interests include Natural Resource Governance, Banking and Financial Markets. She is an Assistant Lecturer with the Department of Business Administration at Academic City University College. She previously worked as a Contract Engineer with ENI Ghana and as a Financial Analyst with Temple Investments Limited.

Amidu Mohammed is a professional accountant, financial policy analyst and Professor of Accounting and Finance with a focus in corporate tax policy, accounting information quality, sustainable banking, development finance, treasury and governmental accounting. He is a researcher with African Economic Research Consortium (AERC), Kenya, and has held Visiting Scholar positions at the International Monetary Fund, Washington DC, USA. He has over 15 years of academic, research and consulting experience and for the past 5 years has been working on various aspects of SMEs management and finance in Ghana in addition to providing services to some organisation including Ghana Revenue Authority (GRA) Millennium Development Authority (MiDA), STAR-Ghana, Ministry of Finance and DANIDA Health Sector Support Office.

Amoah Lordina is a Senior Lecturer at the Department of Finance, University of Ghana Business School. She has a Ph.D. in Development Finance from the University of Stellenbosch, South Africa. Lordina is a researcher with the African Economic Research Consortium and has published articles in reputable international journals. Her areas of research interest include green finance, small business finance, corporate finance and financial market development. She has extensive knowledge in green finance. She participated in the Global Academy on Green Economy organised by the International Training Centre of the ILO and the ESRM programme by the International Finance Corporation.

Anarfo Ebenezer Bugri is a Senior Lecturer in Finance at the Department of Accounting and Finance, Ghana Institute of Management and Public Administration (GIMPA) Business School and a consultant at Corporate Support Group (CSG). Dr. Anarfo's research interests are in the areas of financial inclusion, financial sector development, monetary policy, financial regulation, remittances, food security, FDI, economic growth, capital structure and mental health. His scholarly works on these areas have been published in reputable journals.

Andani Alhassan holds the positions, CEO of LVS Africa, Chairman of Council for Scientific and Industrial Research and Chairman of SOS Children's Villages Ghana. He was also appointed by Gold Fields Limited as an independent non-executive director at its Board of Directors. Until now, he was the CEO/Executive Director of Stanbic Bank Limited and the president of the Ghana Association of Bankers (GAB). He holds a master's degree in Banking and Finance from Finafrica Institute in Milan, Italy. Andani is also an alumnus of the Oxford Strategic Leadership Programme, and holds an International Management Certificate from INSEAD, Chartered Bank.

Antwi Stephen is the Director of Studies and Training at the National Banking College (NBC).

Dr. Antwi is an Economist, a Banker, Lecturer and an International Motivational Speaker. His expertise are in the areas of Banking Operations, Credit Delivery and Risk Analysis. He has held various positions such as Deputy Managing Director, in Charge of Operations and Credit, Area Manager in Charge of Cluster of Branches, Branch Manager and Branch Operations Manager.

He holds a Ph.D., M.Phil. in Agricultural Economics, M.Sc. in Economics, M.B.A. in Finance, B.A. in Economics and a Diploma in Education. Additionally, Dr. Antwi is also a Member of the Chartered Institute of Bankers.

Arun Thankom is a Professor of Global Development and Accountability at the Essex Business School. Currently, he is a Professor Extraordinaire at the Stellenbosch Business School, South Africa, and a Research Fellow at IZA, Bonn. He is also Chairing an academic steering group on Financial inclusion in the International Cooperative and Mutual Insurance Federation (ICMIF). He is a Fellow of Academy of Social Sciences and a Fellow of the Royal Society of Arts, Manufactures and Commerce. Thankom's recent research interests are in the areas of Fintech, financial inclusion, climate change and sustainability.

Asante-Amponsah Daniel is a finance and accounting professional with a working experience with entities across oil and gas, mining and financial services industries. Skilled in statutory and group audits subject to Sarbanes-Oxley (SOX) compliance, ISAs and IFRS standards. An experienced accountant with an accreditation from the Institute of Chartered Accountant, Ghana. He is currently an assistant manager with Corporates, Regulated and Listed Entities Audit at KPMG UK. Prior to joining KPMG UK, he worked with PricewaterhouseCoopers, Ghana as an Experienced Senior Associate with the Energy Utility and Resources Industry Group. Daniel served as a Teaching and Research Assistant to Prof. Joshua Abor in the Department of Finance, University of Ghana Business School. He holds an M.Phil. Finance and B.Sc. Administration (Accounting) degrees from the University of Ghana Business School.

Asomaning Kwamina Koranteng is the Chief Executive of Stanbic Bank Ghana. He began his professional banking career in 1997 at the Cal Merchant Bank and has since worked with several international organisations including JP Morgan Chase & Co and Goldman Sachs & Co in New York.

He is also a Chartered Certified Accountant with a Master's degree in Finance from the Wharton School, University of Pennsylvania, and a Bachelor of Science degree in Business Administration (Accounting option) from the University of Ghana. Kwamina has extensive expertise in International Banking, Corporate Finance and Emerging markets. He serves on the Boards of Stanbic Investment Management Services, Stanbic Holdings, SBG Securities Group and the Advisory Board of the College of Humanities, University of Ghana. He is also an independent Non-Executive Director of Chirano Gold Mines.

Asongu Simplice A. is a Professor and holds a Ph.D. from Oxford Brookes University. He is currently the Lead Economist and Director of the African Governance and Development Institute (Yaoundé, Cameroon); Distinguished Visiting Professor at the University of Johannesburg (Johannesburg, South Africa), the Lead Economist and Director of the European Xtramile Centre of African Studies (Liège, Belgium) and Lead Economist and Co-director of "Centre de Recherche pour le Développement Economique" (Bangui, Central African Republic). He is also a: Senior Research Fellow at the Africa Growth Institute (Cape Town, South Africa).

Assefuah Kathryn A. A. O. is a lecturer in the Banking and Finance Department of the University of Professional Studies, Accra. She holds B.Sc. in Mathematics and Computer Science and M.Phil. in Risk Management and Insurance. He is currently a Ph.D. candidate in Finance. She previously worked at Prudential Life Insurance Company. Her interests are in the areas of pensions, the informal sector, financial inclusion, risk management and insurance.

Azu Gabriel has an M.Phil. in Finance from the University of Ghana and a B.Sc. in Accounting also from the University of Ghana. He is also an associate member of the Institute of Chartered Accountant, Ghana (ICAG). He is currently a teaching and research assistant at the University of Ghana Business School. He has served in the capacity as a teaching and graduate assistant in the University of Ghana Business School for two years.

His research interests are in the area of Financial Inclusion and Financial Development, Corporate Governance, Financial Institutions and Economic Growth and Development.

Banyen Kannyiri Thadious holds a Ph.D. in Development Finance from the University of Cape Town, South Africa, and an M.Phil. Finance and B.Sc. Administration degrees both from the University of Ghana. He has over ten (10) years of teaching and research experience and is currently a senior lecturer in the Department of Banking and Finance at the School of Business, S.D. Dombo University of Business and Integrated Development Studies, Ghana. Kannyiri serves on several administrative committees and boards of the University and has published in and reviewed for several internationally accredited peer-reviewed journals.

Boateng Sarah Serwah is a Lecturer in Finance at Ghana Institute of Management and Public Administration (GIMPA)—Business School, Accra. She holds B.Sc. Administration (Banking and Finance), M.Phil. Finance and Ph.D. Finance from the University of Ghana. Her research interests are in the areas of corporate governance, financial structure, development finance, ethical and sustainable investment.

Bundoo Sunil K. is an Associate Professor in the Department of Economics and Statistics at the University of Mauritius. He has published widely in trade and financial liberalisation; pro-poor macroeconomics; capital markets in particular stock markets and competition policy. He has completed several research and consultancy projects/papers for international organisations such the World Bank; the African Economic Research Consortium (AERC); the World Institute for Development Economics Research (WIDER); the United Nations Research Institute for Social Development (UNRISD); the Consumer Unity Trust Society (CUTS); the UNU-Institute of Advanced Studies (UNU-IAS) and the Melbourne Centre for Financial Studies.

Chipeta Chimwemwe is an Associate Professor of Corporate Finance and Head of the Finance division in the School of Economics and Finance at the University of the Witwatersrand. He was a Visiting Scholar at the J. Mack Robinson College of Business at Georgia State University in USA, and former Bank of Zambia Chair in Banking and Finance at Mulungushi University. He is NRF rated (C2 rating) and has published numerous papers in the field of Finance and Investments. His work appears in high-impact journals. Chimwemwe is a recipient of several awards including the Research Excellence Award and has presented his research findings at numerous national and international conferences. He has several years of practical experience in areas relating to Executive Education, Business Plan development and Digital Asset Investments.

Coffie William is an Associate Professor of Accounting and Finance and the Head of the Department of Accounting at the University of Ghana Business School. He holds a Ph.D. in Financial Economics and a Master's Degree in Finance from Birmingham City University, UK. Prof. Coffie is a Certified Chartered Accountant. He was previously a Senior Lecturer in Accounting and Finance and Programmes Director for M.Sc. Finance and Accounting and M.Sc. International Banking and Finance at University of Wolverhampton, Lecturer in Finance at Birmingham City University, Lecturer in Business and Taxation at Staffordshire University and Visiting Professor at Hong Kong City University.

Doku James Ntiamoah holds a Ph.D. in Finance from the University of Ghana, Legon. Dr. Doku is a Senior Lecturer at the Department of Banking and Finance, University of Professional Studies, Accra (UPSA) where he teaches finance courses and research methods. His main areas of research interest and collaborations are Banking Sector Development, Industrial Organisation of Banking Firm, Capital Structure, Public

Debt and Economic Growth, Institutional Quality and Growth; Institutions and Economic Growth. He has published several articles in peer-reviewed/ranked journals.

Donkor George N. Agyekum is currently the President (CEO) and Chairman of the Board of Directors of the ECOWAS Bank for Investment and Development (EBID). Dr. Donor is a Lawyer and a Banker with over twenty-eight (28) years of experience in senior management positions. He is the author of the book "*Customer Relationship Management Practices within the Rural Banking Industry in Ghana*". He also co-authored several publications including "*Organizational Learning Capability and Family Businesses Performance: Does Innovativeness Matter?*", "*Strategic Planning and Performance of SMEs in Ghana, The moderating effect of market dynamism*", among others. He currently serves on several Boards including the ECOBANK Transnational Incorporated (ETI), WAICA RE-Capital and WAICA RE-Insurance.

Dzeha Gloria Clarissa O. is a Senior Lecturer at the Banking and Finance Department, Central Business School, Central University and currently the Dean of Students. Gloria holds a Diploma in Statistics; Bachelor of Science degree in Banking and Finance; Master of Philosophy in Finance and Doctor of Philosophy in Finance from the University of Ghana. Her research interest includes International Finance, Remittances and Central Banking. She has considerable teaching experience in courses including International Finance, Investment Management, Financial Markets, Commercial Banking and Contemporary issues in Finance. Gloria Clarissa has written several academic papers.

Fanta Ashenafi is a senior lecturer and head of the Ph.D. development finance program at the University of Stellenbosch Business School where he teaches project finance and infrastructure finance. Dr. Fanta's research interests include financial development, infrastructure finance and small business finance, among others. Dr. Fanta holds a doctoral degree in Corporate Finance from Johannes Kepler University of Linz, Austria, and a Master's degree in accounting and finance from Addis Ababa University, Ethiopia.

Fiador Vera is a Senior Lecturer at the Department of Finance of the University of Ghana Business School. She holds a Ph.D. in Finance from the Graduate School of Business, University of Cape Town, South Africa. She has expertise in corporate finance, corporate governance, gender diversity, enterprise risk management and environmental and social risk management. She has a number of peer-reviewed publications to her name and has consulted for a number of reputable entities Vera's current consulting portfolio spans business and financial strategy development and interventions. Vera is a member of the African Economic Research Consortium and was a Visiting Scholar at the International Monetary Fund (IMF), Washington, DC.

Gossel Sean J. is an Associate Professor and the Research Director at the University of Cape Town Graduate School of Business. His expertise lies in the areas of financial economics and financial globalisation. His research focuses on the effects of financial globalisation and democratisation on African economies. On the basis of his publications, Gossel is an editorial member of the Journal of African Business, and a peer reviewer for over 30 international journals. He is also a research collaborator at UCT's Institute for Democracy, Citizenship and Public Policy and the UCT GSB's Development Finance Centre.

Graham Michael is a Professor of Finance at the Stellenbosch University Business School, South Africa. He holds a B.Sc. and M.Sc. in Economics from the University of Tampere, Finland, and a Ph.D. in Finance from the University of Vaasa, Finland. Prior to being appointed Professor of Finance at the Business School, Stellenbosch University, he held academic positions at the University of Vaasa, Finland, Deakin University, Australia, RMIT University, Australia, and Stockholm University, Sweden. He has also held visiting positions at academic institutions in Ghana, Hong Kong, Malaysia, and Singapore. Additionally, he was a Research Associate at the United Nations University, World Institute of Development Economics (UNU/WIDER) and a resident finance expert at the Australian Competition and Consumer Commission (ACCC). He is widely published in leading and internationally ranked peer-reviewed journals.

Green Christopher J. is Emeritus Professor of Economics and Finance at Loughborough University. He has a B.A., B.Phil. (Oxford University), M.Sc., M.Phil. and Ph.D. (Yale University). He has worked in the IMF African Department, at Manchester University, the Bank of England and The University of Wales, Cardiff. He was a Professor of Economics and Finance at Loughborough University for 23 years. He held visiting appointments at Yale University and the African Economic Research Consortium; and has acted as consultant to the UN Food and

Agriculture Organisation, the African Development Bank and the African Economic Research Consortium. His research interests are in portfolio analysis, financial markets and company finance in industrial and developing countries, and he has published more than 100 refereed journal articles and books in these areas.

Gyeke-Dako Agyapomaa has a Ph.D. in Economics from the University of Nottingham (UK), M.Sc. in Economics and Financial Economics from the University of Nottingham (UK) and a B.A. in Economics with Geography from the University of Ghana. She is currently a senior lecturer at the University of Ghana Business School.

Prior to her joining the University of Ghana Business School, she worked with Durham Business School (UK) as a Teaching Fellow. She also worked as the Country Programme Manager of the Bloomberg Media Initiative Africa, Financial Journalism Training Programme on part-time.

Her interests are in Micro, Small and Medium Enterprises (MSME) development, Financial Inclusion and Financial Development, Economic Growth and Development, International Capital Flows, Corporate Governance and Gender Diversity.

She has also consulted for a number of organisations She is also an ad hoc reviewer for some journals.

Harvey Simon K. holds a Ph.D. in Economics from the University of Nebraska-Lincoln, USA. He is currently the head of Macroeconomic Modeling and Forecasting Unit of the Research Department of Bank of Ghana. He was a Senior Lecturer at the Department of Finance of the University of Ghana Business School and has held Visiting Scholar position at the International Monetary Fund (IMF).

Ibrahim Abdul-Jalil has over 12 years of varied experience in academic research and financial services. He has worked as a researcher at Hamad Bin Khalifa University and Qatar University, both in Doha. Abdul-Jalil has also consulted for Government of Ghana projects and other international institutions, including the SNV Netherlands Development Organisation. He previously worked with Standard Chartered Bank Ghana and Coface Ghana. Abdul-Jalil has published in reputable international peer-reviewed journals over the past few years in Islamic letter of guarantee, Islamic venture capital, Islamic finance and circular economy and Islamic financial development and energy intensity. Abdul-Jalil is a Ph.D. candidate (finishing in April 2022) in Islamic Finance and Economy at Hamad Bin Khalifa University in Doha, Qatar, where he previously pursued a second Master's degree in Islamic Finance. He earlier received an M.Sc. in Oil and Gas Economics from the University of Dundee, UK. He also received B.Sc. Business Administration (Accounting) from KNUST.

Iddrisu Abdul Ganiyu holds a B.A. in Economics and Mathematics and M.Phil. in Economics, all from the University of Ghana. He was a teaching and research assistant at the University of Ghana Business School. He is currently pursuing a Ph.D. at the University of Aberdeen, UK. Abdul Ganiyu's research interests are in the areas of development economics, energy economics and financial economics. He has worked on issues related to economic growth, human development, political cycles and corruption, among others.

Iddrisu Khadijah holds a B.Sc. in Accounting from the University of Development Studies and an M.Phil. Finance from the University of Professional Studies Accra, Ghana. She is currently a Ph.D. candidate at Simon Diedong Dombo University of Business and Integrated Development Studies Wa-Ghana. Her research interests include sustainable finance, economics, modern banking practices and property tax.

Idun Anthony Adu-Asare holds a Bachelor of Management Studies from the University of Cape Coast, and an M.Phil. and Ph.D. in Finance from the University of Ghana. He is a lecturer in Finance at the Department of Finance, University of Cape Coast. He has been researching issues patterning to the finance-growth nexus and sustainable development, helping to pinpoint areas that financial intermediation should focus on to minimise systemic risk and promote sustainable development. He teaches Finance, Economics and Research at both undergraduate and graduate levels. He has been a reviewer for some academic journals.

Issahaku Haruna is an Associate Professor of Applied Economics and Finance and the Head of the Department of Economics and Entrepreneurship Development, University for Development Studies, Ghana. Haruna is an international Visiting Scholar at Covenant University, Nigeria. He is a development finance and economics expert whose current research focuses on remittances, digital finance, financial inclusion, agricultural finance and economic development. He has several publications to his credit. He is a member of several professional associations, including the Econometric Society, Africa, Finance and Economics

Association and Society for the Study of Emerging Markets. Haruna is a recipient of the 2020 Emerald Literati Awards, Highly Commended Paper category.

Isshaq Zangina is a Senior Lecturer in the Department of Accounting, University of Ghana Business School, where he teaches courses in both accounting and finance. He has Ph.D. (Finance) from The University of Queensland, Australia. His research interests include the role of accounting information in regulation, financial markets and institutions and empirical corporate finance. He was previously a Senior Lecturer at the Department of Finance, School of Business, University of Cape Coast and Head of the Department of Accounting, School of Business, University of Cape Coast.

Karimu Amin is a trained economist with a strong background in energy economics, public finance, econometrics, and development policy. He holds a Ph.D. and an M.Sc. in Economics from Umea University, Sweden, and a bachelor's degree from KNUST, Ghana. He is currently an Associate Professor in Economics at the School of Economics, University of Cape Town. He also regularly visits the Centre for Environmental and Resource Economics (CERE), Umea University, Mistra Centre for Sustainable Markets (MISUM) at Stockholm School of Economics, Sweden. Prof. Karimu has consulted for organisations such as the UN (UNU-WIDER), the International Growth Centre (IGC), Swedish Energy Agency, Sida, GIZ and IDRC.

Kusi Baah Aye holds an M.Phil. in Finance and is currently awaiting the determination of his Ph.D. thesis. Baah is a Chartered Financial Economist and a fellow member of Global Academy of Finance and Management, USA. He lectures at the Department of Applied Finance and Policy management, University of Education Winneba in the fields of corporate finance, financial management, business finance, electronic banking, investment and portfolio management, credit management and elements of banking. He is a research affiliate at the Dean of the University of Ghana Business School office and affiliated to other universities in Ghana.

Kuttu Saint is a Senior Lecturer in Finance and Risk Management at the University of Ghana Business School, University of Ghana, Legon. He holds B.Sc. (Administration) Banking and Finance, M.Sc. Computational Finance and Ph.D. Finance. He has presented and discussed research papers at several international conferences. He has also chaired conference sessions on emerging market finance. He has published in high-ranking international finance journals hosted by Elsevier, Taylor and Francis and Springer. He has held a lectureship (assistant professorship) position at Hanken School of Economics, Finland, and the Ghana Institute of Management and Public Administration (GIMPA). At Hanken School of Economics.

Mathuva David is a Senior Lecturer and Director, Undergraduate Programmes at Strathmore Business School, Kenya. David also serves as the Academic Director for the M.Sc. in Development Finance programme. David has worked at KPMG Kenya. He has published several research articles in peer-reviewed journals such as *Journal of Applied Accounting Research*, *Journal of Accounting in Emerging Economies*, *Journal of Financial Reporting and Accounting*, *Journal of Co-operative Organization and Management* and *Journal of Money Laundering Control* among others. He serves on the Editorial Boards of *Journal of Accounting in Emerging Economies*, *Emerging Markets Case Studies* and the *African Accounting and Finance Journal*.

Mensah Emmanuel is Head of Capital and Balance Sheet Management with the ABSA Bank, Ghana. He holds a Ph.D. in Finance from the University of Ghana, Legon, with strong interest in Banking and Economics. Dr. Mensah teaches Banking and Finance courses at the University of Ghana Business School on part-time basis. His main research interests include Banking Sector Efficiency, Treasury Management and Economic Growth.

Mensah Sam holds M.B.A. and Ph.D. degrees in Finance from the University of Toronto, an M.A. in Economics from the University of Ottawa, M.A. (Political Science), from McMaster University, B.A. (Political Science) from the University of Ghana. He is the founder and Managing Consultant of SEM International Associates, a financial services consulting firm based in Ghana. From 2006 to 2017, he served as Technical Advisor to Ministry of Finance in Ghana where he led key initiatives such as the Financial Sector Strategic Plan and bond market development. He recently completed a five-year term as Chairman of the Ghana Stock Exchange. Dr. Mensah and is an adjunct lecturer at the University of Ghana Business School. Prior to his consulting career, he was Assistant

Professor of Finance at the University of Michigan and has published extensively in peer-reviewed journals.

Misati Roseline works as a Researcher with the Central Bank of Kenya. Her main responsibilities involve analytical and technical analysis of monetary policy and economic and policy research. She has previously worked with different government ministries for over ten years, including Ministries of Finance, National Planning and Agriculture and the Kenya Institute for Public Policy Research and Analysis (KIPPRA). She has also worked as a Senior Researcher at the African Institute for Remittances and as a guest lecturer at the University of Nairobi. Roseline holds a Ph.D. in Economics and has published widely in internationally peer-reviewed journals.

Murinde Victor is the AXA Professor in Global Finance and the Director of the Research Centre for Global Finance, at SOAS University of London. He is a Fellow of the Econometric Society; he is also a Fellow of the Academy of Social Sciences. He has contributed over 100 research papers, mainly in the area of banking and finance. His other roles include Chair of Group C (Finance) for the African Economic Research Consortium (AERC) and Board of Trustees of British Institute in Eastern Africa. He was the founding Director of the African Development Institute, at the African Development Bank, 2011–2014.

Muriu Peter W. holds a Ph.D. in Financial Economics from the University of Birmingham, UK. He is a senior lecturer in monetary and financial economics at the Department of Economics and Development Studies, University of Nairobi. He is a researcher and an external reviewer, finance and resource mobilisation thematic research for the African Economic Research Consortium (AERC). He is also an external reviewer for Oxford Development Studies, Financial Regulation and Compliance and Transnational Corporations Review Journals. As an independent consultant, he has spearheaded various research projects with the aim to ignite new policies on microfinance; financial inclusion; financial stability; banking concentration; provisioning behaviour and risk management in the banking industry.

Mohammed Jabir Ibrahim holds a Ph.D. in Finance, M.Phil. in Finance and Bachelor of Arts in Economics and Political Science all from the University of Ghana. He is a Lecturer at the Department of Banking and Finance, University of Professional Studies Accra and a Consultant with

Corporate Support Group Limited, a management consultancy firm. His areas of interest are Energy Finance, Financial Markets and Institutions, Fintech, Macroeconomics and Financial Economics.

Moleko Nthabiseng is a Development Economist with a Ph.D. in Development Finance from Stellenbosch Business School. She is a faculty member at the University of Stellenbosch Business School where she teaches Economics and Statistics as a Senior Lecturer. She has worked in senior-level roles within economic development prior to becoming an academic. Her core research interests are in the areas of development finance, economic development and growth. Moleko continues to serve as a Commissioner and Deputy Chairperson of the Commission for Gender Equality, board member and Chairperson of the National Empowerment Fund and a Strategic Advisory Committee Member to the Development Bank of Southern Africa's Infrastructure Fund.

Mumuni Zakari is an Assistant Director and Head of the Modelling and Forecasting Office at the Research Department of the Bank of Ghana. Prior to this, Zakari had served as Special Assistant to the Governor and also performed various roles including providing analytical support to the Bank's Monetary Policy Committee. Zakari Mumuni holds a Ph.D. in Economics from the School of Economics, University of Nottingham, UK.

Nellis Joseph G. is a Professor of Global Economy specialising in macroeconomic analysis and policy, business environmental analysis and strategic thinking for managers. He is also Deputy Dean and the longest serving member of Cranfield School of Management's Executive Board. He has previously served as the Director of the School and Pro-Vice-Chancellor of the University. He has held Visiting Professorial appointments at various universities in Germany, Belgium, Austria, The Netherlands, Hungary, the USA and Ghana. Joe has published 19 research and subject-based books and over 200 academic and practitioner journal articles. He is an experienced contributor to a wide range of national and international conferences and is a consultant to organisations in the areas of strategy and business environmental analysis, strategy formulation and management development. He has served two years in Ghana as a VSO teacher and was formerly Chairman of Wellingborough Homes Housing Association.

Ntim Collins G. is a Professor of Accounting at the Centre for Research in Accounting, Accountability and Governance (CRAAG), Department of Accounting, Southampton Business School, University of Southampton, UK. His research focuses on how and why accounting, finance and governance can global development and sustainability, which has attracted competitive external and internal research funds of over £500,000. He has published extensively in the leading international academic journals, as well as taught accounting, finance and governance subjects to a large number of undergraduate, postgraduate, research, especially Ph.D., executive and professional accounting and finance students in a wide variety of institutions and countries around the world. He has also held several academic, leadership and consulting roles in different reputable institutions in the UK and worldwide.

Ntuli Miracle (nee Ntuli) is an Associate Professor in the School of Economics and Finance at the University of the Witwatersrand. Her research interests are in applied micro-econometrics with a special focus on labour and development economics. She has done work on (i) income distribution and the potential of redistributive systems in Africa, (ii) intra-household resource allocation, (iii) gender differentials in health and labour market outcomes, (iv the economics of education, (v) crime and subjective well-being and (vi) multidimensional poverty and spatial heterogeneity in well-being.

Nyeadi Joseph Dery is a senior lecturer and a chartered accountant with the SD-Dombo University of Business and Integrated Development Studies (SDD-UBIDS) in Ghana. Before joining SDD-UBIDS), Joseph worked with Wa Polytechnic and the University of Mines and Technology as a Senior Lecturer. He holds a Ph.D. in Development Finance from the University of Stellenbosch, South Africa, M.Sc. in Finance from the University of St. Andrews, UK and B.Sc. in Land Economy from KNUST. His areas of interest range from Corporate Finance to Corporate Governance in African context. He has published widely in a number of renowned journals.

Ocran Matthew Kofi is a Professor of economics at the department of economics and Deputy Dean for academic planning and assessment at the Faculty of Economics and Management Sciences, University of the

Western Cape, South Africa. His current research interests lie in macroeconomics, development economics, development finance and economic history.

Oduro-Afriyie Emmanuel is a corporate credit manager with Absa Bank Ghana Limited. He holds a Ph.D. in Development Finance from Stellenbosch University in Cape Town—South Africa. His doctoral research focused on monetary policy and the estimation of aggregate and sectoral threshold inflation rates, inflation inertia, expected durations and switching probabilities of inflationary regimes in African economies. Dr. Oduro-Afriyie is a Moody's Certified Commercial Credit Analyst and has presented several of his academic papers at the Centre for the study of African Economies (CSAE) at the University of Oxford, UK, the University of St. Gallen in Switzerland and the University of Cape Town in South Africa as well as at numerous international conferences.

Ofoeda Isaac is a Lecturer in the Department of Accounting at the University of Professional Studies, Accra (UPSA). He holds a Bachelor's degree in Business Administration (Banking and Finance Option), an M.Phil. in Finance and a Ph.D. in Finance from the University of Ghana Business School. He is also a member of the Institute of Chartered Accountants, Ghana (ICAG). He currently coordinates the M.Phil. Finance and M.Sc. Insurance Risk Management programmes at the UPSA. His research focuses on anti-money laundering regulations, financial inclusion, financial sector development, corporate governance, financial markets and institutions regulations and foreign direct investment.

Ofori-Sasu Daniel is an emerging financial economist and a Ph.D. candidate at the University of Ghana Business School. He holds an M.Phil. in Finance and B.Sc. degree in Agricultural economics from the University of Ghana. His research interests include banking, regulation, corporate finance and governance issues, capital structure and investment decisions, dividend policy, financial development, business development, economics, monetary economics and policy, insurance policy, efficiency modelling, sustainability, econometrics and financial analysis. He is currently a lecturer at Central University and an adjunct lecturer at Accra Business School. He is an independent business, financial and economic consultant.

Ojangole Patricia A. is a professional accountant with 17 years' experience in Banking and Finance. She is the Managing Director of Uganda

Development Bank Limited. Prior to becoming the Managing Director, she worked as a Chief Audit Executive at Uganda Development Bank and a Senior Internal Audit Manager at Standard Bank Group. She holds a first-class M.Phil. in Development Finance from the University of Stellenbosch, South Africa, Executive Master's in Business Administration from Eastern and Southern Africa Management Institute, Tanzania; a Bachelor of Commerce (Hons) Degree from Makerere University. She is currently undertaking her Ph.D. studies in development finance at the University of Stellenbosch. Patricia is a Fellow of the Association of the Certified Chartered Accountants (UK); the Certified Public Accountants of Uganda (ICPAU) as well as The Institute of Internal Auditors Uganda (IIA).

Opoku-Afari Maxwell is currently the First Deputy Governor of the Bank of Ghana. He was appointed to this position on August 7, 2017, and was re-appointed for a second term in August 2021. Previously, Maxwell Opoku-Afari worked at the International Monetary Fund (IMF) from December 2009 to July 2017, serving as Deputy Division Chief in the Regional Studies Division in the African Department, where he led and supervised the production of one of the IMF's flagship publication—the Regional Economic Outlook for sub-Saharan Africa. He also served as Mission Chief to both Sao Tome and Principe and Mauritius.

Oppong Kwame A. is the Head of FinTech and Innovation at Bank of Ghana. His background spans management, technology, digital financial services (DFS) operations, policy development and regulation. He has consulted for several governments, public sector institutions, international development organisations and private corporations globally. He holds a B.Sc. in Business Administration, an M.Sc. in Business, Executive Education certification in policy design and other certifications in blockchain, cloud computing, virtualisation and financial inclusion among others. Kwame is a passionate advocate for financial inclusion, innovation and the development of digital economies.

Osei Jephthah O. holds a B.A. Economics and M.Phil. Economics from the University of Ghana. He is the GS-CUPE graduate scholar at York University, Toronto, Ontario, Canada. He has previously worked as a research assistant in the Department of Finance, University of Ghana Business School, and teaching assistant in the Department of Economics, University of Ghana. Jephthah is a graduate teaching assistant in the Department of Economics, York University, Toronto, Canada.

Otchere Isaac is a Professor of Finance at the Sprott School of Business, Carleton University in Canada. He has extensive international research and teaching experience and expertise in corporate finance, financial economics, development finance and banking. He has held Visiting Scholar positions at the University of Dubai, University of Cape Town Graduate, University of Stellenbosch, University of Ghana Business School, GIMPA, and many other universities. Dr. Otchere has published extensively in highly ranked peer review finance journals. He is a Resource Person for the African Economic Research Consortium (AERC) based in Nairobi, Kenya, and a Fellow of the Carnegie African Diaspora Programme based in New York. His scholarship has received international recognition from prominent international financial institutions including the World Bank, IMF/African Institute.

Quartey Peter is a Professor of Economics with more than 18 years expertise, mainly in development finance, private sector development, monetary and financial sector development with senior-level roles at practitioner, policy and consulting services. He holds a Ph.D. in Development Economics from the University of Manchester (UK) and M.Sc. in Quantitative Development Economics from the University of Warwick (UK). He also holds M.Phil. and BA degrees in Economics from the University of Ghana. He is currently the Director of the Institute of Statistical, Social and Economic Research (ISSER), University of Ghana. He has held Visiting Scholar positions at the International Monetary Fund (IMF), Washington DC, USA, and the Brookings Institution, African Growth Centre.

Sa-Aadu Jarjisu is currently Chester A. Phillips Professor of Finance and Real Estate in the Henry B. Tippie College of Business, the University of Iowa, USA. He teaches fixed income securities, real estate finance and investments, international finance, corporate finance and structured finance. He has written extensively on mortgage choice, mortgage pricing, housing vouchers and REITs. His current research focuses on central banks independence, unconventional monetary policy, the geography and distributional consequences of quantitative easing (QE) and of effects of funding liquidity, and market liquidity induced by QE on new residential housing investments.

Salami Iwa is a Reader in Financial Regulation at the School of Business and Law, University of East London (UEL). She is the Co-Director of the UEL Centre of FinTech and the Programme Leader for the LL.M. in FinTech Law. She has published extensively in the field of FinTech regulation and her list of publications includes a book: *Financial Regulation in Africa* (Ashgate, 2012). She is currently researching regulatory frameworks for Web 3.0 application in finance including crypto-assets, stablecoins, decentralised finance (DeFi), Non-fungible tokens (NFTs) and the metaverse; Central Bank Digital Currencies (CBDCs) and legal dimensions of DLT/Blockchain Technology.

Salia Samuel has over 13 years of experience in academia and industry in the UK and internationally. As a Senior Lecturer in Finance, he has extensive teaching and research presence, with publications in high-rated international journals. His areas of expertise are within the dispora and entrepreneurial finance. He has served as a keynote speaker at national and international conferences. He also actively provides consultancy services for international organisations such as the African Union-Economic, Social and Cultural Council.

Sarpong-Kumankoma Emmanuel is a Senior Lecturer in Finance at the University of Ghana Business School. Dr. Sarpong-Kumankoma's research interests include financial regulation, bank performance, corporate governance, financial literacy, financial management, financial market development, microfinance and international finance. He has publications in journals such as *International Journal of Productivity and Performance Management*, *Managerial and Decision Economics*, *Review of Behavioral Finance*, *Journal of Financial Economic Policy*, *Journal of Financial Regulations and Compliance*, *Journal of Economic Studies* and *Journal of Property Research*, among others.

Sheefeni Johannes Peyavali Sheefeni is an associate professor of economics at the Department of Economics, University of the Western Cape. He holds B.Econ., B.EconHons., M.Econ. and Ph.D. in Economics. Johannes also worked at the University of Namibia, Namibia University of Science and Technology, Central Bank of Namibia, commercial banks such as Nedbank Namibia and First National Bank Namibia. His research interests cover Applied Econometrics, Monetary Policy, Macro-econometric Modelling, International Finance and Banking. He has also published in local and international academic journals.

Sissy Aisha Mohammed holds a B.Sc. in Administration and an M.Phil. in Finance, both from the University of Ghana. She was a teaching and research assistant at the University of Ghana Business School and Ashesi University College. She was a Multimedia Broadcast Journalist with the BBC World Service. She is currently a Director of Administration and Human Resource under the Office of the President of Ghana. Her research interests are in the areas of Development Finance, Financial Inclusion and Banking. She has worked on issues related to economic growth, human development, political cycles, corruption, Human rights and Social Justice among others.

Wolfe Simon is a Professor of Banking and Finance. His Ph.D. in Finance is from Southampton University 1997. Professor Wolfe is the Director of the Centre for Digital Finance (CDF) and Director of the Doctor of Business Administration (DBA) Programme within Southampton Business School at the University of Southampton. He has contributed to the financial economics literature, mainly in the areas of banking and finance, development finance and financial market development. Prior to becoming an academic, Professor Wolfe worked in the industry for a number of years. Simon designed and set up the M.Sc. Finance degree Programme. His core teaching interests lie in the areas of international banking and corporate finance.

Yawson Alfred is a professor in corporate finance at the University of Adelaide Business School, Adelaide, Australia.

List of Figures

List of Tables

PART I

Overview of Banking and Finance

CHAPTER 1

Introduction: An Overview of Africa's Financial Systems

Joshua Yindenaba Abor and Charles Komla Delali Adjasi

1.1 Introduction

The financial system allows for financial transactions to take place between surplus economic units and deficit economic units. It is composed of money, financial instruments, financial markets, financial institutions, and financial regulators that facilitate the interactions between the surplus units and deficit units. The financial system ensures the efficient allocation of economic resources by distributing funds to economic entities for investments that will generate appropriate returns. The functions of the financial system include mobilising savings and allocating resources, facilitating access to debt finance by governments, offering opportunities

J. Y. Abor (✉)
Department of Finance, University of Ghana Business School, Accra, Ghana
e-mail: joshabor@ug.edu.gh

C. K. D. Adjasi
University of Stellenbosch Business School, Cape Town, South Africa
e-mail: Charles.adjasi@usb.ac.za

J. Y. Abor and C. K. D. Adjasi (eds.), *The Economics of Banking and Finance in Africa*, Palgrave Macmillan Studies in Banking and Financial Institutions, https://doi.org/10.1007/978-3-031-04162-4_1

for investments, providing means of managing risk, providing a system for clearing and payments/settlements, and providing means of monitoring investment (Abor, 2018; Amoah et al., 2020). The depth of the financial system demonstrates the extent to which economic agents are able to use it. However, sub-Saharan Africa's financial systems are seen as shallow and tend to experience a financial development gap relative to other developing economies (Abor et al., 2019; Allen et al., 2014; Aryeetey, 2003).

The financial system may be bank-based or market-based.[1] Africa's financial systems tend to be bank-based, implying that the banking sectors play a more significant role compared with the capital markets. However, banking sector indicators in Africa are still lower than in other regions of the world. Banking penetration is still low in many African countries, with banking services largely restricted to urban communities. Though financial inclusion (i.e. in terms of the percentage of adults in sub-Saharan Africa (SSA) with bank accounts) has increased, the percentage is still low compared with emerging countries and the rest of the world. A number of factors have been identified to contribute to the low level of financial inclusion, and these include inadequate supportive infractursture, high transaction costs, unfavourable regulatory regime, low level of financial literacy, high poverty rates, and behavioural biases (see Abor et al., 2020).

The banking sector is also highly inefficient (see Beck & Cull, 2014; Bazot, 2018) and dominated by foreign banks (Banya & Biekpe, 2017; Doku et al., 2012; Fosu, 2013). This high level of inefficiency is often demonstrated by the high bank overhead costs and high-interest margin. The increased presence of foreign banks in the African banking space is a result of the financial sector reforms that a number of African countries carried out, which resulted in the opening of African markets to foreign entry. Government-owned banks also dominate the banking sector in some African countries. It is important to mention that many African countries have taken some initiatives aimed at promoting banking sector development to ensure efficient allocation of capital to finance growth. The banking sectors in Botswana, Malawi, Nigeria, Seychelles, and South Africa are relatively well-capitalised and dynamic, which encourages more innovative practices in banking than those in other African countries (Allen et al., 2011).

[1] A market-based financial system is one in which the capital market plays a more significant role compared with the banking sector.

Like African banks, African stock markets are also confronted with challenges in respect of financial depth (measured by market capitalisation and number of listings) and liquidity. The stock markets in SSA are among the smallest with regard to stock market capitalisation and number of firms listed on stock exchanges. African stock markets are generally characterised by thin trading with low level of turnover or liquidity (Senbet & Otchere, 2010). This issue has gained the attention of policymakers, hence policy initiatives are being undertaken with the aim of building integrated regional stock markets. These initiatives include privatisation of state-owned organisations through public offerings on the stock exchanges (e.g. the privatisation of SIC Insurance Company Limited in Ghana), the introduction of alternative stock exchanges for small and medium enterprises (e.g. the Ghana Alternative Market, the Alternative Securities Market in Nigeria, and the Growth Enterprise Market Segments in Kenya), and the establishment of regional stock exchanges. Examples of regional stock exchanges are the Bourse Régionale des Valeurs Mobilières (BRVM) situated in Abidjan, Cote d'Ivoire, for the Francophone West African countries, and the Bourse Régionale des Valeurs Mobilières d'Afrique Centrale (BVMAC) located in Libreville, Gabon. There are also considerations regarding the need for the Economic Community for West African States (ECOWAS) to also create a regional stock exchange for the Anglophone countries in West Africa. In the same vein, the Southern African Development Community (SADC) and the Eastern African Community (EAC) may form regional exchanges for their respective regions.

The stock markets in Africa have, however, witnessed some increase in the number of stock exchanges over the past two decades. With only 5 stock exchanges in SSA and 3 in North Africa, there are currently about 29 stock exchanges in the continent and the two regional stock exchanges mentioned earlier: the BRVM and the BVMAC. The BRVM serves the Francophone countries in West Africa (i.e. Benin, Burkina Faso, Guinea Bissau, Côte d'Ivoire, Mali, Niger, Senegal, and Togo), while the BVMAC serves the countries in Central Africa (i.e. Central African Republic, Chad, Democratic Republic of Congo, Equatorial Guinea, and Gabon). The past two decades have also been characterised by growth in assets, number of listings, and market capitalisation.

The private equity market has seen some increase; however, this is at a low pace. Private equity investments are estimated at less than 1% of Africa's GDP. The market is dominated by regional and domestic firms.

It is also witnessing increased interests from large foreign firms, which wish to take advantage of the growing investment opportunities in Africa. The modest growth of the private equity market can be attributed to the stable macroeconomic environment in most African countries.

The bond markets are mainly underdeveloped in Africa, and in many countries, they represent less than 10% of GDP. This is far lower than the size of the global bond market, which accounts for about 140% of global GDP African bond markets are dominated by trading in government bonds. The public issuance of corporate bonds is not a common feature in Africa, as these tend to be very small, representing an insignificant composition of the overall local bond market. Corporate bond issues are essentially done through private placement. A number of factors, including limited number of individual and institutional investors, capital gains, high returns in risk-free government instruments, alternative sources of debt financing, weak regulations and market infrastructure, and unfavourable macroeconomic environment tend to adversely impact bond market development in Africa (Abor, 2018). The little progress made so far in this regard is evidenced by the corporate bond market in the regional market in French West Africa, a secondary bond market and a bond index in Nigeria, and a well-developed market for government bonds in South Africa. African countries have typically relied on foreign private capital flows for financing long-term projects. Therefore, they have not paid much attention to developing the domestic bond markets.

The insurance market in Africa is also relatively undeveloped compared with other developing economies. Access to insurance products is restricted and Africa's share of the world insurance market is low, representing about 1.3% of the total world premium. The market is very diverse and fragmented, with only 11 countries controlling about 92% of total insurance premiums in Africa (Balcilar et al., 2020). The insurance penetration rate is low and a number of reasons have been given for this. These include low level of income, lack of human capital and expertise, lack of trust in providers of financial service, and accessibility of informal types of insurance (KPMG, 2017). Mauritius, Namibia, and South Africa tend to have relatively well-developed insurance markets, with insurance penetration rates of 6.4, 6.9, and 14.3%, respectively. The size and impact of the other African countries' insurance sectors are relatively small (Balcilar et al., 2020). However, some steady growth is being recognised, with growth rate in Africa's insurance market surpassing the world average (KPMG, 2015).

The pensions industry in Africa tends to have very low coverage, usually below 5% of the population, mainly made up of civil servants or a few well-paid formal sector employees. In addition to this are the problems of unemployment, a large informal sector, and lack of appropriate vehicles to invest in infrastructure. A number of African countries have implemented reforms, including the participation of the private sector in the pension space.

Africa's financial system is beginning to experience inclusive finance, driven largely by financial technology (FinTech) innovation. FinTech is expanding access to financial services to households and SMEs, which can play a very significant role in economic recovery and boost a more inclusive participation. The form of FinTech which has mostly dominated Africa's financial sector is mobile money, and it is regarded as the most successful innovation in promoting inclusive finance in the region. The other forms, especially mobile banking and crowdfunding, are gaining traction in Africa. The COVID-19 pandemic has significantly improved the adoption of FinTech, but at the same time increased the risks associated with cybercrime activities (see Abor, 2020).

Africa's financial systems are generally confronted with a number of challenges including financial volatility and economic shocks, weak regulations, undeveloped capital markets, weak governments and institutions, international trade barriers, and limited integration with the international financial system. The global financial and economic crises have also presented some uncertainties for emerging and frontier economies, such as African countries. The current COVID-19 pandemic introduces even more serious challenges and new uncertainties, which have implications for Africa's financial systems and its FinTech space (see Abor, 2020; Agbloyor & Abor, 2020). These developments require more research to inform SSA countries on the innovations they need to address these challenges and how to position their financial systems to be resilient to these shocks.

1.2 Purpose of This Book

The banking and the financial markets play a significant role in the growth of various economies. A number of handbooks on banking and finance exist on Europe, America, and Asia. Banks and financial markets in Africa are confronted with different challenges and therefore present a unique case for understanding Africa's financial systems. A number of African countries have experienced banking crises and it is important to examine these issues as well as the regulatory regimes required to address them. This edited book contributes to the limited texts in the area by providing a comprehensive resource on banking and finance for students, scholars, researchers, policymakers, and financial market practitioners. It contains various theoretical and empirical chapters on banking and finance in Africa. The COVID-19 pandemic has had devastating effects on Africa's financial systems, requiring further research and new thinking on how to reform them.

The Economics of Banking and Finance in Africa, which is made up of contributions from scholars in finance and economics as well as financial market practitioners, provides an essential resource and a guide to Africa's financial systems. It is composed of seven parts and thirty chapters. Below is an overview of the chapters.

1.3 An Overview of the Chapters

The book is divided into seven parts. Part I is an Overview of Banking and Finance. Part II focuses on FinTech, Financial Inclusion, and Banking Section Development; Part III looks at Central Bank and Monetary Policy; Part IV looks at Structured Finance, Sustainable Finance, and Islamic Banking; Part V examines Banking Crises and Global Banking; Part VI examines Banking Regulation and Supervision; and Part VII focuses on Non-Bank Financial Markets.

Part I: Overview of Banking and Finance

Having introduced the book by providing an overview of Africa's financial systems and the purpose of the book, we now provide an outline of the rest of the chapters.

Part II: FinTech, Financial Inclusion, and Banking Sector Development

In Chapter 2, Matthew Ocran, Johannes Sheefeni, and Emmanuel Oduro-Afriyie discuss the relationship among inflation, interest rates, and exchange rates in Africa. They suggest that these variables constitute a set of macroeconomic fundamentals that underpins the performance of small open economies, including those in Africa, and that stable outcomes of these variables lie at the core of efforts to ensure a stable macroeconomic environment conducive for growth and development. The authors provide the key stylised facts regarding the behaviour of the variables. They also provide a review of the relevant theories that explain the behaviour of inflation, interest rates, and exchange rates, as well as salient empirical literature associated with each of the variables. The last section of the chapter shows how the variables relate to one another.

Chapter 3 examines the effect of bank market structure on the competition in Africa. Using a panel data approach, James Ntiamoah Doku, Emmanuel Mensah, Zangina Isshaq, and Charles Adjasi found that the African banking sector is characterised by monopolistic competition. They indicate that, though banks produce homogenous products, they have the ability to adjust their prices upward using unique strategies of image branding and product and service offerings, and good customer relationships. They recommend that regulatory reforms should be geared towards introducing credit information sharing among participants in the banking sector in order to reduce the monopolistic power of banks, thereby enhancing competitive behaviour and the efficiency of banking operations.

Chapter 4 focuses on financial inclusion, banking sector development and financial stability in Africa. In this chapter Ebenezer Anarfo, Miracle Nthuli, Sarah Serwah Boateng, and Joshua Y. Abor explore the causal links among financial inclusion, banking sector development, and financial stability. Using a panel vector autoregressive (VAR) estimation approach, they found that financial inclusion, banking sector development, and financial stability all have a reverse causation. This finding suggests that these variables are complements rather than substitutes. Accordingly, financial institutions and central governments should not pursue any of these variables separately as a policy objective but rather consider them as complements when modelling or implementing economic policies for development.

In Chapter 5, Joshua Y. Abor, Peter Quartey, Ahmad H. Ahmad, and Maxwell Opoku-Afari discuss the role of FinTech in transforming the delivery of banking and financial services and its potential for promoting financial inclusion in Africa. The chapter discusses the main types of FinTech which include mobile money, mobile banking, crowdfunding, blockchain technology and cryptocurrencies and their market development in Africa. It looks at the challenges facing FinTech in Africa as well as the impact of the COVID-19 pandemic on Africa's FinTech space, including the dearth of infrastructure—electricity and internet, interoperability between service providers and fraud. The chapter also highlights the importance of optimum regulation, which should be beneficial to both innovations and participants—providers and users.

PART III: Central Bank and Monetary Policy

Chapter 6 by Abel Agoba, Vera Fiador, Emmanuel Sarpong-Kumankoma, and Jarjisu Sa-Aadu looks at how the independence of central banks, exchange rate regime, and monetary policy impacts on inflation in Africa. The study employs a Two-Step GMM, Two-Stage Least Squares, and Fixed Effects estimation methods. The results show that fixed exchange rate regimes have lower inflation rates than systems with floating exchange rates. However, the impact of central bank independence on inflation is higher in floating exchange rate regimes when compared to fixed exchange rate regimes. Also, monetary policy effectiveness is higher in Non-CFA Zone countries relative to those in the CFA Zone. Its impact is enhanced by higher levels of central bank independence.

Chapter 7 by Joshua Abor, Abel Agoba, Zakari Mumuni, and Alfed Yawson analyses the role of central bank independence (CBI) in explaining the impact of monetary policy on financial development in Africa using a 2 Stage GMM estimation technique, 2 Stage Least Squares, and Fixed Effects. The findings show that monetary policy effectiveness on financial development is higher for the banking sector than for capital markets. Central bank independence has a significantly positive impact on both banking sector and capital market development. The effect of monetary policy on financial development is enhanced by CBI. This is because monetary policy has a higher impact on financial development in the presence of higher levels of CBI in Africa. The policy implication of this finding is that monetary policy credibility is essential for financial development in Africa. This credibility could be found in making central banks in Africa independent of political control.

In Chapter 8, Anthony Adu-Asare Idun, Samuel Kwaku Agyei, Sean J. Gossel, and Joshua Abor examine how monetary policy and institutions affect bank market power in Africa. The results of persistent first difference dynamic GMM show that banks with market power can augment the effort of central banks, which use monetary policy to induce the stability of prices and real interest rates. The evidence also shows that the emergence of credit information sharing institutions complements the effect of banks with market power to channel monetary policy transmission into the stability of prices and interest rates. Finally, the results indicate that the conduct of banks with market power has different impacts across the sub-regions.

Chapter 9 examines the relationship between monetary policy and bank risk-taking in Africa. Agyapomaa Gyeke-Dako, Simon Harvey, Gabriel Azu, and Haruna Issahaku found that expansionary monetary policy induces African banks to take excessive risk. They suggest that central banks strengthen their monitoring schemes when accommodative monetary policies become necessary to ensure the stability of banks.

Chapter 10 focuses on bank pricing behaviour, monetary policy, and inclusive financial development in Africa. Mohammed Amidu, Abdul Ganiyu Iddrisu, Alhassan Andani and Benjamin Agyeman looked at the role of monetary policy in the link between bank pricing behaviour and financial development. They found that loan price increases when monetary policy is contracted and bank prices reduce when general price level is stable (effective monetary policy). Their results also indicate that high bank pricing in the light of contractionary monetary policy tends to increase financial inclusion and that high bank pricing reduces financial inclusion when monetary policy is effective.

Part IV: Structured Finance, Sustainable Finance, and Islamic Banking

In Chapter 11, Ashenafi Fanta, Michael Graham, and Daniel Asante-Amponsah discuss structured finance in Africa. This chapter covers what structured finance is, structured finance and conventional bank finance, structured finance instruments, Africa's experience in structured finance, and preconditions for enhancing the use of structured finance in Africa. They indicate that a structured finance market is largely absent in Africa except in Nigeria, Ghana, South Africa, and Cote D'Ivoire. Within these countries, structured finance is largely used to respond to the financial needs of infrastructural development. The chapter identifies the unstable nature of the macroeconomic environment and low level of sophistication of the financial market to account for the underdeveloped nature of structural finance in Africa. They provide useful recommendations.

Chapter 12 discusses Sustainable Finance and Banking in Africa. Lordina Amoah, Gloria Clarissa O. Dzeha, and Thankom Arun examine sustainable finance, the sustainable development goals (SDGs) and sustainable finance, financial institutions, and the 'Triple Bottom Line', socially responsible investment of banks in Africa, and sustainable finance and banking policies and practices in Africa. They argue that SDGs still seem far-fetched in most African countries and this has been further worsened by the COVID-19 pandemic. They suggest that financial sector leaders explore complementary financing options like green bonds and adhere to international best practices in sustainable finance and banking. Also, African countries need to develop national policy measures to spearhead the advancement of a green financial sector.

Chapter 13 provides a general overview of Islamic banking and finance in Africa as an important alternative to conventional models, due to the experiences of recent financial crises. Amin Karimu, Samuel Salia, Abdul-Jalil Ibrahim, and Imhotep Paul Alagidede explain that there is increasing evidence of some significant difference between the two banking models, particularly their performance under shocks. They suggest Islamic banking and finance models have higher asset quality and are better capitalised relative to conventional banking models but also less cost-effective. It provides the possibility to leverage on the strength of the two models to better accommodate impacts of shocks on the global financial system. They cover the principles and models of Islamic banking and finance, an overview of Islamic banking and finance in Africa, as well as the challenges and opportunities it presents.

Part V: Banking Crises and Global Banking

In Chapter 14, Joshua Abor, Sam Mensah, Baah Aye Kusi, and David Mathuva examine banking failures in Africa. They explain the causes of banking failures, including unfavourable economic conditions, regulatory failures, poor corporate governance practices, mismanagement, huge non-performing loans, fraudulent and corrupt dealings, and poor risk management. The chapter also discusses the consequences or effects of banking failures in Africa. It draws on cases from the recent failures of indigenous banks in Ghana and other African countries. They suggest that central banks strengthen their capacity for effective supervision and monitoring, pursue regulatory reforms to anticipate emerging risks, and focus on the soundness of the overall financial and economic system.

Chapter 15 by Charles Adjasi, Isaac Ofoeda, Khadijah Iddrisu, and Foluso Akinsola examines the impact of cross-border banking on the probability of a banking crisis in Africa. Employing logit regression, they found that foreign bank presence and participation in the domestic banking sector are likely to result in a banking crisis in Africa. However, the probability of a banking crisis in Africa as a result of cross-border banking is not significant.

Chapter 16 is also an examination of the effects of cross-border banking and bank pricing on financial inclusion in Africa. Using a System GMM estimator with 330 banks across 29 African countries, Mohammed Amidu, Aisha Sissy, Joshua Abor, and Simon Wolfe found that cross-border banking affects bank pricing behaviour. Also, inclusive finance can be influenced by the pricing behaviour of banks. On the sensitivity analysis, their results suggest that financial inclusion is not responsive to the interaction of cross-border banking and bank pricing mechanisms. These findings have important policy implications.

In Chapter 17, Vera Fiador, Kannyiri Thadious Banyen, Mohammed Amidu, and Victor Murinde examine current developments, challenges, and opportunities in global banking, the future of global banking and implications for African banks. They employ thematic content analysis to examine the changes that have occurred in global banking since the 2008 global financial crisis, including power shifts, regulatory changes, corporate governance issues and operational strategies. They also discuss the current challenges and opportunities in global banking and the role of information communication technology and financial integration. The implications of these changes for future banking in Africa are also highlighted in the chapter.

Part VI: Banking Regulation and Supervision

Chapter 18 discusses risk management and compliance in banking in Africa. In this chapter, Joseph Akotey, Emmanuel Sarpong-Kumankoma, Kwamina Koranteng Asomaning, and Oluseye Samuel Ajuwon cover compliance and how it affects the banking sector in Africa. They explain that compliance is a governance system that equips a bank to act in accordance with the internal and external regulatory and supervisory requirements. They explain that compliance helps a bank to act within the law and survive through growth and profitability. Partial compliance is the same as total non-compliance, which has caused large banks to collapse, and others to be fined millions of dollars.

Chapter 19 is by Elikplimi Komla Agbloyor, Baah Kusi, Patience A. Abor, and Collins G. Ntim. The authors examine how country-level corporate governance structures affect the nexus between financial sector transparency regulations and banking stability in Africa. Employing a Prais-Winsten panel data across 30 African economies, they show that corporate governance structures are crucial in shaping how financial sector transparency regulations affect banking stability in Africa. Specifically, they find positive and negative synergies between financial sector transparency regulations and corporate governance structures on banking stability. Additionally, the net effect results show that the negative effects of public and private sector-led financial sector transparency regulations on banking stability are suppressed when interacted with corporate governance structures.

Chapter 20 by Joshua Abor, Daniel Ofori-Sasu, Joe Nellis, and Christopher Green examines how monetary policy stance affects the link between measures of macro-prudential regulation and banking crises. Using a panel logit regression of 532 banks in 29 African countries over the period 2006–2018, they confirm that macro-prudential regulation and monetary policy play significant roles in reducing the probability of systemic banking crises. They find evidence to support the point that tightening monetary policy alters the negative effect of macro-prudential policy action on systemic banking crises, and that a tight monetary policy stance magnifies the negative effects of both countercyclical capital requirement and reserve requirement on systemic banking crises. They also show that the interaction effect between measures of macro-prudential regulation and monetary policy in reducing systemic banking crises seems to favour countries with strong institutions compared to those with weak ones.

In Chapter 21, Jessie A. Abugre, Roseline Misati, Iwa Salami, and Stephen Antwi discuss recent developments in banking regulation and supervision in Africa, the roles of central banks and regulatory strategy. They argue that regulations and supervision have had to catch up with the fast advancement of technology. Central banks have had to amend their laws to make provision for licensing and regulating non-banking financial institutions that hitherto did not fall under traditional banking services. The role of central banks has also been expanded to include regulation and supervision of technology firms that offer certain financial services. The chapter examines global banking regulations, as well as the Basel's Principles and Africa's banking system. It also discusses how to build effective regulatory and supervisory structures to ensure robust banking systems across the continent.

In Chapter 22, Playing Catch-up: SupTech and RegTech Developments in Africa, Maxwell Opoku-Afari, James A. Abugre, and Kwame Agyapong Oppong assess the effectiveness of supervisory technology (SupTech) and regulatory technology (RegTech) adopted by regulatory authorities for supervisory administration and guidance to FinTech innovations in Africa. The chapter examines the overview, use, and importance of SupTech and RegTech and how the financial system stands to gain when the various tools of SupTech and RegTech are employed to supervise and regulate the FinTech revolution. Regulatory mechanisms of FinTech and the adoption and implementation of RegTech and SupTech are discussed extensively. The authors also identify the challenges confronting the adoption of these technologies in Africa and suggest ways of making them effective in the continent.

Part VII: Non-bank Financial Markets

Chapter 23 provides a review the sustainability, growth, and impact of MFIs in Africa. Elikplimi Komla Agbloyor, Simplice A. Asongu, Peter W. Muriu, and Alfred Yawson discuss the sustainability and quality of loans of microfinance institutions in Africa. They explain that there has been a significant growth in microfinance in the continent and identified a number of factors that have influenced this widespread growth. They also argue that the impact of microfinance on improving welfare in the continent is inconclusive at best.

In Chapter 24, Richard Addae-Manu and Michael Graham provide a review of the nature and characteristics of insurance markets in Africa. Although insurance has many tangible and intangible economic benefits, the African market, seemingly, lags behind many other regional markets. The chapter also discusses the role of Africa's insurance sector and recent developments in statistical trends and observations as a prelude to determining what needs to be done. The authors propose market and regulatory recommendations for greater outreach and penetration in Africa's insurance markets.

Chapter 25 by Kathryn A. A. O. Assefuah, Nthabiseng Moleko and Joshua Y. Abor looks at the pension markets in Africa. The authors give an overview of pension systems in Africa and discuss the role of pension reforms, pension markets and capital market development, and challenges affecting pension markets in the continent. They explain that the pension markets play a number of important roles in the economy, including establishing attractive pension schemes, mobilising and pooling national savings, facilitating financial market development, ensuring corporate governance and monitoring of firms, supporting infrastructure development and the housing finance market, and financing green growth initiatives. Africa's pension markets are also confronted with a number of challenges, including a high unemployment rate, a large informal sector, and a scarcity of appropriate investment vehicles. They recommend policies to improve coverage, given the large informal sector in Africa.

Charles Adjasi, Jabir Ibrahim Mohammed, Joseph Dery Nyeadi, and Sunil K. Bundoo investigate the determinants of stock market development in Africa in Chapter 26. Using a panel fixed effect model, the study finds that stock market liquidity, investment, and savings are significant and positive determinants of stock market development in Africa. The study finds that banking sector development is a substitute rather than a complement to stock market development. The findings of the study also show that strong institutional quality such as control of corruption supports the development of the stock market in Africa.

Isaac Otchere, Daniel Ofori-Sasu, and Joshua Abor look at bond market development in Africa in Chapter 27. The authors discuss the importance of the bond markets, the constraints they face as well as their determinants. Africa's bond markets are relatively shallow and less penetrated, but they are as competitive as those in other developing economies. Also, Africa's bond markets are less integrated than those in the industrialised and developed regions of the world. The authors suggest a comprehensive regulatory framework and progressive regional integration of capital markets to help achieve bond market development goals. In addition, a more inclusive partnership with developed markets is needed in the ongoing and planned sustainable bond development initiatives in order to leverage synergies and maximise effectiveness.

In Chapter 28, Jephthah Osei, Joseph Abor, Patricia A. Ojangole, and Joshua Abor examine the relationship between private capital flows and energy use in Africa, considering the moderating role of domestic financial markets. Their results suggest that domestic financial markets play a significant role in establishing the connection between private capital flow and energy use. Specifically, they find that private capital inflows conditioned on favourable financial markets environment enhance energy use in Africa.

Chapter 29 by Saint Kuttu, William Coffie, Chimwemwe Chipeta, and Ekow Afedzie investigates the relationship between Foreign Direct Investment (FDI), stock market development, and inclusive growth in SSA. They utilise dynamic panel data models using the vector error correction model (VECM) Granger causality framework and document that FDI has a positive effect on stock market development. However, they do not find evidence suggesting that FDI and stock market development exert a significantly positive influence on inclusive growth. Also, inclusive growth, FDI, and stock market development tend not to converge to their long-run equilibrium path in response to changes in any of the variables. They find that human capital and the female labour force play a significant role in fostering inclusive growth. They further show that the availability of natural resources and domestic infrastructure attract FDI, while savings exert a significantly negative influence on FDI.

In the final chapter, Joshua Abor, Elikplimi Komla Agbloyor, George N. Agyekum Donkor, and Angela A. Alu discuss the COVID-19 pandemic and Africa's financial systems. The authors provide an overview of the COVID-19 pandemic and previous pandemics and discuss African governments' response to the pandemic. They then examine how the pandemic has impacted various aspects of Africa's financial systems. The authors also make a case for how to reform post-COVID-19 financial systems in Africa.

1.4 Concluding Remarks

In this chapter we have provided an overview of Africa's financial systems. We note that financial systems play an important role in the economic growth process. They ensure the efficient allocation of economic resources by distributing funds to economic entities for investments that will generate appropriate returns. Their functions include mobilising savings and allocating resources, facilitating access to debt finance by governments, offering opportunities for investments, providing means of managing risk, providing a system for clearing and payments/settlements, and providing means of monitoring investment. Africa's financial system is recognised as bank-based, suggesting the banking sectors play more significant roles than the capital markets. The chapter has identified the various challenges confronting the development of various aspects of Africa's financial systems, notable among them being the impact of the COVID-19 pandemic that has had a great impact on Africa's financial systems. The chapter has also provided an outline of the various chapters in the book.

References

Abor, J. Y. (2018). *Financial markets and institutions: A frontier market perspective* (2nd ed.). Digibooks.

Abor, J. Y. (2020). *Exploring the impact of COVID-19 pandemic on Africa's FinTech space* (Working Paper Series No. 7). Centre for Global Finance, SOAS University of London. https://www.centreforglobalfinance.org/2020-working-papers

Abor, J. Y., Gyeke-Dako, A., Fiador, V., Agbloyor, E., Amidu, M., & Mensah, L. (2019). *Money and banking in Africa*. Springer International Publishing.

Abor, J. Y., Issahaku, H., Amidu, M., & Murinde, V. (2020). Financial inclusion and economic growth. In J. Y. Abor, C. K. D. Adjasi & R. Lensink (Ed.), *Contemporary issues in development finance*. Routledge.

Agbloyor, E. K. & Abor, J. Y. (2020). *The COVID-19 pandemic and its impact on African economies and financial markets: A review* (Working Paper Series No. 13). Centre for Global Finance, SOAS University of London. https://static1.squarespace.com/static/5aeb20ab297114b0c238a685/t/5f96b6957 36e6b08083edfe8/1603712666687/2020+WP+13+-+Final.pdf

Allen, F., Otchere, I., & Senbet, L. W. (2011). African financial systems: A review. *Review of Development Finance, 1*(2), 79–113.

Allen, F., Carletti, E., Cull, R., Qian, J., Senbet, L. W. & Valenzuela, P. (2014). Improving access to banking: Evidence from Kenya. *World Bank Policy Research Paper, 70,* 19–32. World Bank.

Amoah, L., Adjasi, C., Soumare, I., Osei, K., Abor, J. Y., Anarfo, E., Amo-Yartey, C. & Otchere, I. (2020). Finance, economic growth, and development. In J. Y. Abor, C. K. D. Adjasi & R. Lensink (Eds.), *Contemporary issues in development finance*. Routledge.

Aryeetey, E. (2003). Recent development in African financial markets: Agenda for further research. *Journal of African Economics, 12*(2), 111–152.

Balcilar, M., Gupta, R., Lee, C. C., & Olasehinde, G. (2020). Insurance-growth nexus in Africa. *The Geneva Papers on Risk and Insurance-Issues and Practice, 45*(2), 335–360.

Banya, R. M., & Biekpe, N. (2017). Bank competition and economic growth: Empirical evidence from selected frontier African countries. *Journal of Economic Studies, 44*(2), 245–265.

Bazot, G. (2018). Financial consumption and the cost of finance: Measuring financial efficiency in Europe (1950–2007). *Journal of the European Economic Association, 16*(1), 123–160.

Beck, T., & Cull, R. (2014). Banking in Africa. In *The Oxford handbook of banking* (2nd ed.). Oxford University Press

Doku, J. N., Abor, J., Adjasi, C. K., & Andoh, C. (2012). Assessing competitive behaviour in emerging banking market: African evidence. *Finance and Development in Africa, 12*, 25–51.

Fosu, S. (2013). Banking competition in Africa: Subregional comparative studies. *Emerging Markets Review, 15*, 233–254.

KPMG. (2015). *KPMG Africa's banking in Africa report*. http://www.blog.kpmgafrica.com/kpmg-africas-banking-in-africa-report-2015/

KPMG. (2017). *Insurance market in Africa: Where is the boom?* http://www.blog.kpmgafrica.com/insurance-market-in-africa-where-is-the-boom/

Senbet, L. & Otchere, I. (2010). African stock markets: Ingredients for development and capacity building. In Q. Marc & V. Genevieve (Eds.), *African finance in the 21th century*. Palgrave Macmillan Publishing.

PART II

FinTech, Financial Inclusion and Banking Sector Development

CHAPTER 2

Inflation, Interest Rates, and Exchange Rates in Africa

Matthew Kofi Ocran, Johannes Peyavali Sheefeni Sheefeni, and Emmanuel Oduro-Afriyie

2.1 Introduction

The three macroeconomic variables: inflation, interest rates, and exchange rates constitute a set of fundamentals that underpins the performance of all economies. The performance of these three dynamic macroeconomic variables determines to a large extent the outcomes of national output,

M. K. Ocran (✉) · J. P. S. Sheefeni
Department of Economics, University of the Western Cape, Cape Town, South Africa
e-mail: mocran@uwc.ac.za

J. P. S. Sheefeni
e-mail: jsheefeni@uwc.ac.za

E. Oduro-Afriyie
Absa Bank Ghana, Accra, Ghana
e-mail: eoafriyie78@gmail.com

J. Y. Abor and C. K. D. Adjasi (eds.), *The Economics of Banking and Finance in Africa*, Palgrave Macmillan Studies in Banking and Financial Institutions, https://doi.org/10.1007/978-3-031-04162-4_2

the labour, and financial markets in national economies. For instance, the monetary authorities often manage the domestic price level with the aid of interest rates as a policy instrument. The exchange rates, like interest rates, also serve as a channel of monetary policy transmission in small open economies. The role of the three policy variables therefore lies at the core of efforts to ensure a stable macroeconomic environment that is conducive for economic growth and development.

The economic crisis that most African countries endured between the middle of the 1970s and the early 1990s was characterized by high inflation, interest rates that were inappropriate to support savings and investment, as well as misaligned exchange rates. The structural adjustment policies that the main international financial institutions, the World Bank and the International Monetary Fund, imposed on African countries in the 1980s were aimed at restoring balance in the three macroeconomic variables among others (Ocran, 2019). The improvement in inflation, interest rates, and exchange rates recorded since the 1990s have augured well for improvements in the real and nominal economies across the continent.

Through a combination of monetary, exchange rate, and fiscal policies, countries all over the world strive to manage the policy variables: inflation, interest rates, and exchange rates in a manner that assists them in attaining their economic objectives. In a globalized world, the performance of the policy variables in the world's major economies also has material effects on African economies through trade and the international capital markets.

A good understanding of the behaviour, theories, and evidence of how these various important macroeconomic variables perform is of great importance in appreciating the challenges and opportunities around banking and finance in Africa. The rest of the chapter provides an in-depth discussion of each of the variables. The approach is to explore the stylized facts around the variable and to highlight the main theories that attempt to explain the behaviour of the given variable. There is also a brief overview of the relevant empirical literature to ascertain how best the theories explain the facts. The last part of the chapter explores the interrelationships among the three variables in Africa. The last section provides some concluding remarks based on the discussions.

2.2 Inflation

Inflation has been and is still one of the many concerns of central banks around the world, including those in Africa. Various theories of inflation have been formulated since the early nineteenth century to try and explain the reasons behind increases in the price levels. They include quantity theory of money, monetary theory of money, demand pull, cost push, structuralism, rational expectations, new-neoclassical synthesis, and new political macroeconomic theory.

Stylized Facts

In simple terms, inflation is defined as a sustained increase in general prices. There has been a decline in the inflation rate on average in Africa over the past decades. Figure 2.1 shows the trend of inflation in Sub-Saharan African countries for the period 1976–2020. However, there was an increase from the early 1990s following the economic recession during this period which officially started around the end of 1992 and the beginning of 1993. The inflation rate peaked in 1994 and then drastically declined. It increased again during the 2007/2008 financial crisis and declined further. One notable issue here is that the inflation rate has been below 10% since 1985, with the exception of the disruptive episodes of 1994, 1995, and 2008. It is also important to note that while the rate of inflation has generally fallen across Africa, there are significant differences in the inflation outcomes across the continent. For instance, the CFA franc currency zone countries in the region have often recorded much

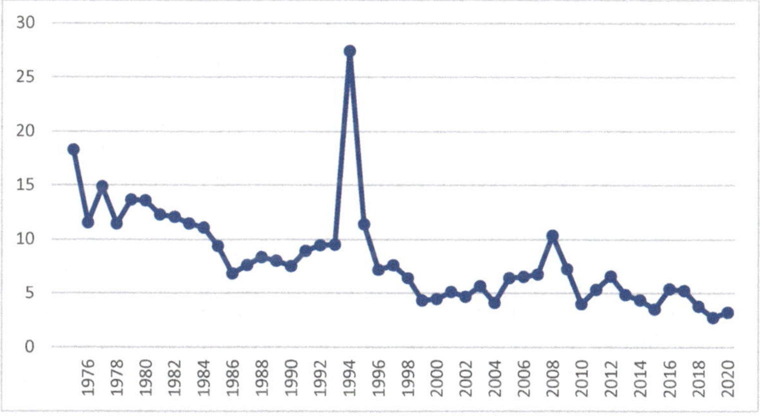

Fig. 2.1 Average inflation rates in sub-Saharan Africa, 1976–2020 (*Source* World Bank. [2021]. World Development Indicators)

lower inflation rates than most countries in Africa. Senegal, Benin, Gabon, and Niger, among many others, recorded annual average consumer price increases of less than 2% between 2010 and 2017. Over the same period, South Africa had a figure of 5.4%, and for Kenya the rate of inflation averaged 7.6%. The rate of inflation in Nigeria between 2010 and 2017 averaged 11.8% (IMF, 2021). On the other hand, there are other countries from the sub-Saharan block that have higher values of inflation, for example, Angola has 17.1%, Ethiopia 15.8%, Liberia 23.6%, South Sudan 29.8%, and Sudan 150.3%. This demonstrates that there are two extremes when it comes to inflation (World Bank, 2021).

The increase in inflation in 1993 could be attributed to the structural theory of inflation, specifically the government budget constraint, the so-called government bottlenecks. Most economies had accumulated so much debt at the time that they found it difficult to finance the programs to resuscitate their economies (Nguyen et al., 2015).

Theories of Inflation

The quantity theory of money (QTM) is one of the ancient theories of economic guidelines. In particular, it forms the epicentre of the nineteenth-century classical monetary policy analysis in the presence of financial events. But most importantly, it provided guidelines for orthodox policy meant to advance and preserve the gold standard. The theory postulates that changes in the quantity of money in circulation largely determine changes in the general level of prices. In other words, inflation is mainly determined by changes in the quantity of money flowing in the economy. The quantity theory of money has been spoken about by early scholars such as David Hume (1711–1776), David Ricardo (1772–1823), Irving Fisher (1876–1947), and Arthur Cecil Pigou (1877–1959).

Monetarism or the monetarist school of thought draws from Milton Friedman (1912–2006). Specifically, they are of the view that the size or quantity of money in the economy is the overriding factor affecting the economy. This view developed around the 1970s and validates changes in the growth rates of monetary aggregates as the core player in explaining the level of economic activities, income (both nominal and real), and prices in the short run. However, it is also said to affect the level of prices in the long run. The modern monetarists put it well by stating that "inflation is always and everywhere a monetary phenomenon that arises from a more rapid expansion in the quantity of money than in total output". Hence, they argue that in the long run, the level of output is not influenced by the quantity of money supply.

Drawing from John Maynard Keynes (1883–1946), demand-pull inflation is said to be a result of increase in aggregate demand. In particular, this happens when the value of aggregate demand exceeds (increases) the value of aggregate supply (remain unchanged), at the full employment level. That is why it is referred to as "too much money chasing too few goods", because demand for goods and services pulls-up the prices. The bigger the gap between aggregate demand and aggregate supply, the faster the rate of price changes in the economy. Demand-pull inflation can be caused by one or more components of the aggregate demand. In particular, an increase in consumption expenditure, investment expenditure, government expenditure, and export earnings. In the same fashion, a decrease in one or more components of total demand is effective in subsidizing pressure of demand and subsequently inflation.

The cost-push inflation was the main type of inflation in the 1950s and 1970s. In principle, cost-push inflation occurs when the cost of production at each level of total production increases. This is so because increases in production cost-push up the price level. There are various known causes of this type of inflation as discussed below. The first cause is increases in wages and salaries, resulting from wage increases enforced by labour unions. The considerable increase in wages raises the cost of production of goods and services. It also enables workers to purchase relatively as much as before irrespective of higher prices. Second, increases in the cost of imported capital and intermediate goods can result in increase in price level (due to increase in price level in the rest of the world or depreciation of the domestic currency vis-à-vis foreign currencies of the exporting countries). Alternatively, some sectors of the economy will be affected by increase in wages and salaries, thus, the prices of their products will be rising. Third, increases in profit margins can cause cost-push inflation. This usually happens when employers (oligopolist and monopolist firms) in turn increase the prices of their products, as a response to wage increment enforced by the labour unions. Sometimes this is referred to as profit-push inflation or administered-price inflation or price-push inflation.

Another important theory is that of structural inflation which explains inflation in the developing countries differently from the traditional theories. This is due to the fact that developing countries are characterized by structural defects which cannot be fully explained by the traditional theories of inflation. That is why the structural theorists are of the view that inflation is a natural outcome of rapid economic development and growth process which purely result from non-monetary factors. In this regard, the structural theory explains three types of bottlenecks: (i) Agricultural bottlenecks, (ii) Government budget constraints, and (iii) Foreign exchange bottlenecks. These three items can be explained as follows: First, the agricultural bottlenecks result in agricultural output being less responsive to increase in income. This is a result of low food supply increment in relation to increase in demand either due to increasing population or income. Thus, aggregate demand will be greater than aggregate supply, implying a gap which in turn pushes up the prices, resulting in inflation. Second, with regard to government budget constraint, it is not a secret that governments are responsible for infrastructural development, heavy and basic industries.

These mega-projects require major funds and investment. However, most developing countries are faced with a resource gap, which in turn results in deficit financing. This implies that there is a gap between demand and supply increases (aggregate demand aggregate supply [AD> AS]) which pushes the prices up, resulting in inflation. Third and last, are foreign exchange bottlenecks. Most developing countries lack sufficient foreign exchange because of relatively low export compared to import, which means payments are higher than earnings. In response to that, these countries implement policies that bridge gaps between exports and imports (i.e., import restrictions, currency devaluations, etc.). Unfortunately, these policies also result in increase in prices in the domestic economy and subsequently inflation. In summary, the view of the structural theory is that the gap between aggregate demand and supply created by the presence of the bottlenecks as discussed leads to inflationary pressures in the economy.

Macroeconomic policy in the 1970s was predominantly under the revolutionary idea of Rational Expectations economists, such as Lucas, McCallum, and many others. The "rational expectations revolution" focussed on the role of expectations. The underlying message here is that people do not necessarily consistently form the same expectations over and over again as suggested by the adaptive expectations. On the contrary, economic agents form their expectations "rationally" based on the information readily available (past/backward-looking and current relevant information) including price expectations. From this viewpoint, the central bank can only be effective in its policy decision if it creates a "price surprise". Otherwise, the "forward-looking" stance of the central bank will successfully deliver a preannounced policy. In the same fashion, if the policymakers announce a disinflation policy in advance, it will only lead to price reduction if the economic agents believe that the government can deliver on such a policy. That is why it is argued that price expectations are related to policy credibility, an important tool for anchoring inflation expectations and for successfully managing inflation in an economy. The point of contention among the schools of thought is the dominance of fiscal policy over monetary policy. This is so because when government funds the current deficits using alternative financing methods, it determines the timing of unavoidable future inflation.

The New Neoclassical Synthesis has become a profound macroeconomic theory in explaining business cycles and price movements. Under this theory, monetary (demand) factors are the major determinants of business cycles on the assumption of price stickiness in the short run as stipulated by the new Keynesian proposition. However, the same theory also adduces more supply shocks in explaining real economic activity as per the new classical real business cycles theory. The NNS uses IS-LM-PC where price level is endogenous. The IS refers to Investment and Saving, i.e. equilibrium of goods and services market; LM refers to demand for and supply of money, i.e. equilibrium of money market; and PC refers to the Phillips Curve. In addition, the NNS accepts expectations as part of the inflation process. The outstanding characteristic of the New IS-LM model behavioural relations can be derived from the decision-making process of the households and firms. Moreover, these relations involve future expectations. The IS curve relates expected output growth to the real interest rate, while the aggregate supply and Phillips curve component relates the current inflation to expected future inflation and output gap.

The new political macroeconomics theory comes from the new classical macroeconomic revolution of the 1970s. It rejects the view that a government has the freedom to manipulate the economy. By incorporating the political incentives, the new political macroeconomics theory focussed primarily on inflation. Specifically, it is of the view that rules-based policies and the depoliticizing of economic policy can lead to a reduction in the inherent amount of inflation in the economic system. Unlike all the prior theories discussed, this theory incorporates the non-economic factors such as institutions, political process, and culture in the process of inflation. The new political economy provides new information on the relations between timing of elections, performance of policy maker, political instability, policy credibility and reputation, and the inflation process itself.

Empirical Evidence

There are various empirical studies on the subject matter that validate and/or nullify the theoretical propositions. For instance, the study by Bleaney and Francisco (2007) examined inflationary performance in sub-Saharan Africa since 1996. The findings from this study revealed that inflation is highly persistent and higher in countries that are less politically stable, in countries without hard peg exchange rate regimes as well as in those with larger fiscal deficits. Moreover, the findings also revealed that inflation typically spiked after a devaluation and was found to be sensitive to supply-side shocks. Particularly, the movements in the real price of oil and rice (but not maize) have significantly affected the inflation rate. The situation was also similar in countries that are reliant on the agricultural sector because of rise in prices when there is no good harvest. The same was also said about countries with fiscal imbalances. These characteristics conform to the structural theory of inflation whereby sources of inflation are non-monetary in nature. Moreover, there are some characteristics leaning towards the new political macroeconomic theory of inflation.

Baldini and Poplawski-Ribeiro (2011) present a model of fiscal dominance with borrowing constraints and shed some light on the relative importance of fiscal and monetary determinants of inflation in SSA. Specifically, the findings show that half of the countries studied had no anti-inflationary policy (monetary and fiscal) for the period 1980–2005. On the contrary, the remaining half had one of the remaining extremes. The one extreme is a fiscal-dominant regime, with weak or no response of primary surpluses to public debt while the other extreme is that of consistent adoption of a monetary-dominant regime. These empirical findings draw from monetary theory of inflation as well as demand-pull theory of inflation. Similarly, Bikai et al. (2016) studied part of SSA, the CEMAC, and investigated the causes of inflation focussing on the monetary aspect. This study also supports the quantity theory of money. Moreover, it also draws from the monetary theory. The findings revealed that the quantity of money supplied (money supply) and imported inflation are the main drivers of inflation in CEMAC countries. The authors further explained that the two factors have more explanatory power than the other variables such as oil prices, budget balance, and output gap. They further stated that the results shed light on some structural problems of slowness of expectations adjustment by the economic agents.

Lastly, Melaku (2021) looked at the determinants of inflation in SSA countries. A number of variables such as GDP, broad money supply, real exchange rate, and interest rate were identified as the main sources of inflation. Additionally, variables such as import prices, inflation expectations, public expenditure, and oil prices were found to be consequential for the determination of inflation. The quantity theory seems to be dominant, so that the hypothesis that inflation is always and everywhere a monetary phenomenon is proven over and over again. Thus, increase in broad money supply aggravates inflation in the long run. Therefore, the control of money supply in the management of inflation should be one of the objectives of monetary authorities in the region.

It is worth noting that different countries in sub-Saharan Africa subscribed to different monetary policies, meaning that monetary operations as well as the transmission mechanism of monetary policies are diverse. This also suggests that the conduct of monetary policy takes place under different monetary policy regimes as means of ultimately managing/controlling inflation. Some of the regimes are exchange rate targeting, monetary targeting, interest rate targeting, discretionary monetary policy, nominal gross domestic product level targeting, inflation targeting, and monetary policy rule (Kavila & Le Roux, 2017).

Monetary policy conduct is a combination of direct instruments, foreign exchange interventions, and open market operations. To start with, there is exchange rate targeting practice which involves the use of the nominal exchange rate as a nominal anchor that can help in controlling domestic inflation. Secondly, monetary targeting or money supply targeting has also been used to control the growth of money supply over time; this in turn results in stable prices. One case in point is Zimbabwe, though this was abandoned at some point. Lastly, inflation targeting requires public announcement of official quantified goals for the inflation rate. South Africa and Ghana are the well-known countries in Africa that explicitly practise this monetary policy regime. The inflation targeting monetary policy regime seems to have yielded successful results.

2.3 Interest Rates

Commercial banks the world over serve as the intermediary between surplus funds and consumers in need of deficit financing. Interest is paid on savings and charged on loans offered. Specifically in sub-Saharan Africa, it has been long noted that the spread between lending and deposit rates is higher than anywhere else (Ahokpossi, 2013; Folawewo & Tennant, 2008; Gyeke-Dako et al., 2018; Musah et al., 2018).

Since the beginning of the 1970s, increasing attention has been paid to the detrimental effects of financial repression in developing countries—following which several African countries sought to liberalize their financial systems, including interest rates. Supported by the International Monetary Fund (IMF), pioneer countries such as Gambia, Ghana, Kenya, Malawi, and Nigeria liberalized interest rates, developed or reactivated indirect monetary instruments, strengthened the regulatory framework, and spurred competition in the financial sector with a view to increasing the efficiency of credit allocation in the economy. The initial effect of interest rate liberalization on the level and variability of lending rates was rather limited. In particular, these rates were only partially responsive to changes in inflation. Deposit rates, on the other hand, tended to decrease after their liberalization. This led to an increase in the spread between lending and deposit rates (Turtelboom, 1991).

In 2017, the World Bank noted that the net interest margin in the median African country was 6.8%. Using data spanning 1996–2017, it was found that of the 47 countries sampled, Sierra Leone had the highest of 21.43% while Libya had the lowest of 0.35%.

More recently, as of May 2021, out of a sample of 51 African economies, Zimbabwe recorded the highest interest rate of 40% compared with a low of 0.25% recorded by Cape Verde in April 2021. A quarter of these countries recorded double-digit rates of interest. The average interest rate across the 51 economies was 7.4% and a median of 4% was recorded (World Bank, 2021).

Figures 2.2, 2.3, and 2.4 display the average and median real interest rates, interest rate spread, and lending rates in Africa spanning the period 1990–2019.

In the early 2000s, in response primarily to cultural or political pressure to keep interest rates low, many African economies established interest rate caps to protect the citizenry from exorbitant interest rates charged by lenders. In low-income populations however, such caps have been

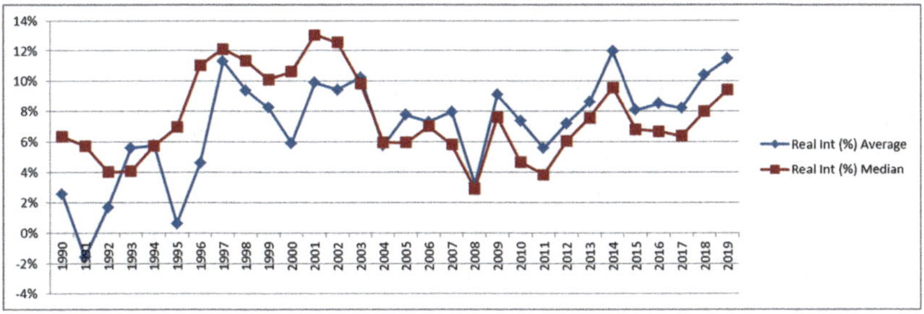

Fig. 2.2 Average and Median real interest rates in Africa (1990–2019) (*Source* World Bank [2021])

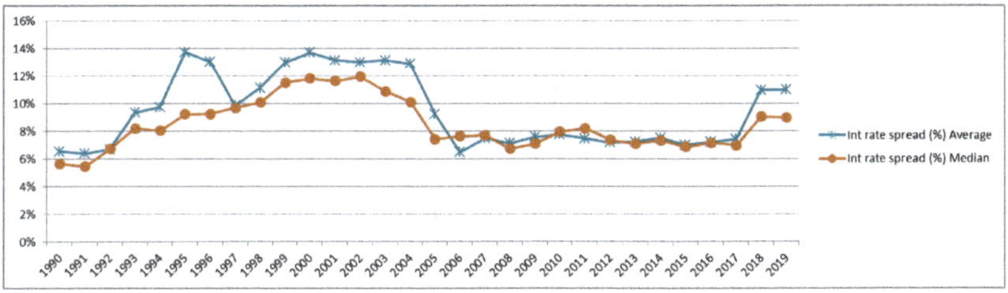

Fig. 2.3 Average and Median Interest rate spread in Africa (1990–2019) (*Source* WDI [2020])

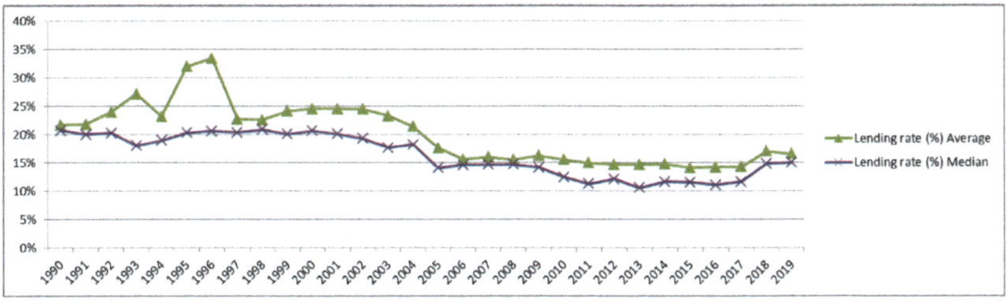

Fig. 2.4 Average and Median Lending rate in Africa (1990–2019) (*Source* World Bank [2021])

known to cause detrimental effects. Price transparency can reduce and access to finance is curtailed. Where governments set the caps too low, lenders are likely to experience slower growth as they struggle to recover costs. Consequently, service delivery to the more remote areas and costlier markets is impacted negatively. Lenders tend to be less transparent about the total cost of funds and may decide in a worst-case scenario to exit the market. Preference for safer investments in government securities such as treasury bills and bonds increases as they become the preferred destination for lenders.

In 2016, the Central Bank of Kenya capped commercial-loan rates at the prevailing policy rate plus 400 basis points. Credit to small businesses plummeted with banks reasoning that the rewards of lending no longer matched the risks. The cap was later scrapped in 2019.

The Central Bank of Nigeria (CBN) penalizes banks for failure to meet stipulated lending targets. With the aim of keeping the naira strong, the CBN inches up interest rates through a tight monetary policy stance. Commercial banks are also mandated to hold copious levels of liquid assets in the form of treasury bills and cash, and keep on hand not less than 27.5% of all deposits, which is noted to be one of the highest on the globe.

Most central banks across SSA have at one point in time conducted monetary policy by pursuing either direct inflation targeting or monetary aggregate targeting. Monetary policy across the continent has evolved in recent years from essentially a monetary targeting approach to an inflation targeting approach.

The monetary targeting approach had two variants. The first was a credit control approach, and the second variant used OMO. The credit control approach targeted domestic credit directly to achieve money supply targets as an intermediate variable and, finally, inflation targets. Under this framework, the opinion was that inflation is primarily a monetary problem and therefore targeting money supply growth was the best method of controlling inflation in the economy. Credit controls involved the imposition of ceilings on the commercial banks' credit to the private sector, and the regulation of borrowing and deposit interest rates. Year after year, the central bank could determine both money supply growth and inflation targets and set the ceilings and rates accordingly.

While it seemed a simple system to implement, there were inherent problems associated with it. The setting of credit ceilings led to excessive liquidity with no vehicles to invest in, and the very low-interest rates meant that the government could borrow money at negligible costs. Indeed, the credit targets were mostly violated due to higher budget financing, leading to breaches of the money supply targets.

The second variant of monetary targeting employed OMO. This involved the sale and purchase of financial instruments as the operating instrument and money supply as the intermediate target. The persistence of excess liquidity in the economy ensured that OMO was invariably unidirectional, involving the sale of instruments.

Undermining factors to the OMO included the lack of a clear demarcation between the sale of instruments to mop up liquidity, and that to raise money to finance the budget. Furthermore, in order to reduce cost, there was some interference with the market process to set both quantity and price (interest rate) targets.

Theories of Interest Rates

Irving Fisher's Theory of Interest has been one of the most durable and influential contributions to economic theory (Carmichael & Stebbing, 1983). Indeed, the origin of most mainstream theories about interest rates goes back to Fisher (1930). A comprehensive view of the theories of interest becomes necessary as for several centuries interest rates have been much a subject of political and economic controversy. In this section, we will briefly delve into the progression of theoretical thought on interest rates with a keen focus on key criticisms of each theory.

There are numerous schools of thought regarding interest rates in the literature and interpretations of these theories have generated several relevant considerations and principles for practical monetary policy.

The Productivity Theory of Interest was expounded by Say (1836), Clark (1895), von-Thünen in 1910 (von Thünen, 1966), and Knight (1936) and posits that capital is demanded due to its productivity. Interest, being its price, must be paid and is the reward paid to capital since labour is generally more productive with capital goods than without them. The borrower, by employing capital, must pay a part of this increased production to the owner of capital in the form of Interest.

The main drawback of this theory is that it focuses solely on the demand of capital, completely ignoring the supply side. The chief argument is that in a scenario of abundant supply of capital, interest will not arise at all, or if it does, will only be minimal, irrespective of how productive capital may be. Furthermore, the theory places emphasis solely on the higher productivity of capital—that interest is payable when productivity of capital is higher. Equally applicable is that if capital is in short supply, its relative scarcity will drive interest rates high. Lastly, the theory is unable to account for interest paid for consumption loans although in practice, interest-bearing loans can very much be taken out for the purposes of consumption.

Another theory of interest is the abstinence theory which was postulated by Marshall (1907) and expounded by Senior (1928) and Bowley (2013). The latter intimates that this theory can be recognized as the most complete of the classical theories.

In this theory, capital is the result of saving which in itself involves a sacrifice or some form of abstinence. As compensation for this abstinence, one must be offered an inducement to save and interest is this inducement. Marshall (1907) noted that saving connotes waiting and should therefore be considered a separate factor of production, equally substitutable for other factors.

Key criticisms against this theory are that although capital can be borrowed and paid for, there is no consideration of the productivity of capital. Also, the opportunity cost of saving cannot be measured, so determining a given rate of interest can be difficult. It has also been noted that in a system where the substantial source of capital is wealthy or rich lenders with surplus income, it becomes difficult to justify the payment of interest because of sacrifice as these lenders may not experience any inconvenience or sacrifice of consumption. Lastly, the theory emphasizes only the supply side of capital, ignoring its demand.

The Austrian Time Preference theory was expounded by Rae (1834) and Bohm-Bawerk (1890). It presents the idea that interest is the reward for agio, i.e., time preference and that there is increased preference for present rather than future goods because future satisfaction undergoes a discount. Interest is this discount (or reward), necessary to induce postponement of present satisfaction to a future date in favour of lending now.

Niehans (1990) criticizes the originality of this theory by noting that the three reasons for the existence of interest per this theory did not demonstrate originality as they already had been very famously listed by prior economists including Rae (1834). Fetter (1902) and Rothbard (1990) also criticize Bohm-Bawerk's reasoning for the existence of a positive rate of interest as faulty.

Postulated and expounded by Fisher (1930), the Time Preference theory is a modification of the Austrian Time Preference theory. With this theory, people's preference to have a certain sum of money now rather than in the future is what drives the supply of loans. A lender will only be prepared to forego present consumption when offered a reward-interest. Consequently, the higher the propensity for present consumption, the higher the interest rate will be.

Criticisms against this theory are that it does not consider the role of credit creation through the banking system on the rate of interest and investments. Also, by ignoring the productivity of capital, it is unable to explain the demand of capital. This theory is noted to have little practical application as it is difficult to identify its precise significance on interest rate determination. Lastly, it may not be entirely accurate to suggest that one will always prefer present to future consumption. Even in the absence of the reward of interest, some may realize greater satisfaction from future than from present consumption.

The Demand and Supply of Capital theory of Interest (a.k.a. Classical Theory of Interest) was expounded by Pigou (1936), Knight (1936), and Walras (2013). Here, interest is the reward for the productive use of the capital. This theory implies that the fundamental determinants of the rate of interest are the forces of supply and demand of capital, productivity in the economy, and thrift habits.

Keynes (1937) criticized this theory by positing that interest is purely a monetary phenomenon and a reward for parting with liquid cash rather than generating a return on savings. Keynes further intimated that merely lending funds which had not been saved but possibly inherited from one's forefathers, can still generate interest. This theory thus neglects the influence of monetary factors as a store of value on the determination of the rate of interest.

Keynes also noted that this theory is confusing and indeterminate as one cannot arbitrarily infer the interest rate unless one knows the savings and investment schedules, which again cannot be inferred unless the interest rate is known. This theory has also been criticized as being narrow in scope because it only focuses on capital used for productive purposes and ignores loans taken for consumption.

The Liquidity Preference Theory of Interest (a.k.a. the Keynesian theory) was postulated by Keynes (1937) who posits that interest is purely a monetary phenomenon and is the reward for parting with liquidity for a specified period. The theory notes that money is liquid and as a result, people like to hoard it. Hence, when one lends money, this liquidity is sacrificed for a specific period and interest becomes the reward offered. Liquidity preference implies a demand for liquid funds which is driven by three motives—transactional, precautionary, and speculative.

Like the classical theory, this theory has been criticized as being indeterminate, inadequate, and misleading, as the liquidity preference is premised on the motive for holding money which is a function of income. However, to determine the level of income, one must first infer the interest rate. Additionally, real factors like time preference and productivity of capital are assumed to have no influence on the interest rate. Keynes also ignored the element of saving even though there can be no liquidity in the absence of saving.

Liquidity is an important determinant of the interest rate and so the theory is noted to present a very narrow explanation of the interest rate as it assumes that there are only 3 main motives (precautionary, transactional, and speculative) that determine the desire for liquidity. All other reasons for desiring liquidity are ignored. The theory also completely ignores the long run and concentrates only on the short term. But in most cases, what is more significant is the long run rather than a short-run interest rate.

The Loanable Funds Theory of Interest was expounded by Knut Wicksell (1907), Ohlin et al. (1937) in an attempt to improve upon the classical theory. Here, the rate of interest is the price of credit which is determined by the demand and supply for loanable funds. Demand for loanable funds has three primary sources: Government, Businessmen, and Consumers who need them for purposes of investment, hoarding, and consumption. Generally, the interest rate and the demand for loanable funds are inversely related. Supply of loanable funds is generated from private savings, individuals and corporates in the form of bank credit, dis-hoardings and savings, and is positively related to the rate of interest.

This theory, like the classical and the Keynesian theories of interest, has been criticized as being indeterminate because interest rate determination depends on savings. But saving depends on income, income depends on investment, and investment itself depends on interest rate. Additionally, the equilibrium between demand for and supply of loanable funds cannot be brought about by the changes in interest rate alone. Both investment and saving are not as influenced by interest as they are by the changes in income levels. This theory also exaggerates the effect of the rate of interest on savings since people usually save not for the sake of interest but out of precautionary motives, thus making savings interest inelastic.

Evidence

While several studies abound on interest rates in sub-Saharan Africa (SSA), there is a paucity of empirical findings as regards the underlying theoretical framework of interest rates. A growing number of studies explore the interaction of interest rates with other macroeconomic themes such as economic growth, budget deficits, monetary policy, and exchange rates. Previous empirical studies on these nexuses have however concentrated mainly on Asia and Latin America. Even where such studies have been undertaken in SSA, findings on the role played by interest rates and their effect on other macroeconomic variables are at best conflicting, inconsistent, or inconclusive. Of these studies, the Keynesian theory was the predominant on interest rate.

The Evans et al. (2018) study on SSA which adopted the St. Louis equation and general method of moments (GMM) approach to data from 1995 to 2016 found that interest rate has a significant negative relationship with GDP per capita while other variables such as money supply, taxation, and primary enrolment have mixed effects. The study supports Keynesian policy assertions that the interest rate is a viable instrument to stabilize output and is a more powerful policy tool than using government spending and taxation. Other studies which support this view but focus solely on Nigeria include Adefeso and Mobolaji (2010), and Nwaogwugwu and Evans (2016).

Other studies have found little evidence for the Keynesian theory. Kelikume (2016) examines the effect of government deficit financing on interest rates by applying panel Vector Auto regression techniques (PVAR) on data from 18 SSA countries spanning 2000–2014. The study shows an initial slow response of interest rate to rising government fiscal deficits, with a subsequent neutral or insensitive response, thus rejecting the conventional Keynesian proposition that rising government deficit reduces the stock of loanable funds and consequently crowds out private sector investment. Odionye and Uma (2013) assert the above in their study on Nigeria.

2.4 Exchange Rates

The nominal exchange rate, the price of foreign currencies in a local currency is an important price in an economy. Exchange rates assume even greater importance in developing countries where local currencies are often not hard currency[1] or vehicle currency.[2] Exchange rates, especially real exchange rates,[3] determine the external competitiveness of an economy. Therefore, the relevance of exchange rates to the broader performance of an economy that is open to the rest of the world cannot be overemphasized.

The IMF, an international financial institution that often provides policy advice to countries regarding their exchange arrangements, suggests that there is no silver bullet regarding the best exchange rate arrangement. The choice of foreign exchange arrangement depends on the peculiar circumstances including the macroeconomic situation in a country (see Ghosh et al., 2010).

The foreign exchange rate market is the largest financial market in the world. The average daily turn-over of the market was estimated at US$6.6 trillion in April 2019. The US dollar is the dominant vehicle currency, and it was estimated to be on one side of 88% of all trades in 2019 (BIS, 2019). The Euro comes second. It accounted for a third of all foreign exchange trades. Clearly, the foreign exchange market is huge. This is because most cross-border trade and financial transactions require foreign currency. It is understandable why people have made strenuous intellectual efforts, since time immemorial, to explain the movements in foreign exchange rates. One of the earliest attempts to do so can be attributed to David Hume's work in 1741. Hume sought to determine exchange rate movements with an approach deeply rooted in the understanding of balance of payments accounts. Over time many models of exchange rate determination have emerged.

[1] Currency that suffers little variation in value over time.

[2] Currency that is widely used in international finance by bankers, Traders, Investors, etc. Examples of such currencies are the US dollar, the British pound, the Euro and the Japanese yen. And to a limited extent the Chinese yuan.

[3] The real exchange rate (RER) between any two countries is the nominal exchange rate multiplied by the ratio of prices between the two countries.

Table 2.1 Classification of exchange rate arrangements. 2019

Type	*Categories*				
Hard pegs	Exchange arrangement with no separate legal tender	Currency board			
Soft pegs	Conventional pegged arrangement	Pegged exchange rate with horizontal bands	Stabilized arrangement	Crawling peg	Craw-like arrangement
Floating regimes (Market driven rates)	Floating	Free floating			
Residual	Other managed arrangements				

Source IMF. AREAER (2019)

Stylized Facts

The exchange rate may also be measured as real effective exchange rate.[4] While the real exchange rate as a concept is useful for ascertaining the competitiveness of an economy in a bilateral relationship, the weighted average of a basket of currencies of trading partners is more pragmatic. Exchange rates are to a large extent influenced by the regime under which they are determined. Exchange rate regimes are broadly categorized into three groups: ***hard pegs***, ***soft pegs***, and ***floating pegs***. Globally, the predominant arrangement is the soft peg. Almost half of 189 countries and 3 territories (47%) that report their exchange rate arrangement to the IMF operate a soft peg regime.

There are five variants of soft peg arrangements: conventional peg, pegged exchange rate with horizontal bands, stabilized arrangements, crawling peg, and crawl-like arrangement (See Table 2.1). Within the

[4] REER is defined as the average of the bilateral real exchange rates between a country and each of its trading partners, adjusted by the respective trade shares of each partner country.

soft peg category, the conventional peg is the most common arrangement. Under the conventional peg, a country formally pegs its currency to another currency or a collection of currencies within margins of ±1% or even less. The collection of currencies may represent the currencies of trading partners or financial partners. The currencies in the collection may then be assigned weights based on many factors such as volume of trade or capital flows. Under a pegged exchange rate with horizontal bands, fluctuations of the currency are maintained at a margin of more than ±1% around a fixed principal rate or the maximum and minimum exchange rate exceed 2%. The stabilized arrangement requires that the exchange rate is maintained within a margin of 2% for at least 6 months. And the currency is not allowed to float during the period. A crawling peg arrangement adjusts the currency in small amounts at a fixed rate or in response to variations in predetermined indicators, such as inflation differentials between a country and its major trading partners, or even between expected inflation differentials between the countries. A crawl-like arrangement is a regime that allows the exchange rate to stay within a narrow margin of 2% relative to a statistically identified trend for at least 6 months. And here the exchange rate cannot be considered as floating.

Hard peg arrangements come in two forms: exchange rate arrangements with no separate legal tender, and currency board arrangements. In the case of the former, another country's currency circulates as legal tender. In most cases, it is the US dollar. So, we have an official dollarization. A currency board system is based on a defined legislative instrument that sets the exchange rate, and it is accompanied by restrictions on the issuing authority to ensure the fulfillment of its legal obligations. Consequently, the domestic currency is backed by holdings of foreign assets; therefore, the traditional role of the monetary policy authority as lender-of-last-resort is completely removed. A currency board arrangement also takes away the independence of a country's monetary authority.

The third group is the *floating* arrangement. The group comprises *free-floating* and *floating* arrangements. A free-floating arrangement is one for which interventions are pursued under extraordinary circumstances with the objective of forestalling disorderly market conditions. A floating exchange rate regime is mostly associated with a market-determined exchange rate with a rate path that cannot be anticipated. These rates are often associated with considerable volatility. Therefore, countries with this arrangement may intervene directly or indirectly in the exchange rate market to moderate the level of volatility. The indicators that inform market intervention by the monetary authority are usually based on judgement around the country's reserves and balance of payments situation among others.

The IMF also provides another kind of classification: *de jure* and de facto. The phenomenon of deeds and words best characterizes the difference between the two classifications. There are instances where the codified exchange rate arrangement is not implemented in practice; this is the de jure regime. By contrast, the de facto classification categorizes regimes based on the behaviour of central banks with the aid of statistical tools and expert judgement of IMF country staff, and engagement with the relevant central banks.

Foreign exchange regimes in Africa have evolved over the years. Pegs are the dominant exchange rate arrangements on the continent. Pegs constitute 60% of the exchange rate arrangements in Africa. For developing and emerging economies, peg arrangement accounts for 47% of the arrangements. The CFA franc currency zone[5] contributes to the dominance of hard pegs in sub-Saharan Africa. The exchange rate in the CFA currency zone is anchored to the Euro. Unlike countries with other exchange rate arrangements, those with peg regimes are more resilient. They hardly move onto other regimes. Instructively, the emerging[6] market economies in Africa use soft pegs. There are only a few of these countries that use hard peg arrangements.

To provide insight into trends in exchange rate movements in Africa, we focus on a sample of 11 countries. The 11 countries are drawn from 3 non-overlapping groups of countries: oil exporters,[7] other resource-intensive countries,[8] and non-resource intensive countries[9] (IMF, 2019).

[5] There are 14 countries in the CFA franc zone: 8 West African countries and 6 Central African countries. Fourteen of the CFA franc zone countries are former French colonies and one Spanish and one Portuguese colonies.

[6] IMF characterises countries that have raised Eurobonds but are outside the emerging market designation such as South Africa, as frontier markets. Frontier markets in Africa include Kenya, Ghana, and Angola.

[7] Countries where net oil exports account for 30% or more of total exports.

[8] Countries where nonrenewable natural resources make up 25% or more of total exports.

[9] These are countries that are neither classified as oil exporters nor other resource-intensive countries.

Table 2.2 Exchange rate regimes in selected African countries

Country name	*Exchange rate arrangement*
Algeria	Crawl-like arrangement
Angola	Other managed arrangement
Congo. Dem. Rep	Stabilised arrangement
Ghana	Floating
Kenya	Other managed arrangement
Mauritius	Floating
Tunisia	Crawl-like arrangement
Nigeria	Stabilised arrangement
Senegal	Conventional peg
South Africa	Floating
Tanzania	Crawl-like arrangement

Source IMF (2019). Survey of Annual Exchange Rate Arrangements 2019

These countries have different exchange rate arrangements. The sample of countries includes Senegal, one of the countries in the CFA franc zone. Also included are two North African countries: Algeria and Tunisia (see Table 2.2).

Changes in annual average of the official exchange rate measured in local currency units per 1 US dollar for the 11 countries under consideration are reviewed for the period 2000 to 2019. The highest rate of change in the mean value of the exchange rate was recorded by DR Congo (77%), followed by Angola (37%) and Ghana (18%). Senegal (0.1%) had the smallest mean value of exchange rate variation. The second best was Mauritius (1.9%), followed closely by Kenya (2.0%).

In order to assess variability in distribution of the changes in the exchange rates, two statistics: standard deviation and variation were used.[10] We assessed the extent of symmetry in the distribution of the change in exchange rate data with the aid of skewness and kurtosis statistics. The distribution of the changes in the South African rand, Tanzanian shilling, and the Tunisian dinar exchange rates are skewed to the left, with the rest recording skewness to the right. The Congolese franc of the DR Congo has a tail distribution that is different from normal distribution.

[10] Variance is measured as the average of the square deviation from the mean. And the standard deviation is obtained by taking the root of the variance.

Table 2.3 Descriptive statistics—Changes in the official exchange rate. 2000–2019

Country/Currency	*Mean*	*Std. Dev*	*Min*	*Max*	*Variance*	*Skewness*	*Kurtosis*
Oil exporters							
Angola/Kwanza (AOA)	**36.7**	**63.4**	**−7.8**	**259.8**	**4023.5**	**2.4**	**8.7**
Nigeria/Naira (NGN)	6.6	10.4	−5.8	31.7	107.3	1.1	3.2
Algeria/Dina (DZA)	3.20	7.4	−6.9	24.9	55.4	1.2	4.8
Other resource-intensive							
South Africa/Rand (ZAR)	5.3	13.8	−0.3	0.2	189.9	−0.8	2.9
Ghana/ Cedi (GHS)	17.8	23.9	0.6	104.4	571.5	2.6	9.7
Tanzania/Shelling (TZS)	5.9	5.6	−3.9	20.5	30.8	−0.2	2.2
DR Congo/Congolese franc (CDF)	76.7	205.9	−1.4	846.9	42,402.6	3.1	11.4
Non-resource intensive							
Mauritius/Rupee (MUR)	1.9	6.5	−9.1	14.5	41.9	0.2	2.3
Senegal*/West African franc (XOF)	0.1	8.4	−16.4	19.7	70.8	0.5	3.3
Tunisia/Tunisia Dinar (TND)	4.9	7.0	−9.4	15.6	49.1	−0.3	2.2
Kenya/Kenya Shilling (KES)	2.0	5.6	−6.6	12.1	35.6	0.4	2.4

Note *Senegal belongs to the CFA franc zone where all countries use the same currency pegged to the Euro

Source World Bank. (2021). World Development Indicators

The Tanzanian shilling and the Tunisian dinar have a distribution that is closer to normal distribution.

The data suggest that Senegal, and by extension the CFA franc currencies, has the most stable currency among the sample considered. It is worthy to note that Senegal's currency is pegged to the Euro in a conventional peg arrangement. Senegal has the best statistics for the many aspects of the distribution of the data representing the changes in the average annual exchange rate data. Standard deviation of the changes in the annual average exchange rate in local currency was 206% for DR Congo and a low of 5.6% for Kenya and Tanzania (see Table 2.3).

Theory

Explaining the determinants of exchange rate movement is a highly contested field in economics. This is because it is incredibly difficult to square exchange rate behaviour with the existing theories and other approaches that purport to explain exchange rate behaviour. Nonetheless, there is unanimity that the vast literature around exchange rate economics is binary in nature. One body of the literature is associated with what has been described as fundamentals. The fundamentals are essentially variables that explain changes in exchange rates. The orthodox exchange rate theories have the singular objective of identifying the variables that explain movements in currency prices. The contestation in the literature of exchange rate economics can be traced to mercantilist and classical perspectives of economic thought (Harvey, 2001). New developments in exchange rate economics have not in any way brought us to the point where we can take comfort in the ability of theory to explain and predict currency price behaviour with certainty.

The frustrations with the theory of exchange rates accounts, in part, for the emergence of the technical or chartist approach. The technical approach relies entirely on historical currency price patterns and trading volumes in forecasting future currency price behaviour. The view here is that there is no rationality in currency price behaviour; therefore it is inconceivable that any theory can predict currency price behaviour (Chang & Osler, 1999). While technical analysis is predominantly used by currency traders to ascertain short-term exchange rate behaviour (Lui & Mole 1996; Menkhoff & Taylor, 2007), most orthodox economists dismiss the approach as mere conjuration (Malkiel, 1990). Studies such as Engel et al. (2007) suggest that while the empirical literature on exchange rate theory does not provide overwhelming evidence of the reliability of the theories in predicting exchange rates, they still hold promise.

Following the discussion above, we present a brief overview of the leading exchange rate models. There are many exchange rate models, but we shall dwell on the four leading theories. The monetary model, while quite basic, serves as a useful benchmark. The Mundell-Fleming, Dornbusch, and the portfolio balance and current account models are the other important exchange rate models. It is important to point out that the workings of exchange rate models are informed by important assumptions, particularly regarding the exchange rate regime which foregrounds a currency exchange market. Another important assumption relates to general price regimes: flexible prices or fixed prices. That said, each model is premised on a set of clearly defined assumptions.

The monetary model is based on the balance of payments account dating back to the work of David Hume, the Scottish intellectual in the eighteenth century. The structure of the model is premised on the Purchasing Power Parity (PPP) and the demand for money theories (Hume, 1741). More importantly, the model assumes that prices in the economy are flexible. This assumption leads to a vertical aggregate supply curve. On the demand for money, the assumption is that real balances are dependent on a handful of domestic macroeconomic variables. Lastly, the model makes a herculean assumption that PPP always holds. The equilibrium representation of the monetary model is developed by drawing on the closed-economy aggregate demand and supply schedules with open-economy features, in the sense that the external sector is accounted for with the PPP framework. So, at equilibrium the nominal exchange rate is given by a ratio of money supply to foreign price level, real income, and a positive parameter. This is the simplest form of the model. One is then able to ascertain the policy implications of changes in real income, money supply, and foreign price level on the exchange rate, other things being equal. In its simplest form, there is no place for interest rates. However, the use of the modified Cambridge quantity theory allows interest rate to enter the model. Through the PPP sub-framework links with the balance of payments account, one can examine the effect of interest rate on the exchange rate as well. The model may be used to ascertain the effect of various policy actions on the exchange rate or the balance of payment. The empirical literature suggests that the monetary model of exchange rate determination is grossly inadequate in explaining exchange rate in the real world (Meese & Rogoff, 1983).

Robert Mundell,[11] then at the IMF, and Marcus Fleming[12] at Edinburgh University independently produced papers in 1962 that elegantly captured how the external and domestic sectors of the economy interact

[11] Mundell (1961).

[12] Fleming (1962).

to explain exchange rate movements. The two frameworks are synthesized and called the Mundell-Fleming (M-F) model in the literature. The model is premised on the assumption that prices are fixed, a Keynesian view of the economy. The M-F model, unlike the monetary model, considers the current and capital accounts of the balance of payments account explicitly. The model assumes that aggregate supply curve is flat since prices are fixed. On the current account, it argues that the PPP theory does not hold even in the long run. Rather, the current account balance depends positively on the exchange rate and negatively on income. On the capital account side, the model assumes that expectations about the exchange rate are static and capital mobility is imperfect. It further argues that equilibrium in the external sector occurs if the flow of capital into an economy is adequate in financing the current account deficit or absorbing the surplus. Therefore, under a floating exchange rate regime the external sector of the economy must always balance. For example, the M-F model suggests that following an expansionary monetary policy, interest rate will fall, capital inflow will increase, and the exchange rate will depreciate. The current account will improve with an increase in income. The effect of expansionary budget policy is the opposite of what pertains under monetary expansion. The M-F model is more attractive than the monetary model because its underlying assumptions are relatively more palatable. That said, it would be naïve to assume that the M-F is perfect. For example, the assumptions around fixed prices and static expectations are patently far from reality. Mundell and Fleming's view on the need for the choice and deployment of the appropriate policy instrument to be cognizant of the relative impact of monetary and budgetary policy is one that cannot be faulted.

The apparent flaws in the monetary model and later, the Mundell-Fleming model that make it unable to meaningfully explain movements in exchange rates led to the search for a more useful model. In 1975, Rudiger Dornbusch proposed a theory of exchange rate that considered rational expectations. The key assumption underlying this macroeconomic framework is that there is a differential in adjustment speeds in the goods and asset markets. The faster adjustment speed in the asset market is because investors are risk-neutral. Therefore, it is assumed that the uncovered interest rate parity theory always holds. The model assumes perfect capital mobility. Dornbusch's model also identifies a perfect foresight path along which monetary expansion leads to an immediate depreciation of the exchange rate. The model suggests that the effect of monetary policy on interest rates and exchange rates is determined by the behaviour of real output. For example, if real output is fixed, monetary expansion will lead to reduction of interest rates, leading to overshooting of the exchange rate over its long-run depreciation. On the other hand, if output responds to aggregate demand, then the response of exchange rate would be subdued. Even though the exchange rate would still depreciate, it may not overshoot, and interest rates may surge (Dornbusch, 1976). The theoretical analysis underpinning the Dornbusch model is consistent with the Mundell-Fleming conclusion that with perfect capital, if a small-open economy pursues a floating exchange rate regime, then it can conduct an effective monetary policy in the short run. Over time there have been many extensions of the original Dornbusch model from Frankel (1978).

William Branson's work (Branson, 1977, 1979, 1983, and extensions by others), provides the basis for the portfolio balance approach to modelling exchange rate movements. Unlike the monetary model which dwells on the demand for money, the portfolio balance approach or asset price approach takes into account many financial assets. The framework expands the range of financial assets considered when compared to the Dornbusch framework. Here, financial assets come in three forms: domestic money supply, domestic bonds issued by government and foreign assets issued by foreign governments. It is also assumed that the domestic economy is small and therefore it takes the interest rates on the assets denominated in foreign currency as given. Domestic agents seek to ensure a balanced portfolio of financial assets by distributing their wealth across the three asset classes. In the short run, prices are fixed. According to the model, current account surpluses lead to increases in the foreign asset holdings. This triggers appreciation of the domestic currency and downward pressure in interest rates. In general, it is quite a challenge to use the approach in empirical analysis, particularly for forecasting because some of the variables in the model are unobservable.

There are a few other models of exchange rate beyond the partial equilibrium models that have not been reviewed thus far. For instance, there are models that can be described as general equilibrium models. These models are based on microeconomic foundations because they consider the behaviour of all the key agents in the economy: consumer, firm, and government. The equilibrium conditions for the various agents are derived to feed into a general equilibrium where all the markets that the agents participate in converge and clear contemporaneously. An example of this is the Redux model of Obstfeld and Rogoff (1995). While the equilibrium models are in some ways an improvement on the partial equilibrium models, their ability to forecast short-term exchange rate movements is doubtful.

Thus far the question of uncertainty has been overlooked. Approaches such as the microstructure models and those that incorporate the value of news into some of the existing models are also popular in the literature. The microstructure models emerged in the nineties (Evans, 2006, Bachetta & van Wincoop, 2006). These models draw on microeconomics to understand the real performance of currency markets. The news modelling approach is much older. Frankel's (1981) and Hartley's (1983) are some of the early papers that present a discussion of the news model.

In sum, all theoretical models have been found wanting in one way or the other, particularly when it comes to prediction of exchange rate behaviour in the short run. The observed behaviour of exchange rate movements including those in Africa shows that the exchange rate regime pertaining in an economy is critical in determining the behaviour of the exchange rate. In Africa, the currencies that exist in conventional peg arrangements, such as the CFA franc in West Africa, perform far better than those that exist in floating regimes.

2.5 Relationship Between Inflation, Interest Rates, and Exchange Rate

The three fundamental macroeconomic variables are all related to one another, theoretically, as has been demonstrated above. However, the seminal work of Irving Fisher in 1930 formally establishes a relationship between the three variables: inflation, interest rates, and exchange rates (Fisher, 1930). The international Fisher effect, as the Fisher hypothesis is now often called, suggests that the nominal interest rate in an economy at any period is consistent with the sum of the real interest rate and the expected inflation. The challenge associated with the empirical testing of the Fisher Effect has been related to the choice of proxy for inflation expectations. The notion of rational expectations has been seen as a good tool in the estimation of expected inflation in recent times.

The less restrictive version of the PPP theory, and the Fisher theory together underpin the International Fisher Effect. The International Fisher Effect theory simply says that the differences in nominal interest rates are associated with the expected changes in the exchange rate between two countries. Consequently, countries that are associated with relatively high nominal interest rates often tend to record a depreciation of the domestic currency because the high nominal interest rate is only a reflection of the expected high level of inflation. In essence, the international Fisher effect provides a theoretical linkage of interest rates, inflation, and exchange rates. The Fisher effect has been tested for many countries and regional blocks with varying outcomes.

2.6 Conclusion

Inflation, interest rates, and exchange rates are important policy variables that have a special place in macroeconomic discourse in policy and academic circles. Each of the variables is associated with a significant volume of literature in as far as the theories that explain the stylized facts are concerned. There is also substantial literature that explores the limits of the theories. Economists have also sought to extensively examine the interrelationships among the three important policy variables: inflation, interest rates, and exchange rates. And this has been so because the formal representation of the theories that explain each of the three variables themselves invariably identifies the other variables as possible determinants.

The initial attempts at explaining movements in exchange rates drew on the relationship between prices, interest rates, and the balance of payments. As early as 1918, Gustav Cassel, a Swedish economist, introduced the theory of purchasing power parity that suggested that exchange rates were associated with the purchasing power of national currencies. Policymakers are often also acquainted with the relationship between interest rates and exchange rates. The relationship between interest rates and exchange rates is formally captured in the interest rate parity theory. Maynard Keynes formalized the interest rate parity concept in 1923. The relationship between exchange rates and balance of payments is used to account for the external influences driven by international capital flow and trade in exchange rate models. This effect is usually built into most modern theories of exchange rate determination for open economies.

Appendix

See Figs. 2.5, 2.6, and 2.7 and Table 2.4.

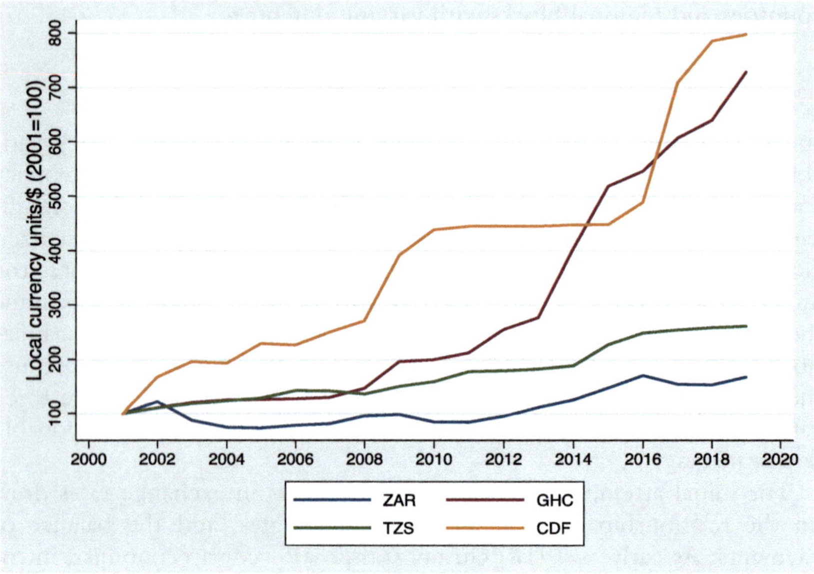

Fig. 2.5 Nominal exchange rate—Other resource-intensive countries

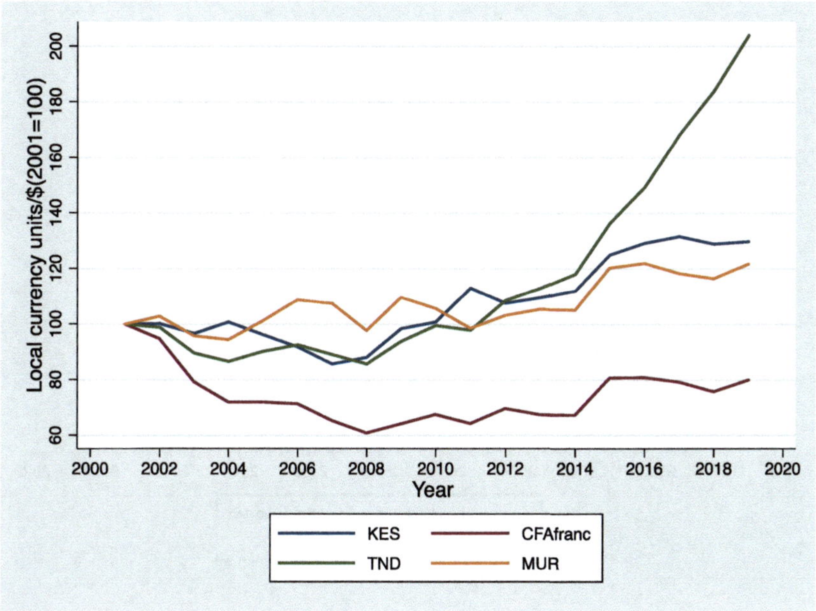

Fig. 2.6 Nominal exchange rate—Non-resource intensive countries

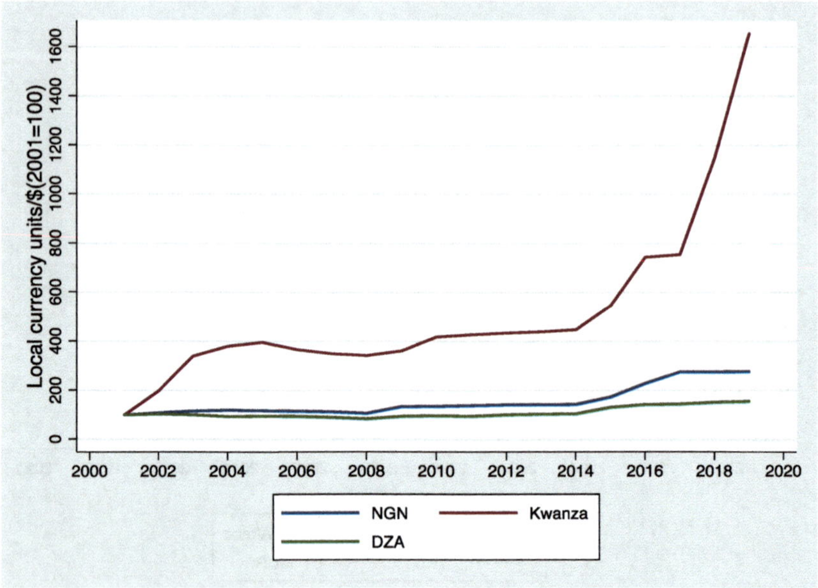

Fig. 2.7 Nominal exchange rate—Resource-intensive countries

Table 2.4 Average Real Interest rates, Lending rates, and Interest rate spread in Africa (2000–2019)

Year	*Real interest rate (%)*		*Lending rate (%)*		*Interest rate spread (%)*	
	Average	*Median*	*Average*	*Median*	*Average*	*Median*
2000	5.92	10.62	24.53	20.65	13.69	11.79
2001	9.91	13.07	24.56	20.06	13.13	11.61
2002	9.44	12.54	24.50	19.28	13.00	11.92
2003	10.24	9.85	23.29	17.64	13.14	10.85
2004	5.77	5.97	21.40	18.17	12.87	10.10
2005	7.78	5.94	17.61	14.07	9.23	7.42
2006	7.32	7.01	15.57	14.57	6.48	7.61
2007	7.99	5.82	15.96	14.59	7.48	7.67
2008	3.23	2.89	15.53	14.62	7.10	6.70
2009	9.11	7.62	16.19	14.08	7.58	7.06
2010	7.38	4.67	15.49	12.42	7.75	7.93
2011	5.59	3.84	14.93	11.19	7.44	8.18
2012	7.21	6.05	14.66	12.03	7.16	7.33
2013	8.62	7.58	14.66	10.52	7.22	7.07
2014	11.97	9.58	14.70	11.57	7.51	7.31
2015	8.10	6.82	14.09	11.46	6.99	6.83
2016	8.52	6.69	14.19	11.04	7.20	7.14
2017	8.21	6.39	14.29	11.58	7.41	6.96
2018	10.40	7.99	17.00	14.79	10.96	9.02
2019	11.47	9.45	16.55	14.95	10.98	8.95

References

Adefeso, H. A., & Mobolaji, H. I. (2010). The fiscal-monetary policy and economic growth in Nigeria: Further empirical evidence. *Pakistan Journal of Social Sciences, 7*(2), 137–142.

Ahokpossi, M. C. (2013). *Determinants of bank interest margins in Sub-Saharan Africa*. International Monetary Fund.

Baldini, A., & Poplawski-Ribeiro, M. (2011). Fiscal and monetary determinants of inflation in low-income countries: Theory and evidence from Sub-Saharan Africa. *Journal of African Economies, 20*(3), 419–462.

Bikai, J. L., Batoumen, M., Hardit & Fossouo, A. (2016). *Determinants of inflation in CEMAC: The role of money* (MPRA Paper No. 89111).

BIS (2019). *Triennial Central Bank Survey of Foreign Exchange Rate and Over-the-counter (OTC) Derivatives Markets in 2019*. Bank for International Settlement.

Bleaney, M. & Francisco, M. (n.d.). *Inflation and fiscal deficits in Sub-Saharan Africa*. World Bank.

Bleaney, M., & Francisco, M. (2007). Exchange rate regimes, inflation and growth in developing countries—An assessment. *The B.E. Journal of Macroeconomics Topics*, *7*(1), 1–20.

Bohm-Bawerk, E. (1890). *Capital and interest*. McMaster University Archive for the History of Economic Thought.

Böhm-Bawerk, E. V. (1906). Capital and interest once more: I. Capital vs. capital goods. *The Quarterly Journal of Economics*, *21*(1), 1–21.

Bohm-Bawerk, E. V. (1907). Capital and interest once more: II. A relapse to the productivity theory. *The Quarterly Journal of Economics*, *21*(2), 247–282.

Bowley, M. (2013). *Nassau Senior and classical economics*. Routledge.

Branson, W. H., Haltunen, H., & Masson, P. (1979). Exchange rates on the short-run: Some further results. *European Economic Review, 12*, 395–402.

Branson, W. H., Haltunen, H., & Masson, P. (1977). Exchange rates in the short-run: The dollar-deutschemark rate. *European Economic Review, 10*, 303–324.

Branson, W. H. (1983). Macroeconomic determinants of real exchange rate risk. In R. J. Herring (Ed.), *Managing foreign exchange risks*. Cambridge University Press.

Carmichael, J., & Stebbing, P. W. (1983). Fisher's paradox and the theory of interest. *The American Economic Review, 73*(4), 619–630.

Cassel, G. (1916). The present situation of the foreign exchanges. *Economic Journal, 26*, 62–65.

Clark, J. B. (1895). The origin of interest. *The Quarterly Journal of Economics, 9*(3), 257–278.

Dornbusch, R., (1976). Expectations and exchange rate dynamics. *Journal of Political Economy*, 84, 1161–1176.

Evans, O., Adeniji, S., Nwaogwugwu, I., Kelikume, I., Dakare, O., & Oke, O. (2018). The relative effect of monetary and fiscal policy on economic development in Africa: A GMM approach to the St Louis equation. *Business and Economic Quarterly, 2*, 3–23.

Fetter, F. A. (1902). The "roundabout process" in the interest theory. *The Quarterly Journal of Economics, 17*(1), 163–180.

Fisher, I. (1930). *Theory of interest: As determined by impatience to spend income and opportunity to invest it*. Augustusm Kelly Publishers.

Fisher's Paradox and the Theory of Interest on JSTOR. (n.d.). Retrieved April 18, 2021, from https://www.jstor.org/stable/1816562?seq=1#metadata_info_tab_contents

Fleming, M. (1962). *Domestic financial policies under fixed floating exchange rates* (Staff Papers, pp. 369–380). International Monetary Fund.

Folawewo, A. O., & Tennant, D. (2008). Determinants of interest rate spreads in Sub-Saharan African countries: A dynamic panel analysis. In *A paper prepared for the 13th Annual African Econometrics Society Conference* (pp. 9–11).

Frankel, J. A. (1978). Purchasing power doctrinal and evidence from the 1920s. *Journal of International Economics, 8*, 169–191.

Franke, J. A. (1981). Flexible exchange rates, prices, and the role of "news": Lessons from the 1970s. *Journal of Political Economy, 89*, 665–705.

Ghosh, A., Ostry, J., & Tsangarides, C. (2010). *Exchange rate regime and the stability of the international monetary system*, IMF Occasional Paper No. 270 (IMF).

Gyeke-Dako, A., Agbloyor, E. K., Turkson, F. E., & Baffour, P. T. (2018). Financial development and the social cost of financial intermediation in Africa. *Journal of African Business, 19*(4), 455–474.

Harvey, J. T. (2001). Exchange rate theory and the "fundamentals." *Journal of Post Keynesian Economics, 24*(1), 3–15.

IMF (2019). *Annual report on exchange arrangements and exchange restrictions 2018*. International Monetary Fund.

IMF. (2021). *Sub-Saharan Africa regional outlook: One planet, two worlds, three stories, world economic and financial surveys*. International Monetary Fund.

Kavila, W., & Le Roux, P. (2017). The role of monetary policy in Zimbabwe's hyperinflation episode. *African Review of Economics and Finance, 9*(2), 132–166.

Kelikume, I. (2016). The effect of budget deficit on interest rates in the countries of sub-Saharan Africa: A panel VAR approach. *The Journal of Developing Areas, 50*(6), 105–120.

Keynes, J. M. (1937). The general theory of employment. *The Quarterly Journal of Economics, 51*(2), 209–223.

Knight, F. H. (1936). The quantity of capital and the rate of interest: I. *Journal of Political Economy, 44*(4), 433–463.

Liu, P. C. (1996). The effects of the fundamentalists' and chartists' expectations on market survey. *Applied Financial Economics, 6*(4), 363–366.

Marshall, A. (1907). The social possibilities of economic chivalry. *The Economic Journal, 17*(65), 7–29.

Meese, R. A., & Rogoff, K. (1983). Empirical exchange rate models of the seventies: Do they fit out of sample? *Journal of International Economics, 14*(1–2), 3–24.

Melaku, M. (2021). Determinants of inflation in Sub-Saharan Africa: A Systematic review. *Developing Country Studies, 11*(3), 16–19.

Mundell, R. A. (1961). A flexible exchange rates and employment policy. *Canadian Journal of Economics and Political Science, 27*, 509–517.

Musah, A., Anokye, F. K., & Gakpetor, E. D. (2018). The impact of interest rate spread on bank profitability in Ghana. *European Journal of Business, Economics and Accountancy, 6*(1), 27–39.

Nguyen, A. D. M., Dridi, J., Unsal, F. D., & Williams, O. H. (2015). *On the drivers of inflation in Sub-Saharan Africa* (IMF Working Paper. WP/15/189).

Niehans, J. (1990). *A history of economic theory: Classic contributions, 1720–1980*. Johns Hopkins University Press.

Nwaogwugwu, I., & Evans, O. (2016). A sectoral analysis of fiscal and monetary actions in Nigeria. *The Journal of Developing Areas, 50*(4), 211–229.

Obstfeld, M., & Kenneth, R. (1995). Exchange rate dynamics redux. *Journal of Political Economy*, 103, 624–660.

Ocran, M. K. (2019). *Economic development in the twenty-first century: Lessons for Africa throughout history*. Palgrave Macmillan. https://doi.org/10.1007/978-3-030-10770-3

Odionye, J. C., & Uma, K. E. (2013). The relationship between budget deficit and interest rate: Evidence from Nigeria. *European Journal of Business and Social Sciences, 2*(1), 158–167.

Ohlin, B., Robertson, D. H., & Hawtrey, R. G. (1937). Alternative theories of the rate of interest: Three rejoinders. *The Economic Journal, 47*(187), 423–443.

Pigou, A. C. (1936). Mr. JM Keynes' General theory of employment, interest and money. *Economica, 3*(10), 115–132.

Rae, J. (1834). *Statement of some new principles on the subject of political economy (1834)*. AM Kelley.

Rothbard, M. N. (1990). Time preference. In *Capital Theory* (pp. 237–242). Palgrave Macmillan.

Senior, N. W. (1928). *Industrial efficiency and social economy* (Vol. 2). Holt & Company.

Turtelboom, M. B. (1991). *Interest rate liberalization: Some lessons from Africa*. International Monetary Fund.

Thünen, J. H. von. (1966). *Von Thünen's isolated state* (C. M. Wartenberg, Trans. & P. Hall, Ed.). Pergamon Press.

Walras, L. (2013). *Elements of pure economics*. Routledge.

Wicksell, K. (1907). The influence of the rate of interest on Prices Economic Journal XVII (pp. 213–220), read before the Economic Section of the British Association, 1906. *Economic Journal, 17*, 213–220.

World Bank. (2021). *World development indicators*. World Bank.

CHAPTER 3

Bank Market Structure and Competition in Africa

James Ntiamoah Doku, Emmanuel Mensah, Zangina Isshaq, and Charles Komla Delali Adjasi

3.1 Introduction

Africa's banking sector today has an ownership mix comprising government-controlled banks, privately owned domestic banks and foreign banks. This has not always been the case. Government involvement in the financial sector in Africa dates back to the 1960s and

J. N. Doku (✉)
University of Professional Studies, Accra, Madina, Ghana
e-mail: jdoku@upsamail.edu.gh

E. Mensah
Absa Bank Ghana, Accra, Ghana
e-mail: ekbmensah@gmail.com

Z. Isshaq
Department of Accounting, University of Ghana Business School, University of Ghana, Legon, Accra, Ghana
e-mail: mzmisshaq@ug.edu.gh

J. Y. Abor and C. K. D. Adjasi (eds.), *The Economics of Banking and Finance in Africa*, Palgrave Macmillan Studies in Banking and Financial Institutions, https://doi.org/10.1007/978-3-031-04162-4_3

1990s, the immediate post-independence years, when there was a high level of state dominance in the banking sector. These years of state dominance in the financial sector led to much economic pain. The way out of the economic difficulties was structural reforms in the 1980s and 1990s. Reforms of the banking and nascent financial sector took the form of loosening state dominance. State ownership of banks may induce conflicts with state regulatory agencies responsible for effective regulation and this may lead to a weak regulatory context in the financial sector. Financial sector reforms across the continent, thus, sought to address these ills. This ushered in a period of financial sector liberalisation. Key to the liberalisation was privatising non-performing (loss-making) state-owned banks and other financial institutions and improving governance and regulation of banks. These actions were aimed at improving the supervision and governance of banks and other financial institutions so as to achieve competition and efficiency in the financial sector.

The financial liberalisation programmes changed the organisation and competitive landscape of the banking sector, which has been further spurred on by advances in communication technology. While the state is no longer the dominant owner in African banking, the industry's structure features a number of dominant banks, which weakens bank regulators' desire to engineer a competitive banking landscape. In relative terms, the degree of financial intermediation efficiency in the banking sector in Africa is behind that of other developing banking sectors, with little financial deepening and inadequate access to finance (Beck et al., 2011). Also, Doku et al. (2012) report that the level of spread of the banking sector in Sub-Saharan Africa is declining, though it is higher than comparator regions such as East Asia & Pacific (EAP), Latin America & the Caribbean (LAC) and South Asia (SAS) regions. The high spread level in the banking system is indicative of competitiveness in the banking sector, which has implications for access to finance and intermediation efficiency.

This chapter of the book assesses the structure of the banking sector and competition in Africa. Towards this end, the chapter is structured as follows: the next section presents stylised facts on bank market structure

C. K. D. Adjasi
University of Stellenbosch, Stellenbosch, South Africa
e-mail: Charles.Adjasi@usb.ac.za

and competition in Africa, followed by a review of existing literature, the methodology, empirical results and policy implications.

3.2 Bank Market Structure and Competition in Africa: Stylised Facts

Bank market structure in Africa has some striking contrasts in the areas of competitiveness, ownership structure and financial deepening across the regional blocks. Doku et al. (2012) find that financial deepening in Southern Africa, West Africa and East and Central Africa seems to lag in growth compared to the banking systems in North Africa. The countries that exhibited enhanced performance in North Africa are Morocco, Algeria, Tunisia, Egypt and Sudan (Doku et al., 2012). These countries share a feature in oil endowment and agricultural resources. The region also sustained constant and remarkable economic growth (Allen et al., 2011). In terms of ownership structure, the banking market in Algeria, Egypt, Libya and Tunisia is largely controlled by the government-owned banks which finance large state infrastructure, agriculture, real estate and allied developmental projects (Allen et al., 2011). In contrast, Morocco, has a banking sector controlled by private ownership, which accounts for a large share of banking market assets (BAM Annual Financial Report, 2010).[1]

Also, the organisational outlook of banks in Central and East Africa appears to be the least developed with respect to financial deepening. Like the North African region, this area is gifted with natural possessions, predominantly agriculture resources and oil. With the exception of Ethiopia and Eritrea, the banking sector exhibits foreign, private local banks and a mix of both. Kenya stands out with a banking sector in which the domestic and privately owned commercial banks control the financial system while the government-controlled banks represent the minority. In Tanzania, the government's control of ownership of banks is less than foreign ownership stake. About half of the banking sector is controlled by foreign-owned banks while state control is largely limited to the minority banks; the same is true for the Ugandan banking system (Allen et al., 2011).

[1] Central Bank of Morocco, Annual Report, 2010.

In Southern Africa, banks in South Africa dominate in the areas of performance and number of banks, followed by Botswana and Namibia. Performance in the banking sector in South Africa has improved in financial deepening over the years. Compared to the other regions in Africa, the Southern African banking sector dominates performance in key areas. But the West African banking sector performs better than East and Central Africa in financial deepening. In West Africa, banking markets in the French-speaking economies are dominated by Ivory Coast and Senegal (Allen et al., 2011) with the formation of a common central bank, known as the Central Bank of West African States (BCEAO). The banking sector in the BCEAO is controlled by foreign-owned banks. Unlike the Francophone countries in the West African region, the Anglophone nations do not have a common central bank. The dominant banking markets among English-speaking countries are in Nigeria, Ghana and Sierra Leone. Similarly, except in Nigeria, foreign-owned banks control the banking sector. As in North and Southern Africa, West Africa's banking sector experienced significant growth in financial deepening measured by private credit to GDP ratio. In terms of distribution of foreign bank ownership in Africa, the West, East and Southern African banking sector has more presence of foreign banks than the North African economies. Foreign banks include Pan-African banks and banks from outside the continent of Africa.

Notwithstanding a substantial growth in the banking sector performance indicators in Africa, compared to comparator regions, the banking sector is still far behind in its intermediation efforts, specifically, in terms of deepening, efficiency and accessibility.

Banking Sector Depth: Africa Versus Comparator Regions

In this section we present a descriptive comparison of the features of the banking system in Sub-Saharan Africa with those of its peer regions on key indicators that have been found relevant in the extant literature. For example, the finance-growth literature, theoretically and empirically, has strongly emphasised the significance of financial development, especially banking sector deepening in enhancing economic growth (Bagehot, 1873; King & Levine, 1993). Others such as Goldsmith (1969), Greenwood and Jovanovich (1990), and Bencivenga and Smith (1991) also emphasise that it is the efficiency and not the volume of resource allocation by financial institutions that drives growth. Thus, efficient allocation of financial resources is regarded as one of the key functions of a well-functioning banking sector. In the banking literature, key measures of efficient intermediation in resource mobilisation and allocation include banking sector's depth (financial deepening) computed as private credit to gross domestic product (GDP), bank assets to gross domestic product and the ratio of liquid liabilities to GDP. Private sector credit to GDP represents domestic private sector lending to the real sector by deposit money banks as a share of GDP. This excludes credit issued to governments, government agencies, and public enterprises in an economy. It provides a measure of allocation of capital to private enterprises from private banks. Total banking assets to GDP ratio measure is different from the private credit to GDP ratio because it includes credit issued to government and bank assets rather than credit to private sectors of an economy. The liquid liabilities to GDP ratio is equivalent to currency plus demand deposits and interest-bearing liabilities of banks and other financial intermediaries divided by GDP. This provides a measure of the banking sector's capacity to assemble private savings for lending.

Figure 3.1 shows the trend in the proxies for financial deepening between Africa and comparator regions. The ratio of private credit to GDP (pcrdbgdp), banks' assets to GDP (dbagdp) and the ratio of liquid liabilities to GDP (llgdp) show significant levels of progress in financial deepening over the period 1960–2017 for all the regions. As noted earlier, private credit to GDP ratio also indicates the size of the banking sector relative to general economy. Economies with high levels of private credit to GDP might experience faster growth since banks may take advantage of scale economies and high productivity.

Banking Sector Intermediation Efficiency & Concentration: Africa Versus Comparator Regions

Another desired key attribute of the banking sector in an economy is the sector's efficiency in intermediation-transforming savings into investment. The intermediation function represents the ability of financial institutions like banks to mobilise savings at low cost while at the same time ensuring sustainable revenues from investment services. Measures of intermediation efficiency in the literature include net interest margin (interest revenue less interest expense as a share of its interest-earning assets), cost-income ratio (total costs as a share of total revenue of banks), overhead expenses to total assets, concentration ratio (assets of three largest banks relative to

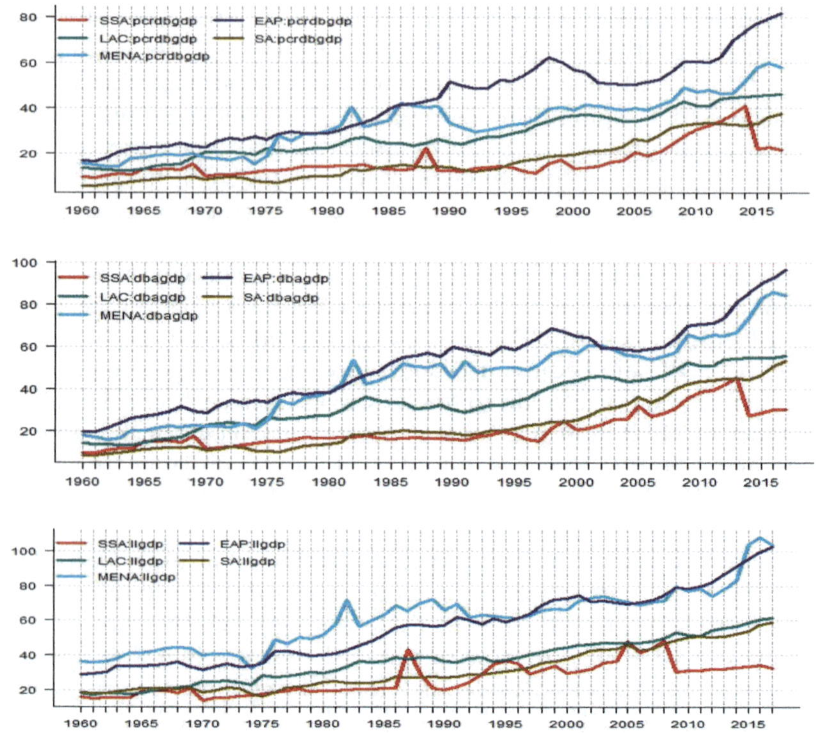

Fig. 3.1 Private Credit/GDP, Deposit Banks' Assets/GDP & Liquid Liabilities/GDP (*Note* EAP [East Asia & Pacific], LAC [Latin America & Caribbeans], MENA [Middle East & North Africa], SA [South Asia], SSA [Sub-Saharan Africa]. llgdp [Liquid liabilities/gdp], dbagdp [Domestic banks assets/gdp], pcrdbgdp [private domestic bank credit/gdp]. *Source* GFDD [2019] and authors' calculations)

assets of all commercial banks) and profitability measures, such as return on assets (ROA) and return on equity (ROE). Figure 3.2 compares SSA and comparator regions on trends in their respective intermediation efficiency proxies. In Fig. 3.2, compared to other regions, the banking sector in SSA has had higher cost-income ratio, net interest margins, concentration and overheads, followed by the Latin American and the Caribbean economies.

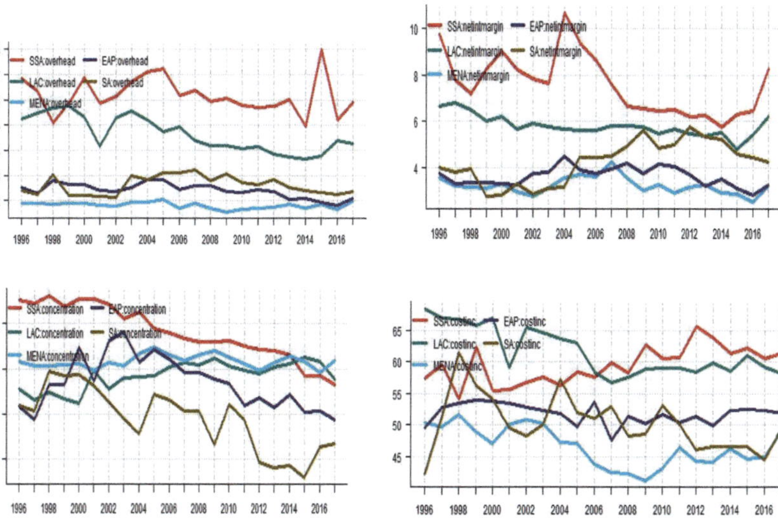

Fig. 3.2 Intermediation Efficiency & Concentration: SSA and Comparator Regions (*Note* EAP [East Asia & Pacific], LAC [Latin America & Caribbeans], MENA [Middle East & North Africa], SA [South Asia], SSA [Sub-Saharan Africa]. Overhead [ratio of overhead costs to total assets], netmargin [ratio of net interest to total assets], concentration [assets of three largest banks as a share of assets of all commercial banks] and costinc [total costs as a share of total income of banks]. *Source* GFDD [2019] and authors' calculations)

Banking Sector Profitability and Stability: SSA and Comparator Regions

Beck et al. (2011) indicated huge profit margins that characterised banking in Africa. There is also a high level of concentration in African banking despite various reforms meant to promote competition in the financial sector. Figure 3.3 shows that ROA and ROE of banks in SSA are higher than those in the comparator regions, but the banking sector's stability, measured as a z-score, is lower. The z-score is one of the measures of banking structure stability and it is represented as the summation of bank capital plus profit on assets ratios scaled with the volatility of profit on assets. Relative to other measures of bank stability, the z-score is more robust and dependable due to the fact that it compares a bank's buffers (capitalisation and returns) against its risk (volatility of returns).

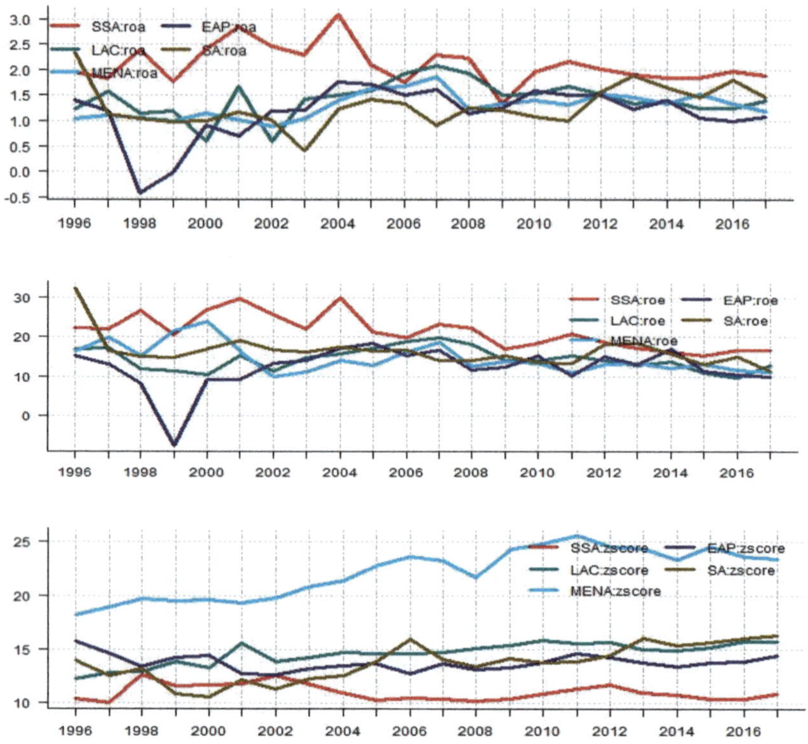

Fig. 3.3 Profitability and Stability: SSA and Comparator Regions (*Note* EAP [East Asia & Pacific], LAC [Latin America & Caribbeans], MENA [Middle East & North Africa], SA [South Asia], SSA [Sub-Saharan Africa]. ROA [ratio of net profit to total assets], ROE [ratio of net profit to shareholders fund], zscore [the sum of bank capital to assets ratio and return on assets ratio, divided by the standard deviation of return on assets]. *Source* GFDD [2019], and authors' calculations)

The African bank market structure characteristics discovered above have implications for policy making. For instance, the relatively low level of financial deepening, high intermediation costs and high concentration among African banks shows that there seems to be a low level of competition among banks in Africa. Second, as noted by Beck et al. (2011), technology application in banking services delivery has drastically influenced and changed the banking sector, but not enough. One of the key drivers likely to influence financial inclusion among banks is competition.

Banking sector competitiveness in Africa is critical for several reasons. First, competition among banks ensures efficient financial resource distribution and superiority of production of financial products and services. Also, the efficiency in resource allocation from banking sector competition heightens economic growth (Vives, 2001). Vives (2001) also notes that the amount of competition in the financial system increases financial inclusion which is necessary for economic growth.

Second, the competitive behaviour of banks has come to the fore after the 2008–2009 worldwide financial disaster. Knowledge gained from the disaster shows that bank market structure affects the level of bank competition and the strength of the financial sector. Stakeholders thus need some level of information about the conduct of banks so that they can design suitable policies to achieve desired results. A number of studies have assessed banks' competitive conduct in developing economies (Gelos & Roldós, 2004), while others focused on developed economies (see Al-Muharrami et al., 2006; Bikker & Haaf, 2002) and the global level (Claessens & Laeven, 2004).

On the continent of Africa, research investigating bank competitive behaviour is limited to country-specific studies (Al-Haschimi, 2007; Beck & Hesse, 2009; Biekpe, 2011; Buchs & Mathiesen, 2005; Flamini et al., 2009; Mlambo & Ncube, 2011; Mwega, 2011; Nannyonjo, 2002; Okeahalam, 1998; Simpasa, 2011;Turk-Ariss, 2009). While these studies are informative about the respective countries, the limitations are that we do not have a continental view of the implications of banking sector competition for financial systems and the economy across the breadth of the African continent. The current study examines bank market structure and competitive behaviour in Africa, which provides a plaftform for assessing the impact of various reforms aimed at enhancing competitive conditions in banking markets in Africa.

3.3 Literature Review

The existing literature explains the implications of bank competition in two strands: the traditional approach and the non-traditional approach. The traditional approach is composed of these hypotheses: the structure-conduct-performance (SCP) paradigm and the efficiency paradigm. The issue that connects these hypotheses is how bank market structure impacts pricing and profits of banks in a market. In the process, the measure of competition is essential to understanding the implications of market structure. We present a review of these approaches to measuring competition and their implications.

Measuring Competition in Banking: The Traditional and Non-traditional Approaches

The traditional approach posits that a very concentrated bank market (a market with few large banks) encourages collusive and anti-competitive behaviour, which leads to superior performance for the dominant banks (Neumark & Sharpe, 1992). Basically, the SCP hypothesis predicts concentrated banking sector to create opportunities for banks to scheme to overcharge for products and services, which results in more profits that the dominants will pass off as superior performance.

Closely related to SCP is the relative-market-power hypothesis (RMP). The RMP hypothesis proposed by Shephard (1986) holds that only banks with huge market shares which have product offerings that are slightly different from competitors may command market power and receive above normal profit. Thus the RMP hypothesis is about a direct link between the performance of a banking sector and its level of concentration. Econometrically, the SCP implies the following model:

$$\mathrm{Perf}_{\mathrm{ijt}} = \alpha_0 + \alpha_1 \mathrm{C}_{\mathrm{jt}} + \sum_{i=1}^{n} \varpi_k \mathrm{X}_{k,\,\mathrm{ijt}} + \varepsilon_{\mathrm{ijt}} \tag{3.1}$$

whereby, *i, j* and *t* designate a bank, market and time respectively. The variable Perf is a measure of bank performance, *C* measures concentration, and X_k is a set of control variables that influence bank performance. One of the key postulations of the SCP is that market structure is exogenous. Thus it is expected that $\alpha_1 > 0$ in line with the SCP hypothesis that the more concentrated a banking system, the more likely is the performance (profit).

The efficiency hypothesis (EH) proposes that what actually makes banks perform highly is the level of bank efficiency (Demsetz, 1973; Peltzman, 1977). This is due to the logic that banks that operate efficiently reduce operational costs and are able to capture more market share and profit. Two types of efficiency can be found: Scale efficiency and

X-efficiency (Berger, 1995). Regarding X-efficiency, banks that possess excellent administration know-how and superior production technology and capacity are able to acquire higher market share, allowing such banks to garner higher profits. The scale efficiency argument is that size matters in enhancing performance, and that explains why some banks perform better than others. The econometric model below can be used to examine, independently, the validity of SCP or EH:

$$\mathrm{Perf}_{\mathrm{ijt}} = \beta_0 + \beta_1 \mathrm{C}_{\mathrm{jt}} + \beta_2 \mathrm{MKTSHARE}_{\mathrm{ijt}} + \sum_{i=1}^{n} \varpi_k \mathrm{X}_{k,\mathrm{ijt}} + \varepsilon_{\mathrm{ijt}} \tag{3.2}$$

where $\mathrm{MKTSHARE}_{\mathrm{ijt}}$ characterises market share of bank i in market j at time t. Thus, EH holds when $\beta_1 = 0$ and $\beta_2 > 0$ whereas the SCP implies that $\beta_2 = 0$ and $\beta_1 > 0$. It can be recognised that Eq. 3.2 contains both SCP and EH that acknowledge the consequence of bank market structure on performance outcome but is unable to settle on which one causes performance. The SCP hypothesis was applied in several empirical studies especially for banks (Barajas et al., 1999; Flamini et al., 2009; Gilbert, 1984; Girardone et al., 2004; Guru et al., 1999; Kosmidou & Pasiouras, 2005; Kosmidou et al., 2006; Maudos, 1998; Rhoades, 1982; Williams, 2003).

Despite its popularity and application in empirical studies, some challenges have been identified with the SCP hypothesis. For instance, Shaffer (2004) noted that the structural approach explores bank competition based on the structure of the marketing segment but ignores how banks behave when the prices of factors used in producing banking products and services change. Additionally, Shaffer (2004) admitted two apprehensions about the SCP: the definition of what constitutes a banking market, which positively impacts the concentration level and need of the types of stability in pricing that join bank market structure and conduct. Shaffer (2004) argued that one needs to recognise and pursue sufficient conditions that link conduct and performance. Likewise, Schmalensee (1989) questioned the appropriateness of using concentration as a proxy for market structure.

Furthermore, the contestability theorists (Baumol et al., 1982) test the reality of SCP and its assumptions. The contestability theory is of the view that even in a concentrated market, one could find behaviour of firms that can be classified as competitive when obstacles to potential entrants are overcome or eliminated (Baumol et al., 1982). When there are possibilities of new firms entering an existing market due to low barriers, incumbent firms may adopt new pricing strategies in a competitive manner. Generally, empirical evidence could not tell whether the direct association between market structure and performance relates to efficiency or collusion (Berger, 1995; Molyneux & Thorton, 1992). Therefore, alternative approaches have been offered: the non-traditional measures of market structure.

Some of the broadly recognised measures of bank competition under the non-traditional (also known as non-structural) approach are the Iwata (1974), Bresnahan (1982), Lau (1982), Panzar-Rose model (Panzar & Rose, 1987), hereafter referred to as PR and Lerner index. These models are rooted in the new industrial organisation theory that examines the competitive behaviour and the use of market power by banks without the use of concentration or market share indicators as proxies for market structure. The Iwata model estimates competitive behaviour by determining conjectural variation coefficients for individual firms supplying a homogeneous product in an oligopolistic market. The Bresnahan (1982), Lau (1982) and Panzar and Rosse (1987) models, on the other hand, evaluate competitive conditions in a contestable banking market. Again, the Bresnahan and Lau models estimate demand, supply and price equations simultaneously while the Panzar and Rosse model accounts for bank-specific differences in production functions examined under long-run equilibrium. Contemporary evidence in the bank competition literature shows alternative measures, the Lerner index and PR-H-statistic. Like the PR, the Lerner index is recognised as a positive measure of market power in the banking literature.

However, the Lerner index has some deficiencies. One notable challenge with the Lerner index is that of non-availability of relevant data to compute its parameters. Usually, the financial statement of banks is not enough to estimate the costs and prices required to calculate the Lerner index. Secondly, different scholars specify differently the marginal cost function in estimating the Lerner index and this leaves more room for subjective specification and estimation. The PR competition assessment is based on the assumption of long-run equilibrium conditions of banks (see Gelos & Roldós, 2002). Goddard and Wilson (2009) modified the static Panzar-Rosse model to account for partial adjustment towards equilibrium, in that bank markets are not in equilibrium always. Thus, the dynamic specification of the PR-H statistic renders the PR-H statistic incorrectly specified.

Despite the identified weakness in the application of the PR-H statistic model, it is one of the mostly used measures of banking sector competition in most of the empirical studies due to its strong theoretical foundation and simplicity. For instance, its estimation requires the use of bank-level financial statements. Shaffer (1982) estimated the PR model and found that the bank market is monopolistic competition among a sample of New York banks. In the Canadian banking system, Nathan and Neave (1989) observed similar results as Shaffer (1989) when they used the PR estimation technique. In Europe, Molyneux et al. (1994a, 1994b) as well as De Bandt and Davis (2000) are testaments to the reliability of the PR model. Generally, the PR approach found banking systems to be in a form of monopolistic competition. However, Casu and Girardone (2006) indicated that there is no correlation between concentration and competition in a banking sector when the PR methodology is used.

Claessens and Laeven (2004) used the PR approach to examine the factors that influence competitive bank behaviour and found that banking sector competition is influenced by the presence of foreign-owned banks, and fewer entry and activity restrictions. From the preceding exposition, it becomes absolutely clear that competition is a complex issue, hence there might be various approaches to estimating competition in banking. Therefore, to provide an inclusive evaluation of competitive bank performance, broader measures of bank competition must be considered.

3.4 Methodology

Analytical Framework: The Panzar and Rosse (1987) Methodology

One of the most widely used methodologies in estimating bank competitive behaviour is that of Panzar-Rosse (1987). The Panzar-Rosse (1987) methodology formulated a reduced-form revenue approach that distinguishes whether the nature of a market can be described as perfect competition, monopolistic competition or monopoly. The Panzar-Rosse (1987) methodology is based on the assumption that banks operate in their long-run equilibrium. Additionally, it assumes the performance of a bank is independent of other market participants, the price elasticity of demand is more than unity, and all banks face a homogenous cost structure. Thus, banks will employ different pricing strategies in response to change in input costs depending on the market structure in which they operate. At equilibrium, profit is maximised at bank and industry level to arrive at equilibrium output and the equilibrium number of banks. Thus, a bank maximises its profit where the difference between marginal revenue and marginal cost of its intermediation is zero:

$$R_i^l(d_i, n, m_i) - C_i^l(d_i, p_i, u_i) = 0 \tag{3.3}$$

R_i^l represents marginal revenue function, with C_i^l being marginal cost function; d_i is the output of bank *i*, while *n* is the number of banks, m_i and u_i consist of exogenous variables that shift a bank's revenue and cost functions respectively whereas p_i is a vector of bank *i*'s factor input prices. By applying the first order condition, the implication is that the zero-profit constraint holds at the industry level:

$$R_i^*(d^*, n^*, m_i) - C_i^*(d^*, p, u) = 0 \tag{3.4}$$

Panzar-Rosse defines the measured competitiveness of a bank as the sum of the elasticities of the reduced-form revenues with respect to factor input prices (the *H*-statistic):

$$H = \sum_{x=1}^{t} \frac{\partial R_i^*}{\partial p_{xi}} \frac{p_{xi}}{R_i^*} \tag{3.5}$$

The Panzar-Rosse (1987) H-statistic differentiates between the main forms of market structure: monopoly/perfect collusion, monopolistic competition and perfect competition/contestable market. For instance, under monopoly, an increase in the input price increases the marginal cost while the equilibrium outputs and total revenue may either reduce or remain unchanged. Therefore, the measured competitiveness is, H - statistic ≤ 0. With respect to monopolistic competition, a change in input price leads to less than a proportionate change in revenue, hence the $0 \leq H$ - statistic ≤ 1, and under perfect competition, the change in input price leads to an equivalent change in revenue, thus the H - statistic $= 1$. Under the assumptions that firms operate with constant price elasticity and a constant return to scale, under the Cobb–Douglas function, Panzar-Rosse (1987) proved that a higher value of H-statistic implies a high competitive measure and that the H-statistic is a continuous measure of competition. The Panzar-Rosse (1987) H-statistic can also be linked to the Lerner index, L, as specified below:

$$L = \frac{H}{H - 1}$$

In its empirical implementation, Bikker and Haaf (2002), among others, adopted a log-linear marginal cost function (dropping bank *i* subscripts):

$$\ln MC = \alpha_0 + \alpha_1 \ln OP + \sum_{i=1}^{m} \beta_{i1} \ln e_i + \sum_{j=1}^{p} \gamma_j EX_{COST j} \tag{3.6}$$

where *OP* is output of the bank, *e* are the factor input prices (*e.g.* funding, personnel expenses and other expenses) and EX_{COST} are other variables exogenous to the cost function C_i^l in Eq. (3.13). Similarly, expressing the marginal revenue function as a log-linear of the form gives:

$$\ln MR = \delta_0 + \delta_1 \ln OP + \sum_{k=1}^{q} \vartheta_k EX_{REVk} \tag{3.7}$$

where EX_{REV} are bank-specific demand function variables. Since banks are profit-maximisers, marginal costs equal marginal revenues in equilibrium, yielding the equilibrium value for output (denoted by an asterisk):

$$\ln OP^* = \frac{\left(\alpha_0 - \delta_0 + \sum_{i=1}^{m} \beta_i \ln e_i + \sum_{j=1}^{p} \gamma_i \ln EX_{COSTj} - \sum_{k=1}^{q} \vartheta_k \ln EX_{REXk}\right)}{(\delta_1 - \alpha_1)} \tag{3.8}$$

The reduced-form equation for income or revenues of bank *i* is the product of the equilibrium values of output of bank *i* and the common price level, determined by the inverse-demand equation, which is expressed in logarithms as:

$$\ln p = \varepsilon + \vartheta \ln(\textstyle\sum_i OP_i^*) \tag{3.9}$$

Like any other specification, the Panzar-Rosse (1987) model has received several attacks by scholars like Shaffer (2004). Other scholars have agreed that the PR model is only as good as the long-run equilibrium condition holds (see Gelos & Roldós, 2002). Goddard and Wilson (2009) further added dynamic estimation to the literature on PR estimation.

The Bresnahan Framework

Bresnahan (1982) and Lau (1982) present a short-run model for determination of the market power of a bank. This model is also known as the conjectural variation (CV) model or mark-up test. It is based on a common opinion that at equilibrium, marginal cost and marginal revenue must intersect (Shaffer, 2004). When the CV was applied to the Japanese banking sector, Uchida and Tsutsui (2005) illustrated this with an assumption that a bank *i* which accepts deposits, d_i from depositors and in turn invests the same in loans q_i and government bonds b_i generates a profit function at time *t* as:

$$\Pi_{it} = P_t(Q_t)q_{it} + r^b_{it}b_{it} - r^d_{it}d_{it} - C_{it}(q_{it}, d_{it}) \tag{3.10}$$

Following first order conditions (see Uchida & Tsutsui, 2005), the following expression represents the revenue of bank *i* earned through credit:

$$R_{it} = \frac{\theta_{it}}{\eta_t}R_{it} + r^d_{it}q_{it} + q_{it}\frac{\partial C_{it}}{\partial d_{it}} + q_{it}\frac{\partial C_{it}}{\partial q_{it}} \tag{3.11}$$

where $R_{it} \equiv P_t q_{it}$, θ_{it} represents the level of competition of an average banking firm, with $\theta_{it} = 0$ signifying perfect competitive outcome; when $\theta_{it} = 1$ monopoly outcome and $0 < \theta_{it} < 1$ for different levels of imperfect competition or market power. The CV approach has been quietly applied in empirical studies (Berg & Kim, 1994; Gelfand & Spiller, 1987; Gruben & McComb, 2003; Shaffer, 1989; Suominen, 1994; Uchida & Tsutsui, 2005). Two main attractions of this approach relate to its being an easily understood test-statistic and the ability to use industry aggregate data (Shaffer, 2004). However, Shaffer (2004) noted one limitation about the CV approach by indicating that the CV may provide an anti-competitive measure of firms if the unit of firms selected is not enough to cover substantial portions of the population or target market, especially cross-country samples where there is cross border competition.

3.5 Empirical Implementation of the Panzar and Rosse (1987) Model

Annual financial statements from the Bankscope database covering 365 banks in Africa were used from year 2000 to 2015 due to data availability. Following the extant literature, we specified the PR (1987) methodology which is specified as a reduced-form revenue equation below:

$$\begin{aligned}\ln(\mathrm{R_{it}}) = {} & \beta_1 \ln(\mathrm{Wf_{it}}) + \beta_2 \ln(\mathrm{Wp_{it}}) + \beta_3 \ln(\mathrm{Wfc_{it}}) + \beta_4 \ln(\mathrm{Size_{it}}) \\ & + \beta_5 \ln(\mathrm{loans/Assets_{it}}) + \beta_6 \ln(\mathrm{Equity/Assets_{it}}) \\ & + \beta_7 \ln(\mathrm{Cos}t - \mathrm{income_{it}}) + \beta_8 \ln(\mathrm{nii}) + \eta_t + \lambda_i + u_{\mathrm{it}} \qquad (3.12)\end{aligned}$$

Following Bikker et al. (2007), Eq. (3.12) is a log-linear estimation where the dependent variable, ln(R), serves as a proxy for the log of total interest revenue (proxy for output price of loans). Bikker et al. (2007) recommended that the estimated H-statistics may be unrealistic if empirical estimations scale total interest revenue which transforms the Panzar and Rosse model into a price rather than a revenue equation. The set of the independent variables used in estimations are the prices of resources (factors) banks used in their productive capacity such as costs of deposits to total deposits (Wf-input which represents deposit costs), employee expenses (Wp-wages cost) to total assets (cost of employee-which also represents labour) and other expenses on fixed assets to stock of fixed assets (Wfc-input price for equipment/fixed capital). The selection of these input variables was guided by the intermediation approach in bank productivity. We also control for a vector of bank-specific variables consistent with existing studies. This includes EQUITYTA (total equity divided by total assets)-that reflects the degree of leverage and differences in risk preference across banks. This variable is expected to be positively related to total revenue since well-capitalised banks might be involved in aggressive riskier operations and thus tend to hold more equity capital, voluntarily or involuntarily. On the other hand, Molyneux et al. (1994a, 1994b) show that the relationship between bank capitalisation and total revenue might be negative because a bank can limit the amount of its capital in order to venture into more revenue generating activities to enhance its income base.

Furthermore, we control for the degree of financial intermediation using loans ratio (loan/assets). It is expected that loans-asset ratio shall positively affect bank revenue since the higher the amount of loans given, the higher the revenue a bank generates. Total assets control for the scale effect is associated with bank size (De Bandt & Davies, 2000; Shaffer, 2002). Another bank-specific variable used is overheads divided by net income ratio (Overheads) as an efficiency measure. Higher values imply that banks are incurring more costs than revenue and are therefore becoming less efficient, and vice versa. The expected coefficient can be negatively related to bank revenue since inefficient banks can be less profitable. The last but not the least is income diversification measured as a share of non-interest income in total revenue income of banks (nii). See Table 3.1 for full descriptions of the variables used in the model.

The η_t represents time fixed effects, λ_i is individual bank fixed effects which capture comparative measures of management efficiency across banks, and u_{it} is the error term. The log-linear form of the model specified above has been identified as suitable in enhancing not only the goodness of fit of the estimation but also reducing simultaneity bias (De Bandt & Davis, 2000). The PR model estimation is based on an H-statistic computed from Eq. 3.12 as:

$$\mathrm{H} = \beta_1 + \beta_2 + \beta_3$$

Table 3.1 Description of variables

Variable	*Description*	*Measurement*	*Scale of measurement*
ROA	Return on Assets	financial & Operational	Ratio
Interest Revenue	Total Interest Revenue	Total Interest Revenue	Absolute Value
Size(Assets)	Total Assets	Total Assets	Absolute Value
Loans/Assets	Loans/assets	Loans/total assets	Ratio
Cost-income	Overheads/net profit	Overhead/net profit	Ratio
Nii	Income diversification	Non-interest income/total revenue	Ratio
W_f	Cost of Deposits	Interest Expense/Deposits	Ratio
W_p	Price of labour	Personnel Expenses/Assets	Ratio
W_{fc}	Price of physical capital	Other Operating Expenses/Fixed Assets	Ratio

Source Authors' computation from Data

A banking system is adjudged to be a monopoly or a perfectly collusive oligopoly when the estimated H-statistic is less than or equal to zero ($H \leq 0$), monopolistically competitive if it is between zero and one ($0 < H < 1$), and a perfect competition when it is one ($H = 1$). Following Bikker and Haaf (2002), we explain measures of the H-statistic as providing a persistent level of competition, with larger values indicating higher competition.

Test of Competitive Long-run Equilibrium

The PR-H-statistic model is based on the principle that the financial market is in the long-run equilibrium. To test for this, we estimate the following equation.

$$\begin{aligned}\ln(\mathrm{ROA_{it}}) = {} & \beta_1 \ln(\mathrm{W_{fit}}) + \beta_2 \ln(\mathrm{Wp_{it}}) + \beta_3 \ln(\mathrm{W_{fcit}}) + \beta_4 \ln(\mathrm{Size_{it}}) \\ & + \beta_5 \ln(\mathrm{loans/Assets_{it}}) + \beta_6 \ln(\mathrm{Equity/Assets_{it}}) \\ & + \beta_7 \ln(\mathrm{Cos}t - \mathrm{income_{it}}) + \eta_t + \lambda_i + u_{\mathrm{it}} \end{aligned} \tag{3.13}$$

We compute the dependent variable (ROA) as earnings before interest and tax divided by total assets. Again, due to the fact that return on average equity can take on negative values, we modify the dependent variable as ROA = ln (1 + ROA) such that ROA is the unadjusted return on equity. Following Claessens and Laeven (2004), we test for the equilibrium, *E,* statistic as:

$$\mathrm{E} = \beta_1 + \beta_2 + \beta_3 = 0$$

Using an F-test, if ***E*** is rejected, the market is supposed not to be in equilibrium. In the empirical estimation of the models (12 and 13), the F-test was performed to determine if the H-statistics are significantly not the same as zero and one. Notice must be given that the equilibrium does not mean that competitive conditions are fixed during the estimation window. It rather communicates a gradual process of change in the banking system. Mathematically, Shaffer (2004) simplified the implication of long-run market equilibrium: when the sum of coefficients on the input costs equals zero, it means there is no association between bank profitability and margins and prices of input in the long run, but where the sum of these relevant coefficients is negative, it implies that any attempt made by the bank to pass along its higher input costs fully to its borrowers and other asset-side customers will result in losing some patronage. On the other hand, when the sum of coefficients is greater than zero, higher input prices are associated with higher margins and profitability.

3.6 Empirical Results

Descriptive and Correlation Analysis

Tables 3.1 and 3.2 report the descriptive statistics of the variables concerned and pairwise correlation matrix analysis. Table 3.2 more specifically shows mean, standard deviation, minimum and maximum values of the variables used in this study. The key input variables used are cost of funds (Wf), personnel cost (Wp) and cost of physical capital (Wfc) with their mean values of 0.368, 0.231 and 21.6% respectively. This shows that other operating expenses on physical equipment and assets constitute large portions of banks' funding cost in Africa. Personnel cost seems to be the least among the units of bank operations and intermediation efforts. Table 3.3 shows the correlation matrix of these variables.

Table 3.3 shows that except cost of funds ratio (lnwf), personnel cost (lnwp) and other operational cost per unit of physical assets (lnwfc) correlate positively with total revenue. The loan-to-asset ratio (lnloanasset) and overheads ratio (lnoverhds) show positive association with total revenue of banks used in the sample. Generally, the correlation coefficients show no sign of multicollinearity and hence they are suitably used in the regression analysis to estimate competitive bank behaviour based on the PR model.

Market Structure (Panzar–Rosse [H-statistic])

The estimated results of bank competitive behaviour (H-statistic) in Africa are provided in Table 3.4 and the associated long-run equilibrium test in Table 3.6. The estimated H-statistic and the corresponding equilibrium test indicate that the E-statistic is not statistically and significantly different from zero, showing that the banking market in Africa is in long-run equilibrium. Also, Table 3.5 shows the H-statistic based on regional classification of the sample. Six estimators were implemented to ensure the robustness of the results arising from the H-statistic. The estimators used are Ordinary Least Square with robust standard errors, full generalised least square (FGLS), panel corrected standard error (PCSE), Prais-Winsten (PRAIS), Newey (NEWEY) and fixed effect estimators. The preferred estimator used in this discussion is the PCSE due to

Table 3.2 Descriptive statistics

Variable	*Obs*	*Mean*	*Std. Dev*	*Min*	*Max*
Total Interest revenue (TR)	4498	15,336.547	44,745.561	−8742.6	864,342
Return on Assets (ROA)	4496	0.052	1.337	−25.02	59.133
Interest Expense/Deposits (wf)	4466	0.368	6.247	0.00	183.613
Personnel Expenses/Assets (wp)	4479	0.231	3.522	−0.004	91.134
Other Operating Expenses/Fixed Assets (wfc)	4462	0.216	399.158	−0.074	12,163.317
Total Assets (Size)	4521	194,801.48	481,950.55	2.700	7,945,772
Loans/assets (loanasset)	4485	0.492	0.205	0.00	2.296
Equity/assets (equityta)	4505	0.145	0.14	−0.959	3.228
Overheads/netincome (overhds)	4424	18.832	306.671	−7308.462	7318.256
Non-interest income/total revenue (nii)	4278	3.359	48.204	−27.749	1830.101

Source Bankscope Database and authors' calculation

Table 3.3 Pairwise correlations

Variables	*(1)*	*(2)*	*(3)*	*(4)*	*(5)*	*(6)*	*(7)*	*(8)*	*(9)*	*(10)*
(1) lnTR	1.000									
(2) lnROA	0.073	1.000								
(3) lnwf	−0.072	0.179	1.000							
(4) lnwp	0.020	0.211	0.164	1.000						
(5) lnwfc	0.019	0.095	0.019	0.300	1.000					
(6) size	0.965	−0.019	−0.208	−0.075	−0.005	1.000				
(7) lnloanasset	0.117	0.048	0.243	−0.010	−0.034	0.080	1.000			
(8) lnequityta	−0.194	0.322	0.138	0.151	−0.056	−0.238	−0.051	1.000		
(9) lnoverhds	0.041	−0.679	−0.108	0.320	0.035	0.052	−0.044	−0.161	1.000	
(10) lnnii	−0.092	0.037	−0.287	0.312	0.220	0.029	−0.188	−0.011	0.151	1.00

Source Bankscope Database and authors' calculation

Table 3.4 Panzar–Rosse H-statistic using total revenue (lnTR) in Africa

	(1)	*(2)*	*(3)*	*(4)*	*(5)*	*(6)*
Ln(TR)	OLS (robust)	FGLS	PCSE	PRAIS	NEWEY	FE
Lnwf	0.1631***	0.2606***	0.2055***	0.2104***	0.1631***	0.2335***
	(0.0576)	(0.0057)	(0.0225)	(0.0073)	(0.0241)	(0.0067)
lnwp	0.3242***	0.251***	0.2695***	0.2421***	0.3242***	0.1147***
	(0.0412)	(0.0067)	(0.0176)	(0.0106)	(0.0181)	(0.0095)
lnwfc	0.0329	0.0472***	0.0467***	0.0545***	0.0329***	0.0179***
	(0.0246)	(0.0043)	(0.0092)	(0.0072)	(0.0093)	(0.0065)
Size	1.0111***	1.0091***	1.0088***	1.0032***	1.0111***	0.9791***
	(0.0099)	(0.0021)	(0.0046)	(0.0053)	(0.0036)	(0.0052)
lnloanasset	−0.0005	0.0473***	0.0393*	0.0614***	−0.0005	0.0957***
	(0.0578)	(0.0083)	(0.0203)	(0.0111)	(0.0221)	(0.0104)
lnequityta	0.0722	0.0999***	0.1067***	0.1269***	0.0722***	0.0906***
	(0.0521)	(0.0086)	(0.0203)	(0.0144)	(0.0202)	(0.0122)
lnoverhds	−0.0538*	−0.0273***	−0.0424***	−0.035***	−0.0538***	−0.0254***
	(0.0305)	(0.0028)	(0.0081)	(0.0045)	(0.013)	(0.0046)
Lnnii	−0.2561***	−0.1635***	−0.1777***	−0.1466***	−0.2561***	−0.1764***
	(0.0472)	(0.0046)	(0.0116)	(0.0051)	(0.0194)	(0.005)
_cons	−0.946***	−0.7149***	−0.8244***	−0.7786***	−0.946***	−1.0395***
	(0.233)	(0.0357)	(0.1052)	(0.0661)	(0.0939)	(0.0605)
Market Structure Wald Test						
H-Statistic	**0.5202**	**0.5588**	**0.5217**	**0.507**	**0.5202**	**0.3661**
Wald F Stat. $H_0 = 0$/Monopoly	64.42***	4277.24***	378.99***	1430.84***	394.73***	767.00***
	Reject	Reject	Reject	Reject	Reject	Reject

(continued)

Table 3.4 (continued)

	(1)	*(2)*	*(3)*	*(4)*	*(5)*	*(6)*
Wald F Stat. $H_0 = 1$/Perf. Comp	54.83***	2666.32***	318.50***	1352.89***	335.95***	2299.21***
	Reject	Reject	Reject	Reject	Reject	Reject
H_0:0 < H < 1	Accept	Accept	Accept	Accept	Accept	Accept
Observations	3690	3687	3690	3690	3690	3690
R-squared	0.9705		0.9689	0.963		0.9275
Time dummy		Yes	Yes	Yes	Yes	Yes
Breusch-Pagan/Cook-Weisberg test for heteroskedasticity				Chi2(1)	12.15	
				Prob > chi2	0.0005	
Wooldridge test for autocorrelation				F(1,344)	62.175	
				Prob > F	0.0000	

Standard errors are in parentheses ***$p < 0.01$, **$p < 0.05$, *$p < 0.1$

NB: *Source* Bankscope Database and authors' calculation. Hausman test (434.69), Prob > $chi^2 = 0.0000$

its superiority over the others. It has the ability to correct for both non-constant variance and autocorrelation, otherwise known as serial correlation in the data (see Table 3.4). Given the large number of banks with varied sizes, which is most likely to produce the above issues in the panel data, the PCSE estimator is justifiably considered as the baseline estimator. With respect to the market structure statistic (H-statistic), Table 3.4 shows that the banking market structure in Africa is characterised by monopolistic competition. This implies that banks in Africa can use their uniqueness in marketing, advertising brand image and unique service offerings to adjust their pricing higher thereby enjoying relatively higher revenue than in a perfectly competitive market.

The empirical results from Table 3.4 show that the coefficients of unit cost of funds (w1), unit cost of personnel (w2) and unit cost of physical assets (w3) are all positively significant in the estimations (FGLS, PCSE, PRAIS, NEWEY & FE). This suggests that unit cost of funds, personnel expenses and other expenses relating to fixed assets are important determinants in the out price of loans by banks in Africa. Using the PCSE, the coefficient of unit price for personnel is found to be larger than the other input costs (w1 & w3), indicating that personnel unit cost is the most critical unit factor cost in the determination of output price of loans among African banks. Thus, cost of personnel matters most for commercial banks which seek to gain competitive advantage over their rivals in the banking system. The coefficient of size of a bank (Size) is also positive and significant in all the estimations, suggesting the existence of scale economies in the out price of loans and generation of revenue. Thus, large banks in Africa can capitalise on their scale economies to generate more revenue from the production of loans and other services. Also, the coefficient of loan-to-asset ratio (lnloanasset) was positive and significant in the PCSE, FGLS, PRAIS and FE estimations. This also implies that customers who benefit from bank loans pay a substantial amount of revenue to the banks. The coefficient of the ratio of equity to asset (lnequityta) is positive and significant in the estimations except the OLS, indicating that well capitalised banks can generate more revenue by engaging in aggressive loan administration strategies even though such efforts could expose them to high risk. High levels of equity to asset ratio (lnequityta) also insure banks against high risk. Again, the coefficient of overhead ratio is negative and significant in all the estimations. This shows that overhead expenses constitute an important cost input in the determination of pricing of loans by banks. Increases in the overhead costs actually reduce bank revenue and profitability. The last but not the least is non-interest income, a proxy for income diversification. Contrary to expectation, the coefficient of income diversification is negative and significant in all the estimations. This may however imply that banks in Africa seem to have a limited scope of income diversifying businesses that would generate more non-interest revenues for them. Table 3.5 presents an H-statistic based on the regional blocks in Africa.

The results from Table 3.5 also confirm the fact that a banking system at regional level as well as non-regional level is operating under monopolistic competition. What essentially it implies is that there exists a conduct of product differentiation in the banking system while banks intensify their unique identity with product quality and advertisement. All the regional H-statistic figures are higher than what pertains in North Africa. This may suggest that the banking system in North Africa is less competitive compared to the other regional blocks (Table 3.6).

3.7 Conclusion and Implications

The banking sector remains the biggest segment of the African financial system. The conduct of banks thus has large implications for financial resources allocation to finance economic growth and alleviate poverty. This chapter has examined the degree of competitive behaviour of banks in Africa using a sample of 365 banks from forty (40) countries in Africa covering the years 2000–2015. Using the Panzar-Rosse (1987) analytical framework, the study found that the banking system in Africa is characterised by monopolistic competition. This further indicates that, though banks produce homogenous products, they have the ability to adjust their prices upward using unique strategies of image branding, unique product and service offerings and good customer relationships.

The economic implications of this nature of bank market structure stems from various arguments that have been advanced in the literature. Following the seminal work of Keeley (1990) and the 2008/2009 financial crisis, bank market structure, especially competitive conduct, has come under strong scrutiny at policy and academic discourse levels. To the opponents of the competition-fragility hypothesis, bank competitive behaviour encourages risk taking. This is partly due to the fact that competitive bank behaviour has strong implications for bank lending and consequently risk-taking tendency. In a competitive bank environment, lending rates are usually lowered due to competitive pressure in the

Table 3.5 Panzar–Rosse H-statistic: regional outlook

Ln(TR)/Region	*(1)* *North Africa*	*(2)* *East Africa*	*(3)* *Southern Africa*	*(4)* *West Africa*	*(5)* *Full Sample*
Lnwf	0.0998***	0.3931***	0.1589***	0.2855***	0.2055***
	(0.0327)	(0.0374)	(0.0223)	(0.0246)	(0.0225)
Lnwp	0.1866***	0.341***	0.2849***	0.284***	0.2695***
	(0.039)	(0.0355)	(0.0196)	(0.0292)	(0.0176)
Lnwfc	0.0894***	0.0661***	0.0074	0.0319*	0.0467***
	(0.0205)	(0.0172)	(0.0132)	(0.0184)	(0.0092)
Size	1.0076***	1.0044***	0.9912***	0.9838***	1.0088***
	(0.0121)	(0.0097)	(0.0072)	(0.0069)	(0.0046)
Lnloanasset	0.0687*	−0.3352***	0.1314***	0.0007	0.0393*
	(0.036)	(0.0649)	(0.0254)	(0.0224)	(0.0203)
Lnequityta	0.1638***	−0.0266	0.0173	0.0982***	0.1067***
	(0.0342)	(0.0374)	(0.0316)	(0.029)	(0.0203)
Lnoverhds	−0.0488***	−0.0439***	−0.0322***	−0.0221***	−0.0424***
	(0.0131)	(0.0127)	(0.0095)	(0.0075)	(0.0081)
Lnnii	−0.1867***	−0.1893***	−0.186***	−0.1161***	−0.1777***
	(0.0209)	(0.0254)	(0.0181)	(0.0127)	(0.0116)
_cons	−1.6051***	−0.356*	−0.8492***	−0.1904*	−0.8244***
	(0.1635)	(0.2137)	(0.1049)	(0.1118)	(0.1052)
Market Structure Wald Test					
H-Statistic	**0.3758**	**0.8002**	**0.4512**	**0.6014**	**0.5217**
Wald F Stat. $H_0 = 0$/Monopoly	83.90*** Reject	167.43*** Reject	277.90*** Reject	250.33*** Reject	378.99*** Reject

(continued)

Table 3.5 (continued)

Ln(TR)/Region	*(1) North Africa*	*(2) East Africa*	*(3) Southern Africa*	*(4) West Africa*	*(5) Full Sample*
Wald F Stat. $H_0 = 1$/Perf. Comp	231.36***	10.44***	411.00***	109.96***	318.50***
	Reject	Reject	Reject	Reject	Reject
H_0:0 < H < 1	Accept	Accept	Accept	Accept	Accept
Observations	906	812	1094	878	3690
R-squared	0.9448	0.9785	0.974	0.9835	0.9689
Time dummy		Yes	Yes	Yes	Yes

Standard errors are in parentheses ***$p < 0.01$, **$p < 0.05$, *$p < 0.1$
NB: *Source* Bankscope Database and authors' calculation

Table 3.6 Long run E-statistic of banking systems in Africa

Ln(ROA)	*(1)*	*(2)*	*(3)*	*(4)*	*(5)*	*(6)*
	OLS (Robust)	FGLS	PCSE	PRAIS	NEWEY	FE
Lnwf	0.0507	−0.0005	0.0422**	0.0397***	0.0507***	0.0115
	(0.0365)	(0.0074)	(0.0174)	(0.0109)	(0.017)	(0.0106)
Lnwp	0.4125***	0.46***	0.3864***	0.3812***	0.4125***	0.1695***
	(0.0834)	(0.0115)	(0.0248)	(0.0144)	(0.0301)	(0.0149)
Lnwfc	−0.0268	0.1027***	0.0756***	0.0972***	−0.0268	0.1143***
	(0.0475)	(0.0068)	(0.0142)	(0.0108)	(0.0163)	(0.0102)
Size	0.0418***	0.016***	0.0388***	0.0371***	0.0418***	−0.0292***
	(0.0122)	(0.0032)	(0.0066)	(0.0063)	(0.0047)	(0.0082)
lnloanasset	0.0268	0.0805***	0.0524***	0.0628***	0.0268	0.0858***
	(0.0406)	(0.0104)	(0.0197)	(0.0162)	(0.0179)	(0.0164)
lnequityta	0.2489***	0.1908***	0.2485***	0.2465***	0.2489***	0.299***
	(0.0578)	(0.013)	(0.0259)	(0.0209)	(0.0247)	(0.0192)
lnoverhds	−0.6934***	−0.7846***	−0.7363***	−0.7434***	−0.6934***	−0.762***
	(0.0549)	(0.0055)	(0.0133)	(0.0072)	(0.0245)	(0.0074)
Lnnii	0.0439	0.0473***	0.0415***	0.0376***	0.0439***	0.011
	(0.0293)	(0.0055)	(0.0103)	(0.008)	(0.0123)	(0.0078)
_cons	−1.2171***	−0.9166***	−1.2966***	−1.3081***	−1.2171***	−1.4274***
	(0.3559)	(0.0538)	(0.1164)	(0.0858)	(0.1149)	(0.0952)
LR E-statistic	**0.4364*** **	**0.5622*** **	**0.5042*** **	**0.5181*** **	**0.4464*** **	**0.2953*** **
LR equilibrium E = 0	Fail to reject	Fail to reject	Fail to reject	Fail to reject	Fail to reject	Fail to reject
Observations	3681	3677	3681	3681	3681	3681
R-squared	0.6945		0.8701	0.8772		0.7883
Time dummy		Yes	Yes	Yes	Yes	

Standard errors are in parentheses ***$p < 0.01$, **$p < 0.05$, *$p < 0.1$
Source Bankscope Database and authors' calculation, Hausman test (276.95), Prob > chi2 = 0.0000

market in order to attract customers. However, the proponents of concentration-stability strongly argue for sustaining a concentrated banking system due to its resilience against crisis. There has never been a consensus both in empirics and in theory on this issue. Banking sector regulators in economies continue to adopt measures that best promote financial stability and economic growth via efficient allocation of financial resources by banks. Thus, bank sector regulators in Africa should pursue sound macro-prudential policies including promoting strong bank governance policies that would ensure banking sector stability and profitability. Additionally, regulatory reforms should be geared towards the introduction of credit information sharing among participants in the banking sector in order to reduce the monopolistic power of banks, thereby enhancing competitive behaviour and efficiency of banking operations.

Appendix

Panzar–Rosse H-statistic using total revenue (LnTR) in North African Banking System

	(1) OLS(robust)	*(2) FGLS*	*(3) PCSE*	*(4) PRAIS*	*(5) NEWEY*	*(6) FE*
Lnwf	0.0357	0.1951***	0.0998***	0.117***	0.0357	0.1853***
	(0.0749)	(0.0125)	(0.0327)	(0.0152)	(0.0367)	(0.0152)
Lnwp	0.2834***	0.1162***	0.1866***	0.1182***	0.2834***	0.1062***
	(0.0504)	(0.0127)	(0.039)	(0.0239)	(0.0307)	(0.0187)
Lnwfc	0.1502***	0.0718***	0.0894***	0.0686***	0.1502***	0.0515***
	(0.0567)	(0.0094)	(0.0205)	(0.0154)	(0.025)	(0.0161)
Size	1.0158***	1.0151***	1.0076***	0.9748***	1.0158***	0.9883***
	(0.0242)	(0.0057)	(0.0121)	(0.0171)	(0.0092)	(0.0159)
Lnloanasset	0.0314	0.0822***	0.0687*	0.0974***	0.0314	0.0946***
	(0.082)	(0.0185)	(0.036)	(0.0255)	(0.0347)	(0.0241)
Lnequityta	0.1868**	0.1018***	0.1638***	0.1693***	0.1868***	0.0595**
	(0.0845)	(0.0172)	(0.0342)	(0.0292)	(0.0364)	(0.0261)
Lnoverhds	−0.0383	−0.0372***	−0.0488***	−0.0461***	−0.0383**	−0.0379***
	(0.0323)	(0.0061)	(0.0131)	(0.0111)	(0.0169)	(0.0128)
Lnnii	−0.3487***	−0.1575***	−0.1867***	−0.1426***	−0.3487***	−0.2345***
	(0.0904)	(0.0092)	(0.0209)	(0.0099)	(0.0341)	(0.0123)
_cons	−1.604***	−1.728***	−1.6051***	−1.5131***	−1.604***	−1.7074***
	(0.2937)	(0.0779)	(0.1635)	(0.1696)	(0.14)	(0.1394)
Observations	906	905	906	906	906	906
R-squared	0.9555		0.9448	0.9023		0.8702
H-Statistic	**0.4693**	**0.3831**	**0.3758**	**0.3038**	**0.4693**	**0.343**

(continued)

(continued)

	(1) OLS(robust)	(2) FGLS	(3) PCSE	(4) PRAIS	(5) NEWEY	(6) FE
Wald F Stat. H = 0/E = 0	49.22***	415.90***	83.90***	98.19***	215.05***	146.51***
Wald F Stat. H = 1/E = 1	62.98***	1078.75***	231.36***	515.57***	275.16***	537.27***

Standard errors are in parentheses
***$p < 0.01$, **$p < 0.05$, *$p < 0.1$

Long run E-statistic of banking systems in North Africa

	(1) OLS(robust)	(2) FGLS	(3) PCSE	(4) PRAIS	(5) NEWEY	(6) FE
lnwf	−0.035	0.0262*	0.0038	0.0062	−0.035	0.0265
	(0.0428)	(0.0156)	(0.0334)	(0.0198)	(0.0281)	(0.0206)
lnwp	0.3215***	0.1928***	0.2455***	0.2434***	0.3215***	0.0986***
	(0.0842)	(0.0222)	(0.0383)	(0.0259)	(0.0612)	(0.0252)
lnwfc	0.0292	0.1029***	0.1455***	0.149***	0.0292	0.1038***
	(0.0573)	(0.0157)	(0.0242)	(0.0214)	(0.0268)	(0.0218)
size	0.0565**	0.0629***	0.0375***	0.0365***	0.0565***	0.0567***
	(0.0216)	(0.0087)	(0.0141)	(0.0134)	(0.0089)	(0.0215)
lnloanasset	0.1077*	0.1108***	0.1251***	0.1254***	0.1077***	0.0548*
	(0.0635)	(0.022)	(0.0322)	(0.0317)	(0.0286)	(0.0327)
lnequityta	0.276***	0.2891***	0.2906***	0.29***	0.276***	0.3532***
	(0.0705)	(0.0283)	(0.0454)	(0.0345)	(0.0385)	(0.0354)
lnoverhds	−0.7064***	−0.7355***	−0.7421***	−0.7435***	−0.7064***	−0.8102***
	(0.0473)	(0.0114)	(0.0195)	(0.0158)	(0.0284)	(0.0174)
lnnii	0.0903**	0.0433***	0.037*	0.0339**	0.0903***	−0.0382**
	(0.0424)	(0.0116)	(0.0206)	(0.0138)	(0.025)	(0.0167)
_cons	−2.1362***	−2.5328***	−2.1814***	−2.1775***	−2.1362***	−2.8725***
	(0.3828)	(0.1262)	(0.1871)	(0.1591)	(0.2032)	(0.1887)
Observations	905	904	905	905	905	905
R-squared	0.7025	.z	0.8847	0.8861	.z	0.788
LR E-statistic	0.3157	0.3219	0.3948	0.3986	0.3157	0.2289
LR equilibrium E = 0	Fail to reject	Fail to reject	Fail to reject	Fail to reject	Fail to reject	Fail to reject

Standard errors are in parentheses
***$p < 0.01$, **$p < 0.05$, *$p < 0.1$

Panzar–Rosse H-statistic using total revenue (LnTR) in East African Banking System

	(1) OLS(robust)	(2) FGLS	(3) PCSE	(4) PRAIS	(5) NEWEY	(6) FE
lnwf	0.3931***	0.2751***	0.3931***	0.3712***	0.3931***	0.2886***
	(0.0916)	(0.0109)	(0.0374)	(0.0147)	(0.0474)	(0.013)
lnwp	0.448***	0.3014***	0.341***	0.259***	0.448***	0.0871***
	(0.0923)	(0.0159)	(0.0355)	(0.0248)	(0.0404)	(0.0176)
lnwfc	0.0597*	0.0572***	0.0661***	0.0749***	0.0597***	0.0564***
	(0.0327)	(0.009)	(0.0172)	(0.0169)	(0.0166)	(0.0121)
size	1.0093***	1.0045***	1.0044***	0.991***	1.0093***	0.9831***
	(0.0169)	(0.0044)	(0.0097)	(0.0103)	(0.0072)	(0.0082)
lnloanasset	−0.4427***	0.0129	−0.3352***	−0.172***	−0.4427***	0.1824***
	(0.1395)	(0.0233)	(0.0649)	(0.0272)	(0.0647)	(0.0253)
lnequityta	−0.1224	0.0183	−0.0266	0.0268	−0.1224***	0.0314
	(0.0921)	(0.0175)	(0.0374)	(0.0319)	(0.0403)	(0.0199)
lnoverhds	−0.0515	−0.0335***	−0.0439***	−0.0375***	−0.0515***	−0.0191***
	(0.0315)	(0.006)	(0.0127)	(0.009)	(0.0151)	(0.0072)
lnnii	−0.223***	−0.1602***	−0.1893***	−0.1496***	−0.223***	−0.1377***
	(0.037)	(0.0103)	(0.0254)	(0.0117)	(0.0478)	(0.009)
_cons	−0.3299	−0.5664***	−0.356*	−0.2969**	−0.3299	−0.8561***
	(0.4813)	(0.082)	(0.2137)	(0.1343)	(0.2321)	(0.1062)
H-Statistic	**0.9008**	**0.6337**	**0.8002**	**0.7051**	**0.9008**	**0.4321**
Wald F Stat. H = 0/E = 0	30.74***	873.73***	167.43***	433.50***	136.49***	276.13***
Wald F Stat. H = 1/E = 1	0.37	291.93***	10.44***	75.83***	1.66	476.56***
Observations	812	811	812	812	812	812
R-squared	0.9777		0.9785	0.9788		0.9704

Standard errors are in parentheses
***$p < 0.01$, **$p < 0.05$, *$p < 0.1$

Long run E-statistic of banking systems in East African Banking System

	(1) OLS(robust)	(2) FGLS	(3) PCSE	(4) PRAIS	(5) NEWEY	(6) FE
lnwf	0.0989	−0.0074	0.0527	0.0476*	0.0989*	0.0134
	(0.1012)	(0.0146)	(0.0433)	(0.0274)	(0.0516)	(0.028)
lnwp	0.456***	0.4724***	0.2874***	0.2458***	0.456***	0.1422***
	(0.1175)	(0.0256)	(0.0589)	(0.0444)	(0.0608)	(0.0381)
lnwfc	0.1255	0.0852***	0.093***	0.0927***	0.1255***	0.036
	(0.089)	(0.0122)	(0.0323)	(0.0314)	(0.0424)	(0.0263)

(continued)

(continued)

	(1) OLS(robust)	*(2) FGLS*	*(3) PCSE*	*(4) PRAIS*	*(5) NEWEY*	*(6) FE*
size	−0.0222	−0.0065	−0.0393	−0.0436***	−0.0222	−0.0498***
	(0.04)	(0.0067)	(0.0243)	(0.0163)	(0.0187)	(0.0178)
lnloanasset	0.0589	0.1109***	0.0688	0.0773	0.0589	0.0936*
	(0.1609)	(0.022)	(0.0577)	(0.0471)	(0.0745)	(0.0546)
lnequityta	−0.074	0.0784***	0.0048	0.037	−0.074	0.147***
	(0.1065)	(0.027)	(0.0633)	(0.0588)	(0.0561)	(0.0432)
lnoverhds	−0.6833***	−0.8087***	−0.7302***	−0.7362***	−0.6833***	−0.8032***
	(0.1407)	(0.0111)	(0.0375)	(0.0177)	(0.0652)	(0.0162)
lnnii	0.0391	0.0494***	0.0023	0.0004	0.0391	0.0183
	(0.0418)	(0.0137)	(0.0219)	(0.0227)	(0.0248)	(0.0194)
_cons	−0.7835	−0.7624***	−1.2097***	−1.2593***	−0.7835***	−1.3061***
	(0.6359)	(0.1251)	(0.3279)	(0.2301)	(0.2995)	(0.2304)
Observations	808	806	808	808	808	808
R-squared	0.7597		0.86	0.8653		0.7884
LR E-statistic	**0.6804**	**0.5502**	**0.4331**	**0.3861**	**0.5550**	**0.1916**
LR equilibrium E = 0	Fail to reject	Fail to reject	Fail to reject	Fail to reject	Fail to reject	Fail to reject

Standard errors are in parentheses
***$p < 0.01$, **$p < 0.05$, *$p < 0.1$

Panzar–Rosse H-statistic using total revenue (LnTR) in Southern African Banking System

Ln(TR)	*(1) OLS (Robust)*	*(2) FGLS*	*(3) PCSE*	*(4) PRAIS*	*(5) NEWEY*	*(6) FE*
lnwf	0.1545***	0.2783***	0.1589***	0.1653***	0.1545***	0.2085***
	(0.0565)	(0.0115)	(0.0223)	(0.0111)	(0.0257)	(0.0098)
lnwp	0.2868***	0.2691***	0.2849***	0.3079***	0.2868***	0.1775***
	(0.0586)	(0.0138)	(0.0196)	(0.0177)	(0.0234)	(0.0182)
lnwfc	−0.0266	0.0039	0.0074	0.0347***	−0.0266*	0.0046
	(0.0417)	(0.0081)	(0.0132)	(0.0106)	(0.0145)	(0.0095)
size	0.9883***	0.9853***	0.9912***	0.9862***	0.9883***	0.936***
	(0.0184)	(0.004)	(0.0072)	(0.0094)	(0.0065)	(0.0078)
lnloanasset	0.1345**	0.0411***	0.1314***	0.124***	0.1345***	0.1232***
	(0.0619)	(0.015)	(0.0254)	(0.0182)	(0.025)	(0.0185)
lnequityta	−0.0471	0.0721***	0.0173	0.0706***	−0.0471*	0.1058***
	(0.0574)	(0.0171)	(0.0316)	(0.0252)	(0.0244)	(0.0222)
lnoverhds	−0.034	−0.045***	−0.0322***	−0.0366***	−0.034**	−0.0325***
	(0.0231)	(0.0063)	(0.0095)	(0.0073)	(0.0147)	(0.0078)

(continued)

(continued)

Ln(TR)	*(1) OLS (Robust)*	*(2) FGLS*	*(3) PCSE*	*(4) PRAIS*	*(5) NEWEY*	*(6) FE*
lnnii	−0.1931**	−0.1715***	−0.186***	−0.1812***	−0.1931***	−0.2177***
	(0.0861)	(0.0104)	(0.0181)	(0.01)	(0.0312)	(0.0099)
_cons	−0.9566***	−0.3972***	−0.8492***	−0.5836***	−0.9566***	−0.4123***
	(0.2516)	(0.0664)	(0.1049)	(0.1108)	(0.0961)	(0.0954)
H-Statistic	**0.4147**	**0.5513**	**0.4512**	**0.5079**	**0.4147**	**0.3906**
Wald F Stat. H = 0/E = 0	22.64***	1138.66***	277.90***	578.29***	153.89***	291.18***
Wald F Stat. H = 1/E = 1	45.07***	754.54***	411.0***	542.91***	306.35***	708.71***
Observations	1094	1093	1094	1094	1094	1094
R-squared	0.9755		0.974	0.9648		0.9473

Standard errors are in parentheses
***$p < 0.01$, **$p < 0.05$, *$p < 0.1$

Long Run E-statistic of banking systems in Southern African Banking System

Ln(ROA)	*(1) OLS (Robust)*	*(2) FGLS*	*(3) PCSE*	*(4) PRAIS*	*(5) NEWEY*	*(6) FE*
lnwf	0.007	0.0095	0.0148	0.015	0.007	0.0348**
	(0.0349)	(0.0155)	(0.0255)	(0.0186)	(0.0181)	(0.0164)
lnwp	0.3646***	0.5591***	0.4343***	0.4529***	0.3646***	0.4254***
	(0.0928)	(0.0221)	(0.0391)	(0.025)	(0.0312)	(0.0305)
lnwfc	−0.1105**	0.0237*	−0.0347	−0.0033	−0.1105***	0.096***
	(0.0431)	(0.0123)	(0.0232)	(0.0168)	(0.0174)	(0.0159)
size	0.0041	−0.0184***	0.0169	0.0184	0.0041	−0.0886***
	(0.0165)	(0.0059)	(0.0109)	(0.0118)	(0.0069)	(0.0131)
lnloanasset	−0.0446	0.0221	−0.0203	−0.0029	−0.0446**	0.1363***
	(0.0345)	(0.0192)	(0.0314)	(0.0275)	(0.0222)	(0.0308)
lnequityta	0.3145***	0.2003***	0.2888***	0.2839***	0.3145***	0.2062***
	(0.0773)	(0.026)	(0.0473)	(0.0395)	(0.0392)	(0.0375)
lnoverhds	−0.5725***	−0.7474***	−0.6649***	−0.6826***	−0.5725***	−0.7066***
	(0.0557)	(0.012)	(0.0207)	(0.013)	(0.0318)	(0.0133)
lnnii	0.0187	0.0687***	0.0367**	0.0427***	0.0187	0.085***
	(0.0376)	(0.0117)	(0.0173)	(0.0165)	(0.0161)	(0.0165)
_cons	−1.1688***	−0.177*	−0.9868***	−0.9131***	−1.1688***	0.0921
	(0.3705)	(0.0924)	(0.1758)	(0.1502)	(0.1288)	(0.1599)
LR E-statistic	**0.4821*** **	**0.5923*** **	**0.4144*** **	**0.4646*** **	**0.2611*** **	**0.5562*** **

(continued)

(continued)

Ln(ROA)	*(1) OLS (Robust)*	*(2) FGLS*	*(3) PCSE*	*(4) PRAIS*	*(5) NEWEY*	*(6) FE*
LR equilibrium E = 0	Fail to reject	Fail to reject	Fail to reject	Fail to reject	Fail to reject	Fail to reject
Observations	1090	1089	1090	1090	1090	1090
R-squared	0.6374		0.8594	0.8701		0.7754

Standard errors are in parentheses
***$p < 0.01$, **$p < 0.05$, *$p < 0.1$

Panzar–Rosse H-statistic using total revenue (LnTR) in West African Banking System

Ln(TR)	*(1) OLS*	*(2) FGLS*	*(3) PCSE*	*(4) PRAIS*	*(5) NEWEY*	*(6) FE*
lnwf	0.2527***	0.297***	0.2855***	0.2884***	0.2527***	0.2559***
	(0.0174)	(0.0145)	(0.0246)	(0.019)	(0.0227)	(0.0186)
lnwp	0.3042***	0.2889***	0.284***	0.2832***	0.3042***	0.208***
	(0.0188)	(0.0182)	(0.0292)	(0.0251)	(0.0223)	(0.0319)
lnwfc	0.0064	0.0455***	0.0319*	0.0343***	0.0064	0.0194
	(0.0113)	(0.0097)	(0.0184)	(0.013)	(0.0136)	(0.0137)
size	0.9823***	0.9837***	0.9838***	0.9841***	0.9823***	0.9882***
	(0.0046)	(0.0044)	(0.0069)	(0.0068)	(0.0049)	(0.01)
lnloanasset	−0.0078	0.0518***	0.0007	0.0011	−0.0078	0.0208
	(0.0133)	(0.0154)	(0.0224)	(0.0166)	(0.0143)	(0.0175)
lnequityta	0.0681***	0.0688***	0.0982***	0.0995***	0.0681***	0.1439***
	(0.0204)	(0.0181)	(0.029)	(0.025)	(0.025)	(0.0271)
lnoverhds	−0.0556***	−0.0138***	−0.0221***	−0.0208***	−0.0556***	−0.0216***
	(0.0081)	(0.0038)	(0.0075)	(0.0071)	(0.0102)	(0.0081)
lnnii	−0.1354***	−0.1414***	−0.1161***	−0.1144***	−0.1354***	−0.1289***
	(0.0081)	(0.0077)	(0.0127)	(0.0081)	(0.017)	(0.0081)
_cons	−0.2523***	−0.1768**	−0.1904*	−0.1847*	−0.2523**	−0.5186***
	(0.0791)	(0.0735)	(0.1118)	(0.1052)	(0.1003)	(0.1567)
Observations	878	878	878	878	878	878
R-squared	0.9881		0.9835	0.9831		0.9303
H-Statistic	**0.5633**	**0.6314**	**0.6014**	**0.6059**	**0.5633**	**0.4833**
Wald F Stat. H = 0/E = 0	387.60***	709.36***	250.33***	338.06***	298.57***	159.70***
Wald F Stat. H = 1/E = 1	232.92***	241.88***	109.96***	143.12**	179.42***	182.53***

Standard errors are in parentheses
***$p < 0.01$, **$p < 0.05$, *$p < 0.1$

Long run E-statistic of banking systems in West Africa

Ln(ROA)	*(1) OLS (robust)*	*(2) FGLS*	*(3) PCSE*	*(4) PRAIS*	*(5) NEWEY*	*(6) FE*
lnwf	−0.114*	−0.030	−0.064*	−0.063**	−0.114***	−0.089***
	(0.057)	(0.019)	(0.034)	(0.028)	(0.03)	(0.024)
lnwp	0.455***	0.484***	0.433***	0.433***	0.455***	0.389***
	(0.073)	(0.022)	(0.042)	(0.034)	(0.032)	(0.041)
lnwfc	0.159***	0.204***	0.186***	0.186***	0.159***	0.222***
	(0.04)	(0.015)	(0.021)	(0.019)	(0.02)	(0.017)
size	−0.01	−0.011**	−0.006	−0.006	−0.01	−0.025*
	(0.013)	(0.005)	(0.01)	(0.009)	(0.007)	(0.013)
lnloanasset	−0.061**	0.021	0.003	0.003	−0.061*	0.08***
	(0.028)	(0.02)	(0.047)	(0.024)	(0.034)	(0.022)
lnequityta	0.225***	0.183***	0.235***	0.235***	0.225***	0.265***
	(0.07)	(0.021)	(0.038)	(0.035)	(0.031)	(0.035)
lnoverhds	−0.811***	−0.832***	−0.809***	−0.809***	−0.811***	−0.781***
	(0.034)	(0.009)	(0.021)	(0.011)	(0.027)	(0.01)
lnnii	0.032	0.014*	0.03**	0.03**	0.032**	0.009
	(0.022)	(0.009)	(0.012)	(0.012)	(0.013)	(0.01)
_cons	−0.912***	−0.498***	−0.812***	−0.811***	−0.912***	−0.767***
	(0.301)	(0.097)	(0.166)	(0.143)	(0.137)	(0.2)
Observations	878	878	878	878	878	878
R-squared	0.887		0.927	0.927		0.887
LR E-statistic	**0.50**	**0.658**	**0.555**	**0.556**	**0.50**	**0.522**
LR equilibrium E = 0	Fail to reject	Fail to reject	Fail to reject	Fail to reject	Fail to reject	Fail to reject

Standard errors are in parentheses
$^{***}p < 0.01$, $^{**}p < 0.05$, $^{*}p < 0.1$

References

Al-Hashimi, A. (2007). *Determinants of bank spreads in Sub-Saharan Africa* (IMF Draft Working Paper, 05/06).

Allen, F., Otchere, I., & Senbet, L. W. (2011). African financial systems. *A Review of Development Finance, 1*, 79–113.

Al-Muharrami, S., Matthews, K., & Yusuf, K. (2006). Market structure and competitive conditions in the Arab GCC banking system. *Journal of Banking and Finance, 30*, 3487–3501.

Bagehot, W. (1873). *Lombard street: A description of the money market*. E.P. Dutton and Company, Reprint 1920.

Barajas, A., Steiner, R., & Salazar, N. (1999). *Interest spread in banking in Colombia, 1974–96* (IMF Staff Papers, Vol.46, [2]).
Baumol, W. J., Panzar, J. C., & Willig, R. D. (1982). *Contestable markets and the theory of industry structure*. Harcourt Brace Jovanovich.
Beck, T., Maimbo S. M., Faye, I., & Triki, T. (2011). *Financing Africa through the crisis and beyond*. IMF, World Bank.
Beck, T. H. L., & Hesse, H. (2009). Why are interest spreads so high in Uganda? *Journal of Development Economics, 88*(2), 192–204.
Bencivenga, V. R., & Smith, B. D. (1991). Financial intermediation and endogenous growth. *Review of Economics Studies, 58*, 195–209.
Berg, S. A., & Kim, M. (1994). Oligopolistic interdependence and the structure of production in banking: An empirical evaluation. *Journal of Money, Credit and Banking, 26*(2), 309–322.
Berger, A. (1995). The profit–structure relationship in banking: Tests of market-power and efficient-structure hypotheses. *Journal of Money, Credit and Banking, 27*(2), 404–431.
Biekpe, N. (2011). The competitiveness of commercial banks in Ghana. *African Development Review, 23*(1), 75–87.
Bikker, J. A., & Haaf, K. (2002). Competition, concentration and their relationship: An empirical analysis of the banking industry. *Journal of Banking and Finance, 26*, 2191–2214.
Bikker, J. A., Spierdijk, L., & Finnie, P. (2007). *The impact of market structure, contestability and institutional environment on banking competition* (DNB Working Paper 156). De Nederlandsche Bank.
Bresnahan, T. F. (1982). The oligopoly solution concept is identified. *Economic Letters, 10*, 87–92.
Buchs, T., & Mathiesen, J. (2005). *Competition and efficiency in banking: Behavioural evidence from Ghana* (IMFWorking Paper No. 05/17). International Monetary Fund.
Casu, B., & Girardone, C. (2006). Bank competition and efficiency in the single European market. *The Manchester School, 74*(4), 441–468.
Claessens, S., & Laeven, L. (2004). What drives bank competition? Some international evidence. *Journal of Money, Credit, and Banking, 36*(2), 563–583.
De Bandt, O., & Davis, P. E. (2000). Competition, contestability and market structure in European banking sectors on the eve of EMU. *Journal of Banking and Finance, 24*, 1045–1066.
Demsetz, H. (1973). Industry structure, market rivalry, and public policy. *Journal of Law and Economics, 16*, 1–9.
Doku, J. N., Adjasi, C. K. D., Abor, J., & Andoh, C. (2012). Assessing competitive behaviour in emerging banking market: African evidence. *Research in Accounting in Emerging Economies, 12B*, 25–51.

Flamini V., McDonald, C., & Schumacher, L. (2009). *The determinants of commercial bank profitability in Sub-Saharan Africa* (IMF WP/09/15).
Gelfand, M., & Spiller, P. (1987). Entry barriers and multiproduct Oligopolies. *International Journal of Industrial Organization, 5*, 101–113.
Gelos R. G., & Roldós J. (2002). *Consolidation and market structure in emerging market banking systems* (IMF Working Paper WP/02/186).
Gelos, G., & Roldós, J. (2004). Consolidation and market structure in emerging market systems. *Emerging Markets Review, 5*, 39–59.
Gilbert, R. A. (1984). Bank market structure and competition: A survey. *Journal of Money, Credit and Banking, 16*(4), 617–645.
Girardone, C., Molyneux, P., & Gardener, E. (2004). Analysing the determinants of bank efficiency: The case of Italian banks. *Applied Economics, 36*(3), 215–227.
Global Financial Development Database (GFDD), 2019.
Goddard, J., & Wilson, J. O. S. (2009). Competition in banking: A disequilibrium approach. *Journal of Banking and Finance, 33*(12), 2282–2292.
Goldsmith, R. W. (1969). *Financial structure and development*. Yale University Press.
Gruben, W. C., & McComb, R. P. (2003). Privatization, competition, and supercompetition in the Mexican commercial banking system. *Journal of Banking and Finance, 27*(2), 229–249.
Greenwood, J., & Jovanovic, B. (1990). Financial development, growth, and the distribution of income. *Journal of Political Economy, 98*, 1076–1107.
Guru, B. K., Staunton, J., & Balashanmugam, B. (1999, December 16–17). *Determinants of commercial bank profitability in Malaysia*. Paper presented at the 12th Annual Australian Finance and Banking Conference.
Iwata, G. (1974). Measurement of conjuctural variations in Oligopoly. *Econometrica, 42*, 947–966.
Keeley, M. (1990). Deposit insurance, risk and market power in banking. *American Economic Review, 80*(5), 1183–1200.
King, R. G., & Levine, R. (1993). Finance and growth: Schumpeter might be right. *Quarterly Journal of Economics, 108*, 717–738.
Kosmidou, K., & Pasiouras, F. (2005). *The determinants of profits and margins in the Greek commercial banking industry: Evidence from the period 1990–2002* (Working Paper [Financial Engineering Laboratory, Department of Production Engineering and Management, Technical University of Crete]).
Kosmidou, K., Pasiouras, F., Doumpos, M., & Zopounidis, C. (2006). A multivariate analysis of the financial characteristics of foreign and domestic banks in the UK. *Omega, International Journal of Management Science, 34*(2), 189–195.
Lau, L. J. (1982). On identifying the degree of competitiveness from industry price and output data. *Economics Letters, 10*, 93–99.

Maudos, J. (1998). Market structure and performance in Spanish banking using a direct measure of efficiency. *Applied Financial Economics, 8*, 191–200.

Mlambo, K., & Ncube, M. (2011). Competition and efficiency in the banking sector in South Africa. *African Development Review, 23*(1), 4–15.

Molyneux, P., & Thorton, J. (1992). The determinants of European bank profitability. *Journal of Banking and Finance, 16*(6), 1173–1178.

Molyneux, P., Lloyd-Williams, D. M., & Thornton, J. (1994a). Competitive condition in European banking. *Journal of Banking and Finance, 18*, 445–459.

Molyneux, P., Lloyd-Williams, D. M., & Thornton, J. (1994b). Competitive conditions in European banking. *Journal of Banking and Finance, 18*, 445–459.

Mwega, F. (2011). The competitiveness and efficiency of the financial services sector in Africa: A case study of Kenya. *African Development Review, 23*(1), 44–59.

Nannyonjo, J. (2002). *Financial sector reforms in Uganda (1990–2000): Interest rate spreads, market structure, bank performance and monetary policy* (Unpublished thesis). Kompendiet-Goteborg.

Nathan, A., & Neave, E. H. (1989). Competition and contestability in Canada's financial system: Empirical results. *The Canadian Journal of Economics, 22*(3), 576–594.

Neumark, D., & Sharpe, S. A. (1992). Market structure and the nature of price rigidity: Evidence from the market for consumer deposits. *Quarterly Journal of Economics, 107*, 657–680.

Okeahalam, C. C. (1998). An analysis of the price-concentration relationship in the Botswana commercial banking industry. *Journal of African Finance and Economic Development, 3*, 65–84.

Panzar, J., & Rosse, J. (1987). Testing for 'monopoly' equilibrium. *The Journal of Industrial Economics, 35*(4), 443–456.

Peltzman, S. (1977). The gains and losses from industrial concentration. *Journal of Law and Economics, 20*(3), 229–263.

Rhoades, S. A. (1982). *Structure-performance studies in banking: An updated summary and evaluation* (Staff Study No. 119). Federal Reserve Board.

Schmalensee, R. (1989). Inter-industry studies of structure and performance. *Handbook of Industrial Organization, 2*(1989), 951–1009.

Shaffer, S. (1982). A non-structural test for competition in financial markets. In *Bank structure and competition. Conference proceedings* (pp. 225–243). Federal Reserve Bank of Chicago.

Shaffer, S. (1989). Competition in the US banking industry. *Economics Letters, 29*(321), 323.

Shaffer, S. (2004). Patterns of competition in banking. *Journal of Economics and Business, 56*, 287–313.

Shaffer, S. (2002). Competitive bank pricing and adverse selection, with implications for testing the SCP hypothesis. *Quarterly Review of Economics & Finance, 42*(3), 633–647.
Shephard, W. G. (1986). Tobin's q and the structure-performance relationship: Comment. *The American Economic Review, 76*(5), 1205–1210.
Simpasa, A. M. (2011). Competitive conditions in the Tanzanian commercial banking industry. *African Development Review, 23*(1), 88–98.
Suominen, M. (1994). Measuring competition in banking: A two product model. *Scandinavian Journal of Economics, 96*, 95–110.
Turk-Ariss, R. (2009). Competitive behavior in Middle East and North Africa banking systems. *The Quarterly Review of Economics and Finance, 49*, 693–710.
Uchida, H., & Tsutsui, Y. (2005). Has competition in the Japanese banking sector improved?. *Journal of Banking & Finance, 29*(2), 419–439.
Vives, X. (2001). Competition in the changing world of banking. *Oxford Review of Economic Policy, 17*(5), 535–545.
Williams, B. (2003). Domestic and international determinants of bank profits: Foreign banks in Australia. *Journal of Banking and Finance, 27*(6), 1185–1210.

CHAPTER 4

Financial Inclusion, Banking Sector Development, and Financial Stability in Africa

Ebenezer Bugri Anarfo, Miracle Ntuli, Sarah Serwah Boateng, and Joshua Yindenaba Abor

4.1 Introduction

In most African economies, inadequate supply of financial services has become a usual occurrence in their economic environment. Over the last decade, the extent to which financial institutions are able to serve low-income earners and rural dwellers has become a main problem that has attracted researchers' attention globally. The phrase "financial inclusion"

E. B. Anarfo (✉)
Department of Accounting and Finance, GIMPA Business School, Ghana Institute of Management and Public Administration, Accra, Ghana
e-mail: eanarfo@gimpa.edu.gh

M. Ntuli
School of Economic and Business Sciences, University of the Witwatersrand, Johannesburg, South Africa
e-mail: Miracle.Benhura@wits.ac.za

J. Y. Abor and C. K. D. Adjasi (eds.), *The Economics of Banking and Finance in Africa*, Palgrave Macmillan Studies in Banking and Financial Institutions, https://doi.org/10.1007/978-3-031-04162-4_4

has been used by researchers to describe this phenomenon (Bhanot et al., 2012). Financial inclusion deals with how the financial institutions of an economy integrate low-income earners and the vulnerable in such a manner that they are not denied access to finance. These services include access to banking services, credit, consulting and insurance services, according to Sinclair (2013).

African economies have over the years made significant improvements toward promoting access to finance. The implementation of some financial technologies, such as the innovation of mobile money in almost all African countries, has offered, especially for young people, the elderly, rural people, and medium-sized enterprises, more opportunities to gain access to finance (Abor et al., 2018). In spite of the impressive and aggressive efforts to introduce these innovative financial tools, the open question of the impact of financial inclusion on African economies remains to be addressed empirically. Policymakers have realized that if vulnerable and poor people are financially included, it will promote social cohesion and alleviate poverty. Yet, in most African economies, the vulnerable, in particular, do not have access to finance (Amidu et al., 2019). Examining the global findex database, Demirguc-Kunt et al. (2015) found that 54.1% of grown ups in middle- and low-income economies had an account at formal financial institutions compared to 90.6% of adults in high-income economies. Ideally, if the vulnerable and poor are financially included, taking themselves out of poverty is made much easier (Amidu et al., 2019). Insufficient access to financial services by the marginalized in society makes them susceptible to external, macro, and microeconomic shocks (Amidu et al., 2019). Hence, financial inclusion can lessen the effect of these shocks on their livelihood and consequently enhance their living standard (Giuliano & Ruiz-Arranz, 2009; Manuamorn, 2007).

According to Sinclair and Bramley (2011), an all-inclusive financial system improves well-being and efficiency, resulting in safe savings, safe

---

S. S. Boateng
Department of Accounting and Finance, GIMPA Business School, Ghana Institute of Management and Public Administration, Accra, Ghana

J. Y. Abor
Department of Finance, University of Ghana Business School, Accra, Ghana
e-mail: joshabor@ug.edu.gh

money transfers, and well-advised financial and investment management practices. As a result, it is no surprise that politicians, scholars, and other development organizations, such as the International Monetary Fund and the World Bank, are paying close attention to financial inclusion around the world. While African development finance institutions and policymakers seek for advice from scholars on how to effectively implement financial inclusion policies, empirical research in the field is still lacking (Anarfo et al., 2019).

The importance of inclusive finance for economic development calls for policymakers and governments in Africa and other developing regions to understand its determinants, among which are banking sector development and financial stability. The extant literature shows that these enhance access to finance by the poor and subsequently promote social and financial inclusion (see Ahamed & Mallick, 2019; Gimet & Lagoarde-Segot, 2012; Machdar, 2020; Vo et al., 2021). However, the existing studies lack simultaneous analysis of the link between financial inclusion, financial stability, and banking sector development. Two strands of literature on this relationship emerge. The first investigates the connection between banking sector development and inclusive finance (see Anarfo et al., 2019; Anarfo, Amewu, et al., 2020; Gimet & Lagoarde-Segot, 2012). The second explores the relation between financial stability and financial inclusion (see Ahamed & Mallick, 2019; Anarfo, Abor, et al., 2020; Danışman & Tarazi, 2020; Frączek, 2019; Machdar, 2020; Neaime & Gaysset, 2018; Siddik et al., 2018; Vo et al., 2021). Although both strands of literature are informative, they ignore the intricate relationship among banking sector development, financial stability, and financial inclusion (see Brouwer et al., 2002).

The empirical literature reveals an affirmative relationship between banking sector development and financial stability (Brouwer et al., 2002). When banking sector development (financial stability) is taken into account, it is uncertain whether the expected association between banking sector development (financial stability) and financial inclusion still holds. The omission of financial stability or banking sector development in financial inclusion studies leads to an omission variable bias and simultaneity problems which result in endogeneity problems, which undermines the results.

This research is different from past research in that it considers the tripartite interconnectedness of financial inclusion, banking sector development, and financial stability. It uses a panel vector autoregressive

(PVAR) approach to simulate the relationships using simultaneous equations. The main goal of this chapter is to explore the possibility of a causal and dynamic link among financial inclusion, financial stability, and banking sector development in African economies. The chapter sought to answer the question, is there a reverse causation among financial inclusion, financial stability, and banking sector development in Africa? The study also looks at whether these variables have complimentary, substitutive, or independent effects on one another. This is critical for policy direction on financial inclusion, whether it should focus on financial stability or banking sector development or both.

The rest of this chapter is outlined as follows: Sect. 4.2 discusses stylized facts about financial inclusion, banking sector development, and financial stability in Africa. A review of empirical literature is presented in Sect. 4.3. The methodology and data sources are reported in Sect. 4.4 and the results and findings are in Sect. 4.5. The study's conclusions and implications for policy are presented in Sect. 4.6.

4.2 Financial Inclusion, Banking Sector Development, and Financial Stability in Africa: Stylized Facts

Stylized Facts on Financial Inclusion in Africa

In an analysis of trends in inclusive finance, Demirguc-Kunt and Klapper (2012) concluded that despite a tremendous achievement over the past few decades, Africa's financial systems are underdeveloped. Domestic credit provided by financial institutions to the private sector as a proportion of GDP, which is an indicator of financial sector development, was 24% in Africa in 2012, compared to 77% in other developing nations and 172% in developed countries, according to a World Bank report. Account penetration, defined as the percentage of account holders aged 15 and upwards, was found to be 39% in Latin America, 24% in Sub-Saharan Africa, 55% in East Asia and Pacific, 33% in South Asia and 45% in Europe and Central Asia, according to Demirguc-Kunt and Klapper (2012).

Deaton (2008) discovered that individuals whose daily living expense is not up to $2 in Sub-Saharan Africa had the highest rate of adults without a bank account, with nearly 60% lacking access to finance. Table 4.1 shows financial inclusion stylized facts in Africa. This shows six key measures

Table 4.1 Financial inclusion stylized facts as at 2017

Country	*ATMs per 100,000 adults*	*Bank branches per 100,000 adults*	*Commercial bank branches per 100,000 adults*	*Bank accounts per 1,000 adults*	*Borrowers from commercial banks per 1,000 adults*	*Depositors with commercial banks per 1,000 adults*
African Sample						
Cote d'Ivoire	7.14	5.25	5.22	234.33		232.96
Egypt	17.63	4.85	4.85	460.08	103.06	460.08
Ghana	11.42	8.60	8.51	627.31	48.93	621.11
Mauritius	43.50	18.60	18.60	2020.00	279.14	1892.11
Nigeria	16.32	4.44	4.44	922.87	21.78	922.87
Rwanda	5.66	6.06	6.18	202.73	19.92	206.57
Seychelles	79.16	52.33	52.33	1795.07	252.61	1795.07
Tunisia	29.95	21.49	21.67	1022.52		1031.34
Zambia	11.45	4.51	4.58	323.53	24.20	328.15
Zimbabwe	6.73	4.74	5.51	392.41	39.99	455.62
Average	22.90	13.09	13.19	800.08	98.70	794.59
European, Asian and Middle-East countries Sample						
China	84.16	8.78	8.78	25.47	426.61	25.47
Italy	92.42	44.63	44.63	667.93	538.36	667.93
Pakistan	9.89	10.07	10.07	350.41	25.02	350.41
Peru	109.02	7.72	7.72	879.00	150.52	879.00
Philippines	28.24	9.05	9.03	510.11		508.87
Poland	71.81	29.29	29.29	1073.07	457.01	1073.07
Singapore	65.16	8.49	8.49	2299.41	1189.52	2299.41
Turkey	77.78	17.39	17.31	1351.02	799.30	1345.07
United Arab Emirates	64.90	11.29	11.19	1065.35	537.76	1055.58
Uruguay	85.22	10.96	11.02	956.13	546.37	961.73
Average	68.86	15.77	15.75	917.79	518.94	916.65

Source Global Financial Development & World Development Indicators Databases and Authors' Compilation

of financial inclusion in selected African countries and a few European, Asian, and Middle-East countries for comparison. The variables include bank branches, ATMs, commercial bank branches, commercial bank borrowers, bank accounts, and commercial bank depositors. The averages of these financial inclusion measures are compared across the countries, over time, to show Africa's relative level of development in these indicators. Table 4.1 indicates that the mean figures of the financial inclusion measures in African countries are far below their European, Asian, and Middle-East counterparts. This implies that financial inclusion is more of an African problem relative to European, Asian, and Middle-East economies.

Stylized Facts on Banking Sector Development and Financial Stability in Africa

Many African economies have made progress significantly in terms of their reforms in the banking sector in order to curtail financial risks and develop the banking industry (Flamini et al., 2009). According to Flamini et al. (2009), Banks in Africa continue to confront uncertainties and risk as they conduct business in the financial markets of the continent which are described largely as having ineffective legal institutions and capricious law enforcement of creditors' rights. Banks play a pivotal function in economic growth and development agendas of many countries in Africa, especially Nigeria and Ghana. These countries increased their banks' capital adequacy requirements to US$486,027 and US$70,796,460, respectively.

Because banks make credit available to real areas of the economy, the banking sector development is critical to the growth of any country's economy. Credit given by banks as a proportion of GDP, M2 to GDP ratio, domestic credit provided by the financial sector as a proportion of GDP, and credit provided to the private sector as a percentage of GDP are only a few examples of banking sector development indicators. In several Sub-Saharan African countries, lending given by the banking sector improved dramatically during the 1990s.

Private sector domestic credit as a percentage of GDP and bank assets ratio scaled by GDP in African economies are currently significantly better than they were ten years ago (Andrianaivo & Yartey, 2010). These increases in credit inflows could be attributed to structural adjustment programs implemented by African economies in the early 1980s and the 1990s. Despite the rapid development of Africa's banking systems, African countries have the lowest metrics of financial growth and depth when compared to other countries across the globe (Andrianaivo & Yartey, 2010).

In African countries, the main supplier of domestic credit is the banking sector. In 2017, Mauritius' banks supplied over 100% credit to the private sector (see Table 4.2). Mauritius' banking system is far more developed, and it offers the most domestic credit scaled by GDP (see Table 4.2). Table 4.2 compares the development of African economies' banking sectors to those of other economies. Because countries differ in terms of financial products access and banking sector growth, it is impossible to make broad statements regarding the advancement of the banking system in Africa. In the previous decade, however, African economies saw

Table 4.2 Banking sector development and financial stability stylized facts as at 2017

Country	*M2 (% of GDP)*	*Domestic credit to private sector by banks (% of GDP)*	*Bank net interest margin (%)*	*Financial stability (Bank Z-score)*
African Sample				
Cote d'Ivoire	28.63	19.56	3.60	15.12
Egypt, Arab Rep	92.30	28.52	3.71	20.84
Ghana	26.10	12.87	11.18	8.98
Mauritius	114.19	102.34	2.63	15.92
Nigeria	24.78	12.78	7.93	16.24
Rwanda	19.71	20.42	9.33	8.17
Seychelles	76.36	28.99	3.72	8.46
Tunisia	73.80	68.56	2.42	38.47
Zambia	21.96	11.14	10.14	9.74
Zimbabwe	35.47	16.76	6.48	3.31
Average	51.33	32.19	6.11	14.53
European, Asian and Middle-East countries Sample				
China	201.41	154.88	2.30	22.93
Italy		79.92	1.77	12.06
Pakistan	57.25	17.00	3.28	9.24
Peru	47.58	42.41	7.29	17.54
Philippines	75.42	45.61	4.06	17.74
Poland	66.57	52.47	3.20	8.98
Singapore	122.87	121.48	1.88	22.21
Turkey	54.25	66.43	4.46	8.15
United Arab Emirates	90.11	78.22	2.51	26.56
Uruguay	48.35	26.09	7.78	6.77
Average	84.87	68.45	3.85	15.22

Source Global Financial Development Database and Authors' Compilation. All Banking Sector Development indicators are expressed as a percentage of GDP an increase in loans to the private sector as a percentage of GDP and bank assets as a percentage of GDP. Table 4.2 also reveals that private sector credit provided by banks accounts for 32.19% of GDP in Africa, whereas it accounts for 68.45% in advanced nations. Despite this difference, African banking systems are relatively stable (Gulde et al., 2006). Table 4.2 shows that financial stability in Africa is 14.53%, compared to 15.22% in other nations, as indicated by the bank Z-score. This conclusion implies that African banks have a somewhat higher risk of default or bank failure than their counterparts in Europe, Asia, and the Middle East. In addition, despite the macroeconomic stability improvement, shared decrease in government intervention and decrease in the non-performing loans ratios, there is variation in the degree of banking development across African economies. This is true because each country has its own unique features.

Financial depth, measured by M2 as a percentage of GDP, is lowest in Africa relative to the rest of the world. Table 4.2 shows that this was averaged 51.33% compared to 84.87% for European, Asian, and Middle-East countries. Only Mauritius (114.19%) and Egypt (92.30%) have M2 to GDP ratios comparable to those of European, Asian, and Middle-East countries. Seychelles and Tunisia also have M2 to GDP ratios above the average for African countries. Rwanda, Zambia, Ghana, and Cote d'Ivoire have the least M2 to GDP ratio (see Table 4.2). In 2003, the M2 to GDP ratios in the majority of Sub-Saharan African countries were from 15 to 30% (Sacerdoti, 2005). Table 4.2 shows that the M2 to GDP ratios of African countries have improved significantly over time.

The average capital adequacy ratio for African banks is 16% of risk-weighted assets. Despite the fact that banks in Africa are not as efficient as those in other economies, they still make a lot of profit. The net interest margins and the costs of overhead are substantially better in Africa than in other low-income nations, according to Honohan and Beck (2007). The financial system in Africa is often concentrated. From Table 4.2, African banks' net interest margin, which measures bank efficiency, averages 6.11% relative to 3.85% for their European, Asian, and Middle-East counterparts. Again, this suggests that African banks are less efficient compared to European, Asian, and Middle-East banks. This is most likely related to the market size being small, as economies of scale result in a greater number of banks in a larger country.

Banking services are normally more readily available in cities, whereas they are scarce or do not exist in rural communities, with banking penetration being just about 5%. As a result, Africa's legal frameworks are ineffective in supporting the banking sector's development and expansion. The enforcement of property rights is an issue because they are not well-defined. Contract enforcement is also a challenge because the legal systems are exceedingly convoluted, making it difficult for the informal sector to be attracted. As a result, Gulde et al. (2006) suggested that even when regulatory standards are met, authorities often lack the power or resources to take corrective action.

4.3 Literature Review

Inclusive finance has become a priority in the policy cycles globally in recent years, as the relevance of having an inclusive financial system has gained international attention. For a country's poverty reduction and long-term economic development, poor and vulnerable people need access to financing. Financial inclusion serves as a tool for providing timely and sufficient credit and other financial services at a reasonable cost to vulnerable people, low-income earners, and the poor. The banking sector is key to spurring on this process. The availability of banking facilities and a strong network of bank branches is essential for growth and expansion of activities. In the last decade, the banking industry has experienced an astronomical volume and complexity of development. Notwithstanding the significant developments in all dimensions of financial stability, sustainability, and competitiveness, there are many concerns from the majority of the population, particularly from deprived communities requesting the much-needed financial and banking services (Chithra, & Selvam, 2013).

Promoting an inclusive access to financial products at a cheaper cost within the context of a thriving consumer protection system is a vital instrument in achieving broad policy goals such as economic and financial empowerment, financial health, financial stability, and long-term growth. This will ensure that individuals can recognize and use the financial tools that are readily available to them to help them accumulate savings, protect themselves from macroeconomic shocks, and fund their enterprises and commercial activities. It should be an important concern for both private and public bodies to ensure that financial tools are made available for individuals so that their present and future welfare can be safeguarded.

Around 350 million persons in Africa lacked access to formal financial services as of 2014. The African continent offers a variety of opportunities to increase access to and use of financial products. The majority of African countries have poor banking infrastructure, financial marginalization, and high poverty rates. Africa, on the other hand, is well-positioned to benefit from digital financial services, thanks to its fast expanding mobile money infrastructure.

The banking sector is a sub-component of the financial sector, and one cannot overemphasize its functions and role in an economy's development agenda. It plays an eminent role in most developed and developing economies' financial intermediation process, suggesting that most economies have a bank-based financial system. Banking is a key sector in most economies, hence there is the need for continuous enactment of appropriate policy initiatives and reforms which ensures that the banking sector performs its role effectively, in which regard financial inclusion is not an exception (Aluko & Ajayi, 2018). Several authors provide empirical support for banking sector development as a determinant of financial inclusion (see Anarfo et al., 2019; Gimet & Lagoarde-Segot, 2012). Anarfo et al. (2019) explored the dynamic and causal relations between financial sector development and inclusive finance in Sub-Saharan Africa using a panel Vector Autoregressive approach. The study discovered a bi-causal association between the development of the financial sector and financial inclusion. According to Guiso et al. (2009), the rise of the banking sector encourages entrepreneurial activities and raises company competitiveness. This implies that the banking sector's expansion will enhance economic efficiency and increase corporate productivity.

Consequently, the aim of the banking sector development policy in emerging and frontier economies is to reduce credit costs to successful businesses, stabilize credit flows, and expand financial services to households (Honohan, 2008). Indeed, banks have a role in identifying and financing successful ventures, keeping an eye on the external and internal interest rate risk, and facilitating transactions. Accordingly, an effective banking sector policy would strive to promote net credit while decreasing interest rate spreads, interest rate risk premiums, and non-performing loans. Therefore, extending financial services access to the majority of the populace is a prerequisite for social and economic growth (see Beck et al., 2007; Klapper et al., 2006). Ultimately, an impressive development framework for the banking sector would strive to expand opportunities for investment for companies and individuals alike (Beck et al., 2008).

The empirical papers discussed above point to the fact that there is a connection between banking sector development and inclusive finance.

The literature on financial stability and inclusion is quite limited, yielding inconsistent and ambiguous results. Financial inclusion has been shown to have both an affirmative and an adverse impact on financial stability in previous studies. Some studies have shown a relation between financial stability and inclusive finance (see Morgan & Pontines, 2018), while others have established a link between financial inclusion and financial instability (see Morgan & Pontines, 2018; Sahay et al., 2015). Scholars and researchers will be able to analyze and evaluate the nature of the link between inclusive finance and financial stability as a result of these mixed findings. Financial stability, on the other hand, may encourage financial inclusiveness. For researchers, this causality from financial stability to financial inclusion seems more significant, as financial stability is not likely to deteriorate financial inclusion.

Morgan and Pontines (2018) conducted an empirical study of the relations between financial stability and financial inclusion. The findings reveal that financial stability is promoted by lending more to small and medium scale businesses which in turn reduces the default probability of financial institutions and their non-performing loans. When medium-sized enterprises have access to credit, the study demonstrates that there is an affirmative association between financial stability and financial inclusion. Adasme et al. (2006) also studied banks in Chile and found that the amount of systematic risk present in small firms is far less than that of larger firms. This suggests that lending to small and medium-sized businesses will decrease banks' overall risk, thereby improving financial stability. Han and Melecky (2013) posit that a 10% rise in the proportion of people who are financially included (bank deposits) reduces withdrawal rate by 3–8%. This further suggests an affirmative connection between financial stability and inclusive finance. Low-income earners are considered largely resilient to macroeconomic shocks. Having them included in the financial sector has the potential to improve financial stability (Hannig & Jansen, 2010). However, financial inclusion can promote financial stability through facilitating the intermediation process of savings-investment. Broadening the client base of banks provides them new market opportunities, which promotes diversification and flexibility to absorb unforeseen losses (Neaime & Gaysset, 2018). Financial stability appears to have a positive unidirectional association with financial inclusion, according to some studies (Cull et al., 2012; Okpara, 2011; Prasad,

2010). Okpara (2011) discovered a strong one-way impact of financial inclusion on financial stability, implying that the two have a long-term relationship. The authors stated that providing banking services to a broader segment of society, particularly the poor, encourages resource mobilization, efficiency, and financial intermediation, all of which increase financial stability.

The debate over whether financial inclusion assists in maintaining financial stability, on the other hand, is still going on. Other empirical works on financial stability and financial inclusion imply that the latter would improve to the former, contrary to the popular belief that it improves financial stability. In the case of reckless rapid credit expansion, Mehrotra and Yetman (2015) argue that more financial inclusion will cause financial instability (sub-prime lending). This rapid unfettered growth could also destabilize the financial system of a country, leading to financial instability (De la Torre et al., 2013). Sahay et al. (2015) found that financial inclusion harms financial stability. The authors argued that when credit facilities are expanded to all segments of the population, this can cause financial instability when there is no proper supervision. Financial stability tends to decrease with credit expansion to vulnerable people, especially in countries where banking supervision is poor. By contrast, strongly supervised countries could see financial stability benefit from increased access to credits.

According to Khan (2011), there are three key ways that boosting financial inclusion can improve financial stability: (i) the inclusion of low-income earners which tends to increase the deposit base of banks. This would minimize the bank's reliance on non-core sources of funds, whose volatility tends to increase during a crisis; (ii) bank asset diversification resulting from loans to small businesses tends to reduce the overall risk of loan portfolios of financial institutions. As the comparative size of a borrower in the overall portfolio decreases, the portfolio's risk decreases as well; (iii) financial inclusion strengthens the effectiveness of monetary policy transmission and this could lead to financial stability. Khan (2011) also examined ways in which promoting financial inclusion could have negative repercussions on financial stability. For example, (i) banks' reputational risk could lead to their financial instability by expanding credit to small borrowers; (ii) loan requirements could be reduced and banks could lend to many borrowers; and (iii) in cases where financial institutions are not regulated properly, increased group lending may dilute the overall efficiency of economic regulation and this will bring about financial instability. This shows that enhancing financial inclusion could lower asset quality which results in sub-prime lending and hence financial instability.

The literature has generally considered financial stability and financial inclusion separately, and the bi-causal relationship between these variables is largely disregarded. Nonetheless, it is necessary to take into consideration whether greater financial inclusion facilitates or hampers financial system stability and vice versa. Any policy recommendation needs to consider their interdependence and potential trade-offs (Čihák et al., 2016). For example, financial expansion by expanding bank loans to more businesses and individuals may, on the one hand, worsen loan portfolio quality, and this can undermine the banking system stability in cases where there is poor banking supervision (Khan, 2011; Sahay et al., 2015). On the other hand, lending more to individuals and companies will encourage stability in the banking system as risk will be diversified (Khan, 2011; Morgan & Pontines, 2018). When the relationship between financial stability and inclusion is overlooked, systemic crises and financial exclusion can occur (Čihák et al., 2016). Morgan and Pontines (2018) highlight the link between financial stability and financial inclusion using empirical evidence. Demirguc-Kunt et al. (2017) stressed how important it is to improve our comprehension of the relevance of inclusive finance, as well as the importance of tailoring financial services. New empirical data is needed on how greater inclusive finance contributes to financial system stability as well as the benefits it offers to society as a whole.

Ahamed and Mallick (2019) examined the effect of financial inclusion on the stability of banks. They posit that due to information asymmetry about risky lenders, the establishment of an all-inclusive financial system may be related to non-performing loans (NPLs). The paper used data from 2004 through 2012 on 2635 banks in 86 countries. The bank z-score was used in their study to proxy financial stability and the demographic and regional indices used as indicators for financial inclusion. Their paper's findings show that financial stability and financial inclusion have an affirmative relationship. They posit that the adoption of an inclusive financial system by banks will lower interest on deposits. As a result of financial inclusion, they have lower marginal borrowing costs and more pricing power on the money market. Financial inclusion is a crucial tool for banks to help stabilize their funding sources, according to Ahamed and Mallick (2019). Financial stability and financial access are linked conditionally, according to Mendoza et al. (2009). According to their findings, financial inclusion and financial stability have a substantial and negative link. Other empirical studies on financial inclusion and stability imply that affirmatively and significantly enhancing financial inclusion by providing banking services increases banking sector stability (Vo et al., 2021).

Danışman and Tarazi (2020) explored how financial inclusion is impacting European banking system stability. They found that promoting financial inclusion stabilizes the banking sector through an increase in digital payments and account ownership. A more in-depth analysis reveals that such financial stability is a result of targeting vulnerable people who are not educated, are unemployed, young, and live in rural communities. Consequently, financial inclusion, together with its well-established importance for the whole society, has the added advantage of promoting financial system stability.

Such mixed evidence, as shown above, provides an opportunity for researchers to analyze and establish relations among financial inclusion, financial stability, and banking sector development. Motivated by results in the extant literature, this chapter analyzes whether there are bi-causal and tripartite connectivenss among inclusive finance, financial stability, and banking sector development in Africa. The findings of this study are key to policymakers, as they serve to inform strategies for financial inclusion.

4.4 Methodology

The causal connections between financial inclusion, banking sector development, and financial stability were investigated using the Panel VAR method in this chapter. Endogeneity issues are a significant obstacle in econometric modeling using panel data analysis, and this technique overcomes them. It also enables the creation of impulse response functions as well as the breakdown of the prediction error variance of the variables. The panel VAR method provides a more flexible framework in which all variables in the system of equations are considered endogenous, making it suitable for the research. Holtz-Eakin et al. (1988) engineered the panel VAR approach, which is currently widely utilized in economics and finance research (Love & Ariss, 2014; Love & Ziccino, 2006). The following is the general model of Panel VAR:

$$Y_{it} = \sum_{k=1}^{p} \alpha_{it} Y_{it-k} + u_{it} \tag{4.1}$$

where Y_{it} is a vector of each country, K denotes endogenous variables, $i = 1, \ldots\ldots N$ over $t = 1 \ldots T$ time periods while Y_{it} is defined as:

$$Y_{it} = \begin{bmatrix} \text{FINDEX}_{it} \\ \text{BSD}_{it} \\ \text{FINSTA}_{it} \end{bmatrix} \tag{4.2}$$

Table 4.3 presents the variables' definitions and sources.

Table 4.3 Data source and variable description

Variable	*Notation*	*Description*	*Data source*
Financial inclusion	ATMS	ATMs per hundred thousand adults	WDI
Financial inclusion	BB	Bank branches per hundred thousand adults	WDI
Financial inclusion	CBB	Commercial bank branches per hundred thousand adults	WDI
Financial inclusion	BAC	Bank accounts per thousand adults,	WDI
Financial inclusion	BFCB	Borrowers from commercial banks per thousand adults	WDI
Financial inclusion	DCB	Depositors with commercial banks per thousand adults	WDI
Bank development	DCPS	Domestic Credit to Private Sector by Banks	GFD
Bank development	NIM	Net Interest Margin	GFD
Financial stability	FINSTA	Bank Z-Score	GFD
Financial inclusion index	FINDEX	A composite index of financial inclusion encompassing the access and usage dimension of financial inclusion	WDI
Banking Sector Development	BSD	A composite index of banking sector development comprising size and efficiency facets of banking sector development	GFD

Note WDI = World Development Indicators: GFD = Global Financial Development

Y_{it-k} represents the lagged figures of the endogenous variables and U_{it} is a $K \times I$ vector of random errors and it is stated as:

$$U_{it} = \left[U_{1t}, U_{2t}, \ldots\ldots U_{Nt}\right] \sim iid\ (0, \delta) \tag{4.3}$$

α_{it} is allowed to be dependent cross-sectional. In situations where exogenous variables exist, Eq. (4.1) will become:

$$Y_{it} = \sum_{k=1}^{p} \alpha_{it} Y_{it-k} + D_{ij} R_t + U_{it} \tag{4.4}$$

where Dij are $K \times M$ matrices for each lag $j = 1, \ldots\ldots p$, and R_t is an $M \times 1$ vector of exogenous covariates similar to all countries i. In the same way, panel VAR can also be defined in a reduced form following Love and Zicchino (2006) as follows:

$$Y_{it} = +\sum_{k=1}^{p} \alpha_{it} Y_{it-k} + \tau_2 R_{it} + \lambda_i + \gamma_t + e_{it} \tag{4.5}$$

If exogeneous variables (R_{it}) are included it makes Eq. (4.4) above different from Love and Zicchino's (2006) specification. Where Y_{it-k} is a vector of three-variables [FINDEX, BSD, FINSTA]. R_{it} captures exogenous variables. Also, λ_i is fixed effect specific to each country which encapsulates time-invariant determinants that are unobservable, γ_t represents time dummies which also account for global economic shocks and e_{it} is the error term.

Specification of Empirical Model

This section specifies the equations empirically involving financial inclusion, banking sector development, and financial stability from Eqs. (4.4) and (4.5) above. There are three empirical equations that constitute the panel VAR framework and these are stated below. The index for financial inclusion, index of banking sector development, and financial stability are modeled in terms of their own lags and the lags of exogenous variables while accounting for time-specific effects and country-specific fixed effects. The models are specified as follows:

$$\text{FINDEX}_{it} = \sum_{j=1}^{p} \delta_{1j} \text{FINDEX}_{it-j} + \sum_{j=1}^{p} \delta_{2j} \text{BSD}_{it-j}$$

$$+\sum_{j=1}^{p}\delta_{3j}\mathrm{FINSTA}_{it-j}+\lambda_i+\gamma_t+\varepsilon_{it} \tag{4.6}$$

$$\mathrm{BSD}_{it}=\sum_{j=1}^{p}\delta_{1j}\mathrm{BSD}_{it-j}+\sum_{j=1}^{p}\delta_{2j}\mathrm{FINDEX}_{it-j}+\sum_{j=1}^{p}\delta_{3j}\mathrm{FINSTA}_{it-j}+\lambda_i+\gamma_t+\varepsilon_{it} \tag{4.7}$$

$$\mathrm{FINSTA}_{it}=\sum_{j=1}^{p}\delta_{1j}\mathrm{FINSTA}_{it-j}+\sum_{j=1}^{p}\delta_{2j}\mathrm{FINDEX}_{it-j}+\sum_{j=1}^{p}\delta_{3j}\mathrm{BSD}_{it-j}+\lambda_i+\gamma_t+\varepsilon_{it} \tag{4.8}$$

FINDEX_{it} is the index for financial inclusion for country i at any time t; BSD_{it} is the banking sector development index for country i at time t; FINSTA_{it} is the financial stability (bank Z-score) for country i at time t; FINDEX_{it-j} is the lag of the index for financial inclusion; BSD_{it-j} is the lag of banking sector development index; FINSTA_{it-j} is the lag of financial stability measured by bank Z-score.

The forecast-error variance decompositions (FEVDs) and impulse response functions (IRFs) are computed using the generalized Cholesky decomposition method after the panel VAR parameters are computed. The forecast-error variance decomposition illustrates each shock's contribution to the source of variation in each endogenous variable at any given forecast period, whereas the impulse response functions demonstrate how endogenous variables respond over time to a shock in another system variable.

Variables Description

Presented in Table 4.3 are the variables description and data sources.

The World Development Indicators (WDI) database was used to get the financial inclusion variables, while the Global Financial Development (GFD) database was used to obtain the banking sector development and financial stability variables. This study makes use of 600 observations or data points from 50 African nations spanning the years 2006 to 2017. The countries were chosen based on the availability of data during the research period. Because the majority of the variables and countries did not have statistics beyond the specified timeframe, the study period did not extend beyond 2017.

Indices Computations and Corresponding Weights

This study constructs indexes for financial inclusion and banking sector development. Levine (2005) laments that the use of poor proxies for financial development is a key problem that has bedeviled the finance-growth nexus. The same issue is evident in the financial inclusion-banking sector development nexus. Financial inclusion is generally recognized as having two main facets—access and usage dimensions (Chakrabarty, 2012; Shah & Dubhashi, 2015). Therefore, financial inclusion measures must take into consideration its multidimensional nature.

Also, single variables such as the ratio of domestic credit from the banking sector to GDP, per capita deposit accounts, ratio of liquid liabilities to GDP, deposits to GDP ratio, number of bank branches, and private sector credit from financial institutions have been used to measure banking sector development (see Brown et al., 2013; Demirgüç-Kunt et al., 2011; Ezeoha, 2013; Nyamongo et al., 2012; Ramirez, 2013). According to several analyses, the above proxies do not effectively represent the financial system's essential operations (Bettin & Zazzaro, 2011; Levine, 2005). Access, size, stability, and efficiency are widely recognized as four fundamental components of banking sector development (WEF, 2013). As a result, it is important that proxies for banking sector development reflect the financial market's multifaceted nature. These multidimensional indicators can be used to analyze the relationships between financial inclusion, banking sector development, and financial stability from a holistic perspective.

The indices for both FINDEX and BSD are calculated as discussed below. Choosing weights is a major issue in indices construction. Panel principal components analysis (PCA) is used to produce the weights so as not to arbitrarily assign weights. Composite financial inclusion index (FINDEX) is calculated as follows:

$$\text{FINDEX}_{it} = \sum_{r=1}^{6} w_r \text{indicator}_{rit}$$

where w_r are the weights or the factor loadings obtained from the PCA; Indicator_{rit} is a measure r for country i at any time t; r represents the 6 constituents of FINDEX where the access aspect of financial inclusion is measured by the number of bank branches, ATMs, and commercial bank branches; while the usage aspect of financial inclusion is measured by the number of borrowers from commercial banks, bank accounts, and depositors with commercial banks.

The analogous index for BSD is:

$$\text{BSD}_{it} = \sum_{r=1}^{6} w_r \text{indicator}_{rit}$$

r represents two metrics of banking sector growth: domestic credit extended to the private sector by banks scaled to GDP, which is the size/depth indicator of banking sector development, and net interest margin (efficiency dimension of banking sector development).

Each indicator is standardized on a scale of 1–7 so that country performance can be easily compared across the various proxies. The worst and best possible results are represented by 1 and 7 respectively. The conversion equation is specified as:

$$6\frac{[\text{country score} - \text{sample minimum}]}{[\text{sample maximum} - \text{sample minimum}]} + 1$$

In this case, the sample minimum and the sample maximum stand for the lowest and highest country scores in the various economies included in this study respectively. In situations where there are variables for which higher figures mean a worse possible outcome, the following conversion equation is used to rescale from 1 to 7, thereby ensuring that the worst and best outcomes are still represented by 1 and 7.

$$6\frac{[\text{country score} - \text{sample minimum}]}{[\text{sample maximum} - \text{sample minimum}]} + 7$$

4.5 Discussion of Results

Summary Statistics

The descriptive statistics for the variables used in this chapter are shown in Table 4.4. We adopt the median as the measure of central tendency in our discussions since the mean is susceptible to outliers. The median ATM value in Africa is 4.81, implying that there are 4.8 ATMs per 100,000 adults in the continent. In Africa, the average number of bank accounts per thousand adults is 154.5. In addition, for every 100,000 adults, there are 3.91 bank branches. This suggests that financial services are not widely available in Africa.

The number of people who borrow from commercial banks (BFCB) and the number of people who deposit with commercial banks (DCB), both indicators of banking sector development's utilization dimension, recorded median values of 27.39 and 155.50, respectively. The median number of commercial bank branches is 3.90. The median values of domestic credit given by banks to the private sector (DCPS) and net interest margin (NIM), both efficiency metrics of banking sector development, are 14.82% and 5.54%, respectively. Thus, domestic credit offered by African banks to the private sector is just 14.82% of GDP, with a net interest margin of 5.54%, indicating low levels of banking sector development. The median Z-score of a bank, which is a measure of financial stability, is 10.18.

Unit Root Test Results

When analyzing panel data, the stationarity of the variables must be taken into account. The order in which the variables are integrated is significant since it allows us to select the best model for calculating the coefficients, making it necessary to test for stationarity. This study used four-panel unit root testing for stationarity to guarantee that the results were reliable and consistent. In Pesaran and Shin (IPS), Levine–Lin Chu (LLC), Philips

Table 4.4 Descriptive statistics

	ATMS	*BAC*	*BB*	*BFCB*	*CBB*	*DCB*	*DCPSB*	*NIM*	*ZSCORE*
Mean	11.38	293.12	7.08	58.24	6.98	296.35	21.40	6.40	12.71
Median	4.81	154.50	3.91	27.39	3.90	155.50	14.82	5.54	10.18
Maximum	79.16	2084.59	53.35	318.17	53.35	2084.59	106.26	60.37	63.41
Minimum	0.00	7.07	0.29	0.13	0.29	1.53	0.50	0.00	2.18
Std. Dev	15.47	383.70	9.11	71.47	9.03	390.22	18.99	4.50	8.88
Skewness	2.05	2.56	2.80	1.70	2.82	2.49	1.96	5.65	1.98
Kurtosis	6.61	9.98	11.51	5.09	11.72	9.41	6.72	62.88	8.09
Jarque-Bera	605.14	1406.00	2406.47	228.83	2560.80	1126.17	703.81	85,859.55	975.99
Probability	0.00	0.00	0.00	0.00	0.00	0.00	0.00	0.00	0.00
Observations	487	450	557	346	570	410	577	555	564

Table 4.5 Panel unit root test

	FINDEX	*BSD*	*FINSTA*
Level			
LLC	−0.717	−7.344***	−6.850**
IPS	3.300	−3.380***	− 2.428***
ADF	41.670	153.866***	131.531**
PP	68.036	162.33***	139.075***
First difference			
LLC	−19.046***		
IPC	−7.153***		
ADF	130.863***		
PP	163.818***		

Note $P < 0.01$***; $P < 0.05$**; $P < 0.10$*

Perron (PP), and Augmented Dickey Fuller (ADF) tests are among them. This is due to the traditional ADF's low predictive power when doing stationary tests in short panels, as in our instance.

The panel unit root test results for stationarity are shown in Table 4.5. The results reveal that the banking sector development index (BSD) and financial stability index (FINSTA) are integrated at order zero I(0), whereas the financial inclusion index (FINDEX) is integrated at first difference I(1) (1). As a result, the data analysis was done using the first difference of the financial inclusion index.

Lag Order Estimation and Selection

The lag order estimate and selection were decided using the Hannan-Quinn information criterion (HQ), Schwarz information criterion (SC), and Akaike information criterion (AIC) once the study used a panel VAR model (AIC). Because the conclusions produced by these information criteria are significantly more robust and resilient, they were chosen (Qu & Perron, 2007). Table 4.6 summarizes the results of the lag order selection. The preferable panel VAR framework is the first order, according to Andrews and Lu's (2001) lag order selection criterion. The first order was chosen since it had the lowest criterion value. As a result, the first order panel VAR is used in the study.

Table 4.6 Panel VAR Lag order computation and selection

Lag	*LogL*	*LR*	*FPE*	*AIC*	*SC*	*HQ*
1	27.23629	NA	6.88e-05	−1.072723	−0.668686*	−0.934935
2	37.75331	17.32215	6.35e-05	−1.161960	−0.353886	−0.886383
3	50.13078	18.20216	5.35e-05	−1.360634	−0.148524	−0.947270
4	66.64309	21.36887*	3.64e-05*	−1.802535	−0.186388	−1.251383*
5	75.81520	10.25118	3.98e-05	−1.812659*	0.207524	−1.123718
6	82.89465	6.663011	5.25e-05	−1.699685	0.724535	−0.872957
7	93.15725	7.847876	6.34e-05	−1.773956	1.054300	−0.809440
8	102.7009	5.613930	9.32e-05	−1.805937	1.426356	−0.703633

*Indicates lag order selected by the criterion
LR: sequential modified LR test statistic (each test at 5% level) FPE: Final prediction error AIC: Akaike information criterion SC: Schwarz information criterion HQ: Hannan-Quinn information criterion

Table 4.7 Granger causality test

Excluded	*Chi-sq*	*Df*	*Prob*
Dependent variable: FINDEX			
BSD	1.483578	1	0.2232
FINSTA	45.26567	1	0.0000
All	48.19391	2	0.0000
Dependent variable: BSD			
FINDEX	2.896705	1	0.0888
FINSTA	2.784536	1	0.0952
All	6.637543	2	0.0362
Dependent variable: FINSTA			
FINDEX	4.861328	1	0.0275
BSD	3.304785	1	0.0691
All	4.920866	2	0.0854

Granger Causality Test

The study used a granger causality test to see if we could model the variables in a panel VAR setup.

The findings of the granger causality test are reported in Table 4.7. Except for the financial inclusion index and banking sector development, which have a one-way link, the data show that the variables granger-cause each other at the standard significant thresholds of 1%, 5%, and 10%. This means that the variables can be put in a Panel VAR setting.

Regression Results

The study's panel VAR findings are reported in Table 4.8. The financial inclusion index lag is statistically significant in affecting banking sector development, according to model 2. This means that financial inclusion encourages the growth of the banking sector. We observe that efforts and legislative measures focused at boosting financial inclusion will lead to the development of the banking industry. Other empirical studies have indicated a positive and significant association between financial inclusion and the development of the banking industry (see Anarfo et al., 2019; Gimet & Lagoarde-Segot, 2012). However, the lag of banking sector development does not influence financial inclusion. The findings in model 1 show that the relations between the lag of banking sector development and financial inclusion is negative, although it is not statistically significant. This suggests that banking sector development that is not pro-poor will not promote financial inclusion. Though the banking sector could be developed, it will still not promote financial inclusion if there are limitations and impediments that constrain the poor and the vulnerable groups in society from having access to finance such as customer identification requirements (Kodongo, 2018).

Table 4.8 Panel VAR results

	(Model 1) *FINDEX*	*(Model 2)* *BSD*	*Model 3* *FINSTA*
FINDEX (−1)	1.039389***	0.031667*	−0.017379**
	(0.01174)	(0.01861)	(0.00788)
	[88.5426]	[1.70197]	[−2.20484]
BSD (−1)	−0.025564	0.920844***	0.025620*
	(0.02099)	(0.03327)	(0.01409)
	[−1.21802]	[27.6805]	[1.81791]
FINSTA (−1)	0.049467***	0.019446*	1.008596***
	(0.00735)	(0.01165)	(0.00494)
	[6.72798]	[1.66869]	[204.299]
R-squared	0.989366	0.909302	0.929906
Adj. R-squared	0.989257	0.908367	0.929183
S.E. equation	0.244938	0.388230	0.164467
F-statistic	9024.838	972.4818	1286.854

Note Standard errors in () & t-statistics in [] and ***, **, * represents significance at 1%, 5% and 10% respectively

The results also show that there is a bi-causal link between the financial inclusion index and financial stability. The lag of financial index is statistically significant in influencing financial stability in model 3, and the lag of financial stability is also statistically significant in influencing financial inclusion. Though the lag of financial inclusion index has a statistically significant influence on financial stability, its sign is negative. This suggests that more financial inclusion is capable of destabilizing the banking sector. The rationale is that if more people, especially the poor and vulnerable, are uncautiously financially included, there is a tendency for banks to provide credit to those who are not creditworthy, which in turn lowers the quality of their assets, leading to sub-prime lending. This would culminate in banking instability. Empirical studies have shown that the global financial crisis was due to sub-prime lending (Khan, 2011). Our result of a negative link between the lag of financial inclusion index and financial stability harmonizes with other empirical studies (see Ahamed & Mallick, 2019; Čihák et al., 2016; Mehrotra & Yetman, 2015; Sahay et al., 2015). However, in model 1, the lag of financial stability positively and significantly relates to financial inclusion. This suggests that more financial stability leads to more financial inclusion. When banks are financially stable, they can provide more credit facilities to a wider segment of the population, including the poor and the vulnerable. This suggests that central governments and policymakers in Africa should aim at initiating and implementing policies that promote financial stability to enhance financial inclusion in their respective economies. This result supports earlier studies (see Khan, 2011; Morgan & Pontines, 2018; Neaime & Gaysset, 2018).

The results reveal that there is a bi-causal relation between banking sector development and financial stability. In model 2 and model 3, the lag of banking sector development positively and significantly influences financial stability and vice versa. This implies that financial stability and banking sector development are complementary rather than substitutes. Hence, policies targeted at enhancing banking sector development would not hamper but rather promote financial stability and vice versa. Also, banking sector development can be achieved without compromising financial stability. This result concurs with other empirical works that investigated the connection between banking sector development and financial instability (Brouwer et al., 2002).

Table 4.9 Variance decomposition of FINDEX

Period	*S.E*	*FINDEX*	*BSD*	*FINSTA*
1	0.244938	100.0000	0.000000	0.000000
2	0.352559	99.86088	0.086089	0.053032
3	0.439794	99.56574	0.258641	0.175622
4	0.517537	99.14417	0.490219	0.365611
5	0.589954	98.62094	0.758486	0.620571
6	0.659153	98.01647	1.045591	0.937944
7	0.726372	97.34734	1.337537	1.315127
8	0.792409	96.62689	1.623582	1.749530
9	0.857813	95.86570	1.895688	2.238614
10	0.922983	95.07206	2.148037	2.779902

Table 4.10 Variance decomposition of BSD

Period	*S.E*	*FINDEX*	*BSD*	*FINSTA*
1	0.388230	1.978264	98.02174	0.000000
2	0.528429	2.274937	97.72142	0.003648
3	0.623650	2.604027	97.38277	0.013201
4	0.694793	2.967205	97.00276	0.030036
5	0.750416	3.365972	96.57835	0.055682
6	0.795131	3.801621	96.10656	0.091822
7	0.831804	4.275204	95.58451	0.140283
8	0.862371	4.787489	95.00948	0.203030
9	0.888221	5.338936	94.37891	0.282151
10	0.910390	5.929661	93.69050	0.379843

Forecast-Error Variance Decomposition of FINDEX, BSD, and FINSTA

The Cholesky forecast-error variance decomposition (FEVD) results are comparable with our findings in the underlying panel VAR framework residual covariance matrix. The results in Table 4.9, based on the computed FEVD, demonstrate that banking sector development and financial stability account for 2.15% and 2.78% of the variation in the financial inclusion index, respectively. Financial stability, rather than banking sector development, appears to explain a slightly higher percentage of variation in financial inclusion over time. Table 4.10 further

Table 4.11 Variance decomposition of FINSTA

Period	*S.E*	*FINDEX*	*BSD*	*FINSTA*
1	0.164467	0.003626	0.405725	99.59065
2	0.233360	0.008147	0.202475	99.78938
3	0.287071	0.033208	0.221837	99.74496
4	0.333265	0.079453	0.433210	99.48734
5	0.374912	0.147381	0.807873	99.04475
6	0.413527	0.237388	1.319438	98.44317
7	0.449998	0.349801	1.944074	97.70612
8	0.484895	0.484910	2.660583	96.85451
9	0.518602	0.642990	3.450344	95.90667
10	0.551393	0.824321	4.297172	94.87851

shows that the financial inclusion index explains 5.93% of the difference in banking sector development, while financial stability explains 0.38%.

The variance decomposition of financial stability in Table 4.11 indicates that 0.82% of the total variation is explained by financial inclusion while banking sector development explains 4.30%. Thus, banking sector development explains more of the variations in financial stability than financial inclusion. The results show that the variables explain themselves more in the long run than the other endogenous variables.

Impulse Response Functions (IRF)

Figure 4.1 shows the endogenous variables' panel VAR framework impulse response functions (IRFs). The financial inclusion index's impulse response to banking sector development (BSD) shocks is positive and statistically significant, confirming our panel VAR results in Table 4.8. The IRF plot shows that a positive shock in financial inclusion has a favorable impact on banking sector development in terms of levels. Figure 4.1 depicts the IRFs of banking sector development and financial stability to shocks in the other endogenous variable.

4.6 Conclusion and Policy Implications

The existing literature has mostly neglected the connectiveness among financial inclusion, banking sector development, and financial stability. As a result, using a panel VAR estimation approach, this research looked into

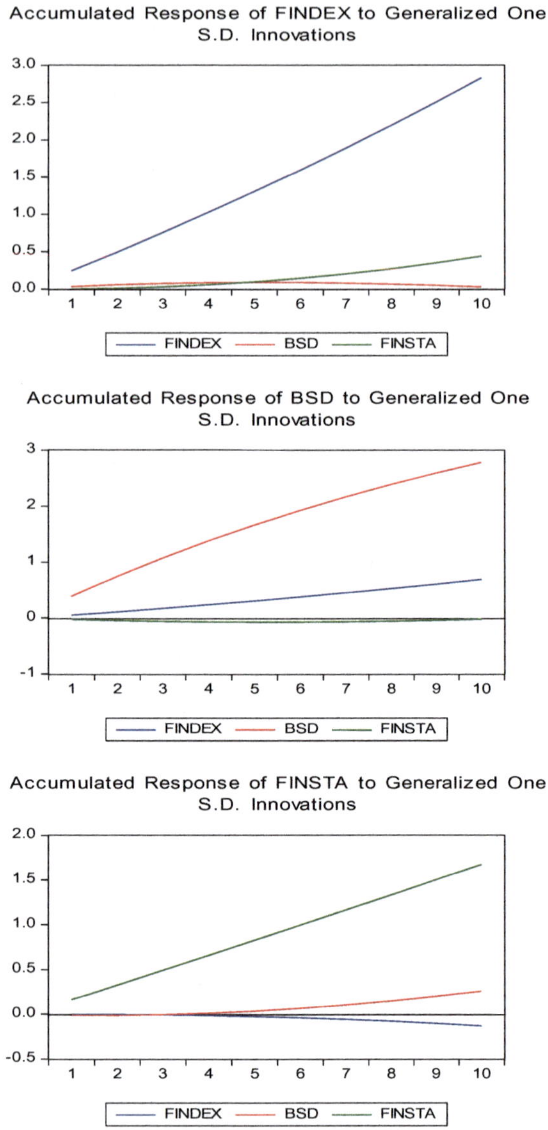

Fig. 4.1 Impulse response functions of FINDEX, BSD, and FINSTA

the dynamic and causal links between financial inclusion, banking sector development, and financial stability in Africa. Financial inclusion, banking sector development, and financial stability are all critical components of most African economies' development agendas and macroeconomic stability, necessitating the study.

Specifically, the results of the study reveal that there is reverse causality among financial inclusion, banking sector development, and financial stability. This suggests that these variables complement each other rather than being contradictory. These results imply that financial institutions and central governments should consider the dependence among these variables when modeling or implementing economic policies. They also imply that pursuing financial stability goals would not compromise or sacrifice the goals of financial inclusion and banking sector development.

The findings also show that increases in financial stability promote financial inclusion. For policy development, central governments and financial institutions in Africa should initiate and implement policies targeted at ensuring financial stability if they are to improve financial inclusion. When financial institutions are stable, they are in a position to provide more finance to businesses, entrepreneurs, and the vulnerable in society. This has the potential of cushioning them from the impact of macroeconomic shocks and volatility on their survival and livelihood (Giuliano & Ruiz-Arranz, 2009; Manuamorn, 2007). The findings also show that financial inclusion enhances banking sector development. Ideally, more people in the banking sector mean an increase in credit provided by banks, more bank branches, savings, investment, and banks' profitability (Issaka Jajah et al., 2020). Financial inclusion plays a key role in most African economies; hence it is expedient that African financial institutions and central governments continue to implement appropriate policies and reforms to enable it. Previous studies also provide empirical support for financial inclusion as a determinant of banking sector development (Anarfo et al., 2019; Anarfo, Amewu, et al., 2020).

Our findings also point to a reverse causality link between banking sector development and financial stability, implying that the two factors are mutually reinforcing. This contrasts with studies that claim that the growth of the banking industry could lead to financial instability as a result of sub-prime lending (Khan, 2011). For policy development, central governments and central banks in Africa can leverage on the affirmative impact of banking sector development on financial stability to promote and enhance financial stability instead of targeting only financial stability as a policy goal.

To conclude, the study adds to the financial inclusion, banking sector development, and financial stability literature from an African perspective. It used a panel VAR methodology to establish the dynamic and causal relations among them, and not between them as has been the focus of other researchers. This is key for informing policies geared at promoting financial inclusion.

References

Abor, J. Y., Amidu, M., & Issahaku, H. (2018). Mobile telephony, financial inclusion and inclusive growth. *Journal of African Business, 19*(3), 430–453.

Adasme, O., Majnoni, G., & Uribe, M. (2006). *Access and risk-friends or foes? Lessons from Chile*. The World Bank.

Ahamed, M. M., & Mallick, S. K. (2019). Is financial inclusion good for bank stability? International evidence. *Journal of Economic Behavior & Organization, 157*, 403–427.

Aluko, O. A., & Ajayi, M. A. (2018). Determinants of banking sector development: Evidence from Sub-Saharan African countries. *Borsa Istanbul Review, 18*(2), 122–139.

Amidu, M., Abor, J. Y., & Issahaku, H. (2019). Left behind, but included: The case of migrant remittances and financial inclusion in Ghana. *African Finance Journal, 21*(2), 36–63.

Anarfo, E. B., Abor, J. Y., & Osei, K. A. (2020). Financial regulation and financial inclusion in Sub-Saharan Africa: Does financial stability play a moderating role? *Research in International Business and Finance*. http://doi.org/10.1016/j.ribaf.2019.101070

Anarfo, E. B., Abor, J. Y., Osei, K. A., & Gyeke-Dako, A. (2019). Financial inclusion and financial sector development in Sub-Saharan Africa: A panel VAR approach. *International Journal of Managerial Finance, 15*(4), 444–463.

Anarfo, E. B., Amewu, G., & Dzeha, G. C. (2020). Financial inclusion and migrant remittances in Sub-Saharan Africa: A panel VAR approach. *International Journal of Social Economics, 47*(7), 809–829.

Andrews, D. W., & Lu, B. (2001). Consistent model and moment selection procedures for GMM estimation with application to dynamic panel data models. *Journal of Econometrics, 101*(1), 123–164.

Andrianaivo, M., & Yartey, C. A. (2010). Understanding the growth of African financial markets. *African Development Review, 22*(3), 394–418.

Beck, T., Demirgüç-Kunt, A., & Levine, R. (2007). Finance, inequality, and the poor. *Journal of Economic Growth, 12*, 27–49.

Beck, T., Demirgüç-Kunt, A., & Peria, M. S. M. (2008). Banking services for everyone? Barriers to bank access and use around the world. *The World Bank Economic Review, 22*(3), 397–430.

Bettin, G., & Zazzaro, A. (2011). Remittances and financial development: Substitute or complement in economic growth? *Bulletin of Economic Research*. https://doi.org/10.1111/j.1467-8586.2011.00398.x.(no-no)

Bhanot, D., Bapat, V., & Bera, S. (2012). Studying financial inclusion in north-east India. *International Journal of Bank Marketing*.

Brouwer, H., De Haas, R., & Kiviet, B. (2002). Banking sector development and financial stability in the run up to EU accession. *Financial Stability and Growth in Emerging Economies*, 97.

Brown, R. P. C., Carmignani, F., & Fayad, G. (2013). Migrants' remittances and financial development: Macro- and micro-level evidence of a perverse relationship. *The World Economy, 36*(5), 636–660. https://doi.org/10.1111/twec.12016

Chakrabarty, K. C. (2012, November). *Financial inclusion: Issues in measurement and analysis*. Keynote Address, BIS-BNM Workshop on Financial Inclusion Indicators, Kuala Lumpur.

Čihák, M., Mare, D. S., & Melecky, M. (2016). The nexus of financial inclusion and financial stability: A study of trade-offs and synergies. *World Bank Policy Research Working Paper*, (7722).

Chithra, N., & Selvam, M. (2013). *Determinants of financial inclusion: An empirical study on the inter-state variations in India*. Available at SSRN 2296096.

Cull, R., Demirgüç-Kunt, A., & Lyman, T. (2012). *Financial inclusion and stability: What does research show?* (World Bank Working Paper No. 9443). World Bank.

Danışman, G. Ö., & Tarazi, A. (2020). Financial inclusion and bank stability: Evidence from Europe. *The European Journal of Finance*. https://doi.org/10.1080/1351847X.2020.1782958

Deaton, A. (2008). Income, health, and well-being around the world: Evidence from the Gallup World Poll. *Journal of Economic Perspectives, 22*(2), 53–72.

De la Torre, A., Feyen, E., & Ize, A. (2013). Financial development: Structure and dynamics. *The World Bank Economic Review, 27*(3), 514–541. https://doi.org/10.1093/wber/lht005

Demirgüç-Kunt, A., Córdova, E. L., Pería, M. S. N., & Woodruff, C. (2011). Remittances and banking sector breadth and depth: Evidence from Mexico. *Journal of Development Economics, 95*(2), 229–241.

Demirguc-Kunt, A., & Klapper, L. (2012). *Measuring financial inclusion: The Global Findex database* (Policy Research Working Paper No. 6025). World Bank.

Demirguc-Kunt, A., Klapper, L., & Singer, D. (2017). *Financial inclusion and inclusive growth: A review of recent empirical evidence*. The World Bank.

Demirguc-Kunt, A., Klapper, L., Singer, D., & Van Oudheusden, P. (2015). *The Global Findex database 2014: Measuring financial inclusion around the world* (Policy Research Working Paper 7255). World Bank.

Ezeoha, A. E. (2013). Financial determinants of international remittance flows to the sub-Saharan African region. *International Migration, 51*, e84–e97. https://doi.org/10.1111/imig.12061

Flamini, V., McDonald, C., & Schumacher, L. (2009). *The determinants of commercial bank profitability in Sub-Saharan Africa* (IMF Working Paper, WP/09/15).

Frączek, B. (2019). Relationships between financial inclusion and financial stability and economic growth—The opportunity or threat for monetary policy? In *Multiple perspectives in risk and risk management* (pp. 261–278). Springer.

Gimet, C., & Lagoarde-Segot, T. (2012). Financial sector development and access to finance. Does size say it all? *Emerging Markets Review, 13*(3), 316–337.

Giuliano, P., & Ruiz-Arranz, M. (2009). Remittances, financial development, and growth. *Journal of Development Economics, 90*, 144–152.

Guiso, L., Sapienza, P., & Zingales, L. (2009). Does local financial development matter? In *The banks and the Italian economy* (p. 31e66). Physica-verlag HD.

Gulde, A. M., Pattillo, C. A., Christensen, J., Carey, K. J., & Wagh, S. (2006). *Sub-Saharan Africa: Financial sector challenges*. International Monetary Fund.

Han, R., & Melecky, M. (2013). Financial inclusion for financial stability: Access to bank deposits and the growth of deposits in the global financial crisis. *World Bank policy research working paper*, (6577).

Hannig, A., & Jansen, S. (2010). *Financial inclusion and financial stability: Current policy issues* (ADBI, Working Paper Series, No. 259). Asian Development Bank Institute.

Holtz-Eakin, D., Newey, W., & Rosen, H. S. (1988). Estimating vector autoregressions with panel data. *Econometrica: Journal of the Econometric Society*, 1371–1395.

Honohan, P. (2008). Cross-country variation in household access to financial services. *Journal of Banking and Finance, 32*(11), 2493–2500.

Honohan, P., & Beck, T. (2007). *Making finance work for Africa*. World Bank Publications.

Issaka Jajah, Y., Anarfo, E. B., & Aveh, F. K. (2020). Financial inclusion and bank profitability in Sub-Saharan Africa. *International Journal of Finance & Economics*.

Khan, H. R. (2011). Financial inclusion and financial stability: Are they two sides of the same coin. *Address by Shri HR Khan, Deputy Governor of the Reserve Bank of India, at BANCON*.

Klapper, L., Laevan, L., & Rajan, R. (2006). Business environment and firm entry: Evidence from international data. *Journal of Finance Econology, 82*, 591–629.

Kodongo, O. (2018). Financial regulations, financial literacy, and financial inclusion: Insights from Kenya. *Emerging Markets Finance and Trade, 54*(12), 2851–2873.

Levine, R. (2005). Finance and growth: Theory and evidence. *Handbook of Economic Growth, 1*, 865–934.

Love, I., & Ariss, R. T. (2014). Macro-financial linkages in Egypt: A panel analysis of economic shocks and loan portfolio quality. *Journal of International Financial Markets, Institutions and Money, 28*, 158–181.

Love, I., & Zicchino, L. (2006). Financial development and dynamic investment behavior: Evidence from panel VAR. *The Quarterly Review of Economics and Finance, 46*, 190–210.

Machdar, N. M. (2020). Financial inclusion, financial stability and sustainability in the banking sector: The case of Indonesia. *International Journal of Economics and Business Administration, VII, I*(1), 193–202.

Manuamorn, O. P. (2007). *Scaling up microinsurance: The case of weather insurance for smallholders in India*. The World Bank.

Mehrotra, A. N., & Yetman, J. (2015). Financial inclusion-issues for central banks. *BIS Quarterly Review*, 83–96.

Mendoza, E. G., Quadrini, V., & Rios-Rull, J. V. (2009). Financial integration, financial development, and global imbalances. *Journal of Political economy, 117*(3), 371–416.

Morgan, P. J., & Pontines, V. (2018). Financial stability and financial inclusion: The case of SME lending. *The Singapore Economic Review, 63*(1), 111–124.

Neaime, S., & Gaysset, I. (2018). Financial inclusion and stability in MENA: Evidence from poverty and inequality. *Finance Research Letters, 24*, 230–237.

Nyamongo, E. M., Misati, R. N., Kipyegon, L., & Ndirangu, L. (2012). Remittances, financial development and economic growth in Africa. *Journal of Economics and Business, 64*(3), 240–260. https://doi.org/10.1016/j.jeconbus.2012.01.001

Okpara, G. C. (2011). Financial inclusion and financial stability: A Toda-Yamamoto causality approach. *Social Sciences (Jamelss), 1*(1), 86–100.

Prasad, E. (2010). *Financial sector regulation and reforms in emerging markets: An overview* (NBER Working Paper No. 16428). National Bureau of Economic Research.

Qu, Z., & Perron, P. (2007). A modified information criterion for cointegration tests based on a VAR approximation. *Econometric Theory, 23*(4), 638–685.

Ramirez, M. D. (2013). Do financial and institutional variables enhance the impact of remittances on economic growth in Latin America and the Caribbean? A Panel Cointegration Analysis. *International Advances in Economic Research, 19*(3), 273–288. https://doi.org/10.1007/s11294-013-9407-2

Sacerdoti, E. (2005). *Access to bank credit in Sub-Sahara Africa: Key issues and reform strategies* (IMF Working Paper, WP/05/166).

Sahay, R., Cihak, M., N'Diaye, P., Barajas, A., Mitra, S., Kyobe, A., Mooi, Y. N., & Yousefi, S. R. (2015) *Financial inclusion: Can it meet multiple macroeconomic goals?* (IMF's Discussion Note). International Monetary Fund.

Shah, P., & Dubhashi, M. (2015). Review paper on financial inclusion—The means of inclusive growth. *Chanakya International Journal of Business Research, 1*(1), 37–48.

Siddik, M., Alam, N., & Kabiraj, S. (2018). Does financial inclusion induce financial stability? Evidence from cross-country analysis. *Australasian Accounting, Business and Finance Journal, 12*(1), 34–46.

Sinclair, S. (2013). Financial inclusion and social financialisation: Britain in a European context. *International Journal of Sociology and Social Policy.*

Sinclair, S., & Bramley, G. (2011). Beyond virtual inclusion–communications inclusion and digital divisions. *Social Policy and Society, 10*(1), 1–11.

Vo, D. H., Nguyen, N. T., & Van, L. T. H. (2021). Financial inclusion and stability in the Asian region using bank-level data. *Borsa Istanbul Review, 21*(1), 36–43.

WEF. (2013). The Financial Development Report 2012. In I. Reuttner (Ed.), *The World Economic Forum.*

World Bank. Development Research Group. Finance & Private Sector Development Team. (2012). *The Little Data Book on Financial Inclusion 2012.* World Bank Publications.

Yartey, C. A., & Adjasi, C. K. D. (2007). *Stock market development in sub-Saharan Africa: Critical issues and challenges* (International Monetary Fund Working Paper, WP/07/209).

CHAPTER 5

FinTech and the Future of Banks and Financial Services in Africa

Joshua Yindenaba Abor, Peter Quartey, Ahmad Hassan Ahmad, and Maxwell Opoku-Afari

5.1 Introduction

The report on the Global Findex Database by the World Bank shows that about 30% of the world's adults do not have an account and a greater percentage of them are in sub-Saharan Africa (SSA) where in 2017, just 38% of male adults and 27% of female adults had accounts with a formal financial institution (Demirgüç-Kunt et al., 2018). Some of the identified factors for this low level of inclusive finance include cost or documentation requirements (Honohan & Beck, 2008), low income

J. Y. Abor (✉)
Department of Finance, University of Ghana Business School, Legon, Accra, Ghana
e-mail: joshabor@ug.edu.gh

P. Quartey
Institute of Statistical, Social and Economic Research, University of Ghana, Legon, Accra, Ghana
e-mail: PQuartey@ug.edu.gh

J. Y. Abor and C. K. D. Adjasi (eds.), *The Economics of Banking and Finance in Africa*, Palgrave Macmillan Studies in Banking and Financial Institutions, https://doi.org/10.1007/978-3-031-04162-4_5

and education levels (Nanziri, 2017) and distance (Demirgüç-Kunt et al., 2018). However, the gap in financial access has been contracting in SSA due to technology adoption, particularly in the field of mobile money. For example, during the period, 2011–2017, the share of mobile money accounts in the region has more than doubled (Demirgüç-Kunt et al., 2018, p. 22). This has been attributed to two factors: limited formal financial and banking systems in the region and the burgeoning of mobile technology systems (Ahmad et al., 2020; Allen et al., 2016). This shows that innovations in FinTech present exceptional opportunities to address obstacles to financial inclusion and to ease the frictions with respect to information, particularly in Africa (AFI, 2018; Demir et al., 2020; Morse, 2015). Therefore, it appears that FinTech will not only introduce the rest of the under-banked population into the formal financial system but will also be able to foster inclusive growth (Demirgüç-Kunt et al., 2018; GPFI, 2016a). FinTech has been changing the financial sector by redefining the manner money is stored, saved, borrowed, invested, remitted, spent, and protected (Skan et al., 2016).

FinTech entails a wide array of technological innovations in the banking and financial services sector that improve and/or alter the approach in delivering financial services. These interventions in technological innovations have transformed the provision of financial services with respect to both personal and commercial finance. There is currently no consensus on what FinTech entails; however, a working definition is provided by the Financial Stability Board as "technologically enabled financial innovation that could result in new business models, applications, processes or products with an associated material effect on financial markets and institutions and the provision of financial services" (Financial Stability Board, 2017). FinTech developments in the financial service sector have been propelled by advances in mobile networks, mobile

A. H. Ahmad
School of Business and Economics, Loughborough University, Loughborough, UK
e-mail: A.H.Ahmad@lboro.ac.uk

M. Opoku-Afari
Bank of Ghana, Accra, Ghana
e-mail: maxwell.opoku-afari@bog.gov.gh

embedded systems, cloud computing, trust management, big data, and data analytic techniques (Gai et al., 2018). FinTech has become one of the major investments for competitive financial firms where its uses have permeated the whole of the financial industry, including loan technology, payments/billing, personal finance/asset management, money transfer/remittances, institutional technology, capital markets, and security technology (Manyika et al., 2016). Examples of FinTech innovations include Automated Teller Machines (ATMs), mobile money integrated payment platforms, mobile banking and mobile finance, short message service (SMS) interactive banking platforms, blockchain technology, cryptocurrency, and crowdfunding.

FinTech interventions affect aspects of the industry and are used for different purposes that include improvement in security, rapid delivery of service, and reduction of operating costs. They can be concentrated on some aspects of the industry, such as mobile sites for internet banking, or can replace established modes of delivery of services, for example, independent online banks and mobile money in the case of developing countries, especially in Africa.

FinTech interventions share similarities with other disruptive innovations in that they can create new markets and value networks that would disrupt existing structures, displace old products with new ones or even create new firms. However, they have some unique features in the financial markets (Philippon, 2016). This is due to the recognition of their potential contributions to the industry. The existing financial infrastructure typically revolves around banks; retail, wholesale, and commercial customers; insurance and pension funds; and foreign exchange, money and capital markets, which are all underpinned by providers of payment systems and other financial markets, in addition to central banks and other financial regulators (Amadou et al., 2019).

FinTech has emerged and is used in the world's major regions. However, in others, it is relatively small (Frost, 2020). For instance, in Africa, the challenges confronting the inclusiveness of financial systems in the region remain formidable, restricting the prospect for more gains in sustained growth, employment, and poverty reduction (Amadou et al., 2019). FinTech is able to perform a crucial role in fostering financial inclusion by allowing households and firms to mobilise resources for investment in a timeous manner to drive productivity. It, therefore, offers opportunities to promote inclusive finance in the continent (Abor et al., 2018). Notwithstanding the benefits associated with FinTech, it is often threatened by security issues, such as fraud and lack of trust. Also, there are concerns regarding vulnerabilities that come with these technologies and business models.

This chapter examines the importance of FinTech in the provision of banking and other financial services and how these promote inclusive finance in Africa. It also weighs the risks of FinTech adoption against its potential benefits. The rest of the chapter is structured as follows: Sect. 5.2 looks at the typology of FinTech in the financial services industry as well as the various types of FinTech in the provision of banking and financial services. Section 5.3 discusses the role of FinTech in driving financial inclusion and Sect. 5.4 examines the developments of FinTech in Africa. Section 5.5 identifies the constraints and challenges to the adoption of FinTech in Africa. Section 5.6 looks at the regulatory implications of the FinTech industry, while Sect. 5.7 concludes the chapter with suggestions on the way forward.

5.2 FinTech: The New Model for Banking and Financial Services

FinTech advancement is less obvious in some countries than others, particularly in the developed ones due to their well-developed and elaborate financial systems. However, technology can easily be adopted and operated in an environment with weak institutions such as in developing countries as well. Although FinTech developments have been growing steadily since the start of the use of the telegraph and telephone in the 1800s, they gained remarkable importance after the 2008 financial crisis, and have permeated many aspects of the financial industry (Arner et al., 2017). Prior to the 2008 financial crisis, FinTech adoption was largely driven by traditional financial institutions in order to support their operations and enhance efficiency. For example, in a bid to promote risk management, traditional financial institutions adopted internet banking, etc. However, FinTech activities and development have been largely outside the traditional financial institutions where they provide alternative sources of finance and investment to firms and households. Some of the driving factors identified include economic growth, level of financial development and quality of legal and other institutions (Demirgüç-Kunt & Levine, 2018).

FinTech innovation is now a ubiquity in all countries, both developed and developing. This is evident in the operations of Amazon, Apple,

Google, Facebook, and Microsoft, which are based in the US and provide a range of financial services such as credit facilities and payment systems. Samsung, Kakao Talk, and Alibaba are Korean firms, and the Chinese have Samsung Pay, Kakao Pay, and Alipay, which provide similar services. Several telecommunication companies offer mobile money services in a number of African countries such as Kenya, Tanzania, Uganda, and Ghana.

FinTech enjoys public confidence relative to traditional institutions. A survey reported in 2015 indicated that US citizens have higher trust in technology-based firms to handle their finances than in traditional banks (Arner et al., 2015). This has also been recognised by the banking industry itself. For example, in response to a survey by Statista in 2017 where bank executives were asked about their strategy in response to FinTech's challenges, 90% stated that they would collaborate with FinTech, 4% said they would acquire them, while another 4% indicated that they would compete with them (see, Fig. 5.1).

In addition, in another survey in 2019 on FinTech adoption rates by SMEs in China, the US, the UK, Mexico, and South Africa, China has the highest rate of adoption of 89%, with the US in a distant second

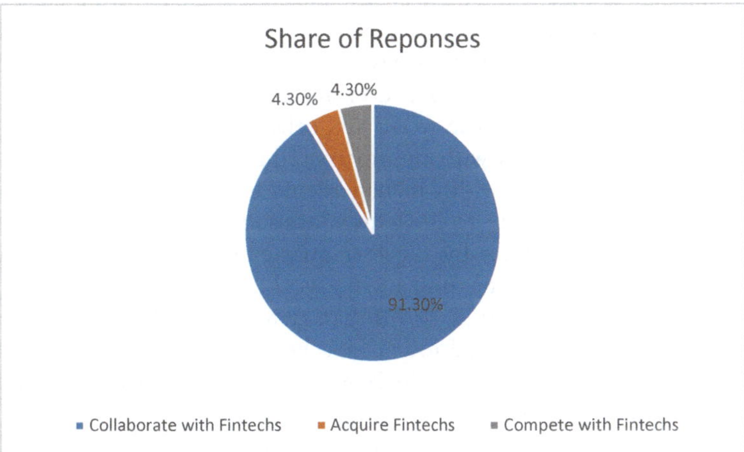

Fig. 5.1 Banks' future strategies for fintech companies (*Source* Authors construction based on Statista Report, 2017)

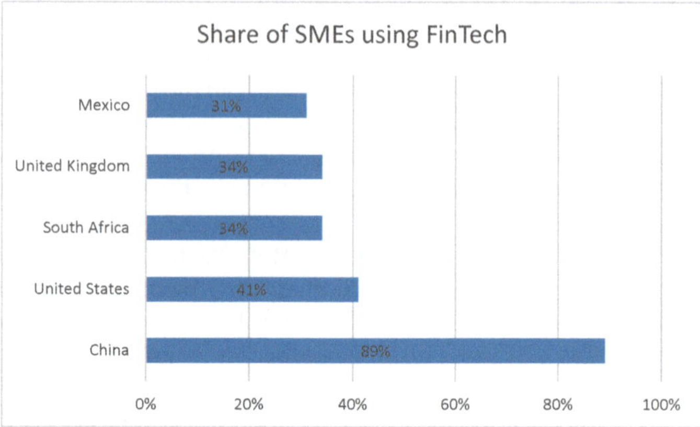

Fig. 5.2 Adoption rates of FinTech in the financial sector (*Source* Authors construction based on Statista Report, 2019)

place of 41%. South Africa and the UK have 34% adoption rates each, while Mexico has 31% as shown in Fig. 5.2.

China is one of the leading countries in this change as the survey found that Alibaba via its Ant Financial established in 2016 dominates. Ant Financial takes care of Alibaba's financial services, and its products include Alipay, which was estimated to have more than 400 million customers as at 2017 (Chen, 2016; Zetzsche et al., 2018). This is more than the active PayPal accounts in the world. Its other products are MyBank and Yu'e Bao. MyBank deals with the microcredit business of the firm while Yu'e Bao manages the wealth management outfit. In 2015, Ant Financial's credit loan portfolio to SMEs was over $100 billion (Chen, 2016), and grew to $165 billion by the first quarter of 2017, which makes it the biggest money market fund in the world. It has exceeded even the traditional providers, such as JP Morgan that had $150 billion under its management by the same period. China has also made a good leap into online insurance. For instance, in November 2015, 308 million policies were sold, the largest number sold in a day in the world.

FinTech is used for various transactions in the financial industry. These include payments, alternative lending and financing, and personal finance. Some uses of FinTech in the world include: digital payment, personal

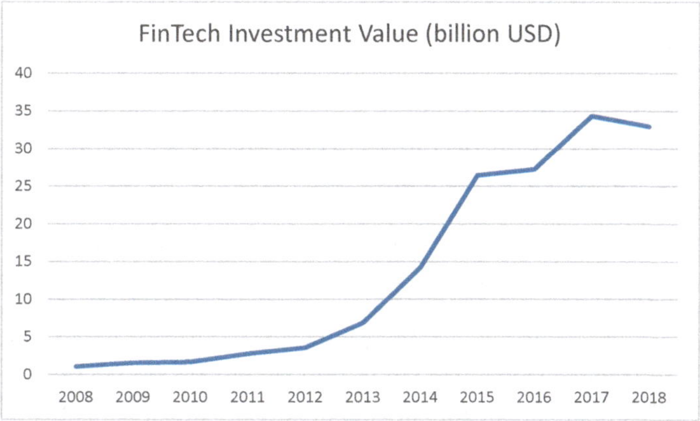

Fig. 5.3 Total global investment value of FinTech—2008–2018 (*Source* Authors construction based on Statista Report, 2019)

finances, alternative lending and financing. Digital payment users are the highest; however, uses for the other services are also gaining importance.

Figure 5.3 shows total investment in FinTech for the period between 2008 and 2018. The figure indicates that FinTech investment rose from about $1billion in 2008 to a phenomenal $34 billion by 2017. This underscores the importance of FinTech and the realisation of its potential by the firms.

Although the number of total values has been substantially growing, the average transaction value per user is generally constant, except for those who use it for digital payments, which rose from about $1600 to $2000 from 2017 to 2019. However, even within that category, the figure is predicted to decline from 2020 to 2023. This suggests that the number of users of FinTech is rising, but the average value of transactions is becoming smaller, which is sometimes encouraged by ease of accessibility of the services as reported for mobile money services in Africa (Ahmad et al., 2020).

The Typology of FinTech in the Financial Services Industry

The FinTech industry has evolved and covered areas that can be broadly grouped into five. These are (i) finance and investments, (ii) operations and risks management, (iii) payments and infrastructure, (iv) data security and monetisation, and (v) customer interface. These are covered below.

Finance and Investments
FinTech provides alternative sources of finance and investment mechanisms. Crowdfunding, including P2P lending, is the most popular FinTech service, but it goes beyond these. Private equity and placements, public offerings, and listings, among others, are all becoming important services provided by FinTech. According to the 2015 Statista report, although P2P recorded a decent growth between 2012 and 2015, it is expected that transactions would increase by more than tenfold by 2025.

FinTech is increasingly becoming important in robo-advisory services. These are financial advisory services provided online with minimal human interventions. The services are based on mathematical rules or algorithms using software. Figure 5.4 shows the growth of crowdfunding and crowd-investing, which have more than doubled in less than a decade and are projected to grow by more than 50% by 2023.

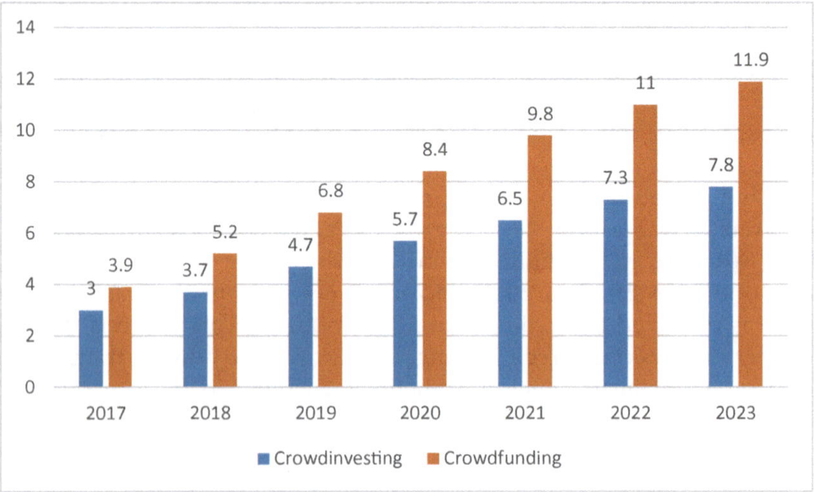

Fig. 5.4 Crowdfunding and crowdinvesting (*Source* Authors construction based on Statista Digital Output Report, 2018)

Operations and Risk Management
FinTech provides additional efficiency to existing firms in their operations, and the use and management of data improves the firms' ability to manage risks better, thereby maximising profit. As discussed above, FinTech makes it possible to provide services at relatively affordable costs, which provides opportunities to extend these services to SMEs and individual customers. It is worth noting that FinTech also faces risks such as regulatory challenges that need to be addressed (Lee & Shin, 2018).

Payments and Infrastructure
Mechanisms for payments have been enhanced by FinTech, particularly by using the internet and mobile telecommunications. Provision of payment systems has been an important function of FinTech in developing countries. FinTech has helped in developing enlarged domestic and cross-border payment systems. This has been very important for both developed and developing countries. For example, it facilitates huge transactions in markets such as foreign exchange, where the daily turnover is $5.4 trillion. Mobile money, which uses mobile telecommunications, has gained ground in several countries of Africa including Kenya, Uganda, Tanzania, and Ghana.

It is not surprising that Asia is leading in this respect, considering the giant leap that has been made with FinTech firms in China, particularly Alibaba (Ahmad et al., 2020; Statista Indices Database, 2017). Africa takes the second position with established mobile money systems in many countries, particularly in Kenya, Tanzania, Uganda, and Ghana (Ahmad et al., 2020). Europe and Latin America are fourth and fifth, respectively, after North America. The Middle East is the region that is lagging in mobile payments.

Data Security and Monetisation
Digitalisation of a financial system exposes it to cyber-attack vulnerability. FinTech, by using big data, can improve the security of the system. Data science techniques are often applied to detect fraud in financial transactions. Fraud detection is typically based on rules, which are used in flagging up fraud in a transaction that is set manually. Big data and analytics techniques as well as previous online fraudulent transactions can be used to flag up or predict fraud in transactions in the future, and data science and machine learning techniques can be used to do this. Business organisations are using innovative ways to manage their data

to generate value. This way of managing data by business firms, which involves identification and marketing data as well as data-based products to produce monetary value, is referred to as data monetisation. FinTech has revolutionised the financial industry in this regard and consequently, data products, such as products based on raw, processed, or analysed data are monetised (Kulhánek, 2019).

Consumer Interface

FinTech is changing the nature of customer interface in the financial industry, where branch networks are declining, particularly in developed countries such as the UK, and interactions via technology have increasingly been used instead. Mobile money in developing countries, particularly in Africa, has made it possible for customers including SMEs to conduct transactions using phones irrespective of whether they are in rural or urban areas.

Role of FinTech in the Provision of Banking and Financial Services

Mobile Money

Mobile money entails using mobile phone networks to carry out financial transactions, where customers' funds are kept by mobile network operators (MNOs). The funds may have originally been bought as airtime or deposited directly into the mobile wallet of the customer for future transactions. The unique feature of mobile money is that customers execute financial transactions directly through the MNOs, and the customers are not required to keep an account with a financial institution. Mobile money generally comes under the regulation of company law as well as the telecommunications regulatory body (Ahmad et al., 2020; Aker & Mbiti, 2010). However, mobile money is gradually coming under the remit of financial regulators in some countries. Mobile money enhances security by minimising the transportation of physical cash and increasing transparency through digital accounting, thus reducing corruption. It provides an entry point into the formal financial system, and as a result, helps in promoting enhanced savings and self-insurance against small adverse shocks (Ahmad et al., 2020; Demirgüç-Kunt et al., 2018).

Mobile money is the most dominant type of FinTech in the financial sector in Africa, and is regarded as the most successful innovation in promoting inclusive finance in the developing world, particularly in Africa. The growth in mobile money usage is promoted by intensifying mobile phones' penetration and their application in rural communities especially. It helps to circumvent the cumbersome bureaucratic processes of bank account opening. The success and general spread of mobile money among the unbanked and underserved is attributed to advances in mobile phone functionality, chip and mobile network technologies, and Point-of-Sale (POS) infrastructure upgrades. These developments have resulted in an improvement in the environment for mobile money solutions and have led to different players within the industry, as mobile money operators and banks collaborate to set up mobile money businesses. The availability of mobile money POS infrastructure and its peer-to-peer (P2P) payments capabilities that allow for the payment of utility bills, transport (Uber and taxi) fares, the purchase of airtime and internet bundles, and money transfer to friends and family have all boosted mobile money adoption rates (GSMA, 2013; Masha, 2016; Quartey, 2020).

Mobile Money in Africa

Mobile money has indeed emerged as the most popular type of FinTech in Africa, transforming the provision of financial services in the region. With the low level of financial development in the region, mobile money signifies an innovative means of attaining financial inclusion and the broader objective of inclusive growth and development. The continent of Africa is regarded as a trailblazer in mobile money adoption and usage, with East Africa setting the pace in the area. In 2019, the number of globally registered mobile money accounts was 1.04 billion, with SSA representing 469 million accounts (about 45%). Surpassing a billion is a remarkable achievement, particularly for an industry that is just over a decade old. The one billion milestone signals the significant role that mobile technology is playing in unlocking access to financial services for the majority of people (GSMA, 2019).

SSA is the epicentre of mobile money, and its expansion in the region indicates no sign of slowing down (GSMA, 2017), providing over 50 million additional registered accounts in 2019 alone (GSMA, 2019). South Africa was the first to issue mobile money licenses in 2004, but the success story is that of M-Pesa in Kenya (Box 5.1 provides further details on M-Pesa). M-Pesa is a mobile money product, which was launched in 2007 by Safaricom in Kenya and Vodacom in Tanzania. These are the two largest MNOs in the respective countries. Both companies are partly owned by Vodafone, UK. M-Pesa services spread quickly in Kenya and by 2015, Kenya had 80,330 M-Pesa agents (retail outlets), and 123,700 mobile money agents, in comparison to about 1,400 bank branches and 2,700 ATMs (Aron, 2018). By the close of 2016, there were about 30 million M-Pesa users globally, of which 20.7 million were in Kenya. Mobile money services quickly expanded to other countries including Tanzania, Ghana, Lesotho, Mozambique, DRC, Egypt, and South Africa and were also found in Albania, Romania, and India. In December 2008, Orange Côte d'Ivoire introduced Orange Money in Côte d'Ivoire, and by 2012, its services had expanded to Senegal, Madagascar, Mali, Niger, Kenya, Botswana, Cameroon, Mauritius, and Jordan. As at 2010, MTN had also launched MTN Mobile Money in Ghana, Côte d'Ivoire, Guinea-Bissau, Benin, Uganda, Rwanda, and Cameroon.

In 2017, 20.9% of the adult population in SSA was reported as having mobile money accounts in relation to the global percentage of 4.4%, according to the World Bank's Findex Database. The percentage of adults with mobile money accounts in 2014 was also higher (11.6%) for SSA compared with the rest of the world, which was 2.1%. SSA is ahead of the other regions in terms of mobile money accounts per 1,000 adults, mobile money outlets per 1,000 adults, and mobile money transactions. In respect of mobile money transactions as a percentage of GDP, SSA records the highest percentage (about 20%) compared to 7% in Middle East and North Africa and less than 6% in the other regions of the world.

Mobile money services were initially focused mainly on person-to-person transactions such as sending and receiving remittances, paying utility bills, receiving wages, paying school fees, as well as paying for general goods and services. However, in recent times, mobile money services have been extended to international remittances, credit, savings, insurance, and trading in securities on the money and capital markets. By June 2016, mobile credit in Kenya, M-Shwari (*shwari* is a Swahili word that means smoothen or make something better or good), had 15 million accounts, while that of Tanzania, M-Pawa (*pawa* denotes the English word power), had recorded 5 million accounts. MTN Ghana and Ecobank launched the Ecobank TBill4All, a mobile money Treasury bill product in 2016. Box 5.1 provides details on this. In June 2017, the Kenyan government introduced the M-Akiba (M for mobile and *Akiba* means savings in Swahili), the first government bond issued through a mobile platform. The bond was targeted at small investors who have mobile money accounts.

Box 5.1: Mobile Money Treasury Bill Product in Ghana
Ecobank Capital Advisors Limited, which is a wholly owned subsidiary of Ecobank, and MTN Mobile Money launched the Ecobank *TBill4All*, with the object of boosting inclusive finance and investment in the country. The Ecobank *TBill4All* is designed as a self-service product that enables Ghanaians to invest in 91-day and 182-day Treasury bills with the use of the MTN mobile money platform. Being the first of its kind in SSA, it is aimed at encouraging the culture of savings and investments as well as ensuring inclusive finance. It allows holders of MTN mobile money wallets to invest amounts from as modest as GHS 5 in Treasury bills as many times as they want. Investors also have the option of discounting their investment any time before maturity.

Source: https://www.ghanabusinessnews.com/2016/10/01/ecobank-launches-mobile-money-treasury-bill-product/

Mobile Banking Services

Mobile banking includes using mobile technology in accessing banking services. It is facilitated by banks and other financial institutions, enabling customers to utilise banking services. It is essentially an extension of regular banking services delivered through mobile technology. The regulatory framework entails the use of the existing banking laws and regulations. The differences between mobile money and mobile banking are in respect of the main service-providers, the procedures for accessing the service, and the regulatory framework. However, the difference between the two is not always obvious. MNOs do not deliver banking services, but they make use of bank accounts to hold customers' funds. In other jurisdictions, banks can provide mobile services like those provided by MNOs. For instance, in Kenya, Safaricom, an MNO, offers M-Pesa, while other MNOs and banks provide competing mobile financial services. In the Kenyan case, under the existing regulatory regime, a formal partnership between the MNO and a bank is not a requirement. However, in other African countries like Uganda and Ghana, a formal partnership between MNO and a bank is required (Ahmad et al., 2020; Aron, 2018).

Crowdfunding Services

Crowdfunding is an internet-enabled method for firms or organisations to raise funds either in the form of investments or donations from various entities. This new method of raising finance emerged in the wake of the 2008 global financial crisis and was in response to the challenges start-ups encountered in raising finance. It entails a pool of individuals or institutions contributing small amounts to raise huge resources to finance some individuals or projects without the involvement of a financial institution using internet or online platforms (known as crowdfunding platforms). It began as an online extension of raising finance from family and friends, with communities pooling funds to support members who wish to start a business. During the early stages of crowdfunding, funds were raised in the form of donations, but over time, it has taken the form of debt or equity investments, focusing on entrepreneurs and micro, small and medium-sized enterprises (MSMEs) that have high growth potential.

The global crowdfunding has expanded rapidly since its inception and in less than a decade, has spread across developed markets, and it is currently also attracting huge interest among developing countries (World Bank, 2013). For instance, in 2012, the global market raised about US$2.7 billion using the various crowdfunding business models and platform types, made up of US$1.6 billion in North America, US$945 million in Europe and US$110 million in the rest of the world (Massolution, 2013). Since 2009, the US and Europe have experienced significant growth in the various types of crowdfunding platforms. Crowdfunding grew at a 63% compound annual growth rate (CAGR) between 2009 and 2012, across all regions. Equity-based platforms showed a CAGR of 114%, with lending-based platforms exhibiting a CAGR of 78%. Donation-based platforms had a CAGR of 43%, while that for reward-based ones was 524% (World Bank, 2013). In 2014, the global crowdfunding market raised US$16.2 billion, representing an increase of 167% over the amount for 2013. The market raised US$34.4 billion in 2015, an increase of 112.3% over the amount raised in 2014. North America leads the market with 50.1% of the global crowdfunding market, followed by Europe (18.8%) and the rest of the world (0.5%), including Oceania, South America, and Africa (Massolution, 2015).

Crowdfunding is made up of four main categories and these are donation-, reward-, debt-, and equity-based. Donation-based crowdfunding allows donors to contribute small amounts of money to support projects or people in need, without expecting a return. This type of crowdfunding is used mainly by the non-profit organisations to support different activities (such as social, environmental, political, other charitable projects, etc.). In reward-based crowdfunding, donors or funders make contributions towards a cause in exchange for a non-financial reward. Rewards usually take the form of tokens of appreciation, or the pre-purchasing of a product or service (the actual invention) based on the amount contributed. Debt-based crowdfunding (which is also referred to as lending-based crowdfunding) allows funders or lenders to grant individual or business loans with the expectation of getting back the principal amount plus a return. In equity-based crowdfunding, individuals and institutions invest in unlisted companies (issuers) in exchange for shares in those companies. It is more appropriate for financing MSMEs and start-ups (Jenik et al., 2017; Kirby & Worner, 2014).

Crowdfunding platforms are usually structured in a way that allows an entrepreneur to post a business pitch or campaign to a website. As part of the pitch, the entrepreneur typically states a target in terms of the amount of funds to be raised. The funders are usually members of the social network of the entrepreneur, but in many instances, they may be members of the public or institutional investors interested in supporting innovative small enterprises. Although much crowdfunding activity in SSA is donation-based, there has been substantial early activity regarding equity- and debt-based platforms in Ghana, Kenya, and South Africa. Some crowdfunding platforms in Africa also focus on promoting projects that are related to social causes. There has been growing interest in crowdfunding in the region, and this may be attributed to the high demand for capital, the increase in mobile technology penetration, the growing African middle class, and the role of Africans in the Diaspora. Crowdfunding offers great potential in terms of supporting entrepreneurs and MSMEs. However, there are challenges including regulatory issues that need serious consideration and addressing.

Crowdfunding Markets in Africa

Crowdfunding is considered a viable and scalable alternative source of raising finance for start-ups and MSMEs in Africa, but it is still at its budding stage. According to a report by Afrikstart in 2016, more than 75 crowdfunding platforms and prototypes have been launched in Africa since 2012, but many of them were shut down in 2014. As of 2015, 57 crowdfunding platforms were headquartered and operating across Africa, with South Africa having the highest number (21), followed by Nigeria with 9 and Egypt with 5. Figure 5.5 shows the number of crowdfunding platforms in African countries. The African crowdfunding market, in 2015, was made up of 21 donation-based crowdfunding platforms,

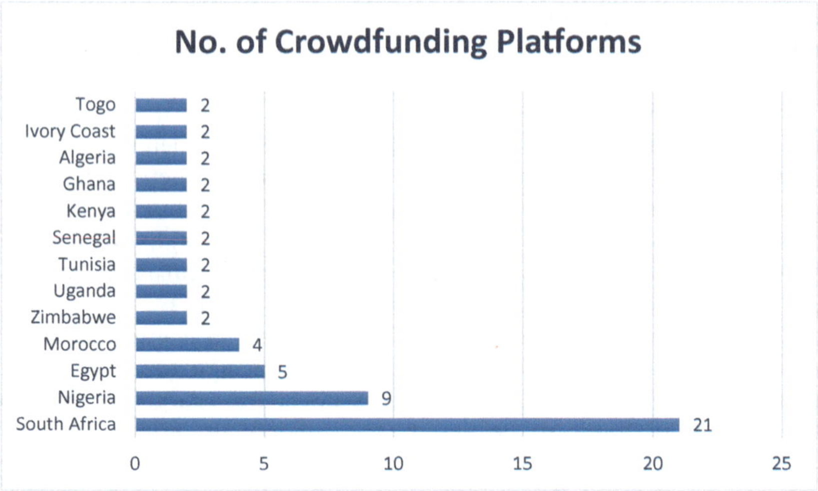

Fig. 5.5 Africa's crowdfunding platforms (*Source* Authors construction based on data from Afrikstart [2016], *Crowdfunding in Africa*)

19 equity-based platforms, 13 reward-based platforms, 2 peer-to-peer lending platforms, and 2 hybrid platforms. Donation-based and equity-based platforms are considered the fastest growing crowdfunding models, as funds raised in 2015 were mainly in the form of donations (37%), equity (33%), and reward-based (23%). Peer-to-peer lending and hybrid models played smaller roles.

It was estimated that in 2015, US$126.9 million was raised for crowdfunded projects through African-based platforms as well as international platforms financing African projects. Out of this figure, only US$32.3 million was raised on Africa-based platforms, with US$94.6 million raised on international platforms in the form of donations and loans. The estimated US$32.3 million raised from Africa-based crowdfunding platforms was used mainly to finance start-ups and small and medium enterprises (SMEs) (US$17.8 million), real estate crowd invested projects (US$13.6 million), travel crowdfunded trips (US$319,434), donation to charity projects and social causes (US$307,860). Figure 5.6 shows how the amounts raised are distributed across the various sectors. South Africa, as the leader in the crowdfunding market in Africa, raised US$30.8 million, and this was followed by Egyptian platforms, raising US$842,000; and

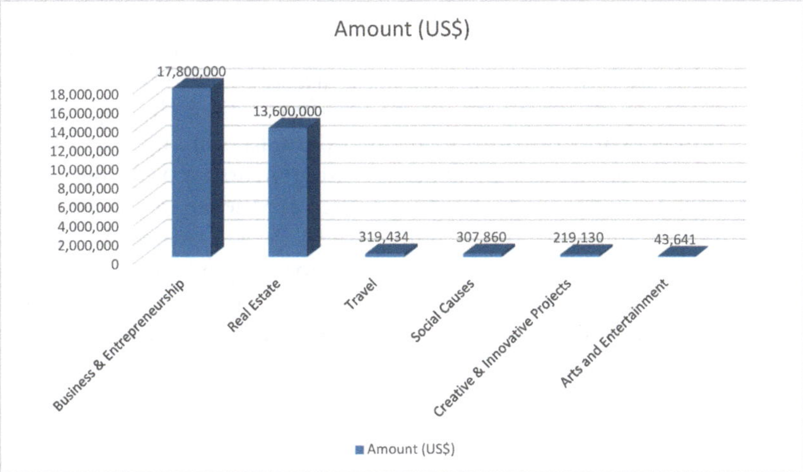

Fig. 5.6 Categories of top crowdfunding projects in 2015 (*Source* Authors construction based on data from Afrikstart [2016], *Crowdfunding in Africa*)

Nigerian platforms, raising US$314,445 in 2015. Crowdfunding platforms in Africa attempt to attract backers (sponsors) to support various projects. For instance, in 2015, a South-African real estate platform, Wealth Migrate, initiated the most funded project raising US$12,700,000 to acquire 4 medical buildings in the USA. RainFin, a South African peer-to-peer lending platform launched thousands of projects to offer loans to support small businesses and individuals. An equity-based crowdfunding platform, Malaik, also raised $250,000 for the Nigerian start-up, i-Drop (Afrikstart, 2016).

Crowdfunding appears to have gained some traction in Africa over the past decade, but it is still among the lowest performing compared with the rest of the world in terms of crowdfunding utilisation (World Bank, 2015). According to the World Bank (2015), the African crowdfunding market in 2015 amounted to about $70 million, representing less than 1% of the size of the global crowdfunding market and about 21% of emerging market activity. The overall crowdfunding market in Africa is projected at between $2.09 and $2.46 billion by 2025 (World Bank, 2013). The low utilisation of crowdfunding in Africa among entrepreneurs is attributable to factors such as unconducive regulatory regimes for debt- and equity-based crowdfunding and technological environments, where e-commerce is not widely utilised. The low internet penetration and low social media use as well as trust issues have been identified to limit the expansion of crowdfunding as an alternative financing option for start-ups and MSMEs in Africa. In spite of these challenges, entrepreneurs are utilising innovative strategies to address the challenges they experience in raising finance through crowdfunding (World Bank, 2015). It is a promising financial innovation with the potential of facilitating financing of entrepreneurs and MSMEs in Africa. It is an emerging alternative form of raising capital in Africa and therefore, most platforms attempt to gain a strong presence within their home country before expanding into other markets.

Cryptocurrency

Cryptocurrency is a digital currency, which is secured by cryptography that makes it difficult to counterfeit or double-spend. The term cryptocurrency was coined from the use of cryptography to improve the network's security (Gandal & Halaburda, 2016; Sovbetov, 2018). Many cryptocurrencies are decentralised networks based on distributed ledger technology (typically a blockchain technology), which serves as a public financial transaction database. A major feature of cryptocurrencies is that a central authority is typically not responsible for issuing them, therefore, they are theoretically exempt from government interference. Cryptocurrency is based on cryptography and peer-to-peer (P2P) online technology. It is generated by computer programmes, distributed, and circulated over the internet. Cryptocurrency investors can buy and sell through online trading platforms. Cryptocurrency can also be described as a virtual currency, since it can be used in exchange for fiat money such as dollars, pounds, and euros, and therefore can be used for carrying out business transactions. The first and most popular blockchain-based cryptocurrency is Bitcoin, which was launched in 2009. Currently, there are about a thousand different cryptocurrencies with several functions and specifications. Apart from Bitcoin, some of the popular cryptocurrencies include Ethereum, Ripple XRP, Bitcoin Cash, Litecoin, NEO, IOTA, Dash, Maker, Byteball Bytes, and Monero. According to a report by Coinmarketcap, in 2017 the most dominant cryptocurrencies in the digital currency market as depicted by their market capitalisation were Bitcoin, Ethereum, Ripple, Bitcoin Cash, and Litecoin. The most prominent of the five is Bitcoin, followed by Ethereum. Some of these cryptocurrencies are clones or forks of Bitcoin, while others are new currencies that were developed from scratch. As of November 2019, more than 18 million Bitcoins had been issued with a total market value of about $146 billion, greater than the GDP of many countries.

Cryptocurrencies are also used as financial securities such as shares. In this sense, they are used by blockchain start-ups to raise capital for projects or business ventures by issuing digital "tokens" or new cryptocurrencies to subscribers who invest using known cryptocurrencies such as Bitcoin or through the use of fiat money to receive voting rights or property rights in the project or business venture. Some start-ups have been able to raise capital through this method, which is typically difficult through the conventional initial public offering (IPO), owing to stringent regulatory requirements. By circumventing regulatory requirements associated with public offerings or other traditional sources of formal finance, start-ups can raise cheaper, easier, and quicker sources of finance for their business activities. Since 2017, blockchain start-ups have been able to raise more than US$ 1.5 billion through initial coin offerings (ICOs) (Salami, 2019).

Cryptocurrencies have the potential of driving inclusive finance. They can help in facilitating easier transfer of funds directly between two entities, without the involvement of a third party such as a bank, a credit card company, or a central authority. Entities that have limited access to the formal financial system are able to engage with other entities in financial transactions using cryptocurrencies. However, the semi-anonymous nature of cryptocurrency transactions makes them susceptible to a multiplicity of illegal activities, such as tax evasion, money laundering, and illicit financial flows. The use of cryptocurrencies raises regulatory concerns, which are more pronounced in Africa, as they can be used to engage in crime, like money laundering and terrorism financing (see Financial Action Task Force, 2015, 2018; Salami, 2018).

Cryptocurrency Markets in Africa

There has been an upsurge of innovation globally with respect to digital currencies and ICOs, following the launch of Bitcoin in 2009. Entrepreneurs have found ICOs to be a quick, unregulated means of raising fresh capital since many of these digital currencies are hosted on decentralised blockchain platforms operating the world over (Yermack, 2018). However, the cryptocurrency markets in Africa are said to be undeveloped. In a virtual currency attitude survey, with Africa representing 7.35% of the total countries surveyed, many countries have clearly stated that investment and trading in virtual currencies are illegal. Figure 5.7 shows an extract of African countries in the survey. The central banks in these countries have indicated that citizens' engagement in the cryptocurrency market is at their own personal risk. Yermack (2018) argues that crypto movement has essentially bypassed SSA to this point. For instance, only 0.3% of the worldwide Bitcoin nodes operate in Africa and almost all of them are in South Africa. Available data shows that the worldwide Bitcoin nodes are almost non-existent in Africa with virtually no Bitcoin ATMs installed in the region. South Africa seems to be assuming a more favourable attitude with respect to virtual currencies.

Despite the risks involved in the cryptocurrency market, some people are actively participating in it. Some African start-ups have been taking advantage of this by raising finance through ICOs. In Nigeria, the official position is that cryptocurrencies are illegal due to criminal activity and in

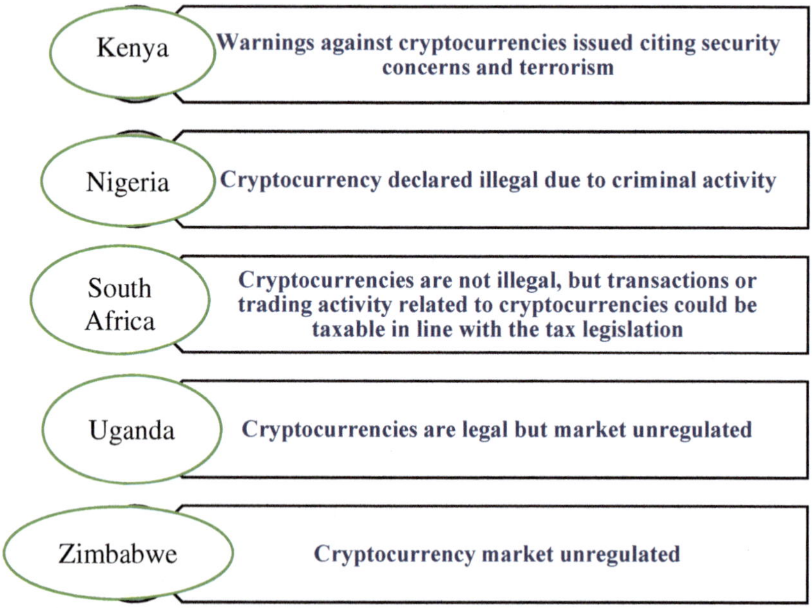

Fig. 5.7 Government position on cryptocurrencies by country (*Source* Authors construction based on data from *Thomson Reuters, 2017*)

2017, the government reviewed its position to place a ban on cryptocurrencies. The Central Bank of Nigeria (CBN) officially banned all financial institutions from participating in the cryptocurrency market. However, citizens could participate in the market at their own risk. For instance, in 2018, SureRemit, a Nigerian blockchain start-up, was able to raise US$7 million through ICO (Ayugi, 2018). The Central Bank of Kenya warned against financial institutions holding or trading in cryptocurrencies issued, citing security concerns and terrorism. There is, however, BitPesa, an exchange and payments platform that serves the East African market and beyond. Box 5.2 provides some details on BitPesa.

Box 5.2: BitPesa

BitPesa was founded in 2013 with its headquarters located in Nairobi, Kenya, and its offices and staff are in cities such as Lagos, London, Luxembourg, Dakar, and Madrid. BitPesa was the first blockchain company to be licensed by the UK's Financial Conduct Authority, and it provides wholesale cryptocurrency liquidity for persons and organisations all over Africa. It launched its beta site with a service in Kenya at the end of May 2012, allowing users to remit money to any mobile money wallet in the country. As of 31st December 2014, Kenyan customers were able to pay for bitcoins on the platform. In May 2015, it launched in Tanzania, permitting customers to remit Tanzanian Shillings to three different mobile networks in Tanzania. It also launched in Nigeria and Uganda in November 2015. By January 2017, BitPesa had closed a US$2.5 million Series A funding round and as at August 2017, it had raised US$10 million Series A funding, which was led by Greycroft Partners. BitPesa purchased TransferZero (an online money transfer company) in Spain in February 2018 and in March 2018, it also launched its services in Ghana.

Source: https://www.bitpesa.co/about/https://en.wikipedia.org/wiki/BitPesa

In Zimbabwe, the financial instability and hyperinflation the country went through in 2008 led to the heightened interest in the investment and trading in cryptocurrencies (Fioramonti, 2017). Bitcoin is said to have traded consistently at an estimated US$10,000 in Zimbabwe (Bianchetti et al., 2018), though, cryptocurrencies have been declared illegal and the central bank has warned against trading in them (Camilla, 2019; Lielacher, 2018; Odhiambo, 2017; Tassev, 2018).

South Africa's official position is that cryptocurrencies are not considered illegal, however, the market is unregulated and the South African Reserve Bank (i.e., the central bank of South Africa) is not responsible for the risks that citizens face with respect to trading in cryptocurrencies (South African Reserve Bank, 2014). However, transactions or trading activity in relation to cryptocurrencies could be taxable in line with the tax legislation. The absence of a regulatory framework on virtual currencies also affects digital tokens, since there are no regulatory requirements with respect to ICOs in South Africa (Timm, 2017). Despite the risks involved in investing and trading in virtual currencies, South African citizens still patronise the cryptocurrency market. Some blockchain-based start-ups such as ProsperiProp have taken advantage of the fact that the market is unregulated in South Africa and have opened the property market to international investors (Timm, 2017). South Africa has two major cryptocurrency exchange platforms: Luno and ice CUBED (Camilla, 2019; Timm, 2017). In April 2020, a group of South African financial regulators, the Intergovernmental FinTech Working Group (IFWG), issued a policy position paper that provides recommendations on developing a regulatory framework for crypto assets. These recommendations are in compliance with the standards set by the Financial Action Task Force (the global money laundering and terrorist financing watchdog). Figure 5.7 summarises the position of some African countries on cryptocurrencies.

5.3 Role of FinTech in Promoting Financial Inclusion

FinTech tends to affect the structure of financial systems by introducing new modes of delivery that lead to reduction in costs of providing financial services, creation of market access opportunities for new entrants (non-bank financial institutions), and broadening access to new segments of the market and customers; these modes can impact the competitiveness of existing financial providers. Such disruptions are likely to bring about enhanced efficiency in the financial sector. He et al. (2017) identified the technologies responsible for transforming financial services to include: mobile access and the internet; distributed ledger technology (DLT), a digital system used to record transactions in which details of the transactions are recorded in different computers at the same time rather than having a centralised database; big data and artificial intelligence (AI); and cryptography, involving the use of strong security systems to support electronic transactions undertaken safely, which is the foundation for smart contracts and cryptocurrencies.

The use of such new technologies in Africa can assist in reducing inefficiencies in the financial system and information costs, ensure transparency, increase trust, and facilitate contract enforcement (AFI, 2017; Amadou et al., 2019; GPFI, 2016b). Since Africa has a lower level of inclusive finance in comparison with other emerging and developing countries, FinTech provides opportunities to bridge the inclusion gap. FinTech facilities, such as mobile money, help in promoting inclusive finance, especially by assisting households to access financial services without a bank account (Donovan, 2012). The relatively huge mobile technology penetration (81 mobile phones per 100 inhabitants) provides new entrants with a unique opportunity, using mobile-based financial services to reach these new customers (Amadou et al., 2019).

The extant literature suggests that FinTech is significant in driving inclusive finance (see Ahmad et al., 2020; Demir et al., 2020; Ghosh, 2016; Gosavi, 2018; Jack & Suri, 2011; Tchamyou et al., 2019; Mbiti & Weil, 2016). Demir et al. (2020) indicate that their results, based on cross-country study, are in tandem with the findings of prior single-country studies that also showed a positive effect of FinTech on inclusive finance in Africa (see Gosavi, 2018; Mbiti & Weil, 2016). Other empirical studies also suggest that the extent of mobile phone penetration has a significant effect on financial inclusion across and within countries. Specifically, mobile money promotes financial inclusion (see Andrianaivo & Kpodar, 2012; Ghosh, 2016). Some studies found that households which have a mobile money account tend to be banked, send/receive remittances more often, and make more savings (see Jack & Suri, 2011; Morawczynski, 2009; Mbiti & Weil, 2016; Ouma et al., 2017). Also, mobile money has a positive effect on the financial inclusion of SMEs, through its effects on enhanced access to bank credit (see Gosavi, 2018). The findings of these studies imply that FinTech has great potential to extend the formal banking system's outreach in countries where a greater part of the population are financially excluded but have a mobile phone (Demir et al., 2020).

The African financial services sector is characterised by low competition (see Banya & Biekpe, 2017; Doku et al., 2012; Fosu, 2013) and a high level of inefficiency (see Bazot, 2018; Beck & Cull, 2013; Philippon, 2016). The low competition is mainly attributed to high entry barriers, while the level of inefficiency is partly a result of higher costs of operation. This feature of the financial system mostly results in high costs of financial services in Africa as compared to other regions of the world. Similarly, African financial systems are bank-based with relatively under-developed capital markets, contractual savings institutions (insurance and pensions), and other non-bank financial institutions. Financial literacy, although not directly under the scope of this chapter, also plays a role in the region's financial exclusion (Abor et al., 2018; Amidu et al., 2018). FinTech devices can be used in facilitating activities such as paying insurance premiums, receiving pension benefits, and investing in financial securities.

FinTech can also help in addressing the problem of asymmetric information and thereby enhance access to credit by MSMEs. The cost of credit risk assessment is still high in Africa. Poor accounting records and lack of credit bureaus are often cited as barriers to MSMEs' access to finance. Big data and machine learning for example can minimise the cost of credit assessments, especially in countries where credit registry is lacking. In this regard, information such as mobile phone usage and payment data can be obtained to assess credit risks probably at lower costs. Amadou et al. (2019) argue that obtaining such alternative information for assessing credit risks is likely to encourage new entrants, such as FinTech firms (peer-to-peer and other crowdfunding platforms) to provide credit.

The opportunities that FinTech offers go beyond mobile money to developing a complete digital financial ecosystem that responds to the needs of both individuals and MSMEs. This is really the next stage in the process of achieving a comprehensive inclusive finance, which is critical to digital economic development and wider financial sector development (AFI, 2018). The Alliance for Financial Inclusion (AFI) proposed a FinTech for inclusive finance framework based on four main pillars (see Box 5.3). They suggest that these four pillars, coupled with supporting infrastructure and an enabling policy and regulatory environment, should provide a basis for an emerging digital financial ecosystem and support economies to maximise the benefits of FinTech-induced financial inclusion, as well as balancing consumer protection, financial integrity, and financial stability.

Box 5.3: Pillars of Framework for FinTech-Induced Financial Inclusion

PILLAR I:
Digital ID and eKYC for Identification and Simplified Account Opening
PILLAR II:
Open Electronic Payment Systems, Infrastructure and an Enabling Regulatory and Policy Environment that Facilitate the Digital Flow of Funds from Both Traditional Financial Intermediaries and New Market Entrants
PILLAR III:
Account Opening Initiatives and Electronic Provision of Government Services, Providing Vital Tools to Access Services and Save
PILLAR IV:
Design of Digital Financial Market Infrastructure and Systems that, in turn, Support Value-Added Financial Services and Products and Deepen Access, Usage and Stability

5.4 FinTech and Africa's Financial Systems

Africa's financial systems are said to be relatively small, shallow, and costly, with limited outreach. This is reflected in the aggregate financial development indicators as well as household and firm data measuring the use of formal financial services (Beck & Cull, 2013). Looking at the indicators of financial development, apart from private sector credit, SSA exhibits the lowest rates in terms of both broad money and bank credit to the private sector compared with other developing regions of the world. With respect to financial inclusion, though the trend seems to suggest some improvement, financial inclusion is still very low compared with the rest of the world. For instance, the percentage of adults in SSA with accounts increased from 23.2% in 2011 to 34.2% in 2014 and subsequently to 42.6% in 2017, compared with the percentage of adults worldwide with accounts, which increased from 50.6% in 2011 to 62% in 2014 and later to 68.5% in 2017 (see Fig. 5.8).

Several factors have been identified to contribute to the low-level financial inclusion in SSA, which include inadequate supportive infrastructure, deterrent transaction costs, unfavourable regulatory regimes, low level of financial literacy, high poverty rates, and behavioural biases (Abor et al.,

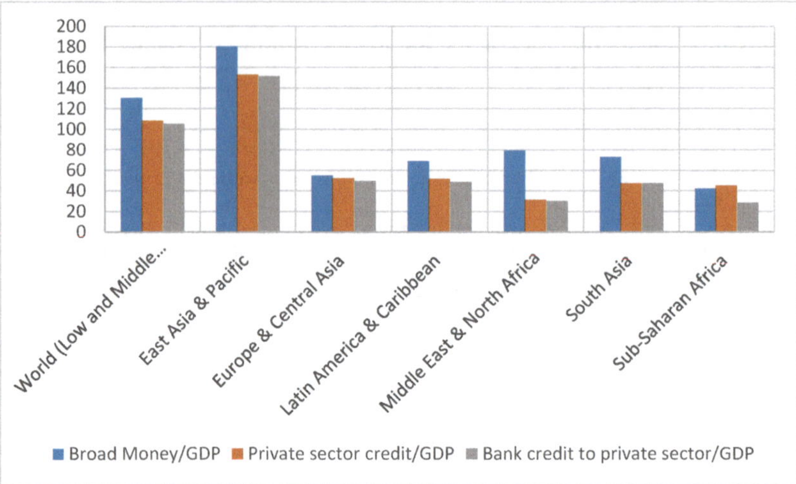

Fig. 5.8 Financial development indicators (*Source* Authors construction based on data from *Global Financial Development Indicators [2019]. *Latest Figures for Middle and North Africa and Private Sector credit/GDP for Sub-Saharan Africa are from 2018*)

2020). Figure 5.9 compares trends in financial inclusion between SSA and the global figures. SSA is lagging in almost all the indicators.

FinTech in Africa: A Comparative Analysis

It is evident from the foregoing that the financial gap in Africa provided a unique opportunity for FinTech in the continent, particularly in sub-Saharan Africa. According to the Global Findex Database 2017, about 70% of the world's adults have an account, but SSA is the laggard region. Africa shares with Asia and Pacific broad features of FinTech development, but its nature as well as its direction in the continent is rather different and mostly ahead in the latter region. This is aided by two factors: the inadequacy of the formal financial and banking system in the continent and the rise of the mobile telephone system (Ahmad et al., 2020; Allen et al., 2016).

A recent survey by Statista showed that personal finance has recorded the highest growth rate, but it is forecast that it will slow down from

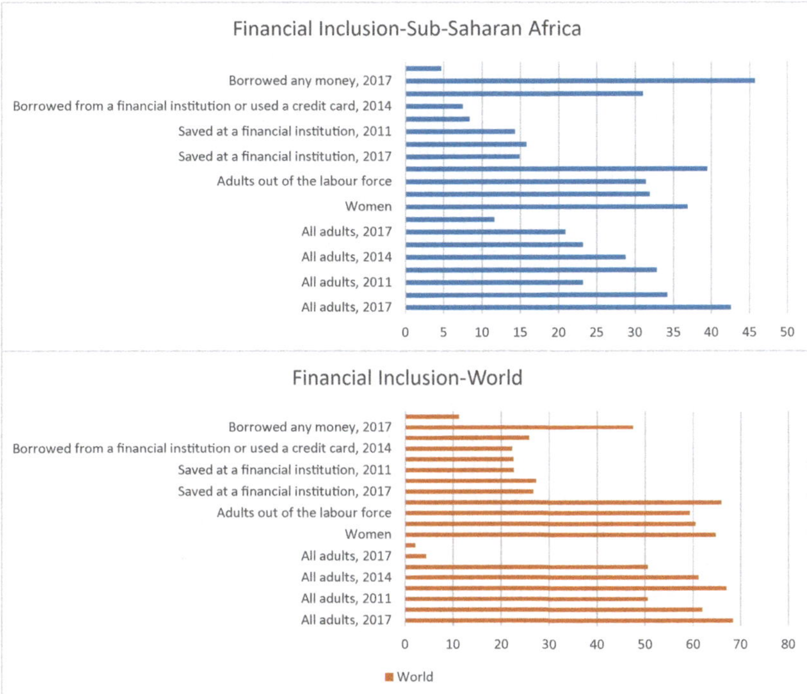

Fig. 5.9 Trends in financial inclusion (*Source* Authors construction based on data from Findex Database, 2014, 2017)

three digits to about 14% by 2023. However, it is still the highest rate. Alternative financing has also been enjoying a very good rate of growth, a double-digit for both 2018 and 2019. However, alternative financing is envisaged to slow down to about 4% by 2023.

According to a recent survey by Statista on the growth rates of crowdfunding and crowdinvesting in Africa for the period, 2017–2019 and projections for 2020–2023 which also reports the growth rates of these transactions and comparison with other parts of the world, crowdinvesting is behind crowdfunding for 2017–2021. However, it is forecast that crowdinvestment will supersede crowdfunding by 2022. It is, therefore, clear that growth projections and forecasts for alternative finance and other crowdsourcing instruments in Africa are very promising.

However, the market experiences the key challenge of controlling fraud. Crowdfunding is only valuable and beneficial to markets if there is trust between borrowers and investors. This means that regulation is essential to obtaining such trust, by instituting binding rules and guidelines. Financial regulation tends to be very complex and slows down the dynamic of an evolving market.

The role social capital plays in crowdfunding has been highlighted in the literature. Particularly, Zheng et al. (2014) found that entrepreneurial social capital that includes social networks has a significant effect on crowdfunding performance in China and the US. A similar conclusion was also reached by Mollick (2014), who used a dataset of 48,500 projects in the US with a total funding of $237 million.

A Statista report on alternative financing using FinTech Asia showed that Africa is far behind and can learn from Asia about exploiting this alternative financing. FinTech is an important alternative source of lending for both businesses and individual consumers in Asia. This shows the leadership of the region not only on the overall adoption of FinTech but also for using FinTech as a source of alternative lending. This requires a further look into the main FinTech market drivers in Africa and other regions. In Africa, the figures for crowdlending for businesses were $278 million in 2017, which rose to $417 million by 2019.

The Statista report also showed the drivers of FinTech markets in the world and in Africa and indicate that the young population, aged 0–14 years, has the highest rate of FinTech adoption in the world, followed by 15–24 and 25–34 years. The group that has the lowest rate is 45–55 years. It is surprising that the older generation, 55 years and above has a higher FinTech adoption rate than the middle-aged group. The pattern is similar for Africa but with a lower magnitude in terms of numbers.

Foodstuffs, beverages, etc. and housing expenditure accounted for most of the consumers' spending for all the periods. Global internet penetration that stood at about 50% in 2017 has increased to 57% by 2019. However, in contrast to the global figures, FinTech drivers in Africa indicate much lower figures for internet penetration in the region. It was 29% in 2017 and marginally increased to 38% in 2019. Broadband subscriptions are generally low in all the tables. As the figures reported are for subscriptions, it is not clear to what extent availability of the broadband affects this low figure. However, smartphone penetration is much higher in all the regions and the world, albeit the figures for Africa are much lower than the rest of the world.

It can be surmised that the established drivers of FinTech in the literature are the changing role of information technology, changing consumer behaviour, changing financial ecosystem and changing regulatory regimes. This is consistent with the literature (for example, see Alt et al., 2015; Kang et al., 2016; Puschmann, 2017). All these seem to be rife in Africa, which suggests that the future of FinTech in the region is bright. However, as noted above, challenges that include fraud, enforcement of the rule of law as well as regulatory issues that are highlighted below are threats to innovation in the continent, which need to be tackled.

5.5 Constraints and Challenges to FinTech Adoption in Africa

From the foregoing, FinTech has made good strides in Africa, especially in the area of mobile finance. This is because of its ability to enhance the delivery of banking and financial services and offer opportunities for promoting inclusive finance in SSA. However, several challenges and constraints have been identified as hindering the growth of the FinTech industry. We discuss some of these challenges.

A major challenge in the FinTech industry is lack of adequate infrastructure. Electricity, telecom, and internet infrastructure are key enablers required to develop the FinTech industry to promote digital financial inclusion. However, in many African countries, the lack of such infrastructure tends to severely limit adoption of new technologies in the financial services sectors. With respect to electricity, Africa seems to be lagging in comparison to the world, with an average of 43% access rate to electricity which is about half of the global access rate of 87%. Also, SSA has about two-thirds of the world's population with electricity access. Internet connectivity is very fundamental to using mobile banking, crowdfunding platforms, and digital currencies, but Africa has the lowest internet penetration, and this adversely impacts the development of these types of FinTech. According to Internet World Stats (2020), as of the first quarter of 2020, the internet penetration rate in Africa stood at 39.3%, compared with the global average of 58.8% and the rest of the world which is 62.9%. Also, Africans represent only 11.5% of total world internet users. Provision of infrastructure was found to be one of the core factors responsible for mobile money success in Kenya and other African countries (Ahmad et al., 2019).

Interoperability between network providers is another barrier to mobile money market development although some countries like Ghana and Kenya have enabled such services. With the rapid growth in mobile money services and the number of active users, the limitations with respect to usage have become even more pronounced. The "closed loop" model does not address the needs of customers any longer. Users now want to be able to send money to more people across different networks and pay for a wider variety of services through their own mobile network or another. The issue of interoperability has been identified by the GSMA as crucial to the development of mobile financial services. Mobile money interoperability is the service that enables direct and seamless transfer of funds from a mobile money wallet to another across different networks. Some mobile money providers in the region are currently putting interoperability initiatives in place in order to enable international remittances. Interoperability minimises the cost of carrying out transactions across different networks since customers will no longer require the services of a third-party payment provider to initiate such transactions across different networks. This allows customers more convenience and security.

Another challenge is the issue of cultural and socio-economic differences in the region. Although Africa is seen as one continent, it is made up of very diverse cultures and socio-economic characteristics. A FinTech firm flourishing in one country is not guaranteed similar success in another, considering that there may be peculiar domestic issues that may inhibit a firm's expansion into that new market. A typical example is the failure of M-Pesa in South Africa. Following its huge success in East Africa, Vodacom in 2010 launched M-Pesa in South Africa, a country with a highly banked population. South Africa has over 80% of its population already having access to traditional banking services. Vodacom lost its competitive advantage in South Africa because it targeted a population that appears to be satisfied with conventional banking services. The size of the market of the financially excluded is also small, thus limiting the volume of transactions. Consequently, in 2016, Vodacom scrapped M-Pesa in South Africa.

The legal environment is another major problem in many African countries. There is the need for effective regulation if the FinTech space is to fulfil its potential of providing access to financial services to many Africans who are financially excluded. The regulatory environment has an important role to play in ensuring that the FinTech ecosystem thrives to promote inclusive finance, and that financial consumers have protection. Though some attempts are being made, there is an urgent need for regulators to do more to speed up the development of the sector. African regulators are generally not as proactive as those in more developed markets. The legal and regulatory responses to innovations and developments in the FinTech industry are often delayed. Also, the existing regulatory frameworks in many African countries are mostly not fit for purpose and not well coordinated.

Similarly, activities in the FinTech industry present a number of challenges for banking supervision. Central banks in Africa tend to have difficulty effectively monitoring micro loans provided by mobile money providers, considering that these micro credits are not captured in the central banks' credit register. This gives rise to increased fraud and cybercrime activities (Makina, 2019). Also, recent FinTech, such as cryptocurrencies and related new financial services, are associated with money laundering and terrorism financing. It creates the atmosphere for criminals and terrorists to launder the proceeds from illegal activities or finance illicit activities (see Financial Action Task Force, 2015, 2018). African central banks often adopt a "wait and see" attitude towards regulation and supervision, so they tend to delay in their response to the developments in the FinTech space, thus undermining the effective supervision of digital financial services and by extension, the entire banking and financial services sector.

Human capital is also important for the success of FinTech. African policymakers along with the regional universities require a well-thought-out programme that can address this, as it will have implications not only for the financial sector but also for the wider macroeconomic performance of the countries, such as employment, productivity, and inequality (Sy et al., 2019; Yemack, 2018).

COVID-19 Pandemic and FinTech Development in Africa

The advent of the COVID-19 pandemic has implications for the development of FinTech in Africa. The use of FinTech offers an attractive choice in accessing financial services in times of pandemics, given the restrictions to movement and social distancing protocols, the risk of infection due to the handling of physical cash, etc. (Arner et al., 2020). FinTech, by providing digital financial access and services, could lessen the social and economic impacts of the COVID-19 pandemic. It will expand access to financial services to individuals and MSMEs, which can play a very important role in economic recovery and boost a more inclusive participation.

The FinTech marketplace, generally, offers providers of financial services more flexibility in order to speedily develop new products and services or modify or upscale existing ones to respond to the crisis (Fuster et al., 2019). A recent study shows that the outbreak and spread of the COVID-19 pandemic and related lockdowns that governments imposed have led to a surge in digital finance and FinTech adoption (Fu & Mishra, 2020). In Africa, the improved FinTech adoption should support in extending financial services and help in driving financial inclusion. This should make it necessary for policymakers to take into consideration the need to invest in infrastructure to provide support for FinTech and also enhance the regulatory regime for FinTech such as mobile money payment systems, crowdfunding, and cryptocurrencies (Abor, 2020).

However, these possibilities may not be realised if the pandemic accentuates the financial exclusion gap that already exists. Also worth noting is the fact that FinTech firms are more vulnerable than conventional financial service providers. Deposit insurance schemes for mobile money users have not yet been adopted in most of the countries, which leaves the depositors vulnerable to any failures of the mobile money providers. This can result in loss of confidence in the system which can affect the whole financial system.

5.6 Concerns and Regulatory Issues of FinTech in Africa

FinTech, just like any new financial, technological, and legal reality, is inherently disruptive for any legal system. Most of the time, it does not easily fit into the existing regulatory framework, and regulatory bodies are challenged to provide the right legal response. The appropriateness and timeliness of such legal response have implications for the sustainability of the FinTech innovation as well as its potential to positively contribute to social change and drive financial inclusion. However, oftentimes, there are delays in providing appropriate legal responses to FinTech innovation, and sometimes the legal response is incomprehensible and inconsistent. Providing a specific legal or regulatory framework for FinTech is very challenging for regulators globally, with countries adopting varying approaches. In the case of SSA, FinTech such as mobile money has contributed immensely to enhancing inclusive finance by reducing the proportion of the unbanked population. In as much as it offers opportunities for promoting financial inclusion in SSA, the region experiences low numbers of successful FinTech firms. Also, new technologies are not evenly adopted (Didenko, 2017).

Regulatory concerns have been expressed regarding operations of FinTech. For example, Alibaba's separation of Ant Financial from its core business was meant to ring-fence the former from risks that can emanate from the latter's other brands: AliPay and Yu'e Bao. This raises the question of the extent to which activities of these firms signal arbitrage opportunities and deficiencies in the current regulatory system. This led to a call for RegTech (Zetzsche et al., 2018). Rapidly growing use of technology in finance is exerting pressure on regulatory institutions to migrate from regulations designed for human behaviour to regulations to supervise automated processes. RegTech is an amalgam of "regulatory" and "technology", and refers to the use of technology in regulation, monitoring, reporting, and compliance. When the financial crisis of 2008 challenged the hitherto assumption of a positive relationship between innovations and benefits in financial industry, regulators reacted by tightening regulatory regimes, and the industry has responded to the regulations, which is evident in the rise in their expenditure with respect to regulation compliance. A report by Fintech Poland reviewed compliance expenses in US banks in relation to the banks' expenses. They found that the amount spent by the banks jumped from less than $35 billion in 2006 to almost $55 billion by 2010.

Some cynics have even gone to the extent of doubting the benefits of innovations in financial industry such as FinTech. Paul Volker, former Chairman of the US Federal Reserve (1979–1987), made the following statement in respect of innovations in the financial industry:

> The most important financial innovation that I have seen in the past 20 years is the ATM (automatic teller machine), that really helps people and prevents visits to the bank, and it is a real convenience.

Therefore, FinTech regulation (RegTech) should be given the proper priorities to ensure that the innovations do not lead to a crisis but to both systemic and overall benefit to economies. There are overlapping authorities with regard to FinTech regulations. For example, mobile money services are provided by mobile telecommunications whose traditional regulatory domain was with commercial laws, but mobile money is supposed to be regulated by the monetary authorities. One way of dealing with such a problem is to disentangle the services, and regulatory arrangements should be based on the kind of services provided. This is similar to what pertains in the UK where financial services provided by traditional non-financial services sectors are still under the oversight of the financial conduct authority.

FinTech activities could present problems for monetary and financial policies as special regulatory instruments may be needed to regulate them, since the conventional regulatory regimes may be inadequate.

The existence and enforcement of property rights also play a crucial role in maintaining a thriving environment for all innovations, but are more important in FinTech. Roma et al. (2017) found that the performance of crowdfunding, among others, depends on obtaining patents in addition to social ties. The literature on FinTech indicates that trust plays an important role in the performance of some FinTech activities, particularly in crowdfunding (Mollick, 2014; Zheng, et al., 2014). Related to this is the issue of optimum regulatory regime, that is, to use an instrument that can strike a balance between maintaining stability and allowing the existence of incentives for innovations. This is particularly important, as regulatory difference has been found to be a key factor in aiding development of FinTech, and lack of risk appetite could also hamper bifacial innovations (Buchak et al., 2018; Zilgalvis, 2014).

There is evidence to suggest a clear difference in the uptake of FinTech services in common law compared to civil law countries in SSA. Common law countries generally tend to have higher FinTech adoption rates compared with civil law countries in SSA. A common law legal system can play an important role in spurring growth (Yermack, 2018). This is supported by the position of Burns (2016) regarding the trend over time for developing countries to emphasise bottom-up, market-driven economic development strategies as opposed to top-down, state-ownership-driven ones. An important achievement of common law systems is the provision of the legal environment for well-functioning markets, which is an essential prerequisite for bottom-up economic development strategies to work effectively. Rather little is known about the optimal type of regulation for promoting FinTech business, and how such regulation might interact with the existing legal regime. SSA countries to a large extent have adopted a hands-off or laid-back approach to regulating FinTech (Yermack, 2018).

Yermack (2018) explains that, generally, FinTech regulation focuses on three general areas: tax collection, financial consumer protection, and financial stability. Another area has to do with compliance with regulations on anti-money laundering, a unique challenge for developing countries like those in SSA that receive international remittances or crowdfunding donations from foreign FinTech platforms. Regulation of FinTech firms is really a challenge even in developed markets, because most of the time, the main motivation for technological innovation is to circumvent or avoid existing regulations. For example, public blockchains can mostly exist in virtual spaces with no physical link whatsoever to countries in which the users live. Therefore, regulators attempting to collect taxes or impose sanctions may not be able to do this directly apart from the blockchain promoters ensuring voluntary compliance.

Obviously, FinTech is an aspect of the financial services sector, and it is an area that has traditionally drawn the attention of regulators and is mostly linked with comprehensive regulatory oversight. Regulators the world over are gradually developing new approaches to regulate FinTech. Didenko (2017) identifies four reasons that justify the need to establish FinTech regulation:

- Threats posed by FinTech to market participants
- Easy access to financial services by unsophisticated customers who may need additional protection
- Rapid developments of FinTech-enabled financial services
- Decentralisation, disintermediation, and anonymisation of financial services delivery, forcing regulatory institutions to develop different ways of exercising control and oversight.

It has been argued that the opportunities FinTech offers provide ample justification for ending certain banking practices in the brick-and-mortar environment, and this has necessitated a completely new regulatory approach to banking. A basic revamp of financial regulation is required to restore a functioning financial system in the digital age. If regulators fail to progress to the digital age, the financial system will remain dysfunctional (McMillan, 2015).

Different approaches have been adopted by different jurisdictions in their regulatory response to FinTech innovation. In some cases, regulatory measures for FinTech are restricted to refining the prevailing law in terms of how it is applied within the context of new technologies, such as including new definitions like “digital or virtual currencies”, clarifying the legal standing of the new concepts (e.g., explaining whether Bitcoin is a currency, a new type of money, a commodity, or something completely different) or ascertaining which regulators are mandated to address the FinTech innovation. In some instances, FinTech regulation tends to become more intrusive. For instance, issues with a FinTech firm may prompt the tightening of the existing rules. In most situations, measures of regulation targeted at FinTech firms do not assume the character of a standalone “FinTech law” or “FinTech statute”. Rather, regulators generally attempt to fine-tune the prevailing legal regime to address the uniqueness of FinTech. This normally will involve dealing with FinTech on a product-by-product basis. In some other instances, regulations focus on FinTech more generally. An example is the notion of a FinTech “sandbox”, a safe supervised environment that is created by regulators to enable innovative firms to try their new products before they are fully implemented. These sandboxes tend to target different firms and are generally not restricted to any product. As a result, underlying sandbox rules tend to be encompassing enough to involve most FinTech firms (Didenko, 2017).

There are four important questions that need careful consideration in shaping a regulatory approach for FinTech. Didenko (2017) suggests that regulators’ clear appreciation and informed legal response to these vital questions help in simplifying and streamlining the process of rulemaking, putting it in perspective and creating a more systematic approach. These questions include:

i. *What is the Overall Objective of FinTech Regulation?*: Regulating FinTech activities can be structured in different ways, depending on the objectives that the regulatory body is pursuing. One objective may be for the regulatory system to perform a prudential function, concentrate on systemic risks and threats to the economy as a whole, and protect financial consumers. Another objective is for the regulation to promote FinTech, either by removing entry barriers or by instituting a preferential system for FinTech firms. In this case, if the objective is to promote FinTech, regulators tend to act as facilitators, and they develop different methods, such as regulatory sandboxes, to facilitate the development of the FinTech industry. As a result, FinTech promotion may be motivated by the need to intensify market competition and the aspiration to realise higher levels of inclusive finance. The two objectives may be conflicting, which will require a policy decision regarding which is the principal objective of regulating FinTech. This decision will be determined by several factors, including the goals of macroeconomic policy, comprising the level of inclusive finance. It is likely that in economies that have a huge unbanked population, the opportunity to make available financial services to those who are financially excluded would outweigh the risks of fraud and the need to protect financial consumers.

ii. *Regulate Now or "Wait and See"*?: In some countries, regulators adopt the cautious approach of "wait and see" to FinTech regulation. Other countries also adopt the forward-looking approach. Whereas both approaches may be beneficial, it is important for regulators to always weigh the expected benefits against the potential risks and costs, following the adoption of the new technologies.

iii. *Which FinTech Areas Require Priority in Terms of Regulatory Attention*?: Two critical factors mostly influence the decision of the regulator regarding where to focus: systemic risks and urgent economic and social issues. Depending on the country involved, some FinTech activities may relate to higher systemic risks, necessitating more intense regulation. Also, some technologies may provide solutions to dealing with certain critical problems in that country, such as enhancing the level of inclusive finance in countries that have higher proportions of unbanked population. A typical example is the case of M-Pesa in Kenya.

iv. *Are the Main Challenges Internal (Domestic) or External (International)*?: Though national regulators' mandates include ensuring the stability of the domestic financial system, FinTech is capable of going beyond a country's borders, considering its nature. For instance, some FinTech firms may want to expand to other countries, especially when there is low demand in the domestic market. Also, the issue of how the operations of foreign FinTech firms affect the domestic financial system raises regulatory concerns.

FinTech activities are receiving much attention from regulators across the globe, and in SSA, regulation of FinTech is extremely crucial because of its potential to spur inclusive finance. In SSA countries, even the FinTech leaders—South Africa and Kenya, do not have a comprehensive legal framework, specifically for FinTech, and they handle several issues as and when they occur. For instance, in 2020 IFWG issued a policy position paper with recommendations on how to regulate crypto assets. By handling issues as and when they occur, SSA countries are unable to keep up with the fast-paced developments in FinTech, but may from time to time issue risk warnings to customers regarding the use of certain types of FinTech (as observed in the virtual currency attitude survey on governments' official position on the use of cryptocurrencies).

Developments in the FinTech ecosystem in Africa also have important implications for the region, which require a coordinated regional approach to ensure effective regulation of these new technologies. According to Salami (2019), a coordinated regional regulatory framework can be achieved against the background of prevailing regional economic communities, as stipulated in the African Union (AU) and the African Economic Community agenda of achieving monetary union for the entire continent by 2028. She suggests that achieving an effective regional regulatory framework for the African member states will require the following:

i. Strengthening prevailing regional cooperation on mobile financial services among African member states
ii. Developing regional standards tailor-made to the point of mobile payment and financial service development of African regional economic communities
iii. Establishing a regional regulatory framework for crowdfunding
iv. Preparing for a robust regional regulatory regime for cryptocurrencies
v. Ensuring strong domestic financial regulation and financial regulatory authorities
vi. Fostering effective coordination among national supervisors
vii. Strengthening the general legal environment, which should form the basis for robust financial and payment systems regime in the continent.

5.7 Conclusion and the Way Forward

FinTech is transforming financial services delivery. It is believed that huge potential gains can be derived from FinTech, and this has heightened the interest in its adoption, as it can improve access and introduction of new services, and thereby enhance efficiency. This chapter examined the importance of FinTech in the provision of banking and other financial services and how it would promote financial inclusion in Africa. The main types of FinTech discussed in this paper include mobile money, mobile banking, crowdfunding, and blockchain technology and cryptocurrencies. The most popular type of FinTech is mobile money, and this is said to play a very significant role in promoting banking and financial services. The African continent is seen as a leader in mobile money adoption and usage, with East Africa being the leading region.

FinTech has the potential to disrupt the financial services sector by introducing new technologies that are associated with a reduction of the costs of providing banking and financial services, the creation of market access opportunities for new entrants (non-bank financial institutions), broadening access to new parts of the market and customers, and impacting the competitiveness of existing financial providers. It also plays a very important role by facilitating inclusive finance in Africa. FinTech, in the form of mobile money, has become known as an innovative means of achieving inclusive finance in Africa, considering the low level of financial development in the region. It is reaching the unbanked population and those who are financially excluded. Mobile money-induced financial inclusion can improve MSMEs' access to financing. Mobile money can facilitate the conduct of effective monetary policy in the sense that it improves inclusive finance. It can also support fiscal development by ensuring the efficient collection of taxes.

For FinTech to achieve its full potential of promoting banking and financial services as well as facilitating improved financial inclusion in Africa, several challenges need to be addressed. Promoting the other types of FinTech—crowdfunding and cryptocurrencies and blockchain technology in Africa will require heavy investment in electricity and internet infrastructure. The issue of interoperability will better position operators to provide new services to customers at reduced costs. Interoperability has the benefit of promoting international remittances. There is also the need to strengthen the existing regulatory framework for FinTech to promote inclusive finance, while protecting financial consumers. Strengthening regulation will mean taking a coordinated and proactive approach to regulatory response to innovation in FinTech. Finally, developing FinTech, given the opportunities provided by COVID-19, is very critical, not only for the poor but also for private sector development.

References

Abor, J. Y. (2020). *Exploring the impact of COVID-19 pandemic on Africa's FinTech space* (Working Paper Series No. 7/2020, Centre for Global Finance, SOAS University of London). https://www.centreforglobalfinance.org/2020-working-papers

Abor, J. Y., Issahaku, H., Amidu, M., & Murinde, V. (2020). Financial inclusion and economic growth. In J. Y. Abor, C. K. D. Adjasi & R. Lensink (Eds.), *Contemporary issues in development finance* (p. 263).

Abor, J. Y., Amidu, M., & Issahaku, H. (2018). Mobile telephony, financial inclusion and inclusive growth. *Journal of African Business, 19*(3), 430–453.

AFI. (2017, July). Defining financial inclusion. *afi-global.org*. https://www.afi-global.org/sites/default/files/publications/2017-07/FIS_GN_28_AW_digital.pdf

AFI. (2018, September 4). FinTech for financial inclusion: A framework for digital financial transformation. *afi-global.org*. https://www.afi-global.org/publications/fintech-for-financial-inclusion-a-framework-for-digital-financial-transformation/

Afrikstart. (2016, September). Crowdfunding in Africa. *afrikstart.com*. http://afrikstart.com/report/wp-content/uploads/2016/09/Afrikstart-Crowdfunding-In-Africa-Report.pdf

Ahmad, A. H., Green, C., & Jiang, F. (2020). Mobile money, financial inclusion and development: A review with reference to African experience. *Journal of Economic Surveys, 34*(4), 753–792.

Ahmad, E., Dowling, D., Chan, D., Colenbrander, S., & Godfrey, N. (2019, April). Scaling up investment for sustainable urban infrastructure: A guide to national and subnational reform. *Report, global commission on the economy and climate*.

Aker, J. C., & Mbiti, I. M. (2010). Mobile phones and economic development in Africa. *Journal of Economic Perspectives, 24*(3), 207–232.

Allen, F., Demirguc-Kunt, A., Klapper, L., & Peria, M. S. M. (2016). The foundations of financial inclusion: Understanding ownership and use of formal accounts. *Journal of Financial Intermediation, 27*, 1–30.

Alt, R., Eckert, C., & Puschmann, T. (2015). Network management and service systems: The case of German and Swiss Banks. *Information Resources Management Journal (IRMJ), 28*(1), 38–56.

Amadou N., Maino, R, Massara, A., Perez Saiz, H., & Sharma, P. (2019). *FinTech in sub-Saharan African countries: A game changer?* International Monetary Fund.

Amidu, M., Abor, J. Y., & Issahaku, H. (2018). *Inclusive finance, financial literacy and livelihood activities of households in Ghana.* Centre for Global Finance.

Andrianaivo, M., & Kpodar, K. (2012). Mobile phones, financial inclusion, and growth. *Review of Economics and Institutions, 3*(2), 30.

Arner, D. W., Zetzsche, D. A., Buckley, R. P., & Barberis, J. N. (2017). FinTech and RegTech: Enabling innovation while preserving financial stability. *Georgetown Journal of International Affairs*, 47–58.

Arner, D. W., Barberis, J., & Buckley, R. P. (2015). The evolution of Fintech: A new post-crisis paradigm. *Georgetown Journal of International Law, 47*, 1271.

Arner, D. W., Barberis, J. N., Walker, J., Buckley, R. P., Dahdal, A. M., & Zetzsche, D. A. (2020). *Digital finance & the COVID-19 crisis* (University of Hong Kong Faculty of Law Research Paper 2020/017).

Aron, J. (2018). Mobile money and the economy: A review of the evidence. *The World Bank Research Observer, 33*(2), 135–188.

Ayugi, W. (2018, February 16) Nigerian blockchain startup SureRemit raises $7 million in biggest African ICO to date. *BitcoinAfrica.io.* https://bitcoinafrica.io/2018/02/16/sureremit-ico/

Banya, R. M., & Biekpe, N. (2017). Bank competition and economic growth: Empirical evidence from selected frontier African countries. *Journal of Economic Studies, 44*(2), 245–265.

Bazot, G. (2018). Financial consumption and the cost of finance: Measuring financial efficiency in Europe (1950–2007). *Journal of the European Economic Association, 16*(1), 123–160.

Beck, T., & Cull. R. (2013). *Banking in Africa* (World Bank Policy Research Working Paper 6684).

Bianchetti, M., Ricci, C., & Scaringi, M. (2018). Are cryptocurrencies real financial bubbles. *Evidence from quantitative analyses. Evidence from quantitative analyses (February 24, 2018). A version of this paper was published in Risk* 26.

Buchak, G., Matvos, G., Piskorski, T., & Seru, A. (2018). Fintech, regulatory arbitrage, and the rise of shadow banks. *Journal of Financial Economics, 130*(3), 453–483.

Burns, S. (2016). *Finance for all: The success of the market-led approach to financial development in the developing world* (AIER Sound Money Project Working Paper Forthcoming.

Camilla, N. (2019). Decentralised monetary systems *Available at SSRN 3498841.*

Chen, J. (2016). The rise and development of internet finance in China: A study on the operation model of Alipay. 전자무역연구 *14*(4), 57–74.

Coinmarketcap. *Cryptocurrency market capitalizations*. https://coinmarketcap.com. Accessed December 2, 2019.

Demir, A., Pesqué-Cela, V., Altunbas, Y., & Murinde, V. (2020) Fintech, financial inclusion and income inequality: A quantile regression approach. *The European Journal of Finance*, 1–22.

Demirgüç-Kunt, A., & Levine, R. (2018). *Finance and growth*. Edward Elgar Publishing Limited.

Demirguc-Kunt, A., Klapper, L., Singer, D., Ansar, S., & Hess, J. (2018). *The Global Findex Database 2017: Measuring financial inclusion and the Fintech revolution*. The World Bank.

Demirgüç-Kunt, A., Honohan, P., & Beck, T. (2008). *Finance for all?: Policies and pitfalls in expanding access*. The World Bank.

Didenko, A. (2017). Regulating FinTech: Lessons from Africa. *San Diego International Law Journal, 19*, 311.

Doku, J. N., Abor, J., Adjasi, C. K. D., & Andoh, C. (2012). Assessing competitive behaviour in emerging banking market: African evidence. In *Finance and development in Africa*. Emerald Group Publishing Limited.

Donovan, K. (2012). Mobile money for financial inclusion. *Information and Communications for Development, 61*(1), 61–73.

Financial Action Task Force. (2018, October 19). Regulation of virtual assets. *fatf-gafi.org*. https://www.fatf-gafi.org/publications/fatfrecommendations/documents/regulation-virtual-assets.html

Financial Action Task Force. (2015, June). Virtual currencies: Guidance for a risk-based approach. *fatf-gafi.org*. https://www.fatf-gafi.org/media/fatf/documents/reports/Guidance-RBA-Virtual-Currencies.pdf

Financial Stability Board. (2017, June 27). Financial stability implications from FinTech: Supervisory and regulatory issues that merit authorities' attention. *fsb.org*. https://www.fsb.org/wp-content/uploads/R270617.pdf

Fioramonti, L. (2017). *Well-being economy*. Pan Macmillan.

Fosu, S. (2013). Banking competition in Africa: Subregional comparative studies. *Emerging Markets Review, 15*, 233–254.

Frost, J. (2020). The economic forces driving Fintech adoption across countries. In *The technological revolution in financial services: How banks, FinTechs, and customers win together* (p. 70).

Fu, J., & Mishra, M. (2020). *The global impact of COVID-19 on Fintech adoption* (Swiss Finance Institute Research Paper 20-38).

Fuster, A., Plosser, M., Schnabl, P., & Vickery, J. (2019). The role of technology in mortgage lending. *The Review of Financial Studies, 32*(5), 1854–1899.

Gai, K., Qiu, M., & Sun, X. (2018). A survey on FinTech. *Journal of Network and Computer Applications, 103*, 262–273.

Gandal, N., & Halaburda, H. (2016). Can we predict the winner in a market with network effects? Competition in cryptocurrency market. *Games, 7*(3), 16.

Ghosh, S. (2016). Does mobile telephony spur growth? Evidence from Indian states. *Telecommunications Policy, 40*(10–11), 1020–1031.

Gosavi, A. (2018). Can mobile money help firms mitigate the problem of access to finance in Eastern sub-Saharan Africa? *Journal of African Business, 19*(3), 343–360.

GPFI. (2016a, July 24). G20 high-level principles for digital financial inclusion. *gpfi.org*. https://www.gpfi.org/sites/gpfi/files/documents/G20%20High%20Level%20Principles%20for%20Digital%20Financial%20Inclusion%20-%20Full%20version-.pdf

GPFI. (2016b, September 4). Progress report to the G20 leaders. *gpfi.org*. https://www.gpfi.org/sites/gpfi/files/documents/GPFI%202016b%20Progress%20Report%20to%20G20%20Leaders.pdf

GSMA. (2013, December). The mobile economy 2013. *gsma.com*. https://www.gsma.com/newsroom/wp-content/uploads/2013/12/GSMA-Mobile-Economy-2013.pdf

GSMA. (2017). State of the industry report on mobile money. https://www.gsma.com/mobilefordevelopment/wpcontent/uploads/2018/05/GSMA_2017_State_of_the_Industry_Report_on_Mobile_Money_Full_Report.pdf

GSMA. (2018, May). State of the industry report on mobile money. *gsma.com*. https://www.gsma.com/mobilefordevelopment/wpcontent/uploads/2018/05/GSMA_2017State_of_the_Industry_Report_on_Mobile_Money_Full_Report.pdf

GSMA. (2019). State of the industry report on mobile money. https://www.gsma.com/sotir/wp-content/uploads/2020/03/GSMA-State-of-the-Industry-Report-on-Mobile-Money-2019-Full-Report.pdf

GSMA. (2020, March). State of the industry report on mobile money. *gsma.com*. https://www.gsma.com/sotir/wp-content/uploads/2020/03/GSMA-State-of-the-Industry-Report-on-Mobile-Money-2019-Full-Report.pdf

He, Dong., Leckow, R. B., Haksar, V., Griffoli, T. M., Jenkinson, N., Kashima, M., Khiaonarong, T., Rochon, C., & Tourpe, H. (2017). *Fintech and financial services: Initial considerations* (IMF Staff Discussion Note SDN/17/05).

IFWG. (2020, April 14). Position paper on Cryto assets regulatory working group. *treasury.gov.za*. http://www.treasury.gov.za/comm_media/press/2020/20200414%20IFWG%20Position%20Paper%20on%20Crypto%20Assets.pdf

Jack, W., & Suri, T. (2011). *Mobile money: The economics of M-PESA* (No. w16721. National Bureau of Economic Research).

Jenik, I., Lyman, T., & Nava, A. (2017). *Crowdfunding and financial inclusion* (CGAP [Consultative Group to Assist the Poor] Working Paper 41).

Kang, M. S., Back, S. J., & Lim, J. I. (2016). A study of self-checklist for personal information protection of FinTech service: For the simple payment service. *Journal of Society for e-Business Studies, 20*(4).

Kirby, E., & Worner, S. (2014). *Crowd-funding: An infant industry growing fast* (IOSCO Research Department).

Kulhánek, O. (2019). *The five rules of data monetization*. KPMG. https://home.kpmg/xx/en/home/insights/2019/04/the-five-rules-of-data-monetization.html

Lee, I., & Shin, Y. J. (2018). Fintech: Ecosystem, business models, investment decisions, and challenges. *Business Horizons, 61*(1), 35–46.

Lielacher, A. (2018, April 17). Zimbabwean cryptocurrency exchange Golix expands to South Africa. *BitcoinAfrica.io*. https://bitcoinafrica.io/2018/04/17/zimbabwean-cryptocurrency-exchange-golix-expands-to-south-africa/

Makina, D. (2019). The potential of FinTech in enabling financial inclusion. In *Extending financial inclusion in Africa* (pp. 299–318). Academic Press.

Manyika, J., Lund, S., Singer, M., White, O., Berry, C. (2016). Digital finance for all: Powering inclusive growth in emerging economies. *McKinsey Global Institute*, 1–15.

Masha, I. (2016). Macroeconomic impact of mobile payment services—A survey of research evidence. In *International Growth Centre/London School of Economics Regional Workshop, Freetown, Sierra Leone*.

Massolution. (2013). 2013CF crowdfunding industry report. *compromisoempresarial.com*. https://www.compromisoempresarial.com/wp-content/uploads/137356857-Massolution-2013CF-Excerpt-Revised-04182.pdf

Massolution. (2015, March 31). *Crowdfunding industry 2015 report. crowdexpert.com*. http://crowdexpert.com/crowdfunding-industry-statistics/

Mbiti, I., & Weil, D. N. (2016). *7. Mobile banking: The impact of M-Pesa in Kenya*. University of Chicago Press.

McMillan, J. (2015, January 20). Banking in the digital age: The failure of financial regulation. *theguardian.com*. https://www.theguardian.com/sustainable-business/2015/jan/20/finance-in-digital-age-while-regulation-stuck-in-industrial

Mollick, E. (2014). The dynamics of crowdfunding: An exploratory study. *Journal of Business Venturing, 29*(1), 1–16.

Morawczynski, O. (2009). Exploring the usage and impact of "transformational" mobile financial services: The case of M-PESA in Kenya. *Journal of Eastern African Studies, 3*(3), 509–525.

Morse, A. (2015). Peer-to-peer crowdfunding: Information and the potential for disruption in consumer lending. *Annual Review of Financial Economics, 7*, 463–482.

Nanziri, E. L. (2017). *Financial inclusion and welfare in post-apartheid South Africa*. African Economic Research Consortium.

Odhiambo, R. (2017, December 1). Reserve Bank of Zimbabwe considers Bitcoin illegal but no regulation has been issued. *BitcoinAfrica.io*. https://bitcoinafrica.io/2017/12/01/reserve-bank-of-zimbabwe-considers-bitcoin-illegal/

Ouma, S. A., Odongo, T. M., & Were, M. (2017). Mobile financial services and financial inclusion: Is it a boon for savings mobilization? *Review of Development Finance, 7*(1), 29–35.

Philippon, T. (2016). *The Fintech opportunity*. No. w22476. National Bureau of Economic Research.

Puschmann, T. (2017). Fintech. *Business & Information Systems Engineering, 59*(1), 69–76.

Roma, P., Petruzzelli, A. M., & Perrone, G. (2017). From the crowd to the market: The role of reward-based crowdfunding performance in attracting professional investors. *Research Policy, 46*(9), 1606–1628.

Salami, I. (2018, April 23). Cryptocurrencies—Cross-border financial regulatory dimensions. *The European Financial Review*. https://www.europeanfinancialreview.com/cryptocurrencies-cross-border-financial-regulatory-dimensions/

Salami, I. (2019). Alternative financing approaches and regulation in Africa. In *Extending financial inclusion in Africa* (pp. 279–297). Academic Press.

Skan, J., Dickerson, J., & Gagliardi, L. (2016, January 15). Fintech and the evolving landscape: Landing points for the industry. *Accenture*. https://www.accenture.com/t20160427T053810__w__/us-en/_acnmedia/PDF-15/Accenture-Fintech-Evolving-Landscape.pdf.

South African Reserve Bank. (2014). *Position paper on virtual currencies* (Position Paper Number 02).

Sovbetov, Y. (2018). Factors influencing cryptocurrency prices: Evidence from bitcoin, ethereum, dash, litcoin, and monero. *Journal of Economics and Financial Analysis, 2*(2), 1–27.

Statista Indices Database. (2017). https://www.statista.com/markets/?kw=statista&crmtag=adwords&gclid=CjwKCAjw2rmWBhB4EiwAiJ0mtSPSLSt8mRQooJ9QAeytsOFKhWM-Cx7gN2jZmABGDrvAvTk-HK7wIxoCifcQAvD_BwE

Sy, A. N., Maino, R., Massara, A., Saiz, H. P., & Sharma, P. (2019). *FinTech in sub-Saharan African countries: A game changer?* International Monetary Fund.

Tassev, L. (2018, June 5). Zimbabwe's Golix exchange enters Kenya, Uganda, South Africa. *Bitcoin.com*. https://news.bitcoin.com/zimbabwes-golix-exchange-enters-kenya-uganda-south-africa/

Tchamyou, V. S., Erreygers, G., & Cassimon, D. (2019). Inequality, ICT and financial access in Africa. *Technological Forecasting and Social Change, 139*, 169–184.

Timm, S. (2017, August 29). SA's ProsperiProp plans to run two ICOs to get around crowdfunding challenge. *Ventureburn*. https://ventureburn.com/2017/08/sas-prosperiprop-plans-run-two-icos-get-around-crowdfunding-challenge/

Quartey, P. (2020). Financial sector landscape in Ghana: Background Paper, Global Finance Programme.

World Bank. (2013, October 24). Crowdfunding's potential for the developing world. *infodev.org*. https://www.infodev.org/crowdfunding

World Bank. (2015, January 1). Crowdfunding in emerging markets: lessons from East African startups. *worldbank.org*. https://documents.worldbank.org/en/publication/documents-reports/documentdetail/820101468186856874

World Bank. (2018, April). *The Global Findex Database 2017*. https://globalfindex.worldbank.org/

Yermack, D. (2018). *FinTech in sub-Saharan Africa: What has worked well, and what hasn't* (No. w25007. National Bureau of Economic Research).

Zetzsche, D. A., Buckley, R. P., Arner, D. W., & Barberis, J. N. (2018). From Fintech to Techfin: Challenges of data driven finance. *Journal of Law & Business, 14*(2), 393–446.

Zheng, H., Li, D., Wu, J., & Xu, Y. (2014). The role of multidimensional social capital in crowdfunding: A comparative study in China and US. *Information & Management, 51*(4), 488–496.

Zilgalvis, P. (2014). The need for an innovation principle in regulatory impact assessment: The case of finance and innovation in Europe. *Policy & Internet, 6*(4), 377–392.

PART III

Central Bank and Monetary Policy

CHAPTER 6

Central Bank Independence, Exchange Rate Regime, Monetary Policy and Inflation in Africa

Abel M. Agoba, Vera Fiador, Emmanuel Sarpong-Kumankoma, and Jarjisu Sa-Aadu

6.1 Introduction

One of the pressing challenges for many African governments, has been the management of price stability. With inflation in countries such as Zimbabwe and Sudan soaring in the recent past to about 319 and 212%, respectively, it is unequivocal that attaining price stability has been a tall order on the continent (IMF, 2019). Relative to other world regions, headline inflation is considerably more volatile in sub-Saharan Africa, given high share of food in the consumer price index (CPI) and more

A. M. Agoba
School of Economics Finance and Accounting, Coventry University, Coventry, United Kingdom

V. Fiador (✉)
University of Ghana Business School, Accra, Ghana
e-mail: vfiador@ug.edu.gh

J. Y. Abor and C. K. D. Adjasi (eds.), *The Economics of Banking and Finance in Africa*, Palgrave Macmillan Studies in Banking and Financial Institutions, https://doi.org/10.1007/978-3-031-04162-4_6

volatile relative food prices—largely due to unstable agricultural production (Nguyen et al., 2017). However, two classes of anchors (nominal and monetary), have generally helped achieve price stability (Frankel & Catão, 2011; Bouoiyour & Selmi, 2013). One is through some level of commitment to a unilateral currency peg. The other highlights delegation of authority to an independent and sufficiently conservative central bank (with or without explicit targeting of inflation).

Some recent works (Abubakar & Ibrahim, 2018; Guellil et al., 2017) have suggested that developing countries which peg their exchange rates achieve lower inflation than those with floating exchange rates (Ghosh, 2002). For countries in the Communauté Financière Africaine (CFA) Franc Zone, there has been a characteristic economic stability, greatly associated with fixed exchange rates and low inflation particularly when compared to their Anglophone counterparts such as Ghana, Liberia and Nigeria. CFA Franc Zone comprises a group of countries in Central and West Africa whose currencies have been linked to the French franc. Strong (2018) asserts that joining the CFA Zone can generate potential economic gains for countries seeking membership by fostering growth and providing price stability. However, in terms of economic growth, non-CFA Zone economies have performed better. This brings to fore the debate on the superiority of the fixed exchange rate regime in terms of its contribution to economic performance (Lohi, 2014).

Other enquiries have focused on the impact of central bank independence (CBI) on inflation performance (Cukierman, 1992). This has gained momentum in Africa since the early 1990s when focus was on improving inflation performance as a precondition for the single currency that the Economic Community of West African States (ECOWAS) and other unions sought to roll out. Ideally, CBI promotes monetary policy effectiveness, as the central bank oversees the determination of the appropriate monetary policy rate and policy tool to achieve a desired price

E. Sarpong-Kumankoma
Department of Finance, University of Ghana Business School, Accra, Ghana
e-mail: ksarpong@ug.edu.gh

J. Sa-Aadu
Tippie College of Business, University of Iowa, Iowa City, IA, USA
e-mail: jsa-aadu@uiowa.edu

level, which is its primary objective (Aguir, 2018). Also, political pressure on the central bank to finance government spending which could be a threat to monetary policy achieving the targeted price level is minimised (Agoba et al., 2019). According to Barro and Gordon (1983), independent central banks promote credible monetary policy as they have no incentives to cheat by reversing announced decisions. The transparency of the central bank appears as the necessary and sufficient condition of its credibility. Monetary policy, if it is to be effective, is based on the sequence of credibility-commitment-transparency-reactivity.

We build on the work of Lohi (2014), who examined the impact of exchange rate regimes on inflation and output growth in Africa. Their paper failing to deal with endogeneity and reverse causality issues could have implications for the findings. We also include several control variables such as fiscal balance, institutional quality, trade openness and central bank independence to minimise the case of omission variable bias. Thirdly, while monetary policy is best identified as a central bank decision, the impact of central bank autonomy, as the final authority in monetary policy decision making, has not been investigated as a possible factor in determining the effectiveness of monetary policy on inflation outcomes globally. However, we maintain that independent central banks are better able to ensure the effectiveness of a monetary policy decision. For example, they can curtail central bank lending that would potentially counter the desired impact of a policy rate on money demand and supply (Agoba et al., 2019; Agoba et al., 2020). They would also ensure that monetary policy decisions are based on sound and objective economic analysis in spite of governments' possible desire to boost economic activities that would increase their chances of winning elections at the expense of price stability (Agoba et al., 2019). Moreover, independent central banks properly regulate financial markets, thereby leading to financial deepening (Agoba et al., 2020). In such a situation, monetary policy is more effective as the transmission mechanism is enhanced in more developed financial markets. As such, monetary policy relies on a clear understanding by financial market participants of central bank actions, both current and likely future (the expectations channel). This is less likely to emerge under dependent central banks. The combination of money target misses, noisy short-term interest rates and incipient communications make it difficult to assess policymakers' intentions. The corollary is that we should expect a strengthening in the monetary transmission as the policy framework becomes clearer with an independent central bank (Adam et al., 2018).

However, it has also been argued that the exchange rate regime within which a central bank operates could stifle the effectiveness of its monetary policy which poses a challenge to achieving price stability (Bouoiyourl & Selmi, 2013). Frankel and Catão (2011) and Copelovitch and Singer (2007) noted that CBI has a more intense influence on lowering inflation under a floating exchange rate system that has a more developed banking sector. Guisinger and Singer (2010), however, argue that monetary authorities' attempt to maintain price stability by adopting a fixed exchange rate system, serves as a signal of government's lower inflation level. This shows some level of inconclusiveness on which exchange rate regime is optimal for effective CBI.

In this study, we firstly, investigate CBI and pegged exchange rate regimes as drivers of inflation in Africa. Specifically, we analyze the link between CBI and the choice of exchange rate regime and inflation performance. We argue that CBI restraints political business cycles. Fixed exchange rate regime also imposes constraints on domestic policy actions. The consequences of these are a disciplined and credible monetary policy framework. This has benefits for price stability. A flexible exchange rate regime, on the other hand, affords freedom of actions and monetary growth which is much more accommodative of inflation. But as to whether CBI is more effective in fixed or floating exchange rate regimes, this study empirically establishes. We utilise the most up-to-date and widest covering data on CBI from Garriga (2016) and Bodea and Hicks (2015b), which capture both *de jure* and de facto CBI measures. Secondly, we examine the effect of exchange rate regimes on inflation in Africa. Currently, economic theory and empirical evidence provide conflicting predictions about this relationship. Hence, our study aims to aid an understanding of this relationship in an African context. The analysis is based on de facto exchange rate classification which is considered to be a better indicator for exchange rate policy. We go beyond previous studies on Africa (e.g., Agoba et al., 2017) in also examining the conditional effects of CBI on inflation given fixed exchange rate regimes with focus on CFA and non-CFA Zones using both *de jure* and de facto CBI measures, unlike previous studies. Intuitively, this study sets to offer new perspectives on the determinants of inflation outcomes. More precisely, we focus on whether the link between inflation dynamics and CBI (e.g., Bodea, 2010) depends intensely on the choice of exchange rate regime and whether the independence of the central bank provides any explanation for monetary policy effectiveness in Africa. Hence, the main purpose here is to verify empirically if better inflation outcomes may be achieved by countries setting up independent central banks and pegged exchange rate regimes and if CBI's and monetary policy effectiveness are conditional on the choice of exchange rate regime and CBI, respectively (e.g., Copelovitch & Singer, 2007).

The remainder of this study proceeds as follows: Sect. 6.2 presents a brief overview of inflation, CBI, monetary policy and exchange rate regimes in Africa. Section 6.3 examines relevant literature on the relationships between and among CBI, exchange rate regimes, monetary policy and inflation while in Sect. 6.4, we describe the datasets and the methodology adopted. Section 6.5 presents and discusses our findings while Sect. 6.6 concludes.

6.2 Overview of Central Bank Independence, Monetary Policy, Exchange Rate Regime and Inflation in Africa

Central Bank Independence

We discuss the number of central bank reforms that have taken place across the globe since the 1970s through 2014. These reforms focus on the extent to which the central bank is made independent from political control.

In Table 6.1, fifty-two (52) countries, had at least one (1) CBI reform between 1970 and 2014. In forty-eight (48) countries, there were at least

Table 6.1 Frequency of CBI reforms by country from 1970 to 2014

Total reforms per country	*Frequency (countries)*	*%*	*Cumulative*
0	14	7.69	7.69
1	52	28.57	36.26
2	48	26.37	62.64
3	43	23.63	86.26
4	21	11.54	97.80
5	3	1.65	99.45
6	1	0.55	100.00

Source Garriga (2016)

two (2) CBI reforms, forty-three (43) countries had at least three (3) CBI reforms, twenty-one (21) countries had at least four (4) CBI reforms, three (3) countries had at least five (5) CBI reforms and one (1) country had at least six (6) CBI reforms within the period. In all, most of the countries in the sample had two (2) and more CBI reforms within the study period. Though there may not be much time variation in the CBI index, there exists significant variations in CBI among countries.

In Fig. 6.1, we observe that out of the 350 CBI reforms that occurred between 1970 and 2014, 116 were in Africa, 242 in developing countries and 108 in developed countries. This means that globally, most CBI reforms have taken place in developing countries. Among developing countries also, a significant portion (48%) of CBI reforms occurred in Africa.

There has been a general increase in CBI in the world as recorded by Garriga (2016) and Bodea and Hicks (2015a) (see Fig. 6.2).

The trend has been an increase in CBI index from 0.35 in 1970 to about 0.68 in 2012 (using the Garriga recoded data). This means that per the charter of most central banks, between 1970 and 2014, they have been made more independent. According to De Haan et al. (2018), 71% of CBI reforms have resulted in increases in CBI.

As seen in Fig. 6.3, average CBI has increased across Africa, other developing countries and developed countries. However, as at 2012, developed countries had higher levels of de jure CBI compared to Africa and other developing countries.

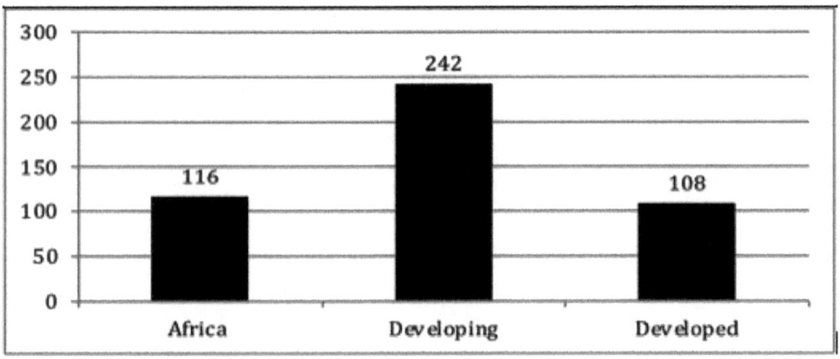

Fig. 6.1 Number of CBI reforms from 1970–2014 (*Source* Author's own computation based on Garriga [2016])

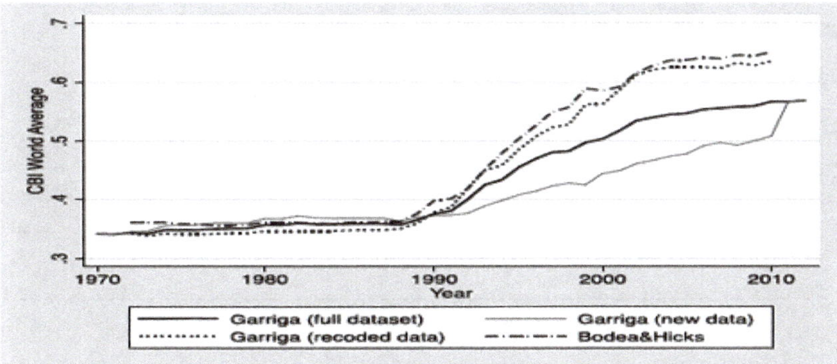

Fig. 6.2 CBI world average for different datasets 1970–2014 (*Source* Garriga [2016])

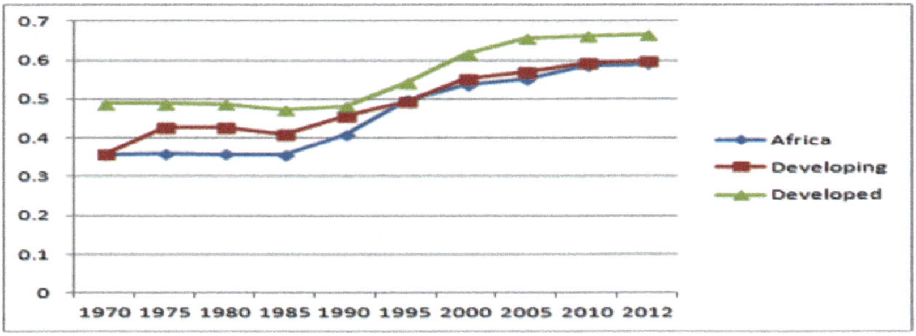

Fig. 6.3 Averages of CBI in Africa, other developing and developed countries (*Source* Garriga [2016])

Inflation

Inflation in Africa

As seen in Fig. 6.4, Africa has had higher average inflation compared to developed and other developing countries since 1970. From about 4.7% in 1970, inflation rose significantly within 5 years to 17.6%. Thereafter, the region experienced a declining inflation rate, though still higher compared to developed countries. Within the period, however, Africa had lower inflation compared to other developing countries. This continued up until 1996 when it went up to a record 27%, the highest compared to

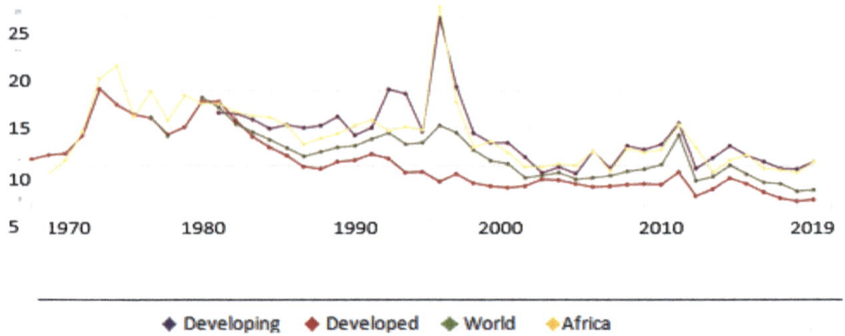

Fig. 6.4 Inflation rate from 1970–2019 (*Source* World Development Indicators [2019])

developed and other developing countries and world averages. However, since then, the average inflation rate for Africa has declined to about 7% in 1998, 8% in 2000 and 5% in 2004. It increased marginally from 2005 to 2010 to about 10.2%. The lowest average inflation for the region in the past 40 years was recorded in 2012 which was about 4.8%. As at 2017, the region's average inflation rate was about 7%.

As of 2019, average inflation rate in emerging markets and developing economies was 4.8% while that of Africa was 11.7%. Headline inflation slowed across the region in 2019 amid stable exchange rates, and amid slowing food price inflation due to higher food production (World Development Indicators, 2019).

Inflation, Monetary Policy and Exchange Rate Regimes

According to an IMF 2018 report on Monetary policy in Africa, in about half of SSA countries, a hard peg provides a nominal anchor. Inflation, over our sample of SSA countries, averaged 9.5% a year (1980–2014), with pronounced differences in various exchange rate regimes. Countries with pegged exchange rates had an average annual inflation rate of 8%, compared with 16% for floating regimes (Fig. 6.5). This implies that inflation in pegs is half as much as in floating regimes.

Over the sample period, nominal interest rates have tended to rise, but the rate of increase for countries with floating rates was almost 6%, as against 2% for countries with pegged rates. It was highest for countries with intermediate regimes, where the growth rate of interest rates was

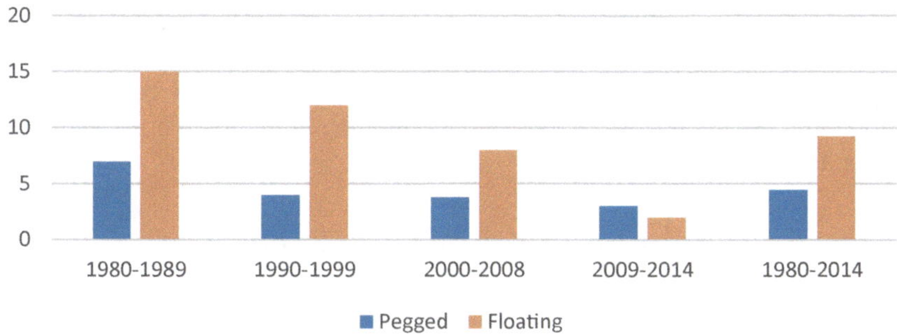

Fig. 6.5 Inflation in SSA by Exchange rate regime (*Source* IMF, AREAER database; and IMF, World Economic Outlook)

almost 9%. A change in nominal interest rates is of importance because a fall in these rates will lead to a stronger demand for money. But the level of real interest rates (i.e., the nominal rates adjusted for inflation) also gives a direct measure of confidence. On average, the real interest rates were 0.2% a year under pegged regimes, 1.8% under intermediate regimes and 2.3% under floating regimes.

6.3 Literature Review

There is a widespread theoretical and empirical literature on CBI, exchange rate regimes, monetary policy and how they affect inflation. In this section, we review these concepts and present a conceptual framework that links and motivates this study.

Time Inconsistency Problem

Kydland and Prescott's (1977), time inconsistency problem, further developed by Barro and Gordon (1983), arises because political authorities have political motivations to exploit the trade-off between unemployment and inflation in the short run (Alesina & Summers, 1993; Phillips, 1958). The relationship between time inconsistency and inflation arises when monetary policy is in the hands of political authorities who utilise opportunities to achieve their political objectives at the expense of maintaining price stability. By creating unexpected inflation, governments reduce real wages and increase output and employment as, for example, elections approach. Rational economic agents, in these circumstances, will adjust their behaviour in line with inflationary expectation, resulting in higher wages and price levels. This was further developed by Barro and Gordon (1983). Empirical evidence, however, does not seem to suggest the existence of this theory.

Central Bank Independence and Inflation

The empirical literature's position on the relationship between CBI and inflation remains debatable. Studies have utilised both the legal CBI index, derived from central bank charters, and the de facto CBI variable, which measures the rate of central bank governor turnover. While legal CBI indices have been found to have significantly negative impact on inflation in developed countries, central bank governor turnover rate has a significantly positive impact on inflation in developing countries. The disparity among these findings is explained by Alpanda and Honig (2014), who suggested that there could be low rate of turnover in central banks that are not independent in situations where the governor of the central bank is subservient to the fiscal authority. This is meant to avoid them being forced to resign. This indicates that lower turnover rates do not always signal high levels of independence.

Iwasaki and Uegaki's (2017) results indicate that a series of study conditions strongly affect the empirical results concerning transition economies. Agoba et al. (2017) and Katseli et al. (2020), find that CBI-inflation nexus is dependent on the model, sample and estimation technique used. This is further buttressed by While, Khan (2018) who find a negative relationship between CBI and inflation, after controlling for several other macroeconomic and policy indicators. Their study indicates that the CBI–inflation relationship varies with the income level of the country. Anwar and Nicolas (2020) observe a positive impact of CBI on inflation stabilisation in their study of 37 countries. They find this relationship to be directional. Zhang and Zheng (2020) also identify a negative impact of CBI on inflation in China. Garriga and Rodriguez (2020) find that higher CBI is associated with lower inflation rates. The study finds that all dimensions included in the measurement of CBI (objectives, personnel, policy and financial independence) contribute to curbing inflation. He and Zou (2018) find that there is no monotonic relationship between CBI and inflation. They find that CBI has a positive effect on inflation when the seigniorage is mainly used to finance non-productive government spending as is common in developing countries. Kim and Lim (2020), study overturned the standard negative inflation-independence relationship. This outcome was accounted for by developing economies and is attributable to political-economy factors: insufficient transparency enables the pursuit of non-price-stabilisation objectives.

CBI, Exchange Rate Regime and Inflation

Some studies attribute the failure to consider the effect of the exchange rate regime on the relationship between CBI and inflation as reason for the mixed and confused results of the empirical literature (Lohi, 2014). The advantage of fixed exchange rate with respect to inflation can first be traced to the elimination of exchange rate risk that impacts the decisions of exporters and importers as well as domestic borrowers in international financial markets. The elimination of this risk means, prices of goods and services would remain relatively stable. Secondly, fixed exchange regimes ensure the alignment of domestic inflation with external inflation, thus anchoring inflation to a certain extent. This makes the fight of inflation less pronounced for independent central banks in such regimes. Monetary authorities do resist floating exchange regimes for reasons that it produces lower policy and institutional credibility and brings along high degree of exchange rate pass-through into domestic prices, among other factors (Calvo & Reinhart, 2002). This leads to more frequent changes in prices thereby making price stability a difficult objective to attain (Bahmani-Oskooee & Saha, 2020; Dong et al., 2020). De Grauwe and Schnabl (2008) analysed the impact of exchange rate regime on inflation in (South) Eastern and Central Europe. The study showed that exchange rate stability positively impacted low inflation. De Grauwe and Schnabl (2004) reveal a significant impact of exchange rate stability on low inflation in Central and Eastern European (CEE) EU candidate countries. Bleaney and Francisco (2007) and Ghosh et al. (2013) suggested a need to separate the effects of monetary union from those of pegging. The study by Bleaney and Fielding find that while a peg reduces inflation by 13 percentage points per year, CFA membership provided an additional gain of 3.9 percentage e points in terms of lower inflation. Lohi (2014) also find that CAEMC and WAEMU countries, respectively had 8 and 10 percentage points lower inflation compared to other low and lower-middle-income countries. However, compared to countries with fixed exchange rate regimes, previous differences slightly decline to 6.2 and 9.4 percentage points for the Central African Economic and Monetary Community (CAEMC) and the West African Economic and Monetary Union (WAEMU) respectively, suggesting potential membership benefits. This was supported by Coulibaly and Davis (2013). Ftiti et al. (2017) in their investigation of the relationship between inflation and CBI across different monetary regimes among emerging and developing economies conclude that inflation is lowered by the exchange rate in the presence of CBI only for non-fixed exchange regimes that are characterised by ineffective monetary policy.

Central Bank Independence and Monetary Policy Effectiveness

Due to the lack of independence among central banks in many developing countries, there are no clearly defined monetary policy objectives. Their stabilisation function would likely be to target growth in output. As a result, in order to expand access to credit, the central bank increases liquidity to stimulate the economy during sluggish growth. Central banks, in order to support governments' pursuit of economic and social development, would provide credit to finance government expenditure. This could potentially crowd out private spending and lead to unproductive financing, thereby not growing the economy and leading to inflation.

Furthermore, there could be a depletion of foreign reserves as a result of government spending financing by the central bank, especially in small open economies. The solution would be to devalue the domestic currency, leading to a vicious cycle of more costly imports, higher depreciation of the domestic currency and high inflation. With the intention to address the issue of accommodating higher government spending, central banks would adopt nominal anchors as guides to monetary policy design.

The objective in small open economies is to defend an exchange rate peg. This could undermine monetary policy independence. This is because variations in the interest rate may be contrary to the exchange rate target and the stock of foreign reserves. For some other countries facing high inflation challenges, the optimal anchor for monetary policy, would not be to have a fixed exchange regime but rather an inflation targeting regime. Within such an arrangement, there are several indicators established by the monetary authority that drive the inflation process. In order to maintain price stability, money supply responds to changes in these indicators under control. This process, however, takes away a lot of independence from the central bank. With a higher level of CBI, however, the central bank may follow a more discretionary approach in which there may be unannounced established priorities, in reaction to economic development. The monetary policy design would usually target exchange rate, the price level or output growth stability.

According to Mahamadu and Abradu-Otoo (2003), there is a positive long-run relationship between inflation, money supply and the exchange rate in Ghana. An earlier study by Chibber and Shafik (1990) in a study covering from 1965 to 1988 also agreed that monetary growth was a key determinant of inflation in Ghana and there was a significant positive relationship between the parallel market exchange rate and the general price level. A study by Canetti and Greene (2000) in which they separated the influence of monetary growth from exchange rate changes on prevailing and predicted rates of inflation, found that monetary dynamics influenced price levels in four countries, while depreciations in exchange rate dominated factors in explaining inflation outcomes in ten African countries that were studied. Earlier, London (1989) concluded that the growth of money supply, expected inflation, exchange rates and real income significantly determined inflation in Africa. Exchange rate was later introduced as one of the explanatory variables in the pure monetarist model. Ndung'u (1997) saw a bidirectional relationship between the rate of inflation and exchange rate. In 1997, a similar conclusion was also reached in the extended version of this study (Ndung'u, 1997). Odusola and Akinlo (2001) in a study for Nigeria, found that having a flexible exchange rate system was not sufficient for output growth in the short term but rather it was factors such as discipline, confidence and credibility on the part of the government (as argued by Dordunoo & Njinkeu, 1997) that were essential.

In summary, the empirical literature has varied conclusions on the impact of monetary policy and exchange rate regime on inflation. The gap exists however on the impact of CBI on the monetary policy-inflation nexus as well as the impact of exchange rate regimes on CBI's inflation performance.

6.4 Methodology

Data and Sample

The sample and data cover the period of the modern exchange rate system following the breakdown of the Bretton-Woods arrangement in 1973. The full sample covers 48 African countries from 1970 to 2014. This is because the CBI data from Garriga (2016) and Bodea and Hicks (2015b), being used, though, being the longest and having the widest coverage, ends in 2014 for our sample of African countries.

Model and Estimation Technique

- **Model**

Our main objective is to study the impact of CBI, exchange rate regime and monetary policy on the level of inflation. We also consider some control and macroeconomic variables.

To identify the effect of CBI, exchange rate regimes and monetary policy on the level of inflation, we specify a cross-country panel model for the period 1970–2014. Given that the number of years for the study (T) is greater than the number of countries (N), there is no threat from cross-country dependence. The model specification is generally given by:

$$\text{Inflation}_{it} = \emptyset_i \text{Inflation}_{it-1} + \lambda_i \text{PEGGED}_{it} + ῆ_i \text{Monetary Policy}_{it} + ß_i X_{it} + \varepsilon_{it} \quad (6.1)$$

Our preferred model is based on Bodea and Higashijima (2015), Lucotte (2012), Acemoglu et al. (2008) and Romer (1993) and can be summarised as follows:

$$\begin{aligned} \text{Inflation}_{it} = {} & \beta_i \text{Inflation}_{it-1} + \beta_2 \text{World Inflation}_{it} + \beta_3 \text{CBI} \\ & + \beta_4 \text{PEGGED}_{it} + \beta_6 \text{Financial Development}_{it} \\ & + \beta_7 \text{LGDPC}_{it} + \beta_8 \text{Political Institutions}_{it} \\ & + \beta_9 \text{Fiscal Deficit}_{it} + \beta_{10} \text{Openness}_{it} + \varepsilon_{it} \end{aligned} \quad (6.2)$$

To capture possible unobserved heterogeneity, and to analyze the impact of exchange rate regime on the CBI-inflation nexus, we specify the following interaction model:

$$\begin{aligned}\text{Inflation}_{it} = {} & \beta_i \text{Inflation}_{it-1} + \beta_2 \text{World Inflation}_{it} + \beta_3 \text{CBI} \\ & + \beta_4 \text{PEGGED}_{it} + \beta_5 (\text{CBI} * \text{PEGGED})_{it} \\ & + \beta_6 \text{Monetary Policy}_{it} + \beta_7 \text{Financial Development}_{it} \\ & + \beta_8 \text{LGDPC}_{it} + \beta_9 \text{Political Institutions}_{it} \\ & + \beta_{10} \text{Fiscal Deficit}_{it} + \beta_{11} \text{Openness}_{it} + \varepsilon_{it} \end{aligned} \quad (6.3)$$

To capture possible unobserved heterogeneity, and to analyze the impact of CBI on the monetary policy-inflation nexus, we specify the following interaction model:

$$\begin{aligned}\text{Inflation}_{it} = {} & \beta_i \text{Inflation}_{it-1} + \beta_2 \text{World Inflation}_{it} + \beta_3 \text{CBI} + \beta_4 \text{PEGGED}_{it} \\ & + \beta_5 \text{Monetary Policy}_{it} + \beta_6 (\text{Monetary Policy} * \text{CBI})_{it} \\ & + \beta_7 \text{Financial Development}_{it} + \beta_8 \text{LGDPC}_{it} \\ & + \beta_9 \text{Political Institutions}_{it} + \beta_{10} \text{Fiscal Deficit}_{it} \\ & + \beta_{11} \text{Openness}_{it} + \varepsilon_{it} \end{aligned} \quad (6.4)$$

where i denotes the country and t denotes the time, ε_{it} is the error term. To properly interpret the interaction terms, we must include the level of conditioning variable i.e., exchange regime and CBI (Brambor et al., 2006). As in the case of CBI, based on Eqs. (6.2 and 6.4), the effects of a change in CBI and monetary policy on our dependent variable are given respectively by:

$$\frac{\partial \text{ Inflation}_{it}}{\partial \text{CBI}_{it}} = \beta_3 + \beta_5 \text{PEGGED}_{it} \text{ and}$$

$$\frac{\partial \text{ Inflation}_{it}}{\partial \text{Monetary Policy}_{it}} = \beta_5 + \beta_6 \text{CBI}_{it}$$

- **Dependent and Independent variables**

Inflation is measured by changes in the GDP deflator as well as changes in the consumer price index. Following Klomp and De Haan (2010), in order to ameliorate potential heteroscedasticity of the error term, our inflation variable is rescaled using:

$$\mathrm{LOG}(1 + \mathrm{Inflation})$$

where inflation is the annual %age change in GDP deflator/CPI Index.

The transformed inflation variable is also more useful for studies on emerging markets and developing countries, which are characterised by hyper-inflationary episodes (Arnone & Romelli, 2013). The GDP deflator is a measure of the price level of all domestically produced final goods and services in an economy. It is sometimes also referred to as the GDP price deflator or the implicit price deflator. The GDP deflator reflects changes in the average price level within the economy. The GDP deflator provides a more comprehensive measure of inflation as it covers all goods and services, unlike the consumer price index (CPI) which has a specific basket of goods and services. We add the lagged value of our dependent variable to correct the potential endogeneity of inflation. It also controls for initial level effects.

CBI represents the annual legal central bank independence measure of a country in one period. Our legal CBI index is from Garriga (2016) and Bodea and Hicks (2015b), who compute CBI indices for 182 countries over the period, 1970–2014. It follows Cukierman, Webb and Neyapti's criteria (CWN). The CWN CBI index is based on a weighted aggregation of 16 legal indicators in four categories regarding the tenure of the bank's governor, policy formation, objectives and limitations on lending to the government. Using the criteria and weights in Cukierman, Webb and Neyapti, the index varies from 0 to 1, with larger values indicating more independence. A central bank is legally more independent when the governor's term in office is longer; the appointment and dismissal procedures are more insulated from the government; the mandate is more focused on price stability; the formulation of monetary policy lies squarely with the central bank and the provisions on direct central bank lending are more restrictive. The index represents the most comprehensive data on CBI that spans the longest period and covers the greatest number of countries, useful for conducting a panel study.

We have highlighted the role of the exchange rate regime in the CBI–inflation relationship. However, different types of exchange rate regimes have been applied across countries and have different effects on the CBI–inflation issue. For example, based on the theory of opportunistic political business cycles, governments employ expansionary economic policies before elections. This occurs in various ways based on the type of exchange rate regime and level of CBI. Under a fixed exchange rate regime, before the election, an expansionary policy is undertaken through tax reductions and/or public expenditure increases. However, under a flexible exchange rate regime, the expansionary policy is applied through interest rate reductions and/or money supply increases. Therefore, our objective is to empirically distinguish among the effects of different exchange rate regimes in explaining the CBI–inflation relationship. The effects are determined by defining the exchange rate regime as either pegged which is captured as *1* and *0* otherwise. *Monetary policy* is captured using the real interest rates.

Financial development is a financial development indicator; measured as the ratio of private credit to GDP to capture banking sector development and the ratio of stock market capitalisation to GDP as a proxy for stock market sector development. These variables are sourced from the World Development Indicators (2015). *Political institutions* are proxied by the political rights score obtained from Freedom House database. The score for the variable ranges from 7 to 1, with 7 representing the least rating and 1 the highest. Following Bodea and Higashijima (2017), we rescale the original score to range between 0 and 6, so that lower scores now correspond to lower political rights rating and higher scores correspond to higher political rights rating. In order to do this, we use the formular −1*(PRS-7), where PRS is the political right score as given by Freedom House.

We also include real per capita income level, Trade *Openness* which is defined as the sum of exports and imports in relation to GDP; *World Inflation* which is proxied by the average inflation rate of industrial countries, computed from the World Bank; the *log of per capita GDP (LGDPC)*, to capture several possible effects; *fiscal deficits*, measured as government expenditure to GDP minus government revenue to GDP (Ismihan & Ozkan, 2012).

We exploit the time dimension of the data and present the regression analysis controlling for country and time-fixed effects. It could be argued that the correlation in the cross-sectional analysis might be driven by time-invariant omitted variables, such as institutional variables, that often are difficult to measure. Country dummies are included to control for omitted variables driven by individual time-invariant effects, thereby eliminating a potential source of omitted-variable bias; period dummies are included to control for period individual invariant variables such as global shocks that might affect aggregate inflation in any period but are not captured by the explanatory variables. This technique, however, does not adjust for all omitted-variable bias since it does not control for omitted variables whose values change over time. However, institutional variables that might affect the inflation–openness relationship, such as CBI, tend to have little time variation.

We also note that, we seek to further evaluate the importance and impact of CFA Zone membership on the impact of CBI on inflation, by distinguishing between the effects of being in a monetary union from those which arise from anchoring the CFA Franc. Indeed, as pointed out by Bleaney and Fielding (2002), the CFA Franc Zone has a special exchange rate regime as it combines two hard peg regimes (monetary union and the pegging of its common currency to the French Franc). These regimes are generally expected to affect economic performance in the same way, the only difference being that monetary union implies greater political commitment and credibility than a peg. Thus, to better estimate the impacts of the CFA Zone exchange rate regime on its economic performance, requires differentiating the effects of the two regimes (Ghosh et al., 2013). To this end, we apply the method used by Bleaney and Fielding (2002) which consists of simultaneously estimating the effects of the peg and that of the CFA using dummy variables (see detail in Sect. 6.3). Therefore, the first dummy will capture the overall effects of the peg while the second will provide the additional effect of belonging to the CFA monetary union. Unlike Bleaney and Fielding (2002), our analysis is based on a panel framework which allows us to consider the joint occurrence of dynamics and unobserved individual heterogeneity. Finally, as previously mentioned, our study focuses on the SSA countries which share most of the salient features of the CFA Zone countries (commodities and oil producers, low or middle-income countries, exposure to external shocks and occurrence of political crisis).

6.5 Estimation Technique

This study uses the two-step System Generalised Method of Moments (SGMM) estimator with Windmeijer (2005) corrected standard errors since this is asymptotically more efficient than the one step-estimator. The autocorrelation test and the robust estimates of the coefficient standard errors assumes no correlation across individuals in the idiosyncratic disturbances.

We use a System Generalised Method of Moments (SGMM) estimator for various reasons. First, due to the relatively small-time duration for some countries in our data, and the use of lagged dependent variable in the model, the SGMM is more appropriate as it avoids the bias that would result from using fixed effects in an OLS regression. Second, because both the CBI index and exchange rate regime dummy vary little within countries, the SGMM leads to a more efficient estimation than fixed effects models (Plümper & Troeger, 2007). Several shortcomings of the data, which include missing data in the sample, fixed individual effects and potential heteroscedasticity and autocorrelation within countries, are adequately addressed by the GMM estimation (Rodman, 2009). The SGMM approach allows us to treat inflation as a dynamic process thus accounting explicitly for the possibility that previous inflation may influence current inflation levels. The inclusion of lagged independent variables may not eliminate potential endogeneity and reverse causation problems. If CBI, exchange rate regimes and monetary policy are correlated with regressors from Eq. (6.1), the main result may not hold. More importantly, fiscal balances may affect the level of independence granted to the central bank. The SGMM allows us to account for these potential effects where CBI, exchange rate regime and monetary policy are treated as endogenous variables.

The study reports two standard specification tests: The Hansen test of over-identifying restrictions tests the overall validity of the instruments. Failure to reject the null hypothesis gives support for the model, including our choice of endogenous variables. The Arellano–Bond test for AR (2) in first differences tests whether the residuals from the regression in differences are second order serially correlated and failure to reject the null hypothesis supports the model specification. In order to deal with the issue of instrument proliferation, we collapse the instrument matrix as suggested by Rodman (2009) and Bontempi and Mammi (2015). The autocorrelation test and the robust estimates of the coefficient standard errors assumes no correlation across individuals in the idiosyncratic disturbances. The study also reports the number of instruments as suggested by Bazzi and Clemens (2013).

6.6 Empirical Results

We present the results of our analysis from Tables 6.2, 6.3, 6.4, 6.5, and 6.6. In Tables 6.7 and 6.8 (Appendix), we present the descriptive statistics and correlation of the variables of interest in this study.

In Tables 6.2 and 6.3, where we measure inflation as the average consumer price index (AVCPI), we examine the impact of CBI, measured as the CBI index as well as the individual components on the CBI index namely personnel independence (CB CEO), which captures the extent to which the central bank governor is free from political control; policy independence (CB POL), which measures the independence of the central bank in deciding on monetary policy and the appropriate policy tool to use; the extent to which price stability is the objective of the central bank (CB OBJ) and the financial independence of the central bank (CB LEND), which measures the extent to which limits are placed on central bank financing of government expenditure. We also use the de facto measure of CBI which measures the central bank governor turnover rate. We rescale this measure so that higher values will correspond to higher independence and lower values would mean low independence of the central bank governor.

Focusing on the impact of CBI on inflation, we observe that CBI, does not have any significant impact on inflation in model 1. This agrees with the literature on CBI, which has not found a significant impact of de jure CBI on inflation; attributing this to a disparity between actual and legal CBI, due to disrespect for CBI provisions (Agoba et al., 2017). This trend can be seen also from models 4, 10 and 13, where the component members of the CBI index namely personnel independence (CB CEO); the extent to which price stability is the principal objective of monetary policy (CB OBJ) and the limits of central bank lending to government (CB LEND) are used as proxies for CBI, respectively.

We also find that fixed exchange rate regimes have lower inflation rates than floating exchange rate regimes. This is shown by the significant negative coefficients of the PEGGED dummy variable as seen in models 1 to 18. To this end, we can tell for example that a shift from a floating to a fixed exchange regime, leads to a 32.5% reduction in inflation rate (model). As explained in the literature, fixed exchange rate regimes preserve the value of currencies as a result of the lack of currency depreciation which should translate into stable prices. This is because a fixed exchange rate regime has the advantage of eliminating the exchange rate risk that affects the decisions of exporters and importers and domestic borrowers in international financial markets, as well as converging domestic inflation with external inflation. The resistance to floating arises from their low policy and institutional credibility and high degree of pass-through of exchange rate changes into domestic prices, among other factors (Calvo & Reinhart, 2002).

The interaction term, which seeks to examine the effectiveness of CBI in fixed exchange rate regimes, indicates that, CBI is less effective in addressing inflation in fixed exchange rate regimes than it does in floating exchange rate regimes. This is indicated by the significantly positive coefficient of the CBI*PEGGED term in the estimation. The interpretation of the coefficient in model 2, for example, is that a change from a floating to a fixed exchange rate regime leads to a 6.2% reduction in the impact of CBI on minimising inflation. A fixed exchange rate regime has a risk of loss of economic policy flexibility in facing external shocks, mainly when economic authorities do not have enough exchange reserves to intervene in the exchange market and/or there is a confidence crisis associated with the lack of government capability in maintaining the pegged exchange rate; under these conditions, the adjustment costs can be very high. This would result in less effective role of the independent central bank in such regimes when compared to floating exchange rate regimes. For example, according to Kappel (1993), total credit to government in the CFA Zone is strictly limited to 20% of the previous year's fiscal receipts. In practice, this is treated as an automatic entitlement. In the absence of specific coordination of fiscal and monetary policy, the credit limit to government is usually insufficient to fund borrowing requirements but there are several routes to render the ceilings ineffective: (a) Reduce government transfers to parastatals and pressurise banks to lend to them without adequate collateral. (b) Delay payment to the private sector. (c) Increase foreign borrowing. In the example of Cameroon "inflationary" Central Bank financing is a small proportion of total financing obtained. We realise that CBI associated with monetary policy decisions (CB POL) produces the most significant result on the difference between the impact of CBI in pegged and floating exchange regimes. That is to mention that, considering the magnitude of the CB*PEGGED term in the model as seen in model 26, where CBI is proxied with the CB POL variable, there is a 7.6% difference in the impact of CBI on inflation in fixed exchange regimes relative to floating exchange regimes. This is the highest compared to the magnitude of the interactive terms for other measures of CBI. This can be attributed to the limit in the use of monetary policy rates in fixed exchange regimes to respond to shocks and influence stability in prices. With floating exchange rates having that advantage, the central bank is more effective as the exchange rate channel is available to them, to influence prices, thereby resulting in a bigger impact on inflation.

For our second objective, we analyse the impact of monetary policy on inflation and the effect of CBI on this impact. As seen in models Tables 6.2 and 6.3, monetary policy has a negative and significant impact on inflation. This means that higher interest rates do result in lower inflation levels. In model 1 for example, a 1% increase in interest rates lead to a 21.8% reduction in inflation rate. This is because higher interest rates mean higher cost of credit and lower demand for money. This leads to less money chasing goods and services and therefore, lower prices.

The interactive term, Monetary Policy*CBI seeks to examine the impact of monetary policy on inflation, given an independent central bank. We see in Tables 6.2 and 6.3, given different measures of CBI, in models 3, 6, 9, 12, 15 and 18, and given the significant negative coefficient of the interactive variable, that CBI improves the effectiveness of monetary policy on inflation. This is because, given a monetary policy decision, independent central banks are better able to ensure its effectiveness as they, for example, would not exceed limits on central bank lending but would also ensure that monetary policy decisions are based on sound and objective economic analysis resulting in lower inflation rates. In such a situation, monetary policy is more effective in more developed financial markets which are products of a better regulated financial market. The understanding of current and expected central bank actions by participants in the financial market is key to monetary policy effectiveness. Such a clear understanding is likely not to emerge under existing dependent central banks: the combination of money target misses, noisy short-term interest rates and incipient communications make it difficult to assess policymakers' intentions. The results in Tables 6.2 and 6.3 are replicated in Tables 6.4 and 6.5, where inflation is measured as the change in the GDP deflator.

In order to further buttress the results in Tables 6.2 and 6.3, where CBI is less effective in fixed exchange rate regimes than in floating

Table 6.2 CBI, Exchange Rate Regime, Monetary Policy and Inflation in Africa

Variables	*(1) CBI Index*	*(2) CBI Index*	*(3) CB Index*	*(4) CB CEO*	*(5) CB CEO*	*(6) CB CEO*	*(7) CB POL*	*(8) CB POL*	*(9) CB POL*
AVCPI $_{t-1}$	0.506***	0.515***	0.517***	0.452***	0.481***	0.483***	0.314***	0.364**	0.371**
	(0.004)	(0.005)	(0.003)	(0.018)	(0.009)	(0.011)	(0.009)	(0.017)	(0.018)
World Inflation	0.270***	0.282***	0.277***	0.150***	0.291***	0.276***	0.308**	0.187***	0.191***
	(0.009)	(0.006)	(0.002)	(0.005)	(0.006)	(0.005)	(0.097)	(0.007)	(0.005)
CBI	−0.203	−0.242**	−0.277**	−0.175	−0.186	−0.182	−0.134*	−0.076**	−0.102**
	(0.195)	(0.072)	(0.069)	(0.254)	(0.312)	(0.312)	(0.091)	(0.033)	(0.041)
PEGGED	−0.325**	−0.378**	−0.355**	−0.267**	−0.138***	−0.122***	−0.117**	−0.246**	−0.255**
	(0.093)	(0.098)	(0.084)	(0.087)	(0.005)	(0.004)	(0.042)	(0.086)	(0.099)
Monetary Policy	−0.218**	−0.162**	−0.168**	−0.113	−0.088	−0.075**	−0.078*	−0.082**	−0.179**
	(0.082)	(0.037)	(0.031)	(0.332)	(0.127)	(0.031)	(0.029)	(0.022)	(0.022)
CBI*PEGGED		0.062*			0.051			0.047**	
		(0.058)			(0.177)			(0.014)	
Monetary Policy* CBI*			−0.091**			−0.052			−0.088***
			(0.035)			(0.098)			(0.011)
Fiscal Deficit	0.074***	0.055**	0.051**	0.123**	0.079	0.083	0.048	0.062*	0.073*
	(0.006)	(0.019)	(0.019)	(0.004)	(0.100)	(0.100)	(0.105)	(0.041)	(0.041)
Openness	0.058***	0.057**	0.069**	0.043*	0.046	0.037	0.073	0.048	0.044**
	(0.006)	(0.027)	(0.032)	(0.031)	(0.165)	(0.257)	(0.163)	(0.079)	(0.021)
LGDPC	−0.081**	−0.105***	−0.108***	−0.179**	−0.179	−0.182	−0.197	−0.211	−0.184
	(0.033)	(0.003)	(0.006)	(0.065)	(0.215)	(0.243)	(0.190)	(0.217)	(0.281)
Political Institutions	−0.192**	−0.067**	−0.079**	−0.061***	−0.093***	−0.101***	−0.186	−0.166***	−0.172***
	(0.056)	(0.022)	(0.038)	(0.031)	(0.011)	(0.048)	(0.128)	(0.004)	(0.005)

(continued)

Table 6.2 (continued)

Variables	*(1)* *CBI Index*	*(2)* *CBI Index*	*(3)* *CB Index*	*(4)* *CB CEO*	*(5)* *CB CEO*	*(6)* *CB CEO*	*(7)* *CB POL*	*(8)* *CB POL*	*(9)* *CB POL*
Private Credit	−0.110*	−0.084**	−0.102**	−0.062**	−0.072**	−0.065**	−0.053**	−0.058**	−0.065**
	(0.072)	(0.041)	(0.039)	(0.025)	(0.012)	(0.012)	(0.028)	(0.022)	(0.021)
Total CBI Effect		−0.18**			−0.135**			−0.029*	
		(0.025)			(0.043)			(0.019)	
Total Monetary Policy Effect			−0.259**			−0.127			−0.267***
			(0.102)			(0.295)			(0.015)
Observations	1023	1023	1018	1023	1023	1018	1023	1023	1018
Number of Index	48	48	48	47	47	47	46	46	46
Number of Instruments	22	22	22	24	24	24	21	21	21
AR (1)	0.018	0.011	0.019	0.012	0.012	0.017	0.012	0.012	0.015
AR (2)	0.106	0.114	0.106	0.118	0.116	0.142	0.115	0.117	0.118
Hansen test	0.121	0.132	0.121	0.176	0.175	0.213	0.128	0.133	0.132

Robust Standard errors in parentheses $^{***}p < 0.01$, $^{**}p < 0.05$, $^{*}p < 0.1$

Notes AVCPI variable is the modified inflation rate computed as: $\text{LOG}(1 + \pi_{\text{AVCPI}})$ where π_{AVCPI} is the annual %age change in consumer price index. CBI is the annual legal CWN central bank independence index measure of a country's central bank independence. CBGTO is the rescaled annualised five-year average central bank governor turnover rate with lower values corresponding to lower independence and higher values corresponding to higher central bank independence. CBCEO is the index for central bank governor legal independence. CBOBJ is the legal central bank objective independence. CBPOL is the legal central bank policy independence and CB LEND is the legal central bank financial independence index. ***Financial Development*** is credit to the private sector as a %age of GDP; measured as the ratio of stock market total value traded to GDP (%), which are proxies for financial development. ***Political Institutions*** is the average of the rescaled political rights score (0–6) which is proxy for political institutional quality. *OPENNESS* is defined as sum of exports and imports in relation to GDP. *PEGGED* is a dummy constructed from the IMF database on de facto exchange regimes, using a one (1) for regimes classified as: "another currency as legal tender," "currency board" or "conventional peg against a single currency," and zero (0) otherwise. Monetary Policy is the central bank policy rate. ***World Inflation*** is proxied by the average inflation rate of industrial countries, computed from the World Bank. *LGDPC* is measured as log of the ratio of real Gross Domestic Product divided by total population. ***Fiscal Deficit*** is government expenditure less government revenue as a % age of GDP

Table 6.3 CBI, Exchange Rate Regime, Monetary Policy and Inflation in Africa

Variables	*(10)* *CB OBJ*	*(11)* *CB OBJ*	*(12)* *CB OBJ*	*(13)* *CB LEND*	*(14)* *CB LEND*	*(15)* *CB LEND*	*(16)* *CBGTOR*	*(17)* *CBGTOR*	*(18)* *CBGTOR*
$AVCPI_{t-1}$	0.465***	0.452***	0.458***	0.550***	0.566***	0.568***	0.617***	0.624***	0.619***
	(0.012)	(0.013)	(0.011)	(0.004)	(0.006)	(0.003)	(0.002)	(0.008)	(0.007)
World Inflation	0.335***	0.137***	0.133***	0.208***	0.195***	0.191***	0.232**	0.237**	0.212**
	(0.012)	(0.006)	(0.004)	(0.003)	(0.013)	(0.015)	(0.061)	(0.065)	(0.047)
CBI	−0.217	−0.221	−0.198**	−0.259	−0.083**	−0.265**	−0.286**	−0.301***	−0.288***
	(0.354)	(0.199)	(0.082)	(0.241)	(0.034)	(0.053)	(0.058)	(0.012)	(0.011)
PEGGED	−0.228**	−0.088	−0.075	−0.175	−0.192**	−0.166**	−0.275**	−0.228**	−0.211**
	(0.079)	(0.083)	(0.091)	(0.219)	(0.067)	(0.032)	(0.085)	(0.073)	(0.076)
Monetary Policy	−0.103**	−0.106**	−0.173**	−0.124*	−0.175**	−0.164**	−0.132**	−0.144***	−0.148*
	(0.056)	(0.058)	(0.057)	(0.099)	(0.038)	(0.038)	(0.046)	(0.019)	(0.099)
CBI*PEGGED		0.064			0.049**			0.071***	
		(0.085)			(0.019)			(0.008)	
Monetary Policy* CBI*			−0.081***			−0.071**			−0.122***
			(0.009)			(0.032)			(0.012)
Fiscal Deficit	0.098**	0.054***	0.058***	0.077***	0.046**	0.049**	0.044	0.038***	0.036*
	(0.027)	(0.008)	(0.008)	(0.008)	(0.011)	(0.011)	(0.061)	(0.002)	(0.019)
Openness	0.054	0.071	0.056	0.052***	0.053***	0.061***	0.084**	0.083**	0.088**
	(0.088)	(0.086)	(0.092)	(0.001)	(0.003)	(0.001)	(0.023)	(0.027)	(0.025)
LGDPC	−0.244	−0.256	−0.197	−0.019	−0.038	−0.026	−0.461	−0.330**	−0.330**
	(0.268)	(0.311)	(0.309)	(0.275)	(0.104)	(0.068)	(0.418)	(0.095)	(0.095)
Political Institutions	−0.145**	−0.107***	−0.113***	−0.182***	−0.164***	−0.164***	−0.192***	−0.101***	−0.088**
	(0.059)	(0.003)	(0.004)	(0.006)	(0.019)	(0.019)	(0.002)	(0.004)	(0.037)

(continued)

Table 6.3 (continued)

Variables	*(10)* *CB OBJ*	*(11)* *CB OBJ*	*(12)* *CB OBJ*	*(13)* *CB LEND*	*(14)* *CB LEND*	*(15)* *CB LEND*	*(16)* *CBGTOR*	*(17)* *CBGTOR*	*(18)* *CBGTOR*
Private Credit	−0.054	−0.072	−0.069	−0.072*	−0.081**	−0.081**	−0.079	−0.099**	−0.113***
	(0.077)	(0.194)	(0.083)	(0.051)	(0.033)	(0.033)	(0.102)	(0.042)	(0.007)
Total CBI Effect		−0.157			−0.034*			−0.23***	
		(0.312)			(0.022)			(0.005)	
Total Monetary Policy Effect			−0.254***			−0.235**			−0.27***
			(0.001)			(0.072)			(0.007)
Observations	1023	1023	1018	1023	1023	1018	1023	1023	1018
Number of Index	46	46	46	46	46	46	46	46	46
Number of Instruments	21	21	21	21	21	21	21	21	22
AR (1)	0.014	0.013	0.009	0.011	0.012	0.018	0.013	0.011	0.013
AR (2)	0.174	0.174	0.173	0.181	0.181	0.122	0.122	0.136	0.141
Hansen test	0.146	0.151	0.155	0.126	0.136	0.119	0.113	0.188	0.226

Robust Standard errors in parentheses $^{***}p < 0.01$, $^{**}p < 0.05$, $^{*}p < 0.1$

Notes The definition of variables are same as in Table 6.2

Table 6.4 CBI, Exchange Rate Regime, Monetary Policy and Inflation in Africa

Variables	*(19) CBI Index*	*(20) CBI Index*	*(21) CB Index*	*(22) CB CEO*	*(23) CB CEO*	*(24) CB CEO*	*(25) CB POL*	*(26) CB POL*	*(27) CB POL*
$GDPDEF_{t-1}$	0.588**	0.502***	0.517***	0.447***	0.348***	0.481***	0.348***	0.351***	0.364**
	(0.004)	(0.008)	(0.003)	(0.005)	(0.003)	(0.009)	(0.003)	(0.009)	(0.017)
World Inflation	0.242**	0.201**	0.282***	0.241*	0.152*	0.291***	0.152*	0.131*	0.187***
	(0.077)	(0.072)	(0.006)	(0.122)	(0.101)	(0.006)	(0.101)	(0.096)	(0.007)
CBI	−0.223	−0.265**	−0.284**	−0.164	−0.135*	−0.187	−0.185*	−0.195**	−0.090**
	(0.348)	(0.070)	(0.072)	(0.243)	(0.092)	(0.312)	(0.092)	(0.063)	(0.033)
PEGGED	−0.378**	−0.352**	−0.378**	−0.180**	−0.168**	−0.138***	−0.168**	−0.253***	−0.246**
	(0.054)	(0.068)	(0.098)	(0.052)	(0.055)	(0.005)	(0.055)	(0.013)	(0.086)
Monetary Policy	−0.287**	−0.290**	−0.162**	−0.164	−0.083*	−0.065	−0.185*	0.192**	−0.051**
	(0.078)	(0.070)	(0.037)	(0.243)	(0.092)	(0.127)	(0.092)	(0.063)	(0.022)
CBI*PEGGED		0.044**			0.038			0.071***	
		(0.045)			(0.237)			(0.008)	
Monetary Policy* CBI*			−0.109**			−0.061			−0.063***
			(0.066)			(0.132)			(0.015)
Fiscal Deficit	0.080**	0.041*	−0.052**	0.072	0.053	0.074	0.053	0.063	0.069*
	(0.023)	(0.031)	(0.019)	(0.097)	(0.064)	(0.100)	(0.064)	(0.063)	(0.041)
Openness	0.072*	0.064**	0.069**	0.022	0.069	0.037	0.069	0.075	0.044
	(0.057)	(0.032)	(0.032)	(0.124)	(0.137)	(0.257)	(0.137)	(0.261)	(0.061)
LGDPC	−0.372*	−0.065	−0.101***	−0.053***	−0.065**	−0.170	−0.065***	−0.078**	−0.219
	(0.236)	(0.157)	(0.002)	(−0.008)	(0.028)	(0.211)	(0.006)	(0.031)	(0.221)
Political Institutions	−0.195**	−0.076**	−0.081**	−0.081	−0.191	−0.095***	−0.191	−0.196	−0.177***

(continued)

Table 6.4 (continued)

Variables	*(19) CBI Index*	*(20) CBI Index*	*(21) CB Index*	*(22) CB CEO*	*(23) CB CEO*	*(24) CB CEO*	*(25) CB POL*	*(26) CB POL*	*(27) CB POL*
	(0.061)	(0.026)	(0.032)	(0.127)	(0.260)	(0.012)	(0.260)	(0.254)	(0.004)
Private Credit	−0.105**	−0.071*	−0.080**	−0.069	−0.062	−0.068**	−0.062	−0.066	−0.051**
	(0.041)	(0.050)	(0.044)	(0.151)	(0.112)	(0.011)	(0.112)	(0.104)	(0.023)
Total CBI Effect		−0.221***			−0.097**			−0.124***	
		(0.017)			(0.034)			(0.011)	
Total Monetary Policy Effect			−0.271***			−0.126			−0.114***
			(0.022)			(0.291)			(0.017)
Observations	1023	1023	1018	1023	1023	1018	1023	1023	1018
Number of Index	48	48	48	47	47	47	46	46	46
Number of Instruments	23	23	22	24	22	24	21	21	21
AR (1)	0.017	0.017	0.019	0.016	0.016	0.018	0.012	0.011	0.016
AR (2)	0.111	0.113	0.109	0.124	0.119	0.142	0.117	0.123	0.148
Hansen test	0.226	0.172	0.124	0.164	0.183	0.213	0.174	0.153	0.152

Robust Standard errors in parentheses ***$p < 0.01$, **$p < 0.05$, *$p < 0.1$

Table 6.5 CBI, Exchange Rate Regime, Monetary Policy and Inflation in Africa

Variables	*(28)* *CB OBJ*	*(29)* *CB OBJ*	*(30)* *CB OBJ*	*(31)* *CB LEND*	*(32)* *CB LEND*	*(33)* *CB LEND*	*(34)* *CBGTOR*	*(35)* *CBGTOR*	*(36)* *CBGTOR*
$GDPDEF_{t-1}$	0.409***	0.420***	0.465***	0.587***	0.543***	0.550***	0.682***	0.676***	0.627***
	(0.007)	(0.006)	(0.013)	(0.008)	(0.007)	(0.004)	(0.004)	(0.007)	(0.009)
World Inflation	0.188**	0.328*	0.137***	0.113**	0.182*	0.195***	0.130*	0.212**	0.107**
	(0.074)	(0.102)	(0.006)	(0.064)	(0.098)	(0.013)	(0.094)	(0.095)	(0.065)
CBI	−0.198	−0.205	−0.221	−0.261	−0.088*	−0.198**	−0.273**	−0.278**	−0.271***
	(0.374)	(1.054)	(0.199)	(0.136)	(0.107)	(0.034)	(0.058)	(0.062)	(0.012)
PEGGED	−0.245*	−0.098	−0.095	−0.141	−0.107**	−0.192**	−0.292**	−0.278**	−0.228**
	(0.072)	(0.101)	(0.083)	(0.124)	(0.059)	(0.067)	(0.071)	(0.054)	(0.073)
Monetary Policy	−0.078**	−0.113**	−0.106**	−0.161	−0.133*	−0.181**	−0.147**	−0.152**	−0.159***
	(0.032)	(0.054)	(0.068)	(0.136)	(0.097)	(0.038)	(0.058)	(0.062)	(0.019)
CBI*PEGGED		0.056			0.039*			0.053***	
		(0.384)			(0.033)			(0.016)	
Monetary Policy* CBI*			−0.098**			−0.116**			−0.127**
			(0.042)			(0.058)			(0.054)
Fiscal Deficit	0.086*	0.051*	0.046***	0.075**	0.025	0.031**	0.039	0.033***	0.032***
	(0.047)	(0.035)	(0.008)	(0.044)	(0.067)	(0.011)	(0.055)	(0.001)	(0.002)
Openness	0.046	0.057	0.056	0.059**	0.044**	0.061***	0.090**	0.072*	0.083**
	(0.104)	(0.107)	(0.092)	(0.021)	(0.019)	(0.001)	(0.044)	(0.057)	(0.027)
LGDPC	−0.069*	−0.057	−0.287	−0.090***	−0.063	−0.016	−0.054	−0.072*	−0.330**
	(0.043)	(0.061)	(0.316)	(0.005)	(0.126)	(0.297)	(0.066)	(0.056)	(0.095)
Political Institutions	−0.165**	−0.131**	−0.115***	−0.161**	−0.157**	−0.164***	−0.181*	−0.195**	−0.101***
	(0.073)	(0.053)	(0.002)	(0.69)	(0.039)	(0.019)	(0.098)	(0.041)	(0.004)

(continued)

Table 6.5 (continued)

Variables	*(28)* *CB OBJ*	*(29)* *CB OBJ*	*(30)* *CB OBJ*	*(31)* *CB LEND*	*(32)* *CB LEND*	*(33)* *CB LEND*	*(34)* *CBGTOR*	*(35)* *CBGTOR*	*(36)* *CBGTOR*
Private Credit	−0.067	−0.044	−0.059	−0.056	−0.046	−0.081**	−0.081**	−0.105**	−0.099**
	(0.122)	(0.135)	(0.083)	(0.081)	(0.126)	(0.023)	(0.021)	(0.042)	(0.042)
Total CBI Effect		−0.149			−0.049*			−0.225***	
		(0.215)			(0.033)			(0.012)	
Total Monetary Policy Effect			−0.204***			−0.297**			−0.398***
			(0.018)			(0.075)			(0.026)
Observations	1023	1023	1018	1023	1023	1018	1023	1023	1018
Number of Index	46	46	46	46	46	46	46	46	46
Number of Instruments	21	21	21	21	21	21	20	20	22
AR (1)	0.017	0.011	0.009	0.013	0.012	0.014	0.011	0.016	0.012
AR (2)	0.177	0.162	0.164	0.186	0.171	0.122	0.134	0.132	0.133
Hansen test	0.142	0.158	0.153	0.148	0.144	0.143	0.157	0.166	0.186

Robust Standard errors in parentheses ***$p < 0.01$, **$p < 0.05$, *$p < 0.1$
Notes The definition of variable are same as in Table 6.4

exchange rate regimes, we estimate the model for CFA franc zone. The estimation is further done for WAEMU and CAEMC. It is evident from the results in Table 6.6, models 25–30, that though CBI has a significant and negative impact on inflation in the CFA Zone, the magnitude of this impact is on average lower than the impact it has in the Non-CFA Zone as shown in models 31–32. This is also the same story for the impact of monetary policy, which though is significant and negative, has a stronger impact in the Non-CFA Zone, than in the CFA Zone. Thirdly, the impact of monetary policy on inflation, given higher CBI is relatively higher in the Non-CFA Zone. In models 33–38, we use alternative estimation methods, the Two Stage Least Squares Instrumental Variables and the fixed effects approaches to examine the objectives of the study. The results of the Two Stage Least Squares instrumental variables estimations are not different from those produced by the Two Step GMM, thus confirming the robustness of our findings.

6.7 Conclusion

In the 1980s, monetary policy in Africa was subordinated to the objective of financing large fiscal deficits in the region. This led to high inflation and, in combination with fixed exchange rates, overvalued real exchange rates. From the mid-1980s to the late 1990s, countries began reform programmes, often with exchange rate unifications and movements towards more market-determined exchange rates, notable reductions in central bank financing of government and financial liberalisations. With substantial debt relief and a favourable external environment, fiscal discipline was re-established in many parts of SSA. This provided support for money-based disinflation programmes to bring down inflation to single digits (or near single) by the late 1990s in the context of higher economic growth and higher international reserves, in line with the experience in other developing countries. With inflation higher in non-CFA zones compared to CFA zones, inflation has still been a burden for most African countries as their levels are higher compared to that of other developing and developed countries. As many African countries switched from fixed to floating exchange regimes and reformed their central banks, this study sought to examine the impact of exchange rate regimes on the inflation rate as the empirical literature has conflicting outcomes. With the argument that CBI improves monetary policy effectiveness, given the objective of price stability for central banks, we also examine the impact of

Table 6.6 CBI, Exchange Rate Regime, Monetary Policy and Inflation in Africa

	CFA zone					
	All CFA countries		*WAEMU*		*CAEMC*	
Variables	*(25)*	*(26)*	*(27)*	*(28)*	*(29)*	*(30)*
GDP DEF $_{t-1}$	0.388***	0.302***	0.375***	0.447***	0.348***	0.451***
	(0.027)	(0.028)	(0.015)	(0.015)	(0.013)	(0.009)
World Inflation	0.142**	0.101*	0.126***	0.141*	0.152**	0.131*
	(0.077)	(0.082)	(0.004)	(0.091)	(0.057)	(0.081)
CBI	−0.113**	−0.112**	−0.117**	−0.114**	−0.115**	−0.111*
	(0.058)	(0.052)	(0.066)	(0.063)	(0.062)	(0.099)
PEGGED						
Monetary Policy	−0.065*	−0.072**	−0.081	−0.091**	−0.064*	−0.−073**
	(0.048)	(0.031)	(0.086)	(0.043)	(0.042)	(0.023)
CBI*PEGGED						
Monetary Policy*CBI		−0.142***		−0.144***		−0.121***
		(0.024)		(0.023)		(0.025)
Fiscal Deficit	0.010**	0.031**	0.116**	0.080**	0.053**	0.063**
	(0.023)	(0.031)	(0.078)	(0.097)	(0.064)	(0.063)
Openness	0.077*	0.072**	0.064**	0.071**	0.087**	0.061**
	(0.052)	(0.024)	(0.129)	(0.202)	(0.029)	(0.025)
LGDPC	0.372*	0.065	0.106	0.153	0.365	0.378
	(0.236)	(0.157)	(0.159)	(0.211)	(0.406)	(0.413)
Political Institutions	0.195**	0.076**	0.059	0.081**	0.094**	0.096**
	(0.041)	(0.036)	(0.108)	(0.017)	(0.022)	(0.024)
Private Credit	−0.105	−0.071*	−0.067	−0.029	−0.022*	−0.036
	(0.146)	(0.053)	(0.169)	(0.163)	(0.012)	(0.104)

	CFA zone					
	All CFA countries		*WAEMU*		*CAEMC*	
Variables	*(25)*	*(26)*	*(27)*	*(28)*	*(29)*	*(30)*
Total CBI Effect						
Total Monetary Policy Effect		−0.214**		−0.235**		−0.194**
		(0.071)		(0.069)		(0.044)
Observations	408	408	238	238	215	215
Number of Index	14	14	7	7	6	6
Number of Instruments	7	7	5	5	4	4
AR (1)	0.012	0.013	0.014	0.016	0.013	0.014
AR (2)	0.104	0.112	0.111	0.118	0.125	0.124
Hansen test	0.177	0.178	0.165	0.162	0.161	0.164
R^2						
Wald Chi^2						
Woolridge's OIR						
p-value						
Woolridge Rob						
Robust Regression						

	Non-CFA		*2SLS (5 year averages) (full sample)*			*Fixed effects (full sample)*		
Variables	*(31)*	*(32)*	*(33)*	*(34)*	*(35)*	*(36)*	*(37)*	*(38)*
GDP DEF $_{t-1}$	0.509***	0.511***	0.587***	0.643***	0.636***			
	(0.017)	(0.016)	(0.028)	(0.027)	(0.022)			
World Inflation	0.188**	0.185**	0.113***	0.122***	0.127***	0.073***	0.052***	0.052***
	(0.064)	(0.064)	(0.014)	(0.019)	(0.011)	(0.007)	(0.007)	(0.007)
CBI	−0.158**	−0.162**	−0.211	−0.215**	−0.227**	−0.226	−0.231**	−0.238**

(continued)

Table 6.6 (continued)

	Non-CFA		*2SLS (5 year averages) (full sample)*			*Fixed effects (full sample)*		
Variables	*(31)*	*(32)*	*(33)*	*(34)*	*(35)*	*(36)*	*(37)*	*(38)*
	(0.372)	(0.331)	(0.366)	(0.067)	(0.073)	(0.358)	(0.054)	(0.052)
PEGGED			−0.333**	−0.347**	−0.351**	−0.292**	−0.278**	−0.278**
			(0.064)	(0.069)	(0.069)	(0.051)	(0.054)	(0.054)
Monetary Policy	−0.202**	−0.211**	−0.137	−0.132**	−0.133**	−0.136	−0.143**	−0.125**
	(0.065)	(0.062)	(0.366)	(0.067)	(0.067)	(0.358)	(0.054)	(0.054)
CBI*PEGGED				0.051**			0.074**	
				(0.053)			(0.056)	
Monetary Policy*CBI		−0.165**			−0.153**			−0.138**
		(0.081)			(0.052)			(0.045)
Fiscal Deficit	0.086***	0.084***	0.075**	0.025**	0.031**	0.083**	0.088***	0.096***
	(0.047)	(0.043)	(0.044)	(0.011)	(0.013)	(0.039)	(0.000)	(0.000)
Openness	0.104**	0.123	0.144**	0.249**	0.278**	0.254**	0.277**	0.265**
	(0.046)	(0.341)	(0.039)	(0.078)	(0.054)	(0.090)	(0.072)	(0.071)
LGDPC	0.369*	0.344**	0.190***	0.123	0.135	0.114	0.172*	0.188*
	(0.123)	(0.092)	(0.005)	(0.126)	(0.188)	(0.166)	(0.096)	(0.091)
Political Institutions	0.065**	0.074	0061***	0.057***	0.063***	0.081***	0.095**	0.107
	(0.023)	(0.134)	(0.005)	(0.009)	(0.005)	(0.008)	(0.031)	(0.168)
Private Credit	−0.057**	−0.065**	−0.036*	−0.046*	−0.038*	−0.131**	−0.105*	−0.075
	(0.022)	(0.028)	(0.021)	(0.026)	(0.022)	(0.065)	(0.082)	(0.089)
Total CBI Effect				−0.164***			−0.157***	
				(0.005)			(0.009)	
Total Monetary Policy Effect		−0.376***			−0.286***			−0.263***
		(0.016)			(0.009)			(0.008)
Observations	672	672	208	208	208	915	915	915
Number of Index	34	34				33	38	38

	Non-CFA		2SLS (5 year averages) (full sample)			Fixed effects (full sample)		
Variables	*(31)*	*(32)*	*(33)*	*(34)*	*(35)*	*(36)*	*(37)*	*(38)*
Number of Instruments	21	21						
AR (1)	0.019	0.019						
AR (2)	0.163	0.163						
Hansen test	0.172	0.172				0.425	0.487	0.487
R^2								
Wald Chi^2			45.26***	45.42***	45.42***			
Woolridge's OIR			0.545	0.549	0.549			
p-value			(0.398)	(0.401)	(0.401)			
Woolridge Rob			8.642**	8.639**	8.639**			
Robust Regression			5.523***	5.5248**	5.5248**			

Robust Standard errors in parentheses ***$p < 0.01$, **$p < 0.05$, *$p < 0.1$

Inflation variable is the modified inflation rate computed as: $\mathrm{LOG}(1 + \pi_{\mathrm{GDPD}f})$ where $\pi_{\mathrm{GDPD}f}$ is the annual %age change in GDP deflator. CBI is the annual legal CWN central bank independence index measure of a country's central bank independence. CBGTO is the rescaled annualised five-year average central bank governor turnover rate with lower values corresponding to lower independence and higher values corresponding to higher central bank independence. CBCEO is the index for central bank governor legal independence. CBOBJ is the legal central bank objective independence. CBPOL is the legal central bank policy independence and CB LEND is the legal central bank financial independence index. ***Financial Development*** is credit to the private sector as a %age of GDP; measured as the ratio of stock market total value traded to GDP (%), which are proxies for financial development. ***Political Institutions*** is the average of the rescaled political rights score (0–6) which is proxy for institutional quality. *OPENNESS* is defined as sum of exports and imports in relation to GDP. *PEGGED* is a dummy constructed from the IMF database on de facto exchange regimes, using a one (1) for regimes classified as: "another currency as legal tender," "currency board," or "conventional peg against a single currency," and zero (0) otherwise. Monetary Policy is the central bank policy rate. ***World Inflation*** is proxied by the average inflation rate of industrial countries, computed from the World Bank. *LGDPC* is measured as log of the ratio of real Gross Domestic Product divided by total population. *Fiscal Deficit* is government expenditure less government revenue as a %age of GDP. CFA (Communauté Financière Africaine) franc zone comprises a group of countries in Central and West Africa whose currencies have been linked to the French franc; West African Economic and Monetary Union (WAEMU)—Benin, Burkina Faso, Côte d'Ivoire, Mali, Niger, Senegal and Togo; Central African Economic and Monetary Community (CAEMC), established in March 1994, whose members are Cameroon, the Central African Republic, Chad, the Republic of Congo, Equatorial Guinea and Gabon

CBI on monetary policy in both fixed and floating exchange rate regimes in Africa.

Focusing on the impact of CBI on inflation, we observe that CBI, measured as the CBI index, does not have any significant impact on inflation in model 1, though it has a negative coefficient as expected. The results are the same when CBI is proxied with the component members of the CBI index namely personnel independence (CB CEO); the extent to which price stability is the principal objective of monetary policy (CB OBJ) and the limits of central bank lending to government (CB LEND). We also find that while fixed exchange rate regimes have lower inflation rates than floating exchange rate regimes, CBI is less effective in addressing inflation in fixed exchange rate regimes than it does in floating exchange rate regimes. This is because, a fixed exchange rate regime has a risk of loss of economic policy flexibility in facing external shocks, mainly when economic authorities do not have enough exchange reserves to intervene in the exchange market and/or there is a confidence crisis associated with the lack of government capability in maintaining the pegged exchange rate; under these conditions, the adjustment costs can be very high. This would result in less effective role of the independent central bank in such regimes when compared to floating exchange rate regimes. We realise that CBI associated with monetary policy decisions (CB POL) produces the most significant result on the difference between the impact of CBI in pegged and floating exchange regimes. This can be attributed to the limit in the use of monetary policy rates in fixed exchange regimes to respond to shocks and influence stability in prices. With floating exchange rates having that advantage, the central bank is more effective as the exchange rate channel is available to them, to influence prices, thereby resulting in a bigger impact on inflation.

We also examined our second objective, where we analysed the impact of monetary policy on inflation and the effect of CBI on this impact. It is evident that, monetary policy, has a negative impact on inflation. This is because higher interest rates mean higher cost of credit and lower demand for money. This leads to less money chasing goods and services and therefore, lower prices. CBI improves the effectiveness of monetary policy on inflation. This is because, given a monetary policy decision, independent central banks are better able to ensure its effectiveness as they, for example, would not exceed limits on central bank lending but would also ensure that monetary policy decisions are based on sound and objective economic analysis resulting in lower inflation rates. In such a situation, monetary policy is more effective in more developed financial markets which are products of a better regulated financial market. In order to further buttress the results, we see that though CBI has a significant and negative impact on inflation in the CFA Zone, the magnitude of this impact is on average lower than the impact it has in the Non-CFA Zone. This is also the same story for the impact of monetary policy, which though is significant and negative, has a stronger impact in the Non-CFA Zone, than in the CFA Zone. Thirdly, the impact of monetary policy on inflation, given higher CBI is relatively higher in the Non-CFA Zone. This implies that the benefits of central bank independence exist for all African countries in spite of their exchange rate regime, but floating exchange rate regimes benefit more from CBI as it improves monetary policy effectiveness even more. The results are robust to different estimation techniques.

Appendix

See Tables 6.7 and 6.8.

Table 6.7 Descriptive statistics

Variable	*Mean*	*Median*	*Max*	*Min*	*SD*	*Obs*
Inflation	2.832	0.992	4.083	−1.229	1.477	917
Financial Development	19.892	14.736	160.125	0.491	19.347	1769
World Inflation	6.787	1.453	16.453	1.867	2.854	1865
CBGTO	0.82	0.68	1.2	0.0	0.03	867
CBI	0.453	0.501	0.866	0.134	0.197	1593
Political Institutions	2.178	2	6	0	1.451	1986
Fiscal Deficit	−7.917	22.521	10.985	−84.508	15.124	1379
Per Capita GDP	1362.7	1568.5	14,749.2	113.7	2129.5	1429
PEGGED	0.311	0.302	1	0	0.454	1259
Monetary Policy	25.651	36.227	99.681	−17.758	0.73	1143
Openness	43.58	45.2	92.9	22.5	16.5	1569

Table 6.8 Correlation matrix

	Inflation	*CBI*	*Financial Development*	*Fiscal Deficit*	*World Inflation*	*PEEGED*	*Monetary Policy*	*LGDPC*	*Political Institutions*	*Openness*
Inflation	1.000									
CBI	−0.1754	1.0000								
Financial Development	−0.3825	0.0416	1.000							
Fiscal Deficit	0.0414	−0.0464	−0.0917	1.0000						
World Inflation	0.2430	−0.3087	−0.0974	−0.0521	1.0000					
PEGGED	0.1094	0.0342	−0.1457	0.0774	0.0794	1.0000				
Monetary Policy	−0.3112	0.2587	−0.1342	0.1657	−0.0876	−0.1132	1.000			
LGDPC	−0.2593	0.2313	0.6313	−0.1995	−0.0380	−0.1512	−0.0422	1.0000		
Political Institutions	−0.2642	0.1458	0.5012	−0.0961	−0.1461	−0.239	0.1532	0.5821	1.0000	
Openness	0.0391	−0.1206	0.1498*	−0.0953	0.0014	−0.0258	0.2232	0.0015	0.0042	1.0000

References

Abubakar, A. U., & Ibrahim, S. (2018). An empirical assessment on the impact of exchange rate on price stability in Nigeria. *4th Social Sciences*, 311.

Acemoglu, D., Johnson, S., Querubin, P., & Robinson, J. A. (2008). *When does policy reform work? The case of central bank independence* (No. w14033). National Bureau of Economic Research.

Adam, C., Berg, A., Portillo, R., & Unsal, F. (2018). Monetary policy and central banking in sub-Saharan Africa. *Research handbook on central banking* (pp. 208–228). Edward Elgar Publishing.

Agoba, A. M., Abor, J., Osei, K. A., & Sa-Aadu, J. (2017). Central bank independence and inflation in Africa: The role of financial systems and institutional quality. *Central Bank Review, 17*(4), 131–146.

Agoba, A. M., Abor, J. Y., Osei, K. A., & Sa-Aadu, J. (2020). Do independent central banks exhibit varied behaviour in election and non-election years? The case of fiscal policy in Africa. *Journal of African Business, 21*(1), 105–125.

Agoba, A. M., Abor, J. Y., Osei, K., Sa-Aadu, J., Amoah, B., & Dzeha, G. C. O. (2019). Central bank independence, elections and fiscal policy in Africa: Examining the moderating role of political institutions. *International Journal of Emerging Markets*.

Aguir, A. (2018). Central bank credibility, independence, and monetary policy. *Journal of Central Banking Theory and Practice, 7*(3), 91–110.

Alesina, A., & Summers, L. H. (1993). Central bank independence and macroeconomic performance: Some comparative evidence. *Journal of Money, Credit and Banking, 25*(2), 151–162.

Alpanda, S., & Honig, A. (2014). The impact of central bank independence on the performance of inflation targeting regimes. *Journal of International Money and Finance, 44*, 118–135.

Anwar, C. J., & Nicholas, O. (2020). Causality relationship between central bank reforms and inflation: Evidence from developing countries. *Signifikan: Jurnal Ilmu Ekonomi, 9*(1), 15–30.

Arnone, M., & Romelli, D. (2013). Dynamic central bank independence indices and inflation rate: A new empirical exploration. *Journal of Financial Stability, 9*(3), 385–398.

Bahmani-Oskooee, M., & Saha, S. (2020). On the asymmetric effects of exchange rate volatility on the trade flows of India with each of its fourteen partners. *Macroeconomics and Finance in Emerging Market Economies*, 1–20.

Barro, R. J., & Gordon, D. B. (1983). Rules, discretion and reputation in a model of monetary policy. *Journal of Monetary Economics, 12*(1), 101–121.

Bazzi, S., & Clemens, M. A. (2013). Blunt instruments: Avoiding common pitfalls in identifying the causes of economic growth. *American Economic Journal: Macroeconomics, 5*(2), 152–186.

Bleaney, M., & Fielding, D. (2002). Exchange rate regimes, inflation and output volatility in developing countries. *Journal of Development Economics, 68*(1), 233–245.

Bleaney, M., & Francisco, M. (2007). Exchange rate regimes, inflation and growth in developing countries—An assessment. *The BE Journal of Macroeconomics, 7*(1).

Bodea, C. (2010). Exchange rate regimes and independent central banks: A correlated choice of imperfectly credible institutions. *International Organization, 64*(3), 411–442.

Bodea, C., & Hicks, R. (2015a). Price stability and central bank independence: Discipline, credibility, and democratic institutions. *International Organization, 69*(1), 35–61.

Bodea, C., & Hicks, R. (2015b). International finance and central bank independence: Institutional diffusion and the flow and cost of capital. *The Journal of Politics, 77*(1), 268–284.

Bodea, C., & Higashijima, M. (2015). Central banks and fiscal policy: Why independent central banks can lead to lower fiscal deficits. *LSE European Politics and Policy (EUROPP) Blog*.

Bodea, C., & Higashijima, M. (2017). Central bank independence and fiscal policy: Can the central bank restrain deficit spending? *British Journal of Political Science, 47*(1), 47–70.

Bontempi, M. E., & Mammi, I. (2015). Implementing a strategy to reduce the instrument count in panel GMM. *The Stata Journal, 15*(4), 1075–1097.

Bouoiyour, J., & Selmi, R. (2013). *The effects of central banks' independence on inflation outcomes in emerging countries: Does the choice of exchange regime matter?*.

Brambor, T., Clark, W. R., & Golder, M. (2006). Understanding interaction models: Improving empirical analyses. *Political Analysis, 14*(1), 63–82.

Calvo, G. A., & Reinhart, C. M. (2002). Fear of floating. *The Quarterly Journal of Economics, 117*(2), 379–408.

Canetti, E., & Greene, J. (2000). *Monetary growth and exchange rate depreciation as causes of inflation in African Countries*. School of Business Montclair State University.

Chhibber, A., & Shafik, N. (1990). *Exchange reform, parallel markets, and inflation in Africa: The case of Ghana* (No. 427). The World Bank.

Copelovitch, P., & Singer, A. (2007). *Financial regulation, monetary policy and inflation in industrialized world*. Annual meeting of the Midwest political science association.

Coulibaly, I., & Davis, J. (2013). *Exchange rate regimes and economic performance: Does CFA zone membership benefit their economies?*

Cukierman, A. (1992). *Central bank strategy, credibility, and independence: Theory and evidence* (p. 393). MIT press.

De Grauwe, P., & Schnabl, G. (2004). EMU entry strategies for the new member states. *Intereconomics, 39*(5), 241–246.

De Grauwe, P., & Schnabl, G. (2008). Exchange rate stability, inflation, and growth in (South) Eastern and Central Europe. *Review of Development Economics, 12*(3), 530–549.

De Haan, J., Bodea, C., Hicks, R., & Eijffinger, S. C. (2018). Central bank independence before and after the crisis. *Comparative Economic Studies, 60*(2), 183–202.

Dong, B., Ma, X., Wang, N., & Wei, W. (2020). Impacts of exchange rate volatility and international oil price shock on China's regional economy: A dynamic CGE analysis. *Energy Economics, 86*, 103762.

Dordunoo, C. K., & Njinkeu, D. (1997). Foreign exchange rate regimes and macroeconomic performance in Sub-Saharan Africa. *Journal of African Economies*, 121–149.

Frankel, J. A., & Catão, L. A. (2011). A comparison of product price targeting and other monetary anchor options for commodity exporters in Latin America [with comment]. *Economia, 12*(1), 1–70.

Ftiti, Z., Aguir, A., & Smida, M. (2017). Time-inconsistency and expansionary business cycle theories: What does matter for the central bank independence—Inflation relationship? *Economic Modelling, 67*, 215–227.

Garriga, A. C. (2016). Central bank independence in the world: A new data set. *International Interactions, 42*(5), 849–868.

Garriga, A. C., & Rodriguez, C. M. (2020). More effective than we thought: Central bank independence and inflation in developing countries. *Economic Modelling, 85*, 87–105.

Ghosh, S. K. (2002). RBI intervention in the forex market: Results from a tobit and logit model using daily data. *Economic and Political Weekly*, 2333–2348.

Ghosh, A. R., Qureshi, M. S., & Tsangarides, C. G. (2013). Is the exchange rate regime really irrelevant for external adjustment? *Economics Letters, 118*(1), 104–109.

Guellil, Z., Marouf, F. Z., & Benbouziane, M. (2017, May). Exchange rate regimes and economic growth in developing countries: An empirical study using panel data from 1980 to 2013. In *Management International Conference, Monastier di Treviso (Venice), Italy* (pp. 24–27).

He, Q., & Zou, H. F. (2018). *Central bank independence and inflation: Schumpeterian theory and evidence* (No. 606). China Economics and Management Academy, Central University of Finance and Economics.

International Monetary Fund. (2019). *World economic outlook*. Washington, D.C: International Monetary Fund.

Ismihan, M., & Ozkan, F. G. (2012). Public debt and financial development: A theoretical exploration. *Economics Letters, 115*(3), 348–351.

Iwasaki, I., & Uegaki, A. (2017). Central bank independence and inflation in transition economies: A comparative meta-analysis with developed and developing economies. *Eastern European Economics, 55*(3), 197–235. https://doi.org/10.1080/00128775.2017.1287548

Kappel, R. (1993). Future prospects for the CFA Franc Zone. *Intereconomics, 28*(6), 269–278.

Katseli, L. T., Theofilakou, A., & Zekente, K. M. (2020). Central bank independence and inflation preferences: New empirical evidence on the effects on inflation. *Economic Issues, 25*(Part 1).

Khan, M. A., & Nawaz, S. (2018). Does Pak-Rupee exchange rate respond to monetary fundamentals? A structural analysis. *The Pakistan Development Review, 57*(2), 175–202.

Kim, Y., & Lim, H. (2020). Transmission of monetary policy in times of high household debt. *Journal of Macroeconomics, 63*, 103168.

Klomp, J., & De Haan, J. (2010). Central bank independence and inflation revisited. *Public Choice, 144*(3), 445–457.

Kydland, F. E., & Prescott, E. C. (1977). Rules rather than discretion: The inconsistency of optimal plans. *Journal of Political Economy, 85*(3), 473–491.

Lohi, J. (2014). Exchange rate regimes and inflation in Sub-Saharan Africa. *Journal of Economics and International Finance, 6*(8), 173–189.

London, A. (1989). Money, Inflation and adjustment policy in Africa: Some further evidence. *African Development Review, 1*(1), 87–111.

Lucotte, Y. (2012). Adoption of inflation targeting and tax revenue performance in emerging market economies: An empirical investigation. *Economic Systems, 36*(4), 609–628.

Mahamadu, B., & Abradu-Otoo, P. (2003). *Monetary growth, exchange rates and inflation in Ghana: An error correction analysis*. Working Paper, WP/BOG-2003/05.

Ndung'u, N. S. (1997). Price and exchange rate dynamics in Kenya: An empirical investigation (1970–1993). *Research Paper/African Economic Research Consortium, 58*.

Nguyen, A. D., Dridi, J., Unsal, F. D., & Williams, O. H. (2017). On the drivers of inflation in Sub-Saharan Africa. *International Economics, 151*, 71–84.

Odusola, A. F., & Akinlo, A. E. (2001). Output, inflation, and exchange rate in developing countries: An application to Nigeria. *The Developing Economies, 39*(2), 199–222.

Phillips, A. W. (1958). The relation between unemployment and the rate of change of money wage rates in the United Kingdom, 1861–1957. *Economica, 25*, 283–299.

Plümper, T., & Troeger, V. E. (2007). Efficient estimation of time-invariant and rarely changing variables in finite sample panel analyses with unit fixed effects. *Political Analysis, 15*(2), 124–139.

Rodman, D. (2009). How to do xtabond2: An introduction to difference and system GMM in Stata. *The Stata Journal, 9*(1), 86–136.

Romer, D. (1993). Openness and inflation: Theory and evidence. *The Quarterly Journal of Economics, 108*(4), 869–903.

Strong, C. (2018, August 14). Did Mali benefit from joining the CFA zone? An analysis using the synthetic control method. *An Analysis Using the Synthetic Control Method.*

The World Bank Group. (2019). World Development Indicators (WDI) Online. http://publications.worldbank.org/WDI/

Windmeijer, F. (2005). A finite sample correction for the variance of linear efficient two-step GMM estimators. *Journal of Econometrics, 126*(1), 25–51.

Zhang, C., & Zheng, N. (2020). Monetary policy and financial investments of nonfinancial firms: New evidence from China. *China Economic Review, 60*, 101420.

CHAPTER 7

Monetary Policy, Central Banks' Independence, and Financial Development in Africa

Joshua Yindenaba Abor, Abel M. Agoba, Zakari Mumuni, and Alfred Yawson

7.1 Introduction

Monetary policy is seen as the process by which a country's government, central bank, or monetary authority controls money supply, availability

J. Y. Abor
Department of Finance, University of Ghana Business School, Accra, Ghana
e-mail: joshabor@ug.edu.gh

A. M. Agoba (✉)
School of Economics Finance and Accounting, Coventry University, Coventry, United Kingdom
e-mail: ad8749@coventry.ac.uk

Z. Mumuni
Bank of Ghana, Accra, Ghana
e-mail: zakari.mumuni@bog.gov.gh

J. Y. Abor and C. K. D. Adjasi (eds.), *The Economics of Banking and Finance in Africa*, Palgrave Macmillan Studies in Banking and Financial Institutions, https://doi.org/10.1007/978-3-031-04162-4_7

of money, and interest rate so as to achieve defined objectives geared towards the growth and stability of the economy and financial systems (Quartey & Afful-Mensah, 2014). Monetary policy is primarily dependent on the cost of borrowing and money supply relationship. Across the sub-Saharan African region, monetary policy has gradually converged in the quest to achieve price stability as the overarching monetary policy objective (Heintz & Ndikumana, 2011; Mishra & Debata, 2020). This is seen in the adoption of inflation targeting regimes by South Africa, Ghana, Mauritius, and Uganda (Klutse et al., 2022). These countries' monetary policy practice focuses on domestic credit control to contain domestic demand with the view to achieving price stability. This aligns with arguments made by monetarists such as Harry G. Johnson, Milton Friedman, and Friedrich Hayek which was that constraining the growth of money supply was a more effective way of keeping inflation in check compared to policies centred on demand-management (Friedman & Schwartz, 1965; Hayek, 1976; Johnson, 1963). With monetary policy being used to control cyclical fluctuations in the economy, the price stability achieved consequently is good for financial development for many reasons.

First, lower levels of inflation translate into lower short-term interest rates, which drive demand for more credit. Subsequently, longer-term rates also decline. The lower interest rates imply higher bond prices which also imply that fixed income earners would have higher principal values for their bonds. This should encourage bond market development (Kang & Pflueger, 2015; Sahoo, 2020). Second, with low inflation, real returns on bonds are higher compared to periods of high Inflation. These high real returns do encourage participation in the bond market. Another significance of price stability for financial development is the stability it provides to financial institutions to properly evaluate viable business projects (Asab & Al-Tarawneh, 2018; Sherraden et al., 2015) thereby growing credit to the private sector. Issahaku (2018) underscored the importance of monetary policy effectiveness to financial development in developing countries.

In spite of the above enumerated impact of monetary policy on price stability and, therefore, financial development, there is a limit on its effect

A. Yawson
The University of Adelaide Business School, Adelaide, SA, Australia
e-mail: alfred.yawson@adelaide.edu.au

on real economic activity (Clouse, 2020; Lacker, 2014). When it comes to the empirical literature on monetary policy effectiveness, the results have been mixed. While some studies conclude that changes in the growth of money result solely in changing the value of nominal but not real gross domestic product, others insist that inflation will result from the growth of money supply (Friedman, 1995; Lacker, 2014). It is in mostly developed countries that this kind of money supply and real economics activities association has been established (Romer & Romer, 2002) but not in developing countries (Lashkary & Kashani, 2011).

Under these circumstances, the focus of discussions has been shifted to the conditions under which monetary policy is effective and credible. One of such conditions that has been argued is the central bank's autonomy (Masciandaro & Romelli, 2015). According to Alavinasab (2016), monetary policy's role in economic development, coupled with changes in aggregate economic activity, are consequences of the conduct of monetary policy and the extent to which the central bank is independent in choosing the appropriate tools of monetary policy to achieve macroeconomic objectives. Central bank independence is the state of having monetary policy delegated to officials who are unelected in a way that restricts the influence of political authorities on monetary policy (de Haan et al., 2018). The impact of central bank decisions on interest rates, exchange rates, and the development of private banks is undisputable.

This chapter's main objective is to examine the conditions under which monetary policy is effective, particularly in Africa in influencing financial development; that is banking, stock market, and bond market development. The focus of our analysis is central bank independence.

Why focus on Africa? Firstly, the role of bank credit in the lives of households and businesses is huge in the sub-Saharan African region (Alfazema, 2020). The deeply embedded information asymmetries, non-existing and poorly developed capital markets, and alternative nonbank credit facilities makes many very reliant on external financing mainly in the form of loans from the banks. The impact of poor and ineffective monetary policy frameworks could post huge and dire consequences for private sector activity and growth (Bernanke & Gertler, 2000). More so, there exist quite significant differences in the ways through which credit in developed countries and developing countries is impacted by monetary policy (Ndikumana, 2014). Whiles in the more advanced financial systems, demand for credit determines the equilibrium quantity of credit extended by commercial banks who accept loan applications at prices that are already determined and conditions that are not related to pricing, the central bank determines policy rates, which subsequently determine the interest rates at which banks stand ready to provide credit. The adjustment made by borrowers with regard to the usage of their lines of credit is based on changes that are made to interest rates. As such, banks' operations are in the form of "retailers of credit" (Flammer, & Ioannou, 2020). In these jurisdictions, the determinants of credit demand, which are independent of monetary policy, ultimately determine equilibrium credit. In this context, there is a limited role of central banks in determining domestic credit. In the case of sub-Saharan African countries, however, it is the component of the credit market which belong to the supply side, specifically banks who in the end are the determinants of who receives and how much credit is disbursed. The typical firm in Africa is credit constrained and does not have an idle line of credit (Fosu & Abass, 2019). The African countries which belong to the emerging markets display what is termed as "financial dualism"; a situation where there are a few who have access to credit from the bank while most of the others (i.e., firms and individuals) lack access to finance. In such countries, it is not demanded that for credit that informs equilibrium credit levels. As such, the responsibility the central bank has in determining the amount of domestic credit using interest rate changes could potentially limit credit is paramount (Bednarek et al., 2021). This raises significant importance for the roles central banks play in Africa's financial development. Furthermore, the low competitive nature of the banking sector found in Africa also means that it is the supply rather than demand that determines the equilibrium level of credit (Adil & Jalil, 2020). This could have implications for the impact of monetary policy on various aspects of financial development, e.g. deposits and credit. Lastly, according to Ndikuma (2014), high cost of credit strengthened local currencies and shallow credit markets constitute significant challenges to making African exports competitive. The primary factor here is that tight monetary policy makes exports expensive and imports cheaper. This deteriorates the balance of payments position, and exchange rate worsens as demand for imports increase. In turn, this potentially creates debt service challenges especially where external debt is sizable with additional pressure on the balance of payments. This has severely constrained the effectiveness of monetary policy. How effective would central bank independence be in making monetary policy more effective in Africa in the face of these challenges?

In the next sections, we present the stylised facts on monetary policy, central bank independence, and financial development in Africa, review the literature, develop the methodology, present the results, and conclude the article.

7.2 Stylised Facts on Monetary Policy, Central Banks' Independence, and Financial Development in Africa

In developed countries, inflation rates have been relatively low compared to developing countries. Inflation rates rose in 1970, from 5.7% to 15.1 in 1976. It, however, declined to 9.1% in 1980 and increased again to 14.2% in 1980. It remained stable up to 1981 after which it fell significantly to 4.9% in 1989. It rose to 6.5% in 1992 and declined to about 3% in 1998. Inflation rates in developed countries have been declining since then to rates close to about 2% as at 2017. As of 2019, average inflation rate in emerging markets and developing economies was 4.8% while that of Africa was 11.7%. Thus, on average, Africa has higher inflation rates than other developing countries. Headline inflation slowed across the region in 2019 amid stable exchange rates, and amid slowing food price inflation due to higher food production. Asia and the Pacific region recorded Inflation of 3.4% compared to that of Europe which was 2.3% (World Development Indicators, 2019). This is depicted in Fig. 7.1.

Over the sample period (1970–2019), nominal interest rates have risen with higher rates in floating exchange rate regimes (6%) compared to 2% for countries with pegged rates. The highest rate, however, is seen in intermediate exchange rate regime countries, which was almost 9%. On average, 0.2% real interest rates (nominal rates adjusted for inflation) under fixed exchange regimes, 1.8% under intermediate regimes, and 2.3% under floating regimes are recorded.

The financial system in Africa is mostly bank sector dominated. The equity and bond markets are either poorly developed or non-existent, thereby constraining access to capital. There exist significant levels of financial exclusion due to limited financial instruments among many other

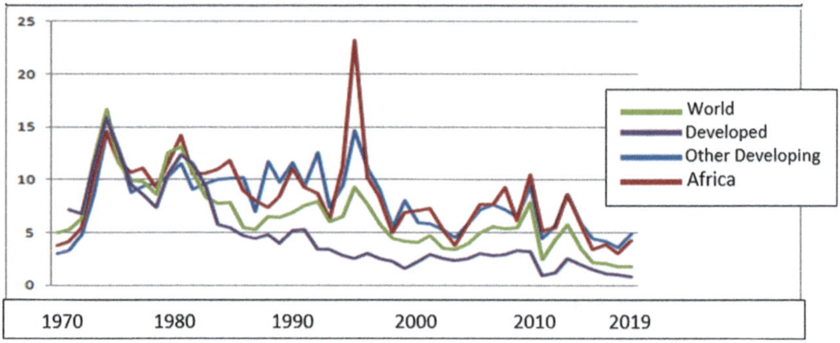

Fig. 7.1 Inflation trend from 1970–2019 (*Source* World Development Indicators [2020])

factors. In addition, interest rates on loans are exorbitantly very high (Bascom, 2016). Table 7.1 depicts details of the above observations. Figure 7.2 indicates that there exist differences in the level of financial development in South Africa (the biggest economy in Africa), Ghana (a small but fast-growing economy), and Uganda (a very small economy). It

Table 7.1 Financial development in Africa, other developing and developed countries

	Financial access and outreach				*Interest rate spread*
	Depositors with commercial banks	*Borrowers from commercial banks*	*Commercial bank branches*	*Automated teller machines*	*Lending rate minus deposit rate*
	per 1,000 adults 2019	*per 1,000 adults 2019*	*per 100,000 adults 2019*	*per 100,000 adults 2019*	*percentage points 2019*
Africa	293	36	5.4	5.79	7.2
Other Developing	660	24	9.5	9.66	4.3
Developed	1,988	.	17.4	62.15	.
World	1,152	.	12.4	47.51	5.6

Source World Development Indicators (2019)

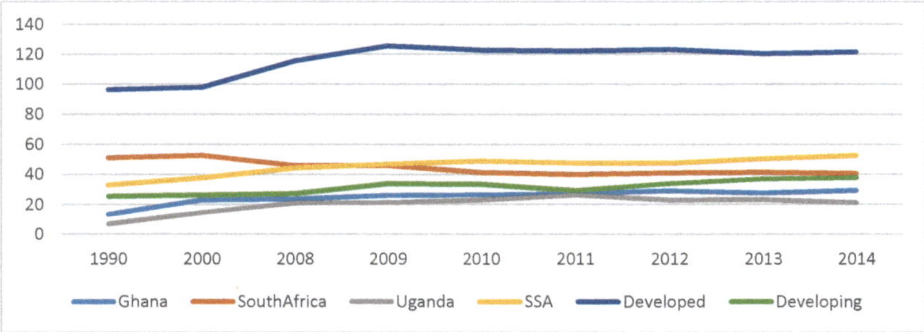

Fig. 7.2 Broad Money (M2) as a percentage of GDP (*Source* Authors own computation, World Development Indicators [2017])

is evident that Uganda and Ghana have shallow financial systems relative to South Africa.

In Fig. 7.3, we see that there exist little differences in the legal independence of central banks in Africa, other developing and developed countries. This could support the assertion CBI's role in determining monetary policy effectiveness in Africa could be significant as it compares equally with the high legal CBI status in developed and other developing countries.

In Fig. 7.4 we also observe that while developed countries have had higher levels of institutional quality, measured by the rescaled civil liberties score (from 0 for least ratings and 6 for highest rating) from Freedom

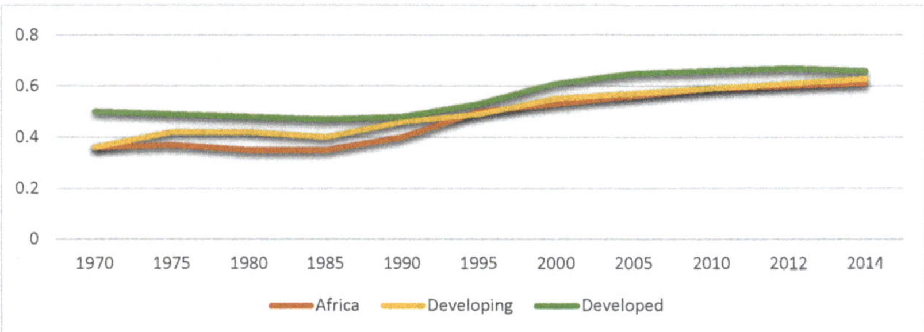

Fig. 7.3 Average CBI 1970–2014 (*Source* Authors' own computation, Garriga [2016]; Bodea and Hicks [2015])

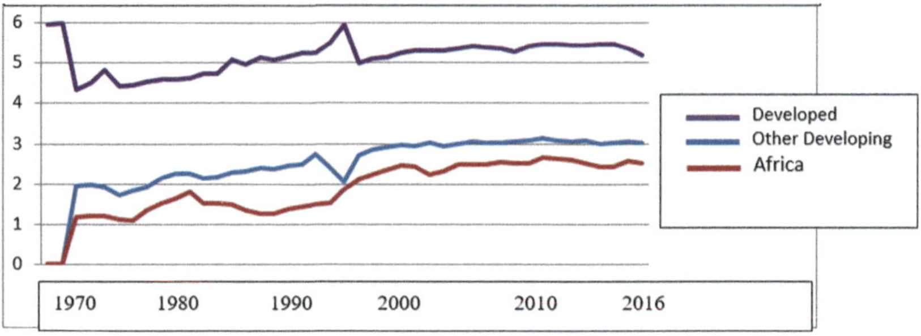

Fig. 7.4 Institutional quality (civil liberties) 1970–2016 (*Source* Freedom House [2017])

House from 1970 to 2016, Africa has had the lowest levels of institutional quality. This has implications for the credibility of central bank independence in these regions.

7.3 Literature Review

Theoretical Foundation

Studies on the effectiveness of monetary policy and its impact on the economy have been abundantly examined by monetary economists and policymakers (Mansor, 2005). When policy rates/money market rates change, it is expected that bank lending rates would also change (Leuvensteijn et al., 2013). There are two (2) competing theories that explain this asymmetric adjustment of interest rate. First is the collusive behaviour hypothesis, which established the relationship between the degree of banking competition and the concentration of the retail market. This hypothesis holds that the likelihood for banks to increase lending rates is non-existent as they seek to maintain their collusive arrangement and as such, when policy rates are reduced, lending rates will be rigid downward (De Bondt, 2005). On the other hand, the customer reaction hypothesis discussed borrowers' reaction when policy rates change. The hypothesis states that in a highly competitive banking environment, the likelihood that bank lending rates will increase is low because banks are aware of the potential negative customer reactions. This hypothesis suggests that when policy rates increase, lending rates will be rigid upward (De Bondt, 2005).

The theoretical argument supporting central bank independence is that, for various reasons, a dependent central bank, is highly biassed in fighting Inflation (Agoba et al., 2020; Fischer, 2015). What accounts for this, according to Drazen (2004), includes pressure from political authorities to have economic activities and productivity boosted in the short run, in order to have an advantage during elections, even at the expense of costs that arise in the long run. The other motivation is the tendency for political authorities to take advantage of the power the central banks have to print and issue money to provide financing for state deficits. The third is what is referred to as time-inconsistency problem of monetary policy making which refers to the lack of credibility of monetary policymakers. It is argued that they renege on their promises to maintain price stability given some incentives. The trust private agents have in the central bank arises when the rules make them accountable and transparent (Masciandaro and Romelli (2015). It has been shown empirically by Lupuşor (2012), however, that CBI is not a sufficient condition in guaranteeing freedom from political pressures in the monetary policy-making space.

The impact of an independent central bank on monetary policy effectiveness can be explained through its impact on bank competition and information asymmetry. Effective central bank independence ensures objective supervision of banks which leads to a level playing field and increased competitiveness in the banking space. This should have an impact on the effectiveness of monetary policy given policy rate changes into changes in lending rates and therefore greater price stability and growth in financial institutions and markets. This would interrupt the operations of the collusive arrangements that impact the effectiveness of monetary policy. The transparency of independent central banks should contribute to minimising the effects of information asymmetry where banks avoid increases in the lending rates and ration credit to circumvent loan default by riskier borrowers.

Independent regulators are professional and consistent when it comes to the supervision of the financial situation of banks (Barth et al. 2013). The independence of the central bank in regulating and supervising the banking sector also achieves stability of the financial system as much as it does for monetary stability (Quintyn & Taylor, 2002). According to Čihák et al. (2010), independent central banks can resist pressures from political interests who have associations with weak and less compliant financial institutions and show professional discretion in the exercise of its powers to discipline such financial institutions. This can lead to a stable financial system and generate confidence in the financial system. "Hutchison and McDill (1999) particularly argue that central bank provides monetary finance to weak financial institutions when those institutions have close association with government, thereby creating an additional channel for the moral hazard problem" (p. 160).

According to Matemilola et al. (2015), the pass-through of the policy rates to bank lending rate is an important subject matter because it measures the effectiveness of monetary policy to control inflation or stabilise the economy. This study argues that the interest rate pass-through of the policy rate to the bank lending rate and asymmetric adjustment of the bank lending rate depends on the credibility of the monetary policy framework which depends on the independence of the central bank. If central banks are not credible, monetary policy changes would not be easily believed since past inconsistencies in monetary policy would feed into the acceptability of current monetary policy changes. If such is the case, financial institutions and markets will be slow in passing-through policy changes into their decisions, thereby leading to no or partial pass-through. This would not bode well for changes in lending and deposit interest rates which should have an impact on supply and demand for credit. However, if a central bank is independent, it eases the pass-through of monetary policy changes and promotes financial development.

According Borys (2011), stock prices are known to be greatly sensitive to economic conditions; highly volatile and as such potentially lead to large swings in the prices and returns on stocks and can negatively impact economic growth. Dividend and interest rate changes as well as individual security risks are factors that have been established to affect investor decision making. These factors are highly impacted by central banks' monetary policy implementation. When central banks change short-term interest rates, signals relating to the present and future outlook of the economy are transmitted to investors whose purchase and sell behaviour subsequently change in the equity market. Consequently, asset prices get affected, and then asset allocation in the broader economy is also affected. Chiarella et al. (2013) note that when there is a decision that signals a riskier macroeconomic environment in the future, there is likely to be a reduction in stock prices When investors expect central banks to increase interest rates, or if investors have an expectation of a more uncertain future cash flow from stocks, then they would have higher expected returns. Bernanke and Kuttner (2005) argued that asset prices are primarily functions of risk and return. The higher the risk, the greater the required return (Nyberg, 2012).

Besides inflation being a monetary phenomenon that tells what happens to the quantity of money per unit of output, it also impacts the stock market (Fama & Schwert, 1977). As such, it has an important place in the relationship between monetary policy and stock market development. Fama (1981), Gertler and Grinols (1982) posit that there is a negative relationship between Inflation and stock prices while the Fisher hypothesis thinks differently.

These included the tax-effect hypothesis and the proxy effect hypothesis (Fama, 1981; Feldstein & Horioka, 1980). There is an argument on reverse causality hypothesis by Geske and Roll (1983), that the stock market's reaction to future economic activity is correlated with government revenue. When there is a government deficit and a reduction in economic activity, domestic borrowing increases or the central bank increases money supply leading to a balanced budget. This increase in domestic borrowing or issuance of money creates Inflation and dampens real economic activity. Stock market returns subsequently falls thus leading to an inverse relationship between stock market returns and Inflation.

Empirical Literature on Monetary Policy and Financial Development

There abound several pieces of literature examining the relationship between monetary policy and financial development. One is by De Bondt (2005) whose study revealed that in South Africa, bank lending rates were responsive to decreases in the money market rate and therefore commercial banks changed their lending rates downwards while the lending rate appeared rigid upward; thus, providing support for the customer reaction hypothesis. In Mauritius, Jankee (2004) also found the presence of asymmetric adjustment for bank lending noting that there was a slow adjustment in bank lending rates when money market rates increased. However, bank lending rates adjusted faster when money market rates decreased. According to Becker et al. (2013), the asymmetric money market rate pass-through is determined by a number of factors such as adjustment costs, volatility, and uncertainty conditions about the future market. In a study by Gerstenberger and Schnabl (2017), it was concluded that the growing concentration of banks in Japan led to a growing gap between deposits above lending, thus compressing interest margins as the traditional source of bank income.

Ndikumana (2014) investigates what monetary policy implies for domestic investment through its effects on bank lending to the private sector and interest rates in sub-Saharan African countries; argued that there are high costs associated with pursuing price stability through contractionary monetary policy. These costs are in the form of reduced investment and ultimately slower economic growth. This was because capital accumulation is constrained by tight monetary policy as it increases borrowing costs through the reduction of loanable funds and the increment in cost of debt as a result of higher interest rates. When the cost of production increases, it translates into higher prices of goods and services which are passed unto consumers. This creates a problem when we focus on the stabilisation of inflation as a gauge of the success of monetary policy. This is the case for many African countries that are still pursuing high growth rates despite the stable inflation levels achieved. The challenge is to raise domestic investment rates. The study found that domestic investment was negatively affected by contractionary monetary policy both indirectly through the bank lending channel and directly through the interest rate or cost of capital channel. The study concluded by suggesting policies geared towards achieving low interest rates to stimulate bank lending to the private sector, which would boost domestic investment.

In a study in Nigeria by Usman and Adejare (2014) covering the period of 1970 to 2010, they concluded that rediscount rate and deposits have positively and significantly affected industrial output while treasury bills have had a negative impact on industrial output. Jimenez et al. (2009) in their study of the impact of decreasing interest on Spanish banks showed that loan defaults were minimised in the short term; while low interest rates led to an increase in lending to highly risky borrowers in order to make some profits. The findings had earlier been confirmed by Lopez-Buenache (2019). According to Altunbas et al. (2010), banks that had low capital, increased risks in lending during the periods of low interest rates. Furthermore, Ioannidou et al. (2015) show that banks offered more loans to risky borrowers at low interest rates compared to less risky borrowers. The presence of securitisation made it possible to increase household and corporate loans during periods of low interest rates (Ciccarelli et al., 2015).

Geng and Zhai (2015) show that interest rates and return on equity had a positive correlation in banks. Bittner et al. (2020) concluded that decreasing interest rates resulted in higher credit to firms and borrowers. The study also found that bigger banks had more capital and the more liquid banks had low chances of lending to risky borrowers and vice versa. Smaller banks were found to have a higher chance of lending to start-ups. According to Mahrous et al. (2020) there is a positive relationship between policy rate and bank risk-taking with long periods of low interest rates leading to more bank risk-taking.

When it comes to stock prices and monetary policy, contrary to Friedman (1956) position, Laopodis (2013) found that stock prices increased whenever the money supply was high. This increase in prices led to more stock market development. According to Friedman (1956) growth in money supply may not lead to higher stock prices because real sector conditions can offset conditions in the money. This is supported by Rigobon and Sack (2004) and Sousa (2010) who show that there exists an inverse relationship between the performance of the stock market and monetary policy which is contractionary. This was in contrast to the findings by Cooper, (1974) where there was no established relationship between money and stock prices. According to Hayford and Malliaris, (2004), there was a rather weak relationship between monetary policy and the stock market. Chatziantoniou et al. (2013) report that stock market performance was affected by innovations in monetary policy instruments and was a means of providing feedback to the central bank on the expected course of the economy by private sector

Empirical Literature on CBI and Financial Development

The financial development literature (Ang & McKibbin, 2007; Chinn & Ito, 2011; Baltagi et al., 2009) has identified institutional factors as key (Tayssir & Feryel, 2017). The high information and transaction cost experienced in many Africa financial systems have been found to be caused by institutional factors as they remain the fundamental roots of these costs (Fernández & Tamayo, 2017; North, 1990). Evidence abounds to the effect that aside political institutions, economic institutions such as central banks independence affect financial development (Masciandaro & Romelli, 2015) through their impact on actual and expected Inflation, government dent and expenditure, as well as interest rates (Agoba et al., 2017; Berger et al., 2017; da Cruz et al., 2016; Eijffinger et al., 2006;

Mbulawa, 2015; Papadamou et al., 2017; Raza et al., 2018; Stiglitz & Weiss, 1981). A study by Doumpos et al. (2016) on the impact of central bank independence on bank soundness, revealed that bank soundness increased with higher independent central banks. This is because when central banks are independent, they execute their regulatory and supervisory role in an objective and professional manner thereby ensuring financial stability (Quintyn & Taylor, 2002). According to Čihák (2010), dependent central banks may be lax in their supervision of financial institutions that have political interested stakeholders and may even provide monetary finance to such firms when they become weak and problematic raising excessive moral hazard issues. In a study by Agoba et al. (2017), CBI had no direct impact of on Inflation in Africa except in the presence of high levels of civil liberties and political rights. An earlier study by Papadamou and Siriopoulos (2014) showed that lower interest rates and higher economic activities were functions of very credible monetary policy frameworks as well as higher effective exchange rates. The conclusion was that since CBI improved the credibility of monetary policy, the lower interest rates generated would spur on higher access to private credit.

Interactive Effect of Monetary Policy and CBI on Financial Development

The impact of an independent central bank on monetary policy effectiveness can be explained through its impact on bank competition and information asymmetry. Effective central bank independence ensures objective supervision of banks which leads to a level playing field and increased competitiveness in the banking space (Agoba et al., 2020). This should have an impact on the effectiveness of monetary policy as changes in policy rate lead to changes in lending rates. Subsequently, we have greater price stability which is good for financial development. This would interrupt the operations of the collusive arrangements that impact effectiveness of monetary policy. The transparency of independent central banks should contribute to minimising the effects of information asymmetry where banks avoid increases in the lending rates and ration credit to circumvent loan default by riskier borrowers (Fernández & Tamayo, 2017).

The argument is that central bank independence makes monetary policy credible and consistent and therefore able to achieve the intended price stability that is favourable for financial development (Klomp &

Sseruyange, 2020). Should a central bank embark on a contractionary monetary policy to achieve price stability, but it is not independent from political control, it's dependent nature could lead it to neutralise the effect of the contractionary monetary policy through a relaxed fiscal policy stance. For example, whereby it lends to central government it increases money supply (contrary to its monetary policy tightening stance), resulting in higher money growth and inflation.

Secondly, apart from price stability, financial development is also a function of regulations such as capital requirement, deposit insurance, private monitoring of bank risk-taking and soundness as well as restrictions on activities, and (e.g., Agoraki et al., 2011; Laeven & Levine, 2009). Studies on the relationship between the supervision system architecture and financial development (Masciandaro & Romelli, 2015) however are lacking. As stated by Doumpos et al. (2016), the theoretical model Berger and Kismer (2013) is contrary to the belief in the importance of CBI in achieving price and financial stability as an independent central bank can create the necessary environment that enables financial institutions to take advantage of the stable macro-environment created by monetary policy.

From the above review, it is evident that though CBI has established benefit for Inflation and financial development, in Africa, its role in improving monetary policy credibility has not been entirely established due to poor political institutional characters. This study seeks to examine if CBI in Africa does improve monetary policy impact on financial development as the region strives to improve it institutions and markets.

7.4 Methodology

Data and Sample

The period for this study spans the years 1970–2014, for 48 African countries. Central bank independence data is obtained from Garriga (2016) and Bodea and Hicks (2015) who compute the Cukierman Web and Neyapti (CWN) index for over the period 1970–2014. The variables identified as control variables are motivated by Tayssir and Feryel (2017) and Chinn and Ito (2006). These variables are trade openness, per capita GDP, annual growth rate of real GDP, public debt, central bank assets to GDP, dummies for inflation targeting regimes and exchange rate regimes.

Model and Estimation Technique

Estimation Technique

Literature has argued that current values of financial development, will be a function of their past values (Agoba et al., 2020; Murinde & Eng, 1994). We include a lag of financial development in the model in order to improve the precision of point estimates (Mizon, 1995). The two-step System Generalised Method of Moments (SGMM) estimator, with Windmeijer (2005) corrected standard errors is used to effectively deal with joint endogeneity and minimise the biases that fixed effects induce. Faced with potential instrument proliferation challenges, we collapse the instrument matrix. This gives us higher point estimates, low number of instruments as well as a Hansen test that can be relied on with low *p*-values (Bontempi & Mammi, 2015; Roodman, 2009). We conduct an autocorrelation test and adopt a robust estimate of the coefficient standard errors on the assumption of zero correlations across individuals in the idiosyncratic disturbances. We also report the Hansen test of over-identifying restrictions, and Arellano–Bond test for AR (2) in first differences, in addition to the number of instruments (Bazzi & Clemens, 2013).

Model

The basic model for the study motivated by our objectives is as follows:

$$\mathrm{FINDEV_{it}} = \beta_1 \mathrm{FINDEV_{it-1}} + \beta_2 \mathrm{MP_{it}} + \beta_3 \mathrm{CBI_{it}} + \beta_4 \mathrm{X_{it}} + \varepsilon_{\mathrm{it}} \quad (7.1)$$

The interactive model is:

$$\begin{aligned} \mathrm{FINDEV_{it}} =& \beta_1 \mathrm{FINDEV_{it-1}} + \beta_2 \mathrm{MP_{it}} + \beta_3 \mathrm{CBI_{it}} \\ &+ \beta_4 (\mathrm{MP} * \mathrm{CBI})_{\mathrm{it}} + \beta_5 \mathrm{X_{it}} + \varepsilon_{\mathrm{it}} \end{aligned} \quad (7.2)$$

where:

i represents the country and *t* the time, $\varepsilon_{\mathrm{it}}$ is the error term, $\mathrm{FINDEV_{it}}$ is financial development, $\mathrm{MP_{it}}$ is monetary policy measured by monetary policy rate, real interest rates, and money supply, $\mathrm{CBI_{it}}$ is central bank independence measured by the CWN index, $\mathrm{X_{it}}$ is a set of control variables which are $\mathrm{GDPR_{it}}$ the real GDP annual growth rate, $\mathrm{POPUL_{it}}$ population size, $\mathrm{LGDPC_{it}}$ log of real GDP per capita, $\mathrm{DEBTG_{it}}$ debt-to-GDP ratio, $\mathrm{CBASSETS}_{it}$ the ratio of central bank assets to GDP. $\mathrm{TRD.OPEN_{it}}$ is trade openness which is the ratio of sum of exports and imports to GDP and $FINOPEN_{it}$ which is financial openness measured as the Chinn-Ito Index.

The total effect of the impact of monetary policy on financial development conditioned on CBI is

$$\frac{\partial FINDEV_{it}}{\partial MP_{it}} = \beta_2 + \beta_4 CBI_{it}$$

This follows the methodologies of Brambor et al. (2006), and Asongu and Nwachukwu (2018).

Definition of Variables

Dependent Variable
Financial development ($FINDEV_{it}$) which is measured by four (4) indicators is our dependent variable. It is first measured as the private credit to GDP ratio ($PRIV.CRE_{it}$). This is a measure of the degree of financial intermediation and the development of the banking sector. It is used to capture the value of all credit issued by financial intermediaries to the private sector as a share of GDP. It however does not include credit given to public corporations and other agencies of government whose allocation may not be done on expected return basis. According to Levine (2000), higher levels of private credit indicate higher levels of financial services and therefore greater financial intermediary development.

The second measure is the domestic credit to private sector by banks($Dom.Crt_{it}$). This refers to "…financial resources provided to the private sector by other depository corporations (deposit taking corporations except central banks), such as through loans, purchases of non-equity securities, and trade credits and other accounts receivable, that establish a claim for repayment. For some countries these claims include credit to public enterprises" (World Development Indicators, 2019).

The third is net interest margin (NIM_{it}). NIMs are defined as "the ratio of net interest income divided by interest-bearing assets, where net interest income is in turn defined as the difference between interest income and interest expense. NIMs can also be defined as the difference between the interest income divided by interest-bearing assets and interest expense divided by interest-bearing assets. It is argued that interest income relative to interest-bearing assets and interest expense relative to interest-bearing assets change with the target policy" (World Development Indicators, 2019).

The fourth measure is a widely used measure in literature; stock market capitalisation ($STOCK.MKCAP_{it}$) which is "the ratio of the value of all stock on the domestic markets to GDP and is an indicator of the size of the economy's stock market" (World Development Indicators, 2019). The stock market provides alternative sources of finance and therefore acts as a substitute of or complement to bank credit (Buttner & Hayo, 2011; Yao et al., 2014). Increases in policy rate, for example, should lead to higher interest income from loans and other forms of credit. However, this would be determined by the elasticity of demand for loans.

Explanatory Variables
The study employs a set of financial, demographical, institutional, and macroeconomic variables as explanatory variables.

We employed three (3) monetary policy measures; monetary policy rate, real interest rate, and money supply (M2) as % of GDP. M2 is the sum of currency outside banks, demand deposits other than those of the central government, and the time, savings, and foreign currency deposits of resident sectors other than the central government. Money supply includes the amount of money in circulation and so determines the level of liquidity in the economy. Increasing money supply due to lower policy rates and real interest rates attracts borrowers. This leads to an expansion in credit to the private sector. According to Chatziantoniou et al. (2013), increases in money supply, lead to inflation, which then negatively affects stock market performance thereby making the stock market unattractive. This further leads to lower stock demands and consequently lower volumes and values of stocks traded (Kyereboah-Coleman & Agyire-Tettey, 2008). In this regard, we expect a negative relationship between money supply and stock returns, a positive relationship however between stock returns and policy rate and real interact rates. Real interest rate is a measure of the cost of capital in an economy. According to Mbutor (2007), the marginal efficiency of capital function, however, posits an inverse relationship between real interest rate and the present value of capital and consumer durable goods. Therefore, a reducing real interest rate should increase the present value of capital and durable consumer goods as well as increase the ratio of the market value to the asset value.

Central bank independence is the annual central bank independence measure of country *i* in period *t*. It represents the degree of CBI measured by the *de jure* indicator (CBI_{it}). This CBI index is given by Garriga (2016), who computes an updated Cukierman, Webb, and

Neyapti (CWN) index for a large set of countries using the International Monetary Fund's Central Bank Law Database. The index varies between 0 and 1, with larger values indicating independence. A central bank is legally more independent when the governor's term in office is longer; the appointment and dismissal procedures are more insulated from the government; the mandate is more focused on price stability; the formulation of monetary policy lies squarely with the central bank; and the provisions on direct central bank lending are restrictive. We expect higher levels of CBI to promote financial development and that monetary policy impact becomes stronger in the presence of higher CBI levels.

We use the Freedom House database to source for civil liberties as our measure of political institutional quality ($PolInst_{it}$). This ranges from 7 to 1, with 7 representing the least rating and 1 the highest. In line with Bodea and Higashijima (2015), we rescale the original score to range from 0 to 6, so that lower scores now correspond to lower civil liberties rating and higher scores correspond to higher civil liberties rating. In order to do this, we use the formular $-1*(CLS - 7)$, where CLS is the civil liberties score as given by Freedom House. We also use the rule of law estimate from the World Governance indicators. We expect the coefficient of political/legal institutional quality to be positive.

The control variables include the log of GDP per capita ($LGDPC_{it}$) which captures the level of economic development; real annual GDP growth rate ($GDPR_{it}$) and Inflation targeting regime (IT_{it}) measured as a dummy variable; with a value of *1* for Inflation targeting countries and periods and *0* otherwise. We also include an exchange rate dummy variable ($FEXRT_{it}$), captured as *1* for fixed exchange rate regimes and *0* otherwise. This is based on the de facto exchange rate regime classification by Reinhart and Rogoff (2004, 2009). This dichotomous variable equals *1* when there is no separate legal tender, when there is a pre-announced peg or currency board arrangement, when there is a pre-announced horizontal band that is narrower than or equal to ±2%, or when there is a de facto peg, and *0* otherwise (Calvo & Reinhart, 2002; Tayssir & Feryel, 2017). Other control variables are public debt($DEBTG_{it}$), which is proxied by the ratio of public debt to GDP. This is calculated as the sum of the accumulated debt-to-GDP ratio for the previous year, discounting it by the interest rate and the ratio of budget deficit to GDP for the current year. It is argued that high public debt leads to a crowding out effect, thereby excluding many potential customers from access to loans (Ismihan & Ozkan, 2012; Kutivadze, 2011). Trade openness ($OPEN_{it}$), is measured as the ratio of the sum of exports and imports of goods and services to GDP. It captures the assessment of the extent to which a country is integrated in global trade. Trade openness is associated with lower inflation volatility (Bowdler & Malik, 2017) which again supports economic activity and hence demand for financial services. Central Bank assets variable ($CBASSETS_{it}$), is measured as the ratio of central bank total assets held to GDP of a country and represents claims on domestic real nonfinancial sector by the central bank. Therefore, the more assets a central bank holds, the more finance it can provide to support the financial system in its drive to expand and provide funds for lending activities at relatively cheaper rates thereby making access to finance much more affordable to many. We include the size of the population ($POPUL_{it}$) to capture the availability of huge number of potential investors and borrowers which means higher savings, investments, and demand for credit. Next is Financial openness,($FINOPEN_{it}$) which is the Chinn-Ito index; an index measuring a country's degree of capital account openness. It is based on the binary dummy variables that codify the tabulation of restrictions on cross-border financial transactions reported in the IMF's Annual Report on Exchange Arrangements and Exchange Restrictions (AREAER). In the binary variable, *1* equals the presence of financial controls, and *0* otherwise. However, unlike Quinn (1997, 531–551) and Quinn (2003, 189–204) which measure the intensity of capital controls, the Chinn-Ito index, does not. Chinn-Ito's correlation with Quinn, though, is 0.84, suggesting that it captures capital control intensity to a reasonable extent. It ranges from −1.90 (least financially open) to 2.37 (most financially open).

Our model includes time periods and country dummies that capture year and country-specific effects correlated with the variables of analysis in particular political stability that may affect all economies in a particular region or economic group.

Empirical Results

Effects of Monetary Policy and CBI on Financial Development

From the descriptive statistics table (Appendix: Descriptive Statistics), we observe that private credit to GDP for Africa, is on average 19.9%. Median CBI values for Africa is 0.50. Average Net Interest Margin is 18.34% and Money supply is 30.02%. Real interest rates average 10.25%.

We separately estimate equations (a) and (b). We use the lagged values of the exogenous variables to explain the exogenous variables in the models (a) and (b). As a result, we estimated these models using the Two Stage System GMM estimator to avoid the problem of endogeneity arising from financial development and CBI. The validity of the model specification determines the effectiveness of the GMM estimator. We employed two main tests. The first one is the test of Sargan. Tables 7.2, 7.3, and 7.4 show that the Sargan test does not reject the null hypothesis of over-identification of the models, thus validating the quality of the internal instruments used. The results of the test of autocorrelation of errors (significant AR (1) and insignificant AR (2)) mean we accept the null hypothesis indicating that there is no correlation between the errors in the second order.

We proceed to analyse and discuss the results of our regressions. As stated earlier, we regress four (4) measures of financial development on three (3) measures of monetary policy. In Table 7.2, we see the results of regressions when we use the monetary policy rate (MPR) as a measure of monetary policy. It is evident from columns (1) to (4) that monetary policy rate changes have a significant impact on domestic credit by banks to the private sector and, private credit to GDP. That is to say that, increases in the monetary policy rate lead to lower credit by banks and other financial institutions in Africa. This is expected as increases in monetary policy rates signal higher cost of borrowing by commercial banks which is translated into higher cost of credit to individuals and business. This leads to lower demand for credit. We, however, do not see any significant impact of the policy rate increase on net interest margin and stock market capitalisation as seen in model (5)–(8). CBI, however, has a significant and positive impact on all measures of financial development in Table 7.2 except net interest margin, where it is negative and significant (models (5)–(6)). That is, higher levels of central bank independence lead to more confidence in the financial system, lower inflation, and proper supervision of the financial systems, thereby enabling improved competition in the banking space. This has the benefits of minimising net interest margins as inefficiencies in monetary policy practices are minimised. This is significant at 5 and 1%. CBI also increases access to credit. This is because CBI ensures price stability and proper regulation and supervision of the financial system, thereby eliciting confidence in the monetary policy framework as argued by Laeven and Levine (2009) and Agoraki et al. (2011). Price

Table 7.2 Effect of Monetary Policy and CBI on Financial Development

	DOM.CRT		*PRIV.CRT*		*NIM*		*STOCK.MKCAP*	
	(1)	*(2)*	*(3)*	*(4)*	*(5)*	*(6)*	*(7)*	*(8)*
Dom.Crt $_{t-1}$	0.527***	0.522***						
	(0.006)	(0.006)						
Priv.CRT $_{t-1}$			0.538***	0.547***				
			(0.003)	(0.004)				
NIM $_{t-1}$					0.414***	0.465***		
					(0.005)	(0.006)		
Stock.Cap $_{t-1}$							0.224***	0.278***
							(0.003)	(0.007)
MPR	−0.138*	−0.143*	−0.136*	−0.142**	−0.119	−0.124	0.076	0.086
	(0.071)	(0.074)	(0.072)	(0.038)	(0.224)	(0.211)	(0.098)	(0.113)
CBI	0.144***	0.151**	0.139**	0.143*	−0.180***	−0.122***	0.072**	0.083**
	(0.009)	(0.025)	(0.021)	(0.048)	(0.007)	(0.007)	(0.017)	(0.019)
PolInst	0.184**	0.177**	0.115***	0.124***	0.099*	0.103**	0.221**	0.245**
	(0.032)	(0.038)	(0.011)	(0.009)	(0.062)	(0.034)	(0.042)	(0.041)
MPR*CBI		−0.108**		−0.102***		−0.089**		0.073**
		(0.033)		(0.013)		(0.018)		(0.019)
DEBTG	−0.033	−0.044	−0.055**	0.045**	−0.039**	−0.022***	−0.037*	−0.069**
	(0.039)	(0.053)	(0.016)	(0.011)	(0.016)	(0.001)	(0.015)	(0.018)
POPUL	0.043**	0.068	0.071**	0.088**	0.057***	0.054**	0.062***	0.063***
	(0.018)	(0.089)	(0.022)	(0.045)	(0.008)	(0.021)	(0.009)	(0.009)
GDPR	0.055**	0.045**	0.069*	0.078*	0.042**	0.044**	0.056***	0.042**
	(0.017)	(0.014)	(0.022)	(0.029)	(0.011)	(0.013)	(0.006)	(0011)
TRD.OPEN	0.083	−0.059	0.129**	0.121**	0.119**	0.122**	0.131*	0.121*
	(0.066)	(0.113)	(0.051)	(0.045)	(0.041)	(0.079)	(0.092)	(0.091)

	DOM.CRT		*PRIV.CRT*		*NIM*		*STOCK.MKCAP*	
	(1)	*(2)*	*(3)*	*(4)*	*(5)*	*(6)*	*(7)*	*(8)*
LGDPC	0.025	0.069	0.564*	0.516**	0.158*	0.253*	0.537**	0.612**
	(0.143)	(0.201)	(0.112)	(0.098)	(0.096)	(0.099)	(0.095)	(0.103)
FEXRT	0.598	0.577**	0.288	1.113*	1.016*	1.208**	0.555*	0.651**
	(0.724)	(0.103)	(1.467)	(0.153)	(0.134)	(0.194)	(0.116)	(0.178)
IT	0.105*	0.333	0.318*	0.225	0.388***	0.335**	0.336*	0.324**
	(0.088)	(0.398)	(0.124)	(0.396)	(0.013)	(0.112)	(0.108)	(0.088)
CBASSETS	0.118*	0.129	0.285	0.238**	0.254**	0.234**	0.115**	0.147**
	(0.078)	(0.231)	(0.302)	(0.079)	(0.064)	(0.066)	(0.076)	(0.049)
FINOPEN	0.355	0.115**	0.228	0.222*	0.133	0.125**	0.179	0.183*
	(0.43)	(0.046)	(0.721)	(0.095)	(0.309)	(0.074)	(0.389)	(0.075)
Total MPR Effect		−0.251**		−0.244***		−0.213*		0.159**
		(0.034)		(0.008)		(0.051)		(0.028)
Observations	1207	1207	1207	1207	1207	1207	1207	1207
Number of Index	48	48	48	48	48	48	23	23
AR (1)	0.007	0.007	0.006	0.006	0.007	0.07	0.007	0.007
AR (2)	0.287	0.274	0.269	0.258	0.289	0.295	0.302	0.328
Sargan test	0.119	0.132	0.138	0.197	0.196	0.186	0.201	0.217

Note The variables are described under Appendix A
Robust Standard Errors in Parentheses ***$p < 0.01$, **$p < 0.05$, *$p < 0.1$

Table 7.3 Effect of Monetary Policy and CBI on Financial Development

	DOM.CRT		*PRIV.CRT*		*NIM*		*STOCK.MKCAP*	
	(9)	*(10)*	*(11)*	*(12)*	*(13)*	*(14)*	*(15)*	*(16)*
Dom.Crt $_{t-1}$	0.542***	0.541***						
	(0.004)	(0.004)						
Priv.CRT $_{t-1}$			0 .629***	0.622***				
			(0.002)	(0.001)				
NIM $_{t-1}$					0.524***	0.566***		
					(0.001)	(0.001)		
Stock.Cap$_{t-1}$							0.318***	0.332***
							(0.004)	(0.008)
RIR	−0.184*	−0.141*	−0.128*	−0.121**	−0.122	−0.134	0.084*	0.092*
	(0.064)	(0.078)	(0.072)	(0.038)	(0.116)	(0.156)	(0.072)	(0.065)
CBI	0.135***	0.181***	0.136**	0.129**	−0.165***	−0.128***	0.069***	0.071***
	(0.013)	(0.011)	(0.041)	(0.043)	(0.007)	(0.008)	(0.007)	(0.005)
PolInst	0.178**	0.164**	0.063**	0.051**	0.128*	0.116**	0.109*	0.191**
	(0.035)	(0.044)	(0.014)	(0.22)	(0.084)	(0.078)	(0.065)	(0.076)
RIR*CBI		−0.111**		−0.148***		−0.083**		0.076**
		(0.032)		(0.013)		(0.019)		(0.025)
DEBTG	−0.029	−0.028	−0.049**	0.045**	−0.033**	−0.032**	−0.028*	−0.055**
	(0.035)	(0.038)	(0.012)	(0.011)	(0.011)	(0.011)	(0.012)	(0.011)
POPUL	0.038**	0.025	0.065***	0.088**	0.051***	0.057**	0.054***	0.054***
	(0.012)	(0.031)	(0.006)	(0.045)	(0.006)	(0.018)	(0.006)	(0.006)
GDPR	0.051**	0.041**	0.066*	0.0 78*	0.045**	0.039**	0.043***	0.044**
	(0.012)	(0.018)	(0.021)	(0.029)	(0.013)	(0.011)	(0.002)	(0019)
TRD.OPEN	0.0768	−0.029	0.135*	0.121**	0.129**	0.118**	0.119*	0.133*
	(0.041)	(0.086)	(0.028)	(0.045)	(0.053)	(0.072)	(0.077)	(0.088)
LGDPC	−0.019	0.039	0.564	−1.111	0.154*	0.269*	1.432**	0.665**
	(0.165)	(0.188)	(0.663)	(0.998)	(0.098)	(0.102)	(0.437)	(0.173)

	DOM.CRT		*PRIV.CRT*		*NIM*		*STOCK.MKCAP*	
	(9)	*(10)*	*(11)*	*(12)*	*(13)*	*(14)*	*(15)*	*(16)*
FEXRT	0.549	0.511**	0.288	1.125*	1.011*	1.221**	0.589*	0.665**
	(0.612)	(0.236)	(1.467)	(0.347)	(0.444	(0.298)	(0.147)	(0.289)
IT	0.117*	0.348	0.318*	0.221	0.391**	0.341**	0.332*	0.328**
	(0.091)	(0.563)	(0.124)	(0.246)	(0.123)	(0.101)	(0.101)	(0.105)
CBASSETS	0.106	0.125	0.285	0.229	0.226**	0.219**	0.115*	0.133**
	(0.225)	(0.221	(0.302)	(0.188)	(0.098)	(0.078)	(0.091)	(0.055)
FINOPEN	0.372	0.111**	0.228	0.235*	0.138	0.108**	0.171	0.178*
	(0.241)	(0.042)	(0.721)	(0.143)	(0.322)	(0.062)	(0.341)	(0.111)
Total RIR Effect		−0.252**		−0.269***		−0.217*		0.168**
		(0.032)		(0.011)		(0.035)		(0.027)
Observations	1207	1207	1207	1207	1207	1207	1207	1207
Number of Index	48	48	48	48	48	48	23	23
AR (1)	0.007	0.006	0.008	0.009	0.008	0.008	0.008	0.008
AR (2)	0.2118	0.212	0.216	0.214	0.210	0.219	0.242	0.238
Sargan test	0.113	0.119	0.128	0.138	0.267	0.288	0.293	0.272

Note The variables are described under Appendix A

Robust Standard Errors in Parentheses $^{***}p < 0.01$, $^{**}p < 0.05$, $^{*}p < 0.1$

PRIV.CRE$_{it}$ *denotes* the ratio of domestic private credit to GDP.$DOM.CRE_{it}$ is domestic credit to private sector which refers to financial resources provided to the private sector by banks.STOCK.MKCAP$_{it}$ denotes the ratio of stock market capitalisation to GDP.NIM denotes net interest margin. *Note* PRIV.CRT$_{it}$ *denotes* the ratio of domestic private credit to GDP. $STOCK.MKCAP_{it}$ denotes the ratio of stock market capitalisation to GDP.$PUBLICBONDS_{it}$ denotes the ratio of public bonds to GDP.CBI_{it} is the central bank independence measured by the CWN index, $GDPR_{it}$ is the real GDP annual growth rate, LGDPC$_{it}$ is log of real GDP per capita, PolInstl$_{it}$ is the rescaled political rights score, from 0–6 where 0 denotes least respect for political rights and 6 highest respect for political rights, and TRD.OPEN is the trade openness measured as the ratio of sum of exports and imports to *GDP*. $FEXRT_{it}$ is a dummy variable for the exchange rate regime measured as *1* for fixed exchange rate regimes and 0 otherwise.IT$_{it}$ *denotes* inflation targeting regime and is a dummy measured as *1* for inflation targeting regimes and *0* otherwise.$POPUL_{it}$ is the size of the population and DEBTG$_{it}$ is the debt to GDP ratio..MPR$_{it}$ is the central bank policy rate. Money and quasi money comprise the sum of currency outside banks, demand deposits other than those of the central government, and the time, savings, and foreign currency deposits of resident sectors other than the central government.RIR_{it} is real interest rates. CBASSETS$_{it}$ is the ratio of central bank assets to GDP and FINOPEN$_{it}$ is Chinn-Ito index for capital openness

Table 7.4 Effect of Monetary Policy and CBI on Financial Development

	AFRICA							
	DOM.CRT		*PRIV.CRT*		*NIM*		*STOCK.MKCAP*	
	5 YEAR AVERAGE (2SLS)				*FIXED EFFECTS*			
	(17)	*(18)*	*(19)*	*(20)*	*(21)*	*(22)*	*(23)*	*(24)*
Dom,Crt $_{t-1}$	0.598***	0.593***						
	(0.002)	(0.002)						
Priv.CRT $_{t-1}$			0.668***	0.672***				
			(0.003)	(0.003)				
NIM $_{t-1}$								
Stock.Cap $_{t-1}$								
M2	0.183**	0.179**	0.164*	0.149**	0.142	0.165	−0.088*	−0.084*
	(0.045)	(0.036)	(0.062)	(0.022)	(0.245)	(0.111)	(0.043)	(0.043)
CBI	0.198**	0.181**	0.194	0.115**	−0.189	−0.143**	0.095***	0.074***
	(0.042)	(0.041)	(0.111)	(0.029)	(0.148)	(0.052)	(0.005)	(0.007)
PolInst	0.173**	0.139**	0.088*	0.096**	0.117*	0.112	0.099*	0.083*
	(0.033)	(0.044)	(0.059)	(0.025)	(0.078)	(0.227)	(0.068)	(0.066)
M2*CBI		0.128**		0.124***		0.096**		−0.072**
		(0.033)		(0.012)		(0.028)		(0.021)
DEBTG	−0.028	−0.024	−0.046	0.048***	−0.038**	−0.037	−0.028**	−0.041***
	(0.033)	(0.033)	(0.057)	(0.002)	(0.013)	(0.055)	(0.009)	(0.005)
POPUL	0.046*	0.034*	0.058***	0.067**	0.055***	0.069*	0.053**	0.054*
	(0.018)	(0.019)	(0.002)	(0.027)	(0.003)	(0.026)	(0.022)	(0.024)
GDPR	0.044*	0.046***	0.062*	0.088*	0.144	0.168**	0.093***	0.094***
	(0.027)	(0.003)	(0.021)	(0.039)	(0.139)	(0.045)	(0.002)	(0.003)
TRD.OPEN	0.098*	−0.076**	0.143	0.125	0.128**	0.119**	0.153*	0.158*

	AFRICA							
	DOM.CRT		*PRIV.CRT*		*NIM*		*STOCK.MKCAP*	
	5 YEAR AVERAGE (2SLS)				*FIXED EFFECTS*			
	(17)	*(18)*	*(19)*	*(20)*	*(21)*	*(22)*	*(23)*	*(24)*
	(0.053)	(0.031)	(0.216)	(0.345)	(0.067)	(0.084)	(0.092)	(0.091)
LGDPC	0.068**	0.072**	0.079	0.096*	0.144**	0.135**	0.145**	0.169**
	(0.019)	(0.032)	(0.99)	(0.044)	(0.051)	(0.058)	(0.057)	(0.052)
FEXRT	0.346	0.348**	0.321	0.339*	0.632**	0.592**	0.643**	0.687**
	(0.366)	(0.099)	(0.776)	(0.097)	(0.179)	(0.158)	(0.136)	(0.179)
IT	0.119*	0.341	0.293*	0.278*	0.391**	0.423*	0.311*	0.315**
	(0.069)	(0.334)	(0.108)	(0.097)	(0.077)	(0.102)	(0.133)	(0.111)
CBASSETS	0.122**	0.126*	0.289	0.226*	0.221*	0.214**	0.117*	0.128**
	(0.068)	(0.068)	(0.63)	(0.74)	(0.141)	(0.071)	(0.087)	(0.066)
FINOPEN	0.247**	0.213*	0.211	0.218*	0.143	0.151**	0.155	0.159*
	(0.079)	(0.078)	(0.543)	(0.111)	(0.342)	(0.043)	(0.243)	(0.071)
Total M2 Effect		0.307**		0.273***		0.261*		–0.156**
		(0.084)		(0.011)		(0.045)		(0.023)
Observations	243	243	245	245	1207	1207	1207	1207
Number of Index	48	48	48	48	48	48	23	23
R^2					0.542	0.578	0.518	0.539
Wald Chi^2	44.56	44.53	45.67	45.98				
Woolridge's OIR	0.534	0.538	0.572	0561				

(continued)

Table 7.4 (continued)

	AFRICA							
	DOM.CRT		*PRIV.CRT*		*NIM*		*STOCK.MKCAP*	
	5 YEAR AVERAGE (2SLS)				*FIXED EFFECTS*			
	(17)	*(18)*	*(19)*	*(20)*	*(21)*	*(22)*	*(23)*	*(24)*
p-value	(0.421)	(0.443)	(0.478)	0.491)				
Woolridge Rob	7.896***	8.135***	8.247***	8.379***				
Robust Regression	5.786**	5.798**	5.896***	5.643**				

Note The variables are described under Appendix A
Robust Standard Errors in Parentheses $^{***}p < 0.01$, $^{**}p < 0.05$, $^{*}p < 0.1$

stability enables banks to properly evaluate loan applications and therefore improve acceptability of loan applications thereby increasing access to credit. We also see a positive and significant CBI coefficient when we measure financial development with stock market capitalisation. This is so because the stable macroeconomic environment created by an independent central bank encourages long-term capital commitment and increase in investment inflows since investment values are preserved in a low inflationary environment. When we proxy monetary policy with real interest rates in Table 7.3, the results are similar to those obtained using the monetary policy rates in Table 7.2.

In Table 7.4, we rely on M2 as our measure of monetary policy. In models 17–24, we use alternative estimation methods, the Two Stage Least Squares Instrumental Variables and the fixed effects approaches to examine the objectives of the study. In applying the 2SLS, we require valid instruments, which are always difficult to get. In the literature, either internal instruments or external instruments are employed. We opt for internal instruments and consequently employ the lags of CBI as instruments. In this regard, we use the lags of CBI as instruments. The lagged values do not themselves belong in the respective estimating equations and they are sufficiently correlated with the explanatory variables. The equations are exactly identified and therefore no need to perform over-identifying restrictions tests. The results of the estimations are not different from those produced by the Two Step GMM, thus confirming the robustness of our findings. The results show that increases in money supply (i.e., lower monetary policy and real interest rates) lead to higher levels of credit by banks and other financial institutions to the private sector. This is seen when we refer to the significantly positive coefficients for M2 in columns (17)–(20). This can be explained as higher levels of deposits, increase the availability of funds for credit intermediation by financial institutions. Credit rationing and other credit limiting practices are stalled when financial institutions have increased supply of funds to dispense as loans. The impact of higher M2 on stock market development is negative and significant. This is because a higher supply of money leads to inflation which reduces the performance of listed stocks minimising their profits. This is seen in models (23–24).

Interactive Effect of Monetary Policy and CBI on Financial Development

As seen in Table 7.2, when we interact the monetary policy rate (MPR) with CBI, we find that the coefficients are negative for domestic credit by banks (model 2), private credit by all deposit taking financial institutions (model 4), and net interest margin (model 6); but positive for stock market capitalisation (model 8). This means that having an independent central bank makes policy rate increases more effective in influencing access to credit. So, in jurisdictions with more independent central banks, the impact of policy rate increases is strengthened. Thus, while the direct effect of policy rate increase on domestic credit by banks and private credit are −0.143 in column (2) and −0.142 in column (4), the total effect of a policy rate increase is −0.251 and −0.244 which are both significant at 5 and 1%, respectively. This can be accounted for by the −0.108 and −0.102 interactive coefficients.

We explain this to mean that monetary policy is more effective at higher levels of central bank independence where credibility of monetary policy decisions is high. This facilitates a higher pass-through rate into interest rates and as such access to credit. Also, the proper regulation of financial institutions also ensures smoother operations of the financial system, leading to an observed impact on lending rates and access to credit. When it comes to net interest margin and stock market capitalisation, the interactive term has a negative and positive coefficient respectively, which is significant (model 6 and 8). Higher monetary policy rate changes, given a more independent central bank, result in a lower net interest margin, because the competitive environment created by the independent central bank will lead to a much lower increase in lending rates compared to less competitive banking sectors, which would mean lower interest incomes. This is on the basis that lending rates respond more to changes in interest rates than deposit rates do. Given a more independent central bank, monetary policy changes are much more able to achieve lower inflation and improve the performance of listed firms. The results are similar when monetary policy is measured with real interest rates (RIR) in Table 7.3. In summary, independent central banks that ensure proper supervision of financial systems, create the necessary conditions that enable market participants to gain confidence to execute financial contracts in the midst of stable prices and low inflation. Financial institutions are compliant, and competition is encouraged in the midst of independent and objective regulation and supervision by the central bank. This helps in expanding credit and financing long-term projects. The competition generates efficiency in operations which translates into lower net interest margins for banks. Alternative estimations in Table 7.4 support the findings using the GMM technique.

The findings generally agree with the theoretical argument this study makes that, the impact of an independent central bank on monetary policy effectiveness can be explained through its impact on bank competition and information asymmetry. Effective central bank independence ensures objective supervision of banks which leads to a level playing field and increased competitiveness in the banking space. This should have an impact on the effectiveness of monetary policy given policy rate changes into changes in lending rates and therefore greater price stability and growth in financial institutions and markets. This would interrupt the operations of the collusive arrangements that impact the effectiveness of monetary policy.

The transparency of independent central banks should contribute to minimising the effects of information asymmetry where banks avoid increases in the lending rates and ration credit to circumvent loan default by riskier borrowers. As argued by Barth et al. (2013) and Quintyn and Taylor (2002), CBI's professional regulation and supervision of financial system ensures financial stability. All the control variables have the apriori expected signs at various levels of significance.

Figures 7.5–7.8, represent the marginal effect of monetary policy on financial development at different levels of central bank independence.

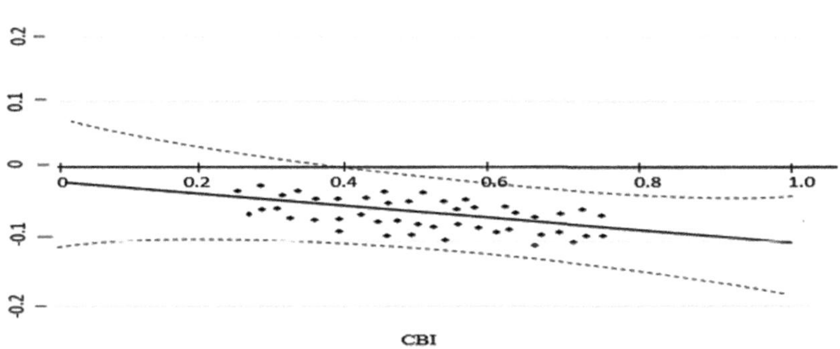

Fig. 7.5 Marginal effects of MPR on Priv.Crt at different levels of CBI

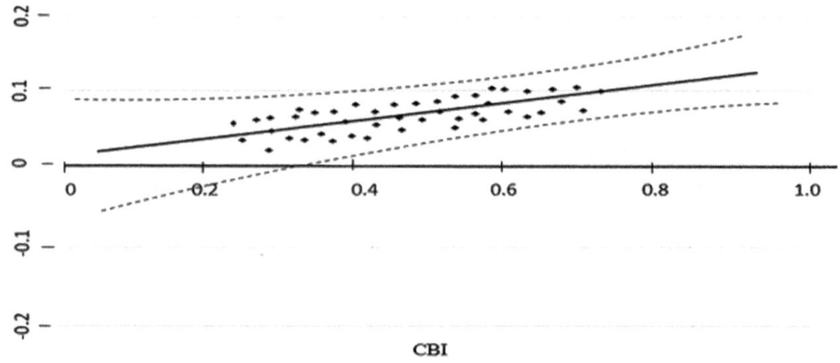

Fig. 7.6 Marginal effect of MPR on STOCK.CAP at different levels of CBI

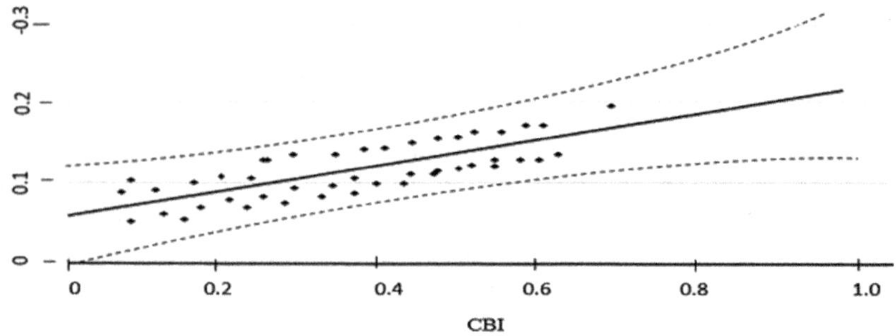

Fig. 7.7 Marginal effect of RIR on STOCK.MK.CAP at different levels of CBI

It is evident from the figures that, monetary policy has a significant impact on financial development, given the conditional variable, central bank independence. It shows that higher levels of CBI have a significant impact on improving the effectiveness of monetary policy on financial development in Africa.

7.5 Conclusion and Implications

This paper examines the impact of monetary policy and central bank independence on financial development. The impact of monetary policy on financial development has been mixed, while that of central bank independence has been established. While monetary policy basically seeks to

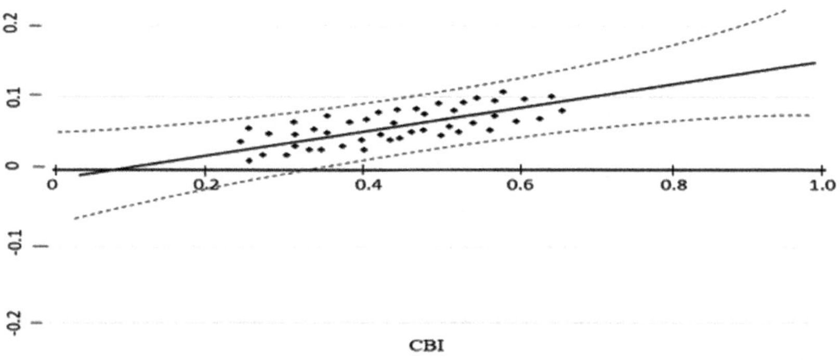

Fig. 7.8 Marginal effect of M2 on NIM at different levels of CBI

achieve price stability, central bank independence does not only seek to achieve price stability but ensures objective and proper regulation and supervision of the financial system, thereby bringing credibility to the monetary policy framework.

We analyse the usefulness of central bank independence on explaining the impact of monetary policy on banking sector and capital market development in Africa using a 2 stage GMM estimation technique, 2 Stage Least Squares, and Fixed Effects, with data spanning 1970–2014 on 48 African countries. Using policy rate, money supply, and real interest rates as measures of monetary policy stance and CBI data from Garriga (2016) and Bodea and Hicks (2015), we find that monetary policy effectiveness on financial development is higher for the banking sector than for the capital markets. Central bank independence has a significantly positive impact on both banking sector and capital market development. Monetary policy effect on financial development is enhanced by CBI as the magnitude of its impact on financial development is higher in the presence of higher levels of CBI in Africa.

The policy implications for these findings are that monetary policy credibility is important for financial development in Africa and this credibility could be found in making central banks in Africa independent of political control. By doing this, central banks can ensure proper regulation and supervision of the financial system, encourage competitiveness among banks and create credibility and confidence in the monetary policy framework, thereby increasing financial institutional efficiency and stability. This provides increased access to finance and improves the availability of long-term capital on the capital markets.

Appendix: Descriptive Statistics

Variable	*Mean*	*Median*	*Max*	*Min*	*SD*	*Obs*
Priv. Crt	19.892	14.736	160.125	0.491	19.347	1769
Dom. Crt	17. 345	12.289	158.093	0.4031	18.921	1769
Stock.MkCap	36.043	13.785	96.939	0.009	76.587	335
NIM	18.3410	16.432	41.220	8.229	24.133	1150
MPR	27.88	30.13	39.12	16.532	26.612	1123
RIR	9.28	10.25	15.23	6.87	5.63	1543
M2	30.02	17.365	67.84	27.54	16.43	1542
CBI	0.501	0.501	0.866	0.137	0.197	1593
PolInst	2.178	2	6	0	1.451	1986
FEXRT	0.311	0.302	1	0	0.454	1259
DEBTG	57.091	43.308	265.128	1.389	47.434	1114
GDPR	4.084	14.736	149.73	−62.08	7.682	1908
Per Capita GDP	1362.7	1568.5	14,749.2	113.7	2129.5	1429
POPUL (log)	5.241	7.736	26.73	2.118	3.37	2013
TRD.OPEN	43.58	45.2	92.9	22.5	16.5	1569
IT	0.019	0.018	1	0	0.0967	1588
FINOPEN	−0.25	−0.0.15	2.37	−1.90	1.45	1986
CBASSETS	2.21	2.35	3.56	1.25	1.451	1986

$PRIV.CRE_{it}$ denotes the ratio of domestic private credit to GDP.$DOM.CRE_{it}$ is domestic credit to private sector which refers to financial resources provided to the private sector by banks.$STOCK.MKCAP_{it}$ denotes the ratio of stock market capitalisation to GDP.NIM denotes net interest margin.NOTES : $PRIV.CRT_{it}$ denotes the ratio of domestic private credit to GDP. $STOCK.MKCAP_{it}$ denotes the ratio of stock market capitalisation to GDP. CBI_{it} is the central bank independence measured by the CWN index, $GDPR_{it}$ is the real GDP annual growth rate, $LGDPC_{it}$ is log of real GDP per capita, $PolInstl_{it}$ is the rescaled political rights score, from 0–6 where 0 denotes least respect for political rights and 6 highest respect for political rights, and TRD.OPEN is the trade openness measured as the ratio of sum of exports and imports to GDP. $FEXRT_{it}$ is a dummy variable for the exchange rate regime measured as *1* for fixed exchange rate regimes and 0 otherwise.IT_{it} *denotes* inflation targeting regime and is a dummy measured as *1* for inflation targeting regimes and *0* otherwise.$POPUL_{it}$ is the size of the population and $DEBTG_{it}$ is the debt to GDP ratio..MPR_{it} is the central bank policy rate. $M2_{it}$*is* Money and quasi money and comprise the sum of currency outside banks, demand deposits other than those of the central government, and the time, savings, and foreign currency deposits of resident sectors other than the central government.RIR_{it} is real interest rates. $CBASSETS_{it}$ is the ratio of central bank assets to GDP and $FINOPEN_{it}$ is Chinn-Ito index for capital openness

References

Adil, F., & Jalil, A. (2020). Determining the financial inclusion output of banking sector of Pakistan—Supply-side analysis. *Economies, 8*(2), 42.

Agoba, A. M., Abor, J., Osei, K. A., & Sa-Aadu, J. (2017). Central bank independence and inflation in Africa: The role of financial systems and institutional quality. *Central Bank Review, 17*(4), 131–146.

Agoba, A. M., Abor, J., Osei, K. A., & Sa-Aadu, J. (2020). The Independence of central banks, political institutional quality and financial sector development in Africa. *Journal of Emerging Markets Finance, 19*(2), 154–188.

Agoraki, M. E. K., Delis, M. D., & Pasiouras, F. (2011). Regulations, competition and bank risk-taking in transition countries. *Journal of Financial Stability, 7*(1), 38–48.

Alavinasab, S. M. (2016). Monetary policy and economic growth: A case study of Iran. *International Journal of Economics, Commerce and Management, 4*(3), 234–244.

Alfazema, A. (2020). *Challenges of the International Financial System in granting bank credit.*

Altunbas, Y., Gambacorta, L., & Marques-Ibanez, D. (2010). Bank risk and monetary policy. *Journal of Financial Stability, 6*(3), 121–129.

Ang, J. B., & McKibbin, W. J. (2007). Financial liberalization, financial sector development and growth: Evidence from Malaysia. *Journal of Development Economics, 84*(1), 215–233.

Arellano, M., & Bond, S. (1991). Some tests of specification for panel data: Monte Carlo evidence and an application to employment equations. *The Review of Economic Studies, 58*(2), 277–297.

Asab, N. A., & Al-Tarawneh, A. (2018). The impact of inflation on the investment: The non-linear nexus and inflation threshold in Jordan. *Modern Applied Science, 12*(12), 1913–1844.

Asongu, S. A., & Nwachukwu, J. C. (2018). Educational quality thresholds in the diffusion of knowledge with mobile phones for inclusive human development in sub-Saharan Africa. *Technological Forecasting and Social Change, 129*, 164–172.

Baltagi, B. H., Demetriades, P. O., & Law, S. H. (2009). Financial development and openness: Evidence from panel data. *Journal of Development Economics, 89*(2), 285–296.

Barth, J. R., Lin, C., Ma, Y., Seade, J., & Song, F. M. (2013). Do bank regulation, supervision and monitoring enhance or impede bank efficiency? *Journal of Banking & Finance, 37*(8), 2879–2892.

Bascom, W. O. (2016). *The economics of financial reform in developing countries.* Springer.

Bazzi, S., & Clemens, M. A. (2013). Blunt instruments: Avoiding common pitfalls in identifying the causes of economic growth. *American Economic Journal: Macroeconomics, 5*(2), 152–186.

Becker, B., Chen, J., & Greenberg, D. (2013). Financial development, fixed costs, and international trade. *The Review of Corporate Finance Studies, 2*(1), 1–28.

Bednarek, P., Dinger, V., te Kaat, D. M., & von Westernhagen, N. (2021). To whom do banks channel central bank funds? *Journal of Banking & Finance, 128*, 106082.

Berger, W., & Kismer, F. (2013). Central bank independence and financial stability. *European Journal of Political Economy, 31*, 109–118.

Berger, A. N., Klapper, L. F., & Turk-Ariss, R. (2017). Bank competition and financial stability. In *Handbook of competition in banking and finance*. Edward Elgar Publishing.

Bernanke, B. S., & Kuttner, K. N. (2005). What explains the stock market's reaction to Federal Reserve policy? *The Journal of Finance*, *60*(3), 1221–1257 (Nyberg, 2012).

Bernanke, B., & Gertler, M. (2000). *Monetary policy and asset price volatility* (No. w7559). National Bureau of Economic Research.

Bittner, C., Bonfim, D., Heider, F., Saidi, F., Schepens, G., & Soares, C. (2020). *Why so negative? The effect of monetary policy on bank credit supply across the euro area*. Unpublished working paper.

Bodea, C., & Hicks, R. (2015). Price stability and central bank independence: Discipline, credibility, and democratic institutions. *International Organization, 69*(1), 35–61.

Bodea, C., & Higashijima, M. (2015). *Central banks and fiscal policy: Why independent central banks can lead to lower fiscal deficits* (LSE European Politics and Policy [EUROPP] Blog).

Bontempi, M. E., & Mammi, I. (2015). Implementing a strategy to reduce the instrument count in panel GMM. *The Stata Journal, 15*(4), 1075–1097.

Borys, M. M. (2011). Testing multi-factor asset pricing models in the Visegrad countries. *Finance a Uver, 61*(2), 118.

Bowdler, C., & Malik, A. (2017). Openness and inflation volatility: Panel data evidence. *The North American Journal of Economics and Finance, 41*, 57–69.

Brambor, T., Clark, W. R., & Golder, M. (2006). Understanding interaction models: Improving empirical analyses. *Political analysis, 14*(1), 63–82.

Büttner, D., & Hayo, B. (2011). Determinants of European stock market integration. *Economic Systems, 35*(4), 574–585.

Calvo, G. A., & Reinhart, C. M. (2002). Fear of floating. *The Quarterly Journal of Economics, 117*(2), 379–408.

Chatziantoniou, I., Duffy, D., & Filis, G. (2013). Stock market response to monetary and fiscal policy shocks: Multi-country evidence. *Economic Modelling, 30*, 754–769.

Chiarella, C., Dieci, R., He, X. Z., & Li, K. (2013). An evolutionary CAPM under heterogeneous beliefs. *Annals of Finance, 9*(2), 185–215.

Chinn, M. D., & Ito, H. (2006, October). What matters for financial Development? Capital controls, institutions, and interactions. *Journal of Development Economics, 81*(1), 163e192.

Chinn, M. D., & Ito, H. (2011). *Financial globalization and China.*

Ciccarelli, M., Maddaloni, A., & Peydró, J. L. (2015). Trusting the bankers: A new look at the credit channel of monetary policy. *Review of Economic Dynamics, 18*(4), 979–1002.

Čihák, M., Harjes, T., & Stavrev, E. (2010). Euro area monetary policy in uncharted waters. In *The European Central Bank at Ten* (pp. 87–117). Springer, Berlin, Heidelberg.

Clouse, J. A. (2020). *Price level risk and some long-run implications of alternative monetary policy strategies.*

Cooper, R. V. (1974). Efficient capital markets and the quantity theory of money. *Journal of Finance, 29*, 887–908.

da Cruz, N. F., Tavares, A. F., Marques, R. C., Jorge, S., & De Sousa, L. (2016). Measuring local government transparency. *Public Management Review, 18*(6), 866–893.

De Bondt, G. J. (2005). Interest rate pass-through: Empirical results for the euro area. *German Economic Review, 6*(1), 37–78.

de Haan, J., Bodea, C., Hicks, R., & Eijffinger, S. C. (2018). Central bank independence before and after the crisis. *Comparative Economic Studies, 60*(2), 183–202.

Doumpos, M., Gaganis, C., & Pasiouras, F. (2016). Bank diversification and overall financial strength: International evidence. *Financial Markets, Institutions & Instruments, 25*(3), 169–213.

Drazen, A. (2004). Fiscal rules from a political economy perspective. In *Rules-based fiscal policy in emerging markets* (pp. 15–29). Palgrave Macmillan.

Eijffinger, S. C., Geraats, P. M., & van der Cruijsen, C. (2006). *Does central bank transparency reduce interest rates?.*

Fama, E. F. (1981). Stock returns, real activity, inflation, and money. *The American economic review, 71*(4), 545–565.

Fama, E. F., & Schwert, G. W. (1977). Asset returns and inflation. *Journal of financial economics, 5*(2), 115–146.

Feldstein, M., & Horioka, C. (1980). Domestic saving and international capital flows. *Economic Journal, 90*, 314–329.

Fernández, A., & Tamayo, C. E. (2017). From institutions to financial development and growth: What are the links? *Journal of Economic Surveys, 31*(1), 17–57.

Fischer, S. (2015, October). *Macroprudential policy in the US economy*. In Speech at "Macroprudential Monetary Policy," The 59th Economic Conference of the Federal Reserve Bank of Boston, Boston, MA (Vol. 2).

Flammer, C., & Ioannou, I. (2020). Strategic management during the financial crisis: How firms adjust their strategic investments in response to credit market disruptions. *Strategic Management Journal, 42*, 1275–1298.

Fosu, A. K., & Abass, A. F. (2019). Domestic credit and export diversification: Africa from a global perspective. *Journal of African Business, 20*(2), 160–179.

Friedman, M. (1995). The role of monetary policy. In *Essential readings in economics* (pp. 215–231). Palgrave.

Friedman, L. (1956). A competitive-bidding strategy. *Operations Research, 4*(1), 104–112.

Friedman, M., & Schwartz, A. J. (1965). Money and business cycles. In *The state of monetary economics* (pp. 32–78). NBER.

Fonseca, G., Cunha, D., Crespo, C., & Relvas, A. P. (2016). Families in the context of macroeconomic crises: A systematic review. *Journal of Family Psychology, 30*(6), 687. Geng and Zhai (2015).

Gerstenberger, J., & Schnabl, G. (2017). *The impact of Japanese monetary policy crisis management on the Japanese banking sector*.

Gertler, M., & Grinols, E. L. (1982). Unemployment, inflation, and common stock returns. *Journal of Money, Credit and Banking, 14*(2), 216–233.

Geske, R., & Roll, R. (1983). The fiscal and monetary linkage between stock returns and inflation. *The Journal of Finance, 38*(1), 1–33.

Hayek, F. A. (1976). *Choice in currency: a way to stop inflation* (Vol. 48). Ludwig von Mises Institute.

Hayford, M. D., & Malliaris, A. G. (2004). Monetary policy and the US stock market. *Economic Inquiry, 42*(3), 387–401.

Heintz, J., & Ndikumana, L. (2011). Is there a case for formal inflation targeting in sub-Saharan Africa? *Journal of African Economies, 20*(suppl_2), ii67–ii103.

Hutchison, M., & McDill, K. (1999). Are all banking crises alike? The Japanese experience in international comparison. *Journal of the Japanese and International Economies, 13*(3), 155–180.

Ioannidou, V., Ongena, S., & Peydró, J. L. (2015). Monetary policy, risk-taking, and pricing: Evidence from a quasi-natural experiment. *Review of Finance, 19*(1), 95–144.

Ismihan, M., & Ozkan, F. G. (2012). Public debt and financial development: A theoretical exploration. *Elsevier Economics Letters, 115*(3), 348e351.

Issahaku, H. (2018). *Remittances, monetary policy and financial development in developing countries* (Doctoral dissertation, University of Ghana).

Jankee, K. (2004). *Testing for nonlinearities in the adjustments of commercial banks' retail rates to interbank rates: The case of Mauritius*. In Paper presented.
Jiménez, G., Salas, V., & Saurina, J. (2009). Organizational distance and use of collateral for business loans. *Journal of Banking & Finance, 33*(2), 234–243.
Johnson, H. G. (1963). A survey of theories of inflation. *Indian Economic Review, 6*(3), 29–69.
Kang, J., & Pflueger, C. E. (2015). Inflation risk in corporate bonds. *The Journal of Finance, 70*(1), 115–162.
Klomp, J., & Sseruyange, J. (2020). Earthquakes and economic outcomes: Does central bank independence matter? *Open Economies Review, 32*, 1–25.
Klutse, S. K., Sági, J., & Kiss, G. D. (2022). Exchange rate crisis among inflation targeting countries in Sub-Saharan Africa. *Risks, 10*(5), 94.
Kutivadze, N. (2011). *Public debt and financial development*. Working Papers, No.2011–13. University of Milan.
Kyereboah-Coleman, A., & Agyire-Tettey, K. F. (2008). Impact of macroeconomic indicators on stock market performance: The case of the Ghana Stock Exchange. *The Journal of Risk Finance, 9*, 365–378.
Lacker, J. M. (2014). Fed credit policy: What is a lender of last resort? *Journal of Economic Dynamics and Control, 49*, 135–138.
Laeven, L., & Levine, R. (2009). Bank governance, regulation and risk taking. *Journal of Financial Economics, 93*(2), 259–275.
Laopodis, N. T. (2013). Monetary policy and stock market dynamics across monetary regimes. Journal of International Money and Finance, 33, 381–406.Friedman, L, 1956 Laopodis, N. T. (2013). Monetary policy and stock market dynamics across monetary regimes. *Journal of International Money and Finance, 33*, 381–406.
Lashkary, M., & Kashani, B. H. (2011). The impact of monetary variables on economic growth in Iran: A Monetarists' Approach. *World Applied Sciences Journal, 15*(3), 449–456.
Levine, R. (2000). Bank-based or market-based financial systems: Which is better? University of Minnesota.
Lopez-Buenache, G. (2019). The evolution of monetary policy effectiveness under macroeconomic instability. *Economic Modelling, 83*, 221–233.
Lupuşor, A. (2012). *Monetary policy or monetary politics? Assessing the impact of electoral cycles on central banks' decisions in advanced and developing economies*. LAP LAMBERT Academic Publishing.
Mahrous, S. N., Samak, N., & Abdelsalam, M. A. M. (2020). The effect of monetary policy on credit risk: evidence from the MENA region countries. *Review of Economics and Political Science, 5*(4), 289–304.
Mansor, A. (2005). Monetary policy and sectoral effect: A case study of Malaysia. *Global Economic Review, 35*, 303–326.

Masciandaro, D., & Romelli, D. (2015). Ups and downs. Central bank independence from the great inflation to the great recession: Theory, institutions and empirics. *Financial History Review, Cambridge University Press*, *22*(03), 259–289.

Matemilola, B. T., Bany-Ariffin, A. N., & Muhtar, F. E. (2015). The impact of monetary policy on bank lending rate in South Africa. *Borsa Istanbul Review, 15*(1), 53–59.

Mbulawa, S. (2015). Determinants of economic growth in Southern Africa development community: The role of institutions. *Applied Economics and Finance, 2*(2), 91–102.

Mbutor, M. O. (2007). The lending channel of monetary policy transmission in Nigeria; vector auto-regressive (VAR) verification.

Mishra, A., & Debata, B. (2020). Does economic policy uncertainty matter for stock market volatility? In *The financial landscape of emerging economies* (pp. 45–53). Springer.

Mizon, G. E. (1995). Progressive modeling of macroeconomic time series The LSE methodology. In *Macroeconometrics* (pp. 107–180). Springer, Dordrecht.

Murinde, V., & Eng, F. S. (1994). Financial development and economic growth in Singapore: Demand-following or supply-leading? *Applied Financial Economics, 4*(6), 391–404.

Ndikumana, L. (2014). Better global governance for a stronger Africa: A new era, a new strategy. *Africa at a Fork in the Road: Taking Off or Disappointment Once Again.*

North, D. C. (1990). *Institutions, institutional change and economic performance.* Cambridge University Press.

Papadamou, S., & Siriopoulos, C. (2014). Interest rate risk and the creation of the Monetary Policy Committee: Evidence from banks' and life insurance companies' stocks in the UK. *Journal of Economics and Business, 71*, 45–67.

Papadamou, S., Sidiropoulos, M., & Spyromitros, E. (2017). Does central bank independence affect stock market volatility? *Research in International Business and Finance, 42*, 855–864.

Quartey, P., & Afful-Mensah, G. (2014). Financial and monetary policies in Ghana: A review of recent trends. *Review of Development Finance, 4*(2), 115–125.

Quinn, D. (1997). The correlates of change in international financial regulation. *American Political Science Review, 91*(3), 531–551.

Quinn, D. P. (2003). Capital account liberalization and financial globalization, 1890–1999: A synoptic view. *International Journal of Finance & Economics, 8*(3), 189–204.

Quintyn, M., & Taylor, M. (2002). *Regulatory and supervisory independence and financial stability.*

Raza, A., Muffatto, M., & Saeed, S. (2018). The influence of formal institutions on the relationship between entrepreneurial readiness and entrepreneurial behaviour: A cross-country analysis. *Journal of Small Business and Enterprise Development.*

Reinhart, C. M., & Rogoff, K. S. (2004). The modern history of exchange rate arrangements: A reinterpretation. *The Quarterly Journal of Economics, 119*(1), 1–48.

Reinhart, C. M., & Rogoff, K. S. (2009). The aftermath of financial crises. *American Economic Review, 99*(2), 466–472.

Rigobon, R., & Sack, B. (2004). The impact of monetary policy on asset prices. *Journal of Monetary Economics, 51*(8), 1553–1575.

Romer, C. D., & Romer, D. H. (2002). *The evolution of economic understanding and postwar stabilization policy.*

Roodman, D. (2009). A note on the theme of too many instruments. *Oxford Bulletin of Economics and Statistics, 71*(1), 135–158.

Sahoo, J. (2020). Financial stress index, growth and price stability in India: Some recent evidence. *Transnational Corporations Review, 13*, 1–15.

Sherraden, M. S., Huang, J., Frey, J. J., Birkenmaier, J., Callahan, C., Clancy, M. M., & Sherraden, M. (2015). Financial capability and asset building for all. *American Academy of Social Work and Social Welfare*, 1–29. Lacker (2014).

Sousa, R. M. (2010). Housing wealth, financial wealth, money demand and policy rule: Evidence from the euro area. *The North American Journal of Economics and Finance, 21*(1), 88–105.

Stiglitz, J. E., & Weiss, A. (1981). Credit rationing in markets with imperfect information. *The American Economic Review, 71*(3), 393–410.

Tayssir, O., & Feryel, O. (2017). Does central banking promote financial development? *Borsa Istanbul Review, 18*, 52–75.

Usman, O. A., & Adejare, A. T. (2014). Money supply, foreign exchange regimes and economic growth in Nigeria. *Research Journal of Finance and Accounting, 5*(8), 121–129.

Van Leuvensteijn, M., Sørensen, C. K., Bikker, J. A., & Van Rixtel, A. A. (2013). Impact of bank competition on the interest rate pass-through in the euro area. *Applied Economics, 45*(11), 1359–1380.

Windmeijer, F. (2005). A finite sample correction for the variance of linear efficient two-step GMM estimators. *Journal of Econometrics, 126*(1), 25–51.

World Development Indicators. (2019). Washington, DC: The World Bank.

World Development Indicators. (2020). Washington, DC: The World Bank.

Yao, J., Ma, C., & He, W. P. (2014). Investor herding behaviour of Chinese stock market. *International Review of Economics & Finance, 29*, 12–29.

CHAPTER 8

Bank Market Power and Monetary Policy Transmission in Africa in the Wake of Information Sharing Institutional Arrangements

Anthony Adu-Asare Idun, Samuel Kwaku Agyei, Sean J. Gossel, and Joshua Yindenaba Abor

8.1 Introduction

The Charter that formed the African Union (AU) in 2002 seeks to achieve a Monetary Union comprising all African countries and to promote sustainable economic development through industrialisation and trade. It is envisaged by the AU that these goals can be achieved through effective monetary policy and a responsive banking system. Central banks across the globe use price stability, interest rates, and money supply as

A. A.-A. Idun (✉) · S. K. Agyei
University of Cape Coast, Cape Coast, Ghana
e-mail: aidun@ucc.edu.gh

S. K. Agyei
e-mail: sagyei@ucc.edu.gh

J. Y. Abor and C. K. D. Adjasi (eds.), *The Economics of Banking and Finance in Africa*, Palgrave Macmillan Studies in Banking and Financial Institutions, https://doi.org/10.1007/978-3-031-04162-4_8

conduits in inducing desirable economic outcomes by facilitating access to credit by the private sector (Gatsi et al., 2020). However, the extent of bank monopoly in the credit market can attenuate the transmission process through which monetary policy induces economic performance. The conduct of banks with market power can also be instrumental in the effectiveness of the monetary policy. Banks with greater market power can catalyse the pass-through effect of monetary policy lending and deposit rates by restricting or boosting credit availability. Banks with market power also decide on the size of private sector credit, which can increase systemic liquidity, reduce non-performing loans (Karadima & Louri, 2020) and stimulate economic activities. Therefore, banks' market power has implications for monetary policy outcomes because banks with market power can attenuate the speed with which monetary policy interventions have desirable economic effects. The bargaining power of these banks can affect money supply or interest rates to stimulate economic activities by changing the lending rates or deposit rates without recourse to the central bank's directives.

Similarly, banks with market power can boost a bank's efficiency because of their economies of scale. Still, they can also pass on their inefficiencies to the detriment of customers by charging higher lending rates. Thus, while the improved efficiencies of the banks can benefit the financial sector and economic development, the inefficiencies can increase the cost of doing business and slow economic productivity.

In addition to price stability, interest rates and money supply, monetary policy also influences the extent to which banks can withstand shocks. In a stable environment, banks can augment the stimulatory policies of central banks. Depositors are thus more willing to save, thereby boosting the liquidity position of banks, while the cost of borrowing will reduce, which encourages investments and economic activities. However, these

S. J. Gossel
Graduate School of Business, University of Cape Town, Cape Town, South Africa
e-mail: sj.gossel@uct.ac.za

J. Y. Abor
University of Ghana Business School, Legon, Accra, Ghana
e-mail: joshabor@ug.edu.gh

effects can only occur in a financial system where banks have the market power to ensure the effectiveness of the monetary policy. Large banks with established relationships with their clients can boost credit availability at the onset of tight monetary policy (Petersen & Rajan, 1995). Still, tighter monetary policies can thwart the effects of tighter monetary policies by banks that want to maintain their relationships in the credit distribution chain. Banks with market power can reduce lending rates and thus neutralise the attempts by Monetary Policy authorities to reduce excess liquidity. On the other hand, banks with market power can also charge competitive lending rates at the onset of loose monetary policy, thereby restricting access to credit intended to boost liquidity and economic activities.

However, the penetration of credit scoring institutions can limit the financial systems' ability to influence monetary policy by reducing information asymmetry, and thus the degree of bank market power. For example, in the U.S., Anti-Trust Laws prevent the collusive conduct of financial firms prohibiting the amalgamation of banks that can result in greater market power. Mergers that can increase the combined firm's Herfindahl-Hirschman Index (HHI) to or beyond 1800 are deemed unacceptable. Strong institutions can also provide a stable banking system, which will better assimilate monetary policies into sustainable development. In Africa, like in other emerging regions, private and public institutions have established information systems that aim to reduce information asymmetry. However, the extent to which the conduct of banks can beneficially transmit monetary policy is an area of ongoing research. This study, therefore, seeks to add to the discussion by exploring whether the emergence of information sharing institutions can mitigate the extent to which banks with market power can dampen the transmission of monetary policy in achieving price stability, reduction in interest rates and currency stability in Africa.

The rest of the chapter is organised as follows: the next section discusses some salient facts about monetary policy in Africa. Section 8.3 reviews the pertinent literature in the research area. Section 8.4 discusses the techniques used to conduct empirical analyses. Section 8.5 summarises the empirical findings, and Sect. 8.6 brings the paper to a close.

8.2 Monetary Policy in Africa

Monetary policy aims to control the growth in money supply to achieve price, exchange rate, financial and interest rate stability while facilitating real output growth. Most African countries adopted financial liberalisation policies between the late 1980s and early 1990s, and since then, monetary policies have increasingly sought to ensure macroeconomic stability (Berg & Portillo, 2018). Table 8.1 contains the mean of some indicators of monetary policy for five-year periods since 2000. On average, the monetary policy rates (MPR) have remained at single digits since 2000. The deposit rate from 8.86% during the 2000–2004 period to 5.57% during the recent 2015–2019 period. However, the figures in Table 8.1 indicate that while policy rates have slightly increased, deposit rates have decreased. On the other hand, following an initial blip in lending rates relative to the monetary policy rate, the two rates have largely tracked each other. As a result, the transmission of policy rates into deposit rates appears to be smoother than that of policy rates into lending rates.

Table 8.1 also shows that African countries have steadily facilitated exchange rate appreciation. Unfortunately, this has not translated into improved inflation, as seen from the significant deterioration from 61.68 during the 2000–2004 period to 150.40 during the 2015–2019 period. Despite improved monetary policy indicators, possible reasons for this Consumer Price Index (CPI) deterioration include a rise in broad money supply above productivity growth.

Over the last decade, Fig. 8.1 shows that some countries have embarked on expansionary monetary policy since their central banks, on average, reduced the monetary policy rates. Over the past decade,

Table 8.1 Macroeconomic averages directly related to monetary policy transmission in Africa

	2000–2004	*2005–2009*	*2010–2014*	*2015–2019*
Average monetary policy rates	7.92	8.36	7.08	8.13
Average deposit rates	8.86	7.30	6.41	5.57
Average lending rates	22.37	15.61	14.25	14.31
Average real exchange rates	106.23	99.44	98.17	96.36
Average Consumer Price Index (CPI)	61.68	83.02	116.62	150.40

Source Authors' estimation for IMF's International Financial Statistics (2020) (Online Edition)

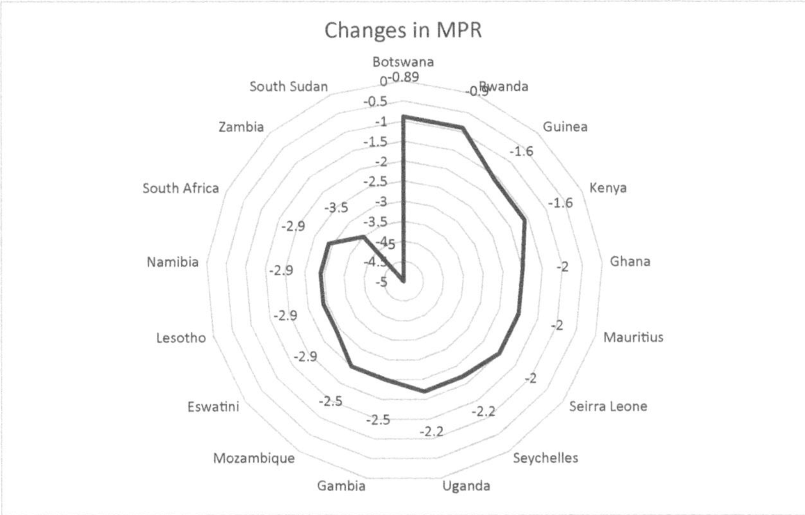

Fig. 8.1 Average changes in the monetary policy rates for some African countries since 2000 (*Source* World Economic Outlook [2020], International Monetary Fund)

Botswana, Burundi, Guinea, Kenya, Ghana, Mauritius, Sierra Leone, Seychelles and Uganda reduced the monetary policy rates by 0.89, 0.9, 1.6, 1.6, 2, 2, 2, 2.2 and 2.2%, respectively. Those countries which recorded higher fall in monetary policy rates include Gambia, Mozambique, Eswatini, Lesotho, Namibia, South Africa, Zambia and South Sudan, with a fall in monetary policy rates of 2.5, 2.5, 2.9, 2.9, 2.9, 3.5, 3.5 and 5%, respectively. The reduction in the monetary policy rates has an impact on the growth in the money supply. Given the output growth, an increase in money supply can translate into price volatility, especially when the growth in the money supply exceeds the output growth. Figure 8.2 shows the dynamics in the growth in broad money and the growth in output from 2000 to 2019.

Figure 8.2 portrays the broad money growth rates for the regional economic grouping in Africa since 2000. It shows that the growth in money supply has been predominantly positive, with the growth range (0–20%) forming the dominating growth in money supply across the regions. The contour floors also show various growth rates in some regions. In

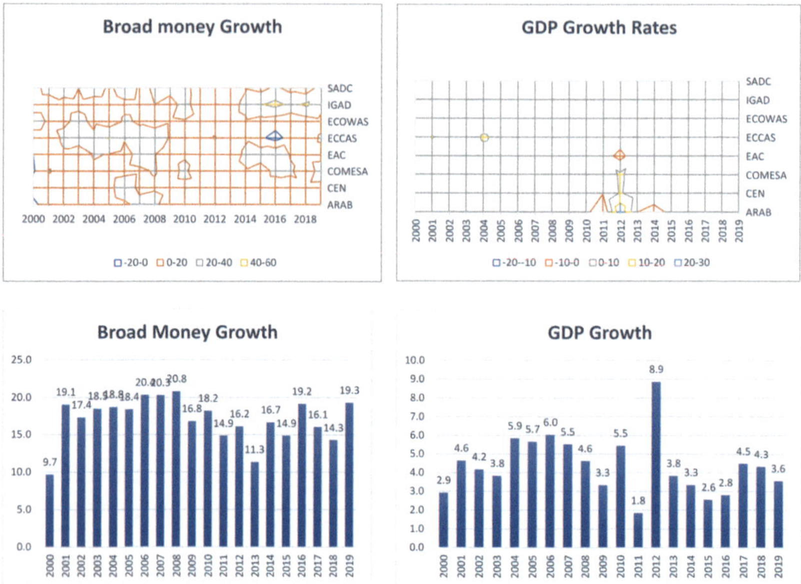

Fig. 8.2 Broad money growth and GDP growth of each regional economic community since 2000 (*Source* Authors, drawn from data from the IMF and the World Bank

2000, Arab-Maghreb (ARAB) and Common Market for East and Central Africa (COMESA) recorded negative growth in money supply just as the Economic Community of Central African States (ECCAS) did in 2016. Some regions have also recorded very high growth in money supply over the period. In 2016 and 2018, the money supply grew by more than 40% in Intergovernmental Authority on Development (IGAD). As shown by the grey-contour lines, the regions have also recorded growth in money supply at a range of 20–40% within the period, especially between 2001 and 2009.

The lower panel of Fig. 8.2 shows that the money supply increased greatly during 2008, 2007 and 2006. The growth in the 2007/2008 period is phenomenal because it indicates that the broad money supply increased in most African economies during the global financial crisis. The growth in broad money reached as high as over 40% in the IGAD region in 2016 and 2018 and as low as below 0% in ARAB and COMESA in

Table 8.2 Average of monetary policy transmission outcomes from 2000 to 2019

	ARAB	*CEN*	*COMESA*	*EAC*	*ECCAS*	*ECOWAS*	*IGAD*	*SADC*
Broad money growth	11.33	15.11	16.59	18.86	17.54	16.35	22.98	19.33
GDP growth	3.88	4.34	4.35	4.90	4.74	4.53	4.43	3.93
Interest rate spread	7.50	7.14	9.60	9.61	19.50	5.76	9.45	11.67
Inflation	3.32	6.95	8.48	12.92	11.34	5.54	15.52	12.61

2000. The grey-contour maps also indicate the growth in broad money supply between 20 and 40% across the regions since 2000. In general, the growth range, 0–20%, dominates the growth in broad money supply across the regions over the period, as indicated by the orange floor. In all, broad money grew by 17.26% for all African countries from 2000 to 2019. Finally, Table 8.2 shows that IGAD experienced the highest growth in money supply (22.98%) over the period, while ARAB experienced the lowest growth in broad money supply (11.33%).

We also analyse the growth in output viz-a-viz the growth in money supply to ascertain the impact of monetary policy transmission on price stability. At the top-right portion of Fig. 8.1, indications are that output grows less than proportionately to the growth of broad money in the subregions, leading to inflationary pressure. In general, output grew between 0 and 10% in the regions, with an overall average growth of 4.39% from 2000 to 2019. The gap between broad money growth and output growth is expected to increase the price levels despite the fall in monetary policy rates. In terms of yearly growth, the right-lower panel of Fig. 8.2 indicates that the continent achieved the highest output growth in 2012 while 2011, 2015, 2016 and 2000 recorded the lowest growth in output. The highest growth in 2012 was influenced by the phenomenal growth average growth rate of 27% recorded by ARAB Maghreb countries. However, the region could not sustain that level of growth in subsequent years. In general, the average output growth has been less than 10% since 2000 and the growth in recent years has been deteriorating. In terms of regional distribution, Table 8.2 shows that EAC recorded the highest growth (4.90%) followed by ECCAS (4.74%), ECOWAS (4.53%), IGAD (4.43%), COMESA (4.35%) and CEN (4.34%). However, ARAB (3.88%) and SADC (3.93) recorded the lowest growth in output over the period. Indications are that the rate of inflation in Africa or its regions can be partly attributed to the gap between the growth rates in money supply and the rate of output growth.

The lower panel of Fig. 8.3 shows the rates of inflation across the regions from 2000 to 2019. The orange floor shows that, in general, the inflation levels have been between 0 and 20% in the regions since 2000. However, IGAD and EAC recorded high inflation rates between 40 and 60% in 2016, while ECCAS and SADC had between 40 and 60% in 2000 and 2001. Similarly, in 2010, the ECCAS region recorded a deflation rate of 2.50%, the lowest across the region. We did not find any extraordinary growth in money supply or output that accounted for the fall in prices in the region, indicating that the decline in prices was not due to the output gap.

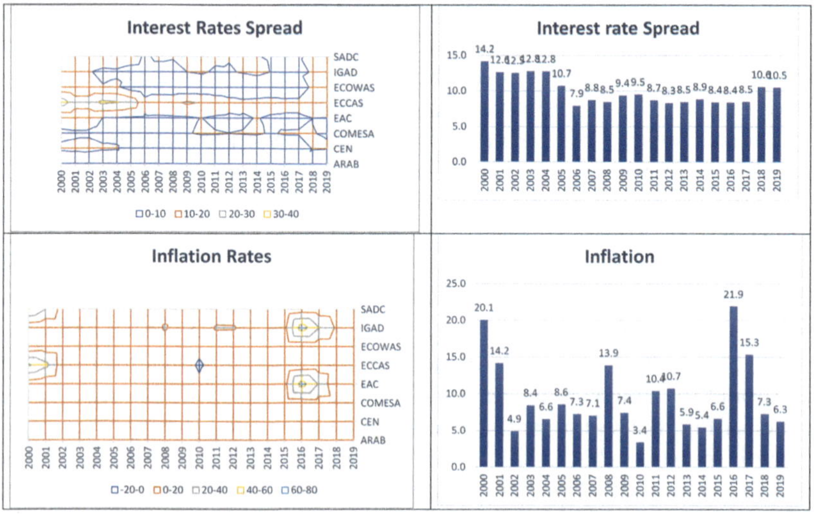

Fig. 8.3 Interest rates spread and inflation rates in regional economic communities in Africa (*Source* Authors, from World Development Indicators' [2020] Data)

From the lower-left panel, the yearly growth in prices indicates that the continent recorded the highest inflation rate of 21.9 and 20.1% in 2016 and 2000, respectively. The inflation rates in IGAD EAC and ECCAS induced the continent's high inflation rates in those years. Similarly, the continent had the lowest inflation rate of 3.4% in 2010, which generated the average deflation rate in the ECCAS region in that year. In the regional distribution (see Table 8.2), IGAD (15.52%), EAC (12.92%), SADC (12.61%) and ECCAS recorded above average rates of inflation, which indicates that these regions still experience price instability. On the other hand, ARAB (3.32%), ECOWAS (5.54%), CEN (6.95%) and COMESA (8.48%) experienced below average rates of inflation, which indicates that the regions are on course in achieving price stability. Overall, the continent recorded an average inflation rate of 9.58%, which is still below the gap between the average growth in money supply and the average growth in output by 12.87%. The gap in money supply and output growth is not the only factor contributing to price instability in Africa. In this paper, we also analyse whether the conduct of banks with market power can induce price stability in Africa and its regional blocs.

In the upper panel of Fig. 8.3, we also examine the extent of bank market power by looking at the interest rate spread across the regions over 2000–2019. Indications are that the ECCAS region recorded a high interest rate spread between 30 and 40% in 2003 and 2009. Most of the spread over the period has been between 0–10 and 10–20%. In general, the average interest rate spread is 10.03% over the decade. Table 8.2 shows that the ECCAS region had the highest spread of 19.50% while the ECOWAS region recorded the lowest spread. This means that market power has been in such areas as ECCAS and SADC and lower in ECOWAS, CEN and ARAB. The spread in EAC, COMESA and IGAD has been around the average spread in the continent. Berg and Portillo (2018) reported that the average spread in developing countries, in general, is around 9%, so the spread in Africa of about 10.03% is higher, which is an indication of higher bank market power in Africa as other studies confirm (Amidu & Wolfe, 2013; Clerides et al., 2015; Idun et al., 2020; Mirzaei & Moore, 2014). In this paper, we test whether the conduct of banks with market power can reduce the transmission process of monetary policy into the price, real interest rate and real exchange rate stability in Africa.

Based on the Figures above, indications are that many African countries have predominantly adopted an expansionary monetary policy over the past decade, which has resulted in growth in the broad money supply. Given the relatively low output growth rates to the growth in money supply, inflationary pressure is still high in some regions even though other regions have maintained some level of price stability. However, due to the higher interest rate spread in the continent, inflation rates cannot be reduced to only the output gap.

In this paper, we analyse the impact of banks with market power on achieving price, interest rates and exchange rates stability as monetary policy anchors in Africa. We also explore the direct effect of bank market power on the broad money supply in Africa and her various economic communities. We also examined how African economies are mitigating the information sharing systems to fastrack the speed with which the conducts of banks with market power induce monetary policy transmission into growth in money supply, price, real interest rates and exchange rates stability.

8.3 Literature Review

In most economies, banks play an essential financial intermediation role by accepting deposits and apportioning them into loan portfolios directly related to credit extension. The central bank's reserve ratio then attenuates the ability to create credit. When the reserve ratio is high, banks can only create credit on limited excess reserves, which reduces loanable funds. In periods of accelerated growth, the demand for loans by firms and other economic agents are likely to rise and banks will then tend to ration the limited loanable funds by the loan rate. Banks also tend to use ration credit in inefficient financial systems due to the high prevalence of information asymmetry at the equilibrium interest rate (Stiglitz & Weiss, 1981). According to the "too big to fail" hypothesis (see Mishkin, 2006; Morgan & Stiroh, 2005; Stern, 2009; Stern & Feldman, 2004), large banks are more likely to be resurrected during a crisis or bank run to avoid the contagious effect of a large bank's crisis on the entire banking system. Through their central banks, there is evidence that most governments directly or indirectly pump liquidity into struggling banks by reducing the reserve requirement. However, a bank with market power can reduce the impact of central banks' expansionary monetary policy.

The literature on the relationship between the degree of bank market power and the effectiveness of monetary policy transmission has commonly been examined from three main perspectives. The first butch of the literature suggests that banks with market power operating in weakly competitive environments can reduce the pass-through effect of changes in monetary policy by manipulating the loan rate in their favour (see Leroy & Lucotte, 2015; Sørensen & Werner, 2006; Van Leuvensteijn et al., 2013). The second strand of literature argues that financial crises or systemic crises affect banks' fundamentals, which in turn attenuate the pass-through effect of interest rates (Acharya et al., 2020; Aristei & Gallo, 2014). The third stream is still emerging and seeks to combine both of the previous streams by contending that the ability of the banking sector to induce interest rates pass-through depends on the equity position of the banks themselves. Hence, banks with excess equity compete for more customers and, in the process, reduce loan rates, thereby speeding up the pass-through effect. On the other hand, banks with less net worth tend to ration credit using loan rates and are thus more likely to reduce monetary policy rate transmission (Zentefis, 2020).

The relationship between the central bank's policy and the banking system can significantly affect the former's ability to achieve price stability. According to the quantity theory of money, the money supply is directly related to prices. Therefore, central banks change the money supply to achieve a specific asset pricing strategy or achieve price stability. Since asset prices and inflation induce the financial system performance, achieving price stability (which is a prime objective of the central bank) also shapes financial stability (Güntner, 2011). The global financial crisis of 2008 showed that an unstable financial system detrimentally affects the long-run performance of banks and other financial institutions. Through their central banks, governments have provided stimulus packages to try to stabilise businesses and financial institutions while also imposing capitalisation and liquidity regulations. Also, by influencing interest rates, central banks can affect banks' risk appetite and reduce the probability of bank failure arising from loan impairments (Özşuca & Akbostancı, 2016).

Central banks also use the banking sector to implement monetary policy depending on the stage of the business cycle. An expansionary monetary policy tends to reduce policy rates to boost economic activity. In an efficient financial system, banks respond to the falling (rising) central bank monetary policy rate by reducing (increasing) their loan rates, which then injects liquidity into (removes liquidity from) the economy. However, the pass-through process from monetary policy into deposit or loan rates depends on the degree of market power in the banking system. The reason is that the greater the banking sector's market power, the greater the banking system's ability to enact or mitigate monetary policy. A competitive banking system can improve the efficiency and effectiveness of monetary policy by fast-tracking the past-through effect of central bank policy rate into interest rates (see Brämer et al., 2013; Güntner, 2011; de Bondt, 2005) and speeds up access to finance (see Pagano, 1993; Boyd & De Nicoló, 2005).

In contrast, banks can insulate their credit extension risk by rationing credit even when facing excess liquidity (Stiglitz & Weiss, 1981). Information sharing, such as the private credit bureaus and public credit registries, can provide information about the borrowers that can make more credit available or reduce non-performing loans (Djankov et al., 2007) and minimise loan contract delinquencies (Doblas-Madrid & Minetti, 2013) by sharing information about borrowers' credit history (Brown et al., 2009).

Information sharing is essential in monetary policy management. Public credit registries supply the central banks with digitalised data about borrowers. By correcting information on borrowers, the central banks can advise the banks to allocate credit into productive sectors. The central banks can also use information from the credit registry to supervise the credit direction of credit creation and monitor economic activities when setting policy rates. Information sharing and creditor protection can increase credit disbursement into the private sector (Djankov et al., 2007). An inducement in private sector allocation can boost investment and future consumption which can increase liquidity in an economy. Information sharing can encourage good loans which in turn can lead to reduction in lending rates (because loans are less risky) (Brown et al., 2009). Credit information sharing can reduce the requirement of collateral and increase credit allocation by ensuring that only credible firms get financing (Beck et al., 2014).

The overall effect is that information sharing provides information to reduce adverse selection and moral hazards to protect creditors and encourage liquidity. By boosting liquidity, information sharing can influence interest rates and general prices. This study explores whether the emergence of information sharing institutions can mitigate the extent to which banks with market power can dampen the transmission of monetary policy in achieving price stability, interest rates reduction and currency stability in Africa.

8.4 Methodology

The paper uses unbalanced country-level bank and monetary indicators covering the period from 2002 to 2017. The start date coincides with the inauguration of the Africa Union. At the same time, the sample period encompasses the time when most African countries moved towards the middle-income stage of economic development, cross-border banking activities have intensified, Pan-African banks have spread across the continent and African countries have embraced private credit bureaus.

The analysis makes use of the dynamic first difference generalised method of moment (GMM) using 17 instruments. These instruments include the transformed first lags of each of the right-hand side variables and untransformed dummies for each of the eight communities in Africa. We had regional integration dummies as instruments because regional integration opens up economies and fosters cross-banking activities that can induce the degree of bank market power and stimulate the extent of monetary policy transmission. The advantage of using dynamic GMM is that this approach efficiently accounts for endogeneity among the monetary policy and bank market power proxies and corrects for serial correlation in the innovation term. The dynamic GMM approach is also appropriate considering the characteristics of our dataset, which include a lesser time-series dimension compared to the number of countries included. The first differencing of the variables also removes unobserved cross-sectional effects in the error term. However, the right-hand variables correlate with the right-hand variables, as shown in Eq. (8.1). Therefore, we used the first independent variable difference, which correlates with the independent variables but is uncorrelated with the error term as instruments. We also included dummies for regional economic blocs, which can influence the right-hand variables but are uncorrelated with the innovation term in Eq. (8.1). To verify that the results of the GMM estimations are correctly specified and stable, we perform Sargan's J-statistics under the assumption that the innovation term correlates with the 17 instruments used in the estimations and the Arellano and Bond (1991) AR(2) serial correlation test.[1] The GMM model for our empirical analyses

[1] In addition to GMM, the analysis also makes use of random effect estimates, which are found to be more applicable than Fixed Effects on the basis of the Hausman test. The results of the RE estimations are not included in this paper due to space constraints but are available on request.

is as follows:

$$\begin{aligned}\Delta \text{MP}_{it} = {} & \beta_1 \text{MP}_{it-1} + \beta_2 \text{BMP}_{it} + \beta_3 \Delta \text{REMIT}_{it} \\ & + \beta_3 \Delta \text{FDI}_{it} + \beta_4 \text{PSC}_{it} + \beta_5 \text{TRADE}_{it} \\ & + \beta_6 \Delta \text{MOB}_{it} + \beta_7 \Delta \text{GDP}_{it} + \beta_8 \Delta \text{EDEBT}_{it} \\ & + \beta_9 \Delta \text{PCB}_{it} + \beta_{10} \Delta \text{INTERACTIONS}_{it} + \Delta \varepsilon_{it} \end{aligned} \tag{8.1}$$

where:

MP is a vector of proxies for monetary policy transmission; BMP is the proxy for bank market power; REMIT is the share of remittances inflows in GDP; FDI is the share of foreign direct investment in GDP; PSC is the share of domestic private sector credit in GDP; TRADE is the share of total trade in GDP (trade openness); MOB is the mobile cellular subscription per 100 people of the population a measure of technological infrastructure); GDP is the real gross domestic product per capita (at 2010 constant prices); EDEBT is the share of external debts in GDP; PCB is private credit bureau coverage, a measure of information sharing system; ε is the error term; $\beta_1 \ldots \beta_{10}$ are the coefficients of the respective regressors to be estimated; i represents each country, and t represents the time-series dimension of the panel structure.

Measures of Monetary Policy

We employ five measures to proxy the outcome of monetary policy. First, we employ the share of broad money (M2) in GDP. The IMF defines broad money as the sum of currency outside banks; demand deposits other than those of the central government; the time, savings, and foreign currency deposits of resident sectors other than the central government; bank and traveller's cheques and other securities such as certificates of deposit and commercial paper. This measure is related to the competitive conduct of banks with market power since it is associated with the credit creation and liquidity of the banks. Banks accept deposits of all forms and translate them into credit creation, increasing the amount of money in circulation. Higher levels of money supply have an attenuating effect on interest rates and, therefore, lending rates. If the central bank increases the money supply through its monetary policy interventions, it boosts liquidity in the financial system, reducing lending rates. However, a bank with market power can still charge higher loan rates in the face of an expansion in the money supply, at least in the short run. Since banks are interconnected, small banks can also mimic the conduct of banks with market power by charging higher loan rates. This explains why loan rates are relatively higher in the banking systems in Africa, where Pan-African banks penetrate (Diallo, 2015). We expect the conduct of banks with market power to induce greater money supply if they sustain a relationship (Petersen et al., 1995) or constraint credit allocation to cause printing of more money by the central bank by reducing the transmission process of the lower policy rates into loan rates or reduce the deposit rate and increase the loan rate simultaneously (Pagano, 1993). The low-interest effect can be the same regarding the growth in money supply, our second measure of monetary policy. In the same measure, we also use the growth in broad money as an alternative measure of the impact of monetary policy since the central bank's expansionary monetary policy directly influences the growth in the broad money supply.

Price stability is a primary goal of monetary policy in most countries in Africa. The general level of price stability is measured by reducing the growth rate in the consumer price index (CPI). Therefore, we measure price stability as a monetary policy target by the inflation rate in various countries. Also, an increase or a decrease in the money supply has implications for interest rates. An increase in the money supply is expected to decrease real interest rates. A reduction in the money supply would increase interest rates since a contractionary monetary policy can reduce loanable funds. Due to this, we also measure monetary policy transmission by real interest rates. By measuring monetary policy transmission by real interest rate, we can examine how banks' conduct with market power can lead to interest rate stability in Africa. We also used real exchange rates as a proxy of monetary policy transmission to determine the impact of a bank with market power on exchange rates stability.

Measurement of Bank Market Power

The structure-conduct-performance hypothesis suggests that the level of concentration in the banking system serves as a placeholder for bank market power. However, the definition of bank concentration is ambiguous since the size of the asset alone does not explain the competitive conduct of banks. Empirical studies often employ the Lerner Index (Beck et al., 2013) to measure bank market power. The Lerner Index (LI) is measured as the difference between the price of banks and their marginal cost as a ratio of the price of banks' output. A higher (lower) LI is an indication of greater (lesser) market power. However, the magnitude of the LI does not explain whether the banks are being efficient or inefficient, which can provide erroneous information on whether the level of bank efficiency induces the extent of market power.

An approach that mitigates the weakness of the LI when measuring the degree of bank market power is the Boone Indicator (see Amidu & Wolfe, 2013; Boone, 2008; Clerides et al., 2015; Mirzaei & Moore, 2014; Stiglitz, 1989). The Boone Indicator (BI) is measured as the coefficient of regression of the banks' market share as the dependent variable and the marginal cost of the banks as the independent variable. Since the performance of banks is negatively related to the marginal costs, a negative BI coefficient indicates that inefficient banks are unlikely to survive increased competition in the banking system. Since the BI incorporates the level of bank efficiency, it indicates the degree of market power that can be ascribed to the banks' level of efficiency rather than merely their size. This study thus uses the Boone indicator to measure the degree of bank market power.

Control Variables

In addition to the factors discussed above, the estimations also include a set of six control factors that have been found to influence monetary policy transmission. The first is foreign direct investments (FDI), which is included to account for private capital inflows, which can increase the foreign deposits to improve broad money supply and reduce real exchange rates volatility. The second is a credit to the private sector (PSC) to account for the resource from the financial sector to the private sector. Since credit to the private sector induces economic growth, which increases money supply on inflation, the inclusion of private sector credit allocation can ascertain the real impact of the conduct of banks with market power on monetary policy transmission. The third factor is external debt (EDEBT) to control foreign inflows to the public sector. Suppose the government receives more resources from other economies. In that case, the influx can reduce the government's domestic borrowings, inducing interest rates stability since the government would not compete with the private sector in the loan market. An inflow of foreign debts would also reduce contractionary monetary policy, which would reduce the money supply through the central banks'nopen market operations. The fourth is trade openness (TRADE) account for the impact of globalisation. The fifth is mobile telecommunication infrastructure (MOB) to account for the infrastructure that can induce electronic financial innovations such as mobile banking, internet banking, cryptocurrency and mobile money penetration in Africa. The final control factor is the national income per capita (GDP), which reflects the level of productivity in the country. An increase in productivity can dampen the effect of increases in the central bank's money supply on inflation and interest rates. When output increases more than proportionately than the growth rate in money supply due to expansionary monetary policy, the economy's price level will decrease and the reverse is also true. An increase in output also has an attenuating effect on real interest rates.

8.5 Empirical Results

Table 8.3 presents the dynamic GMM of regressing money supply, measured as the share of broad money in GDP, against the impact of bank market power. Column 3–1 shows that bank market power has an insignificant effect on money supply when the impact of private credit bureaus (PCB) are excluded. The interaction between private credit bureaus and bank market power in columns 3–2 is highly significant, indicating that private credit bureaus complement the extent to which bank market power speeds up monetary policy transmission. This result thus accords with the view that information sharing systems reduce the loan rate (Brown et al., 2009; Djankov et al., 2007) and the credit risk of non-performing loans (Acharya et al., 2020; Doblas-Madrid & Menitte, 2013).

Subsequently, we examine the impact of banks with market power on money supply across the eight regional economic communities under the Africa Union. Economic communities facilitate trade and cross-border banking, which can expand the operating frontier of banks and increase their market share. By increasing banks' market share, regional economic communities can increase the degree of market power of Pan-African banks. As can be seen, the interaction coefficients are significant and positive for the Common Market for Eastern and Southern Africa (COMESA) (column 3–5), Intergovernmental Authority on Development (IGAD) (column 3–9) and the Southern African Development Community (SADC) (column 3–10). Thus, the level of bank market power significantly improves the transmission of monetary policy in those regions.

Table 8.3 Bank market power and broad money supply (2002–2017)

Eq Name	*1*	*2*	*3*	*4*	*5*
M2(−1)	0.339***	0.302***	0.329***	0.287***	0.327***
	(0.014)	(0.022)	(0.017)	(0.022)	(0.027)
REMIT	−0.578***	−0.520***	−0.615***	−0.466***	−0.546***
	(0.047)	(0.064)	(0.057)	(0.048)	(0.059)
FDI	−0.054	−0.148	−0.010	−0.101	−0.08
	(0.074)	(0.106)	(0.098)	(0.110)	(0.105)
FD	0.244***	0.267***	0.235***	0.243***	
	(0.039)	(0.038)	(0.063)	(0.048)	
TRADE	0.119***	0.123***	0.110***	0.113***	0.120***
	(0.012)	(0.012)	(0.019)	(0.015)	(0.007)
MOB	0.074***	0.076***	0.084***	0.078***	0.089***
	(0.008)	(0.008)	(0.009)	(0.009)	(0.010)
GDP	−0.004***	−0.002	−0.004**	−0.001	0.000
	(0.001)	(0.002)	(0.002)	(0.002)	(0.001)
EDEBT	0.017	0.014	0.023	0.024**	0.020**
	(0.010)	(0.008)	(0.012)	(0.009)	(0.009)
BMP	−0.505	−2.093***	−0.026	32.806***	−3.483***
	(1.805)	(1.048)	(2.118)	(3.418)	(1.145)
PCB		−0.033	−0.026	−0.081	−0.143***
		(0.045)	(0.040)	(0.050)	(0.041)
BMP*PCB		0.796***			
		(0.134)			
BMP*ARAB			−131.583**		
			(54.238)		

Eq Name	*1*	*2*	*3*	*4*	*5*
BMP*CEN				−34.657***	
				(3.901)	
BMP*COMESA					39.345***
					(4.611)
BMP*EAC					
BMP*ECCAS					
BMP*ECOWAS					
BMP*IGAD					
BMP*SADC					
Observations	483	483	483	483	483
Sargan	0.459	0.530	0.497	0.531	0.450
AR(2)	0.9652	0.4234	0.9657	0.2696	0.8531

Eq Name	*6*	*7*	*8*	*9*	*10*
M2(−1)	0.367***	0.299***	0.291***	0.341***	0.295***
	(0.015)	(0.026)	(0.023)	(0.011)	(0.019)
REMIT	−0.626***	−0.604***	−0.520***	−0.599***	−0.495***
	(0.058)	(0.061)	(0.054)	(0.054)	(0.046)
FDI	−0.017	0.084	−0.113	−0.077	−0.101
	(0.088)	(0.175)	(0.122)	(0.056)	(0.100)
FD		0.255**	0.240***	0.244***	0.248***
		(0.110)	(0.055)	(0.051)	(0.044)
TRADE	0.122***	0.085***	0.114***	0.107***	0.119***
	(0.011)	(0.027)	(0.016)	(0.015)	(0.015)
MOB	0.087***	0.069***	0.079***	0.079***	0.079***
	(0.012)	(0.011)	(0.010)	(0.008)	(0.008)
GDP	−0.001	−0.001	−0.001	−0.003**	−0.002
	(0.001)	(0.002)	(0.002)	(0.002)	(0.001)

(continued)

Table 8.3 (continued)

Eq Name	*6*	*7*	*8*	*9*	*10*
EDEBT	0.021	0.038***	0.021**	0.020**	0.026***
	(0.011)	(0.013)	(0.010)	(0.009)	(0.008)
BMP	−1.461	−2.016	27.54***	−1.252	−2.165
	(1.487)	(2.319)	(3.492)	(1.524)	(1.519)
PCB	−0.092***	−0.028	−0.079	0.002	−0.089**
	(0.032)	(0.073)	(0.051)	(0.028)	(0.043)
BMP*PCB					
BMP*ARAB					
BMP*CEN					
BMP*COMESA					
BMP*EAC	22.236				
	−50.312				
BMP*ECCAS		−10.479			
		−37.995			
BMP*ECOWAS			−29.477***		
			(3.930)		
BMP*IGAD				69.634**	
				(30.185)	
BMP*SADC					29.478***
					(3.536)
Observations	483	477	483	483	483
Sargan	0.564	0.725	0.510	0.494	0.505
AR(2)	0.5112	0.9763	0.8162	0.999	0.7816

In comparison, the coefficients for the Arab-Maghreb (column 3–3), the Community of Sahel-Saharan States (CEN) (column 2–4), and the Economic Community of West Africa (ECOWAS) (column 3–8) are significant and negative, indicating that the level of bank market power reduces the money supply, increasing interest rates and loan rates. Furthermore, the negative coefficients associated with the Arab-Maghreb and CEN regions suggest that Islamic banking minimises monetary policy transmission. Lastly, the coefficients are insignificant for the East African Community (EAC) (column 3–6) and Economic Community of Central African States (ECCAS) (column 3–7). Possible reasons for this insignificant include the uncompetitive nature of the banking system in those regions and a higher degree of state interference in the central bank policy in those regions.

Table 8.4 presents the results of the estimations using the growth in the money supply (M2G) as the dependent variable. Unlike the results in Table 4.3, the results below in column 4–1 shows that the level of bank market power in Africa reduces the growth in money supply regardless of whether private credit bureaus (PCB) are excluded. The interaction effects in columns 4–2 further show that information sharing institutions substitute for the degree of bank market power in stimulating expansionary monetary policy.

The results of including the regional interactions (columns 4–3 to 4–10) produce slightly different results to the regional effects in Table 4.3. The interaction terms are significant and positive for the community of Sahel-Saharan States (CEN) (column 4–4), Economic Community of Central African States (ECCAS) (column 4–7). This suggests that bank market power has a strong positive impact on growth in the money supply in these regions. The banks can boost liquidity by relaxing restrictions on access to credit. Large banks can also afford the services of credit referencing institutions which can help reduce the risk of lending.

In comparison, the interaction coefficients are significant and negative in the Common Market for Eastern and Southern Africa (COMESA) (column 4–5), the Economic Community of West Africa (ECOWAS) (column 4–8), and the Southern African Development Community (SADC) (column 4–10), implying that the level of bank market power in these regions dampens the growth of money supply. A reason for this is that a greater degree of market power in these regions (Bempong & Sy, 2015) which is induced by the penetration of large pan-African banks which in turn mimic each other (Diallo, 2015) to reduce the speed with

Table 8.4 Bank market power and growth in broad money supply in Africa

Eq Name	*1*	*2*	*3*	*4*	*5*
M2G(−1)	0.089***	0.090***	0.075***	0.098***	0.098***
	(0.018)	(0.018)	(0.028)	(0.023)	(0.023)
REMIT	−0.179	−0.670**	−0.335	−0.311	−0.280
	(0.202)	(0.335)	(0.303)	(0.239)	(0.246)
FDI	0.114	0.053	−0.211	−0.023	−0.049
	(0.272)	(0.291)	(0.362)	(0.251)	(0.266)
FD	−2.104***	−2.430***	−2.291***	−2.295***	−2.332***
	(0.097)	(0.385)	(0.382)	(0.346)	(0.361)
TRADE	0.329***	0.341***	0.362***	0.381***	0.387***
	(0.062)	(0.087)	(0.126)	(0.078)	(0.082)
MOB	0.067	0.104	0.076	0.078	0.085
	(0.035)	(0.056)	(0.086)	(0.047)	(0.051)
GDP	−0.001	0.002	−0.003	0.000	−0.001
	(0.005)	(0.009)	(0.008)	(0.008)	(0.009)
EDEBT	−0.152***	−0.135***	−0.221***	−0.164***	−0.170***
	(0.035)	(0.044)	(0.075)	(0.042)	(0.045)
BMP	−4.066**	−2.889	−2.257	−32.943***	−3.722
	(1.672)	(2.673)	(3.548)	(9.656)	(3.045)
PCB		−0.381	−0.330	−0.061	−0.112
		(0.442)	(0.569)	(0.422)	(0.430)
BMP*PCB		−2.757***			
		(0.660)			
BMP*ARAB			−3393.88		
			−3771.34		

Eq Name	*1*	*2*	*3*	*4*	*5*
BMP*CEN				30.379***	
				(9.650)	
BMP*COMESA					−18.79**
					(9.512)
BMP*EAC					
BMP*ECCAS					
BMP*ECOWAS					
BMP*IGAD					
BMP*SADC					
Observations:	476	476	476	476	476
Sargan	0.310	0.323	0.439	0.233	0.246
AR(2)	0.694	0.517	0.940	0.637	0.728
Eq Name	*6*	*7*	*8*	*9*	*10*
M2G(−1)	0.095***	−0.042**	0.091***	0.103***	0.095***
	(0.021)	(0.017)	(0.023)	(0.020)	(0.024)
REMIT	−0.154	0.766***	−0.267	−0.273	−0.319
	(0.256)	(0.227)	(0.242)	(0.231)	(0.247)
FDI	−0.014	0.408	0.009	0.084	−0.014
	(0.256)	(0.272)	(0.255)	(0.289)	(0.259)
FD	−2.334***	−1.495***	−2.237***	−2.179***	−2.259***
	(0.365)	(0.329)	(0.345)	(0.314)	(0.355)
TRADE	0.380***	0.231***	0.371***	0.300***	0.376***
	(0.083)	(0.085)	(0.077)	(0.104)	(0.079)
MOB	0.100**	0.024	0.067	0.083	0.071
	(0.050)	(0.055)	(0.047)	(0.043)	(0.049)
GDP	0.000	0.000	0.001	0.001	0.000
	(0.009)	(0.006)	(0.008	(0.008)	(0.008)

(continued)

Table 8.4 (continued)

Eq Name	*6*	*7*	*8*	*9*	*10*
EDEBT	−0.138***	−0.089	−0.160***	−0.154***	−0.172***
	(0.045)	(0.050)	(0.044)	(0.051)	(0.044)
BMP	−4.097	1.352	−31.826***	−3.521	−2.899
	−2.629	−2.49	(9.706)	(2.319)	(2.910)
PCB	−0.106	−0.143	−0.069	0.120	−0.068
	(0.421)	(0.393)	(0.412)	(0.385)	(0.437)
BMP*PCB					
BMP*ARAB					
BMP*CEN					
BMP*COMESA					
BMP*EAC	−25.844				
	−158.753				
BMP*ECCAS		25.050***			
		(8.782)			
BMP*ECOWAS			28.763***		
			(9.523)		
BMP*IGAD				205.171	
				−138.198	
BMP*SADC					−29.61***
					(9.320)
Observations	476	476	476	476	476
Sargan	0.263	0.354	0.246	0.276	0.256
AR(2)	0.152	0.943	0.824	0.152	0.704

***, **, *Represents significance at the 1, 5, 10% levels respectively

which monetary policy translates into broad money growth (Vooren & Baarsma, 2018; Gunji et al., 2009; Olivero et al., 2011;). The interaction coefficients of the remaining regions of the Arab-Maghreb (Arab) (column 4–3), the East African Community (EAC) (column 4–6) and the Intergovernmental Authority on Development (IGAD) (column 4–9) are insignificant, which is a reflection of less-integrative nature of the banking structure in these regions. Finally, the insignificance of the private credit bureau coefficients in the regional estimations indicates that the conduct of banks with market power induces the growth in the money supply regardless of the depth of information sharing across the financial sectors.

Table 8.5 sets out the results of regressing changes in the consumer price index as the dependent variable to assess whether bank market power affects price stability in Africa. The results show that bank market power (BMP) and private credit bureaus (PCB) are insignificant for all the estimations. Hence, this suggests that policymakers should consider the uniqueness of the various regional groupings in Africa when manipulating the behaviour of banks with market power towards price stability. However, when we include the interaction terms, the coefficients are significant and positive for the community of Sahel-Saharan States (CEN) (column 5–4) and the Economic Community of West Africa (ECOWAS) (column 5–8), which suggests that the level of bank market power drives increased inflation and therefore causes price instability in these two regions.

In addition to considering the effects of inflation, Table 8.6 presents the results for real interest rates. In comparison, the coefficient for bank market power (BMP) is insignificant in Table 8.5 (column 5–1) as in Table 8.4 (columns 4–1), the interaction between the level of bank market power and private credit bureaus becomes positive and significant in Table 8.6 (column 6–2), which suggests that banks in Africa use the information sharing systems to induce changes in the real interest rates, thereby speeding up the transmission of monetary policy into real interest rates.

Regarding the regional associations, many of the interactions are less significant than the coefficients in Table 8.5. Still, they are positive and meaningful for the Common Market for Eastern and Southern Africa (COMESA) (column 6–5) and the Southern African Development Community (SADC) (column 6–10), significant and negative for the community of Sahel-Saharan States (CEN) (column 6–4) and the Economic Community of West Africa (ECOWAS) (column 6–8). Hence, this suggests that in place of information sharing systems, banks with

Table 8.5 Bank market power and inflation in Africa

Eq Name	*1*	*2*	*3*	*4*	*5*
INF(−1)	0.183***	0.195***	0.184***	0.201***	0.199***
	(0.026)	(0.018)	(0.024)	(0.021)	(0.020)
REMIT	0.134	0.105	0.124	0.175	0.191
	(0.153)	(0.110)	(0.140)	(0.150)	(0.154)
FDI	0.043		0.050	0.087	0.066
	(0.056)		(0.068)	(0.065)	(0.061)
FD	−0.082		−0.093	−0.033	−0.039
	(0.161)		(0.155)	(0.176)	(0.182
TRADE	0.015	0.025**	0.010	0.020	0.018
	(0.022)	(0.011)	(0.027)	(0.026)	(0.025)
MOB	−0.017	−0.02	−0.012	−0.022	−0.026
	(0.019)	(0.011)	(0.025)	(0.016)	(0.019)
GDP	0.005	0.004	0.004	0.005	0.006
	(0.003)	(0.002)	(0.007)	(0.005)	(0.005)
EDEBT	0.029***	0.031***	0.028**	0.032***	0.028***
	(0.010)	(0.007)	(0.012)	(0.009)	(0.009)
BMP	−0.621	−0.422	−0.458	−27.484***	1.134
	(0.990)	(0.640)	(1.307)	(2.177)	(1.152)
PCB		−0.059	−0.014	0.003	−0.007
		(0.099)	(0.111)	(0.134)	(0.131)
BMP*PCB		−1.093			
		(0.648)			
BMP*ARAB			−33.535		
			(785.862)		

Eq Name	*1*	*2*	*3*	*4*	*5*
BMP*CEN				29.24***	
				(2.708)	
BMP*COMESA					−21.548**
					(2.103)
BMP*EAC					
BMP*ECCAS					
BMP*ECOWAS					
BMP*IGAD					
BMP*SADC					
Observations	467	467	467	467	467
Sargan	0.386	0.351	0.285	0.275	0.284
AR(2):	0.4919	0.7487	0.7357	0.7805	0.861
Eq Name	*6*	*7*	*8*	*9*	*10*
INF(−1)	0.174***	0.189***	0.204***	0.169***	0.202***
	(0.021)	(0.020)	(0.021)	(0.039)	(0.020)
REMIT	0.335***	0.172	0.162	0.148	0.128
	(0.126)	(0.147)	(0.154)	(0.151)	(0.151)
FDI	0.049**	0.066	0.074	0.051	0.072
	(0.023)	(0.058)	(0.065)	(0.061)	(0.063)
FD		−0.004	−0.032	−0.1	−0.062
		−0.138	−0.187	−0.158	−0.161
TRADE	0.032	0.043	0.024	0.021	0.016
	(0.017)	(0.027)	(0.028)	(0.032)	(0.025)
MOB	−0.034**	−0.034**	−0.025	−0.014	−0.020
	(0.014)	(0.016)	(0.017)	(0.024)	(0.019)
GDP	0.005	0.004	0.006	0.005	0.005
	(0.003)	(0.004)	(0.005)	(0.006)	(0.005)

(continued)

Table 8.5 (continued)

Eq Name	*6*	*7*	*8*	*9*	*10*
EDEBT	0.036***	0.024***	0.033***	0.033***	0.028***
	(0.008)	(0.009)	(0.009)	(0.010)	(0.010)
BMP	0.632	2.286**	−27.149***	−0.254	0.788
	(0.910)	(1.051)	(2.240)	(1.364)	(1.156)
PCB	−0.015	0.117	0.009	−0.042	−0.003
	(0.057)	(0.102)	(0.137)	(0.115)	(0.115)
BMP*PCB					
BMP*ARAB					
BMP*CEN					
BMP*COMESA					
BMP*EAC	−71.122***				
	(10.477)				
BMP*ECCAS		−22.916***			
		(3.249)			
BMP*ECOWAS			29.038***		
			(2.784)		
BMP*IGAD				−86.075**	
				(35.167)	
BMP*SADC					−22.119***
					(2.071)
Observations	467	461	467	467	467
Sargan	0.293	0.248	0.298	0.287	0.284
AR(2):	0.7309	0.5399	0.685	0.9893	0.9169

***, **, *Represents significance at the 1, 5, 10% levels respectively.

Table 8.6 Bank market power and real interest rate in Africa

Eq Name:	*1*	*2*	*3*	*4*	*5*
RINTR(−1)	0.232***	0.224***	0.235***	0.215***	0.232***
	(0.002)	(0.007)	(0.002)	(0.003)	(0.003)
REMIT	−23.927***	−23.597***	−24.254***	−24.197***	−22.071***
	(0.315)	(0.424)	(0.425)	(0.316)	(0.331)
FDI	−3.372***	−2.72***	−3.354***	−3.353***	−3.534***
	(0.611)	(0.252)	(0.498)	(0.711)	(0.599)
FD	−2.534***	−3.501***	−2.616***	−3.447***	
	(0.168)	(0.669)	(0.785)	(0.459)	
TRADE	4.139***	4.186***	4.247***	4.176***	4.137***
	(0.133)	(0.160)	(0.125)	(0.168)	(0.121)
MOB	0.594***	0.748***	0.634***	0.723***	0.411***
	(0.059)	(0.137)	(0.118)	(0.074)	(0.058)
GDP	−0.038***	−0.01	−0.027***	−0.037***	−0.048***
	(0.010)	−0.015	(0.010)	(0.012)	(0.011)
EDEBT	0.583***	0.631***	0.608***	0.562***	0.596***
	(0.042)	(0.055)	(0.039)	(0.030)	(0.027)
BMP	−6.267	−3.792	−10.90***	189.452***	−10.914***
	(4.989)	(7.044)	(5.359)	(25.496)	(2.997)
PCB		−0.98	−0.747	−0.938**	0.086
		(0.602)	(0.595)	(0.391)	(0.138)
BMP*PCB		4.724**			
		(1.708)			
		(1.708)			
BMP*ARAB			4122.244		
			−2495.23		

(continued)

Table 8.6 (continued)

Eq Name:	*1*	*2*	*3*	*4*	*5*
BMP*CEN				−217.913***	
				(29.180)	
BMP*COMESA					201.885***
					(22.971)
BMP*EAC					
BMP*ECCAS					
BMP*ECOWAS					
BMP*IGAD					
BMP*SADC					
Observations	483	483	483	483	483
Sargan	0.447	0.551	0.165	0.193	0.880
AR(2)	0.005	0.993	0.989	0.999	0.999
Eq Name	*6*	*7*	*8*	*9*	*10*
RINTR(−1)	0.234***	0.232***	0.236***	0.234***	0.215***
	(0.002)	(0.003)	(0.002)	(0.002)	(0.003)
REMIT	−24.266***	−26.32***	−22.34***	−24.056***	−23.738***
	(0.359)	(0.448)	(0.371)	(0.340)	(0.374)
FDI	−3.155***	−2.217***	−3.553***	−3.351***	−3.279***
	(0.611)	(0.621)	(0.579)	(0.627)	(0.506)
FD	−2.993***	−2.379***		−2.863***	−3.213***
	(0.649)	(0.566)		(0.861)	(0.597)
TRADE	4.181***	3.987***	4.106***	4.191***	4.136***
	(0.109)	(0.195)	(0.123)	(0.129)	(0.149)
MOB	0.690***	0.559***	0.427***	0.647***	0.675***
	(0.069)	(0.103)	(0.067)	(0.066)	(0.078)
GDP	−0.038***	−0.039**	−0.048***	−0.028**	−0.027***
	(0.014)	(0.015)	(0.011)	(0.012)	(0.009)

Eq Name	*6*	*7*	*8*	*9*	*10*
EDEBT	0.603***	0.556***	0.560***	0.611***	0.586***
	(0.037)	(0.041)	(0.038)	(0.049)	(0.032)
BMP	−10.702	−26.96	148.135***	−6.536	−23.559***
	−5.474	−13.834	(19.605)	−7.29	(6.053)
PCB	−0.812	−0.494	0.028	−0.797	−1.026**
	(0.590)	(0.526)	(0.122)	(0.661)	(0.493)
BMP*PCB					
BMP*ARAB					
BMP*CEN					
BMP*COMESA					
BMP*EAC	−59.129				
	−74.994				
BMP*ECCAS		183.598			
		−118.268			
BMP*ECOWAS			−157.557***		
			(21.177)		
BMP*IGAD				−19.271	
				−171.818	
BMP*SADC					228.061***
					(23.392)
Observations:	483	477	483	483	483
Sargan	0.199	0.312	0.483	0.340	0.316
AR(2)	0.586	0.999	0.999	0.999	0.999

***, **, *Represents significance at the 1, 5, 10% levels respectively.

the market can still induce changes in real interest rates in CEN and ECOWAS. These two regions are characterised by a greater degree of competition, as shown in Table 8.2 by their lower interest rate spread since 2000. The remaining coefficient for the Arab-Maghreb (Arab) (column 6–3), the East African Community (EAC) (column 6–6), Economic Community of Central African States (ECCAS) (column 6–7) and the Intergovernmental Authority on Development (IGAD) (column 6–9) are all insignificant, which indicates that information sharing systems augment the conducts of banks with market power to induce monetary policy transmission into changes in real interest rates in Africa.

Finally, Table 8.7 assesses the relationship between bank market power, information sharing, and the real exchange rate. Column 7–1 shows that the level of bank market power has a significant and positive effect on exchange rates in Africa. This implies that the conduct of banks with market power induces exchange rate divergence between African countries' currencies and the United States dollar, irrespective of the emergence of the private credit bureaus. Higher levels of uncompetitive behaviour of banks in Africa can stifle the monetary authorities' effort on currency stability. Banks that have created lending relationships with importing firms can use letters of credits to extend more dollar-dominated credits to those firms, thereby putting pressure on the domestic currencies. The banks would prefer supporting the import sector if they find the industry less risky but profitable due to higher patronage of importing products, as evidenced in most African economies. Conversely, when the export sector does not generate enough innovations to attract banks' funding, banks with market power would be discouraged to provide financing to the industry. The flow of dollar-dominated currency into imports without the corresponding generation of inflows from the export sector is the primary cause of exchange rate depreciation in most developing economies.

Regarding the sub-region interactions, the coefficients for all of the estimations (columns 7–3 to 7–10) are all insignificant, which indicates that central banks in the subregions directly induce exchange rate (in)stability without recourse to the structure of the banking systems. However, in the East African Community (EAC) results (column 7–6), the bank market power coefficient is significant and positive, which implies that economic activities in the region have a more substantial positive impact on the ability of banks with market power to induce real exchange rates differentials compared to the other areas of Africa.

Table 8.7 Bank market and real exchange rate in Africa

Eq Name	*1*	*2*	*3*	*4*	*5*
REXR(−1)	0.495***	0.391**	0.442***	0.521***	0.455***
	(0.047)	(0.197)	(0.127)	(0.073)	(0.085)
REMIT	−0.428	−0.137	−1.444	−0.553	−0.272
	(0.789)	(1.547)	(1.898)	(1.399)	(1.674)
FDI	−0.158	−0.217	−0.493**	−0.144	−0.122
	(0.108)	(0.264)	(0.246)	(0.219)	(0.279)
FD	−0.318**	−0.476	−0.402		−0.304
	(0.115)	(0.479)	(0.298)		(0.228)
TRADE	−0.062	−0.035	−0.042	−0.063	−0.084
	(0.047)	(0.103)	(0.096)	(0.060)	(0.072)
MOB	−0.054***	−0.028	−0.026	−0.069***	−0.014
	(0.017)	(0.099)	(0.065)	(0.027)	(0.046)
GDP	0.004	0.025	0.01	0.003	−0.001
	(0.003)	(0.038)	(0.018)	(0.004)	(0.012)
EDEBT	−0.127***	−0.130***	−0.145***	−0.114***	−0.118***
	(0.009)	(0.037)	(0.038)	(0.022)	(0.026)
BMP	6.569***	14.703	12.298	12.963	5.56
	(1.412)	(11.824)	(9.547)	(11.548)	(4.586)
PCB		−0.842	−0.537	−0.06	−0.166
		(0.769)	(0.369)	(0.264)	(0.229)
BMP*PCB		1.308			
		(1.832)			
BMP*ARAB			−694.66		
			(563.29)		

(continued)

Table 8.7 (continued)

Eq Name	*1*	*2*	*3*	*4*	*5*
BMP*CEN				−6.354	
				(12.281)	
BMP*COMESA					
					9.442
BMP*EAC					(14.29)
BMP*ECCAS					
BMP*ECOWAS					
BMP*IGAD					
BMP*SADC					
Observations	323	323	323	323	323
Sargan	0.263	0.425	0.357	0.235	0.238
AR(2)	0.999	0.864	0.996	0.859	0.785
Eq Name	*6*	*7*	*8*	*9*	*10*
REXR(−1)	0.545***	0.447***	0.441***	0.436***	0.446***
	(0.042)	(0.100)	(0.083)	(0.079)	(0.087)
REMIT	−0.475	0.807	−0.675	−0.396	−0.869
	(0.706)	(1.700)	(1.835)	(1.643)	(1.806)
FDI		0.104	−0.182	−0.056	−0.251
		(0.362)	(0.231)	(0.277)	(0.235)
FD		−0.346	−0.253	−0.215	−0.261
		(0.327)	(0.231)	(0.204)	(0.230)
TRADE	−0.062**	−0.143	−0.064	−0.117	−0.051
	(0.031)	(0.136)	(0.067)	(0.077)	(0.057)
MOB	−0.053**	−0.023	−0.011	−0.005	−0.017
	(0.027)	(0.077)	(0.049)	(0.051)	(0.049)
GDP	0.000	0.002	−0.004	−0.006	−0.002
	(0.005)	(0.013)	(0.011)	(0.010)	(0.011)

Eq Name	*6*	*7*	*8*	*9*	*10*
EDEBT	−0.097***	−0.114**	−0.125***	−0.115***	−0.127***
	(0.016)	(0.053)	(0.029)	(0.022)	(0.029)
BMP	8.071***	5.638	14.97	4.46	4.916
	(2.265)	(5.667)	(11.522)	−4.214	−4.676
PCB	−0.012	−0.156	−0.225	−0.146	−0.273
	(0.184)	(0.333)	(0.263)	(0.267)	(0.265)
BMP*PCB					
BMP*ARAB					
BMP*CEN					
BMP*COMESA					
BMP*EAC	−58.513				
	(30.297)				
BMP*ECCAS		10.973			
		(17.049)			
BMP*ECOWAS			−10.304		
			(13.807)		
BMP*IGAD				−64.44	
				(75.729)	
BMP*SADC					12.847
					(14.728)
Observations	323	319	323	323	323
Sargan	0.252	0.276	0.251	0.269	0.252
AR(2)	0.998	0.932	0.854	0.853	0.879

***, **, *Represents significance at the 1, 5, 10% levels respectively

A possible reason for this differentiation is the highly concentrated nature of the East African financial system, which is closed to the level of concentration in the continent, as shown by the spread in the third row of Table 8.2.

8.6 Conclusion

We contribute to the monetary policy and bank market power discourses by infusing the effect of the permeating private credit information systems within an economic policy regime characterised by the predominantly expansionary policy. We contended that within an expansionary monetary policy, banks with market power can reduce the impact of monetary policy transmission into lower interest rates, price stability, and exchange rate stability, especially for emerging countries with opaque financial systems. The paper further argues that since banks rather rely on interest credits rationing in opaque credit markets for an adequate supply of credits (Stiglitz & Weiss, 1981), the emergence of credit information sharing institutional arrangements can assuage the fear of banks with market power in distributing credits to the extent that they would no longer solely rely on interest rates to ration credits. This would reduce the attenuating effect of banks with market power in monetary policy transmission in Africa. We were also not oblivious of the intuition that the impact of bank market power on monetary policy transmission in the wake of private information sharing coverage can differ across the various economic communities under the African Union. Therefore, we expanded the analyses to incorporate the impact of the economic communities in the nexus between market power and monetary policy transmission, given the degree of information sharing institutional arrangements.

We found some thought-provoking results by including policy measures such as remittances inflows, FDI inflows, external debt, credit to the private sector, trade openness, mobile technology infrastructure and national income. In the first instance, we found that banks with market power reduce the growth of money supply, inflation and real interest rates, especially in the advent of information sharing systems and other policy fundamentals. This information suggests that banks with market power promote price and interest rate stability in Africa. The result is in line with those of the extant studies that stipulate that banks with market power help promote economic and financial stability (see Karadima & Louri, 2020; IJtsma et al., 2017). In the same token, banks with market power increase the rate of exchange rate volatility, which suggests that the banks can reduce the smooth transmission of monetary policy into exchange rate stability. In the second instance, we also found that banks with market power leverage private information sharing systems to reduce the money supply's growth and level. However, in the absence of information sharing systems, banks with market power increase real interest rates. This confirms our assumption and those of many studies (see Brown et al., 2009; Djankov et al., 2007; Doblas-Madrid & Minetti, 2013) that information sharing systems damping the impact of the conduct of banks with market power in monetary policy transmission regarding ensuring interest rates stability. We did not find statistically meaningful evidence that banks with market power leverage private information sharing arrangements to induce price stability and exchange rate stability in Africa. When we applied the public credit registry as a proxy for information sharing institutions, the results were generally similar to that of the private credit bureau. The results for the public credit registry have been withheld to conserve space.

Concerning the impact of regional economic communities, we found that banks with market power reduce the level of money supply in the Arab-Maghreb, CEN and ECOWAS. Similarly, banks in COMESA, IGAD and SADC induce a greater money supply. Regarding the growth in money supply, banks with market power increase the growth in money supply in CEN, ECCAS and ECOWAS, while banks with market power mitigate the impact of monetary policy transmission in the evolution of money supply. Similarly, banks with market power induce price stability in CEN, COMESA, EAC, ECCAS, IGAD and SADC. However, in ECOWAS, the banks with market power stimulate inflation which suggests that the conduct of the banks induces price instability in the sub-region. Moreover, the behaviour of banks with market power reduces real interest rates in CEN and ECOWAS but increases real interest rate instability in COMESA and SADC. The results suggest a multifaceted approach to monetary policy in Africa, given the conduct of banks with market power.

Given the impeccable involvement of banks with market power in ensuring price and interest rates stability, we advocate that credit market regulation should be tailored to reduce banks' risk of market power failure. Central or reserve banks should support ailing big pan-African banks to sustain the soundness of the credit market since their collapse can adversely affect the effectiveness of monetary policy to boost systemic liquidity and economic activities. Based on the findings in the study, we advocate for greater penetration of information sharing institutional arrangements since such arrangements complement the conducts of banks with market power to stimulate monetary policy transmission in Africa. In CEN, banks with market power should be supported to control the growth in money supply and interest rates stability. In the ARAB Maghreb communities, the central banks should liaise with the banks only to manage the money supply. In COMESA, banks with market power can be used to control inflation and money supply growth. In EAC, the central banks can rely on banks with market power to reduce inflation and ensure price stability.

Similarly, in ECCAS, the central banks can use banks with market power to control price stability. Also, in ECOWAS, the conduct of banks with market power can aid the efforts of the central banks in controlling the growth in money supply and interest rate stability. Moreover, in the IGAD, the behaviour of banks with market power can be encouraged to control inflation and maintain price stability. Finally, the central banks should work with banks with market power to manage the growth in money supply and maintain price stability in the SADC region. Further studies can incorporate the role of political institutions in the analyses since central banks in Africa are not wholly immune to political influences.

Appendix

See Table 8.8

Table 8.8 Descriptive statistics

	Mean	*Median*	*Maximum*	*Minimum*	*Std. Dev*	*Observations*
BI	−0.07	−0.05	0.27	−2.54	0.16	656
PCB	5.44	0.00	66.20	0.00	14.51	656
EDEBT	45.63	34.38	175.85	0.00	33.22	624
FD	21.87	14.51	106.26	0.00	19.50	647
FDI	3.76	2.56	39.46	−1.30	4.42	656
INF	6.53	5.12	44.36	−27.79	6.70	631
M2	38.13	26.08	251.62	0.00	29.04	656
M2G	16.39	14.32	191.80	−58.17	15.41	637

(continued)

Table 8.8 (continued)

	Mean	*Median*	*Maximum*	*Minimum*	*Std. Dev*	*Observations*
MOB	52.17	41.19	175.87	0.07	42.91	652
REMIT	3.44	1.55	50.10	0.00	5.60	622
RINTR	13.53	6.01	1158.03	−34.21	66.20	466
TRADE	68.50	61.69	348.00	19.10	32.72	631
GDP	2183.71	1102.53	12,064.78	194.87	2554.93	641
REXR	75.08	96.12	181.40	0.00	45.20	404

References

Acharya, V. V., Imbierowicz, B., Steffen, S., & Teichmann, D. (2020). Does the lack of financial stability impair the transmission of monetary policy? *Journal of Financial Economics*. https://doi.org/10.1016/j.jfineco.2020.06.011

Amidu, M., & Wolfe, S. (2013). The effect of banking market structure on lending channels: Evidence from emerging markets. *Review of Financial Economics, 22*(4), 146–157.

Arellano, M., & Bond, S. (1991). Some tests of specification for panel data: Monte Carlo evidence and an application to employment equations. *Review of Economic Studies, 58*, 277–297. https://doi.org/10.2307/2297968

Aristei, D., & Gallo, M. (2014). Interest rate pass-through in the Euro area during the financial crisis: A multivariate regime-switching approach. *Journal of Policy Modeling, 36*(2), 273–295. Elsevier.

Beck, T., De Jonghe, O., & Schepens, G. (2013). Bank competition and stability: Cross-country heterogeneity. *Journal of Financial Intermediation, 22*(2), 218–244. https://doi.org/10.1016/j.jfi.2012.07.001

Beck, T., Lin, C., & Ma, Y. (2014). Why do firms evade taxes? The role of information sharing and financial sector outreach. *The Journal of Finance, LXIX*(2), 763–817.

Berg, A., & Portillo, R. (2018). Monetary policy in Sub-Saharan Africa. In A. Berg, & R. Portillo (Eds.), *Monetary policy in sub-Saharan Africa* (pp. 1–33). Oxford Scholarship.https://doi.org/10.1093/oso/9780198785811.001.0001

Bempong, E., & Sy, M. (2015). The banking system in Africa: Main facts and challenges. *African Economic Brief, 6*(5), 1–16.

Boyd, J. H., & De Nicoló, G. (2005). The theory of bank risk-taking and competition revisited. *The Journal of Finance, 60*, 1329–1343.

Brämer, P., Gischer, H., Richter, T., & Weiß, M. (2013). Competition in banks' lending business and its interference with ECB monetary policy. *Journal of*

International Financial Journal of International Financial, 25, 144–162. https://doi.org/10.1016/j.intfin.2013.01.009

Boone, J. (2008). A new way of measuring competition using the profit elasticity: American sugar industry, 1890–1914. *The Economic Journal, 118*(531), 1245–1261. https://doi.org/10.1111/j.1468-0297.2008.02168.x

Brown, M., Jappelli, T., & Pagano, M. (2009). Information sharing and credit: Firm-level evidence from transition countries. *Journal Financial Intermediation, 18*, 151–172. https://doi.org/10.1016/j.jfi.2008.04.002

Clerides, S., Delis, M. D., & Kokas, S. (2015). A new data set on competition in national banking markets. *Financial Markets, Institution & Instruments, 24*(2–3), 267–311. https://doi.org/10.1111/fmii.12030

Diallo, B. (2015). Bank competition and crises revisited: New results. *Economic Letters, 129*(1), 81–86. https://doi.org/10.1016/j.econlet.2015.02.015

Djankov, S., McLiesh, C., & Shleifer, A. (2007). Private credit in 129 countries. *Journal of Financial Economics, 84*(1), 299–329.

Doblas-Madrid, A., & Minetti, R. (2013). Sharing information in the credit market: Contract-level evidence from U.S. firms. *Journal of Financial Economics, 109*(1), 198–223. https://doi.org/10.1016/j.jfineco.2013.02.007

de Bondt, G. (2005). Interest rate pass-through: Empirical results for the Euro area. *German Economic Review, 6*(1), 37–78.

Gatsi, J., Idun, A.A.-A., & Mensah, F. (2020). Monetary policy and financial development in Africa: Do governance mechanisms matter. *Journal of Economic and Financial Sciences, 13*(1), 1–13. https://doi.org/10.4102/jef.v13i1.419

Gunji, H., Miura, K., & Yuan, Y. (2009). Bank competition and monetary policy. *Japan and the World Economy, 21*(1), 105–115. https://doi.org/10.1016/j.japwor.2007.11.001

Güntner, J. H. (2011). Competition among banks and the pass-through of monetary policy. *Economic Modelling, 28*, 1891–1901. https://doi.org/10.1016/j.econmod.2011.03.015

Idun, A. A.-A., Aboagye, A. Q. Q., & Bokpin, G. A. (2020). The effect of bank market power on economic growth in Africa: The role of institutions. *Cogent Economics & Finance, 8*(1), 1799481. https://doi.org/10.1080/23322039.2020.1799481

IJtsma, P., Spierdijk, L., & Shaffer, S. (2017). The concentration–stability controversy in banking: New evidence from the EU-25. *Journal of Financial Stability, 33*, 273–284. https://doi.org/10.1016/j.jfs.2017.06.003

International Monetary Fund. (2020). International Financial Statistic: Real-time date series. International Monetary Fund.

International Monetary Fund. (2020). World Economic Outlook. International Monetary Fund.

Karadima, M., & Louri, H. (2020). Non-performing loans in the Euro area: Does bank market power matter? *International Review of Financial Analysis, 72*, 101593. https://doi.org/10.1016/j.irfa.2020.101593

Leroy, A., & Lucotte, Y. (2015). *Structural and cyclical determinants of bank interest rate pass-through in Eurozone*. NBP Working Papers 198, Narodowy Bank Polski, Economic Research Department.

Mirzaei, A., & Moore, T. (2014). What are the driving forces of bank competition across different income groups of countries? *Journal of International Financial Markets, Institutions & Money, 32*(3), 38–71. https://doi.org/10.1016/j.intfin.2014.05.003

Mishkin, F. S. (2006). How big a problem is too big to fail? A review of Gary Stern and Ron Feldman's too big to fail: The hazards of bank bailouts. *Journal of Economic Literature, 44*, 988–1004. https://doi.org/10.1257/jel.44.4.988

Morgan, D. P., & Stiroh, K. J. (2005). *Too big to fail after all these years* (Staff Report No. 220, Federal Reserve Bank of New York).

Olivero, M. P., Li, Y., & Jeon, B. N. (2011). Consolidation in banking and the lending channel of monetary transmission: Evidence from Asia and Latin America. *Journal of International Money and Finance, 30*(6), 1034–1054. https://doi.org/10.1016/j.jimonfin.2011.06.006

Özşuca, E. A., & Akbostancı, E. (2016). An empirical analysis of the risk-taking channel of monetary policy in Turkey. *Emerging Markets Finance & Trade, 52*, 589–609. https://doi.org/10.1080/1540496X.2015.1047300

Pagano, M. (1993). Financial markets and growth: An overview. *European Economic Review, 37*(2–3), 613–622. https://doi.org/10.1016/0014-2921(93)90051-B

Petersen, M. A., & Rajan, R. G. (1995). The effect of credit market competition on lending relationships. *Quarterly Journal of Economics, 110*(2), 407–443. https://doi.org/10.2307/2118445

Sørensen, C. K., & Werner, T. (2006). *Bank interest rate pass-through in the Euro area: A cross country comparison* (Working paper no. 580. European Central Bank, Frankfurt am Main, Germany).

Stern, G. H. (2009). *Better late than never: Addressing too-big-to-fail*. Brookings Institution Press,

Stern, G. H., & Feldman, R. J. (2004). *Too big to fail: The hazards of bank bailouts*. Brookings Institution Press. ISBN: 0-8157-8152-0.

Stiglitz, J. E. (1989). Markets, market failures, and development. *American Economic Review, 79*, 197–203.

Stiglitz, J. E., & Weiss, A. (1981). Credit rationing in markets with rationing credit information imperfect. *The American Economic Review, 71*, 393–410.

Van Leuvensteijn, M., Sørensen, C. K., Bikker, J. A., & Van Rixtel, A. A. (2013). Impact of bank competition on the interest rate pass-through in the Euro area. *Applied Economics, 45*, 1359–1380.

Vooren, M., & Baarsma, B. E. (2018). Bank competition and the transmission of unconventional monetary policy in the euro area. *European Competition Journal, 14*(1), 174–193. https://doi.org/10.1080/17441056.2018.1463688

Zentefis, A. K. (2020). Bank net worth and frustrated monetary policy. *Journal of Financial Economics*, 1–25. https://doi.org/10.1016/j.jfineco.2020.06.007

CHAPTER 9

Monetary Policy and Bank Risk-Taking Behaviour in Africa

Agyapomaa Gyeke-Dako, Simon K. Harvey, Gabriel Azu, and Haruna Issahaku

9.1 Introduction

Protracted low interest rate which can expand economies can also come at the cost of making banks unstable (Fisher, 1933; Hayek, 1939; Kindleberger, 1991). Protracted low interest rates can cause bank instability

A. Gyeke-Dako (✉) · G. Azu
University of Ghana Business School, Legon, Ghana
e-mail: AGyeke-Dako@ug.edu.gh

G. Azu
e-mail: gabrielazu7@gmail.com

S. K. Harvey
Bank of Ghana, Accra, Ghana
e-mail: siarvey@gmail.com

H. Issahaku
University for Development Studies, Tamale, Ghana
e-mail: iharuna@uds.edu.gh

J. Y. Abor and C. K. D. Adjasi (eds.), *The Economics of Banking and Finance in Africa*, Palgrave Macmillan Studies in Banking and Financial Institutions, https://doi.org/10.1007/978-3-031-04162-4_9

by reducing the risk aversion of banks and other investors, and, indeed, research (see Dell'Ariccia et al., 2017) has suggested that banks become less stringent in their lending practices during periods of protracted low interest rate. This risk-taking channel works through three mechanisms that suggest that monetary policy stance has a negative effect on risk-taking appetite of banks.

The first of these mechanisms points to banks' desire to search for yield in periods of low interest rates. Financial institutions with long-term obligations have to match the return they promise on their liabilities with what they gain from their assets (Rajan, 2005). Thus, in the presence of high interest rates, banks can easily obtain the necessary revenue to take care of their promised returns by investing in safe assets. However, when interest rates are low, banks that have already promised high interest rates would have to renegotiate their long-term commitments and switch to riskier investments with high returns to help match their obligations. This increases demand for risky assets and sends a 'fake' signal on the quality of these assets. The increased demand for risky assets causes a decline in the returns of these assets. Consequently, the general decrease in returns, coupled with the illusion of asset quality, stimulates banks to assume more risks.

Second, protracted low interest rates can also cause banks to assume more risk through the effect on cash flows, incomes and real valuations. The persistent accommodative monetary policy raises the value of assets and collateral and reduces banks' perception about the likelihood of default, thereby encouraging a higher risk appetite (Borio & Zhu, 2008).

Third, protracted low interest rate can influence the risk-taking of banks through the response of central banks to negative shocks. For instance, when central banks commit to prolonged lower interest rates, it reduces the probability of credit risks, which therefore stimulates banks to take on greater risk by increasing their exposure.

Several empirical studies have investigated the relationship between monetary policy and the risk-taking appetite of banks. For instance, Chen et al. (2017) examined the nexus between monetary policy and risk-taking behaviour using 29 emerging countries from Eastern and Central Europe, Asia and Latin America. They used different proxies of monetary policy. They measured monetary policy stance using first-order difference of short-term interest rate, interest rate gap and an exogenous innovation of monetary policy, estimated as the residuals of the interest rate equation. Their results concur with the 'bank risk-taking channel' of monetary policy. Aboyadana (2021) also provides empirical evidence on the relationship between monetary policy and bank risk-taking in Sub-Sahara Africa (SSA) from 2001 to 2015. The study measures monetary policy using monetary policy rates. The result provides evidence contrary to the risk-taking channel. Our study improves on the measure of monetary policy stance used by previous studies by incorporating possible channels of monetary policy transmission. Specifically, we create an index which captures real monetary conditions by incorporating real effective exchange rate in the estimation of monetary policy stance. We incorporate exchange rate in the estimation of monetary policy stance because of the important role it plays in the conduct of monetary policy.

Our study focuses on Africa, although the debate on whether an accommodative monetary policy is responsible for the risk-taking appetite of banks can barely be applied to Africa because of the persistently high levels of absolute and relative interest rates that characterise African countries as compared to the USA and the EU. Sub-Saharan Africa has three of the six countries with the highest interest rates in the world, which is reflective of high interest rate in the region. Interest rate in the region average around 20% annually for borrowers and spread between lending and borrowing (8%–10%) is extremely high compared with the spreads in other regions of the world (Almani, 2016). This notwithstanding, a study of this sort is relevant in the African setting for three reasons. First, with the surge of the Covid-19 pandemic globally, many countries including African countries have resorted to reducing their interest rates to historically low levels and therefore it is important to understand what the implications of this would be for African countries. Second, some African countries have experienced instability in the financial sector in recent times as a result of excessive risk-taking behaviour; examples are Ghana (between 2017 and 2018), Guinea-Bissau (2014–Date), South Africa (2015), Nigeria (between 2009 and 2012) and many others as indicated by Laeven and Valencia (2018); therefore it is important to formally establish whether this was caused by excessive accommodative monetary policy and what lessons can be obtained from this. Third, since most African economies are bank-based (Oima & Ojwang, 2013), Africa provides an ideal setting for examining the risk-taking channel. Below, we present some stylised facts that provide more justification for the study.

9.2 Monetary Policy and Risk-Taking Behaviour of Banks in Africa: Stylised Facts

Using data before and after the 2007/2008 Global Financial Crisis (GFC) and including data on the inverse of the *Z*-score (which estimates the distance a firm is away from financial distress) and a measure for monetary policy stance across different regions, some interesting, stylised facts emerge.

Figure 9.1 shows that banks in developed countries increased their risk-taking behaviour before the 2008 financial crisis compared to those in developing countries. After 2008, a consistent decline in the risk-taking behaviour of banks is seen in developed countries. This indicates the level of consciousness of banks in developed countries after the 2007/2008 financial crises, contradicting what is observed for African countries. On average, banks in Africa appear to have taken on more risk than developed and emerging regions after the 2007/2008 financial crisis.

Regarding the trend of monetary policy over the period under consideration, Fig. 9.2 shows that monetary policy rates in Africa have been well above those of developed countries. This is not surprising, given

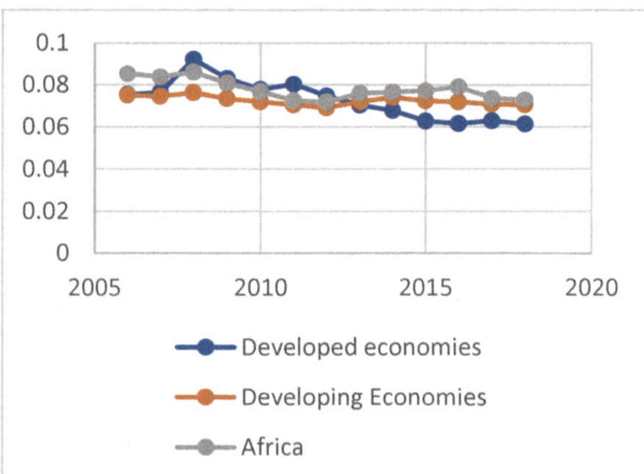

Fig. 9.1 Risk taking (*Note* Computed by authors based on data from Global Financial Development Database and the IMF Database. Risk-taking is measured as inverse of *Z*-score and Monetary Policy is measured as the central bank policy rates)

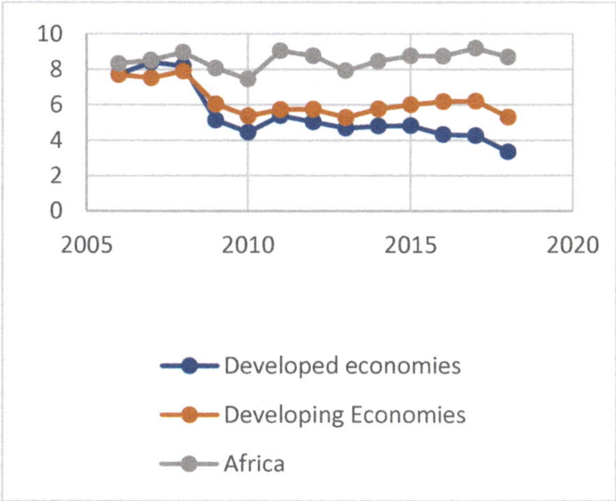

Fig. 9.2 Monetary policy rates (*Note* Computed by authors based on data from Global Financial Development Database and the IMF Database. Risk-taking is measured as inverse of Z-score and Monetary Policy is measured as the central bank policy rates)

Fig. 9.3 Monetary policy and risk taking (Africa) (*Source* Authors)

the consistently high levels of inflation that characterise African countries relative to developed economies. Despite the persistently high monetary policy rate and thus, interest rates in African economies, Fig. 9.2 shows that monetary policy rates in Africa have experienced relative stability since the global financial crisis. In Fig. 9.3, we present some graphics that establish a relationship between monetary policy and risk-taking behaviour. The graphical presentation of the nexus between monetary policy and risk-taking behaviour as shown in Fig. 9.3 generally suggests an inverse association between monetary policy rate and risk-taking appetite of banks, providing informal evidence of risk-taking appetite of banks. This gives reason for a formal investigation of the relationship between the two.

Thus, this study provides empirical evidence on the nexus between monetary policy and bank risk-taking behaviour from 2006 to 2018 using 532 banks in 29 African economies. That is, this study investigates how the monetary policy stance of central banks in Africa affects the risk-taking behaviour of commercial banks operating in Africa, employing the Generalised Method of Moments (GMM) estimation technique. The findings of this study provide useful information on whether there exists a trade-off between prolonged accommodative monetary policy and the stability of banks in order to guide policymakers in their bid to address recessions in their economies.

The remaining chapter is organised as follows: an overview of literature on the bank risk-taking and monetary policy nexus is presented in Sect. 9.3 to help situate the study and inform the methodology used. We present the methodology in Sect. 9.4 and the results in Sect. 9.5. We end the chapter with conclusions and some policy recommendations in Sect. 9.6.

9.3 Monetary Policy and Risk-Taking: Evidence

In this section, we review empirical studies on the nexus between monetary policy and risk-taking behaviour. Jiménez et al. (2014) use data from 1984 to 2006 on the Spanish Credit Register to examine whether monetary policy has an effect on banks' risk-taking behaviour. They found that interest rate has a positive effect (short term) on bank portfolio risk. Thus, their study revealed that reducing interest rate lowers the default risk of borrowers in the short run, since the interest expense is reduced, which therefore enhances their repayment and lowers the probability of default. Conversely, they found that in the medium term, low interest rates increase the value of collateral and search for yield, which causes banks to soften their lending standards and give out riskier loans. Jiménez et al. (2014) also found that when interest rates are low, banks that are well-capitalised assume more risks than those that are not.

Ioannidou et al. (2009) examine whether the risk-taking channel works on the quantity of new loans, employing data on banks in Bolivia over the period 1999–2003. They found that an expansionary monetary policy leads to banks giving out more risky loans to borrowers at a relatively lower interest rate compared to what they charge less risky borrowers. They also found that the lending conditions among Bolivian banks soften when the interest rate shock is expansionary.

Altunbas et al. (2009) take a different turn and provide international evidence on the nexus between monetary policy and banks' risk-taking behaviour. Employing data from 600 European and US listed banks over the period 1999–2008, they provide evidence of an inverse relationship between protracted low interest rates and high risk-taking by banks.

Similar to Altunbas et al. (2009), Maddaloni and Peydró (2011) also provide international evidence by using data for USA and countries in the European Union. They show robust results for the protracted easing of monetary policy rates on the lending behaviour of banks and the associated increase in their asset riskiness. Delis and Kouretas (2011) rather use interest rate to measure monetary policy rate and find that protracted accommodative monetary policy induces a high risk-taking behaviour among banks in the EMU region for the period 2001–2008.

Other empirical studies reveal that the effect of accommodative monetary policy on bank risk-taking may not be constant across banking groups, banking systems or time. De Nicolò et al. (2010), for instance, provide evidence for the risk-taking channel of monetary policy but indicate that it is based on the market conditions of the banking sector and factors that influence these market conditions. They explain that, for example, when the charter values of banks and their capitalisation are sufficiently high in good times, an expansionary monetary policy stimulates more risk-taking. By contrast, the effect of monetary policy on risk-taking of banks is less profound during financial distress. In addition, Buch et al. (2014) employed aggregate data from theUSA. They adopted factor-augmented vector autoregressive models (FAVARs) to show the potential joint identification of bank risk-taking and monetary policy. The results revealed that diverse banking groups react differently to monetary shocks that are expansionary. They also revealed that while domestic banks that are small have a higher risk exposure in terms of new loans, foreign banks seem to reduce their exposure. However, large domestic banks do not change their risk behaviour significantly. Chen et al. (2017) study is the closest to ours. They used a benchmark model to examine the relationship between monetary policy and bank risk-taking using 29 emerging countries from Eastern and Central Europe, Asia and Latin America. They used different proxies of bank risk-taking behaviour and monetary policy. They measured monetary policy stance using the interest rate gap, first-order difference of short-term interest rate and an exogenous innovation of monetary policy, estimated as the residuals of the interest rate equation. They modelled bank risk as a function of monetary policy indicators, bank characteristics, regulation, macroeconomic and some other supplementary variables. Their findings indicate that monetary policy has an adverse effect on the risk-taking behaviour of banks. Thus, their study provides evidence of the existence of the bank risk-taking channel in Eastern and Central Europe, Asia and Latin America.

Although these studies have investigated the nexus between monetary policy and risk-taking behaviour, their measurement of monetary policy has been narrow, as it has not considered the different channels through which monetary policy influences banks' risk-taking behaviour. Thus, this chapter tries to fill this gap by creating an index for real monetary conditions which captures the effect of real effective exchange rate on banks' risk-taking behaviour in addition to the effect of real interest rates.

9.4 Data and Methodology

Data

Data on the bank-specific variables was obtained from Bankscope. The advantage of using data from Bankscope is that it is very comprehensive and provides information on financial statement for more than 32,000 banks and about 200 data items. For the purposes of this study, 532 banks from 29 African countries over a period of 13 years from 2006 to 2018 are used. The long duration provides a proper examination of the changes in banks' risk-taking behaviour to be made since it accommodates years of both economic downturn and economic expansion. The data employed is an unbalanced panel data with gaps since some banks in the dataset may not have existed at a point or possibly ceased operations. Having an unbalanced panel is advantageous because it takes away survivor bias. Data on the macroeconomic variables were obtained from the IMF database.

Model Specification

We modify the model presented by Chen et al. (2017) in two main ways. First, with regard to the monetary policy stance, we measure monetary policy considering the various ways it can be transmitted into the economy. Thus, we cater for the exchange rate channel, traditional interest rate channel and the credit channel in measuring monetary policy stance.

The specification of the functional form is given by:

$$\begin{aligned}\text{BankRisk}_{it} = \beta_0 &+ \beta_1 \text{BankRisk}_{it-1} + \beta_2 \text{MonetaryPolicyStance}_{jt} \\ &+ \text{Efficiency}_{it} + \beta_4 \text{Liquidity}_{it} \\ &+ \beta_5 \text{Income Diversification}_{it} + \beta_6 \text{ROA}_{jt} \\ &+ \beta_7 \text{BankCapitalization}_{it} + \beta_8 \text{GDP per capita growth}_{jt} \\ &+ \beta_9 \text{FinancialDevelopment}_{jt} + \beta_{10} \text{RegulatoryQuality}_{jt} + \varepsilon_{it}\end{aligned} \tag{9.1}$$

where: $i = 1 \ldots m \text{and} j = 1 \ldots n$ where m is the number of banks in the sample and n is the number of countries. t represents the time period.

BankRisk$_{it}$ measures individual bank risk-taking. The selection of an appropriate proxy for bank risk-taking behaviour has been debatable, as several studies have utilised different measures for it. For instance, Gambacorta (2009) and Altunbas et al. (2010) employ the difference in the Expected Default Frequency (ΔEDF) as a measure of the risk-taking appetite of banks. The ΔEDF obtained from Moody's KMV estimates the likelihood that a firm will default within an observable period. From Moody's KMV's perspective, when the assets' market value is lower than the market value of the liabilities, a default is said to have occurred. Thus, the ΔEDF is seen as a forward-looking proxy of credit risk. However, this measure looks at risk-taking from the perspective of the banks and thus, using it to measure bank risk-taking appetite ignores the fact that the variation could result from the side of the loan demand instead of the bank's risk-taking appetite.

To resolve this, Jiménez et al. (2014) and Ioannidou et al. (2009) measure the risk-taking of banks with the easing of credit standards acquired from the central banks' credit register of the countries observed. However, this proxy also has its limitations. These limitations include, the fact that credit registers are accessible only for countries that keep it, and the fact that the proxy also considers just one aspect of banks' risk-taking appetite.

Some empirical studies have resorted to the use of the ratio of non-performing loans to total loans. The ratio of non-performing loans to total loans is a widely employed accounting-based measure of bank fragility which provides evidence of asset quality in terms of market values of equity and the potential adverse exposure to earnings as a result of worsening loan quality. Consequently, the non-performing loans ratio generally reflects the loan portfolio or credit risk of a bank. Since the numerator of the non-performing ratio measures losses on loans, higher non-performing loans indicate a riskier loan portfolio (Delis & Kouretas, 2011). Thus, a higher non-performing loans ratio indicates a high risk-taking appetite of banks. Despite the simplicity of estimating the non-performing loans ratio, it is considered as backward-looking and might be subject to managerial judgement or manipulation (Fiordelisi et al., 2011).

Others have also employed the Z-score to measure the risk-taking appetite of banks. The Z-score or its natural logarithm is widely employed to estimate the insolvency or financial soundness of banks (De Nicolo, et al., 2006; Delis et al., 2014; Lepetit & Strobel, 2013, 2015). The proxy of bank risk-taking is negatively associated to the likelihood that a bank will become insolvent. This suggests that lower (higher) Z-score of banks indicates a higher (lower) risk of insolvency. One main merit of employing the Z-score is that it is obtained from the decision taking of the bank. Another benefit of the Z-score is that it demands less data, and it also uses important financial information as it combines in a single estimate the profitability, leverage and return volatility. The objective of this study is to examine the potential impact of monetary shocks on banks' risk-taking behaviour and not to provide an exact estimation of the risk of banks. Hence, the traditional Z-score is well-suited for the objective of our study.

The Z-score is formally expressed as

$$Z_{it} = \frac{\mathrm{ROA}_{it} + \mathrm{EA}_{it}}{\sigma \mathrm{ROA}_{it}}$$

where $\mathrm{ROA}_{\mathrm{it}}$ represents the return on assets of bank i in year t, $\mathrm{EA}_{\mathrm{it}}$, represents the ratio of equity to total assets and $\sigma \mathrm{ROA}_{it}$ represents the standard deviation of return on assets. The Z-score is seen as the inverse of the likelihood of bank insolvency and can be explained as the number of standard deviations by which returns would have to fall to erase all of the bank's equity (Roy, 1952).

Given that almost all measures of banks' risk-taking have their limitations, the study considers two measures of risk-taking behaviour: the Z-score and the ratio of non-performing loans to total loans, to ascertain the consistency in the variable used.

The study also includes the lag of the bank risk-taking behaviour measures. These are supposed to check the persistence of risk-taking in banks.

Measuring Monetary Policy Stance

Our main explanatory variable is ***Monetary Policy Stance***. Changes in monetary policy rate, apart from directly impacting interbank trading activity through the interbank interest rates, trigger international capital movements that reflect in the exchange rates. These exchange rate pressures in turn have implications for banks' risk perception; therefore a more comprehensive measure of monetary policy stance is one that takes these exchange rate pressures into consideration in addition to the interest rate. Thus, this chapter employs a more comprehensive measure of monetary policy that takes into account the possible channels through which monetary policy can be transmitted and creates an index which can capture the monetary policy stance. We define this index as Real Monetary Conditions Index (RMCI) measured by using the monetary policy stance as a weighted average of real interest rate gap and real exchange rate gap.

The real interest rate gap, $\hat{r}$, is measured as the deviation of the real interest rate r from its long-term trend $\overline{r}$, that is,

$$\hat{r}_{it} = \overline{r}_{it} - r_{it}$$

The real interest rate is approximated as

$$r_{it} = R_{it} - \pi_{it}$$

where π is inflation and R_{it} is the nominal interest rate.

The long-term trend is estimated using the Hodrick–Prescott (HP) filter developed by Hodrick and Prescott (1997) and we use the real interest rate in our estimation. As with the real interest rate gap, we derive the real exchange rate gap from the real effective exchange rate using the HP filter.

Finally, the Real Monetary Conditions Index for country i at time t (RMC_{it}) is estimated as

$$\text{RMC}_{it} = w\hat{r}_{it} + (1 - w)\hat{e}_{it}$$

where w is the weight of real interest rate in determining monetary conditions in the domestic economy, $\hat{r}_{it}$. A positive RMCI is an indication of a tight monetary policy stance while a negative RMCI shows an expansionary monetary policy stance. We assign a weight of 0.8 to real interest rate and a weight of 0.2 to real effective exchange rate because the effect of real effective exchange rate still works through the interest rate.

Bank-Specific Variables

The study includes a number of bank-specific control variables which may impact bank risk-taking behaviour.

Liquidity$_{it}$, which measures bank liquidity is also included in the model. Liquidity is explained as the ratio of liquid assets to the total assets of banks. The relationship between liquidity and bank risk is not clear cut. While on the one hand, more liquid asset insulates a bank from monetary shocks (Cornett et al., 2011), on the other hand, banks may keep more liquid assets to take care of the volatility on returns (Alger & Alger, 1999).

The study also includes a measure of ***Bank Profitability***$_{it}$ (Dong et al., 2016). Bank profitability is commonly measured using two main accounting ratios: return on asset (ROA) and return on equity (ROE). However, ROA is preferred to ROE in this study because it represents a more comprehensive measure of profitability. The study expects more profitable banks to take on more risk than banks with low profitability.

Following Demirgüç-Kunt and Huizinga (2010), we include ***Income Diversification***$_{it}$ to show how diversified banks are in their sources of income and funding. Income diversification is measured as the ratio of non-interest income to total operating income (Chen et al., 2017; Demirgüç-Kunt & Huizinga, 2010). Although it is expected that banks that are well-diversified are less risky and have stability in their returns (Boyd & Graham, 1988; Rose, 1989), some empirical studies have found contrary evidence (De Young & Roland, 2001; Demetz & Strahan, 1997; Stiroh, 2004).

The study also includes a measure of ***Efficiency***$_{it}$. Operating cost to asset ratio is used to proxy bank efficiency. It measures the operating efficiency of banks by calculating the ratio of operation cost of a bank to its asset base. This helps to know how the banks manage their operating expenses as compared to their assets. A higher (lower) ratio implies that the bank has a low (higher) operating efficiency. It is expected that banks with a better efficiency will take on more risk compared with those with low operating efficiency.

Finally, we incorporate ***Bank Capitalisation***$_{it}$ following works by Delis and Kouretas (2011) and Chen et al. (2017). Bank capitalisation is proxied by the ratio of equity to assets. The capitalisation usually represents an inverse of bank leverage. The literature provides that higher bank capitalisation may effectively prevent banks from taking more risk. Delis and Kouretas (2011) found that lower (higher) equity ratio results from higher (lower) risk-taking behaviour of banks.

Macroeconomic Variables
Bourkhis and Nabi (2013) and Festić et al. (2011) suggest that changes in the macroeconomic environment have implications for bank risk-taking behaviour. In particular, a favourable macroeconomic environment translates into lower risk-taking behaviour of banks. Thus, the study includes some macroeconomic variables in the model. These include proxies for growth, inflation, real effective exchange rate, financial development, and regulatory quality.

Economic Growth$_{jt}$ is seen as an important determinant of risk-taking behaviour. In recessions, for example, the quality of loans declines because of the inability of people to pay, whereas the opposite is true for booms. Therefore, we expect countries with high GDP growth to have a more stable banking system, compared to countries with low GDP growth (Soedarmono et al., 2011).

Inflation$_{jt}$ is another variable we consider in this study, and it is measured using the consumer price index. The effect of inflation on banks' risk-taking is ambiguous. Higher inflation can reduce the real value of outstanding loans, making debt servicing easier. Conversely, high inflation can also make it difficult for borrowers to repay their debt by reducing their real income (Baselga-Pascual et al., 2015; Klein, 2013). Thus, the nexus between inflation and bank risk can be negative or positive.

Also, we include ***Financial Development***$_{jt}$ in our models as it can also influence banks' risk-taking behaviour. The amount of credit to the private sector is a proxy for the level of financial development. This variable reflects the ease with which credits are obtained by the private sector (Kattai, 2010). The study envisages that higher levels of credit may increase defaults in the future as riskier loans may be approved in the process of increasing the loans.

Finally, the study includes ***Regulatory Quality***$_{jt}$ as a factor that can affect banks' risk-taking appetite. Generally, an improved regulatory environment should minimise the risk-taking appetite of banks. Levine (1999) and Chen et al. (2017) argue that institutional environment also affects financial development. Thus, we follow the literature and include regulatory quality in our model.

Table 9.1 provides a more comprehensive description of the variables.

Econometric Technique

The models are estimated using a dynamic system Generalised Methods of Moments (GMM) estimator to control for firm-specific, time-invariant effects and endogeneity. The lags of each of the regressors are used as instruments. To ensure the model is correctly specified, the study uses two criteria: the Sargan test which checks the validity of instruments, and the test for second-order autocorrelation. If the model is correctly specified, the variables that are used as instruments should not be correlated with the error term. The Sargan test is asymptotically distributed as a chi square with degrees of freedom equal to the number of instruments minus the number of parameters. The AR (2) test checks whether the model has been correctly specified. It is distributed as a standard normal under the null of no second-order autocorrelation and of the residuals and provides an additional check on the validity of the lagged variables used as instruments in the equation. We employ within-panel and heteroscedasticity serial correlation robust standard errors in the estimations.

9.5 Empirical Results and Discussions

Summary Statistics

The summary statistics presented in Table 9.2 reveal that data for some of the variables are missing for some countries and banks, which has

Table 9.1 Variable selection and justification

Variable	*Measurement*	*Source*
Dependent variable		
Bank risk-taking	$Z-\text{ score} = \frac{\text{ROA}_{it}+\text{EA}_{it}}{\sigma\text{ROA}_{it}}$ ROA_{it} represents the return on total assets of bank i in year t. EA_{it} represents ratio of equity over total assets. σROA_{it} represents the standard deviation of the return on asset	Bankscope
Independent/control variables		
Monetary policy stance	$\text{RMC}_{it} = w\hat{r}_{it} + (1-w)\hat{e}_{it}$ (see methodology for explanation)	IMF and authors' own calculation
Bank Profitability (ROA)	Ratio of profit after tax to total assets $\text{ROA} = \frac{\text{Profit after tax}}{\text{Total assets}}$	Bankscope
Liquidity	The ratio of liquid assets to total assets $\text{Liquidity} = \frac{\text{liquid assets}}{\text{Total assets}}$	Bankscope
Operating efficiency	The ratio of operating cost to total assets $\text{Efficiency} = \frac{\text{Operating cost}}{\text{Total assets}}$	Bankscope and authors' own calculation
Income diversification	The ratio of non-interest income to total operating income income diversification = non-interest income total operating income	Bankscope
Bank capitalisation	The ratio of total equity to total assets $\text{Capitalisation} = \frac{\text{Total equity}}{\text{Total assets}}$	Bankscope
Macroeconomic variables		
Economic growth	GDPper capita growth	IMF
Inflation	Annual Consumer Price Index (CPI)	IMF
Financial development	Domestic credit to private sector (% of GDP)	IMF
Governance indicator		
Regulatory quality	Estimate of regulatory quality	WGI

Note IMF represents International Monetary Fund Database; WGI represents World Governance Indicator Database. *Source* Authors' compilation

Table 9.2 Descriptive statistics

Variable	*Obs*	*Mean*	*Std. Dev*	*Min*	*Max*
Z-score	6900	1127.082	1044.978	1	3577
Ln*Z*-score	6900	6.574	0.986	0	8.182
NPL	4808	9.958	7.443	0.078	45.3
LnNPL	4808	1.956	0.985	−2.549	3.813
RMCI	1083	0.001	5.407	−21.846	14.913
Inflation	6009	7.74	6.259	−2.409	44.357
Efficiency	4687	45.97	179.124	−337.805	1127.168
Income diversification	4687	−31.874	225.869	−1311.448	355.099
ROA	5664	−0.4595	11.8168	−51.222	40.687
GDPPCG	6300	2.66	3.529	−22.312	18.066
Liquidity	3765	5.845	1.755	0	7.836
Financial development	5866	123.822	230.164	−678.449	922.278
Regulatory quality	6312	−4.343	7.413	−36.619	8.939
Bank capitalisation	6900	1296.702	1249.758	1	3872

Note NPL is non-performing loans ratio which is also a measure of bank risk-taking. LnNPL is the natural logarithm of the NPL. *Z*-score is proxy for bank risk-taking. Ln*Z*-score is the natural logarithm of the *Z*-score. RMCI represents the real monetary policy stance. GDPPCG represents GDP per capita growth. ROA represents bank profitability

accounted for lower observation for some of the variables. For brevity, only the key variables are discussed. Table 9.2 shows an average log of the Z-score of 6.57 and a standard deviation of 0.99. The average log of the *Z*-score reveals that most banks in Africa are risk averse (take less risk). Table 9.2 also shows that the average non-performing loans is 9.96 and its standard deviation is 7.44. With regard to the monetary policy stance (RMCI), the average RMCI is 0.001 and the standard deviation is 5.41. A positive average RMCI indicates that most central banks conduct a contractionary monetary policy stance. Notwithstanding the average RMCI, the minimum RMCI of −21.85 indicates that some central banks conducted an expansionary monetary policy stance over the period of study. The maximum RMCI of 14.91 indicates a contractionary monetary policy stance.

Correlation Analysis

Before estimating the econometric model, the study performs correlation analysis to determine the potential relationship between the variables and also ensure there are no possible issues of multicollinearity. Table 9.3 provides the pairwise correlation between the variables. In general, the figures for the pairwise correlation are low, eliminating any potential source of multicollinearity. This provides justification for including all the variables in the model. This further indicates that the standard errors of the estimates obtained from the regression are unbiased.

Empirical Relationship Between Monetary Policy and Risk-Taking of Banks

Turning to the formal econometric analysis, the GMM estimation results are reported in Table 9.4. The first column provides the results for *Z*-score as the dependent variable while the second model provides the results for NPL as the dependent variable. Column 1 shows that the coefficient of monetary policy stance is positively and statistically significant. This indicates that as monetary policy stance increases (decreases) the *Z*-score of banks increases (decreases). Thus, the results demonstrate that an expansionary (contractionary) monetary policy stance increases (reduces) bank risk-taking in African economies. When the *Z*-score is replaced with NPL, which is an alternative measure of bank risk-taking also often used in related studies, the result provides consistent evidence that confirms the proposition made by the bank risk-taking channel. These results are consistent with Chen et al. (2017) whose work also supports the bank risk-taking channel of monetary policy. The results suggest that in Africa, an expansionary monetary policy drives up the value of collateral, assets and banks' income and raises their risk-taking behaviour. These findings contradict Aboyadana (2021) who found that high (low) monetary policy rate increases (reduces) credit risk-taking.

The results for the bank-specific determinants and macroeconomic determinants using both *Z*-score and NPL are consistent with a priori expectations. The relationship between inflation and NPL is positive and significant. The results indicate that high inflation increases banks' NPLs which in turn increases their risk-taking. This could be explained in two ways. First, high inflation increases the volatility of bank returns or income, making them unstable. Second, high inflation also increases the probability of default by firms and individuals.

Operating efficiency has a positive and significant relationship with *Z*-score and a negative relationship with NPLs. The results suggest that high operating efficiency leads to low risk-taking behaviour. Put differently, this

Table 9.3 Pairwise correlations

Variables	*LnZ-score*	*LnNPL*	*RMCI*	*Inflation*	*Operating efficiency*	*Income diversification*	*GDPPCG*	*Liquidity*	*Financial development*	*Regulatory quality*	*Bank capitalisation*
LnZ-score	1.000										
lnNPL	0.025	1.000									
RMCI	−0.034	0.094*	1.000								
Inflation	0.032*	0.227*	−0.121*	1.000							
Operating efficiency	−0.095*	−0.358*	0.136*	−0.262*	1.000						
Income diversification	0.004	−0.008	0.196*	−0.054*	0.377*	1.000					
GDPPCG	0.023	0.036*	−0.113*	0.030*	−0.064*	0.041*	1.000				
Liquidity	−0.009	−0.039	−0.031	−0.038*	−0.042*	0.001	−0.014	1.000			
Financial development	0.058*	−0.130*	−0.111*	−0.043*	0.068*	0.511*	−0.035*	0.026	1.000		
Regulatory quality	−0.088*	−0.011	0.078*	−0.133*	0.218*	0.311*	0.007	−0.022	−0.063*	1.000	
Bank capitalisation	0.469*	0.050*	−0.108*	0.077*	−0.113*	0.007	0.014	0.005	−0.013	−0.048*	1.000

Note *Shows significance at the 0.05 level. LnNPL is the natural logarithm of the NPL. Ln*Z*-score is the natural logarithm of the *Z*-score. RMCI represents the real monetary policy stance. GDPPCG represents GDP per capita growth. ROA represents bank profitability

Table 9.4 Monetary policy and banks' risk-taking

Variables	*(1)* *LnZ-score*	*(2)* *LnNPL*
LnZ-score$_{t-1}$	0.465***	
	(0.0629)	
LnNPL$_{t-1}$		−0.813***
		(0.219)
RMCI	0.0161*	−0.128**
	(0.00822)	(0.0522)
Inflation	−0.0132	0.141**
	(0.0158)	(0.0716)
Efficiency	0.00428***	−0.00493***
	(0.000882)	(0.00151)
Income diversification	0.0135***	−0.00218
	(0.00356)	(0.0119)
Bank capitalisation	0.000731***	−0.000234
	(6.11e-05)	(0.000221)
ROA	0.0954***	−0.0269
	(0.0292)	(0.0656)
GDPPCG	−5.10e-05	0.214***
	(0.0134)	(0.0604)
Liquidity	0.246***	0.0823
	(0.0509)	(0.0944)
Financial development	−0.0135***	0.00985
	(0.00356)	(0.0110)
Regulatory quality	−0.415***	−0.0792
	(0.129)	(0.450)
Model summary		
AR(1)/AR(2)	0.004/0.199	0.003/0.050
Hansen J	0.980	0.981
Observations	573	304
Number of banks	79	67

Note Robust standard errors in parentheses. ***, ** and * denote statistical significance at the 1, 5 and 10% levels, respectively. LnZ-score is the natural logarithm of Z-score which is proxy for bank risk-taking. NPL is non-performing loans ratio which is also a measure of bank risk-taking. RMCI represents monetary policy stance. GDPPCG represents GDP per capita growth. Efficiency represents operating efficiency. ROA measures return on asset which is a proxy for profitability

indicates that bank risk decreases when banks become more efficient. This is consistent with Chen et al. (2017) and Fiordelisi et al. (2011).

Consistent with a priori expectations, Table 9.4 indicates that income diversification reduces bank risk-taking. Although the relationship was negative and insignificant for the NPL, it was positive and significant for Z-score. Income diversification's relationship with Z-score suggests that when banks in Africa properly diversify their sources of funds, their returns are stabilised. This lowers bank risk (Stiroh, 2004).

Capitalisation has an insignificant relationship with NPL, but a significant relationship with Z-score. The positive and significant relationship between capitalisation and Z-score suggests that banks' risk-taking behaviour reduces when they are well capitalised. This is consistent with Khan et al. (2017) who found that banks with high capital cushion have low risk-taking.

The impact of profitability measured as ROA was significant and positive for Z-score but insignificant for the NPL. This indicates that more profitable banks have low volatility of their returns, thereby reducing their risk-taking behaviour. This result is consistent with Khan et al. (2017).

The relationship between real GDP growth rate and NPL is positive and significant. The relationship with NPL suggests that bank risk-taking increases in booming economies, contrary to the argument that borrowers in booming economies are more likely to pay back their debt in time, leading to a low default risk (Brana et al., 2019). The explanation could be that in booming economies, banks would give out more loans without proper loan assessment (adverse selection), which may increase default risk.

Financial development is also found to have a negative and significant effect on bank risk-taking when measured by Z-score. This suggests that growth in credit to the private sector increases the rate of default, which in turn increases the credit risk of banks due to moral hazard problems.

The results also show that liquidity is positively and significantly related to Z-score. This suggests that highly liquid banks have low risk-taking behaviour. Specifically, banks holding more liquid assets are able to insulate themselves from being impacted by monetary shocks (Cornett et al., 2011). This is contrary to the argument by Acharya and Naqvi (2012) that banks take on more risk when they are very liquid.

The result also revealed that high regulatory quality increases bank risk-taking. This is shown by the adverse relationship between regulatory quality and Z-score. This could be explained by banks' confidence that the quality of regulation would reduce moral hazard issues that underlie the excessive risk-taking of banks (Chen et al., 2017). Thus, low regulatory quality reduces bank risk-taking.

9.6 Conclusion and Policy Recommendations

In this chapter, we have examined the impact of monetary policy stance of central banks on the risk-taking appetite of banks in Africa using data on 532 banks from 37 countries in Africa for a period of 13 years from 2006 to 2018. After controlling for bank-specific and country-level variables, the results from this study revealed that banks in Africa assume more risk when the monetary policy is expansionary. These results are consistent when alternative measures of bank risk are used. The findings are consistent with the bank risk-taking channel which suggests that lowering monetary policy rate for a protracted period encourages banks to take on more risk.

Important policy implications emerge from the findings. First, the findings suggest that monetary authorities should balance the trade-off between bank stability and a protracted loose monetary policy stance in order not to expose banks to risk. This is especially important because a fragile banking system has negative repercussions for the other sectors of the economy. In particular, banks in Africa should be closely monitored by the central banks when an expansionary monetary policy stance is implemented since it serves as an incentive for banks to take on more risks. Taking up more risk is not bad since it is associated with high expected returns. However, close monitoring is required to ensure banks do not assume unreasonable risk which may result in their collapse and have a systemic effect on other sectors of the economy. Moreover, central banks in Africa should adopt complementary policies such as monetary policy transparency to counteract the negative effect that an expansionary monetary policy has on the risk-taking appetite of banks.

References

Aboyadana, G. (2021). Monetary policy and bank risk-taking in Sub-Sahara Africa. *The European Journal of Applied Economics, 18*(1).

Afonso, G., Santos, J. A., & Traina, J. (2014). Do 'too-big-to-fail' banks take on more risk? *Economic Policy Review*.

Acharya, V., & Naqvi, H. (2012). The seeds of a crisis: A theory of bank liquidity and risk taking over the business cycle. *Journal of Financial Economics, 106*(2), 349–366.

Almani, A. (2016). Accounting and business magazine of ACCA, October 2016 ed., p. 23.

Altunbas, Y., Gambacorta, L., & Marqués-Ibanez, D. (2009). An empirical assessment of the risk-taking channel. Available at SSRN 1459627.

Altunbas, Y., Gambacorta, L, & Marqués-Ibáñez, D. (2010, March). *Does monetary policy affect bank risk-taking? Centre for Economic Policy Research (CEPR)*. Paper presented at the conference on "Procyclicality and Financial Regulation".

Alger, G., & Alger, I. (1999). *Liquid assets in banks: Theory and practice*. Universite des Sciences Sociales.

Baselga-Pascual, L., Trujillo-Ponce, A., & Cardone-Riportella, C. (2015). Factors influencing bank risk in Europe: Evidence from the financial crisis. *The North American Journal of Economics and Finance, 34*, 138–166.

Borio, C., & Zhu, H. (2008). *Capital regulation, risk-taking and monetary policy: A missing link in the transmission mechanism* (BIS Working Paper No. 268). Retrieved from Bank or International Settlements website: http://www.bis.org/publ/work268.pdf

Borio, C., & Zhu, H. (2012). Capital regulation, risk-taking and monetary policy: A missing link in the transmission mechanism? *Journal of Financial Stability, 8*(4), 236–251.

Bourkhis, K., & Nabi, M. S. (2013). Islamic and conventional banks' soundness during the 2007–2008 financial crisis. *Review of Financial economics, 22*(2), 68–77.

Boyd, J. H. & Graham, S. L. (1988). The profitability and risk effects of allowing bank holding. *Federal Reserve Bank of Minneapolis. Quarterly Review-Federal Reserve Bank of Minneapolis, 12*(2), 3.

Brana, S., Campmas, A., & Lapteacru, I. (2019). (Un) Conventional monetary policy and bank risk-taking: A nonlinear relationship. *Economic Modelling, 81*, 576–593.

Buch, C. M., Eickmeier, S., & Prieto, E. (2014). In search for yield? Survey-based evidence on bank risk taking. *Journal of Economic Dynamics and Control, 43*, 12–30.

Chen, M., Wu, J., Jeon, B. N., & Wang, R. (2017). Monetary policy and bank risk-taking: Evidence from emerging economies. *Emerging Markets Review, 31*, 116–140.

Cornett, M. M., McNutt, J. J., Strahan, P. E., & Tehranian, H. (2011). Liquidity risk management and credit supply in the financial crisis. *Journal of Financial Economics, 101*(2), 297–312.

Delis, M. D., & Kouretas, G. P. (2011). Interest rates and bank risk-taking. *Journal of Banking & Finance, 35*(4), 840–855.

Delis, M. D., Hasan, I., & Tsionas, E. G. (2014). The risk of financial intermediaries. *Journal of Banking and Finance, 44*, 1–12.

Dell'Ariccia, G., Laeven, L., & Suarez, G. A. (2017). Bank leverage and monetary policy's risk-taking channel: Evidence from the United States. *The Journal of Finance, 72*(2), 613–654.

Demirgüç-Kunt, A., & Huizinga, H. (2010). Bank activity and funding strategies: The impact on risk and returns. *Journal of Financial Economics, 98*(3), 626–650.

Demsetz, R. S., & Strahan, P. E. (1997). *Size, diversification and risk at bank holding companies* (Federal Reserve Bank of New York Research Paper [9506]).

De Nicolò, G., Dell'Ariccia, G., Laeven, L., & Valencia, F. (2010). *Monetary policy and bank risk taking* (IMF Staff Position Note SPN/10/09).

De Nicolo, M. G., Boyd, J. H., & Jalal, A. M. (2006). *Bank risk-taking and competition revisited: New theory and new evidence*. International Monetary Fund.

DeYoung, R., & Roland, K. P. (2001). Product mix and earnings volatility at commercial banks: Evidence from a degree of total leverage model. *Journal of Financial Intermediation, 10*(1), 54–84.

Diamond, D. W., & Rajan, R. G. (2005). Liquidity shortages and banking crises. *The Journal of Finance, 60*(2), 615–647.

Dong, Y., Firth, M., Hou, W., & Yang, W. (2016). Evaluating the performance of Chinese commercial banks: A comparative analysis of different types of banks. *European Journal of Operational Research, 252*(1), 280–295.

Festić, M., Kavkler, A., & Repina, S. (2011). The macroeconomic sources of systemic risk in the banking sectors of five new EU member states. *Journal of Banking & Finance, 35*(2), 310–322.

Fiordelisi, F., Marques-Ibanez, D., & Molyneux, P. (2011). Efficiency and risk in European banking. *Journal of Banking & Finance, 35*(5), 1315–1326.

Fisher, I. (1933). The debt-deflation theory of great depressions. *Econometrica: Journal of the Econometric Society, 1*(4), 337–357.

Gambacorta, L. (2009). Monetary policy and the risk-taking channel. *International Banking and Financial Market Developments, 3*, 43–53.

Greenspan, A. (2005). Risk transfer and financial stability. In *Federal Reserve Bank of Chicago Proceedings* (No. 968).

Hayek, F. A. (1939). *Profits interest and investment and other essays on theory of industrial fluctuations*. George Routledge and Sons Limited.

Hodrick, R. J., & Prescott, E. C. (1997). Postwar US business cycles: An empirical investigation. *Journal of Money, credit, and Banking*, 1–16.

Ioannidou, V., Ongena, S., & Peydró, J. L. (2009). *Monetary policy and subprime lending: A tall tale of low federal funds rates, hazardous loans and reduced loan spreads* (European Banking Centre Discussion Paper, 45).

Jiménez, G., Ongena, S., Peydró, J. L., & Saurina, J. (2014). Hazardous times for monetary policy: What do twenty-three million bank loans say about the effects of monetary policy on credit risk-taking? *Econometrica, 82*(2), 463–505.

Kattai, R. (2010). *Credit risk model for the Estonian banking sector*. Eesti Pank.

Khan, M. S., Scheule, H., & Wu, E. (2017). Funding liquidity and bank risk taking. *Journal of Banking & Finance, 82*, 203–216.

Kindleberger, C. P. (1991). Bubbles. In *The world of economics* (pp. 20–22). Palgrave Macmillan.

Klein, N. (2013). *Non-performing loans in CESEE: Determinants and impact on macroeconomic performance*. International Monetary Fund.

Laeven, M. L., Dell'Ariccia, M. G. & Marquez, M. R. (2010). *Monetary policy, leverage, and bank risk taking*. International Monetary Fund.

Laeven, M. L., & Valencia, M. F. (2018). *Systemic banking crises revisited*. International Monetary Fund.

Laeven, L., Ratnovski, L., & Tong, H. (2016). Bank size, capital, and systemic risk: Some international evidence. *Journal of Banking & Finance, 69*, S25–S34.

Lepetit, L., & Strobel, F. (2013). Bank insolvency risk and time-varying Z-score measures. *Journal of International Financial Markets, Institutions and Money, 25*, 73–87.

Lepetit, L., & Strobel, F. (2015). Bank insolvency risk and Z-score measures: A refinement. *Finance Research Letters, 13*, 214–224.

Lepetit, L., Nys, E., Rous, P., & Tarazi, A. (2008). Bank income structure and risk: An empirical analysis of European banks. *Journal of Banking & Finance, 32*(8), 1452–1467.

Levine, R. (1999). Law, finance, and economic growth. *Journal of financial Intermediation, 8*(1–2), 8–35.

Maddaloni, A., & Peydró, J. L. (2011). Bank risk-taking, securitization, supervision, and low interest rates: Evidence from the Euro-area and the US lending standards. *The Review of Financial Studies, 24*(6), 2121–2165.

Nkusu, M. M. (2011). *Nonperforming loans and macrofinancial vulnerabilities in advanced economies*. International Monetary Fund.

Oima, A., & Ojwang, C. (2013). Market-based and bank-based financial structure on economic growth in some selected Ecowas countries. *Journal of Education and Research, 41*(2), 34–41.

Rajan, R. (2005). *Has financial development made the world riskier?* (NBER Working Paper Series No. 11728).

Rose, P. S. (1989). Diversification of the banking firm. *Financial Review, 24*(2), 251–280.

Roy, A. D. (1952). Safety first and the holding of assets. *Econometrica, 20*, 431–449.

Soedarmono, W., Machrouh, F., & Tarazi, A. (2011). Bank market power, economic growth and financial stability: Evidence from Asian banks. *Journal of Asian Economics, 22*(6), 460–470.

Stiroh, K. J. (2004). Diversification in banking: Is non-interest income the answer? *Journal of Money, Credit, and Banking, 36*, 853–882.

Svensson, L. E., & Woodford, M. (2004). Indicator variables for optimal policy under asymmetric information. *Journal of Economic Dynamics and Control, 28*(4), 661–690.

Terraza, V. (2015). The effect of bank size on risk ratios: Implications of banks' performance. *Procedia Economics and Finance, 30*, 903–909.

CHAPTER 10

Bank Pricing Behaviour, Monetary Policy and Inclusive Finance in Africa

Mohammed Amidu, Abdul Ganiyu Iddrisu, Alhassan Andani, and Benjamin Agyeman

10.1 Introduction

The connection between monetary policy and inclusive finance has been of persistent interest to policy makers (Mbutor & Uba, 2013). However, literature on this is skewed to assessing the role of inclusive finance on monetary policy effectiveness (see Lenka & Bairwa, 2016; Mbutor & Uba, 2013; Mehrotra & Yetman, 2015). There is no doubt that the monetary policy of a country largely determines the evolution of its

M. Amidu (✉) · B. Agyeman
University of Ghana Business School, Accra, Ghana
e-mail: mamidu@ug.edu.gh

A. G. Iddrisu
University of Aberdeen, Aberdeen, Scotland, UK

A. Andani
LVS Africa, Accra, Ghana

J. Y. Abor and C. K. D. Adjasi (eds.), *The Economics of Banking and Finance in Africa*, Palgrave Macmillan Studies in Banking and Financial Institutions, https://doi.org/10.1007/978-3-031-04162-4_10

general pricing behaviour of banks, and that banks' pricing behaviour influence financial inclusion (Dev, 2006). Empirical literature has shown that financial inclusion is a significant determinant of national development. According to some strands of the literature, access to finance by vulnerable communities increase savings, investments as well as consumption and female empowerment (Ashraf et al., 2010).

There is evidence of how monetary policy through the pricing behaviour of banks (interest rate) influence non-financial economic activity (see Friedman, 1999; Iddrisu et al., 2022). However, given the elevated role financial inclusion is playing in terms of national development, empirical literature on its determinants are scarce. It has now been recommended that monetary policy is capable of influencing banks' pricing behaviour, which in turn influences inclusive finance (see Amidu, 2006; Ciccarelli et al., 2015) and most empirical studies have shown that a change in lending behaviours of banks (bank's interest rate) is greatly influenced by monetary policy of the central banks (see Iddrisu et al., 2022). In turn, Iddrisu and Turkson (2020) found that a decrease in the interest rates of banks increase financial inclusion. Drawing from the above relationships, this study aimed to empirically fill the monetary policy and financial inclusion nexus gap in Sub-Saharan Africa (SSA).

Using bank-specific and country-level data from 29 SSA countries, this study examines financial inclusion in SSA, exploring the role of monetary policy and banks' pricing behaviour. We first examine the influence of monetary policy on banks' pricing behaviour in SSA. For the purpose of economic policy, it is vital to identify monetary policy determinants of banks' pricing behaviour so as to take action to reduce economic shocks that may arise as a result of banks' price distortion. Secondly, we assess the influence banks' pricing behaviour (loan price, deposit price and fees price) has on financial inclusion. This has not been given empirical attention. Financial inclusion is proxied by two types of indicators: financial usage and access. Finally, we analyse the effect of monetary policy on financial inclusion conditioned on banks' pricing behaviour.

The results of this study show that, monetary policy affect banks' pricing behaviour in SSA. The results suggest that when monetary policy is contracted, banks' loan price is high. Secondly, it indicated that high loan price decreases financial access. Finally, the study, however, found that high banks' pricing induced by contractionary monetary policy tend to increase financial inclusion.

The remaining sections are organized as follows: Sect. 10.2 reviews literature, comprising a theoretical overview of bank pricing behaviour and empirical literature. Section 10.3 presents the evaluating methodology consisting of data sources, variable measurements, the model and estimation strategy. Section 10.4 contains the empirical findings and analysis, while Sect. 10.5 provides conclusion and recommendation.

10.2 Literature Review

Theoretical Overview

Kovanen (2011)'s model of interest rate and monetary policy better explains banks' pricing behaviour. Accordingly, the level of operation of the Central Bank (CB) targets the interbank money market interest rate (denoted by, i^{IB}); the risk-neutral bank determines its loan (L) and deposit (D) portfolios and the level of reserves $\left(R^d\right)$ it plans to hold by close of the day and how competitive the banking system is. We argue that the banking system of developing countries is imperfectly competitive. Therefore, banks have some level of monopoly power in retail credits and deposits pricing but all (banks) behave as price-takers in the interbank money market. We integrate costly intermediation into the model which is a function of the bank's loan portfolio size. Consequently, the profit maximization problem of a risk-neutral bank is as follows:

$$\pi = i^L L - i^D D - c(L) + i^{IB}\left[(D - L) - R^d\right] + \frac{i^{CB,D}}{2v}\int_{-R^d}^{v+u}(R^d + x)dx + \frac{i^{CB,L}}{2v}\int_{-v+u}^{-R^d}(R^d + x)dx \tag{10.1}$$

where $i^L(L)$ is the bank's lending interest rate and decreases with the loan portfolio, $i^D(D)$ is the bank's deposit interest rate and increases with deposits (assuming there are no statutory reserve requirements) and $c(L)$ is the intermediation cost function where the marginal cost of lending is an increasing function of the loan portfolio ($c' > 0 \,\text{and}\, c'' > 0$). The difference $(D - L) - R^d$, is the net interbank market position of the bank and can either be positive or negative. In Eq. (10.1), the last two terms represent the overnight credit and deposit operations with the CB. The close-of-day liquidity shock is assumed to be normally distributed with a zero mean. Further assumption is that the CB has adopted an asymmetric band around its policy rate (i^{CB}); thus, the deposit rate equals $i^{CB,D} = i^{CB} - h'$ and the lending rate equals $i^{CB,L} = i^{CB} + h''$, where h' and h'' are positive constants. Each bank maximizes its profits Eq. (10.1) with respect to L, D and R^d, which gives us the following first-order conditions:

$$i^L = \frac{1}{\left(1 + \frac{1}{\varphi L}\right)}\left[i^{IB} + c'(L)\right] \tag{10.2a}$$

$$i^D = \frac{1}{\left(1 + \frac{1}{\varphi L}\right)} i^{IB} \tag{10.2b}$$

$$i^{IB} = i^{CB} + \frac{h'' - h'}{2v}\left(R^d + u\right) + \frac{h'' - h'}{2} \tag{10.2c}$$

The interest rate on bank's lending (i^L) depends on the term $\left(1 + \frac{1}{\varphi L}\right)$, which is mark-up over the loanable funds' marginal cost, where the last part is given by the interbank market interest rate $\left(i^{IB}\right)$ and the marginal intermediation cost, $C'(L)$. The mark-up size reflects the lack of banking system competition; thus, it is smaller in more competitive banking systems. The marginal cost of intermediation is assumed to reflect the lending activities of the banks. Hence, banks with higher operation costs would charge higher loan prices. The pass-through from interbank market rates to lending interest rates $\left(\frac{\partial i^L}{\partial i^{IB}}\right)$ is also linked to the marginal intermediation cost. Thus, banks are less likely to adjust their lending rates to changes in the policy rate when the costs of intermediation are steeply rising (when $c'' > 0$). Again, deposit prices are determined by the interbank interest rate, therefore, they are lower when the reserve requirements is higher. Further, the deposit price in this model does not directly enter Eq. (10.2a).

With regards to Eq. (10.2c), the model creates a link between the interbank market interest rate and the policy rate. Thus, policy rate level would reflect in the interbank market interest rates. The *liquidity effect* and the impact it makes on interbank interest rates is in the model, as shown by the terms R^d and u. Consequently, the demand and supply for reserves must be equal. By lowering available reserves, the CB can push interbank interest rates higher by increasing the money market demand for liquidity. When the band around the policy rate is symmetric, that is,

$h' = h''$, then the second term drops out and the spread between the interbank and policy rates will equal h.

Linking interest rate of banks to inclusive finance, the model proposed by Cúrdia and Woodford (2016) on financial frictions and aggregate demand is used. We, however, replace household with individual and discard the assumption that each individual owns an equal share in the intermediary sector, as well as the assumption that individuals have access to insurance agency at all periods. Hence, the individual makes his borrowing, spending and saving decisions as in any other period but considering his post-transfer financial wealth.

The nominal net financial wealth $A_t(i)$ of individual i's beginning of period (post-transfer) is as follows;

$$A_t(i) = \left[B_{t-1}(i)\right]^+\left(1 + i^d_{t-1}\right) + \left[B_{t-1}(i)\right]^-\left(1 + i^b_{t-1}\right) + T_i(i), \quad (10.3)$$

where $B_{t-1}(i)$ is the individual's nominal net financial wealth at the end of period -1;

$$[B]^+ \equiv \max(B, 0), \quad [B]^- \equiv \min(B, 0); \quad (10.4)$$

Here, i^d_t is the interest rate at the beginning of period $t + 1$ for savers on their savings deposited with intermediaries at the end of period t, while i^b_t is the interest rate at which borrowers are correspondingly able to borrow from intermediaries in period t for repayment at the beginning of period $t + 1$. Note that the final term $T_t(i)$ is certainly zero in any period in which individual i have no access to the insurance agency. An individual's end-of-period nominal net financial wealth $B_t(i)$ is similarly given by:

$$B_t(i) = A_t(i) - P_tC_t(i) + \int W_t(j)h_t(j;i)dj + D_t + T^g_t, \quad (10.5)$$

where P_t is the Dixit–Stiglitz price index in period t; $W_t(j)$ is the wage of labour of type j in period t; D_t represents the individual's share in the distributed profits of goods-producing firms and T^g_t is the net nominal (lump-sum) government transfer received by each household in period t. Because the individual do not have insurance against income shock, if the financial intermediary set higher interest rate spread (difference between i^d_{t-1} and i^b_{t-1}), it will lead to lower individual's end-of-period nominal net financial wealth $B_t(i)$, which will in turn discourage financial inclusion. Similarly, lower interest rate spread will encourage financial inclusion.

Empirical Literature Review

Empirical literature on the link between monetary policy and pricing behaviour of banks (interest rates) is quite copious but the link between these variables and their impact on financial inclusion is yet to be examined. The extant literature has investigated the relationship between monetary policy and banks' pricing behaviour. Cook and Hahn (1989) and Radecki and Reinhart (1994) analyse the response of short-term and long-term rates to changes in loanable funds, suggest that the policy actions have a significant positive effect on interest rates of all maturities. Kleimeier and Sander (2006) find a faster pass-through in loan markets when interest rate changes are anticipated correctly. In contrast, they also find deposit markets to be more rigid. On the contrary, Ananchotikul and Seneviratne (2015) find that Asia's bank lending channel of domestic monetary policy is not very strong at the aggregate level. Recently, Iddrisu et al. (2022) found in Africa that effective monetary policy (high monetary freedom rate) translates to high banks' loan and deposit prices. In single country analysis, Amidu (2006) suggest that changes in money supply and the Ghana's economic activities significantly affect banks' lending behaviours. The study of Kelilume (2014) evaluating the cause effect relationships between monetary policy rate and short-term and long-term rates in Nigeria pointed out evidence of the effectiveness of monetary policy only in the relationship between monetary policy rate and interbank rates. It is also argued that, there is a significant, although slow pass-through of policy rate changes to bank interest rates in India (Das, 2015). Studies that have also tried to see the combined effect of monetary and fiscal policy on interest rates are as follows. Dell'Erba and Sola (2016) noted that global monetary and fiscal policy stances explain more than 60% of the variation of long-term interest rates in Organization in Economic Cooperation and Development (OECD) countries. However, Mang'ang'a (2014) finds that monetary policy has a more influence on interest rates than the fiscal policy with the Central Bank rate being a significant determinant of interest rates in Kenya.

Literature on how bank pricing behaviour affect financial inclusion is scarce. Iddrisu and Turkson (2020) found that high loan prices decrease financial access. However, quite a number of studies have dealt with the inclusive finance-monetary policy nexus, mainly focusing on the role of financial inclusion in monetary policy effectiveness. For instance, Mbutor and Uba (2013), in Nigeria, concluded that growing financial inclusion enhances the effectiveness of monetary policy. In a related study, Lapukeni (2015) find an inverse relationship between inclusive finance and monetary policy and attribute that to the fact that accounting of monetary aggregates does not include the activities of those outside the banking system. Similarly, Lenka and Bairwa (2016), in a study of the South Asian Association for Regional Cooperation (SAARC) countries, found a significant impact of financial inclusion on monetary policy, arguing that increased financial inclusion reduces the inflation rate in an economy and hence monetary policy will be effective. The work of Ma and Lin (2016) noted that monetary policy is essentially a financial process, which relies on the financial system to transmit impacts into an economy. Evans (2016) establishes that financial inclusion is not a significant driver of monetary policy effectiveness in Africa, rather, monetary policy effectiveness is the driver of financial inclusion. Brownbridge et al. (2017) using four African countries (Ghana, Mauritius, South Africa and Uganda) find that economies with higher levels of financial inclusion exhibit stronger impulse responses.

Considering the above discussions, one can say that the relationship between monetary policy, pricing behaviour of banks and inclusive finance is firm in the literature. However, examining monetary policy pass-through to financial inclusion is limited. This is the gap that this paper addresses.

10.3 Evaluating Methodology

Data Sources

The paper uses both bank and country-level data. The bank data is sourced from the Bank scope database preserved by Fitch/IBCA/Bureau Van Dijk. The data is yearly and covers a sample of 330 banks in 29 African countries for which data was available. To avoid data aggregation bias in our analysis, we use unconsolidated banks' financial statements. Included in the sample are all commercial banks, development banks, cooperative banks, savings banks, real estate and mortgage banks based on availability of data. Macroeconomic data are obtained from the World Development Indicators.

Variable Measurements

Financial inclusion is measured by ***financial access*** (the number of branches per 100,000 adults and access to the capital market) and ***financial usage*** (percentage of adults that own an account in regulated institutions).

Following Brewer and Jackson (2006), ***loan price*** measured by total interest income as a percentage of total earning assets, ***deposit price*** measured by total interest cost divided by total interest-bearing liabilities and price of providing non-interest related services (***Fees price***) are used as indicators of pricing behaviour of banks in Africa.

Monetary policy is measured by the respective countries' money market interest rate and monetary freedom index from the heritage foundation, as used in other works of Amidu and Wolfe (2013). Monetary freedom is a weighted average of price stability and price controls. It is measured from 0 to 100, 100 being the most effective monetary policy framework.

We also add as covariates bank-specific, macroeconomic and monetary environment variables. Bank-level controls included bank age, Loan size is the ratio of loan to total assets, market share is the individual bank loan to total market loan, efficiency is the cost to gross income ratio, Funding source is measured by the total liability to total assets. Inflation (consumer price index) and GDP growth are the macroeconomic variables.

Model and Estimation Strategy

To address the issue of financial inclusion, monetary policy and bank's pricing behaviour, the study examines the effect of monetary policy on financial inclusion conditioned on bank's pricing behaviour. We refer to the work of Iddrisu and Turkson (2020) and subsequently estimate the following empirical model;

$$FI_{t,c} = \alpha_1 FI_{t,c-1} + \alpha_2 PP_{it,c} + \alpha_3 PBB_{it,c} + \left(PP_{t,c} * PBB_{it,c}\right) + \sum_{j=3}^{k} \alpha_j X_{ij} + \varepsilon_{it} \tag{10.6}$$

$$\varepsilon_{it} = \mu_i + \nu_{it}$$

$$E[\mu_i] = E[\nu_{it}] = E[\mu_i \nu_{it}] = 0$$

where $FI_{t,c}$ is financial inclusion of country c at period t, and $FI_{t,c-1}$ is the financial inclusion of the same county in the previous year. $PP_{t,c}$ is the monetary policy of country c in period t, $PBB_{it,c}$ is the pricing behaviour of bank i in country c in period t, $(PP_{t,c} * PBB_{it,c})$ is the interaction between monetary policy and the pricing behaviour of bank i in country c at period t, the variable $X_{i,j}$ is a set of $\{k\}$ variables controlling for bank and respective countries' macroeconomic environments, α's are the parameter vectors and ε_{it} is the unobserved time-invariant error term. Here the disturbance term ε_{it} has two components: the μ_i is an unobserved time-invariant bank-specific effect, and v_{it} is the disturbance term.

This study uses the system generalized method of moments (GMM) estimator in estimating Eq. (10.6). In particular, we use the methodology proposed by Blundell and Bond (1998) and Alvarez and Arellano (2003) in estimating systems of equations both in first difference and at levels. The system GMM estimator combines the standard set equations in first difference with a suitable lagged level as instruments, and an additional set of equations in levels with suitably lagged first differences as instruments (Roodman, 2009). Two-step System GMM is used, Windmeijer (2005) correct standard error, small sample adjustments, and orthogonal deviation. The two-step variant uses residuals from the one-step estimates and is asymptotically more efficient than the one-step.

10.4 Empirical Results

This section presents summary statistics, correlations and the analysis of the regression results in Tables 10.4–10.7. For the regression results, the analyses are based on columns that are not second order autocorrelated and/or has no indication of overidentification of instruments (i.e., columns with insignificant coefficients of second order autocorrelation [AB2] and overidentification (Hansen's test) coefficients). This is because, the presence of second order autocorrelation and/or overidentification of instruments may produce spurious results.

Summary Statistics

In Table 10.1, we present summary statistics of the country-level variables used in this study over the period 2002–2013. The variables are categorized as macroeconomic, monetary policy and inclusive finance.

Table 10.1 Averages for the country-level variables

Macroeconomic variables			*Monetary policy variables*		*Financial inclusion variables*		
	GDP growth	*Inflation*	*Monetary freedom*	*M. Mkt. Int. rate*	*Financial access*	*Financial usage*	*St. Mkt. access*
Algeria	0.03925	3.989149	79.47622	–	–	–	–
Egypt	0.052965	8.990811	71.10271	–	371.6584	4.49596	47.51479
Morocco	0.048018	1.829395	81.9879	3.059355	–	16.91693	56.77411
Sudan	0.066118	12.79251	64.5	–	–	–	–
Tunisia	0.046245	3.815263	80.9962	4.810191	700.128	14.50709	14.49663
Benin	0.04	3.174899	79.4125	–	–	–	–
Burkina Faso	0.051667	3.199441	78.52857	–	76.72372	1.731433	–
Cameroon	0.032076	2.43566	76.20833	–	–	–	–
Cote d'Ivoire	0.010678	2.828464	79.60833	–	115.9514	3.043622	22.77924
Ethiopia	0.08327	14.58635	69.33333	–	–	–	–
Ghana	0.058935	14.29811	64.53622	15.76173	265.7059	4.632849	12.11618
Kenya	0.039952	10.59747	75.02468	–	328.767	4.088392	31.10169
Mali	0.0487	2.663761	80.85938	–	–	–	–
Mauritania	0.041629	6.825447	76.58824	–	–	–	–
Nigeria	0.066873	11.85653	71.12414	–	397.1476	5.456959	18.23843
Rwanda	0.074875	8.137947	73.93438	–	–	–	–
Senegal	0.039721	2.137373	80.98333	–	–	–	–
Sierra Leone	0.092374	12.89041	79.25313	–	–	–	–
Uganda	0.079374	8.370174	79.9	–	135.9226	1.929845	11.78324
Angola	0.133823	40.67299	51.325	–	–	–	–
Botswana	0.038526	8.52434	74.33409	–	437.8815	8.113323	30.1995
Malawi	0.05625	12.81765	67.19167	–	151.1452	1.954094	18.3066

Macroeconomic variables			Monetary policy variables		Financial inclusion variables		
	GDP growth	Inflation	Monetary freedom	M. Mkt. Int. rate	Financial access	Financial usage	St. Mkt. access
Mauritius	0.038917	5.653335	73.03529	–	–	–	–
Mozambique	0.075442	8.486622	72.61667	–	–	–	–
Namibia	0.049842	6.01191	74.54167	8.400417	310.7661	8.239515	7.333862
South Africa	0.036893	5.926116	76.99521	7.752014	–	8.411995	186.7442
Swaziland	0.024524	7.245928	74.50357	–	–	–	–
Tanzania	0.07074	8.189333	74.55417	–	–	1.718701	4.487716
Zimbabwe	−0.06845	2899.289	6.856786	–	–	–	–

Table 10.1 presents the mean value of country-level variables

Note The data comprises of 330 banks across 29 countries over the period 2002–2013—Information is not available

Source Bankscope and authors' own calculation

Under financial inclusion, Tunisia is the highest in terms of financial access with an average of about 700 number of branches per 100,000 adults while Burkina Faso records the lowest average of about 77 number of branches per 100,000 adults. Morocco tops for financial usage of about 17 number of accounts while Tanzania records the lowest of about 2 accounts per 100,000 adults. For stock market access, South Africa recorded the highest mean of about 187 capitalizations and Tanzania again takes the lowest mean of about 4 capitalizations. This indicates the strengths of countries in financial inclusion differ across indicators and justify the alternative use of financial inclusion specifications in the analysis to check robustness. Similarly, for monetary policy variables, the results show that Tunisia is the country with highest monetary freedom of about 90 on average and the least was about 7 for Zimbabwe. Among the money markets of the countries in the sample, Ghana on average charged the highest money market interest rate of about 16% over the period with Morocco recording the least of about 3%. With regards to the macroeconomic controls, Angola is the highest in terms of economic growth with about 0.13% GDP growth while Zimbabwe recorded a negative GDP growth of about −0.68% with an alarming price instability (inflation). Morocco recorded lowest inflation of about 1.8%.

Table 10.2 presents summary statistics for the bank-level variables in the study over the same time period as above. For the banks' pricing variables, banks in Zimbabwe on average charge high loan, fees and deposit prices of about 0.36, 0.10 and 0.22%, respectively. This may be as a result of the high inflation rate in Zimbabwe over the period. Botswana, Morocco and Mali recorded the various low prices of about 0.03, 0.0098 and 0.015% loan, fees and deposit, respectively. For the bank-level control variables, Morocco has the older banks in the sample as she recorded an average of 63 years bank age, while Angola recorded the lowest average of about 12 years. Tunisian banks on average give more loans while Angolan banks recorded the least in the sample. With efficiency, Egyptian banks are more efficient with banks in Rwanda being the least efficient in the sample, probably because of higher rate of financial access and usage in Egyptian banks compared to banks in Rwanda. Cameroonian and Namibian banks have the highest and lowest funding sources respectively, which can be attributed to difference in assets and liabilities. Finally,

Table 10.2 Averages for the bank-level variables by country

	Bank pricing variables			*other control variables*				
	Loan price	*Fee price*	*Deposit price*	*Bank age*	*Loan/Total assets*	*Efficiency*	*Funding sources*	*Mkt. share*
Algeria	0.04017	0.022249	0.019455	22.55953	0.440736	0.319414	0.848434	0.084508
Egypt	0.065758	0.015652	0.055094	34.38334	0.478219	0.240519	0.891071	0.038027
Morocco	0.050658	0.009863	0.024206	62.86364	0.552603	0.341447	0.912198	0.104348
Sudan	0.046127	0.049864	0.05804	19.16667	0.351919	0.50077	0.864544	0.177419
Tunisia	0.052546	0.015254	0.042021	49.38726	0.760904	0.363356	0.861213	0.067073
Benin	0.056296	0.027444	0.025003	12.375	0.552656	0.490792	0.906864	0.244898
Burkina Faso	0.067622	0.038943	0.024481	28	0.600794	0.494454	0.918967	0.212766
Cameroon	0.056169	0.0324	0.023662	21.92857	0.523423	0.425458	0.928634	0.164384
Cote d'Ivoire	0.055063	0.042519	0.022802	29.34722	0.611757	0.551225	0.906209	0.181818
Ethiopia	0.046788	0.032674	0.022612	25.625	0.511628	0.268839	0.888373	0.127907
Ghana	0.123045	0.042696	0.075898	30.22222	0.450323	0.424849	0.879703	0.068024
Kenya	0.09155	0.033274	0.043818	35.02778	0.563299	0.432365	0.841996	0.042187
Mali	0.054804	0.033927	0.015545	17.51389	0.578961	0.532492	0.896227	0.206897
Mauritania	0.053593	0.041531	0.025202	28.5	0.564532	0.488026	0.782448	0.20339
Nigeria	0.096554	0.045141	0.05834	33.80953	0.38526	0.451825	0.834976	0.058201
Rwanda	0.087468	0.038188	0.052689	17.55556	0.54723	0.568237	0.846952	0.222222
Senegal	0.060858	0.028696	0.022034	32.20238	0.618218	0.514865	0.907938	0.322
Sierra Leone	0.108884	0.079976	0.034262	28.38889	0.314371	0.548089	0.817128	0.26087
Uganda	0.11066	0.025986	0.034518	42.95454	0.446809	0.452914	0.852696	0.116678
Angola	0.061864	0.045289	0.030207	11.91667	0.310697	0.403912	0.870597	0.103448
Botswana	0.034132	0.024345	0.097455	23.08333	0.549747	0.282539	0.837013	0.15
Malawi	0.12974	0.073634	0.062926	26.55	0.411407	0.513189	0.857273	0.134831
Mauritius	0.056394	0.038375	0.048575	42.50758	0.576895	0.305189	0.804573	0.110092
Mozambique	0.112419	0.044445	0.042651	22.01042	0.485435	0.533189	0.859407	0.141176

(continued)

Table 10.2 (continued)

	Bank pricing variables			*other control variables*				
	Loan price	*Fee price*	*Deposit price*	*Bank age*	*Loan/Total assets*	*Efficiency*	*Funding sources*	*Mkt. share*
Namibia	0.091608	0.028271	0.085022	58.01389	0.732214	0.340321	0.662757	0.188679
South Africa	0.107579	0.052537	0.117903	33.375	0.6516	0.334845	0.820412	0.083932
Swaziland	0.087107	0.044077	0.042339	31.7	0.691535	0.478065	0.848358	0.229167
Tanzania	0.077844	0.032307	0.032737	23.56018	0.47033	0.490193	0.878589	0.074182
Zimbabwe	0.355246	0.102527	0.224294	51.5	0.401217	0.388544	0.841196	0.238095

Table 10.2 presents the mean value of bank-specific variables of the selected banks
Note The data comprises of 330 banks across 29 countries over the period 2002–2013
Source Bankscope and authors' own calculation

banks in Sierra Leone had market shares of about 26%, with banks in Egypt having the lowest market share of about 0.04% in the sample.[1]

Effects of Monetary Policy on Bank Pricing Behaviour

In this sub-section, we analyse the empirical results on monetary policy and banks' pricing behaviour in SSA. Table 10.4 contain the regression results that use bank-specific variables and accounts for countries' interest rates and monetary freedom, level of growth and inflation. The first two columns (columns 1 and 2) relate to the loan price, the next two columns (columns 3 and 4) relate to fees price while the last two (columns 5 and 6) are related to deposit price. The estimations are done using dynamic panel-data estimation technique (System GMM) corrected for Windmeijer standard error, small sample adjustments and orthogonal deviation.

The results show that for the first column, the coefficient of monetary policy variable (money market rate) is positively and significantly affecting loan price. This suggests that when contractionary monetary policy is implemented, commercial banks tend to increase their loan prices, which is intuitive. To be specific, the results show that, for each additional percentage increase in money market interest rate, loan price increase by 0.003%, all else equal. On the other hand, decrease in money market interest rate reduces loan price. For the effect of monetary freedom as an alternative monetary policy measure, the coefficients are negative and statistically significant across all regressions indicating that higher levels of monetary freedom enable banks' loan and fees prices to reduce.[2] Therefore, the results suggest that higher price stability tend to reduce commercial banks' loan and fees prices, all else equal. On the contrary, lower price stability result in banks exhibiting high pricing behaviour. In conclusion, the results support the hypothesis that monetary policy influences banks' pricing behaviour in SSA. The results support the argument that a country's monetary policy does largely determine the evolution of its general pricing behaviour of banks. This is consistent with the findings of Amidu (2006), Ciccarelli et al. (2015) and Iddrisu et al. (2022)

[1] Table 10.3 presents the pair-wise correlation coefficient among the variables in the study.

[2] As stated above, the estimates of columns 6 can however not be relied on since there is an indication of the existence of second order autocorrelation.

Table 10.3 Pair-wise correlation coefficient between selected variables

Variables	*Loan price*	*Fees price*	*Deposit price*	*M. M. I. rate*	*M'try freedom*	*Financial access*	*Financial usage*	*St. Mkt. access*	*Bank age*	*Loan*	*Mkt. share*	*Efficiency*	*Fund source*	*Inflation*	*GDP growth*
Loan price	1														
Fees price	0.16*	1													
Deposit price	0.60*	0.11*	1												
M.M.I. Rate	0.51*	0.19*	0.19*	1											
M'try freedom	−0.40*	−0.19*	−0.24*	−0.79*	1										
Financial access	−0.23*	−0.32*	0.05*	−0.71*	0.10*	1									
Financial usage	−0.27*	−0.14*	−0.002	−0.73*	0.26*	0.79*	1								
St. Mkt. access	0.03	0.07*	0.21*	−0.12*	0.10*	0.03	0.20*	1							
Bank age	0.03	−0.12*	−0.02	−0.25*	−0.004	0.15*	0.27*	0.002	1						
Loan	0.02	−0.17*	0.11*	−0.34*	0.28*	0.30*	0.34*	0.14*	0.17*	1					
Mkt. share	0.02	0.04*	−0.04*	−0.06	−0.01	−0.17*	0.03	−0.04	0.17*	0.14*	1				
Efficiency	−0.03	0.28*	−0.21*	0.16*	0.012	−0.28*	−0.20*	−0.23*	−0.11*	−0.08*	0.05*	1			
Fund source	−0.10*	−0.31*	−0.27*	−0.03	0.01	−0.02	−0.003	−0.01	0.08*	−0.08*	0.17*	−0.06*	1		
Inflation	0.19*	0.08*	0.16*	0.89*	−0.28*	−0.17*	−0.36*	−0.13*	0.03	−0.06*	0.06*	−0.03	−0.04*	1	

Variables	*Loan price*	*Fees price*	*Deposit price*	*M. M. I. rate*	*M'try freedom*	*Financial access*	*Financial usage*	*St. Mkt. access*	*Bank age*	*Loan*	*Mkt. share*	*Efficiency*	*Fund source*	*Inflation*	*GDP growth*
GDP growth	−0.23*	−0.04	−0.20*	0.15*	−0.01	−0.076*	−0.21*	−0.17*	−0.10*	−0.19*	−0.08*	0.08*	0.05*	−0.07*	1

Note Pair-wise correlation coefficient estimated on sample of 330 banks across 29 African countries. *implies significance at 5% or more
Source Bankscope and authors' own calculation

Table 10.4 Monetary policy and bank pricing behavior

Variables	*Loan price*		*Fees price*		*Deposit price*	
	(1)	*(2)*	*(3)*	*(4)*	*(5)*	*(6)*
Loan price-1	0.980***	0.640***				
	(0.050)	(0.113)				
Fees price-1			0.940***	0.506***		
			(0.037)	(0.118)		
Deposit price-1					0.603***	0.392**
					(0.180)	(0.193)
M.M.I. rate	0.003***		−0.000		0.002	
	(0.001)		(0.001)		(0.004)	
Monetary freedom		−0.003***		−0.0004**		−0.001**
		(0.001)		(0.000)		(0.001)
Bank age	−0.000	−0.001	−0.000	−0.000	−0.000	−0.000
	(0.000)	(0.001)	(0.000)	(0.000)	(0.000)	(0.000)
Loan/Total assets	0.041***	0.024	0.005	0.017	0.128**	0.006
	(0.013)	(0.043)	(0.007)	(0.013)	(0.059)	(0.029)
Mkt. share	0.003	−0.013	−0.002	0.041	−0.380**	−0.018
	(0.033)	(0.087)	(0.013)	(0.037)	(0.168)	(0.053)
Efficiency	−0.055***	−0.096***	0.013	−0.015	−0.074	−0.072***
	(0.018)	(0.032)	(0.013)	(0.015)	(0.055)	(0.025)
Funding sources	−0.032	−0.722**	0.009**	−0.033	0.106	−0.115
	(0.026)	(0.322)	(0.004)	(0.043)	(0.114)	(0.127)
Inflation	−0.001	−0.000	0.001	−0.000	−0.001	−0.000
	(0.001)	(0.000)	(0.000)	(0.000)	(0.003)	(0.000)
GDP growth	0.120	0.247	−0.038	−0.034	−0.304	0.050

Variables	*Loan price*		*Fees price*		*Deposit price*	
	(1)	*(2)*	*(3)*	*(4)*	*(5)*	*(6)*
	(0.081)	(0.157)	(0.045)	(0.044)	(0.208)	(0.104)
Observations	341	1,568	337	1,551	328	1,552
No. of instruments	62	45	45	45	45	45
AB2	−0.397	−0.351	0.087	1.579	−1.096	−1.812*
Hansen's Test	57.033	26.788	36.222	45.022	39.804	33.911
F-test	122.648***	12.679***	443.774***	10.081***	11.179***	4.180***

Table 10.4 reports the two-stage system GMM regression result, Windmeijer-corrected standard error, small sample adjustment and orthogonal deviation. Standard errors in parentheses; ***, ** and * indicate statistical significance at 1, 5 and 10%, respectively

who maintained that a change in lending behaviours of banks is greatly influenced by monetary policy of the central banks.

For the controls, the results of loan to total asset are significant showing in columns 1 and 5 that increase in loan/total assets tend to increase loan and deposit prices. This follows logic with the intuition that higher loan and deposit prices trigger the amount of money banks give out as loans for more profit. It is also consistent with findings of Iddrisu and Turkson (2020) and Iddrisu et al. (2022). Market share is also negative and significant in column 5, which indicates that market share increases with decrease in deposit price. The coefficient of efficiency also supports the results of Iddrisu and Turkson (2020) and Iddrisu et al. (2022) as it indicates in columns 1, 2, and 6 that more efficient banks reduce their loan and deposit prices. Coefficient of bank funding sources indicates in column 2 that an increase in the funding sources of banks reduces their loan price but increases the price of fees as in column 3. However, the rest of the controls were not statistically significant across all regressions.

Effects of Bank Pricing Behaviour on Financial Inclusion

On the relationship between financial inclusion and banks' pricing behaviour in SSA, Table 10.5 presents the regression results that use financial inclusion as the dependent variable. The results from the table show a negative and significant (at 1% level) relationship between loan price and financial access and deposit price also has a significant (at 5% level) negative relationship with financial access.[3] These suggest that when loan and deposit prices increase, financial access (bank branches per 100,000 adults) decreases. The finding for loan price supports the work of Iddrisu and Turkson (2020) and it follows logic since an increase in loan price is likely to reduce the number of loan accounts and subsequently the need for more bank branches. The result of deposit price indicates that higher deposit price reduces financial access. This finding is logical because higher deposit prices reduce banks' net interest margins and consequently their ability to open more branches. In other words, high deposit price may not encourage bank branch expansion. In sum,

[3] Here again, there is an indication of the existence of second order autocorrelation in column 8. We therefore, will not rely on those estimates.

Table 10.5 Bank pricing behaviour and financial inclusion

Variables	*Financial usage*			*Financial access*			*Stock market access*		
	(1)	*(2)*	*(3)*	*(4)*	*(5)*	*(6)*	*(7)*	*(8)*	*(9)*
Financial access-1	0.925***	0.919***	0.946***						
	(0.023)	(0.022)	(0.019)						
Financial usage-1				0.750***	0.749***	0.762***			
				(0.024)	(0.028)	(0.027)			
Stock Mkt. access-1							0.892***	0.890***	0.899***
							(0.023)	(0.025)	(0.022)
Loan price	0.146			−1.834***			−0.529		
	(0.400)			(0.551)			(0.971)		
Fees price		0.849			−1.711			3.614**	
		(0.643)			(1.510)			(1.799)	
Deposit price			−0.018			−0.412**			−0.092
			(0.535)			(0.170)			(0.244)
Bank age	0.000	0.000	0.000	0.001	0.001**	0.001	0.001**	0.001*	0.001**
	(0.000)	(0.000)	(0.000)	(0.000)	(0.001)	(0.001)	(0.001)	(0.001)	(0.001)
Loan/Total assets	0.316***	0.331***	0.381***	0.772***	0.629***	0.799***	−0.263	−0.115	−0.168
	(0.107)	(0.108)	(0.104)	(0.106)	(0.111)	(0.109)	(0.273)	(0.264)	(0.301)
Mkt. share	0.251	0.262	0.179	−0.332*	−0.592**	−0.573***	−0.166	−0.400	−0.153
	(0.285)	(0.285)	(0.274)	(0.175)	(0.234)	(0.197)	(0.328)	(0.383)	(0.349)
Efficiency	−0.102	−0.173*	−0.028	−0.223**	−0.327**	−0.466***	−0.424*	−0.661**	−0.652**
	(0.085)	(0.090)	(0.088)	(0.108)	(0.126)	(0.105)	(0.237)	(0.273)	(0.255)

(continued)

Table 10.5 (continued)

Variables	*Financial usage*			*Financial access*			*Stock market access*		
	(1)	*(2)*	*(3)*	*(4)*	*(5)*	*(6)*	*(7)*	*(8)*	*(9)*
Funding sources	−1.034***	−1.123***	−0.744***	−0.343	−0.787**	−0.552*	−0.466	0.971**	−0.744**
	(0.259)	(0.278)	(0.209)	(0.230)	(0.329)	(0.280)	(0.405)	(0.470)	(0.358)
Inflation	0.008***	0.008***	0.008***	0.006***	0.003	0.004**	0.005	0.005	0.002
	(0.001)	(0.001)	(0.001)	(0.002)	(0.002)	(0.002)	(0.006)	(0.006)	(0.005)
GDP growth	−0.793**	−0.662*	−0.932***	0.469	0.132	0.087	4.281***	3.406***	3.360***
	(0.387)	(0.374)	(0.351)	(0.316)	(0.331)	(0.332)	(1.416)	(1.205)	(1.071)
Observations	890	888	884	1,099	1,097	1,092	1,063	1,061	1,056
No. of instruments	155	155	155	207	207	207	173	190	173
AB2	4.123***	4.073***	4.049***	0.785	−0.019	0.223	−3.420***	−3.647***	−3.713***
Hansen's test	147.903	146.608	145.853	190.995	189.074	187.847	185.269	185.853	182.350
F-test	602.561***	568.888***	841.787***	260.433***	187.680***	245.570***	366.684***	282.220***	373.545***

Table 10.5 reports the two-stage system GMM regression result, Windmeijer-corrected standard error, small sample adjustment and orthogonal deviation. Standard errors in parentheses; ***, ** and * indicate statistical significance at 1, 5 and 10%, respectively

our results fail to reject the hypothesis that banks' pricing behaviour influences inclusive finance in SSA. This finding supports the argument that banks' pricing behaviour significantly influences financial inclusion (Dev, 2006).

For the control variables, the banks' age significantly and positively related to financial access (bank branches per 100,000 adults), contrary to that of Iddrisu and Turkson (2020). Loan to total asset is also positive and significant suggesting that an increase in banks' loan portfolio increases financial access, which is intuitive because large loan portfolio will lead to banks' expansion. For market share, the results indicate that higher market share reduces financial access. Again, the results reveal that high banks' efficiency reduces financial access, suggesting that highly efficient banks may not need many bank branches to serve their clients. Results of the bank funding sources indicate in columns 5 and 6 that decrease in funding sources of banks increase financial access. Inflation positively affects financial access in columns 4 and 6, indicating that financial access increases with high inflation level.

Financial Inclusion and Bank Pricing Behaviour: The Role of Monetary Policy

Finally, this sub-section presents evidence of how monetary policy affect inclusive finance conditioned on banks' pricing behaviour. To avoid possible influence of multicollinearity because of the high correlation (0.79) between monetary policy variables (money market interest rate and monetary freedom), we presented the results in two separate tables (Tables 10.6 and 10.7).[4] In Table 10.6, the results of the money market interest rate across all columns show that, all other things being equal, expansionary/contractionary monetary policy tends to increase/decrease financial inclusion. Loan and deposit prices individually exert significantly negative influence on financial access which is in line with the findings in Table 10.5. The results of fees price also suggest that higher fees price discourages account opening and therefore, decreases financial access (number of bank branches). Importantly, in Table 10.6, the coefficients of the interaction terms were all positive and significant, indicating

[4] Again, columns 1, 2, 3, 4 and 11 of Table 10.6 and columns 3, 4, 6, 7, 8, 9, 10, 11 and 12 of Table 10.7 are not relied on because of the existence of second order autocorrelation and/or overidentification of instruments.

Table 10.6 Bank pricing behaviour and financial inclusion: The role of monetary policy (Money market interest rate)

Variables	*Financial usage*				*Financial access*	
	(1)	*(2)*	*(3)*	*(4)*	*(5)*	*(6)*
Financial usage-1	0.880***	0.810***	0.884***	0.864***		
	(0.042)	(0.049)	(0.030)	(0.036)		
Financial access-1					0.242***	0.578***
					(0.082)	(0.075)
Stock market access-1						
M.M.I. rate	−0.063*	−0.087***	−0.072***	−0.054*	−0.121***	−0.120***
	(0.035)	(0.027)	(0.020)	(0.032)	(0.028)	(0.018)
Loan price	0.376			2.325	−18.058***	
	(1.175)			(3.305)	(3.849)	
M.M.I. rate * Loan price	−0.086			−0.323	0.847***	
	(0.138)			(0.254)	(0.236)	
Fees price		−5.542		−6.036		−11.173*
		(3.386)		(4.894)		(5.718)
M.M.I. rate * Fees price		0.254		0.560		0.942***
		(0.235)		(0.381)		(0.328)
Deposit price			0.414	1.858		
			(1.463)	(2.598)		
M.M.I. rate * Deposit price			−0.012	−0.043		
			(0.114)	(0.161)		
Bank age	0.000	0.000	0.001	0.001	−0.001	−0.002***
	(0.001)	(0.001)	(0.001)	(0.001)	(0.001)	(0.000)
Loan/Total assets	0.216	0.118	−0.056	0.035	0.491**	0.460**
	(0.187)	(0.122)	(0.155)	(0.101)	(0.193)	(0.187)

Variables	*Financial usage*				*Financial access*	
	(1)	*(2)*	*(3)*	*(4)*	*(5)*	*(6)*
Efficiency	0.092	0.033	−0.119	−0.002	−0.832***	−0.341
	(0.217)	(0.148)	(0.246)	(0.167)	(0.287)	(0.302)
Funding sources	−0.354*	−0.127	−0.665**	−0.266	0.025	0.320
	(0.210)	(0.208)	(0.295)	(0.425)	(0.286)	(0.216)
Inflation	0.062***	0.064***	0.057***	0.054***	0.039**	0.058***
	(0.019)	(0.017)	(0.016)	(0.017)	(0.015)	(0.011)
GDP growth	1.334*	1.150**	1.341**	1.193	−2.799***	−1.571
	(0.696)	(0.564)	(0.583)	(0.721)	(0.870)	(1.136)
Observations	226	222	216	212	364	360
No. of instruments	64	64	62	80	77	77
AB2	3.714***	3.764***	3.348***	3.146***	−1.219	0.593
Hansen's test	40.485	40.554	38.486	33.733	62.926	64.390
F-test	546.023***	776.526***	700.493***	441.773***	138.619***	190.502***
Variables	*Financial access*		*Stock market access*			
	(7)	*(8)*	*(9)*	*(10)*	*(11)*	*(12)*
Financial usage-1						
Financial access-1	0.461***	0.240***				
	(0.095)	(0.086)				
Stock market access-1			0.974***	0.981***	0.951***	0.967***
			(0.026)	(0.026)	(0.026)	(0.021)
M.M.I. rate	−0.107***	−0.121***	0.015	0.055***	0.087***	0.009
	(0.027)	(0.029)	(0.024)	(0.019)	(0.020)	(0.025)

(continued)

Table 10.6 (continued)

Variables	*Financial access*		*Stock market access*			
	(7)	*(8)*	*(9)*	*(10)*	*(11)*	*(12)*
Loan price		−16.822***	−4.318*			−8.340*
		(3.695)	(2.224)			(4.728)
M.M.I. rate * loan price		0.771*	0.560***			0.829**
		(0.428)	(0.186)			(0.414)
Fees price		8.629		−10.053**		−9.555
		(12.466)		(4.434)		(8.606)
M.M.I. rate * Fees price		−0.588		0.880**		0.614
		(0.781)		(0.339)		(0.549)
Deposit price	−10.446***	−5.054*			−2.275	7.757
	(3.838)	(2.701)			(1.784)	(5.648)
M.M.I. rate * Deposit price	0.866***	0.420*			0.168	−0.677
	(0.307)	(0.244)			(0.146)	(0.471)
Bank age	−0.001	−0.000	−0.001	−0.002*	−0.001	−0.001
	(0.001)	(0.001)	(0.001)	(0.001)	(0.001)	(0.001)
Loan/Total assets	0.749***	0.509***	0.360*	0.449**	0.201	0.283
	(0.281)	(0.161)	(0.200)	(0.186)	(0.262)	(0.205)
Efficiency	−0.644*	−1.083***	−1.208***	−0.990***	−1.361***	−0.783***
	(0.369)	(0.364)	(0.426)	(0.285)	(0.450)	(0.294)
Funding sources	−0.720	−0.427	−0.236	−0.157	−0.094	0.131
	(0.985)	(0.656)	(0.255)	(0.250)	(0.397)	(0.382)
Inflation	0.025	0.034*	−0.071***	−0.078***	−0.092***	−0.060***
	(0.018)	(0.017)	(0.014)	(0.016)	(0.017)	(0.018)
GDP growth	−1.321	−2.222***	0.331	−0.775	−1.052	−1.646*
	(1.126)	(0.826)	(1.106)	(1.102)	(0.953)	(0.972)

Variables	*Financial access*		*Stock market access*			
	(7)	*(8)*	*(9)*	*(10)*	*(11)*	*(12)*
Observations	351	347	364	360	351	347
No. of instruments	76	96	77	77	76	96
AB2	−0.035	−0.430	−0.106	1.589	3.037***	0.356
Hansen's test	64.277	61.075	65.657	65.296	63.710	61.168
F-test	126.661***	80.931***	282.032***	233.609***	314.738***	396.502***

Table 10.6 reports the two-stage system GMM regression result, Windmeijer-corrected standard error, small sample adjustment and orthogonal deviation. Standard errors in parentheses; ***, ** and * indicate statistical significance at 1, 5 and 10% respectively

that high/low banks' pricing in the light of contractionary/expansionary monetary policy tend to increase/decrease financial and stock market access. This means that when there is no liquidity in the system due to monetary policy tightening, people resort to financial institutions for credit regardless of the banks pricing. For stock market access, the reasoning is that, high fee charges by banks may avoid keeping their money in banks but rather participate in holding investments in stocks, even when these prices are induced by contractionary monetary policy.

In Table 10.7, the result with respect to the effect of monetary freedom on financial usage indicates a negative relationship between them. However, the interaction between monetary freedom and banks' loan and fees prices has a significant positive effect on financial usage. This suggests that high bank pricing in the light of high price stability (effective monetary policy framework) tend to increase financial usage.

To conclude, the findings support the hypothesis that the interaction terms (M.M.I rate*Loan Price, M.M.I rate*Fees Price, M.M.I rate*Deposit Price, Monetary freedom*Loan Price, Monetary freedom*Fees Price and Monetary freedom*Deposit Price) significantly affect financial inclusion. Thus, monetary policy plays a role in inclusive finance through banks' pricing behaviour in SSA.

Some covariates such as age of the bank exerts negative and significant effect on financial usage only in column 6. Also, loan to total asset is positive and significant only for columns 5, 6, 7 and 8 under financial usage. This is intuitive because the more banks give out loans, the more clients they will attract leading to banks' expansion. The results also show that more efficient banks have less bank branches. In columns 1 and 3, decrease in the funding sources of banks increases financial access (open more accounts). Inflation positively affects financial inclusion across all columns except column 7, suggesting that high level of inflation increases financial usage and access. Finally, the economic growth variable indicates that high economic growth increases financial access but reduces usage.

10.5 Conclusion and Policy Implications

There is an empirical gap in the literature regarding the nexus between monetary policy and financial inclusion. Whereas there is evidence of monetary policy through banks' pricing influencing non-financial economic activity, little is known about how financial inclusion is affected. This study provides empirical analysis on the effect of monetary policy in

Table 10.7 Bank pricing behaviour and financial inclusion: The role of monetary policy (Monetary freedom)

Variables	*Financial usage*				*Financial access*	
	(1)	*(2)*	*(3)*	*(4)*	*(5)*	*(6)*
Financial usage-1	0.552***	0.626***	0.739***	0.823***		
	(0.123)	(0.117)	(0.049)	(0.042)		
Financial access-1					0.916***	0.888***
					(0.174)	(0.055)
Stock market access-1						
Monetary freedom	−0.070**	−0.043*	−0.028**	−0.052***	−0.104***	−0.036***
	(0.033)	(0.024)	(0.011)	(0.010)	(0.038)	(0.008)
Loan price	−37.502*			−16.515***	−96.420	
	(20.278)			(5.699)	(59.761)	
Monetary freedom * Loan price	0.587**			0.245***	1.184	
	(0.295)			(0.079)	(0.798)	
Fees price		−55.632**		−35.357***		−88.567***
		(27.580)		(11.419)		(23.458)
Monetary freedom * Fees price		0.735**		0.512***		1.202***
		(0.359)		(0.156)		(0.308)
Deposit price			−37.273**	−24.457***		
			(16.351)	(7.443)		
Monetary freedom * Deposit price			0.510**	0.357***		
			(0.231)	(0.108)		
Bank age	0.001	0.001	0.001*	0.001	−0.003	0.000
	(0.002)	(0.001)	(0.001)	(0.001)	(0.002)	(0.001)
Loan/Total assets	0.586	0.602	−0.209	0.127	0.923	0.591**
	(0.833)	(0.719)	(0.182)	(0.131)	(1.549)	(0.235)

(continued)

Table 10.7 (continued)

Variables	*Financial usage*				*Financial access*	
	(1)	*(2)*	*(3)*	*(4)*	*(5)*	*(6)*
Efficiency	−0.006	−0.578	−0.795***	−0.246	2.878	0.079
	(0.894)	(0.965)	(0.271)	(0.210)	(1.793)	(0.289)
Funding sources	−1.886	−2.804**	−1.645***	−0.912***	4.633	0.955
	(1.234)	(1.208)	(0.470)	(0.336)	(3.475)	(0.835)
Inflation	0.003	0.005**	0.005***	0.005***	0.003	−0.001
	(0.003)	(0.002)	(0.002)	(0.001)	(0.005)	(0.002)
GDP growth	0.335	1.036	−1.440**	−0.779**	−3.022	1.275**
	(1.582)	(1.899)	(0.607)	(0.393)	(5.576)	(0.573)
Observations	900	900	894	884	1,115	1,115
No. of instruments	20	20	52	110	16	48
AB2	−0.094	−0.004	0.596	2.266**	−0.709	0.788
Hansen's test	12.808	13.391	70.469***	124.895**	4.147	100.311***
F-test	21.202***	33.095***	174.114***	266.866***	9.319***	144.367***

Variables	*Financial access*		*Stock market access*			
	(7)	*(8)*	*(9)*	*(10)*	*(11)*	*(12)*
Financial usage-1						
Financial access-1	0.806***	0.827***				
	(0.044)	(0.047)				
Stock market access-1			0.554**	0.851***	0.826***	0.751***
			(0.266)	(0.057)	(0.056)	(0.050)
Monetary freedom	−0.012***	−0.039***	0.037	0.045***	0.055***	0.033*
	(0.004)	(0.008)	(0.111)	(0.015)	(0.013)	(0.017)

Variables	*Financial access*		*Stock market access*			
	(7)	*(8)*	*(9)*	*(10)*	*(11)*	*(12)*
Loan price		15.366	23.508			54.652***
		(10.154)	(68.878)			(19.218)
Monetary freedom * Loan price		−0.209	−0.466			−0.824***
		(0.133)	(1.125)			(0.265)
Fees price		−92.045***		61.330		−132.937**
		(20.367)		(42.184)		(54.980)
Monetary freedom * Fees price		1.253***		−0.543		1.931**
		(0.266)		(0.561)		(0.748)
Deposit price	−6.771	−21.007**			12.310	−13.159
	(4.451)	(8.346)			(13.770)	(10.900)
Monetary freedom * Deposit price	0.088	0.273**			−0.160	0.175
	(0.058)	(0.108)			(0.177)	(0.139)
Bank age	−0.000	0.001	0.003	0.001	0.003*	0.004*
	(0.001)	(0.001)	(0.011)	(0.003)	(0.001)	(0.002)
Loan/Total assets	0.984***	0.688***	−0.821	−0.770	−1.344***	−0.688**
	(0.175)	(0.223)	(2.702)	(0.582)	(0.379)	(0.310)
Efficiency	−0.106	−0.039	−0.912	−1.744**	0.268	−0.414
	(0.218)	(0.197)	(9.493)	(0.716)	(0.644)	(0.655)
Funding sources	0.273	0.553	−0.972	0.654	−2.228*	−1.929**
	(0.597)	(0.542)	(30.943)	(1.687)	(1.302)	(0.878)
Inflation	0.003***	0.001	0.008	−0.000	0.011**	0.011**
	(0.001)	(0.002)	(0.013)	(0.005)	(0.005)	(0.005)
GDP growth	1.125**	−0.329	7.231	3.283*	2.314*	2.249**
	(0.491)	(0.428)	(5.296)	(1.754)	(1.305)	(1.086)

(continued)

Table 10.7 (continued)

Variables	*Financial access*		*Stock market access*			
	(7)	*(8)*	*(9)*	*(10)*	*(11)*	*(12)*
Observations	1,106	1,096	1,079	1,077	1,070	1,060
No. of instruments	80	114	16	48	81	115
AB2	0.042	−1.077	−1.710*	−2.076**	−2.408**	−2.804***
Hansen's test	130.24***	168.818***	22.245***	95.288***	154.616***	162.549***
F-test	116.67***	105.172***	4.351***	40.510***	117.665***	93.482***

Table 10.7 reports the two-stage system GMM regression result, Windmeijer-corrected standard error, small sample adjustment and orthogonal deviation. Standard errors in parentheses; ***, ** and * indicate statistical significance at 1, 5 and 10%, respectively

the light of pricing behaviour banks on financial inclusion in SSA. Using panel data of 330 banks in 29 SSA countries from 2002 to 2013, and employing system GMM estimator, the study first examines how monetary policy affects pricing behaviour of banks, second, it examines how the pricing behaviour of banks affects financial inclusion. Finally, it examines the effect of monetary policy on financial inclusion conditioned on the pricing behaviour of banks. Financial inclusion is measured by financial usage and access. Money market interest rate and monetary freedom are used to measure monetary policy, while loan, fees and deposit prices are used to measure the pricing behaviour banks.

The findings were: First, the results suggest that contractionary monetary policy translates to high bank loan price. This result is consistent with the argument that monetary policy of a country does largely determine its general pricing behaviour of banks. Secondly, the study finds that financial access decreases with high loan price. This suggests that the expectation of some clients is to acquire low interest loans to invest. Therefore, high loan price may push them to finding alternative ways to finance their businesses, hence, loan accounts and the need for more bank branches will reduce. Finally, the results also showed that, high banks' pricing in the light of contractionary monetary policy tend to increase financial inclusion. We thus, conclude that in SSA, high banks' pricing (particularly loan price) may decrease financial inclusion, however, when the high pricing behaviour of banks is induced by contractionary monetary policy, financial inclusion increases. On the policy implications monetary policy makers of SSA countries should continue to be mindful of financial inclusion when they are using monetary policy to target other macroeconomic indicators such as inflation.

References

Alvarez, J., & Arellano, M. (2003). The time series and cross-section asymptotics of dynamic panel data estimators. *Econometrica, 71*(4), 1121–1159.

Amidu, M. (2006). The link between monetary policy and banks' lending behaviour: The Ghanaian case. *Banks and Bank Systems, 1*(1), 38–48.

Amidu, M., & Wolfe, S. (2013). The impact of market power and funding strategy on bank-interest margins. *The European Journal of Finance, 19*(9), 888–908.

Ananchotikul, N., & Seneviratne, M. (2015). *Monetary policy transmission in emerging Asia: The role of banks and the effects of financial globalization*. International Monetary Fund.

Ashraf, N., Karlan, D., & Yin, W. (2010). Female empowerment: Impact of a commitment savings product in the Philippines. *World Development*, *38*(3), 333–344.

Blundell, R., & Bond, S. (1998). Initial conditions and moment restrictions in dynamic panel data models. *Journal of Econometrics*, *87*(1), 115–143.

Brewer, III., & Jackson, III. (2006). A note on the "riskadjusted" price–concentration relationship in banking. *Journal of Banking & Finance*, *30*(3), 1041–1054.

Brownbridge, M., Bwire, T., Rubatsimbira, D., & Tinyinondi, G. A. (2017). The impact of financial inclusion on the interest rate channel of the monetary policy transmission mechanism. *Bank of Uganda, Working Paper Series*, (05).

Ciccarelli, M., Maddaloni, A., & Peydró, J. L. (2015). Trusting the bankers: A new look at the credit channel of monetary policy. *Review of Economic Dynamics*, *18*(4), 979–1002.

Cook, T., & Hahn, T. (1989). The effect of changes in the federal funds rate target on market interest rates in the 1970s. *Journal of Monetary Economics*, *24*(3), 331–351.

Cúrdia, V., & Woodford, M. (2016). Credit frictions and optimal monetary policy. *Journal of Monetary Economics*, *84*, 30–65.

Das, M. S. (2015). *Monetary policy in India: Transmission to bank interest rates*. International Monetary Fund.

Dell'Erba, S., & Sola, S. (2016). Does fiscal policy affect interest rates? Evidence from a factor-augmented panel. *The BE Journal of Macroeconomics*, *16*(2), 395–437.

Dev, S. M. (2006). Financial inclusion: Issues and challenges. *Economic and Political Weekly*, *41*, 4310–4313.

Evans, O. (2016). The effectiveness of monetary policy in Africa: Modeling the impact of financial inclusion. *Iranian Economic Review*, *20*(3), 327–337.

Friedman, B. M. (1999). The future of monetary policy: The central bank as an army with only a signal corps? *International Finance*, *2*(3), 321–338.

Iddrisu, A. G., Andani, A., & Abor, J. Y. (2022). Effective monetary policy, bank pricing behavior and human development in Africa. *International Banking, Accounting and Finance*, *13*(1), 61–87.

Iddrisu, A. G., & Turkson, F. E. (2020). Political business cycles, bank pricing behaviour and financial inclusion in Africa. *Cogent Economics & Finance*, *8*(1), 1762286.

Kelilume, I. (2014). Effects of the monetary policy rate on interest rates in Nigeria. *The International Journal of Business and Finance Research*, *8*(1), 45–55.

Kleimeier, S., & Sander, H. (2006). Expected versus unexpected monetary policy impulses and interest rate pass-through in Euro-zone retail banking markets. *Journal of Banking & Finance, 30*(7), 1839–1870.

Kovanen, A. (2011). *Monetary policy transmission in Ghana: Does the interest rate channel work?* (IMF Working Paper, WP/11/275).

Lapukeni, A. F. (2015). The impact of financial inclusion on monetary policy effectiveness: The case of Malawi. *International Journal of Monetary Economics and Finance, 8*(4), 360–384.

Lenka, S. K., & Bairwa, A. K. (2016). Does financial inclusion affect monetary policy in SAARC countries? *Cogent Economics & Finance, 4*(1), 1127011.

Ma, Y., & Lin, X. (2016). Financial development and the effectiveness of monetary policy. *Journal of Banking & Finance, 68*, 1–11.

Mang'ang'a, S. R. (2014). *The effect of monetary and fiscal policy on interest rates in Kenya* (Doctoral dissertation, University of Nairobi).

Mbutor, M. O., & Uba, I. A. (2013). The impact of financial inclusion on monetary policy in Nigeria. *Journal of Economics and International Finance, 5*(8), 318–326.

Mehrotra, A. N., & Yetman, J. (2015, March). Financial inclusion-issues for central banks. *BIS Quarterly Review*, 83–96.

Radecki, L. J., & Reinhart, V. (1994). The financial linkages in the transmission of monetary policy in the United States. *National differences in interest rate transmission* (pp. 291–337). Bank for International Settlements.

Roodman, D. (2009). How to do xtabond2: An introduction to difference and system GMM in Stata. *The Stata Journal, 9*(1), 86–136.

Windmeijer, F. (2005). A finite sample correction for the variance of linear efficient two-step GMM estimators. *Journal of Econometrics, 126*(1), 25–51.

PART IV

Structured Finance, Sustainable Finance and Islamic Banking

CHAPTER 11

Structured Finance in Africa

Ashenafi Fanta, Michael Graham, and Daniel Asante-Amponsah

11.1 Introduction

Over the years, the financial intermediation role played by financial intuitions has evolved with the development of complex financial solutions to meet the growing and complex needs of businesses, projects, and governments. Indeed, for many organizations and projects, traditional or conventional lending tools, based on the conditions and strength of the borrower, have been sufficient. However, the inability of traditional financing mechanisms to address the complex and changing financing

A. Fanta (✉) · M. Graham
University of Stellenbosch Business School, Cape Town, South Africa
e-mail: ashenafi@usb.ac.za

M. Graham
e-mail: michael.graham@usb.ac.za

D. Asante-Amponsah
PwC Ghana, Accra, Ghana

J. Y. Abor and C. K. D. Adjasi (eds.), *The Economics of Banking and Finance in Africa*, Palgrave Macmillan Studies in Banking and Financial Institutions, https://doi.org/10.1007/978-3-031-04162-4_11

needs of businesses and governments has led to the emergence of structured finance solutions. As indicated in the literature, structured finance solutions encompass all advanced private and public financial arrangements that refinance and hedge any profitable economic activity in an efficient way beyond the scope of on-balance sheet securities at a lower capital cost. These involve a combination of traditional asset classes with contingent claims. Applying structured finance solutions enables entities in need of complex financing solutions to raise funding based on cash flow prospects of projects or assets and not on the financial strength of the borrower. There is a thin line between conventional finance and structured finance because of the flexible nature of structured finance. Despite this, a functional differentiation must be made. In this chapter, we do not only present such a distinction between the two but also respond to some burgeoning question on structured finance in Africa. These include:

- What is the state of the structured finance market in Africa?
- What prominent structured finance techniques are in use across Africa?
- What are the requisite conditions for the structured finance market to grow in Africa?

The rest of the chapter is structured as follows: Sects. 11.2 and 11.3 discuss conventional finance and structured finance, respectively. Section 11.4 presents the general structuring process. In Sects. 11.5 and 11.6, the chapter discusses the incipient structured finance market in Africa and the requisite conditions to support its development, respectively. Section 11.7 concludes the chapter.

11.2 Conventional Financing

In contemporary times, the ability to provide a sufficient source of financing that is tailored to the needs of a firm can be challenging. This is due to the changing nature of operating activities as a result of internal and external factors. In order to address the challenges that hinder the ability to secure appropriate forms of financing for firms of all categories, there is a need to understand the nature of the firm in question. A firm is, essentially, a nexus of contracts that transfigures defined inputs into outputs (Culp, 2006; Jensen & Meckling, 1976). The transformation

Table 11.1 Economic balance sheet of the firm

Real Capital	Financial Capital	
Assets	Unsecured Debt	↑ Seniority
	Common Stock	

process requires capital which can be in two distinct forms. Firstly, capital can be deemed as a factor of production and plays the role of an asset that facilitates the transformation process. Thus, the value of assets is derived from the firm's ability to use capital efficiently to generate cash flows over time. In order to acquire assets necessary for the transformation process, there is the need to allocate the risks associated with these assets among a pool of investors by issuing securities. The other form is the accumulation of capital through the issuance of a combination of equity and debt securities (the second type of capital) to finance assets and the transformation processes. Table 11.1 depicts the firm's sources and the usage of capital.

In order to elucidate the issues that arise from business financing using the second type of capital, we assume a simple case of the representative firm's assets being funded by a single class of unsecured debt and a single class of common equity. This is depicted in the economic (mark-to-market) balance sheet[1] of the firm in Table 11.1. In the table, real capital includes all physical assets used by the firm to generate cash flows while financial capital is the sum of the market value of shareholders' equity and the market value of debt. It is assumed here that the financial capital is unsecured on the real assets of the firm. Consequently, should the firm become insolvent, debt holders have a senior claim on the firm's assets. Thus, when the firm's assets are sold off, should such an event eventuate, the proceeds would first be used to retire the debts on a pro rata basis. The residual claimants (common shareholders) receive a share of

[1] Note that the economic or mark-to-market balance sheet of the firm is not an accounting concept. Typically, items that would be considered "off balance sheet" under accounting rules would be captured in the economic balance sheet.

the liquidated assets only when the value of the assets exceeds the total value of debts. In this setting, all the firm's risks arising from its assets are transferred from the firm as a legal entity to the two categories of security holders (debt and equity).

We further assume that the single class of unsecured debt in Table 11.1 is a zero-coupon bond, where both the interest and principal are paid at the end of the investment period. This could invariably lead to certain concerns with regard to postponing consumption in the current period for a higher consumption at the end of the investment, given the inherent risk involved.[2] There is also the concern of whether or not the representative investor is aware of the true risk of the investment. Questions that arise from this concern include the following: what if the return expected on the debt is too low for the debt investors or too high for the firm? Is there any information gap between the firm's investment decisions and the goal of investors, with a potential instance of adverse selection that may occur in such financing arrangement? In this context, the buyer of a security does not know the true value of the security, but the issuer is aware of such value.

According to Myers (1984) and Myers and Majluf (1984), information asymmetry between corporate insiders and investors about the true quality of the firm's real investments may lead investors to assume that the firm's managers only raise new funds from the market when they have bad news about an investment. Further, Fama and French (2002, 2004) suggest that the financing decision is impacted by adverse selection costs. This shows up in heightening investor concerns about the financial status of the firm when they cannot verify costlessly the quality of a firm's investment decisions. It reduces the price investors would be willing to pay for new securities issued by the firm and they would demand a discount on the corporate securities. The firm, thus, has two choices: issue new securities at a discount (they know the value of the security) or avoid such financing models. The likely scenario is the latter where a firm embraces securities that can be issued to the market at a cost of capital that matches the true risk profile of the firm. In addition, the representative firm will opt, wherever possible, to signal its financial health with corporate financing decisions, thereby reducing the adverse selection cost of issuing securities in certain markets.

[2] It is also possible that the firm may question whether the instrument used is an effective financing solution for the projects undertaken by it.

The foregoing suggests that the representative firm will need to devise innovative financing solutions to reduce adverse selection possibility in new security offerings. This implies providing a structure of the debt that matches the needs of investors. For example, the new financing solution may cater for a class of investors who have a preference for a higher expected return even at the cost of higher risk as well as investors whose investment outcomes are contingent on the payoff of the firm's project. The structure of such a deal would be more sophisticated than the financing product depicted in Table 11.1. This brings to the fore the utilization of structured financing solutions, using non-traditional methods, to reduce the adverse selection problems.

We next discuss structured finance solutions, whose specific examples include receivables securitization, trade finance, and project finance.

11.3 What Is Structured Finance?

Structured finance is, essentially, an off-balance-sheet contractual arrangement. It is designed as a tool to finance a specified asset, or an isolated pool of assets or cash flow stream. This financing technique can also be conceptualized as a "nexus of contracts" put together to restrain asymmetric information problems, alleviate agency conflicts, and stimulate risk sharing between borrowers and lenders (see Caselli & Gatti, 2005; Corielli et al., 2010). In structured finance, financial engineering of a firm's liabilities is applied to achieve specific financing and/or risk management objectives of a single or a group of borrowers or to meet the risk-return preferences of target investors. This includes altering the risk profile of the firm and raising funds at a cost that is independent of the firm's overall risk profile.

The extant literature suggests that structured finance techniques can be used in a variety of ways including funding projects which otherwise could not be financed, lowering cost of capital, allowing originators to maintain their financial flexibility, and promoting efficient risk sharing (see e.g., Caselli & Gatti, 2005; Fabozzi et al., 2006; Leland, 2007). In the example of the zero-coupon bond assumed in Table 11.1, it may well be that a target debt investor prefers risk-return characteristics that are different from what the firm is offering. In this instance, the design of financial capital claims may be insufficient. Consequently, the firm's assets must be repackaged with an end goal of meeting the defined objectives of the firm undertaking the structuring. With such structuring, it is seen that the corporate financial structure goes beyond the basic debt-equity choice mix and encompasses, within the debt claims class, security design features, for example maturity structures and placement, as is the case of normal corporate bond issuances *vis-à-vis* structured finance transactions.

Referring to the firm as the issuer or originator in a structured financing deal, we now have a working definition of structured finance as follows[3]:

> … techniques employed whenever the requirements of the originator or the owner of an asset, be they concerned with funding, liquidity, risk transfer, or other need, cannot be met by an existing, off-the-shelf product or instrument. Hence, to meet this requirement, existing products and techniques must be engineered into a tailor-made product or process. Thus, structured finance is a flexible financial engineering tool. (Fabozzi et al., 2006)

Using the above definition and the economic balance sheet of the firm as illustrative device, we next discuss the various forms of structured finance deals and the typical motivations for originators to undertake them. This discussion is largely based on Culp (2006).

Securing Specific Liabilities with Specific Assets

It can be suggested that the issuance of secured debt provides an elementary form of structured finance. In Table 11.2, we can observe that the firm issues secured liabilities by setting some identifiable assets aside as collateral to back the cash flows on specific secured liabilities. The intent of the provision of collateral is to secure the performance of the liabilities. Lenders, generally, match the type of collateral with the liability, with the useful life of the collateral typically exceeding the term of the liability. Thus, the quality of the collateral is important and tests are performed to examine whether or not the collateral meets the criteria of the lender. Additionally, lenders discount the value of the collateral so that it does not reflect a hundred percent of its highest market value (loan-to-value ratio). Moreover, lenders have a perfected security interest in the collateral assets. As priority lien holders, this guarantees the proportion of asset value due to them in the event of any foreclosure proceeds.

[3] It is important to note that structured finance does not have a universal definition.

Table 11.2 Economic balance sheet of a firm with secured claims

Real Capital	Financial Capital
Collateral Assets	Secured Liabilities
Residual Assets	Unsecured Debt
	Common Stock

Seniority

One of the key reasons why a firm may engage in asset repackaging of this nature is to promote a form of credit enhancement. This is arrived at by the pledging of a specific asset or a collection of assets as collateral against the performance of specified liabilities. This implies that investors in these secured liabilities are eliminated from the seniority line in the firm's typical capital structure. This situation is valuable in a non-M&M world[4]; that is, securing the performance of specified assets is advantageous to the firm, is critical to place liability, or both. For example, information asymmetries are stumbling blocks for counterparties to monitor the firm's ability to honor long-term commitments (e.g., long-dated swaps and derivatives). In order to bridge the information asymmetry gap, the firm sets aside a percentage of its assets as collateral covenanted to ensure performance on the corresponding secured liabilities.

Asset Securitization

In this section we discuss asset securitization, distinct from secured liabilities, as a second form of structured finance. Assets securitization and secured liabilities are alike in many respects and the motivations that

[4] The Modigliani-Miller (1958) capital structure theorem suggests that the capital structure of a company does not affect its overall value.

underline the isolation of assets are similar. However, there are important structural differences between them.

In asset securitization, the firm disposes off some specified real assets. As shown in Table 11.3, the purchasing entity finances this pool of asset acquisition by issuing new securities whose principal and interest obligations are backed by the newly acquired assets as collateral and any form of credit enhancement provided by third parties. The underlying assumption here is that the money received is used by the original firm to retire a corresponding amount of debt, consequently shrinking its balance sheet. As can be observed, there is a noticeable similarity between the first instance of isolating specific assets as collateral for new security issues (see Table 11.2) and this instance of arranging a sale of the same assets for cash, with the new owners of the asset issuing new securities collateralized by those assets. Nevertheless, there are some important distinctions between the two approaches that must be discussed.

First, the purpose of achieving a "true sale" of the assets by the original owner in order to ensure the bankruptcy remoteness of the assets from the rest of the firm may not be served by using them as collateral on a secured liability. This is because the collateral assets will remain on the firm's balance sheet. The second distinction between the two forms of structured finance relates to achieving a credit rating for the disposed asset that is independent and, potentially, higher than the firm's credit risk and credit rating. The independent credit ratings, in most cases, are achieved only when the assets are first sold. Third, asset securitization is a conduit through which the firm can effectively shrink its balance sheet, decrease leverage or increase debt capacity. When the firm pledges assets as collateral against a security issue, it does not necessarily accomplish any of these objectives.

The vehicle through which information asymmetry between corporate insiders and outside investors can be reduced suggests a fourth distinction between isolating specific assets as collateral for new security issues and arranging a sale of the same assets for cash, and then issuing new securities collateralized by the assets. Where investors are unable to monitor or verify costlessly the quality of a firm's investment decisions, repackaging the asset can greatly improve the transparency and verifiability of a given pool of assets. That can more definitely be accomplished when the assets are sold to a new entity and are taken off the balance sheet of the original asset owner.

Table 11.3 Economic balance sheet of a firm with asset securitization

(a) Before Securitization

Original Asset Owner

Real Capital	**Financial Capital**
Assets	Unsecured Debt
	Common Stock

Seniority

Seniority

(b) After Securitization

Original Asset Owner

Real Capital	**Financial Capital**
Assets	Unsecured Debt
	Common Stock

Seniority

Third Party

Real Capital	**Financial Capital**
Securitized Assets	Securitized Products (Liabilities)

Ring-Fencing Assets

Ring-fencing assets, an alternative method of asset repackaging, encompasses the creation of a separate legal entity by isolating specific assets or even a whole line of business inside the firm. The new legal entity may take two forms. It may be a wholly owned subsidiary of the parent company or may be financed in whole or part by external investors. This is demonstrated in Table 11.4, where the parent company retains a substantial equity interest in the subsidiary. Thus, the new legal entity remains consolidated on the parent company's economic balance sheet. However, the new legal entity has the possibility to issue debt backed by the new ring-fenced assets.

The advantages of this sort of arrangement can be viewed from numerous contexts. For instance, there are cases where specific assets of a firm pose specific risks to the firm. Such risks do not automatically influence the decisions of the holding firms to sell such assets off. Alternatively, these assets may be thought of as deserving better creditworthiness than the firm can achieve. Ring-fencing such assets in a bankruptcy-remote enterprise in such situations provides an effective solution.

Reducing Agency Cost and Meeting Specific Investor Demand

Firms may be subjected to high agency cost due to the remoteness of managers and security holders. In such a situation, structuring on the liability side of the economic balance sheet to mitigate such agency cost may be beneficial to the various security holders and also enhance the credibility of management.

With the assumed zero-coupon bond in Table 11.1, we noted that the expected return on the bond may be different from the risk-return characteristics investors may have in mind. Investors who view such investments as too risky may not wish to invest in the company. For example, institutional investors have constraints, in terms of risk-return characteristics, of securities they invest in and would not patronize any that are not of a specific investment grade or do not have principal protection over returns. Thus, designing securities to meet their demand would be necessary, especially for large-scale projects that require a larger amount of financing, and as such, institutional investors become the appropriate alternative source of financing. Generally, a better design of securities to

Table 11.4 Economic balance sheet of a firm with ring-fenced business

(a) Before Ring-Fencing

Original Asset Owner

Real Capital	Financial Capital
Assets	Unsecured Debt
	Common Stock

Seniority

Seniority

(b) After Ring-Fencing

Original Asset Owner

Real Capital	Financial Capital
Assets	Unsecured Debt
	Common Stock

Seniority

Third Party

Real Capital	Financial Capital
Ring-Fenced Assets	New Debt
	Stock Held by Parent Company

meet investor demand may also result in a relatively lower cost of capital for the firm.

11.4 The Structuring Process

The preceding sections discussed investor needs and preferences which, to a large extent, influence the development of structured financing solutions. In the case of the zero-coupon bond, as explained above, it can be suggested that the return may be low for the investors. Perhaps, investors may have a preference for a higher expected return, even at the cost of higher risk, because their portfolios are completely diversified. We also noted that structured finance may bring about a lower cost of capital for the firm.

The "structurer" must understand the issues at hand and design a bespoke product that provides a solution that meets the needs of the two parties (the providers of finance and borrowers). There are different parts of the structuring process, with each part varying in complexity and importance depending on the type of structuring problem. Obviously, one must respond to the question of why structured finance techniques are proposed instead of using traditional finance techniques and/or risk transfer. Given the specific needs of firms, the response to this question is expected to differ. We, thus, provide an overview of the structuring process.

Structuring a financial product is about the design of three vital objects (see Cherubini & Lunga, 2007). The initial choice is centered on the set of maturity dates that represent the due dates of the cash flow payments, $\{t_1, t_2, \ldots t_n\}$. The second and third relate to the design of a set of cash flows reflecting interest payments to be made on the capital, $\{c_1, c_2, \ldots c_n\}$, (*waterfalls*) and the debt repayment plan, $\{k_1, k_2, \ldots, k_n\}$. Rules determining each one of these must be in place to allow for an unambiguous definition of each. Generally, these may either be deterministic or stochastic. For example, the structurer can design a deterministic payment schedule in accordance with standard amortizing schedules on a set of predefined maturities. On the other hand, the design of the rules for stochastic payments, where the creative nature of the structurer function comes into play, may involve coupon payments being contingent on varied risk factors.

The structurer must also determine the specific type of risk exposure characterizing the financial product and address three fundamental questions. First, what are the technical features, or the risk profile, of the product (e.g., the kind of risk factors, the sensitivity to the identified risk factors, and the dimensions of the risk factors)? Second, the structurer must ascertain if there is a class of investors or borrowers that may, potentially, be interested in the risk profile of the product (the demand side of the structured product). In addition, the structurer must determine if it is possible for the investor or borrower to realize the same risk profile, in an alternative, relatively cheaper way. That is, an assessment must be made of the competitors of the product. The next section discusses the specific example of non-traditional methods used to reduce the adverse selection costs embedded in project finance and trade finance.

Project Finance

Among the alternative applications of structured finance, the technique may be used to finance large-scale and capital-intensive investments (e.g., power plants, toll roads, industrial plants) such that the lenders to the project would be content with looking to the cash flow from the project being financed as a source of funds for reimbursement (principal plus interest) rather than the entity seeking to access the funding. Such projects are highly levered and the project's assets serve as collateral. This is known as project finance and the arrangement is an off-balance sheet non-recourse financing one. The financial objectives of the financing arrangement are accomplished through the use of a special purpose vehicle. We present in Fig. 11.1 a sample structure.

Due to its contractual peculiarities, project finance arrangements are also useful in separating sponsors' credit risk from the project's (Gatti et al., 2013; John & John, 1991). The economic drivers for using the project finance technique include decreases in the funding cost brought about by the mitigation of the deadweight costs of principal-agent conflicts and asymmetric information problems, and the safeguarding of project sponsors' financial flexibility (see Corielli et al., 2010; Esty, 2004; Kleimeier & Megginson, 2000).

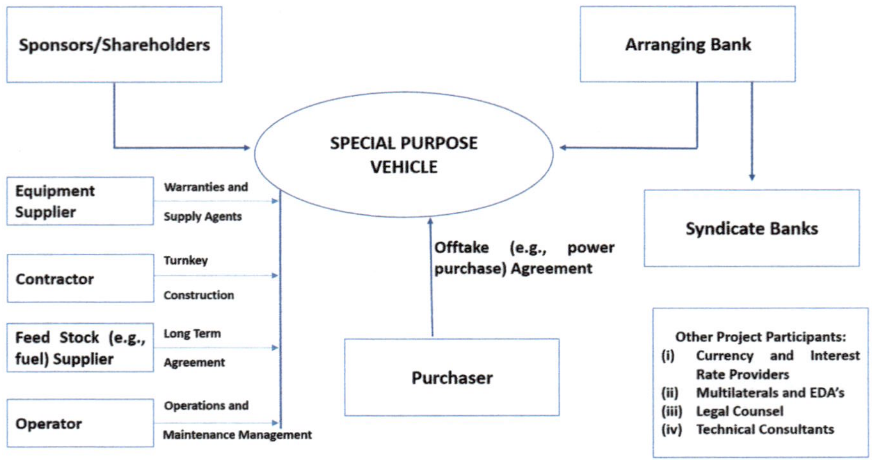

Fig. 11.1 A sample structure of project financing arrangement (*Source* Giddy [2003])

Structured Trade Finance

Structured trade finance, an alternative to conventional lending, is a form of debt finance which aims to promote trade by using non-standard security. It can be defined as *the art of transferring risks (credit risk mainly) in trade financing from parties less able to bear those risks to those more equipped to bear them in a manner that ensures automatic reimbursement of the advances from the underlying assets. Such assets include inventory and export receivables* (UNCTAD, 2001). The architecture of structured trade finance is formulated so that doing business across different borders and specific country risk may be diminished. In these transactions, the strength of the borrower is not in focus compared to a conventional loan. Rather, lenders look at the structure and underlying cash flows. Also, the structures in structured trade finance deals aim to provide an enhanced security mechanism, to act as an improvement on the borrower's position. This is done by segregating the assets that have relatively predictable cash flows and pricing from the perspective of the lender. This enables the corporate borrower to mitigate risk associated with the investment which enables them to secure credit from a lender as and when needed. Among others, there are two important characteristics of structured trade finance that can be noted. First, these arrangements ensure automatic reimbursement of the financier (automatic repayments through deductions at source), if the transaction proceeds normally. Second, such deals guarantee that should anything go wrong, the financier has recourse to some assets as collateral (usually commodities). As with any structured finance product, these financing arrangements are tailored for specific needs of the client.

Structured trade finance products vary and extend across the supply chain, from raw material purchase to customer delivery, to facilitate production and trading activities. They include uncommitted trade facilities, inventory finance, pre-export finance, countertrade, tolling financing, accounts receivable financing, and borrowing base facilities.

- **Uncommitted trade facilities**: This is an agreement between funds providers and users or borrowers where the funds providers (lenders) agree to make short-term funding available to the borrower (user) without clearly defined terms and conditions;
- **Inventory finance**: It is sourcing for funds to pay for the products and consumables for the firm's warehouse. The sources of financing

are collateralized by the products and consumables. This source of financing is mostly used by smaller entities.

- **Pre-export finance**: This involves the request for financing to produce goods for the purpose of exporting. The borrower seeks for funding for goods against proven orders from overseas buyers.
- **Countertrade**: It is a reciprocal form of international trade in which commodities are exchanged for other commodities rather than foreign currency. This type of trade is very common among developing economies with limited foreign exchange.
- **Tolling financing**. A source of financing secured for the construction of roads. The road tolls collected serve as the cash flows to retard the loans and form of collateral.
- **Accounts receivable financing**. This is a form of financing where a firm enters into an agreement that involves the firm obtaining early payment on its invoices outstanding. The accounts receivable serve as assets that may be, at least, equal to the outstanding balances of the billed invoices.
- **Borrowing Base facilities** are types of trade finance or working capital that are structured on the principle that the value of money a borrower can borrow is based on the value of a particular pool of assets held by the company, which is referred to as the "borrowing base".

11.5 Structured Finance Markets in Africa

Despite important strides many African countries have made in reducing poverty and improving quality of life over the last decade, recent years have seen reversals in the trends engendered by a pandemic that imposed an unprecedented burden on the economy and society. Although there is no silver bullet to guide Africa out of the dire situation, empirical evidence suggests that investment in infrastructure such as transport, energy, water, and ICT is likely to help in economic recovery by boosting private sector activity as well as attracting foreign direct investment. Given that Africa has a large infrastructure gap estimated by the African development bank at US$130–170 billion a year, the continent will make a significant gain by investing in infrastructure. However, the infrastructure financing gap to the tune of US$68–108 billion is a major setback.

In economies where the financial sector is well-developed, the domestic financial market serves as a primary source of funding for infrastructure projects. In those markets, funding can be raised using traditional sources such as syndicated loans and infrastructure bonds as well as innovative techniques such as structured finance. Prominent among structured finance techniques are project finance and securitization. Both project finance and securitization necessitate a special purpose vehicle (SPV), albeit with different purposes. In securitization, the SPV is needed to issue asset-backed securities to the investment community whereas in project finance the SPV's mandate goes beyond raising debt. The SPV serves as a project implementing entity by concluding contractual agreements with stakeholders such as Engineering, Procurement, and Construction (EPC) contractors, suppliers, Off-takers (buyers), operation and maintenance (O&M) contractors, etc. The other difference between the two SPVs lies in the fact that while project finance SPV can raise funds through equity and debt, a securitization SPV mainly depends on sales of asset-backed securities (mainly bonds or other debt securities) to investors. The two also differ by their time span.

The structured finance market emerged as an alternative avenue to raise funding when doing so is expensive or the funding is unavailable. The market was created due to regulatory constraints imposing restrictions on the ability of a bank to invest in certain asset classes. While project finance was popularized in the UK, securitization has its roots in the US. Securitization reached its peak prior to the global financial crisis but the market almost collapsed following the mortgage market meltdown. In Africa, development of the structured finance market took a different trend depending on the level of economic development of a country and its financial sector sophistication. For instance, while countries such as South Africa exhibit a greater degree of financial sophistication with a more conducive environment for structured finance transactions, others lack the requisite legal and institutional framework to execute successful structured finance transactions. Discussed in the ensuing paragraphs are the origins, trends, and challenges in project finance and securitization markets in the continent.

Project Finance Market in Africa

The evolution of a project finance market in Africa dates back to the establishment of oil and gas projects sponsored by big energy companies based in North America and Europe. Notable among such projects is the Chad-Cameroon Petroleum Development and Pipeline Project in which US-based ExxonMobil and Chevron participated as sponsors and off-takers. The project was the culmination of years of oil exploration by the energy companies in Chad since the 1970s and it bore fruit only in 2000 through funding from the International Finance Corporation (the World Bank Group). Subsequent years have seen project finance deals in the oil and gas sector in a number of Central and West African countries.

Figure 11.2 traces the trends in value and number of project finance transactions in Africa compared to the world. One can note disparity in the trends between the global and the African project finance market. The global project finance market has been rapidly expanding with the number of deals more than doubled and transaction values tripled between 2003 and 2007. The 2007/2008 financial crisis was a major blow to the global project finance market as both the values and number of transactions exhibited a significant decline afterward. In Africa, on the other hand, the increase in the number of transactions is unremarkable. Generally, the continent exhibited a sluggish growth as evidenced by 14 project finance

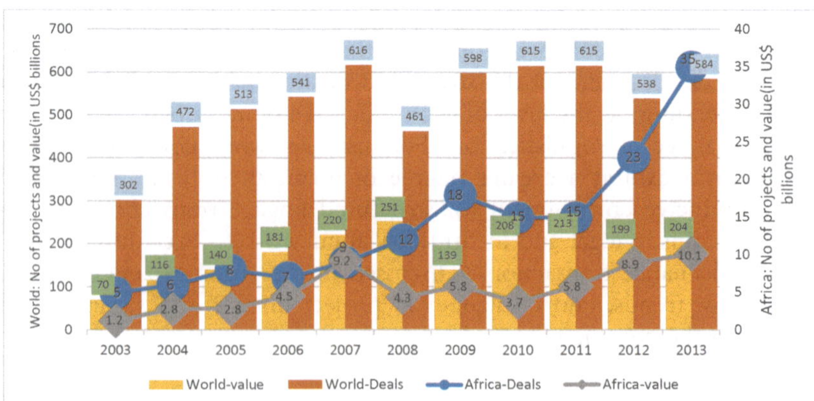

Fig. 11.2 Project finance deals and value: Africa vs World (*Source* Authors' own rendition based on data from Dornel [2014])

deals a year compared to the annual average of 532 projects globally. Similarly, in terms of value, contracts with an average value of US$176 billion were concluded globally compared to US$5 billion in Africa.

Another notable difference in the project finance market in Africa relates to sectoral composition. While projects in Europe and North America are investments in infrastructure assets in sectors such as transportation and power as well as industrial projects, project finance deals in Africa mostly focus on natural resources, with oil and gas being the most prominent ones, followed by mining. Such projects are a commonplace, particularly in Central and West African countries. For instance, Angola, Cameroon, Gabon, and Cote d'Ivoire hosted a handful of projects in the oil and gas sector. There is a notable disparity even within Africa, with central and western African economies having more resource-based projects while countries in East Africa had infrastructure projects (Fig. 11.3).

However, project finance exhibits a different level of development in each country. We present in the following paragraphs the development of the project finance market in three selected countries, namely South

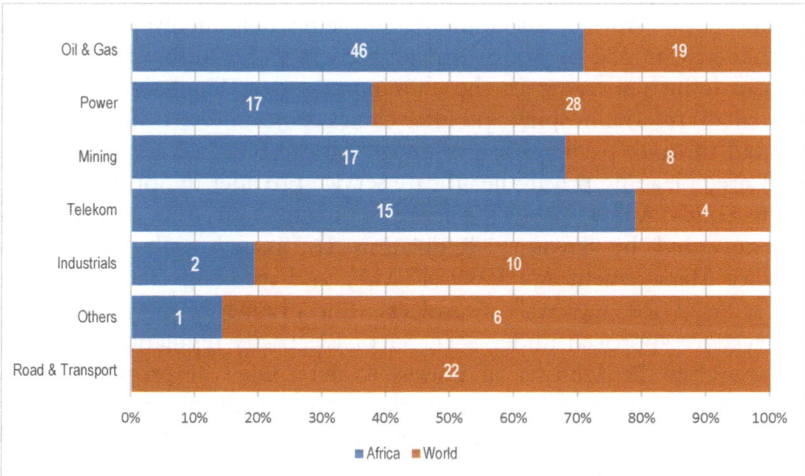

Fig. 11.3 Project finance transactions in Africa and the world (2003–2013) (*Source* Authors' own rendition based on data from Dornel [2014])

Africa, Nigeria, and Egypt, for which we could obtain information about their respective markets.

South Africa

South Africa has the most mature project finance market in Africa and as such the country has successfully implemented a number of project finance transactions over the past few decades in the health, transport, and energy sector. Notable transactions include the Inkosi Albert Luthuli Hospital PPP project implemented right after the country introduced a PPP law in 1999. The hospital is the first PPP project in the health care sector in Africa; it attracted local and international firms that participated as lenders, sponsors, and suppliers. South Africa also successfully rolled out PPP projects in the energy sector through Independent Power Producer (IPP) contracts supplying renewable energy to the power utility. Over the last two decades, the country closed renewable energy IPPs with over US$10 billion investment. In addition, the Gautrain light train project, completed prior to World Cup 2010, is another example of a project finance transaction in South Africa.

Interestingly, the South African project finance market also covered projects in neighboring countries such as Mozambique and Lesotho. For instance, the Mozal project in Mozambique that involved aluminium smelter was funded by South African lenders and sponsored by a South African industrial leader in the aluminium sector. Similarly, the Queen Mamahato referral hospital and filter clinics project in Lesotho was implemented through participation of South African financial institutions and NetCare, a leading private healthcare service provider in South Africa.

In South Africa, project finance transactions in the public sector are governed by Treasury Regulation 16, issued under the Public Finance Management Act 1999 (PFMA), and sector-specific regulations are referred for approval of projects. For instance, renewable energy projects are approved under Sect. 34 of Electricity regulation Act 2006 that requires the Minister of Energy to determine the propriety of the proposed project in terms of technology, number of megawatts, identity of the procurer, and the off-taker. For private sector projects, approval will be made by the relevant government body that regulates the sector. For instance, projects in the extractive industry are regulated by the Mineral and Petroleum Resources Development Act 2002.

A highly sophisticated financial sector provides South Africa an edge over other countries in the region in attracting project finance transactions. The country has more developed financial markets and institutions than both Nigeria and Egypt. As shown in Fig. 11.4, the indices for overall financial development as well as financial markets and institutions are by far greater than the two comparator countries. South Africa has better funded institutional investors, namely insurance companies and pension funds that participate in project finance markets by investing on long-term securities issued by project companies. This is evident from Global Financial Development data (World Bank, 2021) that shows that pension fund asset to GDP for South Africa stands at 99.7% compared to 1.8% for Egypt and 5.6% for Nigeria. Similarly, while insurance company assets to GDP for South Africa stand at 69%, the figure for Egypt is 2.4% and that for Nigeria is 0.96%. This implies that while institutional investors in South Africa are in a better position to actively participate in the project finance market, those in Egypt and Nigeria lack funding to invest in project-related assets that require investment with a long-term maturity.

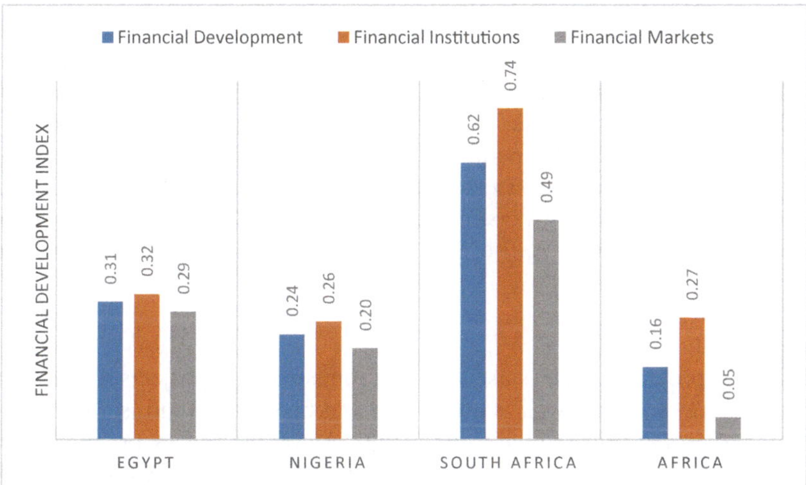

Fig. 11.4 Financial development in South Africa vs Egypt and Nigeria (*Source* Authors' own rendition based on IMF Financial Development Index [see Svirydzenka, 2016])

Nigeria
Project finance is used in Nigeria mostly to finance investment in infrastructure and specifically energy. In addition, public–private partnership (PPP) contracts have been rolled out by the federal and state governments in the country besides a few private sector projects. Examples include a new deep seaport in the Lekki Free Trade Zone in Lagos, the Abuja-Kaduna-Kano gas pipeline project by the Nigerian National Petroleum Corporation (NNPC), and an Engine oil project by Total Nigeria Plc.

The first project finance transaction in Nigeria is Azura IPP—a power IPP with 469 MW capacity. Azura had a financial close in 2015 and it was funded through a US$900 million syndicated loan from 15 banks across nine countries including in Europe. The project received partial risk guarantee and political risk insurance from Multilateral Investment Guarantee Agency (MIGA). The project also involves a put option with the government of Nigeria, allowing sponsors to sell the plant to the government in certain default cases in exchange for a price that covers at a minimum the outstanding debt raised to finance construction of the plant.

Banks are the major financiers of project finance transactions in Nigeria, and this led to limited growth in the market because banks did not have a strong balance sheet to fund projects. About US$3.3 billion of funding for energy projects was obtained from local banks and much of the loans were not recovered due to liquidity problems in the power sector. The establishment of InfraCredit, a credit guarantee company, in 2017 is expected to change the project finance market in the country as the guarantee is likely to encourage risk-averse investors toward investing in project finance related assets such as infrastructure bonds. InfraCredit was set up through partnership between GuatantCo and the Nigerian Sovereign Investment Authority (NSIA) to encourage investment in long-term projects.

Egypt
In Egypt, project finance is used to fund infrastructure projects specifically in the energy sector as well as green field and brown field industrial investment projects in private sector companies. A notable energy project is the development and operation of a wind farm in the Gulf of Suez tendered by the Egyptian Electricity Transmission Company. With the county's commitment to increase reliance on renewable energy, planned green projects are likely to provide an impetus for increased project finance transactions in the country. In Egypt, project finance transactions are

regulated in various ways depending on whether they are undertaken by the private or public sector.

Securitization Market in Africa

Securitization holds the promise to provide Africa with the resources it needs to realize sustainable development goals (SDGs) whose price tag is estimated to be between $500 billion and $2 trillion annually (Harwood, 2021). According to the IMF (2019), countries in sub-Saharan Africa need to invest, on average, 19% of their GDP to achieve the SDGs. However, traditional sources of finance are inadequate to meet such a large demand for funding and as a result countries need to resort to innovative financing techniques such as securitization. Securitization allows countries to raise funds based on expected future cash flows and this helps to finance development projects with a potential to generate returns over an extended period. Two forms of securitization are prevalent: the conventional loan-based securitization and future flow securitization (FFS).

Loan-based securitization (or Asset-Backed Securitization) is used to raise funding by creating structured securities by pooling loans such as credit cards, mortgages, and car loans. The streams of cash flows that accrue to the originating financial institution will be diverted toward payment of returns to investors of securities. A good example of this is raising money based on a pool of mortgages held by a bank, allowing the bank to recover its loan much sooner, hence freeing tied-up capital for use in future lending transactions. Another example is securitization of a pool of car loans by a bank to raise money to invest in other transactions. In both cases, the financial institutions use a pool of loans to create securities with different tranches to sell to the investor community through insolvency remote SPVs.

Box 11.1: Securitization in South Africa

South Africa concluded the first securitization transaction in 1989 when United Building Society Ltd securitized a pool of mortgages valued at R 250 million (approx. US$17 million). This was followed by another transaction later in 1991 where SASFIN, a JSE listed financial service company, securitised instalment rental loans for asset backed securities issued by a special purpose vehicle (SPV) (see for details Saayman & Styger, 2003). However, the securitization market remained inactive until 1999 when Retail Apparel Group (RAG) securitized R 600 million (approx. US$98 million) of its debtors' accounts and Unibank securitised R430 million (approx. US$70 million) of term loan accounts.

The South African securitization market has picked up since 2004 in tandem with sustained economic growth and increased activity in the corporate bond market. The country has the most sophisticated securitization market with a strong regulatory framework. Securitization in South Africa has been stable with average annual transactions of R11billion (approx. USD725 million) since 2013. The market is dominated by residential mortgage-backed securities followed by car loans. Other assets used in securitization include equipment rentals, consumer receivables, instalment leases and commercial mortgages. Recent notable transactions include securitization of mortgage loans, vehicle finance receivables and equipment rental receivables with a total amount of R 30.5 billion (approx. US$2.1 billion). The securities were issued by SA Home Loans Proprietary Limited, Sasfin Bank Limited, SA Taxi Holding Proprietary Limited and First Rand Bank Limited.

Interestingly, some securitization transactions involved placement of securities in European markets mainly because the transactions may not raise the needed funding from the local market. The first such case was completed in 2006 when a Nitro 2 vehicle loan securitization valued at more than R 4 million (approx. USD660 million) was issued by Rand Merchant Bank in partnership with Morgan Stanley & Co International Limited acting on behalf of Wesbank Limited. The second transaction took place in 2007 when Standard Bank partnered with Royal bank of Scotland Plc to set up Blue Granite 4, securitization of residential mortgage loans with a value in excess of R 4 billion (approx. USD560 million).

In South Africa, the securitization market is governed by securitization regulation issued in 2008 as an amendment to the Banks Act 94/1990 because securitization falls beyond the traditional business of banks. In addition, the establishment of a special purpose vehicle is governed by Sect. 8(2) of the Companies Act. The regulation exempts special purpose vehicles from registering as banks as long as securitization transactions are concluded following the required conditions that relate to credit enhancements, liquidity facilities and ownership of the SPV. The SPV can be established as a public or private company depending on whether the securities are traded on the stock exchange. Under the companies' Act, SPVs must be established as public companies if the securities are traded on the Johannesburg Stock Exchange (JSE) or unlisted securities are issued to the public.

Source Based on von Schirnding et al. (2020) and Saayman and Styger (2003) and Byron (2021).

While the traditional loan-based securitization is often used by financial institutions that originate loans, FFS involves creating securities using future cash flow streams based on revenue-generating assets. FFS can be used by any entity owning assets that generate streams of future cash flows. For instance, municipalities can securitize utility accounts to raise funding to invest in new utility projects. Similarly, in resource-rich countries royalties collected from mining and oil companies can be securitized with proceeds to be used in infrastructure financing or other development projects.

FFS has many advantages over the traditional asset-based securitization. FFS can be easily created at a cheaper cost than ABS. In addition, securitization of future cash flows is less complicated than ABS because the latter involves creating waterfalls of different tranches of asset pools. To create ABS, there must exist banks with pools of loans, but FFS can be created even where there are no banks. This is important in Africa where the banking sector is not well-developed in many countries and as a result creating a successful ABS is difficult if not impossible.

The development of securitization in Africa differs across countries depending on various factors including macroeconomic stability, strength of the legal framework, development of institutional investors, and overall development of the financial market. Therefore, we present in the ensuing paragraphs the securitization market in selected countries starting with South Africa which has a more developed market in Africa.

Box 11.2: Future Flow Securitization in Africa

Cote d'ivoire

The Ivorian electricity company, a well-established utility company with a good track record, securitized receivables worth CFA 35 million (approx. US$50 million). The proceeds are needed to meet the company's cash flow and liquidity requirements.

Ghana

The Ghanaian government raised funds using tax related flows while maintaining its fiscal balance. The government used petrol tax to pay off debt in the energy sector that arose due to energy imports becoming too expensive following depreciation of the Ghanaian Cedi. In 2017, two bonds with 7 year and 10-year terms were issued backed by the tax receivables. The government has so far issued six bonds with a total of GHS 8 billion (over US$1.3 billion), and bonds were bought by local institutional investors. Over-collateralization and cash reserves were the two important credit enhancements used in the transaction where the government of Ghana acted as a sponsor. The bonds are listed in the Ghana Stock Exchange on the Fixed Income Market.

Nigeria

Through securitization of receivables from the sale of Expatriate resident Permits and Alien cards in 2017, Nigeria conducted the first future flow securitization transaction raising a total of N25 billion (US$65 million). The transaction was sponsored by Continental Transfer Technique Limited (CTTL), a private sector company operating as a technical partner to the Federal Government of Nigeria in processing resident permits. Prior to securitization of the receivables, CTTL relied on short term bank loans which were relatively expensive to fund its projects. The company wanted to raise long term funds to take advantage of new investment opportunities as well as expand its operation. The transaction was successfully concluded due to (1) bond payment obligations that are tied to stable cash flow receivables (2) CTTL's business that involves sale of permits with stable demand in the foreseeable future due to a good number of expatriates expected to travel and work in Nigeria (3) CTTL having a strong track record of collection of resident permit fees (4) CTTL receiving a guarantee from the Federal Government of Nigeria, giving it the right to cash flow from sale of CERPAC.

Source DLM (2019) CERPAC: First future flow securitization in Nigeria Successfully takes off

11.6 Requisite Conditions to Support the Development of Structured Finance Market in Africa

From what has been presented in the foregoing sections, one can imply that the structured finance market, whether it is project financing or securitization, is not well-developed in Africa except in a few countries. However, given that the continent needs funding to meet sustainable development goals that are critical in pulling millions out of poverty through economic transformation, a concerted effort is needed to develop the market. We highlight in the ensuing paragraphs requisite conditions that must be created for the development of the structured finance market in the continent. Project finance and securitization, the two structured finance techniques featured in this chapter, are organized differently involving different stakeholders, and hence the specific requisite conditions that apply to each will be highlighted under each heading.

Macroeconomic and Political Stability

A stable macroeconomic and political condition is important for doing business in general because instability in these sectors is likely to turn a promising project into a commercially worthless venture. Macroeconomic and political environments are even more important for the development of the structured finance market because adverse developments in the economy and politics can lead to significant loss in the value of a project or asset backed security. In project finance markets, sponsors and financiers require assurance that the project will be able to generate the projected cash flow that will enable the project company to service the loan and pay dividends. Where there is no macroeconomic and political stability, financiers and investors require credit guarantee schemes from national governments and international agencies. In the absence of a guarantee, promising development projects will remain on a paper.

Securitization equally depends on stable macro-economic and political conditions because a securitized asset will fail to generate the stream of cash flow needed to pay investors if conditions are not suitable. A significant shortfall in cash flow may cause a chain of events similar to the one that led to the 2007/2008 global financial crisis triggered by default in the sub-prime mortgage market.

Development of the Financial Sector

The structured finance market is providing an alternative way of raising finance that is unavailable in the financial markets and institutions. Banks that dominate the African financial sector are not ideal for raising long-term capital because they hold deposits that mature over the short term. The structured finance market therefore serves as an alternative way of raising long-term capital by directly interacting with the investment community. However, development of the financial sector serves as a bedrock of project finance as well as securitization transactions. For instance, well-capitalized banks can act as arrangers in project finance transactions by facilitating a project finance deal where they provide a line of credit to the project company when additional funds are needed.

In addition, adequately funded institutional investors such as pension funds and insurance companies can participate in project finance deals by investing in project assets. Similarly, these institutions are critical as investors in assets-backed securities as well as future flow securitizations. Asset-backed securities are used in markets where there are banks holding pools of assets such as mortgage loans, vehicle loans, or credit cards. Securitization is unlikely to succeed in markets where banks have a few assets in their portfolio because securitization, like insurance, works based on the law of large numbers.

Legal Framework to Ensure Investor Rights

Structured finance transactions fall beyond the operational scope of a single financial institution and hence they are concluded based on the strength of the legal and regulatory framework in a country. A strong legal and regulatory system is needed to allow investors to assess risk of the investment venture as well as ensure protection of lenders' and investors' rights. In addition, investors draw confidence from the strength of the legal system for resolving disputes as they arise. Arrangers need a well-formulated legal framework and clear regulations to organize project finance and securitization transactions.

Lack of regulatory frameworks in many countries in Africa is engendered by low level of awareness and understanding of the nature of structured finance transactions. In addition, market participants such as central bankers, security regulatory agencies, and regulators of institutional investors need to develop a common understanding of the nature, risks, and economic benefits of structured finance. Experience from past transactions in Africa suggests that demonstrative structured finance transactions are likely to pave the way for building regulatory capacity because they provide an opportunity for regulators and other stakeholders to have first-hand experience of the transactions.

Tax Incentives

Provision of tax incentives in the form of exemption for structured finance transactions will reduce transaction costs and encourage participation of investors in the market. In project finance transactions, some countries provide SPVs a tax holiday to entice sponsors and financiers to participate in transactions with paramount economic significance. A levy on the other hand increases transaction cost and as a result discourages investment in structured finance assets.

Local Rating Agencies and Service Providers

Rating agencies play a pivotal role in the structured finance market, particularly in selling asset-backed securities by vouching independently for the quality of a structured asset. In the securitization market, less sophisticated investors rely heavily on the rating of the agencies in the investment decision while more sophisticated ones use the rating as a complement to their independent assessment of the valuation of the asset. Three rating agencies, namely Standard and Poor, Moody's, and FITCH, dominate the global rating market. Local rating agencies that understand the local conditions are needed.

11.7 Concluding Remarks

This chapter has reviewed both theoretical and empirical resources on the need to focus much attention on structured finance as an alternative approach to conventional financing to meet the changing financing demands of firms and governments. The risks and the benefits of the various methods of financing have been discussed. Additionally, the chapter has presented the various institutions and procedures, such as the role of rating agencies in enhancing the effectiveness of structured financing as an innovative approach to enhance the value of firms. The chapter has also presented examples in the African financial market that make structured finance a good fit for the continent. Structured financing is largely absent in Africa except a few economies, namely Nigeria, Ghana, South Africa, and Cote D'Ivoire. Within these economies, structured finance is commonly used to finance infrastructure development, thus, narrowing the gap in infrastructure financing within these economies on the continent. The underdeveloped nature of structured finance in Africa is due to its unstable macroeconomic environment and the less sophisticated nature of the financial system of several economies to respond to the relative financial needs and underdevelopment of the regulatory systems. There is therefore a need for working regulatory institutions and decisions that seek to promote innovation and improve the macroeconomic environment to enable the development of structured finance. Governments should seek to provide incentives such as tax cuts and create the environment necessary for the development of structured finance in Africa.

References

Byron, B. (2021). *Structured finance and securitisation in South Africa: Overview*. Accessed on August 30, 2021 from https://uk.practicallaw.thomsonreuters.com/4-521-4150?transitionType=Default&contextData=(sc.Default)&firstPage=true. Thomson Reuters Practical Law.

Caselli, S., & Gatti, S. (2005). *Structured finance: Techniques, products and market*. Springer.

Cherubini, U., & Lunga, G. D. (2007). *Structured finance: The object oriented approach* with CD. Wiley.

Corielli, F., Gatti, S., & Steffanoni, A. (2010). Risk shifting through nonfinancial contracts: Effects on loan spreads and capital structure of project finance deals. *Journal of Money, Credit and Banking, 42*, 1295–1320.

Culp, C. L. (2006). *Structured finance and insurance*. Wiley.

DLM. (2019). *CERPAC: First future flow securitization in Nigeria successfully takes off*. DLM Transaction Report. Accessed on July 30, 2021 from https://dlm.group/wp-content/uploads/2020/09/CERPAC-First-Future-Flow-Securitisation-in-the-Nigerian-Debt-Capital-Market-_V4-19072019_Final.pdf

Dornel, A. (2014). *Project finance for infrastructure in Africa, Presentation at the conference on infrastructure development in Africa*. Accessed on July 23, 2021 from https://www.imf.org/external/np/seminars/eng/2014/CMR/pdf/Dornel_ENG.pdf

Esty, B. C. (2004). Modern project finance: A casebook. John Wiley & Sons Incorporated.

Fama, E. F., & French, K. R. (2002). Testing trade-off and pecking order predictions about dividends and debt. *Review of Financial Studies, 15*, 1–33.

Fama, E. F., & French, K. R. (2004). The capital asset pricing model: Theory and evidence. *Journal of Economic Perspectives, 18*, 25–46.

Fabozzi, F. J., Davis, H. A., & Chuodhry, M. (2006). *Introduction to structured finance*. Wiley.

Gatti, S., Kleimeier, S., Megginson, W., & Steffanoni, A. (2013). Arranger certification in project finance. *Financial Management, 42*, 1–40.

Giddy, I. (2003). Project financing, teaching note, stern school of business, Retrieved July 14, 2022, from https://pages.stern.nyu.edu/~igiddy/dakar/project.pdf

Jensen, M. C., & Meckling, W. H. (1976). Theory of the firm: Managerial behaviour, agency costs and ownership structure. *Journal of Financial Economics, 3*, 305–360.

John, T., & John, K. (1991). Optimality of project financing: Theory and empirical implications in finance and accounting. *Review of Quantitative Finance and Accounting, 1*, 51–74.

Kleimeier, S., & Megginson, W. (2000). Are project finance loans different from other syndicated credits? *Journal of Applied Corporate Finance, 13*, 75–87.

Leland, H. (2007). Financial synergies and the optimal scope of the firm: Implications for mergers, spinoffs, and structured finance. *The Journal of Finance, 62*, 765–807.

Modigliani, F., & Miller, M. H. (1958). The cost of capital, corporation finance and the theory of investment. *The American Economic Review, 48*(3), 261–297.

Myers, S. C. (1984). The capital structure puzzle. *Journal of Finance, 39*, 575–592.

Myers, S. C., & Majluf, N. S. (1984). Corporate financing and investment decisions when firms have information that investors do not have. *Journal of Financial Economics, 13*, 187–221.

Saayman, A., & Styger, P. (2003). Securitisation in South Africa: Historic deficiencies and future outlook. *South African Journal of Economic and Management Sciences, 6*(4), 744–764.

Svirydzenka, K. (2016). *Introducing a new broad-based index of financial development* (IMF Working paper WP/16/5). International Monetary Fund.

von Schirnding, S., Borg-Jorgensen, V. L., & Bromham, B. (2020). *Structured finance and securitisation in South Africa: Overview*. Accessed on July 25, 2021 from https://content.next.westlaw.com/4-5214150?__lrTS=20210529063615843&transitionType=Default&contextData=(sc.Default)&firstPage=true

UNCTAD. (2001). *Potential applications of structured commodity financing techniques for banks in developing countries*. Retrieved July 14, 2022, from https://unctad.org/system/files/official-document/poitcdcomd31.en.pdf

World Bank. (2021). *Global financial development database*. Accessed on July 12, 2021 from https://datacatalog.worldbank.org/search/dataset/0038648

CHAPTER 12

Sustainable Finance and Banking in Africa

Lordina Amoah, Gloria Clarissa O. Dzeha, and Thankom Arun

12.1 Introduction

Sustainable finance and banking incorporate environmental, social and governance (ESG) considerations in financial services delivery. It includes the provision of financial services, the design of products and processes and the concomitant institutional and market arrangements that address issues of sustainable growth and development. The spurt in industrialization across the globe has resulted in increased rates of polar ice caps

L. Amoah (✉)
University of Ghana Business School, Accra, Ghana
e-mail: loamoah@ug.edu.gh

G. C. O. Dzeha
Central University, Miotso-Tema, Ghana
e-mail: gloriadzeha@gmail.com

T. Arun
Essex Business School, Essex University, Essex, UK
e-mail: t.g.arun@essex.ac.uk

J. Y. Abor and C. K. D. Adjasi (eds.), *The Economics of Banking and Finance in Africa*, Palgrave Macmillan Studies in Banking and Financial Institutions, https://doi.org/10.1007/978-3-031-04162-4_12

melting, pollution, collapsing biodiversity, cataclysmic weather events, rising global sea levels and many other environmental problems. Consequently, since the last three decades, several agreements and treaties have been formulated and endorsed by countries around the world to curb the excessive degradation of business activities on the environment and society. These include, the United Nations Framework Convention on Climate Change (UNFCCC) in 1992 (popularized as the Earth Summit); the Kyoto Protocol in 1997 and the Paris agreement in 2015. In addition to these environmental issues, there are a myriad of social issues that have sprung up including rising unemployment, poor education and health, rising inequality and poverty among many others. The role of the financial sector in the transformative change needed to repair, restore and conserve nature and create a better society cannot be overemphasized. Transforming the financial sector into one that is more sustainability-oriented (in order to contribute to achieving a greener future and a resilient economy, stronger society and sustained development) has become a very critical issue in this millennium. Against the foregoing background, this chapter seeks to provide a discussion on sustainable finance and banking with a specific focus on Africa. It brings to light trends in sustainable finance and banking in Africa and points out areas that require further attention.

The next section provides an expose on the Sustainable Development Goals (SDGs) and sustainable finance. The third section provides a discourse on financial institutions and the Triple Bottom Line. Section four explains the concepts and discusses the policies and practices underlying sustainable finance and banking in Africa. In section five, the various green growth financing mechanisms and inherent challenges are discussed. Section six concludes the chapter.

12.2 Sustainable Development Goals and Sustainable Finance

The SDGs (popularly referred to as the Global Goals) were launched in 2015 with the aim to address the precarious environmental, political and economic setbacks that face the world. The SDGs comprise a set of mutual goals, seventeen in number, targeted at ending poverty and hunger, reducing inequality and addressing climate change challenges, among others, by 2030. Clearly, most countries around the world are facing environmental, social and economic challenges that the SDGs can help address. The United Nations (UN) perceives the SDGs as "a blueprint for peace and prosperity for people and the planet, now and into the future". Indeed, the large majority of governments in Africa have made noteworthy efforts to ratify the SDGs by incorporating them into their national strategies and developmental plans. Notwithstanding the extensive advancement made toward attaining the Sustainable Development Goals and their espousal systems, achieving these developmental goals still seems far-fetched in most African countries. The records in the 2020 Africa SDG report show that the best performing region is North Africa while Central Africa is the worst performing. The SDGs record the greatest challenge to be Goal 3 (good health and well-being) and Goal 9 (infrastructure). On the other hand, overall, the countries in Africa have recorded improved performance on Goal 13 (climate action) and Goal 12 (responsible consumption and production). In the area of climate change, Africa contributes to around 4% of global CO2 emissions, but is most vulnerable to the dire impact of climate change, particularly in agriculture and healthcare (Ayompeet al., 2021; Tyson, 2021). According to the African Development Bank, seventy percent of the world's ten most climate vulnerable countries are in Africa. This is because the nations within the continent have low levels of adaptation capacity, resulting from low levels of investment. There is an urgent need for substantial financial resources to support the adaptation to and mitigation of climate change risks and address critical development targets across various sectors of the economy. In Tyson (2021), sub-Saharan Africa urgently needs to mobilize $50 billion every year to address climate adaptation in agriculture, power and urban infrastructure.

Despite the relative gains of some of the SDG goals, the global pandemic, COVID-19, which has negatively impacted the economies and societies of the world, may pose risks in making significant progress on the aggregate in Africa. The Africa SDG report (2020) indicates that over 100 million children and youth have dropped out of school, friable health care systems are being tested and vulnerable groups are at the risk of being excluded even more. According to the report, poverty and food insecurity are predicted to worsen significantly for about 60million Africans. The report indicates that serious challenges exist, with inadequate funds and resources being the foremost challenge in the implementation of the SDGs. Official Development Assistance (ODAs), Remittances and Portfolio Flows have recorded a sharp decline in the face of COVID. The majority of countries in Africa are heavily dependent on external income and earnings from exports and tourism operations, which have seen a significant drop arising from the pandemic (Shipalana, 2020). Apparently, the slowdown in domestic economic activity implies lower revenues for governments. The financing gaps for the SDGs in Africa are likely to get bigger and the absence of financial resources will make sustainable development impossible to achieve. Apparently, more finance is needed to achieve the SDGs. This is supported empirically by Ziolo et al. (2021) who find a strong linkage between their sustainable finance model and environmental sustainability (Goals 11, 12, 13, 15), social sustainability (Goals 1, 3, 4, 5, 10, 16) and economic sustainability (Goals 8, 9, 17). Increasingly stretched public balance sheets demand an escalation of private finance for the SDGs to be implemented successfully. It has become even more critical to explore innovative financing to bridge the financing gap. While financing the SDGs within this region, financial institutions are also expected to adopt and adhere to sustainable finance and banking tenets. There is the need to adopt workable interventions that are consistent with the priorities of financial institutions and those of the SDGs.

12.3 Financial Institutions and the "Triple Bottom Line"

In the foregoing section, it has been well articulated that one of the key challenges to achieving a green and sustainable economy in Africa is financing. Whereas public finance is important in this regard, it is insufficient. Private finance is a significant catalyst in addressing the financing gap. Hence, in this section we turn our attention to the theoretical discourse on the role private finance can play and other considerations financial institutions need to make in order to achieve a green economy. The Triple Bottom line (TBL) proposed by Elkington (1998) (encompassing the 3Ps, planet, people and profits) argues that firms should critically consider social and environmental issues just as they take profits seriously. The "people" or "social bottom line" considers the human development and the welfare of the people within the society; the "planet" or "environmental bottom line" variable considers the engagement with natural resources, land and all other variables that lead to wealth acquisition through profits—and the "profit" variable considers operations of firms that result in increased finance and economic growth. The social bottom line identifies the interdependence between the interest of a business (financial) institution and the interest of its workers essentially. The implementation of the environmental bottom line signifies controlling, managing, observing and reporting on consumption, waste and emissions (Fig. 12.1).

Carter and Rogers (2008) developed the TPL model further to consider the economy, the environment and society. In their view, sustainability must consider and include economic performance, the natural environment and society, such that the convergence of these considerations can help the firm's activities affect the natural environment and society positively and also result in long-term economic benefits and competitive advantage. Over time, several studies have evolved which indicate that the elements of the traditional TBL are not sufficient to adequately cover sustainability in its entirety (Tseng et al., 2020; Wu et al. 2016). Consequently, further dimensions including processes, resilient attitude, long-term goals and stakeholders are vital for promoting sustainability. Tseng et al. (2018) further argues that the subject of sustainability infuses certain complexities. Thus, to ensure the promotion of successful solutions, incorporating qualitative information, quantifiable

Fig. 12.1 The interconnectivity among essentials of the Triple Bottom Line Theory (*Source* Dalibozhko and Krakovetskaya [2018])

data and social media engagement in aspects of the TBL argument is indispensable. Additionally, Tseng et al. (2020) suggest that the dimensions of TBL should be stretched to cover six aspects including economic, environmental, social, operations, technology and engineering.

In practice, the TBL model has influenced the management strategies through the inclusion of sustainability as a part of management agenda on corporate programs. Klewitz and Hansen (2014) show that businesses ensure systematic management that brings a balance in their performance socially and environmentally in a manner that is aligned with economic goals. Increasingly, the TBL has become a measure for sustainability. It depicts the aggregate maximization of profit, social and ecological aspects of sustainability (Isil & Hernke, 2017). Thus, institutional managers embrace business models which require them to evaluate their communal and environmental effect—besides their economic performance—instead of exclusively concentrating on profit generation to ensure sustainability. Notwithstanding the debate on the variables needed to be included to adequately address sustainability, there is some evidence that business organizations that concurrently situate their performance within all three features of TBL do much better than businesses that seek to intensify their performance socially and environmentally without clearly taking cognizance of financial profit (Carter & Rogers, 2008).

Milne and Gray (2013) raise concerns that sustainability reportage is deprived of careful thought as reporters only cherry-pick some aspects and fail to notice the key concerns triggered by firms' actions and inactions. To ensure successful implementation of the TBL, it is expedient that sustainability committees are established to ensure that they communicate sustainability solutions and goals across all organization sections. Indeed, beyond the three constituents in the TBL model, all other aspects must play a role in the sustainability of a business as a going concern and in generating profit. By embracing the TPL method, firms gain insight into its position in the current economy and its ability to survive in the future.

12.4 Sustainable Finance and Banking in Africa

The preceding discussions have first established the importance of financing in achieving sustainable development in Africa and as well explained why it is essential for financial institutions to adopt the Triple Bottom Line Model, which ensures that these institutions adopt sustainable finance and banking principles. Going forward, it is important for us to understand the concepts underlying sustainable finance and banking, which the next sub-section addresses. We then explore general trends pertaining to sustainable finance and banking in Africa, bringing to light some of the policies and practices within the context.

Explaining the Concepts

Spinaci (2021) defines green finance as any financial activity involving the collection of funds for the purpose of addressing issues pertaining to climate and environmental degradation (green financing), on the one hand, and the improvement in the management of financial risk associated with climate and the environment (greening finance), on the other hand. Per his definition, sustainable finance is merely an offshoot of green finance, given that it considers ESG issues and risks with the objective of increasing long-term investments in sustainable economic activities and projects. According to the Swiss Sustainable Finance (SSF), sustainable finance encompasses any form of financial service integrating the three elements of ESG criteria into business activities and investment decisions so that consumers, businesses and society at large reap long-term benefits. According to Blok et al. (2012, p. 471), "sustainable finance refers to financial investments flowing into sustainable development projects and initiatives, environmental products and policies that encourage a more sustainable economy". Overall sustainable finance ensures that benefits reaped from the activities that businesses are engaged in today and in the long run are derived in such a manner that contributes to the protection and restoration of ecological systems and the enhancement of cultural and social well-being. In Spinaci (2021), sustainable finance will play a key role in "building back better" and contribute to achieving a sustainable and resilient recovery from the Covid-19 pandemic.

According to the UNEP FI (2004), "sustainability banking incorporates the evaluation of E&S risk and the application of a comprehensive set of E&S guidelines towards the decision to finance a project". Sustainable banking integrates ESG criteria into traditional banking operations (Deloitte, 2017). It is also referred to as green banking. It focuses on complementing profit maximization with social and environmental concerns, unlike traditional banking. Sustainable banking emphasizes sustainable development, ethical practices, social responsibility, reducing carbon footprints and adopting new technologies in banks' financing activities. With growing advocacy on sustainable development, banks are now required to adopt and incorporate sustainability ethics in funding decisions, product definition processes and corporate strategy. In this way, banks tend to magnify their lenses on environmental and social risks posed by potential projects to be financed by applying some set of guidelines in order to inform their decision. This also means that banks put in place an efficient system to be able to identify, assess and manage such risks in their operations and processes. By implication, banks will fund only projects which satisfy all requirements imposed by the guidelines that ensure that projects are executed in the most environmentally friendly and socially responsible manner (IFC, 2014).

Sustainable Finance and Banking in Africa—Policies and Practices

In Africa, several financial institutions, including banks, investment companies, pension funds and insurance companies are embracing sustainable finance and banking policies and practices. A report by the United Nations Environment Program-Finance Initiative (UNEP FI) asserts that the implementation of sustainable banking practices internationally has placed much demand on the African banks to rise to the occasion. Accordingly, governments have been urged to take more serious and practical measures in the adoption of sustainable banking and finance to safeguard the environment, society and the overall economy (see Shipalana & O'Riordan, 2020). Accordingly, in Africa, to some extent central banks have played the leading role in developing and overseeing the adoption, enactment and monitoring of sustainable banking principles, supported by the IFC.

There are only four African countries associated with the Sustainable Banking Network that have launched and adopted national policies aimed at Sustainable Banking under the IFC. These countries are Ghana, Nigeria, Kenya and South Africa. The Central Bank of Nigeria (CBN) commissioned the Sustainable Banking Principles in Nigeria in 2012. In 2015, the Kenyan Sustainable Finance Initiative was launched with three priorities: comprehensive risk management; business practice, leadership and governance; and growth through inclusivity, innovation and technology. It has five guiding principles which are financial returns vs economic viability; growth through inclusivity and innovation; managing and mitigating associated risks; resource scarcity and choice; and business ethics and values. In November 2019, the Bank of Ghana (BOG) also publicly outdoored the Sustainable Banking Principles and Sector Guidance Notes. As at 2020, twenty-four (24) commercial banks in Ghana had ratified the environment and social sustainability principles. The principles specifically focus on five sectors among the most seriously prone to the environmental and social (E&S) standards. These sectors also constitute a substantial percentage of banks' portfolio exposure. These sectors are Oil & Gas and Mining; Agriculture & Forestry; Power & Energy; Manufacturing and Construction & Real Estate. There are seven principles and five sector-specific guidance notes. They portray sustainable banking as a two-way interconnected imperative. The first seeks to improve the contribution of bank financing to sustainable and inclusive growth by funding society's long-term needs. The second aims at improving and strengthening financial stability through the incorporation of ESG factors in lending decisions. The themes of these Principles are shown in Table 12.1.

Key influencers of the adoption of sustainable banking practices have been justified on the basis of improved access to funding from both domestic and international development agencies, potential for competitive advantage, better community relations and reputation, pressure from various stakeholders, reduction in credit risk and liability risk as well as regulatory requirements (IFC, 2014; UNEP FI, 2004). The UNEP FI report also points out some challenges to the successful implementation of sustainable banking. These include political risk, capacity at the government level, the regulatory environment and the capacity of the financial sector to fully operationalize the sustainable banking model. The

Table 12.1 Ghana sustainable banking principles

Principle	*Consideration*
Principle 1	Environmental and social risk management (ESRM) in banks business activities
Principle 2	Internal environment social and governance (ESG) in banks operations
Principle 3	Commitment to corporate governance and ethical Standard
Principle 4	Commitment to promote gender equality
Principle 5	Commitment to financial inclusion
Principle 6	Commitment to promote resource efficiency, sustainable production and consumption
Principle 7	Commitment to measure and Report on the implementation of the principles

report, therefore, recommends that capacity building should be enhanced so that stakeholders can appreciate the interconnection between the core operations of banks and sustainability. It is also recommended that governments should make E&S liability legislation more comprehensive for all financial sector participants and create incentives for these participants to pursue sustainability. Exploring innovative ideas to improve banking and financial services in general to the underserved and excluded should be taken seriously.

Statistics from IFC and Deloitte (2017) show that a number of banks in sub-Saharan Africa are incorporating Environmental and Social Risk Management (ESRM) into their operations. ESRM generally involves the incorporation of environmental and social considerations in operational processes of financial institutions (FI). The business case for ESRM hinges on the mitigation of three main kinds of business risks. These are credit, liability and reputational risk, shown in Table 12.2.

In line with the implementation of the ESRM, there are a number of global principles and standards that financial institutions may adopt. These include the IFC performance standards and the Equator Principles (EPs). The EPs is a credit risk management framework, employed

Table 12.2 Risks financial institutions face when E&S issues are ruled out

Type of risk	*Description*	*Impacts*
Credit risk:	The likelihood that clients will not be able to repay interests and loan principal as a result of social and environmental issues	• Escalation of project costs • Increased insurance costs • Loss of production capacity • Fines/penalties due to non-compliance with E&S national requirements
Liability risk	The likelihood that financial institutions will face legal complications (fees/fines) in rectifying social and environmental damage by virtue of taking possession of collateral	• Obtaining ownership of contaminated collateral • Direct liability in the case of strict lender liability • Class action suits if FI made responsible for negative impacts
Reputational risk	The likelihood that the public image of FIs is damaged as a result of the negative aspects of project financed	• Negative media coverage • Local resistance or consumer campaigns • Government investigations

Source IFC (2014)

by banks to determine, assess and manage environmental and social risk in project finance transactions. It is a voluntary code of conduct with a primary objective to provide a minimum standard for due diligence to support responsible risk decision-making. The IFC performance standards are also an international benchmark for identifying and managing environmental and social risk. Many financial institutions have adopted it as a major component of their ESRM. The ESRM requires financial institutions to put in place a policy showing their commitment to principles and standards as well as E&S capacity that clearly stipulates the roles and responsibilities of key personnel and training where need be. They are to ensure that they have in place the appropriate procedures for assessing E&S risk through transaction screening, risk categorization, due diligence and associated conditions for financing. At the implementation of the project stage, it is important for FIs to also put in place mechanisms for monitoring E&S risks through reviews of client E&S performance and managing non-compliance where necessary. Ultimately there should also be structures for reporting E&S performance. The Global Reporting Initiative (GRI) is one of the extensively used sustainability reporting frameworks. The GRI provides an avenue for financial institutions to communicate and report traction gained on key standards and indicators bordering on economic, environmental, social and governance issues.

12.5 Green Growth Financing Mechanisms in Africa

While the need to transition to a green economy is increasingly gaining momentum, current levels of private capital targeted toward green projects are relatively limited. However, in order to realize the SDGs, it is critical that sustainable investments increase substantially from current levels. Current flows are woefully inadequate (UNCTAD, 2014). The UNCTAD estimates that investment between US$5 trillion and US$7 trillion is needed every year to achieve the SDGs by 2030. Particularly, in Africa, the AfDB approximates that about $20–$30 billion is needed every year to address climate change issues, which may be achieved using different financing mechanisms and sources (Hauman & Hussain, 2018). Thus, the discourse around sustainable finance and banking is not only focused on the quantum needed but also the type of finance. Financial institutions are now required to develop new and innovative products and green financial instruments to achieve a green financial system. A key question here is, what are the statistics and trends in the development of these green finance and bank products in Africa? The following section discusses this subject and associated challenges.

Green Bonds

Green bonds are used primarily for financing or refinancing green projects or green assets. Other related bonds on the market are sustainability bonds, sustainability-linked bonds, blue bonds and social bonds. They are fixed-income instruments issued by governments, municipalities and corporations to raise money from domestic and international capital markets for new or existing projects intended to have positive environmental and social impacts. The financing of such projects might have as part of its objectives the renewable energy, prevention of pollution, clean water, clean transportation and energy efficiency, sustainable agriculture, responsible waste management, fishery and forestry, protection of aquatic ecosystems or some social objective.

The green bond revolution is gradually catching on in Africa in recent years, even though the green bonds market in the continent is still in its primitive stage. The question is: why are green bonds gaining so much attention? First, the green bond market provides the opportunity for the financial institutions in Africa to make a statement on their commitment to pursuing a green economy.[1] Green bonds are one notable novelty in the sustainable finance space which provides additional funds for projects that would otherwise be excluded from financing. Thus, these bonds are a major tool for unlocking and mobilizing significant capital for sustainability-related investments, given the widening financing gap in the region. In addition, issuing green bonds enables financial institutions in the region to gain access to the large pool of fixed-income capital across the globe, while attracting investors with specific interest in sustainable development. The higher requirements of transparency and institutional accountability in the green bonds market are a good catalyst for driving sustainable development in Africa (Duru & Nyong, 2016). This is especially true in the context of Africa where there is a relatively higher demand for veracity and accountability in the use of proceeds in achieving specific objectives. Aside from the pricing benefit associated with green labels, green bonds also have the potential to improve

[1] A number of financial institutions are already party to sustainable development initiatives like the UNEP FI.

sustainable investing (and in particular sustainable infrastructure investments) for institutional investors such as insurance companies, mutual funds, pension funds and sovereign wealth funds (Bhattacharya et al., 2015; OECD, 2016). Some of the incentives for issuing green bonds in the literature include widening the investor base, lowering cost of capital and the intention to meet investors' demand for sustainable investment products. Hence green bonds are being considered as an alternative source of financing because they are typically designed to be a relatively low-risk financial instrument that affords both issuers and investors to contribute to green projects at a fairly low cost (Maltais & Nykvist, 2020). Particularly on the side of investors, some of the incentives include the opportunities to bolster reputation, status and visibility.

Over the last decade, green bond issuance in Africa seems to be gaining traction (see Table 12.1) as a complementary source of raising finance for sustainability-related projects. According to Moody 2021, the global green bonds market is expected to exceed US$650 billion by the end of 2021 and Africa has mobilized about US$2.2billion for development since 2012, less than one percent of the global value. The limited number of green bonds issued makes measurement of performance relatively difficult (Amundi—IFC, 2020). Apparently, there are key challenges impeding the development of green, and in general bond markets in Africa. In the view of Ntsama et al. (2021), the main barriers inhibiting the growth of the green bonds market in Africa are mainly financial, institutional and political. They further raise concerns about the small capital markets with unsatisfactory liquidity and excessive transaction costs. There is also the issue of the accuracy and accessibility of information to categorize, assess and track green investments. To Tyson (2021), there is lack of appetite by international investors for green bond issues in Africa and this has been attributed to the perceived riskiness of the region relative to other emerging economies. On the other hand, domestic investors tend to be mainly governments and very few private sector participants. Another issue emphasized in Tyson is the substantial mismatch between sectors requiring climate financing and the sectors with a somewhat investor appetite. A typical example is the financing[2] needed for the agricultural sector, given that economies in the region heavily depend on this sector.

[2] An example is financing targeted at building irrigation projects, developing climate-friendly inputs, reversing environmental degradation etc.

Clearly, in order to realize the goal of green bond market development, the stakeholders of the green bond market need to address outstanding challenges pertaining to lack of capacity, absence of appropriate incentives and tailored policies to stimulate private sector participation (Tyson, 2021). Generally, green bonds are usually asset-linked and hence backed by the credibility of the issuing entity. Hence, consideration of the credit rating of issuers in this region is an important subject. Issuers will also have to consider the quality of the pipeline of projects selected for funding. There is yet to be any official all-encompassing regulation or standards that define a green bond. Practically the majority of green bond issuers follow the Green Bond Principles (GBP). These principles are, however, voluntary. The GBPs provide prescriptions pertaining to project suitability, project appraisal and choice, how the funds from the issuance of the bond should be appropriately applied and managed as well as guidelines on disclosure and assurance. For a bond to gain recognition as a green bond, it has to be certified by a third party such as the Climate Bond Standard Board (Maltais & Nykvist, 2020, FSD Africa, 2020). The GBP, other standardization initiatives[3] and the active participation of central banks and regulators[4] present good prospects, incentives as well as the underlying structures for the development of the green bond market in Africa. Table 12.3 provides some information on Africa's cumulative Green Bond issues as at 2019.

Box 12.1: A Peek into the Green Bond Space in Africa

The African Development Bank (ADB) has played an active role in the green bond market since 2010. It issued AAA (investment grade) green bonds totaling US$500 million in 2013. Socially responsible investors purchased 84% of the bond issue. These include 43% asset managers, 28% central banks and official institutions, 28% insurance companies and pension funds and 1% retail and private banks. 52% were bought by

[3] The African Development Bank (AfDB), the European Investment Bank (EIB), the International Finance Corporation (IFC), and the World Bank have established working groups to harmonize the framework for reporting impact on projects to which green bond proceeds have been assigned (Duru & Nyong 2016). The Sustainable stock exchange is a United Nations Partnership Program with the objective of providing a global platform that permits stock exchanges to explore how to promote sustainable investments.

[4] In south Africa, Nigeria and Kenya, the legal and regulatory frameworks are being strengthened through the introduction of national green bond programs.

Table 12.3 Africa's cumulative Green Bond issues

Country	*Green bonds*	*Amount (US$m)*	*First issuance*	*Certified climate bonds (#)*	*Certified climate bond amount (US$m)*	*Use of proceeds*
Kenya	1	41	September 2019	√ (1)	41	Buildings
Namibia	1	5	December 2018			Energy, buildings, transport, water, waste, land use, adaptation and resilience
Seychelles	1	15	October 2018			Land use and marine resources
Nigeria	4	136	December 2017	√ (2)	71	Energy, transport, water, land use
Morocco	4	356	November 2016	Yes—1	117	Energy and buildings
South Africa	6	1,554	April 2012	Yes—2	193	Energy, buildings, transport, water, waste
Total	17	2,107		6	422	

Source Climate Bonds Initiative, October 2019

Americans, 39% by Europeans and 9% by investors from the Middle East and Africa. The bank had allotted significant funds toward various projects across African countries which include investments in energy efficiency, clean transport, biogas, forestry conservation, water and wastewater management. The Nigerian Access Bank issued a five-year green bond in 2019, offering a coupon rate of 15.50%. The bond with a value of $41.1 m is listed on the Nigerian Stock Exchange. The Nigerian Stock Exchange (NSE) and the Luxembourg Stock Exchange (LuxSE) have also signed a Memorandum of Understanding (MoU) to promote cross-listing and trading of green bonds in Nigeria and Luxembourg. The Kenyan government issued a $42.7 m green bond medium-term note (MTN) in 2019 which is listed on the London Stock Exchange (LSE) international securities market. This is the first project to receive green certification in Kenya. In South Africa, the Nedbank issued $100 m of renewable energy bonds in April 2019. This is the first Certified Climate Bond to be issued in South Africa. The Black Rhino Bond arranged by Conservation Capital to raise $50 m is a five-year outcome-based bond. That is, investors will receive the principal and coupon payments based on the increase in the number of black rhinos across five locations in Kenya and South Africa. The IFC and Ghana's Securities and Exchange Commission (SEC) in May 2021 announced a partnership to expedite investments in sustainability projects through the issuance of green bonds.

Green Climate Fund

Climate finance has gained prominence as one of the channels for achieving climate change and sustainable development objectives. One hundred and ninety-four (194) governments adopted the Green Climate Fund (GCF) as a financial mechanism of the United Nations Framework Convention on Climate Change in 2011. The overarching aim is to curb and moderate greenhouse gas emissions in developing countries and facilitate the adaptation of vulnerable societies to the impacts of climate change. GCF funds are received through accredited national and sub-national implementing entities. These generally comprise NGOs, government ministries, national and development banks and domestic and regional organizations that can meet the GCF's standards. It is also possible for countries to access the fund through qualified international and regional development banks and some UN agencies under international access. Some of the funds are distributed through the Enhanced Direct Access (EDA), in which developing country-based accredited institutions receive an allocation and make their own decisions on how to utilize the funds. This is different from other arrangements where the funds can only be accessed through discrete projects and programs approved by the GCF Board. The GCF fund board focuses on eight main mitigation and adaptation results areas. The four mitigation areas are energy generation access; transport; forests and land use; and buildings, cities, industries and appliances; whereas the other four adaptation areas are health, food and water security; livelihoods of people and communities; infrastructure and built environment; and ecosystems and ecosystem services.

As at March 2021, total funding of the GCF Africa amounted to USD3.1b (representing 37%) out of a total of USD8.4b. The African Development Bank (AfDB) is one of the 18 accredited entities in Africa through which the GCF allocates funds to recipient countries. Fonta et al. (2018) report that many African countries have faced diverse challenges in accessing the GCF. Savvidou et al. (2021) point out that the amount of climate finance (adaptation and mitigation) from bilateral and multilateral funders to Africa between 2014 and 2018 is significantly below the quantum required for Africa. Further, they note that, on aggregate, distribution of climate-related finance to African countries hardly meets the urgent demand for adaptation. Evidently, the majority of climate-related finance committed to the region has targeted mitigation (US$30.6 billion representing 61%) relative to adaptation (US$16.5 billion representing 33%). Afful-Koomson (2015) raises concerns about the fact that the majority of climate funds received were mostly small and associated with huge transaction costs.

Clearly, the extent of impact that climate finance will make in the economies of Africa depends on the amount of funds mobilized and the areas targeted. Fonta et al. (2018) reveal that the inability of African countries to get much approval for requests and secure funding stem from lack of readiness and the dependence on Internationally Accredited Entities (IAE). In addition, these countries hardly pay any attention to the GCF critical result or priority areas, probably due to lack of capacity. Some of these areas include the use of land, forest and transport which have high potential for low carbon development transitions. There is also the issue of adherence to international commitments. These challenges need to be addressed in order to improve the effective and impartial distribution of funds for climate actions in the region. Nakhooda et al. (2011) makes some recommendations that require policy attention. First of all, it is important to strengthen and scale up financing for adaptation, which hitherto has received the least funding, and additionally, direct it to critical areas. Measures should be put in place to allocate resources and enhance the equitable distribution of funds among the countries in the SSA region, with emphasis on the sectors and groups that are most susceptible. However, practical strategies need to be put in place to draw in the much-needed climate finance. In the AfDB-OECD (2013) enabling green growth in Africa report, it is emphasized that in order for African countries to attract significant volumes of green and climate financing, governments must be adept at creating the infrastructure required to access such funds, prepare an authentic and potent pipeline of funding prospects and build a cross-departmental discourse on the prospects. Hence, it is crucial that institutional capacity be strengthened to enable them develop and carve out unique climate-related development projects and to gain direct access to the fund. Further, proper and judicious management of secured climate finance is very crucial. That said, good governance of climate finance will play an indispensable role. Afful-Koomson (2015) also adds that African countries need to collaborate well with the GCF to shift the main instruments for financing from grants to loans as well as private capital in order to support the financing of medium- and large-scale projects.

Green Deposits and Loans

The burgeoning focus on sustainability has led to the introduction of green deposit and green loan instruments introduced by responsible banks as a way to mobilize additional capital to fund sustainability projects. Responsible banking implies the movement away from traditional financial instruments to environmentally and socially oriented products. In Miroshnichenko and Brand (2021), responsible banking has resulted in the shift toward the modification of traditional products and services of banks into environmentally and socially focused sets. Thus, green deposits refer to funds that are mobilized in fixed-term accounts for financing green initiatives and projects, that is, projects with positive environmental impacts. On the other hand, a green loan is a type of financing directed toward green projects. Such loans are meant explicitly for investments into the development, operations, maintenance and expansion of renewable and circular solutions with the main aim of mitigating climate change by reducing greenhouse gas emissions. Green loans may be used to purchase energy-efficient homes, finance energy-efficiency projects in businesses, buy electric vehicles, fund the development of wind farms, install solar panels and serve a wide range of environmentally sound purposes. There are various green loan instruments in the green loan market. These are green syndicated loans, sustainability-linked loans (SSLs), green revolving facilities, green asset finance and green supply chain finance. The green loans are expected to align with the Green Loan Principles (GLP). The GLP are a set of non-mandatory guidelines that define the framework for classifying green loans, hence providing some sort of market standard and consistency. Essentially, the GLP set out the guiding taxonomy which should be applied in identifying, selecting and managing green loans. The principles were issued by the Loan Market Association (LMA) in 2018 and accompanied by the Guidance note published in May 2020. The GLP framework stipulates four major criteria for the purposes of establishing what defines a green loan. These are (i) the use of proceeds; (ii) Green project evaluation and selection; (iii) management and monitoring of use of proceeds; and (iv) reporting.

The green loan market is gaining traction in financial markets around the globe and countries in Africa are yet to follow suit. Given the dominant role the banking sector plays in developing economies, measures should be put in place to leverage the sector to shore up green deposits and loans. To date there is only one record of a certified green loan in South Africa, introduced in May 2021. The IFC advanced a loan to the tune of US$150 million to Absa Bank Limited to fund projects in the biomass and renewable energy space. Particularly in Africa, for the green deposit and green loans market to develop and progress effectively, it is important that regulators of the financial sector and central banks in general coordinate their policies to ensure that the credit and monetary system is targeted at transitioning to a green economy by creating incentives for banks to offer such services. A study by Punzi (2018) of the transmission mechanism of monetary, technology and financial shocks to green firms shows that it is only in the scenario of a positive financial shock to green firms that credit to the green sector is boosted. The study also recommends that differentiating capital requirements for green and nongreen activities should be considered. Specifically, capital requirements for green activities (or responsible banks) should be lowered, which should go a long way to sustain green financing. A typical example is the introduction of separate reserve requirement ratios in Lebanon by Banque du Liban. Here, commercial banks' mandatory reserve requirements have been reduced by an amount equivalent to 100–150% of the value of the loan for energy-saving projects. There is also the case of India and Bangladesh. In India, the Reserve Bank is implementing a policy where a minimum percentage of banks' lending is required to flow to green financing. The Bank of Bangladesh has also been supporting commercial banks with liquidity in order to increase the extension of green loans (Punzi, 2018).

In concluding this section, it is important to note that, whereas the aforementioned sources of green funds are important catalysts in achieving a green economy, there is also the urgent need to scale up public finance specifically targeting green projects in order to reduce investment risk. This will help create the platform for long-term green investments while leveraging private finance to enable the implementation of green projects and the SDGs in general. Again, given that the financial needs of large areas of most developing economies are not adequately catered for by formal financial intuitions, some innovative approaches need to be explored. One option that could be explored domestically is crowdfunding. This has been relatively successful in Kenya and Uganda, where retail investors invest directly through the use of mobile platforms rather than through financial intermediaries.

12.6 Conclusion

Sub-Saharan Africa is the world's most susceptible region to climate change, even though it has contributed the least to climate change. This is because of the low levels of adaptation capacity, resulting from low levels of investment. Increasing finance to address climate change adaptation is a fundamental issue for climate justice. Accordingly, the UN Economic Commission for Africa and the IMF have estimated that $50 billion is required each year to address climate adaptation. Expected public finance from governments and international donors is less likely to foot this bill. Consequently, the financial sector is progressively seen as critical for accelerating the transition to sustainability and climate neutrality, with private finance playing a key role. The main reason is the need to mobilize significant amounts of private capital to meet the investment needed to achieve the UN Sustainable Development Goals (SDGs) as well as the climate targets of the Paris Agreement. Another paramount reason rests on the financial sector's ability to put allocated capital to the most efficient use. Consequently, the concept of sustainable finance and banking has received attention through increased advocacy at both the global and national levels.

In shifting from traditional financing and banking to sustainable options, financial institutions are expected to incorporate new systems into their operations to aid in the identification, evaluation and effective management of activities that pose enormous risk to society and the environment. Indeed, as is increasingly becoming the norm, financial institutions are keenly managing environmental and social risk through their funding decisions, corporate strategy and product definition processes. Some progress has been made in the area of adoption of Sustainable Banking and Finance tenets by banks spearheaded by central banks. This is evident in the growing bond market and other innovative finance tools, and the launching of the Sustainable Banking Principles by some countries in the region including Ghana, Nigeria, Kenya and South Africa. Green bonds in particular are one of the most notable innovations in the area of sustainable finance. On the one hand, it is an investment instrument; on the other hand, it is a sustainable development instrument. It is, however, imperative that financial sector leaders pursue best practices (such as those spelt out in the Green Bond Principles) in order to ensure that the investment and sustainability objectives underpinning green bonds are achieved and safeguarded.

Despite the progress made in this region, there is still more to be done in order to bridge the gap between international best practices on sustainable finance banking and what remains to be done in Africa. For example, the Network for Greening the Financial System is a network of the world's central banks with the aim of examining the impacts of climate change on financial stability and regulation. Some Central banks in Africa (Central Bank of West African States and the South African Reserve Bank) are already members. It is important for the other central banks in the region to join to expand and deepen the discourse. It is imperative for every country in the region to develop national policy measures in order to support the development of a green financial sector. In addition, the countries in the region should ratify and strictly adhere to the tenets of the United Nations' Principles for Responsible Investment and the Financial Stability Board's Task Force on Climate-related Financial Disclosures which are initiatives targeted at ensuring that the finance sector contributes its quota toward achieving sustainable development.

In order to mobilize more capital to address the funding gap, it is imperative for the countries in Africa to address the challenges regarding the perception of risk associated with investments in this region so as to expand and grow the green finance market to attain a greener economy. In that respect, Stock exchanges should be more proactive in product design. In addition, they should actively promote green bonds internationally and domestically to deepen investor base, explore cross-listing potentials and as well implement additional initiatives such as creating a dedicated green bond section. To scale up climate finance in the region, good governance of climate finance that ensures judicious management of funds and allocation to the most needed countries, sectors and vulnerable groups is of key importance.

Questions

1. What factors account for the increasing importance of Sustainable Development?
2. Sustainability is about putting measures and policies in place to ensure that businesses are profitable over time. Discuss.
3. What is sustainable finance and banking?
4. Discuss the assertion that it is impossible for financial institutions to have any environmental or social impacts.
5. What are some of the key challenges facing the growth of sustainable banking and finance in developing countries?
6. Discuss the kinds of risks banks face in not considering the environmental and social implications of their funding activities.
7. What is the role of central banks and other regulators in promoting sustainable banking and finance in Africa?
8. Explain the difference between traditional bonds and green bonds.
9. Discuss the concept of the triple bottom line.
10. Discuss the different sources of green finance in Africa.

References

AfDB, A. D. B., & EBRD, I. (2018). *The future of work: Regional perspectives*. A Joint Publication of the African Development Bank Group, Asian Development Bank, European Bank for Reconstruction and Development, Inter-American Development Bank, Washington DC.

AfDB, O. (2013). *Structural transformation and natural resources*. African Economic Outlook.

Afful-Koomson, T. (2015). The Green climate fund in Africa: What should be different?. *Climate and Development, 7*(4), 367–379.

Ayompe, L. M., Davis, S. J., & Egoh, B. N. (2021). Trends and drivers of African fossil fuel CO2 emissions 1990–2017. *Environmental Research Letters, 15*(12), 124039.

Bhattacharya, A., Oppenheim, J., & Stern, N. (2015). Driving sustainable development through better infrastructure: Key elements of a transformation program. *Brookings Global Working Paper Series*.

Blok, K., Höhne, N., Van Der Leun, K., & Harrison, N. (2012). Bridging the greenhouse-gas emissions gap. *Nature Climate Change, 2*(7), 471–474.

Carter, C. R., & Rogers, D. S. (2008). A framework of sustainable supply chain management: moving toward new theory. *International Journal of Physical Distribution & Logistics Management*.

Dalibozhko, A., & Krakovetskaya, I. (2018). Youth entrepreneurial projects for the sustainable development of global community: evidence from Enactus program. *SHS Web of Conferences*, *57*, 1009. EDP Sciences.

Deloitte. (2017). *Sustainable banking as a driver for growth—A survey of Nigerian Banks*.

Duru, U., & Nyong, A. (2016). Why Africa needs green bonds. *Africa Economic Brief, 7*(2), 8.

Elkington, J. (1998). Accounting for the triple bottom line. *Measuring Business Excellence*.

Fonta, W. M., Ayuk, E. T., & Huysen, T. (2018). Africa and the Green climate fund: Current challenges and future opportunities. *Climate Policy, 18*(9).

Hauman M., & Hussain T. (2018, February 7). *Green finance in Africa*. White & Case LLP. https://www.whitecase.com/publications/insight/green-finance-africa

International Finance Corporation. (2014). *IFC Annual Report 2014 : Big Challenges, Big Solutions*. Washington, DC: World Bank Group. © International Finance Corporation. https://openknowledge.worldbank.org/handle/10986/20257 License: CC BY-NC-ND 3.0 IGO-

Isil, O., & Hernke, M. T. (2017). The triple bottom line: A critical review from a transdisciplinary perspective. *Business Strategy and the Environment, 26*(8), 1235–1251.

Klewitz, J., & Hansen, E. G. (2014). Sustainability-oriented innovation of SMEs: A systematic review. *Journal of Cleaner Production, 65*, 57–75.

Maltais, A., & Nykvist, B. (2020). Understanding the role of green bonds in advancing sustainability. *Journal of Sustainable Finance & Investment*, 1–20.

Milne, M. J., & Gray, R. (2013). W (h) ither ecology? The triple bottom line, the global reporting initiative, and corporate sustainability reporting. *Journal of Business Ethics, 118*(1), 13–29.

Miroshnichenko, O. S., & Brand, N. A. (2021). Banks in green economy financing: Overview of modern research. *Finance: Theory and Practice , 25* (2), 76–95.

Nakhooda, S., Caravani, A., Bird, N., Schalatek, L., & America, H. B. S. N. (2011). Climate finance in sub-Saharan Africa. *Climate Finance Policy Briefs, Heinrich Böll Stiftung North America, Washington, DC, USA and Overseas Development Institute (ODI), London, UK.*

Ntsama, U. Y. O., Yan, C., Nasiri, A., & Mboungam, A. H. M. (2021). Green bonds issuance: Insights in low-and middle-income countries. *International Journal of Corporate Social Responsibility, 6*(1), 1–9.

OECD. (2016). *Green bonds: Mobilising the debt capital markets for a low carbon transition.*

Punzi, M. T. (2018). *Role of bank lending in financing green projects: A dynamic stochastic general equilibrium approach.*

Savvidou, G., Atteridge, A., Omari-Motsumi, K., & Trisos, C. H. (2021). Quantifying international public finance for climate change adaptation in Africa. *Climate Policy, 21*(8), 1020–1036.

Shipalana, P., & O'Riordan, A. (2020). *Impact of COVID-19 on Financial Stability in Africa.*

Spinaci, S. (2021). Green and sustainable finance. *EPRS, European Parliament.*

Tseng, M.-L., Chang, C.-H., Lin, C.-W. R., Wu, K.-J., Chen, Q., Xia, L., & Xue, B. (2020). Future trends and guidance for the triple bottom line and sustainability: a data driven bibliometric analysis. *Environmental Science and Pollution Research*, 1–25.

Tseng, M.-L., Lim, M. K., Wong, W.-P., Chen, Y.-C., & Zhan, Y. (2018). A framework for evaluating the performance of sustainable service supply chain management under uncertainty. *International Journal of Production Economics, 195*, 359–372.

Tyson, J. (2021). *Financial-sector development and inclusive and sustainable economic growth in sub-Saharan Africa.*

UNEP FI. (2004). *Sustainability banking in Africa. AICC centre for sustainablity investing.*

UNCTAD (UN Conference on Trade and Development). (2014). *World Investment Report 2014.*

World Bank. (2017, November). A UN environment—WORLD BANK GROUP INITIATIVE. Roadmap for a Sustainable Financial System.

Wu, K.-J., Liao, C.-J., Tseng, M., & Chiu, K. K.-S. (2016). Multi-attribute approach to sustainable supply chain management under uncertainty. *Industrial Management & Data Systems.*

Ziolo, M., Bak, I., & Cheba, K. (2021). The role of sustainable finance in achieving Sustainable Development Goals: Does it work? *Technological and Economic Development of Economy, 27*(1), 45–70. https://doi.org/10.3846/tede.2020.13863

CHAPTER 13

Islamic Banking and Finance in Africa

Amin Karimu, Samuel Salia, Abdul-Jalil Ibrahim, and Imhotep Paul Alagidede

13.1 Introduction

The Islamic financial system has been in existence since the seventh century as noted by Chapra and Khan (2000). In the early stages of Islamic civilization, Muslims were able to establish a financial system that mobilizes resources to finance productive activities and consumer needs without the use of interest as payment for capital. This system however became dormant after western civilization swept through the world along

A. Karimu (✉)
University of Cape Town, Cape Town, South Africa
e-mail: amin.karimu@uct.ac.za

S. Salia
De Montfort University, Leicester, UK
e-mail: samuel.salia@dmu.ac.uk

A.-J. Ibrahim
Hamad Bin Khalifa University, Doha, Qatar
e-mail: Abdibrahim@hbku.edu.qa

J. Y. Abor and C. K. D. Adjasi (eds.), *The Economics of Banking and Finance in Africa*, Palgrave Macmillan Studies in Banking and Financial Institutions, https://doi.org/10.1007/978-3-031-04162-4_13

with western financial systems and associated institutions referred to in this chapter as conventional banks.

There has been a renewed interest in the Islamic financial system and its institutions in recent years due to many factors including the wake of Muslims' desire to stay clear of interest, which is prohibited according to the Islamic Shariah, the increasing severity of financial crisis, especially the recent 2007/2008 global financial crisis, the sheer volume of the financial system that is not backed by any real underlying assets, and the likely implications of a crash of such a system for the world economy. Furthermore, the recent global financial crisis has not only created some doubts among the population on how well the conventional banking is functioning, but also increased interest in Islamic banking due to the observation that they tend to have superior performance during crisis (Hasan & Dridi, 2010).

Some countries in recent years (e.g., Iran, Pakistan, and Sudan) are trying to eliminate the role of interest from their financial systems, whereas other countries such as Malaysia have allowed the establishment of Islamic banks alongside conventional ones. According to Iqbal & Llewellyn (Eds., 2002), there are now more than 200 Islamic financial institutions around the world working under different legal systems. There are examples of western multinational banks such as Citibank, HSBC, Barclays and Shanghai Banking Corporation offerings that have incorporated some Islamic financial products.

Though Islamic financial assets constitute a small fraction of the global banking assets (1.5%), its importance has been rising rapidly. For instance, as noted by Beck et al. (2013), between 2006 and 2011, total assets in Islamic financial institutions doubled to USD 900 billion (*Financial Times*, 2011). In 2019 the value rose to USD 2.44 trillion (IFSB, 2020) with a significant market share in several emerging markets (e.g., several Middle Eastern Countries) and some least developed countries (e.g., Sudan, Pakistan, Egypt) and with significant prospects in both North Africa and Sub-Saharan Africa. Currently there are about 80 Islamic financial institutions operating in Africa (Moody's Investor Services, 2020). Close to 30% of the global Muslim population is in Africa (IFSB, 2020),

I. P. Alagidede
University of the Witwatersrand, Johannesburg, South Africa
e-mail: imhotep.alagidede@wits.ac.za

but the continent accounts for only 1.52% of the USD 2.44 trillion value of the global Islamic finance assets, suggesting a low penetration of Islamic banking in Africa despite the huge Muslim population.

The structure of the chapter is as follows: The next section presents a brief overview of Islamic banking and finance. The principles and models of Islamic banking and finance are presented in Sect. 13.3, while in Sect. 13.4 an overview of Islamic banking and finance in Africa is presented. Section 13.5 provides a discussion on opportunities and challenges of Islamic banking and Sect. 13.6 presents the conclusion.

Islamic Banking and Finance

In theory, Islamic banking is a banking system that operates strictly in accordance with the Shariah law, specifically the *muamalaat* branch of Shariah that provides laws governing business transactions and contracts.

Shariah refers to the commands, prohibitions, guidance and principles derived from the primary sources of Islam, the Quran and Sunnah (Kettell, 2011). Shariah in general can be grouped into five main branches:

1. Rituals and worship branch that is referred to in Arabic as Ibadah
2. Transactions and contracts branch referred to in Arabic as Muamalaat
3. Morals and manners branch referred to in Arabic as Aadaab
4. Beliefs branch referred to in Arabic as Itiqadaat
5. Punishments branch referred to in Arabic as Uqubaat

Islamic banking is governed by one of these five branches contained in Shariah, specifically the second branch, which is the transaction and contract branch (Muamalaat in Arabic). The law under the Muamalaat branch of Shariah prohibits any business transaction and contract that violates any of the following as presented in (Beck et al., 2013):

- Not charging interest payments (riba), as only goods and services are allowed to carry a price and not money (capital),
- does not allow for speculation or gambling,
- prohibits financing of specific illicit activities such as drugs, pornography, tobacco-related products and weapons. Non-involvement is

not only limited to buying or selling but also includes all chains of production and distribution, such as packaging, transportation, warehousing and marketing of these prohibited goods and services
- relies on the idea of profit and loss sharing (risk sharing) among parties, and
- that all transactions must be backed by real transaction (involves tangible assets).

Any transaction or contract that fulfils all the above rules stipulated under the Muamalaat branch of Shariah is permissible under Islamic banking.

It is clear from the explanation provided on Islamic banking, that there are clear differences between Islamic banking and conventional banking. The differences generally hinge on interest charges, risk sharing, types of investment activities that can be financed and speculation as deduced from prior literature on Islamic Banking (Abedifar et al., 2013; Cihak & Hesse, 2010; Hasan & Dridi, 2010; Zaher & Hassan, 2001). Table 13.1 highlights the differences from current account to lending activities.

Islamic Banking and Agency Problem

Information is central to all financial transactions and contracts. However, perfect information is often not available and equally distributed among economic agents involved in a financial transaction. In general, three key problems are pertinent: not everyone has the same information; everyone has less than perfect information; and some economic agents have "inside" information which is not made available to counterparties involved in a financial transaction. In practice, decisions are generally made based on less than complete information among all counterparties involved in a transaction.

One of the problems associated with lack of equal distribution of perfect information among counterparties is the agency problem, where the agent has more information than the principal and can utilize this additional information to his benefit. The question one may ask is: "is the agency problem more pervasive under the profit-sharing rule of Islamic Banking relative to interest payment under conventional Banking?".

In theory the risk-sharing component of Islamic banking results in the equity-like nature of Savings and Investment Deposits. This suggests that on the one hand, the equity-like nature of the products might increase depositors' incentives to monitor and discipline the bank, thereby

Table 13.1 Differences between conventional and Islamic banking

Conventional banking	*Islamic banking*
Current account	
• The bank can use the funds for investment and other purposes regardless of Shariah prohibition	• The bank can use these funds for investment and other purposes if they are in compliance with the Shariah rules
Savings Account	
• The Bank can use the funds for investment and other purposes regardless of Shariah prohibition • There is a debtor–creditor relationship between the depositor and the Bank • Interest charges are involved	• Funds deposited are invested in an investment pool and the depositor fund is therefore a share of the total investment in the pool • The depositor has partnership relationship with the Bank • Profit sharing is involved here between the Bank and the depositor
Leasing	
• Lease commences on the day the Bank pays the price and not when the customer has taken the delivery • All expenses incurred in the purchase of the asset are paid by the Customer	• Lease starts after the delivery of the asset and not from the day the price has been paid by the Bank • The Bank is the owner of the asset, and therefore responsible in paying for all expenses
Lending	
• Conventional Banks are in the business of lending and borrowing money based on interest • There is no restriction to interest payments and speculative transactions under conventional Banking • All types of industries are financed except if the business is deemed illegal by the law of the land • Almost all the financing and deposit side products are loan based • Money is treated as a commodity and therefore lent at a price (interest)	• Islamic Banks work as trading/investment houses and are not involved in money lending activities • Islamic Banking prohibits charging and paying interest and all forms of speculative transactions • Non-Shariah compliance business activities are excluded from Islamic finance such as activities that cause harm to society such as alcohol, tobacco, illicit drugs, etc • Loans are considered as non-commercial and therefore excluded from commercial transaction • Banking products are usually asset backed

Source Authors' summary from various sources including Obaidullah (2005), Abedifar et al. (2013), and Khan and Ahmed (2001)

reducing the agency problems. Similarly, the equity-like nature of deposits might distort the bank's incentives to monitor and discipline borrowers as it does not face the threat of immediate withdrawal by depositors (Beck et al., 2013), which increases the agency problem. Whether the risk-sharing nature of Islamic banking leads to less agency problems than conventional banking depends on the net effect of these opposing mechanisms on depositors and banks. If the effect on banks is larger than on depositors, the agency risk would increase relative to conventional banking, and the reverse is true if depositors' effect is larger than that of the bank.

In practice, however, it has been observed that most Islamic banking products are not based on profit-loss sharing but resemble very much debt instruments. This, according to Aggarwal and Yousef (2000) and Khan (2010), is a rational response by Islamic banks to the weak contractual framework prevalent in most countries with Islamic banks. As a consequence, debt-like rather than equity-like instruments tend to work well under such environments. Abedifar et al. (2013) found that small Islamic banks have lower credit risk relative to conventional banks for a sample of 24 countries between 1999 and 2009.

Similarly, Beck et al. (2013) sampled 500 banks (both Islamic and conventional) from 22 countries for the period 2005–2009 and found that generally Islamic banks have better asset quality via the non-performing loan channel of the asset quality measure. Furthermore, the authors found evidence that the asset quality effect tends to be significant for small and medium sized Islamic banks but not for large ones. Other studies such as Baele et al. (2014) find lower defaults for Islamic than for conventional loans.

In summary, there is some evidence that Islamic banks tend to have lower default rates which translate to better asset quality than conventional banks and that the asset quality aspect of Islamic banking varies across the size of the bank, where smaller and medium size Islamic banks tend to have better asset quality than conventional banks. It is however not very clear what specifically drives these effects.

Sharia-Compliance Financing Products

Islamic finance can mainly be categorized broadly into three financing classes of product, which are debt-based, lease-based and profit-loss sharing financing (Abedifar et al., 2013) as explained below.

Debt-Based Financing

In the case of debt-based financing, the Islamic bank purchases the underlying asset that the customer has demanded, which is then sold to the client (customer). The sale would be on a deferred-payment basis with one or several instalments. This, unlike the case of a debt instrument in conventional banks, which is a form of financial loan contract to facilitate demand for liquid assets, is provided in response to demand by customers to purchase an asset by deferred payment. In general, according to Kettell (2011), the mechanism for such Islamic debt financing contracts is as follows:

1. A customer needs certain goods and promises the Islamic bank to purchase the goods (asset) if the bank buys these goods from the supplier and takes possession of them.
2. The Islamic bank purchases the goods on the spot payment basis from the supplier and takes possession (either constructive or physical).
3. The Islamic bank sells the goods to the customer after adding its profit markup, generally on deferred payment basis for an agreed period.
4. The customer makes the deferred payment to the Islamic bank after or during the agreed period.

Debt financing is currently the most widely used type of financing contract in Islamic banking and investment and it is generally applied to the following products: home financing, vehicle financing, working capital financing, project financing, goods financing, trade financing, profit rate swaps and credit cards.

Lease-Based Financing

The Islamic bank under this mode of financing would purchase the underlying asset and then rent it out to the client (customer). At the end of the rental period, ownership would be transferred wholly or partially to the client. A lease contract is generally in three forms, which are: normal lease, lease to own and lease of a specified but unidentified asset.

The normal lease involves the lessor leasing an asset for a specific period against the periodic lease rentals to lessee. At the end of the lease period, the lessee returns the asset to the lessor. In the case of a lease to own contract, the contract includes a promise that the lessor will transfer the ownership of the leased asset to the lessee at the end of the lease period, whereas in the lease of a specified but unidentified asset, the lease contract is concluded before the asset is delivered to the lessee. However, an agreement is reached to make the described (according to accurate specifications) asset available on a specific future date. The mechanism for a lease contract is as follows:

1. A customer who needs a certain asset visits the Islamic bank and promises to lease the asset.
2. The Islamic bank purchases the asset from the supplier and pays the full amount on the spot as per the quotation.
3. Both parties agree on the terms and conditions and execute the lease contract against the predefined periodic lease rent for a specific lease period.
4. In a normal lease, after the completion of the lease period, the Lessee would return the asset to the Lessor.
5. In case of lease to own, the ownership of the leased asset is transferred to the customer at the end of the lease period, in which case the rental paid by the customer includes the cost of the asset as well.

Profit-Loss Sharing Financing (PLS)
The financier, which is the Islamic bank, is a partner of the client and the realized profit or loss would be shared according to pre-agreed proportions (Khan & Ahmed, 2001). The PLS contract is based on equity orientation, implying that all parties involved in the contract share both profit and losses.

13.2 Principles and Models of Islamic Banking and Finance

Islamic finance involves investment and/or financing based on Islamic principles. The main principle of Islamic financing is the prohibition of riba (interest) and excessive risk taking such as gambling and ambiguity in contracts (gharar) (Obaidullah, 2005), moral screens such as prohibition of financing pornography (Usmani, 2002) and realism (Kahf, 2016).

Riba prohibition is the foundation of Islamic finance, as it is clearly stated in the Qur'an[1] 2:275–276 that "But God has permitted the sale and forbidden the Riba"; "God destroys/eliminates the Riba"; and, in the Qur'an 2: 278–279 "O ye who believe, fear God and quit what remains of the Riba if ye are indeed believers; but if ye do it not, take notice of war from God and His Messenger". The gravity of the sin of Riba is manifested in the use of the phrase "war from God" in the canonical text.

Financial intermediation in conventional banking mainly involves paying interest to depositors and charging interest on borrowers. Islamic banks on the other hand have to avoid interest and thus use more than one Islamic finance contract as the basis of their intermediary activities (Ayub, 2013). Even though Islamic banks do financial intermediation, the difference is that risks in Islamic banking remain with the ownership of assets, which allows them to share profit or loss arising on investments, earn returns on their trading and leasing activities and create value in the real economy. Islamic banks mobilize deposits through current account or savings/investment accounts.

Current account operations allow Islamic banks' customers to place funds into their account for holding and payment services. The contract used in current accounts is usually Qard Hassan (non-interest loan) and this does not attract any return to the customer. Islamic banks shall guarantee the principal amount of deposits. The Islamic bank may use the funds in permissible business subject to agreement with the depositor.

The Mudarabah mode of financing is used to bind the relationship between the savings/investment deposits and the Islamic bank. The investment depositor acts as the Rab al Mal (capital provider) whereas the Islamic banks act as the Mudarib (asset manager). The profit sharing is agreed and this can be varied from the capital contribution, but capital loss is shared according to capital. The "earning asset base" comprises the funds raised from the Islamic bank's capital contribution and the customer's deposit, and this provides the conduit for value creation to justify the earning of return.

According to Kahf et al. (1998), financing according to Shariah requires that the finance contract satisfy two conditions. Firstly, the contract relationship must be morally acceptable according to Islamic teachings. This criterion means that financing based on unbalanced

[1] Mustafa Khattab, the Clear Quran. Translation of the Holy Quran. Accessed on October 5, 2021 at https://quran.com/2.

contract relationships, contracts with imbedded substantial ignorance and uncertainty and the like are prohibited. Secondly, the object of financing must be acceptable under Shariah. Activities which are deemed impermissible such as alcohol, pornography, casinos and pork are prohibited. Another important principle of Islamic finance is realism. Realism postulates that Islamic finance transactions are linked to "real" transactions or exchange of values. The realism principle is manifested in situations where Islamic finance institutions finance sale of goods on deferred terms, lease financing of assets with utility or sharing in innovative projects to create value in the real economy (Kahf & Mohomed, 2016).

Islamic Banks mobilize funds from surplus economic units and transform these through size packaging and maturity matching into financial assets using sale, lease and sharing contracts. The sale contracts mode of financing used by Islamic banks includes Murabahah (deferred payment sale or cost-plus), Salam (forward sale) and Istithn'a (forward sale of manufactured goods). The Murabahah financing mode allows Islamic banks to finance clients on a deferred sale basis where the price of the commodity or item is deferred to a future date and the client pays this price in instalments. The asset-backed financing, coupled with the deferred price, allows the Islamic bank to charge a profit on the original price in the form of a mark-up. This is permissible according to Islamic law as stated in the Qur'an: "But Allah has permitted trading and forbidden interest" (Quran 2: 275). The distinction between a Murabahah financing and a conventional loan is that the former is linked to the real economy as there is an underlining asset, but this is not necessarily the case with the latter.

A Salam contract allows an Islamic financial institution to finance an object of sale contract before its actual existence. This contract allows an Islamic bank to finance a producer, usually a farmer, against the delivery of definite produce or object on an agreed future date. This contract can also be used in trade financing of standard merchandize goods such as crude oil and some importers have used this financing mode to import crude oil in some countries. In the Istithn'a mode of financing, a manufacturer can get financing for a fully described good from an Islamic bank ex ante of the existence of the good. This means that, similar to the Salam contract, the object of the transaction is deferred to future delivery but only for manufactured goods or non-raw material goods. It is important to note that it is permissible to defer both the object and the price to a future date in an Istithna transaction. Unlike Murabahah where price is deferred, in

Salam, the object is deferred whereas in Istithn'a the object and price are deferred.

Mudarabah (silent partnership) and Musharakah (active partnership) are the major contracts used in financing sharing projects. Musharakah is partnership between two or more parties to undertake a project to share profit as well as losses. Profit is negotiated according to the agreement of the parties whereas losses are shared based on the extent of financing by a party. In Musharakah, all parties contribute capital and are active in management. Mudarabah allows a partnership between a Mudarib (manager or entrepreneur) and Rab al Mal (capital owner). Profit is shared between partners while loss is borne by the capital owner. Musharakah and Mudarabah modes of financing do not fix profit, as it is determined ex post. Sharing modes of financing represent the ideal for financing in Islamic finance, but in practice these modes have been limited due to monitoring and agency costs.

The Ijarah (lease) financing mode involves an agreement between an Islamic financial institution and a client to finance a well-defined usufruct or services at a given price. A usufruct is the utility of an asset, machine or building, and the price of the usufruct must be known at the start of the contract (Kahf, 2013). The Ijarah contract allows Islamic banks to finance rental-earning assets such as real estate (usufruct ijarah and tuition fees of schools (service ijarah).

Islamic finance instruments are designed to finance the real economy through a variety of short-term liquid, low-risk financing of trade contracts to long-term financing of real sector investment (Iqbal & Mirakhor, 2013). Risk sharing provides the foundation of the spectrum. The spectrum of financing provides that at one end, it provides the funds for the purchase and sale of already produced goods for further production or consumption. Financing of yet-to-be goods motivates the other end of the spectrum. Islamic financing ensures that financing is backed by real economy activity and thus there is no room to profit from pure financial transactions without a link to real economic activity.

According to Usmani (2002), the asset-backed characteristics of Islamic financing make it more impactful. Commoditizing of money is the cornerstone of the conventional concept of financing where money is traded. This makes the trading in real goods by financial institutions forbidden, in most countries. Islamic law on the contrary does not recognize money as having intrinsic value and thus it cannot be a subject-matter of trade, except in some special cases. The Islamic principle of realism holds that apart from money's function as a store of value and unit of account, earning of a return on trading of units of money is not permissible (Kahf, 2013; Usmani, 2002).

Justification of returns in Islamic finance hinges on the notion of ownership risk and increment in wealth (Kahf, 2013). What this means is that a loan contract creates a debt between a lender and a borrower without any underlining asset. Transfer of money from the lender to the borrower means that the ownership of the loaned funds now rests on the borrower and thus the lender cannot be entitled to increment therein because of the use of the loaned funds. It is important to note that the loaned funds alone will not be able to increase in value without being combined with other factors of production. This allows a borrower to bear ownership risk as well as risk of loss if the borrower will also be entitled to increment in the loaned funds in the value creation process. This means that a financial institution can only have a claim on the increment if it also bears ownership and risk of capital loss through a profit and loss sharing contract.

13.3 An Overview of Islamic Banking and Finance in Africa

"Muslims are more likely than non-Muslims to report religion as a barrier to account ownership; however, this result appears to be mainly driven by respondents in Sub-Saharan Africa" (Beck et al., 2013). Despite this conclusion, Africa has been left behind in the global development of Islamic finance, contributing less than 2% of the global assets of Islamic finance.

The Islamic finance industry comprises Islamic banks, sukuk (Islamic bonds), Islamic funds and takaful (Islamic insurance). The total worth of the industry was estimated at USD 2.44 trillion in 2019 (IFSB, 2020). There is huge potential for growth in Islamic finance assets, as the industry has seen a double-digit growth over the years, as evidenced in the growth of 11.4% in 2019 despite geopolitical and economic factors (IFSB, 2020). The Islamic banking segment experienced a higher growth rate of 12.7% compared to the 0.9% growth recorded in 2018.

The growth and coverage of Islamic finance has not been globally encompassing across the Muslim world, as some significant populations of Muslims are left behind in Africa. Africa is host to some 27.8%

(480 million) Muslims of the 1.7 billion people under the IDB 56-Member countries. The figure is even larger when Muslims in the 32 non-IDB member African countries are considered. Despite representing close to 30% of the global Muslim population, Africa has not witnessed the benefits of Islamic finance, with only 1.8%, 0.33%, 1.56% and 2% of global Islamic banking assets, outstanding sukuk, Islamic funds and Takaful respectively (see Fig. 13.1). Thus, the continent shares only 1.52% of global Islamic finance assets of 2.44 trillion. This raises legitimate concerns of financial inclusion of the growing Islamic finance in sub-Sahara Africa.

There are about 80 Islamic financial institutions operating in Africa as full-fledged Islamic banks and Islamic banking windows of incumbent banks (Moody's Investor Services, 2020). Nigeria, Senegal and Kenya have recently commenced the implementation of their Islamic banking legal and regulatory framework (Moody's Investor Services, 2020). Morocco has seen the entry of Islamic banks since 2017 and Tunisia is also putting in place a regulatory framework to drive further expansion of the industry in the country.

There are already 3 Islamic banks in Kenya with a number of Islamic windows, and the country is currently putting together a regulatory framework to attract more foreign direct investment through the entry of new capital from Islamic banks. Other African countries where there is Islamic banks presence include Ethiopia, Benin, Ivory Coast, Mali and

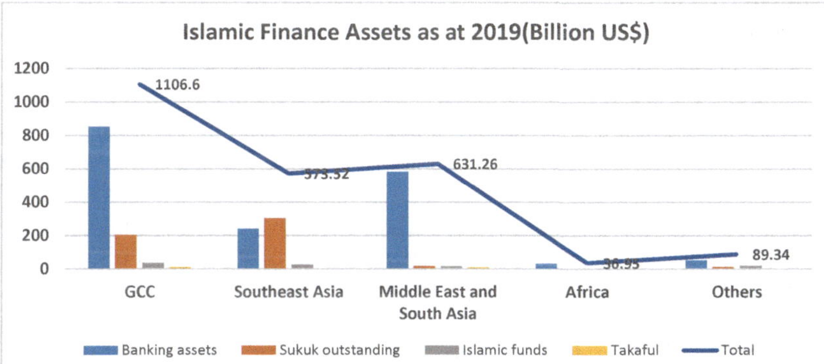

Fig. 13.1 Islamic finance assets (*Source* IFSB [2020])

Senegal. According to Moody's Investor Service (2020b), Egypt and Morocco will lead growth in North Africa, while Sudan, South Africa, Nigeria and Senegal will lead in Sub-Saharan Africa, as most have large Muslim populations, along with existing and rapidly evolving regulatory and supervisory structures in place to support growth.

13.4 Challenges and Opportunities

Islamic banking has gained traction due to the opportunity it provides for financial inclusion (Akhter et al., 2019; Banna et al., 2020). Built on Sharia-driven principles, it prohibits charging and payment of interest on financial transactions (Hassan & Aliyu, 2018). In this regard, the Islamic financial system addresses a major financial inclusion problem, the lack of access to affordable finance. In developing countries, where a significant population lacks the ability to raise finance, high interest payments have proven detrimental to business survival, giving rise to further financial inequalities and worsened poverty (Abdul-Majeed et al., 2018; Sun & Liang, 2021).

In line with the view that Islamic banking abolishes interest payment, it enables the poor to borrow from banks, a strategy that has proved attractive to the achievement of the Sustainable Development Goals (SDGs)(Jan et al., 2021). For example, Islamic finance aligns with the UN's SDGs 8 &16, in that it promotes affordable finance for the poor, which has implications for inequality, poverty and social cohesion. This is a major paradigm shift in that the alignment of Islamic banking to the SDGs provides an opportunity to grow the concept so long as its original binding principles are intimately maintained (Gundogdu, 2018; Hassan et al., 2021; Laldin & Djafri, 2021; Shinkafi et al., 2019). These assertions are consistent with evidence that associates Islamic banking with the sustainability paradigm as related to the Ismaili and Chapra models of Islamic banking (Aliyu et al., 2017).

Furthermore, the Islamic banking system, since its renewed development in about 1975, has recorded a growth rate of 15–20%. This, coupled with the evidence of its strong performance during the 2007 financial crisis, has enhanced the reputation of Islamic banking as a legitimate opportunity to fill a finance gap and provide practical insights into a banking system that is resilient to financial shocks. For example, according to Asmild et al. (2019), the market of sharia compliant equities during the financial crisis outperformed conventional markets and showed less variability, thereby making them less risky. There is also evidence that Islamic banks have higher intermediation ratio and higher asset quality, and are better capitalized (Beck et al., 2013). There is also evidence in the banking literature that suggests Islamic banks have lower credit risk compared to conventional banks (Abedifar et al., 2013). Supporting this stance, Belanès et al. (2015) concluded that such information can provide important insights to managers and regulators in financial market development. Drawing evidence from the features of the Islamic banking system, the evidence suggests that such a system is robust to financial crisis. Therefore, there is an opportunity to develop and adapt banking approaches that align with this concept to avoid significant future shocks from financial crisis.

However, Islamic banking is confronted with challenges. Firstly, the success of Islamic banks during and following the financial crisis has attracted a lot of interest within the banking sector; conventional banks have realized that Islamic finance provides opportunities to venture into new markets (Karbhari et al., 2004). Therefore the approach has experienced significant uptake across the global and conventional banks such as HSBC, Barclays and Citibank which offer Islamic banking services (Mrowiec & Jurkiewicz, 2021). This practice raises an important question about mission drift. Practitioners have dominated the Islamic banking sector in countries where Shariah principles do not apply; hence, it is difficult to assess the extent to which the products and services delivered align with the concept of Islamic banking. For example, Islamic banking in Gulf States such as Saudi Arabia and Oman easily adapt and evolve around a regulatory system that is compliant with Shariah principles.

Previously established Islamic institutions, such as Al-Baraka in the UK (Abdul, 2008), show that progress has been made to champion the concept of Islamic banking as a means of addressing financial needs of the UK-based Muslim community. However, this alone, is not sufficient to test the efficient practice of Islamic banking in the UK. In fact, Islamic scholars have argued that almost 85% of Sukuks in the market are not Shariah-compliant (Lahsasna & Sze Lin, 2012) and this could be further exacerbated in markets where Sharia regulations to not abound. Therefore, problems of regulatory hurdles, competition from conventional banks, and lack of adequately qualified and trained personnel exist (Riaz et al., 2017) and have the potential to cause a mission drift and challenge the concept of financial inclusion which underpins Islamic banking.

Secondly, Islamic banks practice a principle of profit and loss sharing (PLS) which is a key feature that distinguishes Islamic banking from conventional banking (Hassan & Aliyu, 2018). Arguably, this approach is problematic. The practice relies on disclosures from the parties involved in the transaction, especially relating to loss/gains made on the transaction that has been entered. The Islamic banking system is therefore confronted with a severe case of the hazard of information asymmetry (Ahmad & Bahrul, 2018). Just like conventional banks (Tran et al., 2019), information asymmetry exists for Islamic banks (Fu et al., 2018). Challenges in information gathering for borrowers impact credit decision-making of banks (Zhu, 2018). In this regard, agency theory, which focuses on the principal–agent relationship, is important in understanding the significance of promoting confidence and reinforcing trust between lenders and borrowers in the Islamic banking sector (Darayseh & Chazi, 2018; Al-Nasser et al., 2017).

As a result of information asymmetries between Islamic banks and borrowers, and differing motives, Islamic banks lack trust in borrowers and may therefore need an assessment mechanism to build up and/or reinforce this trust (Nicholson-Crotty et al., 2018). This implies that the lack of an approach to assessing borrower creditability is a key barrier against Islamic bank lending.

Thirdly, borrowers have incentives for engaging in undesirable activities, making them likely to invest loans contracted from Islamic banks in non-compliant Shariah ventures (Mili & Abid, 2017). These behaviours are often motivated by the desire to gain higher profits; subsequently, the resulting profit is shared under the profit/loss arrangements in Islamic finance. This moral hazard of funds mingling dilutes the tenets of Islamic finance and constrains the principle of interest abolishment, which remains a major challenge for Islamic banking.

Finally, the terminology of Islamic finance products, dis-interest in internet banking facilities and branch networks as well as a generalized lack of interest in marketing by Islamic banks are at variance with banking innovation (Yafiz et al., 2019). According to Riaz et al. (2017), although some coincidence of perception is evident, the views of practitioners within Islamic banking are shown to be out of line with those of the other parties in a number of key areas. This is further buttressed by the view that Islamic bankers appear to see less potential in the role of the internet as a medium for spreading awareness than do either potential customers or religious scholars (Riaz et al., 2017).

13.5 Conclusion

The various episodes of financial crises experienced over the years, and particularly the recent 2007/2008 crisis, have generated significant interest in Islamic banking. Some have argued that the business model of Islamic banking guided by the Shariah law enables it to withstand such crisis and that it has more stability due to asset quality and high capitalization relative to conventional banking. Though such a banking model has been in the world for many centuries, it is still not well understood by the majority of people around the world, especially the non-Muslim population.

This chapter has presented a clear and non-technical material to clarify what Islamic banking is, the differences between Islamic banking and conventional banking, Sharia-compliance financing products, the principles and models of Islamic banking, an overview of Islamic banking in Africa and the challenges and opportunities of Islamic banking.

The recent financial crisis suggests that the world needs a diversified financial business model to be able to serve different interests of the population and to safeguard the financial system of the world from being exposed to similar risk due to a single financial business model. It is therefore imperative that a significant aspect of the financial system conducts transactions that are backed by real underlying assets and not non-real assets. Also, there is a need to avoid the situation where a significant part of the financial system is driven by speculative activities and gambling.

These aspects (transactions being backed by real underlying assets and not based on speculative activities) of Islamic banking are even more useful for parts of the world with underdeveloped financial systems, where asset quality is low due to high non-performing loans and the risks for defaults are high, and where regulation is so weak that it generates significant information asymmetry problems, so that the likelihood of withstanding financial crisis is low.

References

Abdul-Majeed Alaro, A. R., & Alalubosa, A. H. (2018). Potential of Sharī'ah compliant microfinance in alleviating poverty in Nigeria: A lesson from Bangladesh. *International Journal of Islamic and Middle Eastern Finance and Management, 12*(1), 115–129. https://doi.org/10.1108/IMEFM-01-2017-0021

Abdul, K. A. (2008). The emergence of Islamic banking in the UK: A comparative study with Muslim countries on JSTOR. *Arab Law Quartely*, *22*(2), 180–198. Retrieved from https://www.jstor.org/stable/27650617

Abedifar, P., Molyneux, P., & Tarazi, A. (2013). Risk in Islamic banking. *Review of Finance, 17*(6), 2035–2096. https://doi.org/10.1093/ROF/RFS041

Aggarwal, R. K., & Yousef, T. (2000). Islamic banks and investment financing. *Journal of Money, Credit and Banking, 32*, 93–120.

Ahmad, R. & Bahrul, Y. (2018). Asymmetric information and non-performing financing: Study in the Indonesian Islamic Banking Industry. *Journal of Islamic Economics*, *10*(2), 403–416. Retrieved from https://smartlib.umri.ac.id/assets/uploads/files/bc8e1-7392-22015-1-pb.pdf

Akhter, W., Majeed, M. U. & Roubaud, D. (2019). Islamic banking and financial inclusion: Evidence from Asian and African markets. *Journal of Islamic Business and Management*, *9*(2), 341–354. Retrieved from https://journals.riphah.edu.pk/index.php/jibm/article/view/171

Al-Nasser Mohammed, S. A. S., & Muhammed, J. (2017). The relationship between agency theory, stakeholder theory and Shariah supervisory board in Islamic banking: An attempt towards discussion. *Humanomics, 33*(1), 75–83. https://doi.org/10.1108/H-08-2016-0062

Aliyu, S., Hassan, M. K., Yusof, R. M. & Naiimi, N. (2017). Islamic banking sustainability: A review of literature and directions for future research. *Https://Doi.Org/*https://doi.org/10.1080/1540496X.2016.1262761, *53*(2), 440–470. https://doi.org/10.1080/1540496X.2016.1262761

Asmild, M., Kronborg, D., Mahbub, T., & Matthews, K. (2019). The efficiency patterns of Islamic banks during the global financial crisis: The case of Bangladesh. *The Quarterly Review of Economics and Finance, 74*, 67–74. https://doi.org/10.1016/J.QREF.2018.04.004

Ayub, M. (2013). *Understanding Islamic finance*. Gramedia Pustaka Utama.

Baele, L., Farooq, M., & Ongena, S. (2014). Of religion and redemption: Evidence from default on Islamic loans. *Journal of Banking & Finance*, *44*, 141–159.

Banna, H., Alam, M. R., Ahmad, R., & Sari, N. M. (2020). Does financial inclusion drive the Islamic Banking efficiency? *A Post-Financial Crisis Analysis*. https://doi.org/10.1142/S0217590819420050

Beck, T., Demirgüç-Kunt, A., & Merrouche, O. (2013). Islamic vs. conventional banking: Business model, efficiency and stability. *Journal of Banking & Finance*, *37*(2), 433–447. https://doi.org/10.1016/J.JBANKFIN.2012.09.016

Belanès, A., Ftiti, Z., & Regaïeg, R. (2015). What can we learn about Islamic banks' efficiency under the subprime crisis? Evidence from GCC Region.

Pacific-Basin Finance Journal, 33, 81–92. https://doi.org/10.1016/J.PACFIN.2015.02.012

Chapra, M. U., & Tariqullah, K. (2000). *Regulation and supervision of Islamic banks* (Occasional Paper No. 3). Jeddah, Saudi Arabia: Islamic Research and Training Institute, Islamic Development Bank.

Cihak, M., & Hesse, H. (2010). Islamic banks and financial stability: An empirical analysis. *Journal of Financial Services Research, 38*, 95–113.

Darayseh, M., & Chazi, A. (2018). Bank specifics, economics environment, and agency theory: Determinants of banking performance In GCC. *The Journal of Developing Areas, 52*(4), 199–212. https://doi.org/10.1353/JDA.2018.0060

Financial Times. (2011). *Islamic finance* (Supplement, May 12).

Fu, H., Yang, J., & An, Y. (2018). Contracts for venture capital financing with double-sided moral hazard. *Small Business Economics, 531*, 129–144. https://doi.org/10.1007/S11187-018-0028-2.

Gundogdu, A. S. (2018). An inquiry into Islamic finance from the perspective of sustainable development goals. *European Journal of Sustainable Development, 7*(4), 381–381. https://doi.org/10.14207/EJSD.2018.V7N4P381

Hassan, M. K., & Aliyu, S. (2018). A contemporary survey of islamic banking literature. *Journal of Financial Stability, 34*, 12–43. https://doi.org/10.1016/J.JFS.2017.11.006

Hassan, M. K., Saraç, M., & Khan, A. (Eds.). (2021). *Islamic finance and sustainable development: A sustainable economic framework for Muslim and Non-Muslim countries*. Springer Nature.

Hasan, M. & Dridi, J. (2010). *The effects of the global crisis on Islamic and conventional banks: A comparative study* (IMF Working Paper # WP/10/201).

IFSB. (2020). *Islamic financial service industry stability report*. IFSB. https://www.ifsb.org/preess_full.php?id=534&submit=more

Iqbal, M., & Llewellyn, D. T. (Eds.). (2002). *Islamic banking and finance: new perspectives on profit sharing and risk.* Edward Elgar Publishing.

Iqbal, Z., & Mirakhor, A. (Eds.). (2013). *Economic development and Islamic finance*. World Bank.

Jan, A., Mata, M. N., Albinsson, P. A., Martins, J. M., Hassan, R. B., & Mata, P. N. (2021). Alignment of Islamic Banking sustainability indicators with sustainable development goals: Policy recommendations for addressing the COVID-19 pandemic. *Sustainability, 13*(5), 2607. https://doi.org/10.3390/SU13052607

Kahf, M. (2013). *Islamic finance contracts*. Al Manhal.

Kahf, M., Ahmed, A., & Homoud, S. (1998). Islamic banking and development: An alternative banking concept. Islamic Research and Training Institute (Islamic Development Bank, Jeddah).

Kahf, M., & Mohomed, A. N. (2016). The principle of Realism in Islamic finance. *Journal of Islamic Economics, Banking and Finance.* https://link.gale.com/apps/doc/A598310341/AONE?u=anon~e3f9415f&sid=googleScholar&xid=edc52fdf

Karbhari, Y., Naser, K., & Shahin, Z. (2004). Problems and challenges facing the islamic banking system in the west: The case of the UK. *Thunderbird International Business Review, 46*(5), 521–543. https://doi.org/10.1002/TIE.20023

Kettell, B. (2011). *Introduction to Islamic banking and finance* (Vol. 551). John Wiley & Sons.

Khan, F. (2010). How 'Islamic' is Islamic banking? *Journal of Economic Behavior and Organization, 76*, 805–820.

Khan, T. & Ahmed, H. (2001). *Risk management: An analysis of issues in Islamic financial industry.* Islamic Development Bank, Islamic Research and Training Institute.

Lahsasna, A., & Sze Lin, L. (2012). Issues in Islamic capital markets: Islamic bond/sukuk. 3rd International conference on business and economic research (3rd icber 2012) proceeding. Retrieved from www.internationalconference.com.my

Laldin, M. A. & Djafri, F. (2021). *The role of Islamic finance in achieving sustainable development goals (SDGs)*, 107–126. https://doi.org/10.1007/978-3-030-76016-8_6

Mili, M., & Abid, S. (2017). Moral hazard and risk-taking incentives in Islamic banks, does franchise value matter! *International Journal of Islamic and Middle Eastern Finance and Management, 10*(1), 42–59. https://doi.org/10.1108/IMEFM-12-2015-0148

Moody's Investors Service. (2020a, March). *Cross-Sector—Islamic Finance: GCC and Malaysia will drive growth across Sharīʿah-compliant products in 2020* (pp. 1–19). https://www.moodys.com/research/Moodys-GCC-and-Malaysia-to-drive-Islamic-finance-growth--PBC_1220868

Moody's Investors Service (2020b). *Africa's vast financing needs will drive Islamic Finance growth* https://www.moodys.com/research/Moodys-Africas-vast-financing-needs-will-drive-Islamic-Finance-growth--PBC_1252105.

Mrowiec, P. & Jurkiewicz, M. W. (2021). Selected characteristics of Islamic banking in context of real sphere development. *Global Journal of Business, Economics and Management: Current Issues*, 11(1), 1–09. https://doi.org/10.18844/GJBEM.V11I1.4692.

Mustafa Khattab, the Clear Quran. Translation of the Holy Quran. Accessed on October 5, 2021 at https://quran.com/2

Nicholson-Crotty, J., Nicholson-Crotty, S. & Li, D. (2018). Recruit screening, Rrpresentation, and the moral Hazard problem in policing. https://doi.org/10.1080/15309576.2018.1470992, *42*(2), 483–503. https://doi.org/10.1080/15309576.2018.1470992

Obaidullah, M. (2005). Islamic Financial Services. Islamic economics research center. *King Abdul Aziz University, Saudi Arabia ISBN*, 9960–06.

Riaz, U., Burton, B., & Monk, L. (2017). Perceptions on the accessibility of Islamic banking in the UK—Challenges, opportunities and divergence in opinion. *Accounting Forum, 41*(4), 353–374. https://doi.org/10.1016/J.ACCFOR.2017.10.002

Shinkafi, A. A., Yahaya, S., & Sani, T. A. (2019). Realising financial inclusion in Islamic finance. *Journal of Islamic Marketing, 11*(1), 143–160. https://doi.org/10.1108/JIMA-02-2017-0020

Sun, S. L., & Liang, H. (2021). Globalization and affordability of microfinance. *Journal of Business Venturing, 36*(1), 106065. https://doi.org/10.1016/J.JBUSVENT.2020.106065

Thaker, M. T., Bin, M. A., Thaker, M. T., Bin, H., Allah Pitchay, A., & Bin. (2018). Public relations activities in Islamic banking industry: An approach of circuit of culture (COC) model. *Journal of Islamic Marketing, 9*(2), 283–295. https://doi.org/10.1108/JIMA-06-2016-0047

Tran, D. V., Hassan, M. K., & Houston, R. (2019). Activity strategies, information asymmetry, and bank opacity. *Economic Modelling, 83*, 160–172. https://doi.org/10.1016/J.ECONMOD.2019.02.008

Usmani, M. T. (2002). *An introduction to Islamic finance* (Vol. 20). Brill.

Yafiz, M., Harahap, I. M., Batubara, C. & Ridwan, M. (2019). Customers' Perception of the Use of Arabic Terminology in Sharia Banking Products. *KnE Social Sciences, 2019*, 505–514. https://doi.org/10.18502/KSS.V3I19.4881.

Zaher, T. S., & Hassan, M. K. (2001). A comparative literature survey of Islamic banking and finance. *Financial Markets, Institutions, and Instruments, 10*, 155–199.

Zhu, Z. (2018). Safety promise, moral hazard and financial supervision: Evidence from peer-to-peer lending. *Finance Research Letters, 27*, 1–5. https://doi.org/10.1016/J.FRL.2018.07.002

PART V

Banking Crises and Global Banking

CHAPTER 14

Explaining Banking Failures in Africa

Joshua Yindenaba Abor, Sam Mensah, Baah Aye Kusi, and David Mathuva

14.1 Introduction

It is evident from the literature that the functions performed by banks are critical for promoting economic growth, development, and welfare. These functions include liquidity creation, matching deficit spending units with surplus spending units, business venture evaluation and effective allocation of resources, facilitating economic and financial transactions, monitoring economic agents and provision of information for making decisions. However, banking systems can also be destructive especially when they are distressed and failing as learnt from the 2007 to 2009 global financial crises. In fact, Crotty (2009) warns that banking systems can make or unmake economies if care is not taken.

J. Y. Abor (✉) · B. A. Kusi
Department of Finance, University of Ghana Business School, Legon, Accra, Ghana
e-mail: joshabor@ug.edu.gh

B. A. Kusi
e-mail: baahkusi@gmail.com

J. Y. Abor and C. K. D. Adjasi (eds.), *The Economics of Banking and Finance in Africa*, Palgrave Macmillan Studies in Banking and Financial Institutions, https://doi.org/10.1007/978-3-031-04162-4_14

As such studies have shown that bank failures are injurious to financial and economic systems, as well as economic agents who operate in these systems (Kerstein & Kozberg, 2013; Öğüt et al., 2012). For instance, loss of investor confidence (Osili & Paulson, 2009), employment, increased cost finance (Borio & Lowe, 2002) and low economic and real sector outputs (Bordo et al., 2010; Dell'Ariccia et al., 2008; Levine et al., 2016) are some of the effects of bank failures mentioned in the literature. Furthermore, banking failures are established to put pressure on the fiscal (Feltenstein & Rochon, 2009; Honohan & Klingebiel, 2003, 2000; Turrini et al., 2012) and monetary (Nakatani, 2016; Dell'Ariccia et al., 2008; Hua-Jiang, 2008; Smith, 2002) policies and thereby increasing the tax burden of economic agents and financial market participants. Thus, cost of banking failures which has adverse implications for governments, market participants, and all economic agents cannot be overemphasized and needs attention.

In response to curbing banking failures and other financial institutions failures, it is evident that while abundant empirical evidence exists in Europe, America, and Asia (Balla et al., 2019; Cole & Gunther, 1995; Pedro et al., 2018; Wheelock & Wilson, 2000), there is limited and scanty empirical evidence on banking failures in Africa. Specifically, empirical studies that investigate factors that influence or lead to banking failures are nonexistent in the context of Africa. Coupled with the recent banking failures which hit Ghana, Nigeria, and Kenya, there is an urgent need to establish factors that influence banking failures in Africa. It is against this background that this study attempts to review literature on banking failures with a focus on Africa to identify possible factors that may have

S. Mensah
SEM Capital Advisors Limited, Accra, Ghana
e-mail: smensah@semcapitaladvisors.com

B. A. Kusi
Department of Applied Finance and Policy Management, University of Education, Accra, Ghana

D. Mathuva
Strathmore Business School, Nairobi, Kenya
e-mail: dmathuva@strathmore.edu

influenced banking failures in the region. We found this to be important because of the increasing incidence of banking failures in Africa and regulators would have to know which factors to target to tame banking failures. The rest of the study is organized into sections captioned as: why do banks fail? consequence or effects for banking failures in Africa, banking failures and crises in Africa, remedies for banking failures in Africa, and conclusions and policy implications.

14.2 Why Do Banks Fail?

Bank failure is a global phenomenon and not unique to specific countries or regions, yet not a customary practice (Benston & Kaufman, 1997; Goodhart, 2005). Whenever banks fail, the ripple effects are also experienced by stakeholders outside the mainstream system including non-banking public. Several factors account for bank failures, prominent among them include unfavorable economic conditions, regulatory failures, poor corporate governance practices, mismanagement (i.e., fraudulent and corrupt dealings and poor risk management procedures), and non-performing loans. These are most common in developing economies such as Africa. The impact of bank failure results in unemployment, reduction in earnings, breakdown in the financial sector development, and many associated public interest (see Smith & Walter, 1997). This can go a long way to distract aggregate economic activities and collapse the entire financial system (Hocks, 1994).

Many advanced nations experienced upsetting bank failures in the late 90s. For example, Banco Ambrosiano in Italy, Herstatt Bank of Germany, Barings Bank in the United Kingdom (Gray et al., 2001; Heffernan, 1996; Smith & Walter, 1997), etc. The Federal Deposit Insurance Corporation (FDIC) reports that 560 bank failures were recorded from 2001 to 2019 (see Fig. 14.1). Notable among these banks include: First City Bank of Florida, Fort Walton Beach, FL; Guaranty Bank, Milwaukee, WI, (BestBank in Georgia & Michigan); Trust Company Bank, Memphis, TN, etc.

Bank failures have greatly been recorded in developing economies especially in Africa over the years owing to several factors such as non-performing loans, regulatory failure, poor governance practices, etc. For instance, from 1988 to 1990, three commercial banks in Benin collapsed due to non-performing loans of 80% of banks' loans advanced. In Côte d'Ivoire, four of the biggest banks which account for 90% of the banking

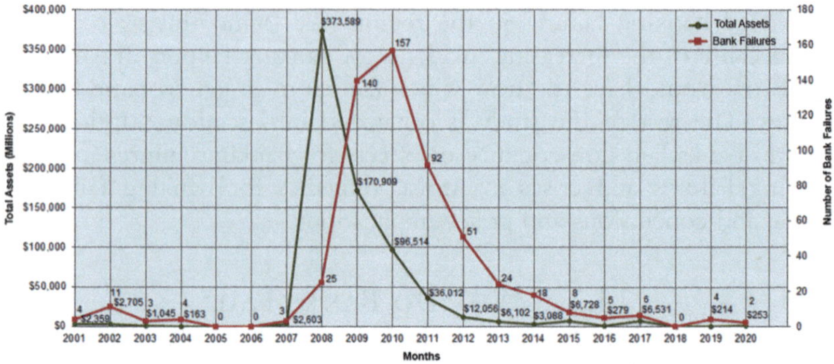

Fig. 14.1 Number of bank failures (*Source* fdic bank failures in brief-summary [available online at: www.fdic.gov/bank/historical/bank])

system loans were liquidated due to poor governance and non-performing loans from 1988 to 1991. The issue has also become rampant in recent times in countries such as Ghana, South Africa, and Nigeria.

Researchers in Economics and Finance have published extensively on the need to address bank failures since the 1930s banking crisis. For instance, Meyer and Pifer (1970) developed a framework that sought to match specific bank failure to a comparable solvent bank that shares similar fundamentals (such as their national economic situations) and propose appropriate financial factors that can resolve the potential insolvency menace. Other studies such as Hwang et al. (1997) have identified the pressing factors likely to cause bank failure. The writers were able to decipher those factors that can be amended over time to avoid bank catastrophe. Yet the issue of bank failures persists up-to-date. As a result of the rippling effects associated with bank failures (from the affected banks to the non-banking public), studying the causes of banking fiascoes have become very relevant in this present age (Kaufman, 1996). We shall focus on the most prominent and prevalent factors casing bank failures in developing world, especially Africa. Therefore, we shall consider how unfavorable economic conditions, regulatory failures, poor corporate governance practices, mismanagement (i.e., fraudulent and corrupt dealings and poor risk management procedures), and non-performing loans lead to banking failure in Africa.

Unfavorable Economic Conditions

Eisenbeis (1986) posits that sudden adverse movement in an economy's terms of trade resulting from global economic shocks (including interest, inflation, and exchange rates volatilities) accompanied by strict bank regulations are key determinants of bank failures. Similar deteriorating economic condition (such as high inflation, interest rates, and exchange rates) on the domestic front can also cause bank failure (Goodhart et al., 1998; Hooks, 1994). A typical example is the South Africa banking crisis in 2002. In that case, poor performance of the Rand coupled with higher interest rate led to the collapse of the then seventh-largest bank in RSA, Saambou Bank. On January 15, 2001, ABSA announced severe losses in its Unifer microlending unit. Saambou's clientele was comparable to Unifer's, and a run on the company began within five weeks, wiping away 20% of its deposits. Other runs were sparked by the collapse of Saambou. Board of Executors, South Africa's fifth-largest bank, folded just a few weeks later. In the end, 22 banks closed, accounting for half of the total number of banks in South Africa and 10% of the banking sector in terms of size. The South African Reserve Bank (SARB) decided against bailing out these institutions. Rather, as the crisis spread, it hiked interest rates, concerned about greater inflation due to exchange-rate depreciation (making the same mistake as the US Fed did during the Great Depression). Given that it was a pure liquidity crisis—all of the impacted banks were solvent and well-capitalized, but their funding systems were shaky—this is shocking and, in retrospect, a bad decision.

Regulatory Failures

The Central Bank oversees bank regulation. The Financial Supervision department is responsible for overseeing banks in order to ensure liquidity, solvency, and appropriate operation of a stable market-based banking system. Moreover, based on the Central Bank internal rating system, the banking sector's audited performance is measured in terms of capital adequacy, asset quality, liquidity, and earnings. In Kenya, an institution must maintain a minimum holding of liquid assets as determined by the Central Bank from time to time under section 19 of the Banking Act. Financial systems might become fragile without sufficient regulation, generating crises that can harm the actual economy (Spratt, 2013). Given that finance's primary goal is to facilitate productive economic activity, regulation's goal is to protect financial stability while also promoting economic growth. When governments intervene to save banks from failure, creditors and consumers tend to trust the government to preserve their interests, according to Hempel and Simonson (1999: 17). Other institutions, creditors, and consumers, on the other hand, are discouraged from successfully monitoring their bank interests in an independent manner as a result of the interference. According to Goodhart et al. (1998), bank failures can be attributed to the following:

(i) Banks may disregard the system if it is characterized by too many superfluous stringent rules.
(ii) The general rules and regulations governing the banking system are unable to resolve certain threats the banks are exposed to.
(iii) A rigid set of standards could prevent banks from choosing the most efficient way to meet the regulatory goals that have been established for them, acting as a deterrent to improvement. Bank failure, according to Spollen (1997), is caused by an inefficient regulatory structure.

Box 14.1: Regulatory Failure in Kenya
A Dubai Bank was placed into receivership in Kenya for a variety of reasons. The first was a declining cash reserve ratio. The bank's failure to meet its financial obligations was the second. The third offense was breaking banking laws and regulations, such as failing to maintain proper capital and liquidity ratios, failing to make provisions for non-performing loans, and failing to have a strong corporate governance structure. Dubai Bank was also cited for failing to follow client instructions and owing the Bank of Africa KES 48 million from a forex transaction. Officials from the Central Bank of Kenya (CBK) have now been accused of assisting top managers of both lenders in concealing the schemes. Since July 14, 2015, when Dubai Bank began violating its daily cash reserve ratio standards, the regulator has been closely monitoring the bank's daily cash reserve ratio. The regulator also stated that its efforts to persuade the small lender to correct the situation had been unsuccessful. Instead, the bank had "failed to comply," and its cash reserve ratios had "continued to erode." "The non-compliance with the cash reserve ratios has to date attracted a total penalty of KES 5,395,721.03. Owing to the consistently deteriorating cash

reserve ratio position of Dubai Bank and its failure to honour financial obligations, including KES 48.18 million due to Bank of Africa Kenya Limited, the CBK is of the considered opinion that the bank will most likely fail to meet its financial obligations in the normal course of business," according to the regulator when deciding to put the lender under receivership.

Poor Corporate Governance Practices

Organizations have a variety of responsibilities in addition to the basic purpose of profit maximization. Corporate governance is defined by the Private Initiative for Corporate Governance as "the system by which stakeholders (shareholders, creditors, employees, clients, suppliers, the government, and society in general) oversee management and insiders to protect their own interests" (Kihumba, 2010). Corporate governance is defined by Sarbanes-Oxley (2005) as proper disclosures to shareholders, regulators, and financial results that are clear. In the general business sense, key stakeholders of corporate governance range from shareholder, board of directors, management, and the Central Bank. Poor corporate governance is one big factor behind bank failures. An empirical study by Bhagat and Bolton (2008) in the United States shows that corporate deficiencies are at the heart of other corporate problems. In Africa, poor corporate governance is the major factor behind bank failures in Africa (Shungu et al., 2014). In Nigeria, Nworji et al. (2011), examine issues, challenges, and opportunities associated with corporate governance and bank failure in Nigeria. The study concludes that poor corporate governance is responsible for the poor functioning of banks. The similar defect is associated with bank failures in countries such as Ghana, Kenya, Zimbabwe, South Africa, and Rwanda (Box 14.2 discusses the role of corporate issues on bank failure in Ghana). Corporate governance is a broad topic with many facets. Issues of fiduciary duty and accountability are fundamental themes in corporate governance. This centers around pushing for the implementation of systems and norms that will ensure proper behavior and shareholder protection.

Box 14.2: Bank Failure in Ghana: Poor Corporate Governance Practices

In a news statement dated August 14, 2017, the BoG announced its approval of GCB Bank LTD's acquisition of two indigenous banks, UT Bank LTD and Capital Bank LTD. The revocation of the banks' operation licenses was mostly due to their insolvency, according to the BoG. Managers of the banks failed, according to BoG, despite multiple agreements with the banks to boost their capital needs. As a result, the banks' licenses were terminated in a Purchase and Assumption deal with GCB Bank LTD to protect clients' deposits. On August 1, 2018, the Bank of Ghana (BoG) announced the merger of five indigenous banks to form the Consolidated Bank Ghana LTD. Unibank Ghana LTD, The Royal Bank LTD, Beige Bank LTD, Sovereign Bank LTD, and Construction Bank LTD were among the five banks that failed. Approximately seven indigenous banks have failed in the last two years. Poor corporate governance has been recognized by BoG and other financial analysts as one of the key causes of the seven banks' failure (According to the 2018 BoG Report). The board of directors and senior management were either inert or engaged in activities that benefited their personal interests rather than the banks' growth. For example, it was discovered that most non-performing loans were given to people who were related to top board members (Debrah, 2018). Furthermore, due to a lack of experience or avarice, bank boards of directors failed to manage bank accounting and corporate reporting systems, as well as the external auditing system (Afolabi Jerry, 2018). Furthermore, the board of directors failed to establish a proper risk management structure. In majority of the failed banks, Chief Internal Auditors lacked independence and integrity, resulting in cover-ups for executive directors during review processes (Afolabi Jerry, 2018). The failure of these banks was mostly due to a general lack of compliance with corporate governance regulations.

Non-performing Loans

Practically, there is no universally accepted global standard for defining non-performing loans (NPLs). A non-performing loan is one that has defaulted or is about to default. When interest and principal payments are 90 days or more past due, or at least 90 days of interest payments have been capitalized, refinanced, or delayed by agreement, or when payments are less than 90 days overdue but there are other good reasons to doubt that payment will be made in full, a loan is considered non-performing (IMF, 2009). NPLs are frequently viewed as undesired outputs or costs to lending institutions, lowering the bank's performance. Some theorists and scholars attribute bank failures to high. For example, a study by Mabvure et al (2012) on the causes of NPLs in Zimbabwe using CBZ Bank as a case study showed that NPLs are one of the biggest factors behind bank closures and have become prevalent in Zimbabwe. Studies in other countries show that most of the bank failures have been caused by a high incidence of NPLs (Brownbridge, 1998). Nishimura et al. (2001) investigated the situation in Japan and determined that after the bubble burst, some of the loans granted to enterprises during the bubble era were non-performing. According to Caprio and Klingebiel (2002), reported in Fofack and Fofack (2005), NPLs accounted for nearly 75% of total loan assets in Indonesia, resulting in the failure of over sixty banks in 1997. In Ghana, NPLs were major contributing factors to the collapse of UT Bank Ltd and UniBank Ltd. Box 14.3 shows the bank failure resulting from non-performing loans in Kenya. Non-performing loans are related directly with commercial bank failure and financial crises. Commercial banks are exposed to the risk of borrowers defaulting due to the nature of their operation. The elimination of non-performing loans (NPLs) is a precondition for improving the banking sector's economic state and stability. If non-performing loans are allowed to continue to exist and be rolled over, resources are locked up in an unprofitable industry, stifling economic growth, and reducing economic efficiency.

Box 14.3: Bank Failure in Kenya: The Role of Non-performing Loans in Kenya

NPLs are loans that are not being serviced as per loan contracts and expose financial institutions to potential losses, according to the Kenyan Central Bank (CBK, 2016). The failed Kenyan banks have been struggling in the red for the past few years, with corporate revenues being sucked up by the sale of non-performing loans (NPLs). According to Chase Bank records, the bank lost KES 742 million. Even though it had produced a profit of KES 2.3 billion the previous year, this transpired. Non-performing loans increased from KES 3 billion in 2014 to KES 11 billion in 2015, according to the statements. The bank's issues stemmed mostly from KES 16.6 billion in "problematic" insider loans, the viability of which was questioned at the time. The unsecured loans included KES 8.7 billion in dubious loans to firms owned or tied to some directors, as well as KES 1 billion in personal loans. Insider lending, according to Kiyai (2003), was the single biggest cause to many of the collapsed local banks' poor loans. Insider loans accounted for a significant share of the bad debts in at least half of the bank collapses. Most of Kenya's bigger bank collapses, such as Chase Bank, Imperial Bank, and Dubai Bank, involved a lot of insider lending, mostly to directors and directors' allies.

Mismanagement

A successful business relies heavily on management. Many banks failed in the 1980s and early 1990s due to poor management. The absence of good managerial ideas in management decision-making is the primary cause of the banking crisis. As a result, expertise and focus are crucial in banking (Spiegel et al., 1996). Mismanagement, particularly excessive risk-taking, is the leading cause of bank failure, according to Pantalone and Platt (1987; Hooks, 1994). On the other hand, White (1993) points out that, while bankers are accused of misbehavior, proving that managerial carelessness is the sole reason of bank failure is challenging. In the area of management failure Spollen (1997) suggested the following:

- Poor Business control and appreciation.
- Poot compliance with stipulated rules.
- Staff deficit especially at the middle management level leading to over-time work and low performance.

Most of the time, organizations are cheated by some of their own employees, usually individuals who have worked for them for a long time and whose work is not supervised. Because they seem to be exceedingly efficient on their timetable, they are given excessive authority. Individuals in this group can be trusted, are dedicated to their jobs, and work long hours under the pretense of demonstrating a high level of devotion. Heffernan (1996) gives an example of a circumstance like this that led to Barings Bank's demise. If worker compensation is related to performance and output falls short of expectations, managers may manipulate productivity for fear of being fired, according to Goodhart et al. (1998). This type of risky behavior could lead to a bank's demise (e.g., Barings

Bank failure). According to Palubinskas and Stough (1999), a shortage of skilled bankers in the areas of loan risk assessment, client financial information inspection, cash flow appraisal, and fundamental profitability calculation contributes to many loan defaults. They go on to state that a lack of skills leads to a system in which there is no credit review and bankers simply enforce and supervise the credit manual, which is not updated to reflect changing periods. Mismanagement is mostly caused by fraud and corruption, as well as poor risk management methods, such as bank lending practices.

Fraudulent and Corrupt Dealings

Fraud leads banks to fail, according to Smith and Walter (1997: 157) and Fitchett (1996), as seen in the cases of Banco Ambrosiano, BCCI, Crédit Lyonnais, and Herstatt. Corruption and fraud, according to Heffernan (1996), have been the root reasons of many collapsed banks. Many people believe that mismanagement, fraud, and deregulation are to blame for bank failures, according to White (1993). However, White claims that fraud was not the fundamental cause of the banking crisis because bank failures were common in the 1930s when there was no fraud.

Poor Risk Management Procedures

According to Hempel and Simonson (1999), the primary function of bank management is not deposit mobilization and loan provision. Credit management that is effective lowers the chance of client default. A bank's competitive advantage is based on its ability to manage credit risk effectively. Bank failure is caused by bad loans. According to Palubinskas and Stough (1999), a bank's collapse is primarily attributed to mismanagement as a result of poor lending decisions such as incorrect credit status assessments, non-performing credit repayment, and an excessive concentration on granting loans to specific customers. Poor credit quality and weak credit risk assessment and measurement methods, according to Akrong (2017), are a primary causes of bank failure; thus, failing to identify or acknowledge an increase in credit risks in a timely manner can cause serious problems. A poor credit management practice was seen as a major reason for the failure of UT Bank Ltd in Ghana. Due to the bank's substantial exposure to insiders and connected parties, the central bank of Ghana discovered that credit management principles and procedures were not being followed. The loan approval process was handled as a tightly connected system that didn't allow for diversity or differing viewpoints, resulting in confirmation biases. Boulders Advisors Limited, one of the auditors, noted in a document that their analysis of "Loans Granted to Related Parties Not Connected to the UT Group" discovered "poor credit management processes, weak credit governance and monitoring."

14.3 Consequences of Banking Failures in Africa

Banking failures has been proven to have hostile implications for financial and economic systems and agents. In this section, the consequences or effects of banking failures are recounted with focus on Africa. The effects of banking failures in Africa include lack of confidence, loss of employment, loss of investible funds, undue fiscal and monetary policy pressures.

Lack of Confidence

Banking failure has contagious effect that leads to panic withdrawals due to reduced confidence of depositors and other financial market participants and investors (Osili & Paulson, 2009). Thus, the failure of one bank leads to a mad rush for deposits by depositors with other banks. While banking failures may induce panic withdrawals by depositors, potential depositors, and other investors and savers may also hold on with the funds and not deposit their surplus funds. This reduces the sustainability of the financial system since the survival banks heavily rely on the concept of the law of large numbers which advances the deposit withdrawals are random and independent hence ensuring banks always have enough funds for the operations. Put differently, the law of large numbers posits that not all depositors will come for the deposits at the same and hence allowing banks to have funds always available for the operation and continuous existence. This is because financial market participants (depositors, savers, and investors) are concerned about safeguarding the funds and investments and hence banking failures possesses a threat to protecting their funds and investment (Gay et al., 1991). Hence, banking failure creates a sense of financial insecurity for financial market participants.

Loss of confidence was particularly evident in the 2017–2018 banking failures in Ghana. During this time, while savers rushed to banking halls to withdraw their savings, new depositors preferred to keep their funds. Thus, the failure of local banks like UT Bank, GN Bank, and Capital Bank led to panics and loss of confidence in banks in Ghana especially local banks.[1]

Loss of Employment

Failed banks are usually liquidated which leads to a discontinuation of the failed bank. The operational discontinuation of failed banks leads to loss of jobs or employment for its workers. Thus, workers are paid for the revenues generated from the operations of the banks and hence, a discontinuation of operations impliedly results into termination of employment contracts for employees who work with failed banks. The loss of jobs has implications for standard of living, government tax revenue, dependence ratio, and national income.

In the case of Ghana, about 2,700 jobs are said to have been lost given the closure of seven (7) banks. This increases the unemployed population and may has serious implications on crime, security, and standard of living. In addition, GCB Bank has laid off 450 employees from the two failed banks it acquired, and had plans to lay off another 250. Consolidated Bank Ghana has laid off 700 former Beige Bank employees as part of a plan to lay off 2,000 people from the five bankrupt banks. The assets that the current bankrupt banks control is valued at $2.1 billion.[2]

Downgrading of Financial and Economic Systems

Banking failure increases uncertainties and risk for both local and international financial participants (Borio & Lowe, 2002). As such, rating agents like S&P Global Rating, Moody's, and Fitch may capture banking failures in their ratings which can result into downgrading of an economy (Derviz & Podpiera, 2008; Kerstein & Kozberg, 2013; Öğüt et al., 2012). Interestingly, downgrading of the economy as a result of banking failure has implications on how foreign investors view the downgraded economy. Additionally, it influences the volumes and cost (or rate) at which government and both natural and artificial entities in the economy can access external financial support.

[1] http://twnafrica.org/wp/2017/?p=546.

[2] http://twnafrica.org/wp/2017/?p=546.

The issuance of bonds together with other expenses by the government of Ghana to address the banking failures have increased government debt to 72.4% of gross domestic product by the end of 2018 from 69.1% in 2017. According to Moody's Investor Services, this has implications for investor confidence given the raise in government debts and can lead to unwilling of investors to assist the Ghana government or charge higher rates.[3]

Increased Cost of Finance

Banking failures create a sense of financial and economic insecurity for economic and financial agents. The financial and economic insecurity created through banking failures is an indication of increased financial instability and uncertainties (Borio & Lowe, 2002). Given that financial market participants look out for safe and sound financial and economic systems in order to safeguard their investments, increased uncertainties resulting from banking failures will induce investors to charge high premiums and cost of finance to compensate for the risk they are assuming in an unsafe banking and economic systems. Likewise, learning from the financial intermediation theory that deposit is the cheapest form of funds for banks and that banking failures can induce banking sector panic withdrawals, this can lead to increased bank funding cost implying that banks will charge higher loan prices. Again, following the literature on banking market structure (Beck et al., 2006; Diallo, 2015), banking failures reduce the number of banks in an economy leading to less competition. Consequently, the reduction in number of banks and competition can induce monopolistic behavior which can lead to increased loan prices. Hence, banking failures have the potential to increase the cost of both local and foreign funds.

With government of Ghana raising bonds to address the banking failure occurrence, the government debts to GDP have increased from 69.1% in 2017 to 72.4% in 2018. Given the rise in government debts to GDP, investor will be less likely to lend to the Ghana government unless the government of Ghana is willing to offer a higher interest rate which will crowd out local investors, increase cost of loan finance and increase non-performing loan.[4]

[3] http://twnafrica.org/wp/2017/?p=546.

[4] http://twnafrica.org/wp/2017/?p=546.

Slowdown in Economic Activities

Banking failure has a direct effect on the real sector which is responsible for promoting productivity which translates into economic growth and development (Bordo et al., 2010). Thus, banks create liquidity, evaluate viable ventures, and efficiently allocate financial resources to the real sector to facilitate the activities of the real sector which is responsible for creating economic value. In fact, prior studies (see Barro, 2001; Dell'Ariccia et al., 2008; Levine et al., 2016) show that the banking and real sectors of most economies complement each and hence the failure of the banking sector has adverse implications for economic activities and value creation. That is, banking failure leads to reduced volumes of loans advanced to the real sector and increased cost of credit to the real sector. Richards (1993) shows that banking failure shock disrupts gross national product while Levine et al. (2016) find that banking failure adversely influence equity issuance, firm profitability, employment, and investment efficiency.

Undue Pressure on Fiscal Policies

Banking failures may induce undue fiscal policy on government especially when government envisages the cost of the banking failure to be greater that the implementing bailout a policy (Honohan & Klingebiel, 2003, 2000; Turrini et al., 2012). That is, tax revenue losses, increased job losses, and loss of investor confidence which are the cost of banking failure can pressure the government to provide funds available for possible bailout. Because, governments are concerned about increasing tax revenue and investor confidence and reducing unemployment, governments may be pressured to make available huge sums of taxpayer money in order to correct the adverse consequences of banking failures. Thus, banking failures which are usually unexpected and unanticipated may unduly put budgetary and fiscal pressure on governments of economies (Feltenstein & Rochon, 2009).

The government of Ghana has had to rise GHC 7.9 billion debt ($ 1.7 billion) to pay for the difference in assets and liabilities of the collapsed banks. The breakdown of the GHC 7.9 billion is that GHC 2.2 billion in bonds was advanced to GCB to meet the difference in the value of UT Bank and Capital Bank after absorbing them while the remaining 5.7 *was advanced to the five banks that merged into Consolidated Bank. This is evidence of how banking failure can put pressure on fiscal behavior of governments.*[5]

Undue Pressure on Monetary Policies

Banking failures may reduce undue monetary policy pressure on the central bank and other related allied regulator. Central banks are responsible for ensuring safe and sound banking and economic systems. Interesting banking failures are usually not expected and hence not planned for. However, once banking failure shows up, central banks are required to make funds available in the form of liquidity support and capital injections in order to salvage the banking and economic systems of the country (Dell'Ariccia et al., 2008; Hua-Jiang, 2008; Nakatani, 2016; Smith, 2002). In the attempt of making these funds available by central banks and related regulators pressures the monetary policy outcome of the central given that banking failures and crises are not anticipated and planned for. Also, central banks who are nicked named "lender of last sort" will have to employ and deploy all available monetary policy measures in order to correct the consequences of banking failures. This situation exerts pressure on the monetary policy policies of central banks and is cost to taxpayer.

Failing banks are extended emergency liquidity support. In the case of Ghana, UT Bank, Capital Bank, and UniBank were given liquidity support of GHC 860 million, GHC 620 million, and GHC 3.1 billion, respectively, as liquidity support which was not paid back. Interestingly, according to the Governor of Bank of Ghana, Dr. Addison, these liquidity supports especially the GHC 3.1 billion posed a serious risk to the central bank and hence putting pressure on the monetary policy of the Bank of Ghana.[6]

[5] http://twnafrica.org/wp/2017/?p=546.

[6] http://twnafrica.org/wp/2017/?p=546.

14.4 Banking Failures and Banking Crises in Africa

The global financial crisis of 2007/2008 led to the collapse of several major banks in developed economies. It appears that such banking (and/or financial) crises do trigger bank failures, and this is demonstrated by the banking crises experienced locally in different countries in Africa. In this chapter, we follow the definition of banking crisis as postulated by Laeven and Valencia (2013) and subsequently by Laeven and Valencia (2018). Leaven and Valencia (2013, 2018) identify a banking crisis using two characteristics:

(i) Where banks demonstrate significant signs of financial distress denoted by bank runs, financial losses, and/or bank liquidations.
(ii) The implementation of significant banking policy reforms in response to the significant losses in the banking system as noted in (i).

Over the period 1970–2016, Africa has experienced a total of 42 systemic banking crises, 82 currency crises, 26 sovereign debt crises, and 24 sovereign debt restructuring instances (Laeven & Valencia, 2020). Figure 14.2 illustrates the banking crises in Africa over the period, 1976–2016.

In the case of banking crises, the failures recorded in Africa alone comprise 27.8% of the world's total bank failures between 1970 and 2016. The bulk of the banking crises (28 in total) in Africa were experienced between 1983 and 1995. Eight countries in Africa (Democratic Republic of Congo, Cameroon, Central African Republic, Chad, Guines, Guinea-Bissau, Kenya, and Nigeria) experienced at least one banking crisis over the period 1970–2016, with 88% of the banking crises happening in the 1980s and 1990s.

Daumont et al. (2004) observe an upsurge in banking crises in Africa in 1980s and 1990s due to reasons such as difficult operating environment (macroeconomic volatility, lending booms, mismatch in bank assets and liabilities, inadequate capital and/or loan-loss provisions, inadequate preparation for financial liberalization, heavy government involvement and loose controls on government-connected banks, weaknesses in accounting, disclosure and legal framework) market structure characteristics (distorted incentives for bank owners, managers and depositors,

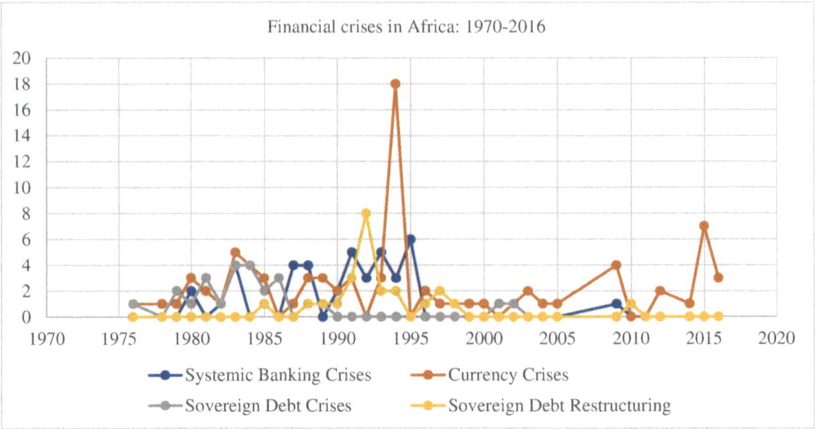

Fig. 14.2 Banking, currency, sovereign debt, and sovereign debt restructuring crises in Africa, 1976–2016 (*Source* Laeven and Valencia [2020])

exchange-rate regimen, ownership, governance, and lending practices), and banks conduct and bank's competitive behavior. Interestingly, only one banking crisis and failure was observed in Africa during and post the GFC, denoting muted impact of the GFC on ban failures.

Mezui et al. (2012) observe that African banking crises tend to match with currency crisis, which is not the case with sovereign debt crises. This seems to be the case based on the data by Laeven and Valencia (2020), a basic (Spearman's) correlational analysis reveals that countries with higher systemic banking crises are characterized by currency crises and sovereign debt restructuring instances. It is interesting to note the negative correlation between systemic banking crises and sovereign debt crises. It appears that in over 50% of the instances, a banking crisis correlates with a currency crisis, while in 9% of the instances, a banking crisis correlates with a sovereign debt crisis as posited by Mezui et al. (2012).[7]

[7] We attempt to perform an ordered probit regression between systemic banking crises in Africa and the absolute nominal GDP in US$ and nominal GDP per capita. The results reveal a significant and negative association between system banking crises and nominal GDP in US$ (0.00513, $p = 0.08$) and a positive association with nominal GDP per capita (−0.00077, $p = 0.06$) over the period 1970–2016.

The banking crises in Africa are often of varying proportions, depending on liquidity, the quality of loans (through NPLs), and bank capital held by the banks. Daumont et al. (2004) note that some affected banks have even experienced negative net worth, a sign of financial distress, implying that they could not afford repaying the deposits funds. This has been the case of Senegalese banks among other countries. It is interesting to note that government-owned and development banks are often casualties of financial distress (Mezui et al., 2012). Mezui et al. (2012) observe that state ownership of banks is associated with 30% of the banking crises, especially in CFA Franc zone. For instance, in the 1980s, 30 state-owned banks faced structural challenges and 27% collapsed in Benin, Burkina Faso, Côte d'Ivoire, Niger, Senegal, and Togo (Powo Fosso, 1999). Cameroon, Côte d'Ivoire, and Nigeria, state-owned banks experienced insolvency and were financially distressed with a huge proportion of non-performing loans. In Nigeria, some of these banks had about 60% of gross loans and advances as non-performing. This led to negative capital and reserves to the tune of N 8.4 billion (about $100 million) in 1994 (Daumont et al., 2004). Still in the 1980s, over 9 banks collapsed in the Central African Economic and Monetary Community (CEMAC). There were 31 other banks facing challenges with weak compliance with standard regulations (1 bank), precarious account balances (20 banks), and insolvency (10 banks) (Njoda & Zolo, 2011). The factors contributing to the banking crises in CEMAC were primarily due to predominance of state-owned banks, weak prudential regulations, and interventionist monetary policies.

Locally owned banks, compared to foreign-owned banks, have experienced more failures in the past. This proposition is supported by Daumont et al. (2004) who argue that foreign banks have over time exhibited profitable operations compared to their domestic peers. However, the foreign equity ownership is no guarantee of good financial health of banks as has been the case in Côte d'Ivoire, Senegal, and Uganda. In Kenya, 24 banks collapsed between 1984 and 1995, with local banks representing 96% of the collapsed banks. Most of the banks that followed till 2006 were primarily domestic banks. There has been an increase in foreign banks in Africa's financial ecosystem since 1995 due to deregulation, the removal/reduction of entry barriers, technological progression, and improved financial integration with other global financial service providers. For instance, in 1995, there was over 50% foreign ownership in banks in 15 African countries which grew to 24 countries

Table 14.1 African countries with most banking crises

Country	*Number of systemic banking crises*	*Systemic banking crisis (year(s))*
Cameroon	2	1987, 1995
Central African Republic	2	1976, 1995
Chad	2	1983, 1992
Congo, Democratic Republic of	3	1983, 1991, 1994
Guinea	2	1985, 1993
Guinea-Bissau	2	1995, 2014
Kenya	2	1985, 1992
Nigeria	2	1991, 2009

Source Laeven and Valencia (2020)

in 2009 (Claessens & van Horen, 2014). In 2009, 3 African countries (Burkina Faso, Madagascar, and Zambia) have 100% foreign ownership of their banks while 3 countries (Botswana, Malawi, and Namibia) reduced foreign ownership in their banking system.

Banks in a select number of African countries (such as Benin, Cameroon, Côte d'Ivoire, Ghana, Guinea, Kenya, Nigeria, Senegal, Uganda, Burundi, Tanzania, and Rwanda) have had a peculiar experience when it comes to crises.

Mlambo et al. (2012) observe that banks in Africa have taken measures to improve their capital quality and risk management following the remarkable banking crises in the 1980s and 1990s. There has been notable growth and diversity in ownership of banks in various African countries with a reduced role of state-owned banks and a focus on running banks as for-profit commercial enterprises. This has led to a general reduction in systemic banking crises in the following years with some crisis emanating in 1995 and sometimes in the 2000s. Table 14.4 illustrates some of the measures undertaken following banking crises in 3 selected African countries: Côte d'Ivoire, Ghana, and Nigeria.

14.5 Remedies for Banking Failures in Africa

The effect of bank failures has several adverse implications for economic systems, agents, and financial market participants as indicated earlier. Following the theories of regulation which seeks to protect public and

Table 14.2 Correlation between systemic banking crises, currency crises, debt crises, and sovereign debt restructuring

	Banking crises	*Currency crises*	*Debt crises*
Currency crises	0.2679		
	0.1142		
Debt crises	−0.0251	0.0807	
	0.8847	0.6398	
Debt restructuring	0.3643**	0.1702	−0.1784
	0.0289	0.3211	0.2978

***Significant at the 1% level. **Significant at the 5% level
Source Based on data by Laeven and Valencia (2020)

private interests and public choice theory which mandates governments as the final decision-maker for an economy, governments and their local (Central Banks, Credit Information sharing Systems, etc.), and international (IMF, Word Bank, IFC, etc.) regulatory agencies have attempted to resolve banking failures using an array of strategies. The remedies for correcting banking failures have been diverse and have different implications. Remedies for correcting banking failures may include bank supervision and monitoring, liquidity and other support systems, bailouts, recapitalization and capital injections, and cleans and reforms. These are discussed in details.

Supervision and Monitoring

Central bank supervision and monitoring have been a key strategic mechanism for curbing banking failures. Central banks around the globe embark on on-site and off-site supervision and monitoring to detect early warning signs of bank failures (Gilbert et al., 1999). These supervision and monitoring strategies ensure banks with financial problems are identified by the regulators and the necessary intervention is taken to curb banking failure. These strategies ensure adherence to safe guidelines and rules of banking in order to avoid banking distress and failure. Central banks over the years have employed an array of supervision and monitory strategies which include Early Warning Signs (EWS) models (CAMEL, CAMELS) (Jagtiani et al., 2003). The EWS models comprise of system to estimate examination rating and system to estimate examination risk ranking. The CAMELS is an internationally recognized rating system used by banking

Table 14.3 Summary of Africa's banking crises in select countries, 1980—2016

Country	*Year of banking crisis*	*Description of the crisis*	*Implications of the crisis*
Benin	1988–1990	There was the collapse of 3 banks in Benin. The banking industry experienced over 78% of bank loans as non-performing by the end of 1988	The non-performing loans comprised 17% of the country's GDP
	2010–2011	Crisis occasioned by sprouting of unauthorized MFIs leading to closure of about 15 institutions by the microfinance supervisor authority	
Burundi	1994–1995	A systemic local banking crisis experienced in 1994. The non-performing loans in the banking system were 25%. The aftermath of the banking crisis led to one bank being liquidated in 1995	
Cameroon	1987–1993	Many banks became illiquid and/or insolvent	Approximately 60–70% of the banking system loans were non-performing as of 1989
Côte d'Ivoire	1988–1991	Four large banks were affected. The four banks accounted for about 90% of the bank loans. The non-performing loans in the four large banks accounted for over 50% of the loans outstanding in the industry	The government incurred up to 25% of the GDP to resuscitate the affected banks
Ghana	1982–1989	Seven banks were insolvent with about 40% of the bank credit issued to non-governmental borrowers being non-performing in 1989	There were restructuring costs associated with the banks affected. This costed up to 6% of the GDP

Country	*Year of banking crisis*	*Description of the crisis*	*Implications of the crisis*
Guinea	1985	Six large banks accounting for about 99% of the bank deposits were found insolvent There were 80% of the bank loans non-performing	The repayment of deposits for the failed banks amounted to 3% of the country's GDP in 1986
Kenya	1980s	4 banks and 24 nonbank financial institutions accounting for 15% of financial system liabilities affected by liquidity and/or solvency problems	
	1984–1989	24 Banks collapsed; all were Kenyan-owned expect 1 foreign-owned bank A local banking crisis experienced. This led to the establishment of the Deposit Protection Fund and the enforcement of the Banking Act (1989)	
	1992–1998	Three banks collapsed. Solvency challenges in banks accounting for more than 30% of financial system assets, 66% of loans of one third of bank loans were non-performing in 1993 The National Bank suffered a bank-run As of 1998, 37 banks had failed	
	2000–2006	6 more banks collapsed. Closures cited to crimes from money laundering to tax evasion	As of 2001, the non-performing loans to total loans was 30% up from 17.6% in 1995
	2014	A later local banking crisis would be experienced in 2014–2016, which led to the failure of 3 banks. The baking failures were due to wide-ranging causes from irregular loans leading to huge non-performing loans, corporate governance weaknesses to bank runs due to negative publicity	

(continued)

Table 14.3 (continued)

Country	*Year of banking crisis*	*Description of the crisis*	*Implications of the crisis*
Nigeria	1991–1995	Eight banks were found insolvent with over 45% of bank loans deemed non-performing as at the close of 1992. 34 banks found insolvent (out of 115 banks) in 1994. The 34 banks accounted for 10% of the bank deposits in 1994	
Senegal	1988–1991	Over 50% of the bank loans were found non-performing in 1988,	This comprised 17% of the country's GDP
Tanzania	1987–1990s	The key financial services players experienced defaults in their portfolios in 1987. State-owned banks which had 95% of bank assets were found insolvent in 1990 In 1194, there were 60–80% of bank loans declared non-performing as at the close of 1994	The resultant losses were estimated at 10% of the country's GDP
Uganda	1990–1994	Over 50% of the banks faced insolvency by 1994	
	1998–1999	Four banks (3 locally owned), which held 12.1% of the Ugandan banking system's deposits, closed between September 1998 and May 1999. This was due to insolvency caused by several causes ranging from failure to meet minimum capital ratios, insider lending, corruption, and corporate governance lapses	

Source: Author's compilation of data gathered from various sources such as Caprio and Klingebiel (2002), Lindgren et al. (1996), World Bank (1991) as cited in Daumont et al. (2004) and Laeven and Valencia (2020)

Table 14.4 Summary of interventions to banking crises in Côte d'Ivoire, Ghana, and Nigeria

Country	*Cote d'Ivoire*	*Ghana*	*Nigeria*
Banking crises start date	1988	January 1982	August 2009
Date when crisis became systemic	1988	January 1982	October 2011
Brief description of crisis	The 1987 recession, along with problems in the cocoa and coffee markets (major exports), resulted in a significant increase in non-performing loans in the private sector. A huge number of non-performing loans in the public sector, a considerable buildup of government payment arrears, a significant fall in public and private deposits in the banking system, a reduction in credit lines from abroad, and bad management in some banks exacerbated these issues. The government thus initiated in late 1991 a financial sector adjustment program (PASFI) supported by a sectoral adjustment loan of the World Bank. The program provided for the rehabilitation of the commercial banking sector through the settlement of government payments arrears, the recapitalization of banks, and	Throughout most of the 1980s, Ghana experienced significant structural imbalances as a result of large budgetary deficits, fast growth in domestic bank credit, a fixed exchange rate, and high inflation, which authorities attempted to control with price controls. The depreciation of capital equipment and insufficient price incentives in the agricultural and export sectors worsened these practices. As a result, actual output in 1981 was 15% lower than it had been in 1974. High fiscal deficits, financed primarily through domestic credit, directed credit policies (since 1981, banks have been required to lend at least 20% of their portfolio to the agricultural sector), a decline in cocoa exports, and a large depreciation of the currently used currency exacerbated the situation in the second half of the 1980s (a 1173% depreciation	The Nigerian banking crisis of 2009–2011, according to the Governor of the Central Bank of Nigeria (CBN), was caused by the creation of an extremely fragile financial system, which resulted in a crisis due to factors such as macroeconomic instability caused by large and sudden capital inflows, major corporate governance failures, and a lack of investor and consumer sophistication considering emerging bank borrowers (Sanusi, 2010: 5)

(continued)

Table 14.4 (continued)

Country	*Cote d'Ivoire*	*Ghana*	*Nigeria*
	the adequate provisioning for their loan losses. The program also involved the liquidation of 6 banks, including the National Agricultural Development Bank (BNDA); the reform of the judicial framework for banking activities; and the restructuring of nonbank financial institutions, including the Abidjan Stock Exchange and the insurance sector	took place in 1983). Banks were faced with liquidity constraints, but there were also flaws in banking oversight and regulation. As a result, 7 of the 11 banks were declared insolvent, and the issues were resolved through capitalization and the purchase of non-performing assets (NPLs). High fiscal deficits, financed primarily through domestic credit, directed credit policies (since 1981, banks have been required to lend at least 20% of their portfolio to the agricultural sector), a decline in cocoa exports, and a large depreciation of the currently used currency exacerbated the situation in the second half of the 1980s (a 1173% depreciation took place in 1983). Banks were faced with liquidity constraints, but there were also flaws in banking oversight and regulation. As a result, 7 of the 11 banks were declared insolvent, and the issues were resolved through capitalization and the purchase of non-performing assets (NPLs)	

Country	*Cote d'Ivoire*	*Ghana*	*Nigeria*
Deposit insurance(Y/N)	No	No	Yes
Deposit freeze (Y/N)	No	No	No
Bank holiday (Y/N)	No	No	No
Significant Bank Liabilities Guarantees	No	No	Yes
Liquidity support	Yes	Yes	Yes (May 2011)
Peak support (in % of deposits)	76.85%	0.19%	25%
Bank restructuring	Yes	Yes	Yes
Nationalizations	No	No	Yes
Asset Purchases and Transfers	Yes	Yes	Yes
Asset management company	1	1	1
Recapitalization	Yes	Yes	Yes
Losses imposed on depositors	Yes	No	No
IMF program put in place	Y	N	N
Peak NPLs (as % of total loans; unofficial estimate)	50.00%	35.00%	30.10%
Fiscal cost net (% GDP)	25.00%	6.00%	11.80%

Source Laeven and Valencia (2020)

supervisory authorities to screen out banks with financial problems for further supervision and monitoring. It is made up of six key indicators for which banking regulators or supervisors rate banks and these indicators capture capital adequacy, asset quality, management quality, earnings, liquidity, and sensitivity to market risk. For each category of indicator, a score between one and five may be signed where one is the best score and indicates strong performance and risk management practices while five is the poorest rating. Interestingly, these early warning detection strategies can help identify failing banks as early as possible for the necessary actions and interventions to be put in place to rescue failing banks.

Regulations and Reforms

Central Banks, who are mandated to ensure financial system soundness and entire economic system efficiency are expected to employ different regulations and reforms to accomplish this mandate. As such Bouyon (2014) advances that banking regulators and reforms are instituted to attain financial stability at the bank system level while attaining economic efficiency at the entire economic system level. This implies that regulation and reforms are employed for the purpose of curbing banking failures and distress by reinforcing financial and economic stability. Interestingly, the theory of regulation shows that regulations are instituted to either protect the interest of the general public or the interest of a private group. Thus, while the theory of public interest of regulation advance that regulations are instituted with the aim of protecting the interest of the general public, the theory of private interest of regulation shows that regulations are instituted with the aim of protecting the interest of the private groups in the society. This theory in sum shows that regulations are tools for correcting or curbing problems that confront societies including banking failures which have several adverse implications for monetary and fiscal policies. Post-2007/2008 global financial crises, financial regulations, and reforms have focused more macro-prudential regulations and reforms than bank level regulations and reforms. Thus, the focus of banking regulators is focused on ensuring entire financial and economic system soundness and not individual banks. Interestingly, regulations and reforms have also taken a “macro-centric” approach. Central banks employ available regulations (capital adequacy requirements, recapitalization, corporate governance reforms, credit information sharing, etc.) and even institute new regulations and reforms that ensure banks are sound and free from financial distress and failure. Hence, through several regulations and reforms at the disposal of central banks, they are able to curb banking failure at the financial system level as well as at the individual bank level.

Central Bank Liquidity Support

In an attempt to rescue failing banks, central banks may advance liquidity support under stringent surveillance to ensure banks confronted with liquidity crises which can result into banking failure is corrected (Djiwandono, 2004). Thus, banking liquidity crisis has been determined to cause bank panic withdrawals which ultimately induces banking failures (Kiss et al., 2018). The mad rush for deposits induced by liquidity crises erodes the confidence of banking market participants and weakens the law of large numbers on which the concept of banking is sustained. Thus, the law of large numbers advances that not all depositors will come for the funds as the same time and that mobilizing "many-small" deposits is preferred to mobilizing "few-huge" deposits. However, in time of panic withdrawal, depositors rush for their funds rendering the concept of law of large number on which banking is sustained useless, hence, inducing banking failure.

Bailouts

Bailout is a general used to describe situations where financial support is extended to a company or country facing potential bankruptcy threat (Keister, 2016). It could take a form of a loan, cash, bonds, and stock purchase. Bailout is usually accompanied by greater oversight and strict regulations from the bailor. Bailout as a remedy for correcting failing banks become popular during 2007/2008 global financial crises in the United States (Panageas, 2010). Induced through by the theory of "too big to fail," the US government found it expedient to provide financial support to failing banks in the United States as a result of the harsh and adverse effect of 2007/2008 global financial crises. The theory of "too big to fail" assumes that the adverse effect of failed banks especially large banks is far more costly than injecting additional capital or funds into the failing banks through bailouts. Hence, the adverse effect of failed banks which have hostile implications for monetary and fiscal policies necessitates bailout actions by governments (Bond & Miller, 1998).

Following the theory of public choice, governments have the mandate to employ available resources at their disposal to help correct social, financial, cultural, and economic crises that may interrupt the smooth running of an economy. While bailout of failed banks has demerits like encouraging moral hazard (of promoters, customers, lenders, and suppliers), it has the power to ensure the continuous survival of failed or failing banks, avoid collapse of the entire financial system and adverse economic effects of banking failure (Bordo & Schwartz, 2000).

Takeovers, Acquisitions, and Mergers

Central banks may direct and encourage strong banks to absorb failing banks or distress banks under some arrangements. Thus, failing or distressed banks that may compromise the financial soundness of the banking and economic systems can be acquired or merged with another bank which is financially sound through recommendation of the central bank. This strategy helps contain failing or distress banks without having to close the failing bank which would have led to job losses and loss of confidence in the banking sector.

14.6 Conclusion and Policy Implications

This paper has been motivated by recognition of the critical role that a banking system plays in the growth of an economy. However, a banking system must be sound to be able to effectively play its intermediation role in an economy. The impact of failure of the banking system is reflected in loss of investor confidence, lower levels of employment, and increased cost of finance.

Although bank failures have been extensively covered in the literature, there is a paucity of studies of bank failures in the African context. This contextual analysis of bank failures in Africa has identified the causes to include unfavorable economic conditions, regulatory failures, poor corporate governance practices, non-performing loans, mismanagement, fraudulent and corrupt dealings, and poor risk management.

Africa has had its share of banking crises. However, compared with bank crises elsewhere, African bank crises have been associated with a peculiar cluster of factors, the key ones being currency crises, sovereign debt restructuring, and state ownership, the latter playing a role in a significant number of cases in the CFA zone. It has also been observed that locally owned banks are more prone to failure compared to foreign-owned banks. This is because foreign banks have tended to be more profitable than local banks.

Bank failures can have devastating consequences. Loss of confidence in the banking system can lead to panic withdrawals and disintermediation as investors and savers decide to avoid the banking system. Loss of employment during bank resolutions can be significant and can worsen unemployment rates which are already significant in African countries. The global credit rating of a country with significant bank failures can fall because of fiscal pressures resulting from the bailout of banks. Monetary policy may also come under stress because of the need for central banks to provide liquidity support to failing banks.

There are lessons to be learnt from what we know so far. Strengthened supervision and monitoring involve building the capacity of central banks. There are time-tested tools of intervention when failure is imminent. These include liquidity support in order to avoid panic withdrawals; bailouts may be used to provide additional financial support to banks facing financial distress; central banks may also promote mergers and acquisitions to stave off bank failure. However, on an ongoing basis, central banks must ensure adherence to safety guidelines and rules to avoid bank distress and failure and costly resolutions. Consistent regulatory reform also enables central banks to be proactive in identifying and anticipating risks to the banking system. Given the interconnectedness of financial institutions, central banks should focus on the soundness of the overall financial and economic system.

An implication of the findings of this study is that policymakers should carefully weigh the benefits of bailouts versus failure. Bailouts may preserve confidence in the banking system while allowing banks to fail may be costly in social and economic terms. The choices are complex and should be guided by global experience and the peculiar circumstances of each country.

References

Afolabi Jerry J. (2018, July 18). *Feature: Why the local banks in Ghana are collapsing*. www.ghanaweb.com

Akrong, E. (2017, August 27). *8 key questions on collapse of UT, Capital Bank (Article)*. www.citifmonline.com

Balla, E., Mazur, L. C., Simpson Prescott, E., & Walter, J. R. (2019). A comparison of community bank failures and FDIC losses in the 1986–92 and 2007–13 banking crises. *Journal of Banking & Finance, 106*, 1–15.

Bank of Ghana. (2018). *Banking sector report*. www.bog.gov.gh/privatecontent/MPC_Press_Releases/Banking_Sector_Report_January_2018.pdf, May 15, 2018.

Barro, R. J. (2001). *Economic growth in East Asia before and after the financial crisis* (No. w8330. National Bureau of Economic Research).

Beck, T., Demirgüç-Kunt, A., & Levine, R. (2006). Bank concentration, competition, and crises: First results. *Journal of Banking & Finance, 30*(5), 1581–1603.

Benston, G. J., & Kaufman, G. G. (1997). FDICIA after five years. *Journal of Economic Perspectives, 11*(3), 139–158.

Bhagat, S., & Bolton, B. (2008). Corporate governance and firm performance. *Journal of Corporate Finance, 14*(3), 257–273.

Bond, T. J., & Miller, M. (1998, January). *Financial bailouts and financial crises*. mimeo, International Monetary Fund.

Bordo, M. D., & Schwartz, A. J. (2000). Measuring real economic effects of bailouts: Historical perspectives on how countries in financial distress have fared with and without bailouts. In *Carnegie-Rochester Conference Series on Public Policy* (Vol. 53, No. 1, pp. 81–167). North-Holland.

Bordo, M. D., Meissner, C. M., & Stuckler, D. (2010). Foreign currency debt, financial crises and economic growth: A long-run view. *Journal of International Money and Finance, 29*(4), 642–665.

Borio, C., & Lowe, P. (2002). Assessing the risk of banking crises. *BIS Quarterly Review, 7*(1), 43–54.

Bouyon, S. (2014, October 7). *The impact of banking structural reform on household retail finance* (ECRI Commentary No. 13).

Brownbridge, M. (1998). Financial distress in local banks in Kenya, Nigeria, Uganda and Zambia: Causes and implications for regulatory policy. *Development Policy Review, 16*(2), 173–188.

Caprio, G., & Klingebiel, D. (2002). *Episodes of systemic and borderline banking crises* (Managing the real and fiscal effects of banking crises, World Bank Discussion Paper 428), pp. 31–49.

CBK. (2016). *Banking supervision annual report*. https://www.centralbank.go.ke/uploads/banking_sector_annual_reports/323855712_2016%20BSD%20ANNUAL%20REPORT%20V5.pdf

Central Bank of Kenya. (2016). *Bank supervision annual report 2016*. http://www.centralbank.go.ke/downloads/acts_regulations/banking_Act.pdf

Claessens, S., & Van Horen, N. (2014). Foreign banks: Trends and impact. *Journal of Money, Credit and Banking, 46*(s1), 295–326.

Cole, R. A., & Gunther, J. W. (1995). Separating the likelihood and timing of bank failure. *Journal of Banking & Finance, 19*(6), 1073–1089.

Crotty, J. (2009). Structural causes of the global financial crisis: A critical assessment of the 'new financial architecture.' *Cambridge Journal of Economics, 33*(4), 563–580.

Daumont, R., Le Gall, F., & Leroux, F. (2004). Banking in sub-Saharan Africa: What went wrong? (pp. 1–49).

Debrah, K. (2018). *Collapse of indigenous banks due to corporate governance failure—Banking consultant*. Available online at www.myjoyonline.com

Dell'Ariccia, G., Detragiache, E., & Rajan, R. (2008). The real effect of banking crises. *Journal of Financial Intermediation, 17*(1), 89–112.

Derviz, A., & Podpiera, J. (2008). Predicting bank CAMELS and S&P ratings: The case of the Czech Republic. *Emerging Markets Finance and Trade, 44*(1), 117–130.

Diallo, B. (2015). Bank competition and crises revisited: New results. *Economics Letters, 129*, 81–86.

Djiwandono, J. S. (2004). Liquidity support to banks during Indonesia's financial crisis. *Bulletin of Indonesian Economic Studies, 40*(1), 59–75.

Eisenbeis, R. A. (1986). 6 regulatory policies and financial stability.

Feltenstein, A., & Rochon, C. (2009). Can good events lead to bad outcomes? Endogenous banking crises and fiscal policy responses. *Journal of Asian Economics, 20*(4), 396–409.

Fitchett, J. (1996, October 3). The credit Lyonnais debacle: The banking scandal that refuses to die. *International Herald Tribune*, Paris.

Fofack, H., & Fofack, H. L. (2005). *Nonperforming loans in sub-Saharan Africa: Causal analysis and macroeconomic implications* (Vol. 3769). World Bank Publications.

Gay, G. D., Timme, S. G., & Yung, K. (1991). Bank failure and contagion effects: Evidence from Hong Kong. *Journal of Financial Research, 14*(2), 153–165.

Gilbert, R. A., Meyer, A. P., & Vaughan, M. D. (1999). The role of supervisory screens and econometric models in off-site surveillance. *Federal Reserve Bank of St. Louis Review, 81*(6), 31.

Goodhart, C. A. E. (2005). Financial regulation, credit risk and financial stability. *National Institute Economic Review, 192*(1), 118–127.

Goodhart, C., Hartmann, P., Llewellyn, D. (1998). Financial regulation: Why, how and where now.

Gray, S. J., Salter, S. B., & Radebaugh, L. H. (2001). *Global accounting & control: A managerial emphasis* (PhD diss.). University of Maribor, Faculty of Economics and Business.

Heffernan, S. (1996). Современное банковское дело в теории и на практике (Modern Banking in Theory and Practice).

Hempel, G. H., & Simonson, D. G. (1999). *Bank management: Text and cases*. Wiley Incorporated.

Honohan, P., & Klingebiel, D. (2003). The fiscal cost implications of an accommodating approach to banking crises. *Journal of Banking & Finance, 27*(8), 1539–1560.

Honohan, P., & Klingebiel, D. (2000). *Controlling the fiscal costs of banking crises* (Vol. 2441). World Bank Publications.

Hooks, L. M. (1994 September). *Risk-based capital and bank failure*. Group of Thirty Occasional Paper Series.

Hua Jiang, J. (2008). Banking crises in monetary economies. *Canadian Journal of Economics/Revue canadienne d'économique, 41*(1), 80–104.

Hwang, D.-Y., Lee, C. F., & Thomas Liaw, K. (1997). Forecasting bank failures and deposit insurance premium. *International Review of Economics & Finance, 6*(3), 317–334.

International Monetary Fund (IMF). (2009). *Risk, measuring systemic, and restoring financial soundness* (Global financial stability report).

Jagtiani, J., Kolari, J., Lemieux, C., & Shin, H. (2003). Early warning models for bank supervision: Simpler could be better. *Economic Perspectives-Federal Reserve Bank of Chicago, 27*(3), 49–59.

Kaufman, G. G. (1996). Bank failures, systemic risk, and bank regulation. *Cato Journal, 16*, 17.

Keister, T. (2016). Bailouts and financial fragility. *The Review of Economic Studies, 83*(2), 704–736.

Kerstein, J., & Kozberg, A. (2013). Using accounting proxies of proprietary FDIC ratings to predict bank failures and enforcement actions during the recent financial crisis. *Journal of Accounting, Auditing & Finance, 28*(2), 128–151.

Kihumba A. K. (2010). Corporate governance, *risk management and bank performance* (Unpublished Theses). Moi University, Kenya.

Kiss, H. J., Rodriguez-Lara, I., & Rosa-Garcia, A. (2018). Panic bank runs. *Economics Letters, 162*, 146–149.

Kiyai, T. K. (2003).*Bad debts restructuring techniques and non-performing loans of commercial banks in Kenya* (PhD diss.). University of Nairobi.

Laeven, L., & Valencia, F. (2020). Systemic banking crises database II. *IMF Economic Review, 68*(4), 307–361.

Laeven, L., & Valencia, F. (2013). Systemic banking crises database. *IMF Economic Review, 61*(2), 225–270.

Laeven, L., & Valencia, F. (2018). *Systemic banking crises revisited* (IMF Working Paper WP/18/206).

Levine, R., Lin, C., & Xie, W. (2016). Spare tire? Stock markets, banking crises, and economic recoveries. *Journal of Financial Economics, 120*(1), 81–101.

Lindgren, M. C.-J., Garcia, M. G., & Saal, M. M. I. (1996). *Bank soundness and macroeconomic policy* (International Monetary Fund).

Mabvure, T., Kamoyo, M., Ndlovu, B., Gwangwava, E., & Manuere, F. (2012). Multinational banks. *Role in Zimbabwe's Economic Development', Journal of Sustainable Development in Africa, 14*(7), 110–129.

Meyer, P. A., & Pifer, H. W. (1970). Prediction of bank failures. *The Journal of Finance, 25*(4), 853–868.

Mezui, C. M., Nalletamby, S., & Kamewe, H. (2012). African systemic financial crises. *Africa Economic Brief, 3*(9), 1–4.

Mlambo, K., Kasekende, L., & Murinde, V. (2012). Comparative overview of bank regulatory experiences and the impact on bank competition and intermediation efficiency in Africa. *Bank Regulatory Reforms in Africa.*

Nakatani, R. (2016). Twin banking and currency crises and monetary policy. *Open Economies Review, 27*(4), 747–767.

Nishimura, K., Kazuhito, I., & Yukiko, O. (2001). The disposal of non-performing loans and its potential influence.

Njoda, T. M., & Zolo, E. A. R. (2011). Commerce international et emploi informel en zone CEMAC. *Journal Statistique Africain, 50*(13), 50–81.

Nworji, I. D., Adebayo, O., & Adeyanju, O. D. (2011). Corporate governance and bank failure in Nigeria: Issues, challenges and opportunities. *Research Journal of Finance and Accounting, 2*(2), 1–19.

Öğüt, H., Doğanay, M. M., Ceylan, N. B., & Aktaş, R. Prediction of bank financial strength ratings: The case of Turkey. *Economic Modelling, 29*(3), 632–640.

Osili, U. O., & Paulson, A. L. (2009). *Banking crises and investor confidence: An empirical investigation* (Policy Discussion Paper FRB of Chicago PDP 9).

Palubinskas, G. T., & Stough, R. R. (1999). *Common cause of bank failures in post-communist countries*. http://www.Sba.Muohio.Edu/Abas/1999/Pal ubigi.Pdf.

Panageas, S. (2010). Bailouts, the incentive to manage risk, and financial crises. *Journal of Financial Economics, 95*(3), 296–311.

Pantalone, C. C., & Platt, M. B. (1987, July). Predicting commercial bank failure since deregulation. *New England Economic Review*, 37–47.

Pedro, C. P., Ramalho, J. J. S., & da Silva, J. V. (2018). The main determinants of banking crises in OECD countries. *Review of World Economics, 154*(1), 203–227.

Powo Fosso, B. (1999). Les déterminants des faillites bancaires dans les pays en développement: le cas des pays de l'union économique et monétaire ouest africaine (UEMOA).

Richards, O. P. (1993). EMU: Outstanding Issues to be resolved. *Butherworths Journal of International Banking and Financial Law, 8*, 6–6.

Sarbanes-Oxley, G. (2005). *The board of directors: Techniques and best practices for corporate governance*. Wiley.
Sanusi, L. S. (2010). The Nigerian Banking Industry: what went wrong and the way forward. *Delivered at Annual Convocation Ceremony of Bayero University, Kano held on, 3*(1).
Shungu, P., Ngirande, H., & Ndlovu, G. (2014). Impact of corporate governance on the performance of commercial banks in Zimbabwe. *Mediterranean Journal of Social Sciences, 5*(15), 93–93.
Smith, B. D. (2002). Monetary policy, banking crises, and the Friedman rule. *American Economic Review, 92*(2), 128–134.
Smith, R., & Walter, I. (1997). *Global banking*. Oxford University Press, Inc.
Spiegel, J., Gart, A., & Gart, S. (1996). *Banking redefined: How superregional powerhouses are reshaping financial services*. Irwin.
Spollen, A. L. (1997). *Corporate fraud: The danger from within*. Oak Tree Press.
Spratt, S. (2013). Food price volatility and financial speculation. *Future Agricultures Working Paper, 47*, 7.
Turrini, A., Röger, W., & Székely, I. P. (2012). Banking crises, output loss, and fiscal policy. *Cesifo Economic Studies, 58*(1), 181–219.
Wheelock, D. C., & Wilson, P. W. (2000). Why do banks disappear? The determinants of US bank failures and acquisitions. *Review of Economics and Statistics, 82*(1), 127–138.
White, L. H. (Ed.). (1993). *The crisis in American Banking*. NYU Press.
World Bank. (1991b). *World Development Report 1991*. The World Bank, Washington, DC.

CHAPTER 15

Cross-Border Banking and Banking Crisis in Africa

Charles Komla Delali Adjasi, Isaac Ofoeda, Khadijah Iddrisu, and Foluso Akinsola

15.1 Introduction

The banking sector plays an essential role in the development of nations across the globe because of its critical role in the financial intermediation process. Generally, banks are mostly depository entities, and also

C. K. D. Adjasi
University of Stellenbosch Business School, Cape Town, South Africa
e-mail: Charles.Adjasi@usb.ac.za

I. Ofoeda (✉)
University for Professional Studies, Accra, Ghana
e-mail: isaac.ofoeda@upsamail.edu.gh

K. Iddrisu
SDD University of Integrated Business and Development, Bamahu, WA, Ghana

F. Akinsola
Department of Economics, University of Lagos, Lagos, Nigeria

J. Y. Abor and C. K. D. Adjasi (eds.), *The Economics of Banking and Finance in Africa*, Palgrave Macmillan Studies in Banking and Financial Institutions, https://doi.org/10.1007/978-3-031-04162-4_15

acting as an intermediary in transferring these surplus funds to deficits units through the provision of loans or the purchase of debt securities and many more (Abor et al., 2019). Therefore, banking sector development is crucial for the growth of economies around the world. This is because cross-border banking promotes banking sector development, financial integration, and globalization. Therefore, the importance of cross-border banking in the global financial landscape cannot be overemphasized as it leads to institutional changes, knowledge transfers, and financial flows (Bara & Abel, 2018). Again, Le and Dickinson (2016) note that cross-border banking promotes diversification and the stability of the domestic lending market. Also, Boyd and De Nicoló (2005) indicate that cross-border banking leads to increased competition which has implications for bank stability (Banyen, 2021). According to Enoch et al. (2015), cross-border banks support the deepening of financial sectors in host countries by increasing competition, increasing access to higher skills and expertise, access to capital, and economies of scale. In addition, cross-border banking improves the transparency of the banking sector and promotes the local supervisory and legal regimes (Amidu, 2020a, 2020b). Undoubtedly, cross-border banking plays a significant role in the development of financial systems across the world.

Nonetheless, in recent times the impact of cross-border banking on the stability of the domestic financial systems has become a focal issue. Cross-border banking is expected to promote the financial system's stability and forestall the possibility of a banking crisis by providing a means for risk diversification and increased competition. Again, cross-border banking may provide access to capital and superior skills and expertise, promote banking sector transparency, improve domestic supervisory and regimes (Amidu, 2020a, 2020b; IMF, 2015). On the other hand, cross-border banking may cause a banking crisis in domestic banking systems as banking failures may be transferred across borders. Also, increased credit supply occasioned by cross-border banking may result in a banking crisis as credit booms are noted as major precursors of a banking crisis (Ganİoğlu, 2016). Banking crises often impose tremendous economic costs on the financial system and may have devastating consequences for the economy. Banking crises often generate huge contagion effects and trigger runs and failures with disruptive consequences for the general economy. Banking crises are associated with significant output losses (Furceri & Zdzienicka, 2012), high and long-lasting unemployment (Bernal-Verdugo et al., 2012), massive trade decline (Abiad et al.,

2012), and contraction of foreign direct investment (Stoddard & Noy, 2015). Again, Uch et al. (2021) report an adverse impact of banking crises on credit growth.

However, empirical studies on the impact of cross-border bank expansion on banking crises have provided mixed results. For a large sample of countries, Demirgüç-Kunt and Levine (2008) report that foreign bank entry was generally associated with a lower incidence of local banking crises. In studying how the differences in bank ownership influence bank behavior, Arena et al. (2010) indicated that foreign bank participation in emerging markets has not led to increased instability in credit markets. In a more recent study, Schnabel and Seckinger (2019) report that foreign banks in a local economy have more than four times growth effects in times of crisis. However, in an examination of US and UK cross-border banking, Degryse et al. (2010) provide evidence that shocks that affect a country's liabilities may undermine the stability of the entire financial system of the other. Also, Jeon et al.,(2013) provide consistent evidence that financial shocks experienced by a parent bank are transmitted to their foreign subsidiaries. Le and Dickinson (2016) submit that there transfer of interbank stress from advanced economies to emerging markets.

Despite the plethora of literature on cross-border bank expansion and banking crises, it appears not much has been done on Africa. The banking landscape in Africa has undergone tremendous transformation over the last few decades. In the 1980s, the African banking system was dominated by state-owned banks. However, following financial liberalization and deregulation, the face of financial systems in Africa has changed. According to the Global Financial Development database, cross-border banking in Africa has been on the ascendency. The share of foreign banks in Africa has increased from 42% in 2000 to 52% in 2013. While cross-border bank penetration in Africa has increased over the years, in the last decade, African banks have increased their geographic footprints across the region and become economically significant beyond their home countries. Today, pan-African banks have a more significant footprint in Africa than banks from outside the region. The influx of foreign banks seems to have several advantages specific to Africa: international banks can help foster governance; they can bring in much-needed technology and experience that should translate into increased efficiency in financial intermediation, and they can help exploit scale economies in small host countries. Therefore, it is important to assess how cross-border bank expansion has influenced the stability of the African financial systems and, by extension, influences the possibility of a banking crisis.

This present study builds on existing literature by examining the impact of cross-border bank expansion on banking crisis in Africa. We structure the rest of the study as follows: in Sect. 15.2 we review relevant literature on the impact of cross-border banking on the banking crisis and the factors that influence the banking crisis. Section 15.3 discusses the empirical approaches and the data used in this study, and we discuss the study's findings in Sect. 15.4. Finally, we conclude from the findings of the study and provide some policy recommendations to inform practice.

15.2 Literature Review

The Link Between Cross-Border Banking and Banking Crisis/Banking Stability

Cross-border banking has become a critical part of the trend toward increased globalization and the integration of financial systems. The impact of cross-border banking on the operations and the stability of the local financial systems has remained a matter of intense debate over the past two decades among researchers and policymakers alike. Although this argument has provided many possible insights into the impact of cross-border banking on the banking crisis or the stability of financial systems, most of the empirical evidence provide conflicting predictions about their relationships. According to the Leckow and Pazarbasioglu (2012), cross-border banking can transform financial systems in countries through institutional changes, knowledge transfers, and financial flows. According to IMF (2015), it promotes financial deepening and financial sector development by increasing competition, providing access to capital and access to higher skills and expertise. It also provides a means for risk diversification and stabilizes the financial sector (IMF, 2015). Cross-border banking introduces new and modern technologies and provides cost and funding spillovers to domestic financial sectors (Bara & Abel, 2018). Amidu (2020a, 2020b) notes that cross-border banking improves the transparency of the banking sector and promotes the local supervisory and legal regimes. This suggests that cross-border banking promotes the banking sector's stability and development, thereby forestalling any banking crisis.

Nonetheless, another strand of literature posits that cross-border banking has negative consequences for the development of the banking sector and may eventually result in a banking crisis. According to the IMF (2015), the complexities of cross-border banks create significant supervision gaps and raise governance issues. Cross-border contagion may be an additional problem that domestic banking systems need to contend with as banking failures, crisis and capital flow volatilities may be transmitted across national borders (Claessens, 2006; Laeven & Valencia, 2013). Also, regulatory arbitrage across countries and competition for safety nets across countries create negative externalities (Laeven, 2011). Additionally, Le and Dickinson (2016) indicate that cross-border banks may reduce credit supply in times of financial distress, thereby worsening the liquidity situation of the domestic financial system.

Empirical studies also provide mixed findings of the impact of cross-border banking on banking sector stability or banking crisis. Sissy et al. (2017) examined how revenue diversification across borders impact banks' risk-taking incentives and performance in Africa. They found that cross-border banking improves the stability of banks. Again, Le and Dickinson (2016) investigated the systematic risk of cross-border banking associated with the sudden stop in international lending and interbank stress contagion in East Asia and provided evidence that there is the transmission of interbank stress from advanced economies to emerging economies. However, Choi et al. (2010) examined how cross-border banking impacts the risk of acquiring banks and report that border bank mergers and acquisitions usually result in risk-increasing activities of banks. Similarly, in a recent study, Dinger and te Kaat (2020) investigated the impact of international capital flows on Euro area bank lending and risk-taking. Their study provided evidence that cross-border capital inflows are associated with increased bank loan volumes, higher loan-to-asset ratios, and higher shares of impaired loans and loan loss provisions. Tonzer (2015) analyzed the interconnectedness of banking systems, bank risk and contagion of 18 advanced economies and report that foreign exposures in banking result in a significant channeling of banking risk. Finally, Zhu and Yang (2016) examined the impact of Chinese banks' cross-border acquisition on risk-taking and found that foreign acquisition reduces state-owned banks' risk-taking. They, however, found that this effect is more pronounced for banks with significant state or government control.

Determinants of Banking Crisis

The banking sector plays a central role in the financial systems of countries across the globe. Given the importance of the banking sector in the development process of nations, banking crisis could generate severe economic and social damage. Therefore, it is essential to promote the development and stability of the banking sector. Factors such as the liquidity, profitability, capital and size of the banking sector, credit growth, competition, economic growth, trade openness, and inflation have been identified as influencing the banking sector's stability or banking crisis. Literature advances that banking crisis is often preceded by credit growth. Angkinand et al. (2010), in a study of the impact of financial liberalization on the likelihood of a financial crisis, found that higher credit growth is associated with a greater probability of banking crisis in 48 countries across the globe. Similarly, Klomp (2010) examined the causes of banking crisis of 110 countries and report that credit growth has significant positive effect in about 51% of the cases. Again, Ganİoğlu (2016) provided evidence that excessive credit growth significantly promotes a banking crisis.

Further, inflation is reported as one of the indicators of impending banking sector problems. The rate of inflation reflects the extent of the stability of the macroeconomy. Higher rates of inflation have adverse effects on the operations of firms as well as the banking sector. Again, a high pre-crisis inflation rate reflects poor macroeconomic policies and imbalances in the financial system. Angkinand et al. (2010) provided evidence that an increased inflation rate increases the likelihood of a banking crisis. Again, Davis and Karim (2016) examined the early warning systems of a banking crisis and found that increased inflation increases the likelihood of a banking crisis. They further report that this probability doubles when inflation exceeds 30%. However, Hamdaoui (2016) and Ganİoğlu (2016) report that inflation plays no significant role in promoting a banking sector crisis. Further, the degree of trade openness of a country largely influences the probability of a banking crisis. The probability of a banking crisis reduces for economies open to trade because such countries can export goods and services when domestic demand falters, which usually precedes a banking crisis. In a diagnostics of banking and currency crisis in 36 advanced economies, Joy et al. (2017) found that trade openness reduces the probability of a banking crisis. Nonetheless, Feldkircher (2014) reports that trade openness can amplify rather than mitigate the impact of a crisis.

Generally, the less competitive or concentrated banking systems imply higher interest rates and lower funds for investment, triggering a banking crisis (Boyd & De Nicoló, 2005). However, competition increases banks' lending and lowers loan default (Amidu, 2020a, 2020b). Also examined financial integration, competition, and bank risk-taking behavior for 47 African countries spanning from 2007 to 2014 found that bank competition has a threshold effect on banks risk-taking behavior. This implies that African economies are not able to fully benefit because of inadequate competition Beck et al. (2006) examined the impact of national bank concentration on the likelihood of a country suffering a systemic banking crisis for 69 countries and found that banking crises are less likely in economies with more concentrated banking systems. Further, the size of the banking sector and the level of financial development may influence banking sector crisis. However, the presence of strong financial banks lessens the probability of a banking crisis. Amaglobeli et al. (2017) report that the pre-crisis banking size impacts the fiscal cost of banking crises. Also, banking crisis is usually preceded by sluggishness in the economy. Low GDP growth is associated with a higher probability of a banking crisis. In a study of the factors related to the emergence of the systemic banking crisis of developed and developing economies, Demirgüç-Kunt and Detragiache (1998) prove that a weak macroeconomic environment (low growth) is a significant trigger of a banking crisis.

15.3 Methodology

This section describes the various methods and procedures that we adopt in the analysis of data. We utilize a wide range of panel data for 52 African countries covering the period 1970–2017.

Empirical Model Specification and Empirical Strategy

Due to the binary nature of banking crisis, the existing empirical literature has used Probit and Logit models to examine the factors that influence the probability of the occurrence of a banking crisis (Berger & Bouwman, 2017; Boyd et al., 2019; Büyükkarabacak & Valev, 2010; Davis et al., 2016; Inekwe & Valenzuela, 2020; Peña, 2017). The Logit model overcomes the limitation of the Linear Probability Model, which may have the fitted probabilities of either being less than zero or greater than one and the partial effect of any explanatory variable (appearing in level form) being constant (Wooldridge, 2012). In line with the literature, we employ logit regression and its marginal effects to examine the impact of cross-border banking on the banking crisis. Precisely, we specify the following regression equation;

$$\text{logit BCRISIS}_{it} = \ln\left(\frac{P\text{ (BCRISIS)}}{1 - P\text{ (BCRISIS)}}\right) = \beta_0 + \beta_1 \text{CBB}_{it} + \beta_2 \mathbf{Z}_{it} + \mu_i + v_t + \varepsilon_{it} \qquad (15.1)$$

Where BCRISIS_{it} is a banking crisis dummy, which takes a value of 1 in a crisis year and 0 if there is no crisis. The subscript i refers to a country, and t indicates time. Again, CBB_{it} is cross-border banking. In line with the literature (Brambila-Macias et al., 2011; Figuet et al., 2015), we measure cross-border banking in using five (5) different proxies. (1) percentage of foreign bank assets among total bank assets, (2) percentage of foreign banks among total banks, (3) percentage of consolidated foreign claims of Bank for International Settlements (BIS) reporting banks to GDP, (4) percentage of external loans and deposits of reporting banks vis-à-vis the banking sector to domestic bank deposits, (5) percentage of loans from nonresident banks (amounts outstanding) to GDP.

In line with the literature, we include some control variables as influencing banking crisis in our model. We denote the control variables by the vector $\mathbf{Z}_{it}$. We control for competition, size, liquidity, capital and profitability of the banking sector, inflation, credit growth, GDP growth, and trade openness (see Levieuge et al., 2021). The banking sector's competitiveness is expected to influence the stability of the banking sector and possibly result in a banking crisis. We measure competition using the Lerner index, which is defined as the gross profit margin of market output price minus marginal cost relative to the market output price. Again, the size of the banking sector and the level of financial development influences the probability of a banking crisis. We expect that a larger banking sector or more developed banking sector is less likely to face crisis. We measure the size of the banking sector using the domestic bank credit to GDP ratio. Also, liquidity indicates how well the banking sector performs and is a major predictor of the banking sector crisis. We, therefore, hypothesize that the more liquid the banking sector, the less likely it is to face problems. We measure liquidity as liquid bank reserves to bank assets ratio.

Further, capital serves as a buffer for the banking system in the event where there are problems. Banks with higher capital levels are considered safe and sound. Hence, the more capital levels of banks, the safer those banks and, therefore, the less likely banking crisis. We use bank capital to total assets to measure bank capital. Again, profits generally indicate a well-performing banking sector. Thus, banking crises are less likely to occur in a profitable banking system. Bank profitability is measured using bank return on assets (Net income divided by total assets). Inflation reflects the extent of the stability of the macroeconomy. We note that a higher rate of inflation is a precursor of a banking crisis. We use the consumer price index to measure inflation. Additionally, excessive credit growth is likely to cause a banking crisis. The more credits banks extend to their customers, the more likelihood of default. Hence, a higher probability of a banking crisis. Credit growth is measured as the growth in domestic credit to the private sector (DCPS) as a percentage of GDP. Slow growth indicates problems with the general economy and could be associated with a banking crisis. We use the GDP growth rate to proxy economic growth. Finally, we control for trade openness. A banking crisis is less likely to occur for open economies. We measure trade openness as the ratio of imports and exports to GDP. All data is sourced from the World Development Indicators and the Global Financial Development Database. Detailed measurement of variables with the source of data is presented in Table 15.1.

To ascertain the marginal effects of the variables, we take the partial differential of Eq. (15.1). That is, the margins give the derivative of the probability that the dependent variable equals one with respect to a conditioning variable. Therefore, each variable's estimated margins coefficient represents the likelihood or probability that the dependent variable will be true, holding all other factors constant.

15.4 Empirical Results

In this section, we discuss the empirical findings of our study. First, we present the descriptive statistics, which enable us to explore the appropriateness of the data for the estimations. Then, we again present the correlation matrix to assess the presence of multicollinearity in our data and the formal empirical analysis that tests our hypothesized relationships.

Table 15.1 Variable descriptions and data sources

Variable	*Measurement*	*Data source*
Cross-border Banking	• Foreign Bank Asset to Total Assets • Consolidated Claims of Foreign banks to GDP • External Loans and Deposits to Domestic Deposits • Loans from Nonresident Banks to GDP • External loans and deposits of reporting banks to domestic bank deposits	Global Financial Development Database
Banking Crisis	• Dummy variable. Takes a value of 1 in a crisis year and 0 if there is no crisis	Global Financial Development Database
Competition	• Lerner Index, that is, gross profit margin of market output price minus marginal cost relative to the market output price	Global Financial Development Database
Bank Liquidity	• Liquid bank reserves to bank assets ratio	Global Financial Development Database
Bank Profitability	• Return on assets (Net income divided by total assets)	Global Financial Development Database
Bank Capital	• Bank capital to total assets	Global Financial Development Database
Bank Size	• Bank credit to GDP ratio	Global Financial Development Database
Inflation	• Consumer Price Index	World Development Indicators Database
Credit Growth	• Growth in domestic credit to the private sector (DCPS) as a percentage of GDP, that is,$DCPS_1 - DCPS_0/DCPS_0$	World Development Indicators
Economic Growth	• GDP growth rate	World Development Indicators Database
Trade Openness	• Sum of exports and imports of goods and services measured as a share of GDP	World Development Indicators Database

Note Both the Global Financial Development Database and the World Development Indicators Database are sourced from the World Bank Group

The descriptive statistics of the variables are presented in Table 15.2. Our study reports a mean of 5.2% for banking crisis. This shows that the probability of a banking crisis in any given country in any given year in our sample is 5.3%. This is in line with the findings of Davis et al. (2016), who reported that there is a 4.5% probability of a banking crisis occurring for a sample of 35 countries. Again, the average foreign banks to total banks in African countries is 47.2%. This indicates that there is a strong presence of foreign banks in the banking systems of most countries in Africa.

However, in terms of the assets controlled by foreign banks, our study reports a mean of 51.2% for foreign bank assets to total assets. This suggests that foreign banks control more of the banking systems of most countries in Africa. Also, the percentage of consolidated foreign claims of Bank for International Settlements reporting banks to GDP reports a mean of 76.8%. This implies the significant importance of foreign banks in African countries. Further, external loans and deposits of reporting banks to domestic bank deposits report an average of 52.7%, while loans from nonresident banks to GDP report a mean of 47.04%. Undoubtedly, all measures of cross-border banking show significant participation of foreign banks in the banking systems of African countries. This is corroborated by the studies of Cull and Peria (2010), who indicated that Sub-Saharan

Table 15.2 Summary statistics

Variable	*Obs*	*Mean*	*Std. Dev*	*Min*	*Max*
Banking Crisis	2494	0.053	0.224	0	1
Foreign Banks to Total Banks	2496	47.204	14.182	0	96
Foreign Bank Asset to Total Assets	2496	51.186	11.175	0	94
Conso Claims of for banks to GDP	2496	76.827	442.018	0.001	8934.19
Ext Loans and Dep to Dom Dep	2496	52.729	149.762	−4.491	5249.35
Loans from Nonresident Banks to GDP	2496	47.043	244.438	0.042	5198.04
Competition	2496	0.299	0.059	−0.386	0.64
Bank Liquidity	2496	23.506	15.199	1.137	390.11
Bank Profitability	2496	1.971	1.268	−14.301	13.842
Bank Capital	2496	10.603	1.404	1.49	23.677
Bank Size	2496	18.6	17.392	0.008	160.125
Inflation	2496	64.245	46.188	15	410.94
Credit Growth	2496	0.045	0.27	−1	7.879
GDP Growth	2496	3.827	6.071	−62.076	123.14
Trade Openness	2496	62.511	29.569	6.32	347.996

Africa ranked among the regions with the highest level of foreign bank presence and participation.

Additionally, the Lerner index as a measure of competition or market power reports a mean of 0.299. The Lerner index is the ability of the firm to set prices above marginal cost, which is and indicates market power. The Lerner index is bounded between 0 and 1, with the extreme value of zero corresponding to perfect competition and the value of one to a pure monopoly. Therefore, a mean of approximately 0.3 implies a fairly competitive banking sector in Africa. This compares with figures from other studies (see Amidu, 2020a, 2020b; Léon, 2016). Further, bank liquidity measured as liquid bank reserves to bank assets ratio reports an average of 23.5%. This shows that the African banking sector is quite liquid. However, our study provides evidence of the low profitability of the banking sector in Africa. The study reports a mean of 1.97% for the return of assets for banks in Africa. Our analysis also suggests a well-capitalized banking sector in Africa as we record an average bank capital to total assets ratio of 10.6%. This is above the 10% capital adequacy ratio required in most African countries. Again, we record an average of 18.6% for domestic bank credit to GDP ratio. This shows that banks significantly contribute to the economies of African countries.

Also, inflation proxied by the consumer price index reports a mean of 64.2. Again, the study reports an average of 4.5% for credit growth and 3.8% for GDP growth rate. Furthermore, our study shows that African countries are pretty opened to trade as we record an average of 62.5% for trade openness. Finally, we present the results of Pearson's correlation in Table 15.3. The correlations show that competition, bank liquidity, bank capital, bank profitability, and bank size are negatively associated with banking crisis. Again, foreign bank to total bank ratio and foreign bank assets to total assets is negatively associated with banking crisis while consolidated claims of foreign banks to GDP and external loans and deposits to domestic deposits are positively correlated with banking crisis. The correlation matrix shows that the problem of multicollinearity is not present in our data.

Further, this study examines the impact of cross-border banking on banking crisis in Africa. Table 15.4 presents the impact of cross-border banking (proxied as 1) percentage of foreign bank assets among total bank assets, (2) percentage of foreign banks among total banks, (3) the percentage of consolidated foreign claims of Bank for International Settlements (BIS) reporting banks to GDP, (4) percentage external loans and

Table 15.3 Correlation matrix

Variables	*(1)*	*(2)*	*(3)*	*(4)*	*(5)*	*(6)*	*(7)*	*(8)*	*(9)*	*(10)*	*(11)*	*(12)*	*(13)*	*(14)*	*(15)*
(1) Banking Crisis	1.000														
(2) Foreign Banks to Total Banks	−0.047*	1.000													
(3) Foreign Bank Asset to Total Assets	−0.068*	0.631*	1.000												
(4) Conso Claims of banks to GDP	0.107*	−0.042*	−0.021	1.000											
(5) Ext Loans and Dep to Dom Dep	0.158*	0.084*	0.023	0.019	1.000										
(6) Loans from Nonresident Banks to GDP	−0.019	−0.032	−0.021	0.586*	0.016	1.000									

(continued)

Table 15.3 (continued)

Variables	*(1)*	*(2)*	*(3)*	*(4)*	*(5)*	*(6)*	*(7)*	*(8)*	*(9)*	*(10)*	*(11)*	*(12)*	*(13)*	*(14)*	*(15)*
(7) Competition	−0.089*	0.595*	0.407*	−0.042*	0.040*	−0.031	1.000								
(8) Bank Liquidity	−0.074*	0.202*	0.222*	0.006	0.009	0.016	0.195*	1.000							
(9) Bank Profitability	−0.096*	0.328*	0.268*	−0.039	0.092*	−0.038	0.423*	0.295*	1.000						
(10) Bank Capital	−0.082*	0.236*	0.283*	−0.031	0.028	−0.028	0.265*	0.171*	0.361*	1.000					
(11) Bank Size	−0.013	−0.009	0.016	−0.046*	0.019	−0.036	0.058*	−0.002	0.009	0.109*	1.000				
(12) Inflation	−0.064*	0.304*	0.281*	−0.010	0.017	0.011	0.306*	0.439*	0.401*	0.475*	0.169*	1.000			
(13) Credit Growth	−0.067*	0.002	0.018	0.010	−0.001	0.021	0.024	0.058*	0.027	0.010	0.033	0.015	1.000		
(14) GDP Growth	−0.068*	0.107*	0.084*	−0.037	0.022	−0.026	0.131*	0.019	0.097*	0.056*	0.041*	0.084*	−0.074*	1.000	
(15) Trade Openness	−0.046*	0.134*	0.116*	0.065*	0.064*	0.131*	0.065*	0.175*	0.153*	0.142*	0.268*	0.296*	0.030	0.191*	1.000

***$p < 0.01$, **$p < 0.05$, *$p < 0.1$

Table 15.4 Logit regression results on the impact of cross-border banking on banking crisis

	(1)	*(2)*	*(3)*	*(4)*	*(5)*
Foreign Banks to Total Banks	0.011**				
	(0.005)				
Foreign Bank Asset to Total Assets		−0.014			
		(0.019)			
Consolidated Claims of Foreign banks to GDP			0.0003***		
			(0.0001)		
External Loans and Deposits to Domestic Deposits				0.003***	
				(0.001)	
Loans from Nonresident Banks to GDP					−0.001
					(0.003)
Competition	−4.391***	−2.47*	−2.751*	−2.865**	−2.796*
	(1.699)	(1.445)	(1.423)	(1.453)	(1.429)
Bank Liquidity	−0.084***	−0.081***	−0.086***	−0.084***	−0.084***
	(0.027)	(0.027)	(0.027)	(0.027)	(0.027)
Bank Profitability	−0.197***	−0.2***	−0.196***	−0.241***	−0.209***
	(0.072)	(0.074)	(0.074)	(0.071)	(0.074)
Bank Capital	−0.152**	−0.14**	−0.151**	−0.149**	−0.149**
	(0.066)	(0.065)	(0.066)	(0.065)	(0.065)
Bank Size	0.004	0.003	0.004	0.003	0.003
	(0.005)	(0.005)	(0.005)	(0.005)	(0.005)
Inflation	0.007***	0.008***	0.008***	0.009***	0.008***
	(0.003)	(0.003)	(0.003)	(0.003)	(0.003)
Credit Growth	−2.299***	−2.32***	−2.406***	−2.362***	−2.308***
	(0.53)	(0.528)	(0.535)	(0.537)	(0.527)
GDP Growth	−0.045***	−0.044***	−0.041***	−0.045***	−0.045***
	(0.015)	(0.015)	(0.015)	(0.015)	(0.015)
Trade Openness	−0.002	−0.002	−0.002	−0.003	−0.001
	(0.003)	(0.003)	(0.003)	(0.003)	(0.003)
Constant	−2.616***	−2.598***	−2.674***	−2.623***	−2.595***
	(0.155)	(0.154)	(0.156)	(0.156)	(0.155)
Observations	2494	2494	2494	2494	2494

(continued)

Table 15.4 (continued)

	(1)	*(2)*	*(3)*	*(4)*	*(5)*
Pseudo R^2	0.101	0.098	0.108	0.126	0.098

Standard errors are in parentheses: $^{***}p < 0.01$, $^{**}p < 0.05$, $^{*}p < 0.1$

deposits of reporting banks to domestic bank deposits, (5) the percentage of loans from nonresident banks (amounts outstanding) to GDP) on banking crisis. We again present the results of the marginal effects in Table 15.5. In models 1–5, we present the logit regression results for our sample, while in models 6–10, we present the marginal effects of our study.

From models 1, 3, and 4, we observe a significant positive relationship between cross-border banking and banking. Specifically, foreign banks to total banks, consolidated claims of foreign banks to GDP, and loans from nonresident banks to GDP show positive coefficients. This suggests that cross-border banking is more likely to cause a banking crisis in Africa. This may be because cross-border banking can transfer banking failures and crises in one country to other countries through interbank markets. Also, cross-border banking affects the stability of the domestic banking system by increasing the supply of loanable funds, which is often associated with increased credit supply. This increased credit supply, in turn, results in the deterioration of loan quality since banks expand the range of loans by providing loans to borrowers, which might otherwise have been rejected. Again, increased cross-border banking activities promote a competitive domestic banking sector, increasing loanable funds' supply and driving interest rates downward. Therefore, this suppresses bank margins and forces banks to engage in more aggressive lending, often resulting in reduced loan screening and monitoring. Our result is in line with the findings of a recent study by Dinger and te Kaat (2020), who found that cross-border capital flows are associated with lower average loan quality. However, the results of the marginal effects as presented in models 6, 8, and 9 show that the probability of cross-border banking resulting in a banking crisis in Africa is negligible.

Also, bank competition measured using the Lerner index report a negative coefficient with banking crisis in all models. Therefore, the result implies that banking crises are more likely with a lower Lerner index

Table 15.5 Logit average marginal effects results on the impact of cross-border banking on banking crisis

	(6)	*(7)*	*(8)*	*(9)*	*(10)*
Foreign Banks to Total Banks	0.001***				
	(0.000)				
Foreign Bank Asset to Total Assets		−0.001			
		(0.001)			
Consolidated Claims of Foreign banks to GDP			0.000***		
			(0.000)		
External Loans and Deposits to Domestic Deposits				0.000***	
				(0.000)	
Loans from Nonresident Banks to GDP					−0.000
					(0.000)
Competition	−0.210**	−0.119*	−0.130*	−0.133**	−0.134*
	(0.082)	(0.070)	(0.068)	(0.068)	(0.069)
Bank Liquidity	−0.004***	−0.004***	−0.004***	−0.004***	−0.004***
	(0.001)	(0.001)	(0.001)	(0.001)	(0.001)
Bank Profitability	−0.009***	−0.010***	−0.009***	−0.011***	−0.010***
	(0.003)	(0.004)	(0.004)	(0.003)	(0.004)
Bank Capital	−0.007***	−0.007**	−0.007**	−0.007**	−0.007**
	(0.003)	(0.003)	(0.003)	(0.003)	(0.003)
Bank Size	0.000	0.000	−0.000	−0.000	0.000
	(0.000)	(0.000)	(0.000)	(0.000)	(0.000)
Inflation	0.000***	0.000***	0.000***	0.000***	0.000***
	(0.000)	(0.000)	(0.000)	(0.000)	(0.000)
Credit Growth	−0.110***	−0.112***	−0.114***	−0.109***	−0.111***
	(0.026)	(0.026)	(0.026)	(0.026)	(0.026)
GDP Growth	−0.002***	−0.002***	−0.002***	−0.002***	−0.002***
	(0.001)	(0.001)	(0.001)	(0.001)	(0.001)
Trade Openness	−0.000	−0.000	−0.000	−0.000	−0.000
	(0.000)	(0.000)	(0.000)	(0.000)	(0.000)
Observations	2494	2494	2494	2494	2494

Standard errors are in parentheses: $^{***}p < 0.01$, $^{**}p < 0.05$, $^{*}p < 0.1$

(more competitive banking sector). This is possible because increased bank competition may inadvertently encourage banks to increase their risk-taking appetite. Also, increased competition drives bank interest margins down, forcing banks to engage in aggressive lending activities to make more profits. This increases the probability of loan default as loan screening, and monitoring efforts of banks are reduced, leading to high default rates. This finding is corroborated by Tongurai and Vithessonthi (2020), who found that bank competition is positively related to banks' risk-taking appetite. Our marginal effect results show that there is between 11.9% and 21% probability of Africa suffering a banking crisis in a highly competitive banking system.

Further, banking sector liquidity reports a negative coefficient with banking crisis in all estimated models. This means that more liquid banking systems are less likely to suffer from banking crises. Therefore, liquidity challenges may result in panic withdrawals from customers, which is considered a major cause of most banking crises. For instance, Jutasompakorn et al. (2014) note that liquidity shortages may have contributed to the 2008 financial crisis. This finding is confirmed by Diamond and Rajan (2005). However, the marginal effect provides evidence that the probability of African banking systems suffering a banking crisis resulting from liquidity problems is 0.4% for all models. Again, we report a negative relationship between banking sector profitability and the likelihood of a banking crisis. This suggests that the more profitable African banking systems are less likely to experience a banking crisis. This is because more profitable banks are well managed and therefore are less likely to fail. Also, more profits serve as capital buffers for banks which improves their stability. However, there is between 0.9% and 1.1% probability of more profitable banking systems suffering banking crisis in Africa.

In addition, bank capital negatively relates to banking crisis. This indicates that well-capitalized banking systems are less likely to experience a banking crisis. This is because higher capital levels provide a cushion against shocks in the banking systems. Therefore, well-capitalized banking systems are safer and less likely to suffer from banking crises. However, the marginal effect results show that the probability of a banking crisis is 0.7% across all models. Also, we find a positive relationship between inflation and the likelihood of a banking crisis. This implies that high inflationary countries are more likely to experience a banking crisis in Africa. This is because inflation is an indication of macroeconomic stability or macroeconomic mismanagement. Therefore, higher inflation adversely affects the economy and the banking system. This is confirmed by the studies of Davis and Karim (2016), who found inflation to increase the probability of a banking crisis. However, the marginal effects show that the likelihood of banking systems suffering a banking crisis in high inflationary periods is negligible. This may be because African countries are characterized mainly by high inflation rates, making banks develop strategies of dealing with them. Therefore, higher inflation rates may not cause too much harm to the banking systems of African countries.

Furthermore, credit growth reports a negative coefficient for all models. This suggests that credit growth is less likely to lead to a banking crisis in Africa. This, although contrary to our expectation, is expected because credit growth is an indication of improved capital and liquidity positions of banks. Therefore, credit growth is less likely to result in a banking crisis. However, this is in contrast with the findings of Ganİoğlu (2016) findings, who find a credit boom promotes a banking crisis. There is, however, between 10.9% and 11.4% probability of African countries experiencing a banking crisis as a result of credit booms. Finally, the study shows a negative relationship between economic growth and the likelihood of a banking crisis. This indicates that strong economies are less likely to result in a banking crisis. However, the marginal effects show a probability of 0.2% for all models.

15.5 Conclusion and Policy Recommendations

This study examines the impact of cross-border banking on banking crisis in Africa. We specifically examine the impact of the percentage of foreign bank assets among total bank assets, percentage of foreign banks among total banks, percentage of consolidated foreign claims of Bank for International Settlements (BIS) reporting banks to GDP, percentage of external loans and deposits of reporting banks to domestic bank deposits and percentage of loans from nonresident banks (amounts outstanding) to GDP on banking crisis. The study relied on data from 52 African countries over the period 1970–2017. We employ the logit regression to estimate our model. As a result, we provide evidence that a banking crisis is more likely with cross-border banking in Africa. In addition, our study suggests that the more foreign bank presence and participation there are, the more likely banking systems in Africa experience a banking crisis. However, our marginal effects show that the probability of cross-border banking resulting in a banking crisis in Africa is negligible. Hence, following the findings of our study, governments, policymakers, and regulators should create the right institutional and regulatory environment for cross-border banking to promote the stability of the banking systems of countries in Africa. Again, policies aimed at promoting competition, improving the capital, profitability, and liquidity levels of banks, promoting economic growth, and reducing inflation will help lessen the probability of a banking crisis in Africa.

References

Abiad, A., Mishra, P., & Topalova, P. (2012, March). *How does trade evolve in the aftermath of financial crises?* (IMF Staff Papers).

Abor, J. Y., Agbloyor, E. K., & Issahaku, H. (2019). The role of financial markets and institutions in private sector development in Africa. *Extending Financial Inclusion in Africa*, 61–85.

Amaglobeli, D., End, N., Jarmuzek, M., & Palomba, G. (2017). The fiscal costs of systemic banking crises. *International Finance, 20*(1), 2–25. https://doi.org/10.1111/infi.12100

Amidu, M. (2020a). Bank competition in Africa: Do institutional quality and cross-border banking matter? *Journal of African Business*, 1–35. https://doi.org/10.1080/15228916.2020.1838833

Amidu, M. (2020b). Bank competition in Africa: Do institutional quality and cross-border banking matter? *Journal of African Business*. https://doi.org/10.1080/15228916.2020.1838833

Angkinand, A. P., Sawangngoenyuang, W., & Wihlborg, C. (2010). Financial liberalization and banking crises: A cross-country analysis*. *International Review of Finance, 10*(2), 263–292. https://doi.org/10.1111/j.1468-2443.2010.01114.x

Arena, M., Reinhart, C., & Vázquez, F. (2010). The lending channel in emerging economies: Are foreign banks different ? *Banks and Bank Systems, 5*(2), 20–50.

Bara, A., & Abel, S. (2018). Cross-border banking, international financial flows and financial deepening. *Studies in Economics and Econometrics, 42*(3), 1–34. https://doi.org/10.1080/10800379.2018.12097337

Beck, T., Demirgüç-Kunt, A., & Levine, R. (2006). Bank concentration, competition, and crises: First results. *Journal of Banking and Finance, 30*(5), 1581–1603. https://doi.org/10.1016/j.jbankfin.2005.05.010

Berger, A. N., & Bouwman, C. H. S. (2017). Bank liquidity creation, monetary policy, and financial crises. *Journal of Financial Stability, 30*, 139–155. https://doi.org/10.1016/j.jfs.2017.05.001

Bernal-Verdugo, L. E., Furceri, D., & Guillaume, D. M. (2012). Crises, labor market policy, and unemployment. *IMF Working Papers*, *12*(65), i. https://doi.org/10.5089/9781463938420.001

Boyd, J. H., & De Nicoló, G. (2005). The theory of bank risk taking and competition revisited. *Journal of Finance, 60*(3), 1329–1343. https://doi.org/10.1111/j.1540-6261.2005.00763.x

Brambila-Macias, J., Massa, I., & Murinde, V. (2011). Cross-border bank lending versus FDI in Africa's growth story. *Applied Financial Economics, 21*(16), 1205–1213. https://doi.org/10.1080/09603107.2011.566179

Boyd, J. H., De Nicolo, G., & Rodionova, T. (2019). Banking crises and crisis dating: Disentangling shocks and policy responses. *Journal of Financial Stability, 41*, 45–54.

Büyükkarabacak, B., & Valev, N. T. (2010). The role of household and business credit in banking crises. *Journal of Banking and Finance, 34*(6), 1247–1256. https://doi.org/10.1016/j.jbankfin.2009.11.022

Choi, S., Francis, B. B., & Hasan, I. (2010). Cross-border bank M&As and risk: Evidence from the bond market. *Journal of Money, Credit and Banking, 42*(4), 615–645. https://doi.org/10.1111/j.1538-4616.2010.00301.x

Claessens, S. (2006). *Competitive implications of cross-border banking* (World Bank Policy Research Working Paper 3854). https://doi.org/10.1142/9789812773418_0011

Cull, R., & Peria, M. S. M. (2010, August). *Foreign bank participation in developing countries what do we know about the drivers and consequences of this phenomenon?* (Policy Research Working Paper).

Davis, E. P., & Karim, D. (2016). Should multivariate early warning systems for banking crises pool across regions? *Review of World Economics, 147*(4), 693–716.

Davis, J. S., Mack, A., Phoa, W., & Vandenabeele, A. (2016). Credit booms, banking crises, and the current account. *Journal of International Money and Finance, 60*, 360–377. https://doi.org/10.1016/j.jimonfin.2015.09.008

Degryse, H., Elahi, M. A., & Penas, M. F. (2010). Cross-border exposures and financial contagion. *International Review of Finance, 10*(2), 209–240. https://doi.org/10.1111/j.1468-2443.2010.01109.x

Demirgüç-Kunt, A., & Detragiache, E. (1998). The determinants of banking crises in developing and developed countries. *IMF Staff Papers, 45*(1), 81–109. https://doi.org/10.2307/3867330

Demirgüç-Kunt, A., & Levine, R. (2008). *Finance, financial sector policies, and long-run growth* (World Bank Policy Research Working Paper, 4469). https://doi.org/10.1596/1813-9450-4469

Diamond, D. W., & Rajan, R. G. (2005). Liquidity shortages and banking crises. *Journal of Finance, 60*(2), 615–647. https://doi.org/10.1111/j.1540-6261.2005.00741.x

Dinger, V., & te Kaat, D. M. (2020). Cross-border capital flows and bank risk-taking. *Journal of Banking and Finance*, 117. https://doi.org/10.1016/j.jbankfin.2020.105842

Enoch, C., Mathieu, P., & Mecagni, M. (2015). Pan-African banks—Opportunities and challenges for cross-border oversight. *Policy Papers, 14*(90). https://doi.org/10.5089/9781498342452.007

Feldkircher, M. (2014). The determinants of vulnerability to the global financial crisis 2008 to 2009: Credit growth and other sources of risk. *Journal of International Money and Finance, 43*, 19–49. https://doi.org/10.1016/j.jimonfin.2013.12.003

Figuet, J. M., Humblot, T., & Lahet, D. (2015). Cross-border banking claims on emerging countries: The Basel III Banking Reforms in a push and pull framework. *Journal of International Financial Markets, Institutions and Money, 34*(2015), 294–310. https://doi.org/10.1016/j.intfin.2014.11.016

Furceri, D., & Zdzienicka, A. (2012). Banking crises and short and medium term output losses in emerging and developing countries: The role of structural and policy variables. *World Development, 40*(12), 2369–2378. https://doi.org/10.1016/j.worlddev.2012.03.021

Ganİoğlu, A. (2016). Financial and political institutional problems as instigators of banking crises. *Developing Economies, 54*(4), 292–312. https://doi.org/10.1111/deve.12113

Hamdaoui, M. (2016, September). Are systemic banking crises in developed and developing countries predictable? *Journal of Multinational Financial Management*, *37–38*, 114–138. https://doi.org/10.1016/j.mulfin.2016.09.002

Leckow, R., & Pazarbasioglu, C. (2012). Resolution of cross-border banks: A proposed framework for enhanced coordination. *Building a More Resilient Financial Sector: Reforms in the Wake of the Global Crisis*, 101.

IMF. (2015, January). *Pan-African banks—Opportunities and challenges for cross-border oversight*. International Monetary Fund, Publication Services. http://www.imf.org/external/pp/ppindex.aspx

Inekwe, J. N., & Valenzuela, M. R. (2020). Financial integration and banking crisis. A critical analysis of restrictions on capital flows. *World Economy, 43*(2), 506–527. https://doi.org/10.1111/twec.12855

Jeon, B. N., Olivero, M. P., & Wu, J. (2013). Multinational banking and the international transmission of financial shocks: Evidence from foreign bank subsidiaries. *Journal of Banking & Finance Journal, 37*, 952–972.

Joy, M., Rusnák, M., Šmídková, K., & Vašíček, B. (2017). Banking and currency crises: Differential diagnostics for developed countries. *International Journal of Finance and Economics, 22*(1), 44–67. https://doi.org/10.1002/ijfe.1570

Jutasompakorn, P., Brooks, R., Brown, C., & Treepongkaruna, S. (2014). Banking crises: Identifying dates and determinants. *Journal of International Financial Markets, Institutions and Money, 32*(1), 150–166. https://doi.org/10.1016/j.intfin.2014.05.004

Klomp, J. (2010). Causes of banking crises revisited. *North American Journal of Economics and Finance, 21*(1), 72–87. https://doi.org/10.1016/j.najef.2009.11.005

Laeven, L. (2011). Banking crises: A review. *Annual Review of Financial Economics, 3*, 17–40. https://doi.org/10.1146/annurev-financial-102710-144816

Laeven, L., & Valencia, F. (2013). Systemic banking crises database. *IMF Economic Review, 61*(2), 225–270. https://doi.org/10.1057/imfer.2013.12

Le, C. H. A., & Dickinson, D. G. (2016). the systemic risk of cross-border banking: Evidence from the sudden stop and interbank stress contagion in East Asia. *Emerging Markets Finance and Trade, 52*(1), 237–254. https://doi.org/10.1080/1540496X.2015.1021643

Léon, F. (2016). Does the expansion of regional cross-border banks affect competition in Africa? Indirect evidence. *Research in International Business and Finance, 37*, 66–77. https://doi.org/10.1016/j.ribaf.2015.10.015

Levieuge, G., Lucotte, Y., & Pradines-Jobet, F. (2021). The cost of banking crises: Does the policy framework matter? *Journal of International Money and Finance*, 110. https://doi.org/10.1016/j.jimonfin.2020.102290

Peña, G. (2017). Money, lending and banking crises. *Economic Papers, 36*(4), 444–458. https://doi.org/10.1111/1759-3441.12195

Schnabel, I., & Seckinger, C. (2019). Foreign banks, financial crises and economic growth in Europe q. *Journal of International Money and Finance, 95*, 70–94.

Sissy, A. M., Amidu, M., & Abor, J. Y. (2017). The effects of revenue diversification and cross border banking on risk and return of banks in Africa. *Research in International Business and Finance, 40*, 1–18. https://doi.org/10.1016/j.ribaf.2016.09.017

Stoddard, O., & Noy, I. (2015). Fire-sale FDI? The impact of financial crises on foreign direct investment. *Review of Development Economics, 19*(2), 387–399. https://doi.org/10.1111/rode.12149

Tongurai, J., & Vithessonthi, C. (2020). Bank regulations, bank competition and bank risk-taking: Evidence from Japan. *Journal of Multinational Financial Management*, 56. https://doi.org/10.1016/j.mulfin.2020.100638

Tonzer, L. (2015). Cross-border interbank networks, banking risk and contagion. *Journal of Financial Stability, 18*, 19–32. https://doi.org/10.1016/j.jfs.2015.02.002

Uch, R., Miyamoto, H., & Kakinaka, M. (2021, March). Effects of a banking crisis on credit growth in developing countries. *Finance Research Letters Journal*.

Wooldridge, J. (2012). Introductory econometrics: A modern approach, 5th edition. In *South Western, Cengage Learning*. https://doi.org/10.4324/9781351140768-8

Zhu, W., & Yang, J. (2016). State ownership, cross-border acquisition, and risk-taking: Evidence from China's banking industry q. *Journal of Banking & Finance, 71*, 133–153.

CHAPTER 16

Cross-Border Banking, Bank Pricing and Financial Inclusion in Africa

Mohammed Amidu, Aisha Mohammed Sissy, Joshua Yindenaba Abor, and Simon Wolfe

Abbreviations

CPI	Consumer Price Index
GMM	Generalized method of moments
LICs	Low-Income Countries
MICs	Middle-Income Countries

M. Amidu (✉) · A. M. Sissy
University of Ghana Business School, Accra, Ghana
e-mail: mamidu@ug.edu.gh

J. Y. Abor
Department of Finance, University of Ghana Business School, Accra, Ghana
e-mail: joshabor@ug.edu.gh

S. Wolfe
University of Southampton Business School, Southampton, UK
e-mail: ssjw@soton.ac.uk

J. Y. Abor and C. K. D. Adjasi (eds.), *The Economics of Banking and Finance in Africa*, Palgrave Macmillan Studies in Banking and Financial Institutions, https://doi.org/10.1007/978-3-031-04162-4_16

OLS	Ordinary Least Squares
PABs	Pan African Banks
SMEs	Small and Medium Enterprises
SSA	Sub-Saharan Africa

16.1 Introduction

Financial inclusion is fast becoming a new paradigm of economic growth (Iqbal & Sami, 2017). Therefore, most governments have made financial inclusion a policy priority (Arun & Kamath, 2015) and it is gaining a lot of interest from researchers. This is because financial inclusion is shown to improve the performance of firms (Chauvet & Jacolin, 2017), increase economic growth (Iqbal & Sami, 2017) and reduce poverty (Mohammed et al., 2017) by positively transforming the production and employment activities of individuals. Furthermore, financial inclusive enables individuals to invest in education, capitalise on promising investment opportunities and unlock entrepreneurship potential. Thus, financial exclusion can lead to the emergence of poverty traps and the perpetuation of underdevelopment (Demirgüç-Kunt & Klapper, 2012b). Financial inclusion involves the provision of a wide range of financial products and services at reduced cost, at high convenience and quality to the vast majority of the population, especially the poor and the marginalised. This is to ensure that no entrepreneur or enterprise is unable to take advantage of good business opportunities because of financial constraints.

Unfortunately, Africa seems to be losing out on benefits of financial inclusion due to the high level of financial exclusion on the continent relative to the rest of the world. According to Demirguc-Kunt et al. (2015), globally, in terms of adults aged 15 and above, 60.7% of them have accounts with financial institutions, 40.1% of them use debit cards to make payments, whiles 17.7% of them receive wages through an account. In sharp contrast to the global statistics, in Sub-Saharan Africa (SSA), only 28.9% of these adults have a formal account, only 8.7% of them use a debit card to make payments and whiles just 7.3% of them receive wages through an account. The story is not much different with regards to other financial inclusion measures including savings capacity and access to credit. Globally, about 27.4%, and 10.7%, respectively of adults aged 15 and above have formal savings, and obtained formal credit in the past year. On the other hand, in SSA, only 15.9%, and 6.3% respectively of adults save with a financial institution, and obtained credit from a financial institution in the past year (Demirguc-Kunt et al., 2015).

There is the hunch that cross-border banking can give the financial inclusion drive in SSA a significant boost. This is because, when banks cross-border they embark on aggressive deposit mobilisation to enable them gain a significant share of the domestic market. Cross-border banks also come with innovation and modern technology they have honed from their original country to their countries of host (Claessens, 2006; Clarke et al., 2006). This financial innovation and cutting-edge technology enable cross-border banks to roll out electronic financial services or financial technology (FinTech) such as ATMs and other smartcards, as well as internet banking to reach out to as many people as possible. Aside electronic banking services, cross-border banks add to the number of brick and mortar bank branches in underserved and unserved areas and for that matter bring banking to the door steps of the financially excluded. Related to this, is the view that the competition brought to the banking system by the entrance of cross-border banks leads to efficiency in the pricing of bank services, therefore making such services affordable (Serrano, 2016).

However, it is argued that some behaviour of cross-border banks may hinder financial inclusion. Cross-border banks may engage in cherry picking of customers, which may expose domestic banks to the riskier customers leading to high non-performing loans in domestic banks. Cross-border can also engage in capital flight, leading to financial instability in the domestic economy. Cross-border banks may also be more committed to the development agenda of their country of origin than they may be to the development goals of the host country and this may make them less incline to promote financial inclusion priorities of the host country (Dages et al., 2000). Cross-border banking increases domestic bank competition. Claessens (2006) and Clarke et al. (2006) "considered that foreign banks add to competition, increase financial service access, bring about great stability and boost financial and economic performance of borrowers". Amidu and Wolfe (2013) however contend "that competition pressurizes banks to adopt strategies to diversify and this decision affects their pricing strategy".

In the light of the lack of clarity regarding the role of cross-border banks in enhancing financial inclusion, this study contributes to the debate by assessing how cross-border banking activities and bank pricing behaviour impacts financial inclusion in Africa. This study is relevant because of the consequences associated with financial exclusion as enumerated by Patwardhan (2018). The financially underserved are prone to the repercussions of financial shocks and emergencies due to their ill preparedness. They are unable to take advantage of viable business opportunities and for that matter lack financial mobility and security. Consequently, this financial fragility affects the physical and mental health of people who are financially unserved and underserved.

The extant literature mostly looks at how foreign bank entry affects their lending behaviour (see Claessens & Horen, 2014; Serrano, 2016) and financial stability (see Angkinand & Wihlborg, 2010; Lee & Zhong, 2015), diversification strategy (Sissy et al., 2017). Meanwhile, the role of banks goes beyond financial stability, diversification strategy and lending concerns. Now, we are more concerned about the ability of banks to reach out to the underserved population, and capital constrained entrepreneurs and extend to them a suite of financial products and services including but not limited to account ownership services, access to affordable credit, saving capabilities, investment alternatives, remittance services, affordable insurance and business mentoring services. This work is also related to the work of (Allen et al., 2016), which examines the effects of banking cost and ownership profile on the ownership and use of accounts. The results showed that lower banking cost encourages financial inclusion as it lowers the cost barrier. The finding on the effect of bank ownership type and the ownership of bank account and its usage was however not robust. Allen et al. (2016) used subjective measures of banking cost such as perceptions about how high or how low the costs of banking services are.

This present paper specifically investigates the effect of cross-border banking on bank pricing behaviour. The paper also examines the effect of bank pricing behaviour on inclusive finance. Finally, it analyses the sensitivity of financial inclusion on the interaction effect of cross-border banking and bank pricing behaviour. The paper makes three main contributions to knowledge. First, we build on the extant literature to contribute to knowledge by simultaneously assessing the roles cross-border banks and bank pricing behaviour play in fostering financial inclusion. The existing literature often assesses the impact of either cross-border banking on financial inclusion or the effect of cost of banking services on financial inclusion, but scarcely both at a time. Second, we employ three objective measures of bank pricing such as loan price, deposit price and fees to enable an objective assessment of the relationships. Again, we assess financial inclusion not just in terms of access, but also in terms of usage of financial services and the quality of those services. Third, we also contribute to the development of cross-border banking literature in Africa. The focus on Africa makes an interesting case study for cross-border banking and financial inclusion for a number of reasons. In the first place, Africa hosts a large proportion of the financially excluded population in the world. Also, there is a high presence of cross-banks all over Africa as compared to places in the world. Lastly, the cost of banking in Africa, in terms of interest rates and charges is generally regarded as very high in Africa (Amidu, 2015).

We employ System GMM estimation technique to overcome endogeneity and reverse causality problems. Cross-border banking is proxied by a dummy variable which takes the value 1 for banks controlled by a foreign shareholder, but 0 if otherwise. Financial inclusion is measured using three indicators: (1) financial access, proxied by the number of branches of a bank (Branch); (2) financial usage which is measured by the proportion of total gross loan to total assets (Loan a/c) and the proportion of total deposit to total liabilities (Deposits a/c); and (3) quality of financial inclusion which is measured by total cost to gross revenue and proportion of earnings assets to total assets. Similarly, bank pricing behaviour is measured using three proxies: lending rate (Loan price), price paid for providing non-interest related services (Fees price), and deposit rate (Deposits price).

The paper makes a number of interesting findings: First, we note that cross-border banking in Africa affects banks' pricing behaviour. For instance, our results suggest that cross-border banks charges lesser fees for non-interest-related services and offers higher deposit prices than their non-cross-border counterparts. This finding is consistent with the argument that cross-border banks may engage in cherry picking of customers, which may influence their pricing behaviour. Moreover, in relation to the effects of bank pricing behaviour on inclusive finance, the results indicate that an increase in loan price results in financial usage increasing. Also, higher fee price reduces financial usage and financial quality (i.e. earning assets to total asset ratio), at the same time increases financial quality by way of increasing cost to income ratio. The results also suggest that higher deposit prices result in the reduction of financial usage but increases financial quality. Furthermore, the results also indicates that financial inclusion is not sensitive to both cross-border banking and bank pricing behaviour.

The remainder of this paper is structured as follows. Section 16.2 presents stylised facts on cross-border banking and financial inclusion in Africa. In Sect. 16.3, we review the theoretical and empirical literature. Section 16.4 describes the empirical strategy, while Sect. 16.5 includes the analysis and discussion of the results. Section 16.6 concludes the paper.

16.2 Stylized Facts on Cross-Border Banking and Financial Inclusion

Cross-border banks have had a very strong presence in Africa over the years. The adoption of financial liberalisation policies in the 1980s encouraged many cross-border banks to enter the African banking terrain. As shown in Fig. 16.1, from the 1990s, government ownership of banks shrunk over the years, giving way to more private participation and greater foreign ownership of banks in Sub-Saharan Africa (SSA). This has engendered competition in the African banking system. In middle-income countries (MICs) in the region, the number of state-owned banks' assets as a percentage of the total assets of the banking sector was 20% in a period between 1990 and 1999 but fell to 10% in a period between 2010 and 2011. For these same countries, foreign-owned banks' share of total industry assets rose from 40% in 1990–1999 to 70% in 2010–2011. Similar trends are observed for low-income countries (LICs) in the region. What is noteworthy of the recent wave in cross-border banking in Africa is an emergence of the Pan African Banks (PABs) (these are African

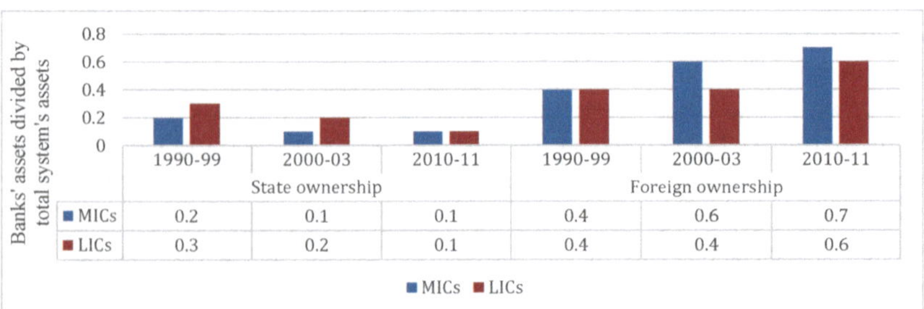

Fig. 16.1 Sub-Saharan Africa: Ownership structure in the Banking Sector, 1990–2011 (*Source* IMF [2015] and sources cited therein)

banks with presence in several African countries). PABs are said to significantly contribute to financial innovation, integration and competition on the continent (IMF, 2015).

Beck (2014) categorises ownership groups in the African banking landscape into five based on leading shareholder: (1) banks which are domestically owned (domestic banks), (2) subsidiaries or branches of banks which have their headquarters located in the sub-region (i.e., East, Southern or West Africa), (3) subsidiaries or branches of banks with parent bank's headquarters not located in the sub-region but elsewhere in Africa (African banks), (4) foreign banks from emerging markets outside Africa and (5) banks with US or Europe parent banks (developed country banks). Shifts in the ownership shares of these ownership categories are shown in Fig. 16.2. For domestic banks, the average stake declined from 54% in 2000 to 43% in 2009. For developed countries foreign banks, the stake remained unaltered at 24% over the period. However, the average stake of African banks expanded from 19% in 2000 to 30% in 2009. This highlights the increasing presence of PABs in the continent's banking system. Some examples of PABs include Ecobank, Absa, Standard Bank, United Bank of Africa. Ecobank for instance, has presence in over 32 countries. United Bank of Africa also has footprints in over 20 countries, while Standard Bank is present in over 16 countries (Beck, 2014).

Despite the increased presence of cross-border banks in SSA, financial inclusion remains very low in the region compared to the global average. This conclusion is based on 2014 Findex data compiled by Demirguc-Kunt et al. (2015) as presented in Table 16.1. For instance, only 34.2%

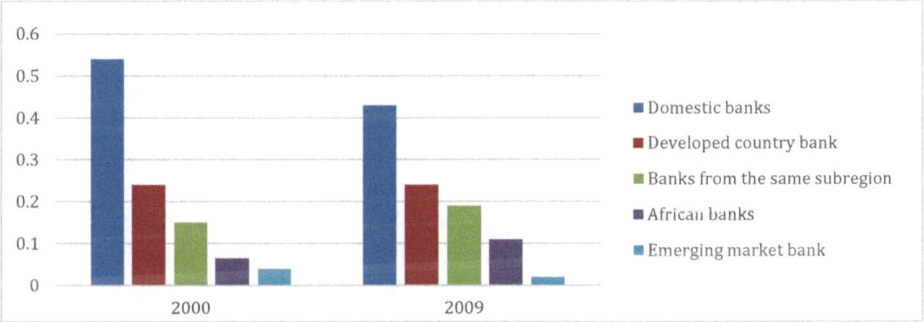

Fig. 16.2 Diverse Bank Ownership Groups across Africa (*Source* Beck [2014] and sources cited therein)

Table 16.1 Financial inclusion indicators in SSA

Financial Inclusion Measure	*SSA*	*World*
Account (% age 15+) All adults	**34.2**	**61.5**
Women	29.9	58.1
Adults belonging to the poorest 40%	24.6	54.0
Young adults (% ages 15–24)	25.9	46.3
Adults living in rural areas	29.2	56.7
Financial Institution Account (% age 15+)		
All adults	28.9	60.7
All adults, 2011	23.9	50.6
Access to Financial Institution Account (% age 15+)		
Has debit card	17.9	40.1
Has debit card, 2011	15.0	30.5
ATM is the main mode of withdrawal (% with an account), 2011	51.7	48.3
Use of Account in the Past Year (% age 15+)		
Used an account to receive wages	7.3	17.7
Used an account to receive government transfers	3.8	8.2
Used a financial institution account to pay utility bill	2.8	16.7
Savings in the Past Year (% age 15+)		
Saved at a financial institution	15.9	27.4
Saved at a financial institution, 2011	14.3	22.6
Saved any money	59.6	56.5
Saved for old age	9.8	23.9
Saved for a farm or business	22.7	13.8
Saved for education or school fees	22.9	22.3
Credit in the Past Year (% age 15+)		
Borrowed from a financial institution	6.3	10.7
Borrowed from a financial institution, 2011	4.8	9.1
Borrowed from family or friends	41.9	26.2
Borrowed from a private informal lender	4.7	4.6
Borrowed any money	54.5	42.4
Borrowed for a farm or business	12.8	7.1
Borrowed for education or school fees	12.3	7.7

Source Demirguc-Kunt et al. (2015)

of adults have any form of account in SSA, which is far lower than the global average (61.5%). The performance is even worse when it comes to ownership of formal bank account. The regional average (28.9%) is less than half of the global average (60.7%). Thus, on the average, over 70% of adults in SSA are unbanked revealing the dearth of financial inclusion in the region. Only 17.9% have a debit card compared to a global average of 40.1%. Though it is good to have an account, how active the account is, is more important. In terms of usage of accounts, only 7.3%, and 2.8% respectively used their accounts to receive wages and settle bills are SSA, which is indicative of low frequency of account usage.

It is not only account penetration and usage that is low in SSA but also formal savings and access to credit from financial institutions. Even though 59.6% of adults saved, only 15.9% saved with a formal financial institution in SSA, which is lower than the world average (27.4%). The relatively high amount of informal savings may be indicative of a lack of access to formal savings opportunities due to barriers such as distance, cost and documentation among others. Again, though 54.5% of adults in SSA borrowed money, only 6.3% borrowed from the formal financial system. Due to the lack of access to formal credit, most African households and enterprises are forced to borrow at high cost from the informal financial sector. This situation stifles entrepreneurship and impedes the growth and development of businesses in Africa. The majority of adults in Africa borrow from family and friends usually in amounts, which are too small to bring about significant change in the capital base.

16.3 Literature Review

Theoretical Overview

The theoretical principles which explain bank pricing behaviour could be further explained in terms of a "monopoly model", "dealership model" or "behavioural model".

Monopoly Model

The monopoly model was developed from a seminal work by Klein (1971), and further adopted by Amidu and Wolfe 2013); Fiador and Amidu (2021). The model "considers the banking firm's main activity as the production of deposits and loans through intermediation services and is represented by the following cost function":

$$C = f(D, L) \tag{16.1}$$

"Where D is the volume of deposits while L is the volume of loans produced by the bank. The assumption in line with Eq. (16.1) is that a banking firm pursues its activities in an environment characterised by the presence of imperfect competition in both deposit and credit markets".

Klein (1971) argues that the "monopoly power of a bank can then be used to explain the scale of operations, its asset and liability structure as well as its decision to affect the price on liabilities (deposits) and assets (loans). Thus, with this approach, a banking firm's price reflects primarily its ability to charge a price higher than the marginal cost of providing the services in both loan and deposit markets". This is illustrated by employing an argument from Oreiro and de Paula (2010) as follows: "assuming that, p is the prevailing interest rate on the inter-bank market; p_L is the price charged on loans generated by the bank and p_D is the price paid to depositors with the bank. α is the reserve requirements imposed by the central bank, and it is computed as a proportion of the deposits; the ε_L is the price elasticity of loan demand; ε_D is the price elasticity of deposit supply; C_L is the marginal cost of loan services; and C_D is the marginal cost of deposits services. If we also assume that a profit maximising bank is risk neutral, the optimal return on loan and deposits" as suggested by Freixas and Rochet (1997) is:

$$\frac{1}{\varepsilon_L^*} = \frac{p_L^* - (p + C_L)}{p_L^*} \tag{16.2}$$

$$\frac{1}{\varepsilon_D^*} = \frac{p(1-\alpha) - C_D - p_D^*}{p_D^*} \tag{16.3}$$

The second and third equations imply that banks set the prices of their loans and deposit services in a manner over marginal costs. This is an inverse of interest elasticity of the loan demand and deposit supply functions. We interpret Eqs. (16.2) and (16.3) as, the lesser the sensitivity of loan demand and deposit supply functions to price variations, the greater a bank's return in both loan and deposit taking, indicating greater the bank profit. However, if banks operate in markets other than an imperfect market, where it grants loans and take deposits, the optimal return on loans and deposits could be given as:

$$\frac{s}{\varepsilon_L^*} = \frac{p_L^* - (p + C_L)}{p_L^*} \tag{16.4}$$

$$\frac{s}{\varepsilon_D^*} = \frac{p(1-\alpha) - C_D - p_D^*}{p_D^*} \tag{16.5}$$

Here, s represents the market share of the nth bank. Equations (16.4) and (16.5) demonstrate "bank return on loan supply and deposit taking and it is a growing function of a bank's market share. It is interpreted to mean that: a reduction in the number of banks resulting from either a merger or acquisition, increases bank concentration" and thus bank profits. From Costa da Silva et al. (2007) and Amidu and Wolfe (2013), the main result from the model translates that, bank profit represents a growing function of the degree of concentration for the entire banking sector.

Dealership Model
We employ dealership model introduced by Ho and Saunders (1981) to explain bank price behaviour. The model sees the banks "as dynamic dealers, setting the price on loans and deposits to balance the asymmetric arrival of loan demand and deposit supplies. The non-synchronous arrival of loans and deposits generates costs for banks given that they have to hold either a long or short position on the money market". This consequently exposes banks to interest rate risks. Here, we use (Amidu & Wolfe, 2013; Estrada et al., 2006; Fiador & Amidu, 2021) intuition to explain the dealership model as follows: "suppose new deposits (loans) are contracted at long-term interest rates, p_D (p_L). If this deposit (loan) arrives earlier than a new loan (deposit), the bank will have to invest (borrow) the funds at the short-term money market interest rate, p. In performing the intermediation function, the bank faces a reinvestment (refinancing) risk at the end of the decision period should the short-term interest rate, p, fall (rise). The bank, therefore, transfers these costs associated with the uncertainty in the provision of deposits and loan operations to the economic agents. Thus, participation of each bank in the market occurs by setting a deposit and loan interest rate, p_D and (p_L) that depends on these costs":

$$p_D = p - a \tag{16.6}$$

$$p_L = p + b$$

Here, "p is the expected interest rate in the money market, a and b are the financial cost related to the provision of deposits and loans respectively. In the dealership model, the profit-maximising bank is expected to maximise its utility of terminal wealth and the set the price of loan and deposits as":

$$s = a + b = \frac{\alpha}{\beta} + \frac{1}{2} R\delta_i^2 Q \tag{16.7}$$

From Ho and Saunders (1981), s represents the price, a is the mark-up on deposits, b the mark-up on loans, α/β measures the relative market power, R is however banks' risk aversion, σ_i^2 is the variance of the interest rate on loans and deposits whiles Q represents banks' transaction size.

Behaviour Model

According to Hanweck and Ryu (2005), monopoly and dealership have two main limitations, thus the "models are single-horizon, static models in which bank assets and liabilities are considered homogenous and accordingly priced at prevailing loan and deposit rates and on the basis of the reference rate". According to Amidu and Wolfe (2013) and Fiador and Amidu (2021), in practice, "bank portfolios are characterised by heterogeneous assets and liabilities with different security, maturity and re-pricing structure that mostly go beyond a single horizon. The second limitation of these models is that the banking sector is treated as either being homogenous or as having heterogeneous traits that are based only on the asset size of banks. Conversely, banks with different products usually differ in terms of their business models, pricing power and more importantly the funding structure and exogenous shock". Possibly, the most-preferred behavioural model on bank pricing is the one developed by Hanweck and Ryu (2005), and further employed by Amidu and Wolfe (2013) and Fiador and Amidu (2021). Their bank behaviour model with regards to price assumes that "at each period, a bank can significantly but not completely select the amount of its investment in assets and liabilities of different re-pricing frequencies, given past choices that are immutable. In modelling bank responses to credit and interest rates risks and share-holders maximisation value, Hanweck and Ryu (2005) argue that 'not only do bank managers have to choose the optimal financial service product mix and geography diversification, they also need to set the loan price and fees, hedge credit quality and volatility changes, manage their liability structure and gauge the moods of the equity and debt markets to favourable or unfavourable news so as to increase or protect share-holder value.' Given these motivations and the ability of banks to change their portfolios and their positions as price takers, and assuming that banks operate to maximise shareholders value over a 12 month horizon, Hanweck and Ryu (2005) model the determinants of price as being the function of changes for different groups of banks in response to credit, interest-rates and term-structural shocks. Another important contribution using a behavioural model on pricing mechanism is that of Lepetit et al. (2008). They test for possible cross-selling behaviour of interest and non-interest products by examining the determinants of the risk premium charged by banks on their loans using the European banking system. Their results reveal that higher reliance on fee-based activities is associated with lower loan price and that borrower default risk is under-priced in the lending rates charged by banks with fee-income shares".

Empirical Literature

Empirical literature on the consequences of cross-border banking and the bank pricing behaviour effects of financial inclusion are reviewed under this chapter. The effects of cross-border banking on the financial sector have been hotly debated. Del Negro and Kay (2002) explains how foreign banks import management expertise and technology to enable them to deliver better banking services in their host countries. Goldberg et al. (2000) have argued that cross-border banks boost capital inflows, they come with superior management skills and are able to acquire and turn around troubled domestic banks. They also import regulatory discipline into the host country, which enables them to operate efficiently in the host country. Detragiache et al. (2008), and Clarke et al. (2005) point out that cross-border banks have comparative advantage in developing and emerging markets with regards to economies of scale, access to capital, risk diversification, managerial skills and lending technologies.

However, the criticisms against cross-border banking are manifold. There is the risk that cross-border banks can transmit shocks from their home country onto the host economy and can also apply domestic deposits to finance project outside the host country (Peek & Rosengreen, 2000). This can cause financial instability in the host country and may harm financial inclusion. Compared to domestic banks, cross-border banks are at a disadvantage when it comes to local knowledge and information and this may cause them to ignore small and opaque borrowers (Mian, 2006), thereby deepening financial exclusion in the host country. Another criticism against cross-border banks is that they may use their superior capital, skills and technology to crowd out domestic banks.

Cross-border banks tend to concentrate on large enterprises and the well-to-do in society, ignoring SMEs and deprived households with little or no access to formal finance (Gormley, 2010). The tendency for cross-border banks to cherry pick less risky borrowers/projects and leave domestic banks with high risk borrowers/projects can lead to financial instability in the host country (Goldberg et al., 2000). Another argument Goldberg et al. (2000) advanced against cross-border banking is that they may encourage capital flight and for that trigger financial instability in the host country.

Zeroing in on the empirics, there are mixed findings regarding the impact of cross-border banking on the financial system. Clarke et al. (2006) finds companies located in higher foreign-bank-dominated jurisdictions to report fewer financing obstacles based on a cross-section of over 3,000 companies from 35 transitioning economies. In a study of cross-border banking in Mexico, Schulz (2006) found that cross-border banks played a critical role in capitalising the banking system in the post crises period and helped to avert the insolvency of the banking system. Furthermore, cross-border banks were also found to have reduced non-performing loan portfolios in the banking system and helped in stabilising the banking sector. However, the author found that cross-border banks failed to transfer managerial expertise and technology to the domestic banking system. Based on a sample of 85 developing countries, Detragiache et al. (2008) revealed that cross-border banks mostly give loans to large firms and government due to their lack of local knowledge necessary for lending to SMEs. Employing a sample of cross-border banks in 137 countries within the period 1995–2009, Claessens and van Horen (2014) found cross-border banks to be more liquid and capitalised but have a smaller proportion of non-performing loans as compared to their domestic counterparts. The authors however found that, in developing countries, the lending portfolio of cross-border banks decreased by up to 6 percentage points relative to domestic banks in countries where cross-border banking is less dominant. The authors concluded that cross-border banks decreased financial deepening in economies where they were less dominant, contract enforcements were unaffordable, and there were limited information-sharing. Employing a sample of 89 low-income countries, Detragiache et al. (2008) found foreign banks with a larger share to experience reductions in the growth of financial sector debt. The work of Serrano (2016) also showed foreign banks not to stimulate credit growth in Mexico after controlling for size, country of origin and institutional quality.

The literature on the impact of cross-border banking on financial development and inclusion in Africa is negligible. This notwithstanding, the findings generally agree with the empirical trends in other emerging and developing economies. Cull and Trandafir (2010) found domestic banks in Uganda to have larger interest spreads which match the riskier portfolios they hold. However, domestic banks were found to have lesser overhead cost. Higher overhead costs and smaller profits of cross-border banks are reflective of the view that cross-border banks cherry pick top level borrowers whose projects are costly to implement and monitor. Employing firm level data across 29 African countries, Beck (2014) revealed that the impact of cross-border banking on Africa is dependent on the banks' region of origin. Thus, foreign banks' share in the banking sector is not a significant determinant of credit access. Also, the proportion of firms with a loan increases with the share of foreign banks originating from emerging and transitioning countries. Furthermore, shares of foreign banks from developed countries do not significantly impact loan growth. Lastly, for smaller firms, having higher share of foreign banks from developed country is negatively related to the probability of obtaining a loan.

Turning to the literature on bank behaviour and financial inclusion, the most notable study is Allen et al. (2016). The authors assessed the impact of account opening costs, its maintenance and usage costs on financial inclusion in a cross-country sample of 124,000 adults in 123 countries. The measures of bank pricing they used include the cost of bank account opening, bank account maintenance cost, as well as direct credit and debit cards costs, as gauged by central banks of the respective countries. All these are dummies variables represented by value 1 for countries whose central banks gauges costs to be between medium and high, but 0 if the central bank gauges the cost to be negligible to low. The results showed the probability of having a bank account to be lower in economies with high cost of account opening and maintenance. In particular, the possibility of having a bank account is 11 percentage points more in countries where cost is perceived to be negligible to low compared to countries where account opening costs are gauged to be medium to high. They further found documentation and distance to be reported most likely in the presence of barriers to financial inclusion in countries with many foreign banks. This means the financially excluded view cross-border banks as having stringent documentation requirements, and being less likely to open branches in deprived locations. Fixed fees and high account opening costs and operating accounts are particularly a huge barrier to financial inclusion in Eastern and Southern Africa. For instance, in Uganda, it costs an equivalent amount of 25% of per capita GDP per annum to maintain a chequing account, and 54% of the unbanked mentioned cost as a reason for not opening an account (Demirgüç-Kunt & Klapper, 2012a).

16.4 Evaluating Methodology

Data Sources

This study focuses on the African banking sector by employing both micro and macro data. The micro data are annual financial statements of 330 banks from 29 African countries from 2002–2013, obtained from the BankScope database, Fitch/IBCA/Bureau Van Dijk. Conducting a research on the banking sector presents an opportunity to make a difference beyond Africa due to the relation between finance and the real economy. The impact and benefits of research on emerging continents like Africa's economic growth would be limited if assessed solely on monetary terms, but rather by the number of people rising from poverty to a higher level of sufficiency (Bekaert & Harvey, 2003). This study looks at stable periods 2002–2006 and 2012–2013, as well as 2007–2011 where there were the global financial crises. The study sample consists of African banks for which there is annual data from 2002–2013. Medium and long-term credit banks, as well as state-owned institutions are included in the sample to ensure that banks (key stakeholders in the deposit and/or loan markets) are not left out. Observations which have outliers like zero or negative are removed from the analysis. Observations which are for capitalisation above the 98th percentile are also removed. Observations showing loan growth rates over the 98th percentile of distribution were also dropped. This is to account for mergers, acquisitions and new start-ups during the period. The macroeconomic data is however obtained from the World Bank's World Development Indicators database.

Measurement Variable

Financial inclusion is measured based on three indicator categories: *financial access* is proxied by the number of bank branches (*Branch*); *financial usage* which is measured by the proportion of total gross loan to total assets (*Loan*), and proportion of total deposit to total liabilities (*Deposits*); *financial quality* which is measured by total cost to gross revenue.

This study follows Brewer and Jackson (2006) by using lending rate (*Loan price*), cost of non-interest services (*Fees price*) and deposit rates (*Deposits price*) as the pricing mechanism of banks in Africa. Lending rate is measured as a percentage of total interest income over total earning assets. The fees price is the cost of non-interest income services such as fees, commission, trading, etc. and the deposit rate is calculated as total interest cost divided by total interest bearing liabilities.

Cross-border banking is measured as a dummy variable which takes value 1 when there is more than 50% foreign stake in local banks by foreign banks, but 0 otherwise. This measure is in line with Beck (2014) and Sissy et al. (2017). If a shareholder from outside the licencing country controls a bank, it is classified to be foreign-owned. For individuals or corporations having more than 50% stake in a bank, being it a subsidiary or a branch, they can exert control over it.

Variables affecting financial inclusion, cross-border banking, and pricing behaviour are also controlled. Such variables include bank and macroeconomic factors like Equity, Size, Market Share, Age, Diversification, Monetary Policy, GDP Growth and Inflation. *Bank Equity* is measured as a ratio of total shareholders' equity to total assets, whiles *Bank Size* is the proxied by the natural logarithm of total assets. *Market Share* on the other hand is measured as a ratio of total individual loans granted to the total loans granted on the market, whiles *Age* is proxied by the number of years the bank has been operating. *Diversification* measures a bank's strategy to delve into generating non-interest income. *Monetary Policy* stance is however proxied by country-specific short-term interest rates, since they affect banks' pricing behaviour and lending. *GDP growth* also controls for the overall state of the economy. When the banking system is subject to excessive inflation, it is less likely to be competitive and results in higher interest rates, this also makes the cost of financial services to be expensive and less informative. To this end, inflation is also proxied by the periodic growth in consumer price index (CPI).

Model and Estimation Strategy

This study adopts regression as a framework to test the relationships between the variables. This starts by first investigating the effects of cross-border banking on bank pricing behaviour in Africa using the model below;

$$\mathrm{BPB}_{it,c} = \alpha_1 \mathrm{BPB}_{it,c-1} + \alpha_2 \mathrm{CBB}_{it,c} + \sum_{j=3}^{k} \alpha_j X_{ij} + \varepsilon_{it} \tag{16.8}$$

where $\mathrm{BPB}_{it,c}$ is pricing behaviour of bank i from country c at time t, $\mathrm{BPB}_{it,c-1}$ however represents the pricing behaviour of bank i from country c at time t in the previous year. $\mathrm{CBB}_{it,c}$ is the cross-border bank i of country c at time t, $X_{i,j}$ also represents a set of $\{k\}$ variables which control for contestability, bank and country-specific variables. The α's represents parameter vectors whiles ε_{it} represents the unobserved time-invariant. The disturbance term ε_{it} also contains two components: thus, μ_i which is the unobserved time-invariant effect on banks, whiles v_{it} represents the disturbance term.

Secondly, and in order to address financial inclusion, cross-border banking and bank pricing behaviour, the study examines the effects of cross-border banking on financial inclusion in the presence of bank pricing behaviour. This study then follows Valverde and Fernandez (2007) to estimate the empirical model below:

$$\mathrm{FI}_{t,c} = \alpha_1 \mathrm{FI}_{t,c-1} + \alpha_2 \mathrm{BPB}_{it,c} + \sum_{j=3}^{k} \alpha_j X_{ij} + \varepsilon_{it} \tag{16.9}$$

$$\varepsilon_{it} = \mu_i + v_{it}$$

$$E[\mu_i] = E[v_{it}] = E[\mu_i v_{it}] = 0$$

After, we then estimate the interaction effect of cross-boarding banking (CBB) and bank pricing behaviour (BPB) on financial inclusion in Eq. (16.10):

$$\mathrm{FI}_{t,c} = \alpha_1 \mathrm{FI}_{t,c-1} + a_2 \mathrm{CBB}_{it,c} + \alpha_3 \mathrm{BPB}_{it,c} + \left(\mathrm{CBB}_{it,c} * \mathrm{BPB}_{it,c}\right) + \sum_{j=3}^{k} \alpha_j X_{ij} + \varepsilon_{it} \tag{16.10}$$

Here, $\mathrm{FI}_{t,c}$ represents inclusive finance in country c at time t, $\mathrm{FI}_{t,c-1}$ represents the same observation for the same county during the initial period. $\mathrm{CBB}_{it,c}$ is the cross-border bank i of country c at time t, $\mathrm{BPB}_{it,c}$ represents pricing behaviour of bank i for country c at time t, $(\mathrm{CBB}_{it,c} * \mathrm{BPB}_{it,c})$ represents an interaction between cross-border bank and the pricing behaviour of bank i in country c during time t. The variable $X_{i,j}$ represent a sets of $\{k\}$ variables which control for country and bank-specific factors, as well as contestability variables, α's which are parameter vectors and ε_{it}, an unobserved time-invariant factor. Here, the unobserved time-invariant ε_{it} contains two components: the μ_i, which has a bank-specific effect and v_{it}, the disturbance term.

A challenge which could come with Ordinary Least Squares (OLS) being adopted to estimate Eqs. (16.8) and (16.9) is the fact that $\mathrm{FI}_{t,c-1}$ has a correlation with fixed effects within the noise term giving rise to "dynamic panel bias". Moreover, when attempting to compensate for unobserved heterogeneity and simultaneity, literature suggests that OLS causes biases. To this end, the methodology suggested by Blundell and Bond (1998) and Alvarez and Arellano (2003) while estimating for both first difference and levels systems of equations are adopted for this study. System GMM estimator, according to Roodman (2009), combines standard equations in first difference with properly lagged-level instruments and additional sets of equations in levels, with adequately lagged first difference instruments. There are one-and-two-step variations of both linear difference and System GMM estimators. This study then adopts two-step System GMM, orthogonal deviation, small-sample adjustments and Windmeijer (2005) correct standard error. The two-step variant is asymptotically more efficient than the one-step since adopts residuals from one-step.

16.5 Empirical Results

Summary Descriptive Statistics

Table 16.2 shows summary statistics for the bank-level variables adopted for this study. The bank-specific variables are classified into bank pricing and other bank-level controls and are averaged per country from 2002 to 2013. Loan price, deposit price and fees price are variables evaluated in bank pricing. According to data from the bank pricing variables, Zimbabwean banks charge high costs on average of 0.36% for loans, 0.10% for

Table 16.2 Averages for the bank-level variables by country

Bank pricing variables				*Bank specific variables*				
	Loan price	*Fees price*	*Deposit price*	*Bank age*	*Divers*	*Bank size*	*Bank equity*	*Mkt. share*
Algeria	0.0402	0.0222	0.0195	22.5595	0.6003	4112.9000	0.1460	0.0845
Angola	0.0619	0.0453	0.0302	11.9167	0.5571	1274.5900	0.6322	0.1034
Benin	0.0563	0.0274	0.0250	12.3750	0.5580	290.9970	0.0931	0.2449
Botswana	0.0341	0.0243	0.0975	23.0833	0.6043	538.5720	0.1618	0.1500
Burkina-Faso	0.0676	0.0389	0.0245	28.0000	0.5250	256.0400	0.0810	0.2128
Cameroon	0.0562	0.0324	0.0237	21.9286	0.5618	515.8300	0.0524	0.1644
Cote d'Ivoire	0.0551	0.0425	0.0228	29.3472	0.5165	566.9930	0.0938	0.1818
Egypt	0.0658	0.0157	0.0551	34.3833	0.5857	3811.3900	0.1089	0.0380
Ethiopia	0.0468	0.0327	0.0226	25.6250	0.5203	538.8540	0.1116	0.1279
Ghana	0.1230	0.0427	0.0759	30.2222	0.5582	248.5590	0.1197	0.0680
Kenya	0.0916	0.0333	0.0438	35.0278	0.5784	337.4840	0.1579	0.0422
Malawi	0.1297	0.0736	0.0629	26.5500	0.5334	99.0982	0.1427	0.1348
Mali	0.0548	0.0339	0.0155	17.5139	0.5396	323.1120	0.1038	0.2069
Mauritania	0.0536	0.0415	0.0252	28.5000	0.5713	124.6070	0.2179	0.2034
Mauritius	0.0564	0.0384	0.0486	42.5076	0.6057	962.9550	0.1909	0.1101
Morocco	0.0507	0.0099	0.0242	62.8636	0.6952	8048.4100	0.0878	0.1043
Mozambique	0.1124	0.0444	0.0427	22.0104	0.5570	331.4960	0.1406	0.1412
Namibia	0.0916	0.0283	0.0850	58.0139	0.5854	899.6940	0.3371	0.1887
Nigeria	0.0966	0.0451	0.0583	33.8095	0.5332	2139.3500	0.1585	0.0582
Rwanda	0.0875	0.0382	0.0527	17.5556	0.5595	76.2154	0.1531	0.2222
Senegal	0.0609	0.0287	0.0220	32.2024	0.5842	426.7850	0.0921	0.3220
Sierra Leone	0.1089	0.0800	0.0343	28.3889	0.5306	36.4171	0.1809	0.2609
South Africa	0.1076	0.0525	0.1179	33.3750	0.6151	18,251.5000	0.1782	0.0839

Bank pricing variables				*Bank specific variables*				
	Loan price	*Fees price*	*Deposit price*	*Bank age*	*Divers*	*Bank size*	*Bank equity*	*Mkt. share*
Sudan	0.0461	0.0499	0.0580	19.1667	0.5782	1561.6900	0.1339	0.1774
Swaziland	0.0871	0.0441	0.0423	31.7000	0.5336	149.8360	0.1517	0.2292
Tanzania	0.0778	0.0323	0.0327	23.5602	0.5454	260.0900	0.1211	0.0742
Tunisia	0.0525	0.0153	0.0420	49.3873	0.5104	1367.0000	0.1388	0.0671
Uganda	0.1107	0.0260	0.0345	42.9545	0.6711	176.8250	0.1473	0.1167
Zimbabwe	0.3552	0.1025	0.2243	51.5000	0.6430	2227.2600	0.1591	0.2381

Table 16.2 shows the mean values of the bank-specific variables of sampled banks. Bank pricing variables represent the measures of the interest income of banks (**Loan Price**), non-interest income (**Fees Price**), as well as interest costs (**Deposit Price**). The bank-specific controls include; **Bank Age** represents the number of years since establishment, **Bank Equity** refers to the ratio of equity to total assets used as a proxy for capitalisation, **Diversification** also refers to revenue diversification, **Market Share** represents a ratio of the individual bank loans to total market loan, **Bank size** refers to the size of the bank. The mean values of sampled banks are in percentage terms with the exception of bank size and bank age which is in years

Source Bankscope and authors' own calculation

fees and 0.22% for deposits. This can possibly be ascribed to Zimbabwe's significant price volatility at the time. For Botswana, Morocco and Mali, however, there are low costs of 0.03%, 0.0098% and 0.015% respectively for their loans. With regards to the other bank-level control variables, Moroccan banks are older than banks from other sampled countries with an average age of 63 whiles Angola has the youngest at 12 years. With regards to bank equity, Angolan banks on average records the highest of about 0.63% with banks in Cameroon recording the least of about 0.05% in the sample. The data also show that banks in Morocco are more diversified in their revenue generation whiles Tunisian banks are less diversify in revenue generation among the countries. In relation to bank size, the data shows that South Africa has the largest banks in the sample with banks in Sierra Leone being the smallest. Finally, firms in Sierra Leone have a market share of 26% while Egyptian banks have the smallest market share of 0.04% among the countries.

Table 16.3 presents summary statistics for key country-level variables adopted in this study. The table shows the averages of the variables over the same time period. The variables have been classified into macroeconomic, cross-border banking and inclusive finance. Those under inclusive finance are; bank branches (financial access), loan and deposit accounts (financial usage) and cost/income and earning/total assets (financial quality). Starting with the country-specific variables; Angola scored 0.13% which is the highest growth rate with regards to the country-specific variables, while Zimbabwe recorded a growth rate of –0.68%, being the lowest, but had an average inflation of 2899.29% within the same period indicating price instability. Morocco on the other hand had the most stable prices since it had an average inflation of about 1.8% within the period. Figures under cross-border banks indicate that all banks (100%) in Benin, Senegal and Mozambique are cross-border banks, with Sudan having about 0.11% cross-border banks representing the lowest in the sample. Regarding the inclusive finance variables, Morocco had the most bank branches of 831, indicating higher financial access. Sierra Leone however had the least with an average of only 12 branches. Tunisia had many loan and deposit accounts with an average of 0.76%, indicating higher financial usage as opposed to Angola which had few at an average of only 0.31%. The highest deposit accounts were recorded by Cameroon of about 0.80% and a low of about 0.46% deposit accounts were recorded by Zimbabwe. Finally, with financial quality represented by cost to income ratio and earning assets to total assets ratio, Rwanda recorded the highest

Table 16.3 Average for macro-country-level variables

Macroeconomic variables			*Cross-Border banking*	*Inclusive finance variables*				
	GDP growth	*Inflation*	*CBB*	*Bank branches*	*Loan a/c*	*Deposit a/c*	*Cost/income*	*Earn/total assets*
Algeria	0.0393	3.9891	0.5714	92.0769	0.4407	0.5828	0.3194	0.7156
Angola	0.1338	40.6730	0.6364	108.5710	0.3107	0.6444	0.4039	0.7396
Benin	0.0400	3.1749	1.0000	29.6667	0.5527	0.6992	0.4908	0.8564
Botswana	0.0385	8.5243	0.7500	25.1429	0.5497	0.7203	0.2825	0.9188
Burkina Faso	0.0517	3.1994	0.8333	35.8000	0.6008	0.7902	0.4945	0.8529
Cameroon	0.0321	2.4357	0.7143	32.7143	0.5234	0.8016	0.4255	0.8784
Cote d'Ivoire	0.0107	2.8285	0.8333	43.5000	0.6118	0.7572	0.5512	0.8466
Egypt	0.0530	8.9908	0.4000	91.7414	0.4782	0.7335	0.2405	0.9070
Ethiopia	0.0833	14.5864	0.1250	255.4290	0.5116	0.7317	0.2688	0.7798
Ghana	0.0589	14.2981	0.5556	48.2778	0.4503	0.6547	0.4248	0.8262
Kenya	0.0400	10.5975	0.2963	43.5185	0.5633	0.7254	0.4324	0.8511
Malawi	0.0563	12.8177	0.6250	22.5000	0.4114	0.7091	0.5132	0.7864
Mali	0.0487	2.6638	0.6667	43.8000	0.5790	0.7235	0.5325	0.8169
Mauritania	0.0416	6.8254	0.3333	23.8333	0.5645	0.5723	0.4880	0.7464
Mauritius	0.0389	5.6533	0.5417	394.6000	0.5769	0.6695	0.3052	0.8248
Morocco	0.0480	1.8294	0.2727	830.7520	0.5526	0.6560	0.3414	0.8768
Mozambique	0.0754	8.4866	1.0000	48.0000	0.4854	0.7149	0.5332	0.7796
Namibia	0.0498	6.0119	0.5000	30.3333	0.7322	0.6515	0.3403	0.9134
Nigeria	0.0669	11.8565	0.2381	271.2220	0.3853	0.6462	0.4518	0.8085
Rwanda	0.0749	8.1379	0.6667	52.3333	0.5472	0.6811	0.5682	0.7961
Senegal	0.0397	2.1374	1.0000	35.7143	0.6182	0.7627	0.5149	0.8717
Sierra Leone	0.0924	12.8904	0.5000	12.0000	0.3144	0.7079	0.5481	0.7178

(continued)

Table 16.3 (continued)

	Macroeconomic variables		*Cross-Border banking*	*Inclusive finance variables*				
	GDP growth	*Inflation*	*CBB*	*Bank branches*	*Loan a/c*	*Deposit a/c*	*Cost/income*	*Earn/total assets*
South Africa	0.0369	5.9261	0.3594	459.9000	0.6516	0.5721	0.3348	0.8355
Sudan	0.0661	12.7925	0.1111	28.0000	0.3519	0.5139	0.5008	0.5786
Swaziland	0.0245	7.2459	0.6000	269.0000	0.6915	0.6741	0.4781	0.8680
Tanzania	0.0707	8.1893	0.7368	31.5000	0.4703	0.7446	0.4902	0.8403
Tunisia	0.0462	3.8153	0.5294	94.8235	0.7609	0.6493	0.3634	0.9124
Uganda	0.0794	8.3702	0.8244	29.2727	0.4468	0.6363	0.4529	0.8564
Zimbabwe	–0.0685	2899.2890	0.6000	27.8000	0.4012	0.4553	0.3885	0.6785

Table 16.3 shows the mean value of country-specific variables including the macroeconomic indicators, cross-border banking variables as well as financial inclusion variables. **Cross-border banking** is proxied by a dummy variable which takes the value 1 if the bank crosses border and 0 otherwise. The **Inclusive finance** variables measure financial access (Bank branches)), financial usage (Loan and Deposits) and **financial quality** (Cost/income and Earning assets/Total assets). **Macroeconomic** variables are; GDP growth measured by the annual growth rate of Gross Domestic Product of a country, and **Inflation** is measured by the annual consumer price inflation

Source Bankscope and authors' own calculation

mean ratio of about 0.57 cost/income and Egypt takes the lowest mean ratio of about 0.24 cost/income. A highest average ratio of about 0.92 earning assets/total assets, whiles a lowest of about 0.58 was recorded by Sudan over the period under consideration. This indicates that countries have varied strengths in relation to inclusive finance indicators and therefore justifies the use of various specifications in the analysis as robustness checks.

Table 16.4 shows the pair-wise correlation coefficient of the study variable to serve as preliminary analysis of the relationships existing between the variables. The pair-wise correlation coefficient between the financial inclusion variables and bank pricing variables are mixed. Bank branches have a negative but significant relationship with loan and deposit prices, but positively and significantly related to fees price. Loan account is negative and significant with fees price but significantly positive with deposit accounts. Deposit accounts are significant and negatively related to all the bank pricing variables. Cost to income ratio is significant with fees and deposit prices with negative and positive signs respectively. The reverse of cost/income is true for earning to total assets ratio. Regarding the correlation between cross-border banks and bank pricing behaviour, we notice that cross-border banks' coefficient is positive and significantly correlated with fees price but negative with deposit price with no significant relationship with loan price, indicating that cross-border banks have higher fees price and lower deposit price. The pair-wise correlation coefficient between the cross-border banks and the different inclusive finance indicators follows. The results show that cross-border bank has a negative and significant correlation with bank branches and loan account but positive with a deposit account and cost/income. This means that cross-border banks have less branches and loan accounts but have more deposit accounts with a high cost to income ratio. However, its relationship with earning assets to total assets was insignificant.

Effect of Cross-Border Banking on Bank Pricing Behaviour

The effect of cross-border banking on the pricing behaviour of African banks is analysed under this section. Table 16.5 shows the regressions results of the bank-specific variables, country-specific monetary policies, the developmental levels and macroeconomic stability. Dynamic panel estimator, two-step system GMM, Windmeijer-correct standard error,

Table 16.4 Pair-wise correlation coefficient between selected variables

	Loan price	*Fees price*	*Deposit price*	*M'try policy*	*Cros Bor. Bk*	*Bank branch*	*Loan A/c*	*Deposit A/c*	*Cost/income*
Loan price	1								
F. price	0.16*	1							
D. price	0.60*	0.11*	1						
M. policy	0.43*	0.46*	0.12*	1					
C.B.B	−0.03	0.05*	−0.17*	0.25*	1				
B. Branch	−0.12*	0.19*	−0.06*	−0.36*	−0.10*	1			
Loan a/c	0.01	−0.17*	0.11*	−0.16*	−0.08*	0.02	1		
Deposit a/c	−0.21*	−0.17*	−0.41*	0.01	0.17*	0.03	−0.09*	1	
Cost/income	−0.03	0.28*	−0.21*	0.27*	0.14*	0.03	−0.08*	0.10*	1
Earn/total ass	0.01	−0.32*	0.09*	−0.14*	−0.03	−0.04*	0.32*	0.06*	−0.29*
Bank age	0.03	−0.12*	−0.02	−0.21*	−0.15*	0.17*	0.17*	0.11*	−0.11*
Mkt. share	0.02	0.04*	−0.04*	0.19*	0.09*	0.11*	0.14*	0.05*	0.05*
Bank equity	0.03	0.23*	0.11*	0.15*	−0.08*	0.14*	−0.11*	−0.34*	0.03
Diversify	0.15*	−0.03	0.16*	−0.16*	−0.09*	0.10*	0.01	−0.20*	−0.12*
Bank size	−0.04*	−0.08*	0.02	−0.43*	−0.12*	0.39*	0.04	0.02	−0.17*
Inflation	0.19*	0.08*	0.16*	0.37*	0.01	−0.01	−0.06*	−0.11*	−0.03
GDP growth	−0.23*	−0.04	−0.20*	0.22*	0.00	−0.01	−0.19*	0.05	0.08*

	Cost/income	*Earn ass/Total ass*	*Bank age*	*Mkt. share*	*Bank equity*	*Diversification*	*Bank size*	*Inflation*	*GDP growth*
Loan Price									
F. price									
D. price									
M. policy									

	Cost/income	*Earn ass/Total ass*	*Bank age*	*Mkt. share*	*Bank equity*	*Diversification*	*Bank size*	*Inflation*	*GDP growth*
C.B.B									
B. Branch									
Loan a/c									
Deposit a/c									
Cost/income	1								
Earn/total ass	−0.29*	1							
Bank age	−0 11*	0.16*	1						
Mkt. share	0.05*	0.02	0.17*	1					
Bank equity	0.03	−0.13*	−0.13*	−0.11*	1				
Diversify	−0.12*	0.03	0.08*	−0.06*	0.15*	1			
Bank size	−0.17*	0.11*	0.15*	0.15*	−0.10*	0.01	1		
Inflation	−0.03	−0.06*	0.03	0.06*	0.03	0.06*	0.02	1	
GDP growth	0.08*	−0.05*	−0.10*	−0.08*	0.30*	−0.08*	−0.03	−0.07*	1

Pair-wise correlation coefficient was estimated using a sample of 330 African banks in 29 countries. * suggests a significant of 5% or more. Bank pricing variables are the measures of bank interest income (Loan Price), non-interest income (Fees Price), as well as interest cost (Deposit Price). Cross-border banking is proxied by a dummy variable that takes a value of 1 if the cross-border and 0 otherwise. The Inclusive Finance variables are the measures of financial access (bank branches), financial usage (number of loan and deposit accounts), as well as financial quality (Cost/income and Earning assets/Total assets). The bank-specific controls include; Bank Age represents the number of years since establishment, Market represents a ratio of the individual bank loans to total market loan, Bank Equity refers to the ratio of equity to total assets used as a proxy for capitalisation, Diversification also refers to revenue diversification, Bank Size refers to the size of the bank. Three macroeconomic controls included are Monetary Policy is the central bank's annual policy rate; GDP growth is the annual growth rate of Gross Domestic Product and Inflation is the annual consumer price inflation

Source Bankscope and authors' own calculation

Table 16.5 Cross-border banking and bank pricing behaviour

Variables	*Loan price (1)*	*Fees price (2)*	*Deposit price (3)*
Loan price–1	0.631***		
	(0.060)		
Fees price–1		0.458***	
		(0.065)	
Deposit price–1			0.824***
			(0.095)
Cross-Border Banking	0.004	−0.005*	0.016**
	(0.005)	(0.003)	(0.007)
Bank age	0.001	0.001	−0.002
	(0.002)	(0.001)	(0.002)
Mkt. share	−0.059***	0.036***	−0.018
	(0.019)	(0.013)	(0.018)
Bank equity	−0.006	0.041	0.004
	(0.027)	(0.025)	(0.034)
Diversification	0.036**	−0.035**	0.002
	(0.016)	(0.015)	(0.015)
Bank size	0.003	−0.001	0.005*
	(0.002)	(0.001)	(0.003)
Monetary policy	0.002***	0.000	0.001**
	(0.000)	(0.000)	(0.000)
Inflation	−0.0000	−0.0000	−0.0000
	(0.0000)	(0.0000)	(0.0000)
GDP growth	0.098***	0.045	−0.004
	(0.036)	(0.028)	(0.045)
Observations	513	515	515
No. of instruments	80	80	80
AB2	0.617	1.416	−1.029
Hansen's Test	70.169	71.933	73.254
F-test	95.315***	41.266***	24.960***

Table 16.5 presents the two-step system GMM regression output, Windmeijer-corrected standard errors, small-sample adjustments and orthogonal deviations. The regressions were conducted adopting a dynamic panel data estimation. The dependent variables are measures of banks' interest income (**Loan Price**), non-interest income (**Fees Price**), and interest cost (**Deposit Price**). **Cross-border banking** is measured by a dummy variable which takes a value of 1 if the bank crosses the border and 0 otherwise. The bank-specific controls in the regression include **Bank Age** represents the number of years since establishment, **Market Share** represents a ratio of the individual bank loans to total market loan, **Bank Equity** refers to the ratio of equity to total assets used as a proxy for capitalisation, **Diversification** also refers to revenue diversification, **Bank size** refers to the size of the bank. Three macroeconomic controls included are **Monetary Policy** is the central bank's annual policy rate; **GDP growth** represents the annual growth rate of Gross Domestic Product; while **Inflation** refers to the annual consumer price inflation. Standard errors in parentheses; ***, ** and * suggests a statistical significance at 1%, 5% and 10% respectively. The following diagnostic tests are reported. (1) The instrument count, (2) number of observations, (3) The Hansen test for identifying restrictions with the null hypothesis of exogenous instruments, (4) the Arellano-Bond test for first and second-order serial correlations within the residuals with the null hypothesis of no second-order serial correlation

small-sample corrections, as well as orthogonal deviations are used to estimate all the regressions. The results suggest that majority of the variables adopted has a significant effect on bank pricing behaviour. Also, all the lagged dependent variables of bank pricing between the independent variables are positive and statistically significant, demonstrating the relevance of taking prior values of the dependent variable into account.

The results show that cross-border bank variable exerts negative and significant effect on fees price at 10% level of significance in column 2, but exerts positive and significant effect on deposit price at 5% significance level. It was however not significant with loan price. This indicates that cross-border banks offer less fees price and high deposit price than their non-cross-border counterparts. To be specific, all things being equal, the results in column 2 show that cross-border banks charge fees price by 0.005 less than non-cross-border banks, while the results in column 3 show that cross-border banks charge deposit price by 0.016 more than non-border-banks. This result suggests that when banks cross-border, they tend to compete with the domestic banks for customers by reducing their fees price and increasing deposit price. These findings are also consistent with the argument that cross-border banks may engage in cherry picking of customers, which may expose domestic banks to the riskier customers leading to high non-performing loans in domestic banks (Goldberg et al., 2000). Again, the results follow the finding of Cull and Trandafir (2010) that local banks have larger interest spreads as compared to foreign banks. In summary, the results from this study support the hypothesis that cross-border banking influences the pricing behaviour of African banks.

Another significant factor that affects loan price and fees pricing is the market share. The results in columns 1 and 2 suggest that banks with larger market share charge low loan prices, but tend to charge high fees price. This may be the reason for controlling a larger share of the market. Diversification is also positive and significant with loan price in column 1 but negative and significant with fees price in column 2, indicating that banks that diversify in terms of their revenue generation tend to charge higher loan price but lower fees price. For bank size, only column 3 was positive and significant at 10% level, indicating that larger banks pay high price on their deposits. This may suggest that larger banks are in a better position to offer favourable pricing on customers' deposits. This study did not find a significant relationship with respect to the other bank-level variables including bank age and equity across all regressions. The results of monetary policy suggest in columns 1 and 3 that contractionary monetary policy leads to high loan and deposit rates. This finding is intuitive to the extent that, as central banks increase the policy rate, banks respond by increasing the rates on loans and deposits. The macroeconomic stability variable (inflation) was not significant across all regressions. From the results also, the economic growth variable (GDP) is positive and statistically significant only in column 1, suggesting that higher growth positively influences loan price.

Effect of Bank Pricing Behaviour on Financial Inclusion

This study also analyses how bank pricing behaviour influences inclusive finance in Africa. Table 16.6 shows the regression output for the dependent variable which is inclusive finance. The various columns refer to the various inclusive finance measures. Financial access is proxied by the number of branches, financial usage by loan and deposit accounts and financial quality by cost/income and earning/total assets ratios. Taking into account the prior values of the dependent variable is of importance and is indicated by the positive and significant lagged financial inclusion variables in Table 16.6. To begin with, loan price is positive and significantly influences loan accounts at 1% as showed in column 2, with the rest of its coefficients being insignificant. This translates that increases in loan price results in financial usage increasing. With respect to fees price, the results show that it is 1% significant in columns 2, 4 and 5 with a positive effect in columns 2 and 5 on loan accounts and earning/total assets respectively, but exerts negative influence on cost/income in column 4. This indicates that higher fees price reduces financial usage and financial quality (using the measure, earnings assets as a ratio of total asset), at the same time increases financial quality by way of increasing cost to income ratio. Deposit price is also found to exert a significantly negative effect on deposit accounts in column 4, but positive and significant in column 5, both at 10% significance level. This suggests that increased deposit rates reduce financial usage while improving financial quality. Our findings signal the fact that the pricing behaviour of banks influences financial inclusion in Africa. These findings are consistent with the position of Dev (2006) that bank pricing behaviour has a substantial impact on inclusive finance.

Some control variables from this study also significantly influence inclusive finance. Bank Age is positive and significant only in column 4, which

Table 16.6 Bank pricing behaviour and financial inclusion

	Financial access	*Financial usage*		*Financial quality*	
Variables	*Bank branches (1)*	*Loan a/c (2)*	*Deposit a/c (3)*	*Cost/income (4)*	*Earn ass/ Tot. ass (5)*
Bank branches–1	0.999***				
	(0.000)				
Loan a/c–1		0.578***			
		(0.066)			
Deposit a/c–1			0.734***		
			(0.065)		
Cost/income–1				0.651***	
				(0.085)	
Earn/assets–1					0.661***
					(0.077)
Loan price	−0.044	1.952***	−0.343	−0.575	−0.098
	(0.129)	(0.524)	(0.453)	(0.451)	(0.270)
Fees price	0.007	−1.955***	0.510	1.641***	−1.169***
	(0.123)	(0.618)	(0.495)	(0.568)	(0.370)
Deposit price	0.048	0.063	−0.582*	−0.654	0.392*
	(0.176)	(0.491)	(0.340)	(0.406)	(0.236)
Bank age	0.001	−0.016	0.005	0.013*	0.001
	(0.005)	(0.011)	(0.007)	(0.007)	(0.003)
Mkt. share	0.018	0.566***	−0.048	0.063	0.051
	(0.060)	(0.146)	(0.090)	(0.122)	(0.080)
Bank equity	−0.004	−0.033	−0.558***	0.100	0.089
	(0.027)	(0.127)	(0.141)	(0.126)	(0.098)

(continued)

Table 16.6 (continued)

Variables	*Financial access*	*Financial usage*		*Financial quality*	
	Bank branches (1)	*Loan a/c* (2)	*Deposit a/c* (3)	*Cost/income* (4)	*Earn ass/ Tot. ass* (5)
Diversification	−0.000	−0.174**	−0.181*	0.096	−0.063
	(0.013)	(0.080)	(0.099)	(0.087)	(0.059)
Bank size	−0.001	0.012	0.000	−0.035***	−0.004
	(0.004)	(0.011)	(0.008)	(0.011)	(0.005)
Monetary policy	−0.000	−0.003	−0.000	−0.007***	0.001
	(0.001)	(0.003)	(0.003)	(0.002)	(0.001)
Inflation	−0.000	0.003***	0.003**	0.003*	−0.002*
	(0.001)	(0.001)	(0.001)	(0.002)	(0.001)
GDP growth	0.004	−0.799***	−0.147	0.083	−0.001
	(0.030)	(0.271)	(0.289)	(0.233)	(0.162)
Observations	511	512	460	498	513
No. of instruments	80.000	80.000	109.000	80.000	80.000
AB2	−0.396	−1.136	−0.260	0.206	1.502
Hansen's Test	3.036	68.549	82.392	72.640	69.373
F-test	5.032e + 09***	14.014***	75.051***	22.088***	29.199***

Table 16.6 presents the two-step system GMM regression output, Windmeijer-corrected standard errors, small-sample adjustments and orthogonal deviations. The regressions were conducted adopting a dynamic panel data estimation. The dependent variables are measures of financial access (**Bank branches**), financial usage (**Loan and Deposits accounts**), and financial quality (**Cost/income and Earning assets/Total assets**). Bank pricing variables represent the measures of the interest income of banks (**Loan Price**), non-interest income (**Fees Price**), as well as interest costs (**Deposit Price**). The bank-specific controls include; **Bank Age** represents the number of years since establishment, **Bank Equity** refers to the ratio of equity to total assets used as a proxy for capitalisation, **Diversification** also refers to revenue diversification, **Market Share** represents a ratio of the individual bank loans to total market loan, **Bank size** refers to the size of the bank. Three macroeconomic controls included are **Monetary Policy** is the central bank's annual policy rate; **GDP growth** represents the annual growth rate of Gross Domestic Product; while **Inflation** refers to the annual consumer price inflation. Standard errors in parentheses; ***, ** and * suggests a statistical significance at 1%, 5% and 10% respectively. The following diagnostic tests are reported. (1) The instrument count, (2) number of observations, (3) The Hansen test for identifying restrictions with the null hypothesis of exogenous instruments, (4) the Arellano-Bond test for first and second-order serial correlations within the residuals with the null hypothesis of no second-order serial correlation

means that financial inclusion (financial quality) inclusion increase with increase in banks age. This means that over time, experienced banks having been in the market for a long time are in a better position to promote inclusive finance, the quality of services improve. Market share positively and significantly affects financial usage only for column 2. This suggests that when banks wield larger market share financial usage increases. The negatively significant relationship between bank equity and financial inclusion (financial usage) only in columns 3, suggests that an increase in banks' equity to total assets tends to decrease financial usage. Diversification is negative and significant in columns 2 and 3 under loan and deposit accounts respectively. This indicates that diversification of revenue has both negative on financial usage. Bank size in column 4 suggests that larger banks tend to decrease financial quality. Regarding monetary policy, the results in column 4 suggest that contractionary monetary policy jeopardises financial quality. Inflation positively influences financial usage and financial quality in columns 2, 3 and 4, at the same time negatively influences financial quality in column 5. GDP growth is also negative but statistically significant in column 2, suggesting that increasing growth usually decreases financial usage.

The Sensitivity of Financial Inclusion to Cross-Border Banking and Bank Pricing Behaviour

In this section, we present the sensitivity of inclusive finance to cross-border banking and bank pricing behaviour. We have established that cross-border banking affects bank pricing behaviour, and that bank pricing behaviour affects African inclusive finance. This study presents evidence on how cross-border banking affects inclusive finance basing on the pricing behaviour of banks as a transmission mechanism. The results are presented in Table 16.7. The lagged dependent variables are also positive and significant indicating the relevance of accounting for the dependent variables' prior values. The results on cross-border banks in all regression results suggest that everything being equal, cross-border banking does not influence financial inclusion. More importantly, the coefficients of the interaction terms are not significant across all regressions in Table 16.7. This suggests that inclusive finance is not sensitive to cross-border banking in the context of African bank pricing behaviour.

Table 16.7 The Interaction effect of Cross-border banking and Bank pricing behaviour on financial inclusion

	Financial access	*Financial usage*		*Financial quality*	
Variables	*Bank branches* (1)	*Loan a/c* (2)	*Deposit a/c* (3)	*Cost/income* (4)	*Earn ass/ Tot. ass* (5)
Bank branches–1	0.999***				
	(0.000)				
Loan a/c–1		0.584***			
		(0.075)			
Deposit a/c–1			0.726***		
			(0.073)		
Cost/income–1				0.644***	
				(0.104)	
Earn/assets–1					0.659***
					(0.084)
Cross-Border Bank	−0.021	0.076	0.005	−0.105	0.035
	(0.089)	(0.085)	(0.075)	(0.109)	(0.053)
Loan price	0.065	2.865***	−0.141	−0.361	0.418
	(0.292)	(0.854)	(0.951)	(0.913)	(0.458)
CBB* Loan price	−0.060	−1.359	−0.173	−0.243	−0.756
	(0.488)	(1.339)	(1.019)	(1.117)	(0.592)
Fees price	−0.057	−2.283***	0.439	0.767	−1.241*
	(0.494)	(0.731)	(0.560)	(0.757)	(0.704)
CBB* Fees price	0.107	1.226	0.420	2.349	−0.715

	Financial access	*Financial usage*		*Financial quality*	
Variables	*Bank branches* (1)	*Loan a/c* (2)	*Deposit a/c* (3)	*Cost/income* (4)	*Earn ass/ Tot. ass* (5)
	(0.717)	(2.041)	(1.398)	(1.786)	(1.331)
Deposit price	−0.447	−0.007	−0.721	−0.686	0.082
	(0.931)	(0.848)	(0.684)	(0.576)	(0.225)
CBB* Deposit price	0.518	0.094	0.116	0.158	0.360
	(1.277)	(1.049)	(0.869)	(1.267)	(0.628)
Bank age	0.003	−0.006	0.003	0.015	0.008
	(0.014)	(0.017)	(0.007)	(0.010)	(0.006)
Mkt. share	−0.017	0.430**	−0.090	0.005	0.069
	(0.067)	(0.216)	(0.118)	(0.131)	(0.090)
Bank equity	−0.007	−0.050	−0.593***	0.083	0.104
	(0.059)	(0.149)	(0.150)	(0.116)	(0.114)
Diversification	0.008	−0.127	−0.179*	0.156	−0.085
	(0.040)	(0.086)	(0.101)	(0.112)	(0.059)
Bank size	−0.000	0.019	0.004	−0.040***	−0.007
	(0.008)	(0.013)	(0.009)	(0.014)	(0.007)

(continued)

Table 16.7 (continued)

Variables	*Financial access*	*Financial usage*		*Financial quality*	
	Bank branches (1)	*Loan a/c* (2)	*Deposit a/c* (3)	*Cost/income* (4)	*Earn ass/ Tot. ass* (5)
Monetary policy	0.000	−0.002	0.000	−0.007**	0.001
	(0.001)	(0.003)	(0.003)	(0.003)	(0.001)
Inflation	−0.000	0.002*	0.003*	0.003*	−0.002**
	(0.001)	(0.001)	(0.002)	(0.002)	(0.001)
GDP growth	0.031	−0.889***	−0.135	0.149	−0.041
	(0.091)	(0.307)	(0.335)	(0.216)	(0.136)
Observations	511	512	460	498	513
No. of instruments	80	80	109	80	80
AB2	−0.457	−1.048	−0.227	0.304	1.641
Hansen's Test	3.556	68.438	82.508	66.390	67.199
F-test	2.411e + 08***	11.959***	48.472***	13.710***	13.694***

Table 16.7 presents the two-step system GMM regression output, Windmeijer-corrected standard errors, small-sample adjustments and orthogonal deviations. The regressions were conducted adopting a dynamic panel data estimation. The dependent variables are measures of financial access (**Bank branches**), financial usage (**Loan and Deposits accounts**), and financial quality (**Cost/income and Earning assets/Total assets**). Bank pricing variables represents the measures of the interest income of banks (**Loan Price**), non-interest income (**Fees Price**), as well as interest costs (**Deposit Price**). The bank-specific controls include; **Bank Age** represents the number of years since establishment, **Bank Equity** refers to the ratio of equity to total assets used as a proxy for capitalisation, **Diversification** also refers to revenue diversification, **Market Share** represents a ratio of the individual bank loans to total market loan, **Bank size** refers to the size of the bank. Three macroeconomic controls included are **Monetary Policy** is the central bank's annual policy rate; **GDP growth** represents the annual growth rate of Gross Domestic Product; while **Inflation** refers to the annual consumer price inflation. Standard errors in parentheses; ***, ** and * suggests a statistical significance at 1%, 5% and 10% respectively. The following diagnostic tests are reported. (1) The instrument count, (2) number of observations, (3) The Hansen test for identifying restrictions with the null hypothesis of exogenous instruments, (4) the Arellano-Bond test for first and second-order serial correlations within the residuals with the null hypothesis of no second-order serial correlation

Conclusion and Policy Implications

This study makes contributions to literature by bringing out empirical evidence on how cross-border banking in the light of African bank pricing behaviour influences inclusive finance. Particularly, adopting a panel dataset which consists of 330 African banks across 29 countries and employing a System GMM estimator, this study first examines how cross-border banking affects bank pricing behaviour. The paper also examines the effect of bank pricing behaviour on financial inclusion. Finally, the study analyses how sensitive inclusive finance is to African cross-border banking and pricing behaviour of banks. The findings of the study revealed that cross-border banking affects African bank pricing behaviour. For instance, the study findings indicate that cross-border banking offers lower fees price and higher deposit prices as compared to non-cross-border banks. This finding is in line with arguments that cross-border banks may engage in cherry picking of customers, which may influence their pricing behaviour. The results of the study also show that bank pricing behaviour significantly explains inclusive finance. This study finds increases in the price of loan to result in financial usage rising, and that higher bank fees price reduces financial usage and financial quality, at the same time increases financial quality by way of increasing cost to income ratio. Also, higher deposit prices lead to financial usage reducing but financial quality falling. Finally, the study finding indicates that inclusive finance is not sensitive to cross-border banking and bank pricing behaviour in Africa. In that, the interaction effect of cross-border banking and pricing behaviour of banks in Africa does not directly explain financial inclusion. We observe that cross-border banking rather influences the pricing behaviour of banks, and bank pricing also plays a significant role in facilitating inclusive finance. Policy initiatives targeted at promoting financial inclusion need to take into consideration the pricing mechanisms of banks. Encouraging cross-border banking may therefore impact the pricing behaviour of banks. Monetary policy interventions are also very important in signalling the direction of bank pricing in Africa.

References

Allen, F., Demirguc-Kunt, A., Klapper, L., & Martinez Peria, M. S. (2016). The foundations of financial inclusion: Understanding ownership and use of formal accounts. *Journal of Financial Intermediation, 27*, 1–30.

Alvarez, J., & Arellano, M. (2003). The time series and cross-section asymptotics of dynamic panel data estimators. *Econometrica, 71*, 1121–1159.

Amidu, M. (2015). Do Sub-Saharan African banks with market power gain from monetary policy? *African Journal Finance, 17*(2), 1–24.

Amidu, M., & Wolfe, S. (2013). Does bank competition and diversification lead to greater stability? Evidence from emerging markets. *Review of Development Finance, 3*(3), 152–166.

Angkinand, A., & Wihlborg, C. (2010). Deposit insurance coverage, ownership, and banks' risk-taking in emerging markets. *Journal of International Money and Finance, 29*(2), 252–274.

Arun, T., & Kamath, R. (2015). Financial inclusion: Policies and practices. *IIMB Management Review, 27*(4), 267–287.

Beck, T. (2014). Cross-border banking and financial deepening: The African experience. *Journal of African Economies*, 24(suppl_1), i32–i45.

Bekaert, G., & Harvey, C. R. (2003). Research in emerging market finance: Looking into the future. *Emerging Market Review, 3*, 429–448.

Blundell, R., & Bond, S. (1998). Initial conditions and moment restrictions in dynamic panel data models. *Journal of Econometrics, 87*(1), 115–143.

Brewer, E., & Jackson, W. E. (2006). A note on the "risk- adjusted" price–concentration relationship in banking. *Journal of Banking & Finance, 30*(3), 1041–1054.

Carbo Valverde, S., & Rodriguez Fernandez, F. (2007). The determinants of bank margins in European banking. *Journal of Banking and Finance, 31*, 2043–2063.

Chauvet, L., & Jacolin, L. (2017). Financial inclusion, bank concentration, and firm performance. *World Development, 97*, 1–13. https://doi.org/10.1016/j.worlddev.2017.03.018

Claessens, S. (2006). Competitive implications of cross-border banking. In G. Caprio, D. D. Evanoff, & G. G. Kaufman (Eds.), *Cross border banking: Regulatory challenges* (pp. 151–182). World Scientific Publishing.

Claessens, S., & Horen, N. (2014). Foreign banks: Trends and impact. *Journal of Money, Credit and Banking, 46*(s1), 295–326.

Clarke, G., Cull, R., & Martinez Peria, M. S. (2006). Foreign bank participation and access to credit across firms in developing countries. *Journal of Comparative Economics, 34*, 774–795.

Clarke, G., Cull, R., & Martinez Peria, M. S., Sanchez, S. (2005). Bank lending to small businesses in Latin America: Does bank origin matter? *Journal of Money, Credit, and Banking, 37*, 83–118.

Costa da Silva, G. J., Oreiro, J .L., Paula, L. F., & Sobreira, R. (2007). *Determinants of Banking Spread in Brazil: An Empirical Evaluation*. Proceedings of the 35th Brazilian Economics Meeting, Brazilian Association of Graduate Programme in Economics.

Cull, R., & Trandafir, M. (2010). *Credit Market Segmentation in Uganda*. World Bank Mimeo.

Dages, B. G., Goldberg, L. S., & Kinney, D. (2000). Foreign and domestic bank participation in emerging markets: lessons from Mexico and Argentina. *Economic Policy Review* (Sep), 17–36.

Del Negro, M., & Kay, S. (2002). Global banks, local crises: Bad news from Argentina. *Econometric Reviews, 87*, 89–106.

Demirgüç-Kunt, A., & Klapper, L. F. (2012a). *Financial inclusion in Africa: An overview*. World Bank.

Demirgüç-Kunt, A., & Klapper, L. F. (2012b). *Measuring financial inclusion: The global findex database*. World Bank.

Demirguc-Kunt, A., Klapper, L., Singer, D., & Van Oudheusden, P. (2015). *The Global Findex database 2014: Measuring financial inclusion around the world* (Policy Research Working Papers, No. 7255). The World Bank.

Detragiache, E., Tressel, T., & Gupta, P. (2008). Foreign banks in poor countries: Theory and evidence. *The Journal of Finance, 63*, 2123–2160.

Dev, S. M. (2006). Financial inclusion: Issues and challenges. *Economic and Political Weekly, 41*(41), 4310–4313.

Estrada, D., Gomez, E., & Orozco, I. (2006). *Determinants of interest margins in Colombia* (p. 393). Banco Dela Republica.

Fiador, V. O. L., & Amidu, M. (2021). Inclusive finance, bank pricing behaviour, and livelihood activities of households in Ghana. *SN Business & Economic, 1*(1), 1–29.

Freixas, X., & Rochet, J. (1997). *Macroeconomics of Banking*. MIT Press.

Goldberg, L., Dages, B. G., & Kinney, D. (2000). Foreign and domestic bank participation in emerging markets: Lessons from Mexico and Argentina. *Economic Policy Review, 6*, 17–36.

Gormley, T. (2010). The impact of foreign bank entry in emerging markets: Evidence from India. *Journal of Financial Intermediation, 19*, 26–51.

Hanweck, G., & Ryu, l. (2005). *The sensitivity of bank net interest margins and profitability to credit, interest-rate and ter-structure shocks across bank Product specializations* (Working Paper 2005-02). Federal Deposit Insurance Corporation.

Ho, T. S., & Sauders, A. (1981). The determinants of bank interest margins: Theory and empirical evidence. *Journal of Financial and Quantitative Analysis, 16*(4), 581–600.

IMF. (2015). *Evolving banking trends in Sub-Saharan Africa*. IMF.

International Monetary Fund. (2006). *Promoting private sector credit in the East African community: Issues, challenges and reform strategies*. IMF.

Iqbal, B. A., & Sami, S. (2017). Role of banks in financial inclusion in India. *Contaduríay Administración, 62*(2), 644–656.

Klein, M. A. (1971). A theory of banking firm. *Journal of Money, Credit and Banking, 3*, 205–218.

Lee, C. W., & Zhong, J. (2015). Financing and risk management of renewable energy projects with a hybrid bond. *Renewable Energy, 75*, 779–787. https://doi.org/10.1016/j.renene.2014.10.052

Lepetit, L., Nys, E., Rous, P., & Tarazi, A. (2008). The expansion of services in European banking: Implications for loan pricing and interest margins. *Journal of Banking and Finance, 32*, 2325–2335.

Mian, A. (2006). Distance constraints: The limits of foreign lending in poor economies. *Journal of Finance, 61*, 1465–1505.

Mohammed, J. I., Mensah, L., & Gyeke-Dako, A. (2017). Financial inclusion and poverty reduction in Sub-Saharan Africa. *African Finance Journal, 19*(1), 1–22.

Oreiro, J. L., & de Paula, L. F. (2010). Macroeconomic determinants of bank spread in Latin America: A recent analysis with special focus on Brazil. *International Review of Applied Economics, 24*(5), 573–590.

Patwardhan, A. (2018). *Chapter 4—Financial Inclusion in the Digital Age Handbook of Blockchain, Digital Finance, and Inclusion* (Vol. 1, pp. 57–89). Academic Press.

Peek, J., & Rosengreen, E. S. (2000, September/October). Implication of the globalization of the banking sector: The Latin American experience. *New England Economic Review*, 45–62.

Roodman, D. (2009). How to do xtabond2: An introduction to difference and system GMM in Stata. *The Stata Journal, 9*(1), 86–136.

Schulz, H. (2006). *Foreign banks in Mexico: New conquistadors or agents of change?* University of Pennsylvania Working Paper.

Serrano, A. (2016). Foreign banks and credit in Mexico. *Global Finance Journal*, 30. https://doi.org/10.1016/j.gfj.2016.01.002

Sissy, A. M., Amidu, M., & Abor, J. Y. (2017). The effects of revenue diversification and cross border banking on risk and return of banks in Africa. *Research in International Business and Finance, 40*, 1–18.

Windmeijer, F. (2005). A finite Sample correction for the variance of linear efficient two step GMM estimators. *Journal of Econometrics, 126*(1), 25–51.

World Bank. (2014). *World development Indicators* (database). Accessed online from www.esds.ac.uk on the 31st of January 2014.

CHAPTER 17

Current Issues in Global Banking and Implications for African Banks

Vera Fiador, Kannyiri Thadious Banyen, Mohammed Amidu, and Victor Murinde

17.1 Introduction

The role of banks in providing the sap of productivity in an economy makes their continued existence and fine fettle a crucial variable in the

V. Fiador · M. Amidu
University of Ghana Business School, Accra, Ghana
e-mail: vfiador@ug.edu.gh

M. Amidu
e-mail: MAmidu@ug.edu.gh

K. T. Banyen (✉)
School of Business, S.D. Dombo University of Business and Integrated Development Studies, Wa, Ghana
e-mail: tbkannyiri@ubids.edu.gh

V. Murinde
School of Oriental and African Studies, London, UK
e-mail: vm10@soas.ac.uk

J. Y. Abor and C. K. D. Adjasi (eds.), *The Economics of Banking and Finance in Africa*, Palgrave Macmillan Studies in Banking and Financial Institutions, https://doi.org/10.1007/978-3-031-04162-4_17

quest for economic development across the globe. The 2008 global financial crisis (GFC), however, served to reveal major shortcomings in the global banking market. The nature and effects of the crisis ignited active debates on issues of market discipline, regulation, corporate governance, and bank stability among practitioners, academics, and policymakers. According to Claessens (2017), these conversations led to a paradigm shift in the global banking space. In Africa and other developing regions with fledgling, bank-dominated economies, however, the power shifts, regulatory, and operational changes occurring in the global banking market since the financial crisis seem to have very far-reaching implications for future banking (Banyen & Biekpe, 2020a), and especially in the wake of the Covid-19 pandemic which also triggered the re-engineering of several operational strategies by banks to adapt to the threats presented by the pandemic and other global trends. Given the changing dynamics within the global financial markets, there is the need for a holistic understanding of the trends in global banking, the opportunities and challenges they present, and how banks in domestic and international markets can pursue performance improvement without exposing the world to a repeat of the 2008 crisis.

The global banking industry consists of a mosaic of agreements, regulations, institutions, networks, and formal and informal players that facilitate the international flow of capital for investment and consumption purposes.[1] The complexity of the global banking system makes it challenging to regulate and control. This is because global banking transcends national regulatory boundaries and given disparities in regulatory and economic regimes among countries, ensuring equitable progress is challenging. The situation is compounded even more by the growing trend of banking digitization and the entry of financial technology (fintech) firms into quasi banking operations. Given the banking regulatory and governance lapses revealed by the 2008 global financial crisis, national and

[1] For the purpose of this chapter global bank/banking is a bank/banking system with presence in all the continent, and/or a bank with a commercial presence outside its home country, by way of at least one branch or subsidiary. Global banks are considered to be foreign owned if they are controlled by a shareholder or group of shareholders from outside the licensing jurisdiction. Control over a bank can be exercised if an individual or entity holds more than 50% of shares in a bank, subsidiary or branch. In case where there is no majority shareholder, the bank is still classified a foreign bank when a foreign minority shareholder has a controlling stake in the bank (Beck et al., 2014). In short a bank with commercial presence outside its home country.

international regulatory bodies must re-evaluate the trends in banking to curtail some of the negative effects of crises (Anginer et al., 2019). For instance, the 2008 financial crisis put a halt to the growth rate of banks in most developed countries, especially in the west, with the then top 1000 banks recording a decline in growth rates from around 24.2% to about 6.8% in 2007/2008, and further down to about 2.7% between 2008 and 2010. Banks in these countries also recorded significant losses, with profits before tax for the top 1000 banks at the time declining by $667 billion between 2007 and 2008 (Capgemini Analysis, 2011). However, these losses were not evenly distributed globally. While bank profit before tax rates in Europe and North America reduced by 143.2% and 174.9%, respectively, between 2007 and 2008, emerging market banks maintained high growth rates, with Asia-Pacific and Latin America recording profits before tax growth rates of 31.4% and 40.1%, respectively (Capgemini Analysis, 2011). These disparities, coupled with the so-called opportunities for growth in underdeveloped banking markets in these emerging economies, have culminated in a rise in the assets and market power of several banks in emerging economies.

In general, the rising importance of banks operating in emerging markets and their growth trajectory is not new in the literature given that similar growth rates were experienced by banks in the West after World War II. What is clear, based on the lessons learnt from the post-World War II banking dynamics, is the need to adequately regulate and monitor these changes taking place within the growing and increasingly complex global banking market to prevent yet another financial crisis (IMF, 2018). Available literature asserts that poor corporate governance and operational lapses were significant variables for the onset of the financial crisis (Blundel-Wignal et al., 2008; Thomsen, 2013) while the spread and magnitude of the crisis were largely blamed on regulatory and supervisory shortfalls, especially for international banking activities (Lane, 2012). The post-crisis period has therefore been characterized by a significant rise in domestic and international banking regulation including increases in bank risk-weighted capital requirements, disclosure laws, and others that seek to reduce bank fragility and improve stakeholder protection and market confidence (Basel III; IMF, 2018). Banks' operational environments have also been sanitized over the years to ensure an easier and efficient flow of capital in domestic and international markets. According to Norman et al. (2018) and Yang, et al. (2019), such improvements in banking regulation promote healthy competitive conduct among banks and reduce their fragility. Lee et al. (2020) add that adequate regulation of the banking sector improves their allocative efficiency and promotes economic growth. Some studies, on the other hand, have found evidence of less desirable effects of excessive banking regulation on bank lending behavior, costs, capital allocation, and economic growth (Kopecky & VanHoose, 2006; Pasiouras et al., 2009). Also, excessive regulation increases bank operational costs, reduces their liquidity, and adversely affects their allocative role and economic growth. These contentions highlight the need for a continuous evaluation of the current issues in global banking to inform policy initiatives that seek to improve global banking performance without exposing the global banking market to another crisis.

As the global banking system continues to go through significant reforms, the effects of these changes on the successes and failures of the global banking industry should equally be continuously evaluated. This chapter, therefore, seeks to consolidate these analyses by reviewing the recent issues and trends in global banking, and how Africa can position its banking system to increase its significance by striking a fair balance between exploiting the opportunities and overcoming the challenges in global banking for greater output growth and economic development. This chapter provides a comprehensive analysis of recent trends in global banking post the 2008 crisis, the challenges and opportunities presented by power shifts, technological advances, regulatory, operational and governance changes, and the implications of these paradigm shifts for Africa's budding banking sector. Given this, the chapter reviews the evolving issues in global banking and analyzes the trends that are determining global banking success in recent times. Secondly, the chapter also examines the challenges and opportunities available in global banking and reviews the future of global banking and the implications for banking in Africa.

The rest of the chapter is outlined as follows: Sect. 17.2 provides an overview of the current issues in global banking, covering power shifts after the crisis, regulatory, operational and corporate governance changes, and the role of technology in global banking. Section 17.3 reviews the challenges and opportunities in global banking, analyzing among other factors, the effects of banking digitization, financial integration, and Covid-19, among others. Section 17.4 reviews issues bordering on the future of global banking and the implications for Africa's banking sector growth and international participation. Section 17.5 concludes the chapter.

17.2 Recent Developments in Global Banking

This section reviews the recent developments in global banking, analyzing pre and post-crisis trends that affect how global banking is done in recent times. The first part is a review of the power shifts that have occurred in global banking since the global financial crisis, then their operating strategy. Over the past decade, there has been a significant shift of banking market power from west to east and in some instances, north to south as emerging markets banking accelerated in periods when Western and more advanced countries took great hits due to the 2008 global financial crisis. Bank capitalization and size have increased significantly in many emerging economies over the past decade, increasing their competitiveness in the global banking market, with the Chinese banking sector leading the pack. According to the Banker Database (2020), the four largest banks by total assets in the world are Industrial and Commercial Bank of China (ICBC), China Construction Bank, Agricultural Bank of China, and the Bank of China, which are all Chinese banks (see Appendix A). The 5th largest bank is a Japanese Bank Mitsubishi UFC Financial Group, also from an Asian country. The Citigroup, which used to be the world's largest bank comes in on 13th while HSBC Holdings Plc. (London, UK), JP Morgan Chase (USA), and Bank of America Corp. (USA) come in 6th, 7th, and 8th places, respectively.

Additionally, two other banks each from China and Japan have made it to the top 25 banks in the world by total assets while banks from Russia (PAO Sberbank of Russia at 60th position), Shinhan Financial Group Co. Ltd (South Korea at 61st and KB Financial Group Inc. at 64th positions), Singapore (DBS Group Holdings Ltd. at 66th), Brazil (Itaú Unibanco Holding SA at 71st), and others are all working their way up the top 100 banks by total assets. The shift in bank market power from the West toward Asia and the Middle East has major implications for the global banking business. Though the shift does not imply an absolute decline in Western banking, most banks from the West are losing their leadership, market share, and control of policy directions in a growing global banking market.

Another notable trend in banking today is the role of the state in the banking business (Frigerio & Vandone, 2018). Looking at the ownership structure of the top 25 banks, it is noteworthy that the banks from emerging economies making their way to the top are largely state-owned.

For instance, the biggest banks that emerged from China are predominantly owned or funded by the state, either directly or through analogous state agencies. For example, about 65.85% of ICBC shares are owned by the Chinese Government.[2] Similarly, China Construction Bank, Agricultural Bank of China, and Bank of China are all largely state-owned. However, Mitsubishi UFC Financial Group Inc. which is the largest bank in Japan and 5th largest in the world, rose to the top 5 as a result of the merger between the Bank of Tokyo-Mitsubishi Ltd and UFJ Bank Ltd in 2006. Though HSBC Holdings Plc (London, UK), JP Morgan Chase (USA), and Bank of America Corp. (USA), the 6th, 7th, and 8th largest banks, respectively, are privately owned banks, these banks are from Western economies with matured banking markets. Also, a number of state-controlled banks from other emerging economies are making their way into the top 100 banks of the world such as State Bank of India. In fact, over three-quarters of the banking industry in India is state-controlled. This suggests that, in emerging markets, state ownership of banking institutions could be a catalyst for banking sector growth (Gerschenkron, 1962). This development view is supported by several studies, such as Delis et al. (2011), Gardener et al. (2011), Hossain et al. (2013), Dong et al. (2014), Wang et al. (2014) as well as Tan and Anchor (2017), who all find significant positive nexuses between state ownership and bank efficiency, asset quality, and asset growth in emerging markets. In contrast, the political view espoused by Kornai (1979) suggests that government participation in banking slows down banking sector development and increases inefficiency in the banking sector. This view is supported by Shaban and James (2018) who found a negative relationship between state ownership and bank efficiency in the Indonesian banking industry. Despite the potentially negative implications, most emerging countries like China have invested heavily in their state-owned banks in their bid to become key players in the global banking space and notwithstanding the significant strides and benefits accrued from the spate of financial liberalization policies in most emerging economies from the mid-to-late 1980s.

In the midst of these changes, competition among banks and the scramble for market share and supremacy has forced banks to revise their

[2] With Central Huijin Investment Company Limited, a Chinese government establishment, owning 34.71% and the Ministry of Finance owning 31.14% of total shares.

operational strategies and focus on more relevant, growth-oriented activities. For instance, banks are beginning to revise their business models to focus on satisfying customers' need for convenience through remote and electronic banking solutions. In a progressively digital world, bank customers are increasingly demanding next-generation digital solutions to their banking needs. According to Gupta (2013) and Ahmad et al. (2020), the rapid rise in mobile phone usage and the increasing availability of internet services across the globe has created a new drive toward the adoption of e-platforms for banking transactions, especially among the youth and most corporate banking clients. Figure 17.1 shows evidence of rising mobile subscriptions in Africa. This rising need for greater convenience in banking through the internet and mobile applications is therefore a major trend in banking today (Abor et al., 2018). Currently, success in banking heavily depends on how efficiently banks meet their customers' demand for autonomy, convenience, and usability of e-banking platforms without compromising customer and bank security. Safe and secure banking digitalization has the potential of increasing bank efficiency, attracting new customers, and enhancing customer loyalty, thus, increasing bank market shares and profitability in an increasingly competitive global banking market (Gomber et al., 2017). According to the extant literature, factors that enhance customer banking

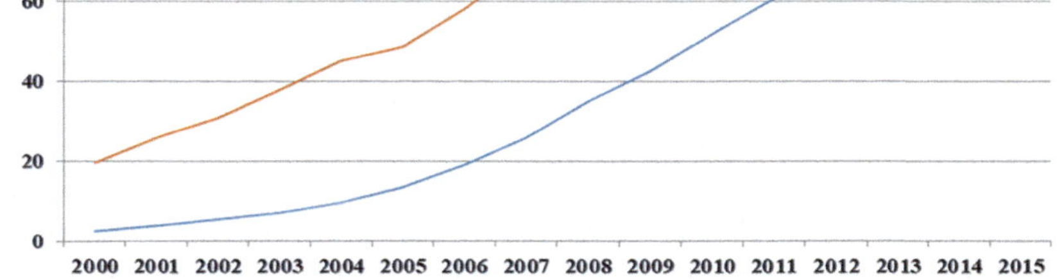

Fig. 17.1 Mobile phone subscriptions per 100 inhabitants (*Source* Ahmad et al. [2020])

experience in terms of convenience, speed, and security increases customer loyalty, increases firm attractiveness, and promotes firm growth (Gupta, 2013; Ling et al., 2016).

Banks are therefore motivated to replace core traditional banking platforms with rich internet applications that enhance the speed and ease of customer service delivery through the internet and mobile applications. This is expected to help banks increase their competitiveness and overall market share by offering customers greater flexibility and convenience. Indeed, banks see remote banking as a cheaper, flexible, and scalable option, compared to the brick-and-mortar banking business models used in the past. It is envisaged that, overtime, remote banking will be the key mode of banking desired by customers and banks which provide superior products will be more attractive to customers.

Another major development in the global banking market today is the rising role of business intelligence and analytics in monitoring customers' behavior. Success in global banking is increasingly influenced by a bank's ability to adequately understand customer behavior and predict their needs. In view of this, banks are increasingly using the transaction history of customers to effectively provide customized products, rewards, and other banking solutions to their clients. According to Ling et al. (2016), success in modern banking is greatly influenced by a bank's ability to meet customer needs and preferences. Therefore, banks seeking to increase their market share are expected to continually offer customized, intelligence-based products that meet the changing needs and preferences of their clientele. For instance, chatbots allow banks to make personalized loan offers to their loan applicants using web-based applications and artificial intelligence. This ensures that customers are provided with specific loan products that fit their profile without wasting their time with offers that are not a good match. The use of business intelligence, analytics, and other performance management systems has therefore seen a significant rise in banking and this trend is expected to rise overtime. Just like Facebook, Google, and other platforms that use historical data to predict and suggest new products to customers, a bank's ability to not only provide the best products to their ever-evolving customers but offer them new product suggestions that meet their tastes and preferences is increasingly becoming critical for banking success and growth. Whether a bank seeks global leadership or not, meta-application services and the use of artificial intelligence is a trend that has come to stay in the global banking market (OECD, 2020).

Also, customers are increasingly demanding consistent product and service offerings across geographic areas in an increasingly globalized financial system to enhance global trade and finance. In view of this, banks involved in international banking are forced to reengineer their operational processes to reduce their payment engines and platforms in different geographic markets to a convenient level to stay competitive. This has led to the establishment of payment hubs in the global banking marketplace. Most banks are adopting strategies to harmonize their international payment systems to meet customer demands for consistent payment and other transaction modalities across countries and economic regions. Besides, establishing payment hubs increases a bank's operational efficiency and helps reduce duplication and infrastructural bottlenecks. Therefore, banks seeking to outcompete other global banks continually examine the scope of products and services against the volume of business expected from their target markets and market segments so as to decide the scope of their payment hubs for improvement. This affords banks greater flexibility in terms of choosing payment systems and payment hubs across their various operational locations at minimum cost and complexity.

In addition to the foregoing developments in global banking is the rise in cooperation among countries through bilateral, multilateral, and other financial integration efforts. The expansion in global banking after the global financial crisis of 2008 has largely been attributed to improvements in emerging market banking systems, greater market coverage, financial inclusion, and financial integration, among others. Emerging market banks have been able to exploit the growth opportunities in these markets because of the significant strides made to integrate their payments systems and expand market opportunities for banks and other financial institutions. According to Banyen and Biekpe (2020a), both *de jure* and de facto financial integration in Africa and other emerging economies have increased significantly over the last decade (Lane & Milesi-Ferretti, 2012). This allowed some banks from these markets to expand their operations across national borders, increase their capital base, and assume global leadership. Banking sector globalization is therefore viewed as a potent catalyst for global banking and general economic growth (Nzioka, 2017).

In spite of the acclaimed benefits of global banks, several studies also argue that its effects are not always desirable. For instance, Laeven and Tressel (2013) show that foreign bank presence and international capital flows could lead to a rise in foreign liabilities, especially in a period of crisis. Also, banking sector globalization and associated competitive conduct of foreign banks could hamper domestic banking sectors of destination countries and reduce economic growth (Cucinelli, 2015). Indeed, foreign banks could crowd out local banks which may not have enough capital to operate a significantly diversified portfolio at competitive prices like their foreign counterparts. Besides, competitive pressure could force banks to engage in risky business practices which could increase their fragility and reduce profitability (Obstfeld, 2015). Proponents of this view, therefore, suggest that countries seeking to improve the global competitiveness of their domestic banks should find an optimal resolution to the so-called financial trilemma.[3]

17.3 Challenges and Opportunities in Global Banking

Global banking has gone through tremendous transformations after the 2008 global financial crisis, and these evolutions are expected to continue to cause major disruptions in the global banking market overtime. Banks are continuously focused on customer satisfaction and general stakeholder protection. In line with this, many advanced regulations such as Basel III, new liquidity requirements, and macro-prudential policies, among others have been introduced to safeguard market participants and ensure stability in banking markets. There is also the issue of Fintech, which both presents a competitive challenge for banks and opportunities for new partnerships in an evolving banking system. These challenges and opportunities are being managed by many banks to help meet customer demands in an increasingly global and highly regulated global banking market. The next few sections discuss these opportunities and challenges and how banks in Africa can respond to them to improve the banking industry for global leadership.

First of all, focusing bank success on customer needs satisfaction provides both great opportunities and significant challenges for banks in the global banking sector. The growing need to satisfy technologically savvy customers in an increasingly digitalized world is a key determinant of success in today's global banking. Globally, banks are motivated

[3] According to Obstfeld (2015) and Claessens (2017), achieving any two of the three objectives of fostering cross-border financial integration, preserving national resolution authority and maintaining financial stability is easy, but achieving all three together has proved to be herculean task for most countries.

to adopt digital banking platforms for their individual and corporate clients in response to their increasing demand for greater convenience and speed using application programming interfaces (APIs). This allows bank customers to personally manage some key transactions from their computers, tablets or mobile phones. By pulling customers away from conventional brick-and-mortar banking toward a more digital realm, bank digitalization has disrupted the global banking business forever. According to Ling et al. (2016), banks must adopt agile digital solutions to banking problems by building partnerships with big-tech firms in order to provide desirable, innovative, and customer-centered products and services if they intend to stay profitable in this digital age.

However, compliance with this new demand can be quite expensive. Consequently, as banks expand the scope and scale of their operations to meet the changing tastes and preferences of customers, they need to continually invest in technology, process re-engineering, and new market explorations that all come at very high costs. Aside from the high cost of technology investments, banks are sometimes forced to give away control of some key processes to big-tech companies to manage and there is also the additional cost of ensuring cyber security for the banks and their customers. The benefits of digitization notwithstanding, banking digitalization could result in job cuts and a general rise in global unemployment rates as firms replace human beings with robotics to stay afloat in a more competitive financial services industry. However, digitalization provides banks with new opportunities and though product and process innovations come at a very high cost, the benefits could be enormous. First, bank technology investments could lead to higher productivity and efficiency (García-Olalla & Vázquez-Ordás, 2020). Banks can now serve more clients at higher speeds, through their agile automated systems and artificial intelligence software, increasing bank productivity overtime (Bons et al., 2012). Technology also reduces operational costs for most banks if properly implemented. Bank technology investments lead to lower per-unit operational cost and higher profitability. Overall, digital banking has been viewed as a panacea to the financial inclusion dilemma in emerging markets (Ozili, 2018).

Another major challenge banks are facing today is competition from Fintech firms and the disruptions they present to banks. Given the stricter regulatory requirements for opening and operating a bank in most industrialized countries, Fintech firms have risen to fill the gaps between what banks offer and the real needs of society for virtual banking services.

These firms have become a major source of competition for banking institutions, taking customers seeking convenience without the regulatory bottlenecks from traditional banks. However, Fintech could offer many opportunities for banks, especially those operating in highly regulated and concentrated banking markets. For example, banks could build partnerships with Fintech companies to offer "banking as a service" (BaaS) and other open banking platforms to their various customers. These platforms allow banks to circumvent many regulatory bottlenecks by allowing Fintech firms to connect with the bank's systems through APIs and offer customers banking solutions that current regulations would not allow either of them to provide. However, Ozili (2018) suggests that Fintech platforms face information asymmetry and adverse selection problems as they often attract clients who might be riskier than bank clients. Building partnerships with banks to leverage bank customer data for client selection could therefore help them obviate this challenge.

In view of the ongoing evolutions in the global banking sector, banking regulation is also becoming more challenging. As global banking business paradigms shift toward automation of business processes and client services in partnerships with big-tech firms, the boundaries of banking become blurred and bank regulation even more intricate. This increased regulatory governance uncertainty, coupled with the fear of weak corporate governance mechanisms may hinder global banking growth. Customers' fear of vulnerabilities, privacy rights breaches, and opportunistic behavior from banks could reduce participation and negate the benefits banks stand to derive from their technology investments. Therefore, inadequate regulation of Fintech and digital banking practices poses a grave danger to the global banking sector. Furthermore, opportunistic banks could explore the grey areas in the current regulatory framework to increase their market share and profits to the detriment of customers and global financial stability (Malady, 2016). For instance, banks in the United States and Europe incurred great losses during the global financial crisis due to excessive risky behavior in their bid to stay competitive and profitable. Several banks invested in novel products through securitization and other strategies, culminating in high losses.

Governments and bank customers are therefore calling for tighter regulation to abate complacency on the part of banks in their pursuit of growth and profitability. Finance ministers of the group of 20 developed and emerging economies have also advocated for stronger capital and liquidity standards and better supervision to promote transparent and responsible banking. However, banks could be adversely affected by new regulations as they compete with Fintech companies and other banks in the digitalization of banking services. Banks will incur additional regulatory compliance costs while pursuing their income and growth goals. However, it is not very certain whether the introduction of new regulations and supervision will equally affect all parts of the world. Policymakers, regulators, and bank managers in Asia and other emerging markets are very much looking up to the West for a clear sense of direction on regulating digital banking amid the rising sophistication in global banking. The main challenge is that while banking globalization has allowed banks to do business internationally, the regulation and supervisory frameworks that govern their activities largely remain national. To ensure global financial stability, countries will need to harmonize their regulatory frameworks to ensure some baseline compliance. Also, national governments could play a stronger role in banking through a blend of greater supervision of the free market and so-called "state capitalism."

Global deregulation is also a major source of opportunity for banks. Most countries have introduced financial sector reforms that have opened up their markets for foreign bank entry in efforts to increase international capital flows and stimulate economic growth (Beck et al., 2013; Claessens & van Horen, 2014; Leon, 2016). There have also been significant efforts to harmonize the financial systems of various economic blocs through bilateral and multilateral agreements. These efforts have increased the growth opportunities of banks. Banks can now open up international branches, set up subsidiaries, acquire or merge with other banks, or set up agencies in foreign countries. These growth opportunities for banks have increased tremendously and so has the need to comply with many global regulations. This could, however, be managed if banks can identify the commonalities in these many regulations and make policy decisions that work for each firm.

There is also the recent challenge of Covid-19, which has adversely affected banks in several ways. Banks played a significant role in stabilizing the economy and transmitting government stimulus and relief packages in most countries. The pandemic has largely accelerated the rate at which banks adopt digital banking services, further compounding the competitive disadvantages of banks still operating traditional banking activities. Covid-19 has also adversely affected branch operations,[4] employee responsibilities, and the general cost of doing business in banking. Bank losses are expected to rise over the next two or so years, especially for small business loans, commercial real estate, and credit cards. For instance, the Deloitte Center for Financial Services estimates such losses at $318 billion in the United States alone, for the period 2020–2022 (Shilling et al., 2020). Additionally, banks' return on equities (ROE) were adversely affected, but this is expected to recover in 2021. However, due to revised capital requirements after the 2008 global financial crisis, banks remained resilient despite the negative impact of Covid-19 on the banking sector globally. Another key effect of the Covid-19 pandemic is a reduction in the global movement of people and goods, which adversely affects international transfers and other banking businesses. Key businesses were also affected as people migrated from urban centers to live and work in more rural areas and firms adopt virtual work options, shift systems, and other workplace redesigns. These issues all reduced the asset bases of banks as business slowed and loan losses accelerated in the wake of the pandemic.

17.4 The Future of Global Banking and Implications for African Banks

The changes occurring in the global banking industry have set a new paradigm that will affect international banking and finance for some time into the foreseeable future. These new trends also have significant implications for Banking in Africa. Before the 2008 global financial crisis, there were moves to adopt some universal supervisory framework to enhance banking globalization and ensure prudence and stability in the market. However, this slowed down significantly after the crisis, partly because banking integration was blamed for the speed and scope of the crisis transmission. However, with a rise in digital banking and the growing confidence in global banking, there is bound to be even greater moves to build consensus on banking supervision. For banks to increase their global presence and boost international transactions, there is a need for national

[4] Banks now focus more on being socially responsible, taking part in the larger effort to ensuring society's safety by boosting surveillance architecture, enhancing safety measures at branches, and increasing their rural services.

regulators to work with one another by way of international agreements, built on home-host principles that are guided by the Basel III accord for effective and responsible global banking (Cihak & Demirgüç-Kunt, 2013; Goyal et al., 2013; IMF, 2015).

According to Claessens (2017), such agreements would ensure that international banks are effectively supervised in the home and host countries, with consensus on how their operations are guided to ensure overall financial stability. This is even more critical with the digitalization of banking as this extends the boundaries of the banking business and contains a lot of grey spots that are not covered by current regulations. This integration has implications as banking sector development in Africa is low, with only 38% of male and 27% of female adults having a bank account in a formal financial institution as of 2017 (Demirgüç-Kunt et al., 2018). Also, the adoption of e-banking platforms is slow and coverage is still small. These factors reduce the speed of Africa's financial integration (Banyen & Biekpe, 2020b; Beck & Cull, 2014) as stakeholders attempt to build local markets and build sub-regional collaborations first before further efforts (Frey & Volz, 2011). This decelerates the process of banking sector globalization in Africa. Besides, many banks on the continent are undercapitalized, compared to banks in other regions and they are generally slow at adopting competitive banking strategies such as digital banking, and revenue diversification strategies, among others (Sissy et al., 2017). These factors are inimical to the growth of banking in Africa. Regulators in African countries, therefore, need to take steps to increase the capital base of local banks to enable them to take advantage of big international banking deals and expand their operations to other foreign markets. Higher risk-weighted capital will also cushion Africa's banking sector against domestic and international shocks. There is also the need to encourage banks to adopt more digital banking platforms to stay competitive. Besides, the Covid-19 pandemic has made banking digitalization a necessity for success in the industry.

The growing importance of emerging and developing markets' banks in global banking also requires the restructuring of regulatory frameworks to meet international standards and ensure compliance. Emerging market banks are increasingly gaining dominance in global banking and their influence on global banking policy will rise overtime. These countries and banks are becoming more active participants in international deliberations on banking reforms and policy. However, the small, weak, and fragmented banking markets in Africa place the continent at a disadvantage. Africa has many rising economies that need finance for development. As incomes in Africa and other emerging markets are rising, there is the expectation of an increase in demand for both consumer and corporate credit. However, with very little influence in global banking, reforms may not always be fair or favorable to the continent, especially the banking sector. Also, going forward, banks in Africa must learn from the current happenings in the global banking market and take steps to position the banking sector on the continent for growth through mergers, acquisitions and recapitalization drives as the continent has a great potential for growth in all sectors. Steps must also be taken to re-evaluate the risk profiles and governance principles of these banks, as the failure of some banks in Africa was due to excessive risk-taking and poor corporate governance practices.

Over time, the dominant role of the dollar in international bank transactions is set to diminish as more countries form monetary unions and adopt common currencies but for a while, the dollar and the United States will continue to play a significant role in global banking, although financial integration, especially banking globalization, will usher in a new era where other nations, their currencies, capital markets and banking firms will increasingly play significant roles. These will present banks in all countries with fresh opportunities and challenges. Banks from new entrants into banking prominence will have to adopt novel strategies to keep their growth trajectory while old and former market leaders will have to find ways to increase their dominance in the global banking space. Specifically, Western banks will need to restructure their operations to regain their former glory and positions in the scheme of banking while banks from emerging markets will need to keep finding innovative ways of attracting and keeping more clients and funding. Also, Western banks operating in saturated banking markets will have to find new markets and deal with toxic assets in their home countries. For instance, in South Africa, FirstRand has entered into a "strategic cooperation" with China Construction Bank focused on growth opportunities in the African continent. And HSBC is looking to acquire a majority stake in Nedbank, South Africa's fourth-largest banking group.

17.5 Conclusion and the Way Forward

Several significant issues emerge from the recent trends and issues in global banking, especially for emerging market economies like Africa. First, the extant literature suggests that banks have realized the need for international cooperation among each other in their efforts to gain global dominance. As Xiao Gang, Chairman of the Bank of China, says: "It is not about who should learn from whom." Instead, it is about learning from each other, strengthening cooperation, and seeking development together.

The literature also points to the increasing trend toward digitalization and remote banking in the years to come. For Africa, which has a significant oral population (70% literacy rate compared to the world average of 90%), this move toward digitalization presents additional complexities on how to enroll the not-so literate populace and foster financial inclusion which is crucial in the quest for reducing poverty and income inequality.

Overall, the evidence from the available literature on the changing dynamics within the global banking space holds relevant implications for policymakers in Africa. In the future, banking in Africa must be predicated on strong corporate governance together with a swift response to customer needs with regard to banking services that are underpinned by appropriate design thinking methodologies and agility. Also, host economies must adequately interrogate the implications of global financial integration with regard to knowledge and technology spillovers, competition and market structure, and regulatory adequacy, among others if they are to fully benefit from the current trends in the global banking industry.

Appendix A: Top 100 Banks by Total Assets

Current rank^	Previous rank^^	Current vs. previous	Company (ticker-exchange)	Headquarters	Accounting principle	Total assets (US$B)
1	1	NC	Industrial & Commercial Bank of China Ltd. (1398-HKG)	China	IFRS	4,324.27
2	2	NC	China Construction Bank Corp. (939-HKG)	China	IFRS	3,653.11
3	3	NC	Agricultural Bank of China Ltd. (1288-HKG)	China	IFRS	3,572.98
4	4	NC	Bank of China Ltd. (3988-HKG)	China	IFRS	3,270.15
5	5	NC	Mitsubishi UFJ Financial Group Inc. (8306-TKS)	Japan	Japanese GAAP	2,892.97
6	7	▲	HSBC Holdings PLC (HSBA-LON)	U.K.	IFRS	2,715.15
7	6	▼	JPMorgan Chase & Co. (JPM-NYSE)	U.S.	U.S. GAAP	2,687.38
8	8	NC	Bank of America Corp. (BAC-NYSE)	U.S.	U.S. GAAP	2,434.08
9	9	NC	BNP Paribas SA (BNP-PAR)	France	IFRS	2,429.26
10	10	NC	Crédit Agricole Group	France	IFRS	2,256.72
11	12	▲	Japan Post Bank Co. Ltd. (7182-TKS)	Japan	Japanese GAAP	1,984.62
12	14	▲	Sumitomo Mitsui Financial Group Inc. (8316-TKS)	Japan	Japanese GAAP	1,954.78
13	11	▼	Citigroup Inc. (C-NYSE)	U.S.	U.S. GAAP	1,951.16
14	13	▼	Wells Fargo & Co. (WFC-NYSE)	U.S.	U.S. GAAP	1,927.56
15	15	NC	Mizuho Financial Group Inc. (8411-TKS)	Japan	Japanese GAAP	1,874.89
16	16	NC	Banco Santander SA (SAN-MAD)[1]	Spain	IFRS	1,702.61
17	18	▲	Société Générale SA (GLE-PAR)	France	IFRS	1,522.05
18	20	▲	Barclays PLC (BARC-LON)	U.K.	IFRS	1,510.14
19	19	NC	Groupe BPCE	France	IFRS	1,501.59
20	22	▲	Postal Savings Bank of China Co. Ltd. (1658-HKG)	China	PRC GAAP	1,467.31
21	17	▼	Deutsche Bank AG (DBK-ETR)	Germany	IFRS	1,456.26
22	21	▼	Bank of Communications Co. Ltd. (3328-HKG)	China	IFRS	1,422.63
23	23	NC	Royal Bank of Canada (RY-TSX)*	Canada	IFRS	1,116.31
24	24	NC	Lloyds Banking Group PLC (LLOY-LON)	U.K.	IFRS	1,104.42
25	26	▲	Toronto-Dominion Bank (TD-TSX)*	Canada	IFRS	1,102.04
26	27	▲	China Merchants Bank Co. Ltd. (600036-SGSE)	China	IFRS	1,065.25
27	35	▲	Intesa Sanpaolo SpA (ISP-MIL)[2]	Italy	IFRS	1,057.82
28	29	▲	Norinchukin Bank	Japan	Japanese GAAP	1,011.14
29	25	▼	ING Groep NV (INGA-AMS)	Netherlands	IFRS	1,000.72
30	33	▲	Goldman Sachs Group Inc. (GS-NYSE)	U.S.	U.S. GAAP	992.97
31	31	NC	Industrial Bank Co. Ltd. (601166-SGSE)**	China	PRC GAAP	976.79
32	28	▼	Crédit Mutuel Group***	France	IFRS	976.14
33	30	▼	UBS Group AG (UBSG-SWX)	Switzerland	IFRS	972.18
34	32	▼	UniCredit SpA (UCG-MIL)	Italy	IFRS	960.21
35	38	▲	China Minsheng Banking Corp. Ltd. (600016-SGSE)	China	IFRS	959.63
36	36	NC	Royal Bank of Scotland Group PLC (RBS-LON)	U.K.	IFRS	957.60
37	34	▼	Shanghai Pudong Development Bank Co. Ltd. (600000-SGSE)**	China	PRC GAAP	950.01
38	37	▼	China CITIC Bank Corp. Ltd. (998-HKG)**	China	IFRS	904.02
39	39	NC	Morgan Stanley (MS-NYSE)	U.S.	U.S. GAAP	895.43
40	40	NC	Bank of Nova Scotia (BNS-TSX)*	Canada	IFRS	872.62
41	41	NC	Credit Suisse Group AG (CSGN-SWX)	Switzerland	U.S. GAAP	812.91
42	42	NC	Banco Bilbao Vizcaya Argentaria SA (BBVA-MAD)[3]	Spain	IFRS	782.16
43	44	▲	Standard Chartered PLC (STAN-LON)	U.K.	IFRS	720.40
44	43	▼	Commonwealth Bank of Australia (CBA-ASX)	Australia	Australian GAAP	688.40
45	49	▲	China Everbright Bank Co. Ltd. (601818-SGSE)	China	IFRS	679.81
46	50	▲	Bank of Montreal (BMO-TSX)*	Canada	IFRS	665.20
47	46	▼	Rabobank	Netherlands	IFRS	662.77
48	45	▼	Australia & New Zealand Banking Group Ltd. (ANZ-ASX)**	Australia	Australian GAAP	661.72
49	51	▲	DZ BANK AG	Germany	IFRS	627.31
50	47	▼	Nordea Bank Abp (NDA SE-OME)	Finland	IFRS	622.66
51	48	▼	Westpac Banking Corp. (WBC-ASX)**	Australia	Australian GAAP	611.47
52	52	NC	National Australia Bank Ltd. (NAB-ASX)**	Australia	Australian GAAP	571.34
53	58	▲	Ping An Bank Co. Ltd. (000001-CNSSE)	China	PRC GAAP	565.72
54	53	▼	Danske Bank A/S (DANSKE-CSE)	Denmark	IFRS	564.83
55	54	▼	State Bank of India (SBIN-NSE)	India	Indian GAAP	561.54
56	55	▼	Resona Holdings Inc. (8308-TKS)	Japan	Japanese GAAP	549.51
57	57	NC	Sumitomo Mitsui Trust Holdings Inc. (8309-TKS)	Japan	Japanese GAAP	509.28
58	59	▲	Canadian Imperial Bank of Commerce (CM-TSX)*[4]	Canada	IFRS	495.99
59	60	▲	U.S. Bancorp (USB-NYSE)	U.S.	U.S. GAAP	495.43
60	66	▲	PAO Sberbank of Russia (SBER-ME)	Russia	IFRS	482.53
61	65	▲	Shinhan Financial Group Co. Ltd. (A055550-KRX)	South Korea	Korean IFRS	478.50
62	56	▼	Commerzbank AG (CBK-ETR)[5]	Germany	IFRS	478.40
63	62	▼	Truist Financial Corp. (TFC-NYSE)	U.S.	U.S. GAAP	473.08

64	64	NC	KB Financial Group Inc. (A105560-KRX)	South Korea	Korean IFRS	449.15
65	61	▼	CaixaBank SA (CABK-MAD)	Spain	IFRS	439.25
66	68	▲	DBS Group Holdings Ltd. (D05-SGX)	Singapore	Singapore FRS	430.45
67	67	NC	Nomura Holdings Inc. (8604-TKS)	Japan	U.S. GAAP	425.50
68	71	▲	Hua Xia Bank Co. Ltd. (600015-SGSE)**	China	PRC GAAP	422.74
69	63	▼	ABN AMRO Bank NV (ABN-AMS)	Netherlands	IFRS	420.89
70	70	NC	PNC Financial Services Group Inc. (PNC-NYSE)	U.S.	U.S. GAAP	410.30
71	69	▼	Itaú Unibanco Holding SA (ITUB4-BSP)	Brazil	IFRS	407.37
72	73	▲	Capital One Financial Corp. (COF-NYSE)	U.S.	U.S. GAAP	390.37
73	75	▲	Bank of New York Mellon Corp. (BK-NYSE)	U.S.	U.S. GAAP	381.51
74	74	NC	Bank of Beijing Co. Ltd. (601169-SGSE)**	China	PRC GAAP	374.97
75	72	▼	NongHyup Financial Group Inc.	South Korea	Korean IFRS	369.92
76	78	▲	Oversea-Chinese Banking Corp. Ltd. (O39-SGX)	Singapore	Singapore FRS	365.57
77	76	▼	Banco do Brasil SA (BBAS3-BSP)	Brazil	BR GAAP	365.51
78	77	▼	Hana Financial Group Inc. (A086790-KRX)	South Korea	Korean IFRS	365.10
79	79	NC	Banco Bradesco SA (BBDC4-BSP)[6]	Brazil	IFRS	345.21
80	83	▲	China Guangfa Bank Co. Ltd.***	China	PRC GAAP	343.26
81	80	▼	Svenska Handelsbanken AB (publ) (SHB A-OME)	Sweden	IFRS	328.59
82	82	NC	KBC Group NV (KBC-BRU)[7]	Belgium	IFRS	327.87
83	81	▼	Caixa Econômica Federal	Brazil	BR GAAP	321.68
84	86	▲	DNB ASA (DNB-OSL)	Norway	IFRS	317.75
85	85	NC	Woori Financial Group Inc. (A316140-KRX)	South Korea	Korean IFRS	313.54
86	84	▼	Nationwide Building Society (NBS-LON)**	U.K.	IFRS	307.45
87	88	▲	Bank of Shanghai Co. Ltd. (601229-SGSE)**	China	PRC GAAP	306.04
88	87	▼	Skandinaviska Enskilda Banken AB (SEB A-OME)	Sweden	IFRS	305.79
89	91	▲	La Banque Postale SA	France	IFRS	304.88
90	89	▼	United Overseas Bank Ltd. (U11-SGX)	Singapore	Singapore FRS	300.68
91	90	▼	Bank of Jiangsu Co. Ltd. (600919-SGSE)	China	PRC GAAP	296.58
92	92	NC	Landesbank Baden-Württemberg	Germany	IFRS	287.99
93	93	NC	Erste Group Bank AG (EBS-WBO)	Austria	IFRS	275.72
94	94	NC	Industrial Bank of Korea (A024110-KRX)	South Korea	Korean IFRS	275.54
95	97	▲	Bayerische Landesbank AöR**	Germany	IFRS	266.27
96	-	▲	Qatar National Bank (QPSC) (QNBK-DSM)	Qatar	IFRS	259.48
97	99	▲	China Zheshang Bank Co. Ltd. (2016-HKG)	China	IFRS	258.63
98	96	▼	Swedbank AB (publ) (SWED A-OME)	Sweden	IFRS	257.79
99	-	▲	Raiffeisen Gruppe Switzerland	Switzerland	Swiss GAAP	256.43
100	95	▼	Banco de Sabadell SA (SAB-MAD)	Spain	IFRS	251.10

Source S&P Global, 2020

References

Abor, J. Y., Amidu, M., & Issahaku, H. (2018). Mobile telephony, financial inclusion and inclusive growth. *Journal of African Business, 19*(3), 430–453.

Ahmad, A. H., Green, C., & Jiang, F. (2020). Mobile money, financial inclusion and development: A review with reference to African experience. *Journal of Economic Surveys, 34*(4), 753–792.

Anginer, D., Bertay, A. C., Cull, R. Demirgüç-Kunt, A., & Mare, D. S. (2019). *Bank regulation and supervision ten years after the global financial crisis* (World Bank Policy Research Working Paper No. 9044). World Bank.

Banyen, K. T., & Biekpe, N. (2020a). Financial integration and bank profitability in five regions of Africa. *International Journal of Emerging Markets*. https://doi.org/10.1108/IJOEM-08-2018-0435

Banyen, K. T., & Biekpe, N. (2020b). Financial integration, competition and bank efficiency in Africa. *Economic Change and Restructuring, 53*(3), 495–518. https://doi.org/10.1007/s10644-019-09262-8

Beck, T., & Cull, R. (2014). Banking in Africa. In A. N. Berger, P. Molyneux, & J. O. S. Wilson (Eds.), *Oxford Handbook of Banking* (2nd ed.). Oxford University Press.

Beck, T., Fuch, M., Singer, D., & Witte, M. (2014 December). Making cross-border banking work for Africa. World bank publications—books. *The World Bank Group*, 20248.

Beck, T., Todorov, R., & Wagner, W. (2013). Supervising cross-border banks: Theory, evidence and policy. *Economic Policy, 28*, 5–44.

Blundell-Wignall, A., Atkinson, P., & Lee, S. (2008). The current financial crisis: Causes and policy issues. *Financial Market Trends*, 11–31.

Bons, R. W. H., Alt, R., Lee, H. G., & Weber, B. (2012). Banking in the Internet and mobile era. *Electron Markets, 22*, 197–202.

Capgemini Analysis. (2011). *Trends in the Global Banking Industry: Key business and technology trends in the banking sector and their implications* (pp. 1–24). https://www.capgemini.com/wp-content/uploads/2017/07/Trends_in_the_Global_Banking_Industry.pdf

Cihak, M., & Demirgüç-Kunt, A. (2013). *Rethinking the state's role in finance.* The World Bank.

Claessens, S. (2017). Global banking: Recent developments and insights from research. *Review of Finance, 21*(4), 1513–1555.

Claessens, S., & van Horen, N. (2014). Foreign banks: Trends and impact. *Journal of Money Credit Banks, 46*(1), 295–326.

Cucinelli, D. (2015). The impact of nonperforming loans on bank lending behaviour: Evidence from the Italian banking sector. *Eurasian Journal of Business and Economics, 8*(16), 59–71.

Delis, M. D., Molyneux, P., & Pasiouras, P. (2011). Regulations and productivity growth in banking: Evidence from transition economies. *Journal of Money, Credit and Banking, 43*(4), 735–764.

Demirgüç-Kunt, A., Klapper, L., Singer, D., Ansar, S., & Hess, J. (2018). *The Global Findex Database 2017: Measuring financial inclusion and the Fintech revolution*. World Bank.

Dong, Y., Hamilton, R., & Tippett, M. (2014). Cost efficiency of the Chinese banking sector: A comparison of stochastic frontier analysis and data envelopment analysis. *Economic Modelling, 36*, 298–308.

Frey, L., & Volz, U. (2011). Regional financial integration in Sub-Saharan Africa—An empirical examination of its effects on financial market development. *South African Journal of Economics, 81*(1), 79–117.

Frigerio, M., & Vandone, D. (2018). Bank ownership and firm-level performance: An empirical assessment of state-owned development banks. In M. García-Olalla & J. Clifton (Eds.), *Contemporary issues in banking: Regulation, governance and performance*. Palgrave Macmillan Studies in Banking and Financial Institutions. https://doi.org/10.1007/978-3-319-90294-4_1

García-Olalla, M., & Vázquez-Ordás, C. J. (2020). Contemporary issues in banking. *Global Policy, 11*(S1).

Gardener, E., Molyneux, P., & Nguyen-Linh, H. (2011). Determinants of efficiency in South East Asian banking. *The Service Industries Journal, 31*, 2693–2719.

Gerschenkron, A. (1962). *Economic backwardness in historical perspective: A book of essays*. Belknap Press of Harvard University Press.

Gomber, P., Koch, J., & Siering, M. (2017). Digital Finance and FinTech: Current research and future research directions. *Journal of Business Economics, 87*(5), 537–580.

Goyal, S., Koeva-Brooks, P., Pradhan, M., Tressel, T., Dell'Ariccia, G., Leckow, R., & Pazarbasioglu, C. (2013). *A banking union for the euro area* (IMF Staff Discussion Note 13/1).

Gupta, S. (2013). The mobile banking and payment revolution. *The European Financial Review, 1*(2), 3–7.

Hossain, M., Jain, P. K., & Mitra, S. (2013). State ownership and bank equity in the Asia-Pacific region. *Pacific-Basin Finance Journal, 21*, 914–931.

International Monetary Fund. (2015). International banking after the crisis: Increasingly local and safer? In *IMF, Global Financial Stability Report* (pp. 55–91). IMF.

International Monetary Fund. (2018). Regulatory reform 10 years after the global financial crisis: Looking back, looking forward. In *Global financial stability report, October 2018: A decade after the global financial crisis: Are we safer?* Downloaded from *IMF e-library* at https://www.elibrary.imf.org/view/IMF082/25319-9781484375594/25319-9781484375594/ch02.xml?language=en&redirect=true

Kopecky, K. J., & VanHoose, D. (2006). Capital regulation, heterogeneous monitoring costs and aggregate loan quality. *Banking and Finance, 6*, 2235–2255.

Kornai, J. (1979). Resource-constrained versus demand-constrained systems. *Econometrica, 47*(4), 801–819.

Laeven, L., & Tressel, T. (2013). Financial integration and fragmentation in the European Union, Technical Note. In C. Enoch, L. Everaert, T. Tressel, & J. Zhou (Eds.), *From fragmentation to integration: EU wide approach to financial oversight* (pp. 139–166). IMF.

Lane, P. R. (2012). The European Sovereign debt crisis. *Journal of Economic Perspectives, 26*(3), 49–68.

Lane, P. R., & Milesi-Ferretti, G. M. (2012). External adjustment and the global crisis. *Journal of International Economics, 88*, 252–265.

Lee, C., Olasehinde-Williams, G., & Olanipekun, I. (2020). Financial Systems, regulatory quality, and economic growth. *The Journal of International Trade and Economic Development*. https://doi.org/10.1080/09638199.2020.1847172

Leon, F. (2016). Does the expansion of regional cross-border banks affect competition in Africa? Indirect evidence. *Research in International Business and Finance, 37*(2016), 66–77.

Ling, G. M., Fern, Y. S., Boon, L. K., & Huat, T. S. (2016). Understanding customer satisfaction of internet banking: A case study in Malacca. *Procedia Economics and Finance, 37*(2016), 80–85.

Malady, L. (2016). Consumer protection issues for digital financial services in emerging markets. *Banking and Finance Law Review, 31*(2), 389–401.

Norman, A. H. M., Gee, C. S., & Isa, C. R. (2018). Does bank regulation matter on the relationship between competition and financial stability? Evidence from Southeast Asian countries. *Pacific-Basin Finance Journal, 48*(2018), 144–161.

Nzioka, O. M. (2017). Investigating the Relationship between financial integration and economic growth in the East African community. *European Scientific Journal, 13*(19), 1857–7881.

Obstfeld, M. (2015). *Trilemmas and tradeoffs: Living with financial globalization* (BIS Working Papers No. 480). Basel.

OECD. (2020). *Digital disruption in banking and its impact on competition*. http://www.oecd.org/daf/competition/digital-disruption-in-financial-markets.htm

Ozili, P. K. (2018). Impact of digital finance on financial inclusion and stability. *Borsa Istanbul Review, 18*(4), 329–340.

Pasiouras, F., Tanna, S., & Zopounidis, C. (2009). The impact of banking regulation on banks cost and profit efficiency: Cross-country evidence. *International Review of Financial Analysis, 6*, 294–302.

Shaban, M., & James, G. A. (2018). The effects of ownership change on bank performance and risk exposure: Evidence from Indonesia. *Journal of Banking and Finance, 88*, 483–497.

Shilling, M., Shaw, G., & Berry, J. (2020, September 10). The path ahead: Navigating financial services sector performance post-COVID-19. *Deloitte Insights*.

Sissy, A. M., Amidu, M., & Abor, J. Y. (2017). The effects of revenue diversification and cross border banking on risk and return of banks in Africa. *Research in International Business and Finance, 40*(2017), 1–18.

Tan, Y., & Anchor, J. (2017). The impacts of risk-taking behaviour and competition on technical efficiency: Evidence from the Chinese banking industry. *Research in International Business and Finance, 41*, 90–104.

The Banker Database. www.thebankerdatabase.com. Accessed on 27 December 2020.

Thomsen, S. (2013). Corporate governance and the financial crisis. In M. Pinedo & I. Walter (Eds.), *Global Asset Management* (pp. 235–246). Palgrave Macmillan. https://doi.org/10.1057/9781137328878_13

Wang, K., Huang, W., Wu, J., & Liu, Y.-N. (2014). Efficiency measures of the Chinese commercial banking system using an additive two-stage DEA. *Omega, 44*, 5–20.

Yang, Z., Gan, C., & Li, Z. (2019). Role of bank regulation on bank performance: Evidence from Asia-Pacific commercial banks. *Journal of Risk and Financial Management, 12*(3), 131–136. https://doi.org/10.3390/jrfm120301

Batch number: 10725847

Printed by Printforce, the Netherlands

Palgrave Macmillan Studies in Banking and Financial Institutions

Series Editor
Philip Molyneux, Bangor University, Bangor, UK

The Palgrave Macmillan Studies in Banking and Financial Institutions series is international in orientation and includes studies of banking systems in particular countries or regions as well as contemporary themes such as Islamic Banking, Financial Exclusion, Mergers and Acquisitions, Risk Management, and IT in Banking. The books focus on research and practice and include up to date and innovative studies that cover issues which impact banking systems globally.

Joshua Yindenaba Abor ·
Charles Komla Delali Adjasi
Editors

The Economics of Banking and Finance in Africa

Developments in Africa's Financial Systems

Volume 2

palgrave
macmillan

Editors
Joshua Yindenaba Abor
University of Ghana Business School
Accra, Ghana

Charles Komla Delali Adjasi
University of Stellenbosch Business School
Cape Town, South Africa

ISSN 2523-336X ISSN 2523-3378 (electronic)
Palgrave Macmillan Studies in Banking and Financial Institutions
ISBN 978-3-031-04161-7 ISBN 978-3-031-04162-4 (eBook)
https://doi.org/10.1007/978-3-031-04162-4

Cover illustration: Timothy Marks

This Palgrave Macmillan imprint is published by the registered company Springer Nature Switzerland AG
The registered company address is: Gewerbestrasse 11, 6330 Cham, Switzerland

Acknowledgements

Joshua Yindenaba Abor
To my wonderful wife, Dr. Patience Aseweh Abor and our lovely children, Ivana, Bastien and Venka for their love, support and encouragement. Also, to my parents, Abor Ndobire and Amina Tobga for their inspiration and commitment throughout my education. I also wish to appreciate my co-editor, Charles, and co-authors of the various chapters.

Charles Komla Delali Adjasi
To my wife Chewe Sakha Adjasi and our boys Delali and Dalitso for their love, support, encouragement and for tolerating Daddy's endless late nights. To my father W.O. K. Adjasi and my late mother D.A.M. Buachie (Auntie Mansah) for your blessings. I would like to thank my co-editor Joshua for the sterling initiatives and collaborative effort in getting this book project completed.

General
We the editors would like to thank all contributing authors for the high quality of their chapters. We wish to thank Prof. Helen Yitah, Dean of School of Languages and the Carnegie Writing Centre, University of Ghana, for the excellent work in proofreading and language editing. We also thank all the reviewers of various chapter as well as Ms. Angela Alu for providing editorial assistance.

The editors wish to specially appreciate the financial support provided by the following banks in completing this book project:

- Ecobank Ghana
- GCB Bank
- Stanbic Bank Ghana
- Agricultural Development Bank, Ghana
- CalBank
- Universal Merchant Bank
- Guaranty Trust Bank

Praise for *The Economics of Banking and Finance in Africa*

"The breadth of themes covered in this book is refreshing and quite extensive, from macroeconomic themes and analyses, through market structures and central bank performance, to such new themes as financial inclusion and FinTech, and the impact of COVID-19 on African financial systems. The scope of the volume is certainly remarkable as it helps us to appreciate recent developments in African financial systems. I am very happy to endorse it and recommend it to all those interested in understanding how finance in Africa works."

—Ernest Aryeetey, *Professor of Economics, Board Chair, African Economic Research Consortium & Former Vice-Chancellor, University of Ghana*

"This volume comes at a critical time to consolidate emerging evidence on the success of financial inclusion in all sectors of African economies. This emerging evidence, supported by the evolution of digital financial services, becomes an important input to development discourse. It now means that we can start formulating strong pillars for financial development in Africa. This book makes interesting contributions to the field of banking and finance."

Prof. Njuguna S. Ndung'u, *Executive Director, African Economic Research Consortium and Former Governor, Central Bank of Kenya*

"This is a welcoming book on banking and finance in Africa. I commend the authors and the editors for covering the landscape and the depth of Africa's financial systems. The book provides an invaluable guide to scholars, policymakers, and graduate students on the theoretical, empirical and policy related issues in banking and finance in Africa. It is a must read for policymakers and researchers seeking to gain a deeper understanding of Africa's financial systems."

—Charles Amo-Yartey, Ph.D., *Senior Economist, International Monetary Fund, Washington DC, USA*

Contents

Notes on Contributors

Abor Joseph is a management and financial professional with over fifteen years of experience. He is currently the managing proprietor of Zuson Services; a business involved in haulage and product distribution. His professional life has largely been in the oil and gas industry as well as the integrated marketing communications industry. He worked as the General Manager of bulk oil distribution companies, such as Rama Energy Limited and Misyl Energy Company Ltd. He also worked as the General Manager of Nick Petroleum Ghana Limited, an oil marketing company. In addition, he worked as a Management and Financial Consultant at Resolve Medical Services. He holds M.Phil. in Finance degree and a Bachelor of Arts Degree in Accounting and Economics from the University of Ghana.

Abor Joshua Yindenaba is a financial economist with many years of expertise, mainly in development finance and economics research, as well as in senior-level practitioner, policy and consulting roles. He is a Professor of Finance and former Dean at the University of Ghana Business School. He is Adjunct Professor of Development Finance at the University of Stellenbosch Business School. He is an External Fellow at the Centre for Global Finance, SOAS University of London and a researcher with the African Economic Research Consortium as well as a Fellow of the Ghana Academy of Arts and Sciences. He has held Visiting Scholar positions at the International Monetary Fund (IMF), in Washington DC, and is a member of the Monetary Policy Committee of the Bank of Ghana.

Abor Patience Aseweh is a Senior Lecturer at the Department of Public Administration and Health Services Management, University of Ghana Business School. She holds a Ph.D. in Management from the Southampton Business School, University of Southampton, UK. Her research interests include issues in corporate governance, leadership and management. She has published in reputable international peer-refereed journals and serves as reviewer for a number of journals. He has also provided capacity building and consulting services for some organisations.

Abugre James Atambilla is a Senior Economic Development Officer in Ghana with vast experience in development finance, development planning and management, public policy administration and local governance and public financial management. He holds an M.Phil. in Economics from the University of Ghana and a Bachelor of Arts Degree in Integrated Development Studies (Economics and Entrepreneurship Development) from the University for Development Studies. He is a Ph.D. student in Finance at the University of Ghana Business School. He is a member of the Ghana Institute of Planners and Commonwealth Association of Planners.

Abugre Jessie A. is a lawyer with extensive experience in legal research, corporate and commercial matters and litigation. Jessie is intrigued by technology, loves everything science and tech and currently works with tech firms and startups. Her practice areas zero in on intellectual property, regulatory compliance and capital markets. She has experience representing high-profile clients in corporate and commercial matters and litigation. She holds a Bachelor of Laws degree from Kwame Nkrumah University of Science and Technology. She has an M.Phil. in Human Resource Management from the University of Ghana. Jessie is a member of the Ghana Bar Association and the International Academy of African Business Development.

Addae-Manu Richard is a nearly qualified Actuary and researcher in Development Finance, with close to twenty years of experience in the insurance industry. Richard's acquired skills include insurance pricing and valuation techniques, software application programming and project management. Richard has a keen interest in developing and growing the insurance sector in Africa and other emerging markets. Hence his research interests include insurance and financial market development. In addition, Richard enjoys family time and following the exploits of his favourite soccer teams.

Adjasi Charles Komla Delali is Professor of Development Finance and Economics at the University of Stellenbosch Business (USB) School in Cape Town South Africa, where he served as Head of Development Finance Programmes from January 2013–June 2017. He is also a Visiting Professor at ENSEA Cote d'Ivoire and an AFREXIM Bank Research Fellow. He has previously been a Visiting Professor at the Department of Economics, Econometrics and Finance, University of Groningen in the Netherlands. His research focuses on financial markets, firm productivity and household welfare development in Africa. He has published widely in reputable journals, a co-edited one book and co-authored another.

Afedzie Ekow is currently the Managing Director of the Ghana Stock Exchange and a member of the Council (Board) of the Exchange. He was educated at the University of Ghana, Legon, Ghana, where he obtained a master's degree in Business Administration (M.B.A.) in 1989 and a Master of Arts degree (M.A.) in Economic Policy Management. He also holds a bachelor's degree in Law (LL.B.) from Mountcrest University College and a Qualifying Certificate from the Ghana School of Law. He is a former Vice President of the African Securities Exchanges Association (ASEA) and currently a member of the Executive Committee of ASEA. He serves on the Boards of the Central Securities Depository (CSD) Ghana Ltd. and Ghana Investment and Securities Institute Ltd. Mr. Afedzie is also a member of the governing committees of Ghana Alternative Market (GAX) and Ghana Fixed Income Market (GFIM).

Agbloyor Elikplimi Komla is an Associate Professor in Finance at the University of Ghana Business School. He is also a research fellow in the Faculty of Economic and Management Sciences, University of Stellenbosch Business School, South Africa. He is a financial economist, chartered accountant and risk management expert. He has several years of teaching, research and consulting experience. Elikplimi has consulted for organisations including the International Finance Corporation (IFC), Ghana, Oil and Gas for Inclusive Growth (GOGIG) and the National Banking College. He is a researcher with the African Economic and Research Consortium (AERC).

Agoba Abel M. is a Lecturer in Finance at Coventry University, UK. He holds a Ph.D. in Finance degree and has over eight (8) years of teaching and research experience. He has developed and acquired extensive experience in outstanding communication, course development, research and publications, online course delivery and conference presentations. He is a member of the Institute of Chartered Accountants Ghana. Abel has experience in facilitating Corporate Finance, Statistical Analysis for Finance, among others. He has a proven excellence in organising short courses and training programs and serves as an external research fellow for Tesah Capital Ghana.

Agyei Samuel Kwaku is a Senior Lecturer of the Department of Finance of the University of Cape Coast. Dr. Agyei holds a Ph.D. and M.Phil. in Finance and Bachelor of Commerce degrees. He is a member, of the Institute of Chartered Accountants (Ghana). Dr. Agyei is currently the Vice-Dean of the School of Business, UCC. He teaches Accounting and Finance courses at both the graduate and undergraduate levels at the University of Cape Coast School of Business. His current research areas include financial literacy, behavioural finance, governance and welfare.

Agyeman Benjamin is a Ph.D. Finance student at the University of Ghana Business School. He holds an M.Phil. in Finance from the University of Ghana, a B.Sc. in Financial Mathematics from the University for Development Studies, and a Post-Secondary Education Certificate (Teachers' Cert 'A') from the University of Cape Coast. His research interests are in the areas of banking and finance, oil and gas finance, and corporate governance and finance. He is currently working on a number of book chapters with some renowned professors in the areas of project finance, sustainable and responsible investment, sustainable energy investment, and international corporate governance.

Ahmad Ahmad Hassan is at the School of Business and Economics, Loughborough University. Ahmad's research is in the areas of mobile money and financial inclusion and development in Africa, exchange rates and economic performance and fiscal policy in developing countries. He has published on these topics in journals including *Economics Letters*, *Journal of International Financial Markets*, *Institutions and Money*, *Review of Quantitative Finance and Accounting*, *Journal of Development Studies*, *The Manchester School*, *Review of Development Economics*, *Open Economies Review* and *Journal of Economic Surveys*.

Ajuwon Oluseye Samuel is a Lecturer in Economics at the University of Lagos, Nigeria. His areas of research are in macroeconomics and development finance, with a special focus on financing small businesses. He holds B.Sc. Economics from Obafemi Awolowo University, Nigeria, M.Sc. and M.Phil. in Economics from the University of Ibadan, Nigeria, and Ph.D. in Development Finance from the University of Stellenbosch Business School, South Africa.

Akinsola Foluso is a researcher and academic with over fifteen years of experience. He is currently a Lecturer in the Department of Economics at the University of Lagos. He obtained Ph.D. in Development Finance at the University of Stellenbosch Business School. He also has a Master's degree and a Bachelor's degree in Economics with honours from the University of Botswana. His areas of specialisation are International Economics, Monetary Economics and Development Finance. Dr. Akinsola has several publications in books and peer-reviewed academic journals.

Akotey Joseph Oscar has a Ph.D. in Development Finance from the University of Stellenbosch. His research interests include Development Finance, Risk Finance and Performance Evaluation. He has published in internationally accredited *3-Star* and *2-Star* journals. He has also made presentations at various international conferences such as the Centre for the Study of Africa Economies, Oxford University, WEI Conference at Harvard University, the Economic Society of South Africa and the Global Development Finance Conferences. He currently teaches *International Finance, Project Finance, Financial Derivatives* and *Corporate Governance* at KNUST School of Business, Kwame Nkrumah University of Science and Technology, Ghana.

Alagidede Imhotep Paul is a metaeconomist, a transdisciplinary scholar and professor at the University of the Witwatersrand, South Africa, and the Simon Diedong Dombo University of Business and Integrated Development Studies, Wa, Ghana. His research and teaching interests transcends traditional academic boundaries, delving into the possibilities and limits of human consciousness. He is an accomplished entrepreneur, a philanthropist and policy maker. Imhotep is the President and Chancellor of the multidimensional network of social enterprises called the Nile Valley Multiversity, the Grand Editor of the Journal of Indigenous and Shamanic Studies, Editor-in-Chief of the Journal of Construction and Built Environment and Executive Director of AREF Consult.

Alu Angela A. is currently awaiting the determination of her Ph.D. with the Department of Finance at the University of Ghana Business School. She holds an M.Phil. in Finance and B.Sc. in Administration (Banking and Finance) from the University of Ghana Business School. Her primary research interests include Natural Resource Governance, Banking and Financial Markets. She is an Assistant Lecturer with the Department of Business Administration at Academic City University College. She previously worked as a Contract Engineer with ENI Ghana and as a Financial Analyst with Temple Investments Limited.

Amidu Mohammed is a professional accountant, financial policy analyst and Professor of Accounting and Finance with a focus in corporate tax policy, accounting information quality, sustainable banking, development finance, treasury and governmental accounting. He is a researcher with African Economic Research Consortium (AERC), Kenya, and has held Visiting Scholar positions at the International Monetary Fund, Washington DC, USA. He has over 15 years of academic, research and consulting experience and for the past 5 years has been working on various aspects of SMEs management and finance in Ghana in addition to providing services to some organisation including Ghana Revenue Authority (GRA) Millennium Development Authority (MiDA), STAR-Ghana, Ministry of Finance and DANIDA Health Sector Support Office.

Amoah Lordina is a Senior Lecturer at the Department of Finance, University of Ghana Business School. She has a Ph.D. in Development Finance from the University of Stellenbosch, South Africa. Lordina is a researcher with the African Economic Research Consortium and has published articles in reputable international journals. Her areas of research interest include green finance, small business finance, corporate finance and financial market development. She has extensive knowledge in green finance. She participated in the Global Academy on Green Economy organised by the International Training Centre of the ILO and the ESRM programme by the International Finance Corporation.

Anarfo Ebenezer Bugri is a Senior Lecturer in Finance at the Department of Accounting and Finance, Ghana Institute of Management and Public Administration (GIMPA) Business School and a consultant at Corporate Support Group (CSG). Dr. Anarfo's research interests are in the areas of financial inclusion, financial sector development, monetary policy, financial regulation, remittances, food security, FDI, economic growth, capital structure and mental health. His scholarly works on these areas have been published in reputable journals.

Andani Alhassan holds the positions, CEO of LVS Africa, Chairman of Council for Scientific and Industrial Research and Chairman of SOS Children's Villages Ghana. He was also appointed by Gold Fields Limited as an independent non-executive director at its Board of Directors. Until now, he was the CEO/Executive Director of Stanbic Bank Limited and the president of the Ghana Association of Bankers (GAB). He holds a master's degree in Banking and Finance from Finafrica Institute in Milan, Italy. Andani is also an alumnus of the Oxford Strategic Leadership Programme, and holds an International Management Certificate from INSEAD, Chartered Bank.

Antwi Stephen is the Director of Studies and Training at the National Banking College (NBC).

Dr. Antwi is an Economist, a Banker, Lecturer and an International Motivational Speaker. His expertise are in the areas of Banking Operations, Credit Delivery and Risk Analysis. He has held various positions such as Deputy Managing Director, in Charge of Operations and Credit, Area Manager in Charge of Cluster of Branches, Branch Manager and Branch Operations Manager.

He holds a Ph.D., M.Phil. in Agricultural Economics, M.Sc. in Economics, M.B.A. in Finance, B.A. in Economics and a Diploma in Education. Additionally, Dr. Antwi is also a Member of the Chartered Institute of Bankers.

Arun Thankom is a Professor of Global Development and Accountability at the Essex Business School. Currently, he is a Professor Extraordinaire at the Stellenbosch Business School, South Africa, and a Research Fellow at IZA, Bonn. He is also Chairing an academic steering group on Financial inclusion in the International Cooperative and Mutual Insurance Federation (ICMIF). He is a Fellow of Academy of Social Sciences and a Fellow of the Royal Society of Arts, Manufactures and Commerce. Thankom's recent research interests are in the areas of Fintech, financial inclusion, climate change and sustainability.

Asante-Amponsah Daniel is a finance and accounting professional with a working experience with entities across oil and gas, mining and financial services industries. Skilled in statutory and group audits subject to Sarbanes-Oxley (SOX) compliance, ISAs and IFRS standards. An experienced accountant with an accreditation from the Institute of Chartered Accountant, Ghana. He is currently an assistant manager with Corporates, Regulated and Listed Entities Audit at KPMG UK. Prior to joining KPMG UK, he worked with PricewaterhouseCoopers, Ghana as an Experienced Senior Associate with the Energy Utility and Resources Industry Group. Daniel served as a Teaching and Research Assistant to Prof. Joshua Abor in the Department of Finance, University of Ghana Business School. He holds an M.Phil. Finance and B.Sc. Administration (Accounting) degrees from the University of Ghana Business School.

Asomaning Kwamina Koranteng is the Chief Executive of Stanbic Bank Ghana. He began his professional banking career in 1997 at the Cal Merchant Bank and has since worked with several international organisations including JP Morgan Chase & Co and Goldman Sachs & Co in New York.

He is also a Chartered Certified Accountant with a Master's degree in Finance from the Wharton School, University of Pennsylvania, and a Bachelor of Science degree in Business Administration (Accounting option) from the University of Ghana. Kwamina has extensive expertise in International Banking, Corporate Finance and Emerging markets. He serves on the Boards of Stanbic Investment Management Services, Stanbic Holdings, SBG Securities Group and the Advisory Board of the College of Humanities, University of Ghana. He is also an independent Non-Executive Director of Chirano Gold Mines.

Asongu Simplice A. is a Professor and holds a Ph.D. from Oxford Brookes University. He is currently the Lead Economist and Director of the African Governance and Development Institute (Yaoundé, Cameroon); Distinguished Visiting Professor at the University of Johannesburg (Johannesburg, South Africa), the Lead Economist and Director of the European Xtramile Centre of African Studies (Liège, Belgium) and Lead Economist and Co-director of "Centre de Recherche pour le Développement Economique" (Bangui, Central African Republic). He is also a: Senior Research Fellow at the Africa Growth Institute (Cape Town, South Africa).

Assefuah Kathryn A. A. O. is a lecturer in the Banking and Finance Department of the University of Professional Studies, Accra. She holds B.Sc. in Mathematics and Computer Science and M.Phil. in Risk Management and Insurance. He is currently a Ph.D. candidate in Finance. She previously worked at Prudential Life Insurance Company. Her interests are in the areas of pensions, the informal sector, financial inclusion, risk management and insurance.

Azu Gabriel has an M.Phil. in Finance from the University of Ghana and a B.Sc. in Accounting also from the University of Ghana. He is also an associate member of the Institute of Chartered Accountant, Ghana (ICAG). He is currently a teaching and research assistant at the University of Ghana Business School. He has served in the capacity as a teaching and graduate assistant in the University of Ghana Business School for two years.

His research interests are in the area of Financial Inclusion and Financial Development, Corporate Governance, Financial Institutions and Economic Growth and Development.

Banyen Kannyiri Thadious holds a Ph.D. in Development Finance from the University of Cape Town, South Africa, and an M.Phil. Finance and B.Sc. Administration degrees both from the University of Ghana. He has over ten (10) years of teaching and research experience and is currently a senior lecturer in the Department of Banking and Finance at the School of Business, S.D. Dombo University of Business and Integrated Development Studies, Ghana. Kannyiri serves on several administrative committees and boards of the University and has published in and reviewed for several internationally accredited peer-reviewed journals.

Boateng Sarah Serwah is a Lecturer in Finance at Ghana Institute of Management and Public Administration (GIMPA)—Business School, Accra. She holds B.Sc. Administration (Banking and Finance), M.Phil. Finance and Ph.D. Finance from the University of Ghana. Her research interests are in the areas of corporate governance, financial structure, development finance, ethical and sustainable investment.

Bundoo Sunil K. is an Associate Professor in the Department of Economics and Statistics at the University of Mauritius. He has published widely in trade and financial liberalisation; pro-poor macroeconomics; capital markets in particular stock markets and competition policy. He has completed several research and consultancy projects/papers for international organisations such the World Bank; the African Economic Research Consortium (AERC); the World Institute for Development Economics Research (WIDER); the United Nations Research Institute for Social Development (UNRISD); the Consumer Unity Trust Society (CUTS); the UNU-Institute of Advanced Studies (UNU-IAS) and the Melbourne Centre for Financial Studies.

Chipeta Chimwemwe is an Associate Professor of Corporate Finance and Head of the Finance division in the School of Economics and Finance at the University of the Witwatersrand. He was a Visiting Scholar at the J. Mack Robinson College of Business at Georgia State University in USA, and former Bank of Zambia Chair in Banking and Finance at Mulungushi University. He is NRF rated (C2 rating) and has published numerous papers in the field of Finance and Investments. His work appears in high-impact journals. Chimwemwe is a recipient of several awards including the Research Excellence Award and has presented his research findings at numerous national and international conferences. He has several years of practical experience in areas relating to Executive Education, Business Plan development and Digital Asset Investments.

Coffie William is an Associate Professor of Accounting and Finance and the Head of the Department of Accounting at the University of Ghana Business School. He holds a Ph.D. in Financial Economics and a Master's Degree in Finance from Birmingham City University, UK. Prof. Coffie is a Certified Chartered Accountant. He was previously a Senior Lecturer in Accounting and Finance and Programmes Director for M.Sc. Finance and Accounting and M.Sc. International Banking and Finance at University of Wolverhampton, Lecturer in Finance at Birmingham City University, Lecturer in Business and Taxation at Staffordshire University and Visiting Professor at Hong Kong City University.

Doku James Ntiamoah holds a Ph.D. in Finance from the University of Ghana, Legon. Dr. Doku is a Senior Lecturer at the Department of Banking and Finance, University of Professional Studies, Accra (UPSA) where he teaches finance courses and research methods. His main areas of research interest and collaborations are Banking Sector Development, Industrial Organisation of Banking Firm, Capital Structure, Public

Debt and Economic Growth, Institutional Quality and Growth; Institutions and Economic Growth. He has published several articles in peer-reviewed/ranked journals.

Donkor George N. Agyekum is currently the President (CEO) and Chairman of the Board of Directors of the ECOWAS Bank for Investment and Development (EBID). Dr. Donor is a Lawyer and a Banker with over twenty-eight (28) years of experience in senior management positions. He is the author of the book "*Customer Relationship Management Practices within the Rural Banking Industry in Ghana*". He also co-authored several publications including "*Organizational Learning Capability and Family Businesses Performance: Does Innovativeness Matter?*", "*Strategic Planning and Performance of SMEs in Ghana, The moderating effect of market dynamism*", among others. He currently serves on several Boards including the ECOBANK Transnational Incorporated (ETI), WAICA RE-Capital and WAICA RE-Insurance.

Dzeha Gloria Clarissa O. is a Senior Lecturer at the Banking and Finance Department, Central Business School, Central University and currently the Dean of Students. Gloria holds a Diploma in Statistics; Bachelor of Science degree in Banking and Finance; Master of Philosophy in Finance and Doctor of Philosophy in Finance from the University of Ghana. Her research interest includes International Finance, Remittances and Central Banking. She has considerable teaching experience in courses including International Finance, Investment Management, Financial Markets, Commercial Banking and Contemporary issues in Finance. Gloria Clarissa has written several academic papers.

Fanta Ashenafi is a senior lecturer and head of the Ph.D. development finance program at the University of Stellenbosch Business School where he teaches project finance and infrastructure finance. Dr. Fanta's research interests include financial development, infrastructure finance and small business finance, among others. Dr. Fanta holds a doctoral degree in Corporate Finance from Johannes Kepler University of Linz, Austria, and a Master's degree in accounting and finance from Addis Ababa University, Ethiopia.

Fiador Vera is a Senior Lecturer at the Department of Finance of the University of Ghana Business School. She holds a Ph.D. in Finance from the Graduate School of Business, University of Cape Town, South Africa. She has expertise in corporate finance, corporate governance, gender diversity, enterprise risk management and environmental and social risk management. She has a number of peer-reviewed publications to her name and has consulted for a number of reputable entities Vera's current consulting portfolio spans business and financial strategy development and interventions. Vera is a member of the African Economic Research Consortium and was a Visiting Scholar at the International Monetary Fund (IMF), Washington, DC.

Gossel Sean J. is an Associate Professor and the Research Director at the University of Cape Town Graduate School of Business. His expertise lies in the areas of financial economics and financial globalisation. His research focuses on the effects of financial globalisation and democratisation on African economies. On the basis of his publications, Gossel is an editorial member of the Journal of African Business, and a peer reviewer for over 30 international journals. He is also a research collaborator at UCT's Institute for Democracy, Citizenship and Public Policy and the UCT GSB's Development Finance Centre.

Graham Michael is a Professor of Finance at the Stellenbosch University Business School, South Africa. He holds a B.Sc. and M.Sc. in Economics from the University of Tampere, Finland, and a Ph.D. in Finance from the University of Vaasa, Finland. Prior to being appointed Professor of Finance at the Business School, Stellenbosch University, he held academic positions at the University of Vaasa, Finland, Deakin University, Australia, RMIT University, Australia, and Stockholm University, Sweden. He has also held visiting positions at academic institutions in Ghana, Hong Kong, Malaysia, and Singapore. Additionally, he was a Research Associate at the United Nations University, World Institute of Development Economics (UNU/WIDER) and a resident finance expert at the Australian Competition and Consumer Commission (ACCC). He is widely published in leading and internationally ranked peer-reviewed journals.

Green Christopher J. is Emeritus Professor of Economics and Finance at Loughborough University. He has a B.A., B.Phil. (Oxford University), M.Sc., M.Phil. and Ph.D. (Yale University). He has worked in the IMF African Department, at Manchester University, the Bank of England and The University of Wales, Cardiff. He was a Professor of Economics and Finance at Loughborough University for 23 years. He held visiting appointments at Yale University and the African Economic Research Consortium; and has acted as consultant to the UN Food and

Agriculture Organisation, the African Development Bank and the African Economic Research Consortium. His research interests are in portfolio analysis, financial markets and company finance in industrial and developing countries, and he has published more than 100 refereed journal articles and books in these areas.

Gyeke-Dako Agyapomaa has a Ph.D. in Economics from the University of Nottingham (UK), M.Sc. in Economics and Financial Economics from the University of Nottingham (UK) and a B.A. in Economics with Geography from the University of Ghana. She is currently a senior lecturer at the University of Ghana Business School.

Prior to her joining the University of Ghana Business School, she worked with Durham Business School (UK) as a Teaching Fellow. She also worked as the Country Programme Manager of the Bloomberg Media Initiative Africa, Financial Journalism Training Programme on part-time.

Her interests are in Micro, Small and Medium Enterprises (MSME) development, Financial Inclusion and Financial Development, Economic Growth and Development, International Capital Flows, Corporate Governance and Gender Diversity.

She has also consulted for a number of organisations She is also an ad hoc reviewer for some journals.

Harvey Simon K. holds a Ph.D. in Economics from the University of Nebraska-Lincoln, USA. He is currently the head of Macroeconomic Modeling and Forecasting Unit of the Research Department of Bank of Ghana. He was a Senior Lecturer at the Department of Finance of the University of Ghana Business School and has held Visiting Scholar position at the International Monetary Fund (IMF).

Ibrahim Abdul-Jalil has over 12 years of varied experience in academic research and financial services. He has worked as a researcher at Hamad Bin Khalifa University and Qatar University, both in Doha. Abdul-Jalil has also consulted for Government of Ghana projects and other international institutions, including the SNV Netherlands Development Organisation. He previously worked with Standard Chartered Bank Ghana and Coface Ghana. Abdul-Jalil has published in reputable international peer-reviewed journals over the past few years in Islamic letter of guarantee, Islamic venture capital, Islamic finance and circular economy and Islamic financial development and energy intensity. Abdul-Jalil is a Ph.D. candidate (finishing in April 2022) in Islamic Finance and Economy at Hamad Bin Khalifa University in Doha, Qatar, where he previously pursued a second Master's degree in Islamic Finance. He earlier received an M.Sc. in Oil and Gas Economics from the University of Dundee, UK. He also received B.Sc. Business Administration (Accounting) from KNUST.

Iddrisu Abdul Ganiyu holds a B.A. in Economics and Mathematics and M.Phil. in Economics, all from the University of Ghana. He was a teaching and research assistant at the University of Ghana Business School. He is currently pursuing a Ph.D. at the University of Aberdeen, UK. Abdul Ganiyu's research interests are in the areas of development economics, energy economics and financial economics. He has worked on issues related to economic growth, human development, political cycles and corruption, among others.

Iddrisu Khadijah holds a B.Sc. in Accounting from the University of Development Studies and an M.Phil. Finance from the University of Professional Studies Accra, Ghana. She is currently a Ph.D. candidate at Simon Diedong Dombo University of Business and Integrated Development Studies Wa-Ghana. Her research interests include sustainable finance, economics, modern banking practices and property tax.

Idun Anthony Adu-Asare holds a Bachelor of Management Studies from the University of Cape Coast, and an M.Phil. and Ph.D. in Finance from the University of Ghana. He is a lecturer in Finance at the Department of Finance, University of Cape Coast. He has been researching issues patterning to the finance-growth nexus and sustainable development, helping to pinpoint areas that financial intermediation should focus on to minimise systemic risk and promote sustainable development. He teaches Finance, Economics and Research at both undergraduate and graduate levels. He has been a reviewer for some academic journals.

Issahaku Haruna is an Associate Professor of Applied Economics and Finance and the Head of the Department of Economics and Entrepreneurship Development, University for Development Studies, Ghana. Haruna is an international Visiting Scholar at Covenant University, Nigeria. He is a development finance and economics expert whose current research focuses on remittances, digital finance, financial inclusion, agricultural finance and economic development. He has several publications to his credit. He is a member of several professional associations, including the Econometric Society, Africa, Finance and Economics

Association and Society for the Study of Emerging Markets. Haruna is a recipient of the 2020 Emerald Literati Awards, Highly Commended Paper category.

Isshaq Zangina is a Senior Lecturer in the Department of Accounting, University of Ghana Business School, where he teaches courses in both accounting and finance. He has Ph.D. (Finance) from The University of Queensland, Australia. His research interests include the role of accounting information in regulation, financial markets and institutions and empirical corporate finance. He was previously a Senior Lecturer at the Department of Finance, School of Business, University of Cape Coast and Head of the Department of Accounting, School of Business, University of Cape Coast.

Karimu Amin is a trained economist with a strong background in energy economics, public finance, econometrics, and development policy. He holds a Ph.D. and an M.Sc. in Economics from Umea University, Sweden, and a bachelor's degree from KNUST, Ghana. He is currently an Associate Professor in Economics at the School of Economics, University of Cape Town. He also regularly visits the Centre for Environmental and Resource Economics (CERE), Umea University, Mistra Centre for Sustainable Markets (MISUM) at Stockholm School of Economics, Sweden. Prof. Karimu has consulted for organisations such as the UN (UNU-WIDER), the International Growth Centre (IGC), Swedish Energy Agency, Sida, GIZ and IDRC.

Kusi Baah Aye holds an M.Phil. in Finance and is currently awaiting the determination of his Ph.D. thesis. Baah is a Chartered Financial Economist and a fellow member of Global Academy of Finance and Management, USA. He lectures at the Department of Applied Finance and Policy management, University of Education Winneba in the fields of corporate finance, financial management, business finance, electronic banking, investment and portfolio management, credit management and elements of banking. He is a research affiliate at the Dean of the University of Ghana Business School office and affiliated to other universities in Ghana.

Kuttu Saint is a Senior Lecturer in Finance and Risk Management at the University of Ghana Business School, University of Ghana, Legon. He holds B.Sc. (Administration) Banking and Finance, M.Sc. Computational Finance and Ph.D. Finance. He has presented and discussed research papers at several international conferences. He has also chaired conference sessions on emerging market finance. He has published in high-ranking international finance journals hosted by Elsevier, Taylor and Francis and Springer. He has held a lectureship (assistant professorship) position at Hanken School of Economics, Finland, and the Ghana Institute of Management and Public Administration (GIMPA). At Hanken School of Economics.

Mathuva David is a Senior Lecturer and Director, Undergraduate Programmes at Strathmore Business School, Kenya. David also serves as the Academic Director for the M.Sc. in Development Finance programme. David has worked at KPMG Kenya. He has published several research articles in peer-reviewed journals such as *Journal of Applied Accounting Research*, *Journal of Accounting in Emerging Economies*, *Journal of Financial Reporting and Accounting*, *Journal of Co-operative Organization and Management* and *Journal of Money Laundering Control* among others. He serves on the Editorial Boards of *Journal of Accounting in Emerging Economies*, *Emerging Markets Case Studies* and the *African Accounting and Finance Journal*.

Mensah Emmanuel is Head of Capital and Balance Sheet Management with the ABSA Bank, Ghana. He holds a Ph.D. in Finance from the University of Ghana, Legon, with strong interest in Banking and Economics. Dr. Mensah teaches Banking and Finance courses at the University of Ghana Business School on part-time basis. His main research interests include Banking Sector Efficiency, Treasury Management and Economic Growth.

Mensah Sam holds M.B.A. and Ph.D. degrees in Finance from the University of Toronto, an M.A. in Economics from the University of Ottawa, M.A. (Political Science), from McMaster University, B.A. (Political Science) from the University of Ghana. He is the founder and Managing Consultant of SEM International Associates, a financial services consulting firm based in Ghana. From 2006 to 2017, he served as Technical Advisor to Ministry of Finance in Ghana where he led key initiatives such as the Financial Sector Strategic Plan and bond market development. He recently completed a five-year term as Chairman of the Ghana Stock Exchange. Dr. Mensah and is an adjunct lecturer at the University of Ghana Business School. Prior to his consulting career, he was Assistant

Professor of Finance at the University of Michigan and has published extensively in peer-reviewed journals.

Misati Roseline works as a Researcher with the Central Bank of Kenya. Her main responsibilities involve analytical and technical analysis of monetary policy and economic and policy research. She has previously worked with different government ministries for over ten years, including Ministries of Finance, National Planning and Agriculture and the Kenya Institute for Public Policy Research and Analysis (KIPPRA). She has also worked as a Senior Researcher at the African Institute for Remittances and as a guest lecturer at the University of Nairobi. Roseline holds a Ph.D. in Economics and has published widely in internationally peer-reviewed journals.

Murinde Victor is the AXA Professor in Global Finance and the Director of the Research Centre for Global Finance, at SOAS University of London. He is a Fellow of the Econometric Society; he is also a Fellow of the Academy of Social Sciences. He has contributed over 100 research papers, mainly in the area of banking and finance. His other roles include Chair of Group C (Finance) for the African Economic Research Consortium (AERC) and Board of Trustees of British Institute in Eastern Africa. He was the founding Director of the African Development Institute, at the African Development Bank, 2011–2014.

Muriu Peter W. holds a Ph.D. in Financial Economics from the University of Birmingham, UK. He is a senior lecturer in monetary and financial economics at the Department of Economics and Development Studies, University of Nairobi. He is a researcher and an external reviewer, finance and resource mobilisation thematic research for the African Economic Research Consortium (AERC). He is also an external reviewer for Oxford Development Studies, Financial Regulation and Compliance and Transnational Corporations Review Journals. As an independent consultant, he has spearheaded various research projects with the aim to ignite new policies on microfinance; financial inclusion; financial stability; banking concentration; provisioning behaviour and risk management in the banking industry.

Mohammed Jabir Ibrahim holds a Ph.D. in Finance, M.Phil. in Finance and Bachelor of Arts in Economics and Political Science all from the University of Ghana. He is a Lecturer at the Department of Banking and Finance, University of Professional Studies Accra and a Consultant with

Corporate Support Group Limited, a management consultancy firm. His areas of interest are Energy Finance, Financial Markets and Institutions, Fintech, Macroeconomics and Financial Economics.

Moleko Nthabiseng is a Development Economist with a Ph.D. in Development Finance from Stellenbosch Business School. She is a faculty member at the University of Stellenbosch Business School where she teaches Economics and Statistics as a Senior Lecturer. She has worked in senior-level roles within economic development prior to becoming an academic. Her core research interests are in the areas of development finance, economic development and growth. Moleko continues to serve as a Commissioner and Deputy Chairperson of the Commission for Gender Equality, board member and Chairperson of the National Empowerment Fund and a Strategic Advisory Committee Member to the Development Bank of Southern Africa's Infrastructure Fund.

Mumuni Zakari is an Assistant Director and Head of the Modelling and Forecasting Office at the Research Department of the Bank of Ghana. Prior to this, Zakari had served as Special Assistant to the Governor and also performed various roles including providing analytical support to the Bank's Monetary Policy Committee. Zakari Mumuni holds a Ph.D. in Economics from the School of Economics, University of Nottingham, UK.

Nellis Joseph G. is a Professor of Global Economy specialising in macroeconomic analysis and policy, business environmental analysis and strategic thinking for managers. He is also Deputy Dean and the longest serving member of Cranfield School of Management's Executive Board. He has previously served as the Director of the School and Pro-Vice-Chancellor of the University. He has held Visiting Professorial appointments at various universities in Germany, Belgium, Austria, The Netherlands, Hungary, the USA and Ghana. Joe has published 19 research and subject-based books and over 200 academic and practitioner journal articles. He is an experienced contributor to a wide range of national and international conferences and is a consultant to organisations in the areas of strategy and business environmental analysis, strategy formulation and management development. He has served two years in Ghana as a VSO teacher and was formerly Chairman of Wellingborough Homes Housing Association.

Ntim Collins G. is a Professor of Accounting at the Centre for Research in Accounting, Accountability and Governance (CRAAG), Department of Accounting, Southampton Business School, University of Southampton, UK. His research focuses on how and why accounting, finance and governance can global development and sustainability, which has attracted competitive external and internal research funds of over £500,000. He has published extensively in the leading international academic journals, as well as taught accounting, finance and governance subjects to a large number of undergraduate, postgraduate, research, especially Ph.D., executive and professional accounting and finance students in a wide variety of institutions and countries around the world. He has also held several academic, leadership and consulting roles in different reputable institutions in the UK and worldwide.

Ntuli Miracle (nee Ntuli) is an Associate Professor in the School of Economics and Finance at the University of the Witwatersrand. Her research interests are in applied micro-econometrics with a special focus on labour and development economics. She has done work on (i) income distribution and the potential of redistributive systems in Africa, (ii) intra-household resource allocation, (iii) gender differentials in health and labour market outcomes, (iv the economics of education, (v) crime and subjective well-being and (vi) multidimensional poverty and spatial heterogeneity in well-being.

Nyeadi Joseph Dery is a senior lecturer and a chartered accountant with the SD-Dombo University of Business and Integrated Development Studies (SDD-UBIDS) in Ghana. Before joining SDD-UBIDS), Joseph worked with Wa Polytechnic and the University of Mines and Technology as a Senior Lecturer. He holds a Ph.D. in Development Finance from the University of Stellenbosch, South Africa, M.Sc. in Finance from the University of St. Andrews, UK and B.Sc. in Land Economy from KNUST. His areas of interest range from Corporate Finance to Corporate Governance in African context. He has published widely in a number of renowned journals.

Ocran Matthew Kofi is a Professor of economics at the department of economics and Deputy Dean for academic planning and assessment at the Faculty of Economics and Management Sciences, University of the

Western Cape, South Africa. His current research interests lie in macroeconomics, development economics, development finance and economic history.

Oduro-Afriyie Emmanuel is a corporate credit manager with Absa Bank Ghana Limited. He holds a Ph.D. in Development Finance from Stellenbosch University in Cape Town—South Africa. His doctoral research focused on monetary policy and the estimation of aggregate and sectoral threshold inflation rates, inflation inertia, expected durations and switching probabilities of inflationary regimes in African economies. Dr. Oduro-Afriyie is a Moody's Certified Commercial Credit Analyst and has presented several of his academic papers at the Centre for the study of African Economies (CSAE) at the University of Oxford, UK, the University of St. Gallen in Switzerland and the University of Cape Town in South Africa as well as at numerous international conferences.

Ofoeda Isaac is a Lecturer in the Department of Accounting at the University of Professional Studies, Accra (UPSA). He holds a Bachelor's degree in Business Administration (Banking and Finance Option), an M.Phil. in Finance and a Ph.D. in Finance from the University of Ghana Business School. He is also a member of the Institute of Chartered Accountants, Ghana (ICAG). He currently coordinates the M.Phil. Finance and M.Sc. Insurance Risk Management programmes at the UPSA. His research focuses on anti-money laundering regulations, financial inclusion, financial sector development, corporate governance, financial markets and institutions regulations and foreign direct investment.

Ofori-Sasu Daniel is an emerging financial economist and a Ph.D. candidate at the University of Ghana Business School. He holds an M.Phil. in Finance and B.Sc. degree in Agricultural economics from the University of Ghana. His research interests include banking, regulation, corporate finance and governance issues, capital structure and investment decisions, dividend policy, financial development, business development, economics, monetary economics and policy, insurance policy, efficiency modelling, sustainability, econometrics and financial analysis. He is currently a lecturer at Central University and an adjunct lecturer at Accra Business School. He is an independent business, financial and economic consultant.

Ojangole Patricia A. is a professional accountant with 17 years' experience in Banking and Finance. She is the Managing Director of Uganda

Development Bank Limited. Prior to becoming the Managing Director, she worked as a Chief Audit Executive at Uganda Development Bank and a Senior Internal Audit Manager at Standard Bank Group. She holds a first-class M.Phil. in Development Finance from the University of Stellenbosch, South Africa, Executive Master's in Business Administration from Eastern and Southern Africa Management Institute, Tanzania; a Bachelor of Commerce (Hons) Degree from Makerere University. She is currently undertaking her Ph.D. studies in development finance at the University of Stellenbosch. Patricia is a Fellow of the Association of the Certified Chartered Accountants (UK); the Certified Public Accountants of Uganda (ICPAU) as well as The Institute of Internal Auditors Uganda (IIA).

Opoku-Afari Maxwell is currently the First Deputy Governor of the Bank of Ghana. He was appointed to this position on August 7, 2017, and was re-appointed for a second term in August 2021. Previously, Maxwell Opoku-Afari worked at the International Monetary Fund (IMF) from December 2009 to July 2017, serving as Deputy Division Chief in the Regional Studies Division in the African Department, where he led and supervised the production of one of the IMF's flagship publication—the Regional Economic Outlook for sub-Saharan Africa. He also served as Mission Chief to both Sao Tome and Principe and Mauritius.

Oppong Kwame A. is the Head of FinTech and Innovation at Bank of Ghana. His background spans management, technology, digital financial services (DFS) operations, policy development and regulation. He has consulted for several governments, public sector institutions, international development organisations and private corporations globally. He holds a B.Sc. in Business Administration, an M.Sc. in Business, Executive Education certification in policy design and other certifications in blockchain, cloud computing, virtualisation and financial inclusion among others. Kwame is a passionate advocate for financial inclusion, innovation and the development of digital economies.

Osei Jephthah O. holds a B.A. Economics and M.Phil. Economics from the University of Ghana. He is the GS-CUPE graduate scholar at York University, Toronto, Ontario, Canada. He has previously worked as a research assistant in the Department of Finance, University of Ghana Business School, and teaching assistant in the Department of Economics, University of Ghana. Jephthah is a graduate teaching assistant in the Department of Economics, York University, Toronto, Canada.

Otchere Isaac is a Professor of Finance at the Sprott School of Business, Carleton University in Canada. He has extensive international research and teaching experience and expertise in corporate finance, financial economics, development finance and banking. He has held Visiting Scholar positions at the University of Dubai, University of Cape Town Graduate, University of Stellenbosch, University of Ghana Business School, GIMPA, and many other universities. Dr. Otchere has published extensively in highly ranked peer review finance journals. He is a Resource Person for the African Economic Research Consortium (AERC) based in Nairobi, Kenya, and a Fellow of the Carnegie African Diaspora Programme based in New York. His scholarship has received international recognition from prominent international financial institutions including the World Bank, IMF/African Institute.

Quartey Peter is a Professor of Economics with more than 18 years expertise, mainly in development finance, private sector development, monetary and financial sector development with senior-level roles at practitioner, policy and consulting services. He holds a Ph.D. in Development Economics from the University of Manchester (UK) and M.Sc. in Quantitative Development Economics from the University of Warwick (UK). He also holds M.Phil. and BA degrees in Economics from the University of Ghana. He is currently the Director of the Institute of Statistical, Social and Economic Research (ISSER), University of Ghana. He has held Visiting Scholar positions at the International Monetary Fund (IMF), Washington DC, USA, and the Brookings Institution, African Growth Centre.

Sa-Aadu Jarjisu is currently Chester A. Phillips Professor of Finance and Real Estate in the Henry B. Tippie College of Business, the University of Iowa, USA. He teaches fixed income securities, real estate finance and investments, international finance, corporate finance and structured finance. He has written extensively on mortgage choice, mortgage pricing, housing vouchers and REITs. His current research focuses on central banks independence, unconventional monetary policy, the geography and distributional consequences of quantitative easing (QE) and of effects of funding liquidity, and market liquidity induced by QE on new residential housing investments.

Salami Iwa is a Reader in Financial Regulation at the School of Business and Law, University of East London (UEL). She is the Co-Director of the UEL Centre of FinTech and the Programme Leader for the LL.M. in FinTech Law. She has published extensively in the field of FinTech regulation and her list of publications includes a book: *Financial Regulation in Africa* (Ashgate, 2012). She is currently researching regulatory frameworks for Web 3.0 application in finance including crypto-assets, stablecoins, decentralised finance (DeFi), Non-fungible tokens (NFTs) and the metaverse; Central Bank Digital Currencies (CBDCs) and legal dimensions of DLT/Blockchain Technology.

Salia Samuel has over 13 years of experience in academia and industry in the UK and internationally. As a Senior Lecturer in Finance, he has extensive teaching and research presence, with publications in high-rated international journals. His areas of expertise are within the dispora and entrepreneurial finance. He has served as a keynote speaker at national and international conferences. He also actively provides consultancy services for international organisations such as the African Union-Economic, Social and Cultural Council.

Sarpong-Kumankoma Emmanuel is a Senior Lecturer in Finance at the University of Ghana Business School. Dr. Sarpong-Kumankoma's research interests include financial regulation, bank performance, corporate governance, financial literacy, financial management, financial market development, microfinance and international finance. He has publications in journals such as *International Journal of Productivity and Performance Management*, *Managerial and Decision Economics*, *Review of Behavioral Finance*, *Journal of Financial Economic Policy*, *Journal of Financial Regulations and Compliance*, *Journal of Economic Studies* and *Journal of Property Research*, among others.

Sheefeni Johannes Peyavali Sheefeni is an associate professor of economics at the Department of Economics, University of the Western Cape. He holds B.Econ., B.EconHons., M.Econ. and Ph.D. in Economics. Johannes also worked at the University of Namibia, Namibia University of Science and Technology, Central Bank of Namibia, commercial banks such as Nedbank Namibia and First National Bank Namibia. His research interests cover Applied Econometrics, Monetary Policy, Macro-econometric Modelling, International Finance and Banking. He has also published in local and international academic journals.

Sissy Aisha Mohammed holds a B.Sc. in Administration and an M.Phil. in Finance, both from the University of Ghana. She was a teaching and research assistant at the University of Ghana Business School and Ashesi University College. She was a Multimedia Broadcast Journalist with the BBC World Service. She is currently a Director of Administration and Human Resource under the Office of the President of Ghana. Her research interests are in the areas of Development Finance, Financial Inclusion and Banking. She has worked on issues related to economic growth, human development, political cycles, corruption, Human rights and Social Justice among others.

Wolfe Simon is a Professor of Banking and Finance. His Ph.D. in Finance is from Southampton University 1997. Professor Wolfe is the Director of the Centre for Digital Finance (CDF) and Director of the Doctor of Business Administration (DBA) Programme within Southampton Business School at the University of Southampton. He has contributed to the financial economics literature, mainly in the areas of banking and finance, development finance and financial market development. Prior to becoming an academic, Professor Wolfe worked in the industry for a number of years. Simon designed and set up the M.Sc. Finance degree Programme. His core teaching interests lie in the areas of international banking and corporate finance.

Yawson Alfred is a professor in corporate finance at the University of Adelaide Business School, Adelaide, Australia.

List of Figures

List of Tables

PART VI

Banking Regulation and Supervision

CHAPTER 18

Risk Management and Compliance in Banking in Africa

Joseph Oscar Akotey, Emmanuel Sarpong-Kumankoma, Kwamina Koranteng Asomaning, and Oluseye Samuel Ajuwon

J. O. Akotey
Kwame Nkrumah University of Science and Technology, Kumasi, Ghana

E. Sarpong-Kumankoma (✉)
University of Ghana Business School, Legon, Accra, Ghana
e-mail: esarpong-kumankoma@ug.edu.gh

O. S. Ajuwon
University of Lagos, Lagos, Nigeria
e-mail: aajuwon@unilag.edu.ng

K. K. Asomaning
Standard Bank, Stanbic Bank Ghana, Accra, Ghana
e-mail: AsomaningK@stanbic.com.gh

J. Y. Abor and C. K. D. Adjasi (eds.), *The Economics of Banking and Finance in Africa*, Palgrave Macmillan Studies in Banking and Financial Institutions, https://doi.org/10.1007/978-3-031-04162-4_18

18.1 Introduction

The financial markets in many countries and across the globe have experienced turbulent moments mainly due to failure to adhere to regulations and internal controls. The collapse of Enron, WorldCom, Auther Anderson, Baring Bank, etc., was due to failure to comply with sound governance structures. Baring Bank—the global second oldest bank and with the Queen as one of its clients—in particular, went down because of the failure of top management to ensure that its employee, Nick Lesson, comply with basic accounting principles, internal controls and audit safeguards. Non-compliance leads to serious financial consequences and "reputational damage that can strategically affect an organisation" (PWC, 2021: 1). For instance, in 2020, some leading global banks were fined US$11.39 billion due to non-compliance with regulations and supervisory requirements (VComply, 2021). In Ghana, failure to comply with compliance structures was the single most destructive weapon that brought down seven (7) universal banks, 23 savings and loans companies, 30 rural and community banks and a staggering 400 microfinance institutions. This crisis had adverse multiplier consequences on many households, business entities and the Ghanaian economy.

Compliance equips financial entities to timely prevent and detect irregularities and illegalities and deal with the same in order to avoid value destruction. The literature shows that certain financial institutions are compliance-reactive while others are proactive (Akotey & Abor, 2013; Dowd et al., 2008) and that proactive compliant firms are resilient and resourceful. Teh (2009) provides evidence that compliance spurs firm's value and Calandro and Flynn (2005) suggest that non-compliance can lead to regulatory risk with consequential effects. Others have, however, argued that compliance has no effect on banks' efficiency (Ayadi et al., 2015). Similarly, Podpiera (2004) reasons that though compliance reduces non-performing loans, it detracts from bank's efficiency by lowering net interest margin.

In this chapter, we delve into the compliance structures of banks in Africa. In particular, we inquire into the link between banks' compliance and risk management and whether compliance has improved banks' value in Africa.

The rest of the chapter covers compliance in banking, management of bank risks through corporate governance, the role of risk management and compliance in micro-prudential oversight, conclusion and recommendations.

18.2 Risk Management and Compliance in Banking

Compliance in Banking

Banking compliance is a water-tight system that ensures that a bank adheres to an approved internal policy designed to guide it to act in accordance with external applicable laws, regulations, supervisory and prudential requirements. Compliance does not only aid a bank to stay abreast in an almost always changing and complex regulatory environment but, most importantly, act proactively to save cost and its integrity. Banking compliance is banking through regulations. It is usually carried out by all employees and customers of the bank under the control and supervision of the Compliance Department (CD). The CD is the police unit of the bank tasked with guiding the bank to keep law and order by being regulatory compliant. It is the quality assurance unit of the bank with the responsibility of facilitating assurance of banking, safeguarding the bank's life (solvency status) and reputation by working within regulations. The CD is also responsible for assisting the bank's customers in interacting with the bank within the law. Thus, any transaction that may cause the bank to be non-compliant must be disclosed and or avoided. For example, the banking law of Ghana restricts lending to one entity, an amount that is not more than 25% of a bank's capital. Thus, a customer wanting a loan of that magnitude must be informed about the law, and the required disclosure and approval must be sought from the regulator.

The responsibilities of the Compliance Department can be summarized under the following: formulate policy to safeguard the bank's data from hacking, virus and theft; protect the bank against sanctions and fines by guiding it to act through and within regulations; avoid tax evasion and money laundering; identify and analyse risk areas; avoid activities that aren't within the bank's ethical policy and loan policy (VComply, 2021).

18.3 Managing Bank Risks Through Corporate Governance

In this section, we discuss the importance and role of corporate governance in managing bank risks. We begin with a brief discussion on traditional and modern approaches to risk management, including Enterprise Risk Management (ERM). This is followed by the theoretical foundation of the concept of corporate governance. The last part of the section focuses on the recent amalgamation of risk and governance to form the new concept of risk governance, and how that can help improve the management of risk in the banking sector.

Traditional and Modern Approaches to Risk Management

Banks face several types of risk in their operations. These include credit risk, interest rate risk, liquidity risk, operational risk, market risk, foreign exchange risk, regulatory risk and fraud risk, among others. Managing these risks has always been challenging and even more so in recent years, following the development of many complex and exotic financial instruments and technologies.

The traditional approach to risk management emphasized managing individual risks identified separately or in "silos". In recognition of the short-sightedness of that approach and its failure to account for the interrelationships among the different kinds of risk facing firms, the concept of ERM was propounded. This has since become quite popular with most large and international firms.

ERM, an enterprise-wide risk management framework, is considered more appropriate than the traditional risk management strategy because of its ability to integrate and coordinate all the risks faced by the firm. However, despite the emergence of ERM and its adoption by several firms, including financial institutions, we continue to observe many corporate failures arising from poor risk management. This underscores the inherent weaknesses in the design and implementation of ERM mechanisms. This could be attributable to the inability to harmonize the approach to risk analysis and corporate governance mechanisms.

Corporate Governance

Corporate governance has attracted greater attention in recent decades following a series of scandals and failures, particularly in the financial sector. Indeed, it is known that weak corporate governance mechanisms and poor supervision and regulation in the banking sector contributed to the global financial crisis in 2007/2008. Corporate governance refers to the arrangements, policies and directives that control and guide the management and operations of a firm. These include setting the strategies and objectives of the firm and assigning responsibilities and lines of authority and accountability.

The Bank for International Settlements (2015) defines corporate governance as "a set of relationships between a company's management, its board, its shareholders and other stakeholders which provides the structure through which the objectives of the company are set, and the means of attaining those objectives and monitoring performance".

Corporate governance also involves catering to the interests and needs of other stakeholders, not just shareholders. These include employees, customers, suppliers, regulators and the community in which the firm operates.

Among the institutions and organizations that have provided widely accepted guidelines for effective corporate governance is the Organisation for Economic Co-operation and Development (OECD). The Principles of Corporate Governance developed by the G20/OECD are aimed at helping policymakers to evaluate and improve the legal, regulatory, and institutional framework for corporate governance to support economic efficiency, sustainable growth and financial stability (OECD, 2015). The principles were originally published in 1999 and have since become the international benchmark for regulators, policymakers, investors, companies and other stakeholders worldwide. The Financial Stability Board and the World Bank have also adopted them as Key Standards for the assessment of governance of Financial Systems (OECD, 2015).

The purpose of corporate governance is to help create an environment that engenders trust, transparency and accountability, in order to promote long-term investment, financial stability and business integrity, thus supporting stronger growth and more inclusive societies (OECD, 2015).

Corporate Governance Theories

One of the principal theories of corporate governance is the agency theory. Agency theory which dates back to Ross (1973) and Jensen and Meckling (1976), highlights the agency problem that arises because ownership of institutions is usually separate from control. Shareholders or principals who are the owners of the firm typically hire managers or agents to take control of the firm. This gives rise to a conflict of interest between the shareholders and managers.

While shareholders expect managers to focus on maximizing their wealth, managers may instead be more concerned about maximizing their own benefits, at the expense of the shareholders. The corporate board structure is the principal means by which shareholders seek to rein in managers by appointing boards of directors to supervise and monitor managers. Boards of directors usually design incentive and compensation schemes that align managers' interests to that of shareholders. This way, managers may be motivated to pursue goals that enhance the benefits of shareholders.

The agency theory framework has been criticized as being parochial in focusing excessively on the interests of shareholders to the disadvantage of other stakeholders, and also for its harmful long-term socio-economic and environmental consequences. Thus, the stakeholders' theory posits that, beyond the interest of shareholders, there are other important groups with a vested interest in corporations, who should not be ignored when crafting the goal of the firm. These groups include employees, suppliers, lenders, regulators, communities, etc. Hence, there is the need to carefully balance the interests of shareholders and the other stakeholders who also contribute to the survival and prosperity of the firm.

Another alternative to the agency theory is the stewardship theory which originated with Davis et al. (1997). This theory considers managers not just as agents for the principals of the firm (shareholders) but also as stewards who aim to faithfully carry out their responsibility of overseeing the interests of shareholders. Thus, managers can be expected to act in the best interests of shareholders instead of pursuing their own selfish interests as suggested by the agency theory.

Impact of Corporate Governance on Bank Risks

Several studies have examined the effect of corporate governance on bank risks. Even so, the results have not always been conclusive. For instance, Fama and Jensen (1983) argue that board independence is required to effectively monitor managers and keep them in check to minimize agency conflicts. This is because executive or inside directors are more likely to be influenced by managers in their decision-making. However, it is also noted that executive directors have more industry, firm-specific and other relevant information than outside or non-executive directors, which can assist the board to make more informed decisions (Harris & Raviv, 2008). Hence, there is the need to have a good blend of both executive and non-executive directors on bank boards. Of course, in order to pursue the overriding role of the board in supervising the activities and decisions of management, and to minimize bank risk-taking, corporate governance directives or codes typically require the majority of bank board members to be non-executive directors and include independent directors. This is the case with the corporate governance directive and code for banks in Ghana and Nigeria, respectively.

Generally, banks have larger boards than the average firm because of their complex organizational structure and the need for several board subcommittees, such as risk, audit and credit committees. However, while some studies suggest that larger boards are more effective in controlling bank risk-taking because of the wide range of perspectives and expertise that come along with larger boards, others argue that extremely large boards may hamper the efficiency and effectiveness of corporate governance mechanisms. Bank risk may decrease as the board gets larger, but if the board becomes too large, it may result in a negative effect on risk-taking due to inefficient monitoring and increased agency conflicts.

In recognition of the need to have a certain minimum number of board members, and to avoid excessively large boards, corporate governance codes for banks usually specify the minimum and maximum number of members for bank boards. For instance, in the case of Ghana, the corporate governance directive for banks specifies a minimum of 5 members and a maximum of 13 for bank boards. For Nigeria, the minimum specified in the corporate governance code for banks is 5 board members, and the maximum is 20 members.

CEO duality, where one person serves as both the CEO and board chairman, is generally considered inappropriate because of the tendency to interfere with the monitoring role of the board, exacerbate agency conflicts, and increase bank risk-taking. Consequently, corporate governance codes require banks to separate the roles of the CEO and the chairman of the board and not allow one person to occupy both positions at the same time. Again, to minimize conflict of interest, some regulators go further to specify that no two related persons or persons from the same family should occupy the position of board chairman and CEO at the same time.

The role of women on boards has been quite controversial. While conventional wisdom suggests that the presence of women on boards should lead to effective monitoring and less risk-taking because women tend to be more meticulous and risk-averse than men, results from some studies show a negative effect of women on bank risk-taking. The latter may be indicative of tokenism, where women are placed on boards for the sake of being women but not necessarily because of expertise (Fiador & Sarpong-Kumankoma, 2021).

The increasing demand for gender diversity in the boardroom may compel some institutions to appoint women who may not have the relevant experience and commitment required for effective monitoring. Also, it may be that the pool of talents from which to select potential female board members, especially in developing countries is rather small. Again, Medland (2004) has noted that the informal social network linking directors consists primarily of men, thereby depriving even qualified women of the opportunity of accessing the corporate boardroom. Moreover, Liu et al. (2014) provide evidence that a critical mass may be needed to have the desired impact of gender diversity. For instance, they found that boards with three or more women have a greater impact on firm performance as opposed to those who had two or fewer women.

This calls into question the argument by some that the inclusion of women on boards should be mandated by legislation as it pertains in some countries. Of course, more research on this issue, especially in developing countries, may help to clarify the implication of gender diversity for bank risk-taking.

Risk Governance

Corporate governance is considered one of the most effective mechanisms that can help address the challenge of managing bank risks. One of the critical roles of corporate governance relates to setting the risk appetite of the bank. This involves determining what types and levels of risk the bank is willing to take or tolerate in pursuit of its strategic objectives and the kind of risk that should be avoided or mitigated. Of course, the nature of the business of banking is such that some measure of risk may be unavoidable if the bank is to maximize the value of its shareholders.

The G20/OECD principles of corporate governance highlight the need to provide financial information on reasonably foreseeable material risks for the benefit of market participants. These include risks that are specific to the industry or the geographical areas where the company operates; its dependence on commodities; market risk (including interest rate or foreign exchange risk); risks arising from derivative contracts and off-balance sheet transactions; business risk; and environmental risk. The principles also include recommendations on providing adequate and comprehensive information to fully advise investors of the material and foreseeable risks of the business. The disclosure should be tailored to the particular company and industry in question, and should also include the system for monitoring and managing risk (OECD, 2015).

In recognition of the complexity and interrelationships among various types of risk and the need for coordination and clarity, a new concept, "risk governance" has recently emerged. The concept has been popularized by the establishment and work of the International Risk Governance Council (IRGC). A White Paper published by IRGC in 2005 was perhaps the first comprehensive scholarly attempt to develop the concept of risk governance. The risk governance framework developed by IRGC has served as the foundation for guidelines and directives issued by many regulatory bodies around the globe, for the management of very complex and ambiguous risks faced by some institutions such as those in the financial sector.

Risk governance is thought of as a more integrative and comprehensive approach to risk management. Risk governance basically involves the linkage between risk management and corporate governance. It seeks to provide a more effective approach to coordinating the processes through which risk is identified, assessed, evaluated, communicated and monitored.

Risk governance is defined by IRGC (2017) in its revised risk governance framework as "the application of the principles of good governance to the identification, assessment, management, evaluation and communication of risks in the context of different stakeholder interests and values". Thus, it involves how critical information on risk is collected, analysed, understood and communicated, and how management decisions are taken and communicated to all relevant parties. The essential principles include transparency, effectiveness and efficiency, accountability, strategic focus, sustainability, equity and fairness, respect for the rule of law and the need for the chosen solution to be politically and legally feasible as well as ethically and publicly acceptable.

The governance of risk is a matter of great concern to regulators. As a result, corporate governance directives issued by central banks usually include specific provisions on the responsibility for risk management in financial institutions. These are in effect, risk governance directives. They provide guidelines on how risk should be viewed in the institution, the process for identifying, analysing and managing risks, as well as the responsibility for risk.

For instance, the 2018 Corporate Governance Directive issued by the Bank of Ghana (BoG) to guide the operations of banks and specialized deposit-taking institutions requires the board of directors to approve and oversee the formulation and implementation of the overall risk strategy of a regulated financial institution, including its risk tolerance/appetite. The board is also responsible for risk policies, risk awareness, risk-taking, risk management and compliance, including anti-money laundering and combating the financing of terrorism (AML/CFT) risk, as well as internal controls system. In addition, financial institutions are required to have at least two board sub-committees, namely, audit committee and risk committee chaired by independent directors (BoG, 2018).

To emphasize the importance of risk management and ensure full implementation of the risk governance directives, the senior management of financial institutions have the responsibility of oversight for the day-day management of risk. They are required to ensure that policies relating to risk management are clearly communicated to all employees and embedded in the culture of the institution. Risk tolerance levels should be communicated as limits to operational management (in the case of quantifiable risks) or as guidelines (in the case of qualitative risk) (BoG, 2018).

Similarly, the Code of Corporate Governance for Banks and Discount Houses in Nigeria requires each bank to have a risk management framework that specifies the governance architecture, policies, procedures and processes for the identification, measurement, monitoring and control of the risks associated with its operations. The board is also given the responsibility for ensuring that the risk management policies of the bank reflect the bank's risk profile and appetite and clearly describe all elements of risk management as well as its internal control system (Central Bank of Nigeria, 2014).

18.4 The Role of Risk Management and Compliance in Micro-Prudential Oversight

Micro-prudential measures centre on ensuring the financial stability of individual banks in order to safeguard the investment of customers and the entire economy. It is a bottom-up approach to financial stability management. It hinges on the biological concept that healthy cell produces healthy organs and healthy body. According to Haan et al. (2019), "Micro-prudential regulation is intended to limit the riskiness of individual institutions". Macro-prudential is however top-down approach that is focused on stabilizing the entire financial system.

Micro and macro-prudential failures can generate systemic shocks and destabilize the entire financial system through what Dill (2020) explains as contagion and interconnectedness of financial institutions, which transmits the failures of one or a handful of entities to their counterparties. Macro-prudential failures almost always lead to a systemic crisis. A financial crisis that does not cause significant disruptions in the real economy is not a systemic risk event (Dill, 2020).

According to Dill (2020), systemic risk may originate from two main transmission points: (1) An external unexpected simultaneous shock to the entire financial system, causing multiple adverse effects throughout the system and drastically disrupting its normal functioning in the transmission of funds and credit extension. "This theory has been called the 'panic view', or more specifically 'illiquidity induced by a contagion of fear" (Dill, 2020: 162). It may occur due to a generalized collapse of bank customers' confidence, a cyberattack on the payments system or a natural catastrophe. (2) Systemic failure may also begin with the failure of a single bank or small group of institutions, which is then transmitted throughout the system through a chain reaction, commonly called the "domino effect". For instance, a single bank with strong interconnectedness to the system can trigger a financial crisis if it experiences significant shocks. Another example is counterparties failures that disrupt the payment system leading to significant increases in settlement risks.

Macro-prudential and micro-prudential measures differ in their coverage and in the skill set pre-requisites for their effective utilization, and the effective use of these tools by bank regulators and other monitory parties involves the availability of adequate information, resources, and qualified personnel. Whereas severe macro-prudential shocks can destabilize the entire financial system, micro-prudential shocks may cause the collapse of the specific banks in question but not the entire financial system. For example, the banking crisis experienced by Ghana in 2017 which led to the folding up of seven banks was due to micro-prudential failures but not macro-prudential shocks.

Micro-prudential regulations can be categorized into the following classes as indicated in Pasiouras et al. (2006) and Klomp and de Haan (2012): activity restrictions, capital regulation, supervisory control, deposit insurance facilities, private sector monitoring, liquidity regulation, and entry regulation. The following discussion covers each category.

Activity restriction is the limitation placed on banks in terms of the financial and investment operations they can engage in. It is a legal requirement that prevents banks from dealing in transactions that can expose customers' deposits to unnecessarily high risks such as investment in junk bonds or lower-grade securities. The theory of activity restriction is as controversial as the inconclusiveness in the empirics. Whereas restricting banking activities reduces diversification (Wagner, 2010) with the possibility of increasing investment concentration which may render banks risky and unstable, opening the floodgates for more activities to allow for increased diversification can also expose banks to severe moral hazards by taking on risky investments (Boyd et al., 1998). Increased activity and diversification across different services can make such banks too powerful to supervise, monitor and discipline (Barth et al., 2004).

The empirical evidence is also non-consensual. Haan et al. (2019) indicate that restricting activities increases individual banks' risk and systemic risk during and after financial crisis. Similarly, Barth et al. (2004) suggest that limiting banks' investment activities is adversely associated with banks' stability, but Demirgüç-Kunt and Detragiache (2011) argue that increased activity in non-core banking operations to raise more non-interest income makes banks unstable.

The effects of the minimum capital requirement on individual bank's risks range from risk reduction through acting as a buffer against loan impairment and bank failure, to the alignment of the interest of equity holders to that of debtholders (Barth et al., 2004; Berger et al., 1995; Dewatripont & Tirole, 1994; Fernandez & González, 2005). However, recent evidence suggests that regulatory capital does not have a strong positive effect on individual bank risk or systemic risk (Haan et al., 2019). Holding bank capital as a buffer can reduce equity returns through a reduction in the equity multiplier, especially if such buffers are held as excess reserves.

Practically, changes in regulatory capital can increase the financing risk of existing banks and compel consolidation in the industry through mergers and acquisitions and the folding up of others. For instance, the 233.33 percentage change in the minimum capital requirement set by the Central Bank of Ghana in 2018 led to the hostile takeover of seven banks and the collapse of several others.

The minimum capital requirement is closely related to the liquid assets that banks are expected to hold in order to meet withdrawals. Liquid assets are vital for equipping a bank to absorb shocks without necessarily re-arranging other parts of its balance sheet. They are insurance against the costs associated with unexpected deposit outflows (Mishkin, 2013). However, liquidity requirement laws can lead to investment herding among banks (Aawaar et al., 2020), a situation that can make the entire financial system susceptible to co-variant risks and lead to fire sales during crisis periods.

Central banks are given powers to supervise and discipline commercial banks in order to minimize the risky behaviours of individual banks and curtail systemic risks and financial crisis. Central banks also conduct a fit and proper person analysis of proposed members of the board of directors and senior managers of banks before such persons are approved. These controls, in addition to the power to take corrective measures such as declaring a bank insolvent and compelling restructuring facilitate a reduction in individual banks' risks. Taking timely actions to restructure distressed banks reduces contagious consequences which could destabilize the entire financial system. Regular and efficient monitoring and supervision enhance financial stability by reducing banks' investment in risky portfolios (Barth et al., 2004). Countries with weak structures for promoting sound accounting and audit standards demand strong central bank supervision to reduce bank risks and financial crisis (Fernandez & González, 2005). Strong supervisory controls can, however, have negative consequences on banks' creativity and product innovation. It is thus not surprising that almost every financial innovation (e.g., mobile money, bitcoin, internet finance, credit and debit cards, etc.) is initiated outside the mainstream banking industry.

Central banks also exert supervisory control on the entry of new banks into the industry. Strict entry regulations can help to eliminate the chaff from the wheat at the gate and thus uphold the soundness of the financial system. However, stringent regulations restricting bank entry may create either a monopolistic or oligopolistic financial structure. According to

Haan et al. (2019) monopolistic financial market is widely diversified but systemically linked and thus vulnerable to systemic linkage failures that can jeopardize the entire financial system. Stringent regulations on bank entry can also reduce industry competition, bank efficiency, technology transfer and, as noted by Boamah et al. (2019), limit proper integration into the global financial system.

Another micro-prudential regulation is the deposit insurance policy which is used to cover the deposits of customers against bank failures by assuring customers of immediate access to their funds. This, according to Helfer (1999), reduces customers incentive to make a "run" for their deposits and thus discourages panic cluster withdrawals from spreading across a financial system which can cause even healthy banks to go down with the distressed ones. Hence deposit insurance schemes can reduce the contagion effect of individual bank failures. The premiums for deposit insurance are usually paid by deposit-taking financial institutions, and its membership is compulsory for depository financial institutions. The core principle of the International Association of Deposit Insurers (IADI) states that "membership in a deposit insurance system should be compulsory for all licensed deposit-taking financial institutions".

However, deposit insurance can generate moral hazard behaviours among banks by incentivizing them to take on risky investments and behave recklessly—without regard to the consequences of their actions. As argued by Helfer (1999), deposit insurance can induce moral hazard by leading financial risk-takers to believe that they will reap the benefits of the risky investments they make while being protected from losses. Such improvident behaviour has the tendency of increasing the possibility of the occurrence of bank failures and systemic crisis. The empirical evidence supports this line of thought that deposit insurance induces bank failures (Barth et al., 2004).

The design of deposit insurance as a safety net can be most effective at limiting moral hazard if the marketplace is permitted to discipline recklessness by letting insolvent banks fail and by imposing costs on those that come close to failing (Helfer, 1999). According to Helfer (1999: 24), "as a rule, the safety net will be a net through which insolvent institutions can fall and not a floor that prevents insolvent institutions from falling far enough to fail".

In Ghana, the law—Ghana Deposit Protection Act, 2016 Act 931—which set up the deposit insurance scheme, protects customers' deposits from loss and promotes the development of a healthy financial system.

In line with IADI standards, its membership is compulsory for banks and specialized deposit-taking financial entities licensed by the central bank (Bank of Ghana). The scheme is financed by compulsory premium payments from members. The premium comprises an initial premium which is zero-point-one percent (0.1%) of the required minimum paid-up capital of each member, and an annual premium determined by the Ghana Deposit Protection Scheme. The annual premium ranges from zero-point-three percent (0.3%) to one-point-five percent (1.5%) of the average deposits insured by the scheme at the end of the preceding year (Act931, 2016). The insurable deposits cover deposits held at the bank or with a specialized deposit-taking institution. In order to prevent conflict of interest, the insurable deposits exclude the deposits of (1) a corporate body that has majority votes of at least 25%, (2) an individual owning at least 5% shares and voting rights of the bank, (3) a director or a member of the management team of the bank (4) an audit firm, a partner of that audit firm and a member of that audit firm who is in charge of performing the external audit of the financial statements of the bank for at least the three years preceding the initiation of official liquidation of the bank (Act931, 2016).

Micro-prudential regulations can also be facilitated by monitoring by private sector actors such as external auditors and rating agencies (Haan et al., 2019). Such external actors help to reduce information opacity and thus improve financial stability. Empirical evidence from Fernandez and González (2005) suggests that private sector monitoring minimizes information asymmetry and moral hazards, which in turn enhances financial sector stability. Some private-sector monitors have, however, been complicit in some financial scandals. For instance, some external auditors have been sanctioned for their commissions and omissions involving some of the banks which failed in Ghana. Haan et al. (2019) suggest that the over-reliance on private sector monitoring may lead to underperforming banks. A report by Barth et al. (2004) implies that private sector monitoring is relatively successful in economies with well-developed capital markets, but jurisdictions with less developed capital markets may not benefit from private sector scrutiny.

18.5 An Overview of Stability of Banks in Africa

The banking industry in Africa has recorded increased market activity in extending access to those who were previously segmented out of the financial system. This has been driven through financial innovations such as mobile money, internet banking, changes in banking regulations and marginal improvement in public infrastructure. However, the sector's efficiency score has declined, and its stability is still fragile (see, e.g., the 2012 and 2020 Global Financial Development Reports). Bank stability is the resilience of an individual bank to withstand systemic shocks. The literature indicates that the z-score is the most significant measure of bank stability (e.g., see Boyd & Runkle, 1993; Demirgüç-Kunt et al., 2008; Čihák & Hesse, 2010). It measures a bank's distance to default by comparing its buffers comprising capitalization and returns with the potential for risk measured by standard deviation or volatility of returns (Čihák et al., 2012). The z-score is calculated as:

$$Z_i = \frac{(k_i + \mu_i)}{\sigma_i}$$

where k_i is equity capital divided by assets, μ_i is return as percent of assets and σ_i is standard deviation of return on assets as a proxy for return volatility (Čihák et al., 2012).

The 2019–2020 World Bank Report on Global Financial Development provides rich and timely information on the banking sector stability within countries and across the globe. In addition to the z-score, it uses other indicators to measure the soundness of the banking sector. These indicators are non-performing loans as a percentage of gross loans, bank capital as a percentage of total assets, regulatory capital as a percentage of risk-weighted assets, bank credit as a percentage of deposits and liquid assets as a percentage of deposit and short-funding. Table 18.1 presents the banking sector stability of the various regions of the globe. It shows that the Sub-Saharan market is below virtually all the other regions. The decline reflects the global trend in financial soundness between 2012 and 2016. The region's stability index has declined from 15.4% in 2010 to 10.4% in 2017.

In order to get a clear picture of the national dynamics, we run another summary statistics for a sample of 15 economies in Africa for the period 2005 to 2017. The 15 economies consist of three (3) countries from

Table 18.1 Bank stability across the various regions, 2015–2017

Bank Z-score						
Region	*Average*	*Median*	*Std dev.*	*Min*	*Max*	*Weighted average world*
	14.2	12.9	8.8	2.8	52.7	20.1
High Income: OECD	15.4	13.4	8.6	3.4	44.1	21.9
High Income: Non-OECD	17.4	16.3	8.7	5.0	43.8	17.5
East Asia and Pacific	12.2	12.8	6.8	2.8	22.7	20.3
Europe and Central Asia	8.8	6.9	5.1	3.0	18.0	6.8
Latin America & CARB	13.9	14.0	7.6	2.8	32.4	16.0
Middle East & North Africa	25.4	20.6	14.1	5.0	52.7	20.7
South Asia	16.0	13.3	7.8	7.1	27.8	15.3
Sub-Saharan Africa	10.4	9.2	5.1	3.0	23.5	13.2

Source World Bank

each of the sub-regions in Africa. The annual mean values are presented in Table 18.2 and the trends are presented in Fig. 18.1.

The results show that banks in North Africa are more stable, with Morocco having the most robust banking sector while those in DR. Congo, Ghana and Botswana are fragile and prone to downturns.

Although the z-score is a very good measure of banks' solvency risk, it is purely based on accounting data. Thus its robustness is based on the relevance and timeliness of the underlying accounting and auditing frameworks. Again, the z-score does not consider the interdependencies of financial institutions within a country. It is therefore not a good measure for systematic risk. Non-performing loan is a better indicator of banks' interdependency and a good pointer of systemic risk. The failure of a customer to honour a debt can create settlement risk and if this is widespread, it can disrupt the payment system, generate systemic risk and financial crisis. Similarly, a bank with a significant level of non-performing loans may default to pay its counterparties. The interconnectedness and interdependences of banks may escalate such defaults into settlement risk and systemic risk. For example, Herstatt Bank of Germany collapsed due to the improper management of settlement risk. Table 18.3 presents the non-performing loans of some African countries. It shows that the

Table 18.2 Summary statistics of bank stability in Africa, 2005–2017

Bank Z-Score

Country	*Sub-region*	*income group*	*Mean*	*Std dev.*	*Min*	*Max*
South Africa	Southern	Upper Middle	13.74	1.35	11.71	16.68
Mauritius	Southern	Upper Middle	15.89	1.85	11.92	19.23
Botswana	Southern	Upper Middle	7.77	1.38	5.37	9.71
Ghana	West	Lower Middle	7.77	0.97	5.78	8.98
Nigeria	West	Lower Middle	16.58	2.19	12.78	20.06
Côte d'Ivoire	West	Lower Middle	17.32	2.47	13.92	21.35
Kenya	East	Lower Middle	17.79	2.20	14.88	21.54
Tanzania	East	Low income	11.03	1.27	9.13	13.05
Rwanda	East	Low income	8.43	1.09	6.42	10.04
Cameroon	Central	Lower Middle	9.65	1.00	8.53	11.69
DR Congo	Central	Low income	4.36	0.58	3.11	5.36
Angola	Central	Lower Middle	11.07	0.94	9.79	12.75
Egypt	North	Lower Middle	17.42	2.78	13.57	20.84
Morocco	North	Lower Middle	39.14	3.88	31.87	44.36
Algeria	North	Upper Middle	16.26	4.80	8.11	21.73

Source World Bank

upper middle-income countries especially those from southern Africa have minimal levels of non-performing loans, an indication of low levels of settlement and systemic risks. However, the other countries in the sample have significant levels of non-performing loans and settlement risks.

18.6 Conclusion and Recommendations

This chapter has delved into compliance and risk management in the business of banking across Africa. It examined how corporate governance structures drive bank compliance and risk management. It also discussed the role of risk management and compliance in micro-prudential oversight. The insight here shows that compliance is extremely vital for the survival of every bank irrespective of its asset size, net worth, customer base, ownership structure, foreign or domestic. Indeed, many banks, both small and big, have failed due to their failure to adhere to compliance measures. The implication of this for the financial sector is this: Comply or fail.

Secondly, the evidence shows that governance is the heartbeat of sound compliance within banking institutions. This suggests that banks with

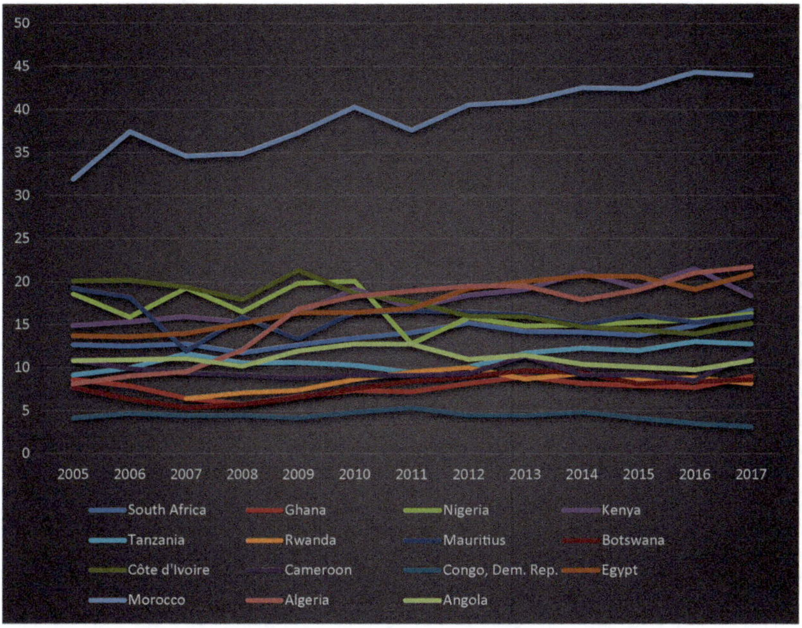

Fig. 18.1 Bank stability in Africa, 2005–2017 (*Source World Bank*)

strong governance structures are most likely to adhere to internal and external compliance structures.

The basic descriptive statistics derived from the 2020 Global Financial Development Database shows marginal improvement in financial depth in the African banking sector. However, the sector's stability and level of efficiency are not just lagging the global average but have even deteriorated. The individual country scores show that the sector in Morocco is the most stable while those in Ghana, Botswana and DR Congo are the weakest. It also shows that southern African countries are better in the management of non-performing loans and settlement risks.

Finally, we have seen that micro-prudential regulation, which includes activity restrictions, capital regulation, supervisory control, deposit insurance facilities, private sector monitoring, liquidity regulation, and entry regulation, may have implications for the stability of individual banks and the entire banking system, through a chain reaction or the domino effect. Even so, micro-prudential oversight must be exercised in a balanced way

Table 18.3 Summary statistics of bank systemic risk in Africa, 2005–2017

Banks' non-performing loans

Country	*Sub-region*	*Income group*	*Mean*	*Std dev.*	*Min*	*Max*
South Africa	Southern	Upper Middle	3.45	1.55	1.10	5.9
Mauritius	Southern	Upper Middle	4.25	2.00	2	7.75
Botswana	Southern	Upper Middle	3.67	0.79	2.62	4.85
Ghana	West	Lower Middle	12.65	3.80	6.4	18.08
Nigeria	West	Lower Middle	10.54	10.21	2.95	37.3
Côte d'Ivoire	West	Lower Middle	N/A	N/A	N/A	N/A
Kenya	East	Lower Middle	7.08	2.22	4.42	10.6
Tanzania	East	Low income	7.63	2.20	5.11	11.52
Rwanda	East	Low income	8.47	4.16	5.10	16.9
Cameroon	Central	Lower Middle	10.43	0.84	9.31	11.55
DR Congo	Central	Low income	N/A	N/A	N/A	N/A
Angola	Central	Lower Middle	N/A	N/A	N/A	N/A
Egypt	North	Lower Middle	13.77	5.73	7.2	26.5
Morocco	North	Lower Middle	7.34	3.47	4.8	15.7
Algeria	North	Upper Middle	13.32	4.30	9.20	21.10

Source *World Bank*

in order to minimize bank risk-taking and also allow for competition, innovation and efficiency in the banking sector.

References

Aawaar, G., Boamah, N. A., & Akotey, J. O. (2020). Investor herd behaviour in Africa's emerging and frontier markets. *International Journal of Financial and Economics Issues, 10*(6), 194–205.

Act 931. (2016). *Ghana Deposit Protection Act, 2016, Act 931.* Parliament of the Republic of Ghana.

Akotey, J. O., & Abor, J. (2013). Risk management in the Ghanaian insurance industry. *Qualitative Research into Financial Markets, 5*(1), 26–42.

Ayadi, R., Naceur, S. B., Casu, B., & Quinn, B. (2015). *Does Basel compliance matter for bank performance?* (IMF Working Paper, WP/15/100). Institute for Capacity Development.

Bank of Ghana. (2018). *Corporate governance directive 2018, Bank of Ghana*. https://www.bog.gov.gh/wp-content/uploads/2019/07/Corporate_Governance

Bank for International Settlements. (2015). *Corporate governance principles for banks*. Bank for International Settlements.

Barth, J., Caprio, G., & Levine, R. (2004). Bank regulation and supervision: What works best? *Journal of Financial Intermediation, 13*(2), 205–248.

Berger, A., Herring, R., & Szego, G. (1995). The role of capital in financial institutions. *Journal of Banking and Finance, 19*, 393–430.

Boamah, N. A., Akotey, J. O., & Aawaar, G. (2019). Economic engagement and within emerging markets integration. *Research in International Business and Finance, 52*(2020), 1–11.

Boyd, J. H., & Runkle, D. E. (1993). Size and performance of banking firms: Testing the predictions of theory. *Journal of Monetary Economics, 31*, 47–67.

Boyd, J., Graham, S., & Hewitt, R. (1998). Bank holding company mergers with nonbank financial firms: Effects on the risk of failure. *Journal of Banking and Finance, 17*, 43–63.

Calandro, J., & Flynn, R. (2005). Premium growth, underwriting return and segment analysis. *Measuring Business Excellence, 9*(4), 27–36.

Central Bank of Nigeria. (2014). *Code of corporate governance for banks and discount houses in Nigeria*. Central Bank of Nigeria. https://www.cbn.gov.ng/out/2014

Čihák, M., Demirgüç-Kunt, A., Feyen, E., & Levine, R. (2012). *Benchmarking financial systems around the world* (Policy Research Working Paper 6175). World Bank.

Čihák, M., & Hesse, H. (2010). Islamic banks and financial stability: An empirical analysis. *Journal of Financial Services Research, 38*(2/3), 95–113.

Davis, J. H., Schoorman, F. D., & Donaldson, L. (1997). Toward a stewardship theory of management. *Academy of Management Review, 22*(1), 20–47.

Demirgüç-Kunt, A., & Detragiache, E. (2011). Basel core principles and bank soundness: Does compliance matter? *Journal of Financial Stability, 7*(4), 179–190.

Demirgüç-Kunt, A., Detragiache, E., & Tressel, T. (2008). Banking on the principles: Compliance with Basel core principles and bank soundness. *Journal of Financial Intermediation, 17*(4), 511–542.

Dewatripont, M., & Tirole, J. (1994). *The prudential regulation of banks*. MIT Press.

Dill, A. (2020). *The role of corporate governance in macro-prudential regulation of systemic risk*. Routledge Publishers.

Dowd, K., Bartlett, D. L., Chaplin, M., Kelliher, P., & O'Brien, C. (2008). Risk management in the UK insurance industry: The changing state of practice. *International Journal of Financial Services Management, 3*(1), 5–23.

Fernandez, A., González, F., & F. (2005). How accounting and auditing systems can counteract risk shifting of safety nets in banking: Some international evidence. *Journal of Financial Stability, 1*, 466–500.

Fama, E., & Jensen, M. (1983). Separation of ownership and control. *Journal of Law and Economics, 26*(2), 301–325.

Fiador, V., & Sarpong-Kumankoma, E. (2021). Does corporate governance explain the quality of bank loan portfolios? Evidence from an emerging economy. *Journal of Financial Economic Policy, 13*(1), 31–44.

Haan, J., Jin, Z., & Zhou, C. (2019, October). *Micro-prudential regulation and banks' systemic risk* (DNB Working Paper No. 656). De Nederlandsche Bank NV.

Harris, M., & Raviv, A. (2008). A theory of board control and size. *Review of Financial Studies, 21*(4), 1797–1832.

Helfer, R. T. (1999). What deposit insurance can and cannot do? *Guest Article. Financial and Development, 36*(1), 1999.

IRGC (2017). *Introduction of the IRGC risk governance framework.* Revised version, IRGC. https://irgc.org/risk-governance/irgc-risk-governance-framework

Jensen, M. C., & Meckling, W. H. (1976). Theory of the firm: Managerial behaviour, agency costs and ownership structure. *Journal of Financial Economics, 3*(4), 305–306.

Klomp, J., & Haan, J. (2012). Banking risk and regulation: Does one size fit all? *Journal of Banking and Finance, 36*(12), 3197–3212.

Liu, Y., Wei, Z., & Xie, F. (2014). Do women directors improve firm performance in China? *Journal of Corporate Finance, 28*, 169–184.

Medland, D. (2004, Winter). *Small steps for womankind.* Corporate Board Member Europe.

Mishkin, F. S. (2013). *The economics of money, banking, and financial markets* (10th ed.). Pearson Publishers.

OECD. (2015). *G20/OECD Principles of corporate governance.* OECD Publishing.https://doi.org/10.1787/9789264236882-en

Pasiouras, F., Gaganis, C., & Zopounidis, C. (2006). The impact of bank regulations, supervision, market structure, and bank characteristics on individual bank ratings: A cross-country analysis. *Review of Quantitative Finance and Accounting, 27*(4), 403–438.

Podpiera, R. (2004). *Does compliance with Basel core principles bring measurable benefits? IMF Working Paper 04/024, 53*(2), 306–326.

PWC. (2021). *Bank regulatory compliance services.* https://www.pwc.com/us/en/industries/financial-services/regulatory-services/bank-regulatory-compliance.html

Ross, S. A. (1973). The economic theory of agency: The principal's problem. *The American Economic Review, 63*(2), 134–139.

Teh, C. T. (2009). *Compliance and impact of corporate governance best practice code on the financial performance of New Zealand listed companies.* Doctor of Business and Administration Thesis. Massey University.

VComply Editorial Team. (2021). *What you need to know about banking compliance*. https://www.v-comply.com/what-you-need-to-know-about-banking-compliance/

Wagner, W. (2010). Diversification at financial institutions and systemic crises. *Journal of Financial Intermediation, 19*(3), 373–386.

CHAPTER 19

Corporate Governance, Regulations and Banking Stability in Africa

Elikplimi Komla Agbloyor, Baah Aye Kusi, Patience Aseweh Abor, and Collins G. Ntim

19.1 Introduction

The financial sector of many economies is heavily scrutinized and regulated, given their ability to destabilize economies as evident from the recent 2007–2009 global financial crisis. Some studies have mentioned weak corporate governance, laxity in supervision, monitoring and regulations as major causes of the recent global financial crisis (Carmassi et al., 2009; Crotty, 2009; Jagannathan et al., 2013; Mazumder & Ahmad, 2010; Poole, 2010a, b). Interestingly, the literature on corporate governance suggests that corporate governance at both firm- and country-levels

E. K. Agbloyor · P. A. Abor
Department of Finance, University of Ghana Business School,
Accra, Ghana
e-mail: ekagbloyor@ug.edu.gh

P. A. Abor
e-mail: pabor@ug.edu.gh

J. Y. Abor and C. K. D. Adjasi (eds.), *The Economics of Banking and Finance in Africa*, Palgrave Macmillan Studies in Banking and Financial Institutions, https://doi.org/10.1007/978-3-031-04162-4_19

promote investor protection and interest, as well as shaping the efficient utilization of resources and maintaining banking stability (Appiah-Kubi et al., 2020a; Globerman et al., 2006; Jones & Pollitt, 2004; Shapiro et al., 2013). Hence, the importance of corporate governance, especially at the country-level cannot be overemphasized although few empirical studies have examined the implications of country-level corporate governance mechanisms in general (see, Appiah-Kubi et al., 2020b; Ernstberger & Gruning, 2013; Hillier et al., 2011; Klapper & Love, 2002; Van Essen et al., 2013), but Africa in particular (Agyemang, Gbettey, et al., 2019a; Agyemang, OSei-Effah, et al., 2019b). In effect, the presence of effective and strong corporate governance can suppress the opportunistic pursuit of corporate insider's interest and serve as a disciplinary measure that guides corporate dealings in order to maximize economic and national outputs, and thereby help reinforce a desirable relationship between regulations and banking stability.

Likewise, financial regulations are instituted to help maintain banking stability and protect the interest of the public. As such, Bouyon (2014a, b) states that regulations and reforms in the financial sector are geared toward the attainment of firm-level banking stability (micro stability) and to reinforce the efficiency of the entire economic system (macro stability). However, existing empirical literature has shown that financial regulations may not always yield or lead to a desired or favorable outcomes of maintaining banking stability and economic efficiency (Allen & Gu, 2018; Hakenes & Schnabel, 2011; Hosono et al., 2004; Uhde & Heimeshoff, 2009). For instance, Hosono et al. (2004) argue that regulations may deprive businesses and institutions of the opportunities of diversifying,

B. A. Kusi (✉)
Department of Applied Finance and Policy Management, University of Education, Winneba, Ghana
e-mail: baahkusi@gmail.com

C. G. Ntim
Department of Accounting, Southampton Business School, University of Southampton, Southampton, UK
e-mail: C.G.Ntim@soton.ac.uk

B. A. Kusi
Department of Finance, University of Ghana Business School, Accra, Ghana

exploiting risky, but profitable opportunities and taking advantage of economies of scale and scope; hence reducing performance and increasing the incidence of institutional instability and failure, especially in the financial sector. Similarly, Hakenes and Schnabel (2011) specifically show that the effect of financial regulation on banking stability is ambiguous and depends on the regulation in question, while Uhde and Heimeshoff (2009) report that financial regulations positively influence banking stability. However, the majority of these studies focused on the effect of capital regulation on banking stability.

Interestingly, Allen and Gu (2018) advance that while macro-prudential regulations represent one of the ways to tame systemic risk and create banking stability, regulatory interventions alone may not be sufficient to create and maintain banking stability. From this, it is clear that for regulations to have a desirable outcome on banking stability, other institutional and corporate governance structures are required to aid effective outcomes of regulation-banking stability nexus. Despite the above assertion, empirical studies on how corporate governance at the country-level help shape the relationship between regulations and banking stability are nonexistent. Hence, this study attempts to present novel evidence on how corporate governance at the country-level influences the relationship between financial sector transparency regulations on banking stability in Africa. Thus, while a number of studies have investigated how corporate governance at the firm-level (see Abdelbadie & Salama, 2019; Anginer et al., 2018; Kusi et al., 2018; Lupu, 2015) and regulations (Edwards, 1996; Goodhart, 2005; Stein, 2012; Ülgen, 2017) individually influence banking stability, very little is known on how country-level corporate governance affect the relationship between financial sector transparency regulations and banking stability, especially in Africa.

Following the literature on financial sector transparency regulations (see Kusi & Opoku-Mensah, 2018; Kusi et al., 2020), the implementation of such regulations may be done with either the private or public sectors leading such initiative. Hence, this study will provide evidence on whether or not financial sector transparency regulation implementation through the private sector is better compared to the public sector as indicated in prior studies (Miller, 2003).

19.2 Overview of Corporate Governance, Financial Sector Transparency Regulation and Banking Stability in Africa

In this section, trends in banking stability, financial sector transparency regulations and corporate governance between 2006 and 2015 are reported and discussed in Table 19.1. Additionally, graphical versions of the figures in Table 19.1 are presented to show the relationships that exist among these variables. Banking stability is measured using z-score, which indicates the distance a firm is away from financial distress, while financial sector transparency regulation is measured using mandatory sharing of bank client information among banks. To measure this, the percentage of adult population who have their credit information with the private information sharing institutions (i.e., private credit bureaus [PrSLFTR]) and the public information sharing institutions (i.e., public credit registries [PuSLFTR]) are used to measure financial sector transparency regulation. With regards to corporate governance, ease of shareholder suit index (ESHS), extent of director liability index (ExD), strength of investor protection (SIP) and extent of business disclosure (ExBD) are obtained

Table 19.1 Trends in banking stability, financial sector transparency regulation and corporate governance in Africa

Years	*Zscore*	*PrSLFTR*	*PuSLFTR*	*CLCG*	*ESHS*	*ExDL*	*ExD*	*SIP*	*ExBD*
2006	13.46	19.70	2.42	7.70	6.44	5.13	5.13	16.69	5.13
2007	13.94	20.24	2.81	7.49	6.21	4.91	5.07	16.18	5.07
2008	13.76	20.05	3.99	7.45	6.33	5.22	4.71	16.32	4.69
2009	14.23	18.21	4.74	7.63	6.29	5.48	4.70	16.52	5.14
2010	14.93	19.45	5.82	7.90	6.28	5.71	5.14	17.19	5.19
2011	14.22	19.16	5.94	7.94	6.26	5.70	5.25	17.27	5.25
2012	14.54	20.30	6.32	8.11	6.57	5.64	5.32	17.60	5.41
2013	14.46	20.91	6.64	8.17	6.64	5.58	5.45	17.74	5.45
2014	14.77	21.06	6.68	8.29	6.73	5.71	5.47	17.99	5.54
2015	15.10	25.86	7.39	8.39	6.87	5.71	5.51	18.13	5.74
Average	14.34	20.50	5.27	7.91	6.46	5.48	5.17	17.16	5.26

Source Graphed by authors based on data from World Development Indicators and Doing Business Databases

Note banking stability (z-score), private sector-led financial transparency regulation (PrSLFTR), public sector-led financial transparency regulation (PuSLFTR), ease of shareholder suit index (ESHS), extent of Disclosure index (ExD), extent of director liability index (ExDL), strength of investor protection (SIP) and extent of business disclosure (ExBD)

from Doing Business database and used as corporate governance variables following prior studies (Appiah-Kubi et al., 2020a; Hillier et al., 2011). Also, the average country-level corporate governance (CLCG) is reported and computed as the yearly average of all the five corporate governance indicators. All the country-level corporate governance indexes are scaled over 10 with the exception of SIP, which is scaled over 25.

From Table 19.1, while the period average banking stability is reported to be 14.34, implying that banking institutions over the 2006–2015 period, are about 14 points away from financial distress, an unstable trend is observed for banking stability over the period. Thus, banking stability is low in Africa given the periods under study.

In terms of financial sector transparency regulation, an average of 20.5 and 5.27% are reported for private and public sector-led financial transparency regulation, respectively. This implies that about 20.5 and 5.27% of adult population have the information captured in private and public sector-led information sharing institutions, which are required by law. Hence, private sector-led financial transparency regulation covers more people compared to the public sector-led financial transparency regulation. However, while public sector-led financial transparency has increased steadily year-on-year, private sector-led financial transparency regulation exhibits frequent fluctuations for the given periods under review. Turning to country-level corporate governance, an overall country-level corporate governance index of 7.91 is reported, while a stable and steady increase in the overall country-level corporate governance index is observed. Specifically, ease of shareholder suit index (ESHS), extent of disclosure index (ExD), extent of director liability index (ExDL), strength of investor protection (SIP) and extent of business disclosure (ExBD) reported period averages of 6.46, 5.48, 5.17, 17.16 and 5.26, respectively. These are indications that country-level corporate governance in Africa is fairly strong over the periods under review.

To fully capture the relationships that exist among the variables of interest on banking stability, Figs. 19.1 and 19.2 are presented to graphically show the relationships that exist among banking stability, financial sector transparency regulations and country-level corporate governance. Specifically, Fig. 19.1 presents the relationships that exist between banking stability and financial sector transparency regulations and banking stability, and country-level corporate governance in Africa between 2006 and 2015. Also, Fig. 19.2 reports on the relationship

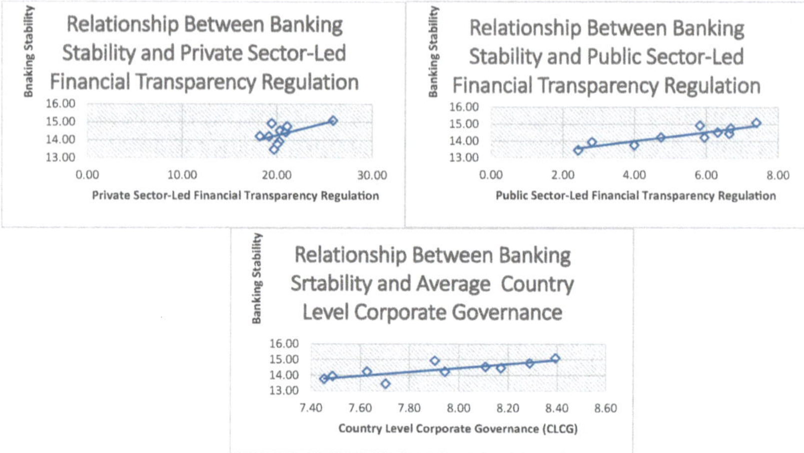

Fig. 19.1 Relationship between banking stability, financial sector transparency regulations and country-level corporate governance (*Source* Graphed by authors based on data from World Development Indicators and Doing Business Databases)

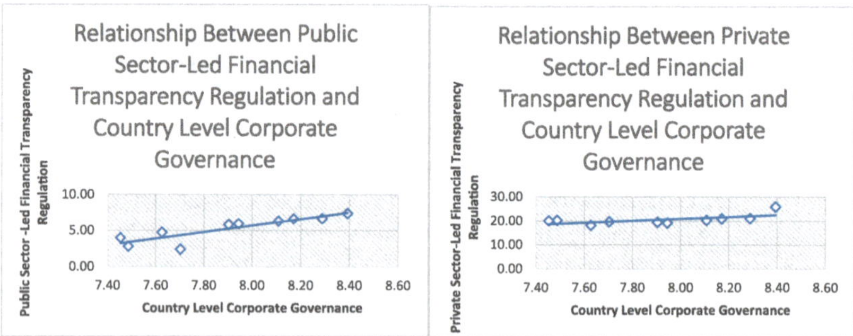

Fig. 19.2 Relationship between financial sector transparency regulations and country-level corporate governance (*Source* Graphed by authors based on data from World Development Indicators and Doing Business Databases)

between financial sector transparency regulations and corporate governance in Africa. From Fig. 19.1, it is observed that the relationship between banking stability and financial sector transparency regulations is a direct relationship, implying that improvements in financial sector transparency regulation positively correlate with banking stability. Similarly, a positive relationship is observed between banking stability and corporate governance at the country-level in Fig. 19.1. Likewise, Fig. 19.2 exhibits a positive relationship between country-level corporate governance and financial sector transparency regulations, implying the improvements in corporate governance may directly correlate with improvement in financial sector transparency regulation. From these graphs, it is evident that both corporate governance and financial sector transparency regulations have a positive association with banking stability, while financial sector transparency regulations are positively associated with corporate governance at the country-level.

19.3 Literature Review: Theory, Empirics and Hypothesis Development

This study draws inspiration from institutional theory. Zucker (1987) advances that institutional theory focuses on the role of social, political and economic systems in which companies operate and gain their legitimacy. It is argued that institutions provide rules of the game and define the appropriate ways to operate by discouraging, constraining or encouraging acceptable behavior (Peters, 2000). Scott (2005) indicates that institutions influence the decision-making process by giving an indication of what is acceptable or not. Hence, corporate governance which defines the framework for corporate dealings and protect the interest of investors and the public at large fall under institutional theory. Interestingly, Scott (2005) suggests that the pillars on which institutions function include normative, cognitive and regulative pillars. Focusing on the regulatory pillar of institutions, it can be argued that institutions under the neo-institutional theory have the responsibility of designing and enforcing rules and regulations in a given society. Following the literature on regulations, the public interest theory of regulation and private interest theory of regulations are the two main theories that explain regulations (Gaffikin, 2005; Hertog, 2012). While the public interest theory of regulations advances that regulations seek to protect and benefit the public at large in terms of the best possible allocation of scarce resources for collective and individual goods (Hantke-Domas, 2007), the private interest theory of regulation argues that regulations promote the interest of dominant individuals and groups in society, but not the public interest (Gaffikin, 2005). From the theory of regulations, it can be inferred that regulations generally improve the interest of the entire society or that of some individuals' or groups' interests. Thus, a number of studies (Avgouleas, 2009; Leuz & Wysocki, 2016; Tadesse, 2006) report that regulations have both economic and financial implications. Also, although regulations may not always yield a desired outcome, strong and effective institutions through corporate governance can enhance how effective financial regulations may influence banking stability. However, this claim remains an assertion which needs to be empirically tested. Specifically, regulations on financial sector transparency aim at reducing the adverse effect of information asymmetry (Freimer & Gordon, 1965; Stiglitz & Weiss, 1981) may better yield desirable outcomes on maintaining banking stability, when corporate governance structures are available and strong.

From an empirical perspective, no study seems to have studied how country-level corporate governance mechanisms influence the relationship between regulations and banking stability. However, while few studies have investigated how institutional quality influences regulations and banking stability, this study takes inspiration from such studies. Additionally, a few studies which are discussed later in this paper show that both country-level corporate governance and disclosure regulations individually influence banking stability and other firms. For the purpose of this study, our empirical literature review focuses first on studies that show the effect of corporate governance on stability. Next, studies on how regulatory disclosure influences banking stability are reported, while studies on how institutional quality affects the relationship between regulatory disclosure and banking stability are also presented.

First, following existing literature on country-level corporate governance and banking stability, Thenmozhi and Narayanan (2016) examine how the rule of law and country-level corporate governance influence the performance of firms post acquisition. Employing a random effect model with year effect controls of 55 acquisitions between 2004 and 2007, their results show that if the rule of law in an emerging market target country is less evolved, but not dismally low, the acquirer from a developed market can gain the opportunity to enforce better discipline at the firm-level in the target firm, and thereby improve post-acquisition performance. However, in the case of emerging market firms' acquisitions, the lower the differencc in country-level corporate governance, the more superior gains are assured. These findings show that country-level corporate governance and rule of law are critical for post-acquisition performance of firms. Similarly, Van Essen et al. (2013) examine corporate governance at the firm- and country-levels on firm performance before and during the 2007–2009 global financial crisis. Employing 1,197 firms across 26 European economies, they show that both country- and firm-level corporate governance promote firm performance in times of crisis. Specifically, firm-level corporate governance, such as chief executive officer duality is associated with better firm performance, while the country-level corporate governance, such as legal systems and creditor rights protection positively affect firm performance, especially during crisis.

Moreover, Mitton (2004) investigates how corporate governance influences dividend payouts using 365 firms across 19 countries. Using fixed effect models, the results show that firms with stronger corporate governance are more profitability. Also, the results report a positive relationship between corporate governance and dividend payouts is limited primarily to countries with strong investor protection, suggesting that firm-level corporate governance and country-level investor protection are complements rather than substitutes. Additionally, Chen et al. (2009) considered how firm- and country-level corporate governance structures interact to influence cost of equity capital in emerging markets. Their results show that firm-level corporate governance reduces cost of equity capital in emerging markets. Additionally, they show that reducing the effect of firm-level corporate governance is more profound in economies with weak country-level corporate governance in the form of legal protection of investors.

In the context of regulated disclosure and banking stability, de Mendonça and de Moraes (2018) relying on the third pillar of Basel Capital Accord, which states that disclosure of information is crucial for banking stability, investigated how central bank transparency through the communication of relevant information by the Brazilian central bank influenced bank financial stability between 1999 and 2014 for 125 banks. Their results suggest that central bank transparency through the communication of expectations regarding credit market improves banking stability, indicating that central bank communications regarding credit development may serve as a good macro-prudential tool for enhancing banking stability. Also, Granja (2018) explored the variations in bank disclosure adoption and supervisory regulation on the development and stability of commercial banks in US. Using a panel of commercial banks in the US, the empirical results show that bank disclosure adoption through local newspapers is associated with improved banking stability and development. Additionally, powerful landowners and small banks were associated with late disclosure adoption regulations.

More so, Akhtaruddin (2005) empirically investigated the extent to which mandatory regulatory disclosure among 94 listed companies in Bangladesh. Their findings show that company specific characteristics is closely associated with mandatory regulatory disclosure. On the whole, they report that companies that have not responded adequately to regulatory requirements disclosed only 44% of the items required to be disclosed. Likewise, Tadesse (2006) exploited the economic consequence of regulated disclosure on banking stability. Using a cross-country panel sample of banks across 49 economies in the 1990s, the results reveal that banking crises are less likely in economies with greater regulated disclosure and transparency. Specifically, banking systems that have more comprehensive disclosure, timely financial reporting, informative reporting and credible financial disclosure are less likely to experience banking crises. Hence, given that banking crises are costly to the entire economy and regulated disclosure reduces banking crises, regulated disclosure has positive economic consequences.

Additionally, Nier (2005) investigated transparency of banking institutions and how it influences the overall stability of banks using 550 banks across 34 economies between 1994 and 2000. Baumann and Baumann and Nier (2004) employed 17 dimensions of accounting reporting disclosures to compute bank-level accounting reporting transparency for listed banks and empirically showed that ex-ante and ex-post effects of transparency on bank stability are positively related. This implies that transparency reduces severe banking problems, and thus improves the overall stability of banks. Finally, Bermpei et al. (2018) examined how institutional quality affects banking regulation and supervision on stability. Employing a panel data of 1,050 commercial banks from 69 developing and emerging economies between 2004 and 2013, their results show that the relationship between banking regulation and supervision on stability largely depends on the level of institutional quality. Specifically, political stability and control of corruption enhance the positive effect of regulation and supervision on banking stability measured with z-score. On the contrary, country-level corporate governance structures, such as creditor rights and rule of law subdue the positive effect of regulations and supervision on banking stability, especially when strong institutions induce loan repayment.

From the theoretical and empirical reviews, it is evident that the relationship between regulations and stability may be influenced by corporate governance structures at the country-level. However, empirical studies to this effect are nonexistent. However, it is worthwhile noting that studies that investigate the individual effects of regulation and corporate governance on banking stability exist. Interestingly, following the literature on regulation, regulated disclosure can be implemented through either the public or private sector. However, the literature is silent on how country-level corporate governance may influence private or public sector-led disclosure (transparency) on banking stability. Furthermore, the existing literature on disclosure or transparency regulations have focused largely on accounting disclosure and transparency. In this study, we attempt to present first time evidence on how private and public sector-led financial transparency and disclosure influence banking stability through corporate governance structures at the country-level.

19.4 Methodology and Data

In this study, the panel data technique is employed to shed insights into the interrelationship between corporate governance and disclosure regulations on banking stability. The data covers 77 banks across 30 economies in Africa between 2006 and 2015. Data used for this study are obtained from three different sources include World Development Indicators, Global Financial Development and World Bank Dong Business databases. Baltagi (2008, 2015) suggests that the panel data technique reports more convincing and conclusive results than the traditional cross sectional and time series data techniques largely because the panel data technique possesses the strengths of both cross sectional and time series and at the same time corrects for the weaknesses. Also, the panel data technique is able to reduce omitted variables compared to the cross-sectional data and captures both time and entity dimensions of variables (Imbens & Wooldridge, 2009), which makes it more robust and preferred. The general panel model is expressed as:

$$Y_{it} = \alpha_i + \pi_j + \gamma_t + \beta X_{it} + \varepsilon_{it} \tag{19.1}$$

$\varepsilon_{it} = \alpha_i + \gamma_t + e_{it} : \alpha_i =$ bank fixed effect $\gamma_t =$ time fixed effect $e_{it} =$ *idiosyncratic term.*

where: subscript 'i' and 'j' denote the cross-sectional dimension of bank and country respectively and runs from 1... N and 't' denotes the time series dimension (time), $t = 1\ldots T$; Υ_{it} is the dependent variable; α_i is a constant term for all periods (t), π_i *is* specific to a country fixed effect (i); γ_t is the time fixed effect t; β *is a k* $\times$ 1 vector of parameters to be estimated on the independent variables for the explanatory variables; X_{it} *is a 1* $\times$ k vector of observations on the independent variables in the model which includes control variables and ε_{it} which is iid is the error term. The study employs Prais-Winsten estimations mainly to correct for autocorrelation and heteroscedasticity. To arrive at this estimation technique, a number of econometric procedures are followed. First, following the Breusch-Pagan lagrangian multiplier test results (Appendix 19.1), there is evidence in favor of estimating generalized least square (GLS) models over ordinary least square (OLS) models. Subsequently, employing the Hausman test (see Appendix 19.2) to choose between the fixed and random effect GLS models, Appendix 19.2 reports result in favor of estimating fixed effect GLS models. However, Appendix 19.3 and 19.4 find evidence of autocorrelation and heteroscedasticity in the fixed effect models and hence models the Prais-Winsten estimation technique to correct the problems of autocorrelation and heteroscedasticity. In modeling banking stability, a number of prior studies (see Beck et al., 2013; Fernández et al., 2016; Ozili, 2018a) are followed. In Eq. 19.2, we estimate the individual effects of disclosure regulation and country-level corporate governance on banking stability while in Eq. 19.3 the interaction effect of disclosure regulation and country-level corporate governance on banking stability. The banking stability equations to be estimated are expressed as follows:

$$\begin{aligned} ZSCORE_{i,t} = {} & \beta_0 + \beta_1 FSTR_{j,t} + \beta_2 CLCG_{j,t} + \beta_3 NIM_{i,t} \\ & + \beta_4 NII_{i,t} + \beta_5 CAP_{i,t} + \beta_6 CI_{i,t} \\ & + \beta_7 HERF_{j,t} + \beta_8 FOREIGNBANK_{j,t} \\ & + \beta_9 SIZE_{i,t} + \beta_{10} GDPC_{j,t} + \beta_{11} LERNER_{i,t} \\ & + \beta_{12} INFLATION_{j,t} + \beta_{13} FINCRISES_t + \varepsilon_{i,t} \end{aligned} \quad (19.2)$$

$$
\begin{aligned}
ZSCORE_{i,t} = {} & \beta_0 + \beta_1 FSTR_{i,t} + \beta_2 CLCG_{i,t} \\
& + \beta_3[FSTR_{i,t} * BCLCG_{i,t}] + \beta_4 NIM_{i,t} \\
& + \beta_5 NII_{i,t} + \beta_6 CAP_{i,t} + \beta_7 CI_{i,t} + \beta_8 HERF_{i,t} \\
& + \beta_9 FOREIGNBANK_{i,t} + \beta_{10} SIZE_{i,t} + \beta_{11} GDPC_{i,t} \\
& + \beta_{12} LERNER_{i,t} + \beta_{13} INFLATION_{i,t} \\
& + \beta_{14} FINCRISES_t + \varepsilon_{i,t}
\end{aligned} \quad (19.3)
$$

To fully capture the effect of firm-level corporate governance on the relationship between disclosure regulations on banking stability, both net and marginal effect approaches are employed following Brambor et al. (2006). In computing the net and marginal effects, the partial derivative of Eqs. 19.2 and 19.3 are taken with respect to disclosure regulations. In the case of net effect Eq. 19.4 is a multiplier with Eq. 19.5 while in the case of marginal effect Eq. 19.5 is used alone. This leads to:

$$\partial ZSCORE_{i,t}/\partial FSTR_{j,t} = \beta_1 \quad (19.4)$$

$$\partial ZSCORE_{i,t}/\partial FSTR_{j,t} = \beta_1 + \beta_3[BCLCG_{j,t}] \quad (19.5)$$

Variable Selection and Justification

Banking stability (ZSCORE) is employed as the dependent variable and computed as a log of capital adequacy ratio plus return on assets all divided by the standard deviation of return on assets (De Nicoló et al., 2006; Ozili, 2018a, b). The resulting value measures how far a bank is away from financial distress and insolvency. Intuitively, Boyd and Runkle (1993) advance that the resulting z-score is interpreted as the number of deviations by which the return of a bank would have to fall from the mean to erode the equity of a bank; hence measuring how stable a bank is from distress.

In measuring financial sector transparency regulation, we follow the prior studies (Kusi et al., 2020) that have employed private bureau and public registry information sharing coverage as transparency variables. This form of transparency in the financial market is backed by law and mandate for all banks to sharing information through information sharing institutions which is led by the private sector (private credit bureaus) and public sector (public credit registries). Ordinarily, improving transparency should lead to improved stability (De Nicoló et al., 2006; Ozili, 2018b). However, following empirical studies that show that financial regulations may not always lead to the desirable outcome of maintaining banking stability and economic efficiency (Allen & Gu, 2018; Hakenes & Schnabel, 2011; Hosono et al., 2004; Uhde & Heimeshoff, 2009), this study argues that the effect of financial sector transparency regulation on banking stability is not straight forward. However, we argue that in the presence of country-level corporate governance, the effect of financial sector transparency regulation may have a more desirable outcome on banking stability. This argument is hinged on prior studies (Bermpei et al., 2018) that show that good institutions and corporate governance strengthens the implementation of regulations to boost banking stability.

Country-level corporate governance indicators are obtained from World Bank Doing Business data. Following prior studies (Appiah-Kubi et al., 2020a; Hillier et al., 2011) five measures which includes ease of shareholder suit index (ESHS), extent of disclosure index (ExD), extent of director liability index (ExDL), strength of investor protection (SIP) and extent of business disclosure (ExBD) are employed as corporate governance indicators at the country-level. The expectation is that corporate governance which is a reflection of good institutional quality Should promote banking stability. Furthermore, we anticipate that corporate governance will positively influence financial sector transparency regulation to promote banking stability.

Net interest margin (NIM) is used as proxy for profitability and measured as the natural log of net interest income. The literature shows that profitable firms have goodwill and improve their corporate image. This induces sustainability and continuity and hence improves the banking stability. Thus, banks that are able to mob up more profits are more financially resilient and stable (Dwumfour, 2017). However, when profits are volatile, it may lead to a decline in banking stability (Islam & Nishiyama, 2016).

Non-interest income (NII) is used as measure of income diversification (Stiroh, 2004a, b). Following the Modern Portfolio theory, diversification is a tool for reducing risk and enhancing banking stability. Hence, one would expect a positive effect of income diversification on banking stability. Bank Capitalization is measured as the natural log of equity and is an indication of a firm's ability to absorb and navigate credit losses. Following the risk-return hypothesis (Berger, 1995), well-capitalized banks have the financial strength to absorb shocks and curtail financial risks to tone down instability. Put differently, well-capitalized banks are able to implement sophisticated risk management strategies to ensure banking stability (Beck et al., 2013).

Bank cost efficiency (CI) is measured as operational cost to operating income and indicates how well a bank is able to manage its cost incurred in relation to its income generated (see Athanasoglou et al., 2008). Hence, higher value of Cost-Income ratio is an indication of poor cost management and thus reduces banking stability. That is the ability to control cost leads to minimization of wastage and risks which translate into improved banking stability (Mensah et al., 2019). Herfindahl-Hirschman is used to compute the concentration of bank loans to show the market structure of banking. Following the concentration-fragility hypothesis, a negative relationship is expected between concentration and banking stability. Thus, concentration is characterized with credit rationing, inefficiencies, credit losses and high interest charges (Kasman & Kasman, 2015), which translates into weakening banking stability (see Schaeck & Čihák, 2010; Turk-Ariss, 2010).

Drawing from past literature, foreign banks are argued to influence banking performance and subsequently banking stability. Foreign banks' presence is measured as the ratio of all foreign banks to total banks in an economy. The presence of foreign banks brings new technologies and financial products and services. These provide a wide range of financial services which deepens the depth and breadth of financial systems and therefore contributes to a more stable financial system (Boateng et al., 2015; Pasiouras & Kosmidou, 2007). Bank size is computed as the natural log of total assets. Following economies and diseconomies of scale, size have both positive and negative effects on banking stability (Mensah et al., 2019). Specifically, economies of scale advance that there are efficiency gains associated with size which promotes banking stability. On the contrary, diseconomies of scale states that large-sized firms have poor supervision and monitoring, duplication of functions and resource and delays in decision-making. These large-sized firm features translate into reduced banking stability. Hence, the relationship between size and banking stability is not straight forward.

Gross domestic product per capita is used as a proxy for standard of living and measures the income attributed to each citizen in an economy (Jimenez et al., 2009). Improvement in gross domestic product per capita implies the ability to settle loans leading to lower credit losses, defaults and banking risks. Hence, a positive relation is expected between gross domestic product per capita and banking stability. Lerner index measured as output price less marginal cost scaled over price is employed to capture the market power of banks (Beck et al., 2013; Carbo et al., 2009). It reflects the extent to which banks are able to price their outputs above the marginal cost hence making them price setters (Tan, 2016). We argue that higher bank market power improves banking stability because ability to price output above the marginal cost leads to higher banking profitability and stability.

Inflation is measured using the consumer price index and measures economic stability (see Castro, 2012). Following empirical literature, both positive and negative effects of inflation on stability is possible. Thus, inflation weakens the ability of bank clients to pay their loans which can lead to worsening financial position of banks (see Castro, 2012) and increase credit losses and defaults to reduce banking stability. However, if banks are able to anticipate inflation changes and factor it to their loan prices, it may improve the banking stability of banks. Hence, the relationship between inflation and banking stability is not straightforward. Financial crises captured as a dummy using the 2007–2009 global financial crises is expected to reduce banking stability given the crises increase the banking distress by increase panic withdrawals and fueling mistrust between banks and their clients. However, in a prolonged financial crisis such as the 2007–2009 crises, regulators may implement crises correcting measures which can lead to crises having a positive effect on banking stability. Following Cubillas and Suarez (2013; 2018), crises induce restructuring (i.e., shutdown, mergers, and acquisition of failed banks) which eliminates weak banks, leaving behind strong and stability banks and hence a positive relationship between crises and banking stability can be expected.

A summary of all the variables is reported in Appendix 19.5.

19.5 Empirical Results and Discussions

In the summary statistics table (Appendix 19.6), outliers which have the potential to adversely influence the consistency, accuracy and efficiency of the coefficients are not detected and observed in the data. Employing Pearson's correlation to detect multicollinearity (see Appendix 19.7), we find no evidence of multicollinearity with the independent variables when we set the multicollinearity threshold to 0.5 following York (2012) and Wichers (1975). Similarly, from Appendix 19.6, the variance inflation factor (VIF) which indicates the acceptability of each variable shows that all the variables are accepted in the model, given that none of the VIF values exceeded the maximum threshold of 10. Hence, there is no evidence of multicollinearity in our model.

From Tables 19.2–19.6 the main results of this study are reported. In Table 19.2, the overall average country-level corporate governance influences the effect of financial sector transparency regulation led by the private and public sector on banking stability in Africa. Similarly, Table 19.3 and 19.4 report on how different country-level corporate governance mechanisms influence how public sector and private sector-led financial transparency regulations affect banking stability in Africa. Additionally, in Tables 19.5 and 19.6, we report the effect of public and private sector-led transparency regulation on banking stability in economies with strong and weak country-level corporate governance in Africa. Specifically, in Table 19.2 there are eight models (Models 1–8), while Tables 19.3 (9–18) and 19.4 (19–28), there are ten models each. Additionally, Tables 19.5 (29–37) and 19.6 (38–47) report ten models each.

From the results, it is evident that country-level corporate governance mechanisms influence the relationship between financial sector transparency regulations and banking stability in Africa. Initially, we observe that private (Models 1 and 3) and public sector-led transparency (Models 5 and 7) regulations reduce and promote banking stability, respectively. This implies that transparency regulation led by the public sector directly promotes banking stability in Africa on its own while transparency regulation led by the private sector impedes banking stability in Africa on its own. Interestingly, once the interactive term of corporate governance and financial transparency regulation is introduced (Model 2), private sector-led transparency regulation improves banking stability, while public sector-led transparency regulation (Model 6) dampens banking stability. These show how important corporate governance is in shaping banking stability. Similarly, observing the signs of the interactive terms of private sector-led transparency regulation and corporate governance and public sector-led transparency regulation and corporate governance, negative and positive synergies are realized between financial transparency regulation (led by private and public sector) and corporate governance, respectively. These show that while public sector-led financial transparency

Table 19.2 Effect of country-level corporate governance and financial sector transparency regulation on banking stability

Variables	*(1)*	*(2)*	*(3)*	*(4)*
	Private sector-led transparency regulation sample			
PrSLTR	−0.0187***	0.0214***	−0.0091***	0.0112
	(0.0020)	(0.0073)	(0.0026)	(0.0135)
PuSLTR				
clcg	0.0680***	0.0915***		
	(0.0158)	(0.0167)		
PrSLTR*clcg		−0.0038***		
		(0.0007)		
PuSLTR*clcg				
NIM	0.0183	0.0180	−0.0145	−0.0199
	(0.0122)	(0.0121)	(0.0163)	(0.0316)
NII	0.1623*	0.1723*	0.2397**	0.0239
	(0.0971)	(0.0979)	(0.0951)	(0.2732)
CAP	0.8619***	0.8603***	0.9051***	0.7018***
	(0.0278)	(0.0275)	(0.0285)	(0.0629)
CI	−0.0276*	−0.0298*	−0.0965***	0.0176
	(0.0161)	(0.0157)	(0.0216)	(0.0195)
HERF	−0.0868	−0.1091*	−0.2112**	0.0536
	(0.0586)	(0.0580)	(0.0955)	(0.1071)
FOREIGNBANKS	−0.0009	−0.0026*	0.0136***	−0.0056**
	(0.0015)	(0.0016)	(0.0028)	(0.0023)
SIZE	−0.8615***	−0.8605***	−0.8985***	−0.6749***

Variables	*(1)* *Private sector-led transparency regulation sample*	*(2)*	*(3)*	*(4)*
	(0.0278)	(0.0275)	(0.0280)	(0.0751)
GDPC	0.2595**	0.2629***	0.0900	0.3838
	(0.1014)	(0.1007)	(0.1047)	(0.3026)
LERNER	0.6189**	0.5763**	−0.3178	0.1990
	(0.2867)	(0.2939)	(0.3843)	(0.5173)
INFLATION	0.0092**	0.0086**	0.0087	0.0174***
	(0.0036)	(0.0037)	(0.0060)	(0.0058)
FINCRISES	0.0580	0.0786*	0.0196	−0.0622
	(0.0411)	(0.0407)	(0.0611)	(0.0683)
Constant	2.9212***	2.8159***	3.3047***	3.2379***
	(0.2362)	(0.2294)	(0.2100)	(0.4010)
Observations	339	339	229	112
R-squared	0.8976	0.9056	0.9207	0.9220
No. of banks	76	76	52	36
Net Effect		**−0.0087****		
Variables	*(5)* *Public sector-led transparency regulation sample*	*(6)*	*(7)*	*(8)*
PrSLTR				
PuSLTR	0.0046*	−0.1135***	0.0062***	−0.0654***
	(0.0027)	(0.0129)	(0.0023)	(0.0129)
clcg	−0.0178	−0.0842***		
	(0.0173)	(0.0179)		

(continued)

Table 19.2 (continued)

Variables	*(5)*	*(6)*	*(7)*	*(8)*
	Public sector-led transparency regulation sample			
PrSLTR*clcg				
PuSLTR*clcg		0.0109***		
		(0.0012)		
NIM	0.0101	−0.0200	−0.0256*	−0.0294
	(0.0138)	(0.0153)	(0.0144)	(0.0242)
NII	0.1856*	0.2241**	0.2526***	0.3061
	(0.1043)	(0.1010)	(0.0977)	(0.2268)
CAP	0.8545***	0.8623***	0.9023***	0.7360***
	(0.0297)	(0.0290)	(0.0296)	(0.0543)
CI	−0.0363**	−0.0512**	−0.0916***	−0.0554
	(0.0177)	(0.0200)	(0.0216)	(0.0348)
HERF	−0.0851	−0.1299**	−0.2289**	−0.0585
	(0.0680)	(0.0654)	(0.0975)	(0.1118)
FOREIGNBANKS	0.0064***	0.0036**	0.0203***	−0.0083***
	(0.0016)	(0.0018)	(0.0017)	(0.0022)
SIZE	−0.8413***	−0.8541***	−0.8938***	−0.7699***
	(0.0296)	(0.0290)	(0.0290)	(0.0636)
GDPC	0.3597***	0.3190***	0.1915*	0.2210
	(0.1201)	(0.1086)	(0.1139)	(0.2481)
LERNER	1.9777***	1.7929***	0.1266	0.8165
	(0.3199)	(0.3205)	(0.4214)	(0.5701)
INFLATION	0.0088**	0.0001	0.0075	−0.0017
	(0.0043)	(0.0043)	(0.0068)	(0.0054)
FINCRISES	0.0924**	0.1111**	0.0736	0.0651
	(0.0471)	(0.0440)	(0.0623)	(0.0546)
Constant	2.4221***	3.6132***	2.6083***	4.1667***

Variables	(5) Public sector-led transparency regulation sample	(6)	(7)	(8)
	(0.2931)	(0.3224)	(0.1613)	(0.4389)
Observations	339	339	229	112
R-squared	0.8727	0.8992	0.9208	0.9302
No. of banks	76	76	52	36
Net Effect		**−0.027**.**		

Standard errors in parentheses—Significance Level: ***$p < 0.01$, **$p < 0.05$, *$p < 0.1$

Source Graphed by authors based on data from World Development Indicators and Doing Business Databases

Note banking stability (z-score), private sector-led financial transparency regulation (PrSLFTR), public sector-led financial transparency regulation (PuSLFTR), ease of shareholder suit index (ESHS), extent of Disclosure index (ExD), extent of director liability index (ExDL), strength of investor protection (SIP) and extent of business disclosure (ExBD)

Table 19.3 Effect of public sector-led transparency regulation and corporation governance on banking stability in Africa

Variables	*(9) Public*	*(10) Public*	*(11) Public*	*(12) Public*	*(13) Public*
PuSLTR	−0.0021	−0.0443***	0.0070***	−0.1140***	0.0041
	(0.0023)	(0.0121)	(0.0026)	(0.0170)	(0.0026)
ESHS	0.1494***	0.115***			
	(0.0231)	(0.0249)			
ExDL			−0.0734***	−0.0924***	
			(0.0131)	(0.0134)	
ExD					−0.0150
					(0.0146)
SIP					
ExBD					
PuSLTR*ESHS		0.00455***			
		(0.00128)			
PuSLTR*ExDL				0.0154***	
				(0.0021)	
PuSLTR*ExD					
PuSLTR*SIP					
PuSLTR*ExBuD					
NIM	−0.0287**	−0.0345**	0.0115	−0.0092	0.0080
	(0.0146)	(0.0153)	(0.0135)	(0.0139)	(0.0138)
NII	0.1243	0.130	0.2077**	0.2140**	0.1738*
	(0.0961)	(0.100)	(0.0997)	(0.0950)	(0.1023)
CAP	0.8630***	0.863***	0.8606***	0.8699***	0.8556***
	(0.0286)	(0.0289)	(0.0295)	(0.0289)	(0.0295)
CI	−0.0390**	−0.0422**	−0.0372**	−0.0478***	−0.0366**
	(0.0158)	(0.0165)	(0.0168)	(0.0157)	(0.0174)
HERF	−0.0591	−0.0673	−0.1129*	−0.1253**	−0.0814
	(0.0618)	(0.0616)	(0.0665)	(0.0637)	(0.0669)
FOREIGNBANKS	0.0129***	0.0110***	0.0075***	0.0075***	0.0072***

Variables	(9) Public	(10) Public	(11) Public	(12) Public	(13) Public
	(0.0017)	(0.00190)	(0.0015)	(0.0017)	(0.0016)
SIZE	−0.8544***	−0.851***	−0.8515***	−0.8681***	−0.8420***
	(0.0286)	(0.0288)	(0.0293)	(0.0288)	(0.0294)
GDPC	0.3103***	0.289***	0.2731**	0.3033***	0.3395***
	(0.1151)	(0.112)	(0.1143)	(0.1078)	(0.1186)
LERNER	1.4591***	1.642***	1.2850***	1.2963***	1.9268***
	(0.2763)	(0.290)	(0.3127)	(0.3111)	(0.3128)
INFLATION	0.0061	0.00644*	0.0053	−0.0019	0.0085**
	(0.0039)	(0.00384)	(0.0042)	(0.0039)	(0.0042)
FINCRISES	0.0881**	0.0706	0.0583	0.1294***	0.0861*
	(0.0435)	(0.0435)	(0.0451)	(0.0434)	(0.0471)
Constant	1.4192***	1.751***	2.9443***	3.3746***	2.3633***
	(0.2022)	(0.229)	(0.2227)	(0.2358)	(0.2320)
Obs	341	341	341	341	341
R-squared	0.8875	0.893	0.8860	0.9030	0.8738
Number of banks	77	77	77	77	77
Net Effect		**−0.0146**		**−0.0295**	

Variables	(14) Public	(15) Public	(16) Public	(17) Public	(18) Public
PuSLTR	−0.0722***	0.0044	−0.1116***	0.0043	−0.0893***
	(0.0084)	(0.0027)	(0.0133)	(0.0027)	(0.0091)
ESHS					
ExDL					
ExD	−0.0867***				

(continued)

Table 19.3 (continued)

Variables	*(14) Public*	*(15) Public*	*(16) Public*	*(17) Public*	*(18) Public*
	(0.0168)				
SIP		−0.0060	−0.0363***		
		(0.0083)	(0.0092)		
ExBD				−0.0326*	−0.1093***
				(0.0170)	(0.0157)
PuSLTR*ESHS					
PuSLTR*ExDL					
PuSLTR*ExD	0.0114***				
	(0.0013)				
PuSLTR*SIP			0.0049***		
			(0.0006)		
PuSLTR*ExBuD					0.0141***
					(0.0013)
NIM	−0.0237	0.0096	−0.0165	0.0089	−0.0314**
	(0.0159)	(0.0138)	(0.0152)	(0.0140)	(0.0151)
NII	0.2277**	0.1830*	0.2300**	0.1818*	0.1759*
	(0.1029)	(0.1042)	(0.1022)	(0.1031)	(0.0972)
CAP	0.8577***	0.8546***	0.8608***	0.8554***	0.8636***
	(0.0295)	(0.0297)	(0.0292)	(0.0296)	(0.0281)
CI	−0.0537**	−0.0366**	−0.0519***	−0.0359**	−0.0482**
	(0.0211)	(0.0177)	(0.0200)	(0.0173)	(0.0197)
HERF	−0.1119*	−0.0825	−0.1283*	−0.0899	−0.1283**
	(0.0641)	(0.0683)	(0.0662)	(0.0662)	(0.0628)
FOREIGNBANKS	0.0054***	0.0066***	0.0036**	0.0068***	0.0057***
	(0.0020)	(0.0016)	(0.0018)	(0.0016)	(0.0019)
SIZE	−0.8528***	−0.8411***	−0.8522***	−0.8435***	−0.8537***
	(0.0292)	(0.0296)	(0.0292)	(0.0295)	(0.0280)

Variables	*(14) Public*	*(15) Public*	*(16) Public*	*(17) Public*	*(18) Public*
GDPC	0.3123***	0.3647***	0.3294***	0.3280***	0.2919***
	(0.1075)	(0.1204)	(0.1095)	(0.1178)	(0.1061)
LERNER	1.5642***	2.0146***	1.9299***	1.7954***	1.2234***
	(0.3339)	(0.3156)	(0.3162)	(0.3211)	(0.3254)
INFLATION	−0.0007	0.0089**	0.0004	0.0085**	0.0019
	(0.0043)	(0.0043)	(0.0043)	(0.0042)	(0.0040)
FINCRISES	0.1217***	0.0954**	0.1185***	0.0863*	0.0764*
	(0.0446)	(0.0472)	(0.0446)	(0.0464)	(0.0415)
Constant	3.4235***	2.3624***	3.4831***	2.5335***	3.6924***
	(0.2790)	(0.2927)	(0.3363)	(0.2548)	(0.2603)
Obs	341	339	339	341	341
R-squared	0.8980	0.8723	0.8965	0.8755	0.9072
Number of banks	77	76	76	77	77
Net Effect	**−0.0133**		**−0.0276**		**−0.0153**

Standard errors in parentheses—Significance Level: ***$p < 0.01$, **$p < 0.05$, *$p < 0.1$

Source Graphed by authors based on data from World Development Indicators and Doing Business Databases

Note banking *stability (z-score)*, private sector-led financial transparency regulation (PrSLFTR), public sector-led financial transparency regulation (PuSLFTR), ease of shareholder suit index (ESHS), extent of Disclosure index (ExD), extent of director liability index (ExDL), strength of investor protection (SIP) and extent of business disclosure (ExBD)

Table 19.4 Effect of private sector-led transparency regulation and corporation governance on banking stability in Africa

Variables	*(19)* *Private*	*(20)* *Private*	*(21)* *Private*	*(22)* *Private*	*(23)* *Private*
PrSLTR	−0.0125***	0.0141***	−0.0132***	−0.0142***	−0.0185***
	(0.0017)	(0.0050)	(0.0021)	(0.0029)	(0.0022)
ESHS	0.1122***	0.1291***			
	(0.0222)	(0.0204)			
ExDL			−0.0172	−0.0201	
			(0.0134)	(0.0210)	
ExD					0.0619***
					(0.0160)
SIP					
ExBD					
PrSLTR*ESHS		−0.0035***			
		(0.0006)			
PrSLTR*ExDL				0.0002	
				(0.0005)	
PrSLTR*ExD					
PrSLTR*SIP					
PrSLTR*ExBD					
NIM	−0.0014	0.0013	0.0198	0.0192	0.0238**
	(0.0130)	(0.0125)	(0.0128)	(0.0127)	(0.0121)
NII	0.1661*	0.1837**	0.1876*	0.1870*	0.1593
	(0.0914)	(0.0921)	(0.0958)	(0.0954)	(0.0980)

Variables	*(19)* *Private*	*(20)* *Private*	*(21)* *Private*	*(22)* *Private*	*(23)* *Private*
CAP	0.8672***	0.8654***	0.8641***	0.8649***	0.8608***
	(0.0275)	(0.0274)	(0.0283)	(0.0283)	(0.0279)
CI	−0.0310**	−0.0297**	−0.0309*	−0.0311*	−0.0295*
	(0.0147)	(0.0145)	(0.0169)	(0.0168)	(0.0162)
HERF	−0.0942*	−0.0999*	−0.1130*	−0.1084*	−0.0993*
	(0.0567)	(0.0560)	(0.0605)	(0.0612)	(0.0575)
FOREIGNBANKS	0.0053***	0.0039**	0.0012	0.0015	−0.0006
	(0.0019)	(0.0017)	(0.0018)	(0.0020)	(0.0016)
SIZE	−0.8693***	−0.8686***	−0.8623***	−0.8630***	−0.8597***
	(0.0274)	(0.0273)	(0.0282)	(0.0282)	(0.0279)
GDPC	0.2020**	0.1869*	0.1800*	0.1790*	0.2446**
	(0.1004)	(0.0996)	(0.1020)	(0.1022)	(0.0996)
LERNER	0.1689	0.0335	0.4251	0.4335	0.6341**
	(0.2823)	(0.2820)	(0.2983)	(0.2988)	(0.2861)
INFLATION	0.0065*	0.0064*	0.0060	0.0058	0.0078**
	(0.0035)	(0.0035)	(0.0038)	(0.0038)	(0.0036)
FINCRISES	0.0301	0.0276	0.0231	0.0233	0.0708*
	(0.0395)	(0.0383)	(0.0414)	(0.0416)	(0.0416)
Constant	2.6073***	2.5677***	3.5040***	3.5098***	3.1153***
	(0.2746)	(0.2517)	(0.2208)	(0.2225)	(0.2136)
Observations	341	341	341	341	341
R-squared	0.9099	0.9146	0.8995	0.8991	0.8965

(continued)

Table 19.4 (continued)

Variables	*(19)* *Private*	*(20)* *Private*	*(21)* *Private*	*(22)* *Private*	*(23)* *Private*
Number of bankcode	77	77	77	77	77
Net Effect		**−0.0085**			
	(24)	*(25)*	*(26)*	*(27)*	*(28)*
Variables	*Private*	*Private*	*Private*	*Private*	*Private*
PrSLTR	0.0396***	−0.0182***	0.0175***	−0.0186***	0.0616***
	(0.0136)	(0.0019)	(0.0067)	(0.0023)	(0.0164)
ESHS					
ExDL					
ExD	0.0764***				
	(0.0174)				
SIP		0.0306***	0.0421***		
		(0.0073)	(0.0078)		
ExBD				0.0547***	0.0753***
				(0.0181)	(0.0195)
PrSLTR*ESHS					
PrSLTR*ExDL					
PrSLTR*ExD	−0.0074***				
	(0.0017)				
PrSLTR*SIP			−0.0016***		
			(0.0003)		
PrSLTR*ExBD					−0.0101***
					(0.0021)
NIM	0.0227*	0.0173	0.0176	0.0242**	0.0221*
	(0.0117)	(0.0122)	(0.0121)	(0.0123)	(0.0120)
NII	0.1793*	0.1667*	0.1771*	0.1640*	0.1989**
	(0.0976)	(0.0972)	(0.0983)	(0.0958)	(0.0942)

Variables	*(24) Private*	*(25) Private*	*(26) Private*	*(27) Private*	*(28) Private*
CAP	0.8563***	0.8616***	0.8601***	0.8641***	0.8646***
	(0.0271)	(0.0279)	(0.0277)	(0.0280)	(0.0271)
CI	−0.0293*	−0.0279*	−0.0294*	−0.0285*	−0.0313*
	(0.0161)	(0.0161)	(0.0158)	(0.0168)	(0.0166)
HERF	−0.0766	−0.0867	−0.1091*	−0.0996*	−0.0934
	(0.0564)	(0.0587)	(0.0583)	(0.0590)	(0.0570)
FOREIGNBANKS	−0.0013	−0.0008	−0.0024	−0.0005	−0.0012
	(0.0016)	(0.0015)	(0.0015)	(0.0016)	(0.0016)
SIZE	−0.8587***	−0.8617***	−0.8611***	−0.8619***	−0.8664***
	(0.0272)	(0.0279)	(0.0277)	(0.0280)	(0.0273)
GDPC	0.2528**	0.2613**	0.2653***	0.2089**	0.2081**
	(0.0984)	(0.1021)	(0.1015)	(0.0991)	(0.0977)
LERNER	0.5145*	0.6060**	0.5371*	0.5487*	0.3831
	(0.2848)	(0.2867)	(0.2946)	(0.2883)	(0.2840)
INFLATION	0.0087**	0.0091**	0.0088**	0.0080**	0.0072**
	(0.0037)	(0.0036)	(0.0037)	(0.0036)	(0.0036)
FINCRISES	0.0975**	0.0606	0.0795*	0.0306	0.0595
	(0.0424)	(0.0412)	(0.0408)	(0.0412)	(0.0413)
Constant	3.0729***	2.9291***	2.8180***	3.1989***	3.1606***
	(0.2079)	(0.2396)	(0.2329)	(0.2160)	(0.2098)
Observations	341	339	339	341	341
R-squared	0.9035	0.8976	0.9059	0.8986	0.9062
Number of bankcode	77	76	76	77	77
Net Effect	**0.0014**		**−0.0099**		**0.0086**

Standard errors in parentheses—Significance Level: $^{***}p < 0.01$, $^{**}p < 0.05$, $^{*}p < 0.1$

Source Graphed by authors based on data from World Development Indicators and Doing Business Databases

Note banking ***stability*** *(z-score)*, private sector-led financial transparency regulation (PrSLFTR), public sector-led financial transparency regulation (PuSLFTR), ease of shareholder suit index (ESHS), extent of Disclosure index (ExD), extent of director liability index (ExDL), strength of investor protection (SIP) and extent of business disclosure (ExBD)

Table 19.5 Effect of public sector-led financial transparency regulation on banking stability in strong and weak country-level corporate governance economies

Variables	*(29)*	*(30)*	*(31)*	*(32)*	*(33)*
	Strong country-level corporate governance sample				
PuSLTR	0.0031	0.0052**	0.0082***	0.0061***	0.0081***
	(0.0020)	(0.0026)	(0.0021)	(0.0022)	(0.0021)
nim	−0.0388**	−0.0314**	−0.0159	−0.0375**	−0.0125
	(0.0168)	(0.0157)	(0.0180)	(0.0185)	(0.0182)
nii	0.1051	0.2460**	0.2584**	0.2191**	0.2609**
	(0.1030)	(0.1241)	(0.1184)	(0.1114)	(0.1187)
cap2	0.9189***	0.8984***	0.9205***	0.9414***	0.9244***
	(0.0293)	(0.0325)	(0.0329)	(0.0307)	(0.0329)
ci	−0.0840***	−0.0940***	−0.0817***	−0.0957***	−0.0688**
	(0.0259)	(0.0328)	(0.0252)	(0.0243)	(0.0271)
HERF	−0.1236*	−0.1282	−0.1756*	−0.2701***	−0.1556
	(0.0679)	(0.0932)	(0.1024)	(0.1006)	(0.1035)
Foreignbanks	0.0138***	0.0155***	0.0199***	0.0223***	0.0207***
	(0.0021)	(0.0022)	(0.0033)	(0.0039)	(0.0033)
size	−0.8988***	−0.8937***	−0.9154***	−0.9335***	−0.9204***
	(0.0294)	(0.0326)	(0.0327)	(0.0307)	(0.0327)
gdpc	0.2508**	0.5355***	0.1404	0.1707	0.1157
	(0.1137)	(0.1795)	(0.1219)	(0.1168)	(0.1227)
Lernerindex	1.7299***	1.1632**	0.1933	−0.0348	0.0492
	(0.3346)	(0.4884)	(0.6172)	(0.5722)	(0.6226)
Inflation	0.0028	0.0075	0.0074	0.0089	0.0024
	(0.0038)	(0.0092)	(0.0067)	(0.0067)	(0.0074)

Variables	(29)	(30)	(31)	(32)	(33)
	Strong country-level corporate governance sample				
fincrises	0.1048*	0.1567***	0.0586	0.0541	0.0521
	(0.0540)	(0.0601)	(0.0677)	(0.0640)	(0.0678)
Constant	2.7254***	2.5981***	2.5692***	2.7932***	2.5933***
	(0.1985)	(0.2036)	(0.2118)	(0.2264)	(0.2119)
Observations	247	217	192	185	194
R-squared	0.9121	0.9109	0.9031	0.9058	0.9003
No. of banks	50	53	41	40	41

Variables	(34)	(35)	(36)	(37)	(38)
	Weak country-level corporate governance sample				
PuSLTR	−0.0278***	−0.0696***	−0.0378***	−0.0390***	−0.0390***
	(0.0072)	(0.0139)	(0.0055)	(0.0050)	(0.0056)
nim	−0.0889**	−0.0375	−0.0193	−0.0202	−0.0210
	(0.0370)	(0.0255)	(0.0242)	(0.0250)	(0.0245)
nii	0.3096	0.1932	0.1317	0.1761	0.1174
	(0.2972)	(0.1865)	(0.1646)	(0.1779)	(0.1626)
cap2	0.5290***	0.6320***	0.7805***	0.7464***	0.7804***
	(0.0632)	(0.0738)	(0.0441)	(0.0472)	(0.0441)
ci	−0.0424	−0.0873***	−0.0118	−0.0171	−0.0108
	(0.0313)	(0.0331)	(0.0212)	(0.0262)	(0.0206)
HERF	0.0894	−0.1014	−0.0077	−0.0100	−0.0084
	(0.1203)	(0.1097)	(0.0720)	(0.0889)	(0.0707)
Foreignbanks	0.0059	−0.0059***	−0.0029	−0.0007	−0.0028
	(0.0038)	(0.0019)	(0.0023)	(0.0022)	(0.0025)
size	−0.5385***	−0.6614***	−0.7774***	−0.7365***	−0.7775***
	(0.0687)	(0.0671)	(0.0479)	(0.0513)	(0.0477)

(continued)

Table 19.5 (continued)

Variables	*(34)* *Weak country-level corporate governance sample*	*(35)*	*(36)*	*(37)*	*(38)*
gdpc	0.3914	0.1912	0.1669	0.1598	0.1520
	(0.3130)	(0.1316)	(0.2205)	(0.2380)	(0.2158)
Lernerindex	1.4391**	1.1823***	0.5798	0.9701*	0.4876
	(0.6486)	(0.4569)	(0.4794)	(0.5381)	(0.4710)
Inflation	−0.0100	−0.0093	0.0075	0.0086	0.0074
	(0.0078)	(0.0057)	(0.0054)	(0.0056)	(0.0053)
fincrises	−0.0822	0.1440**	−0.0208	−0.0072	−0.0226
	(0.0773)	(0.0726)	(0.0585)	(0.0632)	(0.0586)
Constant	2.6301***	3.8374***	3.6722***	3.2313***	3.7282***
	(0.3979)	(0.3489)	(0.3638)	(0.3791)	(0.3600)
Observations	94	124	149	156	147
R-squared	0.9235	0.9138	0.9262	0.9214	0.9251
No. of banks	27	35	38	42	36

Standard errors in parentheses—Significance Level: ***$p < 0.01$, **$p < 0.05$, *$p < 0.1$

Source Graphed by authors based on data from World Development Indicators and Doing Business Databases

Note Banking *Stability (z-score)*, private sector-led financial transparency regulation (PrSLFTR), public sector-led financial transparency regulation (PuSLFTR), ease of shareholder suit index (ESHS), extent of Disclosure index (ExD), extent of director liability index (ExDL), strength of investor protection (SIP) and extent of business disclosure (ExBD)

Table 19.6 Effect of private sector-led financial transparency regulation on banking stability in strong and weak country-level corporate governance economies in Africa

	(39)	*(40)*	*(41)*	*(42)*	*(43)*
Variables	*Strong country-level corporate governance sample*				
PrSLTR	−0.0176***	−0.0084**	−0.0092***	−0.0130***	−0.0079***
	(0.0016)	(0.0033)	(0.0028)	(0.0023)	(0.0029)
nim	−0.0242	−0.0246	−0.0109	−0.0295	−0.0091
	(0.0157)	(0.0167)	(0.0182)	(0.0182)	(0.0182)
nii	0.1438	0.2720**	0.2493**	0.2100*	0.2444**
	(0.0915)	(0.1182)	(0.1163)	(0.1105)	(0.1159)
cap2	0.9223***	0.9001***	0.9229***	0.9495***	0.9271***
	(0.0268)	(0.0307)	(0.0323)	(0.0288)	(0.0322)
ci	−0.0814***	−0.1000***	−0.0948***	−0.1017***	−0.0784***
	(0.0210)	(0.0332)	(0.0251)	(0.0220)	(0.0268)
HERF	−0.1200*	−0.1445	−0.1687*	−0.2424**	−0.1450
	(0.0630)	(0.0890)	(0.1013)	(0.1005)	(0.1024)
Foreignbanks	0.0027	0.0109***	0.0150***	0.0091**	0.0159***
	(0.0022)	(0.0036)	(0.0053)	(0.0041)	(0.0055)
size	−0.9141***	−0.8972***	−0.9203***	−0.9457***	−0.9242***
	(0.0269)	(0.0308)	(0.0321)	(0.0290)	(0.0319)
gdpc	0.0476	0.3044*	0.0412	0.0444	0.0329
	(0.0913)	(0.1727)	(0.1125)	(0.1027)	(0.1136)
Lernerindex	0.2709	0.3440	−0.2188	−0.2664	−0.2625
	(0.2826)	(0.5047)	(0.5997)	(0.4745)	(0.6072)
Inflation	0.0023	0.0024	0.0108*	0.0114*	0.0044
	(0.0028)	(0.0080)	(0.0062)	(0.0059)	(0.0069)

(continued)

Table 19.6 (continued)

Variables	*(39)*	*(40)*	*(41)*	*(42)*	*(43)*
	Strong country-level corporate governance sample				
fincrises	0.0146	0.1108*	0.0108	−0.0106	0.0145
	(0.0488)	(0.0584)	(0.0660)	(0.0637)	(0.0659)
Constant	4.1068***	3.3368***	3.2776***	3.8714***	3.2132***
	(0.2140)	(0.3248)	(0.3251)	(0.2698)	(0.3325)
Observations	247	217	192	185	194
R-squared	0.9314	0.9071	0.8849	0.9033	0.8810
No. of banks	50	53	41	40	41

Variables	*(44)*	*(45)*	*(46)*	*(47)*	*(48)*
	Weak country-level corporate governance sample				
PrSLTR	0.0033	−0.0008	0.0294**	0.0421***	0.0299**
	(0.0037)	(0.0114)	(0.0132)	(0.0157)	(0.0140)
nim	−0.0438	−0.0114	0.0626***	0.0671***	0.0632***
	(0.0404)	(0.0278)	(0.0192)	(0.0210)	(0.0196)
nii	0.6063*	0.0602	0.2612	0.3485*	0.2535
	(0.3516)	(0.2264)	(0.1852)	(0.2009)	(0.1848)
cap2	0.5262***	0.6491***	0.7787***	0.7380***	0.7761***
	(0.0664)	(0.0895)	(0.0479)	(0.0534)	(0.0486)
ci	0.0013	−0.0749**	0.0236	0.0328*	0.0221
	(0.0256)	(0.0382)	(0.0181)	(0.0186)	(0.0186)
HERF	0.1617	−0.0910	0.0896	0.1016	0.0818
	(0.1420)	(0.1031)	(0.0937)	(0.0996)	(0.0929)
Foreignbanks	0.0118***	−0.0015	−0.0018	−0.0005	−0.0020
	(0.0039)	(0.0020)	(0.0019)	(0.0020)	(0.0019)
size	−0.5773***	−0.6120***	−0.7914***	−0.7530***	−0.7890***
	(0.0760)	(0.0867)	(0.0515)	(0.0574)	(0.0521)

Variables	(44) Weak country-level corporate governance sample	(45)	(46)	(47)	(48)
gdpc	0.6668*	0.3073*	0.4298	0.4708	0.4145
	(0.3895)	(0.1743)	(0.2659)	(0.2894)	(0.2638)
Lernerindex	0.0296	0.7925	0.1759	0.0887	0.1110
	(0.8313)	(0.5037)	(0.5229)	(0.5683)	(0.5279)
Inflation	0.0168**	0.0060	0.0174***	0.0231***	0.0168***
	(0.0082)	(0.0058)	(0.0057)	(0.0063)	(0.0056)
fincrises	−0.0563	−0.0754	0.0812	0.1050	0.0802
	(0.0884)	(0.0846)	(0.0701)	(0.0783)	(0.0705)
Constant	2.1183***	2.7835***	2.8475***	2.5220***	2.8818***
	(0.5239)	(0.3668)	(0.3380)	(0.3514)	(0.3392)
Observations	94	124	149	156	147
R-squared	0.9041	0.8853	0.9192	0.9061	0.9158
No. of banks	27	35	38	42	36

Standard errors in parentheses—Significance Level: *** $p < 0.01$, ** $p < 0.05$, * $p < 0.1$

Source Graphed by authors based on data from World Development Indicators and Doing Business Databases

Note Banking Stability (z-score), private sector-led financial transparency regulation (PrSLFTR), public sector-led financial transparency regulation (PuSLFTR), ease of shareholder suit index (ESHS), extent of Disclosure index (ExD), extent of director liability index (ExDL), strength of investor protection (SIP) and extent of business disclosure (ExBD)

regulation and corporate governance complement each other to promote stability, private sector-led financial transparency regulation and corporate governance are substitutes in promoting stability and one should be used in place of the other. Additionally, in Models 3, 4, 7 and 8 in able 19.2 where the study splits the sample into economies with strong and weak country-level corporate governance, we find that while public sector-led financial transparency regulation improves and weakens banking stability in African economies with strong country-level corporate governance, respectively, private sector-led transparency weakens banking stability in economies with strong country-level corporate governance structures, but has no significant effect in African economies with weak country-level corporate governance. From these findings, it is clear that corporate governance at the country-level helps shape how financial sector transparency regulations affect banking stability in Africa.

Furthermore, computing the net effect of financial sector transparency regulations through country-level corporate governance (Models 2 and 6), the result reports $-0.0087 = (0.0214 + [-0.0038*7.908])$ and $-0.0273 = (-0.1135 + [0.0109*7.908)$ net effect of private sector and public sector-led financial transparency regulation, respectively. These computed net effects show that corporate governance structures restrict the dampening effect of both private and public sector-led financial transparencies on banking stability in Africa. Similar results are reported in Tables 19.3 and 19.4 when the net effects of financial sector transparency regulation through different country-level corporate governance structures on banking stability in Africa are computed. That is, we observe that while the negative effects of public sector-led financial transparency regulation on banking stability reduces in the presence of country-level corporate governance, the negative effects of private sector-led financial transparency regulation on banking stability also reduces. These provide clear indications that country-level corporate governance tames the negative effects of public and private sector-led financial transparency regulations on banking stability in Africa.

To further our understanding of the relationship between financial sector transparency regulations on banking stability in Africa, we further split our sample into economies with strong and weak country-level corporate governance as observed in Tables 19.5 (Models 29–38) and 19.6 (Models 39–48). Interestingly, we find that economies with strong country-level corporate governance experience negative effects of private sector-led financial transparency regulation on banking stability, while the same economies experience positive effects of public sector-led financial transparency regulation on banking stability. These presuppose that private sector-led financial transparency regulation dampens banking stability in African economies with strong country-level corporate governance structures, while public sector-led financial transparency regulation promotes banking stability in African economies with strong country-level corporate governance structures. On the contrary, in economies with weak country-level corporate governance, public sector-led financial transparency regulation dampens banking stability, while private sector-led financial transparency regulation promotes banking stability in African economies with weak country-level corporate governance structures. Put differently, while we report that public sector-led financial transparency fosters banking stability in economies with strong country-level corporate governance in Africa, private sector-led financial transparency fosters banking stability in economies with weak country-level corporate governance in Africa. These findings demonstrate clearly that country-level corporate governance structures are crucial for promoting the relationship between financial sector transparency regulations and banking stability in Africa and that financial sector transparency regulations may have different outcomes on banking stability depending on the strength of country-level corporate governance. These findings are consistent with studies (see Bermpei et al., 2018) that show that institutions are important in shaping regulations to promote banking stability.

19.6 Conclusions and Recommendations

In this study, we present evidence on how country-level corporate governance structures affect the relationship between financial sector transparency regulations led by the private and public sectors, and banks stability using banks in Africa. This study is motivated by the lack of empirical studies on how corporate governance at country-level influences the relationship between financial disclosure or transparency regulations and banking stability with a specific focus on Africa. Employing a Prais-Winsten panel of over 77 banks across 30 African economies between 2006 and 2015, insightful and interesting findings are reported.

Overall, our results show that corporate governance at the country-level is crucial in shaping how financial sector transparency regulations led by the private and public sector affect stability of banks in Africa. Specifically, we find that financial sector transparency led by the private sector dampens banking stability, while financial sector transparency led by the public sector enhances banking stability. Also, we report a positive synergy between financial sector transparency led by the public sector and corporate governance structures at the country-level on banking stability, while a negative synergy between financial sector transparency led by the private sector and corporate governance structures at the country-level on banking stability. Additionally, employing net effect techniques, the results show that while the negative effect of public sector-led financial transparency regulation on banking stability is dampened when interacted with corporate governance structures at the country-level, we additionally observe that the negative effect of private sector-led financial transparency regulation on banking stability reduces when interacted with different corporate governance structures at the country-level. Splitting our sample into economies with strong and weak country-level corporate governance structures in Africa, we report that public sector-led financial transparency regulation fosters banking stability in economies with strong country-level corporate governance structures in Africa, private sector-led financial transparency fosters banking stability in economies with weak country-level corporate governance mechanisms in Africa.

These findings provide clear indications that country-level corporate governance helps tame the repressing effects of private and public sector-led financial transparency regulations on banking stability in Africa. Thus, regardless of whether financial transparency regulations are led by the private or public sector, strong country-level corporate governance structures are crucial in ensuring financial sector transparency regulations promote banking stability. More so, the findings suggest that economies with strong corporate governance structures enjoy the desired effect of regulations on banking stability in Africa. Hence, building strong corporate governance at the country-level is critical in improving banking stability. Specifically, public sector-led financial transparency regulation yields more desirable effects on banking stability in economies with strong country-level corporate governance structure, while private sector-led financial transparency regulation yields more desirable effects on banking stability in economies with weak country-level corporate governance structures. The later implies that economies must be selective in the implementation, adoption and establishment of financial sector transparency regulations depending on the strength of their country-level corporate governance structures. In terms of future research direction, further studies are required in the area of country-level corporate governance structures and how they are related to other banking sector variables, such as efficiency and profit maximization. Examining how country-level corporate governance structures affect banking stability in transparent economies will be interesting.

Appendix 19.1: Breusch and Pagan Lagrangian Multiplier Test for Random Effects

Test: Var(u) = 0.
chibar2(01) = 495.33.
Prob > chibar2 = 0.0000.

Appendix 19.2: Hausman (1978) Specification Test

	Coef
Chi-square test value	55.6
P-value	0

Appendix 19.3: Modified Wald Test for Groupwise Heteroskedasticity in Fixed Effect Regression Model

H0: sigma(I)^2 = sigma^2 for all i
chi2 (77) = 1.7e + 05.
Prob > chi2 = 0.0000.

Appendix 19.4: Wooldridge Test for Autocorrelation in Panel Data

H0: no first order autocorrelation
F(1, 60) = 4.664.
Prob > F = 0.0348.

Appendix 19.5: Summary of Variables Employed

Variables	*Measurement*	*Source*	*Expected Sign*
Bank Stability (ZSCORE)	capital ratio + return on assets/standard deviations of return on assets	computed by authors based on data from BankScope	
Country-Level Corporate Governance (CLCG)			

(continued)

(continued)

Variables	*Measurement*	*Source*	*Expected Sign*
Ease of Shareholder suits (ESHS)	The ease of shareholder suits index measures how likely plaintiffs are to access internal corporate evidence. It has six components: (i) whether shareholders owning 10% of the company's share capital have the right to inspect the Buyer–Seller transaction documents before filing a suit; (ii) whether shareholders owning 10% of the company's share capital can request that a government inspector investigate the Buyer–Seller transaction without filing a suit; (iii) what range of documents is available to the shareholder plaintiff from the defendant and witnesses during trial; (iv) whether the plaintiff can obtain categories of relevant documents from the defendant without identifying each document specifically; (v) whether the plaintiff can directly examine the defendant and witnesses during trial (0–2) and (vi) whether the standard of proof for civil suits is lower than that for criminal cases	World Bank, Doing Business project (http://www.doingbusiness.org/)	+
extent of Disclosure index (ExD)	extent of disclosure index measures the approval and disclosure requirements of related-party transactions. It has five components: (i) whether it is the managing director alone, the board of directors, or the general meeting of shareholders the corporate body who can provide legally sufficient approval for the transaction (points are assigned depending on whether interested directors are permitted to vote or not); (ii) whether an external body (an independent auditor, for example) must review the transaction before it takes place; (iii) whether disclosure by Mr. James to the board of directors or the supervisory board is required; (iv) whether immediate disclosure of the transaction to the public, the regulator or the shareholders is required and (v) whether disclosure in periodic filings (for example, annual reports) is required	World Bank, Doing Business project (http://www.doingbusiness.org/)	+

(continued)

(continued)

Variables	*Measurement*	*Source*	*Expected Sign*
extent of director liability index (ExDL)	The extent of director liability index measures when board members can be held liable for harm caused by related-party transactions and what sanctions are available. It has seven components: (i) whether shareholders can sue directly or derivatively for the damage the transaction causes to the company; (ii) whether a shareholder plaintiff can hold Mr. James liable for the damage the Buyer–Seller transaction causes to the company; (iii) whether a shareholder plaintiff can hold other executives and directors (the CEO, members of the board of directors or members of the supervisory board) liable for the damage the transaction causes to the company; (iv) whether Mr. James pays damages for the harm caused to the company upon a successful claim by the shareholder plaintiff; (v) whether Mr. James repays profits made from the transaction upon a successful claim by the shareholder plaintiff; (vi) whether Mr. James is disqualified upon a successful claim by the shareholder plaintiff and (vii) whether a court can void the transaction upon a successful claim by a shareholder plaintiff	World Bank, Doing Business project (http://www.doingbusiness.org/)	+
strength of investor protection (SIP)	The strength of investor protection index is the sum of the extent of disclosure index, extent of director liability index and ease of shareholder suits index	World Bank, Doing Business project (http://www.doingbusiness.org/)	+
extent of business disclosure (ExBD)	Disclosure index measures the extent to which investors are protected through disclosure of ownership and financial information. The index ranges from 0 to 10, with higher values indicating more disclosure	World Bank, Doing Business project (http://www.doingbusiness.org/)	+
Profitability (NIM)	Natural log of net interest margins	computed by authors based on data from BankScope	±
Non-Interest Income (NII)	Non-interest income/total income	computed by authors based on data from Bank Scope	+
Capitalization (CAP)	Natural log of total equity	computed by authors based on data from Bank Scope	+

(continued)

(continued)

Variables	*Measurement*	*Source*	*Expected Sign*
Efficiency (CI)	operating expenses/total operating income	computed by authors based on data from BankScope	–
Concentration (HERF)	(GrossLoans/sum(GrossLoans))^2	computed by authors based on data from BankScope	–
Foreign bank	number of foreign banks/total number of banks	Global Financial Development	+
Size	natural log of total assets	computed by authors based on data from data	–/+
Gross Domestic Product per Capita (GDPC)	sum of gross value added by all resident producers in the economy plus any product taxes and minus any subsidies not included in the value of the products/total population	World Development Indicators	+
Lerner Index (Lerner)	(Price – Marginal Cost)/ Price	Global Financial Development	+
Inflation	changes consumer price index	World Development Indicators	–/+
Financial Crises (FINCRISES)	Dummy which assumes a value of 1 for years 2007, 2008 and 2009 and 0 otherwise	Dietrich and Wanzeried, 2011; Goddard, Molyneux and Wilson, 2009	–/+

Appendix 19.6: Descriptive Statistics

Variable	*Obs*	*Mean*	*Std. Dev*	*Min*	*Max*	*VIF*
ZSCORE	945	1.64	1.027	−4.228	4.524	
PRSLTR	777	20.436	25.479	0	66.2	7.56
PUSLTR	777	5.366	13.842	0	82.6	2.31
CLCG	939	7.908	0.236	1.8	11.400	3.70
ESHS	947	6.449	2.138	1	10	1.90
EXDL	947	5.488	2.337	1	9	1.85
EXD	947	5.164	2.312	0	8	1.75
SIP	939	17.148	4.948	4	25	1.91
EXBD	947	5.248	2.244	0	8	2.30
NIM	739	7.587	2.646	−0.511	13.535	3.32
NII	947	39.500	45.9	−3.333	559.4	7.36
CAP	965	6.798	3.103	−2.303	13.827	2.30
CI	939	1.476	8.871	−190.559	129.267	2.95
HERF	968	7.10	21.60	0	1	1.06
FOREIGNBANKS	656	41.419	21.388	0	94	1.74
SIZE	972	8.994	3.178	1.163	17.198	3.07
GDPC	716	6.90	14.1	−53.6	136.00	1.25
LERNERINDEX	634	29.00	10.40	−8.40	58.00	3.27
INFLATION	840	8.221	5.618	−0.25	47.305	1.49
FINCRISES	973	0.307	0.462	0	1	1.24

Standard errors in parentheses—Significance Level: $***p < 0.01$, $**p < 0.05$, $*p < 0.1$
Source Graphed by authors based on data from World Development Indicators and Doing Business Databases

Note financial stability (z-score), private sector-led financial transparency regulation (PrSLFTR), public sector-led financial transparency regulation (PuSLFTR), ease of shareholder suit index (ESHS), extent of Disclosure index (ExD), extent of director liability index (ExDL), strength of investor protection (SIP) and extent of business disclosure (ExBD)

Appendix 19.7: Pairwise Correlations

Variables	*(1)*	*(2)*	*(3)*	*(4)*	*(5)*	*(6)*
(1) ZSCORE	1.000					
(2) PRSLTR	−0.350*	1.000				
(3) PUSLTR	0.059	−0.308*	1.000			
(4) ESHS	−0.021	0.094*	0.226*	1.000		
(5) EXDL	−0.279*	0.456*	0.206*	0.291*	1.000	
(6) EXD	−0.137*	0.664*	−0.050	0.199*	0.398*	1.000
(7) SIP	−0.197*	0.577*	0.166*	0.658*	0.780*	0.748*
(8) EXBD	−0.148*	0.656*	−0.041	0.170*	0.401*	0.973*
(9) NIM1	−0.120*	0.379*	−0.258*	0.279*	0.087*	0.191*
(10) NII	0.094*	−0.315*	0.127*	0.048	0.002	−0.127*
(11) CAP2	0.197*	−0.226*	0.070*	0.219*	−0.061*	−0.042
(12) CI	−0.049	−0.049	0.021	−0.022	0.008	−0.055*
(13) HERF	0.079*	−0.106*	−0.027	−0.117*	−0.080*	−0.079*
(14) FOREIGNBAN	0.234*	−0.508*	0.203*	−0.010	−0.121*	−0.202*
(15) SIZE	0.102*	−0.238*	0.081*	0.233*	−0.039	−0.051
(16) GDPC	0.074*	−0.210*	−0.085*	−0.043	−0.169*	−0.132*
(17) LERNERINDEX	0.311*	−0.754*	0.402*	0.146*	−0.456*	−0.469*
(18) INFLATION	0.095*	−0.243*	−0.271*	−0.116*	−0.165*	−0.225*
(19) FINCRISES	−0.063*	−0.025	−0.068*	−0.053	−0.078*	−0.101*

Variables	*(7)*	*(8)*	*(9)*	*(10)*	*(11)*	*(12)*
(1) ZSCORE						
(2) PRSLTR						
(3) PUSLTR						
(4) ESHS						
(5) EXDL						
(6) EXD						
(7) SIP	1.000					

(continued)

(continued)

Variables	*(7)*	*(8)*	*(9)*	*(10)*	*(11)*	*(12)*
(8) EXBD	0.725*	1.000				
(9) NIM1	0.253*	0.161*	1.000			
(10) NII	−0.042	−0.126*	−0.613*	1.000		
(11) CAP2	0.047	−0.063*	−0.184*	0.615*	1.000	
(12) CI	−0.032	−0.055*	−0.075*	−0.264*	0.084*	1.000
(13) HERF	−0.123*	−0.088*	−0.058	0.045	0.127*	0.072*
(14) FOREIGNBAN	−0.143*	−0.207*	0.041	−0.035	0.041	0.007
(15) SIZE	0.059*	−0.072*	−0.193*	0.629*	0.972*	0.080*
(16) GDPC	−0.168*	−0.149*	−0.086*	0.048	0.030	0.014
(17) LERNERINDEX	−0.388*	−0.466*	−0.258*	0.219*	0.214*	0.015
(18) INFLATION	−0.251*	−0.221*	−0.128*	0.138*	0.113*	0.052
(19) FINCRISES	−0.109*	−0.085*	−0.068*	0.024	−0.025	0.023

Variables	*(13)*	*(14)*	*(15)*	*(16)*	*(17)*	*(18)*	*(19)*
(1) ZSCORE							
(2) PRSLTR							
(3) PUSLTR							
(4) ESHS							
(5) EXDL							
(6) EXD							
(7) SIP							
(8) EXBD							
(9) NIM1							
(10) NII							
(11) CAP2							
(12) CI							
(13) HERF	1.000						

(continued)

(continued)

Variables	*(13)*	*(14)*	*(15)*	*(16)*	*(17)*	*(18)*	*(19)*
(14) FOREIGNBAN	0.061	1.000					
(15) SIZE	0.115*	0.041	1.000				
(16) GDPC	0.023	0.131*	0.028	1.000			
(17) LERNERINDEX	0.031	0.453*	0.217*	0.099*	1.000		
(18) INFLATION	0.052	0.031	0.121*	−0.023	−0.006	1.000	
(19) FINCRISES	0.004	−0.037	0.002	0.030	−0.136*	0.159*	1.000

Standard errors in parentheses Significance Level: $^{***}p < 0.01$, $^{**}p < 0.05$, $^{*}p < 0.1$
Source Graphed by authors based on data from World Development Indicators and Doing Business Databases
Note banking *stability (z-score)*, private sector-led financial transparency regulation (PrSLFTR), public sector-led financial transparency regulation (PuSLFTR), ease of shareholder suit index (ESHS), extent of Disclosure index (ExD), extent of director liability index (ExDL), strength of investor protection (SIP) and extent of business disclosure (ExBD)

References

Abdelbadie, R. A., & Salama, A. (2019). Corporate governance and financial stability in US banks: Do indirect interlocks matter? *Journal of Business Research, 104*, 85–105.

Agyemang, O. S., Gbettey, C., Gatsi, J. G., & Acquah, I. S. K. (2019a). Country-level corporate governance and foreign direct investment in Africa. *Corporate Governance: The International Journal of Business in Society, 19*(5), 1133–1152.

Agyemang, O. S., Osei-Effah, M., Agyei, S. K., & Gatsi, J. G. (2019b). Country-level corporate governance and protection of minority shareholders' rights: Evidence from African countries. *Accounting Research Journal*, 32(3), 532–552.

Akhtaruddin, M. (2005). Corporate mandatory disclosure practices in Bangladesh. *The International Journal of Accounting, 40*(4), 399–422.

Allen, F., & Gu, X. (2018). The interplay between regulations and financial stability. *Journal of Financial Services Research, 53*(2–3), 233–248.

Anginer, D., Demirguc-Kunt, A., Huizinga, H., & Ma, K. (2018). Corporate governance of banks and financial stability. *Journal of Financial Economics, 130*(2), 327–346.

Appiah-Kubi, S. N. K., Malec, K., Maitah, M., Kutin, S. B., Pánková, L., Phiri, J., & Zaganjori, O. (2020a). The impact of corporate governance structures on foreign direct investment: A case study of West African countries. *Sustainability, 12*(9), 3715.

Appiah-Kubi, S. N. K., Malec, K., Kutin, S. B., Maitah, M., Chiseni, M. C., Phiri, J., ... & Maitah, K. (2020b). Foreign ownership in Sub-Saharan Africa: Do governance structures matter? *Sustainability, 12*(18), 7698.

Ariss, R. T. (2010). On the implications of market power in banking: Evidence from developing countries. *Journal of Banking & Finance, 34*(4), 765–775.

Athanasoglou, P. P., Brissimis, S. N., & Delis, M. D. (2008). Bank-specific, industry-specific and macroeconomic determinants of bank profitability. *Journal of International Financial Markets, Institutions and Money, 18*(2), 121–136.

Avgouleas, E. (2009). The global financial crisis and the disclosure paradigm in European financial regulation: The case for reform. *European Company and Financial Law Review, 6*(4), 440–475.

Baltagi, B. H. (2008). Forecasting with panel data. *Journal of Forecasting, 27*(2), 153–173.

Baltagi, B. H. (Ed.). (2015). *The Oxford handbook of panel data*. Oxford Handbooks.

Baumann, U., & Nier, E. (2004). Disclosure, volatility, and transparency: An empirical investigation into the value of bank disclosure. *Economic Policy Review, 10*(2), 31–45.

Beck, T., De Jonghe, O., & Schepens, G. (2013). Bank competition and stability: Cross-country heterogeneity. *Journal of Financial Intermediation, 22*(2), 218–244.

Berger, A. N. (1995). The relationship between capital and earnings in banking. *Journal of Money, Credit and Banking, 27*(2), 432–456.

Bermpei, T., Kalyvas, A., & Nguyen, T. C. (2018). Does institutional quality condition the effect of bank regulations and supervision on bank stability? Evidence from emerging and developing economies. *International Review of Financial Analysis, 59*, 255–275.

Boateng, A., Huang, W., & Kufuor, N. K. (2015). Commercial bank ownership and performance in China. *Applied Economics, 47*(49), 5320–5336.

Bouyon, S. (2014a). A review of policy options for monitoring household saving. *European Credit Research Institute, 16*, 1–24.

Bouyon, S. (2014b, October 7). *The impact of banking structural reform on household retail finance* (ECRI Commentary No. 13).

Boyd, J. H., & Runkle, D. E. (1993). Size and performance of banking firms: Testing the predictions of theory. *Journal of Monetary Economics, 31*(1), 47–67.

Brambor, T., Clark, W. R., & Golder, M. (2006). Understanding interaction models: Improving empirical analyses. *Political Analysis, 14*(1), 63–82.

Carbo-Valverde, S., Rodriguez-Fernandez, F., & Udell, G. F. (2009). Bank market power and SME financing constraints. *Review of Finance, 13*(2), 309–340.

Carmassi, J., Gros, D., & Micossi, S. (2009). The global financial crisis: Causes and cures. *JCMS: Journal of Common Market Studies, 47*(5), 977–996.

Castro, V. (2012). Macroeconomic determinants of the credit risk in the banking system: The case of the GIPSI. *Economic Modelling, 31*, 672–683.

Chen, K. C., Chen, Z., & Wei, K. J. (2009). Legal protection of investors, corporate governance, and the cost of equity capital. *Journal of Corporate Finance, 15*(3), 273–289.

Crotty, J. (2009). Structural causes of the global financial crisis: A critical assessment of the 'new financial architecture.' *Cambridge Journal of Economics, 33*(4), 563–580.

Cubillas, E., & Suárez, N. (2013). Bank market power after a banking crisis: Some international evidence. *The Spanish Review of Financial Economics, 11*(1), 13–28.

Cubillas, E., & Suárez, N. (2018). Bank market power and lending during the global financial crisis. *Journal of International Money and Finance, 89*, 1–22.

de Mendonça, H. F., & de Moraes, C. O. (2018). Central bank disclosure as a macroprudential tool for financial stability. *Economic Systems, 42*(4), 625–636.

De Nicoló, M. G., Jalal, A. M., & Boyd, J. H. (2006). *Bank risk-taking and competition revisited: New theory and new evidence* (No. 6–297). International Monetary Fund.

den Hertog, J. (2012). *Economic theories of regulation*. Edward Elgar Publishing Limited.

Dwumfour, R. A. (2017). Explaining banking stability in Sub-Saharan Africa. *Research in International Business and Finance, 41*, 260–279.

Edwards, F. R. (1996). *The new finance: Regulation and financial stability*. American Enterprise Institute.

Ernstberger, J., & Grüning, M. (2013). How do firm-and country-level governance mechanisms affect firms' disclosure? *Journal of Accounting and Public Policy, 32*(3), 50–67.

Fernández, A. I., González, F., & Suárez, N. (2016). Banking stability, competition, and economic volatility. *Journal of Financial Stability, 22*, 101–120.

Freimer, M., & Gordon, M. J. (1965). Why bankers ration credit. *The Quarterly Journal of Economics, 79*(3), 397–416.

Gaffikin, M. (2005). *Regulation as accounting theory, school of accounting & finance, university of wollongong*, Working Paper 9.

Globerman, S., Shapiro, D., & Tang, Y. (2006). Foreign direct investment in emerging and transition European countries. *International Finance Review, 6*(6), 431–459.

Goodhart, C. A. (2005). Financial regulation, credit risk and financial stability. *National Institute Economic Review, 192*(1), 118–127.

Granja, J. (2018). Disclosure regulation in the commercial banking industry: Lessons from the national banking era. *Journal of Accounting Research, 56*(1), 173–216.

Hakenes, H., & Schnabel, I. (2011). Capital regulation, bank competition, and financial stability. *Economics Letters, 113*(3), 256–258.

Hantke-Domas, D. (2007). Common legal principles of advanced regulatory systems. *Agua y Libre Comercio: Impacto e Implicaciones de los Acuerdos de Libre Comercio Sobre el Agua y sus Servicios*, Forthcoming.

Hillier, D., Pindado, J., De Queiroz, V., & De La Torre, C. (2011). The impact of country-level corporate governance on research and development. *Journal of International Business Studies, 42*(1), 76–98.

Hosono, K., Iwaki, H., & Tsuru, K. (2004). Bank regulation and market discipline around the world. *Research Institute of Economy, Trade and Industry (RIETI) Discussion Paper Series, 4*.

Imbens, G. W., & Wooldridge, J. M. (2009). Recent developments in the econometrics of program evaluation. *Journal of Economic Lliterature, 47*(1), 5–86.

Islam, M. S., & Nishiyama, S. I. (2016). The determinants of bank net interest margins: A panel evidence from South Asian countries. *Research in International Business and Finance, 37*, 501–514.

Jagannathan, R., Kapoor, M., & Schaumburg, E. (2013). Causes of the great recession of 2007–2009: The financial crisis was the symptom not the disease! *Journal of Financial Intermediation, 22*(1), 4–29.

Jiménez, G., Lopez, J. A., & Saurina, J. (2009). Empirical analysis of corporate credit lines. *The Review of Financial Studies, 22*(12), 5069–5098.

Jones, I., & Pollitt, M. (2004). Understanding how issues in corporate governance develop: Cadbury report to Higgs review. *Corporate Governance: An International Review, 12*(2), 162–171.

Kasman, S., & Kasman, A. (2015). Bank competition, concentration and financial stability in the Turkish banking industry. *Economic Systems, 39*(3), 502–517.

Klapper, L. F., & Love, I. (2002). Corporate governance, investor protection and performance in emerging markets. *Investor Protection and Performance in Emerging Markets* (March 2002).

Kusi, B. A., Agbloyor, E. K., Gyeke-Dako, A., & Asongu, S. A. (2020). Financial sector transparency and net interest margins: Should the private or public sector lead financial sector transparency? *Research in International Business and Finance*, 101260.

Kusi, B. A., Dzeha, G. C., Ofori-Sasu, D., & Ansah-Addo, L. (2018). Corporate governance structures and bank risk taking behaviour: Evidence from Africa using income bracket approach. *International Journal of Business Governance and Ethics, 13*(2), 138–169.

Kusi, B. A., & Opoku-Mensah, M. (2018). Does credit information sharing affect funding cost of banks? Evidence from African banks. *International Journal of Finance & Economics, 23*(1), 19–28.

Leuz, C., & Wysocki, P. D. (2016). The economics of disclosure and financial reporting regulation: Evidence and suggestions for future research. *Journal of Accounting Research, 54*(2), 525–622.

Lupu, I. (2015). The indirect relation between corporate governance and financial stability. *Procedia Economics and Finance, 22*, 538–543.

Mazumder, M. I., & Ahmad, N. (2010). Greed, financial innovation or laxity of regulation? A close look into the 2007–2009 financial crisis and stock market volatility. *Studies in Economics and Finance, 27*(2), 110–134.

Mensah, L., Andoh, C., Kuttu, S., & Kusi, B. A. (2019). Do banking institutions respond to incentives? Banking awards and stability evidence from an emerging economy. *African Finance Journal, 21*(1), 23–49.

Miller, M. J. (Ed.). (2003). *Credit reporting systems and the international economy*. Mit Press.

Mitton, T. (2004). Corporate governance and dividend policy in emerging markets. *Emerging Markets Review, 5*(4), 409–426.

Nier, E. W. (2005). Bank stability and transparency. *Journal of Financial Stability, 1*(3), 342–354.
Ozili, P. K. (2018a). Banking stability determinants in Africa. *International Journal of Managerial Finance, 14*(4), 462–483.
Ozili, P. K. (2018b). Impact of digital finance on financial inclusion and stability. *Borsa Istanbul Review, 18*(4), 329–340.
Pasiouras, F., & Kosmidou, K. (2007). Factors influencing the profitability of domestic and foreign commercial banks in the European Union. *Research in International Business and Finance, 21*(2), 222–237.
Peters, B. G. (2000). *Institutional theory: Problems and prospects*. Institute for Advanced Studies (IHS).
Poole, W. (2010a). A libertarian perspective on the financial crisis and financial reform. *SAIS Review of International Affairs, 30*(1), 17–26.
Poole, W. (2010b). Causes and consequences of the financial crisis of 2007–2009. *Harvard Journal of Law and Public Policy, 33*, 421.
Schaeck, K., & Čihák, M. (2010). *Competition, efficiency, and soundness in banking: An industrial organization perspective*. European banking center discussion Paper, (2010–20S).
Scott, W. R. (2005). Institutional theory: Contributing to a theoretical research program. *Great Minds in Management: The Process of Theory Development, 37*(2), 460–484.
Shapiro, D., Tang, Y., Wang, M., & Zhang, W. (2013). The effects of corporate governance on innovation in Chinese firms. *Journal of Chinese Economic and Business Studies, 13*(4), 311–335.
Stein, J. C. (2012). Monetary policy as financial stability regulation. *The Quarterly Journal of Economics, 127*(1), 57–95.
Stiglitz, J. E., & Weiss, A. (1981). Credit rationing in markets with imperfect information. *The American Economic Review, 71*(3), 393–410.
Stiroh, K. J. (2004a). Diversification in banking: Is noninterest income the answer? *Journal of Money, Credit and Banking, 36*(5), 853–882.
Stiroh, K. J. (2004b). Do community banks benefit from diversification? *Journal of Financial Services Research, 25*(2–3), 135–160.
Tadesse, S. (2006). The economic value of regulated disclosure: Evidence from the banking sector. *Journal of Accounting and Public Policy, 25*(1), 32–70.
Tan, Y. (2016). The impacts of risk and competition on bank profitability in China. *Journal of International Financial Markets, Institutions and Money, 40*, 85–110.
Thenmozhi, M., & Narayanan, P. C. (2016). Rule of law or country level corporate governance: What matters more in emerging market acquisitions? *Research in International Business and Finance, 37*, 448–463.

Uhde, A., & Heimeshoff, U. (2009). Consolidation in banking and financial stability in Europe: Empirical evidence. *Journal of Banking & Finance, 33*(7), 1299–1311.

Ülgen, F. (2017). Financialization and vested interests: Self-regulation vs. financial stability as a public good. *Journal of Economic Issues, 51*(2), 332–340.

Van Essen, M., Engelen, P. J., & Carney, M. (2013). Does "good" corporate governance help in a crisis? The impact of country-and firm-level governance mechanisms in the European financial crisis. *Corporate Governance: An International Review, 21*(3), 201–224.

Wichers, C. R. (1975). The detection of multicollinearity: A comment. *The Review of Economics and Statistics, 57*(3), 366–368.

York, R. (2012). Residualization is not the answer: Rethinking how to address multicollinearity. *Social Science Research, 41*(6), 1379–1386.

Zucker, L. G. (1987). Institutional theories of organization. *Annual Review of Sociology, 13*, 443–464.

CHAPTER 20

Macro-Prudential Regulation, Monetary Policy and Systemic Banking Crises in Africa

Joshua Yindenaba Abor, Daniel Ofori-Sasu, Joseph G. Nellis, and Christopher J. Green

20.1 Introduction

The financial system plays a very significant role in the growth process of any economy. However, prior to the global financial and economic crises, the global financial system witnessed fast and unsustainable growth, leading to a series of macroeconomic and financial imbalances. The global financial and economic crises have worsened these imbalances.

J. Y. Abor
University of Ghana Business School, Legon, Accra, Ghana
e-mail: joshabor@ug.edu.gh

D. Ofori-Sasu (✉)
Central University, Miotso, Tema, Ghana
e-mail: dofori.sasu@central.edu.gh; dofori-sasu@st.ug.edu.gh

J. G. Nellis
Cranfield School of Management, Bedford, UK
e-mail: j.g.nellis@cranfield.ac.uk

J. Y. Abor and C. K. D. Adjasi (eds.), *The Economics of Banking and Finance in Africa*, Palgrave Macmillan Studies in Banking and Financial Institutions, https://doi.org/10.1007/978-3-031-04162-4_20

This necessitated the need for regulation and supervision from both macro-prudential and micro-prudential perspectives (Tomuleasa, 2015). Before the global crisis in 2007/2008, financial stability was looked at primarily from a micro-prudential perspective. The focus of banking supervision was on reducing the risk that individual banks would collapse, without clear regard for the effect on the entire financial system or the economy as a whole (Altunbas et al., 2017). Doojav and Batmunkh (2018) suggest that the global financial crisis has revealed that the challenges in the financial system can harm the real economy, and that monetary policy measures targeted at achieving price stability coupled with micro-prudential regulations are not adequate in ensuring financial stability.

As a result, both policy makers and researchers have started focusing on the significance of macro-prudential regulation in restricting the extreme volatility in the financial system and its resultant impact on the economy. Macro-prudential regulation is recognised to be appropriate for the entire financial system. It is an approach to financial regulation, which aims at mitigating risk to the entire financial system (i.e. systemic risk). It involves the design and implementation of policies aimed at preventing or mitigating crises. Macro-prudential policies are designed with the intention of identifying and mitigating systemic risks, in order to reduce the cost to the economy as a result of disruption in financial services that support the functioning of financial markets. These include the provision of payment and settlement services, credit and insurance (FSB/IMF/BIS, 2009). They are aimed at ensuring the proper functioning of the financial system, in addition to preventing a series of imbalances, so as to support financial stability and to avert systemic risk.

Previous empirical studies have examined the issue of macro-prudential regulation and systemic risk mainly within the context of developed and emerging economies (see Akinci & Olmstead-Rumsey, 2018; Altunbas et al., 2018; Butzbach, 2016; Claessens et al., 2013; Gauthier et al., 2012; Zhang & Zoli, 2016), with little focus on developing countries. Apart from the direct impact of macro-prudential regulation on banking

C. J. Green
School of Business and Economics, Loughborough University, Loughborough, UK
e-mail: c.j.green@lboro.ac.uk

risk, it has also been recognised that monetary policy has an effect on risk-taking and financial stability (see Agur & Demertzis, 2010; Altunbas et al., 2014; Borio & Zhu, 2012; Dell'Ariccia et al., 2010; Gambacorta, 2009). Other studies have also examined macro-prudential and monetary policy interactions (see Angelini et al., 2014; Doojav & Batmunkh, 2018; Quint & Rabanal, 2014; Rubio & Carrasco-Gallego, 2014; Suh, 2012; Yellen, 2011). The limited focus on developing countries, such as those in Africa, calls for empirical investigation on how to design macro-prudential regulation to prevent or mitigate banking crises, considering that unexpected banking crises have impacted a number of African countries. Severe systemic banking crises have been recorded in Africa during the period, prior and subsequent to the global financial and economic crises (Laeven & Valencia, 2018). Systemic banking crises are recognised as having occurred when many banks in a particular country are insolvent at the same time, either because they are all affected by economic and financial shocks or because the failure of one or a group of banks spreads to other banks in the financial system (World Bank, 2012).

Though banking regulators in Africa have used macro-prudential policies, there is scanty empirical evidence on the effectiveness of these policies. Also, it is not clear how the use of macro-prudential policies work with monetary policy in a coordinated manner to impact systemic banking crises in Africa. Africa presents an interesting case for the study, given the changing institutional behaviour and different regulatory frameworks across the continent. This present study contributes to our understanding by providing empirical evidence on how macro-prudential policies and monetary policy impact systemic banking crises within the African context. Specifically, we examine the effect of macro-prudential regulation on systemic banking crises episodes in Africa. We also assess the impact of monetary policy on systemic banking crisis. Finally, we investigate the interaction effect of macro-prudential regulation and monetary policy on systemic banking crisis in Africa.

The rest of the chapter is structured as follows. Section 20.2 presents the stylized facts on macro-prudential regulation, monetary policy and banking crises in Africa. Section 20.3 provides a review of the extant literature on the subject matter. Section 20.4 includes a description of the methodology we employed in the study. Section 20.5 discusses the empirical results of the study. Finally, Sect. 20.6 concludes the study with some policy implications.

20.2 Stylized Facts on Macro-prudential Regulation, Monetary Policy and Banking Crises in Africa

The extant empirical literature suggests that banks that are hit by external shocks experience high peaks of non-performing loans and that these have negative repercussions on banking system stability (Laeven & Valencia, 2018). Most banks in Africa that experienced banking crises or instability were associated with higher non-performing loans and bank runs. After the outbreak of the 2007/2008 global financial and economic crises, banks in African countries still experience banking system instability, which often leads to systemic banking crises (Laeven & Valencia, 2018). In recent years, some African countries have experienced banking instabilities; examples are Ghana (between 2017 and 2018), Guinea-Bissau (2014 to date), South Africa (2015), Nigeria (between 2009 and 2012) and many others (Laeven & Valencia, 2018). These were associated with higher non-performing loans. During this period, monetary policy operated in some cases through direct controls on banks' interest rates, reserve requirements and other balance sheet restrictions in these African countries. Again, for some of these countries, there were no institutions holding the official responsibility of implementing macro-prudential policy. Until recently, the central banks as regulator and supervisor of the banking system and also the monetary authority have been performing the important role in mitigating the effect of external shocks on the banking sector. This situation has led to the implementation of many financial reforms (such as the monetary policy tools) and macro-prudential regulation among many African economies. Moreover, reforms of the banking sector have been initiated together with flexible macro-prudential regulation coupled with a tight monetary policy stance to stabilise these economies.

Macro-prudential policy aims at avoiding macroeconomic costs, arising from the instability of the financial system, but also to reduce systemic banking crises. It is considered complementary not only to micro-prudential regulations but also to monetary policy. In addition, observing the interaction between macro-prudential and monetary policies can have important implications for financial stability. Given that macro-prudential regulation and monetary policy are increasingly becoming popular tools for responding to systemic banking crisis, this study employs different measures of macro-prudential regulation and monetary policy to understand their association with banking system (instability) crises. Examination of the data before and after the 2007/2008 global financial and economic crises, including data on implementation of measures of regulations in Africa, some interesting stylised facts emerge (see Fig. 20.1). Figure 20.1 shows trends of average values of banking system instability, monetary policy (average values of central bank policy rates) and some macro-prudential indicators such as the average values of macro-prudential policy action index, countercyclical capital requirement, reserve requirement and bank liquid reserves over the period, 2006–2018.

From Fig. 20.1, it can be seen that banks in Africa were unstable between 2006 and 2008 due to the outbreak of the 2007/2008 global financial and economic crises. After the crisis, the banks became relatively stable until 2009 when they started experiencing instability between 2009 and 2011. Moreover, trends in banking instability have been fluctuating from 2011 to 2016. Banking instability began to rise from 2016 to 2018. Similarly, monetary policy rates increased marginally from 2006 to 2008, but decreased from 2008 to 2010 due to the 2007/2008 global financial and economic crises. It is observed that monetary policy rates have been unstable between 2010 and 2018.

Macro-prudential policy action is an index based on an aggregate of 17 indicators.[1] Higher average values show the extent (limit) to which the policy was tightened (strengthened) in a particular year while zero (0) indicates that the policy was loosened (relaxed) in a particular country. From the figure, the limits of macro-prudential policy show that the policy was strengthened in 2008, 2011 and 2012 but at different base

[1] The iMaPP database is constructed by Alam et al. (2019), integrating information from major existing databases2/ and national sources. It provides (1) the average regulatory limit on the loan-to-value (LTV) ratio, (2) the dummy-type indexes of tightening and loosening actions over 17 instruments and their subcategories and (3) the description of each policy action, including: countercyclical capital buffer, requirements for banks to maintain a capital conservation buffer, capital requirements, limits on leverage of banks, loan loss provision requirements, limits on foreign currency, limits to the loan-to-value ratios, debt service-to-income ratios, minimum requirements for liquidity coverage ratios, limits to the loan-deposit ratio, limits to net or gross open foreign exchange positions, reserve requirements, loan restrictions, risk measures, taxes and levies applied to specified transactions and macro-prudential measures not captured in the above categories. The iMaPP database is also sourced from national sources, the IMF official documents and the websites of the Bank for International Settlements (BIS) and the Financial Stability Board (FSB). See Alam et al. (2019) for more details.

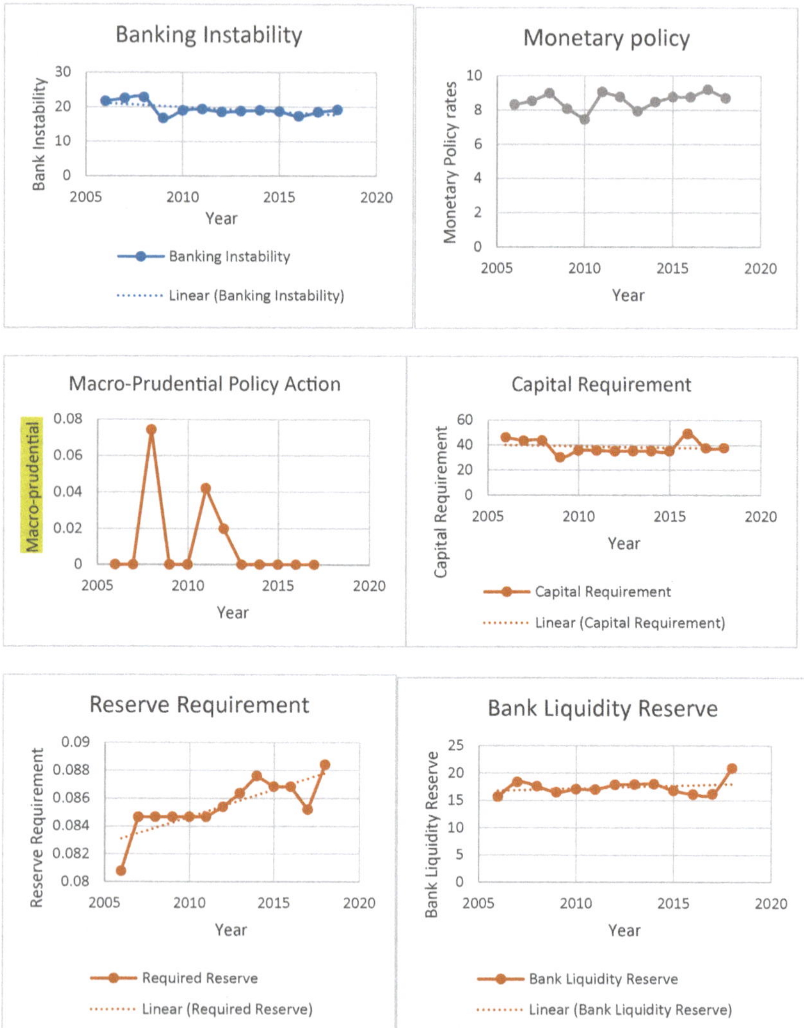

Fig. 20.1 Macro-prudential Indicators, Monetary Policy and Banking Crisis (*Note* Banking Instability [non-performing loans to total loans (NPL)]; Monetary Policy [central bank policy rates]; Macro-prudential policy action is the sum of dummies for 17 Macro-prudential regulations; Capital Requirement is the ratio of bank regulatory capital requirement to risk weighted assets; Reserve requirement is the specified percentage of the amount of deposits held by banks; Bank Liquid Reserve is the ratio of bank liquid reserve to bank total assets over the period 2006–2018. Data obtained from the Global Financial Development Database)

points. However, the policy action in Africa was relaxed in the period 2006–2007, 2009–2010 and 2013–2018. Globally, there has been a trend towards increasing minimum regulatory capital requirements in order to improve resilience of banking systems. However, the case of Africa has been contradictory. From Fig. 20.1, countercyclical capital requirements decreased from 2006 to 2007, and then increased in 2008. We observe that capital requirement decreased steeply from 2008 to 2009 and then increased by a smaller margin between 2009 and 2010. The trend shows that capital requirement became relatively stable between 2010 and 2015 but began to increase from 2015 to 2016. They decreased from 2016 to 2017 and then increased by a small margin in 2018. The unstable trend of countercyclical capital requirements over the years has translated into different levels of actual holdings of capital requirements in Africa. Reserve requirements, on the other hand, have increased from 2006 to 2007 and became relatively stable between 2007 and 2011. They then increased steadily from 2010 to 2014, decreased annually from 2014 to 2016 and finally increased from 2017 to 2018. Similarly, bank liquid reserves have increased from 2006 to 2007 and decreased steadily from 2007 to 2008 but became relatively stable between 2009 and 2014. The trend shows that bank liquid reserves decreased gradually from 2014 to 2017, and then inched up greatly in 2018.

Between 2009 and 2018, limits on macro-prudential policy actions in Africa were relaxed and trends of monetary policy and macro-prudential regulation have been unstable over time. The capital holdings for banks in Africa decreased from a mean of 46.10% of risk weighted average (RWA) in 2006 to 37.68% of RWA in 2018. Limits on reserve requirements increased by a small margin from an average of 8.07% in 2006 to an average of 8.84 in 2018. Bank liquid reserves have increased tremendously from an average of 15.65% in 2006 to an average of 20.85 in 2018. African countries have made several adjustments in their monetary policy rates over the years giving an average of 25.68% in 2006 to an average of 26.41% in 2018.

In general, an examination of the trends in these variables depicts that banking instability, monetary policy rates and regulation on capital requirements in Africa have been decreasing over the period, while regulations on reserve requirement and bank liquid reserves have been increasing over the period. However, macro-prudential policy actions have been inconsistent over the entire period of this study. The overall decreasing trend in banking instability in Africa over the years reflects not only the decreasing trend in regulation on capital requirements but also increasing trends in reserve requirements and bank liquid reserves. Based on the trends of the variables, it is interesting to empirically understand the implications of macro-prudential regulation and monetary policy for banking crises.

20.3 Literature Review

Systemic banking crisis episodes have been seen to be very damaging, contagious and rapidly spreading to other developed and developing economies (Laeven & Valencia, 2018). These have negative repercussions for the financial systems of these economies (Claessens et al., 2001; IMF 2013a; 2013c, Yasnur & Kurniasih, 2017). While some studies have highlighted the dangers resulting from a systemic banking crisis (see Rajan, 2005; Laeven & Valencia, 2013a, 2013b), others have provided policy responses to resolve possible systemic banking crises through macro-prudential regulation (see Barth et al., 2013; Deniz, Demirgüç-Kunt, and Zhu, 2012; Klomp & de Haan, 2014). Some studies have emphasised the need for macro-prudential regulations, which are capable of supporting the whole financial system and which can reduce both existing risks (Tomuleasa, 2015) and the occurrence of banking crises (Claessens et al., 2005, 2011). Since the 2007/2008 global financial and economic crisis, the vulnerability of the global economy to the distress of single banks in different economies has been of key interest to regulators, monetary authorities and policy makers. The prolonged impact of the global financial crisis taught many policymakers a valuable lesson, particularly the central banks around the world. Prior to the crises, many international regulatory approaches were focussed on micro-prudential regulations. After the global financial crisis, efforts have been made to find a way to stabilise most economies and prevent the crisis from reoccurring (Lubis et al., 2019). Subsequently, debate continues among policy makers, practitioners and academics regarding the formulation and measures of macro-prudential policy in ensuring the soundness of the financial system (Claessens, 2015; Mishkin, 2009; Tomuleasa, 2015).

In the quest to promote financial stability, the central banks around the world have implemented macro-prudential policies. These macro-prudential policies have been used intensively in advanced and emerging economies, particularly following the recent financial crisis (Andriushin & Kuznetsova, 2013; Blanchard et al., 2010; Buiter, 2014; Cagliarini,

2016; Claessens, 2015; Mishkin, 2009). Banks finance their assets with government-insured deposits and while this insurance has the effect of preventing bank runs, it creates an incentive for managers of banks to accommodate excessive risks. The goal of macro-prudential regulation such as capital regulation is to push banks to protect deposit insurance, mitigate moral hazard and internalise losses (Hanson et al., 2011). It is also the goal of macro-prudential regulation to prevent banks from excessively contracting their balance sheets in adverse global conditions. For instance, when a bank is hit with a shock that reduces its capital, (1) it can raise capital to replace what has been lost or (2) cause the capital-to-asset ratio to decline. Macro-prudential regulations are used to limit systemic risk that can seriously cause adverse consequences for the real economy (Laeven & Valencia, 2013b; IMF, 2013a, 2013b, 2013c). These include an array of instruments such as regulatory capital (traditional tool), measures for addressing sector specific risks (such as loan-to-value [LTV], debt-to-income [DTI] ratios), counter-cyclical capital requirements, reserve requirements regulation, liquidity tools, dynamic provisions and foreign-currencyreserve regulations. These measures have been used frequently in advanced economies (Chantapacdepong & Shim, 2014; Kuttner & Shim, 2012; Lim et al., 2011). For instance, Lim et al. (2011) assessed the effectiveness of tightening individual instrument in curbing procyclicality of financial risks and found that macro-prudential instruments are effective in lowering financial risks. Also, Zhang and Zoli (2016) established that housing-related macro-prudential instruments like loan-to-value ratio caps are important in reducing house price inflation, growth in credit and bank leverage among Asian countries.

Conversely, the implementation of macro-prudential policies as a means of promoting financial system stability, has raised many questions regarding the interaction between monetary and macro-prudential policies (Lubis et al., 2019). Lubis et al. (2019) shed light on the existing ambiguity surrounding the coordination issues between monetary and macro-prudential policies. According to Lubis et al. (2019), monetary policy alone is not sufficient to maintain financial stability and thus, macro-prudential policies are needed to supplement monetary. They posit that a relatively new approach has been adopted to handle surges of financial imbalances in both advanced and emerging economies, and this approach is to implement both monetary and macro-prudential policies. Furthermore, they argued that monetary policy is adopted to achieve price stability while macro-prudential policies target the soundness of aggregate financial sector.

Previous studies have examined the direct link between macro-prudential policy and financial stability and the relationship has been found to be positive (Tomuleasa, 2015; Zhang & Zoli, 2016). For instance, FSB/IMF/BIS (2009) documents that macro-prudential policies are designed with the aim of identifying and mitigating systemic risks, while Zulkhibri (2019) empirically emphasises the need to foster financial stability through better financial institutions. Further, intervention policy responses to the recent financial crisis in attempt to reduce the probability of another crisis have taken place in many countries (Lu, 2017). This supports the work by Claessens et al. (2005), who found that macro-prudential policies are negatively related to banking crises. Thus, macro-prudential policies support the banking system and reduce the output cost of banking crises. The extant literature has built cross-country databases on the use of macro-prudential measures. For instance, a range of macro-prudential measures, such as capital requirements, reserve requirements, dynamic provisions, liquidity tools and other prudential tools have been used to assess the effectiveness in reducing systemic risks and possible crises. According to Basso and Costain (2016), macro-prudential policy measures that take into consideration traditional capital requirements as policy instruments weaken the likelihood of a banking crisis. Lu (2017) found that capital regulatory stringency is positively linked with lower probability of a systemic banking crisis.

fvFrom the monetary policy literature, Jimenez et al. (2012a, 2012b) observe that reducing monetary policy rates can cause an increase in banks' appetite for credit and liquidity risk as a result of moral hazard problems. Adrian and Shin (2010) analyse the risk-taking channel of monetary policy and observe that expansive monetary policy leads to an increase in banks' lending and their risk-taking behaviour when their value at risk is binding in capital. Thus, a lower interest rate increases the demand for credit by customers and may trigger banks' credit risk exposure. On the other hand, generally, an upsurge in interest rates may increase banks' risk-taking incentives, and may generate profits for the banks. These countervailing effects make the impact of monetary policy on banking crises ultimately critical. Svensson (2017) found a positive effect of monetary policy on the likelihood of a banking crisis. Herrero and del Rio (2003) used a sample of 79 countries over the period, 1970–1999 to examine the impact of monetary policy on the occurrence of banking crises. They found that the bank-lending channel of monetary policy reduces the likelihood of banking crises.

Although, different macro-prudential tools have been explored in isolation, previous studies assert that the objectives of macro-prudential policy should protect the independence of monetary policy (Beau et al., 2012). Others argue that it is better to combine monetary and macro-prudential policies (Blanchard et al., 2010), and that the coordination between the two policies should aid to avoid shocks in the economy (Claessen, 2014 & Tomuleasa, 2015). They provide evidence to support that coordinating the use of monetary and macro-prudential instruments is important in improving stability and mitigating the pro-cyclical consequences in the financial system (Mishkin, 2009). Maddaloni and Peydro (2013) analyse the effect of lending standards of short-term interest rates and macro-prudential policy on a possible credit crunch. They found that the effect of low monetary policy rates on the relaxing of standards might be minimised by tight macro-prudential policies on either banks' capital or loan-to-value ratios. They also show that monetary policy rates and central bank provision of long-term liquidity serve as complements in reducing a likely credit crunch. Thus, macro-prudential policies or regulations interact strongly with other policies including monetary policy to enhance banking system stability (Aikman et al., 2019). However, the empirical evidence relating to these interactions is scanty in the literature. Furthermore, the notion that macro-prudential regulation and monetary policy have different effects on systemic banking crisis, depending on the quality of institutions in a given country is somewhat an emerging issue in the literature. Therefore, having contradictory findings on the issue is to be expected.

Moreover, macro-prudential and monetary policies relationships with the probability of a banking crisis cannot be looked in isolation or independently. In view of this, Lubis et al. (2019) reviewed some studies on the relationship and build their explanation of the interaction of monetary and macro-prudential policies through the role of the financial sector in magnifying shocks to the economy. They revealed that the financial sector forms the conduit through which the interlinking mechanism between monetary and macro-prudential is explored (Barnea et al., 2015; De Paoli & Paustian, 2013; Rubio & Carrasco-Gallego, 2014). Angelini et al. (2014) provide evidence that lack of coordination between macro-prudential and monetary policy may lead to unnecessary volatility of the policy instruments. They explained that the unnecessary volatility occurs because these policy instruments work on the same channel with different objectives, and therefore, the effect of one policy may cancel out the other's action. Empirically, Greenwood-Nimmo and Tarassow (2016) argue that in the absence of monetary policy, macro-prudential policy may not only be able to reduce financial fragility in the short run but when used together, the joint effect may diminish financial fragility.

Following this review of the literature, it is clear that research on the interaction effect of macro-prudential regulation and monetary policy on banking crises in countries with different institutional quality in Africa is still developing. Apart from analysing the independent and interaction effects of macro-prudential regulation and monetary policy on the predicted probability of a systemic banking crisis, we also hypothesise that the impacts may vary across countries with different institutional frameworks.

20.4 Methodology

The study employs a panel dataset of 532 banks in 29 African countries covering the period, 2006–2018. The panel approach allows us to account for continuously evolving country-specific differences in technology, institutional frameworks and economic factors. We utilise the baseline model, which is expressed as:

$$\text{Systemic Banking Crisis} = f\begin{pmatrix}\text{Macro - Prudential Regulations,} \\ \text{Monetary Policy, Control Variables}\end{pmatrix} \tag{20.1}$$

The nature of the measure of a systemic banking crisis allows us to use a qualitative response logit model to estimate the probability of the occurrence of a systemic banking crisis as a function of a vector of independent variables.[2] This is expressed as:

$$\Pr(\mathrm{Y}_i = 1) = \mathrm{F}[\mathrm{H}(\mathrm{X}_i, \theta)] = \frac{1}{1 + e^{-H}} \tag{20.2}$$

[2] The logit model is widely used by many scholars, problems of out of range estimates are avoided (Hosmer et al. 2013) and it gives parameter estimates, which are asymptotically consistent, efficient and normal (Buis 2010).

where Y_i is the dependent variable (predicted probability of systemic banking crisis), which takes the value of one (1) for period(s) when the national banking system of an African country is in crisis (distress), or zero (0) otherwise; F is the probability function, which has a logistic functional form.

Model Specification

Effects of Macro-prudential Regulation and Monetary Policy on Systemic Banking Crisis

Following our baseline equation, we specify Eq. (20.3) that estimates the independent effect of macro-prudential regulation and monetary policy on the predicted probability of a systemic banking crisis.

$$\begin{aligned}\text{SysBankCrisi}_{\text{jt}} &= \sum_{l=1}^{4} \begin{array}{l}\alpha_1 \text{MacroPrudential Regulation}_{\text{jt}} \\ +\alpha_3 \text{Monetary Policy}_{\text{jt}}\end{array} \\ &+ \sum_{k=1}^{N} \beta_k \text{X}_{\text{ijt}} + \lambda_i + \gamma j + \mu t + \varepsilon_{\text{ijt}} \end{aligned} \qquad (20.3)$$

The dependent variable, Systemic Banking Crisis (*SysBankCrisis*), is constructed as a dummy with data obtained from the World Bank Global Financial Development Database as well as Laeven and Valencia (2018).

The subscript i denotes the cross-sectional dimension (bank), $i = 1$, ..., Z; j denotes cross-sectional dimension (country specifics), $j = 1$, ..., M; $_t$ denotes the time series dimension (time), $t = 1$, ..., T.

$\alpha_1 : l = 1, \ldots, 4$, represent the regression coefficients of a vector of four macro-prudential regulation variables; α_3 denotes the coefficient of monetary policy rates;$\beta_k : k = 1, \ldots, N$, are regression parameters for the vector X (control variables) to be estimated; λ_i is the bank fixed effect i; γ_j is the country fixed effect j; and μ_t is the time fixed effect t; and ε_{ijt} is an idiosyncratic error term, which controls for unit-specific residuals in the model for the ith *bank* in the jth *country* at *period t*.

We decompose macro-prudential regulation variables into four: (1) aggregate of macro-prudential policy actions (2) countercyclical capital requirements; (3) reserve requirements and (4) bank liquid reserve ratios.

The macro-prudential policy action variable is an index of dummies, while the individual traditional instruments are expressed in ratios.

We obtained macro-prudential policy action data from the iMaPP database constructed by Alam et al. (2019), integrating information from major existing databases (the Global Macro-prudential policy instruments and IMF annual macro-prudential policy survey) and national sources (Alam et al., 2019; Lim et al., 2011, 2013). We also obtained countercyclical capital requirement data from the World Bank (i.e. data from Financial Soundness Indicators). Reserve requirements and bank liquid reserves data were obtained from the World Bank Global Financial Development Database. Data on monetary policy rates (proxy for monetary policy) were obtained from World Development Indicators.

Macro-Prudential Policy Action is the policy change indicator for the instrument which records tightening actions (+1) (i.e. strengthening), loosening actions (−1) (i.e. relaxing), and no changes (0), and it is cumulated over the past four quarters to account for potential lagged effects. We focus on the aggregate or the sum of all instruments since the aggregate values have relatively more variations across countries in Africa. Macro-prudential policy (MaPP) index is the sum of dummies for all 17 categories: countercyclical capital buffer, requirements for banks to maintain a capital conservation buffer, capital requirements, limits on leverage of banks, loan loss provision requirements, limits on foreign currency, limits to the loan-to-value ratios, debt service-to-income ratios, minimum requirements for liquidity coverage ratios, limits to the loan-deposit ratio, limits to net or gross open foreign exchange positions, reserve requirements, loan restrictions, risk measures, taxes and levies applied to specified transactions and macro-prudential measures not captured in the above categories. We expect a negative effect of macro-prudential policy index on systemic banking crisis. This suggests that strengthening of the policy action translates into curbing the next possible crisis. The strengthening of the macro-prudential policy action reflects higher interest rates and lower credit supply. Thus, strengthening macro-prudential policy action offers banks the opportunity to take higher risk, generate higher profits and mitigate possible defaults or moral hazards, resulting in lower probability of a systemic banking crisis. On the other hand, relaxing macro-prudential policy action leads to the next systemic banking crisis. This suggests that banks may want to reduce interest rates on credits against higher loan demand. This may then lead to higher exposures to risks such as insolvency, moral hazards and liquidity problems, which may increase the likelihood of banking crisis.

Countercyclical Capital Requirement is the minimum capital requirement or Basel III countercyclical capital buffer a financial institution is required to hold. This is the ratio of bank regulatory capital requirements to risk weighted assets. We anticipate a negative effect of regulatory capital on systemic banking crisis, as evidenced in the work of Lu (2017). This is because countries with capital regulatory stringency are more likely to reduce the likelihood of a systemic banking crisis (Laeven & Valancia, 2013b).

Reserve Requirement is regulation by the central bank or monetary authority that sets the minimum amount of reserves that universal or commercial banks are required to hold. It is measured as the specified percentage of the amount of deposits held by banks. We anticipate a negative relationship between reserve requirements and the predicted probability of a systemic banking crisis. This supports the argument by Geng and Zha (2015) who show that the reserve requirement ratio exerts a direct effect on bank risk taking in order to increase profits, leading to greater banking stability.

Bank Liquid Reserve is the minimum amount of liquid assets (domestic currency and deposits with monetary authorities to claims on other governments, the private sector, non-financial public enterprises and other banking institutions) that must be kept on hand by financial institutions to meet the requirements of the central bank. This is expressed as the ratio of bank liquid reserves-to-bank total assets. This suggests that a macro-prudential approach to the liquid reserve requirements of banks is important in minimising the probability of a systemic banking crisis.

Monetary Policy is the regulation or policy actions taken by the monetary authority or central bank to control the interest rate payable on short-term borrowings. We employ monetary policy rates as a proxy for monetary policy. We expect a negative effect of monetary policy rates on systemic banking crisis. During a contractionary or tight monetary policy stance, an increase in monetary policy rates offers the banks a greater incentive to increase profits and reduce credit risk—thus, reducing the next possible banking crisis. The opposite is true, namely that loosening the monetary policy stance, such as lowering interest rates, may lead to excessive credit expansion and this largely explains the financial imbalances and economic shocks, leading to a banking crisis (De Nicolo et al., 2010).

In Eq. 20.3, X (a vector of control variables which includes: bank funding (ratio of total deposits to total assets ratio); credit risk (ratio of nonperforming to gross loans); bank concentration (the ratio of asset of the three largest commercial banks to total commercial banking assets in a country); bank risk taking, measured as the inverse of the Z-score (ratio of the sum of return on asset and capital adequacy relative to the standard deviation of return on asset); private sector credit (ratio of private sector credit-to-gross domestic product (GDP)); exchange rate (natural logarithm of a country's currency rate in terms of the US dollar) and gross domestic product (GDP) per capita. Data on these control variables were obtained from the World Bank Global Financial Development Database. We also control for institutions, which is measured as an aggregate of six indicators (rule of law, government effectiveness, control of corruption, political stability, regulatory quality and voice and accountability) from the Global Financial Development Database. This ranges between −1 and 1 with higher values indicating strong institutions.

We anticipate a negative effect of bank funding on a systemic banking crisis. This suggests that banks with greater funding sources are able to reduce the probability of banking crisis. We expect credit risk to positively affect banking crises. We anticipate a negative relationship between bank concentration and banking crises, as supported by Shehzad et al. (2009). We expect bank risk taking to negatively affect banking crises. This indicates that banks that take excessive risk reduce the possibility of a banking crisis. We expect a positive relationship between private sector credit and the probability of a banking crisis. Countries with strong macroeconomic fundamentals (i.e. stable exchange rates, high GDP per capita) are less likely to experience crises, hence we expect negative effects of the exchange rate and GDP per capita on banking crisis. We also expect countries with strong institutions to reduce the possibility of a crisis, and thus a negative relationship between institution and banking crisis.

Interaction Effect of Macro-Prudential Regulation and Monetary Policy on Systemic Banking Crisis

We specify a model that explains the interaction effect of monetary policy on the relationship between macro-prudential regulation and predicted banking crisis probability. This is specified as follows:

$$
\begin{aligned}
\text{SysBankCrisis}_{\text{jt}} &= \sum_{l=1}^{4} \begin{matrix} \lambda_1 \text{MacroPrudential Regulation}_{\text{jt}} \\ +\alpha_1 \text{Monetary Policy}_{\text{jt}} \end{matrix} \\
&+ \sum_{q=1}^{p} \delta_q \begin{pmatrix} \text{Monetary Policy}_{jt} \\ *\text{MacroPrudential Regulation}_{\text{jt}} \end{pmatrix} \\
&+ \sum_{k=1}^{N} \beta_k \text{X}_{\text{ijt}} + \phi_i + \sigma j + \theta t + \mu_{ijt} \qquad (20.4)
\end{aligned}
$$

where

$\delta_q : q = 1, \ldots, p$ denote the coefficients of the interaction terms between monetary policy and macro-prudential regulation.
α_1 represents the coefficient of monetary policy rate; $\beta_k, k = 1, \ldots, N$ are the coefficients of the control variables (for vector X); $\lambda_l : l = 1, \ldots, 4,$ r epresent the coefficients of macro-prudential regulation variables.
ϕ_i is the individual bank effect; σ_j is the individual country effects; θ_t is the time fixed effects and μ_{ijt} is the composite error term.

We expect a negative interaction effect of macro-prudential regulation variables and monetary policy on systemic banking crises.

Following Compton and Giedeman (2011), the study considers the conditional effect of macro-prudential regulation variables which indicates the marginal change associated with the levels of monetary policy rates when accounting for interaction effects. Before we interpret the findings, let us first take into consideration the expected signs of the individual coefficients. Based on the extant literature on macro-prudential regulation and stability, we would expect negative coefficients between macro-prudential regulation variables and systemic banking crises. That is, higher levels of regulations should reduce the possibility of a banking crisis. We also expect a negative coefficient between the monetary policy variable and banking crisis because better monetary policy should curb a banking crisis. However, we must consider the interaction effect as well as the overall (net) effect of macro-prudential regulation on banking crises. Again, Compton and Giedeman (2011) have interpreted their results by considering the signs associated with the coefficient of the interaction terms. In our case, an interaction of macro-prudential regulation with monetary policy, which results in a negative coefficient, would suggest that macro-prudential regulation and monetary policy are complements in reducing a crisis. A positive interaction term would be interpreted as macro-prudential regulation and monetary policy being substitutes in curbing banking crises.

In terms of the net effect of the macro-prudential regulation variables, we expect monetary policy to alter by either amplifying or reducing the relationship between macro-prudential regulation and the predicted probability of a banking crisis. A negative net effect suggests that monetary policy amplifies the negative impact of macro-prudential regulation on a systemic banking crisis. A positive net effect indicates that monetary policy alters the negative relationship between macro-prudential regulation and a systemic banking crisis. Our interpretations are close to the work of Brambor et al. (2006) and Compton and Giedeman (2011).

We also expect interesting results when considering the interactions for countries with strong and weak institutions. We argue that in designing regulatory framework that is robust in reducing a possible systemic banking crisis, the economy needs strong institutions to play a major role. To do this, we extend our model to predict how macro-prudential and monetary policies interact to affect systemic banking crisis across strong and weak institutions. We expect regulations interactions to further reduce a possible banking crisis in countries with strong institutions compared to countries with weak institutions.

For robustness checks we predict how the lag effects and adjustments of macro-prudential regulation and monetary policy (changes in the macro-prudential regulation and monetary policy variables) affect a banking crisis outcome. We expect a dynamic impact of these variables on banking crisis.

Estimation Technique

The logit regression is a linear regression technique that gives room for correcting heteroskedastic and serial correlation. It follows the standard logistic distribution and results are much easier to interpret. For the logit model, problems of out of range estimates are avoided (Hosmer et al., 2013) and it gives parameter estimates, which are asymptotically consistent, efficient and normal (Buis, 2010). The robust standard errors of the logit model were used to correct for heteroskedasticity and autocorrelation, while the year trend dummies were employed to control for omitted variable biases and time effects (e.g. used in the study is the 2007/2008 Global Financial Crisis). Following Blaydes and Kayser (2011), we conduct robust estimations by transforming Eq. (20.3) and introducing the lag effects (lead-lags) of macro-prudential regulation and monetary policy on systemic banking crisis as well as the effect of macro-prudential regulation or monetary policy changes on systemic banking crisis. Finally, the logit regression results allow us to interpret the estimated coefficients based on the direction and the magnitude of the predicted probability of the outcome variable (i.e. systemic banking crises).

20.5 Empirical Results

This section includes presentation and discussion of the empirical findings. We first present and discuss the summary descriptive statistics, followed by the correlation matrix and then the regression results.

Summary Descriptive Statistics

The descriptive results are presented in Table 20.1. From Table 20.1, the macro-prudential policy action index recorded an average of 0.012, given a range between 0 and 1. This suggests that the aggregate macro-prudential policy action in Africa is relatively low compared to an average of 0.081 in the world as a whole, 0.051 in advanced economies and 0.132 in emerging and developing economies (Alam et al., 2019). The mean of countercyclical capital requirements is 37.47. This suggests a high capital requirement for banks in Africa compared to the world average capital holding of 18.6% of risk weighted average in 2016 (2019/2020 Global Financial Development Report). The mean of reserve requirements is

8.6%, which is relatively lower than the world average of 9.02 for regulatory restrictions of banking activities (Lu, 2017). Bank liquid reserves recorded an average of 18.47, which is close to the world average of 18.7 in recent times (World Bank, 2021). Monetary policy rates recorded a mean of 8.54%. This suggests that countries in Africa have low monetary policy rates, ranging from 0 to 26%.

On the bank-specific variables, bank funding recorded a mean of 75.16%. Credit risk recorded a mean of 8.1% and a standard deviation of 0.128, which indicates high variability of credit risk exposure across the sample. Bank concentration recorded a mean of 55.32%. The inverse of Z-score, which measures bank risk taking recorded an average of 0.016. Higher values of Z-score suggest lower risk banking environment and lower Z-scores values imply more riskier banking condition. Given a range between −0.0036 and 0.14, banks in Africa operate in a risky environment.

For the macroeconomic indicators, private sector credit recorded a mean of 22.88% of GDP of African countries, which is comparatively low compared to other regions. Exchange rates in Africa recorded an average of 4.171 rate to the dollar, while GDP per capita recorded a mean of 2.76. The aggregate institutional indicator recorded an average of −0.483, suggesting that the quality of institutions in Africa is low or poor, ranging between −0.66 and 0.853.

Correlation Matrix

The correlation results for the explanatory variables are presented in Table 20.2. The correlation matrix results generally do not suggest that multi-collinearity is a problem in our data. This is confirmed by Variable Inflation Factor (VIF) below threshold of 10. The correlation analysis only shows the relationship between the two variables without controlling for the effects of the other variables. We therefore present and discuss the regression results as follows.

Regression Results

In Table 20.3, we present the results of the effects of macro-prudential regulation and monetary policy on systemic banking crisis. Macro-prudential regulation variables employed in our study are the aggregate of macro-prudential policy actions, countercyclical capital requirements, reserve requirements and bank liquid reserves. Models 1–4 show the independent effects of macro-prudential regulation on systemic banking crisis conditioned on monetary policy. Model 5 shows the joint effect of macro-prudential regulation and monetary policy on systemic banking crisis.

Effect of Macro-Prudential Regulation and Monetary Policy on Systemic Banking Crisis

In terms of macro-prudential regulation, we show that macro-prudential policy action has a negative and significant effect on the predicted probability of a systemic banking crisis (model 1). This supports the findings of Alam et al. (2019) that macro-prudential policies are able to reduce household credit and house prices. This can be explained from our results that higher value of the macro-prudential index shows the strengthening of policy regulations, which reflects an increase in interest charges on household credits. This may create an incentive for banks to make higher profits and reduce possible default of housing credit. Thus, leading to a lower likelihood of a systemic banking crisis. Countercyclical capital requirement has a significantly negative effect on predicted probability of systemic banking crisis (see model 2). This suggests that more stringent capital requirements are important in lowering the predicted probability of a systemic banking crisis. This supports the work by Lu (2017) who found a significantly negative effect of capital regulation on banking crisis. We show a significantly negative relationship between reserve requirement regulation and the probability of banking crisis (model 3). This is in line with a direct effect of reserve requirement on bank risk indicated by Geng and Zha (2015). The implication is that countries that increase their stringency on the reserve requirement ratio, put pressure on managers of banks to increase their risk taking in order to make more profits for a stable banking system. We also observe that bank liquid reserve enters the regression with a negative coefficient (model 4). This suggests that banks react to lower likelihood of crisis in terms of a higher level of bank liquid reserves to absorb shocks. The implication is that banks with higher liquid reserves are able to reduce the possibility of a systemic banking crisis.

The results of our study also show that the monetary policy rate is negatively and significantly linked to the predicted probability of a banking crisis. The sign attached to the coefficients of the monetary policy rate is consistent (negative) across the model. This suggests that a tight monetary policy stance (increased monetary policy rate) minimises the probability of systemic banking crisis. This supports the argument by Steenkamp (2014) that monetary policy may have implications for financial stability by setting the benchmark of short-term interest rates. Tightening monetary policy reflects a surge in short-term interest rates, which makes money supply and credit less attractive. This increases the incentive for banks to reduce credit default and enhance financial stability.

In terms of the controls, we found a negative relationship between bank funding and banking crisis (see models 2, 4, 5). This shows that banks with greater funding sources are able to reduce the probability of a banking crisis. Credit risk was positively and significantly linked to systemic banking crises (models 1 and 3). This is because banks that have higher levels of non-performing loans (credit risk exposures) suffer banking crises. We found a negative effect of bank concentration on banking crises. This is because a concentrated banking system has the incentive to make profits, decrease insolvency risk and curb the probability of a systemic banking crisis (Shehzad et al., 2009). Bank risk-taking behaviour has a negative effect on the likelihood of a banking crisis. Thus, banks that take excessive risk are able to decrease the likelihood of a systemic banking crisis. Private sector credit has a significantly positive effect on the likelihood of a banking crisis across the models. This suggests that rapid growth in private sector credit is one of the predictors of a banking crisis (Davis et al., 2019). We found a negative effect of exchange rate on banking crises. This suggests that countries that are able to realign their currency reforms have the incentive to curb the buildup of macroeconomic imbalances or possible shocks and therefore reduce a possible banking crisis. We found a negative effect of GDP per capita on the likelihood of a banking crisis. This suggests that a banking crisis is likely to be reduced by countries with higher income levels when households are able to supply funds to the financial institutions. We found institutions to negatively influence banking crisis in all models. This suggests that countries with strong institutions reduce the possibility of a banking crisis. Model 5 which combines all macro-prudential measures shows that aggregate macro-prudential policies have been less significantly used relative to capital requirement, reserve requirement and bank liquid reserves.

Interaction Effect of Macro-prudential Regulation and Monetary Policy Systemic Banking Crisis

From Table 20.3, we have established that strengthening macro-prudential regulation variables (with respect to aggregate macro-prudential policy actions, countercyclical capital requirements, reserve requirements and bank liquid reserves) and higher monetary policy rates reduce the predicted probability of systemic banking crises. In what follows, we argue that monetary policy either complements or substitutes macro-prudential regulation in curbing the predicted probability of systemic banking crisis. We introduce into the baseline model, an interaction term between the macro-prudential regulation and monetary policy. This is conducted to observe both the interaction effect and net effect of macro-prudential regulations and monetary policy. For net effect we observe whether monetary policy magnifies or reduces the negative impact of macro-prudential regulation on systemic banking crisis.

Next, we interpret the signs of the interaction terms by following the work by Compton and Giedeman (2011). From Table 20.4, the coefficient of the interaction term between macro-prudential policy actions and monetary policy rates is positive (model 6). This suggests that aggregate macro-prudential policy action substitutes monetary policy rates in reducing possible systemic banking crises. For the purpose of our study, we interpret that the effect of macro-prudential policy action in reducing the possibility of a crisis falls with higher levels of monetary policy rates. From model 7, an interaction of countercyclical capital requirements with monetary policy rates gives a negative coefficient. This suggests that countercyclical capital requirements and monetary policy rates are complements in reducing systemic banking crises. For our purposes, we explain that the effect of countercyclical capital requirements in reducing the probability of banking crises is greater with higher levels of monetary policy rates. We found that the coefficient of the interaction term between reserve requirement and monetary policy rates is significantly positive (model 8). This suggests that reserve requirement is a substitute for monetary policy rates in reducing the possibility of a crisis. That is, the effect of reserve requirements in reducing the probability of banking crisis falls with higher levels of monetary policy. The insignificant interaction term, as shown in model 9, suggests that bank liquid reserves and monetary policy effects on systemic banking crises are independent and the interaction effect is neutral.

Consistent with Brambor et al. (2006) on pitfalls of interactive regressions, we cannot establish macro-prudential regulation implications exclusively on independent impacts. Hence, there is the need to compute the overall effect or net effects as follows: (1) the net effect for aggregate macro-prudential policy action is (−0.10708) [−0.108 + (0.0107*0.0854)] (see model 6). The negative net effect suggests that monetary policy rates magnifies the negative impact of macro-prudential policy action on the predicted probability of systemic banking crises. Banks should be able to strengthen stability seeking policies in line with macro-prudential actions and monetary policy regime; (2) The net effect for countercyclical capital requirement is −0.00185 [−0.00185 + (−0.00000795*0.0854)]; (3) The net effect for reserve requirements is −0.2425 [−0.243 + (−0.00532*0.0854)]. The interpretation for the negative net effects, as shown in models 7 and 8 respectively, suggests that monetary policy rates amplify the negative effect of countercyclical capital requirements and reserve requirements on the predicted probability of systemic banking crises. The implication is that banks should be able to reduce possible systemic banking crises with stringent macro-prudential regulation on capital and reserve requirements conditioned on an effective monetary policy stance.

Following Klomp and de Haan (2014) as well as Marchionne and Pisicoli (2017), the effect of macro-prudential regulation on banking crises is sensitive to institutional quality. For this reason, we run models showing the interaction effect of macro-prudential regulation and monetary policy on banking crises in an institutional framework. We experimented these relationships and observe interesting results. However, we are interested in observing the signs attached to the coefficient of the variables and the net effects after including the interaction terms. We split the data into countries (country observations) with weak and strong institutions. This is shown in Table 20.5. Weak and strong institutions were constructed with dummies. We classify countries as having weak institutions if they strictly fall below the median value of the institutions variable for a particular year. Countries that fall above or equal the median value were classified as having strong institutions for that specific year. As was found earlier, generally, the coefficients of macro-prudential regulation and monetary policy rates are negative and significant (i.e. the unconditional effect). However, for countries with weak institutions, increasing reserve requirements may lead to the next banking crisis when an interaction term was introduced (model 13). In Table 20.5, macro-prudential policy action and bank liquid reserves are substitutes with monetary policy in reducing banking crises in countries with weak institutions (models 11 and 14) whereas countercyclical capital requirement and reserve requirements complement monetary policy rates in reducing banking crises in countries with weak institutions (models 12 and 13).

The results indicate that for countries with strong institutions, aggregate macro-prudential policy action, countercyclical capital requirements and bank liquid reserves, all complement monetary policy in reducing banking crises (models 15, 16 and 18). However, reserve requirements and monetary policy are substitutes in reducing banking crises in countries with strong institution (model 17). For countries with weak institutions, the net effects of monetary policy rates in explaining the negative impact of macro-prudential regulation (macro-prudential policy action, countercyclical capital requirements and bank liquid reserves) on systemic banking crises are negative (models 11, 12 and 14), while the net effect for reserve requirements is positive (model 13). The negative net effects show that monetary policy rates enhance the negative impact of countercyclical capital requirements, macro-prudential policy action and bank liquid reserves on the possibility of systemic banking crises in countries with weak institutions. The positive net effect shows that monetary policy rates alter the negative effect of reserve requirements on the possibility of systemic banking crises in countries with weak institutions. For countries with strong institutions, the net effect of all the macro-prudential regulation variables is negative. This shows that monetary policy rates amplify the negative effect of macro-prudential regulation on the predicted probability of systemic banking crises. Most of the interaction terms are significant at 1 or 5%.

In order to check for the robustness of our results, we rerun our regressions by introducing the lag effects and adjustments in macro-prudential regulation and monetary policy on banking crisis. Prior to that, first, we argue that if macro-prudential regulation influences the next systemic banking crisis, then it is expected that there are lags between establishing new regulations and that it takes time for these regulations or initiatives to translate into more sound banking practices. We interact with the lags of both monetary policy rates and macro-prudential regulation and introduce the interaction terms into the baseline model to capture the net effects of the relationship between lags of macro-prudential regulation and monetary policy in explaining the probability of a systemic banking crisis. Second, we argue that countries in Africa make adjustments to their regulations and policies by some basis points within a year, which may likely affect the possibility of a systemic banking crisis. For this reason, we introduce changes in macro-prudential regulation and monetary policy in our model to capture the adjustments made by governments and monetary authorities. We then regress these variables on systemic banking crisis. These are presented in Appendix B.

We do not report the independent effect of the lags and percent changes of the variables because of space. However, the conditional effects show that the lags of both macro-prudential regulation and monetary policy rates are negatively and significantly associated with systemic banking crises (see model 19–22). Moreover, changes in monetary policy rates have a negative and significant relationship with the predicted probability of a systemic banking crisis (models 23–26). The results suggest that the previous year's initiative of macro-prudential regulation and monetary policy rates are important in reducing the next systemic banking crisis. Moreover, changes in both macro-prudential regulation and monetary policy independently induce a negative predictability of the next systemic banking crisis.

In terms of the interaction effects, we estimate the net effects of macro-prudential regulation variables (with lags and without lags) conditioned on either monetary policy rates or percent changes in monetary policy rates. In Table 20.6, the net effects for the lags of reserve requirements and bank liquid reserves are negative (models 21 and 22). This suggests that monetary policy rates amplify the negative effect of the previous year's reserve requirements and bank liquid reserves on a systemic banking crisis. However, the net effect for the lag of macro-prudential policy action is positive (model 19). This suggests that monetary policy rates alter the negative impact of the previous year's macro-prudential policy action on a systemic banking crisis. From Table 20.7, we found the net effects for macro-prudential policy action and countercyclical capital requirements to be negatively conditioned on changes in monetary policy (see models 23 and 24). This suggests that adjustments made to monetary policy rates magnify the negative impact of macro-prudential policy action and countercyclical capital requirements on a systemic banking crisis.

Finally, in Table 20.8, we observe a negative net effects for the lags of macro-prudential regulation conditioned on changes in monetary policy rates except for the lag reserve requirements (insignificant interaction term), as shown in models 27 and 28. This indicates that changes in monetary policy rates by basic points or percent change, amplify the negative effect of the previous years' initiatives and actions of macro-prudential regulation on a systemic banking crisis.

20.6 Conclusion and Policy Implications

In this study, we have examined whether the effect of macro-prudential regulation on the predicted probability of a systemic banking crisis depends on monetary policy. Using a logit panel regression and several measures of macro-prudential regulation and monetary policy, we find that macro-prudential regulation and monetary policy independently reduce the likelihood of a systemic banking crisis to occur. By introducing interaction terms into the baseline model, we find that macro-prudential policy action and reserve requirements are substitutes with monetary policy in reducing a possible systemic banking crisis while countercyclical capital requirements and monetary policy are complements in reducing a crisis. We interpret our results based on the net effects as indicating that a tight monetary policy stance alters the negative effect of macro-prudential policy action on a systemic banking crisis. However, monetary policy rates amplify the negative effects of countercyclical capital requirement and reserve requirements on the probability of a systemic banking crisis. We then split the sample based on the quality of institutions, arguing that the relationships may be contradictory in countries with varying levels of institutional quality. We found that monetary policy rates enhance the negative effect of macro-prudential regulation on the predicted probability of a systemic banking crisis in countries with strong institutions. On the other hand, reserve requirements and monetary policy rates are independent of each other in their effect on a systemic banking crisis in countries with weak institutions. We show that the negative net effect estimates of the lagged macro-prudential regulation suggest a high degree of persistence in yearly reduction of the likelihood of a systemic banking crisis. As expected, policy adjustment of monetary policy rates enhances the negative effect of macro-prudential regulation and their lags on predicted probability of a systemic banking crisis.

The major implication of this study is that macro-prudential regulation and monetary policy matter for reducing systemic banking crisis outcomes, in terms of how monetary policy interacts with macro-prudential regulations. However, this effect is effective in countries with strong institutions. In general, the corresponding low net effects in these countries imply that macro-prudential regulation needs to be improved in order to curb the likelihood of systemic banking crises when a tight monetary policy stance is taken. Thus, for poor countries, efforts at strengthening macro-prudential regulation, particularly reserve requirements will be helpful in overcoming the constraints and complex relationship between these regulations and systemic banking crisis outcomes.

Appendix A

See Tables 20.1, 20.2, 20.3, 20.4, and 20.5.

Table 20.1 Descriptive statistics

Variables	*Obs*	*Mean*	*Std. dev*	*Min*	*Max*	*p1*	*p99*	*VIF*
Macro-Prudential Policy Action	4444	0.012	0.143	−1	1	0	1	1.36
Capital Requirement	3929	37.465	48.325	−137.042	156.559	−90.011	148.358	2.36
Reserve Requirement	6903	0.086	0.06	0.009	0.275	0.01	0.275	2.15
Bank Liquid Reserve	4859	17.471	16.327	2.088	115.719	2.259	93.301	1.48
Monetary Policy Rate	6764	8.54	5.68	−4.13	26	−10.73	25.61	2.10
Bank Funding	4274	0.752	0.218	−0.465	2.608	0.001	1.109	1.11
Credit Risks	2340	0.081	0.128	−0.584	1.519	−0.15	0.536	1.06
Bank Concentration	5681	55.32	27.69	0.28	100	3.563	91.533	2.45
Bank Risk Taking	5749	0.016	3.856	−0.0036	0.14	−0.553	0.711	3.53
Private Sector Credit	6724	22.877	23.37	0	94.519	0	87.979	1.53

(continued)

Table 20.1 (continued)

Variables	*Obs*	*Mean*	*Std. dev*	*Min*	*Max*	*p1*	*p99*	*VIF*
Exchange Rate	6245	4.172	2.421	−0.087	10.266	0.056	9.179	1.39
GDP per cap	6242	2.76	4.042	−17.473	24.215	−7.908	17.69	1.23
Institutions	6300	−0.483	0.545	−0.66	0.853	−1.608	0.823	2.89
							Mean VIF	1.89

Macro-Prudential Policy Action Policy action is the sum of dummies for all 17 categories: countercyclical capital buffer, requirements for banks to maintain a capital conservation buffer, capital requirements, limit on leverage of banks, loan loss provision requirements, limits on foreign currency, limits to the loan-to-value ratios, debt service-to-income ratio, minimum requirements for liquidity coverage ratios, limits to the loan-deposit ratio, limits to net or gross open foreign exchange positions, reserve requirements, loan restrictions, risk measures, taxes and levies applied to specified transactions and other Macro-Prudential Policy Action measures not captured in the above categories; **Capital Requirement** is the **Countercyclical** Capital Requirement which is the ratio of bank regulation capital to risk weighted assets; **Reserve Requirement** is the specified percentage of the amount of deposits held by banks; **Bank Liquid Reserve is** the ratio of bank liquid reserve to bank total assets; **Monetary Policy Rate (MPR)** is the central bank policy rate of a country; **Bank Funding** is the ratio of total deposits to total ratio; **Credit Risk** is the ratio of nonperforming to gross loan; **Bank Concentration** is the industry asset concentration of banks, measured as the ratio of asset of the three largest commercial natural logarithm of total bank assets; **Bank Risk Taking** is measured as the inverse of Z-score (ratio of the sum of return on asset and capital adequacy relative to the standard deviation of return on asset); **Private Sector Credit** is the ratio of private credit of deposit money banks to GDP; **Exchange rate** is the natural logarithm of a country's currency rate to the dollar; **GDP per capita** is the natural logarithm of GDP per capital; **Institutions** is measured as an aggregate of six indicators (rule of law, government effectiveness, control of corruption, political stability, regulatory quality and voice and accountability) from the World Governance Indicators

Table 20.2 Matrix of correlations

Variables	*(1)*	*(2)*	*(3)*	*(4)*	*(5)*	*(6)*	*(7)*	*(8)*	*(9)*	*(10)*	*(11)*	*(12)*	*(13)*
(1) Macro-Prudential Policy Action	1.000												
(2) Capital Requirement	−0.093	1.000											
(3) Reserve Requirement	−0.005	−0.415	1.000										
(4) Bank Liquid Reserve	0.337	−0.252	0.265	1.000									
(5) Monetary Policy Rate	−0.046	0.379	−0.371	−0.057	1.000								
(6) Bank Funding	−0.037	0.065	−0.032	−0.145	0.029	1.000							
(7) Credit Risk	0.032	0.053	0.352	0.367	0.156	0.006	1.000						
(8) Bank Concentration	0.100	−0.513	0.173	0.067	−0.250	−0.025	0.004	1.000					
(9) Bank Risk Taking	0.025	−0.041	0.077	0.025	−0.042	−0.038	0.069	0.194	1.000				
(10) Private Sector Credit	−0.053	−0.111	−0.168	0.076	0.262	−0.101	−0.023	0.178	0.052	1.000			
(11) Exchange Rate	−0.016	0.053	0.032	−0.177	−0.297	0.084	−0.126	0.175	−0.022	−0.304	1.000		
(12) GDP per capita	−0.063	0.119	0.089	0.045	0.163	0.032	0.208	−0.215	0.017	−0.252	0.057	1.000	

Variables	*(1)*	*(2)*	*(3)*	*(4)*	*(5)*	*(6)*	*(7)*	*(8)*	*(9)*	*(10)*	*(11)*	*(12)*	*(13)*
(13) Institutions	−0.131	0.160	−0.395	−0.261	0.016	−0.044	−0.281	−0.432	−0.042	−0.119	0.064	0.258	1.000

Macro-Prudential Policy Action Policy action is the sum of dummies for all 17 categories: countercyclical capital buffer, requirements for banks to maintain a capital conservation buffer, capital requirements, limit on leverage of banks, loan loss provision requirements, limits on foreign currency, limits to the loan-to-value ratios, debt service-to-income ratio, minimum requirements for liquidity coverage ratios, limits to the loan-deposit ratio, limits to net or gross open foreign exchange positions, reserve requirements, loan restrictions, risk measures, taxes and levies applied to specified transactions and other Macro-Prudential Policy Action measures not captured in the above categories; **Capital Requirement** is the **Countercyclical** Capital Requirement which is the ratio of bank regulation capital to risk weighted assets; **Reserve Requirement** is the specified percentage of the amount of deposits held by banks; **Bank Liquid Reserve is** the ratio of bank liquid reserve to bank total assets**;** **Monetary Policy Rate(MPR)** is the central bank policy rate of a country; **Bank Funding** is the ratio of total deposits to total ratio; **Credit Risk** is the ratio of nonperforming to gross loan; **Bank Concentration** is the industry asset concentration of banks, measured as the ratio of asset of the three largest commercial natural logarithm of total bank assets; **Bank Risk Taking** is measured as the inverse of Z-score (ratio of the sum of return on asset and capital adequacy relative to the standard deviation of return on asset); **Private Sector Credit** is the ratio of private credit of deposit money banks to GDP; **Exchange rate** is the natural logarithm of a country's currency rate to the dollar; **GDP per capita** is the natural logarithm of GDP per capital; **Institutions** are measured as an aggregate of six indicators (rule of law, government effectiveness, control of corruption, political stability, regulatory quality and voice and accountability) from the World Governance Indicators

Table 20.3 Independent effects of macro-prudential regulations and monetary policy on systemic banking crisis

Variables	*Model 1*	*Model 2*	*Model 3*	*Model 4*	*Model 5*
Macro-Prudential Policy Action	**−0.150***** **(0.0406)**				−0.0310 (0.118)
Capital Requirement		**−0.00202***** **(0.000253)**			−0.00337*** (0.000270)
Reserve Requirement			**−0.227***** **(0.0632)**		−0.784*** (0.108)
Bank Liquid Reserve				**−0.00497***** **(0.000738)**	−0.00711*** (0.00110)
Monetary Policy Rate (MPR)	−0.00259*** (0.000275)	−0.00201*** (0.000213)	−0.00214*** (0.000239)	−0.00247*** (0.000268)	−0.00225*** (0.000209)
Bank Funding	−0.0394 (0.0470)	−0.110*** (0.0393)	−0.0135 (0.0305)	−0.167*** (0.0510)	−0.237*** (0.0540)
Credit Risk	0.235** (0.0945)	0.0984 (0.0673)	0.204*** (0.0684)	0.118 (0.0732)	0.0413 (0.0628)
Bank Concentration	−0.000374*** (4.70e−05)	−0.000601*** (6.32e−05)	−0.000350*** (4.49e−05)	−0.000394*** (4.42e−05)	−0.000713*** (5.60e−05)
Bank Risk Taking	−0.00127*** (0.000166)	−0.000710*** (0.000145)	−0.00105*** (0.000127)	−0.000810*** (0.000174)	0.000778** (0.000320)
Private Sector Credit	0.00151*** (0.000406)	0.00175*** (0.000374)	0.000498* (0.000284)	0.00185*** (0.000382)	0.00107** (0.000430)
Exchange Rate	−2.67e−05*** (4.84e−06)	−9.43e−06* (4.90e−06)	−2.64e−05*** (4.81e−06)	−3.03e−05*** (4.84e−06)	−1.27e−05** (5.41e−06)
GDP per capita	−0.00100 (0.00194)	−0.00482** (0.00227)	−0.000498 (0.00160)	−0.00307 (0.00193)	−0.00293 (0.00273)
Institutions	−0.0999*** (0.0186)	−0.0850*** (0.0184)	−0.0665*** (0.0164)	−0.129*** (0.0193)	−0.200*** (0.0291)

Variables	*Model 1*	*Model 2*	*Model 3*	*Model 4*	*Model 5*
Year Effect	Yes	Yes	Yes	Yes	Yes
Country Effect	Yes	Yes	Yes	Yes	Yes
Constant	0.0887**	0.179***	0.0942***	0.252***	0.507***
	(0.0426)	(0.0404)	(0.0330)	(0.0511)	(0.0600)
Observations	824	807	1,055	786	598
R-squared	0.253	0.326	0.223	0.350	0.567
p-value	0.00	0.00	0.00	0.00	0.00

Capital Requirement *is the* ***Countercyclical*** *Capital Requirement which is the ratio of bank regulation capital to risk weighted assets;* ***Reserve Requirement*** *is* the specified percentage of the amount of deposits held by banks*;* **Macro-Prudential Policy Action Policy action** *is the sum of dummies for all 17 categories: countercyclical capital buffer, requirements for banks to maintain a capital conservation buffer, capital requirements, limit on leverage of banks, loan loss provision requirements, limits on foreign currency, limits to the loan-to-value ratios, debt service-to-income ratio, minimum requirements for liquidity coverage ratios, limits to the loan-deposit ratio, limits to net or gross open foreign exchange positions, reserve requirements, loan restrictions, risk measures, taxes and levies applied to specified transactions and other Macro-Prudential Policy Action measures not captured in the above categories;* **Bank Liquid Reserve** *is the ratio of bank liquid reserve to bank total assets;* ***Monetary Policy Rate(MPR)*** *is the central bank policy rate of a country;* ***Bank Funding*** *is the ratio of total deposits to total ratio;* ***Credit Risk*** *is the ratio of nonperforming to gross loan;* ***Bank Concentration*** *is the industry asset concentration of banks, measured as the ratio of asset of the three largest commercial natural logarithm of total bank assets;* ***Private Sector Credit*** *is the ratio of private credit of deposit money banks to GDP;* ***Exchange rate*** *is the natural logarithm of a country's currency rate to the dollar;* ***GDP per capita*** *is the natural logarithm of GDP per capital;* **Bank Risk Taking** *is measured as the inverse of Z-score (ratio of the sum of return on asset and capital adequacy relative to the standard deviation of return on asset).* **Institutions** *are measured as an aggregate of six indicators (rule of law, government effectiveness, control of corruption, political stability, regulatory quality and voice and accountability) from the World Governance Indicators*

Robust standard errors in parentheses

***$p < 0.01$, **$p < 0.05$, *$p < 0.1$

Table 20.4 Interaction effect of macro-prudential regulations and monetary policy on systemic banking crisis

Variables	*Model 6*	*Model 7*	*Model 8*	*Model 9*	*Model 10*
Macro-Prudential Policy Action	**−0.108***** **(0.0390)**				0.106 (0.102)
Capital Requirement		**−0.00185***** **(0.000274)**			−0.00372*** (0.000313)
Reserve Requirement			**−0.243***** **(0.0634)**		−0.827*** (0.116)
Bank Liquid Reserve				**−0.00511***** **(0.000817)**	−0.00629*** (0.00105)
Monetary Policy Rate (MPR)	−0.00260*** (0.000276)	−0.00159*** (0.000264)	−0.00254*** (0.000326)	−0.00281*** (0.000351)	0.00191* (0.00115)
Macro-Prudential Policy Action*MPR	**0.0107***** **(0.00306)**				0.0322*** (0.0103)
Capital Requirement*MPR		**−7.95e−06**** **(3.42e−06)**			−1.41e−05*** (4.72e−06)
Reserve Requirement*MPR			**0.00532**** **(0.00260)**		− 0.0647*** (0.0250)
Bank Liquid Reserve*MPR				2.43e−05 (1.49e−05)	8.79e−05 (7.39e−05)

Variables	*Model 6*	*Model 7*	*Model 8*	*Model 9*	*Model 10*
Bank Funding	−0.0383	−0.110***	−0.0145	−0.164***	−0.198***
	(0.0470)	(0.0390)	(0.0306)	(0.0511)	(0.0492)
Credit Risk	0.235**	0.101	0.201***	0.118	0.0533
	(0.0945)	(0.0675)	(0.0687)	(0.0730)	(0.0560)
Bank Concentration	−0.000376***	−0.000621***	−0.000352***	−0.000392***	−0.000840***
	(4.71e−05)	(6.47e−05)	(4.54e−05)	(4.42e−05)	(7.31e−05)
Bank Risk Taking	−0.00128***	−0.000733***	−0.00113***	−0.00149***	−0.000336
	(0.000169)	(0.000149)	(0.000137)	(0.000195)	(0.000451)
Private Sector Credit	0.00152***	0.00187***	0.000545*	0.00171***	0.000725
	(0.000406)	(0.000387)	(0.000289)	(0.000394)	(0.000477)
Exchange Rate	−2.68e−05***	−6.71e−06	−2.62e−05***	−3.13e−05***	−7.43e−06
	(4.85e−06)	(5.19e−06)	(4.83e−06)	(5.09e−06)	(5.91e−06)
GDP per capita	−0.00110	−0.00565**	−0.00132	−0.00426**	− 0.00149
	(0.00195)	(0.00226)	(0.00175)	(0.00203)	(0.00352)
Institutions	0.0997***	0.0890***	0.0777***	0.141***	0.249***
	(0.0187)	(0.0199)	(0.0178)	(0.0187)	(0.0267)
Year Effect	Yes	Yes	Yes	Yes	Yes
Country Effect	Yes	Yes	Yes	Yes	Yes
Constant	0.0880**	0.170***	0.0988***	0.259***	0.448***
	(0.0426)	(0.0410)	(0.0334)	(0.0519)	(0.0559)

(continued)

Table 20.4 (continued)

Variables	*Model 6*	*Model 7*	*Model 8*	*Model 9*	*Model 10*
Observations	824	807	1,055	786	598
R-squared	0.254	0.328	0.224	0.351	0.605
p-value	0.00	0.00	0.00	0.00	0.00
Net Effect	**−0.1071**	**−0.00185**	**−0.2425**		

Capital Requirement *is the* ***Countercyclical*** *Capital Requirement which is the ratio of bank regulation capital to risk weighted assets;* ***Reserve Requirement*** *is* the specified percentage of the amount of deposits held by banks; **Macro-Prudential Policy Action Policy action** *is the sum of dummies for all 17 categories: countercyclical capital buffer, requirements for banks to maintain a capital conservation buffer, capital requirements, limit on leverage of banks, loan loss provision requirements, limits on foreign currency, limits to the loan-to-value ratios, debt service-to-income ratio, minimum requirements for liquidity coverage ratios, limits to the loan-deposit ratio, limits to net or gross open foreign exchange positions, reserve requirements, loan restrictions, risk measures, taxes and levies applied to specified transactions and other Macro-Prudential Policy Action measures not captured in the above categories;* **Bank Liquid Reserve** ***is*** *the ratio of bank liquid reserve to bank total assets;* ***Monetary Policy Rate(MPR)*** *is the central bank policy rate of a country;* ***Bank Funding*** *is the ratio of total deposits to total ratio;* ***Credit Risk*** *is the ratio of nonperforming to gross loan;* ***Bank Concentration*** *is the industry asset concentration of banks, measured as the ratio of asset of the three largest commercial natural logarithm of total bank assets;* ***Private Sector Credit*** *is the ratio of private credit of deposit money banks to GDP;* ***Exchange rate*** *is the natural logarithm of a country's currency rate to the dollar;* ***GDP per capita*** *is the natural logarithm of GDP per capital;* **Bank Risk Taking** *is measured as the inverse of Z-score (ratio of the sum of return on asset and capital adequacy relative to the standard deviation of return on asset).* **Institutions** *are measured as an aggregate of six indicators (rule of law, government effectiveness, control of corruption, political stability, regulatory quality and voice and accountability) from the World Governance Indicators*

Robust standard errors in parentheses

***$p<0.01$, **$p<0.05$, *$p<0.1$

Table 20.5 Interaction effect for countries with different AI framework

	Weak institutions			
Variables	*Model 11*	*Model 12*	*Model 13*	*Model 14*
Macro-Prudential Policy Action	−0.0020645 (0.0033619)			
Capital Requirement		**−0.00431***** **(0.000406)**		
Reserve Requirement			**1.243***** **(0.369)**	
Bank Liquid Reserve				**−0.00762***** **(0.00175)**
Monetary Policy Rate (MPR)	−0.00188*** (0.000213)	8.33e − 05 (0.000613)	3.65e − 05 (0.000751)	−0.00403*** (0.000738)
Macro-Prudential Policy*MPR	**0.0288**** **(0.0141)**			
Capital Requirement*MPR		**−9.92e − 05***** **(1.13e − 05)**		
Reserve Requirement*MPR			**−0.0339***** **(0.0103)**	
Bank Liquid Reserve*MPR				**0.000123***** **(3.80e − 05)**
Bank Funding	−0.176*** (0.0395)	−0.0953 (0.0979)	−0.00134 (0.0629)	−0.173*** (0.0377)
Credit Risk	0.000859 (0.0485)	−0.101** (0.0494)	0.00494 (0.0914)	−0.0129 (0.0474)
Bank Concentration	−0.000628*** (2.89e − 05)	−0.00101*** (5.74e − 05)	−0.000462*** (4.84e − 05)	−0.000595*** (2.72e − 05)

(continued)

Table 20.5 (continued)

	Weak institutions			
Variables	*Model 11*	*Model 12*	*Model 13*	*Model 14*
Bank Risk Taking	−0.0107***	−0.00123***	−0.00270***	−0.00899***
	(0.000628)	(0.000384)	(0.000436)	(0.000621)
Private Sector Credit	0.00444***	0.00230***	0.00215***	0.00412***
	(0.000471)	(0.000668)	(0.000572)	(0.000561)
Exchange Rate	6.69e − 05***	1.52e − 05**	3.02e − 06	3.18e − 05***
	(4.49e − 06)	(7.00e − 06)	(4.82e − 06)	(8.95e − 06)
	0.00362	0.00853***	0.000793	0.00207
	(0.00247)	(0.00302)	(0.00252)	(0.00290)
Year Effect	Yes	Yes	Yes	Yes
Country Effect	Yes	Yes	Yes	Yes
Constant	0.241***	0.205**	0.0123	0.343***
	(0.0404)	(0.0856)	(0.0556)	(0.0463)
Observations	390	331	479	381
R-squared	0.726	0.652	0.424	0.744
p-value	0.00	0.00	0.00	0.00
Net Effect	**n.a**	**−0.00432**	**1.2399**	**−0.000761**

	Strong institutions			
Variables	*Model 15*	*Model 16*	*Model 17*	*Model 18*
Macro-Prudential Policy Action	**−0.0491*****			
	(0.0174)			
Capital Requirement		**−0.000394****		
		(0.000186)		

	Strong institutions			
Variables	*Model 15*	*Model 16*	*Model 17*	*Model 18*
Reserve Requirement			**−1.301***** **(0.304)**	
Bank Liquid Reserve				**−0.00234***** **(0.000472)**
Monetary Policy Rate (MPR)	−0.00105*** (0.000269)	−5.45e − 05 (0.000177)	−0.00358*** (0.000825)	0.000618** (0.000299)
Macro-Prudential Policy*MPR	**−0.00411**** **(0.00176)**			
Capital Requirement*MPR		**−8.29e − 06*** **(4.67e − 06)**		
Reserve Requirement*MPR			**0.0169***** **(0.00467)**	
Bank Liquid Reserve*MPR				**−0.000144***** **(1.96e − 05)**
Bank Funding	0.0584 (0.0450)	0.00826 (0.0240)	0.0672** (0.0274)	−0.116*** (0.0424)
Credit Risk	0.291*** (0.110)	0.202** (0.0867)	0.201** (0.0783)	0.0724 (0.0688)
Bank Concentration	−0.000300*** (8.15e − 05)	−0.000349*** (0.000117)	−0.000280*** (6.79e − 05)	−0.000360*** (4.67e − 05)
Bank Risk Taking	−0.00110*** (0.000285)	−0.000929*** (0.000272)	−0.000997*** (0.000240)	−0.00149*** (0.000195)
Private Sector Credit	0.000896 (0.000702)	0.00134** (0.000678)	−0.000892* (0.000496)	0.00274*** (0.000459)
Exchange Rate	−4.16e − 05***	−1.77e − 05**	−4.52e − 05***	−2.34e − 05***

(continued)

Table 20.5 (continued)

Variables	*Strong institutions*			
	Model 15	*Model 16*	*Model 17*	*Model 18*
	(1.40e − 05)	(6.93e − 06)	(1.11e − 05)	(6.31e − 06)
	−0.00105	0.000248	7.29e − 05	−0.00238
	(0.00239)	(0.00191)	(0.00178)	(0.00196)
Year Effect	Yes	Yes	Yes	Yes
Country Effect	Yes	Yes	Yes	Yes
Constant	0.0329	0.0498	0.276***	0.262***
	(0.0446)	(0.0354)	(0.0733)	(0.0443)
Observations	434	476	576	786
R-squared	0.142	0.123	0.225	0.515
p-value	0.00	0.00	0.00	0.00
Net Effect	**−0.049**	**−0.0003947**	**−1.2996**	**−0.00235**

Capital Requirement *is the* ***Countercyclical*** *Capital Requirement which is the ratio of bank regulation capital to risk weighted assets;* ***Reserve Requirement*** *is* the specified percentage of the amount of deposits held by banks; **Macro-Prudential Policy Action Policy action** *is the sum of dummies for all 17 categories: countercyclical capital buffer, requirements for banks to maintain a capital conservation buffer, capital requirements, limit on leverage of banks, loan loss provision requirements, limits on foreign currency, limits to the loan-to-value ratios, debt service-to-income ratio, minimum requirements for liquidity coverage ratios, limits to the loan-deposit ratio, limits to net or gross open foreign exchange positions, reserve requirements, loan restrictions, risk measures, taxes and levies applied to specified transactions and other Macro-Prudential Policy Action measures not captured in the above categories;* **Bank Liquid Reserve** ***is*** *the ratio of bank liquid reserve to bank total assets;* ***Monetary Policy Rate(MPR)*** *is the central bank policy rate of a country;* ***Bank Funding*** *is the ratio of total deposits to total ratio;* ***Credit Risk*** *is the ratio of nonperforming to gross loan;* ***Bank Concentration*** *is the industry asset concentration of banks, measured as the ratio of asset of the three largest commercial natural logarithm of total bank assets;* ***Private Sector Credit*** *is the ratio of private credit of deposit money banks to GDP;* ***Exchange rate*** *is the natural logarithm of a country's currency rate to the dollar;* ***GDP per capita*** *is the natural logarithm of GDP per capital;* **Bank Risk Taking** *is measured as the inverse of Z-score (ratio of the sum of return on asset and capital adequacy relative to the standard deviation of return on asset).* **Institutions** *are measured as an aggregate of six indicators (rule of law, government effectiveness, control of corruption, political stability, regulatory quality and voice and accountability) from the World Governance Indicators*

Robust standard errors in parentheses

***$p < 0.01$, **$p < 0.05$, *$p < 0.1$

Appendix B: Robust Results

See Tables 20.6, 20.7, and 20.8.

Table 20.6 The lag interaction effect of macro-prudential regulation and monetary policy

PANEL A	*Model 19*	*Model 20*	*Model 21*	*Model 22*
Macro-Prudential Policy Action$_{t-1}$	**−0.116*** **			
	(0.0393)			
Capital Requirement$_{t-1}$		**−0.00186*** **		
		(0.000277)		
Reserve Requirement$_{t-1}$			**−0.201*** **	
			(0.0628)	
Bank Liquid Reserve$_{t-1}$				**−0.00420*** **
				(0.000730)
Monetary Policy Rate (MPR)	−0.00255***	−0.00183***	−0.00252***	−0.00271***
	(0.000272)	(0.000284)	(0.000321)	(0.000341)
MPR*Macro-Prudential Policy Action$_{t-1}$	0.0105***			
	(0.00299)			
MPR*Capital Requirement$_{t-1}$		−4.21e−06		
		(3.87e−06)		
MPR*Reserve Requirement$_{t-1}$			0.00535**	
			(0.00249)	
MPR*Bank Liquid Reserve$_{t-1}$				2.56e−05*
				(1.31e−05)
Bank Funding	−0.0438	−0.104***	−0.0164	−0.124**
	(0.0474)	(0.0400)	(0.0309)	(0.0499)
Credit Risk	0.226**	0.120*	0.202***	0.135*
	(0.0901)	(0.0698)	(0.0689)	(0.0724)

(continued)

Table 20.6 (continued)

PANEL A	*Model 19*	*Model 20*	*Model 21*	*Model 22*
Bank Concentration	−0.000371***	−0.000588***	−0.000353***	−0.000388***
	(4.67e−05)	(6.39e−05)	(4.56e−05)	(4.51e−05)
Private Sector Credit	0.00130***	0.00167***	0.000548*	0.00153***
	(0.000390)	(0.000393)	(0.000295)	(0.000378)
Exchange Rate	−2.61e−05***	−1.02e−05*	−2.54e−05***	−2.49e−05***
	(4.90e−06)	(5.48e−06)	(4.76e−06)	(4.78e−06)
GDP per cap	−0.00121	−0.00573**	−0.00156	−0.00496**
	(0.00193)	(0.00228)	(0.00176)	(0.00199)
Institutions	0.176***	0.105***	0.126***	0.193***
	(0.0386)	(0.0369)	(0.0292)	(0.0345)
Year Effect	Yes	Yes	Yes	Yes
Country Effect	Yes	Yes	Yes	Yes
Constant	0.0962**	0.174***	0.0959***	0.209***
	(0.0431)	(0.0426)	(0.0339)	(0.0496)
Observations	831	798	1,049	787
R-squared	0.251	0.319	0.223	0.338
Net Effect	**−0.1151**		**−0.2005**	**−0.004197**

Capital Requirement is the **Countercyclical** Capital Requirement which is the ratio of bank regulation capital to risk weighted assets; **Reserve Requirement** is the specified percentage of the amount of deposits held by banks; **Macro-Prudential Policy Action Policy action** is the sum of dummies for all 17 categories: countercyclical capital buffer, requirements for banks to maintain a capital conservation buffer, capital requirements, limit on leverage of banks, loan loss provision requirements, limits on foreign currency, limits to the loan-to-value ratios, debt service-to-income ratio, minimum requirements for liquidity coverage ratios, limits to the loan-deposit ratio, limits to net or gross open foreign exchange positions, reserve requirements, loan restrictions, risk measures, taxes and levies applied to specified transactions and other Macro-Prudential Policy Action measures not captured in the above categories; **Bank Liquid Reserve is** the ratio of bank liquid reserve to bank total assets; **Monetary Policy Rate(MPR)** is the central bank policy rate of a country; **Bank Funding** is the ratio of total deposits to total ratio; **Credit Risk** is the ratio of nonperforming to gross loan; **Bank Concentration** is the industry asset concentration of banks, measured as the ratio of asset of the three largest commercial natural logarithm of total bank assets; **Private Sector Credit** is the ratio of private credit of deposit money banks to GDP; **Exchange rate** is the natural logarithm of a country's currency rate to the dollar; **GDP per capita** is the natural logarithm of GDP per capital; **Bank Risk Taking** is measured as the inverse of Z-score (ratio of the sum of return on asset and capital adequacy relative to the standard deviation of return on asset). **Institutions** are measured as an aggregate of six indicators (rule of law, government effectiveness, control of corruption, political stability, regulatory quality and voice and accountability) from the World Governance Indicators

Robust standard errors in parentheses

***p<0.01, **p<0.05, *p<0.1

Table 20.7 Effect of changes in monetary policy and macro-prudential regulations

PANEL B	*Model 23*	*Model 24*	*Model 25*	*Model 26*
Macro-Prudential Policy Action	−0.134**			
	(0.0573)			
Capital Requirement		−0.00282***		
		(0.000318)		
Reserve Requirement			0.137***	
			(0.0424)	
Bank Liquid Reserve				−0.00446***
				(0.000839)
ΔMPR	−0.000124*	−0.000607*	−6.98e−05*	0.000137
	(6.67e−05)	(0.000316)	(3.87e−05)	(0.000587)
ΔMPR*Macro-Prudential Policy Action	−0.00120*			
	(0.000629)			
ΔMPR*Capital Requirement		0.000245**		
		(9.88e−05)		
ΔMPR*Reserve Requirement			0.000154	
			(0.000646)	
ΔMPR*Bank Liquid Reserve				−9.83e−06
				(2.12e−05)
Bank Funding	−0.0776	−0.111***	−0.0312	−0.193***
	(0.0542)	(0.0422)	(0.0328)	(0.0607)
Credit Risk	0.194**	0.0187	0.171**	0.0762
	(0.0896)	(0.0615)	(0.0703)	(0.0723)
Bank Concentration	−0.000305***	−0.000603***	−0.000317***	−0.000325***
	(5.12e−05)	(7.12e−05)	(4.95e−05)	(4.72e−05)
Private Sector Credit	3.65e−05	0.00114***	0.000286	0.000397
	(0.000317)	(0.000359)	(0.000262)	(0.000279)

(continued)

Table 20.7 (continued)

PANEL B	*Model 23*	*Model 24*	*Model 25*	*Model 26*
Exchange Rate	−8.01e−06**	4.41e−06	−4.62e−06	−1.15e−05***
	(3.84e−06)	(5.12e−06)	(3.38e−06)	(3.76e−06)
GDP per cap	−0.00251	−0.00756***	−0.00270	−0.00353*
	(0.00223)	(0.00248)	(0.00181)	(0.00206)
Institutions	0.106*	0.0360	0.0874**	0.243***
	(0.0594)	(0.0474)	(0.0400)	(0.0310)
Year Effect	Yes	Yes	Yes	Yes
Country Effect	Yes	Yes	Yes	Yes
Constant	0.0747	0.183***	0.0179	0.222***
	(0.0476)	(0.0424)	(0.0319)	(0.0579)
Observations	809	796	1,040	771
R-squared	0.122	0.270	0.124	0.214
Net Effect	**−0.13632**	**−0.002345**		

Capital Requirement is the **Countercyclical** Capital Requirement which is the ratio of bank regulation capital to risk weighted assets; **Reserve Requirement** is the specified percentage of the amount of deposits held by banks; **Macro-Prudential Policy Action Policy action** is the sum of dummies for all 17 categories: countercyclical capital buffer, requirements for banks to maintain a capital conservation buffer, capital requirements, limit on leverage of banks, loan loss provision requirements, limits on foreign currency, limits to the loan-to-value ratios, debt service-to-income ratio, minimum requirements for liquidity coverage ratios, limits to the loan-deposit ratio, limits to net or gross open foreign exchange positions, reserve requirements, loan restrictions, risk measures, taxes and levies applied to specified transactions and other Macro-Prudential Policy Action measures not captured in the above categories; **Bank Liquid Reserve is** the ratio of bank liquid reserve to bank total assets**;** **Monetary Policy Rate(MPR)** is the central bank policy rate of a country; **Bank Funding** is the ratio of total deposits to total ratio; **Credit Risk** is the ratio of nonperforming to gross loan; **Bank Concentration** is the industry asset concentration of banks, measured as the ratio of asset of the three largest commercial natural logarithm of total bank assets; **Private Sector Credit** is the ratio of private credit of deposit money banks to GDP; **Exchange rate** is the natural logarithm of a country's currency rate to the dollar; **GDP per capita** is the natural logarithm of GDP per capital; **Bank Risk Taking** is measured as the inverse of Z-score (ratio of the sum of return on asset and capital adequacy relative to the standard deviation of return on asset). **Institutions** are measured as an aggregate of six indicators (rule of law, government effectiveness, control of corruption, political stability, regulatory quality and voice and accountability) from the World Governance Indicators

Robust standard errors in parentheses

***p<0.01, **p<0.05, *p<0.1

Table 20.8 The lag interaction effect of macro-prudential regulations and changes in monetary policy

PANEL C	*Model 27*	*Model 28*	*Model 29*	*Model 30*
Macro-Prudential Policy Action$_{t-1}$	−0.135**			
	(0.0573)			
Capital Requirement$_{t-1}$		−0.00278***		
		(0.000324)		
Reserve Requirement$_{t-1}$			0.145***	
			(0.0439)	
Bank Liquid Reserve$_{t-1}$				−0.00396***
				(0.000765)
Δ Monetary Policy Rate (MPR)	−6.74e−05	−0.00341*	−0.000251	0.000603***
	(6.16e−05)	(0.00201)	(0.000166)	(0.000182)
ΔMPR*Macro-Prudential Policy Action$_{t-1}$	**−0.00108****			
	(0.000454)			
ΔMPR*Capital Requirement$_{t-1}$		**0.000277*****		
		(0.000101)		
ΔMPR*Reserve Requirement$_{t-1}$			0.00309	
			(0.00224)	
ΔMPR*Bank Liquid Reserve$_{t-1}$				**−2.98e−05*****
				(7.60e−06)
Bank Funding	−0.0795	−0.106**	−0.0318	−0.188***
	(0.0538)	(0.0427)	(0.0334)	(0.0618)
Credit Risk	0.192**	0.0426	0.170**	0.0923
	(0.0870)	(0.0626)	(0.0702)	(0.0711)
Bank Concentration	−0.000304***	−0.000568***	−0.000318***	−0.000324***
	(5.08e−05)	(6.89e−05)	(4.96e−05)	(4.73e−05)
Private Sector Credit	−1.68e−05	0.000969***	0.000312	0.000439
	(0.000310)	(0.000361)	(0.000266)	(0.000269)

(continued)

Table 20.8 (continued)

PANEL C	*Model 27*	*Model 28*	*Model 29*	*Model 30*
Exchange Rate	−7.32e−06*	8.49e−07	−4.65e−06	−6.96e−06*
	(3.94e−06)	(5.33e−06)	(3.37e−06)	(3.64e−06)
GDP per cap	−0.00251	−0.00775***	−0.00271	−0.00391*
	(0.00221)	(0.00253)	(0.00181)	(0.00205)
Institutions	0.0890***	0.0777***	0.0997***	0.141***
	(0.0199)	(0.0178)	(0.0187)	(0.0187)
Year Effect	Yes	Yes	Yes	Yes
Country Effect	Yes	Yes	Yes	Yes
Constant	0.0772	0.185***	0.0170	0.206***
	(0.0472)	(0.0433)	(0.0325)	(0.0581)
Observations	822	793	1,040	778
R-squared	0.123	0.261	0.124	0.213
Net Effect	**−0.13629**	**−0.002449**		**−0.00397**

Capital Requirement is the **Countercyclical** Capital Requirement which is the ratio of bank regulation capital to risk weighted assets; **Reserve Requirement** is the specified percentage of the amount of deposits held by banks; **Macro-Prudential Policy Action Policy action** is the sum of dummies for all 17 categories: countercyclical capital buffer, requirements for banks to maintain a capital conservation buffer, capital requirements, limit on leverage of banks, loan loss provision requirements, limits on foreign currency, limits to the loan-to-value ratios, debt service-to-income ratio, minimum requirements for liquidity coverage ratios, limits to the loan-deposit ratio, limits to net or gross open foreign exchange positions, reserve requirements, loan restrictions, risk measures, taxes and levies applied to specified transactions and other Macro-Prudential Policy Action measures not captured in the above categories; **Bank Liquid Reserve is** the ratio of bank liquid reserve to bank total assets**; Monetary Policy Rate(MPR)** is the central bank policy rate of a country; **Bank Funding** is the ratio of total deposits to total ratio; **Credit Risk** is the ratio of nonperforming to gross loan; **Bank Concentration** is the industry asset concentration of banks, measured as the ratio of asset of the three largest commercial natural logarithm of total bank assets; **Private Sector Credit** is the ratio of private credit of deposit money banks to GDP; **Exchange rate** is the natural logarithm of a country's currency rate to the dollar; **GDP per capita** is the natural logarithm of GDP per capital; **Bank Risk Taking** is measured as the inverse of Z-score (ratio of the sum of return on asset and capital adequacy relative to the standard deviation of return on asset). **Institutions** are measured as an aggregate of six indicators (rule of law, government effectiveness, control of corruption, political stability, regulatory quality and voice and accountability) from the World Governance Indicators

Robust standard errors in parentheses

***$p<0.01$, **$p<0.05$, *$p<0.1$

References

Adrian, T., & Shin, H. S. (2010). Financial intermediaries and monetary economics. In B. M. Friedman & M. Woodford (Eds.), *Handbook of monetary economics*. Elsevier.

Agur, I., & Demertzis, M. (2010). *Monetary policy and excessive bank risk taking* (Working Paper No. 271).

Aikman, D., Bridges, J., Kashyap, A., & Siegert, C. (2019). Would macro-prudential regulation have prevented the last crisis? *Journal of Economic Perspectives., 33*(1), 107–130.

Akinci, O., & Olmstead-Rumsey, J. (2018). How effective are macroprudential policies? An empirical investigation. *Journal of Financial Intermediation, 33*, 33–57.

Alam, Z., Alter, M. A., Eiseman, J., Gelos, M. R., Kang, M. H., Narita, M. M., ... & Wang, N. (2019). *Digging deeper—Evidence on the effects of macroprudential policies from a new database*. International Monetary Fund.

Altunbas, Y., Gambacorta, L., & Marques-Ibanez, D. (2014). Does monetary policy affect bank risk? *International Journal of Central Banking, 10*(1), 95–135.

Altunbas, Y., Binici, M., & Gambacorta, L. (2017). *Macro-prudential policy and bank risk, Monetary and Economic Department* (BIS Working Papers No 646).

Altunbas, Y., Binici, M., & Gambacorta, L. (2018). Macroprudential policy and bank risk. *Journal of International Money and Finance, 81*, 203–220.

Andriushin, S., & Kuznetsova, V. (2013). Macro-prudential policy instruments of central banks. *Problems of Economic Transition, 56*(7), 75–94.

Angelini, P., Neri, S., & Panetta, F. (2014). The Interaction between capital requirements and monetary policy. *Journal of Money, Credit and Banking, 46*(6), 1073–1112.

Barnea, E., Landskroner, Y., & Sokoler, M. (2015). Monetary policy and financial stability in a banking economy: Transmission mechanism and policy tradeos. *Journal of Financial Stability, 18*, 78–90.

Barth, J. R., Caprio, G., & Levine, R. (2013). Bank regulation and supervision in 180 countries from 1999 to 2011. *Journal of Financial Economic Policy, 5*, 111–219.

Basso, H., & Costain, J. (2016). *Macro-prudential theory: Advances and challenges* (Banco de Espana Occasional Paper, 1604).

Beau, D., Clerc, L., & Mojon, B. (2012). *Macro-prudential policy and the conduct of monetary policy Document De Travail, N° 390.*

Blanchard, O., Ariccia, G. D., & Mauro, P. (2010). Rethinking macroeconomic policy. *Journal of Money, Credit, and Banking, 42*(1), 199–215.

Blaydes, L., & Kayser, M. A. (2011). Counting calories: Democracy and distribution in the developing world. *International Studies Quarterly, 55*(4), 887–908.

Borio, C., & Zhu, H. (2012). Capital regulation, risk-taking and monetary policy: A missing link in the transmission mechanism? *Journal of Financial Stability, 8*(4), 236–251.

Brambor, T., Clark, W., & Golder, M. (2006). Understanding interaction models: Improving empirical analyses. *Political Analysis, 14*(1), 63–82.

Buiter, W. H. (2014). The role of central banks in financial stability: How has it changed? In D. D. Evanoff, C. Holthausen, G. G. Kaufman, & M. Kremer (Eds.), *The role of central banks in financial stability: How has it changed?* Hackensack, NJ: World Scientific.

Buis, M. L. (2010). Stata tip 87: Interpretation of interactions in nonlinear models. *The Stata Journal, 10*(2), 305–308.

Butzbach, O. (2016). Systemic risk, macro-prudential regulation and organizational diversity in banking. *Policy and Society, 35*(3), 239–251.

Cagliarini, A. (2016). Macro-prudential policy: More questions than answers. *The Australian Economic Review, 49*(1), 89–92.

Chantapacdepong, P., & Shim, I. (2014). *Correlations across Asia-Pacific bond markets and the impact of capital flow measures* (BIS working paper no. 472).

Claessens, M. S. (2014). An overview of macroprudential policy tools.

Claessens, S., Demirgüç-Kunt, A., & Huizinga, H. (2001). How does foreign entry affect domestic banking markets? *Journal of banking & finance, 25*(5), 891–911.

Claessens, S., & Laeven, L. (2005). Financial dependence, banking sector competition, and economic growth. *Journal of the European Economic Association, 3*(1), 179–207.

Claessens, S., Pazarbasioglu, C., Laeven, L., Dobler, M., Valencia, F., Nedelescu, O., & Seal, K. (2011). *Crisis management and resolution: Early lessons from the financial crisis* (International Monetary Fund Staff Discussion Note no. 11/05). Viewed 7 June 2017. https://www.imf.org/external/pubs/ft/sdn/2011/sdn1105.pdf

Claessens, S. (2015). An overview of macro-prudential policy tools. *Annual Review of Financial Economics, 7*, 397–422.

Claessens, S., Ghosh, S. R., & Mihet, R. (2013). Macro-prudential policies to mitigate financial system vulnerabilities. *Journal of International Money and Finance, 39*, 153–185.

Compton, R. A., Giedeman, D. C., & Hoover, G. A. (2011). Panel evidence on economic freedom and growth in the United States. *European Journal of Political Economy, 27*(3), 423–435.

Davis, E. P., Liadze, I., & Piggott, R. (2019). Assessing the macroeconomic impact of alternative macroprudential policies. *Economic Modelling, 80*, 407–428.

De Nicol'o, G., Dell'Ariccia, G., Laeven, L., & Valencia, F. (2010). *Monetary policy and bank risk taking* (IMF Staff Position Notes SPN/10/09). International Monetary Fund Home.

De Paoli, B., & Paustian, M. (2013), *Coordinating monetary and macro-prudential policies* (Federal Reserve Bank of New York Staff Report [653]).

Dell'Ariccia, G., Laeven, L., & Marquez, R. (2010). *Monetary policy, leverage, and bank risk-taking* (IMF Working Paper, n 276).

Deniz, A., Demirgüç-Kunt, A. & Zhu, M. (2012). *How Does Bank Competition Affect Systemic Stability?* (Policy Research Working Paper 5981). World Bank.

Doojav, G., & Batmunkh, U. (2018). Monetary and macro-prudential policy in a commodity exporting economy: A structural model analysis. *Central Bank Review, 18*, 107–128.

Financial Stability Board, International Monetary Fund, and Bank for International Settlements (FSB/IMF/BIS). (2009). *Guidance to assess the systemic importance of financial institutions, markets and instruments: Initial considerations* (Report to the G-20 finance ministers and central bank governors [Basel]).

Gambacorta, L. (2009, December). Monetary policy and the risk-taking channel. *BIS Quarterly Review*, Bank for International Settlements.

Gauthier, C., Lehar, A., & Souissi, M. (2012). Macroprudential capital requirements and systemic risk. *Journal of Financial Intermediation, 21*(4), 594–618.

Geng, Z., & Zha, X. (2015). *Effects of the interest rate and reserve requirement ratio on bank risk in China: A panel smooth transition regression approach discrete dynamics in nature and society.*

Greenwood-Nimmo, M., & Tarassow, A. (2016). Monetary shocks, macro-prudential shocks and financial stability. *Economic Modelling, 56*, 11–24.

Hanson, S. G., Kashyap, A. K., & Stein, J. C. (2011). A macroprudential approach to financial regulation. *Journal of Economic Perspectives, 25*(1), 3–28.

Herrero, A. G., & del Río, P. (2003). *Financial stability and the design of monetary policy* (1) Documento de Trabajo n° 0315.

Hosmer Jr, D. W., Lemeshow, S., & Sturdivant, R. X. (2013). *Applied Logistic Regression (Vol. 398).* John Wiley & Sons.

International Monetary Fund (April. (2011). *Regional economic outlook: Asia and Pacific.* International Monetary Fund.

International Monetary Fund. (2013a). *The interaction of monetary and Macro-prudential policies.* International Monetary Fund.

International Monetary Fund. (2013b). *The interaction of monetary and Macro-prudential policies.* In Background paper. International Monetary Fund.

International Monetary Fund. (2013c). *Key aspects of Macro-prudential policies.* International Monetary Fund.

Jiménez G., Ongena, S., Peydró, J.-L., & Saurina, J. (2012a). *Hazardous times for monetary policy: What do twenty-three million bank loans say about the effects of monetary policy on credit risk?* (UPF working paper).

Jiménez G., Ongena, S., Peydró, J.-L., & Saurina, J. (2012b). Credit supply and monetary policy: Identifying the bank balance-sheet channel with loan applications. *American Economic Review, 102*(5), 2301–2326.

Klomp, J., & de Haan, J. (2014). Bank regulation, the quality of institutions, and banking risk in emerging and developing countries: An empirical analysis. *Emerging Markets Finance and Trade, 50*(6), 19–40.

Kuttner, K., & Shim, I. (2012). *Taming the real estate beast: The effects of monetary and Macro-prudential policies on housing prices and credit*. Reserve Bank of Australia Conference.

Laeven, L., & Valencia, F. (2013a). The real effects of financial sector interventions during crises. *Journal of Money, Credit, and Banking, 45*(1), 147–177.

Laeven, L., & Valencia, F. (2013b). Systemic banking crises database. *IMF Economic Review, 61*(2), 225–270.

Laeven, L., & Valencia, F. (2018). *Systemic banking crises revisited* (IMF Working Paper, 18/206).

Laeven, L., & Valencia, F. (2013b). Systemic banking crises database. *IMF Economic Review, 61*(2), 225–270.

Lim, C., Columba, F., Costa, A., Kongsamut, P., Otani, A., Saiyid, M., Wezel, T., & Wu, X. (2011). *Macro-prudential policy: What instruments and how to use them? Lessons from country experiences* (In IMF working paper 11/238). International Monetary Fund.

Lim, C. H., Krznar, M. I., Lipinsky, M. F., Otani, M. A., & Wu, M. X. (2013). *The macroprudential framework: Policy responsiveness and institutional arrangements*. International Monetary Fund.

Lu, W. (2017). Banking crises, bank regulation and intervention. *Journal of Business and Policy Research, 12*(2), 58–74.

Lubis, A., Alexiou, C., & Nellis, J. (2019). What can we learn from the implementation of monetary and macro-prudential policies: A systematic literature review. *Journal of Economic Surveys, 33*(4), 1123–1150.

Maddaloni, A., & Peydró, J. L. (2013). *Monetary policy, macro-prudential policy and banking stability, evidence from the Euro area* (Working PaPer SerieS no 1560). Macro Prudential Research Network.

Marchionne, F., & Pisicoli, B. (2017). Banking regulation, institutional quality, and financial crises. *Kelley School of Business Research Paper*, (17–15).

Mishkin, F. S. (2009). Is monetary policy effective during financial crises? *The American Economic Review, 99*(2), 573–577.

Quint, D., & Rabanal, P. (2014). Monetary and macro-prudential in an estimated DSGE model of Euro Area. *International Journal of Central Banking, 10*(2), 169–236.

Rajan, R. (2005). *Has financial development made the world riskier?* Proceedings of Federal Reserve Bank of Kansas City, pp. 313–69. Federal Reserve Bank of Kansas City.

Rubio, M., & Carrasco-Gallego, J. A. (2014). Macro-prudential and monetary policies: Implications for financial stability and welfare. *Journal of Banking and Finance, 49*, 326–336.

Shehzad, Z., Kelly, A. C., Reiss, P. T., Gee, D. G., Gotimer, K., Uddin, L. Q., ... & Milham, M. P. (2009). The resting brain: Unconstrained yet reliable. *Cerebral Cortex, 19*(10), 2209–2229.

Steenkamp, J. B. (2014). *How global brands create firm value: The 4V model.* International Marketing Review.

Suh, H. (2012). *Macro-prudential Policy: Its effects and relationship to monetary policy* (Working Paper No. 12–28). Federal Reserve Bank of Philadelphia.

Svensson, L. E. (2017). Cost-benefit analysis of leaning against the wind. *Journal of Monetary Economics, 90*(Supplement C), 193–213.

Tomuleasa, I. (2015). Macro-prudential policy and systemic risk: An overview. *Procedia Economics and Finance, 20*, 645–653.

World Bank. (2012). *Global financial development report 2013: Rethinking the role of the state in finance*. World Bank.

World Bank. (2021). *Central bank reserve management practices: Insights into public asset management*. World Bank.

Yasnur, M., & Kurniasih, A. (2017). Factors Affecting bank lending growth: Cases in Indonesia. *International Journal of Scientific and Research Publications, 7*(11), 69–76.

Yellen, J. L. (2011). Macro-prudential supervision and monetary policy in the post-crisis world. *Business Economics, 46*, 3–12.

Zhang, L., & Zoli, E. (2016). Leaning against the wind: Macro-prudential policy in Asia. *Journal of Asian Economics, 42*, 33–52.

Zulkhibri, M. (2019). Macro-prudential policy and tools in a dual banking system: Insights from the literature. *Borsa İstanbul Review, 19*(1), 65–76.

CHAPTER 21

Recent Developments in Banking Regulation and Supervision in Africa

Jessie A. Abugre, Roseline Misati, Iwa Salami, and Stephen Antwi

21.1 Introduction

Recent debate and discussion of the scope for regulatory reforms in Africa have been characterized by concerns that most of these economies in Africa, particularly the financial sector, were severely hit by the 2007/2008 Global Financial Crisis (GFC) and the recent COVID-19

J. A. Abugre (✉)
Accra, Ghana
e-mail: jessieatuama@gmail.com

R. Misati
Central Bank of Kenya, Nairobi, Kenya
e-mail: rosenyamisa@hotmail.com

I. Salami
Royal Docks School of Business and Law, University of East London, London, UK
e-mail: i.salami@uel.ac.uk

J. Y. Abor and C. K. D. Adjasi (eds.), *The Economics of Banking and Finance in Africa*, Palgrave Macmillan Studies in Banking and Financial Institutions, https://doi.org/10.1007/978-3-031-04162-4_21

pandemic. The literature reflects on the causes, impacts, and regulatory remedies adopted to prevent future crises that may lead to distress in the banking system (Agbloyor & Abor, 2020; Global Financial Development Report, 2019/2020; Lu, 2018). In response to major shortcomings from previous crises, some countries have employed a broad range of intervention policies to restore the banking system to health. In the aftermath of various crises, emphasis is placed on better regulation of banking systems and on enhancing the tools available to supervisory agencies to oversee banks and intervene quickly in the case of distress. Thus, the chapter is motivated by the developments of key reforms in regulation and supervision over the years, specifically the experience and lessons for African countries.

Africa's financial system has evolved and undergone several transformations, yet the continent faces major challenges in terms of governance, regulation, and supervision (Global Financial Development Report, 2019/2020). This is reinforced by the fact that banking crises seem to be a recurrent phenomenon. Today, there is widespread agreement that failure in the banking system in Africa was caused by excessive risk-taking by financial institutions and a weak governance system. For instance, banks in some Sub-Saharan African (SSA) countries like Ghana and Nigeria have suffered a number of distress events like high levels of non-performing loans (NPLs), credit risk exposures, exchange rate volatility, structural and institutional failures, weak governance, and risk management tactics (Beck & Cull, 2013; Ozili, 2018), which have led to the collapse of some banks, particularly in Ghana between 2017 and 2018.

Following the evolution of Africa's financial system, it is evident that intermediation rates remained low and monetization of rural regions in Sub-Saharan Africa (SSA) remained elusive due to the form and direction of finance (IMF, 2016). Following independence, a number of African countries announced ambitions to nationalize their banking industries in order to make credit more available to their citizens and they established government-sponsored national banks. These national and development banks did not satisfy the high standards expected of

S. Antwi
National Banking College, Accra, Ghana
e-mail: santwi@nbc.edu.gh

other banks, and as a result, they were not at par with their international counterparts on a worldwide scale. Further, commercial banks grew in popularity over time. Central banks and deposit-taking organizations make up a chunk of Africa's banking system. The Central banks were created with the goal of being self-contained and free of government meddling. In practice, however, central banks collaborate with government finance ministerial arms to assist in the formulation and implementation of macroeconomic policies by state governments. Local banks and international bank branches or subsidiaries make up the majority of deposit-taking institutions. These banks are critical to Africa's financial and banking growth.

Given the role that banks play in financial and economic development, researchers, policymakers, and regulators continue to explore ways to stabilize the banking system. In view of that, policymakers of the African banking industry have highlighted the need for central banks and regulatory bodies to formulate more adequate regulatory and supervisory mechanisms in order to address the sector's difficulties and enhance overall banking sector stability, growth and resilience. The chapter aims to give an overview of recent developments in banking regulation and supervision in Africa against the backdrop of worldwide initiatives to restructure regulatory and supervisory systems. The following is how the rest of the chapter is organized: Bank Regulation and Supervision in Africa is discussed in Sect. 21.2. The Central Bank's Roles and Regulatory Strategy are discussed in Sect. 21.3; the Global Banking Regulations in part 21.4, and the Basel Principles and Africa's Banking System in Sect. 21.5. Section 22.6 examines recent regulation and supervision, and Sect. 21.7 concludes the chapter.

21.2 The Regulation and Supervision of Banks in Africa

African countries have made a significant headway in recent years in changing banking legislation and supervision. Governments have worked hard to conform to international standards and interact with global markets. More complex financial services and products are being adopted as a result of innovation. In recent years, technological advancements have significantly extended access to financial services in Sub-Saharan Africa (SSA) (IMF, 2016). The flood of mobile money and the development of mobile payment technologies have aided in the integration of huge segments of the people into the financial system. Financial development and financial inclusion in Sub-Saharan Africa are being aided by digital financial services. These developments show the effective implementation of banking supervision over the years. However, financial crises that frequently occur at some intervals reveal the flaws in banking legislation and supervision. For instance, when the financial industry is affected by a crisis, faults in the design and execution of rules imposed by central banks and governments are exposed. As a result, African governments and authorities have recognized the need to integrate financial regulatory and supervisory frameworks with worldwide best practices and have faced greater pressure to do so (e.g., Basel Core Principles, Basel II, Basel III, IFRS, and FATF Recommendations).

In emerging nations, a strong financial system is critical for economic progress and poverty alleviation (World Bank, 2001: 76). African regulators must find out and comprehend how to apply these foreign models to the realities of low-income countries. The main challenge for regulators and politicians is determining which specific types of bank regulation and supervision will work best in low-income nations' settings.

The global financial crisis of 2008 serves as a stark reminder that insufficient regulation and supervision in nations with significant economic and financial power may have global consequences, and it has served as a rallying cry for standardized worldwide regulatory cooperation (Bauerle Danzman et al., 2017). It should be underlined that banking laws do not have to be as complicated as the Basel committee intended. Indeed, according to Haldane and Madouros (2012) and Hoenig (2012), those complicated regulations are not only ineffective but also often harmful. The critique focuses on two key points: the effectiveness of complicated laws in preventing bank collapses and financial crises, and the sheer magnitude of resources required in terms of sophisticated risk assessment models, massive databases, and the number of regulators in each jurisdiction. The new capital adequacy rises in the areas of design, data quality, reporting, and operations, according to a working paper by McKinsey on the Basel III. These critiques and results are essential for industrialized nations' financial institutions, but much more so for emerging and low-income countries, which lack the financial, technological, and human resources to implement these regulations.

Why and How to Regulate

In the financial services sector, regulatory reform has increased efficiency and reduced costs. First, regulatory constraints were lifted, allowing financial institutions to adopt more efficient procedures and produce new products and services. Second, regulatory change strengthened the role of competition, which led to lower financial service margins and greater efficiency by forcing the exit or consolidation of inefficient businesses, thus stimulating innovation.

Regulatory reform also aided in the reduction of comparable financial service pricing. In addition, it improved the economy's overall productivity by significantly improving the quality, variety, and accessibility of new financial instruments and services; enhancing global resource allocation by removing barriers to international capital flows; and significantly boosting the growth performance of several developing countries.

The growing variety and sophistication of financial products revealed the shortcomings of the 1988 capital adequacy framework's possibly too simplistic design. Financial crises throughout the world show that the phrase "too big to fail" used to characterize banking behemoths is not totally accurate. As a result, authorities must guarantee that banks are adequately and effectively supervised. Since banks cannot eliminate all information asymmetry, financial institutions must be regulated (Heremans & Pacces, 2000).

One of the most important aims of bank regulation is to guarantee financial system stability. Other reasons for regulating and supervising banks include protecting depositors, preventing excessive risk-taking by banks that can harm depositors and creditors in order to avoid systemic banking crises, ensuring the soundness and stability of the banking system, controlling money supply and monitoring credit, avoiding financial power concentration in a few banks, maintaining public confidence in the banking system, and ensuring healthy coexistence (see Abor, 2018; Nyantakyi & Mouhamadou, 2015). As financial intermediaries, banks play a critical role in African economies. A violation of their responsibility as middlemen will almost certainly send shockwaves across the economic system.

Regulators can employ a variety of tools to control and monitor banks. Such tools include restriction on assets and operations, capital requirements, competition restraints, separation of conventional banking from other financial service industries, risk-based deposit insurance premiums and transparency requirements, bank chartering, and bank examination (Mishkin, 2016). Safety and soundness regulation, monetary policy regulation, credit allocation regulation, consumer protection regulation, investor protection regulation, and entrance and chartering regulation are all examples of banking regulation.

The State of Regulation and Supervision in Africa

The expansion of foreign-owned banks in Africa is a result of globalization. Cross-border access to international banks has been significantly liberalized. GATS, NAFTA, and the EC, in particular, have put in place various international accords on financial services trade. In the European Union, the second banking regulation (89/646/EEC) abolished the requirement for banks founded in one Member State to obtain permission from other Member States before opening a branch in their territory. Outside of these Unions, international banks continue to face more barriers to entering into local markets than domestic banks in most nations. The financial systems of emerging nations vary significantly from those of developing countries on the continent. African banking systems are less developed, as evidenced by their lack of financial depth and access. In African nations, loans to the private sector account for just 21% of GDP on average, compared to 50% in other emerging countries. According to Mlachila et al. (2016), bank assets to GDP in developing nations is just 57%, which is less than half of what it is in developing countries outside Africa. In terms of private finance, even within African nations, there are significant differences. For example, private credit to GDP is 141% in South Africa, 87% in Mauritius, and 61% in Cape Verde, but barely 5% in Chad (Beck et al., 2014).

Licensing and Supervision

The banking industry in SSA was not supervised as early as the rest of the globe. However, significant progress has been made in modernizing banking regulations. A number of SSA nations have recently passed or are about to enact new or additional legislation. Laws today consider the fit and appropriate test, not only for directors and senior management but also for shareholders. To be regulated, banks must fulfill more stringent regulatory standards.

Central banks have been wary of allowing commercial banks to collapse for a variety of reasons, the most serious of which may be the potential of a financial system catastrophe. As a result, banks are expected to have safety nets in place in the event of their insolvency. Regulators use capital requirements to monitor the banking system. This is generally a sum of money that is stored with the regulator and is weighted against the bank's assets as a buffer against unexpected losses. The resources required to capitalize the bank at its beginning are also specified in capital requirements.

SSA nations have sought to delegate certain supervision and regulatory authority to their central banks. However, in most circumstances, the governors of these banks report to the minister in charge of finance, who is sometimes a stand-in for the ruling government. Although significant efforts have been made to provide effective supervision (Table 21.1 shows the efficacy of supervision in several SSA countries), problems persist. The area remains vulnerable, which might be attributed to a late start and early infiltration of foreign banks into the global financial scene, as well as previous bank failures and political instability.

To align with global markets, SSA countries will need to strengthen supervision by adhering to the Basel Core Principles; revising their regulatory framework to strengthen and tighten licensing and dispel the widely held belief that African laws are lax; improving on-site inspection programs; and strengthening their judicial systems to quickly adjudicate on matters and ensure accountability.

Table 21.1 Selected SSA Countries classified by the IMF on basis of the status of Banking System Supervision

Group 1	*Group 2*	*Group 3*
Angola	Ghana	Botswana
Ethiopia	Madagascar	Kenya
Lesotho	Malawi	South Africa
Mozambique	Mauritius	
Rwanda	Namibia	
Swaziland	Tanzania	
	Uganda	
	Zambia	
	Zimbabwe	

1-initial stage of building supervisory structures
2-basic structures and regulatory systems in place
3-Well designed and effectively implement a system with supervisory authority well supported at the political level

21.3 The Roles of the Central Bank and Regulatory Strategy

The regulatory duties of central banks are discussed in this section. In addition, the regulatory strategy is examined in terms of breadth, intensity, and cost.

The Regulatory Roles of the Central Bank

The country's central bank, often known as the reserve bank, is in charge of all financial institutions. It has the responsibility of ensuring that banks perform their operations in an ethical and secure way. In doing so, the central bank fulfills a variety of regulatory functions. The following is a breakdown of these positions.

Issuance of the Charter/License for New Banks

A bank must get the proper documentation and records before it can start doing business. The central bank decides whether or not new banks are permitted. Although court authorities in certain nations produce legal papers, central banks and reserve banks play an essential role in advising judicial authorities on the issue of these documents. In the United States, the federal or state agencies may grant the banking license that allows the new bank to function. The Federal Reserve, on the other hand, cannot grant banking licenses on its own, but it may affect the number of new banks that join the existing ones. This is done in to guarantee that there is healthy and beneficial competition that protects both customers and banks.

Reserve Requirements

By law, the central bank is responsible for setting reserve requirements, putting it in a position to have a substantial effect on member banks' activities and earnings. The necessary reserve ratio is the proportion of total commercial bank deposits that must be held or deposited with central banks. This is usually done as a toll in order to absorb surplus liquidity from the economy. When the central bank believes there is too much money in the economy, generating inflation, the reserved ratio is raised to decrease the percentage of money available for lending. As the amount of money in circulation decreases, interest rates rise. A drop in the reserved ratio, on the other hand, increases the number of loanable funds available to commercial banks. As a result, the central bank supervises commercial bank activity in conformity with national interests through the required reserve ratio.

Control Over Monetary Policy/Rate

Modern monetary policy has shifted from the realm of governments to that of central banks. The central bank decides how much money and credit will flow in the economy at any particular time. The central bank is also responsible for disclosing the country's monetary policy's main interest rate. The monetary policy rate (MPR) is an interest rate established by the monetary authority (i.e., the central bank) to reflect changes in important monetary variables in the economy (such as consumer prices, exchange rates, credit expansion, etc.). MPR is the benchmark against which other lending rates in the economy are measured, and it is frequently employed to maintain price stability. Because it is the rate at which private actors, mostly private banks, receive money from the central bank, the MPR controls the level of other interest rates in the economy. These banks then provide financial products to their clients at an interest rate that is generally dependent on the interest rate. The important interest rates in various nations are varied. Overnight, discount rates and refund rates are the most frequent (with different maturities). The key interest rate is often used by central banks to conduct either a restrictive or expansionary monetary policy. Inflation, currency depreciation, excessive loan expansion, and capital outflows are frequently addressed by raising interest rates. In order to become more competitive, the central bank may strive to boost economic activity by lowering interest rates, stimulating credit growth, or depreciating the currency.

Deposit Insurance

The economy loses when depositors lose faith in commercial banks' solvency. This is because people with surplus cash to deposit with banks refuse to do so if they are unsure about the banks' capacity to satisfy withdrawal requests. For this reason, the central banks place a high value on financial stability in the economy. As a result, the central bank may directly guarantee deposits, or there may be a separate entity supervised by the central bank to do so. Central banks across the globe guarantee commercial bank deposits up to a specific level. Deposit insurance is a type of insurance that helps commercial banks spend their deposits wisely.

Sole Issuer of Currency

Central banks have sole authority to produce and issue their countries' currencies and notes. This function precludes any other organization or individual from entering the economy with any currency or commodity that can be considered as currency. Central bank notes are legal tender, which means they may be used as a medium of a trade by anybody. As a result, modern central banks have a monopoly on banknote issuance. The central banks are able to secure or ensure their acceptability and keep their worth without the intervention of forces in the competitive market. People in the economy will have more faith in the currency as a result of this. The bank can also keep inflation under control by ensuring that national income, output, and spending all have the same value. Even though central banks have the sole authority to print the currencies of their respective countries, criminal activities and the introduction of sophisticated technologies in modern times have made it possible for others to print counterfeit money and other quasi-cash, making it difficult to distinguish between genuine and counterfeit notes. Central banks, on the other hand, are always on the lookout for such crooks and fraudsters.

Monitoring and Measurement of Risk Taken by the Banks

Banks are profit-driven organizations that, if left uncontrolled, may easily engage in any dangerous enterprise that would help them generate the required profit in the shortest amount of time. However, it is the obligation of central banks to ensure that they do not take on disproportionate risks that might result in depositor money being frozen in long-term/risky projects, preventing depositors from accessing their funds when they are needed. Central banks keep an eye on their commercial banks' risks by inspecting their assets, liabilities, and even monetary activities on a regular basis. Risk is measured by the central bank using specifically created models like the value at risk (VaR). Commercial banks that are regarded to have inappropriate levels of risk are investigated and, in certain circumstances, sanctioned. Central banks must guarantee that commercial banks have enough capital to satisfy depositor requirements when they arise. The competition will drive commercial banks to take unjustified risks if central banks do not regulate them. Even in highly competitive markets, central banks are the ones that help keep the risk-reward balance in check.

Enforcing Anti-Discrimination Laws

Anti-discrimination regulations are also enforced by central banks to ensure that domestic and racial agendas do not obstruct access to money and credit. Central banks are implementing regulations prohibiting banks from excluding local communities from financial services. There have been reports that banks are "ringing" in specific communities in the United States, for example. This means that banks will refuse to lend to people in certain areas. This was deemed prejudice since the majority of the residents of these communities were Hispanic or African American. As a result, the Federal Reserve was forced to act to guarantee that credit was not dispersed based on the profile of national creditors. Central banks are responsible for ensuring that money and credit are available to everyone who qualifies. In Ghana, the central bank has made it such that where universal banks are unwilling to go due to cost concerns, rural and community banks, microfinance institutions, and savings and loans firms are given permission to serve certain segments of the economy.

Conflicts of Interest

Commercial bank operations are strictly monitored by the central bank, which looks for conflicts of interest. This implies that when commercial bank executives or the corporations they oversee make large bank loans, central banks can intervene to prohibit and control the practice. Mutual conflicts of interest were one of the primary causes of non-performing assets (NPA). Depositor funds are safeguarded against dangerous and distorted loans because of the central bank's regulatory duty.

Payment Mechanism

Central banks also made it possible for the economy to have a quick and effective payment system. This is because central banks have the ability to guarantee payments and make them irreversible. When a bank makes a payment to another bank, the central bank debits one account and credits another. Commercial banks are immune from counterparty concerns because the central bank acts as an intermediary. Not every commercial bank has to be concerned about not receiving promised payments from a third party. The payment is guaranteed by the central bank when it expires. As a result, the central bank tacitly guarantees the quick operation of the express payment system that we have today, as well as electronic payment and electronic money.

Management of Foreign Exchange

On behalf of the government and the people, the central bank controls foreign exchange reserves. The central bank is also responsible for ensuring that the government always has adequate foreign currency for imports. In the foreign exchange markets, the central bank has the financial strength and capacity to keep the value of its currency stable. When the central bank detects a speculative attack on its currency, it resorts to open market operations to maintain the value. The central bank's capacity to conduct this duty effectively, however, is contingent on the population's willingness to use the financial system for FX management. Rather than using banks or regulated forex bureaus, the majority of traders utilize the black market. It is also widely known that certain banks collude with black market dealers to sell foreign currency at a higher rate outside the banking system.

Government's Bank

The central bank is also the bank of the government. It is in charge of completing deals on behalf of the government. It receives all revenue, such as taxes, dividends, and royalties, and it also makes payments on behalf of the government, such as public sector wages and salaries, and payments to contractors. Central banks/reserves lend to governments, and in some countries, the central bank is responsible for managing the national debt. It raises cash for the government by selling government treasury notes and bonds (Abor et al., 2019).

Lender of Last Resort

The central bank's role as a lender of last resort for banks is also essential. This implies that central banks serve as the ultimate safety net for banks in times of liquidity shortages, allowing them to offer credit to the market. The safety net is known as emergency liquidity support. For example, when terrorists attacked the World Trade Center in New York City in September 2001, several banks were unable to access their customers' checks. As a result, bank reserves decreased. Repurchase agreements and discount loans were used by the Federal Reserve to help the banking system (Abor et al., 2019). Africa's central/reserve banks also assist banks with liquidity problems. However, a bank's ability to get emergency liquidity support from its national central bank is not guaranteed (Freixas et al., 2000, 2004), as there are specific guidelines and requirements that must be followed. Only banks that are illiquid but solvent are eligible for emergency liquidity assistance. When banks are illiquid, it may be impossible for them to repay all their depositors. They can do this in the long run because they are solvent (Tucker, 2009). Because its finances are connected to long-term loans issued to its clients, a bank can run out of liquidity while staying viable. Because it is only given in unanticipated circumstances, emergency liquidity support is only brief. When things return to normal, the emergency liquidity assistance will end, and loans will have to be paid back.

Regulatory Strategy: Scope, Intensity, and Cost

The financial system in Sub-Saharan African countries is at various stages of development, with some regions, such as East Africa, being more advanced in the adoption of technologically innovative financial products and the integration of commercial banks and other new non-bank players into the financial system (Amadou et al., 2019; Baicu, 2011). While such advances continue to create potential for African nations to improve their financial inclusion, they also raise worries about new vulnerabilities, necessitating policymakers' attention to effective regulatory policies. Quintyn and Taylor (2007) point out that developing a regulatory strategy entails determining the breadth, intensity, and costs of regulation and monitoring. The scope of a financial system segment is defined as the moment at which it is brought into the supervisory net. The evaluation of possible systemic risk, relative size, and societal consequences of institutional failure determines the criteria used to prioritize a particular section. The weight of prudential regulation put on priority segments for regulation and supervision is referred to as regulatory intensity. In order to achieve an ideal balance between regulation and boosting competition, innovation, and financial development in Sub-Saharan Africa, both indirect and direct costs should be considered when adopting a regulatory policy.

According to Nhavira et al. (2013), supervisory regimes are grouped along four models (i) the functional model which is characterized by functions performed by financial firms (ii) the vertical/silos model which follows the legal status of the institutions or business type viz banking, securities, insurance, and pension sector, with each sector being supervised by a different agency; (iii) the horizontal (or peaks) model which is identified by objectives of regulation and where each objective is supervised by a separate authority (the twin peaks model, Taylor, 1995); and

(iv) the unified (or integrated) model, in which a single authority supervises the whole financial system and all the public objectives. The majority of African nations have implemented vertical or silos-model/sectoral regulation, in which one financial sector body is in charge of bank prudential and conduct-of-business supervision. For insurance firms, another authority has the same mandate. Market integrity and the securities industry are overseen by a third body (Calvo et al., 2018).

A number of African countries have also increased their attention to effective risk-based supervision and the need for early intervention and prompt supervisory measures. Supervisors evaluate the risk profile of financial institutions or sectors of financial institutions in terms of the risks they face, the effectiveness of their risk management, and the hazards they pose to banking and financial systems in this scenario. This strategy allows supervisors to use restricted resources to effectively minimize hazards they have identified and that are aligned with national goals. This method assures that supervisory actions do not impose undue burdens on lower-risk sectors, entities, or activities. A comprehensive risk-based strategy comprises solutions to address the complete range of hazards, from higher to lower-risk sectors and organizations. A risk-based strategy, when effectively implemented, is more responsive, less onerous, and delegates more choices to those who are most suited to make them (Dordevic et al., 2021; FATF, 2021). A MEFMI (2016) report found that countries in Africa, and MEFMI members, in particular, are still at different stages of development and implementation of risk-based supervision principles, with a few countries having fully implemented and even gone further to incorporate new supervisory developments, while others are still at the entry-level or are only implementing partial provisions of the principles. Kenya and South Africa, for example, have completely adopted risk-based supervision in various financial system sectors, including insurance, while Nigeria is slated to establish a risk-based supervisory framework for the insurance sector in 2021.

Many African nations' regulatory and supervisory strategies encompass deposit-taking institutions as well as non-deposit-taking institutions such as insurance, pensions, and capital markets. Commercial banks and microfinance institutions are primarily regulated by central banks, with distinct regulatory agencies for each of the other sectors. Microfinance institutions, for example, are not subject to the same prudential rules as banks when it comes to serving sectors of the public at the retail level. Non-bank financial institutions are subject to fewer restrictions and less supervision in the analyzed nations, with the majority focusing on certain sectors of the economy or elements of the financial system in order to deepen the financial sector (see Table 21.2).

While our examination of existing practice and structures in many African countries reveals a broad coverage of traditional financial system sectors, African central banks must grapple with the development and implementation of regulatory and supervisory strategies for the non-traditional financial sectors (such as mobile money services, credit-only institutions, digital money lenders, and fintech) that are rapidly developing in these countries. While the fast rise of credit-only financial services providers and mobile financial services continues to expand the financial system in African nations, particularly at the retail end of the market, no unified regulatory policy has been devised. According to the GSMA Report (2018), various countries in Eastern, Southern, and Western Africa have embraced non-bank regulatory regimes, in which case the corresponding companies, such as mobile network operators, have a greater regulatory burden (MNOs). Non-bank mobile money providers are allowed to enter the market and issue e-money in this instance (or equivalent). In some countries, such as Nigeria, South Africa, Cameroon, and Egypt, the regulatory approach is based on the bank-only model, in which the MNO's role is more peripheral, confined to supplying communications infrastructure and/or agency services. Other nations, such as Sudan, have a centralized approach in which the central bank is heavily involved in the mobile money industry. The central bank issues e-money and runs the central processing platform within this tightly regulated framework, thereby making it a market actor (Maina, 2018). For instance, Benin, Mozambique, Senegal, and Zambia have both MNO and Bank-led models (EIB-UNCDF, 2014) regulated by the central bank. However, current country experiences demonstrate that the MNO model is the most flexible, allowing for the creation of suitable regulations in concert with the expansion of products and services.

According to the findings of the preceding investigation, most nations have only succeeded in enacting different types of legislation pertaining to mobile financial services. Credit-only institutions and digital money lenders, on the other hand, are not regulated in many countries, and even when they are, regulation is patchy at best (Bowmans, 2017; Didenko, 2017). Although digital loans and credit supplied by credit-only financial institutions account for a modest part of bank sector lending in many countries, country experience demonstrates that digital credit has not only

Table 21.2 Scope and intensity of the regulatory framework in selected African countries

Country	*Scope/priority*	*Intensity*	*Evolving segments with potential risks*	*Risks*	*Measures/recommendations*
Ghana	Banks Rural and Community Banks Specialized Deposit-Taking Institutions Micro finance institutions Individual SUSU collectors and money lenders Dedicated Electronic Money Issuers	Different regulatory agencies Lighter prudential guidelines No minimum capital and supervision requirement for some entities	Fintech	Cyber Risk and fraudulent activities	Issued crowd funding policy in 2021 Launched a Regulatory and Innovation Sandbox Pilot in 2021 Cybersecurity Act 2020 Anti-Money Laundering Act, 2020
Nigeria	Banks Development Finance Institutions Micro finance banks Insurance Sector Capital Markets	Development Finance Institutions under different laws but licensed by the Central Bank Lesser prudential guidelines	Some activities of Fintech not regulated	Cyber security	Mobile money services framework issued in 2021 Need to consider Fintech firms under regulatory purview of CBN
Kenya	Banks Deposit taking MFI Other sectors e.g. Insurance sector Credit cooperative societies	Different regulatory agencies -Lesser prudential guidelines	Credit only institutions Digital Lending Apps	Mainly related to consumer protection and market conduct of non-deposit taking institutions	Central Bank of Kenya Amendment Bill, 2021 seeking to regulate digital/credit only institutions passed into law in December 2021 Exploring a regulatory sandbox framework

Country	*Scope/priority*	*Intensity*	*Evolving segments with potential risks*	*Risks*	*Measures/recommendations*
Uganda	Banks MFI SACCOs Credit institutions Self-help groups Insurance	Lower prudential guidelines	Fintech	Consumer protection and data privacy	Data Protection and Privacy Act Need for consumer protection legislation Introduced a National Payments System (sandbox) Regulations in 2021
South Africa	Banks (commercial; Mutual and cooperative) Insurers Cooperative financial institutions Financial conglomerates	Lighter regulation for non-deposit taking institutions	Fintech	Cybersecurity	Need for Cybercrime regulatory framework Consideration of regulatory Sandboxes
Zambia	Banks Deposit and non-deposit taking MFI	Lower prudential guidelines	Digital financial services	Vulnerability of consumers	Need to develop consumer protection laws and data governance of DFS
Mauritius	Banks Insurance sector	Lighter regulatory requirements	Cross border transactions	Contagious transmission	Issued crowd funding rules in 2021 Signed many MOU Need for regional regulatory frameworks Regulatory sandbox
Egypt	Banks Digital Banks Non-Bank Micro Finance Institutions	Different regulatory agencies Lighter regulatory requirements	Digital Financial Services	Cyberattacks	Issued new Central Bank and Banking Sector law in 2020 Microfinance Law amended in 2020 Regulatory Sandbox Framework in place since 2019

increased consumer debt but also introduced new concerns. According to research, users of credit-only financial institutions and digital lending are required to give over an excessive quantity of personal information as part of the loan application and usage process, raising worries about consumer protection and data privacy. Furthermore, digital loan providers charge excessive interest rates, employ unfair and unlawful debt collection practices, and often submit unfavorable information to credit agencies, potentially leading to blacklisting and exclusion from the credit market (Afi, 2017; Johnen et al., 2021; Lopez, 2019). As a result of these new dangers, measures to manage market behavior in this financial area must be developed.

Some African nations have already encountered some of the developing hazards and/or predicted the need to adopt a regulatory plan in response to such threats. The Central Bank of Kenya (CBK) has drafted the CBK Amendment Bill, 2021, which aims to provide the CBK the authority to regulate digital lenders. The CBK Amendment Act passed its second reading and was signed into law in September 2021. It now awaits its third and final reading. Furthermore, in 2019, the CBK released the Banking Industry Charter, which outlines a commitment to establishing a responsible and disciplined banking sector. The Charter's implementation continues to improve banking practices, and it is projected to further entrench the: (i) banks' adoption of customer-centric business models, (ii) risk-based credit pricing, (iii) more openness and information disclosures, and (iv) a bank's ethical culture. The National Credit Act of 2016 in South Africa encourages credit market accountability by promoting responsible borrowing to reduce over-indebtedness and prevent irresponsible lending (Brits, 2018; Government Gazette, 2005; Schmulow, 2016). The credit provider is required by the Act to conduct a proper assessment of each consumer's ability to meet their obligations, including taking reasonable steps to investigate and evaluate the consumer's understanding, appreciation of the proposed agreement's obligations, and the ability to meet those obligations in a timely manner. To comply with the Act's requirements and avoid entering into a reckless credit agreement, the credit provider must ensure that the consumer understands and appreciates the risks, costs, and obligations of the agreement, as well as conduct an affordability assessment to ensure that the consumer will be able to meet the proposed agreement's obligations.

The same nations (Kenya, South Africa) are at the forefront of either creating or exploring the adoption of regulatory sandboxes in order to efficiently manage developing and changing areas of the financial system without suffocating innovation. A variety of perceived regulatory hurdles to innovation and entrance in financial services industries have prompted the construction of regulatory sandboxes. Sandboxes have proven successful in some advanced economies and offer promising prospects in Africa in terms of effective use of public resources, ensuring financial inclusion through innovation, and developing appropriate regulatory frameworks for segments, activities, or evolving financial products. This benefits innovators by reducing the time and expense of bringing new ideas to the market, as well as increasing engagement with regulators to better understand their regulatory duties. Regulatory sandboxes have also been used by regulators to test new legislation in a controlled environment and on a limited scale and to collaborate with innovators to ensure adequate consumer protection of new goods and services (CCAF, 2018).

21.4 Global Banking Regulations

The financial sector is increasingly being recognized across the world as a key component in fostering economic and financial growth. As a result, international economies are being pushed to do everything possible to avoid harming financial markets, particularly the banking sector. Banks play an important role in the implementation of monetary and economic policy (Beck et al., 2018).

Banks, for example, serve as delegating monitors for investors, offer liquidity and payment services, lower transaction costs in the services they provide, convert deposits into loans, provide external capital for businesses, and develop banking relationships with consumers. However, excessive risk-taking behavior; increased use of financial leverage; overreliance on wholesale funding; financial intermediaries lowering their lending standards and relying on erroneous credit ratings; and investments in complex structured finance instruments—all contribute to financial distress in the banking system. It is also evident that these behaviors in the banking sector led to the Global Financial Crisis of 2007/2008. The crisis has exposed serious flaws in market discipline and regulation, as well as reignited important policy discussions about financial rules around the globe. Following that crisis, the focus has been on enhancing banking system regulation and the instruments available to monetary and regulatory authorities to oversee banks and respond rapidly in an emergency

(BCBS, 2016a, 2016b, 2018). Regulations are a set of laws and norms that apply to the banking industry (Nyantakyi & Mouhamadou, 2015). Every government in the world regulates and supervises the banking industry. It is undeniable that banking's function has evolved in response to changes in the way banks are regulated (Barth et al., 2003).

The recent crises have demonstrated that all countries require a robust financial sector. In the context of financial interdependence, an international regulatory coordination system is of national and public interest, as the failure of a bank in one country may swiftly spread to other nations. As a result, regulators will need to agree on uniform criteria in order to reassure one another that the financial industry they oversee is adequately regulated. Furthermore, the expansion of emerging nations and globalization have drastically increased the variability of financial sectors that must be governed by international standards (BIS, 2017; IMF Annual report, 2017). Most crucially, the rise of international banks has provided strong incentives for regulators in developing nations, even if they are not members of the Basel Committee, to adopt international norms (Jones, 2020). However, it is difficult to agree on universal principles since various economies have distinct regulatory interests and capacities (Barth, Caprio et al., 2013; Barth, Lin et al., 2013). While the Basel Banking Principles are simplified, the combination of market incentives and transformational regulatory frameworks drives emerging nations to adopt complicated standards based on "global best practices" that are insufficiently standardized for their area (FSI, 2015; Jones, 2014; Jones & Zeitz, 2017). Furthermore, nations outside of the standards organizations are frequently impacted by regulatory decisions due to their strong integration into the global financial system.

The next section discusses international rules on regulation, as guided by the Basel Committee, and Africa's Banking System.

21.5 Basel's Principles and Africa's Banking System

Following the global financial crisis, the Basel Committee and other major standard-setting bodies developed worldwide rules for banking regulation. As a result of the global financial crisis that began in the late 2000s, an increasing number of nations throughout the world have assumed responsibility for banking regulation (Barth et al., 2012; Levine, 2010). Not only has the crisis raised serious concerns about the soundness of the global regulatory system anticipated at the outset, but it has also spurred authorities to explore significant regulatory and supervisory adjustments. As a result of the crisis, regulatory and supervisory practices in nations all over the world have changed. Under the third Basel framework, the Basel Committee on Banking Supervision (BCBS) has imposed additional capital and liquidity criteria for banks as part of its regulatory reform program (i.e. Basel III). Many economies have enacted or are in the process of passing new laws and regulations in response to lessons from the crisis. Banking is based on leverage, in which banks borrow from the market and depositors and then lend to borrowers. In actuality, a bank's lending surpasses its deposit base, and the types of money mobilized and loan portfolios differ. The primary goal of banking regulation is to safeguard against losses caused by payment failures or a decline in the asset portfolio's quality. The Basel I model implies that banks will be able to recover their assets in order to recompense depositors and market participants. Basel I had three main components: the BCBS standardized regulatory minimum figure for internationally active banks, the Basel Committee, which established a basic definition of regulatory capital (Tier 1 and Tier 2), and the BCBS, which established a uniform process for banks to calculate their regulatory capital ratios. However, because to a lack of agreement on universal definitions of Tier 1 and Tier 2 capital, as well as other omissions, Basel II was enacted as a partial reform of the framework. As a result, the Basel Committee, which aims to provide a more comprehensive and risk-sensitive approach to capital management, has formally accepted the new Basel II standards. Minimum capital requirements, the supervisory review procedure, and market discipline are all part of this. While Basel I focused solely on the credit and market risks of a bank's assets for calculating risk-weighted assets (RWA), Basel II added provisions for operational risks as a third element in calculating RWA. Despite Basel II's focus on key risk assessment models for banks' assets, the recent global financial crisis exposed the model's limitations, including ambiguity in defining Tier 1 capital, concerns about banks' liability structuring, and critical flaws in risk management models used by most active international banks. Basel III was enacted as a result of this. While the Basel I and II reforms are nearly entirely focused on microprudential that deals with systemic risks in the global banking sector, Basel III attempts to improve the fundamental concept of capital by focusing on its quality, openness, and consistency in general.

Capital and liquidity requirements are significant tools for banking sector regulation. Increased bank capital requirements help to maintain market discipline and keep shareholders from taking unnecessary risks. Sufficient capital provides a cushion to withstand losses in the event of a financial crisis. To supplement risk-weighted minimum capital requirements, BCBS is proposing liquidity ratios, countercyclical capital buffers, systemic premiums, and a minimum leverage ratio as part of the Basel III rule. According to Basel III, a bank's overall capital requirement must be at least 8% of RWA (BCBS, 1998, 2004, 2006, 2017). According to Basel III, a bank's total capital must consist of at least 75% Tier 1 capital (Common Equity Tier 1 (4.5%) and Tier 1 Additional (1.5%)) and 25% Tier 2 capital (2%). Basel III's goal is to increase Basel II's capital standards by raising the total capital ratio from 8 to 10.5% in 2019 and raising tier 1 capital from 4.5 to 6% in 2019 (Nyantakyi & Mouhamadou, 2015). Some banks continued to pay dividends and incentives to workers throughout the early stages of the crisis, depleting capital reserves and reducing the institutions' ability to absorb more losses. With this in mind, BCBS added two extra capital buffers, a capital conservation buffer and a countercyclical buffer, to absorb additional losses.

Both buffers are based on the same principle: banks must accumulate capital reserves that may be utilized to absorb unexpected losses and shocks to the industry. The maintenance buffer requires banks to keep 2.5% of total capital, with a second pool of zero to 2.5% extra capital required in periods of significant loan growth. Several banks accrued excessive leverage during the pre-crisis period, forcing Basel to adopt a target leverage ratio of at least 3% of total exposure. Many of the changes concentrated on affluent nations rather than underdeveloped countries, notably in Africa, because the crisis began in developed countries. As a result, systematic research on detailed changes in African nations is lacking. While nations debate whether or not to implement Basel III, most African regulators and supervisors continue to use Basel I, with Basel II principles still waiting in several African countries (Barth et al., 2009; Beck et al., 2011). The capital requirement is used to compare how much capital in Africa is regulated to how much capital is controlled in other parts of the world. Few African nations have specific deposit guarantee programs that adhere to the Basel Committee on Banking Supervision's key guidelines for efficient deposit guarantee schemes (Demirguc-Kunt & Detragiache, 2002, 2011; Demirguc-Kunt et al., 2013). Limiting banking operations such as loans, bonds, insurance, and real estate businesses is an essential strategy to govern the banking sector in Africa. Despite the fact that Basel III appears to be a work in progress, Basel IV is undoubtedly on the way. African countries that have implemented Basel III have demonstrated that the adoption of leverage ratios, capital buffers, and pro-cyclicality management provide significant elements for banking stability in their economies (BCBS, 1998, 2004, 2006, 2017; Blundell-Wignall & Atkinson, 2010). Basel III was implemented with the intention of addressing the financial system's flaws in industrialized countries. Although Africa's banking sector is far behind that of the industrialized world, African countries must implement the Basel Principles. The African banking system is found to be fairly liquid and well-capitalized, but it needs to focus on improving asset quality and increasing financial system transparency, training its employees, increasing competition through the adoption of innovation and information technology, and providing an effective banking sector governance mechanism.

The next section presents trends in some regulatory indicators by employing data from the Global Financial Development Database. This was used to assess the situation of banking regulation in Africa over the period 2006–2018. Figure 21.1 illustrates changes in average values of equity to asset ratio, countercyclical capital requirement, reserve requirement, capital buffer, and bank liquid reserves.

Globally, there has been a tendency toward increasing minimum capital requirements to strengthen banking system resilience, and Africa is no exception. As seen in Fig. 21.1, post-crisis trends in countercyclical capital requirements have risen dramatically. Banks in Africa have grown their capital holdings from 17.05% of risk-weighted average (RWA) in 2006 to 20.06% of RWA in 2018. Following the global financial crisis of 2007/2008, reserve requirements have been on the rise. Reserve requirement limits climbed slightly from an average of 8.07% in 2006 to an average of 8.84% in 2018. Although the capital buffer climbed from 4.87 in 2006 to 16.19 in 2018, it has shown inconsistent tendencies from 2006 to 2018. Similarly, bank liquid reserves have stayed quite consistent throughout time (see Fig. 21.1). From an average of 15.65% in 2006 to an average of 20.85% in 2018, bank liquid reserves have risen dramatically.

In terms of the development of Africa's banking regulations relative to other regions, Fig. 21.2 shows the stylized facts on the average 2006–2018 period of capital requirement, capital buffer and reserve requirement for three regions (developed, developing and Africa) in the world.

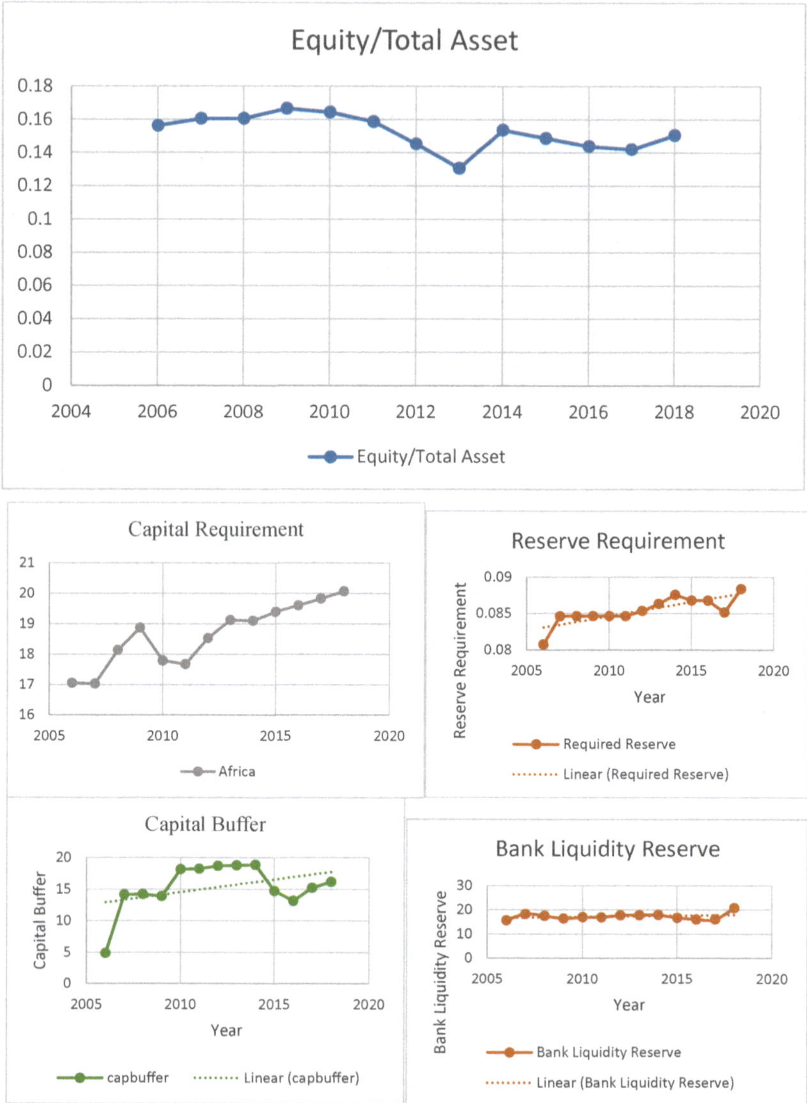

Fig. 21.1 Capital regulations (*Note* Capital Requirement is the ratio of bank regulatory capital requirement to risk-weighted assets; Reserve requirement is the specified percentage of the number of deposits held by banks; Bank Liquid Reserve is the ratio of bank liquid reserve to bank total assets over the period 2006–2018)

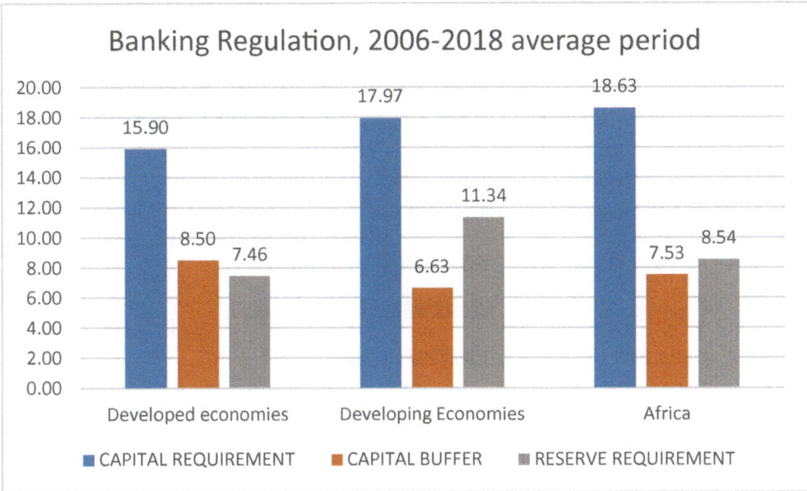

Fig. 21.2 Comparison of banking regulation with other regions (*Note* Capital Requirement is the ratio of bank regulatory capital requirement to risk-weighted assets; Reserve requirement is the specified percentage of the amount of deposits held by banks and Capital Buffer is the difference between total capital ratio [Tier 1 and Tier 2] and the minimum required ratio)

From Fig. 21.2, Africa recorded the highest capital requirement (18.63) compared to developing regions (17.97) and developed regions (15.90) in the world. It was observed that the average capital buffer over the 2006–2018 period for Africa (7.53) lies between countries in developing (6.63) and developed regions (8.50). While developed regions recorded the highest capital buffer, developing regions recorded the lowest. Similarly, the average reserve requirement over the 2006–2018 period for Africa (8.54) lies between countries in developing (11.34) and developed regions (7.46).

In Fig. 21.3, Sub-Saharan Africa recorded the highest geographic coverage of banking regulation and supervision in 2019, representing 33 countries. This is followed by countries in Europe and Central Asia (18), Latin America and the Caribbean (17), East Asia and Pacific (12), South Asia (7) and MENA countries (6). This shows that countries in Sub-Saharan Africa are showing significant interest toward the development

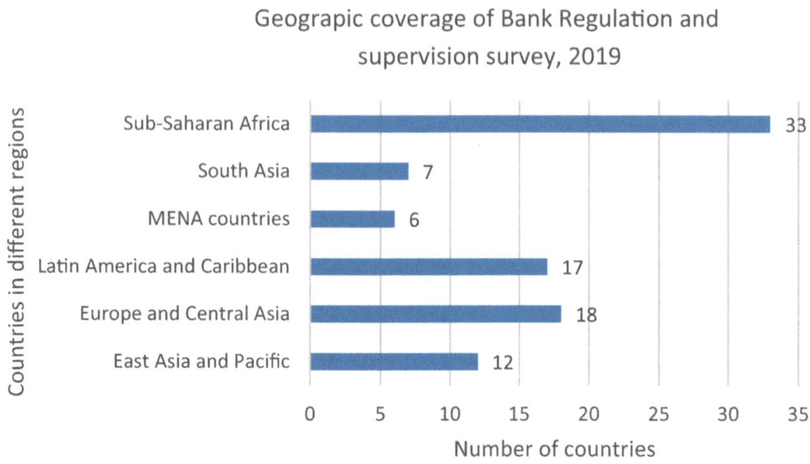

Fig. 21.3 Geographic coverage of Bank Regulation and supervision survey, 2019 (*Source* Global Financial Development Survey Report, 2020)

of banking regulation and supervision compared to other developing countries in the respective regions.

In general, the average of banking regulation indicators in Africa shows some moderate level of development over the 2006–2018 period and greater coverage in banking regulation and supervision.

21.6 Recent Challenges in Regulation and Supervision

In the last two decades, banking rules and regulatory systems have advanced significantly, particularly in African countries. A considerable movement has occurred toward global integration and innovation, as well as the adoption of increasingly complex financial products. Year after year, the number of people who utilize online banking services grows. Regulations have dramatically changed the banking industry during the previous two decades. Even more so, technology, particularly mobile banking services, has aided financial inclusion in Africa, which has the lowest internet penetration of any continent. Regulations and supervision have had to keep up with technological advancements. Governments and central banks have had to establish legislation in order to license non-banking financial companies that did not previously come under the standard financial services umbrella. Central banks' responsibilities have been expanded to encompass not only regulating banks but also monitoring and regulating technological companies that provide certain financial services. In addition, international rules have been developed to govern the banking industry in the aftermath of financial crises, which frequently have worldwide ramifications. The globalization of banking has created concerns about who is responsible for regulating huge international banks that operate in several countries. African regulators have had to embrace international methodologies and standards to control banks (for example, the Basel Committee's Core Principles). To strengthen resilience, global trends have been toward increasing minimum capital requirements. However, new product and service offerings, financial integration and inclusion, and stronger ties with global financial markets all come with heightened risks as a result of the banking sector's far-reaching developments.

The COVID-19 pandemic brought the whole planet to a halt. As a result, most economic sectors were impacted. To combat the spread, governments throughout the world implemented mitigating techniques such as closing down non-essential companies. When it comes to recuperating from the pandemic's consequences, the financial sector has played and will continue to play a critical role in absorbing the shock by providing much-needed money (Acharya & Steffen, 2020; Borio, 2020). Governments and central banks have devised regulations and different policies with the aim of reducing the sharp contraction of economic conditions in the short term, while others sought to support the flow of credit to businesses, either through direct intervention in credit markets (such as government-sponsored credit lines and liability guarantees) or by loosening bank capital buffer restrictions.

Countries had various monetary policies prior to the pandemic. However, the virus's spread has prompted a synchronization of measures that appear to give liquidity to mitigate the pandemic's impact. Most central banks have poured money into the banking system and have utilized unorthodox instruments such as temporary loan repayment suspensions. On the other hand, the acute bankruptcy that many firms and people are experiencing might expose the banking industry to major vulnerabilities owing to the inability to repay loans in full, even in the medium to long term. Non-performing loan suspension over an extended period of time may jeopardize the sector's planned recovery. Regulators have the difficult task of finding a balance between maintaining a sound financial system and supporting and keeping economic activity afloat. When done incorrectly, this is a critical task that can compound the pandemic's detrimental impacts. Regulators can collaborate with banks to achieve a healthy balance and ensure that restructured loans are handled in a transparent and timely manner.

Governments and central banks across the globe have been forced to refocus on financial stability as a result of the COVID-19 pandemic. The pandemic has brought to light flaws in the way the financial industry is governed and controlled. COVID-19 has also emphasized the urgent need for more comprehensive financial inclusion initiatives, given the relatively high pace of digitalization of banks and other financial services. The pandemic has brought attention to the rise of FinTech and other digital financial systems, as well as their acceptance. Some governments offered incentives at the peak of the pandemic to encourage the use of digital services for payment of goods and services, notably through the usage of electronic money or mobile money. Uganda's government, for example, reduced mobile money transfer rates, whereas Egypt, Liberia, and Myanmar raised transactional limits. In response, nations such as Cameroon, the Democratic Republic of the Congo, Ghana, Kenya, Mozambique, Rwanda, Senegal, and Zambia reduced mobile transfer costs while also increasing transactional size restrictions. The usage of digital services has not slowed as economies have opened up, and it is reasonable to assume that digital services are here to stay.

FinTech adoption, in general, has the potential to aid economic recovery following COVID-19, but African nations would need to embrace suitable regulatory and policy frameworks to make this happen (Salami, 2020). Nonetheless, recent advancements in the FinTech sphere have consequences for banking and financial sector legislation and oversight, as detailed in Chapter 22 of this book.

21.7 Conclusion

Globalization has increased the pressure on African banks to meet international banking norms. As a result, nations have been pushed to create laws that conform to international standards. Central banks are progressively embracing international concepts such as the Basel Committee Principles and other international standards-setting bodies. Basel III is being adopted by a large number of countries. For instance, there has been a tendency toward increasing minimum capital requirements to strengthen banking system resilience. The chapter has shown that the post-crisis trends in countercyclical capital requirements and bank liquid reserves have risen dramatically. Following the global financial crisis of 2007/2008, reserve requirements have been on the rise. However, there have been some changing trends in the capital buffers of banks in Africa. Also, the COVID-19 pandemic and the shift toward remote banking and other forms of e-banking platforms provide enough incentive for an evaluation of current banking regulation and supervisory systems in Africa and the world at large.

In general, banking regulation in Africa has been improved and there has been some moderate level of development of banking regulations and supervision over the 2006–2018 period. The chapter has demonstrated that Africa, in recent years, has shown some level of development in banking regulation and supervision.

The strength and stability of African countries' financial and economic systems depend on regulation and supervision by the central bank, and these are effective and appropriate in building a resilient banking system.

References

Abor, J. Y., Gyeke-Dako, A., Fiador, V. A., Agbloyor, E. K., Amidu, M., & Mensah, L. (2019). *Money and banking in Africa*. Springer.

Abor, J. Y. (2018). *Financial markets and institutions: A frontier market perspective* (2nd ed.). Digibooks.

Acharya, V. V., & Steffen, S. (2020). The risk of being a fallen angel and the corporate dash for cash in the midst of COVID. *The Review of Corporate Finance Studies, 9*(3), 430–471.

AFI (Alliance for Financial Inclusion). (2017). *Digitally delivered credit: Consumer protection issues and policy responses to new models of digital lending*. Accessed November 14, 2017. https://www.afi-global.org/publications/digitally-delivered-credit-consumer-protection-issues-and-policy-responses-to-new-models-of-digital-lending/

Agbloyor, E. K., & Abor, J. Y (2020). *The COVID-19 pandemic and its impact on African economies and financial markets: A review. Centre for Global Finance*. Working Paper Series, SOAS, University of London.

Amadou, N. Sy. et al. (2019). *Coping with falling oil prices: The different fortunes of African banks*. IMF Working Papers 2019/129, International Monetary Fund.

Baicu, C. G. (2011). The impact of financial innovation on banking regulation. Evidence from the global financial crisis. *Annals of Spiru Haret University. Economic Series, 11*(4), 31–40.

Barth, J. R., Nolle, D. E., Phumiwasana, T., & Yago, G. (2003). A cross-country analysis of the bank supervisory framework and bank performance. *Financial Markets, Institutions & Instruments, 12*(2), 67–120.

Barth, J. R., Caprio, G. Jr., & Levine, R. (2012). *Guardians of finance: Making regulators work for us*. MIT Press.

Barth, J. R., Lin, C., Ma, Y., Seade, J., & Song, F.M. (2013a). Do bank regulation, supervision and monitoring enhance or impede bank efficiency? *Journal of Banking & Finance, 37*(8), 2879–2892.

Barth, J. R., Caprio, G., & Levine, R. (2013b). Bank regulation and supervision in 180 countries from 1999 to 2011. *Journal of Financial Economic Policy, 5*(2), 111–219.

Barth, J. R., Caprio, G., Levine, R., & Gertler, M. (2009). Banking systems around the globe. In *Prudential Supervision* (pp. 31–96). University of Chicago Press.

Basle Committee on Banking Supervision (1998). Internationa Convergence of Capital Measurement and Capital Standards.

Bauerle, D., Winecoff, K. W. S., & Oatley, T. (2017). All crises are global: Capital cycles in an imbalanced international political economy. *International Studies Quarterly, 61*(4), 907–923.

BCBS (Basel Committee on Banking Supervision). *Global systemically important banks: Revised assessment methodology and the higher loss absorbency requirement*. Accessed July 5, 2018. https://www.bis.org/bcbs/publ/d445.htm

BCBS (Basel Committee on Banking Supervision). *Literature review on integration of regulatory capital and liquidity instruments* (Working Paper No. 30). Bank for International Settlements, Basel. Accessed March 9, 2016a. https://www.bis.org/bcbs/publ/wp30.htm

BCBS (Basel Committee on Banking Supervision). *Literature review on integration of regulatory capital and liquidity instruments*. Accessed March 9, 2016b. https://www.bis.org/bcbs/publ/wp30.htm

BCBS (Basel Committee on Banking Supervision). (2017). *Basel III: Finalising Post-crisis reforms.* Bank for International Settlements. Basel. Accessed December 7, 2017. https://www.bis.org/bcbs/publ/d424.htm

BCBS (Basel Committee on Banking Supervision). *Basel II: International convergence of capital measurement and capital standards: A revised framework.* Basel. Accessed June 10, 2004. https://www.bis.org/publ/bcbs107.htm

BCBS (Basel Committee on Banking Supervision). *Basel II: International convergence of capital measurement and capital standards: A revised framework—Comprehensive version*. Accessed June 30, 2006. https://www.bis.org/publ/bcbs128.htm

Beck, T., Jones, E., & Knaack, P. (2018). Basel standards and developing countries: A difficult relationship. *VoxEU*. Accessed October 15, 2018. https://voxeu.org/article/basel-standards-and-developing-countries

Beck, T., & Cull, R. (2013). Banking in Africa. https://doi.org/10.1596/1813-9450-6684

Beck, T., Cull, R., & Valenzuela, P. (2014). Banking in Africa. *In The Oxford Handbook of Banking*.

Beck, T., Maimbo, S. M., Faye, I. & Triki, T. (2011). Financing Africa: Through the crisis and beyond. *The World Bank*. https://doi.org/10.1596/978-0-8213-8797-9

BIS (Bank for International Settlements). *Consolidated banking statistics*. Accessed March 6, 2017. http://www.bis.org/statistics/consstats.htm

Blundell-Wignall, A., & Atkinson, P. (2010). Thinking beyond Basel III: Necessary solutions for capital and liquidity. *OECD Journal: Financial Market Trends., 1*, 9–33.

Borio, C. (2020). *The prudential response to the Covid-19 crisis, speech on the occasion of the presentation of the Bank's Annual General Meeting*. Bank for International Settlements Accessed 24 July 2020. https://www.bis.org/speeches/sp200630a.htm.

Bowmans. (2017). Fintech in Africa: Unpacking the risks and regulation. *Conference Proceedings*. Johannesburg, South Africa. Accessed May 25, 2017. https://www.bowmanslaw.com/wp-content/uploads/2017/10/Fintech-In-Africa-Conference-Summary.pdf

Brits, R. (2018). The National Credit Act's remedies for reckless credit in the mortgage context. *Potchefstroom Electronic Law Journal/potchefstroomse Elektroniese Regsblad, 21*(1), 1–23.

Calvo, D., Crisanto, J. C., Hohl, S., & Gutiérrez, O. P. (2018). *Financial supervisory architecture: What has changed after the crisis?*. Bank for International Settlements, Financial Stability Institute.

CCAF (Cambridge Centre for Alternative Finance). (2018). *Fintech in Uganda: Implications for regulation*. Judge Business School, University of Cambridge. Accessed November, 2018. https://www.jbs.cam.ac.uk/faculty-research/centres/alternative-finance/publications/fintech-in-uganda-implications-for-regulation/#.YaX5-vHP1E4

Deloitte. *The National Credit Act—Reckless credit*. Accessed 2013. https://www2.deloitte.com/content/dam/Deloitte/za/Documents/governance-risk-compliance/ZA_RecklessCreditUnderTheNationalCreditAct_16042014.pdf

Demirgüç-Kunt, A., & Detragiache, E. (2011). Basel core principles and bank soundness: Does compliance matter? *Journal of Financial Stability, 7*(4), 179–190.

Demirgüç-Kunt, A., & Detragiache, E. (2002). Does deposit insurance increase banking system stability? An empirical investigation. *Journal of Monetary Economics, 49*(7), 1373–1406.

Demirguc-Kunt, A., Detragiache, E., & Merrouche, O. (2013). Bank capital: Lessons from the financial crisis. *Journal of Money, Credit and Banking, 45*(6), 1147–1164.

Didenko, A. (2017). Regulating FinTech: Lessons from Africa. *San Diego International Law Journal, 19*, 311.

Dordevic, L., Ferreira, C., Kitonga, M., & Seal, K. (2021). Strengthening bank regulation and supervision: National progress and gaps. *Departmental Papers, 2021*, 005.

EIB-UNCDF. (2014). *Digital financial services in Africa: Beyond the Kenyan success story*. Accessed December, 2014. https://www.eib.org/attachments/country/study_digital_financial_services_in_africa_en.pdf

FATF (Financial Action Task Force). (2021). *Guidance on risk-based supervision*. Accessed March 4, 2021. https://www.fatf-gafi.org/publications/fatfrecommendations/documents/guidance-rba-supervision.html

Freixas, X., Giannini, C., Hoggarth, G., & Soussa, F. (2000). Lender of last resort: What have we learned since Bagehot? *Journal of Financial Services Research, 18*(1), 63–84.

Freixas, X., Rochet, J. C., & Parigi, B. M. (2004). The lender of last resort: A twenty-first century approach. *Journal of the European Economic Association, 2*(6), 1085–1115.

FSI (Financial Stability Institute). (2014). *FSI survey—Basel II, 2.5 and III implementation*. Accessed July, 2014. https://www.bis.org/fsi/fsiop2014.pdf

FSI (Financial Stability Institute). (2015). *FSI Survey—Basel II, 2.5 and III implementation*. Accessed June 29, 2015. https://www.bis.org/fsi/fsiop2015.htm

Global Financial Development Report. (2019/2020). *Bank regulation and supervision a decade after the global financial crisis*.

Government Gazette. (2005). *National Credit Act, (2005). Republic of South Africa*. Accessed March 15, 2006. https://www.justice.gov.za/mc/vnbp/act2005-034.pdf

GSMA Report. (2018). *2018 mobile money policy and regulatory handbook*. Accessed September 28, 2018. https://www.gsma.com/mobilefordevelopment/wp-content/uploads/2018/09/GSMA-Mobile-Money-Policy-Handbook-2018.pdf

Haldane, A. G., & Madouros, V. (2012). The dog and the frisbee. *Revista de Economía Institucional, 14*(27), 13–56.

Heremans, D., & Pacces, A. M. (2000). *Regulation of banking and financial markets*. Edward Elgar Publishing Limited.

Hoenig, T. M. (2012). *Back to basics: A better alternative to basel capital rules*. In speech to the American Banker Regulatory Symposium (vol. 14). https://www.eib.org/attachments/country/study_digital_financial_services_in_africa_en.pdf

IMF (International Monetary Fund). (2016). *Time for a policy reset*. In regional economic outlook: Sub-Saharan Africa. Accessed April 5, 2016. https://www.imf.org/en/Publications/REO/SSA/Issues/2016/04/05/Time-for-a-Policy-Reset

Johnen, C. M. P., & Mußhoff, O. (2021). Promises and pitfalls of digital credit: Empirical evidence from Kenya. *PlosOne, 16*(7), e0255215.

Jones, E., & Zeitz, A. O. (2017). The limits of globalizing Basel banking standards. *Journal of Financial Regulation, 3*(1), 89–124.

Jones, E. (2020). The challenges international banking standards pose for peripheral developing countries. *The Political Economy of Bank Regulation in Developing Countries*, p. 2.

Jones, E. (2014). *Global banking standards and low income countries: Helping or hindering effective regulation?* (No. 2014/91. GEG Working Paper).

Levine, R. (2010). An autopsy of the US financial system: Accident, suicide, or negligent homicide. *Journal of Financial Economic Policy, 2*, 196–213.

Lopez, M. (2019). *Digital credit for mobile money providers*. GSMA.

Lu, L. (2018). *Decoding Alipay: Mobile payments, a cashless society and regulatory challenges*.

Maina, J. (2018). *Mobile money policy and regulatory handbook*. GSMA.

MEFMI (Macroeconomic and Financial Management Institute of Eastern and Southern Africa). (2016). *Annual report 2016*. Accessed 2016. http://mefmi.org/wp-content/uploads/2018/11/2016-MEFMI-ANNUAL-REPORT.pdf

Mishkin, F. S. (2016). *The economics of money, banking, and financial markets*. Pearson Education.

Mlachila, M. et al. (2016). *Financial development in Sub-Saharan Africa: Promoting inclusive and sustainable growth*. International Monetary Fund, African Department.

Montfort, M., Jidoud, A., Newiak, M., Radzewicz-Bak, B., & Takebe, M. (2016). *Financial development in Sub-Saharan Africa: Promoting inclusive and sustainable growth*. International Monetary Fund.

Nhavira, J. D., Mudzonga, E., & Mugocha, E. (2013). Financial regulation and supervision in Zimbabwe: An evaluation of adequacy and options. *Zimbabwe Economic Policy Analysis and Research Unit*.

Nyantakyi, E. B., & Mouhamadou, S. (2015). The banking system in Africa: Main facts and challenges. *Africa Economic Brief, 6*(5), 1–16.

Ozili P. K. (2018). Banking Stability Determinants in Africa. *International Journal of Managerial Finance*, 14.

Quintyn, M., & Taylor, M. (2007). *Building supervisory Structures in Sub-Saharan Africa-An analytical framework* (IMF Working Paper, WP/07/18).

Salami, I. (2020). COVID-19 crisis in Africa: Leveraging FinTech and RegTech for economic recovery. *Journal of International Banking Law and Regulation, 35*(10), 410–420.

Schmulow, A. (2016). Curbing reckless and predatory lending: A statutory analysis of South Africa's National Credit Act. *Competition and Consumer Law Journal, 24*(3), 220–246.

Shi, D. (2010). China's energy developments, problems and countermeasures since outbreak of global financial crisis. *Sino-Global Energy,* 6.

Sy, A. N., Rodolfo Maino, R., Massara, A., Saiz, H. P., & Sharma, P. (2019). *FinTech in Sub-Saharan African countries: A game changer?* International Monetary Fund.

Taylor, J. B. (1995). The monetary transmission mechanism: An empirical framework. *Journal of Economic Perspectives, 9*(4), 11–26.

Tucker, P. (2009). *The repertoire of official sector interventions in the financial system: last resort lending, market-making, and capital*. In Remarks at the Bank of Japan 2009 International Conference "Financial System and Monetary Policy: Implementation" (pp. 27–28). Bank of Japan.

World Bank. (2001). *Finance for growth: Policy choices in a volatile world* (A World Bank Policy Research Report). World Bank and Oxford University Press. © World Bank. Accessed April 2001 https://openknowledge.worldbank.org/handle/10986/13895. License: CC BY 3.0 IGO.

CHAPTER 22

Playing-Catch Up: SupTech and RegTech Developments in Africa

Maxwell Opoku-Afari, James Atambilla Abugre, and Kwame A. Oppong

22.1 Introduction

Various formidable challenges prevent the financial system from being inclusive, especially in emerging economies like Africa. These problems hamper sustainable growth, employment creation and poverty alleviation (Amadou et al., 2019).FinTech is able to perform a crucial role in fostering an inclusive financial system by enabling firms and households to mobilize resources and invest prudently and timeously to engender

M. Opoku-Afari (✉) · K. A. Oppong
Bank of Ghana, Accra, Ghana
e-mail: maxwell.opoku-afari@bog.gov.gh

K. A. Oppong
e-mail: Kwame.oppong@bog.gov.gh

J. A. Abugre
University of Ghana Bussiness School, Accra, Ghana

J. Y. Abor and C. K. D. Adjasi (eds.), *The Economics of Banking and Finance in Africa*, Palgrave Macmillan Studies in Banking and Financial Institutions, https://doi.org/10.1007/978-3-031-04162-4_22

productivity. It, therefore, offers opportunities to promote inclusive finance in the continent (Abor et al., 2018). FinTech emerged in recent years and is considered by financial inclusion advocates in Africa as a major breakthrough. FinTech makes possible the distribution of capital resources through access to the unserved in the remotest parts of Africa, thereby creating a fertile ground for the achievement of sustained inclusive growth and the empowerment of the hitherto marginalized in society. FinTech developments in the financial industry have been driven by innovations in mobile and telecommunication networks, mobile embedded systems, trust management, cloud computing, big data and data analytic techniques (Gai et al., 2018).

Notwithstanding the immense imperatives of FinTech innovations in the emerging and developing economies' financial system, its adoption and applicability have exposed the already weak financial architecture to a myriad of risks and threats. Cybersecurity threats to participants in FinTech innovations and users of its products have remained one of the hurdles for regulators and other national authorities.

This chapter, therefore, assesses the effectiveness of Supervisory technology (SupTech) and Regulatory technology (RegTech) adopted by regulatory authorities including Central banks for supervisory administration and regulatory guidance to users of FinTech innovations in the financial system across Africa. The chapter is organized as follows: Sect. 22.2 looks at the use of SupTech and RegTech in the regulatory framework of FinTech in Africa. Section 22.3 deals with the emergence of FinTech and its adoption in Africa. Section 22.4 elaborates on the importance of adopting SupTech and RegTech in supervising and regulating FinTech in general and how the financial system stands to gain. Regulatory mechanisms of FinTech and the adoption and implementation of RegTech and SupTech are discussed in Sects. 22.5 and 22.6, respectively, while the challenges confronting their adoption in Africa are discussed in Sect. 22.7. Ways of making SupTech and RegTech effective in Africa are explained in Sect. 22.8 and conclusions and policy implications are presented in Sect. 22.9.

22.2 SupTech and RegTech: A Conceptual Overview

Several regulatory reforms adopted and imposed in the aftermath of the Global Financial Crisis (GFC) of 2007–2008 have resulted in significant structural changes in financial administration across the financial world. Following the Global Financial Crisis, there has been a globally coordinated regulatory reform programs aimed at decreasing risk-taking and systemic risks in the financial industry. These reforms have had a significant negative impact on the world economy. They have also been a major determinant in the development and usage of new technology innovations in the financial sector, especially those that help with regulatory compliance—concepts known as RegTech and SupTech (Pearlman, 2018).

It is crucial to distinguish between RegTech and FinTech. The term RegTech refers to a subset of the term FinTech. Their basic origins of emergence, however, were distinct. RegTech arose as a result of: (1) after-crisis regulatory reforms demanding massive additional data disclosures from supervised entities; (2) improvements and advances in data science (such as AI and machine learning) that can restructure unstructured data; (3) economic opportunities for market participants to reduce rising compliance costs; and (4) regulators' efforts to improve the efficiency of regulatory mechanisms to create competition and maintain their mandates of financial stability (both at the macro and micro levels) and market integrity.

FinTech's emergence, on the other hand, is due to: (1) financial market inefficiencies resulting from the financial crisis and how to use regulatory reforms to address them; (2) public mistrust in the financial system, particularly in the United States and the EU region as well as in developing countries; (3) political influence for different sources of financing mechanisms for small and medium enterprises; (4) redundant financial professionals yearning to utilize their talents; (5) increasing demands for access to quality financial services and inclusion especially among the underserved banking population; and (6) access to new technology and market penetration of the internet and telephony tools, particularly smart phones.

Supervisory tasks for regulators and compliance for supervised institutions are two distinct but interconnected segments of RegTech needs and solutions. RegTech adoption entails the automation of primarily manual operations and/or the use of new technology by regulators and supervisors to increase their abilities to monitor and control their respective industries and to be more efficient. RegTech is often referred to as "SupTech" or supervision technology when it is utilized by supervisors for oversight and monitoring. Regulators can use SupTech solutions to automate and simplify common administrative operations and mechanisms as well as improve and fasten complex decision-making, management and enforcement procedures.

RegTech has recently been fueled by the introduction of fresh technology innovations such as machine learning (ML), artificial intelligence (AI), cloud computing, Application Programming Interfaces (APIs), Know Your Customer utilities, distributed ledger technologies and some of the fastest developments in data analysis orientated "big data" solutions (Pearlman, 2018).

RegTech and SupTech are becoming a means of deploying emerging innovations to decrease costs of compliance for financial institutions and other market participants and to improve regulators' internal reporting and supervisory capabilities (Pearlman, 2018). Many RegTech and SupTech solutions are created and adapted from current and known financial technology solutions, with new technologies being developed de novo to take care of identified regulatory and/or compliance-related supervisory gaps.

In the developing world such as Africa, the ever growing use of FinTech including mobile money and crowdfunding has occasioned the urgent need for regulatory, supervisory and policy reforms in the financial system to meet the demand and supply factors as well as deal with the threats that come with it. Adoption, however, requires a favorable environment with the right infrastructure, technical fitness, robust policy making mechanism and supervision expertise to lead the initiative.

The use of SupTech and RegTech has become imperative to regulators and policy makers in this advent of FinTech due to the large number of non-bank participants and the subsequent huge amount of data that are turned out. The data sets need to be analyzed to inform policy makers about the happenings in the financial market and how the general economy responds to the use of FinTech. The use of RegTech solutions, therefore, enables regulators track, monitor and identify consumer transactions, and manage risks and threats to the financial system, among others. RegTech is more than just a time-saving and efficiency technology; it is a key change that will lead to a paradigm shift in financial services regulation.

22.3 An Overview of Fin Tech in Developing Economies: The Case of Africa

In the absence of asymmetric information, transaction costs and other market defects, financial institutions and markets are central in the efficient allocation of capital resources, according to finance theory. The flow of funds conceptual framework is based on this idea and explains how capital resources are allocated between households and businesses to support economic growth. Indeed, research from both developed and emerging economies reveals that the flow of funds, interest rate and asset price determination, and hence, incomes and expenditures are all interconnected (Murinde, 2012).

Despite its critical role, however, over the years the financial service sector has not been able to efficiently allocate resources in the manner it ought to have done, especially in developing economies like Africa. The report on the Global Findex Database by the World Bank indicates that about 30% of the world's economically active group do not own bank accounts and most of them are in Sub-Saharan Africa (SSA), where in 2017, just 38% of male adults and 27% of female adults owned bank accounts with a recognized formal financial institution (Demirgüç-Kunt et al., 2018). Some of the identified factors responsible for this financial exclusion include cost or documentation requirements (Abor, 2020; Allen et. al., 2016; Beck et al., 2007), low income and education levels (Nanziri, 2015), distance (Demirgüç-Kunt et al., 2018), underinvestment and poor infrastructure (Amadou et al., 2019).

These social and economic bottlenecks have caused much inequality in access to financial services among market participants and its attendant problems of low-income levels and ballooning poverty in Africa (Demirgüç-Kunt et al., 2017). The low-income levels stem from the fact that households' and firms' access to credit has been costly and the requirement procedures are cumbersome, thereby limiting the investment of the needed capital in the productive sectors of the African economy which are dominantly found in the peri-urban areas and periphery of African countries. Poor harvest yields due to subsistence farming and dependence on rain-fed agriculture, loss of perishable farm produce due to low investment in the transport sector and industrialization, dependence on imported finished products, absence of financial services in rural parts of the continent or high cost and cumbersome requirements of credit to households and the private sector, among others, account for the huge unbanked population in Africa. This multiplicity of demand and supply factors of the financial systems does not allow for the mobilization of domestic resources to invest, redistribute and save to bolster the African economies to take off and reengineer their collective transformation.

To mitigate the impact of these factors, there have been many technological innovations to address the barriers to financial inclusion and close the gap in access to financial institutions and ownership of bank accounts. Prominent among these innovations is Financial Technology (FinTech). FinTech, a portmanteau of Financial Technology, is defined variously by international bodies, governments and national authorities as well as researchers. FinTech is distinguished from other technological innovations due to its ability and seemingly adaptive flexibility to become a vehicle of revolution rather than evolution, thereby having a significant impact on the spectrum of financial services and the global economy at large.

FinTech has become one of the major investments for competitive financial firms where its uses, which include loan technology, payments/billing, personal finance/asset management, money transfer/remittances, institutional technology, capital markets and security technology, have permeated the whole of the financial industry (Manyika et al., 2016). FinTech innovations include the Automated Teller Machine (ATM), mobile money integrated payment platforms, mobile banking and mobile finance, short message service (SMS) interactive banking platforms, blockchain technology, cryptocurrency and crowdfunding (Abor et al., 2020). Mobile money, for example, has revolutionized the way financial services are delivered in Sub-Saharan Africa. As a result, the region is on top of the global ranking when it comes to mobile money innovation, adoption and usage, with almost 40 out of 54 countries in the region of Africa vigorously utilizing this new financial technology led by East Africa. FinTech propels growth and serves as a technical catalyst that encourages financial inclusion and economic development in Africa, notwithstanding that overall financial penetration and inclusivity remain low as compared to other regions in the world (Amadou et al., 2019).

22.4 The Demand Factors for the Adoption of SupTech and RegTech by Regulators of FinTech

National regulatory authorities across developed, emerging and developing economies, especially central banks, remain under intense pressure to use technology to promote and ensure inclusive financial and supervisory innovations while preserving financial stability, growth and integrity within the fast evolving financial revolution.

Too many requirements, the need for more human capital, the need to introduce and update information technology systems, ambiguous and outmoded requirements, and too many/too frequent adjustments are among the primary drivers of the current regulatory regime. This can cause central banks and other regulatory authorities to limit innovativeness in the digital financial ecosystem and can impact negatively on financial inclusion which is at its low ebb in Africa. Digital technology can solve many of these challenges and this constitutes one of the main factors that have ignited calls for and given prominence to the adaptation of RegTech and SupTech solutions in Africa.

Hundreds of millions of new consumers are being brought into the formal financial system as a result of technologically driven innovation that is opening up financial inclusivity for consumers at the "bottom of the financial services pyramid" across the globe. By expanding competition and providing options for choice, cutting transaction costs for customers and widening the scope and space of reach, the surge of new FinTech product opportunities promises to further liberalize the financial industry.

Major platforms such as Facebook, Google and Alibaba (also known as "TechFins") are making gains in the payments arena and are even focused on other services (Simone et al., 2018). These cogent reasons, coupled with the demands for efficiency from stake actors, are cardinal pointers for regulators to also adopt technologically driven solutions geared toward ensuring that the above enumerated challenges and opportunities that come with digital financial services and FinTech in general are adequately regulated in the interest of the service providers and consumers.

Automated Report Submission and Data Quality Management

In developed countries, there has emerged a trend for automated reporting and streamlining data quality management by employing integrated rules and validations. RegTech solutions that meet these goals can include a master data management system, regulatory transaction and license review and approval, supervisory data collection and analysis with quality safeguards, risk examination of market players and data exchange with financial systems and other regulators. The automated collection, validation, analysis and exchange of data will check and smoothen reporting demands and procedures, thereby saving time and money for both regulators and market players.

Notwithstanding the advantages of RegTech, manual data submission using templates, spreadsheets, emails and paper is still common in developing nations, which confront a variety of unique problems ranging from technology, infrastructure, human and capital resources to policy and institutional frameworks (Perlman et al., 2018).

Access to a more diverse supply and demand side data provides an avenue for financial inclusion surveys, creating more holistic and clearer picture of the extent of financial exclusion in a specific market. Thus, RegTech and SupTech mechanisms of transmitting data through reporting at any given time set by the regulators are automated, programmed and easily accessed on real-time basis, which usually is convenient and secure. Such data can then be used to establish verifiable trademarks against which gains toward financial accessibility targets can be measured. Disaggregating high-quality supply-side data by gender (how many men and women have access to a specific channel or service) can reveal gender inequalities in financial service inclusion. Because women are more likely than males to be excluded from the financial system, focusing on gender-based indicators could result in unequal returns on investment in financial inclusion programs.

It is often noted that quality data and its management is the panacea toward well thought out and informed policy formulation and implementation. This, however, cannot be said of most African institutions including financial ones, and this has been one of the setbacks toward ensuring that operational activities of the financial institutions are monitored regularly through available untampered data that are accurate, valid and reliable for purposes of ensuring compliance to laid down rules and regulations within the financial ecosystem. The compliance will ensure the protection of consumers' investments and the sustenance of the financial institutions to help mobilize savings and reallocate resources to the needed sectors of the national economies to engender growth.

Financial institutions must comply with laws and regulations, not only to save money, but also to maintain market stability. Regulatory restrictions have an impact on the economy's and markets' overall health. They have been put in place to protect clients while also preserving the financial system's integrity. Regulations also limit the likelihood that central banks may be forced to bail out non-compliant financial firms such as banks, as was identified as one of the key reasons for Ghana's banking crisis between 2016 and 2020. In a way, automated regulatory reporting is a preventative measure. Non-compliance by a bank could lead to reputational damage, a loss of investor trust and imposed fines including penalties, trade halts and the loss of the bank's banking license.

Reporting (e.g. capital and liquidity returns); transactional monitoring (e.g. Money Laundering and Fraud); customer identity management (e.g. Know Your Client); risk management (e.g. scenario analysis and stress testing); and others are all covered by RegTech financial rules. RegTech solutions have an impact on practically every aspect of the financial system, among which include finance, trading, customer-facing businesses and treasury. Due to this wide range of financial instruments that RegTech and SupTech cover and the fact that data produced by the FIs are quality assured and the reporting process automated, regulators are able to transactions on real-time basis to enforce compliance in case of breaches and violations of regulatory requirements.

Collection of Granular Data

Most regulators expect market participants to obtain aggregated data via their reporting platforms and mechanisms where numerous data sources in several templates demand for information for diverse purposes. The acquisition of aggregated data allows for various diversified analysis, uses, consistent reporting and source-validation to overcome the constraints of using aggregated data and template-based reporting. "Push" and "pull" approaches can both be used to obtain granular data. The "push approach" allows market players to electronically submit standardized amounts of granular data on to a central database through an API. In the "pull approach," unrefined data is obtained directly from market participant's information technology systems by the regulator through compulsory means and enforcement. Because the data is not tabulated ahead of time, it eases the load on market players while increasing the burden on regulators. Additional mechanisms to the aforementioned approach-based technology enable automation of raw data processing to be valuable to regulators so as to reduce the cost burden and time to processing and consuming granular data. The use of granular data may be inadequate in Africa due to the non-robustness of technology application by most regulators owing to the huge costs associated with the implementation of such data collection frameworks.

Easy and Quick Access to New Flows of Information for Decision-Making

Financial institutions and regulatory agencies can use RegTech and SupTech solutions to solve the problems created by digital finance and digital globalization and at the same time consolidate the growth of their responsibilities as a result of greater volumes of FIs and data. They are especially well-suited to the execution of modern risk-based, data-driven supervision. They do this by: (i) offering authorities the needed tools that allow them to collect larger and more diverse datasets from a wider range of sources, (ii) automating administrative processes and (iii) digitizing, accelerating and augmenting their analytical skills.

Financial authorities may gain better insights and utilize ecosystem linkages through RegTech/SupTech, which benefits all of their core competencies including financial stability, financial crime fighting and prevention, market behavior, competition dynamics and variations, financial inclusion and access and innovation. Market efficiency, consumer welfare and governance can all benefit from the implementation of RegTech and SupTech. These advantages arise from their ability to cut transactional costs for market players seeking to make entry into the financial services industry and to reduce market information distortions among regulators, providers and customers quickly and efficiently. Supervisory and regulatory authorities are able to achieve all these enumerated results due to the automated nature of RegTech solutions and their quick responsiveness to the needs of all market participants. Among the advantages that may arise from the deployment of new technologies are improved financial sector monitoring and supervision—both domestically and across boundaries, while others include the introduction of new policy and regulatory methods as well as open data platforms.

Enhanced Prediction and Effective Supervision

Manual data collection and processing slow down regulatory responses and hinder data modeling's ability to adequately handle developing financial challenges with a focus on FinTech. RegTech/SupTech solutions, on the other hand, open up new sources of information by obtaining data from unutilized sources, compelling access to real-time analyzed data for decision-making and providing details from unstructured data to quickly respond to any lapses and accurately model regulatory and supervisory solutions to maintain the financial ecosystem's integrity, confidence and stability. If regulators have the capacity to analyze, an increase in the volume, velocity and variety of data can cause improved monitoring and supervision.

Box 22:2
The Bank of Ghana is currently implementing a consumer chatbot to handle complaints in partnership with BFA Global and Sinitic Africa (now Proto), and sponsored by the African Digital Financial Inclusion (ADFI). The chatbot will serve as a central platform for receiving and managing consumer complaints in order to improve confidence in the digital financial service ecosystem.

An enabling regulatory environment is crucial to allowing inclusive and resilient business models to emerge and grow. RegTech/SupTech solutions can help policy makers and rule makers build a stronger evidence base. When designing prudential regulations, for example, richer datasets with multiple applications allow for more extensive modeling and effect assessments. The feedback loop between financial regulators, financial service providers and consumers can be improved by adding new data gathering channels. Such automation helps the regulators and supervisors to receive, process, analyze and take action on a higher volume of financial regulatory and supervision inquiries in a timelier manner. For instance, new ways of gathering and analyzing customer feedback (e.g., chatbots) and understanding their conduct (e.g., Artificial Learning) can offer customers a wider platform to contribute their suggestions in shaping regulations. The consideration of these inputs by regulators and service providers could trigger user flexibility and customer-oriented regulations that comprehensively address the quest for quality service which is affordable, accessible and inclusive.

Firms seeking entry into emerging markets and lines of business can use RegTech/SupTech solutions to streamline licensing and compliance procedures, thereby further lowering regulatory barriers to entry. The verification of application documents and qualifications can be aided by an artificial intelligence solution for licensing. Computers should be able to swiftly parse applications utilizing machine reading (MR) and optical character recognition (OCR). The necessary information may then be extracted and transferred into databases where it could be cross-referenced against license requirements for consideration.

Machines can already read, understand, interpret, extract and summarize the content of complicated documents relevant to financial analysis and decision-making, for example. Thus, this greatly reduces the bureaucracy that characterizes business application, license acquisition and entry requirements in Africa which can limit competition and promote corruption within the financial sector. Hence, the adoption of RegTech/SupTech solutions in Africa could be a turning point for attracting investors in its economy, in that the human interference and involvement in processing entry requirements for new entrants from the international market is significantly reduced. Data submission accuracy could be enhanced and associated costs reduced, regulatory requirements could be adjusted easily to reflect changing demands and compliance cost cut, thereby lowering bottlenecks to market entry and promoting competition. This boosts confidence and guarantees a business-friendly environment in a less costly system for investment.

Big Data Analytics (BD) is one of the developing digital technologies that can be used to fulfill the growing needs of the regulatory regime. It can be used to get more insight from structured and unstructured data as well as provide programmable reporting. This technology can assist in gaining a better understanding of client behavior and interdependence. Most regulatory difficulties such as financial crimes are caused by activities or transactions which are very difficult to detect using typical risk and control mechanisms.

Simplification of Regulations for Easy Understanding by Market Participants

Due to low literacy levels, complex regulatory requirements, and weak control systems, market participants, especially in emerging regions such as Sub-Saharan Africa, face difficulties in obtaining, tracking and interpreting regulatory guidelines as well as identifying and enforcing regulations that concern them. Currently, most market participants, particularly financial institutions, manually apply and interpret rules and regulations in ways that best serve their interests, then manually input those rules and regulations into their systems to generate reports for submission to the regulator(s). This covers the specification of basic data points as well as the factors to be excluded when determining them, such as who is an "active customer," a "churned customer" and a "dormant customer." In this respect, there is a considerable likelihood of service providers abusing their discretion, which can be arbitrary and illegal.

Market participants need some time to identify, understand and practice applicable regulations which can result in serious discrepancies in interpretation, application of the rules and implementation due to human errors and self-seeking motives of business owners and managers of financial institutions. This effect of the agency problem emanating from the open interpretational biases that the market stakeholders are exposed to, can complicate and endanger the financial system, as has been witnessed in the banking and financial crisis in Ghana between 2016 and 2020, which is estimated to have cost the Ghanaian economy nearly 13 billion Ghana cedis (International Monetary Report, 2020).

Market participants can undoubtedly benefit from regulatory contents and frameworks written in a machine-readable language—that can be directly developed and uploaded into market participants' information technology systems without the need for human interference, to automatically implement compressed rules and narrow the gap between intention and interpretation. This could ensure that regulatory requirements are implemented correctly and quickly, decrease the cost and inefficiencies of outside consultations, ameliorate the agency problem for market actors and improve the reliability of data reporting and submission.

Integration of Regulators' Internal Processes

Regulatory agencies within the financial environment have a variety of functions including overseeing the financial system and institutions, providing essential financial infrastructure, ensuring monetary and financial stability and acting as instruments for innovation. Locally tailored RegTech/SupTech could offer a digital ecosystem that integrates the various regulatory mandates as a substitute for the disintegrated components with a fully digitized and institutionalized system to operate real-time monitoring, provide automated analytics and submit progress reports to the regulatory bodies.

Other software including networks and systems such as SWIFT, automated clearing houses (ACH) and the real-time gross settlement (RTGS) system, could be interfaced with the digital architecture to provide real-time information to central banks. RegTech, on the other hand, can be used to solve a specific internal problem and improve internal central bank processes such as automating central bank procedures, optimizing statistical processes, electronically managing employee access rights according to their roles and assisting with worker onboarding and even human resource management (Pearlman et al., 2018).

Within the regulatory and supervisory system, automation may reduce labour effort while preserving scarce time and resources for analytical work. Externally focused RegTech/SupTech solutions can automate data collection whereas internally focused ones can automate data analysis, interpretation and publication. Within the financial regulatory environment, such analytical tasks may necessitate collaboration among several technical and functional authorities. In Africa's already replicated supervisory institutions, a shared and automated RegTech/SupTech solution can decrease cyclical interferences and rifts between work settings, engagements, utilizations and databases.

The use of APIs in open banking, for example, could foster collaboration between central banks and technical service providers, allowing for effortless aggregation of innovative tools into the traditional system of the central bank. Legacy banking systems, on the other hand, have limited scalability and flexibility. Banks are looking into using blockchain-based technology to improve their traditional core systems which include deposit, loan, withdrawal and credit processing as well as data sharing between branches and other financial institutions. Vault, for example, is a centralized, permissioned cryptographic ledger that replaces legacy core banking systems and processes transactions across financial institutions in a more proactive and effortless manner. It uses smart contracts, data analysis, real-time databases and customer relationship management to provide a wide range of retail banking solutions.

22.5 Regulatory Mechanisms of FinTech in Africa

Despite the significant progress in recent years, financial intermediation, growth and inclusion in Sub-Saharan Africa remain among the lowest in the world. The penetration and coverage of financial systems in Sub-Saharan Africa measurable by standard financial development indicators, such as the ratios of private sector credit to Gross Domestic Product and broad money to Gross Domestic Product, have significantly increased between 1995 and 2016 (Amadou et al., 2018, Kasenkende, 2010). However, Sub-Saharan African countries continue to witness a lower financial development than countries in other emerging regions of the world. This has deprived the continent of the impact that a deep financial system brings to bear on the economy and the general wellbeing of the citizenry. Just 20 percent of the population in the subregion own a bank account as against 92 percent in developed economies and 38 percent in other developing regions' economies such as East Asia (World Bank Report, 2018). The region's underbanking is worsened by under-investment in capital accumulation, poor infrastructure and low levels of financial literacy.

However, mobile money has introduced a fundamental and dramatic shift in the way financial services are delivered in the African subregion. Consequently, the area has surged, putting Africa on top of the world when it comes to mobile money penetration, innovation, adoption and application, with nearly three-quarters (40) of Sub-Saharan Africa's 54 countries adopting and using this emerging financial technology (FinTech). In terms of adoption and usage, East Africa continues to lead Sub-Saharan Africa. Despite the fact that overall financial inroads remain below those of other regions, FinTech is becoming a growth bolster and technical catalyst that promotes financial inclusion and economic development on the continent.

Notwithstanding the numerous opportunities that come with the innovations of financial technology in Africa, its adoption and usage are beset with a myriad of challenges that need urgent attention. The adoption of RegTech/ SupTech is, therefore, seen as welcome news for many watchers of the FinTech revolution in Africa, to curtail the potency of the several threats that could erode its impact on the continent.

Adoption of SupTech and RegTech in Regulating FinTech in Africa

Prior to the 2008 financial crisis, the extent and complexity of RegTech advances and other important regulatory service areas were substantially less onerous, and they were frequently managed on a quasi-manual basis. The Liquid Coverage Ratio (LCR) is a 30-day horizon metric that analyzes all contingent cash outflows and liquidity strains for on- and off-balance sheet exposures. In recent years, it has become nearly impossible to quantify and track complex prudential metrics, and to project aggregated cash flow forecasting and automated reporting mechanisms without using dedicated information technology systems and the participation and coordination of larger interested parties.

A variety of factors are impacting the continued demand for technology regulatory systems for FinTech activities across the African continent, and the adoption of RegTech and SupTech is one of the most obvious choices. These factors include, but are not limited to:

a. **A large number of complex regulatory changes**—the number of rules has expanded dramatically in recent times, making it impracticable for financial institutions to examine and monitor all liquidity and transactional changes.
b. **Inefficient legacy design setup**—many financial institutions have fragmented regulatory and compliance operations and information technology systems which sometimes necessitate a great deal of manual involvement.
c. **Enabling technology**—while some digital technologies and innovations such as Artificial Intelligence have existed for some time now, recent advances in processing capacity have made distributed computing a more viable choice.
d. **Several advantages**—a variety of advantages for businesses including:

- **Increased revenue**—by completing Know Your Client (KYC) and Anti-Money Laundering (AML) regulations more quickly, RegTech automation can improve open market competition while also enhancing client satisfaction, loyalty and confidence.
- ***Reduced Cost***—streamlined and automated processes minimize the number of employees required to manually alter data and check for errors, cutting total compliance costs.

- Increased efficiency and productivity—RegTech flexibility allows banks to respond more quickly to regulatory volume and adjustments as well as deliver more frequent reports. They also allow employees to concentrate on higher-value services such as strategic tasks.
- ***Lower risk/better governance***—when financial institutions can simply adhere to rules and a plethora of other compliance obligations, they are less likely to suffer reputational harm, penalties and fines as a result of compliance errors.

e. **Supervisory improvements**—most regulators are studying the advantages and opportunities that RegTech can provide from a supervisory standpoint which could help regulators make decisions more quickly. For example, the huge number of regulatory reports filed to the regulator by banks and other financial institutions must be evaluated and assessed, which is typically a time-consuming and slow procedure for the regulator (s).
f. **Wider digital adoption**—Integration of RegTech as part of a digital technology strategy can result in a more stable financial system and actual economies of scale. All areas of the financial system's activity and jurisdictional footprint are covered by financial rules. As a result, it is critical to try to comprehend and investigate the many regulatory emphases or service sectors. This is to determine which form of digital technology is most suited to solving a certain problem.

Huge et al. (2020) identified five main service areas that RegTech/SupTech development is identified with, namely:

- Regulatory reporting: It is a requirement for financial organizations to submit data to a regulator in order to bring transparency into their operations and ensure that they adhere to all regulatory requirements. This must be done on a regular basis, usually monthly, quarterly and annually. However, for some risks such as intraday liquidity, daily reporting will be required. Financial, prudential (BASEL III), and transactional reporting are only some of the financial disciplines that can be covered by reporting (e.g. MiFID II).

- Regulatory compliance: This comprises adhering to prudential regulations as outlined in specifications, policies, standards, or laws as well as taking the necessary procedures to comply with all relevant directives. Organizations are increasingly using harmonised sets of compliance measures as the number of rules grows and the requirement for operational transparency expands. This method is employed to ensure that all relevant governance standards are completed without duplication of effort and activity.
- Transaction monitoring: This is the analysis of legacy and current customer information and interactions in order to provide a comprehensive view of customer activity. Transfers, deposits and withdrawals are all examples of this. It is a crucial safeguard against money laundering (AML).
- Identity management and control: Know Your Customer (KYC) is a financial industry standard check that ensures that investment consultants and financial institutions have extensive information about their clients' identities, risk aversion levels, investment knowledge and financial behavior. Clients and financial institutions are both protected by KYC which often includes regulations and policies such as risk control and management, customer acceptance of policies and transaction monitoring.
- Risk management: This entails the quantitative management of various hazards across organizations as well as scenario analysis, exposure computation and exposure reporting. In terms of complexity, extent and frequency, financial institutions are under growing pressure to manage these regulatory requirements. Emerging RegTech/SupTech digital solutions can play a critical role in assisting with these growing regulatory management activities and needs.

SupTech and RegTech as Regulatory tools for FinTech in Africa

While RegTech is concerned with the innovative solutions to regulated institutions in FinTech, SupTech is aimed at tackling the challenges faced by supervisory agencies. Following the global financial crisis, innovations in financial supervision are increasingly shifting away from approaches based on historical data, lengthy onsite inspections and often delayed supervisory action toward a more proactive, forward-looking supervision that relies on better data collection and sophisticated data analysis intertwined with greater storage and mobility using cloud computing. Many regulatory agencies are looking into how DLT could help them reach their objectives. SupTech can help reduce time-to-report, collect much more granular financial and transactional data without incurring unnecessary expenditures, increase data usage beyond institution-reported data and reduce or eliminate human data aggregation and collection processes. Currently, supervisory agencies (and other financial authorities) gather aggregate business data (the majority of which is financial data) in the form of standard reporting templates on a regular basis (daily, monthly, quarterly and annually).

The data may be arranged and reported in legacy forms in some circumstances. Even though much of the underlying data is likely to be the same, each unit within the financial authority may have their own format for reporting with distinct algorithms. The present attention is on documents and reporting designs and not the underlying data that is used to create the required reports. The challenges with the present "template-based" approach are:

- The supervisor's ability to edit data and construct customized indications to assist differentiated analyses is limited.
- The data tabulation procedure within the financial institutions, particularly big institutions with various platforms from which data is gathered, could be expensive, time-consuming and laborious.
- There are high expenses of reporting aggregated data while employing reporting designs owing to the system adjustments that reporting institutions must do;
- There are differences in indicators across multiple reporting designs due to calculation and coding errors, or misreading of data points and biasness;
- Data confirmation at the aggregate level creates an avenue for omissions and misrepresentation;
- Huge volumes of templates often overlap with one another and escalate compliance costs.

Collecting raw data characterized by pre-formatted templates allows supervisors the freedom to create customized indicators and ensure harmonization across reporting institutions in any format for a broader range of analyses. Granular data could provide an enriched and prompt supervisory overview if modern data analytics tools are employed. SupTech, thus, helps supervisory agencies to, among other things, maintain efficiency, compliance, productivity and transparency through the following measures.

i. Data-pull strategy—through automated operations managed by a supervisory agency such as the central bank, raw (non-analyzed) business data is obtained straight from financial institutions' operational systems which are then standardized by the agency using the SupTech solutions.
ii. Real-time access—By having direct access to the institutions' operational systems, which may include real-time transaction monitoring, the supervisor can pull or "see" operational data whenever necessary (rather than at predetermined reporting intervals). Regular monitoring of financial institutions and consumer transactions allows supervisory institutions and national governmental bodies to track financial-related crimes and offences such as money laundering, cybercrime and fraud activities within the financial digital space, allowing them to take swift action in order to maintain the system's sanctity and integrity which in most cases is compromised in Africa. For instance, the European Union in 2019 cited 15 African countries out of the 32 nations in its annual report on financial cybercrimes including money laundering and terrorism financing. This was followed by various sanctions to those countries which included Ghana, Nigeria and Burkina Faso.
iii. Reporting utilities—SupTech can provide reporting utilities which have central structures that act as a shared database of reported granular data as well as a repository of computer-readable interpretations of reporting rules (a "semantic reporting utility"). Reporting utilities may minimize the current reporting arrangement in which each reporting institution develops and introduces its own mechanisms and interpretations of the reporting standards and procedures, often depending on external legal guidance for intricate laws. When paired with machine-readable regulations, reporting utilities have the potential to completely automate the reporting value chain. FinTech has been investigated by certain regulators as a way to improve supervision, increase surveillance and minimize the compliance requirements imposed on financial institutions.

iv. Gathering intelligence from unstructured data—SupTech is helping supervisory bodies to gather and deduce meaning from unstructured data (material that is not organized in databases) more quickly, potentially saving supervisors time by reducing time-consuming tasks such as reading several PDF files and searching the Internet. Inspection reports, emails, official communications, meeting minutes, licensing applications and other information created by the supervisory agency but stored in unstructured formats are all examples of relevant data.

v. Regulatory submissions and data quality control—Many regulatory bodies, particularly in developing economies like Africa, lack completely automated methods for handling reporting institution submissions and executing validation tests in order to assure the accuracy of the reported data. SupTech is introducing new tools and services aimed primarily at submission and data quality management.

On the other hand, RegTech solutions leverage on innovative technologies to eliminate the traditional data architecture in order to mine new data sources. Artificial intelligence (AI), machine learning (ML), machine reading (MR), distributed ledger technologies (DLTs), biometrics, natural language processing (NLP), Big Data analytics, smart contracts, cloud computing, cryptography and other technologies are among them. They have the opportunity to automate or speed up manual operations as well as generate insights that may elude or outperform human analysis. The potential applications for financial sector regulation and supervision are numerous, some of which are currently in use while others are in the exploratory or experimental stages of development. Below are some application challenges confronting regulators/supervisors and the corresponding opportunities presented by RegTech solutions.

Automated Regulatory Reporting, Forecasting and Modelling

RegTech solutions improve data analytics by automating and restructuring administrative and operational procedures and by digitizing data and working tools. Regulatory agencies are increasingly looking for ways to automate regulatory processes and establish reporting tools. These are centralized structures that serve as a repository for the interpretation of reporting rules in a computer-readable format as well as a shared database of reported granular data. AI and machine learning (AI/ML) approaches can be used to detect patterns in vast amounts of data from a growing number of sources. AI is a large field, and machine learning is a subset of it. Customer-focused ("front-office") uses such as credit scoring, insurance and client-facing chatbots; operations-focused ("back-office") uses such as capital optimization, model risk management and market impact analysis; and trading and portfolio management in financial markets.

Big Data

"Big Data" refers to the storing and processing of huge and/or complex data collections utilizing a number of data elaboration techniques. In a Big Data setting, AI/ML techniques are commonly employed to enable the creation of new data management platforms that can acquire, store, analyze and interpret massive amounts of structured and unstructured data. Financial businesses can feed data from both internal and external sources into converged data platforms. Customer data is one of the most common types of confidential internal data, as is data on all internal activities (assets, liquidity, loans, payments, etc.). Whether from internal or external sources, personal data are subject to strong privacy safeguards under common law countries. Many datasets in Africa's financial institutions are unstructured, making standard infrastructure challenging to operate with. External sources include a variety of third-party specialized data providers for certain situations which are often accessed using open real-time software interfaces and standardized query methods.

Financial businesses can use Big Data technologies to tap into this vast volume and variety of data sources to improve business, ensure regulatory compliance and analyze trends. Fraud detection by banks and financial organizations utilizing analytics to recognize fraudulent transactions is one of the most popular RegTech applications used by banks and financial services providers.

Risk Management

Regulatory schemes require financial firms to put in measures to manage a variety of risks in a proper way (e.g. liquidity risk, operational risk, sentiment analysis, auditing market conduct) to reduce, if not eliminate entirely, the possibility of their occurrences and the attendant impact on the financial system. RegTech applications by regulators are increasingly harnessing the benefits of technology to stem the tide of agency problems that characterize most financial institutions in Africa as well as the behaviors of management that pose systematic threats to investments within the financial environment. Compliance reporting, for example, has not always been as efficient as desired. Financial firms are frequently required to respond to regulators' ad hoc demands for information. Regulators' use of data analytics is complicated and time-consuming due to the non-machine-readable data given by financial firms.

Applications of Artificial Intelligence/Machine Learning

The application of AI/ML is an area of interest for regulators. Natural Language Processing, a type of AI, is being used by authorities such as the European Central Bank and the Federal Reserve System of the United States to help them identify financial stability issues. Another potential use of AI/ML in the securities market is to detect trade syndicates. Traditional approaches can be particularly difficult to use to detect collusive behavior and price manipulation such as share pricing or circular trading to create a misleading appearance of market activity and other market abuses. Rule-based systems, such as transaction monitoring systems, have a high rate of false positives, which costs both exchanges and regulators time and money. Regulators' detection of market abuses by market participants is seen as a breakthrough in helping to prevent collusive syndicates between dishonest officers of the regulatory institutions and management of financial institutions which have been identified as one of the main causes of the banking crises in Ghana from 2016 to 2020 and in Nigeria in the early 2000s. Complicated network analysis is another difficulty that AI/ML tools may be able to aid with, especially when the network is huge and varies over time (Table 22.1).

Market Participants and the Use of SupTech and RegTech by Regulators

Financial Institutions

Financial institutions across the world suffered with various levels of post-Global Financial Crisis with strict compliance demands, monitoring and restrictions on financial participants from regulators and other national authorities. This made it urgent to develop and apply more innovative and technologically inclined solutions such as RegTech and SupTech as a means to reduce the cost of compliance and to promptly deal with emerging demands of the financial market and manage risk.

Table 22.1 Key Technologies of RegTech innovation and of impact on regulatory processes

Technologies	*Definition*	*RegTech impact*	*Examples*
Artificial Intelligence (AI), Machine Learning	Technology that accomplishes tasks that require human intelligence in the past. Machine Learning is a subtype of artificial intelligence that learns from data and recognizes patterns in order to modify existing algorithms to better fit the data	Fraud prevention and detection	MAS is developing machine learning algorithms
Application Program Interfaces (API)	Protocols and technologies that allow various systems to communicate with one another	Central bank supervision systems and monitored entities' integration and interoperability. E.g. mobile money interoperability in Ghana and Kenya from different telecommunication networks	BSP is using API for regulatory reporting
Big Data Analytics	Extrapolate meaning from big datasets containing both organized and unstructured data. It is mainly based on artificial intelligence (AI) or other technologies	Support for transaction and risk monitoring	
Biometrics	Authentication of people's identities based on their distinct physical and behavioral features	Robust ways to verify identity	BVN in Nigeria is based on biometrics

(continued)

Table 22.1 (continued)

Technologies	*Definition*	*RegTech impact*	*Examples*
Cloud computing	Computing services such as storage and analytics are delivered over the internet. It lowers capital costs, improves processing speed by allocating vast numbers of computer resources, and provides elastic resources for scalability, to name a few benefits	Access to innovative software, data harmonization, and the formation of common processes at a cheaper cost	
Distributed Ledger Technology (DLT)	Distributed databases that store and encrypt verified data and allow it to be safely shared and managed across the internet	Client data exchange in real time	Estonia is using blockchain technology for ID purposes
Semantic technology and data point models	Regulatory text is converted into programming language using technology	Machine-readable regulations provide for quick and low-cost adaptation to regulatory changes	FCA plans to develop machine-readable regulations
Shared Utilities	Central repository that allows concerned parties within the industry to share services	KYC utilities consolidate data and reduce replication	MyInfo in Singapore is a KYC utility

Source Authors' compilation, 2021

Financial firms' regulatory compliance costs and difficulties were exacerbated by uncoordinated timeframes, diverse and duplicated reporting requirements, the implementation of overlapping legislations and the ongoing changes in regulations. This, combined with the loss of trust in the financial system, has made financial institutions in industrialized countries more unwilling to extend loans and retain relationships that have poor returns with increased risks (Amadou et al., 2018). This credit freeze and low-risk appetite impacted several emerging countries. Trade, investments, remittance flows, aid, and capital and technical inflows into developing regions such as Africa were all affected within the last two decades as a result of the aforementioned.

While the RegTech/SupTech market is still evolving, the following RegTech/SupTech solution categories have been identified as being used in Africa.

Compliance

This has been one key fundamental area that has been a heavy burden on both regulators and regulated financial institutions across the globe, both before and after the global financial crisis. Supervisory and regulatory institutions have adopted RegTech and SupTect in recent times to ensure an effortless achievement of compliance with requirements within the financial environment. Enterprise-wide solutions for detecting and keeping track of changes in regulatory requirements at local and international levels include automatic real-time monitoring of compliance levels and compliance risk based on the analysis of operational and other data. These include employee performance and target setting, historical email correspondences, human conduct analysis, trade, investment and communication analysis. To maintain a continued adherence and assess whether the data presented to supervisors are accurate, valid, reliable and fit for purpose, regulatory requirements are built into information technology protocols. "Dynamic compliance" is the term for this form of automatic compliance. This type of RegTech/SupTech solution can significantly reduce the costs of manual compliance procedures.

Figure 22.1 shows compliance expenses in US banks in relation to the banks' expenses. It is evident from the figure that the amount spent by the banks jumped from less than $35 billion in 2006 to almost $55 billion by 2010. This evidently shows the huge amount of resources spent on compliance issues even in the developed financial market which has fewer regulatory complexities compared to those that bedevil Africa's weak market system, characterized as it is by duplicated institutional architecture and requirements.

Identity Management and Control

Counterparty due diligence and KYC procedures, anti-money laundering (AML) controls and fraud detection are all significant aspects of RegTech. For example, digitizing customer or partner entry processes, digitizing and sharing customer/partner data, gathering, monitoring and

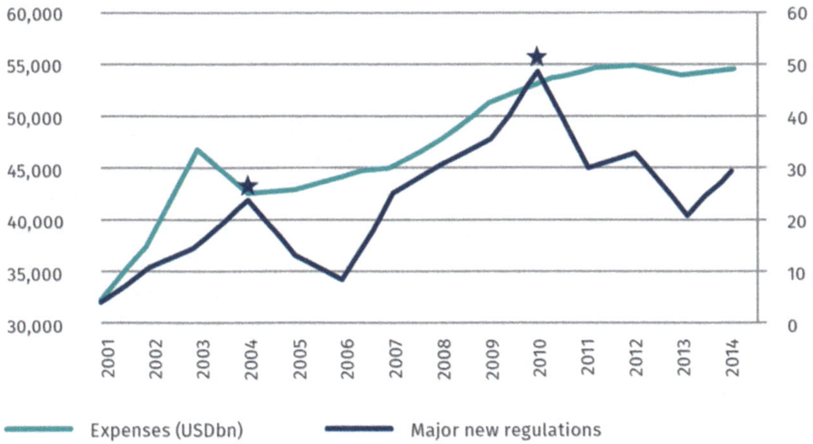

Fig. 22.1 Compliance-related expenses on the US market (*Sources* Fin Tech Poland [2017])

reviewing customer and transaction data, identifying suspicious transactions based on automated triggers and constantly updating and reviewing customer/partner profiles are all examples of digitalization. This field of RegTech including KYC utilities is based on DLT or other technologies.

The automation of several procedures associated with trading in financial markets such as quantifying margins, selecting central counterparts and trading centers, assessing exposures and adhering to standard business practices can serve as a catalyst for creating a congenial atmosphere in Africa's financial system for investment as human interaction is drastically minimized and possible under dealings completely eliminated. Thus, RegTech solutions, when adopted, could be a major breakthrough in the fight against terrorism and the financing of it in Africa, which has become a security threat to the region in recent years.

Risk Management

This section focuses on tools that help financial institutions improve their risk management processes by bringing efficiencies to risk data generation, risk data aggregation, internal risk reporting, automatically identifying and monitoring risks based on internal mechanisms or regulatory definitions and developing red flags and automated actions that are triggered when predetermined risk levels are achieved.

Transaction monitoring on conduct-of-business requirements and solutions include DLT, integrity validation, anti-fraud and market abuse detection systems and back-office automation (post-transaction settlement, closing process) and risks alerts. These solutions could depend on sophisticated data analytics, machine learning or other AI applications to anticipate and model simulations that use historical data to influence financial institutions' operational activities and choices as well as those of regulators and other market participants.

Regulatory Reporting

This is an essential component for supervisory authorities to concentrate on as well as a critical part of regulatory compliance and enforcement. RegTech products automate and consolidate regulatory reporting standards to save time and money, speed up and enhance reporting accuracy and even enable real-time reporting. Individual financial institutions can design and deploy RegTech solutions through multilateral co-operations with FinTech firms, or financial institutions collaborated can jointly acquire or employ a third-party solution—the "shared utility model". Regulatory reporting utilities and KYC utilities are two examples of shared utility models.

Digital Financial Service Providers

Digital financial services have been identified as an effective financial mechanism that opens the scope of financial participation by all financial consumers across the globe and narrows the distance of financial access and trade among the market participants irrespective of the geographical location or economic classification of the region (Work Bank Report, 2017). In developing regions such as Asia and Africa, the growth of digital financial services promotes financial inclusion and economic development. Their ease, user-friendliness and flexible requirements have positioned the digital financial services well in Africa as the most preferred financial service patronage among the larger populace despite the region's high illiteracy rate and inadequate digital support-based infrastructure.

However, the rapid adoption of digital financial services and the introduction of new users and suppliers into the African financial system have created new concerns. Due to low financial literacy, lack of proper legal regime and regulations, a developing digital ecosystem and poor infrastructure base, risks linked to data security and consumer protection can be an obvious hurdle in developing countries.

Multiple regulators including those in the financial and telecommunication sectors are involved in the provision of digital financial services, thereby increasing compliance burdens and complexities, resulting in duplication in digital financial service reporting demands and formats among the different authorities. Increasing the size of a financial institution's risk management and compliance procedures with the necessary human and material resources has been a traditional reaction to high compliance requirements. While this may be a solution for old-aged and well-to-do service providers, it may not be feasible for smaller digital financial service providers—usually startups—with limited financial and human resources.

RegTech solutions, built in-house or by technical service providers, can help digital financial service providers minimize costs by addressing various regulatory and compliance challenges. Market and operational risks, personnel surveillance systems, reporting and compliance, anti-money laundering/countering the financing of terrorism (AML/CFT), know your customer (KYC), customer due diligence (CDD) and risk management are among the top issues that can be addressed (Table 22.2).

22.6 SupTech and RegTech Development and Implementation in Africa

Needs Assessment

A clear regulatory and supervisory purpose to promote efficiency, stability and growth within the financial ecosystem might fuel the ambition to implement RegTech/SupTech. In any financial setting, the necessity to build tools to implement and/or manage a regulatory policy, or to reduce compliance obligations while increasing regulatory reporting frequency, could be a compelling reason to employ RegTech/SupTech solutions.

Embracing emerging technology could also induce policy adjustments as was the case in Nepal, where geospatial information about financial access sources such as bank outlets and agents to increase financial inclusion helped to identify the need for policy prescription on how many

Table 22.2 Market participants and their roles in the adoption of RegTech/SupTech in Africa

Ecosystem participants	*Examples*	*Potential Roles*
Financial Regulators	• Central Banks • Security and Exchange commissions • Insurance Commissions	• Use RegTech to enhance supervisory oversights on supervised entities • Facilitate the introduction of new innovations in the financial industry • Engage with technology providers to develop tailored solutions • Foster collaboration across the RegTech ecosystem • Make rules and regulatory processes to encourage and guide innovation and engagement
Technology Service Providers	• Vizor • Bearing Point • Telecommunication providers	• Understand the regulatory and business frameworks in order to develop innovative solutions that align with the regulatory challenges faced by regulators and market participants
Market Participants	• Financial Institutions • FinTechs • PSP • Digital Financial Service Providers	• Use RegTech to improve their compliance processes • Develop RegTech solutions in-house or outsource development to Technical Service Providers • Adhere to regulatory requirements laid down by regulators (for example, regulatory reporting using Information technology processes outlined by the regulator)

(continued)

Table 22.2 (continued)

Ecosystem participants	*Examples*	*Potential Roles*
Consultants	• BFA Global • R2A • RPA • World Bank, IMF	• Provide expert advice for ideation, development, and/or implementation of RegTech solution

Source Authors' Compilation, 2021

outlets or agents should be stationed in each geographic location in order to achieve financial inclusion goals (Trade Ready report, 2017).

A cloud-based survey across the financial system may bring to the fore the areas that need solutions and other regulatory interventions, and subsequently specific technical groups can be formed to liaise with management and industry players to gather and scrutinize the data to comprehensively evaluate the system for possible policy interventions. The results, when assessed and a choice made of the solution that addresses the desired expected outcome and the ability of a RegTech/SupTech solution to solve the pain points, guarantee a stable financial system of integrity and inclusivity. Thus, needs assessment is fundamental in identifying the needs of the financial market and how RegTech/SupTech solutions(s) can be designed to address the expectations of the financial agents. The identification and design of the appropriate required RegTech/SupTech solution through market participant engagement is as crucial as the success of the product itself.

It is instructive to indicate that most consumers of FinTech products, especially in rural areas in Africa, have low levels of financial knowledge and are usually among the unserved population. These localities also have a weak infrastructure base and are often deprived of internet services and electricity. In view of this, the design and implementation of any RegTech/SupTech solutions in these localities must consider a framework that can work within these dynamics, suitable to the capacity of the users, infrastructure base, financial needs and/or gaps, and without compromising on high standards and regulatory requirements of both the supervised institutions and the consumers of the FinTech products.

Development Strategy

Regulators and supervisors of financial service providers should assess the fundamentals for a RegTech/SupTech program and its applicability, effectiveness and efficacy within the financial ecosystem. This may include designing a roadmap with timelines on how to integrate the already identified products, as discussed above, for implementation with the supervised institutions. The design of a roadmap and strategy for implementation by RegTech and SupTech authorities should be collaborative, consultative and inclusive for all the stakeholders, i.e. the supervised institutions (financial institutions), consumers, enforcement agencies, policy makers and researchers.

The following considerations should be taken into account when developing the strategy to harmonize the various reporting designs and templates:

- Do the regulatory and supervisory bodies have the needed ability to select and superintend over the development of a solution?
- Who are the actors to participate in the development process? Thus, identification of key stakeholders is necessary for the design, development, implementation and users of the RegTech/SupTech solution(s).
- What are the specific roles and responsibilities of each identified stakeholder?
- How long does it take to complete each process of development?
- What is the cost and how much of it should be transferred to the consumers, financial institutions and the regulators?
- Who will pay for it? i.e. assessing the sustainability of the products and regulatory compliance and to what extent the solutions can work vis-a-vis the financial strength of the consumers and supervised institutions.
- How is the new solution going to replace or integrate with legacy systems?

Central banks in Sub-Saharan Africa can form strategic alliances with one another to share information on existing legacy technology solutions and how efficient their development processes are, so as to organize collaborative engagements like the United Kingdom Financial Conduct Authority's (FCA) TechSprint, where recognized players, new FinTech firms and regulators collaborated to identify the benefits of RegTech and e-commerce in the country.

Development of Capacity for Assessment, Execution and Operationalization

The ability to take initiatives, undertake the needed assessments, implement and operationalize each element of the RegTech development process is required to implement the agreed-upon RegTech strategy. To begin the process, a technical expert professional with a basic understanding of regulatory and supervisory processes, project management experience and decision-making power should lead the initiative. By controlling key stages of the development process, additional technical working groups can supplement the core team to evaluate needs, infrastructure requirements and gap analysis, procurement, development and development plan, implementation and adoption. Each technical working group and the core teams should be able to fulfill their jobs while also collaborating with others. However, internal capacity might not be accessible, and this would warrant external support—so that technical assistance from donors and consultants may be requested.

As each jurisdiction may have specific needs, regulatory bodies along with development agencies can catalyze the development of a RegTech solution by promoting a local innovation center, as with the business model of a RegTech regulatory solution. The center can foster collaboration between technical service providers and regulators, ensuring that both parties are aware of the technology, the issues it seeks to address and the context in which it will be implemented. Collaboration among all stakeholders is also essential in developing and implementing an appropriate governance process framework for the operationalization of solutions.

A regulatory sandbox system that curates novel RegTech, SupTech and other FinTech innovations can also be used to test and adopt RegTech and SupTech solutions. Regulators and developers can actively assess the impact of RegTech/SupTech using sandboxes before it is broadly deployed in the financial industry. The results of the prototype testing methods can be utilized to design, experiment and evaluate the solution. Regulatory and supervisory bodies would be able to explore and evaluate prospects to scale the technology for deployment now that they are better informed. The adoption phase follows the development process comprising comprehensive integration of the RegTech and/or SupTech solutions into the relevant ecosystem of the current procedures used for the same purpose and closely monitoring its effectiveness.

22.7 Challenges of SupTech and RegTech in Africa

While there are prospects for RegTech in Africa, emerging and advanced nations vary in terms of their industrialization base, income levels, literacy rate and inequality levels, all of which lead to disparities in ability and hinder regulators' efforts to integrate new technology in a variety of ways. Some of the barriers that can pose challenges to RegTech and SupTech adoption in Africa are discussed below.

Cost Factor

Development and implementation of RegTech and SupTech solutions by regulatory authorities and industry players involve and require high costs of financial and human resources, time and effort. The emergence of FinTech in Africa is quite new and most regulators are still struggling with how to operationalize it fully into the mainstream financial system.

There is low technical know-how on the part of most regulators to effectively adopt and even implement RegTech and SupTech solutions in the developing world including Africa. The financial cost involved to acquire the tools and technology for the purposes of RegTech and SupTech is undoubtedly high. In Africa, where central banks and other regulatory authorities lack the financial resources as compared to their counterparts in the industrialized world, upfront capex expenses to deploy RegTech or SupTech solutions can limit investments. The development process of any RegTech/SupTech solutions, whether in-house or through technical Service provider(s), is a herculean one involving fundamental requirements such as internal and external needs assessment, analyzing the procedures of development, undertaking tendering activities of a RegTech solution, knowing the regulatory environment, developing and experimenting a suitable generic type, scaling up solutions, strategizing long-term RegTech adoption and monitoring implementation.

If the RegTech and SupTech solution depends on outside assistance for smooth implementation, for example, on market players for data input, market participants may need to embrace the system properly in order that regulators may reap the benefits of the investments. Regulatory authorities may be restraining their investment of limited resources by extending the time between inception and implementation. The bureaucratic nature of African public administration will further exacerbate the already long time period needed to fully develop, approve and adopt regulatory mechanisms within the financial environment. And this constitutes a potential barrier to the expeditious adoption of RegTech and SupTech solutions in the regulatory regime of Africa's financial system due to the cost that comes with these saddled systems.

Capacity of Regulators and Market Participants

Regulators need to upgrade their capacities to comprehend and properly apply the technology solutions to supervise and regulate FinTech activities in Africa. If a RegTech or SupTech solution automates data utilization mechanisms or even collects granular data for financial activity such as real-time or item-by-item data analysis, regulators must focus on analytical and technical abilities to process relevant information for decision and policymaking from this data. Consequently, various skills will be required from any regulatory body than was the case during the legacy technologies period.

The technology-focus supervisory regime may thus require a more remarkable shift in the regulators' technical abilities and skills than their initial legacy experience. Though RegTech and SupTech could enhance the productivity and efficiency of FinTech regulators by automating processes or increasing transparency, their impact may be limited if central banks lack the capacity and technical know-how to manage the technologies and their limitations efficiently and analyze output data from them to inform policy decisions. It is worthy of mention that regulators in Africa may lack the various required competencies to be able to effectively adopt and utilize the full potentials that RegTech and SupTech solutions offer within the digital economy.

Because both regulators and market participants have different mandates in the application of RegTech and SupTech, market participants' inability to adopt RegTech and SupTech solutions in their efforts to embrace FinTech can reduce the utility of RegTech and SupTech for regulators and other national authorities. It is self-evident that if market players are unable to accept a reporting solution, they will be unable to supply meaningful data and information to the regulators' solution, thereby defeating the purpose of the solution itself. The solution may not have enough data inputs to satisfy the regulator's supervisory tasks in the digital financial system without data and information from market actors. In the eyes of the participant, his/her inability to apply and utilize the solution may place it at an inappropriate position relative to other market participants who do.

This phenomenon could push out participants, especially start-up firms, which have the tendency of promoting monopoly and oligopoly within the FinTech revolution. Thus, that the African telecommunications market has been dominated by a few giant companies that have the financial and human resource muscle to acquire the needed skills and machinery for adoption of FinTech can be attributed to the above reason. The low literacy and financial knowledge of the African region has the tendency to stampede and slow down the progress of RegTech and SupTech adoption, in that regulators require information on the experience and user needs satisfaction from consumers in order to streamline the operations of the FinTech industry.

Weak Cybersecurity

Globally, technology advancements are projected to improve cybersecurity, but developing regions with emerging technological components such as digital financial services may not be able to transform their infrastructure accordingly as digital access grows (Pearlman, 2018). According to Amadou et al. (2020), addressing cyber-risks, particularly those posed by FinTech, has become so vital that the FSB included monitoring of cyber-risk from FinTech companies in its 2017 work plan and the BIS issued guidelines for cyber mitigation in financial market infrastructure to ensure consistency in ongoing efforts. These regulatory measures could help developed countries protect their financial systems. However, the increased demand for technology applications in the financial industry, along with a lack of adequate internet connectivity, infrastructure, security and regulatory framework, exposes African countries to cyber-risks and attacks. For secure RegTech installations, adequate cybersecurity and cyber-resilience strategies are essential.

Collecting "Big Data" about consumers and their behaviors undoubtedly helps FinTech providers to tailor their solutions to the needs of each individual, thus enhancing the quality of their services and potentially offering a better price. At the same time, this data access and consequent data ownership give rise to risks related to data security (cyber) and the eventual hacking and data breaches (Bates, 2017). Data security has always been a concern for all economic agents. The increased digitization and interconnectivity that is driven by FinTech creates more access points for cyber attackers to take advantage of (Lukonga, 2018). For individuals and households, data stacks may lead to identity theft and personal data invasion for illegal activities or unauthorized financial transactions. In the banking context, a combination of identity theft and simultaneous financial transactions or theft of assets may have a calamitous impact on the victim, especially combined with the ambiguous regulatory landscape regarding liability which directly maps onto consumer protection and infringement of privacy concerns regarding FinTech (IMF, 2020).

More importantly, the increased intermediation because of third parties' involvement in the financial services supply chain, coupled with the complexity of certain FinTech products and the consequent confusion about them (Vezzoso, 2018), may create the perfect environment for exploitation and further facilitate existing fraudulent activities and predatory practices, especially against vulnerable groups. For example, FinTech providers could, based on the information collected by different sources, employ specific designed advertisements for low-income or less tech savvy households when the latter could have been eligible to receive a better offer.

Vasek and Moore identify more than 190 scams and group them into four different categories, namely, Ponzi schemes, mining scams, scam wallets and fraudulent exchanges. They report that 13,000 unique victims lost in total $11million because of these scams. Vasek et al. (2016) discover that several "brain wallets," a form of Bitcoin wallets, were emptied by attackers who were able with brute force to find the passphrase to unlock them. This is facilitated by the fact that FinTech platforms do not share information about their customers or there is less information sharing between FinTech lenders and financial institutions.

One of the most infamous examples involving theft of Bitcoin is that of Mt.Gox, which accounted for more than 70% of Bitcoin transaction worldwide back in 2013. The exchange collapsed in 2014, when cyber attackers drained more than $450 million worth of Bitcoin from its virtual vaults due to certain vulnerabilities in its systems and this reduced its price (Böhme et al., 2015). Gandal et al. (2018) examine several trades taking place on Mt.Gox and find that the exchange rate between USD and

Bitcoin increased by 4% in the days where questionable trading activity occurred. All these illustrations of cyber invasion in the FinTech industry even in the developed world where there are robust and resilient cybersecurity shocks demonstrate that Africa's FinTech market is susceptible to cyber threats. In recent times, mobile money service in Ghana has been so much engulfed in numerous scams and attacks that nearly half a million fraud cases were reported to the Criminal Investigation Department of the Ghana Police Service between 2016 and 2017. This is not peculiar to Ghana but pertains in other African countries with fast developing FinTech industry such as Kenya, Rwanda, Nigeria and Tanzania.

Sustainability Issues

Many regulatory institutions in Africa have over the years been resorting to donors, external bodies and experts to fund and fully set up RegTech and SupTech solutions due to the huge funding requirements and the generally limited logistical and human resources of regulatory institutions. Financial resources, gap analysis or expert advice and other technical support are the major drivers in spearheading RegTech and SupTech initiatives in any environment. Significant influence of and reliance on external bodies in instrumental initiatives such as RegTech and SupTech innovations amounts to artificial dependence on foreign knowledge. This raises concerns over the control of patent rights by foreign authorities, leading to infiltration in the management of the solutions and compromise of data privacy and security. Continuous involvement of external parties in the development of RegTech or SupTech solutions is counterproductive and unsustainable, in that the long-term existence of any RegTech or SupTech initiatives and subsequent solutions may be affected by their exit. A corrective measure approach that takes care of the long-term dependency problem with a catalytic impetus is the R2A initiative. This initiative works collaboratively with regulators and technical service providers to develop RegTech and SupTech solutions so that the dependency challenges are mitigated with the involvement of regulators in the development process.

Over-Reliance on Outmoded Technology by Regulators and Financial Institutions

The continuous use of traditional technologies such as Excel and XML templates for reporting as a compliance requirement by institutions in Africa could stifle the fast adoption of RegTech and SupTech solutions to match with the geometric growth of the FinTech revolution in the financial system. Regulators and central banks will have to examine the effect of legacy technology, cultural dynamics, infrastructure development level and staff competencies when determining the best RegTech and RegTech solution that addresses their gaps and develop a clear strategy for adoption.

These constraints limit RegTech and SupTech adoption or at the very least make the development process more difficult. Central banks, for example, may need to consider transferring huge amounts of data from traditional practices to RegTech platforms or providing access to data that is still held in legacy practices after the implementation of RegTech and SupTech. RegTech and SupTech adoption may not be cumbersome in Africa because legacy practices and supervisory processes are less firmly embedded in financial systems, making it easy to improve upon it. RegTech and SupTech solutions may help financial institutions and FinTech firms such as digital financial service providers maintain compliance in Africa. However, many RegTech and SupTech companies rely on large amounts of reliable and valid data which are difficult to come by in developing regions due to lack of uniform financial infrastructure and proper identification systems.

22.8 Factors to Consider in Promoting SupTech and RegTech Effectiveness and Efficiency in Africa

Collaboration among numerous parties is typically required to develop efficient RegTech and SupTech solutions in any section of the global FinTech industry. In diverse regions of the world, collaborative initiatives such as regulatory sandboxes are emerging with the goal of promoting FinTech innovation while reducing risks and increasing the network of financial opportunities for all economic agents. Several factors need to be considered to ensure that SupTech and RegTech solutions intended to mitigate the threats of FinTech revolution are easily dealt with to promote financial stability and confidence.

Collaboration Among Industry, Market Participants and Regulators

Security concerns arise when market participants, industry players and regulators are not interconnected through regulatory reporting and systemic alignment. Furthermore, the system's dependence on APIs, cloud computing and other emerging solutions that facilitate higher interconnection could further expose it more to cyber threats and place enormous amounts of confidential data under threat of potential breaches. As a result, regulators and market players will have to build and adopt robust solutions to deal with these operational risks.

In lieu of this, it is imperative that market actors cooperate to promote effective responses to cyber threats and intelligence gathering. State actors such as the cyber departments of investigative bodies should team up with market participants, FinTech firms and regulators to ensure that any threats and attacks on service providers, consumers and data centers of regulators are prevented and acted upon with swiftness.

Consumers and suppliers as well as the central bank and supervised firms are all involved in compliance and reporting. Technical service providers and, to some extent, ecosystem members help with technology development and may also play an operational role. Each of these ecosystem members has a specific role to play, but information sharing among them is critical for RegTech development since it aids in the understanding and resolution of hidden difficulties, the selection of relevant tools and the development of contextual solutions. The success of RegTech and SupTech solutions is determined by their smooth integration into the proper ecosystem as well as requisite innovation, despite being led basically by technical service providers.

To maximize efficiencies, RegTech and SupTech solutions must integrate with market participants' systems. Therefore, solutions should be built with the regulator's and market participants' goals and capacities considered while adhering to regulatory standards for confidentiality and integrity of cybersecurity.

Interoperability between network providers is another barrier to mobile money market development, although some countries like Ghana and Kenya have enabled such services. With the rapid growth in mobile money services and the number of active users, the limitations with respect to usage have become even more pronounced. The "closed loop" model does not address the needs of customers any longer (Abor et al., 2020). Users now want to be able to send money to more people across different networks and pay for a wider variety of services through their own mobile network or another.

Mobile money interoperability (MMI) is the service that enables direct and seamless funds transfer from a mobile money wallet to another across different networks. Some mobile money providers in the region are currently putting interoperability initiatives in place in order to enable international remittances. Interoperability reduces the cost of carrying out transactions across different networks since customers will no longer require the services of a third-party payment provider to initiate such transactions across different networks.

Cross-Border and Regional Integration

Developments in the FinTech ecosystem in Africa have important implications for the region, which require a coordinated regional approach to ensure effective regulation of these new technologies. According to Salami (2019), a coordinated regional regulatory framework can take place within the background of prevailing regional economic communities, as stipulated in the African Union (AU) and the ECOWAS agenda of achieving monetary union for the entire continent by 2028. She suggests that achieving effective regional regulatory framework for the African member states will require the following:

- Strengthening prevailing regional integration on mobile financial services among member states
- Developing regional standards tailored toward mobile payment and financial services development of African regional communities
- Establishing a regional regulatory framework for crowdfunding
- Preparing for a robust and resilient regional regulatory regime for cryptocurrencies
- Ensuring independent domestic financial regulation and financial regulatory authorities
- Fostering effective coordination among national supervisors
- Strengthening the general legal frameworks as a basis for robust financial and payment systems regime in Africa

In recent times, the formation of formal monitoring platforms among regulators in nearby countries to promote data sharing and maintain the safety and security of the digital financial and telecommunications economy is encouraging. Kenya, Rwanda, Uganda and South Sudan, for example, are working on a cross-border mobile Subscriber Identity Module (SIM) card registration framework in order to combat the rise in mobile-related crimes. As a result of this RegTech/SupTech solution, unregistered SIM cards will be terminated and service providers will be able to match accounts and transactions to specific individuals. The project is part of the East African Community's (EAC) One Network Area (ONA) agreement which was designed to reduce roaming expenses by unifying call tariffs, and has expanded to include data and digital financial services. The goal is to standardize cross-border DFS transfer regulations and rate costs. The four countries have signed a pact to integrate their national Identification systems, in addition to a common SIM card registration system to ensure that people cannot construct fraudulent nationalities and identities when they migrate from one country to another. This effort has the potential to improve DFS by assisting in the identification of users as well as the prevention of fraud and money laundering (ML) and terrorism financing on the continent.

Effective and Robust Legal Framework and Regulatory Institutions

FinTech activities are receiving much attention from regulators across the globe and in Sub-Saharan Africa. Regulating FinTech is extremely crucial because of the potential of its spurring inclusive finance and job creation and its general impact on the overall economic wellbeing of the market participants. In Sub-Saharan African countries, even the FinTech leaders—South Africa and Kenya, do not have an overarching legal framework specifically for FinTech and how it should be regulated and supervised. However, several issues on the operations of FinTech firms are handled as and when they occur or at best merely by guidelines without a legal direction on handling such matters in accordance with the law. Regulators are therefore rendered ineffective to carry out their compliance and enforcement mandate merely based on guidelines and a knee-jerk approach to emerging challenges associated with FinTech.

Building a Relevant and Sustainable Human Resource Capital Base Across the Continent

Human capital is important for the success of FinTech. African policy makers along with the regional universities require a well-thought-out program that can address this, as it will have implications not only for the financial sector but also for the wider macroeconomic performance of the countries in areas such as employment, productivity and inequality (Yermack, 2018; Sy, et al., 2019). Policy makers and regulators alike should endeavor to train personnel and build their capacities to match up with the complexities of the FinTech era in order that they can apply the solutions required in supervising the activities of the industry. Deliberate efforts will have to be made to ensure that the needed resources are made available to make the human capital base in the FinTech regulatory regime in the region a reality, for this is the only way to minimize the adverse impact of the risks and threats posed by the digital finance environment and to harness the opportunities that come with it.

Investment in Digital Infrastructure Across Africa

Technological innovations wholly hinge on infrastructure that is resilient, compatible and secure. Digital financial services depend heavily on digital infrastructure such as internet connectivity, satellite aerospace signaling and electricity, among others. It is therefore no wonder that FinTech and regulatory solutions in the developed world are more robust due to the enabled environment through the provision of digital infrastructure as mentioned above. Digital infrastructure, seen as the vehicle of technological innovation, is generally inadequate and in some instances non-existing in the region. This has the potential of slowing down the evolution of FinTech in countries with this infrastructure deficit and the subsequent adoption of SupTech and RegTech in the supervisory efforts of national authorities.

Governments within the region should therefore consciously make significant investments of financial and capital resources in digital infrastructure to lubricate the multifaceted parts of FinTech and solutions to regulate its operational conduct. Internet penetration which is at its lowest in most rural parts of Africa should be given the needed boost through investment to connect them to the digital space since most of the FinTech products are wireless-based. In this regard, countries in the region can collaborate to make this a reality by having international wireless cable mega projects that transcend boundaries such as what Ghana and Burkina Faso embarked on in 2016 on the 3G project. Expansion of electricity coverage and creating an enabling environment are key to getting activities of FinTech firms extended to and monitored in rural communities. Provision of good road networks, potable water, connection to power grids and other social amenities will attract investors to every part of the continent irrespective of the location. This will widen the scope of economic activities including digital financial services and achieve the objectives of financial inclusion.

22.9 Conclusions, Policy Implications and Way Forward

The prevailing regulatory and supervisory environment vis-a-vis market dynamics for financial authorities is highly complicated and unpredictable. Several regulations have been revised and new technologies are being discovered in the aftermath of the financial crisis in 2008 to respond to the weaknesses in the conduct, risk identification and management of the financial system, and to increase supervisory effectiveness. In furtherance to this, a surge in FinTech innovation is sweeping the globe, bringing with it new risks and threats associated with innovations, business structures and products. FinTech, on the other hand, has a lot of prospects to help achieve goals of improving the efficiency of financial services and financial inclusion. Authorities must respond in a balanced manner in this regard. This new reality necessitates a review of regulations and a determination of whether current supervisory procedures are acceptable or a revision is required.

FinTech's progress in Africa could be hampered by regulatory uncertainties. Regulators are faced with a conundrum as a result of the dramatic transformation that FinTech is bringing to the banking and financial services industry: how to maintain a balance between regulatory approaches and regulations that create barriers to entry, versus a touch that allows any newcomers to obstruct consumer protection. The range and scale of companies, the mosaic of business models and the categorization of the types of activities, products and transactions are all conundrums. Thus, one business entity with apparently one service type could concurrently fall within a variety of regulatory domains with a number of regulators and regulations covering its operations and services through the employment of diverse technologies.

Clearly, given the complexity of FinTech advances, authorities will be unable to anticipate all of the possible outcomes and their regulatory implications for the financial system. That brings us back to the dialectical approach, in which regulators who lack the capacity to provide comprehensive regulatory mitigation measures can, in the interim, resort to ancillary regulations if necessary at the policy level to narrow the regulatory deficiencies arisen out of the intersection of RegTech/SupTech and FinTech.

In a digital revolution era, however, financial authorities will increasingly need to deploy all or a combination of these regulatory actions to retain policy coherence, comprehensiveness and credibility. Regulators and supervisors will be obliged to adapt to a fast-changing regulatory environment in which conventional borders are blurring, digitization and datafication introduce more risks and complications and larger mandates encompassing both financial stability and inclusion (Simone et al., 2018). Non-compliance to this could encourage regulatory arbitrage, or, worse, lead to oversight lapses and the accumulation of systemic vulnerabilities already prevalent in the African region.

Combining appropriate technology and implementing consumer-centered risk-based supervision and embracing high-quality data to accommodate product innovation is undoubtedly a significant step to take. This approach requires technological tools that are either in use or in a rapidly developing stage. Indeed, in Africa, the use of cloud computing, artificial intelligence, machine learning, blockchain and smart contracts in financial regulation and oversight is still largely untapped and unexplored.

RegTech/SupTech has significant implications for financial inclusion and financial sector growth. Regulatory compliance often implies large expenditures for enterprises, which function as hurdles to entry for firms (especially FinTechs) and increase costs to customers, particularly in the informal sector or for low-income households. Furthermore, financial service providers may be more risk-averse due to concerns about penalties and reputational damage as a result of onerous rules. By streamlining and rationalizing regulatory approval, reporting and compliance processes as well as establishing an enabling regulatory environment for FinTechs, RegTech/SupTech can help to reduce costs and alleviate worries of market participants.

References

Abor, J. Y. (2020). Exploring the impact of COVID-19 pandemic on Africa's FinTech space (Working Paper Series No. 7/2020). Centre for Global Finance, SOAS University of London. https://www.centreforglobalfinance.org/2020-working-papers

Abor, J. Y., Aminu, M., & Issahaku, H. (2018). Mobile telephony, financial inclusion and inclusive Growth. *Journal of African Business, 19*(3), 430–453.

Abor, J. Y., Issahaku, H., Amidu, M., & Murinde, V. (2020). Financial inclusion and economic growth. In J.Y. Abor, C.K.D. Adjasi and R. Lensink. *Contemporary issues in development finance*. London: Routledge.

Access to New Flows of Information, World Bank Group. (2018). Blockchain & Distributed Ledger Technology (DLT). available at https://bit.ly/2yvQHzS

AFI. (July 2017). Defining financial inclusion. Guidance Note No. 28.

AFI. (2018). FinTech for financial inclusion: A framework for digital financial transformation. https://www.afi-global.org/publications/2844/FinTech-for-Financial-Inclusion-A-Framework-for-Digital-Financial-Transformation

Afrikstart. (2016). Crowdfunding in Africa. Report by Afrikstart Crowdfunding Africa. http://afrikstart.com/report/wp-content/uploads/2016/09/Afrikstart-Crowdfunding-In-Africa-Report.pdf

Ahmad, A. H., Green, C., & Jiang, F. (2020). Mobile money, financial inclusion and development: A review with reference to African experience. *Journal of Economic Surveys*. https://doi.org/10.1111/joes.12372

Aker, J. C., & Mbiti, I. M. (2010). Mobile phones and economic development in Africa. *Journal of Economic Perspectives, 24*(3), 207–232.

Allen, F., Demirgüç-Kunt, A., Klapper, L., Peria, S. M., & M. (2016). The foundations of financial inclusion: Understanding ownership and use of formal accounts. *Journal of Financial Intermediation, 27*, 1–30.

Amadou, N. R., Maino, R., Massara, A., Perez-Saiz, H., and Sharma, P. (2019). A game changer? (Working Paper No. 19/04). International Monetary Fund.

Amidu, M., Abor, J. Y., & Issahaku, I. (2020). *Inclusive finance, financial literacy and livelihood activities of households in Ghana*. Edward Elgar. forthcoming.

Ahmad, H. A., Llewellyn, D. T. and Murinde, V. (eds). *Financial literacy and livelihood activities in Ghana*. London: Edward Edgar Publishing.

Andrianaivo, M., & Kpodar, K. (2012). Mobile phones, financial inclusion, and growth. *Review of Economics and Institutions, 3*(2), 30.

Amadou N. R., Maino R., Massara, A., Perez-Saiz, H. & Sharma, P. (2018). *A game Changer? Working paper No. 19/04*, International Monetary Fund.

Arner, D. W., Barberis, J. N., Walker, J., Buckley, R. P., Dahdal, A. M., & Zetzsche, D. A. (2020). Digital finance & the COVID-19 crisis. Available at SSRN 3558889.

Ayugi, W. (2018). Nigerian blockchain startup SureRemit raises $7 million in biggest African ICO to date. Bitcoin Africa.io., https://bitcoinafrica.io/2018/02/16/sureremit-ico/

Bates, A. (2017). Fintech and Suptech in a Nutshell and the Future in a Sandbox, available at https://cfa.is/2POCyV1

Bazot, G. (2018). Financial consumption and the cost of finance: Measuring financial efficiency in Europe (1950–2007). *Journal of the European Economic Association, 16*(1), 123–160.

Beck, T., & Cull, R. (2014). Banking in Africa. In *The Oxford Handbook of Banking* (2nd ed.). Oxford University Press.

Beck, T., Demirgüç-Kunt, A., & Honohan, P. (2007). Finance for all? *World Bank Policy Research Report,* Washington DC, The World Bank.

Bohme, L., & Jack, A., (2015). *Mobile money: The economics of the M-PESA.* NBER Working Paper series, No. 16721. https://www.nber.org/papers/w16721

Arner, D., Barberis, J. & Buckley, R. (2017). FinTech and RegTech in a nutshell, and the future in a Sandbox. Available at https://cfa.is/2POCyVl

Daily Nation. (2013). East African States to share sim card, National Id Data. available at https://bit.ly/2EIZleU

Demirguc-Kunt, Beck, T., & Honohan, P. (2017). Finance for All? *World Bank Policy Research Report*. The World Bank.

Demirgüç-Kunt, A., Klapper, L., Singer, D., Ansar, S., & Hess, J. (2018). *The global Findex database 2017: Measuring financial inclusion and the FinTech revolution*. The World Bank.

Enriques, L. (2017). Financial supervisors and RegTech: Four roles and four challenges. Available at https://goo.gl/akR8by

FCA. (2016). Feedback statement call for input on supporting the development and adopters of RegTech, available at https://bit.ly/2bXLSrg

Gai, A. H., Green, C., & Jiang, F. (2018). Mobile Money, Financial Inclusion and Development : A Review with Reference to African Experience, *Journal of Economic Surveys*.

Gandal, T., & Suri, W. (2018). *Croud-funding and financial inclusion: An infant industry growing fast*. Madrid: IOSCO, https://www.iosco.org.research/pds/swp/crowd-funding

GPFI. (2016a). G20High-level principles for digital financial inclusion. https://www.gpfi.org/sites/gpfi/files/G20%20High%20Level%20Principles%20for%20Digital%20Financial%20Inclusion.pdf.

GPFI. (2016b). "Progress report to the G20 leaders", above n 35; GPFI (December 2016b) (German 2017 Priorities Paper). Available at: http://www.bmz.de/de/zentrales_downloadarchiv/Presse/Prioritaetenpapierzur-G20-Arbeit-der-globalen-Partnerschaft-fuer-finanzielle-Einbindung-GPFI.pdf

GSMA. (2013). The mobile economy 2013, ATKearney. http://gsma.com/newsroom/wp-content/ uploads/2013/12/GSMA-Mobile-Economy-2013.pdf

GSMA. (2017). State of the industry report on Mobile Money, https://www.gsma.com/mobilefordevelopment/wpcontent/uploads/2018/05/GSMA_2017State_of_the_Industry_Report_on_Mobile_Money_Full_Report.pdf

GSMA. (2019). State of the industry report on mobile money. https://www.gsma.com/sotir/wp-content/uploads/2020/03/GSMA-State-of-the-Industry-Report-on-Mobile-Money-2019-Full-Report.pdf

Huge, K., & Nanziri E. L. (2020). Financial inclusion and welfare in post financial crisis. *African Economic Research Consortium.*

IFWG. (2020). Position Paper on Cryto Assets Regulatory Working Group, http://www.treasury.gov.za/comm_media/press/2020/20200414%20IFWG%20Position%20Paper%20on%20Crypto%20Assets.pdf

International Monetary Report. (2020). *Central banks in a digital world: The perspective of Africa*, http://www.imf.report.org/research/file/pdf

Lielacher, A. (2018). Zimbabwean cryptocurrency exchange Golix expands to South Africa. *BitcoinAfrica.io.*

Lukonga, I. (2018). Cryptocurrencies–cross-border financial regulatory dimensions. *The European Financial Review*. https://www.europeanfinancialreview.com/cryptocurrencies-cross-border-financial-regulatory-dimensions/

Jack, W., & Suri, T. (2011). Mobile money: The economics of M-PESA (NBER Working Paper Series, No. 16721). https://www.nber.org/papers/w16721.

Jenik, I., Lyman, Y., & Nava, A. (2017, March). Crowdfunding and financial inclusion (Working Paper, CGAP). https://www.cgap.org/sites/default/files/Working-Paper-Crowdfunding-and-Financial-Inclusion-Mar-2017.pdf

Kasenkende, O. (2010). "Exploring the usage and impact of "Transformational" mobile financial services: The case of M-PESA in Kenya. *Journal of Eastern African Studies, 3*(2), 510–526.

Kirby, E., & Worner, S. (2014). Crowdfunding: An infant industry growing fast. IOSCO, http://www.iosco.org/research/pdf/swp/Crowd-funding-An-Infant-Industry-Growing-Fast.pdf

Makina, D. (2019). The potential of FinTech in enabling financial inclusion. In D. Makina, *Extending financial inclusion in Africa* (299–318) 1st Edition, San Diego; United States, Journal of Financial Research.

Manyika, J., Lund, S., Singer, M., White, O., & Berry, C. (2016). *Digital finance for all: Powering inclusive growth in emerging economies*. McKinsey Global Institute.

Massolution. (2013). *CF crowdfunding industry report*. http://crowdsourcing.org/l/20898

Massolution. (2015). *CF crowdfunding industry 2015 report*. http://crowdexpert.com/crowdfunding-industry-statistics/

McMillan, J. (2015). Banking in the digital age: The failure of financial regulation. *The Guardian*, https://www.theguardian.com/sustainablebusiness/2015/jan/20/finance-in-digital-age-while-regulation-stuck-in-industrial [https:// perma.cc/Y7ED-SB9H]

Mbiti, I., &.Weil, D. N. (2011). *Mobile Banking: The impact of M-Pesa in Kenya* (NBER Working Paper Series, No. 17129).

Morawczynski, O. (2009). Exploring the usage and impact of "transformational" mobile financial services: The case of M-PESA in Kenya. *Journal of Eastern African Studies, 3*(3), 509–525.

Morse, A. (2015). Peer-to-Peer crowdfunding: Information and the potential for disruption for consumer lending. *Annual Review of Financial Economics, 7*, 463–482.

Murinde, L. (2012). *Digital finance for all: Powering inclusive growth in emerging countries*. Mckinsey Global Institute.

Nanziri, E. L. (2015). Financial inclusion and welfare in post-apartheid South Africa. *African Economic Research Consortium.*

Odhiambo, R. (2017). Reserve Bank of Zimbabwe considers Bitcoin illegal but no regulation has been issued. *BitcoinAfrica.io.*

Ouma, S. A., Odongo, T. M., & Were, M. (2017). Mobile financial services and financial inclusion: Is it A Boon for savings mobilization? *Review of Development Finance, 7*(1), 29–35.

Perlman, L.1. & Gurung, N. (2018). Use of RegTech by Central Banks and its impact on financial inclusion evidence from India, Mexico, Nigeria, Nepal and the Philippines. *Journal of the European Economic Association*

Philippon, T. (2016a). *The FinTech opportunity* (NBER Working Paper 22476) http://www.nber.org/papers/w22476.

Philippon, T. (2016b). *The FinTech opportunity* (Unpublished).

Predictive and Algorithmic Supervision, Definition combined from FSB. (2017). Artificial Intelligence and machine learning in financial services. Available at https://bit.ly/2h1h8UT; Rodriguez, J (2017) Types of Artificial Intelligence Learning Models, available at https://bit.ly/2qpDQeq

Quartey, P. (2020). *Financial sector landscape in Ghana: Background Paper.* Global Finance Programme.

Salami, I. (2018, April–May). Cryptocurrencies—Cross-border financial regulatory dimensions. *The European Financial Review*. Available from: https://www.europeanfinancialreview.com/cryptocurrencies-cross-border-financial-regulatory-dimensions/

Simone di Casri, S., Grasser, M., & Kulenkamff, A. (2018). Financial authorities in the era of data abundance: Regtech for regulators and suptech solutions. *Journal of the European Economic Association. 16*(1), 123–160.

Skan, J., Dickerson, J., & Gagliardi, L. (2016). *FinTech and the evolving landscape: Landing points for the industry*. Accenture.

Sovbetov, Y. (2018). Factors influencing cryptocurrency prices: Evidence from Bitcoin, Ethereum, Dash, Litcoin and Monero. *Journal of Economics and Financial Analysis, 2*(2), 1–27. https://ojs.tripaledu.com/index.php/jefa/article/view/36

South African Reserve Bank. (2014). Position paper on virtual currencies. *Position Paper number 02/2014.*

Tassev, L. (2018). Zimbabwe's Golix exchange enters Kenya, Uganda, South Africa. *Bitcoin.com.*

Tchamyou, V. S., Erreyger, G., & Cassimon, D. (2019). Inequality, ICT and financial access in Africa. *Technological Forecasting and Social Change, 139*, 169–184.

Timm, S. (ed.). (2017a). ProsperiProp plans to run two ICOs to get around crowdfunding challenge. *Ventureburn.*

Timm, S. (ed.). (2017b). Everything you need to know about the South African cryptocurrency ecosystem. *Ventureburn.*

Vezzoso, B. (2018). Financial consumption and the cost of finance: Measuring financial efficiency in Europe (1950–2007). *Journal of the European Economic Association, 16*(1), 123–160.

World Bank. (2013). *Crowdfunding's potential for the developing world.* Washington DC, https://documents.worldbank.org/en/publication/documents-reports/documentdetail/18806928

World Bank. (2015). *Crowdfunding in emerging markets: Lessons from East African startups.* Washington, DC. https://documents.worldbank.org/en/publication/documents-reports/documentdetail/820101468186856874

World Bank. (2018, April). *The global Findex database 2017.*

Yermack, D. (2018). *FinTech in Sub-Saharan Africa: What has worked well, and what hasn't* (Working Paper 25007, NBER Working Paper Series). http://www.nber.org/papers/w25007

PART VII

Non-Bank Financial Markets

CHAPTER 23

Sustainability, Growth and Impact of Microfinance Institutions in Africa

Elikplimi Komla Agbloyor, Simplice A. Asongu, Peter W. Muriu, and Alfred Yawson

23.1 Introduction

Microfinance refers to the provision of financial services to the poor or those at the bottom of the economic pyramid. These services include savings, loans, remittances, insurance, investment and pensions. Muhammad Yunus is often credited with pioneering modern microfinance. Yunus came up with the idea of microfinance when he was working at the University of Chittagong. He tested a lending scheme whereby he

E. K. Agbloyor (✉)
Department of Finance, University of Ghana Business School, Accra, Ghana
e-mail: ekagbloyor@ug.edu.gh

S. A. Asongu
Department of Economics, University of South Africa, Pretoria, South Africa
e-mail: asongus@afridev.org

P. W. Muriu
Department of Economics, University of Nairobi, Nairobi, Kenya

J. Y. Abor and C. K. D. Adjasi (eds.), *The Economics of Banking and Finance in Africa*, Palgrave Macmillan Studies in Banking and Financial Institutions, https://doi.org/10.1007/978-3-031-04162-4_23

was giving small loans to vulnerable people/groups. The scheme proved to be successful and Yunus formed the Grameen (Village) Bank which expanded this scheme across Bangladesh and other parts of the world. Muhammad Yunus and Grameen Bank were awarded the Nobel Peace Prize in 1996 for their contribution to the microfinance revolution in the 1970s. In Africa, particularly West Africa, microfinance has existed for centuries through susu (Rotating Savings and Credit Associations, ROSCAs). Each member of the group contributes an amount which is given to one member. When this member pays, the amounts are given to the next member until the cycle is completed. Susu is thought to have originated in Nigeria and spread to Ghana through Yoruba traders in the early 1900s.

There are two schools of thought as to how microfinance should be provided. These are the welfarist and capitalist approaches. The welfarist/poverty lending approach focuses on social objectives and is aimed at improving the livelihood of the customers and therefore low interest rates are charged. The institutionalist/capitalist approach/financial systems approach focuses on the economics or making profits and is thus aimed at making an economic return that is sufficient to cover operational expenses and to provide a return to the shareholders of the MFI (see Chikalipah & Makina, 2019). Microfinance intrinsically pursues both social and economic objectives. It is important to note that MFIs who pursue solely social objectives may not be sustainable in the long run. This is because the income they generate may not be sufficient to cover their expenditure. MFIs such as non-governmental organizations who pursue solely social objectives will have to rely on the benevolence of donors or providers of subsidies to keep operating. On the other hand, MFIs who pursue solely economic objectives may for example lend larger amounts and concentrate on urban areas and consequently not focus on

---

A. Yawson
University of Adelaide Business School, Adelaide, SA, Australia
e-mail: alfred.yawson@adelaide.edu.au

E. K. Agbloyor
Faculty of Economic and Management Sciences, Stellenbosch Business School, Cape Town, South Africa

lending to the poor. Thus, MFIs must find a delicate balance between their social and economic objectives.

The pursuit of financial sustainability may reduce the outreach potential of MFIs (see Cull et al., 2007; Hermes et al., 2011). Pursuing financial sustainability and charging realistic interest rates to poor borrowers could mean that fewer borrowers can access microfinance services, thus reducing the ability of MFIs to reach many more borrowers. Apart from providing financial services such as loans to their clients, MFIs also provide services such as education and training on business management (examples include working capital management, marketing and bookkeeping), financial literacy, as well as other information on areas such as education and health to their clients.

Microfinance is important because without it the poor may not be able to access financial services and live a decent and fulfilling life. One of the biggest contributions of microfinance to the development agenda in Africa is its contribution to promoting financial inclusion with its attendant benefits. This is particularly important given the low levels of financial inclusion in Africa. Microfinance also allows the poor to educate their children, take care of their health, housing, and nutritional needs and to get out of poverty (see Dunford, 2006). This is because the poor are able to borrow and invest in productive assets. Further, microfinance has helped to empower women (see Abor, 2017; Rai & Ravi, 2011) by giving them access to financial services. In some traditional African settings, women are marginalized and are not able to own assets such as land and other properties. Microfinance allows women to access financial services such as loans, thus promoting their economic empowerment since they do not have to depend on their husbands or partners. Indeed, women tend to be one of the largest groups of recipients of support from MFIs. This is because women have been known to be more faithful borrowers compared to men and they are largely found in the informal sector where MFIs are more active. In sum, those at the bottom of the economic pyramid may not be able to accumulate assets, smooth consumption across time and manage risk without access to the financial services provided by MFIs.

Traditional financial institutions shun the poor because they consider them to be very risky. This is because these people usually operate in the informal sector with irregular income patterns. In addition, many poor people live in rural areas with very low population densities, making it expensive and uneconomical for traditional providers of financial services such as banks and insurance companies to reach them. Further, the poor usually have little or no collateral that they can offer to a financial institution as a backstop if they default on a loan. In a way, modern microfinance helps to overcome some of these challenges. MFIs for example usually do not require collateral when they lend to the poor. Further, they are flexible in terms of loan repayment schedules, which suits the irregular cash flow patterns of those operating in the informal sector. Unlike traditional financial institutions, they send their officers to their clients or the field to mobilize savings and to collect loan repayments. This provides convenience to their clients as they may not have to leave their work places to access financial services.

The advent of mobile money which has become very popular and prominent across the continent has also made it easier for MFIs to connect and interface with their clients. Another key feature of modern microfinance is the concept of group lending. Some MFIs lend to a group. The group members are ultimately liable for the loan. The members of the group may not receive a loan unless a member who has taken a loan has repaid it, or the members of the group may borrow jointly and be responsible for servicing the loan. Thus, the members of the group monitor each other and may place social pressure on a member who has taken a loan and is not willing to repay it. Thus, group lending serves as a substitute for collateral.

Microfinance is not without its demerits. Some argue that microfinance may make it difficult for the poor to come out of poverty because of the very high rates of interest that they charge due to the high-risk nature of their clientele. Further, MFIs do not lend to the 'poorest of the poor' (see Skully, 2004), since they are unlikely to pay back any loans. Further, the 'poorest of the poor' may find it difficult to join group lending programs (see Marr, 2004), as the other members may view them to be risky and thus likely to jeopardize their own chances of receiving credit. In this chapter, we examine some critical areas of the operations of MFIs in Africa such as their sustainability, their growth and impact. The rest of this chapter is structured as follows: Sect. 23.2 examines the sustainability of microfinance institutions in Africa. Section 23.3 examines the growth of microfinance institutions in Africa. Section 23.4 examines the impact of microfinance institutions in Africa. Finally, Sect. 23.5 concludes the chapter.

23.2 Sustainability of Microfinance Institutions in Africa

MFI sustainability refers to the ability of the MFI to survive in the long term. An MFI is likely to be sustainable when it has low reliance on subsidies, has a high-quality loan book and its revenues are sufficient to cover its costs. The sustainability of an MFI is important because it is one of the key drivers of the institution's long-term survival. The sustainability of an MFI is important for a number of reasons. An MFI that is sustainable can continue to support the financial inclusion and poverty reduction agenda. It can also easily attract funding from private providers of capital because it is profitable and can cover its operational costs. Finally, a sustainable MFI can balance the goals of achieving efficiency with reaching as many poor people as possible.

Measures of MFI Sustainability

Since MFIs may receive subsidies from donors or governments to support their operations, traditional measures of financial performance such as the return on assets (ROA) and the return on equity (ROE) are unlikely to reflect their true performance. There are a number of measures of MFI sustainability proposed and developed in the literature. For example, Yaron and Manos (2007) discuss some indicators of MFI sustainability. These include the Financial Self Sufficiency (FSS), Subsidy Dependence Index (SDI) and Portfolio at Risk (PaR). In this section, we discuss a broad array of indicators of MFI sustainability.

Financial Self-Sufficiency (FSS)

In simple terms, the FSS index measures the ability of the income of the MFI to cover its expenses. An MFI that can continuously use its income to cover its expenditure is said to be financially self-sufficient.

The FSS index is computed as follows:

$$S = \frac{\text{Adjusted Financial Revenue}}{\text{Adjusted (Financial Expense} + \text{Net Loan Loss Provision Expense} + \text{Operating Expense)}}$$

For example, the financial expense should be adjusted to reflect the cost of subsidies. If an MFI receives a subsidized loan, then the difference between a loan at a market interest rate and the loan obtained at the subsidized cost should be added to the financial costs. A similar adjustment should be made for other subsidies such as grants and subsidies in kind (such as free training for the MFI's staff, MFI staff who work for free and technical advice that is provided at below market rates).

If the FSS ratio is greater than 1, then it implies that the revenues of the MFI are more than enough to cover its expenditure and therefore the MFI is sustainable. On the other hand, if the FSS is less than 1, then it suggests that the revenues of the MFI are not sufficient to cover its expenditure and therefore the MFI is not financially self-sufficient. The FSS has a number of weaknesses. For example, it does not account for the cost of equity or the opportunity cost of capital. By ignoring the cost of equity, the FSS overstates the self-sufficiency of the MFI. Further, it does not account for the size of equity (equity as a proportion of total assets). All else equal, an MFI with a higher equity base is likely to be less self-sufficient because the opportunity cost of capital will be higher. Another weakness of the FSS methodology is that it does not account for the investment decisions of an MFI. That is, it does not distinguish between MFIs which lend to the poor (small loan amounts), those that lend to relatively wealthy clients and therefore have drifted from the mission (mission drift) of serving the poor, and those that invest in financial assets such as treasury instruments and commercial paper.

In terms of the factors that drive FSS, Henock (2019) finds that the MFIs in Ethiopia that have a higher return on assets are more financially sustainable compared to MFIs that have low return on assets. Henock (2019) also finds that MFIs that are operationally more efficient are more financially sustainable compared to those with low operational efficiency. On the other hand, Henock (2019) finds that MFIs that receive higher donations are less financially sustainable compared to those that receive lower donations. In the case of Ethiopia, Henock (2019), contrary to expectations, finds that deposit mobilization is negatively related to the financial sustainability of MFIs. That is, MFIs that have a higher deposit mobilization drive are less financially sustainable compared to those with a lower deposit mobilization drive. Henock (2019) further finds that MFIs which employ a higher level of debt or leverage in their operations are less financially sustainable compared to those that employ lower levels of debt in their operations.

Subsidy Dependence Index (SDI)
The SDI in simple terms compares the subsidy received by an MFI to the income generated on its loan portfolio. It is indicative of how much the return on the MFI's loan portfolio should change for the MFI not to be reliant on subsidies. It also measures the amount of subsidy provided (numerator) for every dollar paid by the clients of the MFI (denominator). The SDI is computed as follows;

$$SDI = \frac{S}{LP * i}$$

where;

S is the annual subsidy received by an MFI
LP is the average size of the loan portfolio.
i is weighted average yield on the loan portfolio.

The annual subsidy can be found as follows;

$$S = A(m - c) + K + [(E * m) - P]$$

where;
A is the average size of concessionary funds received by an MFI
m is the market cost, assuming these funds were obtained in the market or on an arms-length basis. Further, m also includes the administrative cost of mobilizing and servicing savings accounts. This cost can tend to be high for MFIs compared to commercial banks because less well-to-do borrowers are likely to save lower amounts and withdraw more frequently.
When an MFI is exempted from holding reserve requirements, *m* is calculated as;

$$m = \frac{\text{Interestrateon savings} + (\text{Adminstrative cost of maintaining savings accounts})}{100 - \text{Reserve Requirement}}$$

Consequently, the effect of the reserve requirement is to reduce the denominator and increase m. An increase in *m* leads to an increase in the SDI or subsidy dependence of the MFI. This is because the exemption from holding reserve requirements is like savings or a subsidy to the MFI.

c is the average annual cost of the concessionary funds received by the MFI

K is the average annual size of the other subsidies (such as grants and subsidies in kind) received by the MFI.

E is the average annual equity.

P is the annual profit before tax adjusted for items such as loan loss provisions and inflation.

Thus, the annual subsidy received by an MFI is broken down into three components. The first component is the interest cost savings that the MFI obtains because it borrows at below market interest rates. In essence, the receipt of below market cost loans is a form of support to the MFI. The second component of the annual subsidy is in the form of cash or non-cash support that the MFI receives from donors. This includes cash grants or donations and support in kind such as free technical training for its employees. The final component measures by how much the cost attributed to equity ($E * m$) compares to the annual profits of an MFI. If the cost of equity exceeds the profits of an MFI, then there is an implicit subsidy. Thus, the SDI accounts for the opportunity cost of capital. In addition, the SDI accounts for other subsidies such as exemptions from reserve requirement ratios through the opportunity cost of capital.

In plain language therefore, the SDI can be written as;

$$\frac{\text{Annual Subsidy Received by an MFI}}{\text{Average Return on the MFIs Loan Portfolio}}$$

An SDI of zero or in the negative suggests that the MFI is self-sufficient. On the other hand, a positive SDI suggests that an MFI is not self-sufficient or is subsidy reliant.

Unlike the FSS where there is no distinction between income generated on loans (the core mission of an MFI) and income generated from investments in securities, the SDI focuses on income generated from the loan portfolio of an MFI and therefore better reflects how an MFI follows its core mission of lending to the poor, assuming loan sizes are not too large and the MFI does not drift to lending to wealthy clients. Further, the SDI accounts for the cost of equity and other subsidies such as reserve requirements whilst the FSS does not. Finally, the SDI accounts for the administrative cost of servicing small savings accounts through m (which accounts for the market cost of borrowing and administrative cost of servicing savings accounts) which is applied to the concessionary loans obtained by the MFI and the equity of the MFI. Thus, by accounting for the administrative cost of servicing small savings accounts, it accounts for the MFI's decision to substitute between concessionary borrowings and raising voluntary savings as its source of funding.

Outreach Indicators (OI)

These indicators focus on how well the MFI is meeting the main objectives for which it was set-up, that is to provide financial services to the poor and marginalized/under-privileged in society. Some of these indicators include the number of clients that the MFI has provided deposit and lending services to, the proportion of women who have received financial services, the proportion of rural dwellers who have received financial services, and the average size of loans provided to borrowers. Donors and governments for example would like to see MFIs reach more clients, lend to more female borrowers, lend to more rural dwellers and provide low sized loans (indicative of lending to less well-to-do borrowers). Consequently, the OI indicators focus on the outputs or 'raison d'etre of the MFI.

In terms of the breadth of outreach measured by the number of active borrowers, Tchakoute Tchuigoua and Soumaré (2019) find that when loan decisions are decentralized or when loan officers have authority to make loans, it increases the outreach of an MFI. In addition, they find that governance effectiveness and strong internal control systems spur the outreach potential of an MFI. Their results also show that the individual lending methodology compared to that of group lending leads to better MFI outreach. These results generally apply to both profit and non-profit MFIs. Barry and Tacneng (2014) show that non-governmental organizations (NGOs) perform better than other types of MFIs such as banks, cooperatives and non-bank financial institutions in terms of social performance (that is lending to women, and the number of borrowers).

In Box 23.1, we provide an example of the computation of the FSS and the SDI. We use a hypothetical MFI that we call the Future is Bright (FIB) Microfinance. The Box presents the financial statements and indicates the key assumptions that we make. It also presents our model solutions. Assume that the figures are in US dollars.

Box 23.1: Computation of FSS and SDI

Example on FSS and SDI

We will use FIB to compute the values of the FSS and SDI. We present its hypothetical balance sheet/statement of financial position as well as its income statement

Hypothetical Balance Sheet of FIB Microfinance

	Assets		*Liability and equity*
Cash	5,000,000.00	Deposits	5,000,000.00
Short-term Securities	2,500,000.00	Savings	15,000,000.00
Loans	40,000,000.00	Concessionary Borrowed Funds	25,000,000.00
Fixed Assets	5,000,000.00	Equity	5,000,000.00
	50,000,000.00		50,000,000.00

Hypothetical Income Statement of FIB Microfinance

Income Statement		
Interest on loans	14,000,000.00	
Interest on securities	450,000.00	
Interest income		14,450,000.00
Interest paid on savings	1,800,000.00	
Interest paid on concessionary funds	1,250,000.00	
Interest cost		3,050,000.00
Gross profit		11,400,000.00
Operational Cost		10,000,000.00
Profit before tax		1,400,000.00

A summary of the key assumptions is given below

The interest rate on the loan portfolio is 30%

The interest rate earned on securities is 18%

The interest rate on demand deposits is 0%

The interest rate on savings accounts is 10%

The reserve requirement is 10%

The administrative and servicing costs on savings accounts is 4% of savings

The interest rate paid on concessionary borrowed funds is 5%
Operational cost is 20% of assets
Inflation is assumed to be 0%
No provisions are made for loan losses
Other subsidies are assumed to be $1,200,000

Computation of FSS

$$FSS = \frac{\text{Adjusted Financial Revenue}}{\text{Adjusted (Financial Expense + Net Loan Loss Provision Expense + Operating Expense)}}$$

FSS	*Amounts*
Adjusted revenue	14,450,000.00
Financial expense	2,750,000.00
Operating expenses	10,000,000.00
Cost of concessionary borrowings (10%–5%)*25,000,000	1,250,000.00
Denominator (Sum of expenses)	14,000,000.00
FSS	1.03

The FSS ratio of 1.03 or 103% suggests that FIB is financially sustainable as its revenue of $14,450,000 exceeds its cost of $14,000,000.

Computation of SDI

Computation of SDI	*Figures*
Concessionary borrowed funds	25,000,000.00
Market interest rate on savings accounts	0.10
Administrative cost on savings accounts	0.04
Reserve requirements	0.10
Market interest rate on savings accounts and administrative cost (10% + 4%)/(100%–10%)	0.16

(continued)

(continued)

Computation of SDI	*Figures*
Interest on concessionary borrowed funds	0.05
Subsidized cost of borrowing (16%–5%)	0.11
Subsidy on borrowed funds (25,000,000* 11%)	**2,638,888.89**
Equity	5,000,000.00
Market interest rate on savings accounts and administrative cost (10% + 4%)/(100%-10%)	0.16
Imputed cost of equity (5,000,000 * 16%)	**777,777.78**
Other subsidy	**1,200,000.00**
Total subsidy (2,638,889 + 777,778 + 1,200,000)	**4,616,666.67**
Profit before tax	**1,700,000.00**
Net subsidy (4,616,667 - 1,700,000)	**2,916,666.67**
Loan Portfolio	40,000,000.00
Average on-lending interest rate on loan portfolio	0.35
Interest income on loan portfolio (0.35 * 40,000,000)	**14,000,000.00**
SDI	**0.21**

The SDI of 21% implies that average yields on FIB's loan portfolio have to increase by 21%. Thus, the yields need to increase from 35% to 42.35% (35%*1.21). The SDI also shows that for every dollar paid by the clients of the MFI (denominator or interest income earned), $0.175 was provided by donors (subsidy or numerator).

Consequently, the SDI shows that FIB is not self-sustainable.

Our computation highlights the potential conflicts between the FSS and the SDI. Whilst the FSS shows that the SDI is self-sufficient, the SDI indicates otherwise.

Portfolio at Risk (PaR)

The portfolio at risk (PaR) examines the proportion of an MFI's portfolio that is overdue and is at risk of going bad. In particular, it relates the principal on overdue loans to the total principal of all loans outstanding in the MFI's loan book. Mathematically, the PaR is defined as follows;

$$\text{Portfolio at Risk} = \frac{\text{Total Principal on Over due Loans}}{\text{Total Principal of Outstanding Loans}}$$

The PaR may be computed for all the principal on overdue loans for all time periods or maturities, for more than 30 days, for more than 90 days, for more than 180 days or for any time periods specified by the decision-maker. The PaR is indicative of the quality of the loan book of an MFI. A higher PaR suggests that an MFI has a higher exposure to credit risk. Consequently, MFIs with higher PaRs are less financially sustainable compared to those with lower PaRs. It is futuristic in nature because it tells us the amounts that are at risk and not just the principal that is overdue or remains unpaid.

Tchakoute-Tchuigoua and Soumaré (2019) find that more profitable MFIs have a lower PaR compared to less profitable MFIs. Tchakoute-Tchuigoua Soumaré (2019) also finds that when loan decisions are decentralized or when loan officers have authority to make loans, it reduces the credit risk or PaR of an MFI. This is because loan officers are able to collect a lot of information on borrowers and consequently reduce information asymmetries between the borrower and the MFI. Their findings further show that MFIs with effective internal controls and governance mechanisms have lower exposure to credit risk (that is lower PaRs). These results, however, were applicable to non-profit MFIs as opposed to profit MFIs. Individual lending was found to increase credit risk across both profit and non-profit MFIs.

23.3 Stylized Facts on MFI Sustainability in Africa

Financial Self-Sufficiency

Figure 23.1 shows that MFIs across the world are generally financially self-sufficient. This is because the FSS index exceeds 1, meaning that revenue more than covers adjusted expenditure. MFIs in the MENA region have the highest financial self-sufficiency whilst those in Africa have the lowest.

Subsidy Dependence Index

We computed the SDI measure manually as this was not available in the MFI MIX dataset. The SDI was computed as follows;

$$SDI = \frac{S}{LP * i}$$

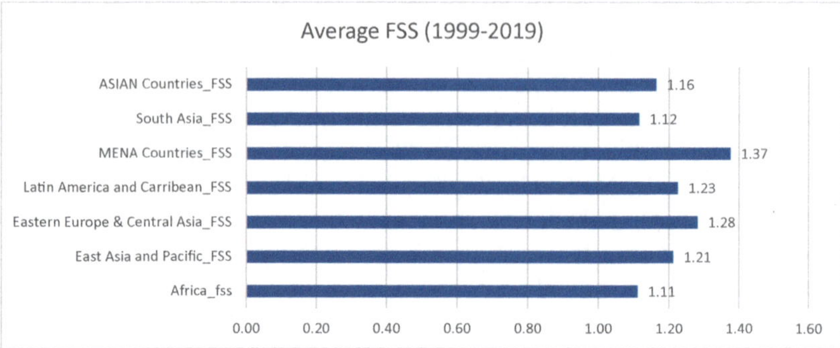

Fig. 23.1 Average financial self sufficiency of MFIs across the world (The data was obtained from MFI MIX)

where $S = K + [(E * m) - P]$

The computation does not include concessionary loans as well as the cost of concessionary loans, as this information was not available from the data. Interestingly, we find that the Latin American and Caribbean region is the most reliant on subsidies whilst the African region is the least reliant on subsidies. In the Latin American and Caribbean region, the average yield on loans has to increase by about 7.43% for MFIs to exit subsidy dependence. On the other hand, the average yield on loan portfolios in the African region has to increase by about 1.5% for MFIs to exit subsidy dependence (Fig. 23.2).

Number of Active Borrowers

Figure 23.3 shows that the number of active borrowers varies widely across the globe. South Asia has the highest number of active borrowers whilst Eastern Europe and Central Asia have the lowest. The average number of active borrowers for Africa for the period was about 32,000. This was only higher than Eastern Europe and Central Asia.

Average Loan Balance Per Borrower/GNI Per Capita

In terms of the average loan balance scaled by GNI, we see wide variations across the world. Eastern Europe and Central Asia have the largest balance whilst countries in the MENA region have the lowest. Lower balances

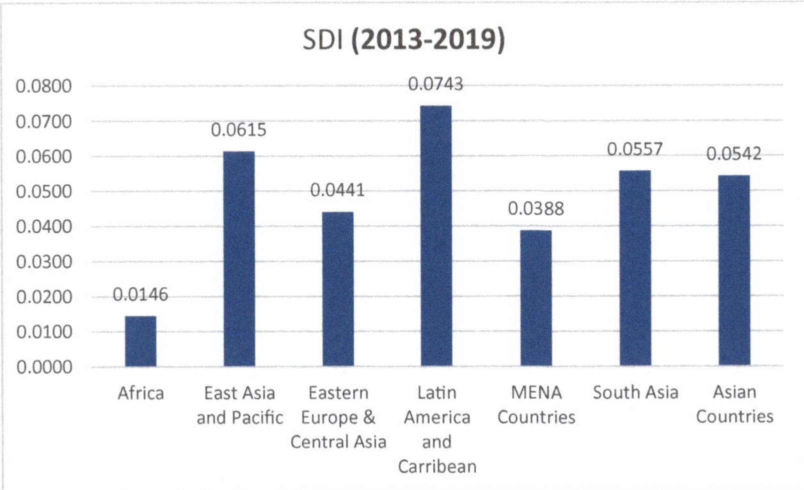

Fig. 23.2 Average subsidy dependence index of MFIs across the world (The index was computed manually by the authors based on data from MFI MIX. We measured donations as K, equity as E, average loan portfolio as LP, nominal yield on the gross loan portfolio as i, net income before taxes and donations as P and interest expense on deposits/deposits as m)

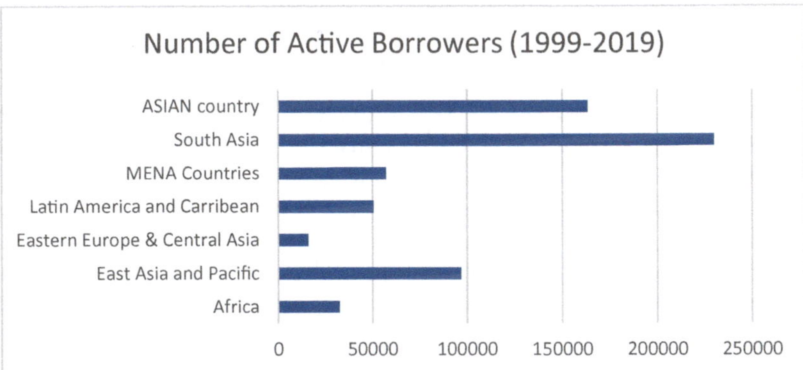

Fig. 23.3 Number of MFI active borrowers across the world (The data was obtained from MFI MIX)

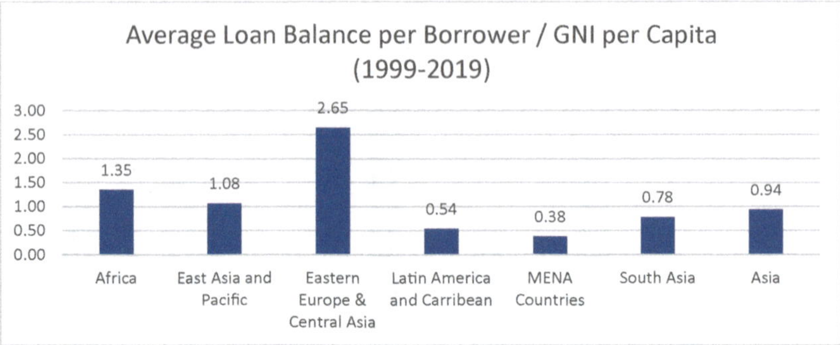

Fig. 23.4 Average loan balance per borrower/GNI per capita across the world (The data was obtained from MFI MIX)

are preferable here because it suggests that the MFI is lending to the poor and has not drifted from its mission. Thus, microfinance institutions tend to stick to their core mandate in the MENA regions and less so in Eastern Europe and Central Asia. Comparatively, there is some evidence of 'mission drift' in Africa, with the continent having the second largest scaled average loan balance. This is unfortunate, as Africa has one of the lowest levels of welfare globally (Fig. 23.4).

Percentage of Female Borrowers

One of the key indicators of MFI outreach and social performance is the percentage of loans granted to female borrowers. Well-performing MFIs in this area lend more to females who tend to be poorer, marginalized and less financially included (Demirgüç-Kunt, Klapper, Singer, Ansar, and Hess, 2020). South Asia had the highest percentage of lending to female borrowers whilst Eastern Europe and Central Asia had the lowest. Africa fared averagely, with lending by MFIs to females being about 60% (Fig. 23.5).

Percentage of Rural Borrowers

The core mission of microfinance is to lend to the poor. Typically, the poor are usually located in rural areas compared to urban areas. Consequently, an MFI that lends more to rural folks is doing better in terms of

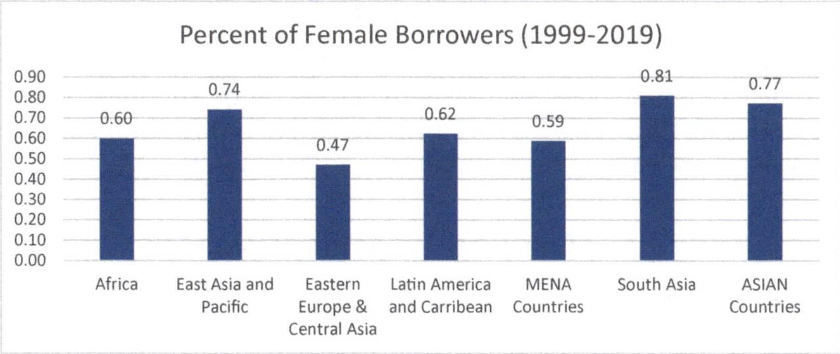

Fig. 23.5 Percentage of MFI female borrowers across the world (The data was obtained from MFI MIX)

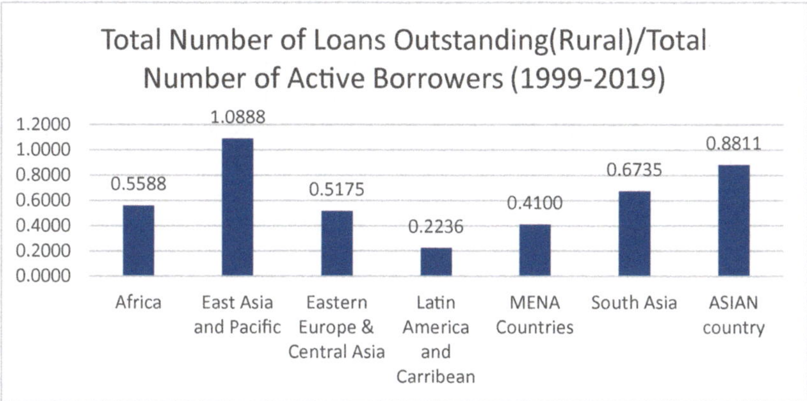

Fig. 23.6 Percentage of MFI rural borrowers across the world (The data was obtained from MFI MIX)

its social performance. The East Asia and Pacific region has the highest lending to rural folks whilst the Latin American and Caribbean region has the lowest. Africa performs averagely in terms of the percentage of loans that goes to rural borrowers (Fig. 23.6).

Portfolio at Risk

The quality of MFI loan books in terms of the principal on loans overdue is largely similar across regions with the exception of Africa which had a PaR of about 14%. This suggests that the quality of MFI loan portfolios in Africa is poor and the worst in the world (Fig. 23.7).

23.4 Growth of MFIs in Africa

Nations in Africa and international governments have been so concerned about the state of development and poverty which exist in Africa, especially in the light of the growing population in the continent (Asongu & le Roux, 2017; Helms, 2006; Human, 2021; Tchamyou, 2019). Therefore, for some years now aid has been rallied to target respective points of intervention and channels established for delivering it to the African population through microfinance institutions (MFIs) such as developmental, agricultural and industrial banking communities.

These MFIs are therefore financial establishments which provide deposit services to customers and other bank-related services such as insurance, custody and asset servicing (Nwachukwu et al., 2018; Wyoming Division of Banking, 2021) and by playing a vital role of

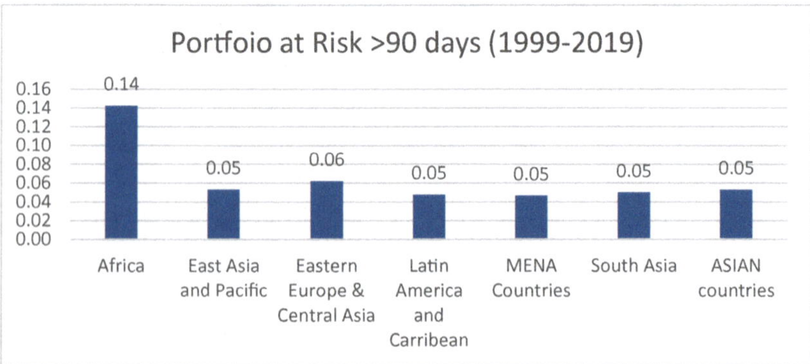

Fig. 23.7 Portfolio at risk (>90 days) across the world (The data was obtained from MFI MIX)

being lenders to small and medium sized enterprises, they vitalize the private sector and assist governments in community development. They are basically characterized in mobilizing informal capital and helping their customers in times of crisis and economic instability.

The Growth of MFIs in Africa

In Africa therefore, the existence of these institutions is quite felt even though the area is shallow in financial advancement (Helms, 2006; Soumaré et al., 2016). According to the narrative, over the years, beginning from the early 1970s, these institutions have in one way or the other registered a level of growth in most African countries, predominantly under the cover of informal business credits and funding formal small enterprises. Inclusive financial services in the African continent are growing substantially. To put this favorable tendency into perspective, between the years 2000 and 2011, according to a Microfinance Information Exchange (MIX) report, MFIs increased from 58 to 397 across the continent. Between 2003 and 2009, borrowers in MFIs in Africa increased from $1.6 million to $8.5 million and from 2000 to 2014, the gross loan portfolio grew about 10 times, reaching $6 billion (Fixler, 2015). For economies that have small financial sectors, these alternative means of funding are relevant in driving economic growth and inclusive development.

The COVID-19 pandemic has affected the performance of MFIs contingent on some dynamics. For instance, according to Zheng and Zhang (2021), the COVID-19 pandemic has led to a reduction of economic activities on a plethora of fronts. However, the corresponding impact of MFIs on targeted outcomes is contingent on such targeted outcomes. As a case in point, Zheng and Zhang (2021) establish that the pandemic-induced effects have decreased the financial efficiency of MFIs whilst increasing the social efficiency of the corresponding MFIs in the light of their enhanced relevance during the pandemic. The FGCA (2021) provides another perspective of the impact of the COVID-19 crises on MFIs. According to the narrative, from a survey of over 100 MFIs in four continents (i.e. Europe, Asia, South America and Africa), the resilience has been clearly noticeable in the sector, especially as it pertains to the adaptability of MFIs which played an essential role in hedging the risk of clients negatively affected by the pandemic, on the one hand, and of institutions rendered unsustainable, on the other hand.

Microfinance institutions have played an important role from the onset in reaching out to the poor population through provision of basic savings accounts, business loans and capital (especially to the female population), educational loans and offers of classes on financial management to their clients (Nwachukwu et al., 2018). Operations of microfinance have existed from as far back as the eighteenth century. These operations became more apparent in the 1970s as more institutions and microlending services were established in Africa and across the world (Mia, 2016; Mia et al., 2019).

Microfinance services have grown in large scale in Africa as their target is to respond to the very poor and financially deprived individuals who do not have the means of providing collateral security and/or a good financial history record.

The Drivers of MFIs' Growth in Africa

Danga and Yusuph (2019) have established that the growth of MFIs have been influenced by the following factors: (i) capacity in managing loans and finances; (ii) adherence to financial guidelines and policies; (iii) appropriate staff training and competent personnel; (iv) robust follow-up on loans; (v) less corruption; (vi) possibility of business training for members and (vii) the capacity of MFIs' stakeholders.

Beyond the above reasons that are directly related to MFI, there are other broader and/or indirect factors worth discussing. MFIs have spread across the world and in Africa for several reasons. In Africa, one of the major drivers of their growth is the persistence of poverty which plagues the continent more than any other region in the world. These institutions are of relevance to poor and financially excluded individuals, especially women, who are usually limited to doing petty jobs in order to increase their families' standard of living (Helms, 2006; Hardy & Dexer-Briggs, 2021; Mersland, 2009). The attendant institutions have therefore been ignited in Africa mainly due to the low level of development and economic fragility of the region, the consequent need to assist the very poor people out of poverty, and by extension, facilitate the overall economic development of the continent.

Another crucial driving point for the existence of these MFIs is the continuous drop and/or fluctuation of prices of agricultural products in the international market. The plight of farmers in Africa and the high dependence of a greater part of the African population on the agricultural sector has been a cause for concern since agricultural growth can reduce poverty rates more effectively (Christiaensen et al., 2011; Ruiz, 2014). Some of these MFIs have therefore been established through the drop in prices of agricultural products both at the regional and international levels. Some of these institutions that are created in response to agricultural development, are also designed to enable farmers get agricultural loans, purchase agricultural inputs at cheaper rates, save money as well as an intermediate between the buyers and farmers to hedge against the exploitation of the latter and unfavorable market price disequilibrium.

The need for new areas to occupy and the desire to undertake risky ventures for eventual yields equally account for the establishment of some of these institutions in Africa. Given the fact that Africa is one of the regions in the world where financial development is still at its infant stage, the desire of businessmen to leverage on potential profit-making opportunities (Lekeet al., 2019) is equally a driving force for the continuous development of these institutions in several African countries. Accordingly, MFIs can invest in areas which the traditional banks find too risky owing to, inter alia, information asymmetry. This formal banking approach to lending is different from some MFIs which also depend on trust and local knowledge of operations to be funded.

Africa is a region with a greater proportion of its population being financially excluded (African Development Bank, 2013; Soumaré et al., 2016). Given the recent improvements in digitalization of almost all activities and sectors across the world, African countries cannot be left out. The need to initiate the African population into the use of these technological and digitalization improvements in carrying out international purchases and payments has brought about the creation of these MFIs, some of which educate on the benefits of being financially included: being actively involved in owning and using financial accounts at the national and international spheres.

The need for foreign aid to reach African governments has equally been a driving force of the growth of these MFIs. In times of economic shocks like the present COVID-19 pandemic, the flow of official development aid from abroad often comes through such specialized agencies to aid governments combat the dire effects of crises. These institutions' ability to pool capital from abroad has been a continuous reason for their existence and persistence (Hardy & Dexer-Briggs, 2021).

In the light of the above, the existence of these MFIs in Africa cannot be ignored because of the role they play in addressing some financing and investment needs that are imperative for socio-economic development. Exclusive growth in most African countries has also motivated the establishment of these institutions which are designed to, *inter alia*, fight poverty and lack of basic infrastructure.

23.5 The Impact of MFIs in Africa

Theory suggests that microfinance outcomes are sensitive to geographic location where group-cohesion, financial literacy, enterprise development and MFIs all vary (Armendáriz & Morduch, 2010). Microfinance initiatives in Africa remain a difficult business. Whilst MFIs operating in other continents have consistently reported positive financial outcomes, those in Africa post negative profits[1] perhaps due to the high operating costs (Muriu, 2012). For MFIs to have a sustainable impact on financial and non-financial outcomes, they must be financially viable so that they can use financial leverage to upscale outreach (Muriu, 2016). This is what Morduch (1999) refers to as the microfinance promise.

Although development aid in Africa is proportionately large (Honohan, 2008), impact assessment of MFIs' operations remains very low. Pointing to the billions of dollars that MFIs advance to the poor, proponents of microfinance argue that microcredit fuels economic growth. Much of the existing literature is anecdotal evidence and has dwelt more on the improvement of the microfinance industry rather than uncovering its impact (Muriu et al., 2017). On the contrary, critics contend that the most vulnerable people are unable to take on the risks of entrepreneurship. Due to the proliferation of MFIs in Africa and the attention the industry has received from private investors, policymakers and donors over the last three decades, existing impact assessments should be re-examined. The robustness of evidence that MFIs reduce poverty should be scrutinized. Thus, we revisit the evidence of MFIs' impact assessments focusing on Africa to test the claims about its successes by considering high-quality studies with methodological rigor.

The overarching question is whether MFIs have made a contribution toward improving the livelihoods of the poor in Africa. But why focus on

[1] https://datacatalog.worldbank.org/dataset/mix-market

Africa? Globally, Africa is the poorest region and therefore has attracted proportionally large development aid.[2] Africa remains underdeveloped in terms of access to finance.[3] In the pre-global financial crisis period, private credit/GDP was only 17% whilst the average for other developing countries ranged from 32 to 43%. Moreover, stock markets are highly underdeveloped.[4] A characteristic of the banking system in Africa is that the majority of the banks invest in government securities, primarily treasury bills. Access to credit by households and small businesses thus remains a challenge. To bridge this financing gap, private investors are therefore targeting their investment at a wide range of microfinance programs.

A vast majority of microfinance impact assessments suffer from inadequate data and weak methodologies which adversely affect the reliability of estimated outcomes (Muriu, 2020). Previous studies have either overlooked or are unable to resolve these challenges, which has increasingly put microfinance industry under scrutiny. Whilst some studies contend that a research design with intervention and control groups is sufficient to establish causality, this may not necessarily hold. Given such hurdles to overcome, the evidence generated by most studies is contestable.

A growing literature comprising quality impact assessments has raised questions regarding the ability of MFIs to reduce poverty amongst households (Attanasio et al., 2015; Angelucci et al., 2015; Augsburg, et al., 2015; Banerjee et al., 2015; Roodman & Morduch, 2014). Previous reviews of evidence on targeted groups, specific regions or outcomes have ignored several factors that may influence the role of microfinance. The delivery mechanisms, duration of loan contracts, the size of loans, repayment schedules, types of financial products and the supplementary services offered can yield different impacts (Awaworyi, 2014; Buera et al., 2020; Duvendack et al., 2011; Maîtrot & Niño-Zarazúa, 2017; Rooyen, et al., 2012 Vaessen et al., 2014). Our point of departure is Rooyen et al. (2012) who reviewed the existing evidence of the impacts of MFIs in Sub Sahara Africa. The authors reveal that microfinance has a positive as well

[2] United Nations, (2020). Sustainable Development Goals Report 2020, Available from:https://unstats.un.org/sdgs/report/2020/

[3] Financial Access Survey, IMF (2020).

[4] https://databank.worldbank.org/source/world-development-indicators.

as a negative impact on the poor, but with a caveat: that there is no sufficient data from the available relevant evidence. They are therefore unable to conclude which microfinance models work best for Africa.

In Ethiopia the evidence remains inconclusive. Using a randomized controlled trial (RCT) on 6,284 rural households, Tarozzi et al. (2015) investigated the impact of two MFIs, Amhara Credit and Savings Institute and Oromiya Credit and Savings Company, on households and small businesses. They did not find any significant impact on income, self-employment activities and health-related expenditures. By contrast, using Fixed Effects estimators to evaluate the impact of the Debit Credit and Savings MFI, Berhane and Gardebroek (2011) found a positive and significant effect on income and per capita consumption. This finding is consistent with Doocy et al. (2005) who showed that microfinance enhances food security and nutrition. These two studies however failed to control for endogeneity.

Along the same vein and using RCT on 5,551 rural households in Morocco, Crépon et al. (2015) examined the impact of Al Amana MFI on individual and group lending mechanisms. Their estimation results found no significant impact on average household consumption since a rise in business profits was offset by a decline in employment income. On the contrary, using a quasi-experimental approach on 500 women who were dependent on agro-processing businesses in the upper east region of Ghana, Annim and Alnaa (2013) found that microfinance boosted household consumption by 40%. Similarly, focusing on Mali and using Propensity Score Matching estimators, Koloma and Alia (2014) found that microfinance impacted positively on poverty reduction but this was more pronounced amongst women.

In rural Kenya, Dupas and Robinson (2013) randomized access to noninterest-bearing bank accounts amongst female market vendors and male bicycle taxi drivers. Although they found no significant impact on business incomes, they nevertheless established that women managed to save more which boosted their investments and consumption expenditures. Overall, the evidence shows that microfinance enhanced accumulation of assets, consumption expenditure and health insurance, and that it increased food quality particularly for women. Although Ashraf et al. (2009) established that microfinance boosted income from export crops, this was not due to the microfinance intervention.

In Egypt, Abou-Ali et al. (2010) evaluated the impact of the Social Fund for Development using a sample of 47,095 borrowers and Propensity Score Matching estimators. The study found that microfinance enhanced consumption expenditure and income levels in urban areas relative to rural areas. In a study of South Africa, Kim et al. (2009) carried out an impact assessment of the Small Enterprise Foundation and found that microfinance boosted borrowers' ability to finance consumption expenditure compared to a control group. The IMAGE trial however fails to control for village effect and is therefore considered not a 'randomized' trial. A key attribute of MFIs has been the focus on women. This is based on the premise that relative to men, they report better financial and non-financial outcomes and their involvement in microfinance programs leads to more development outcomes. On this attribute, Kim et al. (2009) found no significant impact.

An interesting finding is that of Shimamura and Lastarria-Cornhiel (2009) who show that in Malawi microfinance reduces primary school attendance amongst the clients' children. Amongst young boys, microcredit accelerates the repetition of primary school grades and lack of enrolment for young girls. In Rwanda, Lacalle Calderon et al. (2008) established that enrolment into the Red Cross credit program and Village Savings and Credit Association enhances meal quality. These two studies nevertheless fail to control for endogeneity.

In this section we provided a rigorous synthesis of the existing evidence on microfinance impact assessment with a focus on Africa. As the policy and academic debate on MFIs' ability to reduce poverty and welfare rages on, the impacts in Africa remain inconclusive. There is still controversy about the financial and non-financial outcomes on the few available quality studies. Producing robust evidence remains crucial. Governments in Africa and donors should therefore direct public resources into effective development interventions. Thus, addressing the critical question of whether microfinance has an impact on poor households and small businesses is important.

Due to the different contexts and socio-economic conditions in which impact assessments have been undertaken, the interpretation of findings remains complex. Moreover, several studies using non-experimental methodology have a tendency of reporting positive impacts which only reflect short-term linear effects. Thus, there is a significant knowledge gap regarding the long-term effects of microfinance initiatives. Having reviewed empirical evidence on Africa, we conclude that there is no compelling evidence that microfinance leads to increases in permanent income, accumulation of assets and therefore poverty reduction; the findings reveal short-term modest impacts which are not homogenous. However, whilst microfinance may not be an effective tool for development and poverty alleviation, it can be integrated within a broader development framework in the quest for poverty reduction but cannot be seen as a panacea for reducing poverty in Africa.

23.6 Conclusion

This chapter investigated issues surrounding the sustainability, growth and impact of MFIs in Africa. This is premised on the fact that microfinance has the potential to reduce poverty in Africa, which has one of the highest levels of poverty in the world. Our review showed that though MFIs in Africa were financially self-sustainable, they had the lowest FSS ratio globally. Surprisingly, we found that MFIs in Africa were not subsidy dependent. They had the lowest SDI ratio globally. The yields on loan books of MFIs in Africa have to increase by about 1.5% for these institutions to exit subsidy dependence. The average number of active borrowers in Africa was low compared to the rest of the world. Africa performed averagely when it comes to lending to women and the population in rural areas. We also found evidence of mission drift amongst African MFIs given that they tend to give relatively large loans. In terms of the quality of the loan book, Africa had the poorest with a PaR ratio of 14%.

The review showed that there has been significant growth in MFI activities in Africa. In addition, the review found that the growth of MFIs has been influenced by factors such as:

> capacity in managing loans and finances; adherence to financial guidelines and policies; appropriate staff training and competent personnel; robust follow-up on loans; less corruption; possibility of business training for members and the capacity of MFIs' stakeholders. The review shows that both positive and negative effects of microfinance on welfare have been documented in the literature. Further, it questions the robustness of studies that have sought to investigate the impact of microfinance on welfare in Africa. We conclude that the evidence of the effects of microfinance is inconclusive at best and consequently microfinance may not be a panacea for reducing poverty in Africa.

References

Abor, J. Y. (2017). *Entrepreneurial finance for MSMEs: A managerial approach for developing markets*. Palgrave Macmillan.

Abou-Ali, H., El-Azony, H., El-Laity, H., Haughton, J., & Khandker, S. (2010). Evaluating the impact of Egyptian social fund for development programmes. *Journal of Development Effectiveness, 2*(4), 521–555.

African Development Bank. (2013). *Financial inclusion in Africa*. https://www.afdb.org/en/documents/document/financial-inclusion-in-africa-34666. Accessed 16 August 2021.

Angelucci, M., Karlan, D., & Zinman, J. (2015). Microcredit impacts: Evidence-from a randomized microcredit program placement experiment by compartamos Banco. *American Economic Journal: Applied Economics, 7*(1), 151–182.

Annim, S. K., & Alnaa, S. E. (2013). Access to microfinance by rural women: Implications for poverty reduction in rural households in Ghana. *Macrothink Institute—Research in Applied Economics, 5*(2), 19–41.

Armendáriz de Aghion, B., & Morduch, J. (2010). *The economics of microfinance* (2nd ed.). MIT Press.

Ashraf, N., Gine, X., & Karlan, D. (2009). Finding missing markets (and a disturbing epilogue): Evidence from an export crop adoption and marketing intervention in Kenya. *American Journal of Agricultural Economics, 91*(4), 973–990.

Asongu, S. A., & Le Roux, S. (2017). Enhancing ICT for inclusive human development in Sub-Saharan Africa. *Technological Forecasting and Social Change, 118*(May), 44–54.

Attanasio, O., Augsburg, B., De Haas, R., Fitzsimons, E., & Harmgart, H. (2015). The impacts of microfinance: Evidence from joint-liability in Mongolia. *American Economic Journal: Applied Economics, 7*(1), 90–122.

Augsburg, B., De Haas, R., Harmgart, H., & Meghir, C. (2015). The impacts of microcredit: Evidence from Bosnia and Herzegovina. *American Economic Journal: Applied Economics, 7*(1), 183–203.

Awaworyi, S. (2014). Impact of microfinance interventions: A meta-analysis. *Business and Economics, 4*(1), 3–14.

Banerjee, A., Duflo, E., Glennerster, R., & Kinnan, C. (2015). The miracle of microfinance? Evidencefrom a randomized evaluation. *American Economic Journal: Applied Economics, 7*(1), 22–53.

Barry, T. A., & Tacneng, R. (2014). The impact of governance and institutional quality on MFI outreach and financial performance in Sub-Saharan Africa. *World Development, 58*, 1–20.

Berhane, G., & Gardebroek, C. (2011). Does microfinance reduce rural poverty? Evidence based on household panel data from NorthernEthiopia. *American Journal of Agricultural Economics, 93*(1), 43–55.

Buera, F.J., Kaboski, J. P., & Shin, Y. (2020). Taking stock of the evidence on microfinancial interventions. Federal Reserve Bank of St. Louis Review, Second Quarter (pp. 173–202).

Calderon, M. L., Garrido, S. R., & Navarro, J. D. (2008). Pilot impact assessment study of the Spanish Red Cross microcredit program in Rwanda. *Journal of World Economy*, (19), 83–104.

Chikalipah, S. & Makina, D. (2019). A Survey of Microfinance Institutions and Informal Finance in Africa. In D. Makina, *Extending Finanical Inclusion in Africa*. https://doi.org/10.1016/B978-0-12-814164-9.00006-2.

Christiaensen, L., Demery, L., & Kuhl, J. (2011). The (evolving) role of Agriculture in poverty reduction: An empirical perspective. *Journal of Development Economics, 96*(2), 239–254.

Crépon, B., Devoto, F., Duflo, E., & Parienté, W. (2015). Estimating the Impact of Microcredit on Those Who Take It Up: Evidence from a Randomized Experiment in Morocco. *American Economic Journal: Applied Economics, 7*(1), 123–150.

Cull, R., Demirguc-Kunt, A., & Morduch, J. (2007). Financial performance and outreach: A global analysis of lending microbanks. *The Economic Journal, 117*(1), 107–133.

Danga, M., & Yusuph, M. L. (2019). Factors Affecting the Growth of Microfinance Institutions in Tanzania: A Case Study of SACCOS in Singida Region. *International Journal of Academic Multidisciplinary Research (IJAMR), 3*(3), 69–79.

Demirgüç-Kunt, A., Klapper, L., Singer, D., Ansar, S., & Hess, J. (2020). The global Findexdatabase 2017: measuring financial inclusion and opportunities to expand access to and use of financial services. *The World Bank Economic Review*, *34*(Supplement_1), S2-S8.

Doocy, S., Teffera, S., Norell, D., & Burnham, G. (2005). Credit Program Outcomes: Coping Capacity and Nutritional Status in the Food Insecure Context of Ethiopia. *Social Science and Medicine, 60*(10), 2371–2382.

Dunford, C. (2006). Evidence of microfinance's contribution to achieving the millennium development goals. Freedom from Hunger. http://microfinance gateway.org/files/35795_file_Evidence_on_MDGs_Dunford.pdf.

Dupas, P., & Robinson, J. (2013). Savings Constraints and Microenterprise Development: Evidence from a Field Experiment in Kenya. *American Economic Journal: Applied Economics, 5*(1), 163–192.

Duvendack, M., Palmer-Jones, R., Copestake, J. G., Hooper, L., Loke, Y., & Rao, N. (2011). *What is the Evidence of the Impact of Microfinance on the Well-being of Poor People?* EPPI-Centre, University of London.

Egyir, I. S. (2010). Rural Women and Microfinance in Ghana: *Challenges and Prospects* (No.308–2016–4989, pp. 1–13).

FGCA. (2021). The impact of the COVID-19 crisis on microfinance institutions—Analyses and perspectives. *European Microfinance Network*. https://www.gca-foundation.org/wp-content/uploads/2021/07/FGCA_Covid-19-Report-web-VF.pdf. Accessed 8 October 2021

Fixler, A. (2015). African Microfinance's Dynamic Growth and the Story of AfriCap. Center for Financial Inclusion, https://www.centerforfinancialinclusion.org/african-microfinances-dynamic-growth-and-the-story-of-africap. Accessed 8 October 2021.

Hardy J. & Derex-Briggs J. (2021). African development Finance institutions. World in transition. www.whitecase.com. Accessed 14 August 2021.

Helms B. (2006). Access for all. Building inclusive financial systems. Consultative group to assist the poor. The international bank of reconstruction and development, World Bank.

Henock, M. S. (2019). Financial sustainability and outreach performance of saving and credit cooperatives: The case of Eastern Ethiopia. *Asia Pacific Management Review, 24*(1), 1–9.

Hermes, N., Lensink, R., & Meesters, A. (2011). Outreach and efficiency of microfinance institutions. *World Development, 39*(6), 938–948.

Honohan, P. (2008). Cross-Country Variation in Household Access to Financial Services. *Journal of Banking and Finance, 32*(11), 2493–2500.

Human, J. K. (2021). *African countries continue to have the highest poverty rates in the world*. Developmentaid.org. Accessed 14 August 2021.

Kim, J., Ferrari, G., Abramsky, T., Watts, C., Hargreaves, J., Morison, L., et al. (2009). Assessing the incrementaleffects of combiningeconomic and health interventions: The IMAGE study in South Africa. *Bulletin of the World Health Organization, 87*(11), 824–832.

Koloma, Y., & Alia, H. (2014). Gendered impact of microcredit in mali: An evaluation by propensity score matching. *Strat Change, 23*, 517–530.

Lacalle, C. M., Rico, G. S., & Duran, N. J. (2008). Estudiopiloto de evaluacion de impactodelprograma de microcreditos de Cruz Roja Espanola en Ruanda. *Revista De Economia Mundial, 19*, 83–104.

Leke, A., Signé, L., & Initiative, A. G. (2019). Spotlighting opportunities for business in Africa and strategies to succeed in the world's next big growth market. *Africa's Untapped Business Potential: Countries, Sectors, and Strategies*, 77–95.

Maîtrot, M., & Niño-Zarazúa, M. (2017). *Poverty and wellbeing impacts of microfinance: What do we know?* (WIDER Working Paper 190/2017). Helsinki: UNU-WIDER.

Marr, A. (2004). A challenge to the orthodoxy concerning microfinance and poverty reduction. *Journal of Microfinance, 5*(2), 1–35.

Mersland, R. (2009). The Cost of Ownership in Microfinance organizations. *World Development, 37*, 469–478.

Mia, A. (2016). Microfinance Institutions and Legal Status: An Overview of the Microfinance Sector in Bangladesh. *Journal of Asian Finance, Economics and Business, 3*(2), 21–31.

Mia, M. A., Lee, H. A., Chandran, V., Rasiah, R., & Rahman, M. (2019). History of microfinance in Bangladesh: A life cycle theory approach. *Business History, 61*(4), 703–733.

Morduch, J. (1999). The microfinance promise. *Journal of Economic Literature, 37*(4), 1569–1614.

Muriu, P. W. (2012). What Explains The Low Profitability Of Sub-Saharan Africa Microfinance Institutions? *African Journal of Social Sciences, 2*(3), 85–115.

Muriu, P. W. (2016). Microfinance Performance: Does financing choice matter? *European Journal of Business and Management, 8*(33), 77–93.

Muriu, P. W. (2020). The Impact of Microfinance Programs: A Review of Data and Methodological Dilemma. *Journal of Economics and Sustainable Development, 11*(22), 100–109.

Muriu, P. W., Murinde, V., & Mullineux, A. W. (2017). Reflections On Microfinance Book Chapter In: Biekpe N., Cassimon D., Mullineux A. (eds.). *Development Finance* pp 109–159. Palgrave Macmillan, Cham

Nwachukwu, J. C., Aziz, A., Tony-Okeke, U., & Asongu, S. A. (2018). The determinants of interest rates in microfinance: Age, scale and organizational charter. *Review of Development Economics, 22*(3), e135–e159.

Rai, A., & Ravi, S. (2011). Do spouses make claims? Empowerment and microfinance in India. *World Development, 39*(6), 913–921.

Roodman, D., & Morduch, J. (2014). The Impact of Microcredit on the Poor in Bangladesh: Revisiting the Evidence. *The Journal of Development Studies, 50*(4), 583–604.

Rooyen, V. C., Stewart, R., & De Wet, T. (2012). The Impact of Microfinance in Sub-Saharan Africa: A Systematic Review of the Evidence. *World Development, 40*(11), 2249–2262.

Ruiz, C. (2014). How can finance influence productivity of agricultural firms? All about finance. Worldbank.org. https://blogs.worldbank.org/allaboutfinance/how-can-finance-influence-productivity-agricultural-firms / (Accessed: 14/08/2021).

Shimamura, Y., & Lastarria-Cornhiel, S. (2009). Credit Program Participation and Child Schooling In Rural Malawi. *World Development, 38*(4), 567–580.

Soumaré, I., Tchana, F. T., & Kengne, T. M. (2016). Analysis of the determinants of financial inclusion in Central and West Africa. *Journal of Transnational Corporations, Review, 8*(4), 231–249.

Tarozzi, A., Desai, J., & Johnson, K. (2015). The Impacts of Microcredit: Evidence from Ethiopia'. *American Economic Journal: Applied Economics, 7*(1), 54–89.

Tchakoute-Tchuigoua, H., & Soumaré, I. (2019). The effect of loan approval decentralization on microfinance institutions' outreach and loan portfolio quality. *Journal of Business Research, 94*, 1–17.

Tchamyou, V. S., & Asongu, S. A. (2017). Information sharing and financial sector development in Africa. *Journal of African Business, 18*(1), 24–49.

Tchamyou, V. S. (2019). Information sharing and financial sector development in Africa. *Journal of African Business, 18*(1), 24–49.

Vaessen, J., Rivas, A., Duvendack, M., Palmer-Jones, R., Leeuw, F., van Gils, G., Lukach, R., Holvoet, N., Bastiaensen, J., Garcia-Hombrados, J., & Waddington, H. (2014). The effects of microcredit on women's control over household spending in developing countries: A systematic review and metaanalysis. *Campbell Systematic Reviews, 10*(1), 1–205.

Wyoming Division of Banking. (2021). *Special purpose depository institutions*. wyomingbankingdivision@wyo.gov. Accessed 14 August 2021.

Yaron, J., & Manos, R. (2007). Determining the self-sufficiency of microfinance institutions. *Savings and Development*, 131–160.

Zheng, C., & Zhang, J. (2021). The impact of COVID-19 on the efficiency of microfinance institutions. *International Review of Economics & Finance, 71*(January), 407–423.

CHAPTER 24

Insurance Markets in Africa

Richard Addae-Manu and Michael Graham

24.1 Introduction

The insurance sector, both life and non-life,[1] plays a critical role in the financial sector of both emerging and developed economies through efficient resource allocation by mitigating financial losses arising from risk and by mobilising savings from individuals and firms to insurers (Das et al., 2003). In addition, the development and growth of the insurance sector contribute to economic development through the transfer of

[1] Life insurance products are classified as pensions, savings, health, and term assurance policies with some degree of death protection and investment benefits. Life insurers are liable to pay claims either on death, on the diagnosis of a specific underwritten illness or health-related problem, or at the end of the policy term as a survival benefit. Non-life insurance products, on the other hand, offer financial protection against specific non-mortality risk events, and contracts are generally over a relatively shorter term, usually one year, and offer no investment benefits to the insured (Das et al., 2003). Typical examples of non-life insurers' protection include industrial injury, vehicle accidents, fire accidents, theft, and home and business protection.

R. Addae-Manu · M. Graham (✉)
University of Stellenbosch Business School, Cape Town, South Africa
e-mail: michael.graham@usb.ac.za

J. Y. Abor and C. K. D. Adjasi (eds.), *The Economics of Banking and Finance in Africa*, Palgrave Macmillan Studies in Banking and Financial Institutions, https://doi.org/10.1007/978-3-031-04162-4_24

funds to both the corporate and public sectors, boosting business and investor confidence, and improving social well-being and the quality of life (UNCTAD, 2007). The literature also notes that insurance encourages productivity, investment, innovation, and competition. Also, it reduces the impact of losses by pooling the risks of households and firms. Further, it promotes good behaviour from economic agents and minimises the financial consequences of accidents and ill-health.

Although insurance has many beneficial outcomes, insurance coverage remains low in many economies. According to the 2017 worldwide statistics, Africa's portion of world premiums in 2017 was about 1.4% (average life and non-life insurance premiums). The combined regions of the Middle East, Central Asia, and Turkey registered only 1.2% of premiums, Central and Eastern Europe contributed 1.4%, and the Oceania region recorded 1.9%. These are low volumes compared to 3.5% in Latin America, 14.5% in emerging Asia, 16% in advanced Asia, 29% in Western Europe, and 31.5% in North America (Sigma, 2018). Several reasons have been put forward for the low insurance coverage. For example, in the KPMG (2014) insurance industry survey, affordability, low cross-border insurance activity due to poverty, mistrust of the industry, lack of reliable market information, scarcity of human resources, and inadequate legal and judicial structures have been put forward as some of the reasons for the low growth of the insurance sector across Africa.

South Africa underwrites the bulk of the insurance business on the African market partly due to its relatively advanced financial sector (KPMG, 2014). This assertion raises pertinent questions concerning insurance markets in Africa, which this chapter explores. To give this chapter contemporary relevance, we structure the discussions around the following questions:

1. What are the exact market patterns between Africa's insurance sector and other financial sector components to inform this assertion?
2. What are the challenges and opportunities facing the growth of the insurance market in Africa?
3. What market and regulatory reforms can correct the distortions to promote greater consumption and demand, leading to inclusive growth in the insurance markets?

This chapter, thus, seeks to provide a market overview of Africa's insurance sector and address some fundamental concerns in the marketplace. In so doing, the chapter offers excellent insight for insurance regulators, policymakers, insurers, and researchers interested in expanding and growing insurance markets in Africa. The remainder of the chapter is structured as follows: Sect. 24.2 presents an overview of the insurance business and reviews the economic growth role of insurance. Next, we illustrate Africa's insurance and financial market development patterns and statistics in Sect. 24.3. Section 24.4 of the chapter discusses some major market concerns and impediments in the insurance sector. This is followed by a discussion of regulatory proposals to address the identified shortfalls in Sect. 24.5. Finally, Sect. 24.6 concludes with several market recommendations.

24.2 Insurance Business Overview

The typical insurer's balance sheet can be conveniently used to describe the insurance business (see Fig. 24.1). An insurer selects its investment portfolio, taking into consideration the products that it underwrites. For example, a life insurer that writes life annuity contracts invests in long-dated bonds with regular payments to match the annuity contract's expected payments. On the other side of its balance sheet, the bulk of its liabilities are in the estimated provisions set up for future claims on existing contracts and policies. Insurers regularly revise their estimates

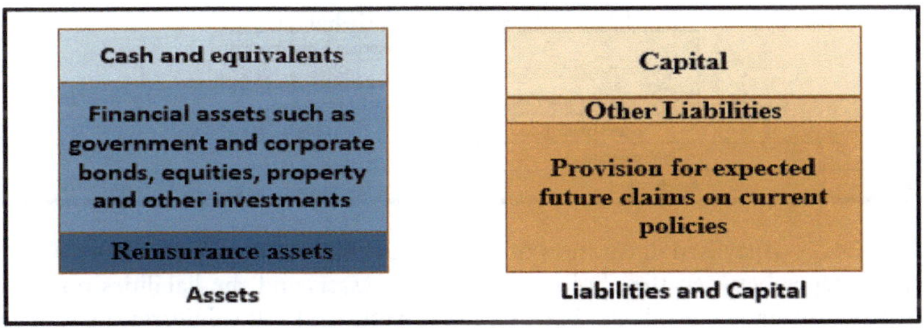

Fig. 24.1 A stylised illustration of the insurer's balance sheet. *Note* This Figure illustrates the key assets and liabilities of a representative insurer (*Source* Swain and Swallow [2015])

of the number of claims and duration of claims to set aside a provision or reserve for the aggregated claims (Swain & Swallow, 2015). As illustrated in Fig. 24.1, the bulk of assets in corporate and government bonds, equity, commercial property, and reinsurance are directly set up to provide for future expected claims. Insurance premiums paid by the insured for the financial protection and business capital reserves are invested in these assets, and proceeds from the assets are used to settle liabilities in the form of claims.

Given the differences in their product offering, life insurers have a greater inclination towards long-term investments, while non-life insurers have a relatively shorter-term outlook and invest more in short-term assets (Arena, 2008). Life insurers mobilise savings by providing attractive medium-to long-term financial products (Webb et al., 2002). A typical life cover product will be an endowment policy designed to pay a specific lump sum on death or on the policy's maturity in return for regular contractual premiums payable by the insured. The insurance policy term could be 10–20 years or up to a specific age limit. In comparison, non-life insurers mobilise funds by offering attractive short-to medium-term non-mortality risk products (Webb et al., 2002). Figure 24.2 shows the matching requirements of a typical insurer in fulfilment of its asset-liability

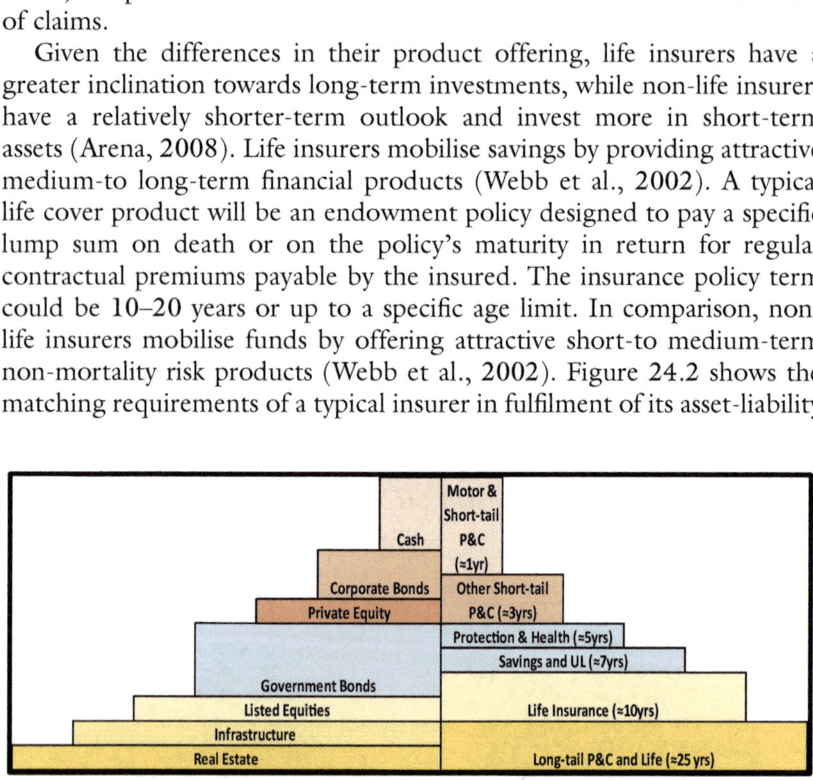

Fig. 24.2 A stylised illustration of the asset-liability strategy. This Figure depicts the linkages between the choice of investment assets and the liabilities posed by different insurance products. For example, savings and UL (Universal Life) products over seven years are matched by long-term government bond investments. In contrast, investments match motor and other short-term P and C (Property and Casualty) insurance products in cash and short-term corporate bonds (*Source* Thimann [2016])

strategy. For instance, life annuities payable until the death of policyholders can match with investments in government bonds that have an income profile suitable in size and timing to the annuity payments. Such investment strategies avoid the refinancing and reinvestment risks when market conditions are unfavourable.

The Role of the Insurance Markets

Insurers act as substitutes for direct investment in capital markets by individuals and corporates. As such, insurers provide financial intermediation and, therefore, contribute to financial market development. Insurance also complements and improves the efficiency and depth of the financial activities of banks. Banks provide liquidity to insurers through their product offering in interest-bearing deposits and loans, letters of credit, and commercial paper. These products are over a fixed term and are shorter than the type of investments required by life insurers with a longer-term perspective than non-life insurance. The provision of liquidity and an effective payment system are prime drivers for depositing cash with banks (Webb et al., 2002). On the other hand, Arena (2008) posits that liquid stock markets provide a channel for the investment of insurance premiums. This is especially so for life insurers that need to match long-term liabilities with long-term assets that are not available through the banking system. Insurers also transfer their market risk to the stock market through stock market investments, depicting a bi-directional relationship between insurers and the capital markets that promotes mutual growth and development. We present a graphical illustration of the critical interactions between the insurance sector, financial markets, and policyholders in Fig. 24.3. The Figure depicts the capital accumulation activities that spur economic growth through the interaction between insurers and financial markets and the dependencies on the commercial environment and policyholders.

To highlight the economic benefits of insurance, we briefly discuss the insurance–economic growth nexus. We do this because the underpinning theoretical literature on the finance–growth nexus provides profound implications for financial sector development policies. For instance, the traditional view (the supply-leading hypothesis [SLH]) suggests that financial development is a precondition for economic growth and stimulates strong national policies that prioritise financial development. On the other hand, the demand-leading hypothesis (DLH) proposes that

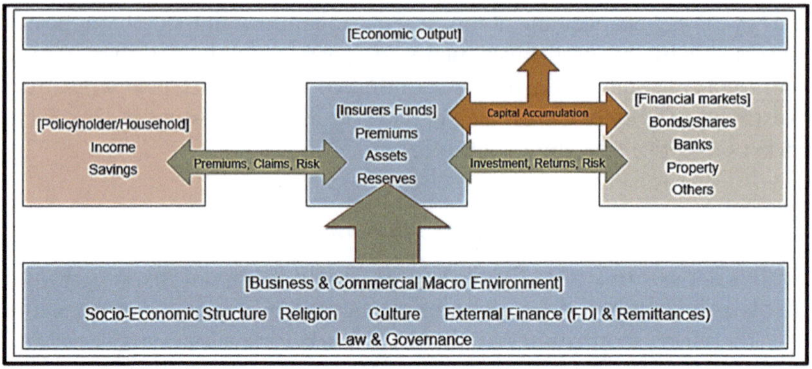

Fig. 24.3 The insurance sector development framework. This Figure illustrates the critical linkages influencing the development of the insurance sector: (1) The interaction between households and insurance in the transfer of risk, (2) The influence of the business and commercial environment that influences insurance business, and (3) The interaction between insurance and the financial markets leading to capital accumulation and potential economic growth benefits

demand from the real economy leads to financial development. This motivates policies that enhance real growth as growth precedes and induces financial sector development (see Darrat, 1999; Levine, 1997). The implications of the contending finance–growth theories, in a sense, make the link between finance and growth an empirical question.

Unambiguous empirical evidence on the insurance–growth nexus may provide guidance to assist policymakers in decision-making. A thread of evidence in the insurance literature confirms the SLH (see e.g., Akinlo, 2013; Alhassan & Fiador, 2014; Arena, 2008; Chen et al., 2012; Haiss & Sümegi, 2008; Han et al., 2010; Muye & Hassan, 2016). Also, Jahromi and Goudarzi (2014) and Lee et al. (2013) find a bi-directional relationship between insurance and real economies. In contrast, mixed results with traces of DLH (economic growth preceding insurance development) have been reported by Ward and Zurbruegg (2000) and Kugler and Ofoghi (2005). Overall, the evidence, although mixed, suggests that the SLH edges DLH behaviour in most economies. This implies that increasing insurance penetration rates can spur economic growth. Therefore, it is essential to monitor the progression and developments in the insurance market so that effective interventions and strategies are put in place to grow the markets.

24.3 Developments in the Insurance Markets in Africa

We next turn our attention to developments in the insurance market in Africa. Recent industry experience of cross-border insurance business reveals that parameters that work well, for instance, in developed insurance markets may not necessarily work well in African markets. This may underscore the national or perhaps regional uniqueness of insurance markets (see Ward & Zurbruegg, 2000) and raises the prospect that certain economic factors facilitate development and growth in specific insurance markets that are unique. For example, Africa has distinct market profiles, such as the demographic dividend from youthful populations. In addition, high external finance from remittances, cultural inclinations, and the developmental gaps in infrastructure could have peculiar influences on insurance penetration and consumption.

Global insurance sector premiums have experienced mixed growth patterns before and after the global financial crisis in 2008. Global life premium income (in real terms) in 2015 was about USD 2.5 trillion, and non-life premiums were approximately USD 2.0 trillion. These represent a real growth rate of 4 and 3.6%, respectively, from the previous year. In the pre-crisis period from 2003 to 2007 average life insurance-growth rates were about 4% globally, 10% for emerging markets, and 2.5% in Africa. The post-crisis period from 2009 to 2014 has seen significantly lower average growth rates globally (close to 0%). However, the growth rates in emerging markets are about 4%, while the growth rates have remained relatively stable in Africa at 2.5% (Sigma, 2016).

The non-life insurance industry has so far registered less drastic growth patterns. Worldwide average premium growth in non-life insurance remained close to 2% before and after the crisis. Whereas emerging market growth rates declined from 10 to 8%, rates dropped from 5 to 3% in Africa. As a direct result of the global financial crisis in 2008, negative global average premium growth of −5% for both non-life and life insurance was registered. Worldwide premium growth rates are increasing again, albeit at a slow pace (Sigma, 2016).

In terms of growth, the African insurance market remains in the doldrums. Life insurance premiums stagnated after declining by 1% in

2016, and non-life insurance increased by only 1% in 2017. South Africa that underwrites about 85% of the total life insurance premiums on the continent has stagnated in recent times. This is due to a structurally weak economy and high unemployment levels that have dwindled the middle-income market. Other markets in Africa have had mixed developments. The fragile economies of the oil-exporting countries, in particular, have experienced adverse insurance growth. In addition, the African non-life insurance market, also led by South Africa with a market share of about 44%, has been negatively affected by the sluggish economic growth in South Africa. In general, the weak economies coupled with intense competition in the African marketplace should strain insurance profits in the short term. However, the longer-term outlook remains buoyant given the infrastructural development gaps and the generally low insurance penetration rates. There is also the need for medical insurance and excellent prospects from the microinsurance market (Sigma, 2018, 2019).

Insurance and Financial Market Trends

The African Insurance Market Characteristics

As earlier indicated, insurance coverage is minuscule compared to other regions. The reason for this may be structural, in that many assets in these economies are, for the most part, not represented in a way that makes them fungible assets (de Soto, 2000). Moreover, a KPMG (2014) insurance industry survey adduces that the financial market development, as a whole, may either spur or constrain growth in the insurance sector. Therefore, this report raises pertinent questions about the relationship between the financial sector, in general, and the insurance industry. We, therefore, examine the insurance market in conjunction with the prevailing banking and stock market trajectories in Africa. We derive the market movements from the Global Financial Development Database (GFDD). We also examine the financial sector development patterns for a group of highly industrialised countries for comparative analysis.

We use three key metrics to gauge the insurance market: the ratio of gross premiums to GDP, the proportion of gross premiums to the size of the population, and the ratio of the size of insurance assets to GDP. Table 24.1 presents the descriptive statistics on the insurance market for the entire Africa region, covering countries with existing data on the GFDD over the 1990–2017 period. Overall, the insurance asset ratios are much higher than the combined life and non-life insurance penetration rates

Table 24.1 Descriptive statistics of insurance market depth

	Mean	*Median*	*Max*	*Min*	*Std. Dev*	*Skewness*	*Kurtosis*	*Obs*
Africa								
ASSETS	7.20	1.91	69.05	0.17	12.25	2.76	11.25	441
LIFE	0.84	0.17	15.38	0.00	2.13	4.16	21.40	782
NON-LIFE	0.84	0.62	14.72	0.00	0.90	9.55	135.42	847
North Africa								
ASSETS	4.50	1.88	18.49	0.44	5.99	1.57	3.77	68
LIFE	0.25	0.12	1.58	0.01	0.30	1.79	6.34	144
NON-LIFE	0.81	0.58	1.69	0.21	0.47	0.51	1.64	144
South Africa								
ASSETS	30.95	31.06	69.05	8.32	17.01	0.87	2.75	57
LIFE	5.78	4.94	15.38	0.44	4.15	0.61	2.13	76
NON-LIFE	1.67	1.80	2.67	0.73	0.56	−0.07	1.84	82
West Africa								
ASSETS	1.69	1.69	3.99	0.46	0.95	0.57	2.36	134
LIFE	0.21	0.13	0.91	0.00	0.20	1.38	4.35	226
NON-LIFE	0.51	0.49	1.20	0.00	0.22	−0.06	3.11	241
East Africa								
ASSETS	6.37	2.48	33.74	0.73	8.33	1.82	5.23	125
LIFE	0.57	0.23	4.22	0.01	0.89	2.41	8.35	214
NON-LIFE	0.88	0.76	2.16	0.02	0.47	0.52	2.11	242
Central Africa								
ASSETS	1.45	1.52	6.50	0.17	0.94	2.77	16.40	57
LIFE	0.11	0.06	0.66	0.00	0.11	1.32	6.66	122
NON-LIFE	0.84	0.60	14.72	0.02	1.88	6.41	44.57	138
5 Highly industrialised countries								
ASSETS	61.35	57.91	119.33	30.39	22.99	0.49	2.25	128
LIFE	5.56	5.35	18.07	2.03	2.99	1.53	5.67	128
NON-LIFE	2.39	2.30	3.71	1.21	0.61	0.25	2.11	131

This table depicts the insurance market depth statistics of countries over the 1990–2017 period. LIFE is the annual ratio of life insurance premium volume to GDP. NON-LIFE is the annual ratio of non-life insurance premiums to GDP. ASSET indicates the annual ratio of the size of insurance company assets to GDP

(7.20% versus the combination of 0.84% and 0.84%). The asset ratios also have a higher variance than the insurance penetration rates. Over the period, the life insurance penetration rate is 0.84% on average, with a low median value of 0.17% and a maximum value of 15.38%. From the skewness statistic of 9.55, the non-life insurance penetration rates are highly positively skewed. The overall mean non-life penetration rate is also 0.84% in Africa.

To better understand the distribution of the overall market statistics in Africa, we further split the statistics by sub-regions. The Southern African region has the highest mean insurance asset ratio of 30.95%, while the lowest mean of 1.45% is registered in the Central African region. The maximum life insurance penetration rate of 15.38% is recorded in South Africa. The Southern African region underwrites the bulk of life insurance business with a mean life insurance penetration average of 5.78%. In comparison, the lowest mean rate of 0.11% is in the central African region. Between the lowest and highest, West Africa has a life insurance penetration rate of 0.21%, North Africa at 0.25%, and East Africa at 0.57%.

The maximum non-life insurance penetration statistic of 14.72 is an outlier recorded in the Central Africa region. The Southern Africa region has the highest mean non-life penetration of 1.67%, and West Africa has the lowest mean value of 0.51%. The mean non-life insurance penetration rates for the North, East, and Central Africa are 0.81, 0.88, and 0.84%.

Compared to the African region, the mean insurance asset statistic of 61.35% from the five highly industrialised economies of the USA, UK, Germany, France, and Japan is more than eight times that in Africa. While the insurance penetration rates are more than six times that of Africa's life insurance penetration rates and close to three times the non-life insurance penetration rates in Africa. Thus, the insurance sector penetration statistics are considerably lower across most parts of Africa than in industrialised markets. The statistics signify a development gap in Africa's insurance markets.

The West African Region

Life insurance penetration rates are on the increase in the West African region. As shown in Fig. 24.4, the market rates drift upwards below 0.5% and are increasing moderately. The market in Togo is expanding rapidly, and together with Côte d'Ivoire, the markets hovered above 0.5% in 2014. The non-life insurance market's progression has been relatively more stable, with most markets moving between 0.4 and 0.8%. Surprisingly, Nigeria, the largest economy within the sub-region, shows market trends below the 0.2% mark for life insurance and is on the decline in terms of non-life penetration.

The depth of the credit market in the region has experienced a u-shaped trend as most markets dip between the late 1990s and the early years of the post-2000 period. Credit penetration rates are on the up and

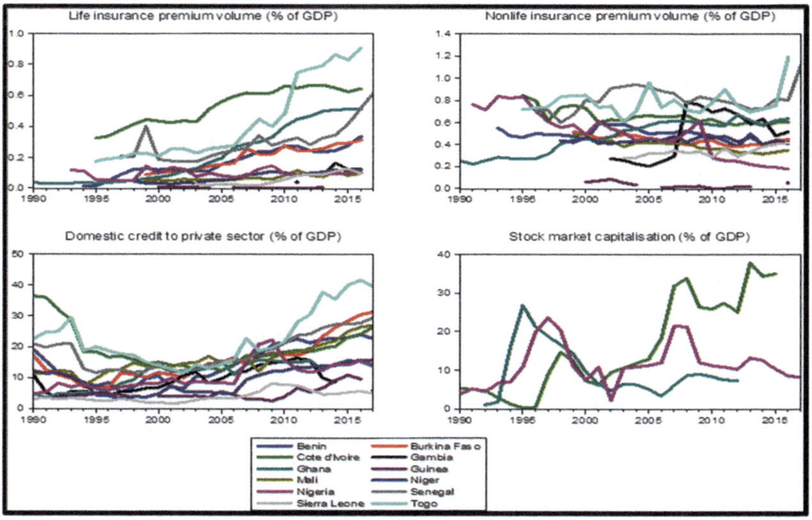

Fig. 24.4 West Africa—insurance and financial market movements between 1990 and 2017 from the GFDD. Steady increasing life insurance and domestic credit. This Figure illustrates the progression of annual market movements in life insurance (LIFE), non-life insurance (NONLIFE), bank credit (CREDIT), and the stock market (STOCK)[2]

fall between 10 and 30% in recent times. The recent increasing trend in credit provision aligns with recent increases in life insurance penetration. This can signal an increase in credit life insurance to protect banks against financial losses arising from the death or disability of debtors. For the three countries in the region with viable stock markets (Côte D'Ivoire, Ghana, and Nigeria), the experience has been mainly volatile.

The KPMG (2014) insurance industry survey report summarises the diverse characteristics of the insurance market in Africa. We present a

[2] The definition of the market indicators in the figures are: CREDIT is an annual measure of the domestic credit in the form of loans, non-equity securities, trade credits and other account receivables provided by financial intermediaries to the private sector, expressed as a percentage of GDP. STOCK represents the total stock market capitalisation value of listed shares expressed as a percentage of GDP. LIFE is the annual ratio of life insurance premium volume to GDP. NONLIFE is the annual ratio of non-life insurance premiums to GDP. PRIBOND and PUBBOND are the total market debt outstanding for private and public bonds, respectively, expressed as a proportion of GDP.

synthesis of this report here. First, the KPMG report demonstrates that the insurance sector in Nigeria is significantly fragmented into 59 insurance companies. The critical economic sector for insurance is the energy sector, where 60% of premiums emanate. Despite the large population of 169 million, only 2.25 million people are insured, and out of the 7 million vehicles, only 14% are comprehensively insured. The key impediment to insurance penetration is the industry's lack of trust due to past industry failures. The oil companies are increasingly looking at opportunities offshore for their insurance needs due to the local insurance industry's lack of capacity and skills.

In Ghana, there has been rapid growth in the insurance industry in recent times. This growth is spurred on by the steep economic growth trajectory and the discovery of oil and gas exploration opportunities. The non-life insurance companies in Ghana outnumber the life insurance companies (26 out of the registered 45). An essential consumer need in the insurance industry in Ghana is funeral insurance cover. The average funeral cost is around $6,000 and can sometimes cost as much as $20,000. As such, there is a growing need for consumers to cede this risk to the insurance industry (KPMG, 2014).

The East African Region

In the East African region, Mauritius leads the way in life insurance penetration as the rates increase rapidly from 2 to 4%, while the rest of the markets are predominantly below 1%. Although Mauritius and Kenya's non-life insurance markets are declining, they are the highest in the region, between 1.2 and 2.0% (Fig. 24.5).

The domestic credit market shows a similar pattern to the movement in the life insurance market. Mauritius leads the region, with credit increasing rapidly from about 40% in 1994 to 100% in 2014. The rest of the credit markets in the Eastern region hover below 20%. The stock markets in Kenya and Mauritius are the largest in market capitalisation: the Kenyan market hovers around 20%, whereas Mauritius's stock market has averaged 60% in recent times, as indicated in Fig. 24.5.

Mauritius has high insurance penetration rates of about 6%. The government is increasingly supportive of the industry and offers tax incentives to spur growth. Even though there are seven life insurers and 12 non-life insurance companies, the insurance market is small and dominated by the top five companies. The Bai insurance company is the largest

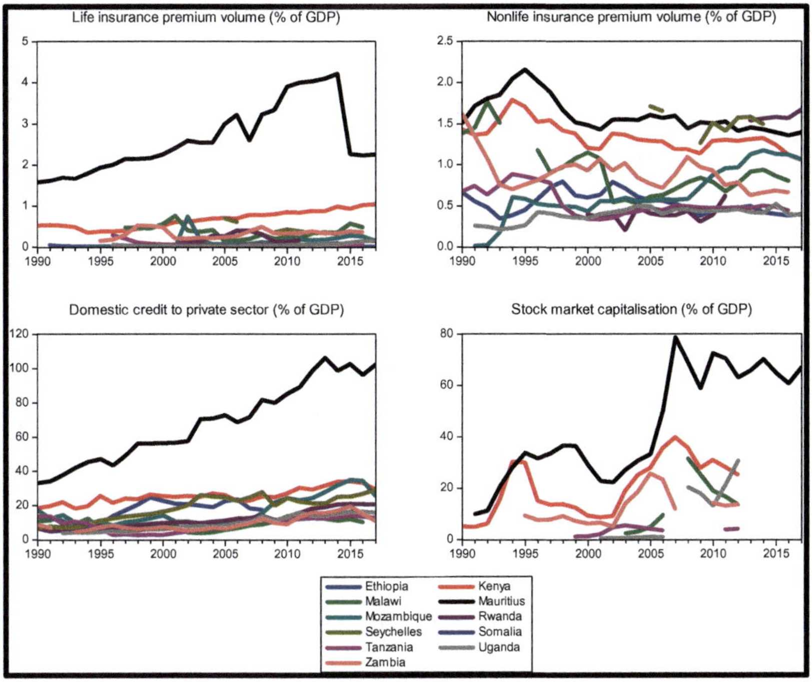

Fig. 24.5 East Africa—insurance and financial market movements between 1990 and 2017 from the GFDD. Mauritius life and credit market soaring, the rest stable. This Figure illustrates the progression of annual market movements in life insurance (LIFE), non-life insurance (NONLIFE), bank credit (CREDIT), and the stock market (STOCK)

life insurance underwriter with a market share of almost 44% (KPMG, 2014).

Kenya has a thriving non-life insurance sector that underwrites almost 66% of the total insurance business. The non-life insurance sector is dominated by vehicle insurance (about 68%), followed by medical insurance (22%) and property insurance (10%) (KPMG, 2014). The insurance industry in Zambia is underdeveloped and hampered by small, undercapitalised insurance companies. This has resulted in most international companies ceding their insurance requirements offshore to the local industry's further detriment. There are 15 general insurers, eight life

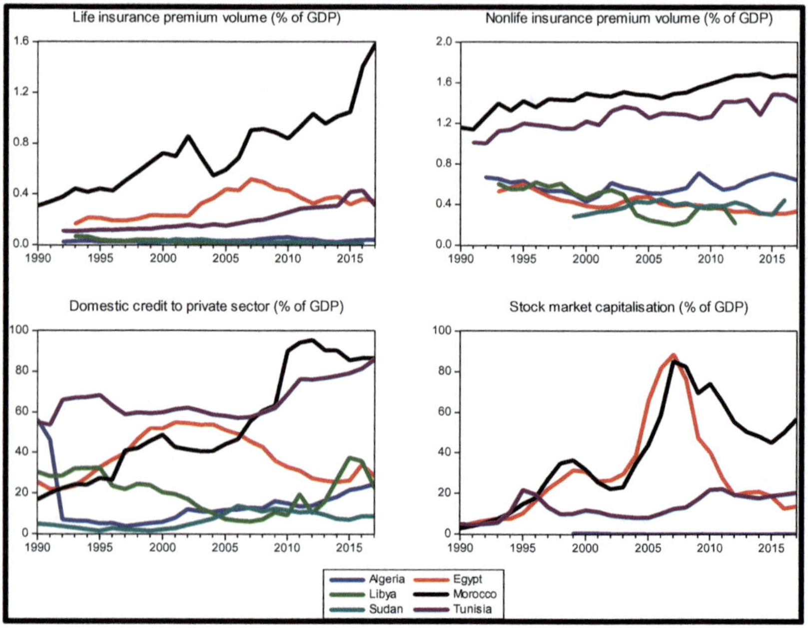

Fig. 24.6 North Africa—insurance and financial market movements between 1990 and 2017 from the GFDD. Morocco market soaring, the rest stable. This Figure illustrates the progression of annual market movements in life insurance (LIFE), non-life insurance (NONLIFE), bank credit(CREDIT), and the stock market (STOCK)

insurers, and three reinsurers in the marketplace. From the recent annual increase of 20% in business volumes, there is excellent potential to increase the insurance penetration rates to support its well-developed financial sector. In addition, the bancassurance distribution model is expected to drive growth in the insurance sector (KPMG, 2014).

The North Africa Region

Life insurance penetration rates are meagre (less than 1%) in this region of Africa. Although Morocco has experienced rapid growth, the rest of North Africa's market has been relatively more stable. In terms of non-life insurance, Morocco, and Tunisia lead with average penetration rates of about 1.5 and 1%, respectively (Fig. 24.6).

The domestic credit time series are relatively more variable than the insurance market development patterns. Again, Tunisia and Morocco lead the region at an average of 60% in 2014. Egypt and Morocco's stock markets peaked at around 80% in 2007, but they declined in recent times. Tunisia is the other country with stock market data records in the region, with stock market capitalisation rates stable at around 20% (Fig. 24.6).

For six years leading to 2010, the insurance sector in Morocco has seen an annual average increase of 10% per annum. As a result, Morocco ranks fourth in Africa in terms of insurance penetration. Penetration is boosted by a world-class banking system that promotes bancassurance partnerships to increase insurance business sales. The market is dominated by four companies that underwrite about 70% of all business. The rest of the market is fragmented with 13 insurers that underwrite 30% of the business (KPMG, 2014).

Egypt's well-developed financial services industry does not seem to augur well for its insurance sector, which has low penetration rates of less than 1%. This low penetration is attributed to the significant population of Moslems that do not support insurance consumption (empirical evidence from Beck and Webb [2003] and Trinh et al. [2016] support the assertion). Another reason is the dominance of state insurance providers relative to private insurance providers required to stimulate the market (KPMG, 2014).

The Southern Africa Region

The dominant insurance and financial hub in the Southern region are in South Africa. In recent times, the life insurance penetration rates in South Africa have hovered between 9 and 12%, at about 16% in 2000. On the other hand, the non-life insurance rates have been more stable, averaging about 2.5 and 2% post the 2005 period for South Africa and Namibia, respectively (Fig. 24.7).

Again, the patterns between the progressions of life insurance rates are similar to that of the credit market. South Africa leads at about 120% of GDP, followed by Namibia at around 40%. The stock market in South Africa experienced massive growth between 2001 and 2007. Post-2007, the rates hover between 200 and 250%. While the stock markets of Botswana and Namibia languish below the 50% mark (Fig. 24.7).

Namibia has a well-structured insurance market comprising sixteen life insurers, twelve general insurers, and two reinsurers. Despite Namibia's small population size, the insurance sector is heavily driven by foreign

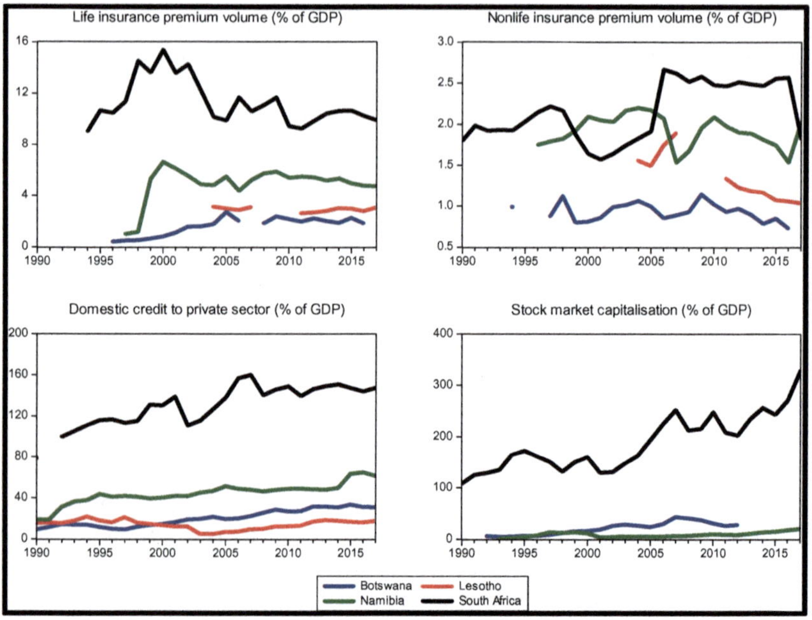

Fig. 24.7 Southern Africa—insurance and financial market movements between 1990 and 2017 from the GFDD. Markets stable, high rates in South Africa. This Figure illustrates the progression of annual market movements in life insurance (LIFE), non-life insurance (NONLIFE), bank credit (CREDIT), and the stock market (STOCK)

direct investments and wealthy citizens. The development and growth of the insurance sector are, however, constrained by the small population size (KPMG, 2014). Botswana's life insurance sector accounts for about 70% of premium income in the insurance market. The market in 2012 is represented by twenty-one general insurers and seven life insurers. The life insurance sector is dominated by the state-owned Botswana Life Insurance Limited, followed by many other companies originating in South Africa. Four companies largely dominate the general insurance market: Botswana Insurance Company, Zurich, Regent, and Mutual and Federal underwrite 75% of total business. The primary short-term insurance products in the market are motor vehicle insurance and property insurance (KPMG, 2014).

In South Africa, the insurance market is the most advanced on the continent. South Africa has a well-developed life and non-life insurance market. It ranks first in Africa in terms of its insurance penetration rate, which is also among the highest globally (KPMG, 2014). The life insurance market is about four times that of the non-life market in terms of premium income. After allowance for inflation, life insurance premium growth in South Africa slowed from 4.6% in 2014 to 2.3% in 2015. This resulted from lower regular and single premiums in a market weakened by a slowing economy and lower household incomes. The short-term outlook for the life insurance business is currently facing challenges from the weak economy. However, it should pick up in the medium term when the economy recovers. Industry practitioners' ongoing strategy is an increased marketing effort to the low-income population groups to increase and deepen life insurance outreach across this group (Sigma, 2016).

Despite the weak economy, non-life premiums in South Africa increased slightly from 0.3% growth in 2014 to 2.5% in 2015. Non-life insurers managed to increase premium rates to curb adverse claims experience from previous years. Apart from the weak economy, rising inflation, and a depreciating currency pose significant challenges to the non-life insurance industry in South Africa (Sigma, 2016).

The Central African Region

The Central African region has no reported data on stock market capitalisation in the sub-region. The life insurance penetration rates are at low levels, hovering around 0.2%. The Cameroon market is the leading indicator for life insurance. Non-life insurance penetration rates are also on average below 2%. The market in Angola shows some distorted high trends in the late 90s. However, it has since declined to low levels, as indicated in Fig. 24.8

Banks' domestic credit shows a U-shaped pattern, transitioning from relatively high levels in the early 90s to lower credit extension levels and then picking up post-2010. In recent times, the credit rates are between 10–20%, with Angola leading the progression (Fig. 24.8).

The Market Characteristics of the Highly Industrialised Nations

To place the discussion into context, we also review the market patterns in five highly advanced industrialised economies: the USA, the UK, Germany, France, and Japan. In terms of life insurance, the UK market

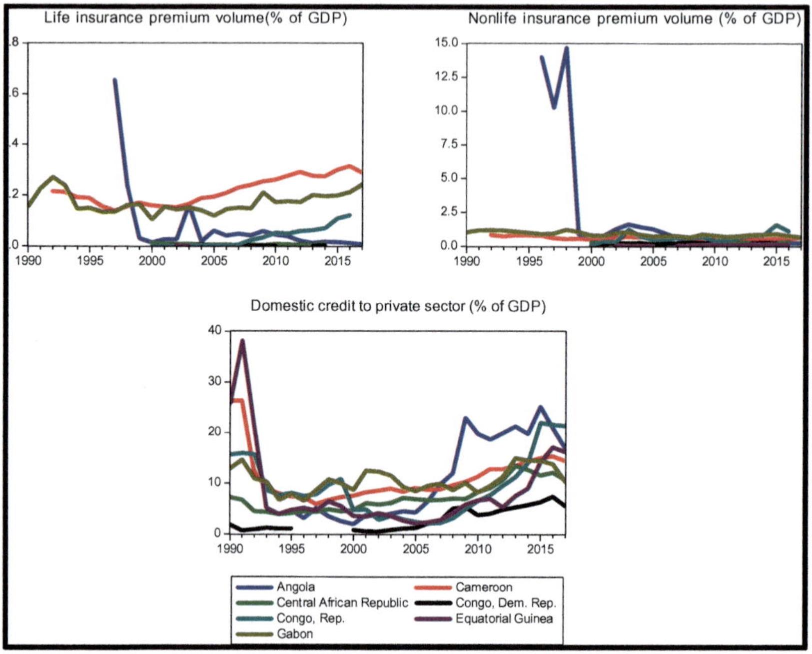

Fig. 24.8 Central Africa—insurance and financial market movements between 1990 and 2017 from the GFDD. Life insurance is climbing, the rest stable. This Figure illustrates the progression of annual market movements in life insurance (LIFE), non-life insurance (NONLIFE), and bank credit (CREDIT)

leads the group of industrialised countries. However, it declined considerably in the aftermath of the global financial crisis in 2008, from over 12% to around the 8% mark in 2015. Markets in France and Japan have also drifted upwards towards the 8% level, while the USA and Germany markets remain stable at around 3%. The time-series pattern in non-life insurance penetration rates shows the USA leading at just above 3% in 2015, followed by the UK market, which is in decline and below 2.5% in 2015. France follows at just above 2.0%, while Germany and Japan are closing in on the 2% mark (Fig. 24.9).

Bank credit extension declined in the UK after the financial crisis, dropping from around 200% to just above 120% in 2015. The decline is similar to that experienced in life insurance penetration rates but at a slower pace.

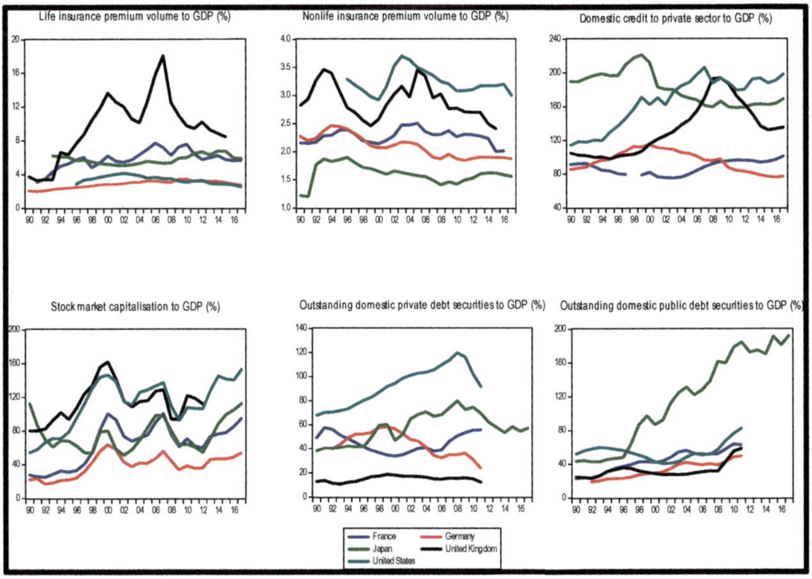

Fig. 24.9 Highly industrialised nations—insurance and financial market movements between 1990 and 2017 from the GFDD. Highest life rates in the UK and highest non-life rates in the USA. Japan's public debt above the rest and growing. US has the largest rates of private bond debt. This figure illustrates the progression of annual market movements in life insurance (LIFE), non-life insurance (NONLIFE), bank credit (CREDIT), private bonds (PRIBOND), public bonds (PUBBOND), and the stock market (STOCK)

The USA and Japan credit markets have remained steady in recent times, just below the 200% point in 2015, while Germany and France have lower credit rates, around 80%. The stock market capitalisation movements present some correlated patterns: the USA and UK markets are closely aligned and have the highest market indicators, averaging around 120% in recent times. France and Japan's markets follow a similar trajectory, drifting upwards to about 80% in 2015. Germany remains stable, hovering around 40% (Fig. 24.9).

Japan has seen rapid growth in the value of public domestic bonds, as shown in Fig. 24.9. The market approached the 200% mark in 2015. The rest of the highly industrialised nations were hovering around 50% in 2010. In terms of the value of outstanding private (corporate) issued

Table 24.2 Correlation matrix of market parameters for Africa

	Bank	*Life*	*Nonlife*	*Stocks*
Bank_Credit	1.00			
Life_Insurance	0.78a	1.00		
Nonlife_Insurance	0.75a	0.70a	1.00	
Stocks	0.83a	0.81a	0.58a	1.00

This table reports the Pearson correlation coefficients. The symbols a, b, and c denote significance at 1, 5, and 10%, respectively of the correlation coefficient (ρ) equal to zero where the null hypothesis is $\rho = 0$, and the alternative is $\rho \neq 0$

bonds, Japan is second among the industrialised countries, declining in recent times to about 50% in 2015. USA private bonds lead the group but decline rapidly after 2008 to low rates below 80% after 2010 (Fig. 24.9).

In comparing the five highly industrialised markets to the market patterns in Africa, we note the following key differences. First, both the insurance sector and financial market statistics are at a much lower scale and can be considered in their primary stages of development across most parts of Africa. Second, there is a more significant correlation between insurance and the other market components in Africa than we note for the panel of highly industrialised countries. This supports the KPMG (2014) assertion of significant integration between the insurance and the financial market components in Africa. In particular, the patterns between insurance and bank credit are substantially significant in Africa. Lastly, we report a greater correlation between the stock market and insurance than between insurance and the progression of bank credit in the advanced industrialised countries (see Tables 24.2 and24.3).

24.4 Challenges and Opportunities in the African Insurance Markets

As earlier noted, insurance coverage has many economic beneficial outcomes that shield against potential financial losses. Hence, this chapter aims to identify policy initiatives leading to greater insurance penetration and consumption in Africa. This is because the development and growth in the insurance industry can contribute to maximising the economic growth potential from insurance protection.

Table 24.3 Correlation matrix of market parameters for the five highly industrialised countries

	Bank	*Life*	*Non-Life*	*Private*	*Public*	*Stocks*
Bank_Credit	1.00					
Life_Insurance	0.11	1.00				
Nonlife_Insurance	−0.01	0.14	1.00			
Private _Bonds	0.47a	−0.50a	0.07	1.00		
Public_Bonds	0.44a	0.004	−0.59a	0.34a	1.00	
Stocks	0.38a	0.51a	0.53a	0.11	0.04	1.00

This table reports the Pearson correlation coefficients. The symbols a, b, and c denote significance at 1, 5, and 10%, respectively of the correlation coefficient (ρ) equal to zero where the null hypothesis is $\rho = 0$, and the alternative is $\rho \neq 0$

An analysis by Trust Re (2014) highlights the key strengths, weaknesses, opportunities, and threats to the African insurance market. We discuss these here. Among the key strengths of Africa's insurance market are the sector's profitability and general support from reinsurers and the government in growing business volumes. On the other hand, the market is weakened by several factors including low insurance penetration rates, low disposable incomes, "undercutting" of premiums, limited appetite and culture for insurance, lack of technical skills in underwriting and pricing, poor regulation of the industry, inconsistency in financial reporting and a general lack of credible claims data for pricing. There are significant challenges to future growth from the lack of skilled insurance professionals, a lack of understanding of insurance benefits, excessive market competition, and inadequate product differentiation (AIB, 2016; Trust Re, 2014; Tyson, 2015).

There are also potential opportunities for growth of the African insurance market stemming from the rapid growth of the middle class and GDP in African economies, new energy exploits, infrastructure development, foreign investments, innovation, and distribution supported through mobile communications and the potential increase in business volumes through legislated compulsory insurance products (AIB, 2016; Nnadozie, 2003; Trust Re, 2014; Tyson, 2015). The AIB (2016) market report further asserts that Africa's low insurance penetration rates present ample growth opportunities. This stems from the report's higher global average insurance penetration rate of about 3% for emerging markets and the lesser rate of 1% reported for most African countries. Thus, the market expects new product development initiatives in agriculture, microinsurance, life insurance, and medical care to close the gap. Furthermore, according to executive opinion from interviewees in the AIB (2016) report, the economic growth boom before 2014 on the African continent has enhanced the insurance sector. The sector made significant strides from tighter regulation, improved distribution channels provided through bancassurance and recent mobile telecommunication networks.

However, potential threats to the insurance industry stem from the impact of regulation on small market players and the effects of high claims incidence crippling the industry. Furthermore, there are ongoing issues around the under-capitalisation and capacity of local players. This is a result of many small market players. Other threats include political and social instability and the repatriation of insurance revenue abroad to the detriment of local economies. The reliance on foreign market players is inevitable in some scenarios but can sabotage the growth of the local insurance industry (AIB, 2016; Tyson, 2015; Trust Re, 2014).

The structural deficiencies in the broader financial sector, in general, is an additional source of concern. Africa's stock (equity) markets are primarily thin and offer little liquidity for African investors. The market depth in market capitalisation and listing is a significant concern. Most of the markets are plagued by inefficient manual operating systems for trading and clearance of sales. The top two markets are in Egypt and South Africa, with the rest of Africa's national stock exchanges burdened by inefficiencies. There is a growing policy directive to grow the national stock exchanges to improve confidence and liquidity (Allen et al., 2011; Yartey & Adjasi, 2007). The stock market can be a source of long-term inflation-protected investment returns, especially for life insurers exposed to long-term liabilities.

The African banking system is primarily dominated by state-owned banks and other large banks that are foreign owned. The central banks and deposit-taking banks are the leading banks. The low levels of credit extension are attributed to the tendency of banks to invest in local treasury bills and other government securities. The sector is undergoing rapid reforms through privatisation and restructuring of state banks to improve the quality of banking services. The banking sectors of Nigeria, Botswana, Malawi, Seychelles, and South Africa are advanced and well capitalised (Allen et al., 2011; Nnadozie, 2003). Bank credit products are significant drivers of the insurance market. As such, the low credit extension in some African markets dampens the insurance market.

Except for the bond markets in Southern Africa, the bond market is at a nascent developmental stage in most African economies. The dearth of the African continent's domestic government and corporate bond markets does not augur well for the region's financial sector. South Africa has a mature bond market originating in the 1980s with a trading platform that is comparable to most advanced nations. Botswana also has a successful bond trading exchange (Allen et al., 2011; Mu et al., 2013; Yartey & Adjasi, 2007). The medium- to long-term fixed-income bond benefits provides guarantees for insurers to manage their medium to long-term risks.

24.5 Regulatory Implications of the Insurance Markets

This section highlights and discusses the extent of Africa's compliance to several regulatory benchmarks and their implications. Insurance markets in Africa that fail to adhere to international regulatory and supervisory standards can lead to the market distortions and inefficiencies identified in Sect. 24.4. Therefore, regulatory reforms are required to correct the market irregularities and instil market confidence. Well-regulated insurance industries provide the necessary support for long-term investments and economic growth Munro and Snyman (1995), Focarelli (2017), and Thels (2015).

The International Association of Insurance Supervisors (IAIS) designs industry benchmarks known as insurance core principles (ICPs). The principles provide guidelines on best practices in insurance sector supervision, including the fair treatment of consumers, the conduct of insurance intermediaries, investment strategies, solvency valuation bases, and capital adequacy requirements. The ICPs provide the highest level of standards for the prudential supervision of financially sound insurers to protect the interest of policyholders and all other stakeholders. IAIS (2018) provides a complete description of all the standards.

Given the market challenges in Africa, most countries are unable to meet the standards of the ICPs. Bhoola et al. (2014) observe the market compliance of several African countries to the IAIS benchmarks. The sample countries included Kenya, Uganda, Tanzania, Rwanda, Burundi, Ghana, Nigeria, and Botswana. Although there were some successes, most countries failed to achieve the standards as set out in Fig. 24.10. From

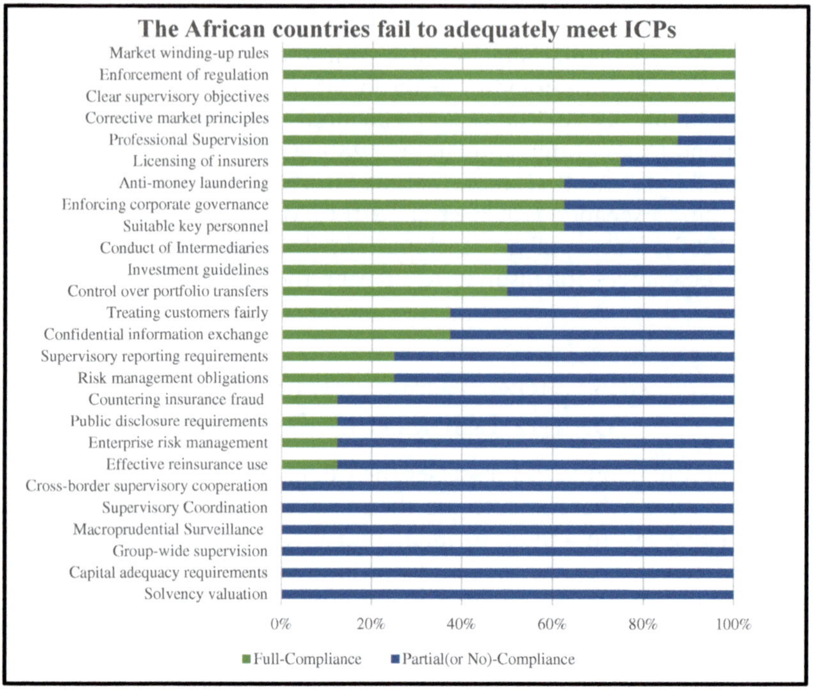

Fig. 24.10 Proportion of countries complying with ICPs. *Note* The Figure illustrates the proportion of compliance to the insurance core principles (ICPs) among 8 African countries. Full compliance indicates that standards are observed or predominantly observed, while partial compliance demonstrates partial or no compliance within the insurance industry

Fig. 24.10, we note that all eight countries failed to meet the supervisory standards for the valuation of assets and liabilities. Without a regular solvency check, insurers run the risk of failing to monitor and reserve adequately for their risks. Insurers may then become insolvent to the detriment of their customers and the stakeholders at large. Moreover, all insurers in the countries sampled fail to hold adequate capital reserves to manage their risks.

Furthermore, the countries did not have the supervisory clout required to manage and oversee large insurance groups. Macroprudential oversight requirements and the coordination of supervision with other supervisory bodies across local and cross-border entities were also lacking. The lack of adequate oversight breeds irregularities and malpractices that lowers confidence in the insurance industry.

Also of some concern is the inadequacies in reinsurance standards, public disclosure of information, fraud management, and enterprise risk management practices in the insurance industry. Only one country out of the eight had suitable processes in place to counter insurance fraud. These shortcomings noticed in the insurance industry for the eight countries that underwrite substantial insurance levels on the continent are a projection of the state of regulation in Africa and, hence, the need for regulatory reforms.

The regulatory shortfalls noted require suitable market interventions to correct the inefficiencies. Even though most African economies' insurance and financial sector are in their primary stages of development, regulatory reforms are critical to instilling public confidence and trust. For example, the statutory solvency valuation of insurers is required at regular intervals to demonstrate to supervisors and the public their ability to counter the liabilities that arise from risks underwritten. Such valuation will encourage insurers to hold assets that are appropriate to their mix of liabilities.

Equally crucial for the insurance industry is the need to comply with the capital adequacy demands of the business. Without adequate capital provision, insurers risk not meeting their policyholder obligations when exposed to unforeseen circumstances. Supervisors therefore need to set standardised capital targets for insurers with appropriate trigger mechanisms for supervisory intervention if breached.

In contrast to the solvency and stability standards of the traditional insurance markets, the regulatory interventions in the vast microinsurance industry in Africa requires a more growth-focused approach. The microinsurance sector has great growth potential for low-income groups that cannot afford traditional insurance products. Hence the industry requires consumer surveys and analyses that create microinsurance awareness and opportunities to structure products and procedures for low-income consumers. Also, the microinsurance distribution channels in Africa, such as mobile networks that are increasing, need to be regulated to maintain the trust of low-income households. Lastly, there is a need for grievance and resolution systems specifically modelled for low-income policyholders to peruse. Given its limited resources, regulatory reforms in the African market should carefully seek to balance out the need for market growth and market solvency (IAIS, 2017).

Therefore, to avoid any unintended consequences, a holistic and balanced approach is required when introducing reforms. This is because market regulation reforms can negatively affect market practice and behaviour, leading to a decrease in insurance consumption. As such, regulatory reforms should avoid the excessive increase in insurers' administrative costs that are likely to be passed on to consumers through higher premiums. In the same way, regulators need to exercise less control over the levels of insurance cover provided or demanded, as this can stifle market innovation and competition. Also, overly restrictive rules over insurance intermediaries can have similar adverse effects. The regulatory framework needs to instigate market conditions that allow insurers to invest efficiently without enforcing stringent product designs that impede investment freedom (Thels, 2015; Van Rossum, 2005).

24.6 Conclusion and Market Recommendations

The insurance industry's growth can fill the gap for long-term domestic capital funding and economic growth in Africa. Although Africa's premium volumes and insurance penetration rates lag behind the more advanced economies, there is ample potential for future growth through the rapid growth of the African middle class, infrastructure development, and other development gaps that exist on the continent. We therefore conclude by discussing market recommendations for more outstanding prospects from the African insurance industry.

As highlighted in the description of the insurance and financial market patterns, the market depth of the African financial sector lags far behind the developed markets. In particular, the absence and low development of the long-term capital markets do not promote growth in the insurance sector and the build-up of substantial long-term capital. All the same, regulators need to enforce insurance asset allocation strategies that reflect the right balance between short and long-term investments in line with their insurance risks. This reduces the risks associated with refinancing and reinvestment of short-term assets. Moreover, it will enable African markets to close the gap on the sale and management of long-term financial risk products. Thus, investment strategies for insurers need to incorporate asset-liability models that ensure that short- and long-term product liabilities are adequately matched with appropriate investments in the financial markets.

In particular, the availability of domestic bond markets can provide new market opportunities to underwrite retirement annuity benefits and other long-term insurance products that require investments in long-term secure tradeable fixed-interest investments. The insurance markets in developed economies have substantial investment allocations in the bond market. Thus, this domestic investment asset's unavailability and inefficiencies of the bond market (and the stock market) can be detrimental to most African markets' insurance industry.

The regulatory enforcement of pricing, reserving, and financial reporting standards is critical in African insurance markets. This will instil greater confidence and trust in the insurance system for consumers, investors, and other stakeholders. In addition, there is a need for skilled insurance personnel, actuarial skills, underwriting, claims management, and appropriate insurance administration and information systems in most African markets. Without these, the insurance sector's value proposition falls further behind the banks leading to greater reliance on precautionary savings than on insurance. This is reflected in the wider margins between insurance and bank penetration rates in African market trajectories relative to those in developed markets.

The usual market practice of seeking out the expertise of global reinsurers is a step in the right direction in closing the skills gap. So is the additional investment in human resource development and training to bridge the skills gap. Regulators can also ensure that certified fit and proper personnel are employed in key positions in the insurance workplace. In addition, the availability and presence of an effective national insurance ombudsman can provide the necessary oversight and boost consumer confidence in making insurance consumption decisions. This will ensure that all market irregularities are adequately reported and investigated to protect vulnerable consumers.

Affordability and accessibility of insurance is a key hindrance for the financially marginalised populace in Africa. Without appropriate structured products for this market, many of the populace will remain excluded and vulnerable to various risks. Thus, to provide inclusive insurance market solutions that increase the risk pool and hence insurance consumption, a structured marketing and management approach is required to develop the microinsurance market. The drive for microinsurance should however not be limited to only agriculture, health, and funeral insurance products. It requires a broader set of insurance products that meet consumers' need for savings, non-life insurance, retirement, and other vital products.

To contain the risk of considerable adverse claims experience due to adverse selection by consumers and moral hazards, insurers require more excellent monitoring of consumer behaviour and superior claims assessment and management. Furthermore, the industry needs a flexible premium regime that adequately provides premium holidays and premium arrangements that do not quickly erode insurance benefits due to the non-payment of premiums. A more client-focused approach is required to identify niche market opportunities that meet the needs of potential consumers to increase the weak insurance penetration rates in Africa.

Furthermore, regulators need to ensure that insurers are adequately capitalised to take advantage of the available market opportunities. Such measures will encourage the merging of smaller players in the market-place and reduce the level of market fragmentation currently experienced. For example, to counter losing business to foreign insurers, local insurers need to increase their capacity to absorb risk from potential foreign direct investments and provide innovative insurance solutions for the ever-growing Africa diaspora market.

For greater outreach and protection, there are justifications for compulsory insurance for consumers that protect the public. For example, third-party vehicle insurance is a minimum mandatory requirement for vehicle owners in some jurisdictions. Compulsory group life or funeral insurance for employees is also becoming a standard provision in remuneration packages.

In addition, the bancassurance distribution model has great potential for the African market. It allows insurers to use the expansive and well-established banking infrastructure and distribution platforms across the African region. These established distribution channels can provide cost savings to insurers to provide greater premium affordability for consumers. The pricing of insurance and establishing adequate reserve estimates for claims and other provisions require a vast data source of historical experiences. Thus, data vendors and data-sharing platforms need to compile and provide periodic pertinent market information on the local insurance industry. Such a database can also help identify niche target groups for increasing the pool of insured risks.

There is a requirement to step up insurance and personal financial education as they are vital to the insurance industry in Africa. The terms and conditions of insurance policies, what is covered and what is not covered, premium affordability, and consumers' needs require proper understanding before consumers' uptake and signage of contracts. Equally relevant is a more excellent grasp of the value of surrender and paid-up benefits on insurance policies and what they mean throughout the insurance contract's cover period. There is also an urgent requirement for greater transparency in the charges and commission payments taken off the insurance policy contracts.

References

AIB. (2016). *Africa insurance barometer [Online]*. https://pdf4pro.com/view/market-survey-african-insurance-e2f20.html

Akinlo, T. (2013). The causal relationship between insurance and economic growth in Nigeria (1986–2010). *Australian Journal of Business and Management Research, 2*(12), 49.

Alhassan, A. L., & Fiador, V. (2014). Insurance-growth nexus in Ghana: An autoregressive distributed lag bounds cointegration approach. *Review of Development Finance, 4*(2), 83–96.

Allen, F., Otchere, I., & Senbet, L. W. (2011). African financial systems: A review. *Review of Development Finance, 1*(2), 79–113.

Arena, M. (2008). Does insurance market activity promote economic growth? A cross-country study for industrialised and developing countries. *Journal of Risk and Insurance, 75*(4), 921–946.

Beck, T., & Webb, I. (2003). Economic, demographic, and institutional determinants of life insurance consumption across countries. *The World Bank Economic Review, 17*(1), 51–88.

Bhoola, K., Madzhadzhi, T., Narayan, J., Strydom, S., & Heerden, H. (2014, October). Insurance regulation in Africa: Impact on insurance and growth strategies. In *Actuarial society of South Africa's 2014 convention, Cape Town, South Africa* (pp. 22–23).

Chen, P. F., Lee, C. C., & Lee, C. F. (2012). How does the development of the life insurance market affect economic growth? Some international evidence. *Journal of International Development, 24*(7), 865–893.

Darrat, A. F. (1999). Are financial deepening and economic growth causally related? Another look at the evidence. *International Economic Journal, 13*(3), 19–35.

Das, U. S., Davies, N., & Podpiera, R. (2003). *Insurance and issues in financial soundness* (International Monetary Fund Working Paper WP/03/138).

De Soto, H. (2000). *The mystery of capital: Why capitalism triumphs in the West and fails everywhere else*. Civitas Books.

Eling, M., Pradhan, S., & Schmit, J. T. (2014). The determinants of microinsurance demand. *The Geneva Papers on Risk and Insurance—Issues and Practice, 39*(2), 224–263.

Focarelli, D. (2017). Why insurance regulation is crucial for long-term investment and economic growth. In *Insurance regulation in the European Union* (pp. 339–359). Palgrave Macmillan.

Haiss, P., & Sümegi, K. (2008). The relationship between insurance and economic growth in Europe: A theoretical and empirical analysis. *Empirica, 35*(4), 405–431.

Han, L., Li, D., Moshirian, F., & Tian, Y. (2010). Insurance development and economic growth. *The Geneva Papers on Risk and Insurance Issues and Practice, 35*(2), 183–199.

IAIS. (2017). *Issues in regulation and supervision of microinsurance [Online]*. https://www.iaisweb.org/file/34275/issues-paper-in-regulation-and-superv sion-of-microinsurancejune-2007

IAIS. (2018). *Insurance core principles.* https://www.iaisweb.org/page/sup ervisory-material/insurance-core-principles/file/77910/all-adopted-icps-upd ated-november-2018

KPMG. (2014). *The South African insurance industry survey 2014.* https:// assets.kpmg/content/dam/kpmg/za/pdf/2016/11/2014-Insurance-survey. pdf

Kugler, M., & Ofoghi, R. (2005, September). Does insurance promote economic growth? Evidence from the UK. In *Money Macro and Finance (MMF) Research Group Conference* (Vol. 8). Retrieved from https://ideas.repec.org/ p/mmf/mmfc05/8.html

Jahromi, P. B., & Goudarzi, H. (2014). The study of co-integration and casual relationship between macroeconomic variables and insurance penetration ratio. *Asian Economic and Financial Review, 4*(7), 853.

Lee, C. C., Lee, C. C., & Chiu, Y. B. (2013). The link between life insurance activities and economic growth: Some new evidence. *Journal of International Money and Finance, 32*, 405–427.

Levine, R. (1997). Financial development and economic growth: Views and agenda. *Journal of Economic Literature, 35*(2), 688–726.

Mu, Y., Stotsky, J. G., & Phelps, P. (2013). Bond markets in Africa. *Review of Development Finance, 3*(3), 121–135.

Munro, A. R., & Snyman, A. M. (1995). The life insurance industry in South Africa. *Geneva Papers on Risk and Insurance: Issues and Practice, 20*(2), 127–140.

Muye, I. M., & Hassan, A. F. S. (2016). Does Islamic insurance development promote economic growth? A panel data analysis. *Procedia Economics and Finance, 35*, 368–373.

Nnadozie, E. (Ed.). (2003). *Africa economic development*. Emerald Group Publishing.

Sigma. (2016). *World insurance in 2015: Steady growth amid regional disparities*. Prepared by Swiss Re [Online]. www.swissre.com/sigma

Sigma. (2018). *World insurance in 2017: Solid, but mature life markets weigh on growth*. Prepared by Swiss Re [Online]. www.swissre.com/sigma

Sigma. (2019). *World insurance: The great pivot east continues*. Prepared by Swiss Re. www.swissre.com/sigma

Swain, R., & Swallow, D. (2015). The prudential regulation of insurers under Solvency II. *Bank of England Quarterly Bulletin Q2, 55*(2), 139–152.

Thels, A. (2015). Regulation in the insurance industry: Opportunities and challenges from an economic perspective. *Economic Issues and Analyses*, 7.

Thimann, C. (2016). Views on insurance, regulation and the macro environment. In J. Ulbrich, C-C. Hedrich, & M. Balling (Eds.), *The SSM at 1, SUERF conference proceedings* 2016/3 (pp. 79–86).

Trinh, T., Nguyen, X., & Sgro, P. (2016). Determinants of non-life insurance expenditure in developed and developing countries: An empirical investigation. *Applied Economics, 48*(58), 5639–5653.

Trust Re. (2014). *The outlook for insurance and reinsurance in sub-Saharan Africa*. Prepared by Trust Re. https://www.trustre.com/uploads/media_centre/research_surveys/TheOutlookForInsurance.pdf

Tyson, J. E. (2015). *Life insurance markets in Sub-Saharan Africa*. Overseas Development Institute.

UNCTAD. (2007). *United Nations conference on trade and development trade and development aspects of insurance* [Online]. https://unctad.org/system/files/official-document/ditctncd20074_en.pdf

Van Rossum, A. (2005). Regulation and insurance economics. *The Geneva Papers on Risk and Insurance-Issues and Practice, 30*(1), 43–46.

Ward, D., & Zurbruegg, R. (2000). Does insurance promote economic growth? Evidence from OECD countries. *Journal of Risk and Insurance, 67*(4), 489–506.

Webb, I. P., Grace, M. F., & Skipper, H. D. (2002). *The effect of banking and insurance on the growth of capital and output* (Center for risk management and insurance working Paper No. 02–1). Robinson College of Business, Georgia State University, Atlanta.

Yartey, C. A., & Adjasi, C. K. (2007). *Stock market development in Sub-Saharan Africa: Critical issues and challenges* (IMF Working Paper No. 07/209). IMF.

CHAPTER 25

Pension Markets in Africa

Kathryn A. A. O. Assefuah, Nthabiseng Moleko, and Joshua Yindenaba Abor

25.1 Introduction

The sustainability of the traditional pay-as-you-go (PAYG) pension systems of many countries across the world has been affected by demographic change in terms of improved life expectancy and reduced fertility rates. Under the PAYG or unfunded scheme, the reduction in pension contributions from the working class does not provide adequate funding

K. A. A. O. Assefuah (✉)
University of Professional Studies, Accra, Ghana
e-mail: assefuah.kathryn@upsamail.edu.gh

N. Moleko
University of Stellenbosch Business School, Cape Town, South Africa
e-mail: nthabisengm@usb.ac.za

J. Y. Abor
Department of Finance, Univeristy of Ghana Business School, Accra, Ghana
e-mail: joshabor@ug.edu.gh

J. Y. Abor and C. K. D. Adjasi (eds.), *The Economics of Banking and Finance in Africa*, Palgrave Macmillan Studies in Banking and Financial Institutions, https://doi.org/10.1007/978-3-031-04162-4_25

to take care of the retirement benefits of the retired. As a result, countries are reforming their pension systems towards partial or full funding schemes. Another rationale for reforms is the fact that funded pension schemes play an important role in the economic development process by promoting capital markets development. It is believed that a well-developed pension market provides the foundation for increased demand for capital market instruments, thus ensuring the development of the capital market.

A number of African countries have also initiated policy reforms of their pension systems in response to the need for introducing systems of social protection to assist in alleviating demographic pressures and poverty amongst the elderly. Also, the need for reform is in response to the fact that the current pension systems in Africa are associated with heavy fiscal burden. That is the existing pension systems tend to crowd out expenditure in other important areas such as education, health, and infrastructure.

The existing pension systems in Africa have very low coverage, usually, below 5% of the population. These are typically made up of civil servants and or a few well-paid formal sector employees. The existing pension systems are also very regressive with cross-subsidies expected from indirect taxes, as payments of pension benefits often outweigh pension contributions (Stewart & Yermo, 2009). Apart from the main rationale of addressing the demographic pressure as well as the fiscal burden of pension benefits, in many of these African countries, an important motivation for pension reform was the need to allow for private participation in the pensions industry and also improve on the governance system and management of the pension system. This was to ensure the effectiveness and efficiency of the entire pension system (Raichura, 2008).

After implementing reforms in various African countries for some time now, it is important to be informed of the landscape of pension systems in Africa. In this chapter, we examine the role of pension markets in Africa, reforms of the pension systems, and an overview of pension systems in Africa. We also discuss the contributions of pension markets to capital market development and the challenges confronting pension markets in Africa. The remainder of the chapter is structured as follows. Section 25.2 discusses the general role of pension markets. Section 25.3 discusses pension reforms in Africa. Section 25.4 provides an overview of pension systems in Africa. Section 25.5 examines pension markets and linkages with capital markets. Section 25.6 investigates the challenges confronting pension markets in Africa, and finally, Sect. 25.7 concludes the paper with some policy recommendations.

25.2 The Role of Pension Markets

The pension markets play a number of important roles in the economy, including establishing attractive pension schemes, mobilising and pooling national savings, facilitating financial market development, ensuring corporate governance and monitoring of firms, supporting infrastructure development, supporting the housing finance market, and financing green growth initiatives. We discuss these in turn.

Establishing Attractive Pension Schemes for Staff

Pension funds play an important role by establishing schemes that assist firms to attract high-quality staff and also minimise employee turnover. The pension schemes can also help in rewarding and retaining competent and high-performing employees (a concept known as business or commercial expediency). Managers can use pension schemes as a negative reward to get rid of old and inefficient staff, whose continuous stay in the organisation constitutes a burden and could result in huge losses to the organisation. In attracting well-qualified staff and also retaining current high-performing ones, for instance, defined-benefit pension plans, which have inherent insurance feature, are often used. Defined benefit plans provide a guarantee for employees' income level during retirement, since their rights to accumulated pension benefits increase depending on their length of service. Also, managers are able to minimise employee turnover by increasing how long an employee must stay in service in order to be entitled to accrued pension benefits. A good pension scheme generally assures employees of future financial stability and this increases their morale for higher productivity.

Mobilising and Pooling of National Savings

An important role of pension funds is to raise long-term savings through pension contributions and allocating them to productive sectors of the economy. Pension funds are required to receive pension contributions from employees and employers and invest these funds to be able to pay future retirement benefits to pensioners upon retirement. Pension funds play an intermediation role by mobilising savings through pension contributions and channelling them for investment. The intermediation role played by pension funds is useful for the efficient allocation of resources to the productive sectors of the economy. A vibrant pensions market will aid an effective mobilisation of savings as well as ensure the efficient allocation of the resources to support productive and economic activities. Pension funds are able to raise more savings under a mandatory pension scheme.

Facilitating Financial Market Development

Pension funds also play a significant role in financial market development, especially in developing countries like Africa, which have underdeveloped financial markets. They facilitate access to finance for production, thus contributing to the economic growth process. Pension funds, like any contractual savings institution, often act as institutional investors. They are very active in the financial market, especially in the capital market and typically invest in instruments like shares and bonds. Through their active participation in the market, they are able to assist in developing the financial market in terms of the level of activity and liquidity. They are also able to help improve financial markets operation by enhancing the efficiency and transparency of the market. For instance, pension funds can push for the modernisation of the markets' trading systems. They can also pressurise banks to introduce financial innovations or adopt innovative banking practices. It is important to however caution that a very high and abrupt demand for domestic assets by pension funds could distort the market and thus needs to be carefully managed. Pension funds also help to improve the performance of life insurance firms as such funds are invested in annuity products for pensioners during retirement.

Ensuring Corporate Governance and Monitoring of Firms

Pension funds have a huge influence on corporate governance because of the size and nature of their portfolios. They mostly manage huge amounts in assets and typically hold diversified portfolio by investing in different sectors of the economy. As institutional investors and blockholders, pension funds engage in shareholder activism to check the opportunistic behaviour of managers of their investee companies. Apart from private negotiations, pension funds often use voting at annual or special shareholder meetings, as one of the most direct means of affecting corporate decisions. They can also push for a change in the composition of the board or even request a seat on the board. Institutional investors like pension funds, generally, tend to be effective monitors of corporate behaviour than individual investors (who often hold a small percentage of companies' shares). Pension funds have the expertise and economies of scale necessary for verifying and monitoring projects and firms. They are capable of monitoring the performance of managers of their investee companies and have investment departments with requisite expertise to track the performance of the investments in the various companies. Therefore, they are able to take appropriate governance actions as and when necessary.

Supporting Infrastructure Development

Infrastructure development is recognised as one of the key determinants of economic development. The continuous need for infrastructure development has led to heightened interest of private sector finance providers in infrastructure projects across the globe. The relatively large size of pension funds, their long-term investment horizon and the focus on domestic assets are gradually attracting policymakers' attention on the need to leverage pension assets to support infrastructure financing (Sy, 2017). With the substantial infrastructure gap and governments' inability to raise enough public finance to support infrastructure development, especially in developing regions like Africa, pension funds are focussing attention in investing in such alternative assets. These investments cover a wide range of infrastructural projects (i.e. from economic infrastructure such as transportation, telecommunication, and energy, to social infrastructure such as health, education, and housing). Pension funds in a number of African countries like Cape Verde, Kenya, South Africa, Swaziland, Tanzania, and Uganda are actively investing in infrastructure projects.

Pension funds are seeking better returns for their investments in order to cater for the retirement benefits of pensioners and therefore are moving into such new asset classes. Considering the long-term nature of pension assets, pension funds are able to match their investments in infrastructure with their assets and at the same time enjoy the benefits of diversification. Pension funds, in the past, invested in infrastructure through listed utility companies or real estate portfolios. However, in recent times, they are investing through private equity funds and sometimes even directly. Investment in infrastructure has now become the new focus of institutional investors like pension funds. They are moving beyond the traditional asset classes like bonds, shares, cash, and real estate and are indeed seeking fresh source of returns and better diversification of risk. Pension funds are spreading their investments across a wider range of investments in infrastructure than they previously did and in the process, they are contributing significantly to infrastructure development, which is necessary for spurring inclusive growth.

Supporting the Housing Finance Market

Access to decent and affordable housing is considered a basic necessity of life and a fundamental human right. However, in many developing countries like those in Africa, a huge housing deficit exists, with many people struggling to find affordable accommodation. The lack of adequate financing for the acquisition and development of housing has significantly contributed to this situation in these countries. The mortgage finance markets, for instance, are well developed in advanced economies and are able to support the housing market, but the situation is different in sub-Saharan Africa (SSA). Mortgage finance is still at its budding stage in Africa and coupled with the stringent requirements, most working people even have difficulty in accessing mortgage finance. Pension funds play an important role in housing provision by supplying the funding to support housing development for the public and especially for pension fund contributors. Most contributors of pension funds in SSA live in poor environments, they are unable to acquire their own houses, and are often exposed to more suffering during retirement. Pension funds are able to pool and accumulate long-term savings and channel such funds in the housing finance market, which can help in alleviating the housing challenges confronting SSA.

Financing Green Growth Initiatives

Pension funds, like other institutional investors, have a significant role to play in financing green growth initiatives (Jones & Hiller, 2010). There are two different types of funds that are considering green projects. One is the growth in "Socially Responsible Investing" (SRI), which has increased the demand for ethical, including green, projects by "ethical funds" (Della

Croce et al., 2011). SRI involves making investment decisions that incorporate Environmental, Social and Governance (ESG) issues. The second is that pension funds may be looking beyond the fact that projects are green to showing interest in projects that offer attractive returns, taking the associated risk into consideration. Some large pension funds are already allocating funds into green investment either directly or through private equity. Such direct investment is often an option for huge pension funds because they tend to have considerable expertise and in-house resources to do this. Smaller pension funds on other hand may make asset allocation into such investment projects through structured finance, green equity or green bonds. Pension fund generally seek lower risk investments, which have steady, inflation-adjusted returns. Though pension funds investment into green projects is currently low, the availability of opportunities and green instruments has the potential of increasing pension funds' asset allocation into such areas.

25.3 Pension Reforms in Africa

The main purpose of pension systems is to encourage the population to smooth consumption over their lives, thus saving income now to provide for their retirement. Where they are unable to save, the state would finance the poor with income through non-contributory schemes (Holzmann, 1999; Rhodes & Natali, 2003; Uthoff, 2006). The structural economic, labour, and political characteristics in many African countries often give rise to specific risks and challenges. In Africa, demographic indicators including old-age dependency rate, median population age, and life expectancy are important considerations for developing pension systems, and in future decisions that would lead to reforms. Pension reform seeks to reduce the demographic, political, and macro-economic risks that arise, reducing the ability to provide income for the old aged in their retirement (Holzmann, 1999). The structural characteristics of a country are important in identification of these risks and the demographic transition of less developed regions shows indicators are not homogenous. Although the entire globe is ageing, the African population is expected to remain stable and is ageing at a far slower pace than the global north.

Issues of inequality and low growth levels reduce the ability to absorb a usually growing working age population into the labour markets and these are predominantly African and Latin American country characteristics. This affects the contribution levels of workers and the number of workers who are fully employed. This will determine the design of pension schemes and extent to which the state bears the burden of reducing poverty.

In contrast, the most common risk in developed and industrialised economies is rising life expectancies presenting the dilemma of an increasingly ageing population. These matched with lower fertility replacement rate equate to higher old age dependency ratios. Germany, Italy, and France show dependency ratios higher than 40%, which means that the number of elderly people in ratio to the working population is rising significantly (Holzmann, 1999; Rhodes & Natali, 2003). The total value of contributions will not be able to meet the rising and current benefits required to pay the nominal pensions of existing pensioners. This simply means in the medium to long term, there will simply not be enough people in the working-age population (15–64) to pay the required contributions to sustain the retirement income of pensioners. There are indications that this will lead to an increase in taxes or debt to finance pension expenditure, putting significant pressure on country budgets. The debate on the long-term fiscal viability becomes relevant at this point.

It is important to indicate that countries are at different stages of the demographic transition and although developing countries are at the incipient and moderate stages where the youth is growing, fertility rates are high and the elderly are low relative to the working population, as evident in most African countries. Some countries (mainly European) are reaching consolidation and exhibiting signs of lower fertility rates and an increasing elderly population towards full demographic transition (Uthoff, 2006), Latin American countries such as Brazil, Peru, Venezuela, and Colombia face these, though not to the same extent of European countries, they are already reaching the advanced stages. Rhodes and Natali (2003) argue financial viability is further worsened by pension schemes that are reaching maturity. When the ratio between the elderly (the beneficiaries) and the working population (contributors) is rising, it is likely to put further pressure on fiscal sustainability. Contributions in PAYG schemes are made by the employed, and in scenarios where nations experience high unemployment rates, the pressure on contribution levels by the working population is further exacerbated. This is two pronged, as the future number of dependents that will require social protection from the state will increase, and there will be further decreases in the number of contributors making contributions to existing beneficiaries in a PAYG.

In PAYG schemes, contributions to pensions are not recognised as savings but are transfers from the young to the old. That means the contribution is seen as a tax due to it being a fraction of funds directly used to pay out the elderly's pensions. In a funded system, contribution to pension schemes is recognised as savings, which are made up of contributions to a pension plan that are returned to a worker at old age. An increase in growth is derived from higher aggregate savings only if individuals were saving less than what was saved in their mandatory pension contributions.

Barr's (2000) simplified pension system model, is an equation comprising the number of pensioners multiplied by the nominal pensions, which is equivalent to the contribution rate of the existing number of workers multiplied by the wage bill. He modifies the model by factoring in a reduction in wages. To balance the equation, it would require either an increased contribution rate or an increase in the number of workers contributing in order to meet the pension payouts for existing pension holders. Reduced productivity and wage levels holds a significant risk for continued sustainability where the number of employed is unlikely to rise or where the contribution levels of the employed are not a feasible option (Rhodes & Natali, 2003). The PAYG system is faced with political risk, market risk, and regulatory constraints when existing workers are unable to meet the existing pensioner obligations; at times, the political conditions and fiscal pressures erode the likelihood of pensioner obligations being met and if the regulatory institutions and framework are unable to ensure economic security amongst other government expenditure priorities. This gives rise to pension reform.

There are three predominant pension reform methods referred to in literature and these reforms are commonly known as systemic, parametric measures, or notional defined contribution. These measures can be implemented as reforms within the specific type of pension system. According to Rhodes and Natali (2003), reform paths within occupational plus purer occupational constitute namely effecting non-parametric changes that converge benefits, improve labour market conditions to increase labour supply in order to reduce the problem of financial instability and intra-generational inequity. Pure universal models suffer financial viability problems, especially where labour market is not producing new jobs.

Pension reform takes place in the context of an existing pension system or scheme, and the nature of reform can take various forms. A commodified regime is where there is a strong push towards privatisation and a decommodified pension system is largely tax-financed, underpinned by the country-specific political economy. It is the prevalence of the state versus the private sector in the provision of pension schemes that determines the route to reform. The question arises of who bears the greater responsibility of providing pension benefits and the prevalence of public versus private schemes, where multiple pension schemes exist? Private schemes provide benefits through occupational arrangements (second or third pillar) and public schemes provide through means-tested or universal systems (first pillar). A mix between the systems arrives at the universal plus occupational scheme (multiple pillar). Barr (2000) proposes an alternative to pillars, and these are developed according to country priorities and referred to as tiers. The difference between tiers and pillars is that tiers place far greater emphasis on objectives of a country versus prescribing a shift before aligning any reform to measures. The second tier he maintains need not be privately managed, against the World Bank view and proposes that publicly managed schemes may face reduced risks.

In the event a country's pension system faces a crisis of financial viability, the World Bank states that country responses have focussed on moving from PAYG to a fully funded scheme (FFS) and in the short term reducing benefits (Holzmann, 1999). Reforms in several countries have been undertaken as a result of weaknesses in the PAYG system, transitioning from PAYG to FFS. Barr (2000) disagrees that a change in pension scheme needs be the only solution to resolving long-term financial viability. He argues that it is possible to increase the savings rate, implement policies that will increase the number of workers, or improve output such that the average nominal wage rises. Other solutions include reducing public expenditure or paying off future debt in advance, a function dependent largely on fiscal discipline. These recommendations will all contribute to the increase in total contributions so that there are adequate reserves to pay pensioners. The labour market participation rate affects all the pension systems, including the universal plus occupational scheme. Policies introduced to reduce the extent to which individuals rely on informal and part-time work would also benefit total contributions.

Box 25.1: Pension Reforms in South Africa

Most pension fund reform research is on developed economies; however, there is a focus on Chile due to the historical significance and reform measures taken in 1981. Its reform was the replacement of PAYG to

FFS partly motivated by an ageing population. It remains a popular case study in the literature for reducing political risk, improving fiscal sustainability, and reducing labour market distortions. A prominent feature in pension reform literature is centred around the privatisation of pension asset managers, focusing on the transition from a publicly to privately managed pillar.

Hendricks (2008) provides a critique of the reforms experienced in South Africa post 1994. Stating that beyond the protection of apartheid era public servants pensions, the downside has been the cost of debt maintenance and opportunity costs of forgoing meeting the social needs the people of South Africa are in dire need for. There remains little evidence found in literature concerning the nature and motivation of the shift from PAYG to FFS. The reform propelled by a demographic transition at advanced stages does not hold for South Africa, in fact National Treasury (2004) agrees that there is no problem of an ageing population as do most developed economies. Therefore, the PAYG to FFS shift propelled by the government has significant debt costs, whose cost has likely outweighed the benefits of privatisation. The argument of political risk cannot be adequate in lieu of the additional investment risk from the stock and bond markets, annuity risk and pension fund management risk that pensioners face under such a scheme. Financing the transition have possibly had major welfare and distributional adverse effects, while it minimised the future fiscal constraints the current reforms for poverty eradication and financing of government economic and social priorities were more urgent.

In the 1980s and mid 1990s, South Africa effected major reforms in the public pension system. The National Treasury's Annual Reports (1998, 1999) reported that the Government Employees Pension Fund (GEPF) was formed after the amalgamation of several funds. A single homogenous fund with standard benefits, retirement provisions, and requirement and management was formed post-1994. As at 1998 the fund had 1.1 million contribution members. It was reported that the pension funds were previously obligated to provide loans to the government using pension assets. These legislative requirements were removed by amendments made to the PIC Act in 1999. The fund is also shown to have improved in the level of unfunded liability levels, which were reduced quite significantly on a yearly basis. The percentage levels of the funded liability increased from 72% in the previous year to 96.5% in the year ending 31 March 1998. The value placed on the unfunded liability was R5.26 billion. Little mention of the nature of the reform and how it was financed is reported. The Annual Report (1999) stated more than a fifth of the fiscal at 21.4% went towards debt repayment in 1998. This cost is due to domestic debt, of which 98% was incurred after 1994 or agreed to during the negotiated or re-negotiated CODESA talks. This debt is domestic debt, with National Treasury stating that 96% of it is recorded as such and the holder of 40% of the domestic debt were the Public Investment Commissioners (PIC), which held the assets of the GEPF.

During pension reform there is a transition period where social security contributions no longer directly offset existing pension payments. They are deposited in a fund, as in the case of South Africa, the GEPF is managed by the PIC. The pension payments to existing pensioners must continue and it is herein that public debt, which is usually raised if the fiscal position is not in surplus. Financing the transition requires selling of state assets, incurring of liabilities or reducing government expenditure or raising taxes. In South Africa, evidence points to issuing of government debt, which is argued by Hendricks (2008) to have had a neutralising and even negative impact on the improvement of aggregate savings. Cuevas et al. (2008) explains broadly that a pension systems change does affect the debt structure of a country. The pensions owed to pensioners are known as implicit debt and this debt when privatisation occurs becomes explicit debt, changing the composition of liabilities with financial debt replacing the implicit which has a direct impact on country credit risk. It no longer is hidden and must be repaid. Empirical evidence (see Cuevas et al., 2008) suggests that financial debt increases the perception of riskiness as the nature of liabilities is amended. Pensioners are afforded equal status on their claims as creditors, equal to bondholders, a far higher status than those offered to PAYG participants, who hold lesser claim than any creditor with government. It has been argued by many that this part of the transition may erode all benefits of reform, as financing costs are too high.

Source (Moleko & Ikhide, 2016; National Treasury, 1998, 1999).

Analysing the measurement of the impact of reform, literature has shown emphasis on Latin American countries like Chile and Columbia with only single measurement on Russia and India (Hauner, 2008; Holzmann, 1999; Poirson, 2007; Schmidt-Hebbel, 1995, 1999; Uthoff, 2006; Vittas, 1999; Walker & Lefort, 2002;). Empirical studies on Sub-Saharan Africa are severely limited. An increase in pension assets in an FFS is argued to have positive effects on growth. Savings is one of the factors pension fund accumulation exhibits growth effects. This accumulation of capital leads to improved resource allocation and investment, leading to capital market development. This in turn has positive consequences for productivity and output. The above-mentioned empirical studies have largely focussed on the impact of funded pensions on savings and more recently on capital market development (Enache et al., 2015; Walker & Lefort, 2002). Other positive pension reform effects on fiscal viability, labour, tax, distribution, and reduced political risks are limited. The fiscal benefits and impacts on taxes and public debt or fiscal viability are usually simulation models and graphical forecasts.

Box 25.2: Micro-Pensions in East Africa

It is important to consider the labour market and economic structure of a country, with the level of development an important consideration for policymakers in developing and emerging market pension systems. The Kenyan pension system has shown growth in the contribution to GDP increasing from 11.5% in 2002 to 14.3% in 2011. The Retirement Benefits Authority currently estimates the assets under management were a value of Kshs. 1,298.74 billion in 2020, having grown from 117.4 billion in 2002 to 432.8 billion in 2011, the growth in pension assets has grown significantly. Despite this it is reported that the financing needs of pensioners remains constrained with the population over 65 million likely to face significant hurdles in meeting their retirement goals. The low pension coverage of 22% of the labour force is due to the type of pension products offered to the informal sector, whose workers comprise a large proportion of the labour force. The level of pension penetration in the informal work sector, when it constitutes more than three quarters of the workforce, is a determinant to the level of worker savings in the economy. Thus, when considering issues of pension reform, African nations should have a strong emphasis on the provision of policies and products that target the majority of the labour force, namely focussing on the informal economy. This differs from developed economies and high to upper-middle-income countries whose financial markets Africa tends to emulate.

Pension reforms that the Kenyan financial sector have adopted to improve the financial market infrastructure also focussed on informal sector contributions. A pension plan known as the Mbao pension plan was established in 2009 and it targeted SMMEs with the intention to increase participation in the informal sector. A minimum of 20 Kenyan shillings was required from participants daily, with a provision pushing out collection of benefits by 3 years or later. An additional use of mobile technology and partnership with the M-Pesa services was encouraged to increase the participation. The following policies were implemented to bring reform to the financial services sector:

- Payment mechanism that do not come through the banking system but enable the rural population to make contributions
- Enabling direct contributions from the beneficiaries rather than employers making contributions
- Cellphone usage and mobile money systems enabling deposits, transfer of funds, and payment of contributions as an alternative to bank payments or cash deposits
- The minimum contribution should be designed to encourage deposits, daily or weekly with the Mbao 20 shillings a day equivalent to US $0.25c
- The costs of service providers need to be monitored and low, with fee structures encouraging savings
- The pension regulators should include financial literacy campaigns and a marketing campaign in an effort to provide the benefits of savings and to demystify the concerns around pension plans and the associated risks to low-income and rural households.

Source (Finance Sector Regulators, 2020; Kwena & Turner, 2013).

25.4 Overview of Pension Systems in Africa

Africa has evolved over time with regards to pensions. Moving from one pension regime to another all in the quest to provide better lives for individuals during their inactive working days. Regulators as well as supervisory teams have migrated from one policy direction to another in terms of pension systems in Africa. African countries have different pension schemes and this may be a result of the different financial systems in place. There exists some form of pension coverage available in only a few African countries and benefits are derived from national, occupational, and public service pension schemes. These benefits are mostly received by formal sector workers. According to Bloom and Mckinnon (2013), Sub-Saharan African countries with lower income have coverage extended to less than 10% of the population and may only cover a number of eventualities (old age, disability, survivorship, work injury, etc.). The public sector worker receives benefits from the Public Pension Scheme. The national (usually) mandatory covers private sector workers as well as public sector workers while the occupational schemes are mostly managed by the employees. However, there exist individual/personal pension schemes which are managed by insurance companies and contribution to this scheme is on voluntary basis. It can however be noted that a larger portion of the African population is employed in the informal sector and this means these formal schemes may not cater for them, an indication that they may need to depend on their own informal provisions, resources, or family assets.

This section provides an overview of pension systems in selected African countries, including Ghana, Nigeria, Senegal, Botswana, South Africa, Zambia, Mauritius, Egypt, Niger, Uganda, Kenya, and Rwanda.

Ghana

Ghana currently is running a three-tier pension system. This consist of two compulsory and one voluntary schemes and these schemes are integrated unlike other sub-Saharan African countries. According to the PwC (2015) report, creating the three-pillar pension system is the most significant development in the pension sector. The 1st Tier, a distinct benefit scheme, is required for workers to have 13.5% contributed on their behalf. The 2nd Tier is a defined contributory Occupational Pension Scheme compulsory for employees with 5% contribution made on their behalf. The 3rd Tier includes all Provident Funds and other Pension Funds outside Tiers I and II and it is an optional scheme covering all employees in the private and public sectors. It is non-mandatory for the business owner (the informal sector worker). Micro pensions for the informal sector through mobile telecommunication platform is a recent development in the Ghanaian Pension Industry. Certain Pensions and Insurance companies have partnered with telecommunication companies to deliver micro pensions to those in the informal sector via mobile phones.

Nigeria

Nigeria introduced the Contributory Pension Scheme in 2004 by the Pension Reform Act which was a fully funded, Defined Contribution and was privately managed. It was a compulsory requirement for all public sector workers and a Retirement Savings Account (RSA) was deployed for all members. For easy access to enrolment, an online enrolment application was designed to get members have easy access to enrolment since the application could register, verify, and enrol individuals unto the scheme.

According to 2019 annual report of the Pension Commission, there was a significant increase (5.72%) in the membership base which translated into the fund base as well. The funds are invested in ordinary shares, bonds, stock, money market instruments, infrastructure, and real estate amongst others. There exist also a Micro Pension Plan launched in 2019 under the RSA.

Senegal

There are two compulsory pension schemes that Senegal currently runs. These are the Retirement Savings Fund of Senegal (IPRES) covering private sector workers, employees in local government and government employees without the civil servant status. This is a Defined Benefit scheme which is centred on a point system, and these points are considered based on three factors: the salary from which contributions are deducted, average salary and number of years contributed. The contribution rate is 14% of salary to which the employee takes 40% (5.6%) and the employer pays 60% (8.4%). The second scheme is the National Pension Fund and it caters for workers in the public sector and those in the armed forces. Contribution to this scheme is 35% of which employee pays 12% and the employer pays 23%. Benefits for this scheme are on a pay as you go basis and to be a beneficiary, one must have worked for at least 30 years and aged 60. Armed forces workers must have to work for 25 years and age 55 to benefit from the scheme.

Botswana

Botswana operates a universal old Age Pension System introduced in 1996 with coverage extending to all citizens above the age of 65 years who resides in Botswana and the cost for this scheme is borne by the government. Benefits provided under this scheme normally get adjusted according to the cost of living. In 2001 the Botswana Public Officers Pensions Fund (BPOPF) which is a funded public sector scheme for employees had a reform where it was moved from Defined Benefit to Define Contribution and this brought about an incredible growth in the funds. Even with this growth, 84% of private formal employees do not have coverage and about 33% of public sector workers are not covered. The pension fund industry is overseen by a Non-Bank Financial Authority.

South Africa

One of both Africa's and the world's largest pension funds is the Government Employees Pension Fund (GEPF) operated in South Africa. With more over 1.2 million active members, the GEPF have over 450 000 pensioners and beneficiaries, and assets worth over R1.61 trillion (GEPF Report, 2020). Established in May 1996 by consolidating different public sector funds the GEPF is a Defined Benefit pension fund that sees to the management and administration of pensions and benefits for workers in the South Africa government. In recent times, R 8,701 per month is the means-tested old age grant for those who cannot support themselves and this is the difference between subsistence and total poverty. Many families, particularly those in rural areas, largely rely on these pensions as their only means of income, and there can be no doubt that access to pensions has had a significant impact on poverty levels.

Aside the contributory occupational pensions and the social non-contributory pensions in the public sector, South Africa has two other funds; the private occupational pensions and the voluntary savings, such as annuities at retirement. On the surface, South Africa appears to have the fiscal and institutional capacity to implement a differentiated system that meets the World Bank's requirement for multi-pillar pension schemes (Van Der Merwe, 2004: 310). The assets from these funds are largely invested in domestic and foreign equity and bonds as it is being managed by the Public Investment Commissioners (PIC).

Zambia

Restructuring of the Zambian National Provident fund took place in 1990 and became a mandatory social insurance scheme managed by the National Pension Scheme Authority (NPSA). This scheme covers local government, civil servants, or employed individuals and voluntary coverage exists for workers in the informal sector and those self-employed. Contribution to the scheme is on a 5% of earnings for employee and 5% of earnings for employer. There is a 10% voluntary contribution too. The system consists of both private and public schemes. And there are three pillars on which these schemes are based. The first pillar is made up of National Pension Scheme Authority, which is a basic compulsory scheme. The second pillar consists of Public Service Pension funds (PSP) and the Local Authority Superannuation Fund (LASF). These two are occupation based and in addition to this are the private occupational schemes, which are managed by insurance and non-insurance companies.

Mauritius

Basic Retirement Pensions (BRP), occupational compulsory pensions, and voluntary pensions are the three types of pension systems that exist in Mauritius. The BRP is a non-contributory pension scheme designed to cater for all citizens of Mauritius who are 60 years and above. The benefits consist of a fixed monthly payment dependant on the age which is reviewed annually. This scheme is managed by the National Pension Fund. The occupational compulsory pensions however entails the Civil Service Defined Benefit (CSDB) scheme which comprises of civil servants who joined before 2012. Employees of this scheme pay 6% of their salaries while the government settles any deficit. However, members who joined after 2012 were enrolled unto another scheme which is a Defined Contribution Scheme (Civil Service Defined Contribution). Again, The National Pension Fund (NPF), a defined benefit funded scheme is compulsory for employees in the private sector. Employee pay 3% of earnings while the employer pays 6%. More so, self-employed workers can join this scheme voluntarily. There is also a National Saving Fund (NSF) which is fully funded with a mandatory contribution of 2% of earning from employees and a lump sum payment is received based on the amount contributed and returns on investment. The NSF is largely invested in government bonds and Treasury bills. Then lastly is the Private Voluntarily Pension Schemes which are privately managed and membership is voluntarily.

Egypt

The structure of Egypt's pension system has public and private schemes. The public pension scheme comprises government employees, military personnel, public and private enterprises employees, and a number of social programmes exist for special groups of population. The Private Pension which is voluntary occupational pension plan exist for those in the private sector. The National Authority for Social Insurance oversees the mandatory social insurance system that comprises employees in both private and public sector including those who work aboard and the workers in the informal sector. The coverage rate of pensions in Egypt is about 80% of the employed population and it is considered as one of the highest in developing countries. There was growth in the number of funds (733–749), number of members (4.8m–4.9m), and assets (77.5m–88.9m) over the period of 2019–2020 according to the annual report of the Financial Regulatory Authority.

Niger

Niger operates a two pensions system namely the "Caisse Nationale de Securite Sociale" (CNSS) which caters for workers in the private sector, and the "Fonds Nationale de Retraite" (FNR) which caters for civil servants, the military personnel, and workers in local government. Total contribution received from the CNSS Scheme is 4% out of which the employer contributes 2.4% and the employee contributes to the rest as a percentage of his earnings. On the other hand, the employer contributes 14% with employee contributing 6% for the FNR Scheme. The coverage of the two schemes is 3% of the labour force which comprises of civil servants and formal sector workers. "la Caisse Autonome des Retraités du Niger" (CARENI), a financially and legally independent institution took over the management of the public sector scheme, something which was initially under the management of FNR. This was due to some administrative and financial management issues with the pension and retirement funds. Government bonds, real estate, and bank deposits are examples of assets that the FNR invests in.

Uganda

Uganda has the National Social Security Fund (NSSF) which is a defined contribution fund for employees in the formal sector, the Public Service Pension Scheme (PSPS), which is a non-contributory defined benefit scheme that caters for civil servants, the Military Pension Schemes as well as other occupational schemes and Individual Savings and Retirement Benefits Schemes. The NSSF is a defined contribution mandatory provident fund that pays a lump sum upon retirement. Contribution is 5 and 10% of earnings between employee and employer, respectively. Benefits to participants are based on adequacy of funds and how investments risks are managed to bring in more returns. The PSPS caters for local government workers, civil servants, judiciary, teachers, doctors, police, and prison officers. Supported by general tax revenues, this Pay As You Go (PAYG) scheme is administered by the Ministry of Public Service. The Military

Pension scheme also called the Armed Forces Pension Scheme covers military officers and it is funded by tax revenues. The Private Occupational and informal schemes comprise formal sector workers whose institutions or companies have the pension plans for their employees as well as individuals who voluntarily want to save towards their retirement and they are regulated by the Uganda Retirement Benefits Regulatory Authority (URBRA) Act. It is worth noting that two informal sector schemes have been established by workers in the informal sector since the (URBRA). These funds are invested in government securities, bonds, equities, and real estate amongst others.

Kenya

Kenya has four different types of pension programmes namely: National Social Security Fund (NSSF), Public Service scheme, Occupational Schemes, and Individual Schemes. The NSSF is a funded and mandatory scheme comprising employees in formal sector institutions with more than five workers excluding those in the Public Service. The Public Service scheme is unfunded and is made of all public service employees, including, teachers, civil servants, and security forces. The occupational scheme is a funded but voluntary scheme comprising formal sector workers in companies that operate retirement schemes. And the individual scheme is open to all on voluntary basis. All the above are regulated by Retirement Benefit Authority except the public service scheme which is regulated by an Act of Parliament. The employer-provided occupational pensions account for 61% of total assets, the NSSF accounts for 38%, and individual pension programmes account for 1%. The accumulated assets in the funded programmes equal 20% of GDP (Odundo, 2004).

There has been a great improvement in the industry with regards to growth in the membership, according to the Kenya National Bureau of Statistics (KNBS) FinAccess Report 2019. In their report there was a significant compounded annual growth rate of 15.7% in membership and 15.8% compounded annual asset growth rate over a ten-year period between 2009 and 2019, and this was attributed to factors like education on the importance of retirement savings, Financial technology, and improvements on communication between schemes and members. Some of the asset classes that funds from pensions are invested in are equities immovable properties, bonds amongst others. The Mbao Pension Plan exists in Kenya to take care of those in the informal sectors; once you are above 18 years and have either a national ID or passport. This is managed through mobile money platform and it reaches a large portion of the population because of its flexibility.

Rwanda

Rwanda's social security scheme has three pension pillars. Rwanda has one mandatory public pension scheme known as "Caissa Sociale du Rwanda" or National Social Security Fund (NSSF) comprising public and private sector workers and it is a plan with a clearly defined benefit. Contribution towards the scheme for both employee and employer is 3 and 5%, respectively. The second pillar is Occupational Pension plan, a fully funded, Defined Contribution or Defined Benefit scheme for the formal sector workers whose employers have the schemes and contributions differ from each employer. Most of the schemes invest in insurance companies and benefits are paid as lump sums. The third scheme, however, is voluntary saving for those who wish to supplement their savings towards retirement. The scheme is a defined contribution and mostly offered by insurance companies (Table 25.1).

25.5 Pension Funds and Capital Market Development

It is important to locate the role of pension funds or assets within the broader financial system. Financial development encompasses the complex interactions between lenders and borrowers of funds in a financial system. Financial institutions act as intermediaries, which provide additional money to markets, transfer funds, create markets, and provide for the efficient allocation of these funds. Financial intermediaries facilitate the flow of these funds from surplus to deficit economic units. There exist depository and non-depository financial intermediaries. Some examples of depository intermediaries in the financial sector include banks, savings, and loans companies, Post Office Savings banks, and credit unions. Non-depository intermediaries include insurance companies, pension, and provident funds, mutual funds, unit and investment trusts, and participation mortgage bond schemes. Insurance companies, pension, and provident funds therefore receive surpluses in the form of insurance premiums and pension contributions and intermediate them to deficit economic units on the equities and securities markets.

Table 25.1 Types of pension systems in selected African countries

Country	*Legal status*	*Contribution from insured person*	*Contribution from employer*	*Contribution from government*	*Contribution from self-employed*	*Statutory retirement age—Men*	*Statutory retirement age—Women*
Ghana	Statutory implemented	5.5%; 18.5% (voluntarily insured)	13%	None	18.5%	60; 55 (if working under hazardous conditions)	60; 55 (if working under hazardous conditions)
Nigeria	Statutory implemented	8%	10%; pays the total cost of a life insurance policy	1% of monthly earnings to subsidise the guaranteed minimum pension for federal public-sector employees; contributes as an employer	n/a	50	50
Senegal	Statutory implemented	2.4%	3.6%	None	n/a	55	55
Botswana	Statutory implemented	None	None	Total cost	None	65	65
South Africa	Statutory implemented	None	None	Total cost	None	60	60

Country	*Legal status*	*Contribution from insured person*	*Contribution from employer*	*Contribution from government*	*Contribution from self-employed*	*Statutory retirement age—Men*	*Statutory retirement age—Women*
Zambia	Statutory implemented	5%; 10% (voluntarily insured)	5%	None	10%	55; 60 (persons whose insurance period began after August 14, 2015)	55; 60 (persons whose insurance period began after August 14, 2015)
Mauritius	Statutory implemented	3%; at least 160 rupees a month (non-employed persons); none (certain low-income agricultural and household workers)	2.5%; none (persons age 65 or older)	Finances any deficit; pays contributions for certain low-income agricultural and household workers	At least 170 rupees a month	60	60
Egypt	Statutory implemented	10% + 3% for lump-sum benefits	15% + 2% for lump-sum benefits	1% (special increment and social solidarity allowance); finances any deficit	None	60	51; at any age
Niger	Statutory implemented	5.25%	6.25%	None	n/a	60; 55 (if prematurely aged)	60; 55 (if prematurely aged)

(continued)

Table 25.1 (continued)

Country	*Legal status*	*Contribution from insured person*	*Contribution from employer*	*Contribution from government*	*Contribution from self-employed*	*Statutory retirement age—Men*	*Statutory retirement age—Women*
Uganda	Statutory implemented	5%; at least 7.5% (voluntarily insured)	10%	None	At least 7.5%	55; 50; before age 55	55; 50; before age 55
Kenya	Statutory implemented	5%	5%	None	5%	50	50
Rwanda	Statutory implemented	3%; 6% (voluntarily insured)	3%	None	6%	60 (younger if prematurely aged)	60 (younger if prematurely aged)

Sources ILO, World Social protection Database, and Authors' own selection of countries

With respect to pension funds, the contributions are invested in various asset classes and limited by each country's regulatory framework. In Ghana, the National Pensions Regulatory Authority provides investment guidelines into the various asset classes for private pension funds. In Kenya, the Retirement Benefits Authority provides the investment limits of each asset class using the Retirement Benefits Regulations, similarly the Nigerian Pension Commission regulates the investments in the pension sector. In South Africa Regulation 28 outlines maximum exposure to the different investment classes that funds must adhere to and limit investment risk across shares, foreign assets, property, cash, bonds, and Krugerrands. It is important to raise that the accumulation of capital through pension funds is referred to as institutional capital due to the regulatory environment required for the interaction between investors, firms, and authorities in the market.

Pension funds trigger innovation in financial systems. New instruments, the modernisation of infrastructure, and improved regulations occur as a consequence of the development of pension funds (Davis, 2006). New product development and demand for new products improves market efficiency. Financial innovation is more specifically described through the development of derivative, securitisation, and equities markets, coupled with indexed instruments, corporate bonds, index futures, zero-coupon bonds, and certificate of deposits (Hu, 2012). Pension funds contribute to the loan and securities market, improving competitiveness as they compete with the banking sector. The outcome of improved efficiency, a reduction of transaction costs and market volatility, as lending rates, and spreads are lowered, reducing firm, and household costs for accessing capital (Davis, 2006). Pension fund assets reduce dividend yields and increase price-to-book ratios, indicating a decline in the cost of capital (Walker & Lefort, 2002). This is also enhanced when concurrently increased corporate governance and liquidity is experienced.

Impavido and Musalem (2000) argue that a benefit of increased pension savings is enhanced competition, efficiency, and modernisation of the securities market. This occurs as fund managers increase their participation in the bond and stock markets, which is followed by competitive bidding on bond and stock issues. Stock exchanges are at times restructured and technology is introduced to manage increased trading volumes. As pension funds and their scale increase on the market, we see settlement systems and professional specialisation. Capital markets make gains from improved governance as a result of increased pension funds activism; this is heightened as at times they represent minority interests putting a focus on companies being more transparent, improving company disclosures and boosting the execution of good governance.

The endogenous growth model theory shows that pension funds have additional benefits that contribute to the development of capital markets, even if they do not lead to an increase in savings. Pension fund savings are therefore able to improve capital markets either through higher savings or a more efficient allocation of savings. A more efficient and liquid stock markets contribute to improved long-term investments, that have a positive growth effect (Pagano, 1993). Pension funds are termed institutional investors as they payout returns on managed funds to fund members upon retirement.

Pension funds are also linked to growth and development via capital market development. The first reason is pension funds accumulate large amounts of wealth, this wealth is then used for investment. In order for investment to take place, the markets develop financial instruments through which investment can take place. Large quantities of institutional investors are accompanied by the development of better regulations for these participants. Pension funds hold greater proportion of assets than households and these asset holdings of bonds and equities enable pension funds to compensate for risk due to pooling and diversifying across assets.

Pension funds hold closer links to investment banks, have access to superior skills than households, and they are able to perform better due to higher levels of specialisation and economies of scale. They thus exhibit a level of specialisation and skill that is not possessed by households. New sectors of the economy such as mutual funds and private equity grow and receive pension fund finance. In other asset classes, long terms securities have been developed to meet the long-term outlook of defined benefit contribution systems. Pension funds make long-term investments in order to match the maturities of assets and liabilities (Hu, 2012; Kim, 2010). The increase of long-term corporate bonds and securitised debt instruments in the markets are reflections of this trend.

Box 25.3: The Case of Pension Assets Used for National Development

The South African pension system has one of the most developed and sophisticated infrastructure globally. It enacted regulation as far back as 1959 with institutional framework and the development of a sector dating back to the early 1900s. The asset classes hold a case for use of pension assets for national development by policymakers. In the case of South Africa, what is referred to as prescribed assets, whereby minimum investment allocation to a specified asset class designated for use through bills and bonds to serve national development priorities, was developed. The asset class is described as ranging between 7 and 25% during the period, 1981–1991. This was discontinued post democracy, despite the significant development needs of the large black majority population, who did not benefit from the infrastructure and other capital allocations. The type of bills and bonds were invested in an infrastructure related bills and bonds allocated to Water Boards, Electricity Supply Commission, Land and Agricultural Bank, and other state authorities.

Table 25.2 shows the distribution of assets of South African pension funds between the years 1959–2016. The last three decades have seen considerable changes in the asset portfolios of privately managed pension funds. According to data from the Financial Services Board Pension Funds Registrar. FSB's annual reports outline the investment pattern for pension funds for each period. Until 1994 the reports reflected only the self-administered, state-controlled, and foreign funds. The annual reports show that from 1994 to date investment patterns remain isolated to self-administered funds.

25.6 Challenges Affecting Pension Markets in Africa

Africa's pension markets are confronted with a number of challenges, including high unemployment rate, large informal sector, and scarcity of appropriate investment vehicles.

High unemployment rate. According to the World Bank report 2020, sub-Saharan Africa had unemployment rate of 6.19% in 2019 which makes it the 4th highest in the world. Current unemployment rate in Africa gives an indication of a high percentage of the labour force that is available and looking for work but do not have one. Unemployment

Table 25.2 Investment by asset class of South Africa pension funds

No	*Asset class*	*1981*	*1987*	*1991*	*1995*	*1999*	*2002*	*2005*	*2008*	*2011*	*2015*
1	Immovable properties	5.8	5.9	4.8	4.3	3.6	1.1	0.6	1.1	0.7	1.2
2	Bills and Bonds	22.4	17.9	9.4	12.6	12.0	10.5	8.6	7.2	7.5	8.5
3	Bills and Bonds issued by the government or provincial administration	9.1	3.6	0.5							
4	Bills and Bonds issued by local authorities and administration boards	8.2	7.0	3.6							
5	Bills and Bonds issued by Rand Water Board or Electricity Supply Commission	7.9	0.3	2.6							
6	Bills and Bonds issued by Land and Agricultural Bank and SARB	4.5	0.7	0.5							
7	Loans	6.3	1.4	0.5	0.3	0.6	0.8	0.1	0.1	–	–
8	Debentures	8.7	6.6	10.2	0.7	0.2	0.6	0.1	1.1	1.1	–
9	Deposits and savings accounts	15.6	19.5	24.4							
10	Equities/Shares in companies				47.7	34.3	29.3	23.3	20	18.8	17.6
11	Collective Investment Schemes/Unit Trusts		24.4	33.3	1.5	5.8	6.2	5.5	6.6	7.9	7.2
12	Insurance Policies				24.6	28.2	35.0	47.6	46	45.9	40.7
13	Deposits and Krugerrands	–			7.5	7.0	6.7	4.3	6.3	5.1	4.3
14	Foreign Investments				–	–		7.8	9.9	11.8	18.8
15	Other Assets	17.0	12.7	10.2	0.8	8.3	9.8	2.1	1.7	1.2	0.11

Source (Financial Services Board, 1959–2016, Moleko & Ikhide, 2016)

seems to be a canker in most African countries. The high level of unemployment is a major challenge affecting the growth of pension funds in Africa as the unemployed cannot contribute to these pension funds. The unemployed with limited resources and the burden of catering for themselves and their families may find it difficult to contribute to such funds. It is only a small number of the populace who are working who are able to contribute to pension funds.

Pension funds offer individuals who contribute to the scheme some kind of consumption smoothening. By contributing to such schemes, the individual can be assured of receiving some benefits upon retirement. With this benefit, even if the amount received does not measure up to the amount received prior to the retirement, the contributor can have some comfort and may be able to cater for some basic needs to some extent. Consumption smoothening is an economic term used to express the desire to have a stable path of consumption. This desire mostly pushes workers to contribute to pension, while in active service when they are earning enough so that in the event when they retire, they will earn some benefits. This would have been the ideal case but the high level of unemployment in Africa poses such a major challenge to pension funds. With the high level of unemployment, where individuals are struggling to meet their basic needs, it is virtually impossible to contribute to such funds. Although social security schemes have the ability to change the lives of the elderly in developing countries, over 342 million of them worldwide do not have income security because they are unemployed and if nothing is done, this figure is expected to rise to 1.6 billion, which is around 80% by 2050 (United Nations Department of Economic and Social Affairs [UN/DESA], 2007).

Another challenge is the presence of large informal sector. It is estimated that 85.8% of Africans are informally employed (ILO, 2018). Also, the Ghana Living Standard Survey (GLSS) (2010), estimates that the informal sector constitutes about 87% of the working population. It is evident that they may have insufficient access to social security, few or no workplace rights and low wages. The high level of the informal sector may be partially duc to the urban migration. As a result of the increasing levels of development in urban areas, a lot of youth have migrated into the cities to seek greener pastures. These young people who may have little or no education and therefore cannot secure jobs in the formal sector end up doing menial jobs. Even though people in the informal sector contribute a lot to the GDP, there is little effort to enrol them unto a formal pension scheme. Those institutions/countries running the 3-tier system of pension make room for the informal sector where the 3rd tier which is a voluntary contributory scheme could be patronised by the informal sector workers. Only 12.3% of African workers are employed in high-skilled labour occupations. This is frightening as it is expected to worsen with the working-age population growing at a faster rate (ILO, 2020 report). Even though there was an improvement in the GDP growth from 2.8% in 2019 to 3.7% in 2020, the economic growth was too low to improve the livelihood of the people due to the strong population growth in the region (UN, 2019). The slight increase in the GDP may be partially due to the improvement in private consumptions, continuous investment in infrastructure, and increasing production of oil (UN, 2019). Pension funds may experience significant growth in their market share if little comes from the informal sector.

Another limitation for pension funds in Africa is the scarcity of the appropriate means for infrastructure investment. However, the increasing interest of private equity funds in African investments, including infrastructure, may aid to alleviate this challenge. Recently, investing in infrastructure has received attention in the area of pensions. Pension funds were mostly invested in the traditional asset classes like bonds, equities, cash, and real estate. However, fund managers seek to look beyond the traditional asset classes so they can diversify their investment and reduce their investment risk. Investing in infrastructure which is considered less risky is gradually becoming an option to consider. This diversification into infrastructure is in search of return so as to meet its primary responsibility. Due to market volatility, inflation, and interest rate risk which pension funds are not protected from, it is just appropriate to spread the funds along a broader spectrum of investment so as to reduce pension liabilities. Again, the long-term nature of infrastructure and its tangibility make fund managers appreciate the underlying value of it rather than the traditional assets which may be affected by other factors. In as much as this may sound good to the stakeholders of pension funds, the dearth of means through which infrastructure investment could be done poses a major challenge to managers. The vehicles are so limited that there is little room to make a good choice for various portfolios. For instance, the fund managers are either investing in roads, social amenities, hospitals, schools, etc.

25.7 Conclusion and Policy Recommendations

Encouraging people to smoothen consumption over their lives so as to accumulate money to provide for the elderly when they retire is the main goal of pension systems. A number of African countries have also introduced policies to restructure their pension systems in response to the need for introducing systems of social protection to assist in alleviating demographic pressures and poverty amongst the elderly.

The pension markets play a number of important roles in the economy, including establishing attractive pension schemes, mobilising and pooling national savings, facilitating financial market development, ensuring corporate governance and monitoring of firms, supporting infrastructure development, supporting the housing finance market, and financing green growth initiatives. A general overview of the pension systems in Africa shows that the system is not matured, coverage is low and contributions are low. Coupled with these are the problems of unemployment, large informal sector, and lack of appropriate vehicles to invest in infrastructure. A few countries including, Ghana, Nigeria, and Kenya have introduced micro pension schemes where the informal sector can subscribe and these may increase the asset base of the pension industry. It is therefore important to get the remaining countries implement some of these policies to improve the coverage since the informal sector in Africa is very large contributing to about 80% of the working population. Pension funds drive financial system innovation. The development of pension funds results in the creation of new instruments, the modernisation of infrastructure, and the improvement of regulations. A few countries invest some of the pension fund assets in infrastructure. Asset managers should expand their portfolio base so that they can earn enough returns to sustain the schemes as the system matures.

References

Barr, N. (2000). *Reforming pensions: Myths, truths, and policy choices*. IMF.

Bloom, D. E., & McKinnon, R. (2013). *The design and implementation of public pension systems in developing countries: Issues and options* (IZA Policy Paper No. 59).

Cuevas, A., Gonzalez, M., Lombardo, D., & Lopez-Mármolejo, A. (2008). *Pension privatization and country risk*. IMF Working paper No. WP/08/195. Washington DC: International Monetary Fund.

Davis, P. (2006, July). *Pension funding, productivity, ageing and economic growth.* Presented at the Third Conference for the Monetary and Stability Foundation, Deutsche Bundesbank, Frankfurt.

Della Croce, R., Kaminker, C., & Stewart, F. (2011). *The role of pension funds in financing green growth initiatives*. OECD Publishing.

Enache, C., Milos, L. R., & Milos, M. C. (2015). Pension reform and capital market development in Central and Eastern European countries. *Economic Research, 28*(1), 75–84.

Financial Sector Regulators. (2020). *The Kenya financial sector stability report* (Issue No. 11).

Financial Services Board (FSB). (1959–2016). *Annual reports of registrar of pension funds*. Pretoria. Accessed online 6 March 2015 from https://www.fsb.co.za/communication/reports.htm

Fourie, L. J., Falkena, H. B., & Kok, W. J. (1992). *Fundamentals of the South African financial system* (1st ed.). Southern Book Publishers.

Ghana Living Standard Survey (GLSS). (2010). *Ghana Living Standard Survey 2010 report*. The Ghana Statistical Service Website.

Government Employees Pension Fund (GEPF). (2020). *Annual report*. https://www.gepf.gov.za/who-is-gepf/. Accessed on 2 August 2021.

Hauner, D. (2008). *Macroeconomic effects of pension reform in Russia* (IMF Working Paper. WP/08/201).

Hendricks, F. (2008). *The private affairs of the public pensions in South Africa: Debt, development and corporatization*. Programme Paper No. 38. United Nations Research Institute for Social Development.

Holzmann, R. (1999). *The World Bank approach to pension reform* (Social protection discussion paper series 9807). Social Protection Unit. World Bank.

Hu, Y. (2012). *Growth of Asian pension assets: Implications for financial and capital* markets (Working Paper Series No. 360). Asian Development Bank Institute.

Impavido, G., & Musalem, A. R. (2000). *Contractual savings, stock, and asset markets* (Working Paper 2490). World Bank Policy Research.

International Labour Organisation. (2018). *Women and men in the informal economy: A statistical picture* (3rd ed.). ILO.

International Labour Oraganisation (ILO). (2020). World Employment and Social Outlook: Trends 2020 International Labour Office—Geneva: ILO. ISBN 978-92-2-031407-4 (web pdf).

Jones, A. W., & Hiller, B. T. (2010). *Achieving scale in investment: Global risk and opportunity from climate change* (Paper No. WP/00/139).

Kenya National Bureau of Statistics (KNBS) FinAccess Report. (2019). https://www.fsdkenya.org/wpcontent/uploads/2019/04/2019-FinAcces-Report-Web-05-JAN-2020.pdf

Kim, H. S. (2010). *Spillover effects of pension funds on capital markets—The mechanism and preconditions*. http://growth-institutions.ec.unipi.it/pages/Pension_system/spillover.pdf. Accessed 15 April 2015.

Kwena, R., & Turner, J. (2013). Extending pension and savings scheme coverage to the informal sector: Kenya's MBAO pension plan. *International Social Security Review, 66*. https://doi.org/10.1111/issr.12010

Moleko, N., & Ikhide, S. (2016). Pension funds evolution, reforms and trends in South Africa. *International Journal of Economics and Finance Studies, 9*(2), 134–151.

National Treasury. (1998). *Republic of South Africa annual report 1998*. Department of National Treasury. http://www.treasury.gov.za/publications/annual%20reports/national%20treasury/default.aspx

National Treasury. (1999). *Republic of South Africa annual report 1999*. Department of National Treasury. http://www.treasury.gov.za/publications/annual%20reports/national%20treasury/default.aspx

National Treasury. (2004). *Retirement fund reform: A discussion paper*. Pretoria: National Treasury.

Nigerian Pension Commission. (2019). *Annual report*. https://www.pencom.gov.ng/wp-content/uploads/2020/10/APPROVED-2019-ANNUAL-REPORT-FINAL-DRAFT.pdf

Odundo, E. (2004). Supervision of a public pension fund: Experience and challenges from Kenya. In A. R. Musalem & R. J. Palacious (Ed.), *Public pension fund management*. The World Bank.

Pagano, M. (1993). Financial markets and growth. *European Economic Review, 37*, 688–726.

Poirson, H. K. (2007). *Financial market implications of India's pension reform* (IMF Working Paper WP/07/85).

PwC (PricewaterhouseCoopers). (2015). *Africa asset management 2020*. http://www.pwc.lu/en/asset-management/docs/pwc-am-africa-2020.pdf

Raichura, A. K. (2008). *Analytical review of the pension system in Kenya*. https://search.oecd.org/finance/private-pensions/41564693.pdf

Rhodes, M., & Natali, D. (2003). *Welfare regimes and pension reform agendas presented at "pension reform in Europe: Shared problems, sharing solutions"*. London School of Economics and Political Science.

Schmidt-Hebbel, K. (1995). *Colombia's pension reform: Fiscal and macroeconomic effects* (World Bank Discussion Papers WDP 314).

Schmidt-Hebbel, K. (1999). *Does pension reform really spur productivity, saving and growth*. The World Bank.

Stewart, F., & Yermo, J. (2009). *Pensions in Africa* (OECD Working Papers on insurance and private pensions No. 30). http://www.oecd.org/finance/private-pensions/42052117.pdf

Sy, A. N. R. (2017). *Leveraging pension funds for financing infrastructure development in Africa*. Africa Growth Initiative, Brookings Institution.

The World Bank. (2018). http://www.worldbank.org/en/topic/financialsector/brief/pension-funds

UN/DESA. (2007). *Development in an ageing world. World economic and social survey*. United Nations.

United Nations. (2019). *World economic situation and prospects 2019*. Department of Economic and Social Affairs.

Uthoff, A. (2006). Gaps in the welfare state and reforms to pension systems in Latin America. Social Development Division of ECLAC. *Cepal Review, 89*, 9–36.

Van der Merwe, T. (2004). The occupational pillar of the South African pension system. *Development Southern Africa, 21*(2), 303–327.

Van Zyl, C., Botha, Z., Goodspeed, I., & Skerrit, P. (2009). *Understanding South African financial markets* (3rd ed.). Van Schaik Publishers.

Vittas, D. (1999, September 21–22). *Pension reform and capital market development: "Feasibility" and "impact" preconditions*. Published paper delivered at OECD conference Privatization and Capital Market Development.

Walker & Lefort. (2002). *Pension reform and capital markets: Are there any hard links?* (Social Protection Discussion Paper Series 0201). Social Protection Unit. World Bank.

CHAPTER 26

On the Determinants of Stock Market Development in Africa

Charles Komla Delali Adjasi, Jabir Ibrahim Mohammed, Joseph Dery Nyeadi, and Sunil K. Bundoo

26.1 Introduction

This chapter analyses the determinants of stock market development in Africa. Globally, the financial markets landscape has changed over the years with African countries' equity capital markets (ECM) witnessing

C. K. D. Adjasi
University of Stellenbosch Business School, Cape Town, South Africa
e-mail: Charles.Adjasi@usb.ac.za

J. I. Mohammed (✉)
University for Professional Studies, Accra, Ghana
e-mail: jabir.mohammed@upsamail.edu.gh

J. D. Nyeadi
SD Dombo University of Business and Integrated Development Studies, Wa, Ghana

S. K. Bundoo
University of Mauritius, Port Louis, Mauritius

J. Y. Abor and C. K. D. Adjasi (eds.), *The Economics of Banking and Finance in Africa*, Palgrave Macmillan Studies in Banking and Financial Institutions, https://doi.org/10.1007/978-3-031-04162-4_26

significant progress. According to the African Equity Market Watch (2020), about 215 firms issued an initial public offer (IPOs) between the period 2010 and 2019 with a market value of US$16.96 billion and further offers (FOs) of 712 firms with a market value of US$71.1 billion. Besides this development, the stock market capitalization in Africa on average rose from 17.4% in 2000 to 32.8% 2010 and down to 28.7% in 2019. This recent development in the African equity markets calls for a better analysis on some of the factors that account for the determinants of the stock market in Africa.

In this study, we build on previous literature on the determinants of stock market development in Africa (see Andrianaivo & Yartey, 2010; Yartey, 2008). This study contributes to three strands of the literature. These are macroeconomics, institutional quality and natural resource revenues determinants of stock market development. Unlike Yartey (2008) and Andrianaivo and Yartey (2010) who study developing countries and African stock markets for the period 1990–2004, this study uses recent data for Africa to analyze the determinants of stock market development. With current development on the African equity markets such as new IPOs and FOs, factors that determine development in the stock market are still needed. Also, most African countries such as Ghana and Tanzania discovered natural resources such as oil and natural gas. Similarly, Africa has relatively progressive institutions and developing macroeconomic fundamentals which are needed to spur-up financial market development and economic growth. According to Yartey and Adjasi (2007), stronger disclosure in the stock market is important in protecting shareholders' interest and investment. So, strong institutions are important in building confidence in the stock market. This study empirically contributes to how institutional quality can facilitate the development of the African equity markets, especially control of corruption.

The study uses unbalanced panel data for the period 2000–2017 with 15 African Equity Capital Markets. Using panel fixed effects model and stock market capitalization as the dependent variable, the study provides very interesting findings. First, the study finds that stock market liquidity,

e-mail: sbundoo@uom.ac.mu

investment rates, inflation and banking sector development are the significant macroeconomic determinants of stock market development in Africa. Contrary to previous literature, that has argued that banking sector development complements stock market development, this study finds the banking sector as a substitute to stock market development. Thus, the development of the banking sector impedes stock market development in Africa. Second, the study finds that among the institutional variables, higher corruption hampers stock market development in Africa. Third, the study finds natural gas rent serves as a powerful determinant of stock market development whilst forest rent hampers stock market development in Africa. Others such as oil rent, mineral rent and total natural resource rent are positive but are not distinguishable from zero. Therefore, policies to increase stock market liquidity, investment, drive banking sector development, natural resource management and control of corruption in African equity capital market are needed to ensure development.

Subsequent sections are organized as follows. Section 26.2 focus on the overview of African stock markets; Sect. 26.3 reviews the literature on theory and empirics. Section 26.4 discusses the data and methodology; Sect. 26.5 discusses the results of the study and finally Sect. 26.6 concludes and provides the policy implications.

26.2 Overview of Stock Market Development in Africa

With the exception of few countries in Africa, the stock market was virtually non-existent in Africa before the late 1980s and the early 1990s. The few countries that had stock markets at the time were: South Africa, Egypt, Zimbabwe, Tunisia, Nigeria, Morocco and Kenya. Before the 1990s they were just only five (5) stock markets in the whole of Africa (Yartey & Adjasi, 2007). Currently, there are 29 stock exchanges in Africa with Egyptian Exchange (EGX) being the oldest, that was established in 1883 followed by Johannesburg Stock Exchange (JSE) founded in 1887. At the moment, the JSE is the largest in Africa in terms of number of firms listed on it and the market capitalization of the listed firms as percentage of GDP as shown in Table 3 below. Though there has been some improvement in the African stock market over the years, some countries in Africa up to date do not have stock exchanges. Some of the countries that joined the market in recent times are Angola, Lesotho and Somalia.

From Table 26.1, 26.2, and 26.3, we have shown the trend of the stock market development using the indicators of stock market development starting from 2000 to 2019. As part of clearer analysis, we have added Thailand, Korea Republic, Japan, Malaysia and Singapore which are from Asia. As shown in the tables, it is clear that there is significant growth in the African stock market by way of increase in the number of listed firms. The increase in the number of listed firms does not however reflect in the other stock development indicators. For instance, market capitalization, total value of stock traded and stock turnover continues to be very low. As per Table 26.3 which is the recent information, the average African stock market is made up of about 95 firms which has a capitalization of 48.6%

Table 26.1 Indicators of stock market development in Africa, 2000

Country Name	*Number of listed companies*	*Total value of stock traded (% of GDP)*	*Stocks traded, turnover ratio of shares (%)*	*Market capitalization of listed companies (% of GDP)*
Botswana	16.0	0.6	36.0	16.9
Egypt, Arab Rep	175.0	4.6	35.5	51.3
Ghana	22.0	0.1	1.4	10.0
Kenya	56.0	0.3	3.0	9.9
Mauritius	31.0	1.4	5.3	26.6
Morocco	53.0	8.1	8.9	62.4
Namibia	12.0	0.5	6.1	8.1
Nigeria	207.0	2.3	11.4	20.1
South Africa	604.0	51.7	34.5	149.8
Tanzania	4.0	0.0	2.1	1.7
Tunisia	44.0	4.5	16.7	13.1
Zambia	8.0	0.0	1.5	8.0
Africa Average	102.7	6.2	13.5	31.5
Africa Average[a]	27.3	1.7	9.0	17.4
Thailand	381.0	15.3	66.2	23.1
Korea, Rep.	1,242.0	86.0	289.2	29.7
Japan	2,055.0	50.8	78.6	64.6
Malaysia	787.0	56.0	46.4	120.6
Singapore	328.0	99.0	62.3	159.1

Source World Bank, World Development Indicators and authors' calculations
[a]Excluding South Africa, Nigeria and Egypt

Table 26.2 Indicators of stock market development in Africa, 2010

Country Name	*Number of listed companies*	*Total value of stock traded (% of GDP)*	*Stocks traded, turnover ratio of shares (%)*	*Market capitalization of listed companies (% of GDP)*
Botswana	31.0	0.7	3.5	17.6
Egypt, Arab Rep.	227.0	17.0	44.2	38.5
Ghana	31.0	0.3	3.5	9.2
Kenya	55.0	2.0	5.5	36.2
Mauritius	62.0	3.6	4.7	77.5
Morocco	73.0	6.5	8.8	74.2
Namibia	7.0	0.2	1.7	10.4
Nigeria	215.0	1.4	10.1	14.0
South Africa	352.0	73.9	30.0	246.4
Tanzania	14.0	0.0	1.8	2.8
Tunisia	56.0	4.2	17.2	24.2
Zambia	11.0	0.1	2.5	42.9
Africa Average	94.5	9.2	11.1	49.5
Africa Average[a]	37.8	2.0	5.5	32.8
Thailand	541.0	65.2	80.1	81.4
Korea, Rep.	1,781.0	142.5	149.3	95.4
Japan	2,281.0	74.9	111.6	67.2
Malaysia	948.0	45.0	28.1	160.3
Singapore	461.0	127.5	47.2	269.9

Source World Bank, World Development Indicators and authors' calculations
[a]Excluding South Africa, Nigeria and Egypt

and 8.1% for both total value traded and turnover. Notwithstanding, the fact that these rates have seen improvement over the years, as compared to the Asian stock market the African stock market is too thin and small in nature. It is worthy to note that the African stock market is dominated by few countries.

When we removed South Africa, Nigeria and Egypt from the sample, we realized a decrease of about 50% in the number of firms listed and the capitalization of the stocks in Africa whereas the reduction in traded stock and stock turnover is over 70%. This indicates that on average, South Africa, Egypt and Nigeria's stock markets are outliers in the African stock market thus these three countries control the stock market in Africa.

Table 26.3 Indicators of stock market development in Africa, 2019

Country name	*Number of listed companies*	*Total value of stock traded (% of GDP)*	*Stocks traded, turnover ratio of shares (%)*	*Market capitalization of listed companies (% of GDP)*
Botswana	36.0	0.5	4.5	19.7
Egypt, Arab Rep.	246.0	3.7	25.3	14.6
Ghana	40.0	0.4	3.2	13.4
Kenya	59.0	0.5	1.9	26.2
Mauritius	95.0	2.5	4.0	61.3
Morocco	74.0	2.7	5.0	54.6
Namibia	11.0	0.8	3.8	21.1
Nigeria	223.0	0.6	6.2	9.8
South Africa	388.0	81.0	33.1	300.6
Tanzania	27.0	0.5	2.6	4.6
Tunisia	81.0	4.3	5.4	21.9
Zambia	24.0	0.1	1.8	35.6
Africa Average	95.6	8.1	8.1	48.6
Africa Average[a]	49.7	1.4	3.6	28.7
Thailand	725.0	67.5	64.5	104.7
Korea, Rep.	2,262.0	117.1	129.8	122.4
Japan	3,704.0	100.3	82.3	121.8
Malaysia	919.0	29.8	26.9	110.8
Singapore	470.0	30.7	16.4	187.4

Source World Bank, World Development Indicators and authors' calculations
[a]Excluding South Africa, Nigeria and Egypt

When it comes to market capitalization, the African market is capitalized mainly by the South African market, which has over 90% of the African market capitalization. It is interesting to note that though the South African stock exchange does not have more firms as compared to the Asian countries we sampled, it is however more capitalized than these Asian stock markets. It is therefore evident that notwithstanding the fact that most African stock markets are too small in size and values and not liquid enough, the South African Exchange (JSE) is well-capitalized, very liquid and sizeable in nature to be able to compete with stock markets in other parts of the world.

Besides, these characteristics the African stock markets have only few stocks been traded daily with informational and disclosure deficiencies. There is equally supervision and regulatory inadequacies in the African stock market (Yartey & Adjasi, 2007). A part from the JSE, the African stock markets are noted to be small, illiquid, few listed firms, lack the needed infrastructure and offer very limited opportunities of trading as compared to developed countries stock markets (Alagidede, 2009). Similarly, the African stock markets are not well integrated (Alagidede, 2009). Notwithstanding these problems facing the African stock market, the African stock markets nevertheless have performed well in terms of absolute returns (Allen et al, 2011). It is also said to have a lot of opportunities for diversification for multinational companies as it does not respond to global news (Alagidede, 2009).

26.3 Theoretical Literature

Macroeconomic Determinants of Stock Market Development

Macroeconomic factors such as economic growth, interest rate, inflation and banking sector development are noted to have some links with the development of financial sector in general. For instance, economic growth is known to have a positive link with financial sector development (Ho & Iyke, 2017). The channel through which economic growth enhances financial sector development is that it helps to reduce the initial fixed cost which is needed to enable the creation of platforms that engender the development of stock market and banking sector participation by people. With the advancement in economy, financial intermediaries are established which thus become major conduits through which individuals participate in the financial market without much cost. In supporting this view, Greenwood and Smith (1997) argue that due to the huge fixed cost needed in the establishment of markets in the financial sector, these markets may become inactive until the economy has developed to a level that they will become cost-effective to operate.

Despite this, banking sector development is one of the macroeconomic variables that is arguably has got a link with stock market development. The link between banking sector development and stock market development is known to be ambiguous. While some argue that banking sector development becomes a substitute to stock market development in propelling economic growth, others are of the view that the two are complementary and hence enhances each other. On the substitutability of stock market with bank market, it is argued that a well-developed stock market quickly disseminates information to the public making the public not able to devote resources in evaluating firms whereas banks privatize their information forcing the public to search properly and hence allocate their resources judiciously for economic growth (Stiglitz, 1985). This makes the banking sector do better in terms of engendering economic growth than the stock market. On the contrary, the banking sector can complement stock market development by facilitating tailor-made risk management services and boosting liquidity (Ho & Iyke, 2017). With high liquidity in the system, investors become reassured that they will be able to cash out from locking into any equity market without fear of not getting market for their investment in the future. This makes many people to participate in the stock market.

One other macroeconomic variable worth mentioning as a determinant of stock market development is inflation. Higher inflation is associated with less liquid and smaller stock markets. Higher inflation reduces the real rate of return on investments and makes investors less eager to invest their money in either the stock market or the banking sector (Boyd et al., 2001). Besides, with the reduction in the real rate of return, creditors are not also willing to give out loans to borrowers thus leading to credit rationing which leads to low capital formation thereby affecting stock market negatively. Another factor in the macroeconomic sector is the interest rate. Theories on the link between interest rate and stock market development have been inconclusive. Whereas a section of studies has shown that interest rate enhances stock market development, others demonstrate that it retards stock market development. The rationale for the positive link between interest rate and stock market development is that stock prices usually reflect investor expectations (Shiller, 1988). An increase in interest rate will entice investors to expect more interest in the future thus pushing up the prices of shares, which will drive in many investors into the market. On the contrary, the higher the interest rate the lower the value of stocks as per the dividend discount model (Gordon & Shapiro, 1956). Besides, it increases the cost of borrowing thus discouraging investors from borrowing to invest in the stock market. It equally increases the cost of doing business with the rise in the cost of capital.

Institutional Determinants of Stock Market Development

Institutional factors in the form of corruption, rule of law, governance effectiveness and political stability certainly have some link with stock market development. For instance, the existence of transparency and effective regulation will affect stock market positively by increasing investor confidence and participation in stock market. In their view, La Porta et al. (1997) show that better legal protection of interest of shareholders and creditors will promote the flow of investment and availability of external finance to firms in the forms of equity. They stress further that rule of law and protection of shareholders' interest are critical predictors of stock market development. Shareholders are often keen on getting their investment protected and their rights guaranteed. Where investors are assured of these by way of the existence of effective and efficient rule of law and proper enforcement mechanism in place, investors will thus be highly motivated to participate in the stock market without any fear. One other issue that attracts investors is the right to vote and select the board members to steer the affairs of the organization. Where there is fairness in the implementation of this without excluding minority shareholders, the stock market is likely to experience growth through participation.

Globerman and Shapiro (2002) in particular argue that investments cannot be protected in environment of poor governance. In an environment where there is no rule of law, investors are very much concerned about how contract terms can be enforced in court with fairness. Court decisions are therefore often influenced in such instances and hence fairness does not prevail. In supporting the influential role of quality institutions on stock market development, Jensen (2003) emphasizes two important reasons. Firstly, good governance prevents bad and undesirable policies which could otherwise be very detrimental to good investment climate. Secondly, in democratic nations, political leaders are accountable not only to their voters but also to businesses operating in their jurisdictions. In such nations, political leaders are very mindful about businesses. They are aware that businesses can retaliate against any obnoxious policies that are inimical to business growth by refusing to invest (Subasat & Bellos, 2013). This therefore means in countries where there are quality institutions, stock market development should be positive.

North (1990) theory of institution explains also the reasons why good governance is a determinant of stock market development. North (1990) believes that institutions such as rule of law, governance effectiveness, control of corruption etc. do not only create opportunism but also build transactional trust in financial transactions and influence investors to engage in cross-border transactions. It is argued that government infrastructure indicates the quality of its investment environment and hence determine the level of capital inflows (Globerman & Shapiro, 2002).

Natural Resource Rents Determinants of Stock Market Development

Natural resource rents (NRR) refers to the profit obtained from natural resources after paying for the cost of production and any opportunity costs of production (Van der Ploeg, 2011). Theoretical literature on the link between NRR and stock market development has been unavailable. The focus in the literature is rather on NRR and economic growth (Khan et al, 2020). On the NRR and economic link, the literature has presented mixed arguments. Some studies have argued that NRR impacts positively on economic growth whereas others believe that it retards economic development. The channel through which NRR spur economic growth is the creation of ample investment and market opportunities in developing economies (Viner, 1952). Brumschweiler (2002) also agree with this assertion by arguing that natural resource endowment enhances economic growth through quality institutions. The inverse relationship between NRR and economic growth is generally described as 'the resource curse hypotheses'. The literature has summarized the reasons for the adverse relation as rent-seeking behaviour of foreign firms extracting natural resources, real exchange rate, exchange rate appreciation (Dutch disease), increase volatility prices of natural resources and weakened institutional quality in resource-endowed countries (see Billmeier & Massa, 2009). The above two arguments in connection with NRR and economic growth can be inferred for that of the NRR and SMD since there is a link between economic growth and SMD in general from the literature.

Empirical Literature on Determinants of Stock Market Development

Our review of the literature is categorized into macroeconomic factors, institutional factors and natural resource rents factors that determine stock market development. On the macroeconomic front, a number of studies exist establishing the link between macroeconomic factors and stock market development (SMD). Naceur et al. (2007) using fixed effect and random effect estimators on 12 Middle East and North African countries established that savings rate, financial intermediaries and stock market liquidity are the main important determinants of SMD. They conclude that stock market and financial intermediaries are complements and not substitutes in growth. In a comprehensive study, Cherif and Gazdar (2010) investigate 14 MENA countries using IV estimation techniques, savings rate, stock market liquidity and interest rates are found to influence SMD in the MENA region. Garcia and Liu (1999) earlier study 15 emerging countries using a panel data of 1980–1995 and conclude that real income, savings rate, banking development and stock market liquidity are important determinants of stock market development in these countries. Their study also establishes that banking sector development and SMD are complementary and not substitute to growth. In a related study, Evrim-Mandaci et al. (2013) examine the stock market determinants in both advanced and emerging countries. Using SUR regression technique, they find that FDI, remittances and bank sector development are influencing factors in SMD.

In a single economy study on the determinants of SMD, Rakhal (2015) establishes that remittances and money supply affect SMD positively while interest rate and exchange rate affect SMD negatively in Nepal. Bayar (2016) examines the determinants of SMD in Turkey and noted that while economic growth and stock market liquidity have a positive impact on SMD, inflation on the other hand had negative impact on SMD. Using Ghanaian economy, Acquah-Sam (2016) investigates the determinants of SMD. This study concludes that gross capital formation and GDP influence SMD while inflation and FDI are found to be insignificant. In a very recent study, Estale and Tabowei (2019) document that GDP has a positive impact on SMD whereas exchange rate has a negative impact on the Nigerian economy. They however noted that inflation and interest rate have insignificant impact.

Empirical literature on institutional quality and SMD determinants are skewed towards positive link direction. Using 8 European Union transition economies, Bayar (2016) realizes that political stability, regulatory quality, rule of law and control of corruption had a positive impact on stock market development. Cherif and Dreger (2016) explore the institutional factors influencing SMD in the Middle East and North Africa. They conclude that control of corruption and rule of law are the main key institutional factors determining the development of stock market in MENA region.

Yartey (2008) study 42 emerging countries from 1990 to 2004 using a robust GMM estimator. He establishes that the macroeconomic factors responsible for SMD are income level, banking sector development, private capital flows and stock market liquidity. He concludes that institutional factors influencing SMD are political risk, law and order and bureaucratic quality. He notes that these factors influence SMD because they enhance the viability of external finance. Similarly, Andrianaivo and Yartey (2010) estimate the link between macroeconomic variables, institutional quality and stock market delopment using system GMM for 17 African countries. They find that the stock market liquidity, domestic savings and banking sector development as the macroeconomic determinants of SMD. They also find political risk as the institutional factor which influences SMD in Africa. These findings were later confirmed by Paul et al. (2017) using 10 SSA countries. In addition, Matadeen (2019) documents that economic growth, banking sector development, stock market liquidity and gross fixed capital formation are the key drivers of SMD in Mauritius whilet institutional factors that influence SMD in Mauritius are political stability, rule of law, governance effectiveness, voice accountability and control of law.

Like the theoretical literature, empirical evidence on the natural resource rents (NRR) factors for SMD are very scanty. One of such studies is Billmeier and Massa (2008). They use a sample of 17 emerging countries in Middle East and Central Asia combining both oil and non-oil economies. They find that in both oil and non-oil countries, institutions and remittances have positive impact on SMD while in the resource-rich countries the SMD is mainly driven by oil prices. In a recent study, Khan et al. (2020) document in Pakistan that natural resources rent negatively influence financial sector development including SMD.

26.4 Methodology

Data Source

The data for the study is taken from Global Financial Development Database for the stock market development data. The macroeconomic variables and natural resources are taken from World Development Indicators of the World Bank. The institutional variables are taken from Global Governance Indicators. The data spans from 2000 to 2017 for 15 countries in Africa which has a functional stock market.

Estimation Strategy

The work of Yartey (2008) and Andrianaivo and Yartey (2010) are followed to model the determinants of stock market development in Africa. For instance, Andrianaivo and Yartey (2010) modify the earlier theoretical model of Calderon-Rossel on stock market development which is a function of income level and stock market liquidity. Our model includes macroeconomic, institutional quality and natural resource revenues. We specified the model, on determinants of stock market development using the panel fixed effect model below:

$$\begin{aligned}\mathrm{STMD_{it}} &= \alpha_\mathrm{i} + \theta_\mathrm{t} + \delta_1 \ln \mathrm{STMLIQ_{it}} + \delta_2 \ln \mathrm{BSD_{it}} \\ &\quad + \delta_3 \ln \mathrm{MACRO_{it}} + \delta_4 \ln \mathrm{INST_{it}} \\ &\quad + \delta_5 \ln \mathrm{NRR_{it}} + \varepsilon_\mathrm{it} \qquad (26.1)\end{aligned}$$

where $STMD$ is stock market capitalization measures as the ratio of total market value traded of listed companies to GDP. STMLIQ is stock market liquidity measures as value of stocks traded as a percentage of GDP. BSD is the banking sector development which is measured as bank credit to the private sector as a percentage of GDP. MACRO are macroeconomic variables such as GDP per capita, inflation, real interest rate, savings, investment and foreign direct investment. $INST$ are institutional variables such as government effectiveness, political stability, voice and accountability, rule of law, control of corruption and regulatory quality. NRRis natural resource rent such as oil rent, mineral rent, natural gas rent, forest rent and total rent. α_i is country fixed effect, θ_t is time fixed effect and ε_{it} is the error term. The details of both dependent and independent variables are discussed below in line with theoritical and empirical literature.

Dependent Variable: Stock Market Development

The main dependent variable for the study is stock market capitalization which is measured as the total value of firms listed on the stock exchange as percentage of GDP. We concentrate on this measure because, overall, all the stocks listed on the stock exchange value shows the total amount of funds available by firms for investment. Also, firms are able to mobilize funds on the basis of the shares they enlist on the stock exchange which enables them to diversify risk on the economy-wide (Amo-Yartey, 2008).

Independent Variables

Stock Market Liquidity

According to Levine and Zervos (1998) stock market liquidity is the value of stock traded as a percentage of GDP. This shows how quickly investors can buy and sell off their securities in the stock market. More liquid stock markets are able to channel funds to productive use which helps to facilitate long-run growth. It also able to improve savings since individuals and investors will have confidence on the stock market and would want to save money through investment in the stock market. This will facilitate development of the stock market. Therefore, a positive relationship is expected between stock market liquidity and stock market capitalization (Amo-Yartey, 2008).

Banking Sector Development

The study includes banking sector development into the model. It is measured as the bank credit to the private sector as a percentage of GDP. Extant literature establishes that banking sector development complements stock market development (Amo-Evrim-Mandaci et al., 2013; Yartey, 2008). This captures the amount of resources that is channelled through the banking sector to the private sector thereby fulfilling one of the key functions of financial intermediation. Thus, channelling funds from surplus units to deficit units. It does not include funds to government and quasi-government institutions. Africa is considered to be a bank-based economy, so the development of the banking sector could be a substitute to the stock market instead of it being a complement. So, the highly developed banking sector may have a negative effect on stock market development since the funds that are supposed to be invested in the stock market may only stay in banks. On the basis of this, we expect a negative relationship between banking sector development and stock market development.

Macroeconomic Stability

Stable macroeconomy facilitates the development of the stock market because it gives an incentive for investors to participate in stock market activities. Some of the macroeconomic variables used in the study include GDP per capita, savings, investment, inflation and real interest rates. GDP per capita measures the income level of citizens within the economy. This expands the economy leading to increase in demand for financial services. So, the higher the level of income the more proactive citizens are willing to part some of their income for investment in the stock market. An increase in savings will facilitate capital flow to the stock market since speculative purpose of holding money will include stock holdings. Also, through the injection cycle in the circular flow of the economy, increase in savings leads to investment in projects which would require firms demanding more capital from the stock market through floating of new shares. This would lead to development in the stock market. Finally, real interest rate and inflation indicate that stocks provide a hedge against inflation because of equity premium and also for real interest rates. There is a negative relationship between stock returns and inflation as well as real interest rates (Yartey, 2008).

Institutional Quality

Domestic stock markets attract both foreign and local investors who face different kinds of risks in the economy. These include economic risk, political risk and financial risk. To be able to mitigate this risk especially political risk, strong institutional quality is needed. Kaufmann et al. (2008) identify six institutional quality indicators that are largely used in the literature (Andrianaivo & Yartey, 2010; Matadeen, 2019; Paul et al., 2017). This is because foreign investors need strong legal protection of their investments so as to prevent the risk of expropriation. Some of these indicators include control of corruption, government effectiveness, political stability, regulatory quality, voice and accountability and rule of law. The values range between 0 and 100 with a zero score being the least and a 100 score being the highest. Countries with higher scores indicate strong institutional quality while countries with lower scores implies low institutional quality. Countries with low corruption levels are more likely to attract foreign direct investors which can support stock market development. Also, when they are strong regulatory quality stock markets are able to enforce rules such as full disclosure by firms, protection of minority and majority shareholders' funds, proper corporate governance practices, filing of annual reports by listed firms which among other things support the development of the stock market. The study expects positive relationship between good institutional quality and stock market development.

Natural Resources

Natural resource revenues provide liquidity for stock market since multinational corporations such as mining companies, International Oil Companies and others list their stocks on the local bourse in a bid to shore up their liquidity. In this study, natural resource rent such as oil, mineral, natural gas, forest and total natural resource rent are used. They are measured as a rent accruing after taken care of all the cost of production as a percentage of GDP. These measures have been used in the extant literature extensively (see Billmeier & Massa, 2008; Khan et al., 2020). The argument is that countries with endowed natural resources, stock markets thrives mainly because natural resources provide enough liquidity for the stock market by making both citizens and multinational corporations to participate in the stock market. This makes such stock markets active thereby developing them. This is in contrast with countries without natural resources. The study expects a positive relationship between natural resources rent and stock market development.

Estimation Technique

The Fixed Effects (FE) estimator is used to estimate the specified model. The FE estimator is a form of Least Squares (GLS) estimator and the FE is also known as the within estimator (Brüderl & Ludwig, 2015). It accounts for time-invariant effects of time-invariant variables (variables that do not change with time). FE explores the relationship between the independent and dependent variables within an entity which could be a country, company or person. FE controls for all discrepancies between observations that do not vary with time and also controls for unobserved heterogeneity when it is correlated with the independent variables. This method is designed to study the causes of changes within a particular entity and it produces consistent estimates. It considers both country and time-specific effects. FE is expected to have a systematic and predictable influence on data. Moreover, FE solves omitted variable problems and also caters for non-continuity in data (Brüderl & Ludwig, 2015). A very important assumption of the FE estimator is that the time-invariant features are unique to the entity and should have no correlation with other entity characteristic. Our study made use of the fixed effects because of the small sample that we are using. The number of countries are 15 which is less than the time frame of 18 years, hence making it difficult to utilize any form of dynamic model such as the GMM (Andrianaivo & Yartey, 2010).

26.5 Results and Discussion

Descriptive Statistics

This section discusses the descriptive statistics of the study. On average stock market capitalization records 25.623% over the sample period. Stock market value traded records an average of 3.32% showing that African stock markets are less liquid. For macroeconomic variables, foreign direct investment records an average of 3.34% indicating that foreign capital inflows to Africa are low.

Similarly, GDP per capita records an average of US$3,016.67 showing that most African countries with equity markets are within lower-middle to middle-income country status and can therefore save to participate in

Table 26.4 Descriptive statistics

Variable	*Obs*	*Mean*	*Std. Dev.*	*Min*	*Max*
Stock market capitalization	161	25.623	21.267	0.053	106.774
Stock value traded	125	3.318	8.037	0.048	58.855
Macroeconomics					
Foreign direct investment	165	3.339	2.408	−0.323	10.154
GDP per capita	165	3016.673	2428.152	315.777	10,484.908
Domestic savings	162	19.064	12.258	−3.368	56.668
Investment	162	23.917	7.788	8.951	43.074
Real Interest	132	6.053	7.904	−34.462	22.686
Inflation	165	120.839	39.828	65.006	340.242
Domestic credit to private	145	33.971	28.379	5.478	106.306
Natural resource revenues					
Natural gas rent	165	0.508	1.010	0.000	4.522
Forest rent	165	3.036	3.598	0.000	16.585
Mineral rents	165	2.391	4.020	0.000	19.175
Oil rent	165	3.167	6.239	0.000	30.489
Natural resource rent	165	9.131	7.538	0.001	34.922
Institutional quality					
Control of corruption	165	40.825	20.398	8.173	82.039
Government effectiveness	165	41.859	18.407	7.177	81.731
Political stability	165	37.274	26.616	2.844	93.75
Regulatory quality	165	42.243	17.402	8.173	83.654
Rule of law	165	44.288	18.664	4.785	82.692
Voice and accountability	165	40.594	17.627	9.005	75.117

Source Authors' computation

stock market activities. The domestic savings rate is 19.064% and investment is 23.917%. Also, the real interest rate is 6.053% and credit to the private sector is 33.971%. The natural gas rent on average is 0.508%, forest rent is 3.036%, mineral rent is 2.391%, oil rent is 3.167% and overall natural resource rent is 9.131%.

Regarding the institutional quality variables, almost all of the term has an average of percentage value below 50%. For instant political stability score in Africa even below 40 averaging 37.272% for the sample period. The low rate of institutional quality in Africa bemoans poor performance of some stock markets in Africa because of the lack of confidence in the quality of institutions by investors.

Determinants of Stock Market Development

This section discusses the results of the study in line with three subsections. First macroeconomic determinants of stock market capitalization are reported and discussed in Sect. 26.5.1. Second, institutional determinants of stock market are discussed in Sect. 26.5.2. Third, natural resource rent determinants of stock market development are analysed and discussed in Sect. 26.5.3.

Macroeconomics

This section discusses macroeconomic determinants of stock market development. The study result is presented in Table 26.5. Stock market development is measured as ratio of market capitalization as a percentage of GDP. In model 1, the study finds that stock value traded which measures the liquidity of the stock market is positive and significant. This means that a unit increase in stock market liquidity will increase market capitalization by 0.284 units all things being equal. This means that liquidity of the stock market is good in improving the capitalization of the stock market. The study also finds that banking sector development measured by private sector credit as a percentage of GDP is negative and significant implying that an increase in private credit by 1 unit leads to a reduction in stock market development by 0.363. Also, investment is found to be positive and significant. This means that increase in investment in the domestic economy promotes stock market capitalization since the investors will buy shares in companies listed in the local bourse which will increase the capitalization of the market. The study also finds GDP

Table 26.5 Macroeconomic determinants of stock market development in Africa

Variables	*Model 1*	*Model 2*	*Model 3*	*Model 4*
Stock Value Traded	0.284***	0.227***	0.299***	0.279***
	(0.071)	(0.065)	(0.076)	(0.089)
Private Credit	−0.363**	−0.012	−0.229	−0.102
	(0.137)	(0.226)	(0.157)	(0.218)
Log GDP per capita	0.362	−0.198	0.164	0.167
	(0.298)	(0.213)	(0.325)	(0.374)
Real Interest rate	−0.077		−0.078	−0.106*
	(0.056)		(0.047)	(0.059)
Investment	0.546***	0.432**		
	(0.162)	(0.151)		
Inflation		−0.443**		
		(0.205)		
Savings			0.243	
			(0.175)	
Foreign Direct Invest				−0.033
				(0.056)
Constant	0.222	5.500**	2.230	2.555
	(2.626)	(2.270)	(2.668)	(2.839)
Observations	88	132	87	90
R-squared	0.621	0.576	0.582	0.500
No of Countries	12	15	12	12
Time Fixed Effect	Yes	Yes	Yes	Yes

Note ***, ** and * are significant levels at 1, 5, and 10%, respectively. The robust standard errors are in parenthesis

per capita to be positive but insignificant and real interest rates variable is negative and insignificant. This implies that an increase in real interest rates have negative repercussions on the stock market since investors will shift their investment on the stock market to other marketable securities such as treasury bills and other short-term investments.

In model 2, we include inflation in the model in line with Amo-Yartey (2008) but we exclude real interest rates since inflation also represents the investment climate of the economy. We find that stock market liquidity in positive and statistically significant. We also find that investment remains positive and significant. Inflation is negative and significant. This means that as inflation increases, it will increase interest rates, which will change speculative motive for holding money from investment in the stock markets to other short-term marketable securities. We also find private credit to GDP to be negative and insignificant as well as GDP per capita.

In Model 3, we include savings in the model while ignoring investment and inflation. The reason is that savings represent the investible amount within the economy while real interest rate account for inflation. We find savings to be positive but insignificant. Thus, increase in savings will make funds available for the purchase of shares in the stock market which will increase stock market capitalization. We find stock market liquidity to be positive and significant, GDP per capita remains positive but insignificant. Private credit is negative and real interest rate are negative and insignificant.

In Model 4, foreign direct investment is included in the baseline model. The study finds foreign direct investment to be negative and insignificant. Thus, inflows of foreign funds into the economy of Africa does not have any effect on stock market capitalization. Thus, those funds are only flown in for direct investment purposes and not for the sake of stock market capitalization.

Furthermore, the study finds that stock market liquidity is positive and significant, private credit is negative, GDP per capita is positive and insignificant. Again, real interest rate is negative and significant. This confirms the fact that an increase in real interest rates does not help with the development of the stock market since funds would be shifted to the investment of short-term marketable securities in Africa. In appendix A1, similar results are presented without South Africa, which is the most liquid and well-capitalize market in Africa. We reported findings that are akin to those reported in Table 26.5. This means that our results are robust to omission of very important stock market. This makes our findings much reliable.

Institutional Quality

Table 26.6 presents results on institutional determinants of stock market while controlling for key other macroeconomic factors, banking sector and stock market liquidity. The institutional variables used are taken from World Governance Indicators (WGI) of the World Development Indicators. These are control of corruption, government effectiveness, political stability, voice and accountability, rule of law and regulatory quality.

In model 1, we estimate for control of corruption which captures the perception of the extent to which public power is exercised for private

Table 26.6 Institutional determinants of stock market development

Variables	*Model 1*	*Model 2*	*Model 3*	*Model 4*	*Model 5*	*Model 6*
Stock Value Traded	0.223***	0.220***	0.227***	0.217***	0.227***	0.223***
	(0.061)	(0.066)	(0.065)	(0.063)	(0.065)	(0.064)
Private Credit	−0.0466	−0.0466	−0.0122	−0.021	−0.014	−0.048
	(0.187)	(0.224)	(0.219)	(0.200)	(0.228)	(0.220)
Log GDP per capita	−0.190	−0.220	−0.199	−0.224	−0.194	−0.219
	(0.202)	(0.208)	(0.248)	(0.219)	(0.215)	(0.223)
Investment	0.496***	0.424**	0.432**	0.360**	0.430**	0.390**
	(0.136)	(0.147)	(0.147)	(0.131)	(0.153)	(0.149)
Inflation	−0.629***	−0.414*	−0.442**	−0.294	−0.438*	−0.424**
	(0.189)	(0.205)	(0.184)	(0.176)	(0.205)	(0.196)
Control of Corruption	−0.012***					
	(0.004)					
Gov Effectiveness		0.004				
		(0.005)				
Political Stability			3.89e-05			
			(0.006)			
Regulatory Quality				0.010		
				(0.006)		
Voice and Accountability					0.001	
					(0.003)	
Rule of Law						0.004
						(0.005)
Constant	6.707***	5.518**	5.501**	4.864**	5.422**	5.654**
	(2.188)	(2.272)	(2.355)	(2.241)	(2.287)	(2.349)
Observations	132	132	132	132	132	132
R-squared	0.609	0.578	0.576	0.591	0.576	0.578
No. of Countries	15	15	15	15	15	15
Time Fixed Effects	Yes	Yes	Yes	Yes	Yes	Yes

Note ***, ** and * are significant levels at 1, 5, and 10%, respectively. The robust standard errors are in parenthesis

gain, including both petty and grand forms of corruption. Essentially, the study finds control of corruption to be negative and statistically significant at a 1% significance level on stock market capitalization. This means that higher perception for corruption impedes on the stock market capitalization. This is generally so, because in most African countries, corruption is rampant which derails investors' confidence in the stock market thereby lowering stock market participation when corruption perception is high. Thus, the study finds that a unit increase in corruption perception reduces stock market capitalization by 0.012 units all things being equal. In essence corruption is considered as a big issue when it comes to stock market development in Africa. The study finds stock market liquidity to be positive and significant, investment is also positive and significant whilst inflation is negative and significant as well. The rest of the variables such as private credit and GDP per capita all show negative and insignificant relationship with stock market capitalization.

In model 2, we estimate government effectiveness. Government effectiveness captures the perception of the quality of public and civil services and the degree of its independence from political pressure, the quality of policy formulation and implementation and the degree to which government commits to such policies. The study finds that government effectiveness is positive but insignificant. The implication is that when public and civil services formulate policies necessary for stock market development such as demutualization, investors protection and digitization policies and implement them very well it will lead in the development of the stock market. The study also finds stock market liquidity and investment to be positive and significant whilst inflation remains negative and significant. The rest of the variables such as GDP per capita and private credit are negative and insignificant determinants of stock market development.

In model 3, we considered political stability. This captures the perception of the likelihood for political instability and politically motivated violence including terrorism. The study finds positive and insignificant effects of political stability on stock market development. Thus, a stable political environment will create a conducive atmosphere for stock market integration to occur. The study also finds stock market liquidity and investment to be positive and significant while inflation remains negative and significant. The rest of the variables such as GDP per capita and private credit are negative and insignificant determinants of stock market development.

In model 4, regulatory quality is estimated. This captures the ability of government to formulate and implement sound policies and regulation that permit and promote private sector development. The study finds regulatory quality to be positive and insignificant depicting that government formulation of good regulations can help to ensure stock market capitalization. This is because investors interests would be protected and the stock market can properly function as a result of quality laws that guide their operations. Again, stock market liquidity and investment are found to be positive and significant while inflation is negative and insignificant. The rest of the variables such as GDP per capita and private credit are negative and insignificant determinants of stock market development.

Model 5 focuses on voice and accountability. This captures the perceptions of the extent to which a country's citizens are able to participate in selecting their government, as well as freedom of expression and of the media. The study finds positive and insignificant effect on stock market capitalization. This gives the freedom to stock market participants to freely express their opinion on matters relating to the stock market. Participation in the stock market gives stockholders the right to ownership of the listed firms, so policies that are enacted to give them the freedom to express their views, both at Annual General Meetings (AGM) and on the media to drive home their demand for accountability will help with the development of the stock market all things being equal. Similarly, with stock market liquidity and investment, the study finds positive and significant relationship with stock market capitalization while inflation remains negative and significant. The rest of the variables such as GDP per capita and private credit are negative and insignificant determinants of stock market development in Africa.

Finally, in model 6, the study estimates for rule of law. The rule of law captures the perception of the extent to which agents have confidence in and abide by rules of society more particularly the quality of contract enforcement and property rights. The study finds positive but insignificant effect of rule of law on stock market capitalization. Since stock markets deal with contract enforcement, it is prudent that African countries develop their courts, policing and other enforceable institutions of state to ensure that the stock market abides by its own rules and regulations. This will enable the stock market in Africa to develop. Again, the study finds positive and significant relationship between stock market liquidity and investment on stock market capitalization with inflation remaining negative and significant in the model. The rest of the variables such as GDP per capita and private credit are negative and insignificant determinants of stock market development.

Natural Resource Rent

Table 26.7 shows the results of the determinants of natural resources on stock market development in Africa. The natural resource revenues studied are the share of natural gas rent as a percentage of GDP, mineral rent as a percentage of GDP, oil rent as a percentage of GDP, forest rent as a percentage of GDP and total natural resource rent as a percentage of GDP.

In Model 1, the study finds that natural gas rent is significant and positive indicating that an increase in natural gas rent makes liquidity available to both government and multinational companies in the extractive sector which intend to invest money in the domestic stock market. This helps to develop the stock exchange. Thus, increase in natural gas rent by 1 unit leads to the development of the stock market by 0.32 units all things being equal. The study finds stock market liquidity and investment to be positive and significant with inflation being negative and significant towards stock market capitalization. Private credit and GDP per capita remain negative and insignificant.

Model 2 shows the results of oil rent as a percentage of GDP. The results show a positive and insignificant effect of oil rent on stock market development. Thus, increase in oil rent improves liquidity position of investors in the oil sector and thus may influence their participation in the stock market. However, this influence is not statistically distinguishable from zero. Again, the study finds all the other variables such as stock market liquidity, investment, inflation, GDP per capita and private credit to remains the same.

In model 3, the study estimates the results of mineral rents. It finds that mineral rent is positive but insignificant on stock market capitalization. This implies that as mineral rents increase, firms in the mining sector are able to increase in their capitalization in the stock market. However, this outcome is not statistically different from zero since it is not significant. Similarly, the study finds stock market liquidity and investment to be positive and significant towards stock market capitalization. Also, inflation remains negative and significant. Finally, private credit and GDP per capita are negative and insignificant in the model.

Table 26.7 Natural Resource Rents Determinants of Stock Market Development

Variables	*Model 1*	*Model 2*	*Model 3*	*Model 4*	*Model 5*
Stock Value Traded	0.208***	0.216***	0.229***	0.236***	0.226***
	(0.058)	(0.063)	(0.066)	(0.062)	(0.064)
Private Credit	−0.000	−0.021	−0.004	0.002	−0.013
	(0.167)	(0.207)	(0.226)	(0.229)	(0.222)
Log GDP per capita	−0.116	−0.228	−0.208	−0.519**	−0.196
	(0.174)	(0.198)	(0.225)	(0.214)	(0.211)
Investment	0.351**	0.404**	0.431**	0.429***	0.422**
	(0.119)	(0.136)	(0.153)	(0.136)	(0.158)
Inflation	−0.282*	−0.368*	−0.444**	−0.363*	−0.429**
	(0.159)	(0.186)	(0.206)	(0.201)	(0.199)
Natural Gas Rents	0.317***				
	(0.043)				
Oil Rents		0.021			
		(0.015)			
Mineral Rents			0.006		
			(0.011)		
Forest Rents				−0.080**	
				(0.034)	
Total Nat. Res. Rents					0.005
					(0.012)
Constant	4.305*	5.466**	5.536**	7.763***	5.413**
	(2.118)	(2.193)	(2.305)	(1.857)	(2.182)
Observations	132	132	132	132	132
R-squared	0.631	0.588	0.577	0.609	0.577
No. of Countries	15	15	15	15	15
Time Fixed Effects	Yes	Yes	Yes	Yes	Yes

Note ***, ** and * are significant levels at 1, 5, and 10%, respectively. The robust standard errors are in parenthesis

In model 4, the study estimates with forest rent as a determinant on stock market capitalization. The study finds negative and significant relationship between forest rent and stock market capitalization. This implies that an increase in forest rent does not facilitate stock market capitalization. Thus, an increase in forest rent by 1 unit reduces stock market capitalization by 0.08 units all things being equal. This negative impact is primarily due to the fact that forest resource revenues come directly to the state which might be used for other things rather than used for stock market capitalization. This means that forest rent has curse on stock market development rather than a blessing. In addition, the study finds stock market liquidity and investment to be positive and significant. GDP per capita and inflation variables are negative and significant. The negative impact of GDP per capita on stock market capitalization depicts that a rise in income in Africa does not have improvement in the stock market capitalization partly because the Africans do not understand the working of the stock market or are not too patient to wait for a long-time to fully benefit from the stock market development.

Finally, in model 5, the total natural resource rent model is estimated. This is the summation of natural gas rent, oil rent, mineral rent and forest rent as a percentage of GDP. The study finds a positive but insignificant relationship between total resource rent and stock market capitalization. The implication is that natural resource rent is a blessing for stock market capitalization since it increases liquidity position of most African countries with endowed natural resources. Again, the study finds stock market liquidity and investment to be positive and significant. GDP per capita and private credit remains negative and insignificant with stock market capitalization. As a robustness to the results presented in Table 26.7, we estimated the model without South Africa. The findings are similar to those reported here. Appendix A3 presents the results.

26.6 Summary and Policy Implications

This chapter empirically examines the determinants of stock market development in the African equity market using data for the period 2000–2017 for 15 African Stock Exchanges. The chapter analyses the key determinants of stock market development in Africa by looking at it in three thematic areas. First, macroeconomic determinants of stock market development. Second, institutional determinants of stock market development. Third, natural resource revenue determinants of stock market development.

The study suggests a number of interesting findings. First, we find that stock market liquidity, investment rate, inflation rate and credit to the private sector which represents banking sector development are the key macroeconomic determinants of stock market development in Africa. In particular, the findings indicate that stock market liquidity facilitates the development of the stock market since investors are aware that when they invest in the stock market, it will be active for them to quickly convert their financial assets into liquid assets all things being equal. Similarly, investment boost stock market development because where there are enough funds for investment, investors will choose active stock market for their investment. However, the study indicates that banking sector development is a substitute to stock market development in Africa instead of a complement. Thus, the development of the banking sector in Africa retards the growth of the stock market all things being equal.

Second, the study finds that institutional quality development is an anchor to the development of the stock market. Control of corruption is found to be negative and significant. The implication is that countries with a higher rate of corruption perception may hamper the development of the stock exchange. The study findings clearly support the fact that in corruption -ridden countries, stock markets are less likely to develop. Other institutional quality variables such as political stability, voice and accountability, government effectiveness, regulatory quality and rule of law are found to be positive but have an insignificant impact on stock market development in Africa.

Third, the study finds that natural resource revenues endowment might have a blessing or a curse on stock market development depending on the type of natural resource rent. In particular, the study finds natural gas rent to be a blessing to stock market development whilst forest rent was noted as a curse to stock market development in Africa. The rest of the natural resource variables such as oil rent, mineral rent including total natural resource rent were positive but insignificant.

These findings have important policy implications for the development of the stock market in Africa. First, stock market liquidity promotes stock market capitalization in Africa. In general, it is important that African countries' stock exchanges initiate policies that can help to support stock market value traded. Thus, the need to develop systems and platforms that can easily facilitate the conversion of stocks into liquidity and this will boost-up investors' confidence to participate in the stock exchanges in Africa. Secondly, policies must be initiated to promote investment climate in African stock exchanges. Investor's protection policies must be encouraged in the African stock exchange such as demutualization policies. Thirdly, institutional quality is important especially control of corruption in Africa if stock exchanges are to progress and develop into international standards. Investors must have a good run for their money and not to end into corrupt hands. The courts should be developed properly and parliamentary laws passed with competent implementing institutions to deal with corrupt issues. Finally, African countries endowed with natural resources should take advantage to develop their stock exchanges. They should encourage the listing of multinational companies in the extractive sector in their respective local bourse. This will help them to take advantage of the natural resource endowment in the development of the stock market.

Appendix Results Without South Africa

Tables 26.8, 26.9, and 26.10.

Table 26.8 Macroeconomic determinants of stock market development-stock market capitalization

Variables	*Model 1*	*Model 2*	*Model 3*	*Model 4*
Stock Value Traded	0.251***	0.203***	0.287***	0.261**
	(0.0689)	(0.0665)	(0.0814)	(0.0929)
Private Credit	−0.261	0.0752	−0.194	−0.0438
	(0.154)	(0.269)	(0.203)	(0.257)
Log GDP per capita	0.557*	−0.120	0.291	0.334
	(0.272)	(0.246)	(0.390)	(0.414)
Real Interest rate	−0.0919		−0.0933	−0.121*
	(0.0575)		(0.0523)	(0.0635)
Investment	0.572***	0.453**		
	(0.164)	(0.151)		
Inflation		−0.421**		
		(0.188)		
Savings			0.213	
			(0.164)	
Foreign Direct Invest				−0.0367
				(0.0714)
Constant	−1.731	4.353	1.141	1.033
	(2.500)	(2.646)	(3.221)	(3.283)
Observations	77	121	76	79
R-squared	0.644	0.579	0.579	0.505
No. of Countries	11	14	11	11
Time Fixed Effects	Yes	Yes	Yes	Yes

Note ***, ** and * are significant levels at 1, 5, and 10%, respectively. The robust standard errors are in parenthesis

Table 26.9 Institutional determinants of stock market development

Variables	*Model 1*	*Model 2*	*Model 3*	*Model 4*	*Model 5*	*Model 6*
Stock Value Traded	0.223***	0.220***	0.227***	0.217***	0.227***	0.223***
	(0.0610)	(0.0662)	(0.0647)	(0.0625)	(0.0650)	(0.0642)
Private Credit	−0.0466	−0.0466	−0.0122	−0.0212	−0.0140	−0.0476
	(0.187)	(0.224)	(0.219)	(0.200)	(0.228)	(0.220)
Log GDP per capita	−0.190	−0.220	−0.199	−0.224	−0.194	−0.219
	(0.202)	(0.208)	(0.248)	(0.219)	(0.215)	(0.223)
Investment	0.496***	0.424**	0.432**	0.360**	0.430**	0.390**
	(0.136)	(0.147)	(0.147)	(0.131)	(0.153)	(0.149)
Inflation	−0.629***	−0.414*	−0.442**	−0.294	−0.438*	−0.424**
	(0.189)	(0.205)	(0.184)	(0.176)	(0.205)	(0.196)
Control of Corruption	−0.012***					
	(0.004)					
Gov Effectiveness		0.00352				
		(0.00516)				
Political Stability			3.89e-05			
			(0.00559)			
Regulatory Quality				0.00938		
				(0.00558)		
Voice and Account-ability					0.000912	
					(0.00305)	
Rule of Law						0.00370
						(0.00548)
Constant	6.707***	5.518**	5.501**	4.864**	5.422**	5.654**
	(2.188)	(2.272)	(2.355)	(2.241)	(2.287)	(2.349)
Observations	132	132	132	132	132	132
R-squared	0.609	0.578	0.576	0.591	0.576	0.578
No. of Countries	14	14	14	14	14	14
Time Fixed Effects	Yes	Yes	Yes	Yes	Yes	Yes

Note: ***, ** and * are significant levels at 1, 5, and 10%, respectively. The robust standard errors are in parenthesis

Table 26.10 Natural resource revenues determinants of stock market development

Variables	*Model 1*	*Model 2*	*Model 3*	*Model 4*	*Model 5*
Stock Value Traded	0.184***	0.196**	0.205**	0.221***	0.200***
	(0.0600)	(0.0651)	(0.0684)	(0.0648)	(0.0651)
Private Credit	0.0869	0.0514	0.0800	0.0310	0.0760
	(0.193)	(0.248)	(0.270)	(0.255)	(0.264)
Log GDP per capita	−0.0371	−0.166	−0.131	−0.525*	−0.115
	(0.209)	(0.246)	(0.263)	(0.260)	(0.251)
Investment	0.370***	0.427***	0.451**	0.449***	0.438**
	(0.121)	(0.139)	(0.153)	(0.134)	(0.157)
Inflation	−0.258*	−0.358*	−0.422**	−0.347	−0.398**
	(0.139)	(0.169)	(0.190)	(0.197)	(0.179)
Natural Gas Rents	0.317***				
	(0.0384)				
Oil Rents		0.0177			
		(0.0137)			
Mineral Rents			0.00559		
			(0.0109)		
Forest Rents				−0.0813**	
				(0.0369)	
Total Nat. Res. Rent					0.00787
					(0.0116)
Constant	3.132	4.529	4.418	7.444***	4.192
	(2.423)	(2.654)	(2.744)	(2.427)	(2.595)
Observations	121	121	121	121	121
R-squared	0.637	0.588	0.580	0.610	0.583
No. of Countries	14	14	14	14	14
Time Fixed Effects	Yes	Yes	Yes	Yes	Yes

Note ***, ** and * are significant levels at 1, 5, and 10%, respectively. The robust standard errors are in parenthesis

References

Acquah-Sam, E. (2016). Determinants of capital market development in Ghana. *European Scientific Journal, 12*(1), 251–270.

Adjasi, C. K. D., & Biekpe, N. B. (2006). Stock market development and economic growth: The case of selected African countries. *African Development Review, 18*(1), 144–161.

Alagidede, P. (2009). Are African stock markets integrated with the rest of the world? *African Finance Journal, 11*(1), 37–53.

Allen, F., Otchere, I., & Senbet, L. (2011). African financial system: A review. *Review of Development Finance, 1*, 79–113.

Andrianaivo, M., & Yartey, C. A. (2010). Understanding the growth of African Financial markets. *African Development Review, 22*(3), 394–418.

Bayar, Y. (2016). Institutional determinants of stock market development in European Union Transition Economies. *The Romanian Economic Journal, XIX*(61), 211–226

Billmeier, A., & Massa, I. (2007). *What drives stock market development in the Middle East and Central Asia—Institutions, remittances, or natural resources?* (IMF Working Paper, WP/07/157).

Billmeier, A., & Massa, I. (2008). Go long or short in pyramids? News from the Egyptian stock market. *International Review of Financial Analysis, 17*(5), 949–970.

Billmeier, A., & Massa, I. (2009). What drives stock market development in emerging markets—institutions, remittances, or natural resources? *Emerging Markets Review, 10*(1), 23–35. https://doi.org/10.1016/j.ememar.2008.10.005

Boyd, J. H., Levine, R., & Smith, B. D. (2001). The impact of inflation on financial market performance. *Journal of Monetary Economics, 47*, 221–248.

Bruderl, J., & Ludwig, V. (2015). Fixed-effects panel regression. In H. Best & C. Wolf (Eds.), *Regression Analysis and Causal Inference* (pp. 327–358). Sage.

Brunnschweiler, C. N. J. W. (2008). Cursing the blessings? Natural resource abundance, institutions, and economic growth. *World Development., 36*, 399–419.

Cherif, M., & Gazdar, K. (2010). Macroeconomic and institutional determinants of stock market development in MENA region: New results from a panel data analysis. *International Journal of Banking and Finance, 7*(1), 138–159.

Cherif, M. and Dreger, C. (2016). Institutional Determinants of Financial Development in MENA countries. *Review of Development Economics, 20*(3), 670–680, ISSN 1467–9361, Wiley, Hoboken. https://doi.org/10.1111/rode.12192 , https://onlinelibrary.wiley.com/doi/abs/https://doi.org/10.1111/rode.12192

Estale, M. L., & Tabowei, P. (2019). Macroeconomic determinants of market capitalization in Nigeria: A further investigation. *International Journal of Quantitative and Qualitative Research Methods.*, *7*(4), 11–25.

Evrim-Mandaci, P., Aktan, B., Kurt-Gumus, G., & Tvaronaviciene,. (2013). Determinants of stock market development: Evidence from advanced and emerging markets in a long span. *Business Theory and Practice, 14*(1), 51–56.

Garcia, V., & Liu, L. (1999). Macroeconomic determinants of stock market development. *Journal of Applied Economics, 2*(1), 29–59.

Globerman, S., & Shapiro, D. (2002). Global foreign direct investment flows: The role of governance infrastructure. *World Development, 30*, 1898–1919.

Gordon, M. J., & Shapiro, E. (1956). Capital equipment analysis: the required rate of profit. *Management Science, 3*(1), 102–110, Reprinted in Management of Corporate Capital, Free Press, Glencoe, IL, 1959.

Greenwood, J., & Smith, B. (1997). Financial markets in development, and the development of financial markets. *Journal of Economic Dynamics and Control, 21*(1), 145–181.

Ho, S.-Y., & Iyke, N. B. (2017). Determinants of stock market development: A review of the literature. *Studies in Economics and Finance, 34*(1), 143–164. https://doi.org/10.1108/sef-05-2016-0111

Jensen, N. (2003). Democratic governance and multinational corporations: Political regimes and inflows of foreign direct investment. *International Organization, 57*, 587–616.

Khan, H., Khan, S., & Zuojun, F. (2020). Institutional quality and financial development: Evidence from developing and emerging economies. *Global Business Review.*

Kaufmann, D., Kraay, A., & Mastruzzi, M. (2008). *Governance matters VII: Aggregate and individual governance indicators 1996–2007*. The World Bank.

La Porta, R., Lopez-de-Silanes, F., & Shleifer, A. (1997). Legal determinants of external finance. *Journal of Finance, 52*, 113–150.

Matadeen, J. (2019). Stock market development: An assessment of its macroeconomic and institutional determinants in Mauritius. *International Journal of Economics and Financial Issues.*, *9*(4), 197–202.

Meon, P. G., & Sekkat, K. (2005). Does corruption grease or sand the wheels of growth? *Public Choice, 122*(1), 69–97.

Naceur, S. B., Ghazouani, S., & Omran, M. (2007). The determinants of stock market development in the Middle-Eastern and North African Region. *Managerial Finance, 33*(7), 477–489.

North, D. C. (1990). A transaction cost theory of politics. *Journal of Theoretical Politics, 2*(4), 355–367.

North, D. C. (1994). Institutional change: A framework of analysis. *Social Rules*, 189–201.

Paul, K. K., Japheth, K., & Linus, O. (2017). Effects of macroeconomic factors on stock market development in Sub-saharan Africa. *International Journal of Business Management and Finance., 1*(4), 52–71.

Rakhal, R. (2015). Determinants of stock market performance. *Nepal Commerce Campus*, 134–142

Shiller, R. J. (1988). Causes of changing in financial market volatility. *The Federal Reserve Bank of Kansas City, 2*(1), 1–22.

Stiglitz, J. E. (1985). Credit markets and the control of capital. *Journal of Money, Credit, Banking, 17*(2), 133–152.

Subasat, T., & Bellos, S. (2013). Governance and FDI in Latin America: A panel Gravity Model Approach. *Latin American Journal of Economics, 50*(1), 107–131.

Van der Ploeg, F. (2011). Natural resources: Curse or blessing? *Journal of Economics Literature, 49*, 366–420.

Viner, J. J. T. P. (1952). *America's aims and the progress of underdeveloped countries* (pp. 175–202). University of Chicago Press.

Wang, X. (2009). *Regulation and corruption in transitional China* (Economics Working Papers EDP-0919). The University of Manchester.

Yartey, C. A. (2007). Well-developed financial intermediary sector promotes stock market development: Evidence from Africa. *Journal of Emerging Market Finance, 6*(3), 269–289.

Yartey, C. A. (2008). *The determinants of stock market development in emerging economies: Is South Africa different?* (IMF Working Paper 08/32).

Yartey, C. A. (2010). The institutional and macroeconomic determinants of stock market development in emerging economies. *Applied Financial Economics, 20*(21), 1615–1625.

Yartey, C. A., & C. K. Adjasi (2007). *Stock market development in Sub-Saharan Africa: Critical issues and challenges.* (IMF Working Paper 07/209).

CHAPTER 27

Bond Market Development in Africa: A Review

Isaac Otchere, Daniel Ofori-Sasu, and Joshua Yindenaba Abor

27.1 Introduction

Financial globalization has stirred up the need for many economies to expand their markets across geographical boundaries. The integrated nature of the financial market has triggered the development of the bond market. Over the past decade, it has become clear that the global bond market plays an important role in the internationalization of capital

I. Otchere (✉)
Carleton University, Ottawa, ON, Canada
e-mail: Isaac.otchere@carleton.ca

D. Ofori-Sasu (✉)
Central University, Miotso-Tema, Ghana
e-mail: dofori.sasu@central.edu.gh; dofori-sasu@st.ug.edu.gh

J. Y. Abor
University of Ghana Business School, Legon, Accra, Ghana
e-mail: joshabor@ug.edu.gh

J. Y. Abor and C. K. D. Adjasi (eds.), *The Economics of Banking and Finance in Africa*, Palgrave Macmillan Studies in Banking and Financial Institutions, https://doi.org/10.1007/978-3-031-04162-4_27

markets. For most developed markets, one of the key aspects of financial market reform, following the 2007/2008 Global Financial Crisis (GFC), has been the development of national and regional bond markets as an alternative to bank financing (Astrauskaite & Paškevicius, 2014; Batten et al., 2009). This has made corporate bonds, an appropriate investment choice (Astrauskaite & Paškevicius, 2014) because of the diversification it provides. The recent global COVID-19 crisis and the attendant deleterious effects on the global financial markets caused yields on deposits and government securities to fall sharply. Emerging debt markets experienced a temporary increase in the inflow of funds from institutional investors (Agbloyor & Abor, 2020). For instance, the IMF has provided US$ 9 billion to African lower-income countries and US$20 billion to African emerging markets since the pandemic evolved (IMF, 2021). Prior to the pandemic and the 2007/2008 GFC, attention was paid to the markets in which governments issued and traded short-term securities, and subsequently to markets in which industrial and financial companies issued and traded short-term securities (Batten & Kim, 2001; Kim, 2000) with less attention on the capital market, in particular bond market. Given that the bond market plays a significant role in capital market development, economic growth and development, policymakers, practitioners, and researchers have taken a holistic approach to investigating the African bond market (Allen et al., 2011; Mu et al., 2013a, 2013b), mainly because of financial globalization and portfolio investments and debt flows in the region (World Bank, 2019).

Africa is economically and culturally diverse and has different regional economic blocs. The development needs in Africa are enormous, and meeting these needs is critical to rapid economic growth across the continent. Economic development and growth are closely linked to capital markets and financial integration. Capital market development provides a source of funding for national and regional development and it is a medium for regional integration. Regional integration and trade reinforce capital market development across the different economies and blocs in Africa. The capital market, particularly bond markets, is increasingly used to raise capital to finance development projects of virtually every country in Africa. As a result, African bond markets have grown steadily in recent years, but the markets are still underdeveloped (Bae, 2012; Batten et al., 2009; Duru & Nyong, 2016; Mu et al., 2013a, 2013b). For example, the African Development Bank (2006) highlighted the growing role of bond markets in funding growth in sub-Saharan Africa. Financial systems in Africa differ from country to country as the continent's 53 countries are economically, culturally diverse with different regional economic blocs (Allen et al., 2011). In view of that, reviewing the development of the bond market for a heterogeneous group of countries may present a challenge. Therefore, we discuss bond market development in Africa based on two criteria. The first is based on geographical lines and the second is on the level of economic development.

Despite the increasing number of studies on bond market development and the growth of the bond markets in Africa, there is very little contribution to the literature in the African space. We do not know much about the state of the bond market in Africa, etc. To attempt to fill this gap, this provides a systematic critical overview of the literature on the development of bond markets in Africa. The purpose of this paper is to provide cogent conclusions and suggest ways that the African bond market can be developed based on a systematic review of empirical works on bond market development. It adds to the discussion on bond market development by exploring its contribution to economic development and the challenges to the development of the government and corporate bond market, among others.

This review attempts to address the question posed earlier and makes concrete contributions. As far as we know, it provides a comprehensive analysis of the theoretical basis and empirical studies on the development of the bond market in Africa for the first time. This records, among other things, the current state of the bond market in Africa (main players in the bond market, pension services, bond market performance); Bond market and infrastructure finance in Africa; Restrictions on the development of the bond market in Africa and how the development of the bond market in Africa can be encouraged.

To achieve the objective of the paper, Sect. 27.1 highlights the features and types of bond market from the African context; Sect. 27.2 provides the country specific examples of bond markets and discusses why the need for bond market development?; Sect. 27.3 discusses bond market development and financing in Africa; Sect. 27.4 highlights the current situation and performance of the bond market in Africa; Sect. 27.5 reveals the constraints to bond market development in Africa; Sect. 27.6 provides the empirical review on the determinants of bond market development; and Sect. 27.7 provides the conclusion for policy implications.

27.2 Bond Markets: Features and Types

A bond is a long-term debt instrument. The issuer (the borrower) is obliged to make periodic payments (coupon payments) to the bondholder (the lender) as well as pay the principal sum (face value) upon maturity of the bond. The types of bonds include government and corporate bonds. Government bonds are bonds that the government sells and guarantees. Government bonds include municipal, sovereign and agency bonds. Government entities issue mainly two types of municipal bonds, and these include obligation bonds (unsecured bonds that are backed in full faith by the issuing government because they have the power to tax citizens and raise money to repay investors) and revenue bonds (revenues from a particular project or source, such as highway tolls or lease fees. Municipal bonds are bonds issued by cities and municipalities to finance their daily activities and the construction of capital-intensive projects, such as roads, schools and hospitals. For the government type of bond, the limited capacity of domestic market to absorb the issue may require the government to issue bonds in foreign currency and sell them to foreign investors. This type of bond is issued in a foreign currency that is stronger than the currency of the issuing country. Diaspora bonds are bonds issued by governments but are aimed at citizens, residents, and individuals who come from the country but live elsewhere. Islamic bonds are bonds issued by governments, Islamic banks and other companies in Islamic countries.

Agency bonds, also known as the state-owned enterprise bonds, are low-risk investments issued by government agencies and government sponsored bodies. It is usually backed by full loyalty and faith of the national government. Government bonds are debt instruments (e.g., Treasury bills, Treasury notes, government Treasury bonds, Treasury inflation-protected securities) issued and backed by the government.

Corporate bonds (short-term, medium-term, or long-term) are bonds issued by private or public companies. Investors who buy these types of bonds usually led to the issuer, who in turn imposes on the issuer the legal obligation to pay interest on the capital (principal) and return the capital (principal) to the investors when the bond expires.

Since not all bonds are the same, governments and corporations have the option of issuing different types of bonds to achieve the best funding channel. Bonds can also be classified based on whether they are secured by collateral and their seniority in terms of corporate default; hence they can be classified as secured bonds, large unsecured bonds or lower (or minor) unsecured bonds. Apart from the government bonds (municipal bonds, agency bonds, sovereign bonds) and corporate bonds, other classifications of bonds include Islamic bonds, diaspora bonds, green bonds and many others (Fabozzi & Fabozzi, 2021). Recently, green bonds are gaining traction in the global financial markets.

There are different types of bonds with different features. Bonds vary depending on the interest rates they offer. They are generally fixed-rate bonds (attracting a fixed coupon rate), floating-rate bonds (with interest set to reference rate such as the LIBOR) or zero-coupon bonds (which don't pay periodic interest) There are also permanent/perpetual bonds and convertible bonds, contingent convertible bonds, callable bonds, retractable bonds, etc. Examples of issuers and their funding needs are grouped into two. The first group includes sovereign entities, governments and government agencies (including countries, states, cities and towns). Their funding needs are usually to raise cash for budgeted public expenditure, operating expenses and funds to repay debt. The other group is corporations. These include financial and non-financial institutions. Their financing needs include cash for operating expenses, capital for growth and expansion.

Country-Specific Examples of Bond Markets

South African Bond Market

Despite 2007/2008 Global Financial Crisis, some markets in Africa have shown considerable development in some specific type of bonds over the years. For instance, the most popular type of bond in the South African domestic bond market is Republic of South Africa government bonds. This is mainly issued to support the state's financial budget and is only open to selected dealers and representatives in the primary auction market. The South African Bond Exchange is a public company that manages and regulates the purchase of long-term bonds and interest rate derivatives in the country. South Africa is the only region in Africa with a developed government bond market. In the 1980s, the country issued its first demand-driven government bonds. While the South African bond market is more advanced in Africa, the secondary bond market in the region is not well developed. This is a big challenge for investors trading bonds in South Africa.

Nigerian Bond Market

Despite the integrated market, there is limited market depth in West Africa. For instance, Nigeria is the only English-speaking country to have a secondary bond market and bond index. The Federal Government of Nigeria (FGN) bond is the most popular type of bond in the Nigerian bond market. It is mainly issued by the Nigeria Debt Management Office, which is responsible for regulating the bond market activities with the view to reducing the country's budget deficit. FGN bonds range from 3 to 20 years in duration and can be purchased in both primary and secondary markets. The Central Bank of Nigeria acts as a bond issuer and registrar, while the Central Securities Clearing Systems Limited is the custodian of the bonds listed on the Nigerian Stock Exchange (NSE). Banks and discount houses are the primary dealers and market makers (PDMMs) in FGN designated by the FGN Debt Management Office. The PDMMs are required to exchange and distribute proceeds of FGN bonds that have been issued and are also responsible for boosting secondary bond market activity in the country. FGN first released the Sovereign Bond Index in December 2006, with fixed interest rate specifications for FGN bonds.

Kenyan Bond Market

As in other parts of Africa, government bond markets in East and Central Africa are not well advanced. Countries in these regions, with the exception of Kenya, do not have a wide range of accounts and bonds. The most popular type of bond in the Kenyan market is the Kenyan government bond. The Central Bank of Kenya acts as the issuing authority for this type of bond. Most of these bonds are classified as fixed-rate, floating-rate bonds, and zero-coupon bonds that are issued primarily to finance government budget deficits. Kenya has a variety of short-term, medium-term and long-term Treasury bills and bonds. In Kenya, corporate and municipal bond issuances are almost non-existent, while the infrastructure bonds are the only issuance bonds.

Other Bond Market Hot Spots in Africa

Apart from Kenya, Nigeria and South Africa, some countries within the continent have begun issuing bonds to raise capital for infrastructure development. These types of bonds include diaspora bonds, Islamic bonds and sovereign bonds. The Ethiopian government exploited Ethiopia's huge diaspora in 2008 and issued millennium corporate bonds (the first diaspora bonds) to cover the cost of a $4.8 billion project when the government found it difficult to raise or borrow money from banks. The country issued the second diaspora bond, the so-called Grand Renaissance Dam Bonds, in 2014. However, if a country issuing diaspora bond opens the bonds to all investors, credit ratings may be necessary to improve its overall capacity to attract large investors. The Nigerian Securities and Exchange Market Commission issued Islamic bonds in 2013 and raised NGN 11.4 billion to develop its infrastructure. The bond is rated "A" by Augusto & Co, a credit rating company in Nigeria. Islamic bonds, also known as sukuk bonds, are traded on the Gambian and Sudan bond markets. Sukuk bonds are a small-scale bond for the citizens of these countries to increase their development capital. For example, the Sudanese government sold $160 million in sukuk bonds in 2012. In addition, Senegal considered issuing $200 million in sukuk in 2014 to develop infrastructure and energy projects. Countries such as South Africa, Mauritania and Kenya are also developing plans to issue sukuk bonds in the near future. The main challenge facing issuers and regulators is how to create attractive conditions for sukuk bonds rather than for the Islamic regions that better understand the principles governing Islamic financing.

Ghana has a less developed but growing bond market, and corporate bond issuance is gaining momentum, although issuers remain small. Similar to most African countries where the corporate bond market is still in its infancy, there is little presence of private sector issuers in the country. As in most African bond markets, government bonds predominate in Ghana and Nigeria in particular. Government bonds were introduced in Ghana in 2007 with the issue of $750 million 10-year bonds in the international capital market. The bond was issued to raise funds for Ghana's energy, electricity and transport infrastructure projects. This was an attempt to diversify Ghana's public debt structure (i.e., the sovereign bond), as the country had previously relied on favorable debt from multilateral agencies. At the time of issue, credit rating agencies like Standard and Poor (S&P) and Fitch had rated the bonds "B+ Stable" and "B+ positive", respectively.

In 2013, the Rwandan government issued a $400 million 10-year government bond with a fixed interest rate of 6.875%. The proceeds from this issue were used to repay government loans, finance a hydropower project and to complete a convention center in Kigali. The sovereign bond of Rwanda was rated "B stable" by the S&P at the time of issue and the major concern was the country's ability to pay since most of the government budget were funded by donors from the international market. Tanzania and Kenya plan to issue government bonds in the international capital market as well. Botswana is one of a few countries in Africa that has a representation in government bonds for both primary and secondary markets. This implies that there is a primary dealership system in government bonds for both the primary and secondary market. The government debt instrument consists of Botswana Certificates, which is mostly used for open market operations. The government bonds are issued to help develop the domestic capital markets.

With respect to North African countries, none of the North African bond markets are concerned with the secondary bond market. In the Francophone countries of West Africa, there is a market for corporate bonds with a maximum maturity of ten years.

Why the Need for a Developed Bond Markets?

The importance of the bond market to economic growth is of significance to policymakers. Bond markets are becoming increasingly important, especially as they offer a number of benefits to investors, as well as to individuals and funds that need stable and predictable income and capital appreciation. The International Capital Market Association (ICMA) (2013)[1] described bonds, especially corporate bonds, as an important means of stimulating private investment and reducing citizens' dependence on the public sector. They have long been a steady source of financing for businesses and investors throughout the global economy. According to the ICMA (2013) report, bonds have been, among a host of financing methods, a reliable and cost-effective source of financing around the world. Bond markets benefit issuing companies by providing secure, stable and flexible financing for their activities, technological development, innovation, economic growth, employment, trade and wealth creation. The ICMA report (2013) shows how important bond markets are to companies, investors, governments, and economies around the world; and why is it important that regulations, laws and policies that affect them avoid any unintended consequences that could stifle the development of these markets.

[1] An international organization that works with market users and global authorities to develop the bond market.

In many African countries it is natural for governments to borrow money by borrowing instead of issuing bonds. In the past, businesses relied on locally generated funds as capital borrowed from family and friends (Goodfriend, 2006). However, as the economy develops, companies need to rely on external financing, first in the form of bank loans. Large companies in good standing seek financing directly from corporate bonds and/or exchanges. Goodfriend (2006) highlights the role of bond financing in addressing the credit crunch period of 1990–1991 (Kaufman, 1991), which is a feature of the short-term credit market. The bond market plays a powerful role in broader development of the financial market. It is important in boosting a credit culture, market discipline, and observable standard for financiers, issuers, bond investors, and other market participants. It provides access to unsecured business finance and economic growth. This can be used by financial institutions such as banks to assess loan market conditions.

27.3 Bond Market Development and Financing in Africa

The literature on financial markets suggests that well-functioning financial markets are required to foster economic growth (see Aryeetey, 2003; Levine, 1997; Senbet & Otchere, 2010) and that inclusive financial development can be inclusive and stimulate development (see Levine, 2004; Park & Mercado, 2015). Financial markets perform a number of functions, including mobilizing and pooling savings, providing information about likely investments and allocating capital, facilitating the exchange of goods and services, facilitating trade, diversifying and managing risk as well the supervision of companies and the exercise of corporate governance (Levine, 1997). Resilient financial markets allow countries to move beyond volatile and short-term capital flows until they are able to attract long-term capital for investments that drive economic growth and development. Financial markets must have clear channels or links to economic growth in order to have the desired effect on economic development. For example, banks need to be able to appropriately distribute the funds they mobilize through lending. Equally, the stock markets must actively produce information and ensure liquidity through well-functioning trading systems (Senbet & Otchere, 2010). Achieving solid, diversified and liquid financial markets requires a good mix of banks, capital markets, and private equity financing and contractual savings institutions. In Africa, however, the financial markets are considered small, cramped and illiquid with limited reach. This is reflected in aggregate indicators on financial development as well as in data from companies and households that assess how formal financial services are used (Beck & Robert, 2014).

Bond markets in Africa are mostly underdeveloped. In many African countries, the bond market represents less than 10% of GDP, well below the global bond market, which represents around 140% of the world's GDP. The bond market is mainly dominated by government bond trading. Public issuance of corporate bonds is not a common feature in African bond markets as they are typically very small and represent an insignificant composition of the global local bond market. Corporate bonds are primarily issued through private placements. A number of factors, including a limited number of private and institutional investors, capital gains, high returns on risk-free government instruments, alternative sources of leverage, weak regulation and market infrastructure, and an unfavorable macroeconomic environment, they all tend to have a negative impact on the development of African bond markets (Abor, 2018). Little progress in bond market development can be seen in the regional corporate bond market in French West Africa, a secondary bond and index market in Nigeria, and a well-developed government bond market in South Africa. African countries typically depend on private foreign capital flows to finance long-term projects. Therefore, they did not pay much attention to the development of domestic bond markets.

Over the past years, Africa has mobilized resources from the international capital markets. For instance, African countries raised about $8.25 billion in 2015 alone. Countries like Ghana, Zambia and Cameroon issued about 10.75, 9.37 and 9.5% coupon Eurobonds respectively. Developing the bond market in the region has benefited the continent, not only as a source of alternative funding, but also by contributing to the financial stability in the continent (AfDB report, 2015). The report from the African Development Bank (2006) shows that the bond market in most African countries is underdeveloped and some are still in their early stage. The market value of government bonds and corporate bonds is much lower in most African countries than in other developing, emerging and industrialized countries. The local currency bond market was dominated by government bonds, but it is not so in other developed parts of the world (Aykut & Blaszkiewicz-Schwartzman, 2018). In 2014, the outstanding stock of African local currency government securities (T-Bill and T-bonds) was 4% more than in 2013, of which five countries (South Africa, Kenya, Nigeria, Morocco and Egypt) accounted for about 85% of an estimated amount of $486 billion. The other countries (including Ghana) are the only countries that had an outstanding amount of $10 billion in 2014.

The African Development Bank noted that North and Southern Africa are the two regions that are most developed in the bond market while East Africa, Central and West Africa lag further behind. The African Fundamental Bond Index reveals the 2015 country ranking and scores of the top ten bond markets in Africa. Following the rankings, a drop in rank suggests that a country's market is not performing well while an increase in a rank suggests that a country's bond market is performing well. The top ten 2015 bond market ranking of African countries, in order of most developed to the least developed are South Africa, Egypt, Nigeria, Namibia, Botswana, Kenya, Mauritius, Ghana, Morocco and Algeria. South Africa has maintained first position of the ranking over the years and the country remains the Benchmark in African bond markets. The Egyptian market has progressively become one of the most top-ranking bond market moving up 6 places. Nigeria's market performed well with an increase of 9.8% compared to its 2014 score. Namibia comes up with an overall score increase of 12%, moving up by three places from the 2014 ranking. In comparison with the 2014 ranking, Botswana fell one place while Kenya maintained its position on the ranking from 2014. Mauritius came down five places in the 2015 African ranking of the bond market. Ghana ranked 3rd but moved 5 places down in the 2015 ranking while Morocco moved four places downward from 2014 in the ranking with a drop in its score by 5%. In 2015, Algeria performed very well by moving up the rank but was placed 10 in 2015 for the first time. This indicates that the country has increased in rank but was last from the bottom of the 2015 country ranking.

The AfDB report indicates that a sound and robust bond market infrastructure is important for effective and efficient development of the bond market. Bond market infrastructure implies the institution of effective automated trading and settlement platforms as well as settlement cycles. The AfDB constructs a bond index for bond market infrastructure by applying scores to the indicators. The report categorized the indicators into (1) availability of clearing and settlement systems; (2) settlement cycles; and (3) availability of electronic trading. In constructing the scores, countries that have scores above 80 are considered as high performers. Those that fall between 60 and 80 are classified as above average performers and those that fall between 50 and 60 are classified as average performers. However, those that come below 50 score point are underperformers.

Following the AfDB report, we present the 2015 bond market infrastructure index of African countries in Fig. 27.1.[2]

From Fig. 27.1, among all the African countries, those that are underperforming in bond market infrastructure are Angola, Burundi, Comoros, Djibouti, Eritrea, Guinea, Lesotho, Liberia, Libya, Madagascar, Mauritania, Sao Tome, Somalia, South Sudan, Zimbabwe, Congo Dem. Republic, Malaysia, Sierra Leone, and Ethiopia.

The global financial crisis of 2007/2008 led to a severe shortage of resources from banks that previously provided resources (loans) for the expansion of public infrastructure. Prior to that, governments had come under severe economic pressure as their ability to use funds for large-scale infrastructural projects was severely reduced. Infrastructure developers have begun to look for an alternative source of funding and an intensified focus on raising capital for this purpose is through capital market borrowing. In Africa, one of the key drivers of growth is infrastructure development. In pursuing the development agenda through infrastructure, and in a steady decline in bank lending, governments, project developers and financiers are increasingly using sources of funding such as bonds, investment funds, pension funds, insurance funds and public–private partnerships to support infrastructure development projects.

African countries are currently pursuing the issue of Green bond to promote inclusive growth. This was necessitated by the problems associated with the changing climate and environmental degradation (Duru & Nyong, 2016). In view of the fact that money will be required to achieve the desired goals, the African market is shifting to green financing. From a global perspective, Standard & Poor's, in 2007 showed that the global green bond market is expected to be worth 100 billion US dollars by the end of 2015 and also predicts that the global green bond market will reach a trillion dollars by 2020. The world estimates of how much money

[2] Countries which are part of monetary union, WAEMU (Benin, Burkina-Faso, Cote d'Ivoire, Guinea-Bissau, Mali, Niger, Senegal and Togo) and CEMAC (Cameroon, Chad, Congo, Equatorial Guinea, Gabon, Republic of Central Africa) are sharing the same scores for some indicators as they are part of Monetary Union with common capital market.

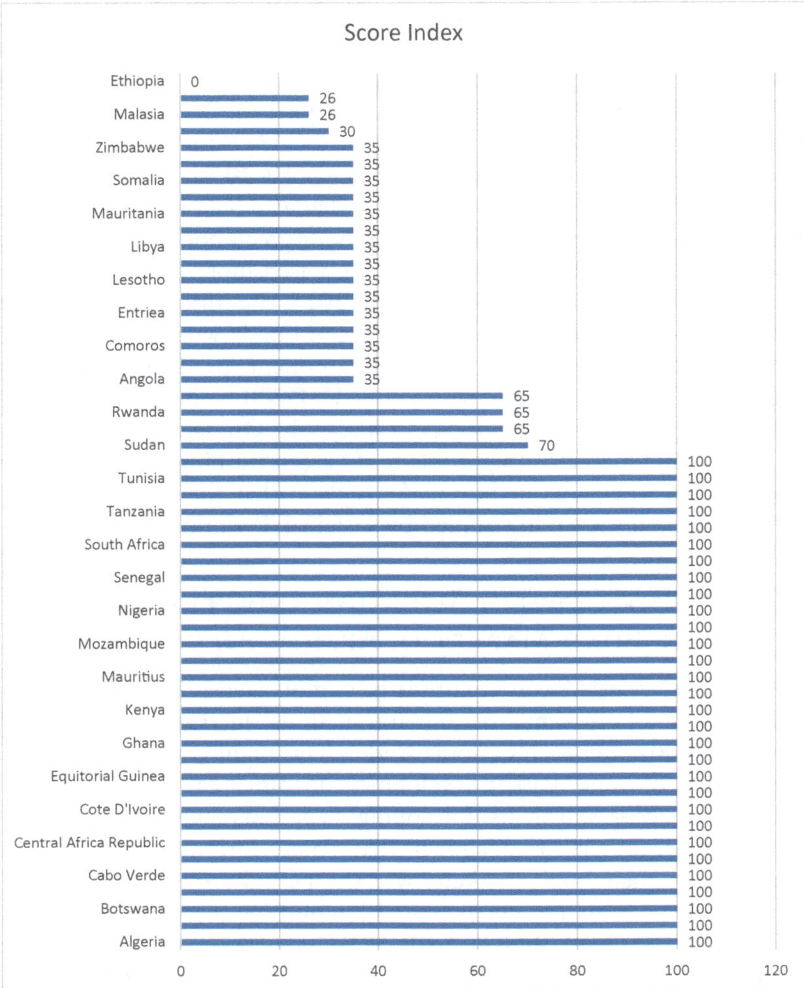

Fig. 27.1 Bond market infrastructure scores (*Source* Authors computation based on data obtained from the African Financial Markets Initiative, African Development Bank Report, 2015. The scores range between 0 [no bond market infrastructure] and 100 [high performers bond market] with high scores indicating high rank for the countries)

it would take to end global climate change range between $300 billion and $50 trillion over the next two decades. The estimated adaptation costs for Africa are considerably higher around US$45–50 billion a year by 2050. Following this average estimates, Duru and Nyong (2016) estimated that the costs associated with climate change adaptation in Africa will drop to US$20–30 billion over the next 10–20 years. Likewise, the cost of the infrastructure sector is estimated at $93 billion annually. These estimates have great potential in the search for green bonds in Africa. The annual global green bond issuance has increased more than 35 times in seven years since its inception in 2007. In 2013, the African Development Bank became active in issuing its first green bonds worth $500 million in Africa. Major players on the African continent, particularly in South Africa are IDC and Nedbank with about USD700 million and USD490 million in issuance of green bonds, respectively. One major challenge of the green bond market is the problem of "green washing". This problem arises when participants in the market ensure that the use of proceeds from green bonds is strictly guided by sustainability principles.

27.4 The Current Situation and Performance of the Bond Market in Africa: An Overview

Over the past year, African countries have mobilized resources from the capital market, both domestic and international markets. Even though before the 2007/2008 GFC, some studies have highlighted the historical performance of bond market development in Africa and have concluded that the market is still in its developing stage (Aryeetey, 2003; Levine, 1997, 2004), others have shown that some African countries have improved on their bond markets over the period (Allen et al., 2011). This section presents the current situation and/or the performance the bond markets between 2000 and 2017. We use data on local government bonds in local currency, corporate bond issuance volume to GDP, Non-financial corporate bond to total bond and notes outstanding, domestic private debt securities to GDP, domestic public debt securities to GDP, the amount of international private debt securities to GDP, international public debt securities to GDP, syndicated loan issuance volume to GDP and portfolio investment bond. The data was obtained from the World Bank's Global Development Index database.

From Fig. 27.2, we observe that government domestic local currency bond increased from 2000 to 2002 by insignificant margin but increased

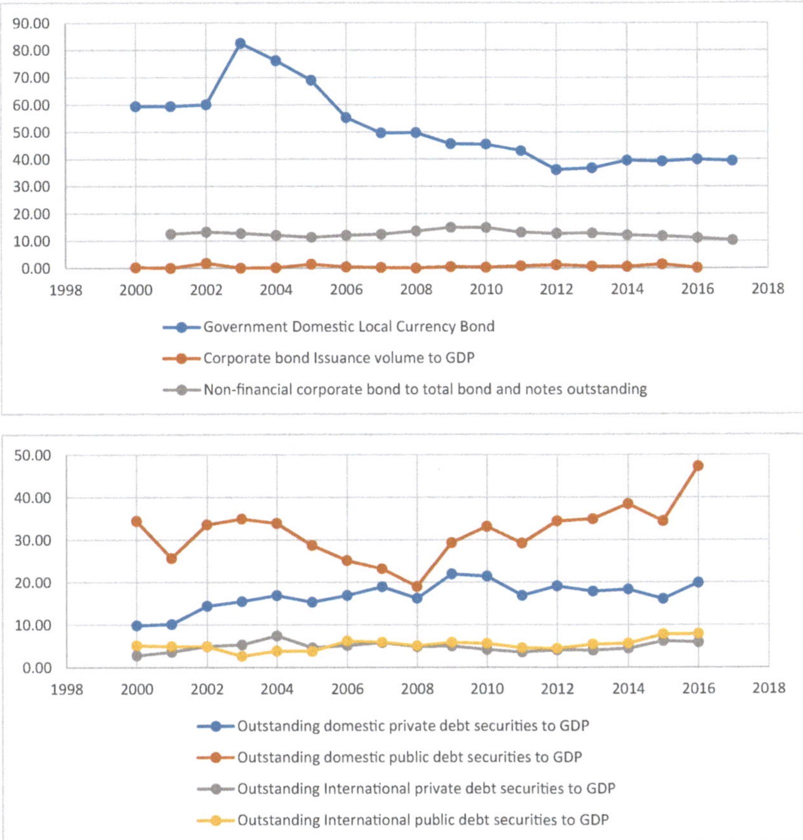

Fig. 27.2 Trends in bond market indicators (*Source* Authors computation based on data obtained from the Global Financial Development Database, 2020)

sharply in 2003. It then declined steeply between 2003 and 2006 and continued to decline gradually from 2006 to 2012. It begun to increase slowly from 2012 to 2014 but the issue has fluctuated between 2014 and 2017 period. Corporate bond volume to GDP fluctuated annually in the period 2000 and 2005 but decreased consistently from 2005 to 2008. It fluctuated again in the year 2008–2017 with greater volatilities. In general, government domestic local currency bond decreased from 59.53

in 2000 to 39.40 in 2017. Similarly, corporate bond issuance volume to GDP decreased from 34.97% of GDP in 2000 to 24.69% of GDP in 2017.

From Fig. 27.2, African countries sought (mobilized) more of domestic public debt securities to GDP over the period 2000–2017 compared with domestic private debt securities to GDP. We highlight that both the (outstanding) international private debt securities to GDP and (outstanding) international public debt securities to GDP were given equal priority as funding sources in Africa. In general, domestic private and public debt securities to GDP and international private and public debt securities were unstable over the period 2000–2017.

Figure 27.3 suggests that government domestic local currency bond and syndicated loan issuance volume to GDP were more developed before the 2007/2008 Global Financial Crisis than after the crisis. Thus, the crisis had a countercyclical effect on government domestic local currency bond and syndicated loan issuance volume to GDP. This suggests that government bonds and syndicated bonds recorded relatively higher before the crisis than during the post-crisis era. In Fig. 27.3, we observe that issuance of corporate bond volume to GDP, outstanding domestic private

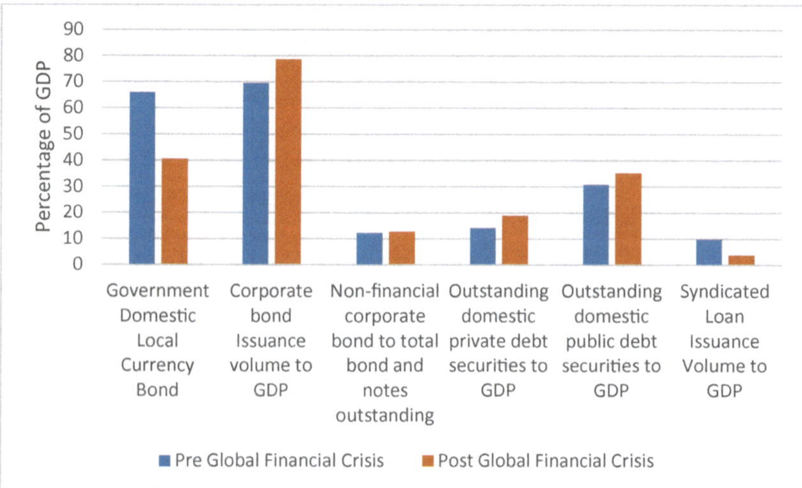

Fig. 27.3 Bond market development in the pre and post global financial crisis era (*Source* Authors computation based on data obtained from the Global Financial Development Database, 2020)

debt securities to GDP and domestic public debt securities to GDP peaked after the crisis compared with pre-crisis era. This suggests that African countries learnt a lot of lessons from the crisis and begun to focus on developing their corporate bond issuance volume to GDP, domestic private debt securities to GDP and domestic public debt securities to GDP. We show that non-financial corporate bond to total bond and notes outstanding remained relatively the same before and after the 2007/2008 Global Financial Crisis.

Bond market indicators differ across Africa due to the different nature of markets or economies within which they operate. In this regard, the government and corporate bond types in Africa will vary across the different income brackets in Africa. Data on the different bond market indicators was obtained from the Global Financial Development database, spanning from 2000 to 2017 over the different income brackets in Africa. Figure 27.4 shows the average level of bond market indicators in lower-income countries, lower middle-income countries, upper middle-income countries and high-income countries. Government domestic local currency bonds recorded the highest in low-income countries, representing 63.86%, followed by high-income countries (54.38%), lower middle-income countries (50.24%) and upper middle-income countries (26.73%). Thus, lower income countries in Africa perform well in terms of government domestic local currency bond market. Corporate

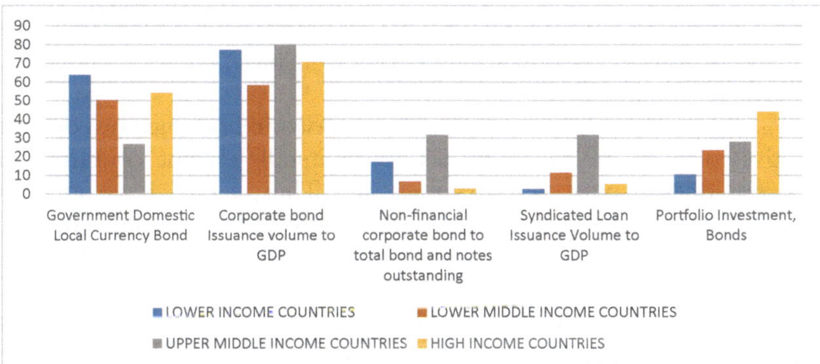

Fig. 27.4 Bond market development in lower, lower middle, upper middle and high-income African countries, 2000–2020 (*Source* Authors computation based on data obtained from the Global Financial Development Database, 2020)

bonds (issuance volume to GDP) in upper middle-income countries in Africa, representing 79.96%, outperformed those in lower-income countries (77.28%), high-income countries (70.66%) and lower middle-income countries (58.27). This is attributed to a relatively well-developed capital market among countries in upper middle-income brackets compared to others. Again, non-financial corporate bonds (to total bond and notes outstanding) recorded better volumes in upper middle-income countries in Africa, representing 31.47%, followed by lower income countries (17.19%), lower middle-income countries (6.66%) and high-income countries in Africa (2.91%). Syndicated bonds, measured as syndicated loan issuance volume to GDP were remarkable in upper middle-income countries relative to lower middle-income countries, high-income countries and lower income countries in Africa. The above shows that countries in upper middle-income brackets have relatively a robust institutional framework that strengthens their capital market compared to countries in other income brackets, hence, leading to greater performance in non-financial corporate bond market and syndicated bond markets. It is quite surprising that in terms of non-financial bond and syndicated bonds, countries in lower-income brackets in Africa perform relatively better compared to those in lower middle income and high-income brackets. This implies that countries in lower middle income and high-income brackets have not paid much attention to strengthening their non-financial corporate bond markets, instead their focus may be driven toward developing other type of bond marketed. The implication is that countries in lower middle income and high-income brackets should put mechanism in place to strengthen non-financial corporate bond and syndicated bond markets.

Finally, portfolio investment bonds increased in high-income countries relative to lower income countries, lower middle-income countries and upper middle-income countries in Africa. Thus, capital flows in terms of portfolio investment bonds penetrate more in high-income countries and could be the reason why those countries are developed in line with portfolio investment bonds.

From Fig. 27.5, government (domestic local currency) bond issuance was high in central African countries, followed by North African countries. East African markets and countries in the West African region were in the same rank while markets in Southern Africa recorded the lowest government domestic bonds over 2000–2017 period. However, in terms of corporate bonds (issuance volume to GDP), countries in Southern

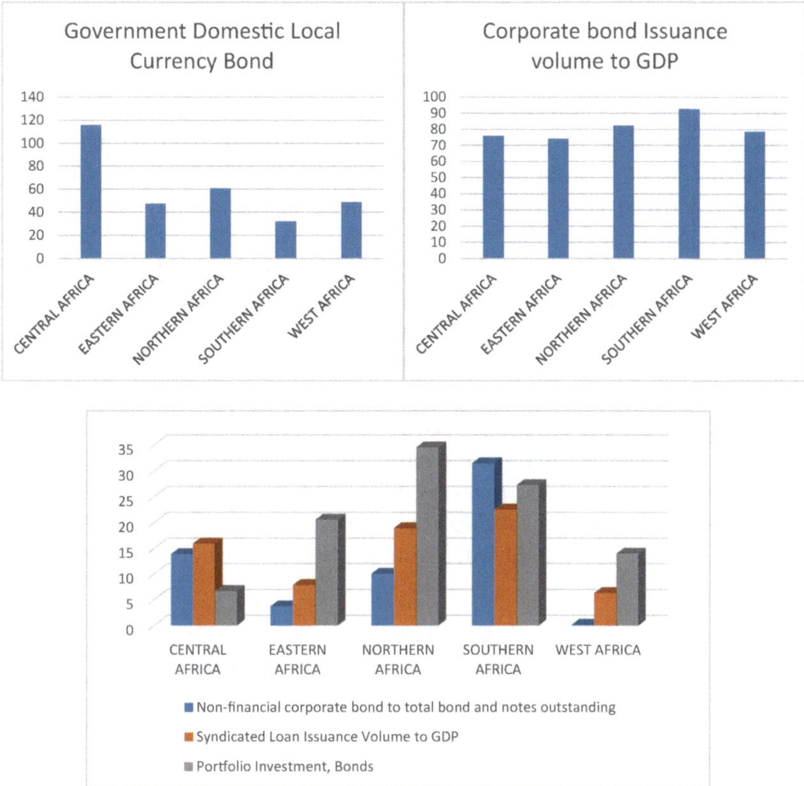

Fig. 27.5 Bond market development in the different regions in Africa, 2006–2020 (*Source* Authors computation based on data obtained from the Global Financial Development Database, 2020)

Africa performed better than their counter parts in the Northern African region, West Africa, Central Africa and Eastern Africa. Again, Fig. 27.5 depicts that countries concentrated in central Africa and southern Africa issued more government bond and corporate bond, respectively. The differences in the performance of specific types of bonds across Africa may be attributed to differences in currency and economic integration or financial globalization. Thus, capital flows to countries in central Africa and southern Africa due to their developed government bond market and corporate bond markets respectively. The implication is that countries with lower average levels of government and corporate bonds in Africa should mirror or benchmark the strategies put in place by leaders in government and corporate bonds.

Next, we observe that non-financial corporate bond market in Southern Africa, outperformed that of Central African countries, Northern African countries, Eastern African countries and West African countries. Syndicated bond market was greatly sourced in Southern Africa countries, followed by Northern African countries, Central African countries, Eastern African countries and West African countries. Thus, countries in southern Africa have relatively well-developed non-financial corporate bond and syndicated bond markets compared to those in other parts of Africa. It can also be that countries in Southern Africa have a well-integrated financial and economic systems that attract investors, hence, leading to greater performance in their non-financial corporate bond and syndicated bond markets. However, more portfolio investment bonds flowed to countries in Northern Africa compared with countries in Southern Africa, Eastern Africa, West Africa and Central Africa.

27.5 Constraints to Bond Market Development in Africa

Capital markets play a very important role in a nation's financial system. However, the bond markets in Africa have faced many constraints. As governments borrow more, pressure on investors such as pension funds and individual investors could reduce demand for government bonds. In addition, previous analysis showed that companies and individuals in Africa are more dependent on short-term debt instruments and bank credit than on bond issuance in the capital markets (Abor, 2018). On the African continent, external shocks, together with internal shocks—affecting the financial system—can disrupt the development process and the development channels of the bond market, which is still at a rudimentary stage. In view of the increased volatility on the capital markets and the decline in bond issuance, it is expected that the current COVID-19 pandemic to further slowdown various aspect of the economy (Abor, 2020) as well as development of the corporate bond market in Africa (Agbloyor & Abor, 2020), at least in the short and medium term. The pandemic is likely to cause companies seeking to exploit or reuse the corporate bond market to rethink their intentions. Even if interest rates fall due to monetary policy, companies are more likely to look to bank finance than bonds. Furthermore, not only has the GFC 2007/2008 impacted the capital market, but the outbreak of the recent pandemic has added momentum and urgency to the need to develop domestic capital markets in Africa due to the deterioration in fiscal space. The crisis resulted in a decline in export earnings and a sudden reversal in capital flows, which until then had helped fund long-term investments. This has worsened fiscal space and created a favorable environment for governments to mobilize resources from domestic capital markets to meet their budget deficits.

The activity of the bond markets in ECOWAS and other parts of the continent is hampered by high transaction costs and asymmetrical taxation. The costs of trade in the bond market include advances in communications, data-handling technology and market frictions. Financial market frictions do not only affect taxes and transaction costs, but it interferes with trade in the capital market. On one hand, financial market friction impedes on the costs of trade and the time needed to make trades. Capital gain taxes, on the other hand, influence decisions to trade bonds (DeGennaro, 2005). Corporations pay income and capital gains taxes, and these payments surely affect their investment decisions and trade in bonds.

In most African markets, foreign investors that contribute to the development of the bond market is lacking. The reason is attributed to the lack of a market for hedging instruments (example is currency swaps) and withholding taxes (Roldos, 2004). For instance, there are restrictions on foreign investors with respect to the maximum shareholding allowed in Kenyan stock market. The investor base for corporate bonds in some African countries tends to be concentrated in government-controlled provident funds, insurance companies and banks. Thus, those who are active traders are missing in these markets, which is indicative of a bond market that is still in its infant stage.

For most African countries, the banking sector continues to provide loans based on the value of collaterals and guarantees by corporations. The credit needs continue to grow rapidly with increasing population, and the private sector as well as state-owned companies spend large amount of time looking for additional debt finance. This could be a fertile ground for the bond markets, especially corporate bonds. Again, the increasing debt financing needs of domestic enterprises and failure to address these needs, create the need for further development of the bond market (IOSCO,

2004). However, African markets are not developed to cater for the financing needs of the economy.

Another major challenge, affecting the bond market in some African countries has to do with poor information flow, and the general public's lack of knowledge of bonds (government and corporate bonds) and the bond market. According to the IMF (2005), many corporate bond markets in Africa seem to have a limited flow of timely information about issuers. It is evidenced that sufficient information flow on the bases of trading offers spillover benefits to investors in the market. However, in most countries in Africa, such information is scarce, posing a critical challenge to bond market development. This also poses a challenge to rating agencies. The poor information flows on bond markets are often more limited in some African markets makes the quality of rating services difficult. Publicly available information may also not be adequate for investors to evaluate the credit worthiness of potential issuers (Fan & Wong, 2002). One reason that could account for the poor information flow is the lack of incentives for timely reporting of bond market information. Although, local credit rating agencies do exist in some African countries, these agencies are quite new and need some time to develop and build reputation.

It appears, that most African countries have no clear and specific guidelines or investment policy documents (EMEAP, 2002). This makes investors to more risk-averse attitude toward investing in the bond market. Moreover, investors put their resources and confidence in firms that have a history of good performance track record, particularly the highly rated security markets. Professional guidelines for effective operations of the bond market lacking in the African bond market (Allen et al., 2011; IMF, 2005; Jin & Loh, 2002). This calls for skills and experienced individuals and investors (private and government) to avail relevant information to the public, in order to develop this market. A study by Moody (2002) reveals that some African legal environment on investment is still in the infancy state. Currently, some African markets still have some challenges with their regulatory environment. The current state of the capital markets demonstrates that the legal frameworks are crucial in the future successful development of the bond market and need attention.

27.6 Determinants of Bond Market Development: An Empirical Review

The financial system in Africa, like other parts of the world, are set of institutions made up of the central banks, financial institutions, financial instruments, financial markets and money as a store of exchange and store of wealth. Central banks are independent of state control but work closely with state institutions such as finance and economic planning ministries (as in the case of Ghana) and drive the agendas of various governments to formulate and implement macroeconomic policies. Financial markets allow the trading of financial instruments (helps to transfer resources and facilitates risk sharing). The provision of services, including access to financial markets, is the responsibility of financial institutions. A feature of the financial system in Africa is that a large number of financial institutions, such as banks, invest in government bonds, mainly in treasury bonds.

Macroeconomic Factors

It appears, that there seem to be scant empirical studies on the determinant of bond market development in Africa. From developed markets perspective, research on the determinants of bond market is growing rapidly. For instance, Eichengreen and Luengnaruemitchai (2008) focused on the determinants of bond market developments in Latin America and show a positive and significant but non-linear (concave) impact of country size, trade openness (not concave but positive) and GDP per capita on bond market development. In terms of country size, countries with large population may have large participants or investors who have the capacity to push their funds in the bond market and may result in bond market development. It can be explained that countries of smaller economy are less likely to have well-developed bond markets because the typical amount of capital raised with the issue may be too small to attract multinational corporations and foreign investors (Eichengreen & Luengnaruemitchai, 2004). However, further enlargement of a country can lead to market inefficiencies and a decline in the bond market. Countries that increase their trading openness can improve their bond markets. This is because the opening of trading attracts capital investment and may ultimately have a positive impact on the bond market. It is argued that more open economies encourage the development of the bond market because self-interest may not be able to insist on policies that suppress competing sources of supply when the economy is exposed to international competition (Rajan & Zingales, 2003). Countries that are less integrated into external economies have more incentives to develop the domestic capital market in order to meet their funding constraints. Moreover, an additional increase in trade openness may cause distractions in the capital market and decrease the performance of the bond market. An increase in GDP per capita leads to bond market development through financial sector development. This implies that higher income levels of households and firms provide incentives for individuals and firms to push more of their income into the capital market through the financial sector. This leads to a positive relationship between GDP per capita and bond market.

Furthermore, Forslund et al. (2011) show that macroeconomic stability, openness, investor protection, contract enforcement and pension privatization costs are decisive for the development of the bond market. For instance, countries with a stable macroeconomic system are able to develop their bond markets. This leads to a positive relationship between stable macroeconomic and bond market development. Countries with large trade openness have larger economies of scale to attract more investors into developing the bond market.

Financial Factors

In terms of financial factors, Eichengreen and Luengnaruemitchai (2008) find a negative and significant relationship between domestic interest rate and government bonds. Domestic credit and interest rate spread are positively related to financial bonds and corporate (not public bond) markets respectively. Countries that expand credits to the domestic market are more likely to develop businesses through the credit market. As businesses develop, they are able to channel their funds into profitable financial markets. This suggests an indirect positive relationship between domestic credit and bond market development. Both demand and supply of bonds depend on prevailing market interest rates. Bond supply is driving prices (interest rates) down, while higher interest rates (prices) attract higher demand for bonds. Thus, higher interest rates provide an incentive for bondholders to invest more funds, while lower interest rates discourage bond investments. This explains the positive relationship between interest rates and the development of the bond market.

Likewise, the market value of corporate bonds is inversely related to higher interest rates and an open checking account. Interest rate volatility was found to be negatively associated with bond market development (Mu et al., 2013a, 2013b; Smaaoui et al., 2017). Interest rate variability can be important if investors have different levels of risk aversion. This can reduce the attractiveness of holding bonds for a risk-averse investor and a high degree of variability, as fixed income assets would tend to impede the development of long-term issues. Tight capital controls are important to correlate with the larger government bond markets but are negligibly related to the corporate bond markets. This is because strict capital regulation gives issuers the incentive to raise interest rates, which encourages investors to hold more bonds that then produce higher yields. This is in line with the work of Forslund et al. (2011), who examined the determinants of public debt in developing and emerging countries and showed that capital controls have a positive effect on public debt.

In emerging Asia, Eichengreen and Luengnaruemitchai (2004) examined 41 developed and developing countries, used panel data from 1990 to 2001, to examine the factors that influence bond market developments. Eichengreen and Luengnaruemitchai (2004) showed that domestic bank lending, exchange rate volatility, lack of capital control and the budget balance are positively related to private debt reserves, while fluctuations in GDP per capita and interest rates are negatively and significantly related to private debt stocks. Further, Eichengreen and Luengnaruemitchai (2004) found that market size, a well-capitalized banking system, and stable exchange rates strengthen the bond market, while inadequate accounting standards, corruption, low bureaucracy, lack of need for public funds and capital controls discourage the development of the bond market. According to Claessens et al. (2007), economies with a larger base of domestic investors have a larger domestic bond market, while economies with less flexible exchange rates are associated with lower domestic debt relative to foreign debt. Using data from 43 developing and developed countries from 1990 to 2009, Bae (2012) found that GDP per capita is one of the main determinants of bond markets, with rising deficits leading to larger bond markets. Again, low interest rates, large banks and well-developed government bond markets are the main determinants of corporate bond market developments.

The variability in interest rates makes it less attractive to hold bonds and can have a negative impact on the bond market (Eichengreen & Luengnaruemitchai, 2004). Exchange rate variability is also important for the development of the bond market. Fixed exchange rates, for example, can induce foreign investors to ask for bonds, which would encourage the development of the bond markets. However, the variability of foreign exchange discourages investors from holding bonds and therefore has a negative impact on the development of the bond market. Some have suggested that opening up to foreign portfolio investment improves the quality of local corporate governance and improves access to domestic debt for foreign investors. Therefore, countries with stricter capital controls can provide incentives for governments and companies to obtain funding in the local market rather than the foreign capital market.

Institutional Factors

Allen et al. (2011) presented a comprehensive overview of the financial systems of the African continent. The review includes central banks, deposit banks and non-banks such as stock exchanges, bond markets, insurance markets and microfinance institutions, among others. Mu et al. (2013a, 2013b) collect a unique data set on the government and corporate bond markets in Africa. In their thesis they presented an economic model for the analysis of the most important determinants of the African state stock market and the capitalization of corporate bonds. They found that good institutions and interest rate volatility are directly related to the government's market capitalization. However, budget deficits, high interest margins, exchange rate fluctuations and the opening of performance and capital accounts are inversely related to the state's market capitalization. The institutional quality turned out to be irrelevant for the bond market as the African market has a weak institutional framework. Earlier studies on the development of the bond market focused on industrialized countries (Adelegan & Radzewicz-Bak, 2009; Claessens et al., 2007; Eichengreen & Luengnaruemitchai, 2004). For example, Eichengreen and Luengnaruemitchai (2004) found that the investment profile, exchange rate volatility, lack of capital controls and the budget balance correlated positively with public debt reserves, while interest rate dispersion and the quality of bureaucracy were negatively and significantly with the linked to public debt.

In terms of investment profile, there are not always high-quality issuers with solid business models and prudent financial records. This means that countries whose investors have a good investment profile are more likely to increase the performance of the bond market. Forslund et al. (2011)

show that countries that have the right laws to protect the interest of investors are able to resolve conflicts of interest and develop the bond market. Again, countries that are able to enforce competitive contracts are able to strengthen their capital market.

In Africa, the main characteristic of financial markets is the lack of bond markets for both government and corporate bonds. According to reviews by Allen et al. (2011), the African bond market is still untapped or, at best, is developing or in its early stages. Although research on the development of the financial sector in Africa is increasing (Anayiotos & Toroyan, 2009; Andrianaivo & Yartey, 2009; Beck et al., 2011; Kablan, 2010; Yartey & Adjasi, 2007), the focus is less on development of bond markets in Africa. On one hand, Machokoto et al. (2020) advanced the literature of Graham and Harvey (2015) and showed that supply-side factors are major determinants of the rising levels of corporate debt faced by African economies. For instance, they show that access to external capital is scarce in the South Africa. On the other hand, Machokoto et al. (2020) found that demand-side factors, including size, tangibility and profitability, have no link with the emergence of corporate debt in South Africa.

In what follows, we analyze the relationship between the bond market and financial, macroeconomic and institutional indicators in Africa. We use data spanning from 2006 to 2020 and data was obtained from the Global Financial Development database. This is done to illustrate the determinants of bond market development based on the association between the individual variables and bond market.

To fully capture the relationships that exist among the variables, Figs. 27.6 and 27.7 are presented to graphically show the relationships that exist among bond market development indicators, financial, macroeconomic and institution variables. Specifically, Fig. 27.6 presents the relationships that exist between government bonds (measured as government domestic local currency bonds to GDP) and other indicators in Africa between 2006 and 2020.

From our sample (see Fig. 27.6), there was a negative correlation between domestic credit to private sector and government bonds, implying that countries that increase domestic credit to private sector may reduce government bond issuance. Foreign direct investment (FDI) has a negative correlation with government bonds from the sample, implying that countries that attract more FDIs pay less attention to government bonds. A positive relationship was observed between government bonds and trade openness from the sample. This shows that trade openness

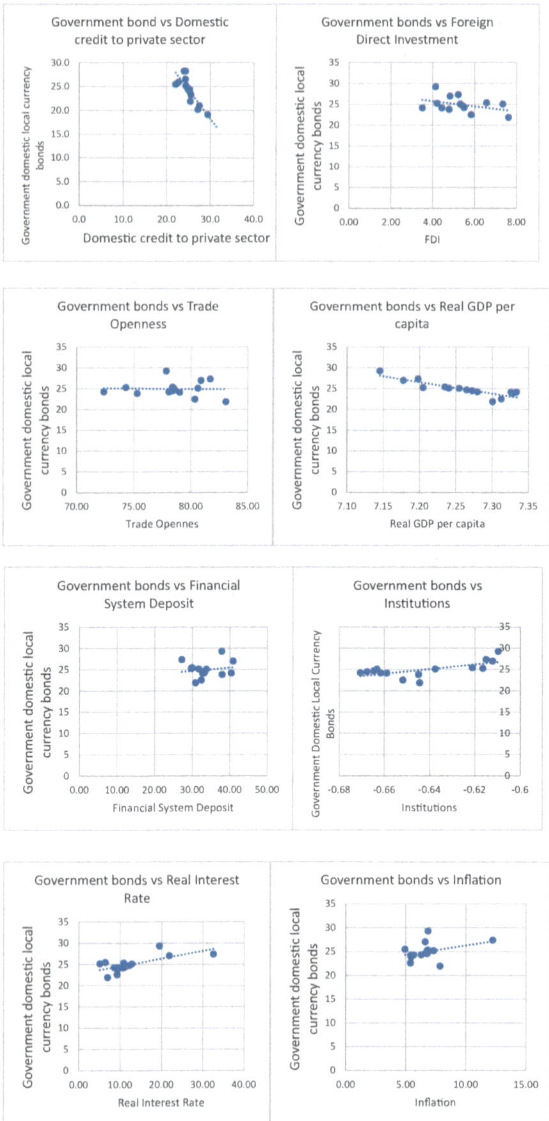

Fig. 27.6 Relationship between government bonds, financial, macroeconomic and institutional factors (*Source* Authors computation based on data obtained from the Global Financial Development Database, 2020)

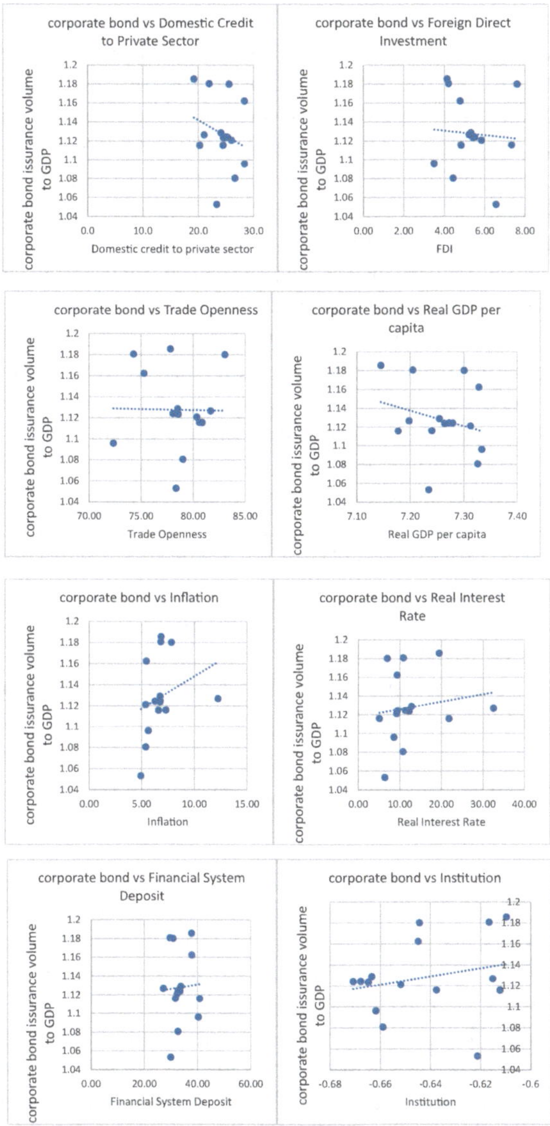

Fig. 27.7 Relationship between corporate bonds, financial, macroeconomic and institutional factors (*Source* Authors computation based on data obtained from the Global Financial Development Database, 2020)

attracts more government bonds. Real GDP per capita was negatively associated with government bonds, implying that an increase in real GDP per capita leads to a decline in government bonds. The figure shows a positive association between government bonds and indicators like financial system deposits, institutional quality, and real interest rate and inflation rates. This implies that an increase in financial system deposits, institutional quality, and real interest rate and inflation rates leads to an increase in government bonds.

Also, Fig. 27.7 reports on the relationship between these indicators and corporate bonds in Africa. From Fig. 27.7, it is observed that the relationship between domestic credit to private sector and corporate bonds was negative, implying that countries that increase domestic credit to private sector focus less on corporate bonds. Foreign direct investment (FDI) has a negative correlation with corporate bonds, implying that countries that attract more FDIs pay less attention to corporate bonds. Corporate bond was positively linked to trade openness. Real GDP per capita was negatively associated with corporate bonds from our sample, implying that an increase in real GDP per capita leads to a decline in corporate bonds. The figure shows a positive association between corporate bonds and financial system deposits, institutional quality, and real interest rate and inflation rates. This implies that an increase in financial system deposits, institutional quality, real interest rate and inflation rates, leads to an increase in corporate bonds.

27.7 Conclusion and Policy Implication

In view of the above discussion, it is crucial that the existing literature on the development of bond markets from an African perspective is still in its infancy. There is still a wide debate among scholars about the need to develop the bond market and the factors that will contribute to the development of the bond market in Africa. In addition, researchers are also considering how the development of bond markets can be integrated into a framework for maintaining the financial and economic system. This document contributes to our understanding of African bond markets. While African countries rely heavily on government bonds to finance budget deficits, the development of corporate bond markets, with the exception of South Africa, is still in its infancy. Most countries in Africa are heavily dependent on foreign credit, capital inflows and bank loans. Recently, the corporate bond markets in Africa have started to grow steadily and it seems that most countries have started to rely on them as a source of finance.

The report suggests that while the bond market in Africa is relatively stable and less permeated, it is as competitive as other developing and emerging countries. The study shows that local currency government bonds in Africa showed an overall downward trend over the 2000–2018 period. The volume of corporate bonds in relation to GDP and the volume of non-financial corporate bonds in relation to the total volume of bonds showed unchanged trends between 2000 and 2018. The study shows that the outstanding domestic private debt as a percentage of GDP has increased over the period 2000–2018, while the circulation of domestic public debt as a percentage of GDP was relatively unstable over the same period. International private and public debt outstanding as a percentage of GDP shows constant trends over the 2000–2018 period.

In most African countries, the public sector dominated debt issuance, mainly very short-dated debt and activities focused on the domestic primary market with limited secondary trade. In addition, local government bonds performed relatively better before the global financial crisis, while corporate bond volume relative to GDP performed relatively well after the global financial crisis.

The study shows that southern African bond markets are, in many respects, less integrated than those in other regions. Therefore, regional communities must take steps to strengthen regional financial integration. Financial sector development plans across the region should aim to develop methodologies in the context of harmonized regulatory frameworks and progressive regional integration of capital markets to contribute to an efficient financial sector.

Given the numerous challenges facing African bond markets, as explored in the study, governments and the private sector must make significant efforts to improve markets in other countries to compete with those in other developed regions of the world. Extensive marketing and awareness campaigns must be carried out to encourage the issuance of bonds and, finally, legal and regulatory reforms must be undertaken to develop the market in Africa. There should be reform aimed at encouraging bond issuance through an improved rating system. Other reforms in Africa should include cost reductions and easier access to financial markets.

In conclusion, while bond markets at the national and regional levels in Africa are still largely underdeveloped, a number of governments, private sector and donor initiatives are underway with limited effectiveness. Therefore, a more inclusive partnership is needed in ongoing and planned initiatives in order to leverage synergies and maximize the effectiveness of the initiatives.

References

Abor, J. Y. (2018). *Financial markets and institutions: A frontier market perspective* (2nd ed.). Digibooks.

Abor, J. Y. (2020). *Exploring the Impact of COVID-19 Pandemic on Africa's FinTech Space* (Working Paper Series No. 7/2020). Centre for Global Finance, SOAS University of London.

Adelegan, J., & Radzewicz-Bak, B. (2009). *What determines bond market development in sub-Saharan Africa* (IMF Working Paper No. 09/213). Inter-national Monetary Fund, Washington.

African Development Bank. (2006). *African development report 2006: Aid, debt relief and development in Africa*. Oxford University Press.

Agbloyor, E. K., & Abor, J. Y. (2020). *The COVID-19 pandemic and its impact on African economies and financial markets: A review* (Working Paper Series No. 7/2020). Centre for Global Finance, SOAS University of London.

Allen, F., Otchere, I., & Senbet, L. W. (2011). Review African financial systems: A review. *Review of Development Finance, 1*, 79–113.

Anayiotos, G., & Toroyan, H. (2009). *Institutional factors and financial sector development: Evidence from sub-Saharan Africa* (IMF Working Paper No.09/258). International Monetary Fund, Washington.

Andrianaivo, M., & Yartey, C. (2009). *Understanding the growth of African financial markets* (IMF Working Paper No. 09/182). International Monetary Fund, Washington.

Aryeetey, E. (2003). Recent development in African financial markets: Agenda for further research. *Journal of African Economies, 12*(2), 111–152.

Astrauskaite, I., & Paškevicius, A. (2014). Competition between banks and bond markets: Hardly impacted or softly complemented. The Economies of Balkan and Eastern Europe Countries in the Changed World (EBEEC 2013). *Procedia Economics and Finance, 9*, 111–119.

Aykut, D., & Blaszkiewicz-Schwartzman, M. (2018). *Shaping the future of Africa: Markets and opportunities for private investors* (No. 125925, pp. 1–4). The World Bank.

Bae, K.-H. (2012). *Determinants of local currency bonds and foreign holdings: Implications for bond market development in the People's Republic of China* (ADB Working Paper Series on Regional Economic Integration No. 97). Asian Development Bank, Manila.

Batten, J., & Kim, Y. H. (2001). Expanding long-term financing through bond market development: A post crisis policy task. *Government Bond Markets in Asia*, 290–360.

Batten, J. A., Hogan, W. P., & Szilagyi, P. G. (2009). *Foreign bond markets and financial market development: International perspectives* (ADBI Working Paper Series No. 173 2009).

Beck, T., & Robert, C. (2014)."Banking in Africa. In *The Oxford handbook of banking* (2nd Ed.). Oxford University Press.

Beck, T., Maimbo, S., Faye, I., & Tiki, T. (2011). *Financing Africa: Through the crisis and beyond*. World Bank.

Claessens, S., Klingebiel, D., & Schmukler, S. (2007). Government bonds in domestic and foreign currency: The role for institutional and macroeconomic-factors. *Review of International Economics, 15*(2), 370–413.

DeGennaro, R. P. (2005). Market imperfections. *Journal of Financial Transformation, 14.*

Duru, U., & Nyong, A. (2016). Why Africa needs green bonds. *Africa Economic Brief Chief Economist Complex | AEB, 7*(2).

Eichengreen, B., & Luengnaruemitchai, P. (2004). *Why doesn't Asia have bigger bond markets?* (NBER Working Paper No. 10576). National Bureau of Economic Research, Cambridge, MA.

Eichengreen, B., & Luengnaruemitchai, P. (2008). Bond markets as conduits for capital flows: How does Asia compare? In *International financial issues in the Pacific rim: Global imbalances, financial liberalization, and exchange rate policy* (pp. 267–313). University of Chicago Press.

EMEAP. (2002). *Payment systems in EMEAP economies*. Available via the internet: http://www.emeap.org/redbook2/redbook.pdf

Fabozzi, F. J., & Fabozzi, F. A. (2021). *Bond markets, analysis, and strategies*. MIT Press.

Fan, J. P., & Wong, T. J. (2002). Corporate ownership structure and the informativeness of accounting earnings in East Asia. *Journal of Accounting and Economics, 33*(3), 401–425.

Forslund, K., Lima, L., & Panizza, U. (2011). The determinants of the composition of public debt in developing and emerging market countries. *Review of Development Finance, 1*(3–4), 207–222.

Goodfriend, M. (2006). *Why a corporate bond market: Growth and direct finance*. Press & Communications. This publication is available on the BIS website: https://www.bis.org

Graham, J. R., & Harvey, C. R. (2015). *The equity risk premium in 2015*. Available at SSRN 2611793.

IMF. (2005, April). *Global financial stability report*. World Economic and Financial Surveys, Washington.

IMF. (2021). Background note for international financing summit for Africa high-level event.

International Capital Market Association, ICMA. (2013). Economic importance of the corporate bond markets.

IOSCO. (2004, May). Transparency of corporate bond markets. Report of the Technical Committee of the International Organization of Securities Commissions.

Jin, N. K., & Loh, L. (2002). *Developing a viable corporate bond market: The Singapore experience* (Economics and Finance No. 2). Institute of Southeast Asian Studies.

Kablan, S. (2010). *Banking efficiency and financial development in Sub-Saharan Africa*. International Monetary Fund.

Kaufman, H. (1991, October 9). Credit crunches: The deregulator were wrong. *Wall Street Journal*.

Kim, Y. H. (2000). Policy agenda for bond market development in Asia. *Bond Market Development in Asia*, 141.

Levine, R. (1997). Financial development and economic growth: Views and agenda. *Journal of Economic Literature, 35*, 688–726.

Levine, R. (2004). *Finance and growth: Theory and evidence* (NBER Working Paper Series, Working Paper 10766).

Machokoto M., Areneke, G., & Maher, B. I. (2020). Rising corporate debt and value relevance of supply-side factors in South Africa. *Journal of Business Research, 109*, 26–37.

Moody's Investor Service. (2002). *Malaysia's debt capital markets assume new importance*. Special Comments (New York, March) National Securities Clearing Corporation 1997, Emerging Markets: Developing Clearance and Settlement Systems.

Mu, Y., Phelps, P., & Stotsky, J. G. (2013a). Bond markets in Africa. *Review of Development Finance, 3*(3), 121–135.

Mu, Y., Phelps, P., & Stotsky, J. G. (2013b). *Bond markets in Africa* (IMF Working Paper No. 12/13). International Monetary Fund, Washington.

Park, C. Y., & Mercado, R. (2015). *Financial inclusion, poverty, and income inequality in developing Asia* (Asian Development Bank Economics Working Paper Series, [426]).

Rajan, R., & Zingales, L. (2003). *Saving capitalism from the capitalists: Unleashing the power of financial markets to create wealth and spread opportunity*. Crown Business.

Roldos, E. (2004). *Pension reform, investment restrictions, and capital markets* (IMF Policy Discussion Paper PDP/04/4). Washington: International Monetary Fund.

Senbet, L., & Otchere, I. (2010). African stock markets: Ingredients for development and capacity building. In Q. Marc, V. Genevieve, & Palgrave (Eds.), *African finance in the 21th century*. Macmillan Publishing.

Smaaoui, H., Grandes, M., & Akindele, A. (2017). The determinate of bond market development: Further evidence from emerging and developed countries. *Emerging Market Review, 32*, 148–167.

World Bank. (2019). *10 years of green bonds: Creating the blueprint for sustainability across capital markets*. World Bank.

Yartey, C., & Adjasi, C. (2007). *Stock market development in sub-Saharan Africa: Critical issues and challenges* (IMF Working Paper No. 07/209). International Monetary Fund, Washington.

CHAPTER 28

Private Capital Flows, Domestic Financial Markets and Energy Use in Africa

Jephthah O. Osei, Joseph Abor, Patricia A. Ojangole, and Joshua Yindenaba Abor

28.1 Introduction

After independence in the 1970s and until the early 1990s, most African countries had feeble growth. Africa is a growth disaster, according to Easterly and Levine (1997). However, since the early 1990s, Africa's growth trends have shifted upwards. Many of the world's fastest-growing economies are now in Africa, and most African countries are expanding

J. O. Osei · P. A. Ojangole · J. Y. Abor
University of Ghana Business School, Legon, Accra, Ghana
e-mail: pojangole@udbl.co.ug

J. Y. Abor
e-mail: joshabor@ug.edu.gh

J. Abor (✉)
Uganda Development Bank Limited, Kampala, Uganda
e-mail: joeabor@gmail.com

J. Y. Abor and C. K. D. Adjasi (eds.), *The Economics of Banking and Finance in Africa*, Palgrave Macmillan Studies in Banking and Financial Institutions, https://doi.org/10.1007/978-3-031-04162-4_28

faster than those in the developed world, with growth rates of around 5.25% in 2011 and 5.75% in 2012. Moreover, Africa was adjudged the world's fastest-growing continent in 2013 (Agbloyor et al., 2014). In 2017, the African Development Bank (AfDB) ranked the continent the second-fastest-growing economy with an average growth of 3.4% in 2017 and 4.3% in 2018.[1] Recent evidence from the International Monetary Fund (IMF) envisages that the region will experience the slowest economic growth due to the COVID-19 pandemic. According to the IMF's 2020 report, the growth rate in the region declined by 1.9% and the overall economy contracted by 2.1 percentage points in 2020. This led to a large increase in fiscal spending through stimulus packages ranging in cost from about 0.02% of GDP in least developed countries such as South Sudan to about 10.4% of GDP in more developed countries such as South Africa.[2] According to AfDB's African Economic Outlook 2021 report, the continent is expected to resume growth in 2021 at 3.4%. This projected recovery is underpinned by the resumption of tourism, the resurgence of commodity prices, a rollback of pandemic-induced restrictions especially in the financial and energy sectors of the African economy.

Energy is paramount because sustainable development in the medium to long term depends largely on stable and affordable energy devoid of environmental defect (Qamruzzaman & Jianguo, 2020). With the persistent growth in energy demand due to rapid urbanisation, there is the need to examine the role domestic financial markets play in enhancing energy consumption in Africa (Dincer, 2000; Qamruzzaman & Jianguo, 2020). Financial market development is essential because it enhances the savings and investment allocation mechanism in the financial sector and triggers economic growth (Agbloyor et al., 2014). Because a vibrant financial market is a necessary condition for private capital inflows (Alfaro et al., 2004), governments deliberately institute policies to attract capital inflows (Alfaro et al., 2004; Azman-Saini et al., 2010) to enhance productivity indirectly through energy and technology transfers (Okada, 2013). Although private capital flows to Africa have increased in recent times, they vary in terms of their components. For instance, Foreign Direct

[1] See AfDB' African Economic Outlook 2017. Available online at https://www.afdb.org/fileadmin/uploads/afdb/Documents/Publications/AEO_2017_Report_Full_English.pdf.

[2] https://www.afdb.org/en/knowledge/publications/african-economic-outlook.

Investment (FDI) inflows outweigh the flows of Foreign Portfolio Investment (FPI) and Private Debt Portfolio. A key question is: how do the domestic financial markets interact with private capital flows to improve energy consumption in the developing world?

Studies have shown a mixed effect of private capital flows on energy consumption (see Çoban & Topcu, 2013; Doytch & Narayan, 2016; Lee, 2013; Mielnik & Goldemberg, 2002; Pao & Tsai, 2011; Sadorsky, 2011). Doytch and Narayan (2016), for example, showed an inverse relationship between energy consumption and private capital flows for developing countries, while Sadorsky (2011) revealed a positive relationship between FDI and energy consumption. Agbloyor et al. (2014) examined the relationship between private capital flows and economic growth using domestic financial markets as a moderating factor. After decomposing private capital flows into their various components, they found that FDI, FPI and PDF all have an inverse effect on economic growth. However, after interacting private capital flows with domestic financial market variables, their results proved that countries with strong domestic financial markets can transform the negative impact into a positive one.

Since energy is a significant factor of sustainable economic growth, this paper seeks to answer the key question of how private capital flows affect energy demand conditioned on domestic financial markets in Africa. This paper is innovative and distinct from earlier studies by Alfaro et al. (2004) and Mohammed et al. (2020) in two ways. First, it uses all three components of private capital flows (i.e. foreign direct investment, foreign portfolio investment and portfolio debt inflows) and not only FDI as in the case of Alfaro et al. (2004). Second, we interact domestic financial markets with private capital flows other than oil revenues as in the case of Mohammed et al. (2020) to examine their impact on energy and not economic growth. However, the paper is similar to the work of Agbloyor et al. (2014) in terms of response variables but different in terms of focus. While they focused on private capital on economic growth in Africa, this paper centres on the impact of private capital flows on energy consumption, considering keenly the moderating role of domestic financial markets. We employ a dynamic Generalised Least Square (GLS) based on the Durbin-Watson autoregression model of order (1) with more current data from 1990 to 2019. The advantage of this method over the static approach used in previous studies by Agbloyor et al. (2014) is the ability to solve endogeneity problems both between the dependent variable and the random term and between the regressors and the unobserved country specific effect so that the stochastic term is freely random and independent. Our empirical results showed that domestic financial markets may not provide conduits for private capital flows in general to influence energy use, but rather serve as absorptive capacities for portfolio investment flows to Africa.

The remaining sections of the study are structured as follows: Sect. 28.2 provides a literature review. Section 28.3 presents the research methodology employed in the study. The empirical findings are discussed in Sect. 28.4, while Sect. 28.5 concludes the paper with policy recommendations.

28.2 Literature Review

The fundamental endogenous growth theory forms the theoretical foundation of this study. The theory is an improvement on the famous Solow Growth theory and provides the opportunity to increase the number of regressors in the neo-classical growth theories. It hypothesises that increasing domestic capital formation directly increases aggregate investment (Bailliu, 2000) with spill overs on the indigenous financial markets (Agbloyor et al., 2014). Thus, countries with robust financial systems exhibit a higher economic growth rate compared to those with weaker financial systems, even when they receive equal proportion of net capital inflows. The literature documents numerous studies that have established a mixed effect of private capital flows, particularly foreign direct investment (FDI) and foreign portfolio investment (FPI) on macroeconomic indicators (see Bekaert & Harvey, 1998; Bekaert et al., 2003; Choong et al., 2010 Durham, 2004; Qamruzzaman & Jianguo, 2020). For example, Soto (2000) reports that developing countries' FDI and FPI inflows directly influence income growth, but bank related inflows, whether short or long term, negatively influence income growth. Choong et al. (2010) studied the economic effect of FDI and FPI on growth in both advanced and developing countries through the domestic stock market channels. Their results show that FDI positively influences economic growth, but FPI negatively influences economic growth.

Other researchers have argued that the influence of private capital flows on a country's growth relies greatly on the performance of the host country's macroeconomic indicators including gross domestic product, human capital, trade openness, oil reserves and financial market development (Agbloyor et al., 2014; Bailliu, 2000; Hermes & Lensink, 2003; Mohammed et al., 2020; Omran & Bolbol, 2003). For instance, Bailliu (2000) showed for forty (40) developing countries that FDI and FPI promote economic growth, but only in countries with developed banking sectors. Durham (2004) also attributes such growth to strong financial development and vibrant legal institutions. Nili and Rastad (2007) observed that although increasing oil reserves promote national growth for oil-producing economies, robust domestic financial markets have a deepening effect on investment in these countries. This finding is confirmed in a recent study by Samargandi et al. (2014) in Saudi Arabia where the researchers revealed that a well-developed financial market fosters economic growth in non-oil production-sectors compared to the oil-production sectors of the economy. According to Agbloyor et al. (2014), these macroeconomic indicators serve as conduits for private capital flows to directly impact economic growth.

Moreover, the flows of capital in the form of foreign direct investment (FDI) and equity have a direct effect on the overall production process in an economy through industrialisation and infrastructural development (Qamruzzaman & Jianguo, 2020). In relation to energy, the use of traditional energy and its adverse environmental and production cost puts the effects of FDI inflows on energy consumption into two major categories: composition and technique effects (Fisher-Vanden et al., 2006; Hübler & Keller, 2010). The former involves structural dynamics in the economy such as reducing one sector and expanding the other. The latter requires the transformation of novel technology capable of ensuring energy efficiency which will replace the outmoded ones (Hübler & Keller, 2010) (Qamruzzaman & Jianguo, 2020). Empirical evidence on the impact of private capital flows and foreign direct investment on energy consumption is mixed. Studies such as Doytch and Narayan (2016) and Mielnik and Goldemberg (2002) show an inverse relationship between energy intensity, defined as energy consumption as a share of GDP, and foreign direct investment. Doytch and Narayan (2016), for example, argue that this negative relationship results from the introduction of new technologies in developing countries. Other studies such as Hübler and Keller (2010) and Sadorsky (2011) failed to find a significant effect of FDI on energy consumption in a longitudinal panel study. Chang (2015) expanded this study to include fifty-three sampled countries within a non-linear analytical framework. Yet the study discovered no statistically significant effects of foreign direct investment on energy consumption. Sadorsky (2011) followed a similar approach but controlled for banking variants to investigate the nexus, with a focus on Central and Eastern European countries. For the nine sampled economies from these regions, the results showed a direct influence of FDI on energy consumption. This direct relationship has also been revealed by other studies (Çoban & Topcu, 2013; Lee, 2013; Mielnik & Goldemberg, 2002; Pao & Tsai, 2011; Sadorsky, 2011).

Ting et al. (2011) provided specific evidence for China's Jiangsu province concerning the direct effect of sector-wide FDI on energy consumption. The results revealed that FDI inflows in the province are largely concentrated in industrial (extraction and manufacturing) energy consumption, but there is also a cumulative share in the service sector. Meanwhile, the impacts of foreign direct investment in agriculture, industry, transport and communications on energy consumption were initially positive but became negative from 2004 onwards, unlike the effects of FDI in construction and 'other industries' that were close to stabilising, with the effect of close to zero. A subsequent study by Jiang et al. (2014) reached a similar conclusion after adjusting for the impact of energy efficiency in the sub-sectors of the manufacturing industry.

We have observed from the ensuing debate that the impact of private capital flows, particularly on economic growth, depends largely on a sound macroeconomic environment with robust financial markets in the receiving country. In addition, we observed that the impact of private capital flows on energy consumption is mixed. However, the literature remains silent on the relationship between domestic financial markets and energy consumption in the presence of private capital flows. Meanwhile, Choong et al. (2010) showed that the interaction between domestic stock market and FDI have a positive effect on economic growth, an assertion that has been confirmed by recent studies such as Agbloyor et al. (2014) and Mohammed et al. (2020). This paper considers the effect of domestic financial markets on energy use, taking into consideration the moderating effect of private capital flows in Africa.

28.3 Methodology

The Model

We specify the Modified fixed effect model based on the feasible Generalised Least Squares (FGLS). This is a biased-correction method due to its ability to solve correlations emanating from within groups across periods as a result of group-specific shocks. The biased-correction process tailors from the *p*th order of the modified Durbin-Watson (pDW) autoregression.[3] The functional forms are presented as follows.

Given that,

$$y_{it} = K_{it}'\beta_o + C_{it} + \varepsilon_{it} \tag{28.1}$$

and

$$C_{it} = X_{it}'\beta_1 + Z_{it}'\beta_2^i + \epsilon_{it} \tag{28.2}$$

Where y_{it} is the outcome variable of interest, K_{it} are covariates that vary at the individual level, C_{it} are group-year effects, X_{it} are the covariates that vary at the group-year level and are assumed to have constant group-specific coefficients, Z_{it} are covariates that vary at the group-year level and have group-specific coefficients assumed to be non-stochastic and identical across groups,[4] $i = 1,..., s$, $t = 1,..., T$ for each i and t, ε_{it} and ϵ_{it} are unobserved random components assumed to be uncorrelated with either the observed explanatory variables or each other and with zero mean. Estimation and inferences can be performed by simultaneously solving the model formed by the combination of (1) and (2) as,

$$y_{it} = K_{it}'\beta_o + X_{it}'\beta_1 + Z_{it}'\beta_2^i + \mu_{it} \tag{28.3}$$

Where $\mu_{it} = \varepsilon_{it} + \epsilon_{it}$. The cluster problem arises from the fact that for all $i \neq j$ that $E[\varepsilon_{it}, \epsilon_{it}] = \sigma_v^2$ and the policy autocorrelation problem arises from $E[\varepsilon_{it}, \epsilon_{it-k}] = \delta(k) \neq 0$ if μ_{it} is serially correlated. It is important to determine whether the correlation is binding, that is, whether fixed effect or random effect is the better estimator of the model specified in Eq. (28.3). We therefore performed the Hausman test that any heterogeneity is uncorrelated. Rejection of the null favours the fixed effect approach and vice versa. The standard errors are adjusted to address the presence of serial correlation between individuals within group-year cells following the modified Durbin-Watson AR(p).

[3] The pDW proposed by Bhargava et al. (1982) cited by Born and Breitung (2016) is the ratio of the sum of squared difference and the sum of squared residuals. The test is based on the linear combination of the DW statistic ratios.

[4] Note that for a fixed effect model, $Z_{it} = 1$ such that $Z_{it} = [1,t]$ is the group-specific effect with time trends.

Empirical Model Estimation

Our empirical model follows directly from Eq. (28.3). We specify a linear regression model showing the relationship among domestic capital mobilisation, private capital flows and energy consumption for some selected African countries[5] as follows.

$$\text{Energy}_{it} = \beta_0 + \theta_i \text{PCF}_{it} + \gamma_i \text{DFM}_{it} + \alpha_i R_{it} + Z_i + \mu_{it} \qquad (28.4)$$

Where the respondent variable *Energy* is energy consumption measured as the overall energy use equivalent per 1000 GDP at constant price. PCF is private capital flows made up of foreign direct investment (FDI), portfolio investment inflows (PFI) and gross portfolio debt inflows (GPDI). DFM is a vector of domestic financial market variables measured by stock market capitalisation, stock market turnover ratio, private credit by deposit money banks percentage of GDP, bank credit to deposit ratio and domestic credit to private sector percentage of GDP. These indicator variables were chosen following studies such as Agbloyor et al. (2014), Kumar and Woo (2010), Imbs and Ranciere (2007), Alfaro et al. (2004) and Pattilo et al. (2002, 2004). *R* is a vector of state variables controlling for financial system variations measured by financial system deposits to GDP ratio (Agbloyor et al., 2014; Kumar & Woo, 2010), energy price measured by oil rents percentage of GDP, and industry demand for energy, and β, γ, and α are parameters estimated following the fixed effect approach. Our goal is to determine whether DFM conditioned on PCF serve as conduits to enhance energy use. We therefore modify Eq. (28.4) by interacting each PCF variable with DFM factors in separate models. This will help to identify those that are substitutes and complements. As such Eq. (28.4) is modified as:

$$\text{Energy}_{it} = \beta_0 + \forall_i (\text{PCF}_{it} * \text{DFM}_{it}) + \alpha_i R_{it} + Z_i + \mu_{it} \qquad (28.5)$$

Where $(\text{PCF}_{it} * \text{DCM}_{it})$ is the interactive term. As mentioned earlier, the policy autocorrelation problem arises when μ_{it} is serially correlated. We predict the level of correlation using the Bonferroni correlation analysis and correct this by estimating Eq. (28.5) based on a Durbin-Watson AR

[5] Based on data availability, participating countries included Algeria, Botswana, Cote D'Ivoire, Egypt, Eswatini, Ghana, Kenya, Malawi, Mauritius, Morocco, Namibia, Nigeria, South Africa, Tanzania, Tunisia, Uganda and Zambia.

(1) disturbance term so that the error term is freely random with mean zero and constant variance. We also conduct a stationarity test using the Fisher-type unit-root test based on the Augmented Dickey-Fuller test.

Data Source

We employed a panel involving seventeen (17) African countries covering the period 1990 to 2019. Data on domestic financial markets were obtained from the Global Financial Development Database (GFDD). The rest were obtained from the World Development Indicators (WDI).

28.4 Empirical Results and Discussion

Table 28.1 presents the summary statistics of the variables employed in this study. The difference in observations is attributed to the nonavailability of data for some countries in some years. To avoid violating the basic least squares assumptions, we conduct the Shapiro–Wilk's *W* test for normality to investigate whether the variables are normally distributed (i.e. independent, and identically distributed). The *W* tests the null hypothesis that the variables are normally undistributed. Column 7 of

Table 28.1 Descriptive statistics

Variable	*Obs*	*Mean*	*Std. Dev*	*Min*	*Max*	*W-Test*
Energy use	379	138.509	72.186	56.602	339.555	0.831***
FDI	510	2.515	2.289	–6.898	10.912	0.898***
PFI	471	–4.856	3.018	–2.390	1.430	0.454***
GPDI	203	10.364	42.533	0.003	395.208	0.228***
Stock market capitalisation	395	31.617	51.428	0.057	328.361	0.567***
Stock market turnover	359	10.961	17.649	0.014	205.443	0.529***
Private credit	508	30.392	31.772	2.292	146.812	0.766***
Bank credit	508	76.735	29.858	16.116	182.507	0.973***
Domestic credit	503	32.804	33.193	2.941	160.125	0.765***
Financial system	507	32.315	22.111	3.653	102.45	0.897***
Industry demand	501	27.562	8.654	10.415	58.884	0.951***
Energy price	510	2.713	5.765	0	30.664	0.689***

Notes *$p < 0.1$, **$p < 0.05$, ***$p < 0.01$; Shapiro–Wilk's *W* test for normal data presented in the last column

Table 28.1 shows the results of the Shapiro–Wilk's W test. Our empirical results reject this claim for all variables statistically at 1% significance level indicating that the variables were all normally distributed around their respective means. We can also observe from Table 28.1 that the variables' ranges do not reveal outliers capable of rendering the coefficients biased by influencing the consistency and efficiency in the dataset. In other words, the standard deviation values reveal that the sample intervals are evenly distributed so that the estimated results are not influenced by relative extrema.

We also examined the persistence of strong correlation in the data using the Bonferroni pairwise correlation matrix. Table 28.2 presents the results of the pairwise matrix of correlation. This ex-ante diagnostic is important because of the likelihood of multicollinearity emanating from fitting five different models of Eq. (28.5) for each PCF variable. We observed significant negative correlation between stock market capitalisation and FDI and PFI, respectively. A similar inference is observed for private credit ratio and domestic credit ratio. However, there exists a strong significant positive correlation between private credit ratio, bank credit and domestic credit on gross domestic debt individually. We correct these anomalies by fitting the final models with adjusted DW-AR (1) standard errors.

Table 28.3 presents the results of the stationarity test following the Fisher-type unit-root test based on the augmented Dickey-Fuller test. The goal here is to determine whether to estimate the results at levels effect or first difference depending on the stationarity. Thus, if variables are stationary at levels, then we proceed to estimate the level regression and difference regression if otherwise. In Table 28.3 the study rejects the null hypothesis of unit roots present and concludes that the variables have no unit roots, follow random walk and are stationary at levels.

Tables 28.4–28.7 present the panel results establishing the private capital flows and energy use nexus moderated by domestic financial market indicators. Table 28.4 presents the base model while Tables 28.5–28.7 show the models with interactions and are divided into 5 columns each depending on the domestic financial variable used. We control for time heterogeneity and the country specific effect. It must be emphasised that each column is reported as a fixed or random effect estimate based on the results of the Hausman test. That is, where the Hausman is statistically significant we report the fixed effect results and random effect if otherwise. In Table 28.4, an effort has been made to demonstrate the independent effect of private capital flows and financial market

Table 28.2 Pairwise correlations matrix based on bonferroni test

Variables	*(1)*	*(2)*	*(3)*	*(4)*	*(5)*	*(6)*	*(7)*	*(8)*	*(9)*
(1) Energy use	1.000								
(2) FDI	0.016	1.000							
	(0.74)								
(3) PFI	−0.184*	0.117*	1.000						
	(0.00)	(0.01)							
(4) GPDI	−0.156	−0.047	0.064	1.000					
	(0.05)	(0.50)	(0.38)						
(5) Stock market capitalisation	0.376*	−0.145*	−0.335*	0.119	1.000				
	(0.00)	(0.00)	(0.00)	(0.12)					
(6) Stock market turnover	−0.017	−0.140*	−0.089	−0.056	0.315*	1.000			
	(0.77)	(0.00)	(0.10)	(0.47)	(0.000)				
(7) Private credit	−0.023	−0.108*	−0.252*	0.264*	0.824*	0.251*	1.000		
	(0.66)	(0.01)	(0.00)	(0.00)	(0.000)	(0.00)			
(8) Bank credit	−0.036	−0.009	−0.155*	0.139*	0.341*	0.035	0.607*	1.000	
	(0.47)	(0.84)	(0.00)	(0.04)	(0.000)	(0.51)	(0.00)		
(9) Domestic credit	−0.023	−0.117*	−0.255*	0.261*	0.831*	0.250*	0.996*	0.604*	1.000
	(0.65)	(0.00)	(0.00)	(0.00)	(0.000)	(0.00)	(0.00)	(0.00)	

Notes *$p < 0.1$, **$p < 0.05$, ***$p < 0.01$; Based on Bonferroni correlation analysis

Table 28.3 Fisher-type unit-root test based on augmented Dickey–Fuller tests

Variable	*Level*
Energy use	4.9997***
Foreign direct investment	33.8383***
Portfolio investment	29.3091***
Gross portfolio debt inflows	9.9427***
Stock market capitalisation	47.0732***
Stock market turnover ratio	70.9558 ***
Private credit deposit	52.2974***
Bank credit to bank deposit ratio	39.9153***
Domestic credit to private sector	53.4629***
Financial system deposit	28.7041***
Energy price	16.0180***
Industry energy demand	11.2349***

Notes $^{*}p < 0.1$, $^{**}p < 0.05$, $^{***}p < 0.01$; Time trend and panel means are included. The asymptotic T-statistic follows the modified inverse Chi-Square p-values. Ho: All panels contain unit roots

indicators on energy use. We observed a negative effect of FDI on energy use. The negative relationship between FDI and macroeconomic variables such as energy use might look strange but is not new in the literature. Studies such as Agbloyor et al. (2014) and Akinlo (2004) observed a similar negative relationship between FDI and economic growth. One plausible explanation for this inverse relationship may be the crowding out of domestic investment by FDI that liquidates most of the local firms especially in the industrial sector that are dominant energy consumers. Conversely, we observed a positive effect of domestic financial market indicators such as stock market capitalisation and private credit to deposit but an inverse relationship for variables such as bank credit and domestic credit to private sector on energy use. In terms of the controls, energy price showed a positive effect on energy use, while industrial demand and financial systems showed negative effects on energy use. These outcomes provide enough motivation for investigating the functional role of financial markets in stimulating private capital flow to influence energy use.

In Table 28.5, FDI is moderated by domestic financial market indicators in all five (5) columns. We observed a similar significant inverse relationship between FDI and energy use in all five columns. The interactive term also showed a significant positive effect in column 4, suggesting that domestic financial markets provide the necessary environment for

Table 28.4 Impact of private capital flow on domestic financial market energy use in Africa: the base model

Energy use	*(1)*	*(2)*	*(3)*
Private capital flows			
Foreign direct investment	−4.525***		
	(−3.96)		
Portfolio investment		1.13e−10	
		(0.13)	
Gross portfolio debt			0.155
			(1.61)
Financial market indicators			
Stock market capitalisation	0.853***	0.639***	0.284
	(5.75)	(4.58)	(1.11)
Stock markets turnover	−0.209	−0.329	0.650
	(−0.74)	(−1.27)	(1.54)
Private credits by deposit	0.770	1.388*	2.049
	(0.96)	(1.70)	(1.56)
Bank credit to bank deposits	−0.104	−0.487***	−1.183***
	(−0.61)	(−2.76)	(−4.16)
Domestic credit to private sector	−1.559**	−1.256*	−1.443
	(−2.21)	(−1.74)	(−1.17)
State variables			
Energy price	2.455***	3.899***	−1.122
	(3.70)	(6.51)	(−1.22)
Industry demand	−0.393	−2.191***	0.348
	(−0.93)	(−5.62)	(0.61)
Financial system deposits	−0.900***	−1.412***	−2.170***
	(−3.16)	(−5.47)	(−4.48)
Constant	310.1***	262.1***	743.8***
	(64.51)	(13.74)	(174.29)
No. of obs	257	269	96
Hausman test	1176.42***	280.30	37.27***

Notes *$p < 0.10$, **$p < 0.05$, ***$p < 0.010$; *t* statistics in parentheses

FDI to directly influence the energy use nexus. This finding supports an earlier claim by Agbloyor et al. (2014) and Alfaro et al. (2004) that strong domestic financial markets positively improve the mechanism through which FDI affects economic growth. Our results also display that the moderation has an incremental effect beyond the variables it interacted with. For example, after the interaction, stock market capitalisation,

Table 28.5 Foreign direct investment and energy use: moderating role of domestic financial markets

Energy use	*(1)*	*(2)*	*(3)*	*(4)*	*(5)*
Foreign direct investment	−4.849***	−5.336***	−5.365***	−4.986***	– 6.147***
	(1.45)	(1.16)	(1.18)	(1.29)	(1.34)
Financial market indicators					
Stock market capitalisation	0.515***				
	(0.82)				
Stock market turnover		0.357			
		(0.25)			
Private credit			0.303**		
			(0.14)		
Bank credit				−0.378***	
				(0.11)	
Domestic credit					0.346**
					(0.14)
Interaction term	0.279	−0.582	−1.697	3.059*	−1.246
	(0.39)	(1.29)	(1.47)	(1.62)	(0.04)
State variables					
Energy price	1.735***	3.558***	4.050***	3.482***	3.763***
	(0.52)	(0.59)	(0.56)	(0.59)	(0.64)
Industry demand	−0.049	−1.421***	−1.207***	−1.052**	−1.265
	(0.39)	(0.38)	(0.38)	(0.43)	(0.44)
Financial system deposits	−1.588***	−1.07***	−1.207***	−1.148***	– 1.342***
	(0.13)	(0.15)	(0.17)	(0.15)	(0.19)
Constant	253.8***	233.17***	219.26***	425.55***	305.38***
	(4.21)	(15.39)	(14.87)	(3.59)	(3.51)
No. of obs	277	257	340	340	339
Time effect	Yes	Yes	Yes	Yes	Yes
Hausman test	**326.86*** **	**1.10**	**0.72**	**0.69**	**0.75**
F Statistic	37.89***	28.14***	32.84***	44.35***	34.51***

Notes $^*p < 0.10$, $^{**}p < 0.05$, $^{***}p < 0.010$; t statistics in parentheses

private credit and domestic credit independently revealed a positive effect on energy use. This revelation is largely consistent with earlier studies such as Adjasi et al. (2012) and Alfaro et al. (2004, 2007) . While bank credit to deposit was independently negative, it became positive after interacting with FDI. In terms of controls, Table 28.5 revealed a significantly direct relationship between energy price and energy use in all columns. A reasonable explanation for this finding is the increasing demand for the limited supply of energy, coupled with the high cost of energy production and distribution in Africa. We also observed an inverse relationship between industry demand and energy use in Africa. Obviously, excessive demand by the industries, coupled with high cost of energy purchase, serves as an impediment to industrial demand, especially for the domestic infant industries. Also, the negative relationship between financial system deposit and energy use suggests that poor financial systems deplete energy use by economic agents and vice versa, ceteris paribus.

In Table 28.6, we report the results of the effect of gross portfolio investment inflows (PFI) on energy use in the presence of domestic financial market indicators. We observed that PFI had no significant effect on energy use for all columns. Unlike the case of FDI, the interactions showed a negative relationship with PFI for financial indicators such as stock market turnover, bank credit and domestic credit as shown in columns 2, 4 and 5. This suggests that domestic financial market variables do not provide a conduit for portfolio investment to positively influence energy use. Hitherto, domestic markets showed an independent significant positive effect for variables such as stock market capitalisation and private credit, but a negative effect for bank credit to deposit ratio. This outcome is consistent with the famous financial growth-nexus paradigm. This theory suggests that financial development in the form of an advanced stock market enhances macroeconomic activities especially in developing economies such as Africa. Like the cases in Table 28.5, energy price showed a positive effect on energy use while industrial demand and financial deposits revealed inverse relationships with energy use in Africa.

The relationship between gross portfolio debt inflows GPDI) and energy use was not different from what was observed for FDI and PFI as shown in Table 28.7. Portfolio debt inflows show a significantly negative effect on energy use as indicated in columns 2 and 4. This finding is not novel in the literature (see for instance, Agbloyor et al., 2014; Alfaro et al., 2004; Imbs & Ranciere, 2007; Kumar & Woo, 2010; Pattilo et al., 2002, 2004). Of key interest is the sufficing role of financial market in

Table 28.6 Portfolio investment inflows and energy use: moderating role of domestic financial markets

Energy use	*(1)*	*(2)*	*(3)*	*(4)*	*(5)*
Portfolio investment inflows	1.634	−1.141	1.971	−9.871	2.251
	(1.49)	(1.17)	(1.99)	(1.14)	(2.03)
Financial market indicators					
Stock market capitalisation	0.688***				
	(0.07)				
Stock market turnover		0.379			
		(0.26)			
Private credit			3.198***		
			(0.14)		
Bank credit				−0.358***	
				(0.10)	
Domestic credit					0.109
					(0.13)
Interactive term	−1.091	−1.711**	−3.711	−2.231***	−3.811*
	(1.27)	(7.85)	(2.32)	(7.75)	(2.19)
State variables					
Energy price	3.118***	4.114***	3.178***	4.364***	3.235***
	(0.58)	(0.61)	(0.61)	(0.55)	(0.60)
Industry demand	−0.418	−2.346***	−1.767***	−2.643***	−1.855***
	(0.47)	(0.61)	(0.46)	(0.42)	(0.46)
Financial system deposits	−1.556***	−1.076***	−1.327***	−0.857***	−1.233***
	(0.13)	(0.13)	(0.20)	(0.11)	(0.19)
Constant	225.2***	240.39**	288.6***	276.73***	293.4***
	(5.89)	(4.16)	(5.02)	(82.52)	(4.82)
No. of obs	255	239	310	310	309
time effect	Yes	Yes	Yes	Yes	Yes
Hausman test	**276.80*** **	**0.89**	**451.05**	**0.76**	**306.18**
F statistic	40.03***	21.61***	24.29***	36.59***	25.0***

Notes *$p < 0.10$, **$p < 0.05$, ***$p < 0.010$; t statistics in parentheses

Table 28.7 Gross portfolio debt inflows and energy use: moderating role of domestic financial market

Energy use	*(1)*	*(2)*	*(3)*	*(4)*	*(5)*
Gross portfolio debt	0.488	−1.421***	−0.936	−2.097***	−1.243
	(0.59)	(0.52)	(0.74)	(0.52)	(1.05)
Financial market indicators					
Stock market capitalisation	0.349***				
	(0.18)				
Stock market turnover		0.861***			
		(0.31)			
Private credit			0.095		
			(0.21)		
Bank credit				−0.519***	
				(0.14)	
Domestic credit					−0.023
					(0.18)
Interaction term	0.414	1.18***	0.728	1.674***	0.015
	(0.44)	(0.38)	(0.56)	(0.39)	(0.01)
State variables					
Energy price	0.918	−0.143	0.132	1.114	0.009
	(0.77)	(0.89)	(1.02)	(0.73)	(1.03)
Industry demand	0.147	0.499	1.653**	0.338	1.491**
	(0.54)	(0.53)	(0.77)	(0.53)	(0.73)
Financial system deposits	−1.658***	−1.682***	−1.349***	−1.430***	– 1.236***
	(0.19)	(0.21)	(0.30)	(0.17)	(0.31)
Constant	185.63***	187.46***	466.36***	236.99***	452.6***
	(18.4)	(4.43)	(4.89)	(28.19)	(4.82)
No. of obs	99	96	119	119	119
Time effect	Yes	Yes	Yes	Yes	Yes
Hausman test	**2.52**	**7.50**	**0.37**	**0.75**	**22.03**
F statistic	6.99***	6.92***	5.82***	9.88***	5.58***

Notes *$p < 0.10$, **$p < 0.05$, ***$p < 0.010$; *t* statistics in parentheses

moderating GPDI. Our results revealed a positive interaction between GPDI and stock market turnover as well as bank credit to deposit ratio as shown in columns 2 and 4. Like the case of FDI, this interaction had an incremental effect beyond the moderation. Thus, beyond the interaction, financial market variables such as stock market capitalisation and stock market turnover were found to have a statistically significantly independent positive effect on energy use. Bank credit on the other hand showed opposing views as in the case of FDI. That is, independently it had a negative influence on energy use, but when interacted with GPDI we observed a positive effect.

These findings support the proposition by Alfaro et al. (2004, cited by Adjasi et al., 2012) that the significance of private capital moderation with financial market indicators unravel crucial allocation functions that financial markets perform in the macroeconomic environment. According to them, the inflows of FDI, and by extension, PFI and GPDI, depends substantially on how well the domestic financial market can allocate financial resources. That is, the development of the internal financial system provides a necessary conduit for capital flows to influence macroeconomic activities such as energy use. As observed from our results, private capital flows can positively influence energy use if domestic financial markets are robust in the mobilisation and allocation of financial resources for efficient use.

28.5 Conclusion

Inflows of private capital remain a significant development agendum for regions of the developing world such as Africa, mainly due to the positive impact of FDI on economic growth. The argument has so far been centred on the role of capital flow in economic growth. The literature is yet to exploit this role for energy use, especially within the African context. In this study, we tried to investigate the effect of private capital flows on energy use by looking at the moderating roles of domestic financial market variables. We defined private capital flows to include FDI, gross portfolio investment and gross portfolio debt inflows. Domestic financial market was represented by five (5) indicators, i.e. stock market capitalisation, stock market turnover ratio, private credit to bank deposit ratio, bank credit to deposit ratio and domestic credit to private sector ratio. To avoid selection biases, we controlled for energy price, industry demand for energy and the financial system's deposit. Our empirical results revealed that the domestic financial market plays a significant role in establishing the connection between private capital flow and energy use. Specifically, it showed that private capital inflows conditioned on a favourable financial market environment enhance energy use in Africa. In other words, the presence of these financial market indicators provides a conduit for private capital flows to improve energy use in Africa. It is therefore highly recommended that fiscal authorities in Africa provide the basic means to strengthen and further develop the domestic financial markets to attract the necessary private capital to enhance energy use. This can be done through overcoming the 'cost' incurred in the financial system such as the reduction in financial cost of acquiring and securing information, contracts, markets and intermediaries.

References

Adjasi, C. K., Abor, J., Osei, K. A., & Nyavor-Foli, E. E. (2012). FDI and economic activity in Africa: The role of local financial markets. *Thunderbird International Business Review, 54*(4), 429–439.

Agbloyor, E. K., Abor, J. Y., Adjasi, C. K. D., & Yawson, A. (2014). Private capital flows and economic growth in Africa: The role of domestic financial markets. *Journal of International Financial Markets, Institutions and Money, 30*, 137–152.

Akinlo, A. E. (2004). Foreign direct investment and growth in Nigeria: An empirical investigation. *Journal of Policy Modeling, 26*(5), 627–639.

Alfaro, L., Chanda, A., Kalemli-Ozcan, S., & Sayek, S. (2004). FDI and economic growth: The role of local financial markets. *Journal of International Economics, 64*(1), 89–112.

Alfaro, L., Chanda, A., Kalemli-Ozcan, S., & Sayek, S. (2007). How does foreign direct investment promote economic growth? Exploring the effects of financial markets on linkages. In *Proceedings of the German Development Economics Conference, 2007 28*, Verein für Socialpolitik, Research Committee Development Economics.

Azman-Saini, W. N. W., Baharumshah, A. Z., & Law, S. H. (2010). Foreign direct investment, economic freedom, and economic growth: International evidence. *Economic Modelling, 27*(5), 1079–1089.

Bailliu, J. (2000). *Private capital flows, financial development, and economic growth in developing countries* (No. 2000-15). Bank of Canada.

Bekaert, G., & Harvey, C. R. (1998). Capital markets: An engine for economic growth. *The Brown Journal of World Affairs, 5*(1), 33–53.

Bekaert, G., Harvey, C. R., & Lundblad, C. T. (2003). Equity market liberalization in emerging markets. *Journal of Financial Research, 26*(3), 275–299.

Bhargava, A., Franzini, L., & Narendranathan, W. (1982). Serial correlation and the fixed effects model. *The Review of Economic Studies, 49*(4), 533–549.

Born, B., & Breitung, J. (2016). Testing for serial correlation in fixed-effects panel data models. *Econometric Reviews, 35*(7), 1290–1316.

Chang, S. C. (2015). Effects of financial developments and income on energy consumption. *International Review of Economics & Finance, 35*, 28–44.

Choong, C. K., Baharumshah, A. Z., Yusop, Z., & Habibullah, M. S. (2010). Private capital flows, stock market and economic growth in developed and developing countries: A comparative analysis. *Japan and the World Economy, 22*(2), 107–117.

Çoban, S., & Topcu, M. (2013). The nexus between financial development and energy consumption in the EU: A dynamic panel data analysis. *Energy Economics, 39*, 81–88.

Dincer, I. (2000). Renewable energy and sustainable development: A crucial review. *Renewable and Sustainable Energy Reviews, 4*(2), 157–175.

Doytch, N., & Narayan, S. (2016). Does FDI influence renewable energy consumption? An analysis of sectoral FDI impact on renewable and non-renewable industrial energy consumption. *Energy Economics, 54*, 291–301.

Durham, J. B. (2004). Absorptive capacity and the effects of foreign direct investment and equity foreign portfolio investment on economic growth. *European Economic Review, 48*(2), 285–306.

Easterly, W., & Levine, R. (1997). Africa's growth tragedy: Policies and ethnic divisions. *The Quarterly Journal of Economics, 112*(4), 1203–1250.

Fisher-Vanden, K., Jefferson, G. H., Jingkui, M., & Jianyi, X. (2006). Technology development and energy productivity in China. *Energy Economics, 28*(5–6), 690–705.

Hermes, N., & Lensink, R. (2003). Foreign direct investment, financial development and economic growth. *The Journal of Development Studies, 40*(1), 142–163.

Hübler, M., & Keller, A. (2010). Energy savings via FDI? Empirical evidence from developing countries. *Environment and Development Economics, 15*(1), 59–80.

Imbs, J., & Ranciere, R. (2007). *The overhang hangover*. Mimeo. IMF.

Jiang, L., Folmer, H., & Ji, M. (2014). The drivers of energy intensity in China: A spatial panel data approach. *China Economic Review, 31*, 351–360.

Kumar, M. S., & Woo, J. (2010). *Public debt and growth*. (IMF Working Paper No. 174). International Monetary Fund.

Lee, J. W. (2013). The contribution of foreign direct investment to clean energy use, carbon emissions and economic growth. *Energy Policy, 55*, 483–489.

Mielnik, O., & Goldemberg, J. (2002). Foreign direct investment and decoupling between energy and gross domestic product in developing countries. *Energy Policy, 30*(2), 87–89.

Mohammed, J. I., Karimu, A., Fiador, V. O., & Abor, J. Y. (2020). Oil revenues and economic growth in oil-producing countries: The role of domestic financial markets. *Resources Policy, 69*, 101832.

Nili, M., & Rastad, M. (2007). Addressing the growth failure of the oil economies: The role of financial development. *The Quarterly Review of Economics and Finance, 46*(5), 726–740.

Okada, K. (2013). The interaction effects of financial openness and institutions on international capital flows. *Journal of Macroeconomics, 35*, 131–143.

Omran, M., & Bolbol, A. (2003). Foreign direct investment, financial development, and economic growth: Evidence from the Arab countries. *Review of Middle East Economics and Finance, 1*(3), 37–55.

Pao, H. T., & Tsai, C. M. (2011). Multivariate Granger causality between CO_2 emissions, energy consumption, FDI (foreign direct investment) and GDP (gross domestic product): Evidence from a panel of BRIC (Brazil, Russian Federation, India, and China) countries. *Energy, 36*(1), 685–693.

Pattilo, C., Poirson, H., & Ricci, L. (2002). *External debt and growth* (IMF Working Paper No. 69). International Monetary Fund.

Pattilo, C., Poirson, H., & Ricci, L. (2004). *What are the channels through which external debt Affects growth?* (IMF Working Paper No. 15). International Monetary Fund.

Qamruzzaman, M., & Jianguo, W. (2020). The asymmetric relationship between financial development, trade openness, foreign capital flows, and renewable energy consumption: Fresh evidence from panel NARDL investigation. *Renewable Energy, 159*, 827–842.

Sadorsky, P. (2011). Financial development and energy consumption in Central and Eastern European frontier economies. *Energy Policy, 39*(2), 999–1006.

Samargandi, N., Fidrmuc, J., & Ghosh, S. (2014). Financial development and economic growth in an oil-rich economy: The case of Saudi Arabia. *Economic Modelling, 43*, 267–278.

Soto, M. (2000). *Capital flows and growth in developing countries: Recent empirical evidence* (Working Paper No. 160). OECD Development Centre.

Ting, Y. U. E., Yin, L. R., & Ying, Z. Y. (2011). Analysis of the FDI effect on energy consumption intensity in Jiangsu province. *Energy Procedia, 5*, 100–104.

CHAPTER 29

Foreign Direct Investment, Stock Market Development, and Inclusive Growth in Selected Sub-Saharan African Countries

Saint Kuttu, William Coffie, Chimwemwe Chipeta, and Ekow Afedzie

S. Kuttu
Department of Finance, University of Ghana Business School, Accra, Ghana
e-mail: skuttu@ug.edu.gh

C. Chipeta
University of the Witwatersrand, Johannesburg, South Africa
e-mail: wcoffie@ug.edu.gh

E. Afedzie
Ghana Stock Exchange, Accra, Ghana

W. Coffie (✉)
Department of Accounting, University of Ghana Business School, Accra, Ghana
e-mail: wcoffie@ug.edu.gh

J. Y. Abor and C. K. D. Adjasi (eds.), *The Economics of Banking and Finance in Africa*, Palgrave Macmillan Studies in Banking and Financial Institutions, https://doi.org/10.1007/978-3-031-04162-4_29

29.1 Introduction

Foreign Direct Investment (FDI) is an important source of external capital for host economies. In particular, FDI could lead to increased capital formation, employment opportunities, knowledge, and technological transfers, which should have significant benefits for the host country's economy. Accordingly, the amount of FDI flowing into Sub-Saharan African (SSA) countries has grown remarkably over the past three decades. For instance, FDI into SSA grew from USD1.16 billion in 1990 to USD31.38 billion in 2019, translating to a compound annual growth of 12%. Likewise, the share of FDI as a percentage of GDP increased from 28% in 1990 to 180% in 2019.[1] At the same time, the annual GDP growth in these countries has averaged 3.56% over the same period, a figure which is considerably higher than the economic growth rates for high-income countries.[2] This steady growth in economic activity coincided with growth in domestic financial markets[3], which has been spurred by a number of policies aimed at liberalising the financial sector. Despite these achievements, Anyanwu and Anyanwu (2017) observe that SSA has lagged behind other developing nations in the quest to mitigate poverty.

Given the above concerns, a considerable amount of research has attempted to document the link between FDI and Economic Growth across the globe (see Iamsiraroj, 2016) and in Africa (see Acquah & Ibrahim, 2020; Malikane & Chitambara, 2017; Onuoha et al., 2018). While these studies yield mixed results, their contributions provide useful avenues to explore the pace and distribution of Economic Growth in SSA. Accordingly, Kraay (2004) contends that Inclusive Growth (IG) is a necessary ingredient for poverty reduction. Our focus on IG is motivated

[1] These growth rates are calculated from data sourced from the World Development Indicators available from https://databank.worldbank.org/source/world-development-indicators. This was retrieved on 24/09/2021.

[2] The annual growth rates in GDP from high-income economies averaged 2.16% over the period 1990 to 2019. These growth rates are calculated from data obtained from the World Development Indicators, available from https://databank.worldbank.org/source/world-development-indicators. This was retrieved on 24/09/2021.

[3] The Domestic Credit to the Private Sector as a percentage of GDP for SSA has increased steadily from 36% in 1990 to 41% in 2019. This figure peaked at 60% in 2007. These growth rates are calculated from data obtained from the World Development Indicators, available from https://databank.worldbank.org/source/world-development-indicators. This was retrieved on 24/09/2021.

by the gloomy poverty statistics in SSA, despite the notable increases in FDI, Economic Growth, and capital market development over the past three decades. We contend that IG better captures equitable access to economic opportunities for all sectors of society. Thus, our paper aims to fill the gap in the IG literature by documenting the link between FDI and IG, as exemplified by SSA. To better understand the forces driving sustainable IG, we explore the role of capital market development in influencing the link between FDI and IG in SSA. By the same token, Acquah and Ibrahim (2020) contend that the financial sector plays an intermediary role between FDI and Economic Growth. In this context, we argue that more developed financial markets should facilitate FDI by providing efficient allocation of capital, thereby fostering inclusive economic growth prospects.

Our paper contributes to the IG literature in the following ways: First, we highlight the importance of FDI in facilitating the development of domestic capital markets. Accordingly, we show that FDI has a positive and significant effect on Stock Market Development (SMD). Second, we conclude that FDI and SMD are not sufficient to achieve IG, particularly in SSA, where the financial sector is relatively underdeveloped and largely concentrated among a few participants. Also, IG, FDI, and SMD tend not to converge to their long-run equilibrium path in response to changes in any of the variables. However, we show that human capital and the female labour force play a significant role in fostering IG. Thus, our findings highlight the importance of human capital and the incorporation of women into mainstream economic activities as part of the solution to achieving IG. Third, our findings reinforce the importance of natural resource availability and the development of domestic infrastructure as important determinants of FDI. Thus, our paper highlights the call for effective mobilisation of domestic natural resources to develop infrastructure as a necessary ingredient for attracting FDI. Lastly, we show that the gross savings of a country exert a significant negative influence on IG. Thus, our study highlights the need to rethink and broaden the scope of domestic savings in order to achieve meaningful IG.

The rest of the chapter is organised as follows: Sect. 29.2 discusses the theoretical and empirical review. Section 29.3 outlines the methodology. Section 29.4 describes the data. Section 29.5 highlights the empirical analysis and discusses the results. Section 29.6 concludes the paper and provides useful policy recommendations.

29.2 Theoretical and Empirical Review

Theoretical Review

The theories that are used to explain the nexus between Foreign Direct Investment, capital market development, and Inclusive Growth include Institutional theory, classical theory, and dependency theory.

The classical theory highlights the benefits, particularly if the initial conditions required for FDI benefits are met by developing domestic economies (Asongu & De Moor, 2017; Gammoudiet al., 2016). The classical theory expounds benefits derived by less developed economies from FDI in the form of development of domestic Infrastructure, foreign exchange income, the balance of payment appreciation, international market integration into the local market, and tax base expansion (Toone, 2012).

The dependency theory views globalisation through the lens of market capitalisation, cheap labour exploitation, and the substitution of primary resources with knowledge of obsolete technology from developed economies. According to the theory, FDI has a negative influence on growth among developing economies due to the following reasons: To begin with, multinational corporations distort domestic investment by creating instability within the domestic economy. This instability occurs by the use of capital induced technology which is a perfect substitute for human labour, hence, promoting unemployment and income inequality and distorting the taste of indigenes for local products (Taylor & Thrift, 2013). These foreign investors exploit local assets and use them to enhance development in their home countries at the expense of less developed countries (Jensen, 2008). Finally, the alliance between foreign investors and local political elites precludes the local indigenes of less developed economies from fully maximising the benefits of FDI (Jensen, 2008).

Institutional theory underlines the duties of the institutions in drawing FDI. FDI arises from the competition or games between governments (Assuncao et al., 2011); hence institutions are responsible for the creation of the rules of the game. The rapid effect of institutions in drawing FDI is extensively expounded by Bénassy-Quéré et al. (2007). Other studies point out that low labour cost and market size do not determine FDI significantly when institutional quality and some policy formulation characteristics are considered (Kinoshita & Campos, 2006; Popovici & Calin 2012, 2013).

These theories are relevant for the study because while the institutional theory expands the relevance of institutions in attracting FDI, the dependency and classical theories point out the merit and demerits of FDI to developing economies, a context within which this study is being conducted.

Empirical Review

The empirical literature has recorded mixed evidence with regard to the relationship between Economic Growth (EG) and Foreign Direct Investment (FDI). The majority of these studies were dynamic in nature in terms of the span of data examined. The impacts of FDI on Nigerian economic growth from 1970 to 2008 was investigated by Umoh et al. (2012). They identified factors such as positive feedback from Economic Growth to FDI as well as FDI to Economic Growth. Buchanan et al. (2012), however, found a negative impact of EG on FDI using data for 164 countries that are members of the Economic and Monetary Community of Central Africa (CEMAC). Agbloyor et al. (2014) also examined the relationship existing between public and private capital flows into Africa and found FDI, foreign equity portfolio investment as well as private debt flows to negatively affect Economic Growth in Africa. They found that economies with stronger financial markets benefit more by reversing the negative effects of private capital flows. Chanegriha et al. (2020) used data from 136 economies but identified no explicit support for the causal relationship existing between FDI and EG in most of the economies under study.

In another related study, Olawumi et al. (2017), in investigating the impact FDI has on African economic growth from 1980 to 2013, provided weak evidence. Zekarias (2016), on the other hand, in examining FDI's influence on Economic Growth across 14 East-African countries from 1980 to 2013, found FDI to positively and significantly impact Economic Growth, despite this being a heterogeneous relationship across many economies. Malikane and Chitambara (2017) also explored the relationship between Economic Growth, democracy, and FDI across eight South-African countries from 1980 to 2014. Their study found that FDI directly and positively affects Economic Growth. They also posited that FDI's impact on Economic Growth depends on the host country's level of democracy. Onuoha et al. (2018) also found FDI to significantly contribute to Economic Growth while exploring the existing relationship between Economic Growth and some macroeconomic indicators across economies in West Africa from 1990 to 2016.

The relationship between FDI and the quality of institutions has also been investigated in the literature. In one study, Sabir et al. (2019) classified 148 countries according to income groups and found that EG enhances FDI across developing economies but negatively affects FDI in developed countries. They stated that their findings could be attributable to foreign investors paying much more attention to high institutional quality (IQ) than growth in developed countries. Fon et al. (2021) also examined the influence of FDI flows on the quality of institutions across economies in Africa, relying on data across 54 countries from 2003 to 2015. Their study found an insignificant impact of FDI on IQ across both developed and developing countries. Yeboua (2021) also investigated the influence of institutional development on the growth of FDI in Africa.

Adjasi et al. (2012) also found FDI to significantly influence economic activity after it interacts with private-sector credit and savings, which are components of financial markets. Relying on a panel smooth transition regression model using a sample of 27 countries in Africa from 1990 to 2017, the results indicate that FDI leads to Economic Growth in countries with higher institutional development above normal standards. Literature has also established a relationship between FDI, Economic Growth, and economic freedom. Ciftcia and Ciftcia (2022) investigated the causal relationships between Economic Growth, Foreign Direct Investment (FDI), and economic freedom among high FDI receiving countries from 1995 to 2019. They found more foreign investments to contribute towards the rise in economic freedom across these countries. Zghidi et al. (2016) also explored the influence of democracy and economic freedom across the FDI-growth nexus over a panel of eight South-African countries from 1980 to 2014, as well as a panel of four countries in Northern Africa from 1980 to 2013. Using the system generalised method of moments (GMM), they found the growth-enhancing effects of FDI to be stronger when high economic freedom and democratic institutions are present.

In a developed economy context, Economou (2019) reports that business, monetary, investment, and financial freedom, as well as property rights and government integrity, have a significantly positive impact on receiving FDI for the South European economies. Agbloyor et al. (2016) examined the role of institutional development on the FDI-growth relationship in Sub-Saharan African countries from 1996 to 2010. Aside not finding a significant relationship between institutional development and Economic Growth, they did not find convincing evidence that institutions alter favourably the effect of FDI on Economic Growth. Agbloyor et al. (2014) also found that strong financial markets are required for private capital flows to positively influence Economic Growth. The findings from Adjasi et al. (2012) also indicate that FDI is very productive in well-functioning markets, and they propose that governments in Africa should place special emphasis on expanding local financial markets in order to reap the full economic benefits associated with FDI inflows. They employed a linear interaction model by interacting FDI and some institutional indicators, adopting the system generalised method of moments (SYS-GMM) estimators. The findings did not indicate any robust evidence with regard to the moderating role of institutions in the FDI and growth nexus. They, however, found a direct positive impact of institutions on Economic Growth.

Sayari et al. (2018) studied the long-run impact of FDI and EG on EF for 36 European countries and found that FDI negatively affects EF in Western European countries. Singh and Gal (2020) found EF to have a significantly positive effect on FDI across North and West Europe, South and East Asia, and Latin America, while it has an insignificant impact in East and South Europe, the Middle East, as well as North Africa. Adams and Opoku (2015) also analysed the effects of the regulatory regimes, that is, business, credit, and labour market regulations, on FDI-growth relations across 22 Sub-Saharan African countries from 1980 to 2011. Adopting a general method of moments (GMM) estimation approach, they found FDI not to directly influence Economic Growth. They found it to positively affect growth upon its linear interaction with the regulatory regime characteristics. Ghazalian and Amponsem (2019) concluded that rule of law, regulations, as well as openness of the market are the major FDI-attracting factors. Moreover, they found that the effect of EF sub-components changes across geo-economic regions and through the economic characteristics of the countries.

FDI and poverty reduction have also been highlighted in the literature. Gohou and Soumaré (2012) examined the direct associations between FDI and welfare across 52 economies in Africa between 1990 and 2007. They identified a significantly positive relationship existing between FDI and poverty reduction and they concluded that FDI influences poverty reduction in underdeveloped countries more than in developed countries.

Dada and Akinlo (2021) also examined the threshold impact environmental degradation has on the FDI and poverty nexus across Sub-Saharan Africa from 1986 to 2018. They found the poverty reduction impact of FDI not to be negatively affected by environmental degradation after employing a threshold regression that adopts diverse measures of poverty and environmental degradation.

Tsaurai (2018) investigated the association between FDI and natural resources when reducing poverty across countries in South and West Africa from 2002 to 2012. Adopting diverse methodologies and proxies for poverty, the findings indicated that the interactive effect of FDI and natural resources reduces poverty levels in Africa. Bilal Khan et al. (2019) also found FDI to significantly contribute to poverty reduction in Pakistan, having adopted an ARDL bounds testing approach from 1985 to 2016.

The connection between Foreign Direct Investment and the Capital Market has also been examined in the literature. Durham (2004) investigated the empirical conditions under which Equity Foreign Portfolio Investment (EFPI) and Foreign Direct Investment (FDI) affect Economic Growth across 80 countries from 1979 to 1998. Adopting a linear interaction model, the results indicated that the benefits of FDI in relation to Economic Growth are enhanced by good institutions and efficient financial systems. Using a threshold regression model on FDI and different kinds of capital flows, Slesman et al. (2015) also found that only countries with the higher quality institutions see increased Economic Growth. They found FDI to have an insignificant or negative impact on Economic Growth across countries below a certain degree of institutional development.

Claessens et al. (2001) studied the causes of the expansion of stock market activities across international financial markets and found FDI to have a positive correlation with the capitalisation of stock markets and traded value. Raza and Jawaid (2012) also examined the impact of FDI on the stock markets of host countries that are developing, adopting an Ordinary Least Square (OLS) regression using time series data from 1988 to 2009. The results showed a positive effect of FDI on the stock markets in Pakistan. Nazir et al. (2010) also explored the relationship between Stock Market Development and Economic Growth in Pakistan from 1986 to 2008. Based on their results, in developing markets like Pakistan, Economic Growth can be achieved through growing the size of a country's stock market as well as market capitalisation.

29.3 Methodology

We follow the panel vector autoregressive (PVAR) model of Love and Zicchino (2006) and describe the causal relationship between Foreign Direct Investment, Stock Market Development, and Inclusive Growth in 11 selected African countries in a matrix form, as shown in Eqs. 29.1–29.3.

$$\Delta\text{FDI}_t = \alpha_1 + \sum_{i=1}^{k-1} \beta_i \Delta\text{FDI}_{t-i} + \sum_{j=1}^{k-1} \beta_j \Delta\text{SMD}_{t-j} + \sum_{m=1}^{k-1} \beta_m \Delta\text{IG}_{t-m} + \delta_1 \text{ECT}_{t-1} + \varepsilon_{1t} \quad (29.1)$$

$$\Delta\text{SMD}_t = \alpha_2 + \sum_{i=1}^{k-1} \beta_i \Delta\text{FDI}_{t-i} + \sum_{j=1}^{k-1} \beta_j \Delta\text{SMD}_{t-j} + \sum_{m=1}^{k-1} \beta_m \Delta\text{IG}_{t-m} + \delta_2 \text{ECT}_{t-1} + \varepsilon_{2t} \quad (26.2)$$

$$\Delta\text{IG}_t = \alpha_3 + \sum_{i=1}^{k-1} \beta_i \Delta\text{FDI}_{t-i} + \sum_{j=1}^{k-1} \beta_j \Delta\text{SMD}_{t-j} + \sum_{m=1}^{k-1} \beta_m \Delta\text{IG}_{t-m} + \delta_3 \text{ECT}_{t-1} + \varepsilon_{3t} \quad (26.3)$$

Where FDI, SMD, and IG are Foreign Direct Investment, Stock Market Development, and Inclusive Growth, respectively, which alternate in taking the dependent and explanatory variable roles; the lag length is reduced by $1(k - 1)$; $t + 1 \ldots T$;$\alpha_{i=(1....3)}$, $\beta_i, \beta_j, \beta_m$ are the short-run dynamic coefficients of the model's adjustment long-run equilibrium. δ_i $(i = 1....3)$ is the speed of adjustment parameter with a negative sign; and $\varepsilon_{it}(i = 1....3)$ are white noise error terms; ECT_{t-1} is the lagged value of the error correction term from the co-integration regression of the dependent variable on the regressor. This contains the long-run information derived from the long-run cointegration relationship while δ_s are the speed of adjustment along the long-run equilibrium path. Short-run causality is inferred from the lagged dynamic variables of the explanatory variable,β, using the partial χ^2 statistics of the Wald test (Wald, 1948), while the long-run causality is tested through the lagged cointegrating vectors,$\delta_s ECT_{t-j}$.

29.4 Data Description

The Inclusive Growth variable consists of data on selected variables spelt out under the various pillars of Inclusive Growth by the Asian Development Bank (2014) based on data availability for the 11 Sub-Saharan African countries sampled (see Table 29.1). For each indicator spelt out in Table 29.1, data were obtained for the period 1992 to 2019 from the World Development Indicators and the World Governance Indicators databases of the World Bank for the eleven African countries (the selection of eleven countries is due to the availability of corresponding stock market capitalisation to gross domestic product data). In view of the wide range of data for the various indicators which ultimately influences Inclusive Growth, we use a data reducing technique to reduce the indicators into a component that can be interpreted. A principal component analysis is used to reduce the dimension and scale of the data. For FDI and SMD, we used Foreign Direct Investment, net inflows (% of GDP), and stock market capitalisation to GDP (%), respectively

From the summaries in Table 29.2, the three variables show minimum variations across the 11 sampled African countries for the period 1992 to 2019. The normality tests for all three variables show positive skewness and are leptokurtic. The Jarque–Bera statistic shows that the three variables are not normally distributed. This suggests that there may be outliers in the data. The Jarque–Bera statistic measures the difference of the skewness and kurtosis of the series with those from the normal distribution.

Table 29.3 shows the Pearson correlation matrix for the three variables used in this study. Clearly, the pairwise correlations between the variables are relatively weak, suggesting no evidence of multicollinearity. To determine whether the variables used for this study are stationary, we use the panel unit root test. This is a key requirement for the panel VECM model in order to determine the order of integration (Pradhan & Arvin, 2015, p. 241). Levin et al. (2002), (LLC) and Im et al. (2003) (IPS) tests are based on the augmented Dickey-Fuller (ADF) principle. However, the

Table 29.1 IG indicators

IG Indicators	*Measures*
Poverty and Inequality	
Income	The annualised average growth rate in per capita real survey mean consumption or income, total population (%)
	Poverty headcount ratio at $1.90 a day (2011 PPP) (% of the population)
	Poverty headcount ratio at national poverty lines (% of the population)
Non-Income	Compulsory education, duration (years)
	Primary education, duration (years)
	Secondary education, duration (years)
	Mortality rate, under-5 (per 1,000 live births)
	Prevalence of underweight, weight for age (% of children under 5)
Growth Expansion of Economic Opportunities	
Economic Growth and Employment	GNI per capita, PPP (constant 2017 international $)
	GDP per capita, PPP (constant 2017 international $)
	Contributing family workers, total (% of total employment) (modelled ILO estimate)
	Employment to population ratio, 15 + , total (%) (national estimate)
	Employment to population ratio, 15 + , total (%) (modelled ILO estimate)
	GDP per person employed (constant 2017 PPP $)
Key Infrastructure Endowment	Electric power consumption (kWh per capita)
	Mobile cellular subscriptions (per 100 people)
	Depositors with commercial banks (per 1,000 adults)
Social Inclusion to Ensure Equal Access to Economic Opportunities	
Access and Inputs to Education and Health	

(continued)

Table 29.1 (continued)

IG Indicators	*Measures*
	Government expenditure on education, total (% of government expenditure)
	Pupil-teacher ratio, primary
	Immunisation, DPT (% of children ages 12–23 months)
	Immunisation, HepB3 (% of one-year-old children)
	Immunisation, measles (% of children ages 12–23 months)
	Domestic general government health expenditure (% of general government expenditure)
	Physicians (per 1,000 people)
	Nurses and midwives (per 1,000 people)
Access to Basic Infrastructure Utilities and Services	Access to clean fuels and technologies for cooking (% of the population)
	Access to electricity (% of the population)
	People using safely managed drinking water services (% of the population)
	People using safely managed sanitation services (% of the population)
Gender Equality and Opportunity	School enrolment, primary (gross), gender parity index (GPI)
	School enrolment, primary and secondary (gross), gender parity index (GPI)
	School enrolment, secondary (gross), gender parity index (GPI)
	School enrolment, tertiary (gross), gender parity index (GPI)
	Ratio of female to male labour force participation rate (%) (national estimate)
	Proportion of seats held by women in national parliaments (%)
Good Governance and Institutions	Voice and accountability
	Government Effectiveness
	Control of Corruption

Data on the Good Governance Indicators were sourced from World Governance Indicators of the World Bank. The rest of the data in the Table were sourced from the World Development Indicators of the World Bank

Table 29.2 Descriptive statistics

Variables	*Obs*	*Mean*	*Std*	*Min*	*Max*	*Skew*	*Kurt*	*JB*	*Prob*
IG	307	1.129	0.867	−0.123	2.914	1.650	5.691	24.366	0.00
FDI	307	2.139	2.204	−6.897	10.663	5.691	5.691	170.862	0.00
SMD	307	39.708	56.879	0.389	343.473	11.663	17.837	1394.634	0.00

The sample comprises 11 African countries, with data for the period 1971–2020. These summary statistics are in levels. The abbreviation IG stands for Inclusive Growth; FDI: Foreign Direct Investment, net inflows (% of GDP); SMD: Stock Market Development (stock market capitalisation as a % of GDP); Obs.: observations; Std.: standard deviations; Min.: minimum; Max.: maximum; Skew.: skewness; Kur.: kurtosis; JB: Jarque–Bera statistics; Prob.: probability

Table 29.3 Correlation matrix

Variable	*IG*	*FDI*	*SMD*
IG	1		
FDI	−0.001	1	
SMD	0.481	−0.054	1

The sample comprises 11 African Countries for the period 1992–2019. The abbreviation IG stands for Inclusive Growth; FDI: Foreign Direct Investment, net inflows (% of GDP); SMD: Stock Market Development (stock market capitalisation as a % of GDP)

main difference between the two is that the LLC test assumes homogeneous unit-roots across all cross-sections, while the IPS test allows for heterogeneity (Baltagi, 2013).

The null hypothesis for both LLC and IPS is that the series is non-stationary against the alternative that each series is stationary. The IPS is preferred due to its ability to cater to individual country heterogeneity. We perform a panel unit root test on each of the three variables at both level and first differences. The Fisher-ADF and Fisher-Phillips-Perron (Fisher-PP) (Choi, 2001; Maddala & Wu, 1999) panel unit root tests are used for a robustness check.

As shown in Table 29.4, we can consider the three panels to be integrated of order one, I (1). Hence, we estimate a co-integration model to determine the long-run relationship.

According to Muye and Muye (2017), one of the key issues to consider when dealing with a panel data Granger causality test is cross-sectional

Table 29.4 Panel unit root

Test	*Variables*					
Statistics	Level data			First difference data		
	IG	FDI	SMD	IG	FDI	SMD
Case 1: No trend and no intercept						
LLC	−12.240	−6.224**	−0.067	−4.526**	−18.503**	−2.128**
IPS	–	–	–	–	–	–
ADF	1.657	65.431**	15.004	88.485**	348.089**	175.009**
PP	0.604	56.538**	14.045	142.190**	852.215**	188.600**
Case 2: With intercept only						
LLC	3.916	−7.298**	−1.558	5.749**	−15.456**	−9.426**
IPS	7.479	−7.341**	−1.366	−8.067**	−18.446**	−8.792**
ADF	5.508	95.213**	30.104	107.644**	236.277**	114.610**
PP	3.567	90.812**	23.561	152.339**	249.678**	127.075**
Case 3: With intercept and trend						
LLC	1.183	−5.582**	0.514	−10.557**	−13.563**	−7.632**
IPS	−1.592	−7.023**	−0.049	−11.967**	−17.591**	−7.087**
ADF	22.615	89.557**	22.040	357.806**	290.894**	87.679**
PP	19.633	81.078**	13.886	731.550**	1224.990**	98.422**

**Denotes significance at the 5% level. The abbreviation IG stands for Inclusive Growth; FDI: Foreign Direct Investment; SMD: Stock Market Development (stock market capitalisation as a % of GDP); LLC: Levine-Lin-Chu statistics; IPS: Im-Pessaran-Shin statistics; ADF: augmented Dickey-Fuller statistics; PP: Philips–Perron statistics

Table 29.5 Panel cross-sectional residual dependence test

Variables	*Test*	*Statistic*	*Probability*
IG/FDI/SMD	Breusch-Pagan LM	642.366**	0.005
	Peseran scaled LM	56.003**	0.006
	Peseran CD	13.872**	0.001

**Denotes significance at the 5% level

Table 29.6 Panel co-integration test

Pedroni (Engle-Granger based)				
Test	*Statistic*	*Dependent variable*		
		IG	*FDI*	*SMD*
Pedroni (1999, 2004)	Panel v-statistic	−2.225**	0.798	1.251**
	Panel rho-statistic	2.668**	−4.167**	−0.701**
	Panel PP-statistic	3.653**	−5.975**	1.333**
	Panel ADF-statistic	3.653**	−6.413**	1.433**
	Group rho-statistic	−4.083**	−3.831**	1.549**
	Group PP-statistic	3.573**	−7.996**	0.529**
	Group ADF-statistic	5.679**	8.618**	0.078**

Fisher (Combined Johansen) *Hypothesised Number of CE(s)*	*Fisher Statistic (Trace test)*	*Probability (Max eigen)*	*Fisher Statistic*	*Probability*
None	62.000**	0.010	46.55**	0.002
At most 1	35.450**	0.014	28.39**	0.016
At most 2	37.97**	0.019	37.97**	0.018

**Denotes significance at the 5% level

dependency. Because of the interconnectedness of the developing countries in our sample due to globalisation, there is the tendency of the propagation of shocks across countries due to upheaval or shock in one country. According to Tekin (2012), the null hypothesis is that there is no cross-sectional dependency (correlation) in residuals, and the test statistic is asymptotically distributed as standard normal. We apply the Pesaran et al. (2004) for robustness check because the Breusch and Pagan (1980) test is used for large T and small N.

As shown in Table 29.5, all the cross-sectional residual dependence tests strongly reject the null hypothesis that there is no correlation (cross-sectional interdependence) in variables or residuals within the sample. This is expected because of the high incidence of poverty and low per capita GDP in developing countries. This also shows that the IG, FDI, and SMD variables appear to reveal some characteristics that are common to developing countries.

To determine whether there is a long-run equilibrium relationship between non-stationary variables, we conduct a panel co-integration test.

Karanfil and Li (2015) contend that the results of the panel co-integration tests influence the panel Granger causality test strategy and model specification. This shows that panel variable co-integration implies that the variables under consideration move together over time so that short-term disturbances are corrected in the long run (Engle & Granger, 1987; Stock & Watson, 1993), and therefore causality should be investigated through the panel VECM framework. On the other hand, Granger (1988) argues that a lack of co-integration suggests that the variables do not have a long-run relation and therefore tend to move randomly away from each other. Hence, a panel VAR should be estimated for causality analysis.

The Akaike information criterion (AIC) (Akaike, 1974) and the Schwarz information criterion (SC) (Schwarz, 1978) are the most common lag length selection methods in the literature. This study, therefore, uses the SC to determine the optimal lag selection. The AIC is also used for robustness checks. Hence, an unrestricted VAR is estimated, and the lags for estimating the co-integration are selected using the *Schwarz information criterion.*

As shown in Table 29.6, panel co-integration tests were conducted on each of the three equations with each of the variables: IG, FDI, and SMD, assuming the role of the dependent variable and the others being explanatory variables. The results show that there is evidence of a long-run equilibrium relationship between the three variables when each of them is made a dependent variable. Therefore, a dynamic panel data model using the VECM Granger causality framework was estimated.

Having established the order of integration through the panel root tests and the presence of a long-run equilibrium through the panel co-integration tests, the next step is to test the direction of causality through dynamic panel causality tests. The tests for causality, however, are dependent on the panel co-integration results (Engle & Granger, 1987; Granger, 1988; Stock & Watson, 1993).

29.5 Empirical Analysis and Discussion

Empirical Analysis

From the results in Table 29.7, only FDI has a positive effect on Stock Market Development. This result is corroborated by results from the panel data random-effect model (29.10 in Appendix 1). For the long-run

Table 29.7 Panel Granger causality based on VECM estimation

Dependent Variable	*Direction of causality/explanatory variable*				*Diagnostics test: serial correlation*
	χ^2 *statistics (p-value)*		*Long- run coefficient (t-statistics)*		*LM-test* p-*value*
	ΔIG	ΔFDI	ΔSMD	*ECT*	
ΔIG	–	0.631 (0.729)	8.361 (0.315)	−0.025 [0.351]	1.555 (0.025)
ΔFDI	0.967 (0.617)	–	2.494 (0.287)	−0.012 [0.598]	0.013 (0.265)
ΔSMD	4.818 (0.090)	7.490** (0.024)	–	−0.011 [0.265]	0.014 (0.658)

The abbreviation IG stands for Inclusive Growth; FDI: Foreign Direct Investment; SMD: Stock Market Development (stock market capitalisation as a % of GDP). Short Run-The sum of the lagged coefficients for the respective short-run changes in the independent variable(s) are shown with their corresponding Wald χ^2 Statistics and *p*-values in brackets (). For the long-run, coefficients of the ECT are reported and in squared-brackets [ ] are the *t*-statistics. The ** denotes a significance of 5%

causality, the coefficients of the ECT were not significant when IG, FDI, and SMD were made the dependent variables. These results mean that IG, FDI, and SMD tend not to converge towards their long-run equilibrium path in response to changes in any of the variables. The diagnostic test on the standardised residuals shows no serial correction. Hence our model is well specified.

Discussion of Results

The Granger causality test establishes the bidirectional causality effects from FDI to SMD. SMD also affects IG Granger, while IG Granger eventually causes FDI. In effect, each of these variables has a causal effect on the other in turn. From the results in Table 29.7, all models (1–3) indicate that IG, FDI, and SMD's coefficients are positive in the short run when each of them is made an outcome variable with the others being independent variables, as found in Umoh et al. (2012). However, only FDI and SMD exhibit significant positive coefficients at the standard level. The positive relationships as established between FDI and IG, SMD in model

(1) are consistent with Zekarias (2016), as well as Malikane and Chitambara (2017). This means that in the short run, IG and SMD attract more Foreign Direct Investment. This is possible because as people are lifted out of poverty through employment, education, and expansion of economic opportunities, their purchasing power increases, which creates stability in business growth, and this will naturally result in capital inflow increasing.

Furthermore, as the stock market develops, it reduces market frictions, improving transparency and liquidity, and these indicators boost foreign investors' confidence to direct funds to such markets. The evidence shows that foreign investors place a premium on SMD as a basis for capital flow across borders, at least in the short term, consistent with results from Ciftcia and Ciftcia (2022). Similarly, in model (2), the positive but weak relationship that exists between SMD and IG, FDI indicates that Stock Market Development is dependent on IG and Foreign Direct Investment, *albeit* with a minimal effect. This is also consistent with Olawumi et al. (2017). Likewise, in model (3), even though the coefficient estimates are statistically insignificant, the positive relationship that exists between IG and FDI, SMD demonstrates that Inclusive Growth is possible in the presence of stock market capitalisation and inflows from foreign capital sources. IG leads to an increase in SMD due to the fact that many individuals will participate in the capital market by investing surplus funds. These findings are consistent with Gohou and Soumaré (2012) but inconsistent with Sabir et al. (2019) in the context of developed countries as well as Adams and Opoku (2015) when growth interacts linearly with regulatory regime variables.

On the contrary, consistent with Sayari et al. (2018), the results as reported in Table 29.7 show that in the long run, the bidirectional coefficients of SMD, IG, and FDI exhibit a negative sign but retain a statistically insignificant sensitivity coefficient at standard levels. These results mean that the existence of SMD, IG, and FDI help improve upon each other in the short run while there is a reduction in each of these variables as a result of their impact on each other in the long run. What that means is that in the long run, FDI will reduce IG and SMD, IG will reduce FDI and SMD, and vice versa. A possible explanation is that in the short term, as FDI flows into the country, economic activities expand, employment and access to basic infrastructure increase, poverty reduces, disposal income increases as well as stock market capitalisation growth, while in the long run, as foreign investors repatriate profit meant for capital reinvestment, the economy shrinks, economic opportunities dwindle, and the stock market will respond accordingly to these economic realities. This is, however inconsistent with Singh and Gal (2020).

The robustness results in Tables 29.8 to 29.10 using panel regression confirm our results in Table 29.7 where all the panel coefficient estimates for variables under investigation are statistically insignificant. However, it is vital to note that FDI is key for African economies developing their capital markets at least in the short term, and therefore, deliberate steps should be taken by the various governments to improve the institutional environment that would attract FDI flow.

Our control variables further show that human capital and the female labour force have a positive statistical relationship with Inclusive Growth, indicating that human capital and the female labour force play an important role in fostering Inclusive Growth. Thus, our findings highlight the importance of human capital and the inclusion of women into mainstream economic activities as part of the solution to achieving Inclusive Growth. We further find that natural resource availability and domestic infrastructure development have a significant positive relationship with FDI. This result reinforces the importance of the availability of natural resources and the development of domestic infrastructure as important determinants of FDI inflow. Therefore, our paper highlights the call for effective mobilisation of domestic natural resources to develop infrastructure as a necessary ingredient for attracting FDI. Lastly, we show that the gross savings of a country exert a significant negative influence on IG. Thus, our study highlights the need to rethink and broaden the scope of domestic savings in order to achieve meaningful, Inclusive Growth.

29.6 Conclusions and Recommendations

The role of FDI and the development of financial markets in fostering Economic Growth has been documented widely in the literature. However, the role of country-specific and macroeconomic factors in influencing the pace and distribution of Economic Growth in SSA has not been adequately documented. To address this gap, we estimated dynamic panel data models using the VECM Granger causality framework to examine the nexus between FDI, SMD, and IG. FDI has a positive effect on SMD, and FDI and SMD are not sufficient to achieve IG, particularly in SSA, where the financial sector is relatively underdeveloped and largely concentrated among a few participants. Also, IG, FDI, and SMD tend not to converge onto their long-run equilibrium path in response to changes in any of the variables. From the panel models that we estimated as a robustness check, we find that human capital and the female labour force play a significant role in fostering IG. Thus, our findings highlight the importance of human capital development and diversity in the workforce, particularly the incorporation of women into mainstream economic activities, as part of the solution to achieving IG. Our findings also reinforce the importance of natural resource availability and the development of domestic infrastructure as important determinants of FDI. Thus, our paper highlights the call for effective mobilisation of domestic natural resources to develop infrastructure as a necessary ingredient for attracting FDI. Furthermore, we show that the gross savings of a country exert a significant negative influence on IG. Thus, our study highlights the need to rethink and broaden the scope of domestic savings in order to achieve meaningful IG. The paper provides useful areas for potential future research, particularly focusing on institutional determinants of IG in SSA. For example, institutional factors such as the rule of law, control of corruption, government effectiveness, media freedom, property rights, trade openness, and ease of doing business could provide useful pointers to the factors that drive IG and FDI.

Appendix: Results from Panel Models[4]

Table 29.8 Random effect Robust panel regression

IG	*Coef*	*St. Err*	t-*value*	p-*value*	*[95% conf interval]*		*Sig*
FDI	−.015	.042	−0.36	.719	−.097	.067	
SMD	.003	.003	1.05	.294	−.002	.008	
DEBT	.022	.042	0.52	.606	−.061	.104	
FEMLAB	.003	.002	1.79	.074	0	.006	**
SAVING	−.033	.01	−3.16	.002	−.053	−.012	**
HC	.384	.174	2.20	.027	.043	.725	**

(continued)

[4] For brevity only the empirical results are presented here. The pre-statistical analyses are available upon request.

Table 29.8 (continued)

IG	*Coef*	*St. Err*	t-*value*	p-*value*	*[95% conf interval]*		*Sig*
Openness	0	.01	0.02	.987	−.02	.02	
TECH	.001	.002	0.28	.776	−.003	.004	
Constant	1.152	.334	3.45	.001	.498	1.805	**
Mean dependent var	0.701			SD dependent var 1.054			
Overall *r*-squared	0.194			Number of obs 308.000			
Chi-square	37.333			Prob > chi2 0.000			
R-squared within	0.203			*R*-squared between 0.193			

**Denotes 5% significant level. IG, FDI, SMD, DEBT, FEMLAB, SAVING, HC, OPENNESS, and TECH denote IG, Net Foreign Direct Investment Inflow, stock market capitalisation, Public Debt, Female Labour Force, Gross Savings, Human Capital, Trade Openness, and Mobile Technology, respectively

Table 29.9 Fixed effect Robust panel regression

FDI	*Coef*	*St. Err*	t-*value*	p-*value*	*[95% conf interval]*		*Sig*
IG	−.105	.477	−0.22	.83	−1.168	.958	
SMD	.017	.01	1.74	.112	−.005	.039	
OPENNESS	−008	.034	−0.23	.823	−.084	.068	
Infra	.001	0	2.76	.02	0	.001	**
Labor	.129	.063	2.05	.067	−.011	.27	**
GCF	.004	.05	0.09	.932	−.107	.116	
NRA	.145	.057	2.56	.028	.019	.271	**
Constant	−6.292	2.93	−2.15	.057	−12.822	.237	**
Mean dependent var	2.144			SD dependent var	2.202		
R-squared	0.162			Number of obs	308.000		
F-test	7.640			Prob > *F*	0.003		
Akaike crit. (AIC)	1203.818			Bayesian crit. (BIC)	1229.929		

**Denotes 5% significant level. IG, FDI, SMD, DEBT, FEMLAB, SAVING, HC, OPENNESS, and TECH denote IG, Net Foreign Direct Investment Inflow, stock market capitalisation, trade openness, infrastructure stock, Labour cost, gross capital formation, and Trade Openness natural resource availability, respectively

Table 29.10 Random effect Robust panel regression

SMD	*Coef*	*St. Err*	t-*value*	p-*value*	*[95% Conf interval]*		*Sig*
IG	−.018	3.617	−0.00	.996	−7.107	7.072	
FDI	1.468	1.274	1.15	.04	−1.028	3.965	**
Growth	−.333	.491	−0.68	.497	−1.295	.628	
Openness	.666	.383	1.74	.082	−.084	1.417	
INFL	.08	.067	1.19	.235	−.052	.212	
Turnover	.003	.004	0.75	.451	−.004	.01	
MANVA	−3.364	2.481	−1.36	.175	−8.225	1.498	
SERVVA	.159	.249	0.64	.524	−.33	.647	
Constant	43.23	39.556	1.09	.274	−34.298	120.758	
Mean dependent var	39.579			SD dependent var	56.832		
Overall *r*-squared	0.013			Number of obs	308.000		
Chi-square	81.861			Prob > chi2	0.000		
R-squared within	0.252			*R*-squared between	0.095		

**Denotes 5% significant level. IG, FDI, SMD, GROWTH, INF, TURNOVER, MANVA, SERVVA and OPENNESS, Economic Growth, Labour cost, inflation, stock market turnover, Value-added from manufacturing, value-added from service, and Trade Openness, respectively

References

Adams, S., & Opoku, E. E. O. (2015). Foreign direct investment, regulations and growth in sub-Saharan Africa. *Economic Analysis and Policy, 47*, 48–56.

Adjasi, C. K., Abor, J., Osei, K. A., & Nyavor-Foli, E. E. (2012). FDI and economic activity in Africa: The role of local financial markets. *Thunderbird International Business Review, 54*(4), 429–439.

Agbloyor, E. K., Gyeke-Dako, A., Kuipo, R., & Abor, J. Y. (2016). Foreign direct investment and economic growth in SSA: The role of institutions. *Thunderbird International Business Review, 58*(5), 479–497.

Agbloyor, E. K., Abor, J. Y., Adjasi, C. K. D., & Yawson, A. (2014). Private capital flows and economic growth in Africa: The role of domestic financial markets. *Journal of International Financial Markets, Institutions and Money, 30*, 137–152.

Akaike, H. (1974). A new look at the statistical model identification. *IEEE Transactions on Automatic Control, 19*(6), 716–723.

Acquah, A. M., & Ibrahim, M. (2020). Foreign direct investment, economic growth and financial sector development in Africa. *Journal of Sustainable Finance & Investment, 10*(4), 315–334.

Anyanwu, J. C., & Anyanwu, J. C. (2017). The Key Drivers of Poverty in Sub-Saharan Africa and What Can be Done About it to Achieve the Poverty Sustainable Development Goal. *Asian Journal of Economic Modelling, 5*(3), 297–317.

Asian Development Bank. Development Indi, Asian Development Bank. Economics, & Re. (2014). *Key Indicators for Asia and the Pacific 2011*. Asian Development Bank.

Asongu, S. A., & De Moor, L. (2017). Financial globalisation dynamic thresholds for financial development: Evidence from Africa. *The European Journal of Development Research, 29*(1), 192–212.

Assuncao, S., Forte, R. & Teixeira, A. A. C. (2011). *Location Determinants of Determinants of FDI: a Literature Review* (FEP working papers: University of Porto. 433).

Baltagi, B. H. (2008). *Econometric analysis of panel data* (Vol. 4). John Wiley & Sons.

Bénassy-Quéré, A., Coupet, M., & Mayer, T. (2007). Institutional determinants of foreign direct investment. *World Economy, 30*(5), 764–782.

Bilal Khan, M., Huobao, X., & Saleem, H. (2019). Direct impact of inflow of foreign direct investment on poverty reduction in Pakistan: A bonds testing approach. *Economic Research-Ekonomska istraživanja, 32*(1), 3647–3666.

Breusch, T. S., & Pagan, A. R. (1980). The Lagrange multiplier test and its applications to model specification in econometrics. *The Review of Economic Studies, 47*(1), 239–253.

Buchanan, B. G., Le, Q. V., & Rishi, M. (2012). Foreign direct investment and institutional quality: Some empirical evidence. *International Review of Financial Analysis, 21*, 81–89.

Chanegriha, M., Stewart, C., & Tsoukis, C. (2020). Testing for causality between FDI and economic growth using heterogeneous panel data. *The Journal of International Trade & Economic Development, 29*(5), 546–565.

Choi, I. (2001). Unit root tests for panel data. *Journal of International Money and Finance*, Elsevier, *20*(2), 249–272.

Ciftci, C., & Durusu-Ciftci, D. (2022). Economic freedom, foreign direct investment, and economic growth: The role of sub-components of freedom. *The Journal of International Trade & Economic Development, 31*(2), 233–254. https://doi.org/10.1080/09638199.2021.1962392

Claessens, S., Klingebiel, D. & Schmukler, S. L. (2001). FDI and stock market development: Complements or substitutes. *World Bank Working Paper*, 1–37.

Dada, J. T., & Akinlo, T. (2021). Foreign direct investment and poverty reduction in sub-Saharan Africa: Does environmental degradation matter? *Future Business Journal, 7*(1), 1–10.

Durham, J. B. (2004). Absorptive capacity and the effects of foreign direct investment and equity foreign portfolio investment on economic growth. *European Economic Review, 48*(2), 285–306.

Economou, F. (2019). Economic freedom and asymmetric crisis effects on FDI inflows: The case of four South European economies. *Research in International Business and Finance, 49*, 114–126.

Engle, R. F. & Granger, C. W. (1987). Co-integration and error correction: representation, estimation, and testing. *Econometrica: Journal of the Econometric Society*, 251–276.

Fon, R. M., Filippaios, F., Stoian, C., & Lee, S.H., (2021). Does foreign direct investment promote institutional development in Africa? *International Business Review, 30*(4), 101835.

Gammoudi, M., Cherif, M. & Asongu, S. (2016). FDI and Growth in the MENA countries: Are the GCC countries Different? *African Governance and Development Institute WP/16/015.*

Ghazalian, P. L., & Amponsem, F. (2019). The effects of economic freedom on FDI inflows: An empirical analysis. *Applied Economics, 51*(11), 1111–1132.

Gohou, G., & Soumaré, I. (2012). Does foreign direct investment reduce poverty in Africa and are there regional differences? *World Development, 40*(1), 75–95.

Granger, C. W. (1988). Some recent development in a concept of causality. *Journal of Econometrics, 39*(1–2), 199–211.

Iamsiraroj, S. (2016). The foreign direct investment–economic growth nexus. *International Review of Economics & Finance, 42*, 116–133.

Muye, I. M., & Muye, I. Y. (2017). Testing for causality among globalization, institution and financial development: Further evidence from three economic blocs. *Borsa Istanbul Review, 17*(2), 117–132.

Im, K. S., Pesaran, M. H., & Shin, Y. (2003). Testing for unit roots in heterogeneous panels. *Journal of Econometrics, 115*(1), 53–74.

Jensen, N. M. (2008). *Nation-states and the multinational corporation*. Princeton University Press.

Karanfil, F., & Li, Y. (2015). Electricity consumption and economic growth: Exploring panel-specific differences. *Energy Policy, 82*, 264–277.

Kinoshita, Y. & Campos, N. F. (2006). A re-examination of determinants of foreign direct investment in transition economies. In *Annual Meeting of the Allied Social Science Associations at the IMF Institute, London Business School* (pp. 1–39).

Kraay, A. (2004). *When is Growth Pro-poor? Cross-country Evidence* (Vol. 3225). World Bank Publications.

Levin, A., Lin, C. F., & Chu, C. S. J. (2002). Unit root tests in panel data: Asymptotic and finite-sample properties. *Journal of Econometrics, 108*(1), 1–24.

Love, I., & Zicchino, L. (2006). Financial development and dynamic investment behavior: Evidence from panel VAR. *The Quarterly Review of Economics and Finance, 46*(2), 190–210.

Maddala, G.S., & Wu, S. (1999). A comparative study of unit root tests with panel data and a new simple test. *Oxford Bulletin of Economics and Statistics, 61*, 631–652.

Malikane, C., & Chitambara, P. (2017). Foreign direct investment, democracy and economic growth in southern Africa. *African Development Review, 29*(1), 92–102.

Nazir, M. S., Nawaz, M. M., & Gilani, U. J. (2010). Relationship between economic growth and stock market development. *African Journal of Business Management, 4*(16), 3473–3479.

Olawumi, D., Awolusi, Olufemi P., & Adeyeye, T. G. P. (2017). Foreign direct investment and economic growth in Africa : A comparative analysis. *International Journal of Sustainable Economy, 9*(3), 183–198.

Pesaran, M. H., Schuermann, T., & Weiner, S. (2004). Modelling regional interdependencies using a global error-correcting macroeconometric model. *Journal of Business and Economics Statistics, 22*, 129–162.

Popovici, O. C., & Călin, A. C. (2013). Ways of attracting fdi in western and eastern European countries: Upgrading institutions' quality. *Young Economists Journal/revista Tinerilor Economisti, 10*(20), 200–207.

Popovici, O. C., & Călin, A. C. (2014). FDI theories. *A Location-Based Approach. Romanian Economic Journal, 17*(53), 3–24.

Pradhan, R. & Arvin, B. M. (2015). Foreign aid, economic growth, FDI, and trade openness in lower middle-income countries: A dynamic panel data analysis. In *Handbook on the economics of foreign aid,* 232–254. Edward Elgar Publishing.

Raza, S. A., & Jawaid, S. T. (2012). Foreign capital inflows, economic growth and stock market capitalization in asian countries: An ARDL bound testing approach. *Quality and Quantity*. https://doi.org/10.1007/s11135-012-9774-4.

Sabir, S., Rafique, A., & Abbas, K. (2019). Institutions and FDI: Evidence from developed and developing countries. *Financial Innovation, 5*(1), 1–20.

Sayari, N., Sari, R., & Hammoudeh, S. (2018). The impact of value added components of GDP and FDI on economic freedom in Europe. *Economic Systems, 42*(2), 282–294.

Schwarz, G. (1978). Estimating the dimension of a model. *The Annals of Statistics* 6 (2), 461–464. https://doi.org/10.1214/aos/1176344136.

Singh, D., & Gál, Z. (2020). Economic freedom and its impact on foreign direct investment: Global overview. *Review of Economic Perspectives, 20*(1), 73–90.

Slesman, L., Baharumshah, A. Z., & Wohar, M. E. (2015). Capital inflows and economic growth: Does the role of institutions matter? *International Journal of Finance & Economics, 20*(3), 253–275.

Stock, J. H., & Watson, M. W. (1993). A simple estimator of cointegrating vectors in higher order integrated systems. *Econometrica: Journal of the Econometric Society*, 783–820.

Taylor, M. & Thrift, N. (2013). *The Geography of Multinationals (RLE International Business): Studies in the Spatial Development and Economic Consequences of Multinational Corporations*. Routledge.

Tekin, R. B. (2012). Economic growth, exports and foreign direct investment in Least Developed Countries: A panel Granger causality analysis. *Economic Modelling, 29*(3), 868–878.

Toone, J. E. (2012). Mirage in the Gulf: Examining the upsurge in FDI in the GCC and its legal and economic implications for the MENA region. *Emory Int'l l. Rev., 26*, 677.

Tsaurai, K. (2018). Investigating the impact of foreign direct investment on poverty reduction efforts in Africa. *Revista Galega De Economia, 27*(2), 139–154.

Umoh, O. J., Jacob, A. O., & Chuku, C. A. (2012). Foreign direct investment and economic growth in Nigeria: An analysis of the endogenous effects. *Current Research Journal of Economic Theory, 4*(3), 53–66.

Wald, A. (1943). Tests of statistical hypotheses concerning several parameters when the number of observations is large. *Transactions of the American Mathematical Society, 54*(3), 426–482.

World Bank. (2020). Global Economic Prospects: Sub-Saharan Africa.

Yeboua, K. (2021). Foreign direct investment and economic growth in Africa: New empirical approach on the role of institutional development. *Journal of African Business, 22*(3), 361–378.

Zekarias, S. M. (2016). The impact of foreign direct investment (FDI) on economic growth in Eastern Africa: Evidence from panel data analysis. *Applied Economics and Finance, 3*(1), 145–160.

Zghidi, N., Mohamed Sghaier, I., & Abida, Z. (2016). Does economic freedom enhance the impact of foreign direct investment on economic growth in North African countries? A panel data analysis. *African Development Review, 28*(1), 64–74.

CHAPTER 30

The COVID-19 Pandemic and Africa's Financial Systems: *How Do We Reform Post-COVID-19 Financial Systems?*

Joshua Yindenaba Abor, Elikplimi Komla Agbloyor, George N. Agyekum Donkor, and Angela A. Alu

30.1 Introduction

The recent COVID-19 crisis has had an influence on many aspects of daily life and has resulted in both economic and non-economic consequences. According to World Health Organization data as of November

J. Y. Abor (✉) · E. K. Agbloyor · A. A. Alu
University of Ghana Business School, Legon, Accna, Ghana
e-mail: joshabor@ug.edu.gh

E. K. Agbloyor
e-mail: ekagbloyor@ug.edu.gh

A. A. Alu
e-mail: aalu002@st.ug.edu.gh

G. N. A. Donkor
ECOWAS Bank for Investment and Development, Lome, Togo

J. Y. Abor and C. K. D. Adjasi (eds.), *The Economics of Banking and Finance in Africa*, Palgrave Macmillan Studies in Banking and Financial Institutions, https://doi.org/10.1007/978-3-031-04162-4_30

29, 2021, there have been more than 260 million COVID-19 cases worldwide, with about 5.2 million fatalities. The terrible loss of countless lives throughout the world is one of the non-economic consequences. In terms of economic impact, the pandemic has wreaked havoc on the lives of millions of people all over the world. Examples include: job losses, high unemployment rates, the closure of many businesses due to lockdown measures, low consumer demand, supply chain disruptions, as well as decline in the liquidity and financial health of several companies, which led to some of them turning to the stock markets for funding and deferring dividend payments in order to save cash.

The steep drop in stock values in major markets across the world, especially beginning in February 2020, was one of the early signs that the crisis would have a serious impact on the global economy and financial markets. The S&P 500, for example, dropped by more than 20% in the United States between February and March 2020. Both the NASDAQ, which is heavily weighted in technology companies, and the Dow Jones Industrial Average (DJIA) dropped by around 17% and 23%, respectively. Other major markets in Australia, China, France, Germany, Japan, Russia, Singapore and the United Kingdom followed a similar pattern. The drop in stock prices resulted in major increases in volatility/uncertainty in global capital markets. Obviously, the pandemic has impacted diverse sectors of the global economy in different ways. Some of the sectors that were affected with substantial market value losses included booking, entertainment and live events, airlines, cruise and casinos and hotels and resorts firms. Financial services and energy businesses were hard hit by the selloff at that time.

During the pandemic, industries such as biotech, consumer staples, health care and technology outperformed others (CFA Institute, 2020). The technology sector has performed well during the pandemic, as demonstrated by the NASDAQ with almost 30% gain on August 31, 2020. According to Damodaran (2020), the pandemic has had a greater impact on the fortunes of older and more mature businesses than on those of younger and faster-growing businesses. To put it another way, younger and higher growing firms have outperformed older and more established companies, mirroring how the pandemic has affected various age groupings of companies.

According to Fan et al. (2018), pandemic risks can have an impact on the global economy corresponding to an average climate change equivalent of 0.2–2% of global income. Given the devastation wrought by

COVID-19, their projection of a $500 billion cost due to losses from a worldwide pandemic appears to be considerably understated. Indeed, governments throughout the world have launched a variety of rescue programs. For example, under the Coronavirus Aid, Relief and Economic Security Act, the United States alone enacted a $2.3 trillion program (IMF, 2020). Among many other initiatives, the Paycheck Protection Programme and Health Care Enhancement Act (IMF, 2020a, 2020b) received an extra $483 billion. As of August 2020, policymakers in the United States were discussing new stimulus packages ranging from $1 trillion to $10 trillion. As a result, total US interventions might range between $4 and $10 trillion by the end of the pandemic. This contrasts with the $700 billion Troubled Asset Relief Program (TRAP), the $200 billion Term Asset-Backed Securities Lending Facility (TALE), and the $787 billion American Recovery and Reinvestment Act of 2009, which were all substantial interventions during the global financial crisis of 2007–2008. Furthermore, contrary to the intervention in 2007–2009, which mostly targeted major financial institutions, the interventions during the current crisis tend to be broader in scope, targeting people and companies of all sizes.

Given the magnitude and scope of the crisis, we examine the pandemic's influence on Africa's financial systems. The chapter also proposes reforms in Africa's financial systems. The rest of this chapter is organized as follows: Sect. 30.2 provides an overview of the COVID-19 pandemic and previous pandemics. Section 30.3 outlines African governments' policy responses to the pandemic. Section 30.4 discusses its impact on Africa's financial systems. Section 30.5 details how to reform Africa's financial systems after the COVID-19 pandemic. Section 30.6 concludes the chapter.

30.2 Overview of COVID-19 and Previous Pandemics

Apart from COVID-19, the world has seen numerous pandemics. The first was influenza A, which caused the Spanish flu (H1N1). Although there was no general agreement on its origins, it did spread around the world between 1918 and 1919. During that period, it was believed that 500 million people, or one-third of the world's population, were infected with the virus, with 50 million people worldwide dying as a result. This led to a 16 percent drop in world GDP. An influenza A (H2N2) virus, which first appeared in East Asia in February 1957, sparked the second pandemic (Asian flu). In February 1957, it was first recorded in Singapore, and in April 1957, it was also reported in Hong Kong. It was estimated that 1.1 million people died. The influenza A (H3N2) virus was responsible for the third pandemic, which occurred in 1968. This was initially reported in the United States in September 1968, with an estimated 1 million fatalities worldwide. The 1957 and 1968 pandemics were very mild (Centres for Disease Control and Prevention, 2019). Mexico witnessed the introduction of a new influenza virus in the form of an H1N1 subtype in March 2009. This affected 214 countries, leading to 18,449 deaths (WHO, 2009).

Major public health issues, such as severe acute respiratory syndrome (SARS), Middle East Respiratory Syndrome (MERS), avian flu (Influenza H5N1), influenza (H1N1), and the current COVID-19 due to SARSCoV-2 (Bhatia & Abraham, 2020; Peeri et al., 2020)—have wreaked havoc on human lives and triggered economic downturns in the last two decades. It is critical to use what we have learned from previous pandemics to prepare better for future ones. The current COVID-19 pandemic, as well as lessons learned from previous pandemics and epidemics such as Ebola in Africa, should equip us to develop pandemic preparedness, coping strategies and response plans that do not disrupt the health system and have a limited economic impact (Khetrapal & Bhatia, 2020).

The new coronavirus struck the whole world eight months after the first case of COVID-19 was discovered in Wuhan, China in November 2019 (named SARS-CoV-2). The WHO labeled the viral outbreak a public health emergency of global concern on the 30th of January 2020, and a pandemic on the 11th of March 2020.

30.3 African Governments' Policy Responses to the COVID-19 Pandemic

The African region reported its first case of COVID-19 on the 14th February 2020 in Egypt (OECD, 2020) and in SSA the first case appeared in Nigeria on the 27th February 2020 (WHO, 2020). The occurrence in Africa was close to two months after the first case was reported in Wuhan, China, providing the region with ample time to put in place preparedness plans. Local transmission of the virus superseded imported cases and the doubling time has been shortened to less than 7 days in over 95%

of affected countries. Therefore, African countries were bracing themselves for the eventual impact of the COVID-19 pandemic.[1] At the end of April 2020, the Africa region had recorded an overall total of 20,652 confirmed cases and 861 related deaths (i.e., case fatality ratio 4.2%) had been reported across 45 countries. The highest mortality rates were reported in Algeria 12.6% (425/3382), Liberia 9.7% (12/124), Democratic Republic of Congo 6.1% (28/459), Mali 5.9% (23/389), Burkina Faso 6.6% (42/632), and Niger 4.2% (29/696) (WHO, 2020).

After the initial cases were reported in the respective countries, a number of governments of African countries responded by implementing public health and social measures in order to curb and contain the spread of the virus. Some of these policy measures include encouraging social distancing, closure of borders and travel restrictions, closure of schools, bans on large gatherings, self-isolation for persons exposed to the virus, the establishment of quarantine centers for confirmed cases, and either a partial lockdown of some cities or full lockdown of the entire country. Apart from these, African countries also implemented a number of economic measures to reduce the human and economic impact of the CoVID-19 pandemic. Table 30.1 summarizes the key economic responses by governments of selected African countries. These are measures taken between March and July 2020.

The COVID-19 pandemic has had an impact on Africa's economic growth through domestic and external channels. Prior to that, it was forecasted that the average GDP in 2020 for African economies would diminish for the first time in 25 years. This had implications for the general well-being and level of poverty in Africa. According to the UN, an estimated 30 million people could fall into poverty and many more could become acutely food insecure. The OECD (2020) has observed that policy measures initiated to mitigate the impact of the COVID-19 pandemic will continue to evolve as countries move to the next stages of the COVID-19 response, including:

- *Surviving the pandemic*: This involves ensuring adequate resources are channeled to addressing basic necessities such as food and

[1] Resolve to Save Lives. Global situation update. 2020. Available from: https://vital.ent.box.com/s/m45vny0o2hhzsosscgbkgem3j8pux4f3.

Table 30.1 Policy responses implemented by selected African countries (March–July)

Policy	*Specific measures*	*African Country*
Fiscal	Postponement of tax payment	Algeria, Angola, Botswana, Burkina Faso, Cameroon, Congo, DRC, Egypt, Rwanda, South Africa, Zambia, Zimbabwe
	Granting grace period for filing tax	Angola, Benin, Botswana, Burkina Faso, Cameroon, DRC, Ghana, Morocco, Namibia, Rwanda, Senegal, Uganda, Zimbabwe
	Lowering taxes/granting tax exemptions or tax holiday	Angola, Burkina Faso, Congo, Cameroon, DRC, Ethiopia, Ghana, Kenya, Malawi, Mali, Morocco, Senegal, South Africa, Tanzania, Uganda, Zambia
	Provision of allowances/cash transfers/wage subsidy	Algeria, Benin, Botswana, Cameroon, Egypt, Gambia, Kenya, Nigeria, Malawi, Rwanda, South Africa
	Provision of business support scheme	Benin, Botswana, Egypt, Ethiopia, Ghana, Kenya, Mali, Morocco, Namibia, Nigeria, Rwanda, Senegal, South Africa, Tanzania, Zimbabwe
	Provision of free food and subsidy on the consumption of utilities (water and electricity)	Burkina Faso, DRC, Egypt, Ethiopia, Gambia, Ghana, Kenya, Mali, Rwanda, Senegal, South Africa

Policy	*Specific measures*	*African Country*
Monetary and macro-financial	Reduction of policy rate	Algeria, Angola, Botswana, Burkina Faso, Cameroon, Congo, DRC, Gambia, Ghana, Kenya, Malawi, Mali, Morocco, Namibia, Nigeria, Rwanda, Senegal, South Africa, Tanzania, Uganda, Zambia, Zimbabwe
	Reduction/elimination of reserve requirement	Algeria, Angola, Benin, Botswana, Congo, DRC, Egypt, Gambia, Ghana, Kenya, Malawi, Morocco, Nigeria, Rwanda, Tanzania, Zimbabwe
	Reduction of capital adequacy/relief on bank capital requirements/ reduction of the capital conservation buffer	Botswana, Cameroon, Congo, DRC, Morocco, Namibia, South Africa, Zambia
	Easing of solvency and releasing liquidity	Algeria, Benin, Botswana, Burkina Faso, Cameroon, Congo, Egypt, Ethiopia, Gambia, Ghana, Kenya, Malawi, Morocco, Nigeria, South Africa, Uganda, Zambia, Zimbabwe
	Revision of provisioning and classification rules for specific loan categories/regulatory forbearance for non-performing loans	Algeria, Botswana, Burkina Faso, Congo, DRC, Ghana, Guinea, Kenya, Malawi, Mali, Senegal, Zambia
	Granting of moratorium by banks on loans to clients/providing debt relief to borrowers	Algeria, Angola, Burkina Faso, Egypt, Ghana, Kenya, Morocco, Mali, Namibia, Nigeria, Rwanda, Senegal, South Africa, Uganda, Zambia

(continued)

Table 30.1 (continued)

Policy	*Specific measures*	*African Country*
	Expansion of the range of instruments accepted as collateral in monetary operations	Botswana, Cameroon, Congo, Morocco, South Africa, Zambia
	Lowering haircuts on government securities used in refinancing operations	Algeria, Cameroon, Congo Tanzania
	Introduction of measures to promote the use of electronic payments	Benin, Burkina Faso, Congo, DRC, Egypt, Ghana, Kenya, Malawi, Mali, Rwanda, Senegal, Tanzania, Uganda, Zambia
Exchange rate and balance of payment	Transitioning to a more flexible exchange rate regime/limiting foreign exchange market interventions	Gambia, Morocco, Rwanda
	Moving from a managed floating exchange rate regime to a fixed exchange rate system	Zimbabwe
	Implementation of a new annual downward rate of crawl	Botswana
	Standing ready to intervene in the foreign exchange market	Uganda
	Cutting import bill and banning exports of several products	Algeria, Benin
	Introduction of electronic platform for foreign exchange transactions	Angola
	Seeking debt service deferral	Gambia, Ghana
Others	President/Vice President donating a salary or taking a pay-cut	Algeria, Ghana, Malawi, Mali, Nigeria, South Africa

Policy	*Specific measures*	*African Country*
	Ministers and top government officials donating a salary or taking a pay-cut	Ghana, Kenya, Malawi, Nigeria, Rwanda, South Africa
	Prohibition of eviction of renters in case of non-payment of rent	DRC, Uganda
	Release of prisoners	Ethiopia, Ghana, Kenya, Nigeria, Somalia, South Africa

Source https://www.imf.org/en/Topics/imf-and-covid19/Policy-Responses-to-COVID-19; https://en.wikipedia.org/wiki/Impact_of_the_COVID-19_pandemic_on_prisons

medicine, and ensuring proper physical and mental health, in addition to safety for the people;

- *Returning to normal*: This entails supporting firms and households to continue their usual activities and repairing the harm or loss suffered in the time of the pandemic; and
- *Re-focusing on the long term*: This means shifting resources and focusing attention toward long-term development.

30.4 Implications of COVID-19 Pandemic for Africa's Financial Markets

The literature suggests that well-functioning financial markets are required for economic growth (see Abor et al., 2020; Amoah et al., 2020; Aryeetey, 2003 Livine, 1997; Senbet & Otchere, 2010). For that reason inclusive financial development can promote inclusive growth and development (see Levine, 2004; Park & Mercado, 2015). Mobilizing and pooling savings, producing information about likely investments and allocating capital, easing the exchange of goods and services, facilitating trade, diversifying and managing risk and monitoring firms and exerting corporate governance—are all functions performed by financial markets (Levine, 1997). Robust financial markets enable countries to advance beyond short-term, volatile capital flows to the point where they can attract longer-term capital for growth and development initiatives. The pandemic has had a severe impact on financial markets. To have the intended influence on economic development, financial markets must have clear pathways or links with economic growth. Banks, for example, must be able to deploy the resources mobilized through credit extension responsibly. Similarly, stock exchanges must be active in providing information and guaranteeing liquidity through well-functioning trading platforms (Allen et al., 2011; Senbet & Otchere, 2010). To establish robust, diverse and liquid financial markets, a good combination of banks, capital markets, private equity finance and contractual savings institutions is required. Finance markets in Africa, on the other hand, are tiny, restricted and illiquid, with limited reach. This is evident in the aggregate financial indicators as well as the use of firm- and household-level formal financial services (Beck and Cull, 2014). We now turn our attention to analyzing the impact of the pandemic on Africa's financial markets by focusing on its effects on banking and microfinance institutions (MFIs), non-bank financial institutions, capital markets, investment firms and FinTech.

Impact of COVID-19 Pandemic on Banking and MFIs

The COVID-19 pandemic has had some effects on African banks. According to the CDC Group (The U.K.'s Development Finance Institution and Impact Investor), the crisis has put severe pressure on African banks as foreign banks withdraw correspondent banking relationships in an effort to 'de-risk' their operations (CDC Group, 2020). Recognizing this challenge, the CDC group pledged an additional \$75 million to enhance its trade facility with ABSA Bank. Further, the COVID-19 crisis is likely to constrain the ability of banks to mobilize deposits and make loans. The reduced ability to raise deposits is likely to affect the liquidity of banks, leading to lower credit expansion by banks to the productive sectors of the economy. Indeed, this conjecture is supported by evidence from the great recession that took place between 2007 and 2010. For instance, Fig. 30.1 shows a drop in deposit taking between 2009 and 2010, probably due to aftershocks of the 2007–2009 global financial

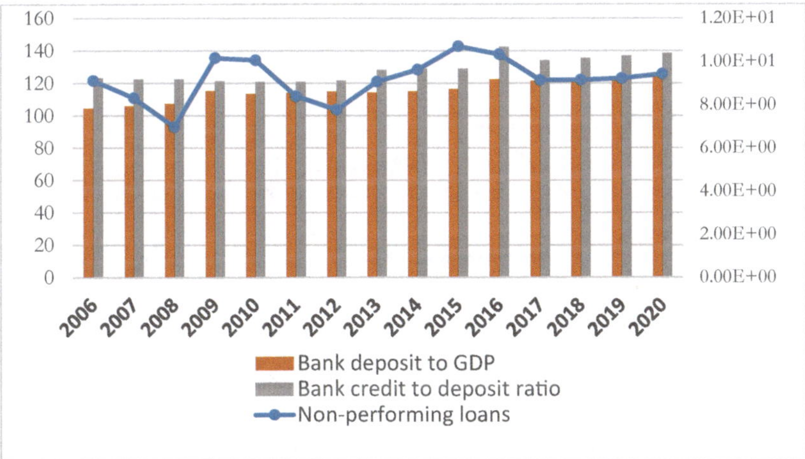

Fig. 30.1 Deposit taking and lending across African banks (*Source* Global Financial Development Database, 2020)

crisis. Lending by banks (bank credit to deposit ratio) declined between 2008 and 2010. The period after 2008 also experienced increasing Non-performing Loans (NPLs). NPLs also increased steadily between 2012 and 2015 for Africa (see Fig. 30.2). However, the NPL ratio declined between 2015 and 2017 and it began inching up afterward, specifically between 2017 and 2020. We expect the NPL ratio across African banks to worsen slightly at least in the short-term due to the pandemic. Depending on how long the pandemic lasts, this effect could linger for between 2 and 5 years before full recovery takes place. The data suggests that the countries that were most at risk in terms of the NPL spike were Mauritania (27.36%), Sierra Leonne (23.48%), Central African Republic (22.37%), Senegal (18.66%), Djibouti (16.31%), Equatorial Guinea (15.25%), Ghana (13.76%) and Tunisia (13.38%).

Apart from deposit taking and lending, the crisis has also affected the profitability and stability of banks across the continent. The Z-score measures the distance from default and has therefore been used in the empirical literature to proxy bank stability. Higher values of the Z-score suggest a safer banking system because banks are farther away from default. The Z-score has been criticized as a measure of banking stability because it did not pick up vulnerabilities in the banking system before the 2007–2009 banking crisis. Newer measures of banking systemic risk such as CoVaR (see Tobias & Brunnermeier, 2016) and Marginal

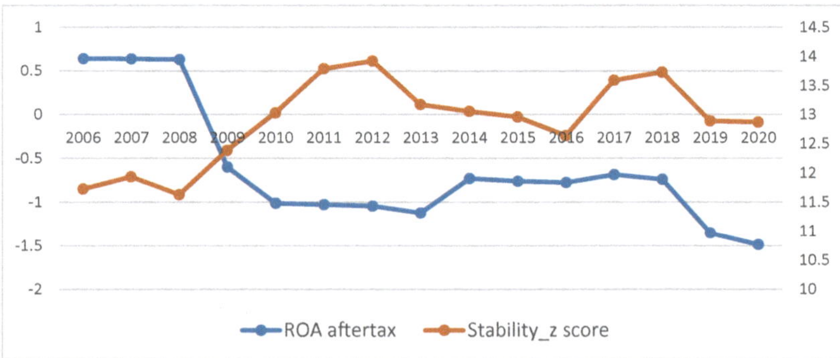

Fig. 30.2 Profitability and stability of African banks (*Source* Global Financial Development Database, 2020)

Expected Shortfall (see Brownlees & Engle, 2012) have been developed to provide a clearer picture of financial system vulnerabilities. These measures however are not widely available for African banks, given that they are mainly market risk indicators that are easier to compute when a bank is traded on a stock exchange. In terms of Marginal Expected Shortfall (MES), data from the New York University Stern Business School VLab show that the banks that pose the most systemic risk in Africa are located in South Africa, Nigeria, Morocco and Egypt. Table 30.2 presents the Top 10 banks based on the MES extracted from VLab. The majority of the banks have South African origins.

We, therefore, resort mainly to the Z-score, being cognizant of its weaknesses. The Z-score as a measure of bank stability declined between 2019 and 2020 and this is expected to reduce further as the pandemic continues. Interestingly, the estimated Z-score (banking stability) was reducing between 2012 and 2016, while NPL was rising. Again, while the Z-score fell between 2018 and 2020, we see the NPL assuming a rising trend.

Table 30.2 Measures of marginal expected shortfall for African banks

No	*Country*	*Bank*	*SRISK T*	*SRISK T-1*	*Change in SRISK*
1	South Africa	Standard Bank Group Ltd	3266.1	-950.7	4216.8
2	South Africa	Absa Group Ltd	2905.4	1772.3	1133.1
3	South Africa	Investec Ltd	2703.7	2485.9	217.8
4	South Africa	Nedbank Group Ltd	2558.4	1378.9	1179.5
5	South Africa	Liberty Holdings Ltd	1408.5	1191.8	216.7
6	South Africa	Momentum Metropolitan Holdings	1220.5	959	261.5
7	Nigeria	FBN Holdings Plc	741	685.1	55.8
8	South Africa	African Phoenix Investments Ltd	−20.7	−48	27.3
9	South Africa	Hosken Consolidated Investments Ltd	−46.5	−165.8	119.3
10	Morocco	Douja Promotion Groupe Addoha	−162.2	−136.8	−25.4

Source Extracted by Authors based on data from New York University's Stern Business School VLab

Impact of COVID-19 Pandemic on Non-Bank Financial Institutions

Just as the pandemic was expected to affect the banking sector, we expect it to affect the non-banking financial institutions. In this review, we attempt to further predict the impact of the pandemic on investment management firms, insurance firms and pension funds. Figure 30.3 shows that in the earlier periods (2004–2014), non-life insurance penetration (non-life insurance premium volume to GDP) and the life insurance penetration (life insurance premium volume to GDP) were of the same trend. By 2015, however, life insurance penetration had begun to outpace non-life insurance penetration, particularly between 2015 and 2020. The data also shows that insurance sector assets generally increased significantly during this period.

We expect that the COVID-19 pandemic will moderate the growth of insurance (both life and non-life) sector penetration in Africa. This is premised on a number of reasons. First, COVID-19 is likely to affect the payment of premiums on a number of insurance policies, especially those that come up for renewal. Some individuals and businesses may decide not to reinsure policies such as motor vehicles because they are not using their vehicles. Due to the effect on income, life insurance policies may be discontinued, or withdrawals made on the policies would have an investment component built in. In Lesotho for example, insurance companies were asked on the 7th of May 2020 to suspend installment payments. Botswana also rescheduled payments on life insurance and

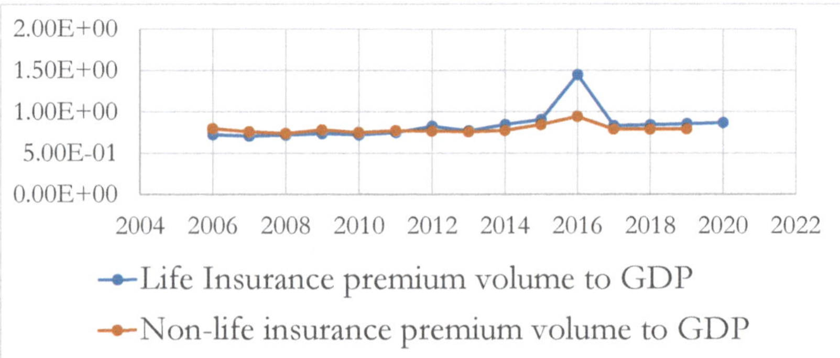

Fig. 30.3 Life and non-life insurance premium (*Source* Global Financial Development Database, 2020)

retirement funds for at least three months. In South Africa, the issuance of new insurance licenses was suspended for six months. Some policies adopted by African governments may help cushion the insurance sector. For example, in Sierra Leonne the government incentives for healthcare workers included a life insurance component. In Ghana, the government announced a GHS 350,000 insurance package for frontline health workers.

Second, the impact of the COVID-19 pandemic on the non-insurance sector is whether insurers are liable to pay claims to businesses that took out business interruption policies. Insurers in South Africa rejected claims by businesses, arguing that even if businesses had taken insurance against infectious or contagious diseases, such policies do not specifically cover the impact of national lockdowns (*Insurance Journal, 2020*). These debates raise an important question as to whether the effect of a pandemic on this scale can be insured. If regulators and law courts force insurers to make payments, this is likely to lead to an increase in premiums. The result may be individuals and businesses being priced out of the insurance market or being under-insured relative to their needs. This may have an impact on the development of the insurance sector across the region. The top insurance markets (based on insurance penetration and insurance company assets) on the continent, which are South Africa, Namibia, Morocco, Mauritius and Kenya, may suffer the most due to a contraction in the insurance market on the continent.

In terms of the potential impact of the pandemic on the pensions sector, it is important to note that the sector on the continent is not well developed, with just a few exceptions. We expected that pension contributions would fall at least in the short- to medium-term due to unemployment and income effects on the ability of individuals and businesses to make regular pension contributions. Another channel through which COVID-19 could affect the pensions industry is the impact of the crisis on the returns of the portfolios of pension funds. For example, in Ghana, pension funds and other asset managers were asked to take a haircut of 200 basis points on their Treasury bill investments, leading to a reduction in the fiscal burden on the government. This amounts qualitatively to a transfer of wealth of over GHS 300 million (approx. $52 million) from these funds to the government. In a number of countries such as Lesotho and Botswana, pension funds were asked to either suspend or reschedule pension payments. This is also likely to adversely affect the fortunes of pension funds. Finally, given the stress on businesses and on governments, the unfunded pension liabilities of businesses and governments on defined benefit schemes are likely to increase significantly in the short-to-medium term.

Impact of COVID-19 Pandemic on Capital Markets

One of the major financial markets that could be affected by the pandemic is the stock market. The stock market is a leading indicator of economic activity as investors discount future cash flows when they attempt to value companies. Consequently, a fall or rise in the stock market can be an indication of an onset of a crisis or the end of one. Stock market development across the continent has been low with a number of markets characterized by illiquidity. Further, various studies have shown that African markets are informationally inefficient, meaning information is not quickly and rapidly reflected in stock markets (Agbloyor et al., 2020; Ntim et al., 2007; Osei, 2002). Figure 30.4 shows that stock market capitalization had been on the decline after the global financial crisis in 2007. Stock market capitalization fell to a trough in 2012 and then generally began to rise again. In Africa, stock market capitalization seems to have been stable between 2013 and 2020, although a significant part of the capitalization is contributed by South Africa. However, after dropping South

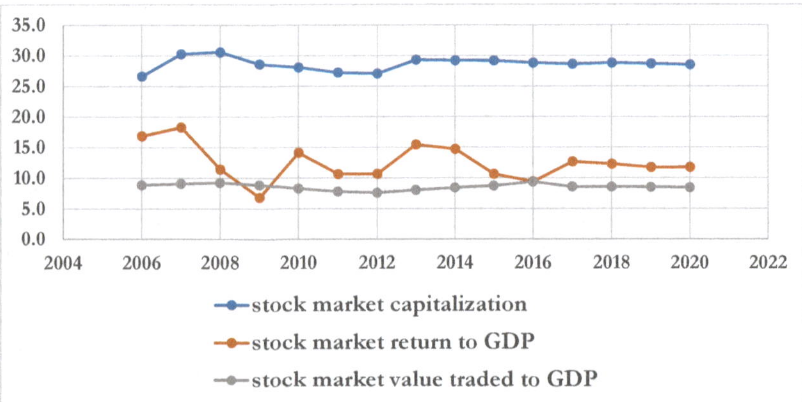

Fig. 30.4 Trends in stock market development in Africa (*Source* Global Financial Development Database, 2020)

Africa, it becomes more apparent that stock markets in the region are not well developed. The biggest markets on the continent are South Africa, Mauritius, Morocco, Cote D'Ivoire, Botswana, Kenya, Uganda, Egypt and Tunisia. Stock markets in Africa have generally underperformed during the COVID-19 period and this may decline further post COVID. In terms of stock market return to GDP, Fig. 30.4 shows a changing trend across the period 2006–2020 and it is expected to decline after COVID. This is because investors are going to pull out their funds from investing in the stock market due to the outbreak of the pandemic. Figure 30.4 shows that stock market value traded to GDP has been stable across the 2006–2020 period and it is expected to decline at least in the short-to-medium term.

As was indicated earlier, the debt markets in Africa are underdeveloped. Bond markets in Africa underperformed during the COVID period and are expected to decline further after COVID. Though governments are borrowing more, the strain on investors such as pension funds and individual investors may reduce the demand for government bonds. Further, our earlier review indicated that firms in Africa rely more on bank lending compared to issuing bonds in the capital markets. Given the increased volatility in capital markets and reductions in IPOs, we expected that the crisis would set back the development of the corporate bond market in Africa at least in the short-to-medium term. The crisis is likely to lead companies that intended to explore or reuse the corporate bond market to reconsider their intentions. We expect that even if interest rates drop due to easing monetary policy stance, firms are more likely to go in for bank finance as opposed to issuing bonds. In Fig. 30.5, corporate bond issuance volume to GDP and government domestic bonds declined between 2006 and 2012 and have been fairly stable between 2014 and 2020. However, it is expected to decline after the pandemic. This is because the government especially is likely to borrow from external sources (international financial market). After showing a changing trend between 2006 and 2017, portfolio investment bonds began to inch up after 2017. This is expected to increase further post COVID.

Investment Firms

The crisis is likely to have an impact on brokerage and asset management firms across the continent. This is likely to be the case because of panic withdrawals by clients, leading to liquidity problems. Investors are

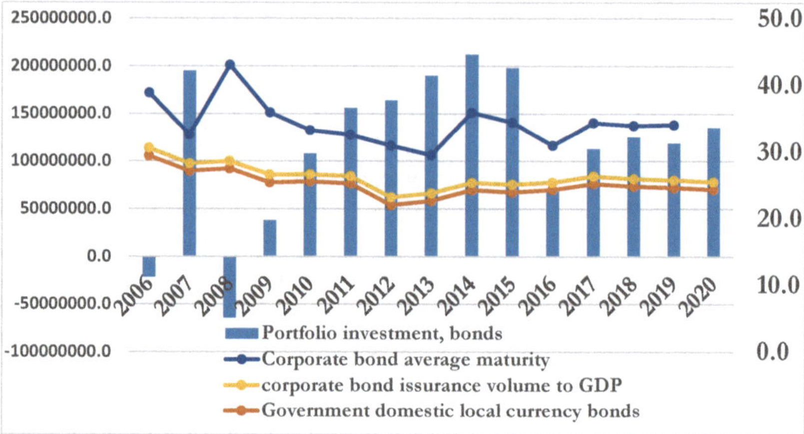

Fig. 30.5 Trends in bond market development in Africa (*Source* Global Financial Development Database, 2020)

likely to also invest less because they want to hold on to their money for precautionary reasons in case things get worse. Further, the increase in unemployment and under-employment is likely to lead to less investments by both businesses and individuals.

Given the negative returns posted by stock markets, investors may shift their funds more into money market instruments for protection and safety. This is likely to adversely affect the ability of businesses to tap into long-term funds, resulting in an increase in productivity and growth. Further, it is instructive to note that the crisis has seriously affected the ability of firms to raise capital on the stock exchange. This has consequences of future economic growth and development as implied by the finance and growth literature (see King and Levine, 1993a, 1993b). A report by EY shows that global IPO activity declined in the first half of 2020. For example, the report shows that IPO activity in the Middle East and North Africa (MENA) declined by 11% in terms of volume and 43% in terms of proceeds (EY, 2020).

Impact of COVID-19 Pandemic on FinTech

The COVID-19 pandemic has affected the FinTech industry in Africa with elevated risks associated with cybercrime due to enhanced adoption

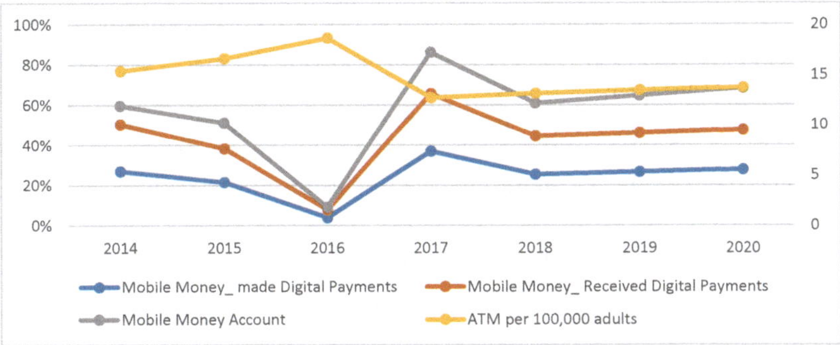

Fig. 30.6 Trends in FinTech Adoption in Africa (*Source* Global Financial Development Database, 2020)

rate. From Fig. 30.6, the adoption of FinTech inched up during COVID and is expected to increase after COVID. The increased risks in connection with FinTech adoption will be more prominent in Africa, given the weak regulatory regime. Considering the vulnerability with respect to the FinTech business, FinTech firms may be confronted with challenges regarding finance since the majority of them have been in business for less than a decade and are yet to make profits. Relying on investor funding will no longer be guaranteed, considering the declining revenues as a result of the effect of the COVID-19 pandemic. The present condition also makes it challenging to establish new FinTech startups. It is important to note that irrespective of these challenges and risks posed by the pandemic, it also presents some opportunities. The FinTech industry appears to be better placed for the digital transformation taking place in Africa's financial services sectors (Abor, 2020).

The technology sector in general, and particularly firms facilitating communication and exchanges of goods and services remotely have witnessed a significant increase in adoption and usage. The provision of such services is crucial for firms and households to lessen some of the health and socio-economic risks of the pandemic (Fu & Mishra, 2020). For instance, FinTech offers an attractive choice of accessing financial services during crisis, given the restrictions to movement and social distancing protocols as well as the risk of infection posed by holding cash (Arner et al., 2020). Additionally, the use of FinTech enables providers of financial services to swiftly respond to shocks by introducing new products or services, changing or upscaling existing ones. The outbreak of the pandemic, coupled with the related lockdowns imposed by governments, have led to a considerable increase in FinTech and digital finance adoption (Fuster et al., 2019). FinTech adoption should improve the extension of financial services and facilitate financial inclusion in the region.

30.5 How to Reform Africa's Post-COVID-19 Financial Systems

Unfortunately, it is now obvious that COVID-19 is here to stay—and so are its impacts. The pressure is on to address the ongoing issues, as well as to deal with the existing challenges in the financial system. There is a need to implement early and ambitious policy responses and reforms in the financial systems. We discuss these measures as follows:

Improving macroeconomic stability: A stable macroeconomic environment is necessary for financial sector development, especially the capital market. An economy with stable and predictable inflation rates, a lower exchange rate, favorable interest rates and high per capita income is likely to attract both domestic and foreign investors into the capital market. This also involves effective monetary policy implementation in the midst of fiscal consolidation. Considering the fact that investments in equity have a longer horizon, investors will look out for stable macroeconomic indicators in order to invest.

Instituting effective regulatory and supervisory regimes: Effective regulation and supervision of the financial system is necessary to ensure its soundness and stability. Development of the stock market for instance requires clear rules and regulations within an efficient judicial system. These rules must follow international best practices and also reflect local structures and needs. Strengthening regulation and supervision should go beyond putting in place the rules to include their enforcement, which is very crucial and requires compliance. Instituting a strong corporate governance system is also important in boosting investor confidence regarding regulatory issues.

Encouraging financial market development: This entails ensuring effective market infrastructure; encouraging institutional investors; improving institutional quality; promoting the demutualization and integration of stock markets; increasing the level of education, public awareness and financial literacy; promoting FinTech adoption to further drive inclusive finance; investing in infrastructure to support FinTech; and improving the regulatory regime for FinTech—RegTech and SupTech.

Attracting private capital flows: Attracting private capital flows in the form of foreign direct investment (FDI) and portfolio inflows, as well as encouraging international remittance flows, is necessary for promoting financial sector development. Such external capital inflows are channeled through the financial system to finance economic activity.

Leveraging natural resources: This involves encouraging natural resource revenue retention in the domestic economy to improve financial market activity. African governments need to obtain the best deals in mining stability agreements. They need to ensure that a lot of the export revenue from precious minerals is retained in the domestic economy to improve financial market activity and develop the financial system.

Curbing illicit financial flows: This will include strengthening the tax system by including tax reforms that improve the efficiency in tax administration and creating synergies between the revenue authority's Act and statutory enactments of other agencies to close all gaps exploited by MNC's through transfer pricing. It also involves negotiating international tax treaties and improving the exchange of information with other countries. Negotiating international tax treaties and the exchange of information among countries will be useful in addressing illicit financial flows by preventing related companies from engaging in trade mis-pricing. The financial resources retained will support the development of the financial system.

Promoting the establishment of Development Finance Institutions (DFIs): Governments need to consider the establishment of DFIs such as National Development Banks (NDBs) to support specific sectors. NDBs play an active role in mobilizing resources from the public and private sectors to support investments in critical sectors of the economy. They perform counter-cyclical and pro-cyclical roles and are active in the market during crises. They provide financing to important sectors that have difficulty accessing finance from traditional financing institutions and also help to de-risk private investment by financing important sectors.

30.6 Conclusion

This chapter examined how the COVID-19 pandemic has affected and is affecting Africa's financial systems. It also discussed how to reform post-COVID-19 financial systems in Africa. Examining the data leads to some intriguing conclusions. To begin with, we saw that a number of countries eased monetary policy in response to the crisis. Governments have also used expansionary fiscal policies, such as borrowing, to offer social assistance and ameliorate the impacts of the crisis. The pandemic has impacted various aspects of Africa's financial systems. African countries must develop measures to minimize the impacts of the crisis and restore growth and prosperity to their economies and financial systems. There is clearly the need to implement early and ambitious policy responses and reforms in Africa's financial systems. This will help to ensure soundness and stability to drive growth on the continent. Some of these measures include: improving macroeconomic stability, instituting effective regulatory and supervisory regimes, encouraging financial market development by ensuring effective market infrastructure, encouraging institutional investors, improving institutional quality, promoting demutualization and integration of stock markets, increasing the level of education and public awareness, promoting FinTech adoption to further drive inclusive finance, and investing in infrastructure to support and improve the regulatory regime for FinTech—RegTech and SupTech. Other measures include: attracting private capital flows, leveraging natural resources by encouraging natural resource revenue retention in the domestic economy in order to improve financial market activity, curbing illicit financial flows by negotiating international tax treaties and improving exchanges of information and promoting the establishment of Development Finance Institutions to support specific sectors of the economy.

References

Abor, J. Y. (2020). *Exploring the impact of COVID-19 pandemic on Africa's FinTech Space*. Working Paper, Paper Series No. 7/2020. Centre for Global Finance, SOAS University of London. https://www.centreforglobalfinance.org/2020-working-papers

Abor, J. Y., Issahaku, H., Amidu, M., & Murinde, V. (2020). Financial inclusion and economic growth. In J. Y. Abor, C. K. D. Adjasi, & Lensink, R (Eds.), *Contemporary issues in development finance*. Routledge.

Agbloyor, E. K., Gyeke-Darko, A., Fiador, V. O. & Kuttu, S. (2020). *COVID–19 and the informational Efficiency of the Ghana Stock Exchange*. https://globalnetwork.io/perspectives/2020/08/covid-19-crisis-and-informational-efficiency-ghana-stock-exchange

Allen, F., Otchere, I., & Senbet, L. W. (2011). African financial systems: A review. *Review of Development Finance, 1*(2), 79–113.

Amoah, L., Adjasi, C., Soumare, I., Osei, K., Abor, J. Y., Anarfo, E., Amo-Yartey, C., & Otchere, I. (2020). Finance, economic growth, and development, In J. Y. Abor, C. K. D. Adjasi, & Lensink, R. (Eds.), *Contemporary issues in development finance*. Routledge.

Arner, D. W., Barberis, J. N., Walker, J., Buckley, R. P., Dahdal, A. M., & Zetsche, D. A. (2020). *Digital finance & the COVID-19 crisis*. Available at SSRN 3558889.

Aryeetey, E. (2003). Recent development in African financial markets: Agenda for further research. *Journal of African Economics, 12*(2), 111–152.

Beck, T., & Cull, R. (2014). *Small-and medium-sized enterprises finance in Africa*. Working Paper 16, Africa Growth Initiative, Brookings, https://www.brookings.edu/wp-content/uploads/2016/06/SME-Finance-in-Africa-Designed_FINAL.pdf

Bhatia, R., & Abraham, P. (2020). Time to revisit national response to pandemics. *The Indian Journal of Medical Research, 151*(2–3), 111.

Brownlees, C. T., & Engle, R. (2012). *Volatility, correlation and tails for systemic risk measurement*. Available at SSRN, 1611229.

CDC. (2020). *CDC Announces additional US$ 75 million trade finance deal with Absa as part of COVID response*. https://www.cdcgroup.com/en/news-insight/news/cdc-announces-additional-us75-million-trade-finance-deal-with-absa-as-part-of-covid-19-response/

Centres for Disease Control and Prevention. (2019). *Past pandemics*. Available from: https://www.cdc.gov/flu/pandemic-resources/basics/past-pandemics.html, accessed on July 29, 2020.

CFA Institute. (2020). *Aswath Damodaron on Valuations amid COVID-19*: "*Go Back to Basics*". https://blogs.cfainstitute.org/investor/2020/05/29/aswath-damodaran-on-valuations-amid-covid-19-go-back-to-basics/

Damodaran, A. (2020, June 19). Musing of markets. A viral market Update X: *A Corporate Life Cycle Perspective*. http://aswathdamodaran.blogspot.com/2020/06/

EY. (2020). *COVID-19 slows down Global IPO Activity YTD 2020*. https://www.ey.com/en_gl/news/2020/06/covid-19-pandemic-slows-global-ipo-activity-ytd-2020.

Fan, V. Y., Jamison, D. T., & Summers, L. H. (2018). Pandemic risk: How large are the expected losses? *Bulletin of the World Health Organization, 96*(2), 129.

Fu, J., & Mishra, M. (2020) *The global impact of COVID-19 on FinTech adoption*. Swiss Finance Institute Research Paper Series N20–38, https://papers.ssrn.com/sol3/papers.cfm?abstrac id=3588453

Fuster, A., Plosser, M., Schnabl, P., & Vickery, J. (2019). The role of technology in mortgage lending. *The Review of Financial Studies, 32*(5), 1854–1899.

IMF. (2020a). *Debt relief under the Heavily Indebted Poor Countries (HIPC) Initiative*. Retrieved from IMF. https://www.imf.org/en/About/Factsheets/Sheets/2016/08/01/11/Debt-Relief-Under-the-Heavily-Indebted-Poor-Countries-Initiative. Retrieved on 3rd August 2020.

IMF. (2020b). *Policy Response to OCVID-19*. Retrieved from IMF. https://www.imf.org/en/Topics/imf-and-covid19/Policy-Responses-to-COVID-19

Insurance Journal. (2020). S. African Insurers are Pushed to Pay COVID-19 Business Interruption Claims. https://www.insurancejournal.com/news/international/2020/07/02/574127.htm

Khetrapal, S., & Bhatia, R. (2020). Impact of COVID-19 pandemic on health system & sustainable development goal 3. *Indian Journal of Medical Research, 151*(5), 395.

King, R. G., & Levine, R. (1993a). Finance and growth: Schumpeter might be right. *The Quarterly Journal of Economics, 108*(3), 717–737.

King, R. G., & Levine, R. (1993b). Finance, entrepreneurship and growth. *Journal of Monertary Economics, 32*(3), 513–542.

KPMG. (2015). *KPMG Africa's banking in Africa report*. http://www.blog.kpmgafrica.com/kpmg-africas-banking-in-africa-report-2015/.

KPMG. (2017). *Insurance market in Africa: Where is the boom?* http://www.blog.kpmgafrica.com/insurance-market-in-africa-where-is-the-boom/.

Levine, R. (1997). Financial development and economic growth: Views and agenda. *Journal of Economic Literature, 35*, 688–726.

Levine, R. (2004). *Finance and Growth: Theory and Evidence*. NBER Working Paper Series, Working Paper 10766.

Ntim, C. G., Opong, K. K., & Danbolt, J. (2007). An empirical re-examination of the weak form efficient markets hypothesis of the Ghana Stock Market using variance-ratios tests. *African Finance Journal, 9*(2), 1–5.

OECD. (2020), *COVID-19 in Africa: Regional socio-economic implication and policy priorities*. Retrieved from OECD. https://read.oecd-ilibrary.org/view/?ref=132_132745-u5ptlrdb5x&tltle=COVID-19-in-Africa-Regional-Socio-economic-implication-and-policy-priorities

Osei, K. A. (2002). Asset pricing and information efficiency of the Ghana Stock Market. AERC Research Paper 115, African Economic Research Consortium, Nairobi.

Park, C. Y. & Mercado, R. (2015). *Financial inclusion, poverty, and income inequality in developing Asia*. Asian Development Bank Economics Working Paper Series, (426).

Peeri, N. C., Shrestha, N., Rahman, M. S., Zaki, R., Tan, Z., Bibi, S., & Haque, U. (2020). The SARS, MERS and novel coronavirus (COVID-19) epidemics, the newest and biggest global health threats: What lessons have we learned? *International Journal of Epidemiology, 49*(3), 717–726.

Senbet, L., Otchere, I. (2010). African stock markets: Ingredients for development and capacity building. In Q. Marc & V. Genevieve (Eds.), *African finance in the 21th century*. Palgrave Macmillan Publishing.

Tobias, A., & Brunnermeier, M. K. (2016). CoVaR. *The American Economic Review, 106*(7), 1705.

World Bank. (2020a). *COVID-19 (Coronavirus) Drives Sub-Saharan Africa towards first Recession in 25 Years*. Retrieved from World Bank. http://www.worldbank.org/en/news/press-release/2020a/04/09/covid-19-coronavirus-drives-sub-saharan-africa-toward-first-recession-in-25-years

World Bank. (2020b). *For Sub-Saharan Africa, Coronavirus Crisis Calls for Policies for Greater Resilience*. Retrieved from World Bank. http://www.worldbank.org/en/region/afr/publication/for-sub-saharan-africa-coronavirus-crisis-calls-for-policies-for-greater-resilience

World Bank. (2020b). *World Bank Predicts Sharpest Decline of Remittance in Recent History*. Retrieved from World Bank. https://www.worldbank.org/en/news/press-release/2020c/04/22/world-bank-predicts-sharpest-decline-of-remittances-in-recent-history.

World Bank. (2020d). *COVID-19 (Corona Virus) Response*. Retrieved from World Bank. https://www.worldbank.org/en/region/afr/coronavirus.

World Health Organization. (2020a). *Weekly bulletin on outbreaks and other emergencies*. Retrieved from World Health Organization. https://apps.who.int/iris/bitstream/handle/10665/331892/OEW17-2026042020a.pdf.

World Health Organization. (2020b). *Coronavirus disease (COVID-19) outbreak situation*. Retrieved from World Health Organization. https://covid19.who.int

World Health Organization. (2010). *Pandemic (H1N1) 2009- update 112*. Available from. https://www.who.int/cst/don/2010%2008%2006/en/, accessed on April 18, 2020.

https://www.imf.org/en/Topics/imf-and-covid19/Policy-Responses-to-COVID-19

https://en.wikipedia.org/wiki/Impact_of_the_COVID-19_pandemic_on_prisons

Index

J. Y. Abor and C. K. D. Adjasi (eds.), *The Economics of Banking and Finance in Africa*, Palgrave Macmillan Studies in Banking and Financial Institutions, https://doi.org/10.1007/978-3-031-04162-4

C

D

N

O

P

GPSR Compliance

The European Union's (EU) General Product Safety Regulation (GPSR) is a set of rules that requires consumer products to be safe and our obligations to ensure this.

If you have any concerns about our products, you can contact us on ProductSafety@springernature.com

In case Publisher is established outside the EU, the EU authorized representative is:

Springer Nature Customer Service Center GmbH
Europaplatz 3
69115 Heidelberg, Germany

Batch number: 10725847

Printed by Printforce, the Netherlands